Library and Book Trade Almanac™

formerly **The Bowker Annual**

2010 | 55th Edition

Library and Book Trade Almanac™

formerly **The Bowker Annual**

2010 | 55th Edition

Editor Dave Bogart
Consultant Julia C. Blixrud

 **Information Today, Inc.**

Published by Information Today, Inc.
Copyright © 2010 Information Today, Inc.
All rights reserved

International Standard Book Number 978-1-57387-382-6
International Standard Serial Number 2150-5446
Library of Congress Catalog Card Number 55-12434

Information Today, Inc.
143 Old Marlton Pike
Medford, NJ   08055-8750
Phone: 800-300-9868 (customer service)
             800-409-4929 (editorial queries)
Fax: 609-654-4309
E-mail (orders): custserv@infotoday.com
Web Site: http://www.infotoday.com

Printed and bound in the United States of America

US $219

ISBN 13: 978-1-57387-382-6

21900

9 781573 873826

Contents

Part 2
Legislation, Funding, and Grants

Part 3
Library/Information Science Education,
Placement, and Salaries

Part 4
Research and Statistics

Book Trade Research and Statistics

Part 5
Reference Information

Bibliographies

Ready Reference

Distinguished Books

Part 6
Directory of Organizations

Directory of Library and Related Organizations

Directory of Book Trade and Related Organizations

Preface

Welcome to this 55th edition of the *Library and Book Trade Almanac,* which continues a long tradition of presenting a broad and useful compilation of information of interest to the library and publishing worlds.

It chronicles a year of deepening challenge as society deals with the most severe economic downturn since the Great Depression. Libraries, faced with shortages, find their services in more demand than ever. Publishers are retrenching and seeking new ways to produce books and do business.

Our Special Reports in this edition examine two areas of interest.

- Harold C. Relyea and Jeffrey W. Seifert look at how the change of administrations in Washington has affected access to government information; the change, they note, "has been neither as thorough nor as rapid as anticipated by some."

- In a companion report, Vikki Gordon discusses the use of National Security Directives by successive presidential administrations over the past half-century to limit what the American people, and Congress, are allowed to know about major executive branch decisions.

- Erin Dorney describes how libraries—from the smallest up to the Library of Congress—are finding creative ways to use social networking services like Flickr, Twitter, and YouTube.

Part 1 also includes reports on the activities of federal libraries, federal agencies, and national and international library and publishing organizations.

Recent and current legislation and regulations affecting libraries are detailed in Part 2, along with the activities of two major funding and grant-making agencies, the National Endowment for the Humanities and the Institute of Museum and Library Services.

Part 3 offers a wealth of professional information for librarians, from advice on finding job opportunities to listings of the year's major scholarship and award winners.

Part 4 presents a varied abundance of research and statistics—tables of book and periodicals prices, library acquisition expenditures, detailed data on publishing, and reports on noteworthy research projects and research tools. Among Part 4 features are an examination of how libraries have kept pace with inflation over the years, Jim Milliot's survey of the year in publishing, and Albert Greco's analysis of the U.S. import/export trade in books.

Reference information makes up Part 5, from lists of bestsellers, major literary prize winners, and recommended books to guidance on how to obtain an ISBN, ISSN, and SAN.

Part 6 is our directory of library and publishing organizations at the state, national, and international levels, plus a calendar of major upcoming events.

The *Library and Book Trade Almanac* represents the efforts of many people, and we are grateful to all those who assembled reports, contributed articles, supplied statistics, and responded to our requests for information. Particular thanks, once again, are due Consultant Editor Julia C. Blixrud, Contributing Editor Catherine Barr, and Christine McNaull, whose skill and diligence in turning it all into a book makes everyone else's job easier.

We believe you will find this 55th *Library and Book Trade Almanac* a valuable resource to which you will often turn, and, as always, we welcome your comments and suggestions for future editions.

Dave Bogart
Editor

Part 1
Reports from the Field

Special Reports

Access to Government Information: The Presidential Transition, 2008–2009

Harold C. Relyea

Congressional Research Service, Library of Congress (Retired)

Jeffrey W. Seifert

Congressional Research Service, Library of Congress

Having served two terms as president, George W. Bush was constitutionally pro-scribed from seeking the same office again in 2008. Moreover, it was unlikely that he could have been returned to the White House. By the fall of the year, his approval rating among the electorate ranged from 19 percent to 34 percent, sec-ond only to the self-disgraced Richard Nixon. Late in Bush's administration, Pulitzer-prize winning journalist Charlie Savage of the *Boston Globe,* reviewing the president's record, observed that the "zone of secrecy surrounding the execu-tive branch has been dramatically widened."[1]

By contrast, the opposition party candidate, Barack Obama, a charismatic and very articulate African American contender for the presidency, expressed strong support for transparency in government operations and seemingly regard-ed accountability within the federal government as an important value. There were many, not just those within the traditional open government community, who considered Obama's position in these regards a welcome return to a legacy of freedom of information and "sunshine."

As we now know, Obama won that contest, becoming the 44th President of the United States. This report reviews and assesses the information access record of George W. Bush in the final year of his administration, and the initial year of his successor in the same regard.

Bush Departs

During his final year in office, President George W. Bush continued to widen the zone of secrecy surrounding the executive branch. While his administration had

Harold C. Relyea, for more than three and a half decades, was a Specialist in American National Government with the Congressional Research Service (CRS) of the Library of Congress, where he held both managerial and research positions. Jeffrey W. Seifert is currently a Specialist in Information Science and Technology Policy and a CRS research manager. The views expressed here are personal, not institutional.

waged some indirect opposition to the legislation, he had signed into law on December 31, 2007, amendments to the Freedom of Information Act (FOIA).[2] His approval was given without ceremony or a statement.

Undermining the FOIA Amendments

Shortly thereafter, it was learned that officials at the Office of Management and Budget (OMB) had indicated that all of the funding authorized by the amendments for a new Office of Government Information Services (OGIS) would be located in the fiscal year (FY) 2009 budget for the Department of Justice. Many regarded this arrangement as an attempt by the administration to give Justice control of OGIS, perhaps to the point of fatally crippling it, or allocating the OGIS funds to its own Office of Information and Privacy, which was the administration's overseer for agency compliance with FOIA policy.

Established within the National Archives and Records Administration (NARA), OGIS was mandated to review agency compliance with FOIA, recommend changes in the statute's administration to Congress and the president, offer mediation services between FOIA requesters and agencies as a nonexclusive alternative to litigation, and issue advisory opinions if mediation failed to resolve a dispute. Congress had deliberately located OGIS outside the Department of Justice, which represented agencies sued by FOIA requesters. In the face of questions about the matter, OMB officials declined to comment prior to the formal presentation of the president's budget to Congress on February 4. What that document revealed was a legislative proposal, to be enacted as a section of the general provisions of the Commerce, Justice, Science, and Related Agencies Appropriations legislation for FY 2009, specifying that the Department of Justice "shall carry out the responsibilities" of OGIS and repealing the new office's statutory mandate.[3] Congress ignored this proposal and subsequently funded OGIS in its status as a NARA component. Named to head OGIS on June 10, 2009, was Miriam Nisbet, who had been a special counsel with NARA, a legislative counsel with the American Library Association, and came to the position from the United Nations Educational, Scientific and Cultural Organization (UNESCO) where she had directed its Information Society Division. OGIS began operations in September 2009.

Facilitating Classification

Like Ronald Reagan before him, President Bush reversed the 30-year trend in security classification policy of narrowing the bases and discretion for making records officially secret by amending the prevailing executive order on classification with E.O. 13292 of March 25, 2003.[4] A few years later, the *New York Times* observed editorially that the "Bush Administration is classifying the documents to be kept from public scrutiny at the rate of 125 a minute. The move toward greater secrecy," it continued, "has nearly doubled the number of documents annually hidden from public view—to well more than 15 million last year [2006], nearly twice the number classified in 2001."[5]

E.O. 13292, among other reversals, eliminated the existing standard that information not be classified if there is "significant doubt" about the need to do so; treated information obtained in confidence from foreign governments as classified; and authorized the vice president, "in the performance of executive duties," to classify information originally. It also added the broad areas of "infrastructures" and "protection services" to the categories of classifiable information; eased the reclassification of declassified records; postponed the automatic declassification of protected records 25 or more years old from the beginning of April 17, 2003, to the beginning of December 31, 2006; eliminated the requirement that agencies prepare plans for declassifying records; and permitted the director of central intelligence (DCI) to block declassification actions of the Interagency Security Classification Appeals Panel (ISCAP), unless overruled by the president. Composed of senior-level representatives of the secretary of state, secretary of defense, attorney general, DCI, archivist of the United States, and national security adviser to the president, ISCAP makes final determinations on classification challenges appealed to it; approves, denies, or amends exemptions from automatic declassification sought by agencies; makes final determinations on mandatory declassification review requests appealed to it; and generally advises and assists the president in the discharge of his discretionary authority to protect the national security of the United States.

Ignoring Declassification

Proposals for fostering the declassification of records were offered by the Public Interest Declassification Board (PIDB) in January 2008. Statutorily established in 2000,[6] the board was a response to the work of the Commission on Protecting and Reducing Government Secrecy, chaired by Sen. Daniel P. Moynihan (D-N.Y.) during 1995–1997.[7] Preparation of *Improving Declassification,* the first PIDB report, began shortly after the panel's initial February 2006 meeting. During that year and into the next, the board, on nearly a monthly basis, took testimony on declassification matters from representatives of the departments and agencies having the largest declassification programs, NARA, including the presidential libraries, and knowledgeable members of the public.[8] The report offered the following comments regarding the board's overall finding.

> Though the Government is committed, as a matter of policy, to making historically significant information available to the public as soon as it can safely do so, there is no common understanding among the agencies of what "historically significant" information is, nor any common understanding of how such information will be treated once identified as such. Rather, it becomes part of the "queue," lost in the shuffle of automatic declassification reviews, FOIA requests, specifically mandated searches, and the like. What of historical significance is actually being declassified is unclear to both the public and to the Government.
>
> Making matters worse, declassification does not necessarily mean that information will be available to the public any time soon. Once declassified, documents undergo archival processing, which includes determining whether they should be withheld for reasons other than security classification, conducting archival description (which may include indexing the documents), and conducting any necessary preservation activities. The National Archives lacks sufficient resources to keep pace with agency declassification reviews, resulting in enormous backlogs. It will likely take years for hundreds of millions of pages of materials declassified over the past 12 years to become available to the public. Moreover, many declassified documents will continue to be withheld from the public because they contain other types of controlled, unclassified information, such as investigative or personal information. Many more years are likely to pass before this protected information is allowed into the public domain.[9]

While recognizing that "manpower is not the sole key to success" in declassification efforts, the PIDB report found that declassification "can and must be done in a smarter way," "needs to be better focused with greater uniformity among departments and agencies," and "needs to use technology to a greater extent to accomplish its mission and institute better strategic planning to address the needs of the future, especially the declassification of information stored in existing as well as emerging digital, optical, and other nontextual formats."[10] With these considerations in mind, the panel identified 15 issues and made 49 recommendations for the declassification of classified national security information, including the following:

- Establishing by executive order or by statute a national declassification program under the supervision of the Archivist of the United States, with a new National Declassification Center (NDC), directed by a deputy archivist for declassification policy and programs, to administer the program

- Requiring departments and agencies to consolidate all of their declassification activities in one office or to bring them under the control of a single office

- Ensuring, by presidential directive, that historically significant classified records are given priority at the 25-year review point, both in terms of what records are taken first and in terms of the quality of the review they receive

- Establishing and appointing, through the Archivist of the United States, a board composed of prominent historians, academicians, and former government officials to determine which events or activities of the federal government should be considered historically significant from a national security and foreign policy standpoint, for a particular year, and so advise the archivist for purposes of setting priorities for declassification activities

- Establishing, through the archivist, a single center within the Washington, D.C., metropolitan area, to house all future classified presidential records from the end of a presidential administration until their eventual declassification and physical transfer to a presidential library for public examination

- Directing agencies, by NDC guidelines or other appropriate executive branch issuance, to dedicate some specific percentage of their declassification review personnel to conducting reviews of classified records less than 25 years old that they know to be historically significant

- Charging the new NDC, through an executive order or other appropriate issuance, with prescribing uniform guidelines to govern the declassification of all executive departments and agencies

- Authorizing NDC to conduct declassification reviews for other departments and agencies on a reimbursable basis

- Requiring that any withdrawal of records that were previously available to the public at the National Archives be approved by the archivist

- Requiring that records identified as being of historical significance undergo a concurrent review for personal privacy or "controlled but unclassified" information at the same time as the review for declassification is conducted

- Developing, through the archivist, a personnel plan, to be funded as part of NARA's annual budget, that would address the current archival processing backlog and otherwise enable the archives in the future to fully process all declassified records within five years of their declassification so that they may be available to the public
- Requiring, by amendment of the operative executive order, that all departments and agencies with significant classification activity establish historical advisory boards, composed of experts within and outside the agency
- Requiring, by appropriate executive branch issuance, that all departments and agencies with responsibilities in the national security area hire an appropriate number of historians, either to select classified records of historical significance for declassification review and publication or to write historical accounts based upon the department's or agency's classified holdings
- Establishing new arrangements to assure the preservation of the President's Daily Brief (PDB) as a presidential record under the Presidential Records Act, and allowing for the protection of the PDB under the terms of the Presidential Records Act
- Establishing formal procedures for the declassification review of classified congressional committee reports and hearing transcripts by NDC[11]

President Bush sent a January 29, 2008, memorandum to cabinet officials and senior presidential assistants having responsibility for national security and homeland security policy soliciting their views on the recommendations in the PIDB report. These were to be submitted in writing no later than April 15. While responses were made, it does not appear that the Bush administration took any further action.

Extending Control over the Records of Former Presidents

During the closing years of the Bush regime, congressional efforts to overturn E.O. 13233 and return to the original intent of the Presidential Records Act were frustrated in the Senate.[12] The president had issued the directive on November 1, 2001, early in his initial term.[13] While the statute authorized a former president to seek a court order to stop the disclosure of particular records by the Archivist of the United States as a violation of the former president's rights and privileges, E.O. 13233 reversed this arrangement and prohibited the archivist from releasing particular records unless and until both the incumbent and former presidents agreed to their disclosure, or until the archivist was directed to disclose the records by a final court order resulting from a lawsuit brought by a person requesting the documentary materials. For the first time, the order also vested a former vice president and a representative or group of representatives of a former president whose records are subject to the Presidential Records Act with authority to prohibit the archivist from releasing particular records.

The policy changes brought by the order met with opposition from, among others, historians, political scientists, journalists, lawyers, and members of Congress.[14] Remedial legislation was introduced, amended, and favorably reported in the House of Representatives in 2002, but did not receive a floor vote prior to the final adjournment of the 107th Congress. The champion of the legislation, Rep. Steve Horn (R-Calif.), did not stand for re-election, and no successor legislation was introduced until the first session of the 110th Congress when the Democrats were in the majority in the House. In March 2007 Rep. Henry Waxman (D-Calif.) introduced legislation revoking E.O. 13233 and allowing the archivist to reassume control of access to the records of recent former presidents. Moved quickly, the bill was approved by the House on March 14 under a suspension of the rules on a 333–93 vote.[15] Sen. Jeff Bingaman (D-N.M.) introduced a companion bill, which was favorably reported, but languished on the Senate legislative calendar without a final vote before the final adjournment of the 110th Congress and the departure of the Bush administration.

Struggling with Information Control Markings

Among the deficiencies that contributed to the surprise terrorist attacks on the World Trade Center and the Pentagon on September 11, 2001, were the failure of intelligence and law enforcement agencies to share relevant information and the secrecy practices attending such information. A national study commission investigating the attacks recommended, in these regards, that "[i]nformation procedures should provide incentives for sharing, to restore a better balance between security and shared knowledge," and called upon the president to "coordinate the resolution of the legal, policy, and technical issues across agencies to create a 'trusted information network'" to facilitate such sharing.[16]

While security classification policy and procedures—such as the unwillingness of agencies to honor the security clearances of personnel from outside their own domains and to otherwise adhere to strict need-to-know practices—contributed to information sharing deficiencies, the use of numerous other information-control markings in addition to the authorized national security protection labels also had a negative effect. Their legal basis was often not clear; their application and authority was not well understood; and their general effect was restrictive. The variety and widespread use of these markings first came to public attention in 1972 when congressional overseers examining the administration and operation of the Freedom of Information Act disclosed their existence.[17] The Nixon administration, at that time and during the remainder of its tenure, made no apparent effort to curb the generation and use of such labels, and the continued practice was inherited by the administration of President George W. Bush.

When legislating the Homeland Security Act of 2002, Congress directed the president to "prescribe and implement procedures under which relevant Federal agencies—"

(A) share relevant and appropriate homeland security information with other Federal agencies, including the Department [of Homeland Security], and appropriate State and local personnel;
(B) identify and safeguard homeland security information that is sensitive but unclassified; and
(C) to the extent such information is in classified form, determine whether, how, and to what extent to remove classified information, as appropriate, and with which such personnel it may be shared after such information is removed.[18]

The president's response came in the issuance of E.O. 13311 of July 29, 2003, in which he largely assigned his responsibilities for the development and implementation of information-sharing arrangements to the secretary of homeland security.[19] By the early autumn of 2004, as Congress turned its attention to legislating intelligence reforms to strengthen the ability of agencies to detect and deter terrorist attacks, there had not been any response from the secretary regarding the development of the anticipated information sharing arrangements. Consequently, Congress revisited the matter in the Intelligence Reform and Terrorism Prevention Act of 2004, which mandated a so-called Information Sharing Environment (ISE)—an arrangement to facilitate, among federal, state, local, and tribal governments, as well as segments of the private sector, the "sharing of terrorism information in a manner consistent with the national security and with applicable legal standards relating to privacy and civil liberties."[20]

A December 16, 2005, presidential memorandum for the heads of executive departments and agencies, in support of ISE, explicitly noted, in one of its guidelines, the need to standardize procedures for sensitive but unclassified information, saying: "To promote and enhance the effective and efficient acquisition, access, retention, production, use, management, and sharing of Sensitive But Unclassified (SBU) information, including homeland security information, law enforcement information, and terrorism information, procedures and standards for designating, marking, and handling SBU information (collectively 'SBU procedures') must be standardized across the Federal Government."[21]

As part of the markings standardization effort, an interagency working group, led by the Department of Homeland Security and the Department of Justice, was formed and, according to testimony by ISE Program Manager Thomas E. McNamara at a May 10, 2006, House hearing, completed an initial inventory of information control markings in March 2006. In his statement, McNamara said:

> Preliminary assessments indicate that there are no government-wide definitions, procedures, or training for designating information that may be SBU. Additionally, more than 60 different marking types are used across the Federal Government to identify SBU, including various designations within a single department. (It is important to note, seventeen of these markings are statutory.) Also, while different agencies may use the same marking to denote information that is to be handled as SBU, a chosen category of information is often defined differently from agency to agency, and agencies may impose different handling requirements. Some of these markings and handling procedures are not only inconsistent, but are contradictory.[22]

During the course of his testimony, McNamara indicated that some legislative action might be needed, possibly to adjust statutorily authorized markings or control regimes, or perhaps to prohibit the use of protection designations not otherwise statutorily mandated.[23]

A few months later, it was reported that the Department of Homeland Security and the Department of Justice were deadlocked over the information control markings to be commonly used to facilitate information sharing, as well as a supporting management structure, and control over who gets information. As a consequence, a mid-June deadline set by the president to propose a new labeling system was missed.[24]

The ISE Implementation Plan, prepared by the ISE Program Manager and issued in November 2006, pointed out that "the growing and non-standardized inventory of SBU designations and markings is a serious impediment to information sharing among agencies, between levels of government, and, as appropriate, with the private sector. Elimination of this impediment," it continued, "is essential to ensure that the future ISE promotes and enhances the effective and efficient acquisition, access, retention, production, use, management, and sharing of unclassified information while also ensuring its appropriate and consistent safeguarding."[25] In accordance with the SBU procedures standardization guideline in the president's December 2005 memorandum, the secretary of homeland security and the attorney general, in coordination with the secretaries of state, defense, and energy, and the director of national intelligence, were to submit for presidential approval recommendations (1) "for government-wide policies and procedures to standardize SBU procedures" and (2) "for legislative, policy, regulatory, and administrative changes," as well as (3) an "assessment—by each department and agency participating in the SBU procedures review process—of the costs and budgetary considerations for all proposed changes to marking conventions, handling caveats, and other procedures pertaining to SBU information."[26]

In early February 2008 it was reported that the new SBU regime was ready for presidential approval and was being shared with some congressional staff in briefings. Information would be rated in three categories concerning "safeguards" as to how it should be stored, handled, and transmitted, and "dissemination" as to who is allowed to see it. The three categories, ranging from the lowest to the highest degree of protection, would be (1) "standard safeguards, standard dissemination," (2) "standard safeguards, specific dissemination," and (3) "enhanced safeguards, specific dissemination." At least four existing categories of SBU information were to be grandfathered into the new system. These included the *Safeguards Information* of the Nuclear Regulatory Commission, *Sensitive Security Information* of the Transportation Security Administration, and *Protected Critical Infrastructure Information* as well as *Chemical-Terrorism Vulnerability Information* of the Department of Homeland Security.[27]

It was not clear how or by whom the implementation and use of these new arrangements would be monitored, or how infractions would be detected and punished. Similarly, the relationship between the three new information protection categories and the exemptions of the Freedom of Information Act was also uncertain due to the lack of more specific details concerning the new regime. Furthermore, the introduction of these new arrangements did not require the departments and agencies, for other administrative purposes, to abandon existing, or cease creating new, information control markings or to better manage their use.

Obama Arrives

Barack Obama came to the presidency after slightly more than three years in the United States Senate. He had previously served three terms in the Illinois State Senate (1997–2004), and earlier had been a community activist in Chicago prior to his entry to Harvard Law School, from which he graduated in 1991. As a legislator, he was not an obvious champion of open government policy, although he supported accountability arrangements in government and, as a U.S. senator, offered legislation to establish greater transparency in federal spending, with one such proposal, which he cosponsored, becoming the Federal Funding Accountability and Transparency Act of 2006.[28] This statute provides a mandate for *USAspending.gov*. During his 2008 presidential campaign, references to accountability and transparency in government became frequent and were well received by an electorate that was suspicious of, if not rather displeased with, the secrecy practices of the Bush administration.

Upon arriving at the White House, President Obama had to contend immediately with a rapidly deepening worldwide recession that was particularly acute for the U.S. economy. Other initial demands included the reduction of American troop levels in Iraq and changing the war strategy in Afghanistan. Nominations to executive and judicial positions, economic recovery, and healthcare reform soon complicated and intensified his interactions with Congress. The Obama administration's close attention to this agenda resulted in both less immediate efforts at open government reform and less actual elimination of Bush administration secrecy policies and practices than some expected or would have liked.

Initial Steps

The day after his January 20, 2009, inauguration, Obama issued a memorandum to all heads of executive branch departments and agencies regarding FOIA. There, he thrilled proponents of open government, who had been stifled and frustrated by eight years of the Bush administration, with a commitment to the basic philosophy and procedures of the statute, saying:

> All agencies should adopt a presumption in favor of disclosure, in order to renew their commitment to the principles embodied in FOIA, and to usher in a new era of open Government. The presumption of disclosure should be applied to all decisions involving FOIA.[29]

The president's memorandum also directed executive branch entities to "take affirmative steps to make information public." Expanding on this premise, he wrote:

> They should not wait for specific requests from the public. All agencies should use modern technology to inform citizens about what is known and done by their Government. Disclosure should be timely.[30]

Later, on March 19, a supporting memorandum from Attorney General Eric H. Holder, Jr., reinforced the president's "openness prevails" policy, identifying two important implications.

> First, an agency should not withhold information simply because it may do so legally. I strongly encourage agencies to make discretionary disclosures of information. An agency should not withhold records merely because it can demonstrate, as a technical matter, that the records fall within the scope of a FOIA exemption.
> Second, whenever an agency determines that it cannot make full disclosure of a requested record, it must consider whether it can make partial disclosure. Agencies should always be mindful that the FOIA requires them to take reasonable steps to segregate and release nonexempt information. Even if some parts of a record must be withheld, other parts either may not

be covered by a statutory exemption, or may be covered only in a technical sense unrelated to the actual impact of disclosure.[31]

Recognizing that "the disclosure obligation under the FOIA is not absolute," the memorandum rescinded predecessor 2001 Attorney General guidance "which stated that the Department of Justice would defend decisions to withhold records 'unless they lack a sound legal basis or present an unwarranted risk of adverse impact on the ability of other agencies to protect other important records'." Under the policy of the Obama administration, it said, "the Department of Justice will defend a denial of a FOIA request only if (1) the agency reasonably foresees that disclosure would harm an interest protected by one of the statutory exemptions, or (2) disclosure is prohibited by law."[32]

Some months later, at a late September Senate oversight hearing on freedom of information, Meredith Fuchs, general counsel of the National Security Archive, observed: "There is no doubt that the Obama Administration has changed the course that the prior administration had set in this area." Noting that, during the past several months, there had been "many decisions to release information that had been withheld by the Bush Administration," she commented that there were, as well, "several high profile refusals to release records, including the continued refusal to release [Office of Legal Counsel] memoranda concerning the warrantless surveillance program and the continued effort to block release of images of detainees at Abu Ghraib that two courts have ruled must be released." Indeed, she said, "many concerns remain among frequent FOIA requesters about the implementation of the Obama policies," and she called for stronger and more supportive leadership in the future from the attorney general regarding FOIA administration and litigation.[33] A few months thereafter, it was reported that more than 300 individuals and groups had filed FOIA lawsuits during the first year of the Obama administration, the plaintiffs contending that little had changed since the years of the Bush administration.[34]

On the same day that the government-wide FOIA memorandum was issued, Obama promulgated E.O. 13489, revoking E.O. 13233 and the Bush administration's expansive policy regarding public disclosure arrangements concerning the records of former presidents.[35] The Archivist of the United States was returned to being the principal decision-maker concerning the public release of such materials; the privilege of the incumbent or affected former president to protect records was narrowed and procedurally clarified; and no role was prescribed for a representative or a group of representatives or an incumbent or former vice president in such matters. Remedial legislation had been approved by the House on January 7 under a suspension of the rules on a 359–58 vote.[36] Sent to the Senate, the bill was cleared with a substituted text and placed on the legislative calendar on May 19, where it remained, however, without further action.

Disappointments

These early actions of the Obama administration—new FOIA policy of presumptive information availability, limiting restrictions on the disclosure of the records of former presidents, and the notable decision to release four memos written by the Office of Legal Counsel at the Department of Justice in 2002 and 2005 providing a legal rationale for harsh interrogation of terrorism subjects—were initial down payments on an anticipated open government effort by the new regime. That prospect, however, soon came into question as a consequence of subsequent developments. In early February, to the surprise of many, the Obama administration pressed ahead with a claim of the state secrets privilege in a lawsuit before the United States Court of Appeals for the Ninth Circuit seeking reinstatement of a claim for damages against an air carrier involved in the transportation of the plaintiffs to a foreign locale where they were allegedly tortured. The government attorney in the case, when specifically asked if the "change of administration has no bearing" in the litigation, responded in the negative. The attorney for the plaintiffs condemned the action of the Obama administration, calling it a ratification of the previous regime's "extreme policies," which he said prevented torture victims from seeking redress.[37] "It would have been hard to distinguish the Obama administration from its predecessor during a San Francisco court hearing this week," the *Washington Post* editorialized shortly thereafter. Observing that "howls of condemnation from some civil liberties advocates were predictable and understandable," it was noted that the entire matter of invoking the states secrets privilege was under review by the attorney general, and the hope was expressed that "he will not be as reflexive in invoking the shield as were his predecessors." The writer concluded, however, that "trust in matters as sensitive as these is not enough, no matter who is president."[38]

Some months later, the plans of Attorney General Holder in this regard were revealed. The new policy would make it more difficult to invoke the state secrets privilege by requiring that the attorney general and a team of Department of Justice lawyers be convinced that the release of sensitive information would present significant harm to national defense or foreign relations, which collectively constitute national security. Nonetheless, the standards involved appeared to be vague, if not nebulous. One sympathetic analyst, Gary Bass, executive director of OMB Watch, reportedly said it was "'enormously consistent with open-government recommendations' from himself and other advocates."[39] The *New York Times* was not so sure. Calling the new arrangement "An Incomplete State Secrets Fix," it editorially warned that the "Obama administration has essentially embraced the Bush approach in existing cases, trying to toss out important lawsuits alleging kidnapping, torture and unlawful wiretapping without any evidence being presented." While the attorney general's new guidelines were viewed as "a positive step forward," they purportedly "did not go nearly far enough," and offered no "shift in the Obama administration's demand for blanket secrecy in pending cases" or "support for pending legislation that would mandate thorough court review of state secrets claims made by the executive branch." In a cautionary conclusion, the editorial said:

> Since assuming office, Mr. Holder has reviewed the administration's position in ongoing cases and has continued broad secrecy claims of the sort President Obama criticized when he was running for president. To the extent that legitimate cases get dismissed as a result, Mr. Holder should make sure allegations of government wrongdoing get referred to an agency inspector general, as his new plan requires.

Assessing the total policy, the editorial concluded that the "need for such safeguards is not theoretical."[40]

In another situation, after initially deciding that it would not ask for court prohibition of the release of photographs showing the abuse of prisoners in Iraq and Afghanistan, the Obama administration changed its position.[41] "The Obama administration," said the *New York Times* editorially shortly thereafter, "has clung for so long to the Bush administration's expansive claims of national security and executive power that it is in danger of turning President George W. Bush's cover-up of abuses committed in the name of fighting terrorism into President Barack Obama's cover-up." Calling the action one of the "reminders of this dismaying retreat of Mr. Obama's passionate campaign promises to make a break with Mr. Bush's abuses of power," the editorial noted that, apart from a court challenge, the secretary of defense had been legislatively given authority to withhold the photos.[42] The editorial concluded with the comment that such photographs should be disclosed "to demonstrate that this nation has turned the page on Mr. Bush's shameful policies," and offering that: "Withholding the painful truth shows the opposite."[43]

In mid-November, Secretary of Defense Robert Gates blocked the public release of the photos in question,[44] and a few weeks later, the Supreme Court vacated a lower court ruling that would have required disclosure of the pictures.[45] Noting that the vacated appellate court ruling "was based on sound precedent and principles of government openness and accountability," the *New York Times* observed that "President Obama managed to void those principles and poke a large retroactive hole in the Freedom of Information Act." Continuing, the observation was offered that:

> disclosure is the best way to demonstrate that this nation has truly broken from the Bush administration's shameful policies. Letting officials decide not to release evidence of those policies is a dangerous step. Under the new law's perverse logic, the more outrageous the government's conduct, the greater the protection from disclosure.
>
> Allowing the executive branch to hide an important category of information without any real review also ignores the core purpose of the Freedom of Information Act. For a president who rose to the White House on promises of transparency and reasonable limits on executive power, this is not a legal victory to be proud of. [46]

Later in the year, after extensive obstruction by both the Bush and Obama administrations, a federal judge dismissed government objections to releasing Federal Bureau of Investigation records concerning statements made by Vice President Richard B. Cheney to the special prosecutor during his investigation of matters concerning the unauthorized disclosure of the Central Intelligence Agency (CIA) status of Valerie Plame. Disclosure of the records, it had been asserted, might chill cooperation by White House officials in such investigations in the future.[47] The records indicated that Cheney did not have clear memories about details surrounding the Plame leak, was ignorant of some pertinent interactions with the press by his chief of staff, and was displeased with the CIA's handling of alleged attempts by Iraq to buy uranium.[48]

Shortly thereafter, the Obama administration better acquitted itself when, in late October, the White House voluntarily posted on its Web site portions of its long-sought visitors log for the first six months of the year. A second installment was provided in November, and monthly releases were planned for the future. Press accounts noted the frequency of visits by some individuals, as well as the variety of personalities listed—entertainers, business executives, labor leaders, lobbyists, fund-raisers, and some celebrities.[49]

Open Government Directive

In compliance with the instructions of President Obama's January 21, 2009, memorandum on "Transparency and Open Government," OMB, on December 8, 2009, issued the long-anticipated Open Government Directive (OGD).[50] Eleven pages long, and accompanied by a report,[51] the directive "was informed by recommendations from the Federal Chief Technology Officer, who solicited public comment through the White House Open Government Initiative," and rooted in three principles: transparency, participation, and collaboration. Collectively, the three principles are described as the "cornerstone of an open government."[52] Transparency is intended to promote accountability. Participation represents the citizens' contribution to policy decision making. Collaboration focuses on cooperation both across federal agencies as well as between federal agencies and other public and private entities. In addition to its attempt to institutionalize a wholesale rebirth of the information practices of the federal government, the OGD is notable for its relatively short deadlines and presumption that agencies have the resources not only to implement the directive, but also to capitalize on, and respond to, the cacophony of information and demands that are implicitly envisioned as a measure of the success of open government.

The actions fall under four major objectives. The first objective is Publish Government Information Online, which directs agencies to make information available online in open formats (platform independent, machine readable, and able to be reused) and with the presumption in favor of openness ("to the extent permitted by law and subject to valid privacy, confidentiality, security, or other restrictions," but with an emphasis on being responsive even in the face of high demand, and using technology to improve the dissemination of information). The objective is operationalized by two deadline-driven mandates. One of these mandates is to "publish online in an open format at least three high-value data sets" within 45 days.[53] The OGD later defines high-value information as "information that can be used to increase agency accountability and responsiveness; improve public knowledge of the agency and its operations; further the core mission of the agency; create economic opportunity; or respond to [the] need and demand as identified through public consultation."[54] These data sets were to have not previously been available online and are to be registered via the *Data.gov* Web site. The second mandate is, within 60 days, to "create an Open Government Webpage located at http://www.[agency].gov/open to serve as a gateway for agency activities related to the Open Government Directive."[55] On these Web sites, agencies are expected to include a means for the public to provide feedback on the agency's OGD activities; respond to such feedback; and publish their annual FOIA reports in an open format. Separately, agencies are directed to take steps to reduce significant backlogs of FOIA requests by 10 percent, and to "comply with guidance on implementing specific presidential open government initiatives such as Data.gov, eRulemaking, IT Dashboard, Recovery.gov, and USAspending.gov."[56]

The second objective is to Improve the Quality of Government Information. The objective is operationalized by three specific deadlines for action. Within 45 days, agencies, in consultation with OMB, are to "designate a high-level senior official to be accountable for the quality and objectivity of, and internal controls over, the Federal spending information publicly disseminated through such public venues as USAspending.gov or other similar websites."[57] Within 60 days, the OMB deputy director for management is directed to issue a "framework for the quality of Federal spending information publicly disseminated." The framework would require agencies to submit plans regarding their internal controls and processes to ensure information quality. There is also reference to a future assessment to consider whether additional OMB guidance should be issued regarding other types of government information that are publicly disseminated. Within 120 days, the OMB deputy director for management is directed to issue a "a longer-term strategy for Federal spending transparency, including the Federal Funding Accountability Transparency Act and the American Reinvestment and Recovery Act."[58]

The third objective is to Create and Institutionalize a Culture of Open Government. This objective contemplates the need to foster opportunities for the three principles of the OGD to become integrated into the everyday business practices of the federal government. Central to this objective is the requirement that each agency develop its own Open Government Plan (OGP). Within 120 days, each agency is to "develop and publish on its Open Government Webpage an Open Government Plan that will describe how it will improve transparency and integrate public participation and collaboration into its activities."[59] The OGD includes considerable guidance to agencies on how to go about developing their OGPs, which are to be updated every two years, describing five major components each plan should contain. The component that appears to be most heavily emphasized is transparency. With eight subparts, the transparency component focuses on a variety of activities agencies are to undertake to publish information online. In summary, they include developing a strategic action plan for transparency that inventories and outlines timelines for making high-value information available; publication of data "as granular as possible"; detailing compliance with other transparency initiatives; details for proposed measures to inform the public of agency actions, such as public meetings, Internet press conferences, and periodic national town hall meetings; providing information to the public about agency compliance with records management requirements; providing information to the public about the agency's staffing and capacity to respond to FOIA requests; providing information to the public about staffing and processes used for responding to congressional requests for information; and providing information to the public about the agency's declassification programs.

The second component of the OGPs focuses on participation. As part of this component, agencies are expected to "explain in detail" how they will improve participation in the decision making process. This includes discussing plans for revising "current practices to increase opportunities for public-participation in and feedback on the agency's core mission activities;" providing descriptions and links to Web sites for public engagement; and "proposals for new feedback mechanisms, including innovative tools and practices that create new and easier methods for public engagement."[60]

The third component of the OGPs focuses on collaboration. For this component, agencies are expected to discuss how they will improve collaboration with "Federal and non-Federal governmental agencies, the public, and non-profit and private entities in fulfilling the agency's core mission activities."[61] The plans are to contain details about technology platforms, Web sites, and "innovative methods, such as prizes and competitions," for facilitating collaboration with various audiences.

The fourth component is the inclusion of "at least one specific, new transparency, participation, or collaboration" flagship initiative that agencies will implement.

The fifth component is a focus on public and agency involvement, and encourages agencies to look beyond the requirements of the OGD for further ideas and opportunities to invite and sustain public engagement.

Three other activities round out the objective to institutionalize a culture of open government. Within 60 days, the federal chief information officer (CIO) and the federal chief technology officer (CTO) are directed to create an Open Government Dashboard, which is to serve as an aggregator of the agencies' Open Government Plans and measure of their progress in meeting the objectives of the OGD. Within 45 days, the OMB deputy director for management, the federal CIO, and the federal CTO are directed to "establish a working group that focuses on transparency, accountability, participation, and collaboration within the Federal Government."[62] The working group, "with senior level representation from program and management offices throughout the Government," is intended to serve as a forum for sharing best practices and coordinating efforts to promote transparency, collaboration, and participation. Within 90 days, the OMB deputy director for management is directed to issue "a framework for how agencies can use challenges, prizes, and other incentive-backed strategies to find innovative or cost-effective solutions to improving open government."[63]

The fourth objective is to Create an Enabling Policy Framework for Open Government. This objective recognizes that the communications technology environment is very dynamic. In recent years, the emergence and popular embrace of social media applications such as blogs, YouTube, Facebook, and Twitter have left both the executive and legislative branches struggling to find ways to engage citizens in their favorite communications mediums while remaining in compliance with a range of privacy, security, and records management laws that long predate Web 2.0. To that end, within 120 days, the administrator of the OMB Office of Information and Regulatory Affairs (OIRA), in consultation with the Federal CIO and Federal CTO, is directed to review OMB implementation guidelines on laws such as the Paperwork Reduction Act and privacy regulations "to identify impediments to open government and to the use of new technologies and, where necessary, issue clarifying guidance and/or propose revisions to such policies, to promote greater openness in government."[64]

At the time of this writing, some of the first deadlines of the OGD have just started to pass and the public's perception of what has been accomplished so far is decidedly mixed. In some cases, data sets posted to Data.gov as part of each agency's requirement to post three high-value data sets were reportedly removed days later with few clues as to why. Although privacy, confidentiality, security, and other restrictions are contemplated as justifications in the OGD, the apparent lack of a clear and open notice from OMB raised eyebrows and made headlines.[65] In other cases, agency choices of what to post revealed that "high-value" is clearly in the eye of the beholder. Some critics—hoping for information on travel logs, spending reports, and oil and gas lease decisions—instead found information such as population counts of wild horses and burros from the Department of the Interior, tire quality ratings from the Department of Transportation, and an accounting of villages damaged or destroyed in the Darfur region of Sudan during 2003–2009 from the Department of State.[66]

Some of this disappointment may be the result of impossibly high expectations, driven in part by the soaring rhetoric of the Obama administration (such as promises of "an unprecedented and sustained level of openness and transparency in every agency"[67]), which was in stark contrast to its predecessor. Some of this may also be the result of an overly optimistic belief that the power of technology would automatically overcome the realities of governing, delivering results at the speed of a Google search. It will likely take considerable time, effort, and persistence to bridge the yawning gap between expectations and reality, and deliver on the fullest potential of open government. However, the OGD is notable for three contributions it makes to the government information landscape. First, it establishes an explicit expectation (although not wholly irreversible under extraordinary circumstances) by which the White House will be held accountable for the duration of its term, and which future administrations will have to address. Second, the emphasis on technology and open standards will likely spur innovation in the area of information sharing and analysis in ways yet unforeseen. Third, it highlights the long-overdue need for a thoughtful re-examination of federal information policy laws in a way that does not throw out the privacy and records baby with the analog era bathwater.

Security Classified and Controlled Unclassified Information

The OMB memorandum of December 8, 2009, setting out the terms of the open government directive, proffers that such prescribed action should occur "to the extent permitted by law and subject to valid privacy, confidentiality, security, or other restrictions." This qualification was understood by most interpreters to exclude security classified information properly designated and many types of SBU records. Reforms regarding both of these types of protected information were addressed separately by the new administration.

On May 27 the White House released a presidential memorandum to the heads of executive departments and agencies reminding the recipients that, "[w]hile the Government must be able to prevent the public disclosure of information where such disclosure would compromise the privacy of American citizens, national security, or other legitimate interests, a democratic government accountable to the people must be as transparent as possible and must not withhold information for self-serving reasons or simply to avoid embarrassment."[68] To this end, the president directed a review of the policy and procedures for the security classification of information and the creation of an interagency task force to review similarly the conditions and arrangements pertaining to SBU or what is called controlled unclassified information (CUI).

Regarding the CUI task force, the memorandum designated Attorney General Holder and Secretary of Homeland Security Janet Napolitano as co-chairs and named other officials as members. Its August 25 report to the president was publicly released by the White House on December 15. The report indicated that SBU information "is identified by over 100 unique markings and at least 130 different labeling or handling regimes," which "collectively . . . reflect a disjointed, inconsistent, and unpredictable system for protecting, sharing, and disclosing sensitive information." It offered the following assessment of current SBU information procedures.

> Regardless of any individual regime's performance, it is clear that as a whole, Executive Branch performance under these measures suffers immensely from interagency inconsistency in SBU policies, frequent uncertainty in interagency settings as to exactly what policies apply, and inconsistent application of similar policies across agencies. Additionally, the absence of effective training, oversight, and accountability at many agencies results in a tendency to overprotect information as SBU, thus greatly diminishing government transparency.[69]

"Current SBU policies are generally ill-suited" to "sharing terrorism-related and other intelligence and law enforcement information with local law enforcement," it was noted, and "the markings are sometimes misunderstood as providing an independent basis for withholding documents from the public, Congress, or the courts, which in turn can undermine transparency, as well as public trust in government."[70]

The report offered 40 remedial recommendations for consideration by the president. Among these were:

- Simplifying the definition of controlled unclassified information (CUI) to "All unclassified information for which, pursuant to statute, regulation, or departmental or agency policy, there is a compelling requirement for safeguarding and/or dissemination controls"[71]
- Expanding the scope of the CUI framework "to include all information falling within the definition of CUI in the possession or under the control of the Executive Branch of the Federal Government"[72]
- Making the expanded CUI framework "the single categorical designation used to identify, safeguard, and disseminate unclassified information"[73]
- Setting a presidentially imposed "moratorium on efforts within the Executive Branch to define or develop new SBU categories outside of the CUI Framework"[74]
- Following a prescribed four-step process for designating CUI
- Establishing "standards for personnel possessing the authority and/or necessary qualifications for identifying information as CUI"[75]
- Requiring each agency to establish a program to manage its CUI, including, at a minimum, "Senior Officials responsible on behalf of the agency head for recommending CUI Designations, providing training, CUI management, and oversight of agency CUI activities"[76]

- Simplifying CUI categories and markings
- Establishing standard markings and guidance
- Clarifying that "the CUI Framework and FOIA are entirely separate and that CUI markings have no bearing on whether records are exempt from release under FOIA"[77]
- Clarifying "that a CUI marking is not a basis for withholding information from Congress or the Judiciary"[78]
- Establishing a life cycle for all CUI information to be, with some specified exceptions, decontrolled after ten years
- Authorizing agencies "to impose administrative sanctions for repeated non-compliance with CUI policies or with CUI safeguard or dissemination control requirements"

The president's May 27 memorandum mandating the CUI task force also directed Assistant to the President for National Security Affairs James L. Jones to review security classification policy and procedures prescribed by E.O. 12958, as amended, and to submit recommendations and proposed revisions to the order, particularly regarding the establishment of a National Declassification Center, addressing overclassification, facilitating greater sharing of classified information, appropriate prohibition of reclassification, and relevant considerations regarding the electronic information environment.[79]

Shortly thereafter, the White House set up an Internet blog—the Declassification Policy Forum—to receive solicited suggestions about the reform of E.O. 12958 and the classification process. These suggestions were to be considered for the final recommendations sent to the president.[80] After the blog was terminated in mid-July, a number of participating public advocacy organizations and individuals became concerned that the resulting recommendations and proposed revisions to E.O. 12958 requested by the president would be delivered by the national security adviser without an opportunity for further comment. Their August 1 request for such a comment opportunity, however, was denied by the national security adviser a month later. Expressing appreciation for the comments received, Jones indicated that "it is essential to preserve the confidentiality of the President's deliberative process regarding these complex issues that stem from the President's constitutional authority to protect the national security" and, for that reason, "we cannot agree to make public a highly deliberative draft containing recommended changes in the order." Shortly thereafter, an August 4 draft of an executive order amending E.O. 12958 was disclosed by *Secrecy News*.[81] Prepared by an interagency task force, the draft, it was noted, remained subject to revision and had not yet been formally transmitted to the White House.

The final version of the new directive was issued on December 29 as E.O. 13526, together with a presidential implementation memorandum and a designation of officials having original classification authority.[82] Among the significant features of the new classified information order are

- Restoring the standards that, where "there is significant doubt about the need to classify information, it shall not be classified," and where "there is significant doubt about the appropriate level of classification, it shall be classified at the lower level"[83]

- Emphasizing the requirement that the "unauthorized disclosure could reasonably be expected to cause identifiable or describable damage to the national security"[84]

- Prescribing a new fundamental principle that "No information may remain classified indefinitely"[85]

- Prohibiting the reclassification of information after its declassification and release to the public under proper authority except when agencies can comply with specified restrictions[86]

- Requiring agency heads to "complete on a periodic basis a comprehensive review of the agency's classification guidance, particularly classification guidelines, to ensure the guidance reflects current circumstances and to identify classified information that no longer requires protection and can be declassified"[87]

- Establishing "within the National Archives a National Declassification Center to streamline declassification processes, facilitate quality-assurance measures, and implement standardized training regarding the declassification of records determined to have permanent historical value"[88]

- Facilitating approved information sharing by promoting maximum possible access to classified information by persons who meet standard criteria for access[89]

- Eliminating an intelligence community veto of declassification decisions made by the Interagency Security Classification Appeals Panel, which had been granted by the prior administration [90]

Asked about the impact of the new arrangements, one close observer, Steven Aftergood, the director of the Project on Government Secrecy at the Federation of American Scientists, reportedly said: "Everything depends on the faithful implementation by the agencies, but there are some real innovations here."[91] In an editorial commending the recent reforms, the *Washington Post* noted that additional recommendations "to design a more fundamental transformation of the security classification system" were expected from the president's national security adviser. Hope was expressed that those recommendations would result "in a balance that significantly increases the openness that the president seeks."[92]

Conclusion

With the election of Barack Obama to the presidency in 2008, there was an expectation in various quarters that he would eliminate or reverse, to some degree, the secrecy policies and practices of the prior administration. The fulfillment of that expectation, however, has been neither as thorough nor as rapid as anticipated by some. Why?

In a campaign for high political office, many issues and policy areas are equal in status for candidates, although some have tactical or strategic importance for winning votes and support in key geographical locales or among particular groups. It is likely that, for candidate Obama, transparency and openness in government was one of those matters, among many, that were sincerely important to him. Arriving at the Oval Office, however, real conditions were in play, and the many considerations of the campaign portfolio suddenly became prioritized. The need for responses to a worldwide recession, a collapsing domestic financial structure, and a failing American economy, along with foreign policy necessities concerning Iraq and Afghanistan, as well as other compelling demands, overrode, at least for the moment, openness commitments of the campaign. To top things off, a marathon effort to reform health care grew into a heated sprint in an unsuccessful effort to deliver legislation to the president's desk late in the year, consuming most of the remaining oxygen in the policy environment.

Handling all of these matters, the new president had little time to deal with a legacy of policy momentum. Sure, there was a pioneering directive on FOIA administration, but, as old sailors well know, it takes planning and time to turn a huge ship (of state). Presciently, Meredith Fuchs, general counsel of the National Security Archive, commenting on the sustained, if not somewhat increased volume of FOIA lawsuits in 2009, said she suspected that the Obama administration reflexively defended decisions made years earlier during the Bush administration to withhold requested records.[93]

It is also possible, in a similar way, that government lawyers were serving the new regime all too well, defending the federal government, the executive branch, or the president, when consideration might well have been given to the American citizenry as their client.

The new president, upon arrival at the institution, found a presidency greatly strengthened by the prior occupant of the position. Although he did not seek such authority, he may well have thought that he could exercise this power in a better way than did his predecessor, and he apparently was not willing to concede any of it to Congress or the courts. This power was to be retained.

Finally, there may be something of a tendency on the part of the Obama administration, seeking, as it does, to better apply information technology (IT) to achieve its objectives, to over-emphasize the use of IT for the proactive output of government information. At worst, this approach was realized in the propagandistic and censorial Committee on Public Information of the World War I era. In a more balanced view, the FOIA was legislated to provide the public with a procedure to gain access to "unpublished" government information. The open government initiative prescribed by the OMB directive of December 8, 2009, provides an offset to such proactive output—allowing the public to contribute ideas to government policymaking. There is, of course, no guarantee that such public input will be of desirable quality or usefulness. Regarding this aspect of the policy statement, Steven Aftergood at the Federation of American Scientists recently commented that "The quality of public comments on the development of the open government directive last summer, which sometimes suffered from digressions into extraneous matters, was not consistently encouraging on that note."[94] Members of Congress have similar experience with constituent communiqués, which sometimes reflect misunderstanding or insufficient knowledge about public policy issues. They have the resources of congressional support agencies to draw upon to provide remedial educational information.

It has been said that fashion is something that goes in one year and out the other. Certainly open government is not a matter of fashion, and certainly the Obama administration has more than one year to accomplish its goals and fulfill its promises.

Notes

1. Charlie Savage, *Takeover: The Return of the Imperial Presidency and the Subversion of American Democracy* (Little, Brown, 2007), p. 329.

2. P.L. 110-175; 121 Stat. 2524.

3. U.S. Office of Management and Budget, *Budget of the United States Government, Fiscal Year 2009—Appendix* (GPO, 2008), p. 239.

4. 3 C.F.R., 2003 Comp., pp. 196–218.

5. Editorial, "The Dangerous Comfort of Secrecy," *New York Times,* July 12, 2005, p. A22.

6. 114 Stat. 2856.

7. See U.S. Commission on Protecting and Reducing Government Secrecy, *Secrecy: Report of the Commission on Protecting and Reducing Government Secrecy* (GPO, 1997).

8. U.S. National Archives and Records Administration, Public Interest Declassification Board, *Improving Declassification: A Report to the President from the Public Interest Declassification Board* (Washington: Dec. 2007), p. 3.

9. Ibid., p. 6.

10. Ibid.

11. Ibid., pp. 8–12.

12. See 44 U.S.C. 2201–2207.

13. 3 C.F.R., 2001 Comp., pp. 815–819.

14. See U.S. Congress, House Committee on Government Reform, Subcommittee on Government Efficiency, Financial Management, and Intergovernmental Relations, *Hearings Regarding Executive Order 13233 and the Presidential Records Act,* hearings, 107th Cong., 1st and 2nd sess., Nov. 6, 2001; Apr. 11 and 24, 2002 (GPO, 2002).

15. *Congressional Record,* daily edition, vol. 153, Mar. 14, 2007, pp. H2496–H2500.

16. U.S. National Commission on Terrorist Attacks Upon the United States, *The 9/11 Commission Report* (GPO, 2004), pp. 417–418.

17. See U.S. Congress, House Committee on Government Operations, Subcommittee on Foreign Operations and Government Information, *U.S. Government Information Policies and Practices—Security Classification Problems Involving Subsection (b)(1) of the Freedom of Information Act (Part 7),* hearings, 92nd Cong., 2nd sess., May 1–3, 5, 8, and 11, 1972 (GPO, 1972), pp. 2477–2500.

18. 116 Stat. 2253; 6 U.S.C. 482.

19. 3 C.F.R., 2003 Comp., pp. 245–246.

20. 118 Stat. 3665; 6 U.S.C. 485.

21. U.S. White House Office, Office of the Press Secretary, *Memorandum for the Heads of Executive Departments and Agencies,* Subject: "Guidelines and Requirements in Support of the Information Sharing Environment," (Dec. 16, 2005), p. 3.

22. U.S. Congress, House Committee on Homeland Security, Subcommittee on Intelligence, Information Sharing, and Terrorism Risk Assessment, *Building the Information Sharing Environment: Addressing the Challenges of Implementation,* hearing, 109th Cong., 2nd sess., May 10, 2006 (GPO, 2007), p. 12.

23. Ibid., p. 24.

24. Siobhan Gorman, "Turf War Hampers War on Terror," *Baltimore Sun,* July 13, 2006, p. 3A.

25. U.S. Office of the Director of National Intelligence, Program Manager, Information Sharing Environment, *Information Sharing Environment Implementation Plan* (Washington: Nov. 2006), p. 94.

26. Ibid., p. 95.

27. Shaun Waterman (UPI), "New Standards to Cover Restricted Data Types," *Washington Times,* Feb. 7, 2008, p. A6.

28. 120 Stat. 1186.

29. U.S. White House Office, Office of the Press Secretary, *Memorandum for the Heads of Executive Departments and Agencies,* Subject: "Freedom of Information Act" (Jan. 21, 2009), p. 1.

30. Ibid., p. 2.

31. U.S. Department of Justice, Office of the Attorney General, *Memorandum for the Heads of Executive Departments and Agencies,* Subject: "Freedom of Information Act (FOIA)," (Mar. 19, 2009), p. 1.

32. Ibid., pp. 1–2.

33. Meredith Fuchs, general counsel, National Security Archive, Statement for the record, Senate Committee on the Judiciary, "Advancing Freedom of Information in the New Era of Responsibility," hearing, Sept. 30, 2009, Washington, D.C., pp. 4–5.

34. Carol D. Leonnig, "Over 300 Public-Records Lawsuits Filed in Obama's First Year," *Washington Post,* Jan. 27, 2010, p. A3.

35. *Federal Register,* vol. 74, Jan. 26, 2009, pp. 4669–4671.

36. *Congressional Record,* daily edition, vol. 155, Jan. 7, 2009, pp. H42–H45.

37. Peter Finn, "Justice Dept. Uses 'State Secrets' Defense," *Washington Post,* Feb. 10, 2009, p. A4; John Schwartz, "Obama Backs Off a Reversal on Secrets," *New York Times,* Feb. 10, 2009, pp. A12, A16.

38. Editorial, "New Team, Old Position," *Washington Post,* Feb. 14, 2009, p. A18.

39. Carrie Johnson, "Obama to Set Higher Bar for Keeping State Secrets," *Washington Post,* Sept. 23, 2009, pp. A1, A7; Charlie Savage, "Justice Dept. Planning to Limit Government's Use of State Secrets Privilege," *New York Times,* Sept. 23, 2009, p. A22.

40. Editorial, "An Incomplete State Secrets Fix," *New York Times,* Sept. 29, 2009, p. A34.

41. Adam Liptak, "Obama's About-Face on Detainee Photos Leads to Supreme Court," *New York Times,* Sept. 15, 2009, p. A17.

42. See 123 Stat. 2184.

43. Editorial, "The Cover-Up Continues," *New York Times,* Oct. 26, 2009, p. A20.

44. Associated Press, "Gates Blocks Photographs of Prisoners," *New York Times,* Nov. 15, 2009, p. 22.

45. Associated Press, "High Court Says U.S. May Withhold Detainee Photos," *Washington Post,* Dec. 1, 2009, p. A6; Adam Liptak, "Justices Void Order Requiring U.S. to Show Photos of Detainee Abuse," *New York Times,* Dec. 1, 2009, p. A23.

46. Editorial, "Photos and Freedom," *New York Times,* Dec. 5, 2009, p. A18.

47. Del Quentin Wilber, "Government Ordered to Release Much of What Cheney Told Leak Investigators," *Washington Post,* Oct. 2, 2009, p. A9.

48. Barton Gellman, "Cheney Was Hazy on Role in CIA Leak, FBI Notes from '04 Show," *Washington Post,* Oct. 31, 2009, p. A4; David Johnston, "In '04 Interview, Cheney Denied Role in C.I.A. Leak," *New York Times,* Oct. 31, 2009, p. A12.

49. Michael D. Shear, "White House Releases Six-Month Log of Visitors," *Washington Post,* Oct. 31, 2009, p. A4; Jeff Zeleny, "White House Visitors Log Includes Stars and C.E.O.'s," *New York Times,* Oct. 31, 2009, p. A11; Helene Cooper, "Additional Names of Visitors Are Released by White House," *New York Times,* Nov. 26, 2009, p. A22; Dan Eggen, "White House Guests Include Friend and Foe," *Washington Post,* Nov. 26, 2009, p. A2.

50. U.S. Office of Management and Budget, *Memorandum for the Heads of Executive Departments and Agencies,* Subject: "Open Government Directive" (Dec. 8, 2009).

51. U.S. Office of Management and Budget, *Open Government: A Progress Report to the American People* (Washington: Dec. 2009), available at http://www.whitehouse.gov/sites/default/files/microsites/ogi-progress-report-american-people.pdf.

52. U.S. Office of Management and Budget, *Memorandum for the Heads of Executive Departments and Agencies,* Subject: "Open Government Directive," p. 1.

53. Ibid., p. 2.

54. Ibid., pp. 7–8.

55. Ibid., p. 2.

56. Ibid., p. 3.

57. Ibid., pp. 3–4.

58. Ibid., p. 4.

59. Ibid., p. 4.

60. Ibid., p. 9.

61. Ibid., p. 10.

62. Ibid., p. 5.

63. Ibid.

64. Ibid., p. 6.

65. Aliya Sternstein, "White House Bars Agencies from Posting Some Statistics," *NextGov,* Jan. 27, 2010, available at http://www.nextgov.com/nextgov/ng_20100127_9912.php.

66. Ed O'Keefe, "Data Released Under Obama Order Criticized," *Washington Post,* Jan. 28, 2010, p. A23.

67. U.S. Office of Management and Budget, *Memorandum for the Heads of Executive Departments and Agencies,* Subject: "Open Government Directive," p. 4.

68. U.S. White House Office, Office of the Press Secretary, *Memorandum for the Heads of Executive Departments and Agencies,* Subject: "Classified Information and Controlled Unclassified Information" (May 27, 2009), p. 1.

69. U.S. Presidential Task Force on Controlled Unclassified Information, *Report and Recommendations of the Presidential Task Force on Controlled Unclassified Information* (Washington: Aug. 25, 2009), pp. 5–6.

70. Ibid., p. 6.

71. Ibid., p. 11.

72. Ibid.

73. Ibid.

74. Ibid., p. 12.

75. Ibid., p. 14.

76. Ibid.

77. Ibid., p. 16.

78. Ibid., p. 20.

79. U.S. White House Office, Office of the Press Secretary, *Memorandum for the Heads of Executive Departments and Agencies,* Subject: "Classified Information and Controlled Unclassified Information," pp. 1–2.

80. Kim Hart, "Obama Seeks Input on Classification of Records," *Washington Post,* June 27, 2009, p. A11.

81. See *Secrecy News,* vol. 2009, Sept. 29, 2009, available at http://www.fas.org with links to both the national security adviser's Sept. 2 letter and the Aug. 4 draft executive order.

82. *Federal Register,* vol. 75, Jan. 5, 2010, pp. 705–736.

83. Ibid., pp. 707, 708.

84. Ibid., p. 709.

85. Ibid.

86. Ibid., pp. 710–711.

87. Ibid., p. 712.

88. Ibid., p. 719.

89. Ibid., p. 720.

90. See Ibid., pp. 724–725.

91. Charlie Savage, "Obama Moves to Curb Secrecy with Order on Classified Documents," *New York Times,* Dec. 30, 2009, p. A18.

92. Editorial, "Classified Material," *Washington Post,* Jan. 18, 2010, p. A16.

93. Carol D. Leonnig, "Over 300 Public-Records Lawsuits Filed in Obama's First Year," p. A3.

94. *Secrecy News,* vol. 2009, Dec. 8, 2009, available at http://www.fas.org.

How Presidential NSDs Affect Access to Information

National Security Directives issued by U.S. presidential administrations can unilaterally put restrictions on information, effectively granting executive control over what the public—and Congress—is allowed to know. This report looks at the ways in which NSDs have been used by U.S. presidents over the past six decades and the efforts that have been made to force greater openness.

Vikki Gordon

National Security Directives (NSDs) are administrative instruments that the president may employ to prescribe policy for the executive branch and, in some instances, to effect national security policy change unilaterally.[1] Some other tools available to the president include executive orders, proclamations, executive agreements, and memoranda.[2]

NSDs are issued through the National Security Council (NSC), and have been employed by every president since the establishment of NSC in 1947. NSDs are usually security classified and have been called different names by different administrations. They are used by the president not only to make national security policy, but also to coordinate and manage national security policy development and implementation across the agencies and departments. President Lyndon B. Johnson described National Security Action Memoranda (as NSDs were called under his administration) as: "a formal notification to the head of a department or other government agency informing him of a presidential decision in the field of national security affairs and generally requiring follow-up action by the department or agency addressed."[3] Administrative instruments, such as executive orders, are subject to the Federal Register Act of 1935, which requires that executive orders and proclamations of "general applicability and legal effect" must be published, and provides, at a minimum, that "every document or order which prescribes a penalty has general applicability and legal effect."[4] The publishing requirement contained in the Federal Register Act is not applicable to NSDs because they have "no legal effect—they are policy declarations, which may be administratively enforceable within the executive branch—and do not prescribe penalties, at least not directly."[5] Consequently, many NSDs remain classified. Unlike executive orders or proclamations, NSDs are not typically issued under any statutory authority conferred by Congress.

This report offers some observations and insights into the character of NSDs; traces the creation and evolution of this tool of unilateral power from its inception during the Truman administration to Barack Obama's presidency; briefly discusses the role of NSDs; and outlines the challenges NSDs present to Congress's constitutionally prescribed policy making and oversight roles.

Vikki Gordon is a doctoral student at Oxford Brookes University. She is researching National Security Directives and how they have been used to unilaterally shape U.S. national security policy.

Creation and Evolution of NSDs

There have been numerous iterations of NSDs, although NSDs have been used for the same purposes over time, to make and implement policy on a wide variety of national security issues and provide guidance and coordination of the national security apparatus. However, when a new administration arrives at the White House, the labeling of NSDs has often been altered as a reflection of the individual style and NSC organizational preferences of each president.[6]

The early NSDs were developed as part of the management of decisions. They were originally a vehicle for discussion at NSC meetings under the Truman administration, and were continued by the Eisenhower administration. NSC policy papers originated from the council's members, executive secretaries, and support staff, with most coming from the Departments of State and Defense.[7] Some policy papers served as information to aid discussion, while others posited a problem or issue, analyzed it, and made recommendations.[8] Those containing policy recommendations made their way to the president, whose signature indicated approval of the proposed policy.[9]

The Kennedy administration developed the NSC policy papers into a series entitled National Security Action Memoranda (NSAM). These NSAM were used to document and communicate presidential decisions on national security policy and, in some cases, for directing the implementing actions for such policies. The NSAM also served as a vehicle for the president to request information or direct studies to be undertaken on national security issues. In later administrations, these studies formed a separate series of documents. The Johnson administration continued with the NSAM series in a similar fashion.

For the duration of Richard M. Nixon's presidency, and Gerald R. Ford's, National Security Directives took on a new name as designated in NSDM-1 (*Establishment of NSC Decision and Study Memoranda Series,* January 20, 1969). Nixon established a separate series of study papers called National Security Study Memoranda (NSSM) that began with a request for a study answering 26 questions on the war in Vietnam (*Situation in Vietnam,* NSSM-1, January 21, 1969). The reports compiled in response to a particular NSSM could then be used as a basis for the president to determine policy. The president's decision was then recorded in a National Security Decision Memorandum (NSDM) and distributed to relevant cabinet members, department leaders, and agency heads.[10]

The Carter administration renamed the two series Presidential Directives (PDs) for decisions and Presidential Review Memoranda (PRM) for studies. President Ronald W. Reagan designated his directives as National Security Decision Directives (NSDDs) and National Security Study Memoranda (NSSM). President George H. W. Bush (Bush I) renamed the two series National Security Directives (NSDs) and National Security Reviews (NSRs). During the tenure of President William J. Clinton, NSDs became Presidential Decision Directives/ National Security Council (PDD/NSC), and NSRs became Presidential Review Directives (PRDs).[11]

During the tenure of President George W. Bush (Bush II), the separate study series that had been used for the previous 40 years was eliminated, returning to the original dual purpose of the directives. He renamed these instruments National Security Presidential Directives in NSPD-1 (*Organization of the National Security Council System,* February 13, 2001). Additionally, after the establishment of the Department of Homeland Security, Bush II created a separate series of instruments called Homeland Security Presidential Directives (HSPDs). In some instances, an NSPD would simultaneously be given an HSPD number. For example, security classified NSPD-17 (*National Strategy to Combat Weapons of Mass Destruction,* September 14, 2002) was also issued in an unclassified version as HSPD-4 (December 11, 2002) with the same title.

President Barack Obama returned to the two separate series, renaming decision directives Presidential Policy Directives (PPD) and study directives Presidential Study Directives (PSD).

NSDs have been used for the same purposes over time, to make and implement national security policy and to manage and coordinate the national security apparatus. However, the change in labeling and decision to use a separate study series reflects the individual style and NSC organizational preference of each president.[12]

Role of NSDs

When presidents arrive at the White House, they are confronted with various iterations of NSDs containing "policies that their predecessors have established, which they may or may not wish to pursue, and, at the same time, confront developing events on the international stage."[13] Policy in existence when a new president arrives at the White House "must be reviewed, modified, or rescinded in considering the preconceived policy preferences and world views that the president, his advisers, and Cabinet come with to the office."[14] For example, basic national security strategy type NSDs, such as Truman's NSC-68 (April 14, 1950) or Reagan's NSDD-32 (May 20, 1982), may expound national security policy goals closely aligned to the president's world view. Typically, a review process is undertaken, usually requested through study directives that require specific questions for the addressees, or a study group, to answer and submit reports to the president by a designated time. "The reports that ensue often provide the basis for a presidential decision that is subsequently issued in the form of a NSD"[15] or the president decides to continue a policy of his predecessor. The president can also issue an NSD to rescind a policy contained in previous NSDs. In addition, NSDs are issued to respond to external events in the international environment, such as international incidents; an example would be Reagan's NSDD-102 (September 5, 1983) responding to the Soviet shooting-down of a Korean Air Lines passenger plane. They may also respond to domestic political concerns, such as congressional and public opinion.

Although NSDs are employed to confront a wide variety of national security issues, it is possible to group NSDs into a number of common themes and topics they have been used to address over time (see Figure 1).[16]

Figure 1 / National Security Directive Topics

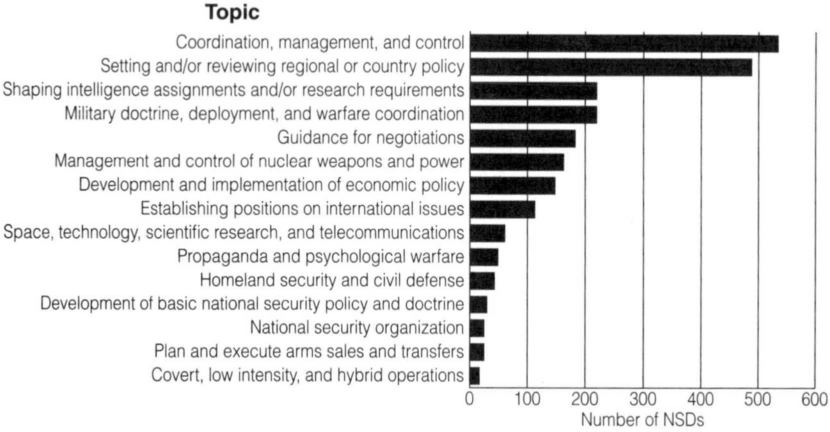

Topic

Source: Gordon, Vikki. 2009. *National Security Directives: Unilaterally Shaping U.S. National Security Policy.* Unpublished Doctoral Dissertation, Oxford Brookes University, Oxford, United Kingdom

As shown in Figure 1, NSDs have covered a variety of topics. The following example illustrates how NSDs have been used to establish policy on an issue and how NSDs may be used to modify or change the direction of a previously established policy. Additionally, the following example illustrates how an NSD may overlap more than a single topic listed in Figure 1.

In 1972 President Nixon issued NSDM-165 (*International Aspects of Weather Modification,* May 2, 1972) announcing the president's decision to continue to support international cooperation for civilian research and development in the field of weather modification, but not to encourage requests for assistance in operations from other countries where there was a "high risk of damage." In terms of climate modification, the NSDM stated:

> the U.S. shall continue research bearing on climate modification but no climate modification operation (civilian or military) shall be conducted until its total impact can be predicted with great assurance and without specific approval from the President.

The NSDM also stated, "the President has decided not to propose at this time legislation for the licensing or regulation of weather modification activities."

Later, President Ford sought international restraints on environmental warfare of this type and employed an NSD to change direction from his predecessor's policy. In NSDM-277 (*International Restraints on Environmental Warfare,* October 15, 1974), he put forward the position that:

> It is in the United States' interests to consider with the USSR restraints on the use of environmental modification techniques for military purposes, and to this end, enter into discussions with the Soviet Union to explore the possibility of such restraints.

Weather modification policy falls into the "Space, technology, scientific research, and telecommunications" category as well as the "Establishing positions on international issues" category in Figure 1.

Challenges and Implications

The use of NSDs to make national security policy poses significant challenges for Congress and, at the same time, illustrates the inherent tensions between the coequal branches of the U.S. government as well as the extent of executive power. NSDs are a tool of unilateral executive power—along with executive orders, proclamations, memoranda, and executive agreements—that enable the president to bypass the usual legislative process and establish policy that otherwise would not exist.[17] The courts have recognized the president's authority to act unilaterally in *Curtis Wright,*[18] *Pink*[19] and *Belmont,*[20] although Congress and the courts may overturn such actions. For instance, in the case of executive orders, Congress may pass legislation to overturn an executive order or it may acquiesce. Also, the courts may overturn an executive order, or certain provisions of it. However, a unique aspect of NSDs, in comparison to the other tools of unilateral action, is their generally secret nature.

The vast majority of NSDs are security classified when issued and remain so for varying amounts of time. Classification policy is prescribed unilaterally by the president through executive orders, which have been modified over time. Congress explicitly recognized the executive's authority to make classification policy in the Freedom of Information Act (FOIA)[21] in the first of the nine exemptions from the statute's rule of disclosure. The executive orders prescribing classification policy, issued since Franklin Roosevelt, have varied over time between a more expansive trend set by Truman and a more limiting trend set by Eisenhower.[22] The former provided "wider discretion to create official secrets, broader classification bases, and more restrictive declassification policy and procedures"; the latter "narrowed the bases for classification, discouraging overclassification and more rigorous declassification procedures with specific time limitations for review and declassification."[23]

Consequently, the variation in classification policy makes predicting how soon any given NSD will be declassified after issuance difficult, and significant periods can elapse before public policy is scrutinized. Indeed, the average lag time between issuance and declassification is 18 years, and lag times have varied from 9 days to more than 40 years.[24] As a result of NSDs being usually marked either "Top Secret," "Secret," or "Confidential" as per security classification policy promulgated in various executive orders over time, only those with the appropriate level of security clearance within the executive branch (often high-ranking officials) are permitted to see NSDs. Their classified status prevents most members of Congress from finding out about or accessing the information contained in any particular NSD. Since relevant congressional committees have not been routinely consulted or informed of the issuance or content of NSDs that establish and direct national policy and many years may elapse before an NSD becomes declassified and available for review, obvious questions are raised about executive accountability and the exclusion of Congress from its constitutionally mandated policy making and oversight roles. Congress cannot make timely responses to policy to which it is not privy, and requests for NSDs in the past have been met with claims of executive privilege.[25]

Indeed, during a period of heightened congressional interest in NSDs during the late 1980s following the revelation of a number of controversial policies originating in NSDs, a number of members of Congress raised concerns about the use of NSDs and some policies the Reagan administration was pursuing through them. Hearings were held concerning policies established in NSDD-84 (March 11, 1983) on safeguarding national security information[26] and NSDD-145 (September 17, 1984) on technology transfers and telecommunication.[27] These NSDs had a potentially broad domestic impact. For instance, NSDD-84 contained a provision requiring all persons with authorized access to classified information to sign a nondisclosure agreement as a condition to access. Those persons with access to Sensitive Compartmented Information (SCI)—classified information concerning or derived from intelligence sources, methods, or analytical processes[28]—were also required to sign nondisclosure agreements that included a provision for prepublication review of private writing. It also became known in 1987 that NSDs had played a role in the Iran-Contra scandal.

Hearings were held, deliberations on the potential separation of powers issues surrounding the use of NSDs took place, and remedial legislation was proposed in Congress to bring an element of control over presidential use of NSDs. Indeed, Congressman Jack Brooks (D-Texas) sponsored legislation several times to address disclosure of NSDs. The first bill Brooks introduced, on July 27, 1988, was H.R. 5092, the Presidential Directives and Records Accountability Act.[29] Brooks further cosponsored and introduced on August 2, 1990, H.R. 5438, the Presidential Directives and Records Accountability Act.[30] The last effort was made when he cosponsored, along with Lee H. Hamilton (D-Ind.), H.R. 2524, the Presidential Directives and Records Accountability Act,[31] which was introduced by John Conyers, Jr. (D-Mich.) on June 4, 1991. However, despite these actions, Congress was unable to overcome the classified status of NSDs and the executive's assertion of executive privilege, and these legislative efforts were unsuccessful.

The assertion by the executive that NSDs are privileged communications and, therefore, subject to a claim of executive privilege is part of a wider debate about congressional access to information and the balance of power between the two branches in the conduct of national security policy.

Conclusions

Since the establishment of NSC, presidents have routinely used NSDs to make national security policy. Often an NSD will record a presidential national security policy decision, set out guidelines, order implementing actions, and sometimes commit federal resources. Almost 60 percent of the NSDs available for review in the period from Kennedy to Bush I fall into one or more of these categories.[32]

The remaining NSDs address internal management issues of the executive branch and do not make substantive policy. In addition, NSDs have played a significant role in shaping U.S. national security policy. NSDs are often security classified, make foreign and military policy, and almost 20 percent of significant NSDs declassified from Kennedy to Bush I had a potentially broad domestic affect.[33] There has been an upward trend in the issuance of NSDs with a potentially broad domestic impact, such as NSDD-84, since the Reagan administration. The domestic aspect of some NSDs is particularly troublesome to Congress as it makes the need for effective congressional oversight more critical to assure accountability and the protection of civil liberties.

Classification of NSDs and the executive branch's unwillingness to routinely share them with Congress, even though Congress has established procedures for the protection of classified information, raises fundamental questions about the balance of power between the two coequal branches.

Notes

1. Gordon, Vikki. 2007. "Unilaterally Shaping U.S. National Security Policy: The Role of National Security Directives." *Presidential Studies Quarterly,* 37(2): 347–367. p. 349.

2. See generally Cooper, Philip. 2002. *By Order of the President: The Use and Abuse of Executive Direct Action* (University Press of Kansas); Howell, William G. 2003. *Power Without Persuasion: The Politics of Direct Presidential Action* (Princeton University Press); Mayer, Kenneth. 2001. *With the Stroke of a Pen: Executive Orders and Presidential Power* (Princeton University Press).

3. Cooper, Philip. 2002. p. 144.

4. 44 USC 1505.

5. Gordon, Vikki. 2009. "National Security Directives: Unilaterally Shaping U.S. National Security Policy." Unpublished Doctoral Dissertation, Oxford Brookes University, Oxford, United Kingdom.

6. Ibid.

7. Relyea, Harold C. 2005. *Presidential Directives: Background and Overview.* CRS Report 98-611 GOV (January 7, 2005), p. 8.

8. Cooper, Philip. 2002. p. 146.

9. Falk, Stanley F. 1964. "The National Security Council Under Truman, Eisenhower and Kennedy," *Political Science Quarterly* 79: 403–34, cited in Relyea, Harold C. 2005. p.9.

10. Relyea, Harold C. 2005. p. 9

11. Relyea, Harold C. 2005. p. 9

12. Gordon, Vikki. 2009.

13. Ibid.

14. Ibid.

15. Ibid.

16. See Gordon, Vikki. 2007. "Unilaterally Shaping U.S. National Security Policy: The Role of National Security Directives," *Presidential Studies Quarterly,* 37(2): 347–367, 353–361. Also, Cooper, Philip. 2002.

17. Howell, William G. 2003. *Power Without Persuasion: The Politics of Direct Presidential Action* (Princeton University Press), p. 13.

18. United States v. Curtiss-Wright Exporting Corp. 299 U.S. 304 (1936).

19. United States v. Pink, 315 U.S. 203 (1942).

20. United States v. Belmont, 301 U.S. 324 (1937).

21. FOIA as amended, 5 U.S.C. § 552

22. Gordon, Vikki. 2010. "National Security Directive Declassification." *Government Information Quarterly,* Special Issue on Open Government, forthcoming.

23. Gordon, Vikki. 2009.

24. Based on those NSDs available for review from Kennedy to Bush II with classification markings present. Gordon, Vikki. 2009.

25. U.S. House of Representatives. 1988. Hearing Before a Subcommittee of the Committee on Government Operations, *Presidential Directives and Records Accountability Act,* 100th Cong., 2nd Sess.

26. U.S. Senate. 1984. Hearing Before the Senate Committee on Governmental Affairs.

27. *National Security Decision Directive 84,* 98th Cong., 1st Sess.

28. Congressional hearings on H.R. 145 and NSDD-145 on February 25 and 26 and on March 17, 1987, by the Subcommittee on Legislation and National Security of the House Committee on Government Operations. Joint hearings were also held on February 26, 1987, by the Subcommittee on Science, Research, and Technology, and the Subcommittee on Transportation, Aviation, and Materials of the House Committee on Science, Space, and Technology.

29. Director of Central Intelligence Directive 1/19, 1995, *Security Policy for Sensitive Compartmented Information and Security Policy Manual,* March 1.

30. 100th Cong., 2nd Sess.

31. 101st Cong., 2nd Sess.

32. 102nd Cong., 1st Sess.

33. Based on research undertaken for the author's Ph.D. thesis. Gordon, Vikki. 2009.

34. Based on research undertaken for the author's Ph.D. thesis. Gordon, Vikki. 2009.

Libraries and Social Networking—
Finding New Ways to Connect

Erin Dorney

Social networking sites have been used by public, special, school, and academic libraries throughout the world with varied success for the past four or five years. Most consider social networking sites to be Web 2.0 tools; Internet applications for which users are actively engaged in creating and distributing content. These sites allow libraries and librarians to create profiles, acquire "friends," build networks, and explore connections that exist between people. Many have found that by embracing these technologies, libraries can reach new users, engage more effectively with users, and enhance library services by providing opportunities for feedback and interaction.

Social networking services on the Web give individuals and institutions a platform to share information and connect with like-minded entities. Users sign up and enter information about themselves (likes, dislikes, interests, activities, profession, geographic location, and so forth), resulting in a personal "profile," which may or may not include images, a collection of links, space for public comment, and additional services. Once they are members, users are given the ability to expose themselves to people with similar interests or characteristics and make selective contact. Access to social networking Web sites is possible across the spectrum of electronic communication—through home computers, laptops and netbooks, personal digital assistants (PDAs), smartphones (iPhone, Blackberry, Droid), and cell phones.

Social networking sites have experienced an explosion in growth since their inception, particularly during the past few years. For example, Facebook.com grew from 12 million active users in 2006 to 100 million in 2008 and to more than 350 million by late 2009 (Facebook, 2009).

Typical Library Social Networks

While the number of social networking sites seems endless, ranging from general to specialized networks, library involvement can be most frequently found on Facebook.com, MySpace.com, and Twitter.com. However, numerous others are in use, including Friendster.com, Bebo.com, LinkedIn.com, Orkut.com, and Ning.com, all offering the opportunity for users to develop their own social network.

In a 2009 study by Curtis Rogers of the South Carolina State Library, 545 library staff members from across the United States answered questions about use of Web 2.0 and social media tools. More than half of the respondents came from public libraries and more than 20 percent from academic libraries. Out of

Erin Dorney is Outreach Librarian at Millersville University of Pennsylvania. She holds an MS in library and information studies with an advanced certificate in digital libraries from Syracuse University and is earning an MA in English from West Chester University of Pennsylvania. She blogs at http://www.libraryscenester.wordpress.com, where her topics include outreach, marketing, academic libraries, next-gen librarianship, and LIS students.

531 respondents to the question "My library uses the following Web 2.0 applications to promote and market library services," social networks (374) and blogs (322) were the highest on the list. Respondents also rated their perception of each application's effectiveness in achieving marketing or promotional goals. On a scale from 1 to 5 (with 5 being very effective), social networks ranked highest with an average of 3.36. Additionally, only 7.3 percent of all respondents said that Web 2.0 tools were unimportant.

In the same survey, respondents were asked to select which Web 2.0 and social media tools their libraries were using from a list of 26 options. The tool most widely used was Facebook at 74.7 percent, followed by blogging tools at 53.1 percent, with Twitter in third place at 50 percent (Rogers, 2009).

Facebook.com

Facebook was created in 2004 by Mark Zuckerberg, a psychology student at Harvard. Membership was initially open to Harvard students only, but grew to 5.5 million active users in 2005 after the site was opened to other schools, and to 12 million active users in 2006 after membership was opened to anyone with a registered e-mail address. Current memberships tops 350 million active users (Facebook, 2009). Although Facebook is a privately owned and operated company—Facebook, Inc.—the site began, and has remained, free of charge to users; profits are gained through advertising revenue. According to Compete, a Web analytics company, Facebook surpassed MySpace in terms of unique monthly visitors in January 2009 to become the top-ranked social network, with Twitter coming in at number three (Kazeniac, 2009).

Once a member, a user can input information to create profiles with photos, personal activities and interests, and contact information. Communication between Facebook "friends" takes place via private or public messages or an internal chat feature. Recently, in order to combat growing concerns about privacy, Facebook enabled users to choose their own privacy settings. These settings restrict who can see what parts of a user's personal profile.

Another popular use of Facebook is to create and join interest and fan groups or pages, some of which are maintained by organizations as a means of advertising. In addition to personal profiles, Facebook allows the creation of pages for places, products, services, stores, restaurants, bars, clubs, organizations, politicians, government officials, nonprofits, television shows, films, games, sports teams, celebrities, public figures, musicians, and Web sites.

A typical library Facebook Fan Page (one of the most popular library presences within social networking sites) includes a logo or image, address, hours, phone numbers, and the library's Web address. Depending on settings, other features may include a list of fans (social network users who have identified themselves as "fans" of the library), video clips, photographs, calendars, and reports or announcements of events. RSS feeds can also be fed directly into Facebook Fan Pages to dynamically update content with little upkeep. Additionally, many libraries and vendors have created "widgets" (stand-alone applications that can be embedded into third-party sites) featuring such functions as catalog searching, chat reference, and database searching. Among these widgets are WorldCat, JSTOR, Google Calendar, LibGuides, and Meebo. While these features may seem to replicate the library Web site, providing information within social networks instead of requiring users to search elsewhere has proven beneficial for many institutions.

Libraries have found social networking channels such as Facebook to be powerful tools for promotion and extension of library services, resources, and events. This includes providing research and reference help, reader's advisory, and community, cultural, and technological programming. Some libraries have utilized Facebook photo galleries to share collections of historic photos or coverage of library renovation projects with users. Libraries and users have the ability to post short videos of library events (often captured on FlipCams or smart phones). Additionally, Facebook pages provide an opportunity to solicit input from library users on such matters as acquisitions, hours, and programming details. When libraries actively monitor and participate in these Facebook-facilitated discussions, learning opportunities develop that contribute to good customer service and the fulfillment of information needs.

Libraries of all types are using Facebook effectively. Among them:

Public Libraries

- DeKalb County (Georgia) Public Library (http://www.facebook.com/dekalblibrary)
- Hennepin County (Minnesota) Library (http://www.facebook.com/hclib)
- Houston (Texas) Public Library (http://www.facebook.com/houstonlibrary)

Academic Libraries

- Harvard Law School Library (http://www.facebook.com/hlslib)
- University of Warwick Library, Coventry, England (http://www.facebook.com/WarwickUniLibrary)
- Duke University Law Library (http://www.facebook.com/dukelawlibrary)
- Michigan State University Libraries (http://www.facebook.com/msu.libraries)

Special Libraries

- Library of Congress (http://www.facebook.com/libraryofcongress)
- Eisenhower Presidential Library and Museum (http://www.facebook.com/pages/Abilene-KS/Eisenhower-Presidential-Library-and-Museum/120299890054)
- Ateneo School of Medicine and Public Health Library (http://www.facebook.com/pages/Pasig-Philippines/Ateneo-School-of-Medicine-and-Public-Health-Library/112449867908)

School Libraries

- The Unquiet Library: Creekview High School Media Center, Canton, Georgia (http://www.facebook.com/pages/Canton-GA/The-Unquiet-Library-Creekview-High-School-Media-Center/31676317923)
- Castilleja School Library, Palo Alto, California (http://www.facebook.com/pages/Palo-Alto-CA/Castilleja-School-Library/128789371278)

- Rainier (Washington) High School Library (http://www.facebook.com/
pages/Rainier-WA/Rainier-High-School-Library/126261583655)

Twitter.com

Created in 2006 by Jack Dorsey and gaining worldwide popularity, Twitter is a "microblogging" and social networking tool that allows users to exchange "tweets" (messages of 140 characters or less). Tweets are displayed on the user's profile page and are delivered to the user's subscribers (known as "followers"). Privacy settings allow users to restrict their tweets to approved friends only or to display them for the entire Twitter population. As with Facebook, many organizations and corporations have joined Twitter to provide an additional method of exposure and advertising. Corporations in particular have adopted the practice of monitoring tweets about their products and services, finding that the ability to respond to and remedy complaints and misunderstandings improves word-of-mouth marketing and customer experience.

A 2009 study by market research firm Pear Analytics of 2,000 tweets separated content into six major categories: pointless babble (40.55 percent), conversational (37.55 percent), pass-along value (8.70 percent), self-promotion (5.85 percent), spam (3.75 percent), and news (3.60 percent) (Kelly, 2009). However, social networking researcher danah boyd urges users and critics to appreciate Twitter for its important contribution to social grooming and awareness (boyd, 2009).

Once libraries have created a Twitter account (featuring an image, a Web site link, location, and a brief "bio"), it can post updates, follow and view updates from other users, and send public replies or private direct messages to connect with other Twitter users. Utilizing third-party services, users can also send images and videos (sometimes directly from their cell phone or smart phone) and shorten lengthy URLS. In addition, Twitter and many other social networking sites (including Facebook and most blogging platforms) integrate fairly seamlessly, allowing updates to be "pushed out" to other platforms simultaneously. Tweets can even be integrated into library home pages to provide dynamic content.

Twitter is frequently used as an outreach channel for libraries of all kinds, including news posts regarding special events, announcements, holiday hours, exhibits, displays, and new materials arrivals. Libraries can also tweet about update resources and new service roll-outs, using the service as a free public relations/marketing tool. Twitter has additional benefits as a multi-directional communication channel; not only can users see what the library is tweeting about, they can tweet back in response. Depending on whether these communications are private or public, others can see the discussion and add their thoughts, providing an avenue for feedback and participation. Users can ask questions using Twitter, resulting in another access point for reference and research support. And with an increased focus on remaining relevant in the age of Google, libraries can use Twitter for customer service, monitoring the conversation and providing solutions for unsatisfactory experiences.

Libraries actively using Twitter include:

Public Libraries

- Skokie (Illinois) Public Library (http://www.twitter.com/skokielibrary)
- Park Ridge (Illinois) Public Library (http://www.twitter.com/prpl)
- Lester Public Library, Two Rivers, Wisconsin (http://www.twitter.com/lesterpublic)

Academic Libraries

- Kansas State Libraries (http://www.twitter.com/kstatelibraries)
- University of Illinois at Urbana-Champaign Undergraduate Library (http://www.twitter.com/askundergrad)
- University of Southern California Libraries (http://www.twitter.com/USC Libraries)

Special Libraries

- Smithsonian Institution Libraries (http://www.twitter.com/silibraries)
- Peace Palace Library, The Hague, Netherlands (http://www.twitter.com/peacepalace)
- Massachusetts Public Law Libraries (http://www.twitter.com/masslawlib)

School Libraries

- New Trier High School Library, Winnetka, Illinois (http://www.twitter.com/newtrierlibrary)
- Hillside Junior High School Library, Boise, Idaho (http://www.twitter.com/HillsideLibrary)
- Skyline High School Library, Longmont, Colorado (http://www.twitter.com/SkylineLibrary)

MySpace.com

MySpace is a social networking Web site owned by Rupert Murdoch's News Corporation (parent company of Fox Broadcasting and numerous other media enterprises). Created in 2003, the site was initially popular with musicians as an avenue to distribute music, photographs, and other information to fans without the need to develop an entire Web site. Similar to Facebook, MySpace is free to use and generates profit through advertising revenue.

After registering, users can input personal information into sections including "About Me," "Who I'd Like to Meet," "Interests," and "Details." Users can also set their "mood" using emoticons to indicate how they are feeling and upload images to use as their profile picture and store in online photo galleries. Blogging features are also available, and users can leave messages in a comments section similar to a Facebook "wall post." MySpace, while sharing many features with Facebook, allows more personal control over the "look and feel" of user profiles. Whereas most social networking interfaces enjoy a consistent graphical layout, MySpace gives users the power to customize layout and colors with very little HTML or Web development experience.

Many libraries have created MySpace pages as a part of their social networking presence online. In addition to providing channels of outreach discussed above, MySpace seems to be particularly popular with teen audiences, lending itself well to interactive teen spaces. Library involvement also gives teens opportunities to learn how to be smart and safe when using Web technology.

Some libraries use their MySpace pages to promote the library, posting bulletins and blog entries with news, updates, and programming details. Library hours changes are often posted, along with publicity for contests and events. Page administrators can integrate Twitter accounts to post updates on MySpace and set up widgets for catalog searching, instant messaging and other chat services, and databases (usually requiring user authentication). Games and YouTube and other video snippets can be integrated into a MySpace page as well.

However, many early MySpace adopters are transitioning to other social networks or simply letting their MySpace profiles die. According to global information services company Experian, MySpace saw a 55 percent drop in users between September 2008 and September 2009 (Experian Hitwise, 2009). This decrease is visible within the library environment as well, with many MySpace library profiles now defunct, riddled with spam, or removed altogether.

However, there are successful and continuing MySpace library sites, among them:

Public Libraries

- Carnegie Library Pittsburgh Teen Department (http://www.myspace.com/clpteens)
- Denver Public Library (http://www.myspace.com/denver_evolver)
- Cudahy (Wisconsin) Family Library (http://www.myspace.com/cudahy libraryteens)

Academic Libraries

- Brooklyn College Library, Brooklyn, New York (http://www.myspace.com/brooklyncollegelibrary)
- Bryant University Library, Smithfield, Rhode Island (http://www.myspace.com/bryantuniversitylibrary)
- Mohawk College Library, Hamilton, Ontario (http://www.myspace.com/mohawkcollegelibrary)

Meeting Users Where They Are

Online presences on social networks such as Facebook, Twitter, and MySpace allow libraries and library workers to communicate with users in a comfortable and familiar environment. Those born between 1982 and 2000 (the "Millennial" generation, also known as "Generation Y") are reaching school and college age and have increasingly high expectations about technology (Howe and Strauss, 2000). Many of these 10- to 28-year-olds—having grown up with cell phones, text messaging, and the Internet—consider social networking sites a part of daily life. Libraries have capitalized on these expectations and abilities and tailored their outreach methods to reach them.

The Young Adult Library Services Association (YALSA), a division of the American Library Association (ALA), has created a toolkit for libraries, "Teens and Social Networking in School and Public Libraries." As benefits of social networking, YALSA cites teen empowerment, improvement of text-based literacy skills, and opportunities for creation and collaboration, community service, and communication (Young Adult Library Services Association, 2009). Clearly, there are educational benefits in this emerging, non-traditional form of communicating.

Brand Awareness and Public Perception

When current library users become a "fan" of a library page, or tweet a question to a library Twitter account, the viral nature of word-of-mouth marketing comes into play. Some libraries have found that these sorts of connections can attract potential library users and encourage them to seek out more information on library services, resources, and events, increasing the library's audience and impact. Many libraries are realizing the importance of managing their public image, and monitoring social networks is an easy way to see what users have to say. While corporate entities are responding to negative publicity via social networks to improve their financial bottom line, libraries have an opportunity to increase their relevance, use, and public perception. The conversational and participatory nature of social networks allows communication to flow both ways, and many libraries view them as useful tools that help create a more meaningful relationship between libraries and their patrons. By investing users in the process of shaping the future of libraries, libraries solidify their own future by improving public perception and relevance.

Professional Development

In addition to libraries using social networks as an outreach tool and for user interaction, many librarians are using social networking sites for professional development. Most conferences (including the ALA Annual Conference, the Association of College and Research Libraries Conference, and Computers in Libraries) have some kind of social networking aspect attached to them. For example, librarians create Facebook "events" to RSVP to social gatherings and meet-ups. Another popular use of social networking at conferences is the creation of a Twitter "hashtag" (a word preceded by a hash mark) that acts as a tag to group together tweets on a similar topic. Hashtags are then searchable and can be viewed by other conference attendees (in different sessions or those who are at home) and archived for future reference. In addition to participating in the physical aspects of a conference or professional development activity, social networks allow librarians to participate virtually, often on-the-go through smartphone technology.

Many librarian interest groups are available through social networking sites and are convenient for communication and collaboration between colleagues who are geographically widespread. Sharing of information that once took place internally has expanded to listservs and is now available through Facebook, Twitter, and other services to an enormous audience. In addition, many national, regional, state, and local professional associations have created pages, profiles, and groups on social networking sites. One example is ALA, which has an "official" MySpace page to update and interact with members and potential members. Such presence enables these organizations to communicate with their constituents, keep a finger on the pulse of trends and attitudes in order to offer relevant support and services, and identify library advocates.

Library Vendors

Library vendors have embraced social networking for a number of reasons. Vendors typically post product information, event dates and details, photos, search widgets, tutorials, job postings, and free trial and representative-contact information. Credo Reference (http://www.facebook.com/credoreference) engages fans via Facebook and Twitter with daily questions that stem from resources held within their database. This is a particularly positive example, as Credo is providing users (in this case, librarians) with the opportunity to engage in conversation surrounding information without pushing for a sale. Other library vendors on social networking sites include LexisNexis Academic (http://www. facebook.com/pages/LexisNexis-Academic-Library-Solutions/61433792931), Brodart Books (http://www.twitter.com/BrodartPulse), EBSCO Publishing (http:// www.twitter.com/EBSCOPublishing), and JSTOR (http://www.facebook.com/ JSTOR.org).

Social Networking Concerns

While many libraries, professional organizations, and vendors have embraced social networking, concerns remain. Some wonder if libraries are invading patrons' space by creating a presence there. A 2008 survey of 366 Valparaiso University freshmen revealed that while most students would be accepting of library contact through social networking, a sizable minority reacted negatively to the concept, citing spamming and a desire to keep academic and personal life separate (Connell, 2009). Other libraries question jumping on the social networking bandwagon simply because it's a popular thing to do. Social networking advocates recommend using tools such as Facebook, MySpace, and Twitter only after first conducting an in-depth review of community standards (what services library patrons are using, how well they adapt to new technologies) and staff comfort level (critical factors are enthusiasm and willingness to engage).

Privacy has always been an issue with social networking. There is concern about third-party data collection, identity theft, hacking and phishing schemes, and viruses. Based on a strong history of intellectual freedom, libraries in particular are sensitive to the idea of storing personal data on remote systems. Technology is another issue, as some social sites may conflict with security settings or bog down processing time by requiring large amounts of bandwidth and computer memory.

Not all libraries have embraced this new form of communication. Some school and public libraries block or filter social networking sites for various reasons, among them student distraction, misunderstandings about use, and the difficulty of exerting control. Other institutions have regulated the use of social sites by their employees.

Guidelines and Best Practices

Although there are no official rules for libraries using social networks (aside from the terms of service of any third-party site), there are many guidelines and best practices, often referred to as "netiquette." For example, librarians from Penn State recommended that institutions avoid "aggressive friending," opting for more subtle publicity such as mentioning the social networking presence during instruction and reference interactions (Mack, Behler, Roberts, and Rimland, 2007). This allows users to determine the amount of privacy that will allow them to remain comfortable. Many librarians also stress that libraries need to actively engage users with the content facilitated through social networking sites. According to Marshall Breeding, director for innovative technologies and research at Vanderbilt University, "It's easy to set up a Twitter account and put out the first tweet or two on behalf of your library. It requires a commitment of resources to ensure a steady stream of interesting content over a sustained period" (Breeding, 2009). Determining what libraries want to accomplish with their social networking presence is essential.

Current Trends

While most social networking began via Web interface, many users are now creating and consuming content on mobile platforms. A 2009 Pew Internet and American Life Project study revealed that 75 percent of teens and 93 percent of adults ages 18–29 now have cell phones (Lenhart, Purcell, Smith, and Zickuhr, 2010). While social networking opened up new lines of communication worldwide, without the constraints of location, users desire local connections as well. A new breed of social networking has emerged called geosocial networking, in which geolocation technology enables location-specific networks to connect. Users can identify themselves as a particular location and geosocial networking sites will tell them what is in the area; whether any of their social networking friends or followers are nearby; and, in some cases, provide activity or venue recommendations.

One popular geosocial networking application is Dennis Crowley's "Foursquare." Not only does the application embrace the typical geosocial features; it turns networking into a game in which users are awarded points for visiting a new place, going out often, and inputting additional information. The addition of a competitive aspect has potential to draw a wide range of users immersed in the gaming lifestyle. For libraries, this may be an interesting tool to add to existing social networking repertoires. Geosocial networking applications like Foursquare enable libraries to add their institution as a place (including hours), add tags (movies, books, and so forth), and add details of special events. Some libraries are also experimenting with setting up contests within Foursquare for their users, awarding prizes to those who "check in" to the library most often. Even if geosocial networking is simply the next technology fad, it is an additional example of libraries meeting user information needs where they are.

Conclusion

The Pew Internet and American Life Project reports that both teen and adult use of social networking has increased significantly, with 73 percent of "wired" American teens now using social networking Web sites (up from 55 percent in November 2006) and 47 percent of online adults (up from 37 percent in November 2008) (Lenhart et al., 2010). While social networking sites continue to develop and gain steam, libraries will likely continue to identify and use unique opportunities to reach both users and current non-users. For the most part free both of cost and of advanced technology requirements, social networking has led to acquiring new library patrons, developing powerful reach and impact, and opening up lines of communication for a more interactive and empowering library experience.

Sources

boyd, d. (2009, August 16). "Twitter: 'Pointless Babble' or Peripheral Awareness + Social Grooming?" Message posted to http://www.zephoria.org/thoughts/archives/2009/08/16/twitter_pointle.html.

Breeding, M. (2009). "Social Networking Strategies for Professionals." *Computers in Libraries,* 29(9), 29–31.

Connell, R. S. (2009). "Academic Libraries, Facebook and MySpace, and Student Outreach: A Survey of Student Opinion." *portal: Libraries and the Academy,* 9(1), 25–36. Retrieved from http://muse.jhu.edu/journals/portal_libraries_and_the_academy/v009/9.1.connell.pdf.

Experian Hitwise (2009, October 9). "Facebook Visits Increased 194 Percent in Past Year." Retrieved from http://www.hitwise.com/us/press-center/press-releases/social-networking-sept-09.

Facebook (2009). Timeline. Retrieved from http://www.facebook.com/press/info.php?statistics#/press/info.php?timeline.

Howe, N. and Strauss, W. (2000). *Millennials Rising: The Next Great Generation* (Vintage).

Kazeniac, A. (2009, February 9). "Social Networks: Facebook Takes Over Top Spot, Twitter Climbs." Message posted to http://blog.compete.com/2009/02/09/facebook-myspace-twitter-social-network.

Kelly, R. (2009). "Twitter Study Reveals Interesting Results About Usage." Retrieved from http://www.pearanalytics.com/wp-content/uploads/2009/08/Twitter-Study-August-2009.pdf.

Lenhart, A., Purcell, K., Smith, A., and Zickuhr, K. (2010). "Social Media and Young Adults: Social Media and Mobile Internet Use Among Teens and

Young Adults." Pew Internet and American Life Project. Retrieved from http://www.pewinternet.org/Reports/2010/Social-Media-and-Young-Adults. aspx?r=1.

Mack, D., Behler, A., Roberts, B., and Rimland, E. (2007). "Reaching Students with Facebook: Data and Best Practices." *Electronic Journal of Academic and Special Librarianship,* 8(2). Retrieved from http://southernlibrarianship. icaap.org/content/v08n02/mack_d01.html.

Rogers, C. (2009). "Social Media, Libraries, and Web 2.0: How American Libraries Are Using New Tools for Public Relations and to Attract New Users." Retrieved from http://www.statelibrary.sc.gov/docs/social_media_survey 2009.pdf.

Young Adult Library Services Association (2009). *Teens and Social Networking in School and Public Libraries: A Toolkit for Librarians and Library Workers.* Retrieved from http://www.ala.org/ala/mgrps/divs/yalsa/aboutyalsa/ Handouts/SocialNetworkingTool.pdf.

Federal Agency and Federal Library Reports

Library of Congress

10 First St. S.E., Washington, DC 20540
202-707-5000
World Wide Web http://www.loc.gov

James H. Billington
Librarian of Congress

Founded in 1800, the Library of Congress is the nation's oldest federal cultural institution and the largest library in the world, with nearly 145 million items in various languages, disciplines, and formats. As the world's largest repository of knowledge and creativity, the library's mission is to make its resources available and useful to the U.S. Congress and the American people and to sustain and preserve a universal collection of knowledge and creativity for future generations. The library serves Congress and the nation both on-site in its reading rooms on Capitol Hill and through its award-winning Web site, http://www.loc.gov.

Legislative Support to Congress

Serving Congress is the library's highest priority, particularly in the area of legislative support. During the past year, the library's Congressional Research Service (CRS) provided Congress with current, objective research and analysis relevant to national security and military law, the economy, energy policy, the H1N1 influenza pandemic, financial reform, healthcare reform, unemployment compensation, employment and training, food safety, climate change, and the continuing situations in Iraq and Afghanistan.

CRS responded to more than 870,000 research requests from Congress. In July it successfully launched the Mercury request and research management tool, which replaces its legacy Inquiry Status Tracking System for congressional requests.

More than a decade after its inception, the Legislative Information System (LIS), developed solely for use by Congress and congressional staff members, continued to provide access to information on past and current legislation through all facets of the lawmaking process. A multi-year project was launched

Report compiled by Audrey Fischer, Public Affairs Specialist, Library of Congress.

to develop a new strategic direction for LIS and identify enhancement opportunities. The project will involve CRS and other Library of Congress stakeholders as well as such external partners as the House Clerk's Office and the secretary of the Senate. CRS launched a redesigned Web site in September 2009 to facilitate congressional access to CRS products, services, and experts.

The Law Library of Congress—the world's largest law library, comprising 2.6 million items—provided Congress with comprehensive international, comparative, and foreign law research based on the most current information available. During 2009 law library staff wrote 611 legal research reports, special studies, and memoranda in response to congressional inquiries.

The *Global Legal Monitor,* a continually updated online publication that covers legal news and developments worldwide, continued to be a popular page on the law library's Web site. The law library launched a redesigned Web site for Congress in January 2009 to facilitate access to online legal resources.

The Global Legal Information Network (GLIN) provided Congress and other participating parliamentary bodies with more than 170,000 laws, judicial decisions, and related legal materials contributed by 34 member nations and international organizations. The use of digital certification was implemented during the year to authenticate the integrity of legal texts found in the database. In an effort to expand its online resources, the law library began offering "blawgs" (legal blogs) on its public Web site. This important new format for publishing legal opinion and commentary offers more than 100 titles covering a broad cross section of legal topics.

The Copyright Office provided policy advice and technical assistance to Congress on important copyright laws and such related issues as statutory licenses for satellite carriers, orphan works (copyrighted works whose owners are unknown or cannot be located), and public performance rights for sound recordings broadcast over the air. In March 2009 the Register of Copyrights submitted a report to Congress analyzing changes in costs arising from the reengineering of the Copyright Office and the introduction of an integrated system for processing copyright applications, including electronic filing. The report recommended changes to fees for copyright services, effective August 1. A complete list of fees is available on the Copyright Office Web site at http://www.copyright.gov.

Inaugural Support

On January 20, 2009, Barack Obama was sworn to office as the nation's first African American president. The former senator from Illinois, who referenced his presidential predecessor Abraham Lincoln throughout his campaign, took the oath of office on the same Bible used by Lincoln for his swearing-in on March 4, 1861. The Lincoln inaugural Bible, which is housed in the library's Rare Book and Special Collections Division, is an 1853 King James translation printed by Oxford University Press, and was probably ordered by then-Supreme Court Clerk William Thomas Carroll for justices officiating at such events; Carroll certified that the Bible was the one upon which Supreme Court Justice Roger Brooke Taney swore Lincoln to office. The Lincoln Bible received special conservation treatment in the library's Preservation Directorate prior to the Obama inaugural.

The library also made available to members of Congress rare Bibles from its collections for their swearing-in ceremonies at the Capitol on January 6, 2009.

Security

Keeping the library's staff members, patrons, facilities, and collections secure remained a high priority in 2009. The focus was placed on enhancing the Emergency Preparedness Program, improving security at the library's Capitol Hill buildings and outlying facilities, and expanding staff security awareness.

In coordination with other agencies on Capitol Hill and elsewhere, the library continued upgrading its emergency preparedness capabilities, facilities security, and internal controls that safeguard the library's collections. Before the library's occupancy of Modules 3 and 4 at its Fort Meade, Maryland, book storage facility, primary and secondary intrusions systems and closed-circuit television coverage were installed in the cold storage areas.

The Office of Security and Emergency Preparedness continued to conduct building evacuation and shelter-in-place drills at all eight of the library's facilities. A new Continuity of Operations (COOP) Management Relocation site was designated where key library personnel can operate in the event that Capitol Hill facilities are compromised. To facilitate emergency communications with staff, the library implemented a Web-based virtual operations center (WebEOC) and a mass-alert notification system (through Everbridge Aware).

The Information Technology (IT) Security Program ensures that the library's mission-critical systems are reliable and secure and that the technology infrastructure that supports these systems is uncompromised. The library's technology infrastructure includes three data centers, more than 350 servers, 250 library-wide systems and applications, 9,500 voice connections, 14,000 data network connections, 5,000 workstations, and 1,000 local printers. Library staff members completed the mandatory annual IT Security-Awareness Training.

The long-planned merger of the Library of Congress Police with the U.S. Capitol Police was fully implemented on September 29, 2009, in accordance with P.L. 110-178.

Strategic Planning

The Librarian of Congress launched his fiscal 2009–2010 management agenda in July, calling for a library-wide approach to updating the institution's strategic plan. The library is also developing coordinated plans to manage its information technology as a shared organizational resource. Other areas under review are human capital management (employees' skills), facilities management, Web site content management, and the acquisition and management of electronic works through mandatory deposit.

The management agenda addresses the findings of a number of internal management-related studies, including a report from a committee on strategic direction, an Office of the Inspector General report on information technology strategic planning, and a library-wide employee survey. The effort will allow the library's executive committee to continue to strengthen library programs, ensure timely decision making, properly allocate resources, and enhance accountability.

Budget

During fiscal year (FY) 2009, the library operated under two continuing resolutions from October 1, 2008, until March 11, 2009, when the president signed the Omnibus Appropriations Act, 2009 (P.L. 111-8). The act provided an appropriation for the library of $646.7 million, including authority to spend up to $39.7 million in offsetting receipts.

Development

During FY 2009 the library's fund-raising activities brought in a total of $14.6 million, representing 661 gifts from 498 donors. Those gifts, including $1.8 million received through the library's Planned Giving Program, were made to 72 separate library funds. The library forged partnerships with 176 first-time donors; these new donors gave $7.1 million, representing 51 percent of the gifts received during the year.

Ten new gift and trust funds were established, including two funds to support the World Digital Library. A $3 million grant from the Qatar Foundation will provide general support and help to include materials from the Central Library of the Qatar Foundation, and a $2 million grant from the Carnegie Corporation will support work with Uganda, South Africa, Central Asia, and the Caucasus.

The James Madison Council—the library's first private sector advisory group—continued to provide substantial support for a number of initiatives. Gifts from Madison Council members in FY 2009 totaled $2 million, bringing the council's total support since 1990 to $190 million. Private gifts supported a variety of new and continuing initiatives throughout the library, including exhibitions, acquisitions, and symposia and other scholarly programs. Private donors gave more than $1.2 million to support the 2009 National Book Festival and $3.9 million in cash and pledges to create a "residential scholars center" to provide a convenient home for scholarly discourse in the nation's capital.

Educational Outreach

At a number of forums throughout the year, members of the library's education outreach staff demonstrated the potential for digital resources to enhance curriculum and spark critical thinking in the classroom. On March 16, 2009, the library sponsored a forum titled "American Education in the Digital Age and Beyond: A Discussion for the 21st Century" in partnership with the group Strong American Schools (whose mission is "to educate Americans on the state of the U.S. public education system and urge them to become advocates for improving the nation's schools") and the Bill and Melinda Gates Foundation. The program included presentations from the library's Teaching with Primary Sources (TPS) program, which instructs educators on how to use the library's online primary source materials in the classroom.

In late June the library and the International Society for Technology in Education (ISTE) hosted a "21st Century Learning with Technology" reception at the library for more than 800 K–12 educators attending ISTE's National Education Computing Conference. The event featured the launch of TPS Direct, a free online professional-development database to aid educators in learning to use digital resources in the classroom.

The library's new Web site for teacher resources, the Teachers Page, was launched in 2009 at http://www.loc.gov/teachers. Primary source presentations on Abraham Lincoln and the Jamestown colony were added to the site. Web presentations were developed to provide educators with ideas for teaching with specific Library of Congress primary source collections. These included "The African-American Odyssey," "The Samuel F. B. Morse Papers," and "The Alfred Whital Stern Collection of Lincolniana."

Literacy Promotion

With its network of affiliates in all 50 states and more than 80 organizational partners, the Center for the Book in the Library of Congress promotes books, reading, libraries, and literacy.

One of the center's activities is the National Book Festival. At the 2009 festival, children's author Jon Scieszka, the library's 2008–2009 National Ambassador for Young People's Literature, announced a new literacy initiative, the "Exquisite Corpse Adventure." This ongoing story, to be written and illustrated by a host of children's authors and illustrators, is featured on the library's new literacy promotion Web site at http://www.read.gov, which also debuted at the book festival.

The library opened a Young Readers Center in the Thomas Jefferson Building on October 23, 2009. Visitors can choose to read a book from an up-to-date collection of noncirculating titles, browse the Web's child-friendly sites, or attend programs especially designed for young readers. The center's media room also provides an opportunity for visitors to view Webcasts of young adult and children's authors who have appeared at the National Book Festival. The Center for the Book provides oversight for the Young Readers Center. [For more on the center's activities, see the following article, "Center for the Book"—Ed.]

Collections

During 2009 the size of the library's collections grew to 144.6 million items, an increase of 2.8 million over the previous year. This figure included more than 33.5 million cataloged books and other print materials, 63.7 million manuscripts, 16 million microforms, 5.4 million maps, 6 million pieces of sheet music, 14.4 million visual materials (photographs, posters, moving images, prints, and drawings), 3 million audio materials, and more than 1 million items in miscellaneous formats.

Important New Acquisitions

The library receives millions of items each year from copyright deposits, federal agencies, and purchases, exchanges, and gifts.

In 2009 the Copyright Office forwarded more than 700,000 copies of works with a net value estimated at $32.3 million to the library. About half were received from publishers under the mandatory-deposit provisions of the copyright law.

Significant acquisitions made possible by the library's James Madison Council included a holograph score of Leonard Bernstein's Symphony No. 3; a unique daguerreotype of Edwin Stanton, Civil War era secretary of war and attorney general; the *London Chronicle* of August 17, 1776; and a Civil War map of the battlefield at Bull Run, dated July 21, 1861.

The library also acquired the following significant items and collections:

- The National Council for Traditional Arts collection of archival folk music recordings
- A rare 1837 edition of the *Atlas of South Carolina* by architect Robert Mills (1781–1855), who designed the Washington Monument
- The Richard Yates Correspondence Collection, consisting of 11 items pertaining to the legal and political career of Abraham Lincoln
- The Strober Presidential Oral History Archive, consisting of 313 cassette interviews, totaling 500 hours, with key figures from the Kennedy, Nixon, and Reagan administrations
- The archives of the American Society of Composers, Authors, and Publishers (ASCAP) Foundation, the not-for-profit arm of the world's largest performing-rights organization

Cataloging

The library cataloged 361,337 new works in FY 2009. Production of full- and core-level original cataloging totaled 210,403 bibliographic records. The library serves as the secretariat for the international Program for Cooperative Cataloging; together, the member institutions created 333,282 name and series authority records and 22,345 subject authorities. Of these, 99,076 name and series authority records and 18,605 subject authorities were created by the library.

During the year the library mounted an Authorities and Vocabularies service on its Web site to provide access to commonly found standards and vocabularies promulgated by the Library of Congress. The Library of Congress Subject Headings (LCSH) is the first offering on the site at http://id.loc.gov/authorities.

In addition to its other cataloging services and products, the library began offering the entire 31 years of the quarterly *Cataloging Service Bulletin,* which includes current, new, and revised information about the library's cataloging and classification practices and policies (http://www.loc.gov/cds/PDFdownloads/csb).

In November the library launched Cataloger's Desktop 3.0, a major upgrade of its popular Web-based subscription service of important cataloging and metadata resources.

Future of Bibliographic Control

During the year the library began implementing many of the recommendations cited in *On the Record: Report of the Library of Congress Working Group on the Future of Bibliographic Control,* which was issued in January 2008. Paired with this report is a study of the creation and distribution of bibliographic data in U.S. and Canadian libraries. The library commissioned R2 Consulting LLC to search and describe the current marketplace for cataloging records in the MARC format. Both reports are available at http://www.loc.gov/bibliographic-future.

The Library of Congress continued to serve as a member of the Joint Steering Committee for Development of a new descriptive cataloging standard, Resource Description and Access (RDA). In June 2009 the steering committee completed the content of RDA and the fiscal year closed with plans to deliver the RDA online Web product in early 2010. The library, with the National Agricultural Library and the National Library of Medicine, designed a test of RDA in the United States and selected 24 additional partner institutions to carry out the test in the next fiscal year. The findings of the test will inform the national libraries' joint decision on whether to implement the new code.

Reference Services

In addition to serving Congress, the library provides reference services to the public in its reading rooms and through its Web site. During FY 2009 the library's staff handled nearly 590,000 reference requests that were received in person, on the telephone, and through written and electronic correspondence. More than 1.1 million items were circulated for use within the library. Library staff also responded to reference questions posed by patrons using the Ask a Librarian feature on the library's Web site.

On April 15, 2009, the new Reader Registration System was implemented. Of the nearly 42,000 reader cards issued in FY 2009, more than half were issued since the implementation of the new system. An automated call slip system was implemented in June, allowing researchers to submit online requests for library materials for use in the reading rooms, through the library's online public access catalog. Automated requests, which can be submitted on-site or off-site, eliminate the need for researchers to submit paper call slips to request materials from the general collections.

In conjunction with the opening of the Capitol Visitor Center in December 2008, the library extended the Thomas Jefferson Building's regular public hours to Monday through Saturday, 8:30 A.M. to 4:30 P.M. Beginning with Presidents Day 2009, the library began remaining open on federal holidays except Thanksgiving, Christmas, and New Year's Day, which in total represents more than an additional 400 hours available to the public each year. Reading room hours for researchers remain unchanged.

Online Resources

Through its National Digital Library Program and digitization efforts by its various divisions, the library has been adding high-quality digital content to its award-winning Web site, http://www.loc.gov. Consistently recognized as one of the top federal sites, the site recorded more than 81 million visits and 630 million page views in FY 2009.

The Web site provides users with access to the library's unparalleled resources, including its online catalog, selected collections in various formats, copyright and legislative information, Webcasts and podcasts of library events, and exhibitions. Special presentations are dedicated to the achievements of African Americans, Asians, Hispanics, Jews, women, and veterans.

As a portal to the library's 19 million online primary source files, the Wise Guide (http://www.loc.gov/wiseguide) continued to introduce new and returning users to the library's Web site. Wise Guide is updated monthly with a series of articles containing links to the library's online resources.

An upgrade to the Integrated Library System allows users to request library materials through the Online Public Access Catalog on the library's Web site, thereby eliminating paper call slips. Also accessible on the site are the public legislative information system known as THOMAS and the Global Legal Information Network (GLIN), which tracks legislative issues and provides legal information.

Enhancements were made to the library's personalized Web site, http://www.myloc.gov, which allows visitors to assemble a virtual tour of the library's exhibitions through bookmarking them on a "passport to knowledge."

By subscribing to the library's RSS feeds and its e-mail update service, users can easily stay up-to-date about areas of the library's site that particularly interest them. To sign up for either service, visit http://www.loc.gov/rss.

The library continued to promote its activities by producing and making accessible Webcasts and podcasts on its Web site at http://www.loc.gov/webcasts and http://www.loc.gov/podcasts.

Web 2.0

To develop new communication channels and new relationships, to reach new audiences and to experiment with and explore new technologies, the Library of Congress is participating in online social networks including Twitter, Facebook, and YouTube. These sites allow users to generate and share content online in a manner collectively referred to as "Web 2.0." The resulting "viral" effect can exponentially increase the number of people who see a particular piece of content.

The library's feed on the popular micro-blogging site Twitter launched in January 2009. In April the library entered the video-sharing site YouTube, offering clips from the National Book Festival, scholarly lectures from the Kluge Center, and historic films from the library's collections. On June 30 the library launched a site on iTunes U, an area of Apple's iTunes Store that offers free educational audio and video content from many of the world's top universities and other institutions. The site allows users to download content to portable devices. More than 40,000 tracks were downloaded within the first week. Just days later, the library's official "fan page" on Facebook went live. The page provides a single place where information about library events, photos, interaction with Facebook users, and other material can be brought together. Little more than a week after the launch, the library had amassed more than 5,500 fans.

The library's participation on the photo-sharing site Flickr remained enormously popular, with approximately 800,000 views per month. The library continued to add images to existing photo sets and to upload new sets, such as a group of Lincoln-related images timed to coincide with the Lincoln exhibition.

The library's blog at http:/www.loc.gov/blog contains links to all Library Web 2.0 sites.

Global Access

The Library of Congress provides access to global resources through cooperative agreements and exchanges with other nations, as well as its overseas offices. The overseas offices (http://www.loc.gov/acq/ovop) collect and catalog materials from 86 countries in some 150 languages and 25 scripts.

World Digital Library

The World Digital Library (WDL) Web site (http://www.wdl.org) was officially launched on April 21, 2009, at UNESCO headquarters in Paris at a reception hosted jointly by Librarian of Congress James H. Billington and UNESCO Director-General Koïchiro Matsuura. Nearly 605,000 users visited the site the day of the launch.

Billington first proposed the creation of a WDL Web site in a speech before UNESCO in June 2005. His vision for the site was to make significant primary materials in various formats from cultures around the world available on the Internet, free of charge and in the United Nations' languages (Arabic, Chinese, English, French, Portuguese, Russian, and Spanish).

The site includes content from or about all 192 UNESCO member countries. Among the 26 institutions from 18 countries contributing content to the WDL site are the national libraries of China, Egypt, France, Israel, Japan, Russia, Serbia, and Sweden; the U.S. National Archives and Records Administration; and major university libraries in several countries. By the end of the fiscal year, a total of 51 partners from 32 countries had joined the project and approximately 5.1 million people had visited the site.

Preservation

Preserving its unparalleled collections—from cuneiform tablets to born-digital items—is among the library's major activities.

During the year the library assessed the preservation needs of nearly 808,000 items from its general and special collections, including books, photographs, maps, audiovisual materials, and other formats. Of these, some 345,000 items were housed in protective containers. Nearly 6.8 million items were repaired, mass-deacidified, or microfilmed or otherwise reformatted. Work continued to document the library's "top treasures" and safeguard them by upgrading their oxygen-free cases.

Notable items treated during FY 2009 included two extraordinary primary source collections of African Americana: the Gladstone Collection of 19th-century photos of notable African Americans, and "Color Town," a one-of-a-kind 52-page album produced by Max Waldman in the late 1940s that dramatically illustrates daily life in a primarily African American community in that era.

To meet the challenges of preserving traditional and new media, renovation work was completed in the Conservation Division's main laboratories. A new optical properties and imaging laboratory opened in the Preservation Research and Testing Division. Using various wavelengths of light, imaging of the L'Enfant Plan for the City of Washington (1791) revealed new details and tracked prior treatments on the map's surface. Imaging of Lincoln's first and second drafts of the Gettysburg Address revealed new details, such as fingerprints and previously hidden pencil marks. Imaging of the Virginia Declaration of Rights (a model for the Declaration of Independence) revealed word changes and watermarks.

Books

With support from Congress, the library continued to fill new units at its book storage facility in Fort Meade, Maryland. On July 7, 2009, a ribbon-cutting ceremony was held at the facility to mark the completion of high-density storage modules 3 and 4. During the year the library accessioned and transferred 308,258 items to the facility, bringing the total to 3 million items stored there. The retrieval rate—within 12 business hours or less—was 100 percent.

The library is nearing completion of its Digitizing American Imprints project, which was funded by a grant of $2 million from the Alfred P. Sloan Foundation. The focus of the project is on at-risk "brittle books" from the library's special collections. At the fiscal year's end, the library had digitized more than 52,600 volumes totaling approximately 9.3 million images.

Working with the Internet Archive, the library developed the open source page-turner, a tool that greatly enhances the usability of digital books. The scanned materials are accessible on the Internet Archive's Web site (http://www.internetarchive.org) with bibliographic links to the digitized books in the library's Integrated Library System.

Newspapers

The library, in partnership with the National Endowment for the Humanities, is participating in the National Digital Newspaper Program (NDNP), a collaborative effort to digitize and provide free and public access to historic American newspapers that are in the public domain. During the year the number of NDNP state projects contributing digitized content grew from 7 to 22.

The library continued its effort to make newspapers accessible on the Web site Chronicling America, a free, searchable database of historic American newspaper pages published between 1880 and 1922 (http://www.loc.gov/chronicling america). A milestone was reached in June 2009 when the site posted its millionth page. At the end of FY 2009, the site contained more than 1.44 million newspaper pages.

Maps

The crown jewel of the library's cartography collection—the 1507 world map by Martin Waldseemüller that first used the name "America"—continued to be preserved and protected while it remained on view in the library's "Exploring the Early Americas" exhibition. Prior to display, the library's Preservation Directorate and Geography and Map Division—in collaboration with the National Institute for Standards and Technology and the Alcoa Foundation—created a permanent, oxygen-free aluminum housing to preserve this rare item. A year-long monitoring of the special map encasement indicated that the oxygen-free seal could last 150 years, far exceeding design requirements of 25 to 30 years. The knowledge obtained through the process of designing and installing this case has been documented and shared with the national and international preservation community on the Preservation Directorate's Web site at http://www.loc.gov/preserv.

Audiovisual Collections

Opened in July 2007, the library's Packard Campus for Audio Visual Conservation in Culpeper, Virginia, consolidated its audiovisual collections—the world's largest and most comprehensive. The collections previously were housed in Library of Congress buildings in four states and the District of Columbia.

Philanthropist David Woodley Packard and the Packard Humanities Institute donated the state-of-the-art facility to the American people, making it the largest-ever private gift to the legislative branch of the U.S. government. The $155 million facility was financed jointly by the gift from Packard and appropriations from Congress totaling $82.1 million.

The Packard Campus comprises a collections building, where 5.7 million items (1.2 million moving images, nearly 3 million sound recordings, and 1.5 million related items, such as manuscripts, posters, and screenplays) are housed under ideal conditions; a conservation building, where the collections are acquired, managed, and preserved; and a separate facility with 124 vaults where combustible nitrate films can be stored safely. Researchers in the library's related reading rooms on Capitol Hill will be able to access derivative copies of the digital files through high-speed fiber optic connections to Culpeper.

In FY 2009, the second year of a multi-year operational ramp-up, work continued to construct and equip three preservation laboratories for film, sound, and video in the Culpeper facility's main Conservation Building. Six film developing machines were built, tested, and certified for use in the laboratory. The second phase of building the sound and video preservation laboratories began; the prototype IRENE (Image, Reconstruct, Erase Noise, Etc.) system—developed by scientists at Lawrence Berkeley Laboratory and using digital imaging technologies to reconstruct damaged sound recordings—was delivered to the Packard campus, and at year's end it was awaiting final acceptance testing.

The 200-seat Mount Pony Theater resumed its popular film screenings in April 2009, expanding to three shows a week with the addition of a Saturday evening program. The Art Deco-style theater is one of only five theaters in the United States equipped to show original classic film prints on nitrate film stock as they would have been screened in theaters before 1950. The theater also features a custom-made organ that provides live music accompaniment for silent movies to enhance viewers' cinematic experience.

Films

It is estimated that half of the films produced before 1950 and 80 percent to 90 percent of those made before 1920 have disappeared forever. The Library of Congress is working with many organizations to prevent such losses and to preserve motion pictures through the National Film Registry.

Under the terms of the National Film Preservation Act of 1992, the Librarian of Congress, with advice from the National Film Preservation Board, began selecting 25 films annually for the National Film Registry, to be preserved for all time. The films are chosen based on whether they are "culturally, historically, or aesthetically significant." The library works to ensure that registry films are preserved by library staff or through collaboration with other archives, motion picture studios, and independent filmmakers.

In December 2009 the librarian named the following 25 films to the registry, bringing the total to 525.

Dog Day Afternoon (1975)
The Exiles (1961)
Heroes All (1920)
Hot Dogs for Gauguin (1972)
The Incredible Shrinking Man (1957)
Jezebel (1938)
The Jungle (1967)
Lead Shoes (1949)
Little Nemo (1911)
Mabel's Blunder (1914)
The Mark of Zorro (1940)
Mrs. Miniver (1942)
The Muppet Movie (1979)
Once Upon a Time in the West (1968)
Pillow Talk (1959)
Precious Images (1986)
Quasi at the Quackadero (1975)
The Red Book (1994)
The Revenge of Pancho Villa (1930–1936)
Scratch and Crow (1995)
Stark Love (1927)
The Story of G.I. Joe (1945)
A Study in Reds (1932)
Thriller (1983)
Under Western Stars (1938)

Sound Recordings

The library is conducting a study on the state of audio preservation, which will be published in FY 2010. The results will have an impact on the development of a comprehensive plan for a national audio preservation program—the first of its kind—as directed by Congress in the National Recording Preservation Act of 2000. That act also tasks the Librarian of Congress with annually choosing recordings that are "culturally, historically, or aesthetically significant."

In June 2009 the following 25 sound recordings were added to the National Recording Registry, bringing the total to 275.

"No News, or What Killed the Dog," Nat M. Wills (1908)

Acoustic Recordings for Victor Records, Jascha Heifetz (1917–1924)

"Night Life," Mary Lou Williams (1930)

Sounds of the Ivory-billed Woodpecker (1935)

"Gang Busters" (1935–1957)

"Bei Mir Bist Du Schoen," Andrews Sisters (1938)

"Que é Que a Bahiana Tem?" Carmen Miranda (1939)

NBC Radio coverage of Marian Anderson's recital at the Lincoln Memorial (April 9, 1939)

"Tom Dooley," Frank Proffitt (1940)

The Mary Margaret McBride Program, featuring Zora Neale Hurston (January 25, 1943)

"Uncle Sam Blues," Oran "Hot Lips" Page with Eddie Condon's Jazz Band (V-Disc) (1944)

"Sinews of Peace" (Iron Curtain) Speech at Westminster College in Fulton, Missouri, Winston Churchill (March 5, 1946)

"The Churkendoose," Ray Bolger (1947)

"Boogie Chillen," John Lee Hooker (1948)

"A Child's Christmas in Wales," Dylan Thomas (1952)

"A Festival of Lessons and Carols as Sung on Christmas Eve in King's College Chapel, Cambridge," King's College Choir, Boris Ord, director (1954)

"West Side Story," original cast recording (1957)

"Tom Dooley," the Kingston Trio (1958)

"Rumble," Link Wray (1958)

"The Play of Daniel: A Twelfth-Century Drama," New York Pro Musica, directed by Noah Greenberg (1958)

"Rank Stranger," Stanley Brothers (1960)

"2000 Years with Carl Reiner and Mel Brooks," Carl Reiner and Mel Brooks (1960)

"At Last!" Etta James (1961)

"The Who Sings My Generation," The Who (1966)

"He Stopped Loving Her Today," George Jones (1980)

Oral History

The American Folklife Center continued its mandate to "preserve and present American folklife" through a number of outreach and oral history programs such as the Veterans History Project and StoryCorps.

Established by Congress in 2000, the Veterans History Project is a major program of the library's American Folklife Center. The program preserves the memories of both those who served in the armed forces and those at home. Congress demonstrated its continued support of the project with a bipartisan resolution establishing Veterans History Project Week to coincide with Veterans Day.

In FY 2009 the project collected more than 7,400 personal recollections, bringing the total to 67,400. More than 7,000 collections are accessible on the project's Web site at http://www.loc.gov/vets. Special presentations added to the site during the year honored disabled veterans, African American veterans, members of the Coast Guard and the Merchant Marine, and commemorated D-Day.

Launched in 2003 by Dave Isay and his documentary company Sound Portraits Productions, StoryCorps is one of the nation's largest oral narrative projects. Isay was inspired by the Works Progress Administration's (WPA) Federal Writers' Project of the 1930s, which recorded oral history interviews with everyday Americans across the country. In FY 2009 more than 7,000 audio files of interviews were added to the collection, bringing the total housed in the American Folklife Center to more than 24,000. In addition to weekly broadcasts on National Public Radio's "Morning Edition," StoryCorps stories are available as downloadable podcasts.

Digital Preservation and Management

The Library of Congress is leading a nationwide program to collect and preserve at-risk digital content of cultural and historical importance. Since 2000 the congressionally mandated National Digital Information Infrastructure and Preservation Program (NDIIPP) has been building a digital preservation network of partners. In 2009 NDIIPP added 20 new partners, bringing the total to 150 participants in the network. These partners are seeking to preserve a wide range of "born digital" records, including those produced in state, federal, academic, and private sector organizations. They are also working collaboratively to establish standards for digital preservation. The project also includes Web capture to address the problem of the limited lifespan of the average online site as well as plans to manage the influx of born-digital collections.

State Records

States face formidable challenges in caring for digital records with long-term legal and historical value. Most states lack the resources to ensure the preservation of the information they produce in digital form only, such as legislative records, court case files, and executive agency records. As a result, much state government digital information—including content useful to policymakers—is at risk.

In 2009 the library expanded its support of the Preserving State Government Information Program, which helps state archives, libraries, historical societies, and other agencies safeguard their digital information. The number of states participating in the effort grew to 35.

Federal Records

The Library of Congress, U.S. Government Printing Office, Internet Archive, California Digital Library, and University of North Texas Libraries continued to collaborate on a project to preserve public U.S. government Web sites at the end of the George W. Bush presidential administration ending January 19, 2009. The project is intended to document federal agencies' online archives during the transition of government and to enhance the existing collections of the five partner institutions. Congressional Web sites, which the library has been preserving on a monthly basis since December 2003, are also part of the project.

Among the library's Web capture projects in FY 2009 was the effort to preserve Web sites pertaining to the 2008 U.S. presidential election. With advice from the Congressional Research Service and volunteer curators across the country, the library identified, captured, and archived more than 2,200 Web sites, totaling 140 million documents or 5 terabytes of data.

Private Sector

Eight private sector partners continued to participate in the Preserving Creative America project to safeguard creative works in digital formats. The project was launched in 2007 with the library's award of $2.15 million to partners in the creative community to preserve photographs, cartoons, motion pictures, sound recordings, and video games. Work on all projects continued in 2009, with a focus on developing and improving standards and practices that will ultimately benefit public archives as well as commercial communities. The use of consistent and standard metadata is key to the long-term management and preservation of digital photographs. Participating partners such as the Society of American Archivists and the Stock Artists Alliance continued their ongoing mission to promote the use of metadata. The latter sponsored a series of seminars titled "getMETAsmart" in major U.S. cities to educate digital photographers on how the use of metadata can benefit their businesses.

Web Capture

Since 2000 the library's Web Capture Team has worked with other library offices to develop thematic or event-based Web archives collections. The library's Web archives expanded to more than 3 billion documents in 24 collections. The archiving team maintained existing collections pertaining to the war in Iraq, the 111th Congress, and law-related blogs. The team captured Web sites pertaining to several topics, including the 2008 U.S. presidential election, comprising more than 2,200 Web sites containing 140 million documents.

Standards

The library continued to lead the Federal Agency Digitization Guidelines Working Group, a collaborative effort by 14 federal agencies to define common guidelines, methods, and practices to digitize historical content in a standard manner. Two separate working groups were formed to address two distinct formats: still images (books, manuscripts, maps, and photographic prints and negatives) and audiovisual material (sound, video, and motion picture film). Guidelines for the digitization of still images and audiovisual materials have been prepared and await public review. The working group continued to share its progress with the private sector, academic community, and libraries and archives, nationally and internationally, through its Web site, http://www.digitizationguidelines.gov.

Digital Collections Management

In 2009 the library launched a Digital Collections Management initiative to more effectively manage the creation, acquisition, and maintenance of its digital collections, and to prepare for the influx of large quantities of externally created digital content acquired through copyright deposit and other means. The first major project will focus on mandatory deposit of electronic journals for the library's collections.

The library has historically received print publications through the copyright deposit system. Electronic scholarly serials, which increasingly have no print equivalents, are widely considered to be at risk of loss. The library is working with external organizations to provide a new service, eDeposit, that will allow copyright owners to electronically deposit their publications into a digital archive maintained by the library. Through eDeposit, the library can continue to preserve cultural heritage for future generations in the era of electronic publishing. In 2009 the Digital Collections Management team worked with the eDeposit Working Group on a first draft of system requirements for the new tools needed to manage the workflow for processing deposited e-serials. The team also began to consider the custodial needs of this new collection.

U.S. Copyright Office

The U.S. Copyright Office in the Library of Congress administers the U.S. copyright law, under which authors of creative works register claims to protect their intellectual property. Congress enacted the first copyright law in May 1790; in 1870 it centralized the national copyright function in the Library of Congress. The collections of the Library of Congress have been created largely through the copyright deposit system.

During FY 2009 the Copyright Office received 532,370 new claims to copyright, covering more than 1 million works. It registered 382,086 of those claims using the new eCO system for electronic copyright registration. The new system accommodates traditional formats as well as items that are born digital.

The Copyright Royalty and Distribution Reform Act of 2004 (Public Law 108-419) replaced the Copyright Arbitration Royalty Panels with an entity comprising three copyright royalty judges and their staff. The judges were sworn to office in January 2006. In their fourth year of operation, the judges set rates and terms for various statutory licenses and distributed royalty fees collected by the Copyright Office. In 2009 the judges directed the distribution of nearly $273 million to copyright owners.

National Library Service for the Blind and Physically Handicapped

Established in 1931 when President Herbert Hoover signed the Pratt-Smoot Act into law, the National Library Service for the Blind and Physically Handicapped (NLS) currently circulates more than 24 million copies of braille and recorded books and magazines to some 800,000 readers through a network of 131 cooperating libraries. NLS also provides a free service known as the 102 Talking-Book Club to more than 3,700 patrons who are 100 years of age or older.

In April 2009, following months of pilot testing, the permanent version of the online Braille and Audio Reading Download (BARD) service was established. The service makes audiobooks available as downloadable files over the Internet. At year's end 7,700 patrons were registered to use the BARD service, which offers more than 16,000 titles.

During the year NLS continued its work toward the next generation of audio technology, digital talking books. The project calls for phasing in digital playback machines and media and phasing out analog tape cassettes and equipment. In preparation for pre-launch testing of the digital talking book system, 5,000 digital talking book players were allocated to eight libraries and the Jewish Braille Institute of America (now known as JBI International) to be distributed to selected patrons in their service areas. These institutions also received and distributed to selected patrons 18,000 copies of 54 digital talking books on cartridges for use during the testing period, which was held May through July. August marked the national launch of the new digital talking book program with the distribution of digital players and audiobooks on flash memory cartridges in newly designed mailing containers to libraries nationwide.

John W. Kluge Center

The John W. Kluge Center was established in 2000 with a gift of $60 million from John W. Kluge, Metromedia president and founding chairman of the James Madison Council (the library's private sector advisory group). Located within the library's Office of Scholarly Programs, the center's goal is to bring the world's top scholars to the Library of Congress, where they can use the institution's resources and can interact with policymakers in Washington.

During the year the Kluge Center continued to attract outstanding senior scholars and postdoctoral fellows. Through their work, scholars, researchers, literary enthusiasts, and the general public were able to deepen their understanding of the cultural, historical, philosophical, scientific, and creative dimensions of the human experience. The center sponsored symposia, lectures, book talks, and conferences. For more information about the John W. Kluge Center, visit http://www.loc.gov/kluge.

Publications

Each year the library publishes books, calendars, and other printed products featuring its vast content, many in cooperation with trade publishers.

Among the titles published in 2009 were works that feature the library's Civil War and World War II era collections: *In Lincoln's Hand: His Original Manuscripts with Commentary by Distinguished Americans*; *Traveling the Freedom Road: From Slavery and the Civil War Through Reconstruction*; and *World War II: 365 Days*. *Baseball Americana: Treasures from the Library of Congress* draws on the world's largest collection of baseball-related items.

To commemorate the 100th anniversary of the birth of political cartoonist Herbert Block, the library and the Herb Block Foundation, in association with W. W. Norton & Company, published *Herblock: The Life and Works of the Great Political Cartoonist.*

Exhibitions

The number of visitors to the library's exhibitions increased by 30 percent in 2009, in large part because of the popularity of the Library of Congress Experience, which comprises several interactive exhibitions: "Creating the United States," "Exploring the Early Americas: The Jay I. Kislak Collection at the Library of Congress," and "Thomas Jefferson's Library." The Library of Congress Experience also offers an opportunity to explore the art and architecture of the library's historic Thomas Jefferson Building. In the Great Hall, interactive kiosks allow visitors to zoom in on details of the space and explore in detail a display of two of the library's most prized objects, the Gutenberg Bible and the Giant Bible of Mainz.

The library's Gershwin Room reopened in January 2009 with an updated version of the exhibition "Here to Stay: The Legacy of George and Ira Gershwin." First mounted in 1998, the exhibition was closed during the construction of the Capitol Visitor Center and passageway connecting the U.S. Capitol to the Library of Congress.

The library commemorated the 200th anniversary of the birth of Abraham Lincoln with a major exhibition, "With Malice Toward None: The Abraham Lincoln Bicentennial Exhibition," mounted in a new gallery in the Jefferson Building.

Other library exhibitions in 2009 marked the 200th anniversary of Louis Braille, the inventor of a tactile system of reading and writing; the 100th anniversary of the birth of political cartoonist Herbert Block; and the 2008 election of President Barack Obama, which featured 50 Obama-related items of memorabilia from Africa.

The Music Division mounted displays in the foyer of the Performing Arts Reading Room to highlight the centennial of Serge Diaghilev's Ballets Russes, to feature presidential campaign songs, and to celebrate the integration of music and animation.

The Geography and Map Division mounted a display of Civil War maps by Jed Hotchkiss, General Stonewall Jackson's chief cartographer.

The library's exhibitions can be viewed online at http://www.loc.gov/exhibits and http://www.myLOC.gov.

Special Events

During the year the library presented hundreds of public events, including poetry and literary programs, concerts, lectures, and symposia, many of which were broadcast live or archived on the library's Web site at http://www.loc.gov/webcasts. For a list of upcoming events, visit http://www.loc.gov/loc/events.

Literary Events

Since its inception in 2001, the library's National Book Festival has become a highly anticipated annual event. More than 130,000 gathered on the National Mall on September 26 to celebrate creativity and literacy at the ninth annual festival. [For more on the festival, see the following article, "Center for the Book"— *Ed.*]

During the year, the library's Poetry and Literature Center sponsored a number of programs featuring new and renowned poets reading from their works. Kay Ryan served as the library's Poet Laureate Consultant in Poetry for the 2008–2010 literary season. During the year Ryan and 30 other noted poets were featured on the public radio series "The Poet and the Poem from the Library of Congress."

Ryan opened the literary season on October 21 with a reading from her works. She announced a national poetry project that embraces community colleges through an online poetry page, "Poetry for the Mind's Joy," and a poetry writing contest. The project, in conjunction with the Community College Humanities Association, also designates April 1 as National Poetry Day on community college campuses.

Concerts

Since 1925 the library's Coolidge Auditorium has provided a venue for world-class performers and world premieres of commissioned works. Sponsored by the Music Division, the annual concert series reflects the diversity of music in the United States and features many genres—classical, jazz, musical theater, dance, pop, and rock.

The 2008–2009 season of concerts presented a lineup of more than 40 free events inspired by the resources of the library's music archive—the world's largest, with more than 22 million items. With a theme of celebration, the library's 83rd season included special events honoring the composers Elliott Carter, George Frederic Handel, Franz Joseph Haydn, Felix Mendelssohn, and Olivier Messiaen.

The American Folklife Center continued its popular concert series "Homegrown: The Music of America," which features diverse musical traditions. Concerts during the year featured cowboy music from Wyoming; Native American music from Maine, New Jersey, Oregon, and Pennsylvania; Cape Breton Island-inspired fiddle music from New Hampshire; and gospel music from Kentucky.

The Library of Congress and baritone Thomas Hampson resumed their acclaimed "Song of America" project with a second season, July 2009 through

February 2010. Hampson presents a unique series of recitals, educational activities, exhibitions, recordings, Webcasts, and interactive online resources.

Symposia and Lectures

Various library divisions sponsored hundreds of programs and lectures on a wide range of topics during the year. The bicentennials of the births of Abraham Lincoln and Charles Darwin—both born February 12, 1809—were marked by a symposium and lectures, respectively. Planned in conjunction with the library's Lincoln bicentennial exhibition, a two-day symposium featured Lincoln scholars and the library's collection of Lincolniana.

In May the library hosted the symposium "The Sound of Broadway Music" in conjunction with the release of a book of the same title by Steven Suskin, who conducted his research in the library's Music Division.

For the first time since its rediscovery in 1901, the 1507 world map by Martin Waldseemüller was the subject of a symposium sponsored by the Geography and Map Division on May 14 and 15. "Exploring Waldseemüller's World" brought together a distinguished group of 400 scholars to discuss the history and production of the map—the first to depict a landmass separated by water from Europe, Africa, and Asia and to name it "America." The map is on display in the library's "Exploring the Americas" exhibition.

To mark the 60th anniversary of the North Atlantic Treaty Organization (NATO), on July 9 the Law Library of Congress hosted a panel discussion on the legal challenges facing the organization. On December 3, the law library marked the 60th anniversary of the Geneva Conventions of 1949 with a program sponsored jointly with the American Red Cross and the Friends of the Law Library of Congress.

The American Folklife Center and the Publishing Office celebrated the publication of *Baseball Americana: Treasures from the Library of Congress* with a symposium October 2–3.

Honors and Awards

Gershwin Prize for Popular Song

Declaring it "Wonder Week in Washington, D.C.," Librarian of Congress James H. Billington began a week of festivities in late February with a press conference announcing Stevie Wonder as the recipient of the second Library of Congress Gershwin Prize for Popular Song.

The prize, which President Obama presented to Wonder at a special concert at the White House on February 25, commemorates composer and lyricist George and Ira Gershwin, whose extensive manuscript collections are held by the library. The prize is awarded to musicians whose lifetime contributions in the field of popular song exemplify the standard of excellence associated with the Gershwins. Paul Simon received the first Gershwin Prize in 2007, and in November Paul McCartney was named the recipient of the third.

Living Legend Award

In recognition of 20 years of service as chair of the Library of Congress National Film Preservation Board, Fay Kanin was presented with the library's 100th Living Legend Award. Kanin, a screenwriter and producer, became an industry leader as the president of the Academy of Motion Picture Arts and Sciences from 1979 to 1983.

Former Chicago Cub Ernie Banks was presented the Living Legend Award at the library's baseball symposium on October 3. Banks was a two-time National League most valuable player, an 11-time all-star, a member of the Five Hundred Home Run Club, and a Baseball Hall of Fame inductee.

Additional Sources of Information

Library of Congress telephone numbers for public information:

Main switchboard (with menu)	202-707-5000
Reading room hours and locations	202-707-6400
General reference	202-707-3399
	TTY 202-707-4210
Visitor information	202-707-8000
	TTY 202-707-6200
Exhibition hours	202-707-4604
Reference assistance	202-707-6500
Copyright information	202-707-3000
Copyright hotline (to order forms)	202-707-9100
Sales shop (credit card orders)	888-682-3557

Center for the Book

Library of Congress, Washington, DC 20540
World Wide Web http://www.loc.gov/cfbook

John Y. Cole
Director

Congress established the Center for the Book in the Library of Congress by statute (Public Law 95-129) in 1977. The center's purpose is to use the resources and prestige of the Library of Congress to stimulate public interest in books and reading. Through the years, its mission has expanded to include literacy and library promotion and encouragement of the historical study of books, reading, libraries, and the printed word.

The center's audience, which is international as well as national, has always included readers and potential readers of all ages. The center is a successful public-private partnership, relying on outside funding for all of its activities; the Library of Congress supports its five staff positions.

Highlights of 2009

During 2009 the Center for the Book

- Assumed responsibility for the new Young Readers Center, located in the Jefferson Building and the first space devoted to the reading interests of children and teens in the library's history
- Played a major role in the most successful National Book Festival ever organized by the Library of Congress
- Coordinated more than 30 public events at the library, many of them talks in the center's "Books and Beyond" series of talks and book signings by authors of new books based on Library of Congress collections or projects
- Continued its recent emphasis on promoting reading to young people

Young Readers Center

Opened on Oct. 23, 2009, the Young Readers Center is a showcase for center projects that encourage reading and literacy among young people. Its overall purpose, however, is broader: to increase public awareness of efforts throughout the Library of Congress to promote reading and learning to the same audience. Young readers of all ages are welcome to browse and use its collection of award-winning books and classics; they need only to be accompanied by an adult.

The Young Readers Center's immediate focus is on providing personal and family "read aloud" experiences, which can be supplemented by demonstrations of the library's online educational projects and films of author presentations aimed at younger audiences at the library's annual National Book Festivals. Future programming will include talks by authors, demonstrations by illustrators, and projects cosponsored with other Library of Congress offices and the center's national reading promotion organizational partners.

National Ambassador

Noted children's author Jon Scieszka completed a lively second and final year as the first National Ambassador for Young People's Literature, a program developed with the Children's Book Council to promote the importance of young people's literature nationwide. Scieszka traveled the country for two years, promoting the ambassadorship, reading, and his books. He was the featured author in two programs during the 2009 National Book Festival, entertaining the audience both during the "Exquisite Corpse Adventure" session (see below) and in the Children's pavilion with illustrator David Shannon.

Scieszka was succeeded in the ambassadorship in January 2010 by Katherine Paterson, two-time winner of the National Book Award and the Newbery Medal. Paterson will serve in the position during 2010 and 2011, and has chosen "Read for Your Life" as the theme for her platform.

Letters About Literature

The six national winners of the 2008–2009 Letters About Literature reading and writing contest were announced in April 2009. To enter, a young (grades 4 through 12) reader writes a personal letter to an author, living or dead, from any genre—fiction or nonfiction, contemporary or classic—explaining how that author's work changed the student's way of thinking about the world or himself or herself. More than 59,000 letters were submitted. The program is cosponsored by the Center for the Book, its state centers, and the Target store chain, which donates $10,000 to each of the schools of the six national winners and $1,000 to each of the schools of the 12 honorable mention winners. The 2009–2010 program was launched in September 2009.

River of Words

The center has cosponsored River of Words, an annual environmental poetry and art competition for students ages 5–19, for 14 years. On May 13, 2009, an awards ceremony was held in the library's Jefferson Building; the master of ceremonies was River of Words cofounder Robert Hass, who was U.S. Poet Laureate for 1995–1997. Young people and their families traveled to the event from across the country and as far away as Sri Lanka, the home of the international winner.

Online Resources

In 2009 the Center for the Book collaborated with the library's Public Affairs Office, Educational Outreach Division, Web Services Office, and the Ad Council on a new multimedia Web site (http://www.read.gov) that was launched during the National Book Festival on September 26. The site offers resources from throughout the Library of Congress designed to stimulate the reading of books and to interest users in learning about the authors and illustrators who create them. The center also began connecting its audiences with both its activities and current books through

- A redesigned and more user-friendly Web site (http://www.loc.gov/cfbook) that provides links to approximately 200 like-minded affiliates, partners, and organizations, nationally and internationally, and the only national listing of One Book projects and their books
- A new Books & Beyond Book Club on Facebook—all Center for the Book public programs, including Books & Beyond talks, are recorded for later Webcasting and are now available on http://www.read.gov

Read.gov offers "audience" pages designed specifically for children, teens, adults, and for educators and parents. These pages contain such resources as Webcasts in which authors discuss their latest works at recent National Book Festivals, digitized classics with classic illustrations such as Dickens's "A Christmas Carol" and Poe's "The Raven," educational resources for parents and teens, and the Young Readers Tool Kit, prepared by educational specialists for each year's National Book Festival.

A highlight of Read.gov is the exclusive story "The Exquisite Corpse Adventure," whose first episode debuted and was read by its author, National Ambassador for Young People's Literature Jon Scieszka, during the opening session in the Children's Pavilion at the 2009 National Book Festival. On the Web site the episode is illustrated by Chris Van Dusen.

"The Exquisite Corpse" is an original sequential story that will be composed of a total of 27 episodes, with the final episode debuting at the 2010 National Book Festival. It is a project of the Center for the Book and one of its reading promotion partners, the National Children's Book and Literacy Alliance. Other authors participating include M. T. Anderson, Natalie Babbitt, Kate DiCamillo, Nikki Grimes, Gregory Maguire, Fred and Patricia McKissack, Linda Sue Park, and Katherine Paterson.

National Book Festival

For the ninth year, the Center for the Book took the lead in organizing the program for the National Book Festival. Held on September 26 and covering seven blocks on the National Mall, the 2009 festival featured 78 nationally known and award-winning authors, illustrators, and poets. More than 130,000 members of the public attended—a new record. President Barack Obama and First Lady Michelle Obama were honorary chairpersons. In addition to an exceptionally strong group of authors and illustrators of books for young people—including Lois Lowry, Judy Blume, Megan McDonald, and Steven Kellogg—the festival highlighted such "blockbuster" writers as John Grisham, John Irving, Paula Deen, and Jodi Picoult. Librarian of Congress James H. Billington opened the

Fiction and Fantasy Pavilion by presenting Grisham with the first National Book Festival Award for Creative Achievement.

The center also organized the Pavilion of the States to highlight its reading and literacy promotion projects and those of the 50 states, the District of Columbia, and the U.S. territories. Representatives of the various state Centers for the Book provided information and answered questions about their states' writers, libraries, book festivals, book awards, and reading promotion activities. In addition, several festival authors and illustrators made scheduled visits to their state's table to greet fans and sign autographs.

An especially popular Pavilion of the State feature among young readers and their families was "Discover Great Places Through Reading," a free map of the United States that visitors could present at each table for an appropriate state sticker or stamp. The map included "52 Great Reads About Great Places," a reading list of books for young people compiled through book recommendations from each state.

State Centers for the Book

The state center affiliates program, which began in 1984, was highlighted in 2009 by the establishment of the Virgin Islands Center for the Book—the first territorial affiliate. The announcement was made on April 16 at Government House in St. Croix by U.S. Virgin Islands Governor John P. deJongh.

The Center for the Book now has 52 official affiliates that renew their partnerships with the national center every three years: the 50 states, the District of Columbia, and the U.S. Virgin Islands. The purpose of the network is to link reading promotion resources and ideas from the Library of Congress with related projects and interests at the local level. The annual "idea exchange" meeting is an important way for representatives from the state centers to learn how their peers around the country promote reading, literacy, and libraries.

At the 2009 state center idea exchange May 11–12, coordinators from 40 state affiliates discussed current and potential projects as well as topics such as fund raising and board development. They also heard about the center's new newsletter and were asked to make contributions to this online publication. Boorstin Awards for innovative reading promotion efforts were also presented. The Indiana and Wisconsin state centers each received a $1,000 award, donated to the Center for the Book by Ruth Boorstin, wife of former Librarian of Congress (1975–1987) Daniel J. Boorstin, who established the center in 1977. During the second day, project directors Catherine Gourley (Letters About Literature) and Pamela Michael (River of Words) met with state centers participating in their respective projects.

The national center cohosted poetry readings with the Oregon and Massachusetts state centers during 2009, both featuring young poets to whom Poet Laureate Kay Ryan had awarded $10,000 Library of Congress Witter Bynner Fellowships. On October 5 Mary Szybist presented a poetry reading at Lewis & Clark College in Portland, Oregon; Christine Davis's presentation was on November 1 in Concord, Massachusetts.

National Reading Promotion Partners

The center's partnership program, which includes more than 80 national nonprofit and governmental organizations, strengthens and supports its reading and literacy projects nationwide. At the 2009 partners idea exchange meeting, guest speakers included representatives from new partner RedRoom.com, a Web site for writers. Other new partners are the Literacy Council of Northern Virginia, the North Texas Future Fund, Guys Read (a project of National Ambassador for Young People's Literature Jon Scieszka), and ReadKiddoRead, a project of the writer James Patterson. Partnership events cosponsored at the Library of Congress during the year included a March luncheon with the National Newspaper Association Foundation; an International Literacy Day program in September with the International Reading Association and featuring Alma Powell, chair of the America's Promise Alliance; a literacy awards dinner in September with the National Coalition for Literacy; and, with the PEN/Faulkner Foundation's Writers in Schools project, a presentation for young people by writer Amy Tan.

International Activities

The center hosted visits by reading promoters and librarians from more than a dozen countries during 2009, most of them arranged by the State Department. In August center director John Y. Cole, as the former chair and a corresponding member of the Literacy and Reading Section of the International Federation of Library Associations and Institutions (IFLA), participated in section activities at the 75th IFLA General Conference in Milan. He also met there with representatives of the center's two international "sister" organizations, the South African Centre for the Book and the Pushkin Library Foundation, the organizer and sponsor of more than 30 "reading centers" in libraries throughout Russia.

National Agricultural Library

U.S. Department of Agriculture, Abraham Lincoln Bldg.,
10301 Baltimore Ave., Beltsville, MD 20705-2351
E-mail agref@nal.usda.gov
World Wide Web http://www.nal.usda.gov

Gary McCone

Associate Director

The U.S. Department of Agriculture's National Agricultural Library (NAL) is the world's largest and most accessible agricultural research library, offering service directly to the public and via its Web site, http://www.nal.usda.gov. The library was created with the U.S. Department of Agriculture (USDA) in 1862 and established as a national library by Congress (7 USCS § 3125a) as the primary agricultural information resource of the United States.

Congress assigned to the library the responsibilities to

- Acquire, preserve, and manage information resources relating to agriculture and allied sciences
- Organize agricultural information products and services and provide them within the United States and internationally
- Plan, coordinate, and evaluate information and library needs relating to agricultural research and education
- Cooperate with and coordinate efforts toward development of a comprehensive agricultural library and information network
- Coordinate the development of specialized subject information services among the agricultural and library information communities

NAL is the only library in the United States with the mandate to carry out these national and international responsibilities for the agricultural community. NAL's vision is "advancing access to global information for agriculture."

The library is located in Beltsville, Maryland, near Washington, D.C., on the grounds of USDA's Henry A. Wallace Beltsville Agricultural Research Center. Its 15-story Abraham Lincoln Building is named in honor of the president who created the Department of Agriculture and signed many of the major U.S. laws affecting agriculture.

NAL employs about 155 librarians, information specialists, computer specialists, administrators, and clerical personnel, supplemented by about 50 volunteers, cooperators from NAL partnering organizations, and contract staff.

The library's expert staff, leadership in delivering information services, collaborations with other U.S. and international agricultural research and information organizations, extensive collection of agricultural information, AGRICOLA bibliographic database of citations to the agricultural literature, and advanced information technology infrastructure contribute to its reputation as one of the world's foremost agricultural libraries.

The Collection

The NAL collection dates to the congressionally approved 1839 purchase of books for the Agricultural Division of the Patent Office, predating the 1862 establishment of USDA itself. Today NAL provides access to billions of pages of agricultural information—an immense collection of scientific books, journals, audiovisuals, reports, theses, software, laser discs, artifacts, and images—and to a widening array of digital media, as well as databases and other information resources germane to the broad reach of agriculture-related sciences.

The library's collection contains nearly 3.6 million items, as reported to the Association of Research Libraries, dating from the 16th century to the present, including the most complete repository of U.S. Department of Agriculture publications and the world's most extensive set of materials on the history of agriculture in the United States. The collection covers all aspects of agriculture and related sciences and is a comprehensive resource for agricultural scientists, policy-makers, regulators, and scholars.

Networks of Cooperation

The NAL collection and information resources are supplemented by networks of cooperation with other institutions, including arrangements with agricultural libraries at U.S. land-grant universities, other U.S. national libraries, agricultural libraries in other countries, and libraries of the United Nations and other international organizations.

AgNIC

The library serves as secretariat for the Agriculture Network Information Center (AgNIC) Alliance (http://www.agnic.org), a voluntary, collaborative partnership that hosts a distributed network of discipline-specific agricultural information Web sites. In 2009 the combined AgNIC partner Web statistics totaled more than 125 million Web hits. AgNIC provides access to high-quality agricultural information selected by AgNIC partners, including land-grant universities, NAL, and other institutions globally. AgNIC's 60 member institutions offer 68 subject-specific sites and reference services. Additional sites and resources are being developed. During 2009 partners continued to build full-text content through a variety of projects such as metadata harvesting. This service uses the Open Archives Initiative (OAI) protocols to harvest metadata for full-text resources from targeted institutional repositories and collections for a single point of access. AgNIC also added social networking capabilities (Web 2.0 options) to the Web site, migrated to new more dynamic technology for the public site, and upgraded the content management system for the partners' work space. AgNIC continues to work with related efforts around the world, such as the Federation of Learning Repositories for Agriculture, through OrganicEdunet, and the CACAO Project in Britain for navigating multilingual textual content in digital libraries.

AGLINET

As the U.S. node of an international agricultural information system, NAL also serves as a gateway to U.S. agricultural libraries and resources. NAL cooperates with other libraries, information centers, and consortia via several reciprocal agreements. It is part of the Agricultural Libraries Network (AGLINET) administered by the Food and Agriculture Organization (FAO) of the United Nations. AGLINET is a worldwide voluntary network of agricultural libraries with strong regional/country coverage and other collections of specialized subject resources. Member libraries provide low-cost interlibrary loan and photocopy service to other AGLINET libraries, bibliographic information, reproductions (fiche or photocopy), and other cooperative activities as appropriate.

Animal Science Image Gallery

The National Agricultural Library and the American Society of Animal Science are collaborators on the Animal Science Image Gallery, a Web site of animal science images at http://anscigallery.nal.usda.gov. The images, animations, and videos, which also have accompanying text, are intended for classroom and educational outreach. The gallery was originally funded through a USDA Higher Education Challenge Grant, and NAL will host it in perpetuity. Gallery editors, reviewers, and submitters come from the membership of the American Society of Animal Science (ASAS), the American Dairy Science Association, the Poultry Science Association, the Equine Science Society, the American Society for Nutrition, the Society for the Study of Reproduction, and the American College of Theriogenologists.

Building the NAL Collection

NAL annually acquires approximately 17,000 serial titles, including more than 7,000 digital journals. More than 1,500 of those digital journals in agriculture and related sciences are purchased with permanent data-storage rights. NAL has primary responsibility for collecting and retaining all publications of USDA and its agencies, and is the only U.S. national library with a legislated mandate to collect comprehensively in the following disciplines: animal sciences, plant sciences, agricultural economics and statistics, agricultural products, agricultural chemistry and engineering, agronomy and soil conservation, forestry and forest products, rural sociology and rural life, food sciences, and nutrition. In addition to these core subjects, the NAL collection contains extensive materials in such related subjects as biology, natural history, wildlife ecology, pollution, genetics, natural resources, meteorology, and fisheries.

Since the mid-1800s NAL has carried out a strong global program to acquire international publications. In the past, direct purchasing was paired with the exchange of USDA publications with foreign partners. Over the last decade, the changes in publishing practice from paper to digital have essentially eliminated the opportunities for exchange. In general, NAL's acquisition program and collection development policy are based upon its responsibility to provide service to the staff of the Department of Agriculture, U.S. land-grant universities, and the general public in all subjects pertaining to agriculture. The NAL Collection Development Policy (http://www.nal.usda.gov/about/policy/coll_dev_toc.shtml) outlines the scope of subjects collected and the degree of coverage for each subject. This policy is regularly revised to include emerging subject areas and incorporate guidelines for collecting new formats, especially digital formats. NAL collection policies reflect and differentiate the collecting responsibilities of the National Library of Medicine and the Library of Congress. These three national libraries have developed cooperative collection development policy statements for the following subject areas: biotechnology, human nutrition and food, and veterinary sciences.

Special Collections

The NAL special collections program emphasizes access to and preservation of rare and unique materials documenting the history of agriculture and related sciences. Items in the library's special collections include rare books, manuscripts, nursery and seed trade catalogs, posters, objects, photographs, and other rare or unique materials documenting agricultural subjects. Materials date from the 1500s to the late 1900s and include many international sources.

Detailed information about NAL special collections is available on the NAL Web site at http://www.nal.usda.gov/speccoll.

NAL special collections of note include the following:

- The U.S. Department of Agriculture History Collection (http://www.nal. usda.gov/speccoll/collect/history.html), assembled over 80 years by USDA historians, includes letters, memoranda, reports, and papers of USDA officials, as well as photographs, oral histories, and clippings covering the activities of the department from its founding through the early 1990s. A guide to this collection is viewable via the NAL Web site.

- The U.S. Department of Agriculture Pomological Watercolor Collection (http://www.nal.usda.gov/speccoll/collectionsguide/mssindex/pomology) includes more than 7,000 expertly detailed, botanically accurate watercolor illustrations of fruits and nuts representing newly introduced varieties, healthy and diseased fruits, and depictions of various stages of development. Created between 1880 and 1915, the watercolor illustrations served as official documentation of the work of the Office of the Pomologist and were used for creation of chromolithographs in publications distributed widely by the department. Although created for scientific accuracy, the works in this collection are artistic treasures in their own right. The library recently received a grant to preserve and digitize the entire collection and put it on the Web.

- The Henry G. Gilbert Nursery and Seed Trade Catalog Collection (http://www.nal.usda.gov/speccoll/collectionsguide/nurserycatalogs.shtml) is a rich collection of historic catalogs of the nursery and seed trade. Started in 1904 by USDA economic botanist Percy L. Ricker, the collection is used by researchers to document the introduction of plants to the United States, study economic trends, and illustrate early developments in American landscape design. The earliest catalogs document the trade to the mid-1700s. NAL continues to collect nursery and seed catalogs.

- The Rare Book Collection (http://www.nal.usda.gov/speccoll/collectionsguide/rarebooks.shtml) highlights agriculture's printed historical record and covers a wide variety of subjects. The collection, international in scope, documents early agricultural practices in Britain and Europe as well as the Americas. In 2009 records of 567 items in the NAL Rare Book and Manuscript collections were added to AGRICOLA (AGRICultural On-Line Access). NAL holdings of Carl Linnaeus, "father of taxonomy," include more than 300 books by or about Linnaeus, among them a rare first edition of his 1735 work *Systema Naturae.*
- NAL offers access to more than 390 manuscript collections (http://www.nal.usda.gov/speccoll/collectionsguide/mssindex1.shtml) documenting the story of American agriculture and its influence on the world.

In recent years, special collections staff have enhanced access to the program's unique materials by putting digitized images on its Web site. NAL provides in-house research and reference services for its special collections and offers fee-based duplication services. Detailed indexes to the content of many manuscript collections are available in print as well as on the Web. AGRICOLA—NAL's catalog and index to its collections—includes bibliographic entries for special collection items, manuscripts, and rare books.

Preservation

NAL is committed to the preservation of its print and non-print collections. It continues to monitor and improve the environmental quality of stacks to extend the longevity of all materials in the collection. The long-term strategy is to ensure that the growing body of agricultural information is systematically identified, preserved, and archived.

The library's program of digital conversion of print material has resulted in a growing collection of USDA publications, including *Home and Garden Bulletin, Agriculture Information Bulletin, Agricultural Economic Report, Journal of Agricultural Research, Yearbook of the United States Department of Agriculture,* and several Agricultural Marketing Service series. Other historical USDA publications include the *Report of the Commissioner of Agriculture,* published from 1862 to 1888, continued by the *Report of the Secretary of Agriculture,* published from 1889 to 1893. *Century of Service: The First 100 Years of the United States Department of Agriculture,* published in 1963, explores the history of the department from its establishment in 1862 through the Kennedy administration. NAL also has completed digitizing the popular Agriculture Handbook series and has begun to digitize the Technical Bulletin series. The library provides online access to these and other full-text publications, including many non-USDA historical materials not restricted by copyright, via the NAL digital repository known as AgSpace.

AgSpace

AgSpace, the library's digital repository, is a combination of several efforts within NAL under various stages of development and implementation. Among them are the following:

- The library has undertaken several projects to digitize, store, and provide online access to historic print documents. The majority of the nearly 650,000 pages currently available online are USDA documents. The full text of these materials and more information about these digitization projects can be found at http://naldr.nal.usda.gov.
- NAL is developing procedures to collect, store, and make publicly available the current research publications of USDA scientists and employees. As of the close of 2009, more than 35,000 articles had been added to the repository. AgSpace does not yet hold all appropriate research publications, but NAL is working to acquire them. Eventually, AgSpace will be the primary source and first resort to identify and use all USDA publications, research, and other resources.

Long-range plans include collecting, maintaining, and providing access to a broad range of agricultural information in a wide variety of digital formats. The end result will be a perpetual, reliable, publicly accessible repository of digital documents, datasets, images, audiovisual files, and so forth relating to agriculture.

AGRICOLA

AGRICOLA catalogs and indexes NAL collections, as well as being a primary public source offering worldwide access to agricultural information. AGRICOLA is searchable on the Web (http://agricola.nal.usda.gov), and also can be accessed on a fee basis through several commercial vendors, both online and on CD-ROM. Users can also subscribe to the complete AGRICOLA file on a fee basis from the National Technical Information Service, part of the U.S. Department of Commerce.

The AGRICOLA database covers materials in all formats, including printed works from the 15th century onward. The records describe publications and resources encompassing all aspects of agriculture and allied disciplines. Tens of thousands of AGRICOLA records contain links to networked Web resources. The AGRICOLA database is organized into the two components noted below, and is updated with records for newly cataloged and indexed materials that are searchable separately or together:

- NAL Public Access Catalog, containing more than 900,000 citations to books, audiovisual materials, serial titles, and other materials in the NAL collection (AGRICOLA also contains some bibliographic records for items cataloged by other libraries but not held in the NAL collection)
- NAL Article Citation Database, consisting of 3.8 million citations to serial articles, book chapters, reports, and reprints

In 2007 NAL implemented a re-scoped AGRICOLA Index to offer more links to full-text articles and limit duplication with other abstracting and indexing services. To be considered for indexing in AGRICOLA, publications must meet at least one of the following criteria:

- Be a U.S. Department of Agriculture publication, or contain articles or chapters authored by USDA personnel
- Support NAL Information Centers
- Contain articles or chapters on core agricultural topics, written in English
- Not be indexed by other abstracting and indexing service

The 2009 list of publications indexed in AGRICOLA can be found at http://www.nal.usda.gov/agricolajournals. The re-scoped AGRICOLA index continues to serve as the search tool to access NAL collections.

Information Management and Information Technology

Over the past quarter century, NAL has applied information technology to support managing and providing access to a diverse array of agricultural information. Technological developments spearheaded by the library date back to the 1940s and 1950s when NAL Director Ralph Shaw invented "electronic machines" such as the photo charger, rapid selector, and photo clerk. NAL has made numerous technological improvements since.

NAL has fully implemented the Voyager integrated library management system (produced by Endeavor Information Systems, now known as the Ex Libris Group). The system supports ordering, receiving, and invoice processing for purchases; creating and maintaining indexing and cataloging records for AGRICOLA; circulation and the online public access catalog. The Voyager system has also been integrated with the Relais (Relais International, Inc.) system for supporting NAL interlibrary loan and document delivery services.

English-Spanish Agricultural Thesaurus and Glossary

NAL is known for its expertise in developing and using a thesaurus, or controlled vocabulary, a critical component of effective digital information systems. The NAL Agricultural Thesaurus (NALT) (http://agclass.nal.usda.gov/agt.shtml) is a hierarchical vocabulary of agricultural and biological terms. Updated annually, NALT broadly defines the subject scope of agriculture, organized according to 17 subject categories and with 2,649 definitions. Biological nomenclature comprises most terms in the thesaurus, although it also includes terminology in the supporting physical and social sciences. Suggestions for new terms or definitions can be sent by e-mail to NAL.thesaurus@ars.usda.gov.

Originally prepared to meet the needs of Agricultural Research Service (ARS) scientists, NALT is now extensively used to aid retrieval in agricultural information systems within USDA and elsewhere. NALT is the indexing vocabulary for NAL's bibliographic database of 4 million article citations to agricultural resources included in the AGRICOLA database.

NAL released the ninth edition of NALT, containing approximately 78,000 terms, in January 2010. Terminology associated with biofuels, agroforestry, bacteria, viruses, insects, and Solanum and other important Latin American plant species was expanded in this edition. The taxonomic classification of bacteria was realigned based on the second edition of *Bergey's Manual of Systematic Bacteriology.* The taxonomic classification of viruses was realigned based on the *Eighth Report of the International Committee on the Taxonomy of Viruses.*

The NAL Glossary is a collection of definitions of agricultural terms developed in conjunction with the creation of NALT. The 2010 edition contains 2,649 definitions ranging across agriculture and its many ancillary subjects, most composed by NALT staff.

NAL publishes Spanish-language versions of NALT and the glossary, which carry the names *Tesauro Agrícola* and *Glosario,* respectively. The Spanish-language versions of NALT and the glossary support increased Spanish-language access to agricultural information throughout the United States and the world.

During 2009 the Inter-American Institute for Cooperation on Agriculture (IICA) (http://www.iica.int) and NAL expanded their extant collaboration to include the Spanish-and English-language versions of the thesaurus and glossary. With the aid of Latin American experts, IICA and NAL cooperatively develop and maintain these terminology tools to support the advancement of agricultural information in the Americas.

The Spanish-language version of NALT is updated concurrently with the annual release of the English-language version of NALT. The 2010 edition contains more than 73,600 terms and 2,649 definitions. The thesaurus Web site is available in both English and Spanish.

Although these compilations are primarily intended for indexers, computer programmers working with Web search engines, and others who gather and organize information, the glossary and thesaurus are also suitable for students—from fifth grade up—as well as for teachers, writers, translators, and people who work in agriculture. Users can download all four publications in a variety of formats (pdf, XML, txt, MARC 21, and RDF-SKOS) from http://agclass.nal.usda.gov/download.shtml.

Library Services

NAL serves the agricultural information needs of customers through a combination of Web-based and traditional library services including reference, document delivery, and information center services. The NAL Web site offers access to a wide variety of full-text resources as well as online access to reference and document delivery services. In 2009 the library delivered more than 90 million direct customer services throughout the world via its Web site and other Internet-based services.

The main reading room in the library's Beltsville, Maryland, facility features a walk-up service desk, access to an array of digital information resources including full-text scientific journals, a current periodicals collection, and on-site request service for materials from NAL's print collection. NAL also operates a walk-in reference and digital services center at USDA headquarters in downtown

Washington, D.C. Services at both facilities are available 8:30 to 4:30 Monday through Friday, except federal holidays. NAL's reference services are accessible online using "contact us" links on the NAL Web pages, by use of email addressed to agref@ars.usda.gov, by postal mail addressed to "Reference, National Agricultural Library ARS/USDA, 10301 Baltimore Avenue, Beltsville, MD 20705," or by telephone at 301-504-5755. The library's research and reader services team covers all areas and aspects of agriculture and provides reference assistance focused especially on subjects and topic areas not addressed by the various subject-focused information centers of the library.

NAL's information centers are reliable sources of comprehensive, science-based information on key aspects of U.S. agriculture, providing timely, accurate, and in-depth coverage of their specialized subject areas. Their expert staff offer extensive Web-based information resources and advanced reference services. Each NAL information center has its own Web site and is a partner in AgNIC (http://www.agnic.org). Presently, NAL has seven information centers:

- The Alternative Farming Systems Information Center (AFSIC) (http://afsic.nal.usda.gov) specializes in identifying and accessing information relating to farming methods that maintain the health and productivity of the entire farming enterprise, including the world's natural resources. This focus includes sustainable and alternative agricultural systems, crops, and livestock.

- The Animal Welfare Information Center (AWIC) (http://awic.nal.usda.gov) provides scientific information and referrals to help ensure the proper care and treatment of animals used in biomedical research, testing, teaching, and exhibitions, and by animal dealers. Among its varied outreach activities, the center conducts workshops for researchers on meeting the information requirements of the Animal Welfare Act.

- The Food and Nutrition Information Center (FNIC) (http://fnic.nal.usda.gov), a leader in food and human nutrition information dissemination since 1971, provides credible, accurate, and practical resources for nutrition and health professionals, educators, government personnel, and consumers. FNIC maintains a staff of registered dietitians, specialists with training in food science and human nutrition who can answer questions on food and human nutrition.

- The Food Safety Information Center (FSIC) (http://foodsafety.nal.usda.gov) provides links to consumer, educator, and research information on a variety of food safety topics. In 2009 in-depth technical fact sheets on popular topics such as aflatoxins, salmonella, and E. coli were released. FSIC also found success in using the social networking site Twitter to engage with those interested in food safety, gaining more than 5,300 followers.

- The National Invasive Species Information Center (NISIC) (http://www.invasivespeciesinfo.gov) is a gateway to invasive species information, covering federal, state, local, and international sources. The Web site provides accessible, accurate, referenced, up-to-date, and comprehensive information on invasive species; information useful to local, state, tribal, and federal managers, policy-makers, scientists, teachers, students, and others.

• The Rural Information Center (http://ric.nal.usda.gov) provides services for local officials, organizations, businesses, and rural residents working to maintain the vitality of rural areas. It collects and disseminates information on such diverse topics as community economic development, small business development, access to health care, finance, housing, environment, quality of life, community leadership, and education.

• The Water Quality Information Center (WQIC) (http://wqic.nal.usda.gov) collects, organizes, and communicates scientific findings, educational methodologies, and public policy issues relating to water resources and agriculture. The center provides access to numerous bibliographies and a database of online documents relating to water and agriculture.

In addition to these information centers, NAL manages the Nutrition.gov Web site (http://www.nutrition.gov) in collaboration with other USDA agencies and the Department of Health and Human Services. This site provides vetted, science-based nutrition information for the general consumer and highlights the latest in nutrition news and tools from across federal government agencies. A team of registered dietitians at NAL's Food and Nutrition Information Center maintains Nutrition.gov and answers questions on food and nutrition issues.

The site is an important tool for developing food- and exercise-based strategies for weight management and for disseminating the work of multiple federal agencies in a national obesity prevention effort. Nutrition.gov includes databases, recipes, interactive tools, and specialized information for infants and children, adult men and women, and seniors. It provides a comprehensive source of information on nutrition and dietary guidance from multiple federal agencies.

Web-Based Products and Services

In 2009 the NAL Web sites collectively received an average of 8 million hits a month from people seeking agricultural information. As NAL continues to improve its Web site functionality, search capability, and content, it anticipates that usage will continue to increase.

NAL was an early adopter of social media/Web 2.0 technologies. It has a growing presence on Twitter and is also utilizing Facebook to increase its user population.

"InfoFarm: The NAL Blog" (http://weblogs.nal.usda.gov/infofarm) has been addressing the topics of agriculture and libraries since October 2007. A few times a week, InfoFarm postings highlight NAL resources that customers might not find on their own. The blog's content keeps its readers informed on a range of issues from farm safety to food safety, from livestock to legislation. The online magazine *Slate* favorably reviewed the NAL blog, commenting that "the best government blogs actually sound like blogs," and *Government Video* crowned InfoFarm "Web Site of the Week" in November 2009.

DigiTop

DigiTop, USDA's Digital Desktop Library, provides online access to thousands of journals in full text, 13 citation databases, hundreds of newspapers from around the world, significant additional digital reference resources, and an array of personalized services. DigiTop is available to the entire USDA work force worldwide—more than 100,000 people—24 hours a day. NAL staff provides help desk services, continuous user education, and training for DigiTop users. During fiscal year 2009 nearly 1,250,000 articles were downloaded from DigiTop.

Document Delivery Services

NAL's document delivery operation responds to thousands of requests each year for agricultural information materials from USDA employees and from libraries and organizations around the world. For USDA employees, NAL also acquires needed information materials that are not otherwise available from NAL collections.

NAL uses the Relais Enterprise document request and delivery system integrated with its Voyager library system, with DigiTop, and other Open-URL and ISO ILL compliant systems to support document delivery. NAL customers can request and receive materials electronically and check on the status of their requests via the World Wide Web. Documents are requested from NAL via the Web, using AGRICOLA or blank request forms. NAL also accepts requests via OCLC (NAL's symbol is AGL) and DOCLINE (NAL's libid is MDUNAL). See http://www.nal.usda.gov/services/request.shtml for details.

Leadership

Simon Y. Liu, formerly an associate director of the National Library of Medicine (NLM) and the director of its Office of Computer and Communications Systems, was named NAL director effective February 14, 2010.

A native of Taiwan, he received his undergraduate training there. In postgraduate training in the United States, he earned master's degrees in computer science, business administration, and government from Indiana University, the University of Maryland, and Johns Hopkins University, respectively. He has received two doctoral degrees (in higher education and computer science) from George Washington University and holds adjunct faculty and graduate school appointments at several institutions.

Before his service with NLM he held information technology and management leadership positions with the U.S. Departments of Justice and Treasury, following private-sector contractor work supporting software development for NASA information systems and space mission studies.

Liu succeeds Peter Young, who left NAL in late 2008 to take a position with the Library of Congress. Eleanor Frierson served as acting director in the interim.

National Library of Medicine

8600 Rockville Pike, Bethesda, MD 20894
301-496-6308, 888-346-3656, fax 301-496-4450
E-mail publicinfo@nlm.nih.gov
World Wide Web http://www.nlm.nih.gov

Kathleen Cravedi

Director, Office of Communications and Public Liaison

Melanie Modlin

Deputy Director, Office of Communications and Public Liaison

The National Library of Medicine (NLM) in Bethesda, Maryland, is a part of the National Institutes of Health (NIH), U.S. Department of Health and Human Services. As the world's largest biomedical library and the developer of trusted electronic information services, NLM delivers trillions of bytes of data to millions of users every day.

NLM is a key link in the chain that translates biomedical research into practice, making the results of research—DNA sequences, clinical trials data, toxicology and environmental health data, published scientific articles, and consumer health information—readily available worldwide. Internationally recognized as a leader in biomedical informatics and information technology, NLM also conducts and supports a wide spectrum of leading-edge informatics research and development in electronic health records, clinical decision support, information retrieval, advanced imaging, computational biology, telecommunications, and disaster response.

In today's increasingly digital world, NLM carries out its mission of enabling biomedical research, supporting health care and public health, and promoting healthy behavior by

- Acquiring, organizing, and preserving the world's scholarly biomedical literature
- Providing broad access to biomedical and health information, in partnership with the 5,800-member National Network of Libraries of Medicine
- Serving—via its National Center for Biotechnology Information—as a leading global resource for building, curating, and providing sophisticated access to molecular biology and genomic information, including that from the Human Genome Project and Genome-Wide Association Studies
- Creating high-quality information services relevant to disaster preparedness, toxicology and environmental health, health services research, and public health computational biology, telecommunications, and disaster response
- Conducting research and development on biomedical communications systems, methods, technologies, and networks and information dissemination and utilization among health professionals, patients, and the general public

• Funding advanced biomedical informatics research and serving as the primary supporter of pre- and post-doctoral research training in biomedical informatics at 18 U.S. universities

The library is open to all and has many services and resources for scientists, health professionals, historians, and the general public. NLM has more than 14 million books, journals, manuscripts, audiovisuals, and other forms of medical information, in more than 150 languages, on its shelves. Patrons also have access to a remarkable collection of books, manuscripts, and art relating to the history of the health sciences. Used not only by scholars, these materials are frequently integrated into exhibitions and displays for visitors. Traveling versions of NLM exhibitions attract crowds across the country.

NLM continues to focus on the goals of its 2006–2016 long-range plan, including key activities in support of interoperable electronic health records, more-effective disaster and emergency response, and development of a robust knowledge base for personalized health care.

Scientific Information Services

The most frequently consulted online scientific medical resource in the world is MEDLINE/PubMed, a publicly available database of references and abstracts for medical journal articles from 1948 to the present. During 2009 PubMed added approximately 825,000 new citations for a total of more than 20 million from 36,000 journals, some dating back to the 1950s. A new and streamlined user interface presents users with additional perspectives on the information retrieved.

Another important part of NLM's vast online holdings is PubMed Central (PMC), a Web-based repository of biomedical journal literature providing free, unrestricted access to the full text of articles. As of September 2009 PMC contained more than 1.8 million articles from nearly 700 journals. A growing number of articles by NIH-funded researchers are now being deposited and made available to the public via PMC, in response to the NIH Public Access Policy.

GenBank, another widely used NLM resource, began modestly, as a collection of 600 DNA sequences for the entire year 1982, and now includes all publicly available DNA sequences—155 million from more than 300,000 organisms. In response to the H1N1 outbreak, a specialized mechanism for contributing influenza sequence data has been established.

Integrated retrieval tools allow seamless searching of the data housed in GenBank and more than 40 integrated biomedical databases, including related literature and curated reference gene and genome databases developed by NLM's National Center for Biotechnology Information (NCBI) to support rapid advances in research.

In addition to the widely known GenBank and MEDLINE/PubMed databases, NCBI continues to expand its resource of more than 40 integrated biomedical databases that support the rapid advances in research.

Launched in fiscal year (FY) 2009, the Sequence Read Archive (SRA) is absorbing the data from the 1000 Genomes Project. It is one of the fastest-growing biological databases in existence, with more than 10 terabytes of sequence data currently under management and a growth rate of about 1 terabyte a month. NCBI's role in organizing these voluminous data is a critical step in the discovery process that detects important new associations between genes and then translates that information into better diagnoses and treatments.

The dbGaP database, which links genotype data with phenotype information from clinical research studies to support identification of genetic factors that influence health, continues to expand and serves as the public repository for the trans-NIH Genome-Wide Association Studies (GWAS) project.

As the central coordinating body for clinical terminology standards within DHHS, NLM works closely with the Office of the National Coordinator for Health Information Technology (ONC) to promote adoption and "meaningful use" of electronic health records (EHRs). NLM supports, develops, and disseminates key data standards that are targets for U.S. health information exchange in ONC's recently published criteria for certification of EHRs. NLM's Lister Hill Center is actively engaged in research on Next Generation EHRs, while also developing tools and frequently used subsets of large terminologies to help EHR developers and users implement health data standards. In addition, the Lister Hill Center leads research to create and improve biomedical communications systems, technologies, and networks.

NLM has a long history of providing health information during times of disaster. Through its Disaster Information Management Resource Center, under the Division of Specialized Information Services (SIS), NLM is building on proven emergency backup and response mechanisms within the National Network of Libraries of Medicine to promote effective use of libraries and specially trained librarians in disaster-management efforts. NLM also investigates new methods for sharing health information in emergencies as its contribution to the unique Bethesda Hospital Emergency Preparedness Partnership, a model of private-public hospital collaboration for coordinated disaster planning. NLM also partners with the Pan American Health Organization and other bodies in the Central American Network for Disaster and Health Information to promote capacity-building activities in the area of disaster-related information management. SIS creates additional information resources and services in toxicology, environmental health, chemistry, and HIV/AIDS.

Information Services for the Public

NLM has extensive information resources to serve the general public, from young children to senior citizens. The library's main portal for consumer health information is MedlinePlus (http://www.medlineplus.gov), available in both English and Spanish with selected materials in nearly 50 other languages. In FY 2009 MedlinePlus had more than 120 million unique visitors from every state in the United States and many countries around the world. In addition to more than 800 "health topics," MedlinePlus has interactive tutorials for persons with low literacy, a medical dictionary, an illustrated medical encyclopedia, directories of hospitals and providers, surgical videos, and links to scientific literature. A "medlineplus4you" Twitter feed makes use of social media to increase the public's awareness of these free resources. In addition, to respond to the large and rapidly growing mobile Internet audience, NLM recently launched Mobile MedlinePlus, which delivers the same authoritative consumer health information to users on the go. For example, users can look up the side effects for their new prescription on Mobile MedlinePlus while they're waiting for the pharmacists to fill their order.

NLM celebrated its third year of producing the quarterly magazine *NIH MedlinePlus,* an outreach effort made possible with support from NIH and the non-profit Friends of the NLM. The free magazine contains no advertising and is widely distributed to the public via physician offices, libraries, and other locations, and has a readership of up to 5 million nationwide. Each magazine focuses on the latest research results, clinical trials, and new or updated guidelines from the various NIH institutes. A Spanish/English version, *NIH MedlinePlus Salud,* was launched in January 2009 with support from the National Alliance for Hispanic Health to address the specific health needs of the growing Hispanic population.

Another information resource for the public is NIHSeniorHealth.gov, a collaborative effort of NLM and the National Institute on Aging, as well as other NIH institutes and centers. NIHSeniorHealth.gov contains information in a format that is especially tailored to seniors' cognitive needs—large type, for example. It also has a "talking" function that allows users to listen as the text is read to them.

ClinicalTrials.gov (http://www.ClinicalTrials.gov), created in 2000 by the Lister Hill Center, provides comprehensive information about all types of clinical research studies. The popular site has more than 86,000 protocol records sponsored by the U.S. government, the pharmaceutical industry, and academic and international organizations from all 50 states and 172 countries. ClinicalTrials.gov receives more than 52 million page views a month and hosts approximately 800,000 unique visitors a month. In 2008 NLM added the capability to submit summary results data on clinical trials of drugs and devices. Required by law, this first-of-its-kind resource includes results data on primary and secondary outcomes of registered trials, as well as information on the patient populations studied. The ClinicalTrialsg.gov registry and results database is a unique resource for scientific and clinical information that can assist in giving patients, healthcare providers, and researchers more-comprehensive information about ongoing and completed research.

NLM exhibitions, large and small, highlight the library's historical resources and expand its audience. Designed to appeal to the public as well as the specialist, most of the shows travel to libraries and other institutions around the nation. The current exhibition "Against the Odds: Making a Difference in Global Health" looks at the revolution in global health that is taking place around the world. This interactive display on the Bethesda, Maryland, campus of NIH also includes an informative Web site and lesson plans for middle school and high school teachers. Traveling versions of NLM exhibitions, provided free of charge to libraries nationwide, explore topics as diverse as African American surgeons, Charles Darwin, Harry Potter's relationship to medieval science, and America's women physicians. NLM's History of Medicine Division's Exhibition Program coordinates these efforts.

NLM's information services and research programs serve the nation and the world by supporting scientific discovery, clinical research, education, health care delivery, public health response, and the empowerment of people to improve their personal health. The library is committed to the innovative use of computing and communications to enhance effective public access to the results of biomedical research.

Administration

The director of the library, Donald A. B. Lindberg, M.D., is guided in matters of policy by a board of regents consisting of 10 appointed and 11 ex officio members.

Table 1 / Selected NLM Statistics*

Library Operation	Volume
Collection (book and nonbook)	14,373,745
Items cataloged	20, 615
Serial titles received	20,096
Articles indexed for MEDLINE	712,675
Circulation requests processed	442,511
For interlibrary loan	271,592
For on-site users	170,919
Computerized searches (MEDLINE/PubMed)	1,281,180,957
Budget authority	$330,771,000
Staff	754

*For the year ending September 30, 2009

United States Government Printing Office

732 North Capitol St. N.W., Washington, DC 20401
World Wide Web http://www.gpo.gov

Gary Somerset

Media and Public Relations Manager
202-512-1957, e-mail gsomerset@gpo.gov

The U.S. Government Printing Office (GPO) is the federal government's primary centralized resource for gathering, cataloging, producing, providing, and preserving published information in all its forms. Since its inception, GPO has offered Congress, the courts, and government agencies a set of centralized services, enabling them to produce printed documents easily and cost effectively according to a uniform set of federal government specifications. In addition, GPO has offered these publications for sale to the public and made them widely available at no cost through the Federal Depository Library Program (FDLP).

Today GPO is at the epicenter of technological change as it embraces its historic mission while looking to the digital future, transforming itself into a digital information processing facility that will follow its mission into the 21st century and beyond.

GPO is part of the legislative branch of the federal government and operates under the authority of the public printing and documents chapters of Title 44 of the U.S. Code. In addition to Congress, all three branches of the federal government rely on GPO's services. Congressional documents, Supreme Court decisions, federal regulations and reports, IRS tax forms, and U.S. passports all are produced by or through GPO.

GPO's headquarters, which includes a bookstore, is located in Washington, D.C. Nationwide, GPO maintains 15 field locations and two major distribution facilities, in Pueblo, Colorado, and Laurel, Maryland.

GPO's information dissemination activities include FDLP, which disseminates information products from all three branches of government to nearly 1,250 libraries nationwide; GPO's Federal Digital System (FDsys), which provides online access to titles on GPO servers, as well as links to titles on other federal Web sites; and a Publications Sales Program that sells government publications to the public.

GPO also administers the Cataloging and Indexing Program, the By-Law Program, and the distribution component of the International Exchange Program of the Library of Congress. To achieve its mission to provide timely, permanent, no-fee public access to federal government publications, GPO coordinates a network of libraries that assist the public in using U.S. government information resources; maintains such tools as the *Catalog of Government Publications* (*CGP*) to identify, describe, locate, and obtain publications; and maintains a permanent collection of government publications.

Together, these activities disseminate one of the world's largest collections of published information.

Federal Digital System

GPO's Federal Digital System (FDsys) was launched in January 2009. FDsys will replace GPO Access after all content within GPO Access is migrated into FDsys, which is scheduled to happen in 2010. FDsys is managing, preserving, providing version control and access to, and disseminating authentic U.S. government information. FDsys will include all known federal government documents within the scope of GPO's FDLP and other information-dissemination programs. The system design is based on the Reference Model for an Open Archival Information System (OAIS) (ISO 14721:2003). FDsys is a one-stop site for authentic published government information. Six months after its launch, it was named one of the top government Web sites by *Government Computer News*.

FDsys allows federal content creators to create and submit content to be preserved, authenticated, managed, and delivered upon request. Content entered into the system is cataloged according to GPO metadata and document-creation standards. This content is available for Web searching, Internet viewing, downloading, and printing, and as document masters for conventional and on-demand printing or other dissemination methods. Content may include text and associated graphics, including print, digital, video, audio, or other forms that may emerge.

In 2009 a new publication, *Daily Compilation of Presidential Documents,* was specifically engineered for FDsys. This online publication, launched in February, contains information released by the White House press office regarding orders, statements, and remarks made by the president. It replaces the printed *Weekly Compilation of Presidential Documents* and can be found at http://fdsys.gpo.gov/fdsys/browse/collection.action?collectionCode=CPD.

In October the White House, GPO, and the National Archives' Office of the Federal Register (OFR) achieved a breakthrough in making government information available and usable by the public. GPO converted the text of the *Federal Register* (2000–2009) into XML (extensible markup language) and placed it online in numerous federal government portals, including GPO's Federal Digital System (http://www.gpo.gov/fdsys/bulkdata/FR), the *Federal Register* Web site (http://www.federalregister.gov), and the government's new portal for government data (http://www.data.gov). In January 2010 the *Code of Federal Regulations (CFR)*—the codification of the general and permanent rules published in the *Federal Register* by the executive departments and agencies of the federal government—was also placed online in XML at these sites. This project began when President Barack Obama challenged federal agencies to create a more open and transparent government.

To search FDsys, visit http://www.fdsys.gov.

Authentication

The increasing use of electronic documents poses special challenges in verifying authenticity because digital technology makes such documents easy to alter or copy, leading to multiple, non-identical versions that can be used in unauthorized or illegitimate ways.

To help meet this challenge, GPO began implementing digital signatures to certain electronic documents on FDsys that not only establish GPO as the trusted information disseminator but also provide the reassurance that an electronic document has not been altered since GPO disseminated it. Continued implementation led to the release of additional authenticated content in fiscal year (FY) 2009 and laid the groundwork for still more content to be authenticated in 2010.

In January 2009 GPO launched authenticated congressional bills. All versions of bills from the 110th and 111th Congresses were authenticated in this application. This is expected to be the last application authenticated on GPO Access; future authenticated content will be released on FDsys.

Also in January 2009 the first group of migrated collections was released. Two collections in this group, Public and Private Laws and Congressional Bills, were authenticated for all years available. In May 2009 the Budget of the United States Government was authenticated and released on FDsys, so that all collections that have been authenticated on GPO Access now are authenticated on FDsys for all years available.

FY 2009 also saw the release of four additional authenticated collections on FDsys: *Congressional Directory,* the *Congressional Record* (bound edition), the *U.S. Government Manual,* and the *Statutes at Large.* Preparations are complete to authenticate four collections already on FDsys in early FY 2010—the *List of CFR Sections Affected (LSA),* the *Weekly Compilation of Presidential Documents,* and the *Daily Compilation of Presidential Documents.*

More information on the authentication initiative can be accessed at http://www.gpoaccess.gov/authentication.

Online Training

During FY 2009 GPO created several educational articles and FAQs. Tutorials were created for the FDLP Desktop, Resources for New Depository Coordinators, Depository Administration, GPO Cataloging, and Self Studies.

As part of its education and outreach mission, GPO has presented several programs on topics relating to FDLP through Online Programming for All Libraries (OPAL), a Web conferencing service. Recent programming from GPO staff, GPO interns, and federal depository staff includes "An Overview of Microfiche, Shipping Lists, and SuDocs Classification," "OSTI: A Very Brief Overview of OSTI Offerings," "Searching for Free Government Full Text Docs Online: Where to Begin," "Disseminating Government Information in Partnership with GPO," "Geology Librarianship and Government Documents," "Geographic Information System Programs in Libraries," "Orientation for New FDLP Depository Staff," "The Conservation Kitchen Returns: Wraps, Jackets, and Boxed Treats," and "Overview of Authentication and Authentication of FDLP Partner Content."

In FY 2010 GPO staff and members of the depository community will continue to present educational sessions in OPAL, and these sessions will remain available as an archive on the OPAL Web site, which can be accessed at http://www.opal-online.org/archiveGPO.htm.

Federal Depository Library Program

Integrated Library System

The overall goal of the implementation of GPO's Integrated Library System (ILS) is the provision of access to bibliographic records of federal government publications, many containing links to the electronic version of the publication. The ILS system's power and capabilities can be utilized to provide needed services. The goal is also to streamline workflow and internal activities in support of FDLP and reduce the use of and dependency on legacy systems.

The enhanced online *Catalog of Government Publications* (*CGP*) is an index of public documents from all three branches of the federal government, currently covering 1976 forward. In the online information environment, *CGP* is essential to GPO's core mission of ensuring that the public has access to federal government information. *CGP* continues to move forward in providing public access. From its launch in March 2006 through FY 2009, nearly 72 million searches of *CGP* were made, an average of more than 58,000 successful requests a day. The enhanced *CGP* is a component of a modernization plan to replace older legacy systems with GPO's state-of-the-art ILS. *CGP* can be found at http://catalog. gpo.gov.

Future enhancements to GPO's ILS will include implementing the MetaLib federated searching product (multi-database searching capability) available from *CGP*, and enhancements to the Federal Depository Library Directory (FDLD), an interface that allows the public to access, search, and export library directory information.

During FY 2009 Library Technical Information Services (LTIS) continued to deploy enhancements to the ILS Aleph 500, with the goal of improving services to the public in addition to providing services to participants in FDLP. The focus of ILS project activities in FY 2009 was database cleanup and maintenance. LTIS entered into an agreement with Library Technologies, Inc. (LTI) to purchase authority control services for *CGP*. LTI evaluated every bibliographic record (more than 500,000) in *CGP* and identified errors in name, series, and subject headings. These errors were corrected, which improved searching and indexing functionality. To continue this maintenance activity for newly created records, GPO contracted with LTI to provide authority control services for *CGP* on a monthly subscription basis. In addition, LTIS undertook a de-duplication project to consolidate and eliminate duplicate records in *CGP* that resulted from the initial data load from *Monthly Catalog* files in 2006.

Growth of *CGP* will be evident in 2010 following the award in September 2009 of a contract to transcribe GPO's historic shelflist cards. The metadata transcription of the pre-1976 cards continued in FY 2009. A reassessment of project workflow and deliverables was completed by GPO's Library Services and Content Management (LSCM). PTFS (Progressive Technology Federal Systems, Inc.), which was contracted in FY 2008 to assist with the project, was tasked with digitization of approximately 300,000 cards in FY 2009. Metadata transcription tasks were incorporated into the routine LTIS workflow. With the assistance of two graduate students in library science hired by LSCM during the summer, more than 6,000 monograph cards were transcribed. Cataloging librarians in LTIS provided the quality control and enhanced the records with valid Library of

Congress subject headings and authorized name authority headings. Additional staffing resources to undertake metadata transcription will continue.

Automated Metadata Extraction Project

In late 2007 GPO entered into an interagency agreement with the Defense Technical Information Center (DTIC), in collaboration with Old Dominion University (ODU), to create cataloging records using automated metadata extraction software tools and processes currently used by DTIC and the National Aeronautics and Space Administration (NASA). In FY 2009 LSCM and ODU continued to evaluate and refine the automated tool using the Environmental Protection Agency (EPA) document collection, and ODU produced a sample batch of metadata records for review by LSCM. Additionally, LSCM delivered a second batch of 1,000 FDLP in-scope congressional pdf files to ODU for analysis. The LSCM project team determined that the records produced for the EPA collection by the automated metadata extraction tool did not meet the minimum requirements and cataloging standards set forth by LSCM absent major or full human modifications to the record. The EPA documents, selected at random from a large EPA Web harvesting project LSCM conducted in early 2007, were published by a variety of EPA offices throughout the country. These documents proved to be problematic from a programming perspective because bibliographic information often was not presented in a standardized format or location on the document, making it hard for the ODU/DTIC tool to identify critical bibliographic metadata.

As part of the second phase of the agreement, ODU analyzed the congressional collection of documents and provided LSCM with a characterization and feasibility report. ODU was preparing a final report on the two-year project, including recommendations as to cost and feasibility of implementation based on the two document collections provided by LSCM. Results of the project will be shared with the FDLP community.

Digitization Efforts

LSCM continues to work with staff at the Library of Congress on the digitization of the bound *Congressional Record* from the 43rd Congress through the 105th Congress. The library is digitizing the material, which then will be ingested and made available as part of FDsys. This material is in addition to the digitization of the *Statutes at Large*. The library has completed the conversion of this material into preservation files, which will also be made available through FDsys.

LSCM staff continued to work with other federal agencies on the Federal Agencies Digitization Guidelines Initiative. LSCM is an active participant in the Federal Still Image Digitization Working Group, established to develop common standards for federal agencies and institutions, and also continues to participate in the federal agencies audiovisual group. A Web site (http://www.digitization guidelines.gov) highlights the work done so far, including a digital imaging framework and content categories and digitization objectives.

LSCM seeks to increase its collaboration in digitization projects by actively seeking partners who possess digitized files that can be ingested into FDsys. This year saw the implementation of an agreement with the National Oceanic and Atmospheric Administration's (NOAA's) coastal zone information center to make its material available through FDsys once the system can ingest converted content. LSCM encourages interested parties to use the partnership Web site to find out more about partnership possibilities and requirements. The partnership inquiry form is available at http://www.fdlp.gov/component/form/?form_id=3.

Registry of U.S. Government Publications Digitization Projects

GPO continues to expand its collaborative digitization effort. LSCM has updated and refreshed the digitization initiatives Web site. Now titled "Federal Publications Digitization and Public Access Files Initiatives," it is located at http://www.fdlp.gov/home/about/453.

The Web site includes an update of the white paper *Priorities for Digitization of the Legacy Collection.* Guidelines on additional file formats acceptable for ingest into FDsys also have been updated. In an effort to increase awareness and participation in LSCM's digitization efforts, a flyer has been developed highlighting partnerships and the registry of U.S. Government Publication Projects. The registry currently lists more than 170 federal government digitization projects from institutions throughout the United States. Additional information about GPO's Digitization and Preservation Initiatives can be found at http://registry.fdlp.gov.

FDLP Partnerships

New partnerships were formed during FY 2009 with GAO and the Association of Schools of Public Health (ASPH). The partnership with GAO provides permanent public access to GAO reports and GAO comptroller general decisions databases available on the GAO Web site. This content previously was duplicated on GPO Access. This agreement eliminated duplication, minimized version control issues, and ensured permanent public access to these comprehensive content collections. LSCM joined with ASPH to provide electronic access to *Public Health Reports,* the official journal of the U.S. Public Health Service published by ASPH. The partnership agreement ensures continued federal depository library access to this journal. During FY 2009 LSCM also renewed its content partnerships with the National Library of Medicine and the National Renewable Energy Laboratory.

Efforts to promote partnerships and encourage depository libraries and federal agencies to enter into partnerships with LSCM expanded during the year. A marketing plan for partnerships was developed and released in May 2009. A partnership logo was made available in June for partners to use in highlighting their relationship with LSCM. Marketing materials highlighting browse topics and the partnership program and its benefits were distributed during depository library council meetings and at various events throughout the year. For the most current list of LSCM partners and additional information, visit http://www.fdlp.gov/outreach/partnerships.

Depository Library Administration and Public Access Assessments

FDLs follow FDLP requirements found in Title 44, United States Code, Chapter 19, as well as those prescribed by GPO. These requirements, as well as guidance to help depository library personnel understand them, are found in the *Federal Depository Library Handbook*. The handbook and periodic updates are disseminated via FDLP Desktop, a Web resource for depository library personnel found at http://www.fdlp.gov/administration/handbook.

GPO reviews how each individual depository library applies the requirements and guidance as it has the responsibility to ensure that libraries receiving federal government publications are fulfilling the responsibility of making the publications freely available to the public (44USC§1909). This is accomplished primarily through the Public Access Assessments program, a review of conditions at each individual depository library. The program emphasizes how FDLs serve the public's information needs by reviewing how each library provides access to and services for U.S. government information resources. Public Access Assessments also offer the opportunity for GPO and individual libraries to share information so as to increase the efficiency and effectiveness of FDLP.

FDLP Marketing Plan and Customer Relations Program

The services provided by FDLs and administered by GPO are unique and essential to the public; together, GPO and FDLs can utilize these services to the fullest.

Many critical calls for help with marketing the services and benefits of FDLs and the FDLP have been made by the Depository Library Council and depository librarians throughout the country. In response to these calls, GPO is proposing a variety of marketing strategies and activities.

The FDLP Marketing Plan is designed to give FDLs the tools they need to market their valuable services to all audiences in the most effective way possible. The FDLP Marketing Plan, Phases 1 and 2, is available at http://www.fdlp.gov/outreach/promotionalresources/98-fdlpmarketingplan.

The performance framework of government is increasingly "customer-centric," yet is still outpaced by the rising expectations of customers. The necessity to understand those whom government serves, and their needs, is therefore of the utmost importance. While GPO has long had channels to obtain feedback and suggestions from the depository library community, these methods have not been cyclical or embedded into the planning and business processes.

During FY 2009 LSCM was asked specifically to develop and implement a formal customer relations program for FDLs that would delineate them by type of library. Establishing such a plan allows LSCM to better serve depository library needs. It also allows LSCM to monitor and document business operations to ensure provision of appropriate customer care, response to mission requirements, and solicitation of feedback from depository libraries on performance.

The Customer Relations Program: Plan for FDL Partners identifies two goals: (1) develop a customer relations program that will identify needed improvements in services to and communication with FDLs, address identified needs, and use quantitative metrics for success measures; (2) develop a customer relations program that will identify and report on needed improvements in business processes that support services provided to FDLs.

The segmentation survey of depository libraries conducted in spring 2009 was the first step in doing research to understand the varied needs of the FDLP's diverse libraries and depository users. A formal customer relations plan is now in place, and work has begun to implement action items from the program.

LSCM *Year in Review*

GPO published the second annual LSCM FY 2009 *Year in Review*. This document recounts LSCM's major accomplishments during the fiscal year in support of FDLP, Cataloging and Indexing Program, International Exchange Service, and By-Law Program. A copy of *Year in Review* was distributed to every FDL. This document will be released annually each October. *Year in Review* is archived on the FDLP Desktop at http://www.fdlp.gov/home/about/533-yir.

Community Outreach

GPO continues to provide outreach to the depository library community. Efforts include travel by GPO staff, public access assessments, partnerships, online training, and GPO-sponsored meetings.

In FY 2009 GPO outreach activities included participation in more than 40 programs, including the Publishers and Librarians Conference; the ILCEP conference for publishers of science/technical information in the Department of Defense; DigCCurr 2009: Digital Curation Practice, Promise and Prospects; the Partnership for Indian Education Conference; the Society of Government Meeting Planners conference; the National Information Standards Organization (NISO) conference; and a variety of 100th and 125th Federal Depository Library anniversary celebrations.

GPO representatives regularly participate in library association and other professional meetings, local regional meetings, and various workshops. Additionally, in 2010 GPO will hold two Depository Library Council meetings and the Federal Depository Library Conference, convene the Interagency Depository Seminar, and continue to support depository anniversary celebrations. Under the newly established public access assessment program, GPO librarians will work with depository libraries to assure free public access to federal government information and consult on best practices.

Distribution and Other Statistics

The following statistics reflect notable LSCM metrics for FY 2009:

New Titles Acquired	20,618
Searches of the Catalog of U.S. Government Publications	22,543,806
Total Titles Cataloged	20,938
Total PURLs Created	13,343
Total Titles Distributed	9,738
Total Copies Distributed	2,222,811
Titles Linked to from GPO Access	73,176
Titles Available on GPO Access	252,823

By-Law Distribution of Documents

LSCM administers the dissemination of certain tangible publications as specified by public law. Under Title 44 of the United States Code, GPO is required to provide copies of publications to certain federal agencies and others at the direction of Congress. Two or more copies of every publication printed are provided to the Library of Congress, regardless of whether the publication is distributed to FDLs. The National Archives and Records Administration (NARA) is entitled to receive three copies of every publication printed. Additionally, on behalf of the Department of State, LSCM distributes copies of publications to foreign legations. LSCM also maintains mailing lists for by-law distribution of specific publications.

A database created in 2008 to track by-law publications more efficiently is being updated daily and is providing excellent results. There is adequate on-site storage for the by-law publications. Also in FY 2009, protocols for by-law publications were established between various GPO business units to ensure that all by-law publications are identified as such by the superintendent of documents and that their costs are identified.

International Exchange Service

Under the direction of the Library of Congress, which manages the International Exchange Service (IES) program, LSCM distributes tangible U.S. government publications to foreign governments that agree to send similar publications of their governments to the United States for the library's collections. LSCM has also been assisting the library in its efforts to modernize the IES program. Activities in FY 2009 included reviewing and updating the list of publications distributed to IES libraries and merging mailing lists to reflect the elimination of the distinction between full and partial libraries. These changes went into effect on October 1.

GPO Access

Under Public Law 103-40, GPO is required to maintain an electronic directory of federal electronic information, provide a system of online access to the *Congressional Record,* the *Federal Register,* and other appropriate publications, and operate an electronic storage facility for federal electronic information. GPO's response to this mandate was the launch of GPO Access in 1994. GPO Access began with three databases; today, it allows worldwide access to more than 4,000 databases and 120 applications. Since its inception, GPO Access has experienced a continuous and steady usage increase. There were approximately 316,445,791 GPO Access retrievals in FY 2009.

With 325,999 available titles, GPO Access contains a wide variety of applications, ranging from congressional and legislative information to federal regulations and presidential materials. GPO also hosts 22 federal Web sites, including that of the Supreme Court, as well as a reference suite of services for finding federal government information.

(As noted earlier in this report, GPO's Federal Digital System—FDsys, launched in January 2009—will replace GPO Access after all content within GPO Access is migrated into FDsys, which is scheduled to happen during FY 2010.)

Ben's Guide to U.S. Government

Ben's Guide to U.S. Government (http://bensguide.gpo.gov), the educational component of GPO Access, strives to introduce and explain the workings of all three branches of the federal government. Through the use of primary source materials, grade-appropriate explanations, and a stimulating site design, Ben's Guide not only increases the public's access to and knowledge of the government, but makes learning fun.

The site is broken down into four grade levels (K–2, 3–5, 6–8, and 9–12) and also provides an area for parents and educators. The material in each of these sections is tailored specifically for its intended audience. Ben's Guide includes historical documents and information on legislative processes, elections, and citizenship. The site also features learning activities and a list of federal Web sites designed for students, parents, and educators.

FDLP Desktop and the FDLP Community

The ongoing success of FDLP is due, in large part, to the collaborative relationship between FDLs and LSCM. Taking the idea of collaboration further, LSCM extends this concept online to libraries and partners through Web sites designed to provide program-related information and tools through the FDLP Desktop at http://www.fdlp.gov as well as networking applications to improve collaboration between depositories through the FDLP community site at http://community.fdlp.gov.

In January 2009 FDLP Desktop was released out of beta and continues to evolve, allowing librarians to reference information and complete FDLP-related tasks. This includes the ability to stay abreast of the latest news regarding FDLP, register for FDLP events, order promotional items, download documents, and utilize tools to optimize a library's selection profile. LSCM continues to refine and enhance the desktop by researching and implementing new Web dissemination methods. Improvements are implemented continually, based on feedback from the depository library council, FDLs, partner institutions, and the evolution of Web technologies.

Also in early 2009 LSCM released a beta library networking site to promote more real-time collaboration between FDLs. Networking technologies have experienced phenomenal growth, and LSCM has recognized the advantages of leveraging these tools. The FDLP community site was launched to give members of the FDL community an opportunity to connect, collaborate, and learn from each other in a secure environment. Through the site, members can express themselves and collaborate with colleagues by creating a profile, forming groups, writing and commenting on blogs, starting online discussions, sharing photos and documents, and sending and receiving private messages. By hosting the service on a federal domain, members are guaranteed a secure environment that is not blocked by their institutions and is locked down to prevent unsolicited materials, advertisements, and other vulnerabilities. The site is improved constantly as networking technologies evolve and through feedback received from the FDL community. The FDLP Desktop is available at http://www.fdlp.gov.

Depository Library Spotlight

Depository libraries serve the public every day by providing free access to a wealth of government information products. In May 2009 LSCM began to share information about these invaluable institutions in a new way. Each month LSCM highlights the services or innovations of a different federal depository library or libraries in an article posted on both the GPO Web pages and FDLP Desktop. By spotlighting the activities that different types of FDLs throughout the country pursue to help their communities find and use government information products, LSCM continues to share the strengths and innovations of its partner libraries and helps its services.

So far, libraries spotlighted include regional depositories (an academic library and a state library), a public library, an academic library, a federal service academy library, and a group of libraries that shares its state's regional depository collection cooperatively. These all represent the diversity of libraries and services within FDLP, as well as representing the dedication and expertise of library personnel at FDLs around the country. The spotlight feature is found at http://www.fdlp.gov/outreach/spotlight.

Selling Government Publications

GPO's Sales Program currently offers for sale approximately 5,500 individual government titles on a broad array of subjects. These are sold principally via the Internet, e-mail, telephone, fax, and mail. The program operates on a cost-recovery basis. Publications for sale include books, forms, posters, pamphlets, and CD-ROMs. Subscription services for both dated periodicals and basic-and-supplement services (involving an initial volume and supplemental issues) also are offered.

GPO's U.S. Government Online Bookstore (http://bookstore.gpo.gov) is the prime source of information on its sales inventory. The online bookstore includes a searchable database of all in-print publications as well as an extensive archive of recently out-of-print titles. It also includes a broad spectrum of special publication collections featuring new and popular titles and key product lines. GPO uses Pay.gov, a secure government-wide financial management transaction portal available around the clock to provide timely and efficient processing of online orders. The online bookstore also gives customers the options of expedited shipping, new and improved shopping cart and order confirmation e-mails, and expanded ordering options for international customers.

Express service, which includes priority handling and expedited delivery, is available for orders placed by telephone for domestic delivery. Orders placed before noon eastern time for in-stock publications and single-copy subscriptions will be delivered within two working days. Call the telephone order desk using the toll-free number 866-512-1800 (or 202-512-1800 within the Washington, D.C., area) for more information.

Consumer-oriented publications also are either sold or distributed at no charge through the Federal Citizen Information Center, in Pueblo, Colorado, which GPO operates on behalf of the General Services Administration.

Members of the public can register free of charge to receive e-mail updates when new publications become available for sale through GPO's New Titles by Topic e-mail alert service, which can be accessed at http://bookstore.gpo.gov/alertservice.jsp.

Standing Order Service is available to ensure automatic receipt of many of GPO's most popular recurring and series publications. Standing order customers receive each new edition automatically as soon as it is published. This service can be set up using a MasterCard, American Express, or Discover credit card, or through a superintendent of documents deposit account. For more information on how to set up a standing order for recurring or series publications, e-mail contactcenter@gpo.gov or call 866-512-1800 (toll free) or 202-512-1800 within the Washington, D.C., area.

The GPO Sales Program has begun using print-on-demand technology to increase the long-term availability of publications and is testing the capabilities of a number of vendors. Sales also has brought its bibliographic practices more in line with those of the commercial publishing sector by utilizing ONIX (Online Information Exchange), the publishing industry's standard electronic format for sharing product data with wholesale and retail booksellers, other publishers, and anyone else involved in the sale of books. ONIX enables GPO to have government publications listed, promoted, and sold by commercial book dealers worldwide. GPO sales titles are listed on Amazon.com, Barnesandnoble.com, and other online commercial book selling sites.

National Technical Information Service

U.S. Department of Commerce, Alexandria, VA 22312
800-553-NTIS (6847) or 703-605-6000
World Wide Web http://www.ntis.gov

Linda Davis

Marketing Communications, Office of Federal Services

The National Technical Information Service (NTIS) is the nation's largest and most comprehensive source of government-funded scientific, technical, engineering, and business information produced or sponsored by U.S. and international government sources. NTIS is a federal agency within the U.S. Department of Commerce.

Since 1945 the NTIS mission has been to operate a central U.S. government access point for scientific and technical information useful to American industry and government. NTIS maintains a permanent archive of this declassified information for researchers, businesses, and the public to access quickly and easily. Release of the information is intended to promote U.S. economic growth and development and to increase U.S. competitiveness in the world market.

The NTIS collection of more than 2 million titles contains products available in various formats. Such information includes reports describing research conducted or sponsored by federal agencies and their contractors; statistical and business information; U.S. military publications; multimedia training programs; databases developed by federal agencies; and technical reports prepared by research organizations worldwide. NTIS maintains a permanent repository of its information products.

More than 200 U.S. government agencies contribute to the NTIS collection, including the National Aeronautics and Space Administration; Environmental Protection Agency; the departments of Agriculture, Commerce, Defense, Energy, Health and Human Services, Homeland Security, Interior, Labor, Treasury, Veterans Affairs, Housing and Urban Development, Education, and Transportation; and numerous other agencies. International contributors include Canada, Japan, Britain, and several European countries.

NTIS on the Web

NTIS offers Web-based access to information on government scientific and technical research products. Visitors to http://www.ntis.gov can search the entire collection dating back to 1964 free of charge. NTIS provides many of the technical reports for purchase on CD, paper copies, or downloaded pdf files. RSS feeds of recently catalogued materials are available in 39 major subject categories at http://www.ntis.gov/RSSNTISCategorylist.aspx.

NTIS Database

The NTIS Database offers unparalleled bibliographic coverage of U.S. government and worldwide government-sponsored research information products acquired by NTIS since 1964. Its contents represent hundreds of billions of research dollars and cover a range of important topics including agriculture, biotechnology, business, communication, energy, engineering, the environment, health and safety, medicine, research and development, science, space, technology, and transportation.

The NTIS Database can be leased directly from NTIS and can also be accessed through several commercial services. For an updated list of organizations offering NTIS Database products, see http://www.ntis.gov/products/commercial.aspx.

To lease the NTIS Database directly from NTIS, contact the NTIS Office of Product Management at 703-605-6515. For more information, see http://www.ntis.gov/products/ntisdb.aspx.

NTIS National Technical Reports Library

The National Technical Reports Library (NTRL) enhances accessibility to the NTIS technical reports collection. Subscription rates are based on institutional full-time equivalent (FTE) enrollment of employees. The NTRL operates on a system interface that allows users to do queries on the large NTIS bibliographic database. The intent is to broadly expand and improve access to more than 2.5 million bibliographic records (pre-1960 to present) and 500k full-text documents in pdf format that are directly linked to that bibliographic database. For more information, go to http://www.ntis.gov/products/ntrl.aspx.

Other Databases Available from NTIS

NTIS offers several valuable research-oriented database products. To find out more about accessing the databases, visit http://www.ntis.gov/products/data.aspx.

AGRICOLA

As one of the most comprehensive sources of U.S. agricultural and life sciences information, the AGRICOLA (Agricultural Online Access) Database contains bibliographic records for documents acquired by the National Agricultural Library of the U.S. Department of Agriculture. To access an updated list of organizations offering AGRICOLA Database products, see http://www.ntis.gov/products/agricola.aspx.

AGRIS

The International Information System for the Agricultural Science and Technology (AGRIS) Database is a cooperative system for collecting and disseminating information on the world's agricultural literature in which more than 100 national and multinational centers take part. References to citations for U.S. publications given coverage in the AGRICOLA Database are not included in AGRIS. To access an updated list of organizations offering AGRIS Database products, see http://www.ntis.gov/products/agris.aspx.

Energy Science and Technology

The Energy Science and Technology Database (EDB) is a multidisciplinary file containing worldwide references to basic and applied scientific and technical research literature. The information is collected for use by government managers, researchers at the national laboratories, and other research efforts sponsored by the U.S. Department of Energy, and the results of this research are transferred to the public. To access an updated list of organizations offering EDB products, see http://www.ntis.gov/products/engsci.aspx.

FEDRIP

The Federal Research in Progress Database (FEDRIP) provides access to more than 150,000 current government-sponsored research projects in several fields, including the physical sciences, engineering, and life sciences. To access an updated list of organizations offering FEDRIP Database products, see http://www.ntis.gov/products/fedrip.aspx.

Online Subscriptions

NTIS offers convenient online access, on a subscription basis, to the following resources:

World News Connection

World News Connection (WNC) is an NTIS online news service accessible only via the World Wide Web. WNC makes available English-language translations of time-sensitive news and information from thousands of non-U.S. media. Particularly effective in its coverage of local media, WNC provides the power to identify what is happening in a specific country or region. The information is obtained from speeches, television and radio broadcasts, newspaper articles, periodicals, and books. The subject matter focuses on socioeconomic, political, scientific, technical, and environmental issues and events.

The information in WNC is provided to NTIS by the Open Source Center (OSC), a U.S. government agency. For more than 60 years, analysts from OSC's domestic and overseas bureaus have monitored timely and pertinent open source material, including gray literature. Uniquely, WNC allows subscribers to take advantage of the intelligence-gathering experience of OSC. WNC is updated every government business day. New information is added hourly.

Access to WNC is available through Dialog Corporation. To use the service, complete the WNC form at http://www.dialog.com/contacts/forms/wnc.shtml.

U.S. Export Administration Regulations

U.S. Export Administration Regulations (EAR) provides the latest rules controlling the export of U.S. dual-use commodities, technology, and software. Step by step, EAR explains when an export license is necessary and when it is not, how to obtain an export license, policy changes as they are issued, new restrictions on exports to certain countries and of certain types of items, and where to obtain further help.

This information is available through NTIS in loose-leaf form, on CD-ROM, and online. An e-mail update notification service is also available.

For more information, see http://www.ntis.gov/products/export-regs.aspx.

Special Subscription Services

NTIS Alerts

More than 1,000 new titles are added to the NTIS collection every week. NTIS prepares a list of search criteria that is run against all new studies and research and development reports in 16 subject areas. An NTIS Alert provides a twice-monthly information briefing service covering a wide range of technology topics.

For more information, call the NTIS Subscriptions Department at 703-605-6060 or see http://www.ntis.gov/products/alerts.aspx.

SRIM

Selected Research in Microfiche (SRIM) is an inexpensive, tailored information service that delivers full-text microfiche copies of technical reports based on a customer's needs. Customers choose between Standard SRIM Service (selecting one or more of the 320 existing subject areas) or Custom SRIM Service, which creates a new subject area to meet their particular needs. Custom SRIM Service requires a one-time fee to cover the cost of strategy development and computer programming to set up a profile. Except for this fee, the cost of Custom SRIM is the same as the Standard SRIM. Through this ongoing subscription service, customers receive microfiche copies of new reports pertaining to their field(s) of interest, as NTIS obtains the reports.

For more information, see http://www.ntis.gov/products/srim.aspx. To place an order, call 800-363-2068 or 703-605-6060.

The SRIM service is also available in CD-ROM format—Science and Technology on CD. Documents are digitized and stored in pdf format that can easily be viewed using free Adobe Acrobat Reader software. With Science and Technology on CD, NTIS can provide more publications—those that cannot be rendered on microfiche, such as colorized illustrations or oversized formats.

For more information, see http://www.ntis.gov/products/STonCD.aspx.

NTIS Customer Service

NTIS's automated systems keep it at the forefront when it comes to customer service. Shopping online at NTIS is safe and secure; its secure socket layer (SSL) software is among the best available.

Electronic document storage is fully integrated with NTIS's order-taking process, allowing it to provide rapid reproduction for the most recent additions to the NTIS document collection. Most orders for shipment are filled and delivered anywhere in the United States in five to seven business days. Rush service is available for an additional fee.

Key NTIS Contacts for Ordering

Order by Phone

Sales Desk   800-553-6847 or 703-605-6000
8:30 A.M.–5:00 P.M. Eastern time, Monday–Friday

Subscriptions   800-363-2068 or 703-605-6060
8:30 A.M.–5:00 P.M. Eastern time, Monday–Friday

TDD (hearing impaired)   703-487-4639
8:30 A.M.–5:00 P.M. Eastern time, Monday–Friday

Order by Fax

24 hours a day, seven days a week   703-605-6900
To verify receipt of fax, call 703-605-6090, 7:00 A.M.–5:00 P.M. Eastern Time, Monday–Friday

Order by Mail

National Technical Information Service
5301 Shawnee Rd.
Alexandria, VA 22312

RUSH Service (available for an additional fee)   800-553-6847 or 703-605-6000
Note: If requesting RUSH Service, please do not mail your order

Order Online

Direct and secure online ordering   http://www.ntis.gov

National Archives and Records Administration

8601 Adelphi Rd., College Park, MD 20740
301-837-2000
World Wide Web http://www.archives.gov

Susan M. Ashtianie
Director, Policy and Planning Staff

The National Archives and Records Administration (NARA), an independent federal agency, is the nation's record keeper. NARA safeguards and preserves the records of the federal government, so that the people can discover, use, and learn from this documentary heritage. NARA ensures continuing access to the essential documentation of the rights of American citizens and the actions of their government.

NARA is singular among the world's archives as a unified federal institution that accessions and preserves materials from all three branches of government. It carries out its mission through a national network of archives and records services facilities including presidential libraries documenting administrations back to that of Herbert Hoover. NARA assists federal agencies in documenting their activities, administering records management programs, scheduling records, and retiring non-current records to federal records centers. It also assists the National Historical Publications and Records Commission in its grant program for state and local records and edited publications of the papers of prominent Americans; it archives the papers of key figures in American history, and state and local government records; publishes the laws, regulations, presidential documents, and other official notices of the federal government through the *Federal Register*; and oversees classification and declassification policy in the federal government through the Information Security Oversight Office.

NARA constituents include the federal government, educators and their students at all levels, the public, family historians, the media, the archival community, and a broad spectrum of professional associations and researchers in such fields as history, political science, law, library and information services, and genealogy.

The size and breadth of NARA's holdings are staggering. Together, NARA's facilities hold approximately 4 million cubic feet (equivalent to more than 10 billion pieces of paper) of original textual and nontextual materials from the executive, legislative, and judicial branches of the federal government. Its multimedia collections include more than 120,000 motion picture films; more than 8 million maps, charts, and architectural drawings; more than 250,000 sound and video recordings; more than 27 million aerial photographs; more than 14 million still pictures and posters; and about 90 terabytes of electronic records.

NARA employs approximately 3,500 people, of whom nearly 2,600 are full-time permanent staff members.

Strategic Directions

NARA's strategic priorities are laid out in *Preserving the Past to Protect the Future: The Strategic Plan of the National Archives and Records Administration*

2006–2016, which was revised in 2009. Success for the agency as envisioned in the plan centers on six strategic goals:

- As the nation's record keeper, NARA will ensure the continuity and effective operation of federal programs by expanding its leadership and services in managing the government's records.
- NARA will preserve and process records to ensure access by the public as soon as legally possible.
- NARA will address the challenges of electronic records in government to ensure success in fulfilling NARA's mission in the digital era.
- NARA will provide prompt, easy, and secure access to its holdings anywhere, anytime.
- NARA will increase access to its records in ways that further civic literacy through its museum, public outreach, education, and grants programs.
- NARA will equip itself to meet the changing needs of its customers.

The plan lays out strategies for reaching these goals, sets milestone targets for accomplishments through 2016, and identifies measurements for gauging progress. The targets and measurements are further delineated in NARA's annual performance plans.

NARA's strategic plan and annual performance plans, together with performance and accountability reports, are available on the NARA Web site at http://www.archives.gov/about/plans-reports or by calling 301-837-1850.

Records and Access

Electronic Records Archives

The Electronic Records Archives (ERA) system is NARA's strategic initiative to preserve and provide long-term access to uniquely valuable electronic records of the federal government, and to transition government-wide management of the lifecycle of all records into the realm of e-government. ERA is being developed in five increments between 2005 and 2012. Each increment will build on prior accomplishments and add capabilities and capacity. Two increments have been completed, with three additional ERA instances expected during 2010.

The ERA system began operating on June 27, 2008, and supports the lifecycle management, transfer, and archival storage of federal electronic records. NARA and four federal agency partners (the U.S. Patent and Trademark Office, Bureau of Labor Statistics, Naval Oceanographic Office, and the National Nuclear Security Administration's Kansas City Plant) tested the system's capabilities in a first pilot phase during 2009.

A second increment of ERA was released in December 2008 for records of the Executive Office of the President (EOP), focusing on ingesting into ERA the presidential records of the George W. Bush administration. By law, NARA takes legal custody of all presidential records of an administration when a president leaves office in mid-January. By September 2009 NARA had ingested all 72 terabytes of Bush administration presidential electronic records, comprising 270 million objects created by 42 White House systems that were in proprietary or unique formats. The system has the capability of indexing the textual content of the records as well as metadata, so that the records are searchable both by full content and by metadata, meeting the needs of the presidential libraries.

In January 2010 NARA deployed a third instance of ERA for the backup and storage of electronic records of Congress. NARA provides archival services to Congress as a courtesy, and handling the records is governed by House and Senate rules.

NARA expects to deploy the Online Public Access (OPA) instance of ERA to support public access to records during 2010. OPA will be a Web site that allows researchers and the public to search available electronic records, digital copies of traditional records, descriptions of NARA's holdings, and the archives.gov Web site. The site will be free and available around the clock, and its ongoing design will be based on extensive feedback from NARA's researchers and the public. The OPA catalog will be a search portal to various NARA information sources and services.

Although the current ERA system is robust, development is a long way from complete. Increment 3 of ERA system development focuses on a preservation framework that will allow NARA to implement a variety of tools for long-term preservation of different formats of electronic records. Also expected is the development of an ERA instance for classified records. For more information about ERA, visit http://www.archives.gov/era.

During 2009 NARA established the National Archives Center for Advanced Systems and Technologies (NCAST), which will serve as its premier center for advanced and applied research capabilities in the fields of computer science, engineering, and archival science. NCAST conducts research on new technologies, both to be aware of new types of electronic records NARA will need to preserve and to evaluate new technologies that might be incorporated into the ERA system or other systems to increase their value. For more information about NCAST, visit http://www.archives.gov/ncast.

National Declassification Center

In an executive order signed in December 2009, President Barack Obama directed an overhaul of the way documents created by the federal government are classified and declassified. The stated aim of the initiative is to promote transparency and accountability of government. The president also directed the creation of the National Declassification Center (NDC), now located within NARA.

NDC will lead the streamlining of the declassification process throughout the federal government. In particular, it will accelerate the processing of historically valuable classified records in which more than one federal agency has an interest. It will oversee the development of common declassification processes among agencies, and it will prioritize declassification based on public interest and the likelihood of declassification.

For more information about NDC, visit http://www.archives.gov/declassification.

Archival Research Catalog

Through NARA's Archival Research Catalog (ARC), anyone with a computer connected to the Internet can search descriptions of NARA's nationwide holdings and view digital copies of some of its most popular documents. A significant piece of the electronic access strategy outlined in NARA's strategic plan, this online catalog of all NARA holdings nationwide allows the public, for the first time, to search for information about NARA's vast holdings, including those in the regional archives and presidential libraries, in a single online data system. Because of the vast amount of NARA holdings, it will take several years to fully populate ARC. At present, the catalog contains more than 4.2 million descriptions of NARA's archival holdings, or approximately 70 percent of the total. Included in the catalog are more than 156,000 digital copies of high-interest documents and descriptions of more than 6.4 billion electronic records. The documents available online include many of the holdings highlighted in the Public Vaults, NARA's permanent interactive exhibition. The catalog is available at http://www.archives.gov/research/arc.

Office of Government Information

The Office of Government Information (OGIS), which began operations in September 2009, is charged with providing services to mediate disputes between Freedom of Information Act (FOIA) requesters and federal agencies; reviewing policies and procedures of administrative agencies under FOIA; reviewing agency compliance with FOIA; and recommending policy changes to Congress and the president to improve the administration of FOIA.

OGIS is soliciting and receiving comments and questions from the public regarding the administration of FOIA, and will use the information to improve FOIA processes and to facilitate communications between federal agencies and the public. OGIS is informally mediating disputes between FOIA requesters and agencies, and will begin offering formal mediation services by the end of the current fiscal year.

For more information about OGIS, visit http://www.archives.gov/ogis.

Internet

NARA's Web site, http://www.archives.gov, provides the most widely available means of electronic access to information about and services from the archives. Feedback from visitors to the Web site, as well as visitors to the National Archives building in Washington, D.C., led to portals designed to support the particular needs of genealogists, veterans and their families, educators and students, researchers, the general public, records managers, journalists, information-security specialists, members of Congress, and federal employees. The site includes directions on how to contact NARA and do research at its facilities; descriptions of holdings in an online catalog at http://www.archives.gov/research/arc; direct access to certain archival electronic records at http://www.archives.gov/aad; digital copies of selected archival documents; an Internet Web form (at http://www.archives.gov/contact/inquire-form.html) for customer questions, reference requests, comments, and complaints; electronic versions of Federal Register publications; online exhibits; classroom resources for students and teachers; and such online tools as the interactive inquiry program at http://www.archives.gov/veterans/evetrecs that allows veterans and the next-of-kin of deceased veterans to complete and print, for mail-in submission, requests for their service records. At http://www.archives.gov/presidential-libraries, visitors can link to individual presidential library Web sites.

Copies of military pension records from the American Revolution through World War I, census pages, land files, court records, and microfilm publications can be ordered online, as well as books, apparel, and accessories at http://www.archives.gov/order. Researchers can also submit reference questions about various research topics online. Visitors to the Web site can also obtain RSS feeds for the "Document for Today" feature, NARA news, and press releases.

In cooperation with several federal agencies, NARA also has established a Web portal, http://www.regulations.gov, providing access to federal rules and instructions for submitting comments on federal regulatory actions.

Digitization Projects

NARA is working to digitize its traditional holdings to benefit their preservation and to provide greater access to the public. ARC provides users the ability to identify what archival holdings NARA has via descriptions; however, except for the relatively small amount of material digitized and made available through ARC, it does not provide online access to the holdings themselves. Most of NARA's holdings currently are available only from the archival facility in which they are stored. By digitizing these holdings, NARA will vastly increase public access to them. In 2008 NARA created a strategy to deal with digitization efforts, which includes working with partners in the private sector. Currently more than 1,300 ARC descriptions link to millions of digital copies on partners' Web sites, and many thousands more will be made available in the future. Further information about NARA's digitization partnerships can be found at http://www.archives.gov/digitization/index.html.

Social Media

NARA launched several social media projects in 2009. Its main goals are to increase awareness about archival holdings and programs and to enrich its relationship with the public through social networking conversations. Social media projects are also a new way for NARA to learn more about its researchers, friends, and the general public and what they would like from the National Archives.

NARA shares historical videos from its holdings and videos of recent public events through YouTube, and photographs and documents from its collections through Flickr Commons. NARA can also be found on Facebook, and regularly "tweets" about news and events via Twitter. A Twitter feed from the John F. Kennedy Presidential Library recreates the 1960 campaign trail experience.

The NARAtions blog focuses on online public access and has sparked conversations about ideas NARA hopes to explore as new paths for online searching and digitization. NARA plans to use the blog to share information and collect feedback from the public on its Open Government plan and activities in the coming year. NARA uses IdeaScale, an idea generation and social voting tool, as a way to get input from the public and stakeholders on its participation in the Open Government initiative.

More information about NARA's Web 2.0 projects is available online at http://www.archives.gov/social-media.

The National Archives Experience

The National Archives Experience, a set of interconnected resources made possible by a public-private partnership between NARA and the Foundation for the National Archives, provides a variety of ways of exploring the power and importance of the nation's records.

The Rotunda for the Charters of Freedom at the National Archives building in Washington, D.C., is the cornerstone of the National Archives Experience. On display are the Declaration of Independence, the Constitution, and the Bill of Rights, known collectively as the Charters of Freedom. The Public Vaults is a 9,000-square-foot permanent exhibition that conveys the feeling of going beyond the walls of the rotunda and into the stacks and vaults of the working archives. Dozens of individual exhibits, many of them interactive, reveal the breadth and variety of NARA's holdings. Complementing the Public Vaults, the O'Brien Gallery hosts a changing array of topical exhibits based on National Archives records. The 290-seat McGowan Theater is a state-of-the-art showplace for NARA's extensive audiovisual holdings and serves as a forum for lectures and discussion. It also is home to the Charles Guggenheim Center for the Documentary Film at the National Archives. Inside the Boeing Learning Center, the ReSource Room is an access point for teachers and parents to explore documents found in the exhibits and to use NARA's records as teaching tools.

A set of Web pages now makes the entire National Archives Experience available online. An illustrated history of the Charters of Freedom can be found, as well as information on educational programs, special events, and exhibits currently at the National Archives. For those planning to visit Washington, it is possible to make on-line reservations for the National Archives Experience at http://www.recreation.gov.

For more information, visit http://www.archives.gov/national-archives-experience.

Research Center

At the Robert M. Warner Research Center, researchers can consult with staff experts on records in the National Archives building and submit requests to examine original documents. The center houses approximately 275,000 rolls of microfilmed records, documenting military service prior to World War I, immigration into the United States, the federal census, Congress, federal courts in the District of Columbia, the Bureau of Indian Affairs, and the Freedmen's Bureau. The center also contains an extensive and expanding system of reference reports, helping researchers conduct research in federal documents.

Archives Library Information Center

The Archives Library Information Center (ALIC) provides access to information on American history and government, archival administration, information management, and government documents. ALIC is physically located in two traditional libraries in the National Archives building in Washington and the National Archives at College Park, Maryland. Customers also can visit ALIC on the Internet at http://www.archives.gov/research/alic, where they will find "Reference at Your Desk" Internet links, staff-compiled bibliographies and publications, and an online library catalog. ALIC can be reached by telephone at 202-357-5018 in Washington and 301-837-3415 in College Park.

Government Documents

U.S. government publications are generally available to researchers at many of the 1,250 congressionally designated federal depository libraries throughout the United States. A record set of these publications also is part of NARA's archival holdings. Publications of the U.S. Government (Record Group 287) is a collection of selected publications of U.S. government agencies, arranged by the classification system (SuDoc System) devised by the Office of the Superintendent of Documents, Government Printing Office (GPO). The core of the collection is a library established in 1895 by GPO's Public Documents Division. By 1972, when NARA acquired the library, it included official publications dating from the early years of the federal government and selected publications produced for and by federal government agencies. Since 1972 the 25,000-cubic-foot collection has been augmented periodically with accessions of U.S. government publications selected by the Office of the Superintendent of Documents as a byproduct of its cataloging activity. As with the federal depository library collections, the holdings in NARA's Record Group 287 comprise only a portion of all U.S. government publications.

NARA Publications

NARA publishes guides and indexes to various portions of its archival holdings; catalogs of microfilmed records; informational leaflets and brochures; general interest books about NARA and its holdings that will appeal to anyone with an interest in U.S. history; more-specialized publications that will be useful to scholars, archivists, records managers, historians, researchers, and educators; facsimiles of certain documents; and *Prologue,* a scholarly journal published quarterly. Some publications are also available on NARA's Web site at http://www. archives.gov/publications/online.html. Many are available from NARA's customer service center in College Park by telephoning 800-234-8861 or 866-272-6272 or faxing 301-837-0483. The NARA Web site's publications homepage, http://www.archives.gov/publications, provides detailed information about available publications and ordering.

Federal Register

The *Federal Register* is the U.S. government's daily gazette, containing presidential documents, proposed and final federal regulations, and public notices of federal agencies. The *Federal Register* is published by the Office of the Federal Register and printed and distributed by GPO. The two agencies collaborate in the same way to produce the annual revisions of the *Code of Federal Regulations* (*CFR*). Free access to the full text of the electronic version of the *Federal Register* and *CFR*—and to an unofficial, daily-updated electronic *CFR* (the *e-CFR*)— is available at http://www.federalregister.gov. Documents scheduled for future publication in the *Federal Register* are available for public inspection at the Office of the Federal Register (800 North Capitol St. N.W., Washington, D.C.) or online at the electronic Public Inspection Desk (http://www.federalregister.gov).

Access to rules published in the *Federal Register* and open for public comment, and a portal for submitting comments, are provided through the multiagency Web site http://www.regulations.gov.

Access to the full texts of other Federal Register publications, including the *Compilation of Presidential Documents, Public Papers of the President,* slip laws, *U.S. Statutes at Large,* and the *United States Government Manual* is available via http://www.federalregister.gov. All Federal Register publications are hosted on GPO Web sites at http://www.fdsys.gov and http://www.gpoaccess.gov (which is scheduled to be retired in 2010). Printed editions of these publications also are maintained at all federal depository libraries.

Public Law Electronic Notification Service (PENS) is a free subscription e-mail service available for notification of recently enacted public laws. The Federal Register Table of Contents Service is a free e-mail service available for delivery of the daily table of contents from the *Federal Register* with direct links to documents.

The Office of the Federal Register also publishes information about its ministerial responsibilities associated with the operation of the Electoral College and ratification of constitutional amendments and provides access to related records. Publication information concerning laws, regulations, and presidential documents and services is available from the Office of the Federal Register (telephone 202-741-6000). Further information, together with additional finding aids for Federal Register publications, the Electoral College, and constitutional amendments, is also available at http://www.archives.gov/federal-register.

Publications can be ordered by contacting GPO at http://bookstore.gpo.gov, and via toll-free telephone at 866-512-1800. To submit orders by fax or by mail, see http://bookstore.gpo.gov/help/index.jsp.

Customer Service

Few records repositories serve as many customers as NARA. In fiscal year 2009 there were more than 128,000 researcher visits to NARA facilities nationwide, including archives, presidential libraries, and federal records centers. At the same time, more than 1.4 million customers requested information in writing. NARA also served the executive agencies of the federal government, the courts, and Congress by providing records storage, reference service, training, advice, and guidance on many issues relating to records management. Federal records centers replied to more than 8.8 million requests for information and records, including more than 1.3 million requests for information regarding military and civilian service records provided by the National Personnel Records Center in St. Louis. NARA also provided informative public programs at its various facilities for more than 17,000 people. More than a million visited the National Archives Experience in Washington, and exhibits in the presidential library museums were visited by more than 2.4 million people.

NARA knows it must understand who its customers are and what they need to ensure that people can discover, use, and learn from their documentary heritage in the National Archives. Customers are surveyed regularly to help NARA align its standards of performance with their expectations. By repeating surveys at frequent, systematic intervals, changes in NARA's performance are measured and appropriate management actions are taken to ensure that service levels reflect an appropriate balance between customer needs and NARA resources. NARA also maintains an Internet Web form (http://www.archives.gov/contact/inquire-form.html) to facilitate continuous feedback from customers about what is most important to them and what NARA might do better to meet their needs.

Grants

The National Historical Publications and Records Commission (NHPRC) is the grant-making affiliate of NARA's national grants program. The Archivist of the United States chairs the commission and makes grants on its recommendation. The commission's 14 other members represent the President of the United States (two appointees), the U.S. Supreme Court, the Senate and House of Representatives, the U.S. Departments of State and Defense, the Librarian of Congress, the American Association for State and Local History, the American Historical Association, the Association for Documentary Editing, the National Association of Government Archives and Records Administrators, the Organization of American Historians, and the Society of American Archivists.

The commission carries out a statutory mission to ensure understanding of the nation's past by promoting the preservation and use of essential historical documents. The commission supports the creation and publication of documentary editions and research in the management and preservation of authentic electronic records, and it works in partnership with a national network of state archives and state historical records advisory boards to develop a national archival infrastructure. NHPRC grants help state and local governments, and archives, universities, historical societies, professional organizations, and other nonprofit organizations establish or strengthen archival programs, improve training and techniques, preserve and process records collections, and provide access to them through finding aids, digitization of collections, and documentary editions of the papers of significant historical figures and movements in American history. For more information about the commission, visit http://www.archives.gov/nhprc.

Information Security Oversight Office

The Information Security Oversight Office (ISOO) is responsible for policy and oversight of the government-wide security classification system and the National Industrial Security Program. ISOO is a component of NARA and receives policy and program guidance from the National Security Council. ISOO oversees the security classification programs (classification, safeguarding, and declassification) in both government and industry. It is also responsible for carrying out NARA's authorities and responsibilities as the executive agent for controlled unclassified information. ISOO contributes materially to the effective implementation of the government-wide security classification program and has a direct impact on the performance of thousands of government employees and contract personnel who work with classified national security information.

For more information on ISOO, visit http://www.archives.gov/isoo.

Federal Library and Information Center Committee

101 Independence Ave. S.E., Washington, DC 20540-4935
202-707-4800, fax 202-707-4818, e-mail flicc@loc.gov

Roberta I. Shaffer
Executive Director

Highlights of the Year

During fiscal year (FY) 2009, the Federal Library and Information Center Committee (FLICC) continued its mission to foster excellence in federal library and information services through interagency cooperation and to provide guidance and direction for the Federal Library and Information Network (FEDLINK).

FLICC membership focused its quarterly meetings on a variety of broad federal information issues, including "Initiatives and Issues in Federal Libraries"; "Leadership in Uncertain Times," presented by Richard Huffine of the U.S. Geological Survey; "The Future of Reference at the Department of Justice," with Mimi Vollstedt of the department and additional team members Jennifer Hammond, Dennis Feldt, and Jim Gernert; and "Information Analytics, An Opportunity to Learn," presented by Edna Reid of Clarion University.

The FLICC working groups completed an ambitious agenda during the fiscal year.

- The Human Resources Working Group began to develop its formal mentoring and coaching initiative and held its second annual career fair for those interested in working as federal librarians.
- The Education Working Group presented a variety of seminars, workshops, and institutes on gray literature, library technician development, mentoring, preservation, and Enterprise 2.0.
- The Libraries and Emerging Technologies Working Group sponsored a program as part of the American Library Association (ALA) Annual Conference on federal library careers, working with ALA's Federal and Armed Forces Libraries Round Table.
- The FLICC Awards Working Group announced the Federal Library/ Information Center of the Year, Federal Librarian of the Year, and Federal Library Technician of the Year.
- The Libraries and Emerging Technology Working Group began developing papers, case studies, and short programs on technology implementation in federal agencies, including scripts for working with information technology (IT) departments, consortial technology acquisition, test beds for new technologies, sharing information policy, cloud computing, and the use of proxy servers. As part of the Computers in Libraries program, the working group supported a series of discussions on such topics as digital preservation and e-government.

- The Preservation and Digitization Working Group planned and sponsored a three-tier preservation program that included online preservation courses and a week-long preservation institute. Work also continued with Safety Net, a group of federal libraries in the Washington, D.C., area that have agreed to aid each other in the event of a regional disaster.

FLICC also continued its collaboration with the Library of Congress general counsel on a series of meetings between federal agency legal counsels and agency librarians. Now in their 11th year, these forums grew out of the recognition that federal attorneys and librarians share many of the same concerns about issues relating to copyright law, privacy law, the Freedom of Information Act, and other legal issues in regard both to using information within the agency and to publishing the agency's own information. The aim of these meetings is to enhance the relationship between agency attorneys and librarians and help them to develop contacts with their counterparts at other agencies. The 2009 series featured discussions on legal issues relating to use policies for Web 2.0 technologies; an annual copyright update; the future of legal scholarship in relation to researching, preserving, and determining the accuracy of legal blogs; and creating a world law library for the 21st century.

FLICC's cooperative network, FEDLINK, continued to enhance its fiscal operations while providing its members with savings of more than $17.4 million in vendor volume discounts and approximately $17.8 million more in cost avoidance.

To meet the requirements of the Fiscal Operations Improvement Act of 2000 (P.L. 106-481) that established statutory authority for FEDLINK's fee-based activities, FEDLINK governing bodies and staff members confirmed that plans were on track for the third year of its rolling five-year business plan developed in FY 2006. They explored the position of the FEDLINK program and its role in the federal sector of the commercial market.

Budgeting efforts projected costs and revenue, looking at both private sector and historic costs adjusted and calculated in line with vendor and Government Accountability Office (GAO) predictions. After examining FEDLINK program growth, realized savings through program management, and program reserves, FLICC/FEDLINK's governing bodies recommended that fees remain the same in FY 2010 but agreed to lower the purchasing threshold at which transfer-pay fees decrease from 6.75 percent to 6 percent from $300,000 to $100,000.

During FY 2009 FEDLINK continued to give federal agencies cost-effective access to an array of automated information retrieval services for online research, cataloging, and resource sharing. FEDLINK members also procured print serials, electronic journals, books, and other publications; document delivery, and digitization and preservation services via Library of Congress/FEDLINK contracts with more than 120 major vendors.

In conjunction with the working groups, FLICC offered a total of 28 seminars, workshops, and lunchtime discussions to nearly 1,200 members of the federal library and information center community. Institutes and workshops looked at professional development, technological developments, and movement toward the semantic Web, gray literature, preservation, and controlled vocabularies.

FLICC also collaborated with other groups by co-promoting educational programs and opening events up to each others' members when possible.

The Learning@Lunch series featured a variety of topics and speakers. The series highlighted a Web service for using controlled vocabularies, using Web 2.0 and social media in the workplace, understanding and using legislative histories, investigating the rising Web 2.0 technologies, near-real-time content aggregation and its implications for food safety information and beyond, and recent developments in the management and re-use of public sector information in the United Kingdom.

Staff members also served as principal speakers and leaders at a variety of national information community and professional association committees and conferences, including the Military Librarians Workshop, Computers in Libraries, Internet Librarian, and the annual conference of the Special Library Association (SLA).

FEDLINK negotiated discounted rates for several national conferences with Information Today, Inc. Nearly 500 attendees registered through FEDLINK to attend brokered conferences, including Computers in Libraries, Internet Librarian, WebSearch University, and the annual conference of the American Association of Law Libraries, saving the government nearly $100,000.

FEDLINK's continuing financial management efforts also ensured that FEDLINK successfully passed the Library of Congress financial audit of FY 2008 transactions.

Executive Board

The FLICC Executive Board (FEB) focused its efforts on a number of initiatives relating to the FLICC/FEDLINK Business Plan and environmental scan, OCLC's suggested revisions to the guidelines for use and reuse of WorldCat records, the EPA Advisory Board's recommendations for EPA libraries, and government policies relating to the use of social networking applications. The board recommended revising the bylaws to reflect changes in agencies, removing the now-defunct U.S. Information Agency (USIA) and National Commission for Libraries and Information Science (NCLIS) from the list of FLICC members, adding the Institute of Museum and Library Services (IMLS) in place of NCLIS, and adding a seat for the Office of the Director of National Intelligence.

Working Group Highlights

Awards

To honor the many ways in which federal libraries, librarians, and library technicians fulfill the information demands of government, business, research, scholarly communities, and the public, the Awards Working Group again administered a series of national awards for federal librarianship. During FY 2009 the working group prepared a Web video on the awards and nomination process and posted it to a newly created awards Web site. The site also offers a number of scanned exemplars from past winner nomination packets.

The winners of the FY 2008 awards, awarded in FY 2009, were:

- Federal library/information center of the year (large organization, with a staff of 11 or more), Information Services Division, National Institute of Standards and Technology (NIST) Research Library, Gaithersburg, Maryland; (small organization) Hurlburt Field Library, U.S. Air Force, Hurlburt Field, Florida.
- Federal Librarian of the Year, Verlene Herrington, U.S. Army Military Intelligence Library, Fort Huachuca, Arizona.
- Federal Library Technician of the Year, Lawana Gladney, Department of Justice, Washington, D.C.

Budget and Finance

The Budget and Finance Working Group developed the FY 2010 FEDLINK budget and fee structure in the spring quarter. The final budget reduced membership fees for transfer-pay customers to 6 percent on amounts exceeding $100,000; fees remain 6.75 percent below $100,000 and 4 percent on amounts exceeding $1,000,000. Direct-pay fees remained at FY 2009 levels, as did Direct Express fees of 0.75 percent for all participating commercial online information services vendors.

The FEDLINK Advisory Council and FEB approved the budget in May, FLICC membership in June, and Library of Congress officials in September.

Consortia and Interagency Cooperative Activities

The Consortia and Interagency Cooperative Activities Working Group provided input as FEDLINK continued market research and negotiations with two science publishers and assisted in defining criteria for assessing member needs.

Disaster Preparedness

The Disaster Preparedness Working Group assists federal libraries and information centers in preparing for disasters by supporting and promoting cooperation among federal agencies, offering education programs, and providing information resources for disaster recovery. The working group oversees Safety Net, the Washington, D.C., regional network for disaster response. The working group sponsored a workshop on disaster response and recovery for 42 Washington-based federal and nonfederal librarians.

Education

The Education Working Group, in concert with other FLICC working groups, sponsored a total of 28 seminars, workshops, and lunchtime discussions during FY 2009 for members of the federal library and information center community. These programs focused on cataloging, taxonomy, preservation and disaster planning, project management, copyright, digital content management, Web 2.0, and career development.

The working group also sponsored a series of orientations to libraries and information centers to help federal librarians become acquainted with a variety of institutions and collections in the Washington area, among them the Census Bureau library, the Daughters of the American Revolution library, the Environmental Protection Agency Headquarters and Chemical Libraries Collaboration, the Edward Bennett Williams Law Library at Georgetown University, and the U.S. Senate Library.

The working group continued to promote federal librarianship to new library school graduates and other job-seekers by cosponsoring the third annual Careers in Federal Libraries preconference event at the 2009 ALA Annual Conference in Chicago, an event that attracted nearly 300 registrants and covered basic advice about federal applications, interviews, and the selection process.

Human Resources

The Human Resources Working Group spent FY 2009 designing the FLICC Mentoring and Coaching program and the FLICC Job Fair.

In August the working group's Careers in Federal Libraries program attracted 350 registrants and vendors from nearly 25 agencies. The program also featured a series of well-attended sessions on such topics as résumé writing.

Integrated Library Systems

FLICC formed an ad hoc working group to help analyze federal libraries' needs and options for replacing integrated library systems. The group identified potential vendors, created a bibliography, and collected technical specifications.

Libraries and Emerging Technologies

The Libraries and Emerging Technologies working group sponsored two specialized streams of programming as part of the Computers in Libraries conference, one focusing on government libraries and the other on special libraries, with presentations on digital preservation, e-government, and electronic records management, IM (instant messaging) reference, cooperative systems vs. integrated systems, federated search, "libraries and return on investment," and the changing physical shape of libraries.

Nominating

The Nominating Working Group oversaw the 2009 election process for FLICC rotating members, FEB members, the FEDLINK Advisory Council, and a FEDLINK delegate to the OCLC Members Council.

Policy and Advocacy

The Policy and Advocacy Working Group reported on policies relating to use of Web 2.0 applications by the government, scientific data preservation and access, and the activities of the White House Innovation and Information Policy Working Group and the National Archives Executive Group on Controlled Unclassified Information.

Preservation and Digitization

The Preservation and Digitization Working Group embarked on a survey of digitization among federal libraries and public presentations. Group member Deborah Keller of the U.S. Army Corps of Engineers presented a poster session conference at Chapel Hill, North Carolina, and facilitated a presentation with FLICC members Patricia Murphy of the National Agricultural Library, Richard Huffine of the U.S. Geological Survey, and Claretta Crawford of the U.S. Army's Fort Leonard Wood.

Executive Director's Office

In addition to the many strategic planning, budgeting, and administrative efforts, the executive director's office hosted visitors from the Netherlands, Denmark, Germany, South Korea, and Japan, all interested in emulating FLICC/FEDLINK concepts in their respective countries. The executive director also served on the search committee for a new National Agricultural Library director and on the OCLC Review Board.

Additional outreach efforts included serving as a program moderator for the ALA Careers Workshop, supporting the American Association of Law Libraries' federal law librarians caucus, and attending sessions on e-Content and the World Future Society.

Publications and Education Office

During FY 2009 FLICC continued its publication program as a digital communication provider and used the FEDLIB listserv to communicate critical advocacy and program information to more than 3,000 electronic subscribers.

The office revised mission-critical materials and developed targeted resources to support the FEDLINK program, including revisions to the online registration process, initial meetings on revising the FEDLINK member handbook, and two FEDLINK Information Alerts. FLICC also produced the minutes of the four FY 2008 quarterly meetings and six executive board meetings, and all FLICC Education Program promotional and support materials. Office staff members also participated in several strategic planning efforts on knowledge navigators and the Library of Congress Librarians Web page.

Staff members continued to convert all publications, announcements, alerts, member materials, meeting minutes, and working group resources into HTML and pdf formats, maintained the many Web links throughout the FLICC/FEDLINK Web site, and enhanced and expanded the site via an inter-unit team of content, design, editorial, and technical personnel. Staff also participated in the Federal Consortium on Second Life as part of ongoing efforts to influence federal agency use of Web 2.0 emerging technologies.

FLICC increased its distance-learning offerings by using Web conferencing software for a number of its free events and routinely incorporated versions of PowerPoint and other presentation materials to enhance access to the resources available at educational programs.

Publications staff members continued to support the Member Services Unit and their Online Registration/Online Interagency Agreement (IAG) system.

FLICC demonstrated its ongoing commitment to library technicians' continuing education by hosting its Institute for Federal Library Technicians and its annual teleconference series, "Soaring to . . . Excellence," produced by the College of DuPage.

Federal and academic librarians also joined FLICC professionals to discuss various areas of librarianship, including peer-reviewed literature, taxonomies, acquisitions, cataloging, copyright laws, reference, and automation.

FEDLINK

During FY 2009 FEDLINK continued to give federal agencies cost-effective access to an array of automated information retrieval services for online research, cataloging, information management, and resource sharing. FEDLINK members also procured print and electronic journals, print and electronic books, sound recordings, audiovisual materials, document delivery, technical processing services, digitization, and preservation and conservation services through contracts with more than 120 vendors. The program obtained further discounts for customers through consortia and enterprise-wide licenses for journals, aggregated information retrieval services, and books.

FEDLINK awarded four new contracts for electronic retrieval services and competed requirements for serials subscription services for four agencies under contracts with seven serials subscription agents. FEDLINK staff assisted 13 agencies in using the preservation contracts to digitize and conserve special collections and to create related metadata. They assisted four agencies in working with Internet Archive to create digital archives, and with another agency to procure the software application that will help it to manage digital collections locally. Four more agencies were assisted in procuring contract cataloging services.

The FEDLINK Advisory Council met six times during the year. In addition to its general oversight activities, the council provided insight into trends in the information industry and supported adoption of the proposed FY 2010 budget.

Suzanne Ryder, chief librarian at the Naval Research Laboratory Library, and Chris Cole, associate director for technical services at the National Agricultural Library, represented FEDLINK on the OCLC Members Council. Cole and FLICC Executive Director Roberta Shaffer participated in a review board formed by OCLC's board of directors to review proposed changes to the guidelines on the use and transfer of WorldCat records. The review board surveyed the community and recommended that rather than implement the proposed policy changes, OCLC seek further input on how best the guidelines might meet the cooperatives' needs.

FEDLINK Fiscal Operations

FEDLINK provided its members with $78.7 million in transfer-pay services, $4.9 million in direct-pay services, and an estimated $42.3 million in Direct Express services, saving federal agencies more than $17.4 million in vendor volume discounts and approximately $17.8 million more in cost avoidance.

Staff members supported business plan goals for improving processes and expanding the market for product and services through the following initiatives: reduced transfer-pay customer fees by 13 percent to 20 percent starting with FY 2009 procurements; promoted, using pay.gov, facilitation of federal customer credit card purchases under $100,000 and vendor Direct Express payments to FEDLINK; streamlined the invoicing and payment process; met with selected vendors and members on requirements and acquisition of company data for electronic invoicing; and re-established partnership agreements to develop and upgrade critical components of the FEDLINK Subsidiary Financial System.

Financial Management, Reporting, and Control

FEDLINK successfully passed the Library of Congress financial audit of FY 2008 transactions and completed vulnerability assessments of program financial risks for library services. It continued to provide central accounting for customer agency account balances to meet Treasury Department reporting requirements, and also completed all aspects of its revolving fund status reporting, including preparation, review, and forecasts of revenue and expenses for the accounting period.

National Center for Education Statistics
Library Statistics Program

U.S. Department of Education, Institute of Education Sciences
Elementary/Secondary and Libraries Studies Division
1990 K St. N.W., Washington, DC 20006

Adrienne Chute and Tai A. Phan

In an effort to collect and disseminate more-complete statistical information about libraries, the National Center for Education Statistics (NCES) initiated a formal library statistics program in 1989 that included surveys on academic libraries, school library media centers, public libraries, and state libraries.* At the end of December 2007, the Public Libraries Survey and the State Library Agencies Survey were transferred to the Office of Library Programs of the Institute of Museum and Library Services (IMLS). The Academic Libraries Survey (ALS) and the School Library Media Centers Survey (SLMCS) continue to be administered and funded by NCES, under the leadership of Tai A. Phan, program director, Library Statistics Program. [For detailed information on the surveys now being handled by IMLS, see "Institute of Museum and Library Services Library Programs" in Part 2. For a sampling of findings from recent surveys, see "Highlights of IMLS and NCES Surveys" in Part 4—*Ed.*]

The library surveys conducted by NCES are designed to provide comprehensive nationwide data on the status of libraries. Federal, state, and local officials, professional associations, and local practitioners use these surveys for planning, evaluating, and making policy. These data are also available to researchers and educators.

The Library Statistics Program's Web site, http://nces.ed.gov/surveys/libraries, provides links to data search tools, data files, survey definitions, and survey designs for each survey. The two library surveys conducted by NCES—ALS and SLMCS—are described below.

Academic Libraries

The Academic Libraries Survey provides descriptive statistics from approximately 3,800 academic libraries in the 50 states, the District of Columbia, and the outlying areas of the United States. NCES surveyed academic libraries on a three-year cycle between 1966 and 1988. From 1988 to 1998, ALS was a component of the Integrated Postsecondary Education Data System (IPEDS), and was on a two-year cycle. Beginning with fiscal year (FY) 2000, ALS is no longer a component of IPEDS, but remains on a two-year cycle. IPEDS and ALS data can still be linked by the identification codes of the postsecondary education institutions. In aggregate, these data provide an overview of the status of academic libraries nationally and by state. ALS collects data on libraries in the entire universe of degree-granting postsecondary institutions, using a Web-based data collection system.

*The authorization for the National Center for Education Statistics (NCES) to collect library statistics is included in the Education Sciences Reform Act of 2002 (PL 107-279), under Title I, Part C.

ALS has an established working group composed of representatives of the academic library community. Its mission is to improve data quality and the timeliness of data collection, processing, and release. NCES also works cooperatively in the collection of the ALS with the American Library Association, the Association of Research Libraries, the Association of College and Research Libraries, and academic libraries.

ALS collects data on the number of academic libraries, operating expenditures, full-time-equivalent library staff, number of service outlets, collection size, circulation, interlibrary loans, number of public service hours, library visits, reference transactions, consortia services, number of presentations, attendance at presentations, electronic services, and information literacy. Academic libraries are also asked whether they provide reference services by e-mail or the Internet, whether they have technology for patrons with disabilities, and whether documents are digitized by library staff.

An NCES First Look report, *Academic Libraries, 2008* (NCES 2010-348), was released on the NCES Web site on December 9, 2009. The final data file and documentation for the 2008 ALS public use data file (NCES 2010-310) were released on the Web site the same day. NCES has developed a Web-based peer analysis tool for the ALS called "Compare Academic Libraries," which currently uses the ALS 2008 data.

Additional information on academic library statistics is available from Tai A. Phan, National Center for Education Statistics, telephone 202-502-7431, e-mail tai.phan@ed.gov.

School Library Media Centers

National surveys of school library media centers in elementary and secondary schools in the United States were conducted in 1958, 1962, 1974, 1978, and 1986, 1993–1994, 1999–2000, 2003–2004 and 2007–2008. Data collection for the 2011–2012 survey was scheduled to begin during fall 2011 and will end in spring 2012.

NCES, with the assistance of the U.S. Bureau of the Census, conducts the School Library Media Centers Survey as part of the Schools and Staffing Survey (SASS). SASS is the nation's largest sample survey of teachers, schools, and principals in U.S. K–12 public and private schools. Data from the school library media center questionnaire provide a national picture of school library staffing, collections, expenditures, technology, and services. Results from the 2007–2008 survey can be found in *Public and Bureau of Indian Education Elementary and Secondary School Library Media Centers in the United States: 2007–08 Schools and Staffing Survey* (NCES 2009-322).

NCES also published a historical report about school libraries titled *Fifty Years of Supporting Children's Learning: A History of Public School Libraries and Federal Legislation from 1953–2000*. Drawn from more than 50 sources, this report presents descriptive data about public school libraries since 1953. Along with key characteristics of school libraries, the report also presents national and regional standards and federal legislation affecting school library media centers.

Data from sample surveys are presented at the national, regional, and school levels, and by state.

NCES has included library-oriented questions on the parent and teacher instruments of its new Early Childhood Longitudinal Study (ECLS). For more information, visit http://nces.ed.gov/ecls. Library items also appear in the National Household Education Survey (NHES) instruments. For more information about that survey, visit http://nces.ed.gov/nhes.

NCES also included a questionnaire about high school library media centers in the Education Longitudinal Study of 2002 (ELS: 2002). This survey collected data from tenth graders about their schools, their school library media centers, their communities, and their home life. The report *School Library Media Centers: Selected Results from the Education Longitudinal Study of 2002 (ELS: 2002)* (NCES 2005-302) is available on the NCES Web site. For more information about this survey, visit http://nces.ed.gov/surveys/els2002.

Additional information on school library media center statistics is available from Tai A. Phan, National Center for Education Statistics, telephone 202-502-7431, e-mail tai.phan@ed.gov.

How to Obtain Printed and Electronic Products

Reports are currently published in the First Look format. First Look reports consist of a short collection of tables presenting state and national totals, a survey description, and data highlights. NCES also publishes separate more in-depth studies analyzing these data.

Internet Access

Many NCES publications (including out-of-print publications) and edited raw data files from the library surveys are available for viewing or downloading at no charge through the Electronic Catalog on the NCES Web site at http://nces.ed.gov/pubsearch.

Ordering Printed Products

Many NCES publications are also available in printed format. To order one free copy of recent NCES reports, contact the Education Publications Center (ED Pubs) at http://www.edpubs.org, by e-mail at edpubs@edpubs.ed.gov, by toll-free telephone at 877-433-7827 (TTY/TDD 877-576-7734), by fax at 703-605-6794, or by mail at ED Pubs, P.O. Box 22207, Alexandria, VA 22304.

Many publications are available through the Educational Resources Information Center (ERIC) system. For more information on services and products, visit the EDRS Web site at http://www.eric.ed.gov.

Out-of-print publications and data files may be available through the NCES Electronic Catalog on the NCES Web site at http://nces.ed.gov/pubsearch or through one of the 1,250 Federal Depository Libraries throughout the United States. Use the NCES publication number included in the citations for publications and data files to locate items in the NCES Electronic Catalog; use the GPO number to locate items in a federal depository library.

Defense Technical Information Center

Fort Belvoir, VA 22060
World Wide Web http://www.dtic.mil

Sandy Schwalb
Public Affairs Officer

The Defense Technical Information Center (DTIC) is the largest central resource available for Department of Defense (DoD) and government-funded scientific, technical, engineering and business-related information. DTIC provides engineers, researchers, scientists, information professionals, those in laboratories and universities, and the military access to more than 2 million publications covering 250 subject areas. DTIC's mission is "to provide essential, technical, research, development, testing and evaluation information rapidly, accurately and reliably to support our customers' needs."

DTIC, a DoD field activity, is in the office of the under secretary of defense for acquisition, technology, and logistics, and reports to the director, defense research and engineering. Some of DTIC's functions include

- Providing secure access to defense-related information
- Leveraging the multibillion-dollar investment in DoD research and engineering
- Ensuring that DoD scientific and technical information gets into the hands of the right people in the defense community
- Offering up-to-date electronic information to the defense community using various technologies, including Web 2.0 tools
- Acting as a primary provider of Web services for organizations within DoD
- Providing information support to the federal and contractor communities

DTIC is located in the Andrew T. McNamara Headquarters Complex Building at Fort Belvoir, Virginia, and has four regional offices, whose addresses appear below.

DTIC is a DoD field activity, which means it is one of several organizations whose work reaches across all segments of the department. In June 2009 DTIC commemorated its fifth anniversary as a field activity. This designation increased its visibility in the department and provided DTIC with a "seat at the table," with others from the Pentagon and throughout the defense community.

Reaching Customers

Over the past several years, DTIC has consolidated its resources into two Web sites—DTIC Online (available to the public) and DTIC Online Access Controlled (a secure site)—and continued to expand its use of Web 2.0 technologies. In 2008 DTIC launched DoDTechipedia, a wiki designed for use by the defense community; DefenseSolutions.gov, a public portal through which innovative companies, entrepreneurs, and research organizations can offer potential solutions to theme areas; and DTIC Online Access Controlled, launched in September 2009, the newest addition to DTIC's suite of services.

DoDTechipedia

DoDTechipedia.mil is a secure online system facilitating the sharing of knowledge and collaboration throughout the U.S. defense community. By the end of 2009 it had more than 10,000 users. DoDTechipedia ensures greater transparency and communication among DoD scientists, engineers, program managers, and the military. This tool helps members of the DoD community to collaborate, identify solutions for technology challenges, and ensure that taxpayer dollars are spent in an efficient manner. Some of its features include a live forum, a quick registration process using a (DoD-issued) Common Access Card, a "sandbox" for users to practice posting and editing content, acronyms/definitions, technology areas where discussions about scientific and technical investment areas or about enabling technology take place, interest area pages for DoD personnel and DoD contractors to work together on challenges and solutions, blog capabilities, hyperlinking of terms, and the ability to upload attachments.

In 2009 DoDTechipedia won the *GCN* (*Government Computer News*) 22nd annual award for "Outstanding Information Technology Achievement in Government." Additionally, the wiki was highlighted on the White House Web site in the Open Government Initiative/Innovations Gallery. The announcement from the White House stated that a benefit of DoDTechipedia was that it "ensures that Combatant Commands have access to the information they need from the science and technology community to make the best investment decisions. This helps keep both our soldiers and the American people more safe."

DefenseSolutions

DefenseSolutions.gov (http://defensesolutions.gov) is a portal through which innovative companies, entrepreneurs, and research organizations that have not considered doing business with DoD in the past can offer potential solutions to defense problems. DoD is looking for concepts that have the potential to advance the military's missions; in addition, this program offers a streamlined process to fund promising ideas.

DTIC Online Access Controlled

DTIC Online Access Controlled provides a gateway to DoD unclassified, controlled science and technology and research and engineering information. This Web site, which went live September 2009, contains the resources from DTIC's former Research and Engineering portal, while providing access to the Total Electronic Migration System (more about this in the section on the Information Analysis Centers), Private Scientific and Technical Information Network (STINET), and DoDTechipedia. Users of DTIC Online Access Controlled can get congressional budget information, DoD scientific and technical planning documents, the Biomedical Research Database, the Militarily Critical Technologies List, more than 2 million technical reports, research summaries, and numerous other resources.

Outreach to the Military

DTIC hosted its second Combatant Commanders Workshop November 3–4, 2009, in Tampa, Florida, with the theme "Real-Time S&T Support for Real-World Solutions." The event attracted more than 175 attendees and provided an opportunity for the combatant command community to hear about how DTIC can assist them. The keynote speaker was Zachery J. Lemnios, who was named DoD director, defense research and engineering, in 2009. He highlighted the latest resources available to help the combatant commands achieve technical superiority on the battlefield. The workshop included a sharing of insight on leveraging scientific and technical research and collaboration tools. Attendees were given in-depth knowledge of DTIC's products and services, while DTIC garnered input on the needs of combatants.

During 2009 DTIC personnel continued to participate and assist in various exercises held by the combatant commands, leading to enhanced information sharing.

Web Hosting Expertise

As a leader in excellence for information storage and retrieval, DTIC has been able to advise DoD components concerning policy, law, best practices, and security strategies that relate to the transmission and use of all types of information. This is an effective support program for senior-level planners and other users of information resources. The shared infrastructure allows many organizations to obtain technologies and resources that no single organization could afford on its own. DTIC hosts more than 100 Web sites sponsored by components of the office of the secretary of defense, military service headquarters organizations, and several defense agencies, such as the Joint Chiefs of Staff, the Federal Voting Assistance Program, and the Defense Prisoner of War/Missing Personnel Office.

Security of Information

While there is much publicly accessible material in the DTIC collection (nearly half of DoD's technical reports are publicly available the day they are published), some information is restricted by security classifications. The DoD's scientific and technical information is always categorized (or "marked") by the office that originates the document. This marking determines how, and to whom, the information can be disseminated.

The information in DTIC's collection is 51 percent "unclassified, unlimited"; 40 percent "unclassified, limited"; and 9 percent "classified."

Resources

DTIC's holdings include technical reports on completed research; research summaries of planned, ongoing, and completed work; independent research and development summaries; defense technology transfer agreements; DoD planning documents; DoD directives and instructions; conference proceedings; security classification guides; command histories; and special collections that date back to World War II. DoD-funded researchers are required to search DTIC's collections to ensure that they do not undertake unnecessary or redundant research.

The scope of DTIC's collection includes areas normally associated with defense research. These are examples of the types of information found in DTIC: air platforms, atmospheric sciences, behavioral and social sciences, environmental quality, human factors engineering, information warfare, mathematics and computer sciences, nuclear science and technology, radiation studies, sensors, virtual reality, and propulsion, engines, and fuels.

Registering for Services

DTIC offers its information services to a diverse population of the defense community; because of the nature of the information that DTIC handles, users must qualify for services, but by the end of 2009 DTIC had close to 30,000 registered users. In addition to individuals in the DoD and federal sectors, DTIC's customers can also be found in academia, the intelligence community, foreign governments (for instance, there are negotiated agreements with Australia, Canada, France, Germany, the Netherlands, the Republic of Korea, and the United Kingdom) as well as military school students and taxpayers.

DTIC's registered users typically include acquisition instructors, active duty military, congressional staff, DoD contractors, faculty and students at military schools, historians, information professionals and librarians, logistics management specialists, small business owners, security managers, and software engineers and developers.

Registered users can order documents directly from DTIC. Those who are not eligible to register with DTIC can order "unclassified, unlimited" documents by contacting the National Technical Information Service (NTIS) at 800-553-NTIS (553-6847) or by visiting http://www.ntis.gov.

DTIC's Primary Collections

The Technical Reports (TR) database contains more than 2 million reports in print, nonprint (CDs, DVDs, software, data files, databases, and video recordings), and electronic formats conveying the results of defense-sponsored research, development, test, and evaluation efforts. It includes journal articles, DoD-sponsored patent applications, studies, analyses, open source literature from other countries, conference proceedings, and theses. Between 25,000 and 30,000 documents are added each year.

The Research Summaries (RS) database contains descriptions of DoD research that provide information on technical content, responsible individuals and organizations, principal investigators, and funding sources at the work-unit level. Available only to certain registered users, this collection is controlled by individual access restrictions. The collection consists of more than 315,000 active and inactive summaries from 1965 to the present.

The Independent Research and Development (IR&D) database contains more than 172,000 descriptions (dating back to the mid-1970s) of research and development projects initiated and conducted by defense contractors independent of DoD control and without direct DoD funding. On average, nearly $3 billion worth of IR&D projects are submitted to DTIC annually. The database includes basic and applied research, technology development efforts, and systems and concept formulation studies. Defense contractors and potential contractors are encouraged to submit project descriptions to the IR&D database. Accessible only to U.S. government organizations, the proprietary IR&D information is used to identify contractors with expertise in areas of interest to DoD and to avoid DoD duplication of industry research and development efforts.

Information Sources

DTIC information is derived from many sources, including: DoD organizations (civilian and military) and DoD contractors; U.S. government organizations and their contractors; nonprofit organizations working on DoD scientific, research, and engineering activities; academia; and foreign governments. DTIC accepts information in print, nonprint (CDs and DVDs), and electronically via the Internet. DTIC gets information from the defense community, for the defense community, about defense, and beyond. Having a full range of science and technology and research and development information within the DTIC collection ensures that technological innovations are linked to defense development and acquisition efforts. New research projects can begin with the highest level of information available. This avoids duplication effort, maximizing the use of DoD project dollars.

Information Analysis Centers

Another facet of DTIC administrative activities is the management and funding of contractor-operated joint service-oriented Information Analysis Centers (IACs), which are research organizations. Chartered by DoD, IACs identify, analyze, and use scientific and technical information in specific technology areas. They also develop information and analysis products for the defense science and engineering communities. IACs are staffed by experienced technical area scientists, engineers, and information specialists who help users locate and analyze scientific and technical information in specific subject areas. They improve productivity in the defense research, development, and acquisition communities. For more information, visit http://iac.dtic.mil.

The DTIC-managed IACs, as of December 2009, were: AMMTIAC (Advanced Materials, Manufacturing, and Testing); CBRNIAC (Chemical, Biological, Radiological, Nuclear Defense); CPIAC (Chemical Propulsion); DACS (Data and Analysis Center for Software); IATAC (Information Assurance Technology Analysis Center); MSIAC (Modeling and Simulation); RIAC (Reliability); SENSIAC (Sensors); SURVIAC (Survivability); and WSTIAC (Weapons Systems Technology).

Many of the products and services produced by the IACs are available free of charge and include announcements of reports relevant to the particular IAC's field of interest, authoritative bibliographic search reports, the latest scientific and engineering information on specific technical subjects, consultation with or referral to world-recognized technical experts, and status of current technologies. The Total Electronic Migration System (TEMS), a gateway to the IAC collection, is available online. TEMS provides DTIC registered users the ability to perform full-text searches and retrieve mission-critical information.

Annual Conference

"Protecting While Sharing Defense Information," was the theme of DTIC's 2009 Annual Conference, held in early April in Alexandria, Virginia. Attendees included engineers; scientists, and professionals in technology, research and development, information science, and acquisition from DoD and from federal and contractor communities. Government and commercial exhibitors demonstrated their latest information services and technologies. The more than 280 registrants represented the Navy, Air Force, Army, DoD, and federal agencies, the contractor community, and academic institutions.

DTIC's 2010 conference took place in late March, again in Alexandria, with the theme "Celebrating 65 Years of Providing Access to Defense Information."

Free Training

DTIC provides free training for customers at its Fort Belvoir headquarters and at the regional offices in Dayton, Boston, Albuquerque, and Los Angeles. Additionally, customized and on-site courses can be provided, with travel expenses paid by the hosting organization. The training curriculum includes searching DTIC databases, and DoD Scientific and Technical Information (STINFO) management. A course about marking documents for distribution is offered only by request. To schedule a session, e-mail stinfo@dtic.mil or call 703-767-8240.

QuestionPoint

DTIC continues to be a participating member of QuestionPoint, a virtual reference service developed jointly by the Library of Congress and the Online Computer Library Center (OCLC) and supported by cooperating institutions worldwide. This collaborative digital reference service allows libraries and information centers to expand reference services with shared resources and subject specialists around the world. DTIC is part of the Global Reference Network, a worldwide group of libraries and institutions committed to digital reference, and the Defense Digital Library Research Service, an around-the-clock electronic reference assistance for DoD libraries.

DTIC Review

DTIC Review (http://www.dtic.mil/dtic/stresources/dticreview/index.html) provides the full text of selected technical reports and a bibliography of other references of interest in a single publication. Each volume provides a sampling of documents from the DTIC collection on a specific topic of current interest. Topics highlighted during 2009 included biomimetics, pandemics, counterinsurgency, and improvised explosive devices.

Cooperation and Collaboration

DTIC works with the information and library communities through many partnerships and affiliations. The following are among them:

- CENDI, an interagency working group of senior scientific and technical information managers from 13 U.S. federal agencies, including the Departments of Commerce, Energy, Interior, and Defense, the National Aeronautics and Space Administration, the Government Printing Office, and the Library of Congress
- SLA, the Special Libraries Association, and its Military Libraries Division
- FLICC, the Federal Library and Information Center Committee
- Science.gov, a collaboration of scientific and technical organizations in the federal government, a free gateway to more than 1,700 government information resources about science including technical reports, journal citations, databases, federal Web sites, and fact sheets
- NFAIS, the National Federation of Advanced Information Services
- ASIDIC, the Association of Information and Dissemination Centers
- NISO, the National Information Standards Organization

Military Libraries Workshop

DTIC staff helped organize and took part in the 53rd annual Military Libraries Workshop, sponsored by the Military Libraries Division of the SLA. Held December 7–11, the workshop was hosted by the Arnold Engineering Development Center (AEDC) at Arnold Air Force Base in Tennessee. The workshop theme, "Toward New Horizons," came from the title of a 1945 report regarding the steps the United States needed to take in order to develop and maintain superior air forces. This report led directly to the establishment of AEDC.

A four-hour pre-conference class on "DTIC for the Research Community: DTIC Online Access Controlled" was presented to a mix of prospective and experienced users and an update on DTIC activities was presented as part of the formal program. Workshop highlights included reports from the chief librarian of each major service and the Library of Congress as well as sessions on innovative uses of Web 2.0 technologies and their implementation by DoD components.

DTIC Regional Offices

DTIC has four regional offices, through which it is able to provide a range of products and services including reference, registration, and assistance in accessing DTIC's numerous offerings. There is also a satellite office in San Diego that focuses on human systems and biomedical research and development and provides information support to small businesses.

Midwestern Regional Office
Wright-Patterson Air Force Base, Ohio
Tel. 937-255-7905, fax 937-986-7002
E-mail dayton@dtic.mil

Northeastern Regional Office
Hanscom Air Force Base, Maine
Tel. 781-377-2413, fax 781-377-5627
E-mail boston@dtic.mil

Southwestern Regional Office
Kirtland Air Force Base, New Mexico
Tel. 505-846-6797, fax 505-846-6799
E-mail albuq@dtic.mil

Western Regional Office
El Segundo, California
Tel. 310-653-2483, fax 310-363-2159
E-mail losangel@dtic.mil

DTIC-A, San Diego
NAS North Island
Box 357011
San Diego, CA 92135-7011
Tel. 619-545-7384
E-mail dticasd@dticam.dtic.mil

Note: DTIC and STINET are registered service marks of the Defense Technical Information Center.

National Library of Education

Knowledge Utilization Division
National Center for Education Evaluation and Regional Assistance
Institute of Education Sciences, U.S. Department of Education
400 Maryland Ave. S.W. Washington, DC 20202
World Wide Web http://ies.ed.gov/ncee/projects/nat_ed_library.asp

Christina Dunn

Director, National Library of Education
202-219-1012, e-mail christina.dunn@ed.gov

The year 2009 marked 15 years of service by the National Library of Education (NLE), the primary resource center for education information in the federal government. As an Institute of Education Sciences (IES) program in the U.S. Department of Education (ED), NLE serves the research needs of the education community through two primary programs: the Education Resources Information Center (ERIC) and the Education Department Research Library/Reference Center. These programs are the center for the collection, preservation, discovery, and retrieval of education information, especially information produced by and for the department.

Public Law 103-227, the Educational Research, Development, Dissemination and Improvement Act of 1994, created NLE; it was then reauthorized under Public Law 107-279, Education Sciences Reform Act of 2002. The legislation requires the director, qualified in library science, to report to the commissioner for education evaluation and regional assistance and to carry out four primary responsibilities:

- Collecting and archiving information, including products and publications developed through, or supported by, the Institute of Education Sciences; and other relevant and useful education-related research, statistics, and evaluation materials and other information, projects, and publications that are consistent with scientifically valid research or the priorities and mission of the institute, and developed by the department, other federal agencies, or entities
- Providing a central location within the federal government for information about education
- Providing comprehensive reference services on matters relating to education to employees of the Department of Education and its contractors and grantees, other federal employees, and members of the public
- Promoting greater cooperation and resource sharing among providers and repositories of education information in the United States

To support its legislated mandate, NLE's programs—ERIC and the Research Library—are designed to share these responsibilities by complementing each other and eliminating duplication of effort. Collecting and archiving information,

George Diez of the National Library of Education's Research Library staff contributed to this article.

and providing a central location within the federal government for information about education, are primarily addressed through ERIC. The provision of comprehensive reference services is the major focus of NLE. Together, they address promoting cooperation and resource sharing, although in different ways. To carry out these responsibilities, the NLE director is assisted by six federal staff, including the ERIC director, as well as ERIC and NLE contractors.

As part of its mission, ERIC (http://www.eric.ed.gov) is committed to providing a comprehensive, easy-to-use, searchable Internet-based bibliographic and full-text database of education research and information for educators, researchers, and the general public. Its digital library is centered around a collection of more than 1.3 million bibliographic records of education resources dating from 1966 to the present, including journal articles, books, research syntheses, conference papers, technical reports, policy papers, and other education-related materials. ERIC users conduct more than 8 million searches each month through the ERIC Web site and commercial and noncommercial sites. Since ERIC is the major public program and outreach arm of NLE, it is covered in the following separate article. This article, while providing a brief overview of NLE, is devoted to the activities of the Education Department Research Library/Reference Center.

ED Research Library/Reference Center

The ED Research Library provides information services to agency staff and contractors, the general public, government agencies, and other libraries. Comprised of 14 staff—five full-time federal staff and nine contract librarians—the library is divided into two units: Technical Services and Serials Management, with an emphasis on electronic resource management; and Reference and Document Delivery. Both staffing and organizational structure are flexible to allow quick and proficient response to changing user needs, institutional initiatives, and advances in technology. Key customers served by the Research Library include approximately 5,000 ED staff nationwide; ED contractors performing research; education organizations and media; and academic, special, and government libraries. All services are supported by the library's budget, which in fiscal year 2009 was $1.5 million.

Located at the department's headquarters building in Washington, D.C., the library houses current and historical collections and archives of information on education issues, research, statistics, and policy, with a special emphasis on agency documents, including contractor and grantee publications, and current and historical federal education legislation. The library also collects journals supporting the ERIC database and research reports supporting the What Works Clearinghouse. The print (paper and electronic) monograph collections now number more than 96,000 titles, while journal holdings exceed 800 titles, including open access journals.

Leveraging technology to support the education research of customers has been a central focus of the NLE since its creation. While these efforts are more apparent in the ERIC program, NLE also employs and explores technology. Currently it provides agency staff with access to a comprehensive collection of digital information resources covering the subjects of education, psychology, sociology, public policy, and law. It also uses commercial electronic document delivery services to improve turnaround time for customer requests and its own internally developed document delivery tracking tool to monitor fulfillment for large requests. To better promote and manage information requests, as well as to create its own information bank, the library employs virtual reference technology to provide reference services to ED staff and contractors, and to support the activities of the IES Regional Educational Laboratories Virtual Reference Desk Program. The virtualization of NLE services has enabled the library to take a greater role in outreach and service to the education community at large.

In addition to digital bibliographic information resources and virtual reference services, the library utilizes digital content management system technology to control archives of ED products and publications, including the working documents of the National Mathematics Advisory Panel and the knowledge base of the Regional Educational Laboratories Virtual Reference Desk Program. In 2009 NLE delivered more than 95 percent of its products and services in digital formats, with usage increasing almost 3 percent over 2008 levels. Promoting and improving services is a continuing factor in achieving library initiatives, with marketing of services and collections being as important as the application of technology.

Use of the Library

During 2009 research library use was similar to that of the previous two years, with a little more than 18,000 requests received. Document delivery and interlibrary loan showed the greatest growth, with requests for reference assistance increasing only slightly. While most information requests continue to come from the general public, most staff time (71.2 percent) is devoted to responding to the information needs of ED staff and contractors as their requests tend to be complex and often require services that extend over several weeks or months. This group generated about 6,500 requests, or 36 percent of all requests received in 2009; it also continued to access more electronic journal articles and conduct more database searches than in 2008, showing an increase in usage of 2.6 percent. Efforts to train staff and contractors in using the library's digital resources appear to have paid off as the majority of information requests, as well as database and journal usage, takes place on the library's portal, with usage of the "Ask a Librarian" feature increasing by more than 30 percent over the course of the year.

The general public generated around 7,100 requests (39.5 percent), down slightly from 2009; most were for reference assistance. Of these, about 22 percent were referrals generated by the department's EDPubs service, the 800-USA-LEARN service, Regional Education Laboratories Virtual Reference Desk, and ERIC Help Desk. The characteristics of public users remained almost the same as in previous years. More than 70 percent of the general public contacting the reference center in 2009 were K–12 educators, students in institutions of higher education, or researchers; 27 percent were parents; and about 3 percent were unknown. As in 2008, the majority of these customers continued to access the library by telephone (55 percent), followed closely by e-mail (43 percent, up from 39 percent in 2008); fewer than 2 percent visited the facility.

Another major user group consists of academic, government, and special libraries; they generated a little over 4,400 requests (24.5 percent), about the same as in 2008; most of these requests—about 3,300—continued to be for interlibrary loan/document delivery services. The most frequently requested items were historical documents of all types, such as policy, research, and contractor reports, including those on ERIC microfiche, and other publications released prior to 1985. Libraries in institutions of higher education accounted for most of the borrowing; the library's strong historical and research collections and a "no charge" lending policy support this community.

Collections

The library's collection focus has remained the same since its creation: education issues, with an emphasis on research and policy; and related topics, including law, public policy, economics, urban affairs, sociology, history, philosophy, psychology, cognitive development, and library and information science. In 2009 about 2,650 print monographs and 404 electronic publications, excluding agency publications, were added to the collection. The number of paid journal subscriptions remained at 322. Approximately 95 percent of current subscriptions are delivered in electronic format; this is the preferred format due to the facility's limited storage capacity and customer demand for desktop accessibility to journal articles.

Historically the library has maintained special collections of documents associated with its parent agency, having a complete collection of ERIC microfiche, research reports supporting the work of the What Works Clearinghouse and special panels, and current and historical publications of or related to the agency including a special collection of federal education legislation. With the digitization of the ERIC microfiche collection of about 340,000 documents, the library now has electronic access to the full text of all ERIC microfiche indexed between 1966 and 1992. In contrast, the ERIC Web site at http://www.ed.eric.gov provides public access to those documents for which copyright clearance was obtained—the full text of nearly 192,000 documents or almost 55 percent of the collection. All documents from the ERIC microfiche collection are available through interlibrary loan upon request.

Other special collections include documents and archives of the former National Institute of Education and the former U.S. Office of Education, including reports, studies, manuals, statistical publications, speeches, and policy papers. Together, these collections represent a resource covering the history of the U.S. Department of Education and its predecessor agencies. The library also serves as a federal depository library under the U.S. Government Printing Office program.

Services

NLE's primary role is to provide reference and other information services, including legislative reference and statistical information services, to the education community at large, as well as to provide document delivery services to ED staff and contractors and interlibrary loan services to other libraries and government agencies. Services to agency staff and contractors continue to grow, resulting in additional library resources being focused on this community in recent years. Through its involvement in the Regional Education Laboratories Virtual Reference Desk, the library provides resources and reference services to researchers and end users alike. Outreach to academic libraries includes a gift books program, interlibrary loan, and document delivery.

Of the more than 7,000 inquiries from the general public received in 2009, most pertained the same issues that were of interest in the previous year: No Child Left Behind requirements, agency programs, student achievement and assessment, charter schools, teacher quality and preparation, early childhood education, and national statistics. Other topics of public interest in 2009 included agency policy and budget; federal funding to states and local school districts; current education issues in the news, such as technology in the schools, community colleges, after-school and summer programming, school choice, academic standards, and failing schools; and teacher certification requirements.

By lending books and other materials from its collection, NLE serves other libraries in a variety of institutions. During the past year it made available more than 3,100 items, mostly agency documents, contractor reports, digitized ERIC microfiche, and recent research in the field of education. Most requests are from institutions of higher education, followed by federal and state agencies, and other libraries. Growth in this service area is attributed to a stronger collection of current education research reports, including those from other English-speaking countries; digitized ERIC microfiche; and government documents, especially historical documents from the department.

Agency staff conducted 28,980 searches of the Library's databases. Results of these searches coupled with ED staff and contractor requests for specific titles generated requests for over 6,800 journal articles and documents. Although more full-text journal articles are available to agency staff online, the number of requests for journal articles and other documents grew slightly over 2008. The library filled around 53 percent of requests from its own collections, with the remaining 47 percent filled from other sources—about 7.5 percent were borrowed from other libraries, 31.5 percent came from document delivery services and 8 percent were purchased from book vendors and sponsoring organizations. In the last few years, the library has been able to fill more requests from its own collections; there has been a concerted effort to fill gaps, especially in the journals collection, and to identify and acquire new publications more quickly than in previous years.

The U.S. Department of Education Research Library can be contacted by e-mail at library@ed.gov. The library's reference desk is available by telephone at 800-424-1616 (toll free,) 202-205-5015, 202-205-5019, or 202-205-7561 (TTY), and by fax at 202-401-0547. Located in the U.S. Department of Education's Headquarters Building, it is open from 9:00 A.M. to 5:00 P.M. weekdays, except federal holidays.

Education Resources Information Center

National Library of Education
National Center for Education Evaluation and Regional Assistance
Institute of Education Sciences, U.S. Department of Education
400 Maryland Ave. S.W., Washington, DC 20202
World Wide Web http://www.eric.ed.gov

Luna Levinson

Director, ERIC Program
202-208-2321, e-mail Luna.Levinson@ed.gov

The National Library of Education's largest program is the Education Resources Information Center (ERIC), a digital library of education materials comprising more than 1.3 million bibliographic records and 321,491 full-text materials spanning the period 1966 to the present. For decades, ERIC has served the information needs of schools, institutions of higher education, educators, parents, administrators, policymakers, researchers, and other public and private entities through a variety of library services and formats—first in paper copy, then in microfiche, and today exclusively in electronic format. ERIC provides service directly to the public via its Web site, http://www.eric.ed.gov. All of the library functions are administered by the U.S. Department of Education's Institute of Education Sciences (IES).

With a 43-year history of public service, ERIC is one of the oldest programs in the U.S. Department of Education. As the world's largest education resource, ERIC is distinguished by two hallmarks: free dissemination of bibliographic records, and the collection of gray literature such as research conference papers and government contractor reports.

The authorizing legislation for ERIC is part of the Education Sciences Reform Act of 2002, Public Law 107-279. This legislation envisioned ERIC subject areas or topics (previously covered by the ERIC Clearinghouses) as part of the totality of enhanced information dissemination to be conducted by the Institute of Education Sciences. In addition, information dissemination includes information on closing the achievement gap and educational practices that improve academic achievement and promote learning.

ERIC Mission

The ERIC mission is to provide a comprehensive, easy-to-use, searchable, Internet-based bibliographic and full-text database of education research and information for educators, researchers, and the general public. Terms defining the ERIC mission are explained as follows:

- *Comprehensive,* consisting of journal articles and non-journal materials, including materials not published by commercial publishers, that are directly related to education
- *Easy-to-use and searchable,* allowing database users to find the information they need quickly and efficiently

- *Electronic,* making ERIC operations accessible to the maximum extent feasible and linking to publishers and commercial sources of journal articles
- *Bibliographic and full-text,* with bibliographic records conveying the information users need in a simple and straightforward manner, and whenever possible including full-text journal articles and non-journal materials free of charge

Following this mission, the overarching goal of ERIC is to increase the availability and quality of research and information for ERIC users.

Activities that fulfill the ERIC mission are broadly categorized as collection development, content authorizations and agreements, acquisitions and processing, database and Web site operations, and communications. These five functions continue to evolve and improve as suggestions and guidance are received from a variety of sources including public comments and the ERIC Steering Committee and Content Experts, recognized authorities tasked with advising the ERIC contractor. All of the ERIC activities are conducted under a single contract awarded to Computer Sciences Corporation (CSC) by the U.S. Department of Education in August 2009.

ERIC Collection

ERIC is one of the few collections to index non-journal materials as well as journal literature. The largest share of the collection consists of citations to journal articles (836,245 records), and a smaller portion consists of non-journal materials (494,203 records). The non-journal materials, frequently called gray literature, are not produced by commercial publishers and are not easy to find. In ERIC, the gray literature consists of research synthesis, dissertations, conference proceedings, and selected papers such as keynote speeches, technical reports, policy papers, literature reviews, bibliographies, congressional hearings and reports, reports on federal and state standards, testing and regulations, U.S. Department of Education contractor reports (e.g., the What Works Clearinghouse and the National Center for Education Statistics), and working papers for established research and policy organizations.

To support consistency and reliability in content coverage, most education journals are indexed comprehensively so that all articles in each issue are included. Currently, ERIC indexes a total of 1,051 journals; 952 journals comprehensively, and a smaller number, 99, selectively. Articles from selectively covered journals are acquired by ERIC subject specialists, who determine individual documents for the ERIC database according to the ERIC selection policy.

The broad selection standard provides that all materials added to the ERIC database are directly related to the field of education. The majority of the journals indexed in ERIC are peer-reviewed, and the peer-reviewed status is indicated for all journals indexed from 2004 forward, when this data began to be documented by the ERIC system. The collection scope includes early childhood education through higher education, vocational education, and special education; it includes teacher education, education administration, assessment and evaluation, counseling, information technology, and the academic areas of reading, mathematics, science, environmental education, languages, and social studies. In addition, the collection includes resources addressing one of the three objectives identified in Section 172 of the Education Sciences Reform Act: closing the achievement gap, encouraging educational practices that improve academic achievement, and conducting education research.

Following that standard, there are three sets of specific criteria providing guidance for document selection. The quality criteria consist of five basic factors: completeness, integrity, objectivity, substantive merit, and utility/importance. Selection is further determined by sponsorship criteria, and preference for inclusion in ERIC is given to those resources with identified sponsorship (for example, professional societies and government agencies). Detailed editorial criteria also provide factors for consideration, especially with regard to journals considered for comprehensive indexing.

ERIC Digitization Project

To increase public access to ERIC records, the Department of Education launched a major initiative in 2006 to convert microfiche full-text documents published by ERIC between 1966 and 1992 to digital format for distribution, and this project was concluded in 2009. The project scope was to digitize and archive microfiche full-text documents containing an estimated 43 million pages and to provide copyright due diligence by seeking permission from the copyright holders to make the electronic version available to users.

The project result was the addition of about 57 percent of the microfiche collection to the ERIC digital library, more than 193,000 of the 340,000 microfiche documents. The National Archive Publishing Company (NAPC), ERIC's partner in this initiative, continues to accept copyright permission to release documents online.

ERIC Web Site

The ERIC Web site is the central location for all information about ERIC and carries the most recent additions and changes in the ERIC collection. All submissions considered for selection must be in digital format and are accompanied by author permission for dissemination. For individual document submissions, authors (copyright holders) register through the ERIC Web site feature "My ERIC"; follow the steps to enter bibliographic information, abstract, and document file; and submit the electronic document release form authorizing ERIC to disseminate the materials. In 2009 almost 30 percent of all non-journal acquisitions were online submissions. Journal publishers, associations, and other entities with multiple documents also submit electronic content following guidance and instructions consistent with provider agreements from ERIC. Once publishers have signed an ERIC agreement, files can be submitted by e-mail or disk or by upload to ERIC's ftp site.

The complete list of journals indexed in ERIC, including the years of coverage and the number of articles indexed, is a tool on the ERIC Web site enabling users to identify more easily specific journal literature. The non-journal list of associations and other entities contributing content to the ERIC digital library is also provided on the ERIC Web site. Another convenience for users that is designed to streamline the process of obtaining full text, is the "Find in a Library" feature, which leverages the Open URL Gateway and WorldCat to provide a link from ERIC records to electronic and print resources available in libraries. For all journals currently indexed in ERIC, there are links to publishers' Web sites if users choose to purchase full-text articles.

The ERIC search capability includes basic and advanced search, field code searching, search within results, and related items. Another feature, designed to address misspellings, is "Would You Like to Try" followed by suggested search terms or phrases. The ERIC Thesaurus offers another approach for ERIC searching. Refinements to ERIC's technical architecture continue to improve system functionality and user satisfaction. Usability tests with participant groups including librarians, researchers, and students provide input on issues such as online submission, the "Help" section, and an extensive range of search operations. With all database enhancements, the development process contributes to increase accessibility, efficiency, and quality.

A series of short, animated tutorials help searchers use ERIC and all its features from basic search functions to using Boolean operators. Other tutorials include: author search, citation management, combining descriptors, keyword versus descriptors search, phrase search, truncating terms in a search, and more. The Web site home page provides specific areas of interest and information to publishers, authors, librarians, and licensors, while a news section offers a menu of recent developments such as the ERIC microfiche digitization project.

Automated systems for acquisition and processing help to reduce the total time required to produce a database record, and most records are processed in less than 30 days. The ERIC bibliographic file is updated multiple times per week on the ERIC Web site, and monthly totals of records published are displayed on the ERIC home page. In 2009 a total of 48,103 new records were published; of this number, 44,436 records were journal articles (called EJs) and 3,667 were non-journal documents (called EDs). ERIC acquired 5,788 more records in 2009 than in 2008.

ERIC Access

The ERIC digital library is accessible through the government-sponsored Web site as well as through Google, Google Scholar, Yahoo, MSN, and commercial services such as Cambridge Scientific Abstracts, EBSCO, OCLC, and ProQuest. There were more than 128 million searches of the ERIC digital library in 2009.

The ERIC digital library can be reached by toll-free telephone in the United States, Canada, and Puerto Rico at 800-LET-ERIC (800-538-3742), Monday through Friday, 8:00 A.M. to 8:00 P.M. eastern time. Questions can also be transmitted via the message box on the "Contact Us" page on the ERIC Web site.

National Association and Organization Reports

American Library Association

50 E. Huron St., Chicago, IL 60611
800-545-2433
World Wide Web http://www.ala.org

Camila A. Alire
President

The American Library Association (ALA) was founded in 1876 in Philadelphia and later chartered in the Commonwealth of Massachusetts; it is the oldest, largest, and most influential library association in the world. ALA has approximately 63,000 members, including not only librarians but also library trustees, publishers, and other interested people from every state and many nations. The association serves public, state, school, and academic libraries, as well as special libraries for people working in government, commerce and industry, the arts, and the armed services or in hospitals, prisons, and other institutions.

ALA's mission is "to provide leadership for the development, promotion, and improvement of library and information services and the profession of librarianship in order to enhance learning and ensure access to information for all."

ALA is governed by an elected council—its policy-making body—and an executive board, which acts for the council in the administration of established policies and programs. Within this context, the executive board is the body that manages the affairs of the association, delegating management of the day-to-day operation to the association's executive director. ALA also has 37 standing committees, designated as committees of the association or of the council. ALA operations are implemented by staff through a structure of programmatic offices and support units.

ALA is home to 11 membership divisions, each focused on a type of library or library function. They are the American Association of School Librarians (AASL); the Association for Library Collections and Technical Services (ALCTS); the Association for Library Service to Children (ALSC); the Association of College and Research Libraries (ACRL); the Association of Library Trustees, Advocates, Friends, and Foundations (ALTAFF); the Association of Specialized and Cooperative Library Agencies (ASCLA); the Library and Information Technology Association (LITA); the Library Leadership and Management Association (LLAMA); the Public Library Association (PLA); the Reference and User Services Association (RUSA); and the Young Adult Library Services Association (YALSA).

ALA also hosts 17 roundtables for members who share interests that do not fall within the scope of any of the divisions. A network of affiliates, chapters, and other organizations enables ALA to reach a broad audience.

Key action areas include diversity, equitable access to information and library services, education and lifelong learning, intellectual freedom, advocacy for libraries and the profession, literacy, and organizational excellence.

ALA offices are units of the association that address broad interests and issues of concern to ALA members; they track issues and provide information, services, and products for members and the general public. Current ALA offices are the Chapter Relations Office (CRO), the Development Office, the Governance Office, the International Relations Office (IRO), the Office for Accreditation (OA), the Office for Diversity (OFD), the Office of Government Relations (OGR), the Office for Human Resource Development and Recruitment (HRDR), the Office for Information Technology Policy (OITP), the Office for Intellectual Freedom (OIF), the Office for Library Advocacy (OLA), the Office for Literacy and Outreach Services (OLOS), the Office for Research and Statistics (ORS), the Public Information Office (PIO), the Public Programs Office (PPO), and the Washington Office.

ALA is headquartered in Chicago; the Office of Government Relations and the Office for Information Technology Policy are housed at ALA's Washington Office. ALA also has an editorial office for *Choice,* a review journal for academic libraries, in Middletown, Connecticut.

ALA is a 501(c)(3) charitable and educational organization.

Focusing on Advocacy and Literacy

During her presidential year, 2009–2010 ALA President Camila Alire, dean emerita at the University of New Mexico in Albuquerque and Colorado State University in Fort Collins, implemented key initiatives to address advocacy and literacy.

"ALA embodies the hard work of all the librarians, information specialists, and library support staff who take serving the information needs of their communities very seriously," Alire said at her inaugural banquet. "One of my goals is to provide another level of advocacy that articulates not only the value of all types of libraries but also the value of our members working in those libraries to their respective communities."

A focus on "member-driven advocacy" content and training—for librarians, library staff, and supporters of all types of libraries—was designed to complement ALA's other efforts targeting local, state, and federal legislative advocacy. Such front-line advocacy features a critical emphasis on the competencies and content needed to advocate for the library and library needs within the library structure and within libraries' respective communities—cities, counties, higher education environments, and schools and school districts.

In addition, Alire brought national attention to libraries and their role as literacy builders, engaged library leaders everywhere to focus on current literacy best practices in building community, and developed programs that incorporate literacy partners to build a comprehensive advocacy for the literacy movement.

"We know that a literate public is an informed public," Alire said, "and that our library users need multiple literacies including reading, information, digital, and cultural literacies in order to access information of all types in all formats. However, not everyone recognizes the crucial role libraries play. Today and for the future, it is not enough to focus only on providing these vital services. We all must advocate for our respective communities' right to have them and for the value of our libraries."

Highlights of the Year

ALA Responds to Economic Crisis

Widespread media coverage of the increase in library usage during tough economic times positioned libraries as trusted and valuable community resources, focusing on how libraries assist job-seekers and help families save money, as well as on how they are changing to meet the demands of the communities they serve.

A virtual toolkit for those seeking library jobs during the economic downturn, the new Web site Get a Job! (http://www.getajob.ala.org) offers resources, links, best practices, and real-life examples from a range of ALA divisions and units. The site also features advice from members as well as career-search professionals.

An ALA Editions Special Report addressed the economy's impact on jobs. *Crisis in Employment* by Jane Jerrard presented advice and methods for providing appropriate training and education to job-seekers. The report, which was also made available in electronic format at a lower price, was published rapidly to ensure timely advice.

The ALA Chapter Relations Office and the International Relations Office supported state library associations as they battled efforts to cut state funding to libraries just when their services—such as workshops on financial planning and investment, technology training, access to valuable databases, free access to computers—were most needed. More than 75,000 library supporters nationwide sent messages directly to their governors and legislators, efforts that helped to stave off or reduce catastrophic cuts in Ohio, Florida, and New Jersey.

RUSA worked with the Financial Industry Regulatory Authority (FINRA) Investor Education Foundation to develop a new resource to help people cope with tough economic times through the Smart Investing @ your library program. FINRA's Investor Alert brochure *Job Dislocation: Making Smart Financial Choices After a Job Loss* offered guidance and tips for the general public on maintaining financial stability during a period of unemployment. Topics included taking the right financial steps, protecting against investment fraud, understanding health insurance options, and asking appropriate questions about employer benefit plans.

ALA's Washington Office responded to the recession by taking action to inform decision-makers—including newly elected President Barack Obama—of the many ways the nation's libraries serve as first responders in times of economic crisis. In addition to economy-related issues, the report "Opening the 'Window to a Larger World': Libraries' Role in Changing America," submitted by 2008–2009 ALA President James Rettig to President Obama's transition team, outlined top ALA issues and concerns. The Open Access Working Group, which includes ALA, ACRL, and eight other library and public-interest groups, also sent a report, "Public Access to the Published Results of Publicly Funded Research Will Benefit the Economy, Science, and Health."

Tributes to Krug, Josey

The library world lost two important leaders in 2009: OIF Director Judith Krug and ALA Past President E. J. Josey.

Krug, director of ALA's OIF and executive director of the Freedom to Read Foundation (FRTF) for more than 40 years, died April 11 at age 69. Known for her steadfast support of writers, teachers, librarians, and students, Krug advised countless librarians and trustees on dealing with challenges to library materials. She was involved in several First Amendment cases that went to the U.S. Supreme Court and was the founder of Banned Books Week. At the 2009 ALA Annual Conference, Krug was awarded Honorary Membership in ALA and recognized with tributes from every ALA state chapter and the ALA Council, the William J. Brennan, Jr. Award from the Thomas Jefferson Center, and the FTRF Founder's Award.

Josey, professor emeritus at the University of Pittsburgh and 1983–1985 president of ALA, died at age 85 on July 3. In 1964 Josey authored a resolution forbidding ALA officers and staff from participating in state associations that denied membership to black librarians. This action led to the integration of the library associations of several southern states, and Josey became the first black librarian to be accepted as a member of the Georgia Library Association.

Supreme Court Denies Review of COPA

In January 2009 the U.S. Supreme Court denied review of the Third Circuit U.S. Court of Appeals' decision to strike down the Child Online Protection Act (COPA), thus ending a decade-long court case. COPA, a congressional effort to overcome the constitutional deficiencies of the Communications Decency Act, would have criminalized the transmission of materials "for commercial purposes" considered to be "harmful to minors" via the Internet if those materials could be accessed by minors. FRTF filed friend-of-the-court briefs at each stage of the litigation, arguing that COPA placed an unconstitutional burden on protected speech between adults.

ALA Files Comments on Broadband

In December ALA submitted comments to the Federal Communications Commission regarding broadband adoption as part of the National Broadband Plan (NBP). ALA's comments highlighted the unique position of the public library as an institution whose mission is to serve the information needs of the community. The implicit goal of NBP is not to have the infrastructure in place to provide access to the Internet but rather to ensure that every individual can benefit from the resources made available by that infrastructure. "As more critical resources, such as job applications and government services, are available primarily online, the societal cost of not being able to access these resources increases dramatically," ALA stated. "It is critical that the FCC includes libraries in the National Broadband Plan in order to ensure that libraries have high-capacity broadband necessary to provide these services."

ALTAFF Unites Voices of ALTA, FOLUSA

On February 1, 2009, the Association for Library Trustees and Advocates (ALTA) and Friends of Libraries U.S.A. (FOLUSA) officially joined forces to become the Association of Library Trustees, Advocates, Friends, and Foundations (ALTAFF). The new division helps library trustees and friends groups to work together at the local, state, and national levels to promote and advocate for libraries, with an ultimate goal to harness the power of hundreds of thousands of library advocates so that libraries will thrive even in times of economic distress.

New @ your library Web Site

ALA soft-launched the @ your library Web site (http://www.atyourlibrary.org) during National Library Week in April 2009. The new site—a two-year pilot project funded by Carnegie Corporation of New York that targets families, children, teens, and such underserved populations as recent immigrants and job-seekers—offers information on topics of general interest to the public and uses interactive technology and social networking to stimulate library usage and raise public awareness of the library as a valuable community resource. The site is designed to work in tandem with the I Love Libraries Web site maintained by OLA.

National Library Legislative Day

More than 400 librarians and library supporters traveled to Washington, D.C., to attend National Library Legislative Day May 11–12, 2009. Participants spent the first day at briefings on a variety of issues including appropriations, telecommunications, and the USAPatriot Act, then took part in a congressional reception overlooking the Capitol Building. On May 12 participants put their knowledge to work while meeting with their elected officials and their staffs.

New Spectrum Initiative

ALA President Alire, Past President Rettig, and President-Elect Roberta Stevens launched the Spectrum Presidential Initiative, a special one-year effort to raise $1 million for the Spectrum Scholarship Program. The initiative will allow ALA to provide 90 to 100 more Spectrum Scholarships as well as increase the Spectrum Endowment to provide future scholars with much-needed support. Established in 1997, Spectrum is ALA's national diversity and recruitment effort designed to address the underrepresentation of critically needed racial and ethnic librarians in the profession.

Banned Books Week

The 28th celebration of Banned Books Week, OIF's long-running censorship awareness effort, promoted the campaign "Read. Speak. Know" using quotes from regularly challenged books in hand-drawn posters to capture the central theme of the annual event: that knowledge is powerful and must not be limited in any way. The 2009 campaign brought in more than $100,000. Also as part of the September 26–October 3 event, OIF hosted its fifth annual Read-Out! September 26. Some 300 enthusiastic audience members saw and heard highly acclaimed authors read from their own or their favorite books that have been banned or challenged. Frequently challenged author Chris Crutcher emceed the event, which included readings and book-signings by some of the top ten most challenged authors of the previous year: Justin Richardson, Peter Parnell, Lauren Myracle, Stephen Chbosky, Sarah Brannen, and Cecily von Ziegesar.

Teen Read Week

Teen Read Week 2009, October 18–24, took the theme "Read Beyond Reality" to encourage teens to read a wide variety of books and graphic novels, particularly science fiction; fantasy; tall tales and myths; nonfiction about careers in science, space exploration, robotics, and artificial intelligence; and books that tie into video games and virtual reality. More than 11,000 teens voted in the 2009 Teens Top Ten list, with *Paper Towns* by John Green (Dutton) as the No. 1 popular young adult book from the previous year; teens also chose the 2010 theme, "Books with Beat."

SummerSlam Reading Jam

In June 2009 YALSA and World Wrestling Entertainment launched the SummerSlam Reading Jam, a pilot project to boost summer reading for teens. Some 500 libraries encouraged young readers to check out two books between June 24 and July 16; each patron who did so was entered into a contest to win a trip to the SummerSlam Pay-per-View wrestling event in Los Angeles in August. YALSA and World Wrestling Entertainment plan to expand the project in 2010.

AASL Initiative Supports Learning Standards

AASL launched Learning4Life (L4L), a national plan to support states, school systems, and individual schools preparing to implement its "Standards for the 21st-Century Learner" and "Empowering Learners: Guidelines for School Library Media Programs." By targeting specific audiences—decision-makers, educators, parents, students, and the public—over the next three to five years, AASL hopes to introduce the standards and guidelines to internal and external audiences, build awareness of the importance of school library media programs, and create an understanding of and commitment to the learning standards and guidelines.

AASL Names Best Sites for Teaching and Learning

In its inaugural year, AASL's "Top 25 Web Sites for Teaching and Learning" program honored sites that foster innovation, creativity, active participation, and collaboration. The list, which will be updated annually, recognizes free, user-friendly sites that offer tools and resources for organizing and managing, content collaboration, curriculum sharing, media sharing, virtual environments, and social networking and communication. AASL also honored an additional 21 landmark Web sites known for their exemplary histories of authoritative, dynamic content and curricular relevance.

ACRL Promotes Scholarly Communication

ACRL continued its efforts to enhance and promote scholarly communication, releasing an updated version of the division's popular Scholarly Communication Toolkit in a new format. In addition, ACRL and the Association for Research Libraries continued to cosponsor the Institute for Scholarly Communication, and the two groups issued the guide "Developing a Scholarly Communication Program in Your Library," which outlines steps for libraries interested in developing scholarly communication programs.

ALCTS to Develop Preservation Week

In early 2009 ALCTS received $15,000 in 2010 funding to develop Preservation Week, scheduled to launch in mid-2010. Modeled after Teen Read Week and National Library Week, Preservation Week is intended to help U.S. libraries provide tools—including a variety of toolkits, programs, and a speakers bureau—for users to preserve their own cultural heritage. Developed in collaboration with the Library of Congress, Preservation Week seeks to bring together a number of preservation and conservation organizations to make preserving and conserving personal cultural heritage a priority. The Institute of Museum and Library Services (IMLS), ALA Graphics, PIO, and ALA's @ your library campaign are also contributing to the program.

PPO Launches ProgrammingLibrarian.org

PPO debuted an online resource to help libraries of all types and sizes create cultural and community programs. The Web site, http://www.Programming Librarian.org, includes a resource library, live learning opportunities, and a blog to keep librarians informed of opportunities and inspire new library programs. As the site continues to develop, users will find more resources, ideas, and opportunities to network with peers and programming experts. Development of the site is funded by a grant from IMLS.

Investing Program Wins Award

Smart investing @ your library, a grant program offered by the FINRA Investor Education Foundation and RUSA, was one of 17 programs receiving an "award of excellence" from the 2009 Associations Advance America Awards program, sponsored by the American Society of Association Executives and the Center for Association Leadership. Begun in 2007, Smart investing @ your library is an ongoing national program that helps public libraries provide effective, unbiased financial and investor education resources and services through grant funding ranging from $5,000 to $100,000, as well as assistance in the areas of marketing, communications, evaluation, and project management.

Campaign for America's Libraries

ALSC officially launched phase two of the Kids! @ your library campaign, which incorporates additional materials into the campaign's online toolkit to help librarians promote the library and library resources to children in grades 5–8. New tools include free downloadable So much to see so much to do @ your library mini-posters and bookmarks as well as print-ready art designed by award-winning children's book illustrator and graphic designer David Diaz. Additional materials include two new readers' theater scripts based on the work of Christopher Paul Curtis and Jerry Spinelli, library activities and games, and two new poetry resources, 15 Ways to Use Poetry @ your library and Poetry Programs @ your library.

Campaign for the World's Libraries

The Latvian Library Association and the Romania Library Association joined Campaign for the World's Libraries in 2009. Campaign for the World's Libraries was developed by ALA and the International Federation of Library Associations and Institutions (IFLA) to showcase the roles played by public, school, academic, and special libraries worldwide. To date, 35 countries have joined the campaign, and the @ your library brand has been translated into each country's language. New logos reflecting the national colors of each member nation were made available for download during National Library Week 2009.

Programs and Partners

Campaign Partnerships

The American Dream Starts @ your library grant, developed by ALA and funded through Dollar General Literacy Foundation, awarded funding to 34 public libraries to add or expand literacy services for adult English-language learners.

Using the Campaign for America's Libraries @ your library brand, Verizon's Thinkfinity.org featured librarian-specific content from ALA and library initiatives in a collection of resources specifically for school library specialists. The Thinkfinity @ your library page showcases materials collected from Thinkfinity content partners and includes discipline-specific, standards-based educational resources on current subject areas. It also highlights events such as Youth Media Month, School Library Media Month, and El Día de los Niños, El Día de los Libros.

The fourth season of the Step Up to the Plate @ your library program, developed by ALA and the National Baseball Hall of Fame and Museum, was launched during Youth Baseball Week April 13–19, 2009, and was a featured program during the week's celebration at the National Baseball Hall of Fame in Cooperstown, New York. The program once again centered on a baseball trivia contest, with this year's questions—developed by the library staff at the Hall of

Fame—focusing on multiculturalism in baseball and baseball around the world. The program concluded with a drawing at the Hall of Fame. Step Up to the Plate spokesperson and Hall of Famer Ozzie Smith chose Oscar Youngquist, 11, of Racine, Wisconsin, as the grand prize winner.

Continuing an eight-year partnership with the Campaign for America's Libraries, *Woman's Day* magazine featured the four winners of its latest library initiative, which asked readers how they used the library to improve a family member's or their own emotional, mental, or physical health. Winners included a woman who found solace in the library when her husband was ill, one who used the resources at her library to learn about her postpartum depression, a woman who was able to make an informed health choice thanks to the research training offered at her library, and a reader who, after losing her eyesight, used books on tape provided by the Library of Congress to rediscover her love of reading. The magazine's next library initiative asked women to submit stories of how the library helped them save money during tough economic times.

PPO Traveling Exhibitions

PPO sent seven ongoing traveling exhibitions across the country in 2009, visiting a total of 88 public, academic, and special libraries: "Alexander Hamilton: The Man Who Made Modern America," "Benjamin Franklin: In Search of a Better World," "Changing the Face of Medicine: Celebrating America's Women Physicians," "Forever Free: Abraham Lincoln's Journey to Emancipation," "John Adams Unbound," "Lewis and Clark and the Indian Country," and "Pride and Passion: The African American Baseball Experience." In addition, PPO announced tours for three additional traveling exhibitions. "Lincoln: The Constitution and the Civil War" offers a fresh perspective on Abraham Lincoln that focuses on his struggle to meet the political and constitutional challenges of the Civil War; it will travel to 25 public, academic, and special libraries through October 2013. "Visions of the Universe: Four Centuries of Discovery," which features astronomy through the ages, from Galileo's early findings to the latest results of the Hubble Space Telescope, was hosted by 40 public libraries for six-week periods from January 2009 through April 2010. The third, "Harry Potter's World: Renaissance Science, Magic, and Medicine," uses materials from the National Library of Medicine to explore Harry Potter's world, its roots in Renaissance science, and the ethical questions that affected not only the wizards in J. K. Rowling's books but also the historical thinkers featured in the series. Twelve libraries were to host the special small-format exhibit for four-week periods between September 2009 and November 2010.

Conferences and Workshops

Annual Conference

Nearly 29,000 librarians and library supporters attended ALA's Annual Conference July 9–14, 2009, at the McCormick Place convention center in downtown Chicago. The total of 28,941—the largest on record—included 22,762 attendees and 6,179 exhibitors.

James Rettig's President's Program focused on the need to restore connections between the federal government and the people. Thomas S. Blanton, director of the National Security Archive at George Washington University, spoke about "The Secrecy Hangover," discussing the loss of access to government information, evaluating actions of the Obama administration, and writing the prescription for additional steps the federal government might take to provide more open access to government information.

The keynote speech at the opening general session was delivered by Christie Hefner, former CEO and chairman of Playboy Enterprises, an advocate of freedom of expression, social justice, and equal rights and opportunities for women. Steve Lopez, *Los Angeles Times* columnist and author of the novel *The Soloist* (Putnam) was the closing general session speaker.

NPR journalist and political commentator Cokie Roberts made the keynote presentation at the 2009 Public Library Association president's program. In addition, PLA sponsored 20 programs and three preconferences.

At the Newbery/Caldecott banquet, more than 1,100 attendees lauded Newbery Medal winner Neil Gaiman, author of *The Graveyard Book* (HarperCollins), Caldecott Medal winner Beth Krommes, author of *The House in the Night* (Houghton Mifflin), and Laura Ingalls Wilder medalist Ashley Bryan.

Participants also had the opportunity to attend the conference from their desktops via ALA's new Virtual Conference. Ten interactive Web sessions covered such topics as accessing stimulus money for broadband deployment, "greening your library," and customer service.

More than 400 turned out for YALSA's fashion show hosted by Steven Rosengard of the television show "Project Runway." Disney-Hyperion Books sponsored the sold-out event.

PPO presented the LIVE! @ your library Reading Stage with a special focus on poetry, offering readings from award-winning, popular, and up-and-coming poets. Featured authors and poets included Sherman Alexie, Cristina Henriquez, Jane Hirshfield, Marlon James, Ed Bok Lee, and Sara Paretsky.

Five hundred library supporters turned out for a sold-out evening with National Public Radio's "Wait Wait . . . Don't Tell Me!" to raise funds for ALTAFF.

The 5th Annual Empowerment Conference attracted more than 200 attendees to its day-and-a-half of programming on the theme "Who's Da Boss: Leadership for Library Support Staff." Cosponsored by Conference Services and HRDR, the conference began with author and professor of business ethics Al Gini speaking on "Lincoln's Ten Critical Tasks of Leadership." The conference offered 13 concurrent sessions; among the highlights was "Lunch with the Famous First Ladies," in which performer Jenny Riddle portrayed three remarkable American women.

2010 Midwinter Meeting

More than 11,000 people—8,526 members and 2,569 exhibitors—attended ALA's 2010 Midwinter Meeting January 15–19 in Boston.

Key themes of the meeting included budget cuts in tough economic times and how libraries provide services in a changing information environment. Librarians also responded to a campaign organized by ALA and the Massachusetts Convention Center Authority (MCCA) to raise funds for relief efforts following the January 12, 2010, earthquake in Haiti. Meeting attendees' donations were matched in kind by MCCA, resulting in a total donation of $27,084.

Former U.S. Vice President Al Gore delivered the Arthur Curley Memorial Lecture, discussing his new book, *Our Choice: A Plan to Solve the Climate Crisis* (Rodale).

Numerous other newsmakers and authors participated in the Midwinter Meeting, including Yohannes Gebregeorgis, founder and executive director of Ethiopia Reads; Elizabeth Gilbert, author of the bestseller *Eat, Pray, Love: One Woman's Search for Everything Across Italy, India and Indonesia* (Penguin); Atul Gawande, author of *Better: A Surgeon's Notes on Performance* (Picador); and Adriana Trigiani, author of *Very Valentine* (Harper).

At the Youth Media Awards announcements of the best in children's and young adult literature, the 2010 John Newbery Medal for the most distinguished contribution to children's literature went to Rebecca Stead for *When You Reach Me* (Wendy Lamb). Jerry Pinkney, author and illustrator of *The Lion and the Mouse* (Little, Brown) received the 2010 Caldecott Medal for the most distinguished American picture book for children, and Libba Bray, author of *Going Bovine* (Delacorte), won the Michael L. Printz Award for excellence in literature for young adults. The inaugural winner of a new award, the Coretta Scott King–Virginia Hamilton Award for Lifetime Achievement, was also announced: Walter Dean Myers, whose books include *Amiri and Odette: A Love Story* (Scholastic), *Fallen Angels* (Scholastic), *Monster* (Amistad), and *Sunrise Over Fallujah* (Scholastic). More than 6,500 people logged on to view the live Youth Media Awards Webcast, 1,900 got the news via Twitter, and nearly 1,000 Facebook fans followed the results.

Other meeting highlights included ALA President Alire's presentation "Advocacy on the Front Lines: How to Make a Difference from Where You Sit," which drew a standing-room-only crowd, and a forum for candidates for ALA president and treasurer.

ACRL National Conference

More than 4,300 library staff, exhibitors, speakers, and guests from every state and 22 countries met in Seattle March 12–15, 2009, for the ACRL 14th National Conference. Combined with the more than 350 people participating online, the conference had the highest registrant participation ever for an ACRL National Conference—3,263. The conference offered more than 300 programs that explored the changing nature and roles of academic and research libraries and librarianship. Poster sessions and the second offering of the Cyber Zed Shed also proved popular.

LITA National Forum

The 12th Annual LITA National Forum, with the theme "Open and Mobile," was held in Salt Lake City October 1–4. Keynote speakers included Joan K. Lippincott of the Coalition for Networked Information; David Weinberger, author of *Everything Is Miscellaneous: The Power of the New Digital Disorder* (Holt); and

Liz Lawley of the Rochester Institute of Technology. Two preconference workshops were offered: "The Future of Mobile" by Jason Griffey, head of library information technology at the University of Tennessee at Chattanooga, and "Accessibility Update: Section 508 and WCAG in a Library 2.0 World" by Nina McHale, assistant professor and Web librarian at the Auraria Library in Denver.

Publishing

New Online Store

Launched in early February 2009, ALA Publishing's new online store drew enthusiastic reviews from customers and resulted in increased interest in all ALA products in the store. The new store offers a contemporary interface for browsing by product/publication type or by area of interest; a feature that remembers the contents of a shopping cart for up to 30 days; a wish list option for storing items of interest for later purchase or e-mailing to others directly from the store; product descriptions for books that include links to Library Thing, WorldCat, and bookmarking sites like Del.ici.ous; RSS feeds for new product alerts; and an area on each product page showing additional products customers may be interested in.

ALA Editions

ALA Editions published a bumper crop of publications in 2009, with 36 new titles and revisions. Among the titles published were *Booktalking Bonanza: Ten Ready-to-Use Multimedia Sessions for the Busy Librarian* by Betsy Diamant-Cohen and Selma K. Levi; *The Hipster Librarian's Guide to Teen Craft Projects* by Tina Coleman and Peggie Llanes; *Privacy and Confidentiality Issues: A Guide for Libraries and their Lawyers* by Theresa Chmara; *Marketing Today's Academic Library: A Bold New Approach to Communicating with Students* by Brian Mathews; *Inside, Outside, and Online: Building Your Library Community* by Chrystie Hill; *The Library PR Handbook,* edited by ALA PIO Director Mark Gould; *The Librarian's Book of Quotes,* compiled by Tatyana Eckstrand; and *The Back Page* by Bill Ott.

American Libraries

American Libraries (*AL*), ALA's flagship news and features magazine, continued to offer readers up-to-the-minute information in a growing variety of formats. *AL*'s suite now includes ten issues of the print magazine, the weekly e-newsletter *American Libraries Direct,* a student version of *AL Direct,* the blog "Inside Scoop," AL Focus videocasts, *American Libraries Online* newsfeed, occasional digital supplements, and classified employment ads through ALA JobLIST. The print magazine offered updates on many issues affecting librarians and libraries, from dealing with dysfunctional staff to a story on tagging, and from the then-upcoming Obama presidency and what it might mean for libraries to a look at training and retooling in tight times. *AL* "Newsmakers" profiled a wide range of people with diverse roles and influences in the library world, including Cory Doctorow, Kay Ryan, Patricia Martin, Richard Gottlieb, Johannes Gebregeorgis, and Cokie Roberts. As a response to the financial crisis, *AL* published a combined August/September issue in 2009.

Booklist Publications

Booklist Publications had a busy year in digital media while maintaining the quality and depth of its print publications. The whole suite of publications offered numerous features, articles, "top ten" lists, and read-alikes and listen-alikes. More than 8,500 titles were reviewed and recommended in adult, youth, media, and reference. *Booklist Online* added three new blogs during the year: "Audiobooker" by teacher librarian and audiobook advocate Mary Burkey; "Bookends," which features middle school librarians Cindy Dobrez and Lynn Rutan; and "Points of Reference" by *Booklist* editor Mary Ellen Quinn and a team of experts from academic, public, and school libraries. In May 2009 *Booklist* announced that *Book Links* magazine would in fiscal 2010 be published as a quarterly print supplement to *Booklist* at no additional cost to subscribers, rather than as a stand-alone magazine.

ALA Graphics

The year at ALA Graphics started with the fastest-moving celebrity READ poster on record, featuring two stars of the movie *Twilight,* Robert Pattinson and Kristen Stewart. Other celebrities featured on READ posters were Hugh Laurie, America Ferrera, Cole Hamels, Yao Ming, Rachel McAdams, Ne-Yo, and the Jonas Brothers. A series of new character posters based on popular young adult and children's books was issued. The diversity poster and bookmark line was expanded to include Latino heritage in the fall, black history in February, women's history in March, and Asian/Pacific American heritage in May. A Celebrate Native American Literature poster and bookmark were published in partnership with the American Indian Library Association. A poster celebrating children's poetry by Mary Ann Hoberman, U.S. children's poet laureate, marked National Poetry Month in April, while a new History Lives poster and bookmark honored the bicentennial of Abraham Lincoln's birthday.

Campaign-related posters, bookmarks, and other items included Banned Books Week, Teen Read Week, Teen Tech Week, and National Library Week. In partnership with AASL, ALA Graphics produced a poster and bookmark highlighting the new Standards for the 21st-Century Learner. A "green" product line with the message "Read Renew Return" debuted and grew to include a bamboo lanyard, a reusable nylon grocery bag, an organic cotton T-shirt, and library card sleeves providing an additional incentive for librarians to promote library card use along with their own library information.

Online Resources

ALA TechSource completed phase two of its Drupal-based Web site update, along with enhanced electronic delivery of *Library Technology Reports* and *Smart Libraries Newsletter* through MetaPress, a leading e-journal host. The ALA TechSource blog continued to offer timely perspectives from academic and public libraries with posts from Jason Griffey, Kate Sheehan, Michael Stephens,

Cindi Trainor, Tom Peters, and ALA TechSource Editor Dan Freeman. ALA TechSource also continued supplementing the print publications with online events and activities, most notably expanding its presence on Twitter, topping 2,000 followers.

Leadership

Camila Alire was inaugurated as ALA president at the 2009 Annual Conference in Chicago.

Alire is dean emerita at the University of New Mexico and at Colorado State University, and is also professor of practice at Simmons College and an adjunct professor at San José University. She has also served as dean/director of libraries at the University of Colorado at Denver. Within ALA, she has served on council, executive board, committees, several presidents' special advisory task forces, and as president of ACRL.

Roberta Stevens, outreach projects and partnerships officer at the Library of Congress and project manager for the National Book Festival, became ALA president-elect in the 2009 election. Stevens, who will be inaugurated as ALA president at the 2010 Annual Conference in Washington, D.C., pledged to advocate tirelessly for all libraries and library employees during challenging economic times. She said she is looking forward to working with everyone in ALA to ensure that all Americans have access to the library collections and services that they have come to rely upon as a critical component of society.

ALA Council elected three new ALA Executive Board members at the 2009 ALA Midwinter Meeting in Denver. Patricia M. Hogan, administrative librarian at the Poplar Creek Public Library District in Streamwood, Illinois; Stephen L. Matthews, librarian at the Currier Library at the Foxcroft School in Middleburg, Virginia; and Courtney L. Young, a reference librarian and professor of women's studies at Pennsylvania State University in Monaca, are serving three-year terms that began in July 2009 and will conclude in June 2012.

Grants and Contributions

Beyond Words Gives $179,000 for Disaster Relief

Beyond Words issued grants to 20 school library media programs nationwide in 2008–2009, providing more than $179,000 for public school libraries that suffered materials losses because of a major disaster. The Beyond Words grants, sponsored by national retailer Dollar General, can be used to buy books, media, and/or library equipment that support learning in a school library environment. AASL administers the program in collaboration with the National Education Association.

Toyota Grant Provides Books on Japanese Culture

Through a $100,000 grant from the Toyota Motor Corporation, ALA provided more than 200 public libraries in 45 states with a set of 50 books on modern

Japanese culture and literature. Half the libraries receiving the books serve populations smaller than 25,000. Many of the libraries highlighted these new collections with programming.

Teen Tech Week

With the theme Press Play @ your library, the third annual Teen Tech Week, held March 8–14, 2009, again encouraged teens to explore the nonprint resources available at their libraries. Through funding from the Verizon Foundation, YALSA distributed $10,000 in mini-grants to 20 librarians. Galaxy Press provided six public service announcements featuring Tom Kenny, the voice of SpongeBob SquarePants, to promote the event. Promotional Partners for Teen Tech Week 2008 were Evanced Solutions, Galaxy Press, Rosen Publishing, Simon & Schuster, Tutor.com, and the Verizon Foundation.

WrestleMania Reading Challenge

More than 1,600 libraries took up the 2009 WrestleMania Reading Challenge, sponsored by YALSA and World Wrestling Entertainment, with support from Mattel. In 2009 participation extended to include those in grades 5–12. The challenge begins Teen Read Week and encourages participating youth to read beyond Teen Read Week by offering prizes and incentives. Fifteen finalists in three categories won trips to WrestleMania XXV in Houston, plus $2,000 for their libraries.

Major Awards and Honors

Honorary Membership

ALA conferred a posthumous Honorary Membership at the 2009 Annual Conference on Judith F. Krug, who served as director of OIF and executive director of the Freedom to Read Foundation for more than 40 years, until her death in April 2009.

Krug was the founder of ALA's Banned Books Week and was involved in multiple First Amendment cases that have gone all the way to the U.S. Supreme Court. She was the recipient of many awards, including the Joseph P. Lippincott Award, the Irita Van Doren Award, the Harry Kalven Freedom of Expression Award, and the William J. Brennan, Jr. Award.

Honorary membership is usually given to a living citizen of any country whose contribution to librarianship or a closely related field is so outstanding that it is of lasting importance to the advancement of the whole field of library service. The honor was bestowed on Krug posthumously upon the recommendation of the ALA Executive Board and by vote of the ALA Council.

James Madison Award

Thomas M. Susman, director of the American Bar Association's Government Affairs Office, was the winner of the 2009 James Madison Award, which honors those who, at the national level, have championed, protected, and promoted public access to government information. ALA Past President Rettig said Susman, who practiced with the Washington, D.C., law firm Ropes and Gray for 27 years before being named to his position at the American Bar Association in 2008, has shown a long commitment to the importance of open access to government information. "Tom has stood shoulder to shoulder with our nation's librarians in our efforts to make government information available to the public and our long, historic fights to protect library patrons' privacy," Rettig said.

Association of American Publishers

71 Fifth Ave., New York, NY 10010
212-255-0200, fax 212-255-7007

50 F St. N.W., Washington, DC 20001
202-347-3375, fax 202-347-3690

World Wide Web http://www.publishers.org

Judith Platt
Director, Communications/Public Affairs

The Association of American Publishers (AAP) is the national trade association of the U.S. book publishing industry. The association was created in 1970 through the merger of the American Book Publishers Council, a trade publishing group, and the American Educational Publishers Institute, an organization of textbook publishers. AAP's more than 300 corporate members include most of the major commercial book publishers in the United States as well as smaller and medium-sized houses, not-for-profit publishers, university presses, and scholarly societies.

AAP members publish hardcover and paperback books in every field including general fiction and nonfiction, poetry, children's books, textbooks, Bibles and other religious works, reference works, scientific, medical, technical, professional and scholarly books and journals, computer software, and a range of digital products and services.

AAP policy is set by a board of directors, elected by the membership for four-year terms, under a chair who serves for two years. There is an executive committee composed of the chair, vice chair, secretary, and treasurer and a minimum of two at-large members. Management of the association, within the guidelines set by the board, is the responsibility of AAP's president and CEO.

Highlights of 2009

Among the highlights of the year in publishing:

- Tom Allen, a former Congressman from Maine, became AAP's president and CEO on May 1, succeeding another former Congress member, Pat Schroeder, who had held the presidency since June 1997.
- The AAP Honors award for 2009 went to Walden Media.
- Will Ethridge (Pearson Education) was elected to a two-year term as AAP chairman.
- AAP's Annual Meeting included a surprise visit and speech by former President Bill Clinton.
- The Professional and Scholarly Publishing Division's R. R. Hawkins Award went to Harvard University Press for *The Race Between Education and Technology* by Claudia Goldin and Lawrence F. Katz.
- Book sales for 2008 were an estimated $24.3 billion, a drop of 2.8 percent from the previous year.

- Tibetan publisher Paljor Norbu received the Jeri Laber International Freedom to Publish Award.
- "Get Caught Reading" celebrated its tenth anniversary.
- AAP's Higher Education publishers launched AccessText Network.
- M. Luisa Simpson became executive director of AAP's International Copyright Enforcement and Trade Policy program, succeeding Patricia Judd.
- AAP continued to press for an exemption for children's books from the Consumer Product Safety Improvement Act's lead-content testing and certification provisions.
- AAP, the Authors Guild, and Google filed an amended settlement agreement on November 16; final resolution of the case, involving Google Book Search, had not been reached at the time this report was prepared.

Government Affairs

AAP's Washington office is the industry's front line on matters of federal legislation and government policy. It keeps AAP members informed about developments on Capitol Hill and in the executive branch to enable the membership to develop consensus positions on national policy issues. AAP's government affairs professionals serve as the industry's voice in advocating the views and concerns of American publishers on questions of national policy.

Consumer Product Safety Improvement Act

A major concern for AAP grew out of passage of the Consumer Product Safety Improvement Act (CPSIA) in August 2008. Enacted in response to a series of highly publicized recalls because of lead contamination of toys, manufactured primarily in China, CPSIA requires that all products intended for children under the age of 12 be certified not to contain lead over prescribed statutory levels. AAP has been pressing to have ordinary paper-based books and other paper-based print materials excluded from the testing and certification requirements, holding that they do not pose a threat of lead exposure to children. While the question of the law's applicability to paper-based books remained unresolved, AAP welcomed the announcement in December 2009 by the Consumer Product Safety Commission that it would extend the stay on enforcement of CPSIA's lead-content testing and certification provisions for an additional year (the original stay was issued in February 2009). AAP, the Printing Industries of America, and the Book Manufacturers Institute petitioned for extending the stay in light of the confusion that still surrounds the testing and certification requirements and the fact that several key rulemaking proceedings necessary for implementing those requirements were not expected to be completed until August 2010. Meanwhile, AAP is lobbying for congressional action that would add amendments to CPSIA to enable the commission to engage in "risk assessment" to determine whether ordinary children's books should be subject to the lead testing and certification requirements.

Communications and Public Affairs

AAP's Communications and Public Affairs program informs the trade press and other media, the AAP membership, and the general public about the association's work and serves as the industry's voice on a host of issues. Through the program's regular publications, press releases and advisories, op-ed pieces, and other means, AAP disseminates the publishing industry's views and provides up-to-the-minute information on subjects of concern to its members. The program has primary responsibility for the AAP Web site, http://www.publishers.org.

In 2009 AAP added tools to the Web site that allow visitors to share information across the Internet. All news releases disseminated by AAP and posted to publishers.org can now be shared via e-mail as well as through more than 40 bookmarking and social networking sites through a "+Share" function. AAP news can also be followed through an RSS feed and saved by printing releases straight from the site.

In addition to the *AAP Monthly Report,* the association's regular newsletter, the communications program publishes a weekly electronic news bulletin for AAP members, the *Insider.*

Get Caught Reading

In 2009 AAP undertook efforts to revitalize the Get Caught Reading campaign, creating a subcommittee chaired by Diana Debartlo (HarperCollins) to oversee the effort. The group includes representatives from the library marketing, digital, publicity, and editorial divisions of various trade houses including Houghton Mifflin Harcourt, Simon & Schuster, Random House, Scholastic, and John Wiley & Sons. Plans call for incorporating new content and taglines for promotion in the digital environment, including development of Facebook pages and video to highlight the importance of reading. New Get Caught Reading celebrities for 2009 included Dora the Explorer and Olympic gymnast Shawn Johnson.

In 2009 Get Caught Reading/Get Caught Listening exhibits were part of the annual book industry trade show BookExpo America and the Brooklyn Book Fair.

The Get Caught Listening audiobooks subcommittee was planning to host a series of author stages at BookExpo America featuring authors and voice-over talent discussing the development of audiobooks. Branded as Get Caught Listening programs, the author stages will highlight the importance of audiobooks as education and entertainment.

Thousands of booksellers, educators, and librarians continue to use the Web site http://www.getcaughtreading.org as a resource to initiate Get Caught Reading campaigns in their communities, to order artwork, and to send electronic cards. Newsletters highlighting educators' activities are distributed through AAP twice a year. AAP continued its reading promotion partnership with the American Booksellers Association.

Copyright

The AAP Copyright Committee coordinates efforts to protect and strengthen intellectual property rights and to enhance public awareness of the importance of copyright as an incentive to creativity. The committee monitors intellectual property legislation in the United States and abroad, and serves as an advisory body to the AAP Board of Directors in formulating policy on legislation and compliance activities, including litigation. The committee coordinates AAP's efforts to promote understanding and compliance with U.S. copyright law on America's college and university campuses. Carol Richman (Sage Publications) chaired the committee in 2009.

Google Settlement

During 2009 the copyright committee continued to monitor copyright issues related to the Google Book Search program, including the lawsuit filed in federal court in the fall of 2005 by five major AAP members (the McGraw-Hill Companies, Pearson Education, Penguin Group USA, Simon & Schuster, and John Wiley & Sons) asserting that the Google Library Project's mass digitization of in-copyright books was not protected by the fair use doctrine. The case was settled in October 2008 with the announcement of a groundbreaking agreement that would expand online access to millions of in-copyright books and other written materials in the United States from the collections of a number of major U.S. libraries participating in Google Book Search. The agreement, reached after two years of negotiations, resolved the class action lawsuit brought by book authors and the Authors Guild, as well as the separate publishers' lawsuit. Heavy opposition to the settlement agreement resulted in postponement of the court hearing and the filing of a revised settlement agreement in November 2009 that addressed major concerns of the U.S. Department of Justice and foreign publishers, among others. In March 2010 resolution of the case was still pending. The agreement promises to benefit readers and researchers, and enhance the ability of authors and publishers to distribute their content in digital form, by significantly expanding online access to works through Google Book Search, an ambitious effort to make millions of books searchable via the Web. The committee also monitored a number of important court decisions in cases filed against Google, along with domestic and foreign news media coverage of Google's views and business transactions.

E-Reserves: Georgia State University Suit

The discovery process continued throughout 2009 in the case filed by three AAP members (Oxford University Press, Cambridge University Press, and Sage Publications) in 2008 to stop widespread copyright infringement at Georgia State University (GSU), one of three state universities that had refused to engage in any dialogue with AAP regarding their e-reserves policies and practices. The complaint charged that GSU officials are violating the law by systematically enabling professors to provide students with digital copies of copyrighted course readings published by the plaintiffs and numerous other publishers without the authorization of those publishers. The lawsuit seeks injunctive relief to bring an end to such practices, but does not seek monetary damages.

While the plaintiffs were proceeding with their deposition phase in early 2009, the Georgia State Board of Regents unilaterally revised the copyright guidelines for the University of Georgia System, and GSU's counsel sought a protective order on grounds that, due to the sovereign immunity considerations that restrict publishers' case to prospective injunctive relief, evidence of practices under the old copyright policies should no longer be considered relevant to the case. The court granted the defendants' motion for a discovery protective order. Additionally, the court refused to exclude GSU's expert report submitted by copyright authority Kenneth Crews of Columbia University, rejecting the plaintiffs' contentions that the report contained inadmissible legal opinion and advocacy, and was not filed in a timely manner under the court's rules. The judge claimed that the report contained a review of the history and development of university electronic reserves systems and a discussion of copyright policies at other universities that "will be helpful to the Court in understanding the evidence presented, determining facts, and crafting relief, if appropriate." In response, three declarations were submitted addressing certain aspects of the opposed expert witness's testimony, while Crews also filed his rebuttal arguments. Resolution of the case was pending as of the end of 2009.

Golan v. *Mukasey*

The Copyright Committee monitored several lawsuits during 2009. After several postponements, the committee approved the filing of an amicus (friend-of-the-court) brief addressing the First Amendment issues on remand from the Tenth Circuit in *Golan* v. *Mukasey*. The appellate court panel had accepted the view of Stanford University law professor Lawrence Lessig and others that First Amendment scrutiny was appropriate for legislative actions through which Congress reportedly "altered the traditional contours of copyright." The AAP brief argued that the statute at issue was not subject to the highest "strict scrutiny" level of First Amendment judicial review because it is content-neutral, and that the statute should easily survive judicial scrutiny under a lower standard of constitutional review.

NIH Public Access Policy

The copyright committee supported the Fair Copyright in Research Works Act (H.R. 801), introduced in February 2009 to repeal the National Institutes of Health (NIH) public access policy that requires government-funded researchers to submit their final peer-reviewed electronic manuscripts to NIH upon their acceptance for publication by a journal, making the article freely available to the public on NIH's PubMed Central Web site.

At the same time, journal publishers participated in a series of roundtable discussions sponsored by the House Science and Research Subcommittee and the White House Office of Science and Technology Policy concerning public access to government-funded research. The roundtable process, with participation from the publishing, library, and university communities, was scheduled to begin in late June and run through the summer. The committee was hopeful that the roundtable discussions would have a positive effect on the continuing debate over the NIH policy and the "public access to government-funded research" issues. While publishers were actively lobbying for the introduction of a Senate counterpart to HR 801, legislation was introduced—the Federal Research Public Access Act (S.1373)—to extend the NIH Public Access Policy to 11 federal agencies that spend $100 million a year on extramural research. S.1373 specifies an even narrower window (six months) than the NIH has required between journal publication of an article and the uploading of the final manuscript of the article to the agency's Web site. The committee will continue to monitor both bills in 2010.

WIPO Proposal on Exceptions for Visually Impaired

Early in 2009 the World Blind Union circulated a draft international agreement that would allow cross-border use of copyrighted works reproduced and distributed in specialized formats without permission from rights-holders for the benefit of users with various disabilities. This set off a chain of events including AAP's submission of comments and participation in a public meeting organized by the U.S. Copyright Office to discuss the issues raised by the print disability community with respect to access to copyrighted works. Recounting publishers' legislative activities and continued efforts since 1996 to address the needs of individuals with print disabilities, AAP's comments argued that harmonizing exceptions and limitations through an international instrument is neither necessary nor desirable because existing international copyright regimes currently provide needed diversity and flexibility by leaving the treatment of these issues at the national level and subject to the Berne and TRIPs Agreements' three-step test for creating copyright exceptions and limitations. As a result of the meeting and the written comments submitted in response to the Copyright Office's notice of inquiry, the U.S. delegation to a subsequent Geneva meeting of the World Intellectual Property Organization (WIPO) Standing Committee on Copyright took the position that a proposed World Blind Union treaty to harmonize "disabilities" limitations and exceptions to copyright would be "premature" and that the standing committee should be examining market-based solutions to accessibility problems. A few months later, however, Brazil, Ecuador, and Paraguay tabled the treaty, which was discussed at a meeting of the standing committee for copyright in December. In preparation for this event, the U.S. Copyright Office asked for public comment on how the treaty was affecting U.S. copyright laws and international obligations, possible benefits or concerns raised by the treaty, and issues that could complicate implementation of the treaty in the United States or elsewhere. AAP filed comments again in November and will continue to monitor further developments in 2010 as well.

Rights and Permissions Advisory Committee

The Rights and Permissions Advisory Committee (RPAC), which operates under the aegis of the AAP Copyright Committee, sponsors educational programs for rights and permissions professionals. Chaired by Bonnie Beacher (McGraw-Hill), RPAC hosted its annual conference in New York City in June, drawing more than 80 professionals to the day-long program. The conference featured sessions on copyright basics, the Google settlement and pertinent legislation, as well as demonstrations of the electronic copyright registration process and the newly developed AccessText Network. The program included an interactive panel discussion, "Your Questions Answered: Permissions Experts Tell All." RPAC maintains the AAP Imprints List, which can be found at http://www.publishers.org/main/Membership/member_03.htm. It provides contact information and information on various imprints for those seeking permission. RPAC members are revising and updating the *Copyright Primer,* expected to be released in 2010, and are working with the American Society of Composers, Authors, and Publishers (ASCAP) to create "best practice" music permissions guidelines and to improve the licensing and permissions process.

Digital Issues

AAP's Digital Issues Working Group (DIWG), a forum for publishers to share information and learn about business opportunities and strategies in the digital world, holds luncheon meetings throughout the year featuring speakers on a range of subjects. Peter Balis (John Wiley & Sons) and Leslie Hulse (HarperCollins) are the working group's co-chairs.

Meeting topics in 2009 included e-book platforms and applications for mobile phones, implementation of the EPUB production and delivery format for e-books, numerical identification of e-book products, and the challenges of converting complex content into reflowable digital formats.

Diversity/Recruit and Retain

AAP's Diversity/Recruit and Retain Committee (DRRC) continued its work to attract a talented and diverse work force to book publishing with its "Book Yourself a Career" campaign. The committee, comprising senior human resource professionals from trade and academic houses, is chaired by Ann Wienerman (Random House).

The committee's focus for 2009 included outreach to New York metropolitan area colleges with diverse student populations, with AAP hosting presentations on book publishing. Campuses visited included Rutgers, City College of New York (CCNY), Queens College, Hunter, Baruch, and Pace. Efforts also included outreach to area high schools, with a special program for students at BookExpo America. The program featured an introduction to publishing presented by Pamela Horn (Sterling Publishing) and a presentation by young adult author Matt de la Pena.

DRRC's annual Introduction to Publishing program, in 2009 titled "What's Behind the Pages of the Book Business," gave industry newcomers an in-depth look at publishing. Speakers included Morgan Entrekin (Grove Atlantic), Jonathan Karp (Twelve), Amy Einhorn (Amy Einhorn Books), Carrie Kania (HarperCollins), Kelly Gallagher (R. R. Bowker), Liz Perl and Mark Compertz (Simon & Schuster), and National Book Foundation Director Harold Augenbraum. Topics ranged from the editorial process to the impact of book awards, the digital revolution, and consumer book buying behaviors.

Young to Publishing Group

The Young to Publishing Group (YPG), a subcommittee of DRRC, has a membership of more than 1,500 young professionals who have been in the industry from one to five years. YPG hosts monthly brown bag lunches with guest speakers from every area of publishing. Speakers in 2009 included Lisa Serra (Scholastic), former *Publishers Weekly* editor-in-chief Sara Nelson (now book editor at *O* magazine), Paul Bogaards (Knopf), and representatives of National Public Radio. YPG hosted a special program at BookExpo America for young professionals in publishing and bookselling, featuring Geoff Shandler (Little, Brown) and Geoff Kloske (Riverhead). Future plans include a program that will bring young publishing professionals together with young agents.

Freedom to Read

The mandate of the AAP Freedom to Read Committee is to protect the free marketplace of ideas for American publishers. The committee serves as the publishing industry's early warning system on issues such as libel, privacy, school and library censorship, journalists' privilege, Internet censorship, government regulation of protected speech, and third party liability for protected speech. The committee coordinates AAP participation in First Amendment court cases, sponsors educational programs, plays an active role in the Media Coalition (a trade association of business-oriented groups concerned with censorship issues), and works with groups within and beyond the book community to advance common interests in the area of intellectual freedom. Elisabeth Sifton (Farrar, Straus & Giroux) chaired the committee in 2009.

Judith Krug

AAP joined colleagues in the book community and beyond in mourning the loss of free speech advocate Judith Krug, director of the American Library Association's Office for Intellectual Freedom and founder of the Freedom to Read Foundation, who died in Chicago on April 11, 2009, after an 18-month battle with cancer.

U.S. v. *Stevens*

In July 2009 AAP, joined by librarians, authors, booksellers and a range of content providers and distributors, filed an amicus brief with the U.S. Supreme Court in the First Amendment case *United States* v. *Stevens*. The brief asked the court to reject arguments by the government that a whole category of speech can be denied First Amendment protection when Congress finds the "value" of the speech to be outweighed by the government's interest in suppressing it.

At issue is a federal statute that prohibits the creation, sale, or possession of "a depiction of animal cruelty." What the government wants to criminalize are not *acts* of animal cruelty, which are already illegal in all 50 states, but *speech* about those acts. Despite the government's assurances that the statute is limited to animal-fighting and videos in which animals are cruelly killed, the law's breadth would put at risk creators of illustrated books, films, or magazine articles graphically depicting such things as slaughterhouse practices, bullfighting, or poaching.

Presidential Records

Publishers welcomed the swift action taken by the House of Representatives in January 2009 in overturning an executive order by President George W. Bush limiting access to presidential records. The order, issued in November 2001, gave incumbent and former presidents, vice presidents, and even members of their families veto power over the release of presidential papers, essentially overturning the Presidential Records Act. AAP took lead on an amicus brief in an unsuccessful legal challenge and cosponsored a public information program featuring noted presidential historians.

Oregon Harmful-to-Minors Law Challenge

A federal judge refused to strike down an Oregon law that could limit minors' access to books and other materials with sexual content. In April 2008 AAP joined with other members of Media Coalition and six Oregon booksellers in a legal challenge to the law, which criminalizes the dissemination of sexually explicit material to anyone under the age of 13 or the dissemination to anyone under the age of 18 of any material with the intent to sexually arouse the recipient or the provider. The Oregon statute makes no provision for judging the material as a whole, or for considering its literary, artistic, or scientific value as required under the Supreme Court's *Miller* and *Ginsberg* rulings. The case is on appeal to the Ninth Circuit.

End of COPA

The U.S. Supreme Court announced in January that it would not re-hear the challenge to the Child Online Protection Act (COPA). Putting an end to a decade of litigation, the Supreme Court left standing a 2008 ruling by the Third Circuit that found COPA to be unconstitutionally vague, overbroad, and not the least restrictive means of preventing minors from accessing harmful-to-minors materials on the Internet.

Enacted by Congress after the Supreme Court struck down the Communications Decency Act, COPA sought to criminalize the transmission of materials considered to be "harmful to minors" via the World Wide Web if those materials could be accessed by minors. AAP filed a number of amicus briefs arguing that the statute placed an unconstitutional burden on protected speech between adults and that filtering technology administered by parents was a more effective, less-intrusive way of protecting minors than criminalizing First Amendment-protected speech on the Internet.

USAPatriot Act Reauthorization

With several USAPatriot Act provisions, including Section 215, due to expire at the end of 2009, AAP joined other organizations in the Campaign for Reader Privacy (CRP) in launching the latest phase of a five-year campaign to restore the reader privacy safeguards that were stripped away by the USAPatriot Act in

2001. (In addition to AAP, CRP members are the American Booksellers Association, the American Library Association, and PEN American Center). CRP conducted an intensive lobbying effort throughout the year, involving face-to-face meetings with Senate and House Judiciary Committee staff and other key congressional personnel, and were heartened when, on November 5, the House Judiciary Committee approved legislation that would effectively prevent government "fishing expeditions" in libraries and bookstores by prohibiting Section 215 searches of library or bookstore customer records unless there are "specific and articulable facts" to show that the person is a "suspected agent of a foreign power" or someone connected to the suspected agent. At year's end, however, the reauthorization bills were tied up in partisan wrangling and it appeared that short-term extensions would keep existing provisions in place.

Libel Tourism

"Libel tourism," the exploitation of plaintiff-friendly libel laws in other countries as a weapon to use against U.S. authors and publishers, is an increasing concern for AAP members.

AAP advocates federal legislation that would protect U.S. authors and publishers from foreign libel judgments that are inconsistent with First Amendment free speech and free press protections. In a statement submitted to House of Representatives oversight hearings in February, AAP told the Judiciary Subcommittee on Commercial and Administrative Law that "the sale of books over the Internet exposes U.S. authors and publishers to the danger of being sued almost anywhere in the world, and libel tourist litigation remains a threat in any country where our strong constitutional free speech protections are absent."

In June 2009 Rep. Steve Cohen (D-Tenn.) reintroduced legislation (H.R. 2765) that would preclude U.S. courts from recognizing foreign defamation judgments that do not satisfy the free speech and free press protections guaranteed by the First Amendment. The bill passed the House on a voice vote on June 15. Before passage, AAP sent a letter to House members pointing out that while the bill was a step in the right direction, it did not go far enough and significantly failed to give U.S. authors and publishers the ability to counter-sue in a U.S. court to deter attempted enforcement of a foreign judgment that is "repugnant to the First Amendment."

Trump v. *O'Brien*

In July AAP welcomed dismissal by a New Jersey judge of Donald Trump's defamation suit against Timothy O'Brien, author of *Trump Nation,* and his publisher, Hachette Book Group. Trump charged that O'Brien's book injured his business reputation by estimating his net worth at a substantially lower figure than he claims.

In May 2007 AAP had joined in asking a New Jersey state appeals court to overturn the ruling of a lower court that would have required O'Brien to turn over research material and to identify confidential sources for his book. The court order was disturbing because the judge denied O'Brien journalist's "shield law" protection because the book was "entertainment" and not "news." In October 2009 the order was overturned in a strongly worded appeals court ruling. In dismissing the case entirely, Judge Michele Fox found insufficient evidence to allow it to go to trial.

Censorship of Valerie Plame Memoir

In November the 2nd Circuit affirmed the ruling of a lower court barring former CIA operative Valerie Plame Wilson from referring in her memoir to her pre-2002 employment with the CIA. In 2008 AAP took the lead on an amicus brief supporting Wilson and her publisher, Simon & Schuster, in a lawsuit claiming that the government's demands constituted a prior restraint of speech in violation of the First Amendment. The CIA had ordered all pre-2002 employment references redacted from her book, *Fair Game: My Life as a Spy, My Betrayal by the White House,* prior to publication in 2007, notwithstanding the fact that the information was contained in an unclassified letter she received from a CIA benefits officer, which had been introduced at House hearings, published in the *Congressional Record,* and widely available on the Internet. The appellate court held that Wilson remained bound by the secrecy agreement she had signed as long as the information was not officially disclosed, and that while the CIA may have been negligent in sending her personnel information without proper classification, it was she, not the CIA, who had made it public.

Video Game Violence

In February the Ninth Circuit Court of Appeals, ruling in *VSDA* v. *Schwarzenegger,* upheld a lower court ruling striking down a California statute that banned the sale or rental of violent video games to anyone under 18 and required manufacturers and distributors to place warning labels on such games. A year earlier AAP had joined with other Media Coalition members in an amicus brief arguing that the language of the statute was unconstitutionally vague and that the district court was right in rejecting the state's attempt to regulate First Amendment-protected material on the basis of violent content.

Book Banning and Censorship

Battles continued across the nation as students, teachers, librarians, and community leaders fought for the right, especially the right of young people, to read a wide variety of books of their own choosing in public and school libraries.

In February 2009 the Freedom to Read Committee joined with booksellers, authors, librarians, and anti-censorship groups in urging members of the Topeka, Kansas, library board to reverse a decision to remove several sex education books, including *The Joy of Sex,* from the open shelves of the library's health section based on a complaint that the material was "harmful to minors." The board subsequently reversed its decision and voted to retain the books on open shelves.

The committee also joined in protesting the dismissal by the city council of four library board members in West Bend, Wisconsin, for their refusal to remove from the library young adult fiction and sex education materials that some members of the community characterized as "pornography." The library board held a hearing that drew 200 people and then voted unanimously to sustain its current policy and retain the books on open shelves.

AAP member publishers enthusiastically participated in the celebration of Banned Books Week, September 26–October 3. A celebration of the right to read freely, Banned Books Week was created in 1982 by the American Library Association, along with the American Booksellers Association and AAP, in response to the growing number of attempts to remove or restrict access to books in public and school libraries, classrooms, and bookstores.

First Amendment Program at ALA Conference

The Freedom to Read Committee joined with ALA's Intellectual Freedom Committee and the Comic Book Legal Defense Fund in sponsoring a First Amendment program at the 2009 ALA Annual Conference in Chicago titled "Ban those @#$*%! Comic Books: Graphic Novels and Censorship." The growing importance of graphic novels in library collections has generated high-profile censorship incidents in libraries and schools across the country and a panel of celebrated creators, including Newbery Award winner Neil Gaiman, spoke about censorship of their work.

Higher Education

AAP's Higher Education group serves the needs and interests of AAP members who publish for the post-secondary educational market. John Isley (Pearson Education) chaired the Higher Education Executive Committee in 2009.

A significant portion of AAP's efforts focused on educating policy-makers about significant strides in the development of course materials that best meet the needs of students and their instructors. These efforts often require responding to legislative initiatives. In 2009 textbook-related legislation was introduced in 29 states and in Congress.

The Higher Education group launched two major initiatives in 2009:

The AccessText Network (ATN)—a national online system that will make it easier and faster for students with print-related disabilities to obtain textbooks needed for their college courses—initiated its beta phase. ATN was developed in conjunction with the Alternative Media Access Center, an initiative of the Georgia Board of Regents and the University System of Georgia.

ATN improves the way electronic versions of print textbooks are delivered from publishers to campus-based disability services to students offices and streamline the permissions process for scanning copies of print textbooks when publisher files are unavailable, and for re-using alternate formats created by the campus-based offices.

Funding for the development of AccessText was provided by eight AAP member publishers: Cengage Learning, CQ Press; John Wiley & Sons, Macmillan, McGraw-Hill, Pearson, Reed Elsevier, and W. W. Norton.

AAP also launched Cost Effective Solutions for Student Success, an initiative to expand publisher outreach to educators and policy-makers, enabling them to provide information about new technologies and options to improve student success, increasing retention and pass rates while reducing students' costs for course materials and reducing per-pupil instruction costs for colleges and universities.

Since the initiative's inception, publishers have crisscrossed the nation sharing information, exploring new business models and cost-saving options to offset funding cutbacks, and analyzing ways in which they can help meet the challenges facing states, university systems, and individual schools and faculty.

Higher Education Critical Issues Task Force

The Higher Education Group's Critical Issues Task Force (CITF), whose members represent publishers of textbooks and other instructional materials for the post-secondary educational market, works exclusively on issues involving the provision of accessible instructional materials to students with print-related disabilities.

CITF also worked with policy-makers in California to write AB 386, landmark legislation enacted in October 2009 to help college campuses provide captioned versions of audiovisual materials to deaf students.

CITF members also helped to fund and develop ATN.

International Copyright Protection

AAP's International Copyright Protection Committee works to combat international copyright piracy, to increase fair access to foreign markets, and to strengthen intellectual property laws. Deborah Wiley (John Wiley & Sons) continues to chair the International Copyright Protection Committee.

AAP's enforcement and advocacy efforts extend to a number of key Asian markets including Hong Kong, Malaysia, the Philippines, the People's Republic of China, South Korea, Taiwan, and Thailand. In several of these, AAP works with local industry representatives to shape policy and strengthen enforcement though engagement with relevant government agencies. AAP and its member publishers have also been engaged in efforts in Brazil, Egypt, India, Japan, and Vietnam.

China remains a primary focus of AAP's ongoing enforcement and advocacy efforts. The past year saw several significant developments, including the successful conclusion of two cases before the World Trade Organization (WTO) on intellectual property protection and market access. The market access case is of particular significance as the WTO Appellate Body upheld findings that restrictions limiting the right of publishers to import and distribute publications into the market contravened China's WTO obligations. In another major development, as a result of U.S.-Chinese government dialogue under the auspices of the Joint Commission on Commerce and Trade, the Chinese government issued a "Notice to Libraries to Strengthen Copyright Protection." While the notice signifies China's recognition of the need to better police the practices of its libraries, how the Chinese government will pursue the objectives remains to be seen.

Collaborative efforts continued between AAP and Britain's Publishers Association to combat infringement of higher education textbooks at institutions of higher learning throughout China. In the coming year, both organizations will intensify engagement with the Chinese government on Internet piracy, particularly online piracy of medical and scientific journals.

Copyright law reform remains a key component of AAP's advocacy efforts. Working through local industry representative and coalitions, AAP has provided input into a number of government consultations on copyright law reform. With online piracy a rapidly expanding threat, legislative reform to facilitate cooperation between rights-holders (particularly publishers) and Internet service providers to combat infringing activity is among the highest priorities for AAP and the International Copyright Protection Committee.

AAP is a founding member of the International Intellectual Property Alliance (IIPA), through which, in February 2009, AAP again provided information and submitted specific recommendations regarding the adequacy of intellectual property protection in a number of countries to the U.S. Trade Representative (USTR) as part of USTR's annual Special 301 review of intellectual property and market access problems worldwide.

International Freedom to Publish

AAP's International Freedom to Publish Committee (IFTP) defends and promotes freedom of written communication worldwide. IFTP monitors human rights issues and provides moral support and practical assistance to publishers and authors outside the United States who are denied basic freedoms. The committee carries on its work in close cooperation with other human rights groups, including the International Publishers Association's Freedom to Publish Committee, Human Rights Watch, and PEN American Center. Hal Fessenden (Viking Penguin) served as committee chairman in 2009.

In 2003 IFTP established the Jeri Laber International Freedom to Publish Award, to be given annually to a book publisher outside the United States who has demonstrated courage in the face of political persecution. The award, which carries a cash prize, is named in honor of human rights activist Jeri Laber, one of IFTP's founding members, who continues to direct its work as an AAP consultant. The Jeri Laber award has been given to publishers in Iran, Turkey, Indonesia, Egypt, Cambodia, and Tibet.

The 2009 Jeri Laber International Freedom to Publish Award went to Paljor Norbu, an 81-year-old Tibetan printer and publisher. Norbu, who had been arrested many times in the past and spent several years in prison, was most recently arrested by Chinese police on October 31, 2008, for allegedly printing "prohibited material," including the banned Tibetan flag. He was tried in secret in November and sentenced to seven years in prison. His whereabouts remain unknown.

The award was presented in April 2009 at the PEN Annual Gala at the American Museum of Natural History in New York City. A film about Norbu was shown at the gala, and his daughter and granddaughter accepted the award in his place.

IFTP continues to monitor events in Iran and the situation of writers and publishers there, especially in light of the many arrests that followed demonstrations protesting the 2009 Iranian election. Committee members have paid special attention to the arrests of two Iranians. One of them is Maziar Bahari, who served as a guide to Nan Graham, Jack Macrae, and Laber when they visited Iran several years ago. Bahari was freed from detention after an international protest. The other is Kian Tajbakhsh, who was arrested after the disputed election and sentenced to at least 12 years detention. Efforts are continuing to obtain his release. Of the 70 Iranian journalists who were rounded up during the protests, about 25 remained in prison at the time this report was prepared, with a heavy impact on Iran's independent press.

IFTP monitors events in Turkey, including the ongoing harassment and persecution of writers, publishers, and journalists. Progress is slow; many trials are still going on, and there are writers in prison on terrorism charges under Article 301 ("insulting Turkishness"). According to changes made in the law, the minister of justice now has to approve all Article 301 cases. The number of cases has diminished. However, Article 216 ("incitement to hatred") is being used.

IFTP members undertake missions to meet with writers, publishers, human rights activists, and others in areas where freedom of expression is seriously threatened. In 2008 committee members Hal Fessenden and Wendy Wolf, together with Larry Siems of PEN and a few others, traveled to Cambodia. In June 2009 Fessenden, Siems, and Joel Simon attended the IFEX Global Forum on Free Expression in Oslo, where they met with, among others, activists from Turkey and representatives of the International Publishers Association.

In March AAP joined with free speech, academic, and civil rights organizations in calling on the Obama administration to end the practice of ideological exclusion—the denial of visas to foreign scholars, writers, artists, and others on the basis of their political views and associations. A Cold War-era strategy originally designed to bar entry to communists and communist sympathizers, the practice ostensibly ended with the repeal of the ideological exclusion provisions of the McCarran-Walter Act but was resurrected by the George W. Bush Administration in the USAPatriot Act, which barred entry to anyone who has "endorsed or espoused" terrorism. Since 2001 the practice has been used to deny entry to prominent foreign academics, human rights activists, and journalists who have been critical of U.S. foreign policy. The Obama administration responded in an April 16 letter from the Department of Homeland Security, offering to meet with representatives of the signatory organizations "to hear your views on this issue." While stressing that the statutory authority to issue visas rests with the State Department, Deputy Assistant Secretary of Homeland Security Richard C. Barth said in the letter that he had "initiated a wide-ranging review of our immigration policies" and that "the Department would benefit from your perspective as we work to improve our immigration policies."

AAP welcomed a ruling in July by the Second Circuit Court of Appeals reversing a lower court ruling and finding that the U.S. government had not justified denial of a visa to a leading Islamic scholar. The court of appeals found that First Amendment rights of U.S. organizations are implicated when foreign journalists, scholars, artists, and others are barred entry into the United States. The case was remanded for further proceedings. In spring 2008 AAP joined in an amicus brief supporting a lawsuit brought on behalf of Islamic scholar Tariq Ramadan, who was denied a visa after being offered, and accepting, a tenured professorship at Notre Dame. The brief focused on the ideological exclusion provisions of the USAPatriot Act.

The committee, together with the AAP president, sends letters of protest to various government officials about violations of free expression in their countries. In 2009 letters were sent to Russia's president, Dmitry Medvedev, and its prosecutor general, Yury Yakovlevich Chaika, concerning the murders of human rights lawyer Stanislav Markelov and journalist Anastasiya Baburova; to Chinese officials calling for the release of Chinese dissident Liu Xiaobo; and to UNESCO concerning the choice of the next UNESCO general director. The committee signed a petition protesting the seizure of materials belonging to the Russian human rights organization Memorial.

In 2009 IFTP hosted a number of speakers on various topics and from different parts of the world. Robert Barnett of Columbia University spoke about the situation in Tibet. Larry Siems of PEN American Center spoke about the plight of Iraqi translators in the United States and about ideological exclusion and kept the committee informed about PEN activities. Joel Simon and Nina Ognianova of the Committee to Protect Journalists (CPJ) described the release of a CPJ report on the unsolved killings of 18 journalists in Russia in the past nine years. Simon also discussed the cases of two American journalists from Current TV imprisoned in North Korea. Elyse Lightman reported on a new PEN Center in Cambodia, the direct result of an IFTPC/PEN mission to Cambodia in 2008; a driving force in its establishment was Kho Tararith, the recipient of the 2008 Jeri Laber award. Minky Worden, communications director of Human Rights Watch, discussed Freedom of Expression in China. Nahid Mozaffari discussed the protests in Iran following the June 12 elections. Jim Ross, Legal and Policy Director of Human Rights Watch, reported on the state of free expression in Sri Lanka. Georgette Gagnon, director of the Africa Division of Human Rights Watch, discussed freedom of expression in Zimbabwe. Carlos Lauria, Americas coordinator for CPJ, reported on the emergence of a blogging community in Cuba. Seref Holle discussed the legal situation of his stepfather, Turkish publisher Ragip Zarakolu.

Professional and Scholarly Publishing

AAP's Professional and Scholarly Publishing Division (PSP) is made up of AAP members who publish books, journals, loose-leaf, and electronic products in technology, science, medicine, business, law, humanities, the social and behavioral sciences, and scholarly reference. Professional societies, commercial organizations, and university presses play an important role in the division. Michael Hays (McGraw-Hill Higher Education) chaired the PSP Executive Council in 2009.

The 2009 PSP Annual Conference, "Focus on the User: Localization, Customization, Personalization," was held in Washington, D.C., in February. Two pre-conferences addressed topical issues—"The Development Cycle for Digitally Enabled Publishing: Technology, Intelligence and Listening to Your Users," organized by the PSP Electronic Information Committee, and "MashUp at the Library: Managing Colliding User Needs, Technologies, and the Ability to Deliver," organized by the PSP American Medical Publishers Committee.

A highlight of the conference was a relaunched awards program. Now called the American Publishers Awards for Professional and Scholarly Excellence (PROSE), the initiative increased the visibility and stature of the awards. More than 35 PROSE Awards for achievement in 2008 were presented at the awards luncheon. The 33rd annual R. R. Hawkins Award, the top PROSE prize, was presented to Harvard University Press for *The Race Between Education and Technology* by Claudia Goldin and Lawrence F. Katz. The award was delivered by Priscilla Hawkins Burns, daughter of award namesake Reginald Robert Hawkins.

Interest in the PROSE Awards was heightened by a new Web site, http://www.proseawards.com, which includes a tape of the PROSE awards luncheon ceremony along with a video, "The Mind of the Judge," which documents the awards selection process from the judges' viewpoint. The launch of the PROSE Awards and related activities are the brainchild of PSP Books Committee Chair John A. Jenkins (CQ Press), who spent the better part of a year redesigning the awards program.

Responding to a publishing world experiencing unprecedented change, the PSP Executive Council convened in November 2009 for a review of strategic priorities to guide the division in the coming two years. Three focus areas identified were:

- *Education as a fundamental component of PSP's mission.* For many years, through its conference and seminars, PSP has fostered education and communication among industry participants. The goal for the coming years is to expand this by exploring new venues for education (Webinars and partnering with other organizations) and investigating new topics that reflect the changing dynamics of the scholarly and professional publishing community.
- *Intellectual property and copyright.* Often misunderstood by the public in a world characterized by instantaneous access to the Web and the expectation that information should be free of charge, the importance of copyright and the value added by publishers needs to be communicated more forcefully. PSP seeks to foster a better understanding of how the continued role of publishers will maintain the integrity of scholarship and protect the expression of ideas.
- *Defining the important role of the publisher.* PSP represents a unique community of members that have embraced technology and made major strides in delivery of e-content, yet the importance and contributions of this community are little understood or appreciated. In looking forward, PSP seeks to define the role and importance of the publisher in the scholarly, professional, and research communication process.

Launched in 2008, *PSP . . . Links* published 22 issues in 2009, providing a semi-monthly information service to help keep individuals at PSP member organizations apprised of industry developments. The e-mail service highlights new items on the PSP and AAP Web sites, announces educational seminars and conferences offered by PSP as well as other organizations with programs of interest, and points readers to articles, Web sites, and job postings relevant to the PSP community. The *PSP Bulletin* is published quarterly and in 2009 introduced a new "Spotlight On . . . " feature that provides a forum for invited organizations to brief PSP members about new developments and services. The PSP Web site, http://www.pspcentral.org, continues to be a resource about the organization and the industry in general. The section "Publishing Facts: Learn More about Scholarly Information" provides a primer on the fundamentals of scholarly publishing.

In seeking a better grasp on data relating to the professional and scholarly community, an effort was undertaken to maximize the response rate and usefulness of the AAP Annual Professional and Scholarly Journals and Books Surveys for 2008. The response rate for 2008 journals data expanded considerably from the 2007 report, with data collected on 5,400 journals in 2008 compared with 4,094 in 2007 (an increase of nearly 32 percent in the number of journals reporting). For the first time in several years, a report on scholarly and professional books publishing was published for 2008.

Education remains a cornerstone of PSP's activities. In 2009 the popular Journals Boot Camp, which takes place every two years, was held in Denver over four days. The one-day Books Boot Camp was given in the spring (New York) and fall (Boston). Successful partnerships with other organizations resulted in a number of well-received programs: Three "Basics of Copyright for Today's Dynamic Publishing Environment" seminars were offered in collaboration with the Copyright Clearance Center in May (New York and Washington, D.C.) and October (Chicago). In conjunction with the International Association of Scientific, Technical, and Medical Publishers (STM), a seminar on "Books 2.X: Making, Selling, Distributing, Discovering, and Using E-Books" was held in New York in May before BookExpo America. A seminar introduced in 2008, "Citation Analysis and Evaluating Research Performance," was repeated in 2009. The PSP Electronic Information Committee introduced two seminar series—four sessions offered in the spring and four different sessions in the fall—titled "Selected Topics in Electronic Publishing" and offered both on-site at AAP's New York offices and via a Webinar. Participants were enrolled for the full spring or fall series, and programs were designed to be both presentational and interactive.

AAP continues to play an active role in legislative matters. Information on AAP communications and comments as well as those from other publishing organizations can be found on pspcentral at http://www.pspcentral.org/publicpolicy. cfm. Coverage can be found in the section dealing with Public Policy Issues and Legislation.

PSP supported or participated in a number of public service programs to make available medical information where it is needed throughout the world. PSP continues to maintain active roles in Research4Life, a United Nations-coordinated global initiative for developing countries. In a joint venture between STM and PSP, patientINFORM collaborates with four virtual health organizations (VHOs) in the United States to provide patients and caregivers with free access to research articles the VHOs have designated as important in helping patients better understand disease and treatment in cancer, diabetes, cardiology, and arthritis. At the end of the year, patientINFORM introduced plans to add new VHOs to the list of participants and expand the number of publishers that would offer article access on a free or low-cost basis. The American Medical Publishers Committee of PSP partnered with the National Library of Medicine (NLM) in early 2009 to launch the Emergency Access Initiative, a partnership between medical publishers and NLM to provide free access to full-text articles from a list of more than 200 critical biomedical serial titles and select reference books to healthcare professionals and libraries following an emergency.

Internationally, PSP continues to cooperate with international publishing associations to find balance between fair use of intellectual property and the need of rights-holders to realize a fair return for their works. The division has worked with STM and Britain's Publishing Association to gather information and produce reports on author/reader behavior and publishing trends in scholarly, professional, and academic research publishing.

Resources for the Book Publishing Industry

AAP-Bowker Webinars on Book-Buying

In 2009, for the first time, AAP and R. R. Bowker partnered to host two Webinars, in October and December, looking at consumer habits and motivation related to book-buying behaviors. The Webinars featured newly released data for the first three quarters of 2009 using both age and gender demographics and looking at the popularity of various genres and formats within each demographic category. Approximately 100 registrants participated in each of the Webinars.

Compensation Reports

AAP continues to provide valuable aggregate data reports, including the annual Survey on Compensation and Personnel Practices in the Book Publishing Industry, widely regarded as the most comprehensive and reliable source of data in this area. AAP's Compensation Committee, composed of senior compensation and human resources professionals, met throughout the year to create job descriptions and manage the survey process. Purchase of the report is contingent upon participation in the survey.

Total Compensation Solutions, which produces the report for AAP, presented highlights of the 2009 report at the AAP's annual human resources seminar, Compensation and Human Resources Practices in the Book Publishing Industry, in November. The seminar featured experts from Mars International addressing sales compensation practices.

AAP also tracks holiday benefits for the publishing community and shares data with a compensation committee comprising publishing industry professionals who independently oversee the holiday and vacation compensation for their respective houses.

Annual Statistics

AAP publishes industry statistics for all segments of book publishing, on a monthly and annual basis. More than 80 publishers participate in AAP's monthly statistical reports, the only resource in publishing that aggregates revenue and compiles raw data on market size on a month-to-month basis and provides year-to-date growth based on a cross-section of the industry. Additional data points were produced for the el-hi and higher education communities. An outreach to journals publishers resulted in representation of 45 percent of total journal articles produced in the marketplace.

School Division

The AAP School Division represents leading developers of instructional materials, technology-based curricula, and assessments and works to create instructional solutions that help students, teachers, and school succeed. The division focuses its work in several key areas: ensuring access to instructional materials; increasing funding for all types of instructional materials; and fostering a fair, competitive, and robust market for education publishers. Paul McFall (Pearson Education) chaired the division's executive committee in 2009.

The year was a challenging one for school publishers. The most severe economic downturn since the Depression led to deep cuts in education spending at state and local levels. Many school districts and states postponed curriculum adoptions. As a result, elementary and secondary (el-hi) net sales tumbled by 13.8 percent, according to AAP statistics. Sales in adoption states were the weakest: down 29.8 percent in 2009 vs. 12.3 percent for non-adoption states. Meanwhile, sales of supplemental el-hi materials showed a 14.9 percent increase in 2009.

Public Policy

Despite difficult economic conditions, the division's advocacy efforts continued to play an important role in assisting school publishers. In Florida AAP was successful in keeping the 2010 math adoption on schedule. In Texas AAP played an important role in securing $465 million in funding for the 2010 reading/language arts curriculum adoption.

At the federal level, AAP and its members in early 2009 continued their advocacy initiative for education spending in the federal economic stimulus package. AAP's efforts, along with those of many other national education organizations, succeeded in securing significant increases. And, at the national (non-federal) level, the division played an important role in developing and communicating an AAP position on Common Core State Standards.

Conferences and Meetings

Among the high points of the division's 2009 Annual Meeting in Naples, Florida, was the presentation of its highest honor, the Mary McNulty Lifetime Achievement Award, to E. Addison "Buzz" Ellis, a 30-year veteran and former McGraw-Hill Education executive and three-time chairman of the division.

The division's Fall Summit on K–12 School Publishing, held October 8, addressed topics including the 2010 economic outlook for K–12 publishing, response to intervention curricula, new state technology initiatives, and the fiscal outlook in the states. In his opening remarks, AAP President and CEO Tom Allen stressed that in the world of education publishers should be proud of their products and their contributions. "Part of our job at AAP needs to be to mount an effective public advocacy campaign to explain the kinds of values publishers add to products that educate our children, define our culture, and move forward our democracy," Allen said.

Smaller and Independent Publishers

AAP's Smaller and Independent Publishing (SIP) Committee was created in 1998 to serve the special needs and interests of the association's small and independent publisher members. Gene Gollogley (Booklight) chaired the committee in 2009.

In an effort to provide educational and networking opportunities consistent with the current economic climate, SIP hosted a new series of early evening educational programs titled "Bright Independent Lights, Big Independent Ideas." The series provided programs on business, sales, marketing, publicity, and digital technology tailored to the needs and interests of smaller and independent publishers.

Trade Publishing

AAP's Trade Publishing Group is made up of publishers of fiction, general non-fiction, poetry, children's literature, religious, and reference publications, in hardcover, paperback, and electronic formats, and is the most senior committee within the trade publishing core of AAP. Bridget Marmion (Houghton Mifflin Harcourt) chaired the committee in 2009.

In 2009 the committee focused its efforts on dialogues relating to the value of book publishing and hosted speakers from within and outside the book industry to address evolving business practices. The committee also initiated dialogue on the evolution of electronic catalogs, inviting various end users including booksellers, librarians, and the media. Speakers included Kathy Smith of HarperCollins; Malcolm Jones of *Newsweek,* Miriam Tulaio of the New York Public Library, and Susannah Hermans, who is owner of Oblong Books in Rhinebeck, New York, and representative of the American Booksellers Association's E-catalog task force.

During the year the committee launched its second annual Books Are Great Gifts campaign. An industry-wide initiative, Books Are Great Gifts featured three promotional videos with popular authors sharing their reasons why books make great gifts. Among the authors in the 2009 campaign were Julie Andrews and Emma Walton, Alec Baldwin, Dan Brown, Sandra Boynton, Neil Gaiman, Nick Hornby, Elmore Leonard, and Danielle Steel. The videos received widespread book retailer support, airing on BookSense.com, Barnes&Noble.com, Amazon.com, and Borders.com Web sites and on YouTube. Snippets were also featured on "Good Morning America" in advance of the TV show's holiday books segment. Books Are Great Gifts has its own Web site (http://www.books aregreatgifts.com) and Facebook pages. The campaign also featured a contest in which consumers were asked to submit their own reasons why books make great gifts for a chance to win a book-filled gift basket.

The Web site also aggregated links to industry resources, including publisher sites that spotlight other creative content marketing books as great gifts. Participating publishers included Hachette Book Group, HarperCollins, Houghton Mifflin Harcourt, Hyperion, John Wiley & Sons, Penguin Group (USA), Random House, Simon & Schuster, St. Martin's Press, and W. W. Norton.

The Trade Group is responsible for the AAP Honors award program, identifying and selecting candidates from outside the publishing industry who have helped promote American books and authors. The honors are presented each year at the AAP Annual Meeting. In 2009 the AAP Honors went to Walden Media, a film production company responsible for bringing children's classic and award-winning literature to the screen that also created an impressive educational outreach program, working with teachers, museums, and national organizations across the country to develop supplemental programs and materials related to the films and to the books they are based on.

Publishing Latino Voices of America

AAP works to increase awareness of Latino books through its Publishing Latino Voices for America (PLVA) Task Force. Among its most prominent initiatives was the launch of the Las Comadres Borders National Book Club. The national Latina organization Las Comadres, in cooperation with AAP and Borders, sponsors the Las Comadres and Friends National Latino Book Club at select Borders stores in Arizona, California, Florida, Illinois, Massachusetts, New Mexico, Texas, and Utah. Membership is open to anyone interested in reading English-language works written by Latina or Latino authors.

PLVA also continues its effort to create recommended reading lists aligned with Latino Books Month in May, as well as with Día de los Niños/Día de los Libros (Children's Day/Books Day). Held each year on April 30, the latter is an annual celebration of the written word for children of all cultural backgrounds created and produced by the Association for Library Service to Children, a division of the American Library Association. Each fall the committee produces a recommended reading list for Hispanic Heritage Month and shares it with bookselling, educator, and librarian communities.

Adopt A School

AAP continued to match authors with schools throughout New York City's five boroughs as part of its Adopt-A-School program. Working with the city department of education, the program brings authors to schools to promote the joy of books and reading, involving schools from pre-kindergarten through high school. Adopt-A-School celebrated its fourth successful year in partnership with the Children's Book Council. Fourteen publishers provided authors to 28 schools. Among this year's authors were Lenore Look, Leslie Margolis, Rob Spillman, Steve Metzger, Natalie Standiford, Roni Schotter, and Michael Rosen. Participating schools were all recipients of REACH grants awarded to their libraries by the New York City Fund for Public Schools for their commitment to literacy.

Trade Libraries Committee

AAP's Trade Libraries Committee, chaired by Talia Ross (Macmillan), is composed of representatives of major book publishing houses in partnership with such organizations as the American Library Association. The committee continued to focus its efforts in 2009 on promoting titles, hosting educational sessions for librarians at various trade conventions including BookExpo America, the ALA Midwinter Meeting, and the Texas Library Association Annual Conference. The committee hosted a second successful author dinner and breakfast at BookExpo America 2009 with speakers including Kathryn Stockett, Elin Hildebrand, Jonathan Letham, and Robert Goolrick.

In fall 2009 the committee hosted a spring catalog preview exclusively for adult collection development librarians in the greater New York area.

Annual Meeting Highlights

Meeting Hears Former President Bill Clinton

Former President Bill Clinton spoke before an audience of more than 200 publishers and guests at the 2009 AAP Annual Meeting in New York. In a 45-minute talk at the Yale Club that covered a wide range of subjects, Clinton spoke about education, health care reform, and the Clinton Global Initiative, which hopes to bring world leaders together to find solutions to the world's pressing problems. The full text of the former president's address is available on the AAP Web site at http://02c494f.netsolhost.com/main/PressCenter/Archicves/2009_March/documents/TranscriptofClintonSpeechtoAAPAnnualMeeting.pdf.

Change of Leadership

At her final AAP Annual Meeting as president and CEO, Pat Schroeder expressed her gratitude for "the energy and dedication of the men and women who serve this association as officers, as members of the board, and as members of the many committees through which our work is carried on." She introduced her successor, Tom Allen, who began his tenure at AAP in early April. Both Schroeder and Allen are former members of Congress.

21st Century Solutions

The 2009 meeting program looked at "Twenty-First Century Publishing Solutions" from a variety of perspectives. David Drummond, Google's chief legal officer and senior vice president for corporate development, and Richard Sarnoff, AAP outgoing chairman, discussed the contentious but interesting process that led up to the Google Book Search settlement, expressing the hope that digital content subscriptions might represent a significant new revenue stream. Looking at the serious threat facing the nation's print newspapers, Dow Jones CEO Les Hinton took the newspaper industry to task for its willingness to give away valuable content without creating a viable business model to compensate for that content, but asserted that "if we're willing to protect our interests, the market does not have to stay irrational forever." Lawyer and author representative Bob Barnett contrasted the publishing models that serve the interests of the celebrity authors he represents with the growing phenomenon of online publishing, including self-publishing.

Walden Media Gets AAP Honors

Walden Media was the recipient of the 2009 AAP Honors, presented by Bridget Marmion (Houghton Mifflin Harcourt), chair of the AAP Trade Publishers Executive Committee, to Walden President Micheal Flaherty. Walden Media chose Reach Out and Read as the recipient of the $5,000 charitable donation that accompanies the award.

New Officers

New officers were elected by the AAP membership at the Annual Meeting. Will Ethridge—president and CEO, higher education, international, and professional publishing, at Pearson Education—was elected to a two-year term as AAP chairman. David Young, chairman and CEO of Hachette Book Group, was elected vice chairman, and John Sargent, CEO of Macmillan, treasurer.

FY 2009–2010 Budget Approved

The membership approved an operating budget of $10.8 million for fiscal year 2009–2010, with $6.7 million allocated to Core, $1.6 million allocated to Higher Education, and $2.5 million to the two divisions ($1.4 million for the School Division and $1.1 million for PSP). A shortfall of $1.1 million will be drawn from cash reserves.

American Booksellers Association

200 White Plains Rd., Tarrytown, NY 10591
914-591-2665
World Wide Web http://www.BookWeb.org

Dan Cullen
Content Officer

2009 Highlights

The American Booksellers Association (ABA) had an active year in 2009, one that saw key changes in senior staff leadership, the further development of the IndieBound national marketing program, sustained participation in industry events and initiatives, and vigorous advocacy efforts on the national, state, and local levels.

Recognizing the difficult economic times ABA bookstore members faced, in February 2009 ABA President Gayle Shanks and the association's board of directors announced cuts to ABA's operating expenses and a 50 percent reduction in 2009 membership dues.

Early in the year, ABA CEO Avin Mark Domnitz announced that he would be stepping down when his current contract ended in July. In making the announcement to members, Shanks noted that Domnitz "has ably led an amazing staff over these past 12 years—an era of many accomplishments, of dramatic litigation, and of creative initiatives," adding that he had "created an organization that is open and responsive to its members, breaking down barriers to communication while encouraging interaction on all levels among booksellers, publishers, wholesalers, the ABA board, association staff, and the book-loving world."

The association announced the establishment of the Avin Mark Domnitz Scholarship to its fifth annual Winter Institute to honor Domnitz's contributions to independent bookselling. The scholarship is open to the owners and regular employees of bookstores that participated in the association's annual ABACUS financial survey.

In April the ABA board announced that the association's chief operating officer, Oren J. Teicher, had been named ABA's new CEO. Teicher's appointment was effective June 1. After assuming the new post, Teicher sent an open letter to ABA membership, saying that ". . . together we can create a business and cultural environment where independent bookstores won't merely survive but will, once again, thrive. I pledge to use all of my energy and best efforts to make that a reality." Teicher announced the appointment of Len Vlahos to fill his former position of chief operating officer.

In May ABA announced the election of three board directors and a new president and vice president. Elected to serve three-year terms as directors beginning June 2009 were Becky Anderson of Anderson's Bookshop in Naperville, Illinois; Betsy Burton of the King's English Bookshop in Salt Lake City; and Beth Puffer of Bank Street Bookstore in New York City. ABA membership also ratified the board's choice of Michael Tucker of Books Inc. in San Francisco to serve a one-year term as ABA president and Anderson to serve a one-year term as vice president/secretary.

Dealing with Challenging Times

The continuing economic downturn and slow recovery of 2009 made for a challenging year for independent booksellers, but one that was not without positive signs. Forty ABA member stores opened in 2009 in 19 states, with California, New York, and Wisconsin leading the way at five openings each. Illinois and Texas followed, each with four. One ABA international member also opened for business in 2009: Coral Reef Bookstore in Anguilla, British West Indies. To meet the current economic challenges, the new owners carefully fashioned business plans, put together curated book inventories, added an array of gift and other non-book items, and sought unique ways to promote their stores. In the three years prior to 2009, more than 100 new stores had opened and joined ABA.

The holiday season saw sales dips at some indie booksellers, but these declines were outnumbered by modest—and sometimes robust—gains at others. To help members, ABA reprised the IndieBound holiday design initiative, which offered member stores innovative marketing materials they could adapt and personalize. Consumer favorites returned from 2008, along with new images and slogans, all emphasizing community and the value of books as gifts.

Booksellers across the country reported that the "Local First" shop-local movement was bearing fruit, and several reaped the benefits of homegrown marketing campaigns. A post-holiday survey of more than 1,800 independent businesses (including bookstores) revealed that holiday sales for independent retailers were up an average of 2.2 percent. That contrasts with U.S. Commerce Department figures that showed overall retail sales were down 0.3 percent in December and up only 1.8 percent in November.

The post-holiday survey also found that for the third year independent retailers in cities with active shop-local campaigns reported stronger holiday sales than those in cities without such campaigns. These campaigns have been launched by local business alliances in more than 100 cities and towns. Independent retailers in these cities reported an average increase in holiday sales of 3 percent, compared with 1 percent for those in cities without an active shop-local initiative. Nearly 80 percent of business owners surveyed said public awareness of the value of choosing locally owned businesses had increased in the past year (16 percent said it had stayed the same). Similar surveys conducted in 2009 and 2008 also found that independent businesses in cities with shop-local campaigns reported stronger sales than those in communities without such initiatives.

Continuing a tradition, ABA senior staff members again spent time working at member stores during the holiday shopping period. With the intent of helping member stores in any way they could, and to learn more about the challenges they face, ABA staff traveled to stores within a few hours of the association's Tarrytown, New York, offices or combined their stints as bookstore helpers with previously planned business trips and vacations in locales across the country. This year staff volunteered at the Flying Pig Bookstore in Shelburne, Vermont; Mrs. Nelson's Toy and Book Shop in La Verne, California; Boulder Book Store in Boulder, Colorado; Northshire Bookstore in Manchester Center, Vermont; and the Book Stall at Chestnut Court in Winnetka, Illinois.

The year also saw important dialog and cooperative efforts between ABA and other associations. The Association of Booksellers for Children (ABC) noted in 2009 that it was exploring a variety of options "to keep the organization viable." In an e-mail sent to ABC's bookseller members, the ABC board suggested that "A possible option would include becoming a division of ABA, a department of ABA, or another configuration that we haven't determined yet." The ABC board stressed that a merger with ABA was just one option that it was exploring in a "period of unprecedented change" involving shifting consumer patterns, technological innovation, and changing publisher priorities. A joint ABC/ABA task force, the ABA board, and the ABC board continued discussions on a possible merger throughout the year. In addition, ABA and the National Association of College Stores announced a new joint promotion that will offer increased benefits and services to members of both associations.

IndieCommerce

ABA continued to update and enhance its business solutions services to members during the year. In April ABA unveiled a new name and a new logo for its former E-Commerce Solution program; now known as IndieCommerce. Throughout the year stores continued to migrate their IndieCommerce Web sites to the IndieCommerce open source content management system that allows for faster development of new features and greater adaptability and ease of use. In September ABA announced that member stores with IndieCommerce Web sites now had the ability to sell more than 220,000 e-books in several formats, including Adobe, Palm, and Microsoft. The new functionality allows consumers to purchase e-books and to have those books downloaded from store sites to consumers' computers or handheld devices.

Because of significant changes in consumer behavior and in ABA Gift Card Program usage, ABA announced in 2009 that it would begin to phase out the program after the 2009 holiday season. With the announcement, ABA outlined the reasons for the change and stressed its commitment to helping members establish alternative programs.

IndieBound

ABA's IndieBound program saw the consolidation and growth of established efforts during 2009 and the launch of several initiatives.

In March ABA was named to the 2009 Associations Advance America Honor Roll, a national awards competition sponsored by the American Society of Association Executives (ASAE) and the Center for Association Leadership. ABA was honored for IndieBound, a community-oriented movement launched in May 2008 that brings together booksellers, readers, independent retailers, local business alliances, and anyone else with a belief that healthy local economies help communities thrive.

In November the Booksellers Association of the United Kingdom and Ireland (BA) announced that it would be launching an IndieBound marketing campaign for members of its Independent Booksellers Forum in early 2010. In the November issue of its magazine *Bookselling Essentials,* BA gave its members a preview of IndieBound and commented that "We are thrilled to be working with the American Booksellers Association to facilitate the IndieBound campaign into the U.K."

Indies Choice Book Awards

Early in 2009 ABA announced that it was launching a new awards program, the Indies Choice Book Awards. Winners were selected by the owners and staff of ABA member stores in seven categories highlighting the type of books that independent booksellers champion best. The Indies Choice Book Awards, which take the place of ABA's BookSense Book of the Year Awards, reflect the spirit of ABA member booksellers in the IndieBound movement and their dedication to handselling engaging fiction, nonfiction, children's, and young adult titles.

The winners of the inaugural Indies Choice Awards were: (best indie buzz book) (fiction): *The Guernsey Literary and Potato Peel Pie Society* by Mary Ann Shaffer and Annie Barrows (Dial); (best conversation starter) (nonfiction) *The Wordy Shipmates* by Sarah Vowell (Riverhead); (best author discovery) David Wroblewski for *The Story of Edgar Sawtelle* (Ecco); (best indie young adult buzz book) (fiction) *The Graveyard Book* by Neil Gaiman (HarperCollins); (best new picture book) *Bats at the Library* by Brian Lies (Houghton Mifflin); and (most engaging author) Sherman Alexie. Five Indies Choice Book Awards honor recipients were also named in each category.

In addition, following voting by independent booksellers, ABA in April announced the first three inductees to the Indies Choice Book Awards Picture Book Hall of Fame: *Where the Wild Things Are* by Maurice Sendak (Harper-Collins); *Make Way for Ducklings* by Robert McCloskey (Viking); and *Don't Let the Pigeon Drive the Bus* by Mo Willems (Hyperion).

To help celebrate the accomplishments of the BookSense Picks List, which first appeared in 1999 and was the precursor to the Indie Next List, ABA in 2009 offered members a monthly downloadable pdf display piece showcasing the top picks for that month over the past ten years. In addition to each monthly list are seasonal lists of ten years of Kids' Picks.

A 2009 survey of ABA member bookstores about the Indie Next List revealed that 90.3 percent of responding booksellers use the list in their stores and 55.8 percent create an in-store Indie Next List display. Of those who reported creating a display, 71.6 percent reported that it generated sales.

New Alliances and Initiatives

As the IndieBound movement gained strength, a new series of successful alliances continued to develop. Working with the American Independent Business Alliance, ABA helped bookstore members participate in Independents Week, a nationwide promotion in July on behalf of independent businesses. ABA also worked with the National Association of Recording Merchandisers in support of Record Store Day, held on April 18. The steps included collaborative advertising and marketing efforts, including independent record stores in IndieBound.org's store search results, and the initiation of a monthly list of the top ten bestselling music-related books at indie bookstores.

During the year ABA also updated its list of notable "Local First" titles. The revised Indie Local First Reading List was given a new design, additional titles and bookseller recommendations were added, and more links to local resources were included.

IndieBound.org—the Internet home page for the IndieBound movement—launched several features focusing on independent bookstores. Content was continually added to the site through the year, including full information pages for individual book titles (allowing authors, publishers, and bloggers to link to IndieBound); highlighted quotes from booksellers featured in the Indie Next List Great Reads and Notables; book reviews from more than 130 alternative and independent newspapers; hundreds of book-related videos; and a new service for other independent retailers and enthusiasts, "IndieBound To-Go." This feature provides the necessary tools for retailers, community groups, schools, and others to download, print, and re-create do-it-yourself IndieBound materials.

Important enhancements were added to the "wish list" functionality of IndieBound.org, making wish lists created by site users easier to compile and share. IndieBound also added book widgets, which allow fans of IndieBound to feature the Indie Next List, the Kids' Next List, and the Indie Bestseller Lists on Web sites and blogs.

IndieBound.org content gained depth in November when ABA introduced a partnership with National Public Radio (NPR). The book information pages on IndieBound.org now feature audio content from NPR's book coverage, adding to the reviews, features, and interviews that are now a part of IndieBound.org's enhanced book data. In November NPR began publishing four bestseller lists weekly: hardcover fiction, hardcover nonfiction, paperback fiction, and paperback nonfiction—using the Indie Bestseller List feeds. NPR.org is also a member of the IndieBound Affiliate Program. Each book review and story on NPR.org links to the book mentioned for sale through independent bookstores. This provides repeat exposure of independent bookstores to NPR.org readers, and an ongoing opportunity to buy from IndieCommerce stores.

With the launch of the IndieBound app for iPhone in April, independent booksellers joined the rapidly growing realm of mobile applications. The new app spotlights three of IndieBound.org's most popular features—bookseller recommendations, book search, and the Indie Store Finder. Three months after its introduction, the app was selected for inclusion in *O'Reilly Media's Best iPhone Apps: A Guide for Discriminating Downloaders.* Only 200 apps were selected for inclusion in the O'Reilly publication from among the approximately 50,000 apps available at the time.

In November ABA released the 2.0 version of IndieBound for iPhone. Consumers can now search for and purchase e-books from independent booksellers across the United States. The Indie Bestsellers, the Indie Next List, and other book lists now feature an "also available as an e-book" sticker where appropriate. The Book Search has also been upgraded with a choice of three searches: all results, books only, or e-books only. In addition, changes to the map function in the app make it even easier to find independent bookstores.

By the end of the year, the app had been downloaded approximately 120,000 times.

Winter Institute and BookExpo America

The fourth annual ABA Winter Institute in Salt Lake City attracted hundreds of independent booksellers who participated in two and a half days of education, peer interaction, and professional rejuvenation. In addition to such sessions as "Using Multimedia to Market Your Store," the institute featured a keynote panel discussion on the state of the book industry hosted by Roxanne Coady of R. J. Julia Booksellers in Madison, Connecticut, with panelists Morgan Entrekin of Grove/Atlantic, Nan Graham of Scribner, and Robert Miller of HarperStudio. Other features were a pre-institute Local First conference, and tours of local bookstores.

ABA and its member bookstores were active participants at BookExpo America (BEA), held May 28–31 in New York City. ABA offered a full day of education and held its annual meeting during the trade show. ABA worked closely with BEA organizers in 2009 on a number of initiatives; importantly, BEA offered limited free convention attendance to ABA bookstore members. Additionally, ABA brought its annual Day of Education back to the convention facility in 2009, and BEA offered a concurrent retailer education track to encourage "crossover" attendance. During its Day of Education, ABA built upon the curriculum begun at the 2009 Winter Institute, with educational sessions and panels on topics ranging from marketing via social media to budgeting and monitoring sales and expenses, and from best practices for handselling to remainder buying. The schedule also included programming for children's booksellers developed by ABC.

Advocacy

Throughout the year ABA continued its advocacy efforts on the part of its bookstore members.

Recognizing the importance of the Small Business Administration to the health of member bookstores, the association wrote to Sen. Mary Landrieu (D-La.), chair of the U.S. Senate Committee on Small Business and Entrepreneurship, in support of Karen Gordon Mills, President Barack Obama's successful nominee to head the Small Business Administration.

As the national debate on health care reform expanded, ABA compiled relevant data from a survey of member bookstores, and in August the ABA board adopted a policy statement on the topic. The statement underscored the need for reforming a system that, it stated, currently limits or precludes "the ability of small businesses to offer health insurance to their employees." The statement also emphasized the board's belief that "any government-imposed mandates on employers to provide insurance must take into consideration the unique financial realities of small businesses. A health care 'solution' that inequitably retards or restricts the growth of small businesses is no business remedy at all."

In August the ABA board issued a statement saying it neither supported nor opposed the proposed Google Book Search Settlement, but did believe that "there are important, related issues involved." The statement stressed that "ABA has long believed that the interests of our members, of writers and readers, and of our democratic society, are best served when the marketplace adheres to a standard of open access to books and other forms of intellectual content," adding that ABA believes that "when any one company's proprietary formats or exclusionary contractual relationships prevent other, competing, members of the supply chain from gaining access to these books and/or other forms of intellectual content, our society as a whole is harmed." Regarding the question of open access and reader privacy, the statement stressed that "Independent booksellers have long been stalwart defenders of First Amendment rights, and we strongly believe that information about what books any individual may be reading should be kept confidential. We vigorously opposed Section 215 of the USAPatriot Act because we believe that allowing government unfettered access to citizens' reading choices has a chilling effect on the free exchange of ideas throughout the entire culture. Concentrating too much power in any one entity and restricting or denying readers' access to content threatens the protection of these essential civil liberties."

In October the ABA board wrote the U.S. Department of Justice requesting that it investigate predatory pricing practices by Amazon.com, Wal-Mart, and Target that had drawn widespread media coverage and that the board believes constitute illegal predatory pricing damaging to the book industry and harmful to consumers.

American Booksellers Foundation for Free Expression

In 2009 the American Booksellers Foundation for Free Expression (ABFFE) filed a friend-of-the-court brief with the Supreme Court urging the court to overturn a law banning the depiction of animal abuse. Under the law, ABFFE held, a bookseller could be sent to jail for five years for selling such books as Ernest Hemingway's classic novel *Death in the Afternoon,* which centers on bullfighting.

The fight to restore the protections for reader privacy eliminated by the USAPatriot Act resumed at the end of the year as Congress again faced the necessity of reauthorizing the act's Section 215, which gives the government the power to secretly search bookstore and library records. ABFFE is urging Congress to limit bookstore and library searches to the records of people who are suspected of terrorism or espionage.

The foundation celebrated the successful challenge of the Child Online Protection Act (COPA), which banned the display of material that is "harmful to minors" on commercial Web sites. ABFFE held that the law could have applied to images of book jackets and excerpts on bookstore Web sites.

ABFFE joined in the successful effort to lift the federal government's ban on the Muslim scholar Tariq Ramadan, who was denied entry into the United States to take a teaching job at the University of Notre Dame because he had contributed to a charity that gave money to the Palestinian Islamic organization Hamas.

The Kids' Right to Read Project, a joint initiative of ABFFE and the National Coalition Against Censorship, continued to fight book censorship at the local level. Since its launch in 2007, the project has opposed challenges to 250 titles in 31 states.

ABFFE was founded by ABA in 1990. Its address is 275 Seventh Ave., Suite 1504, New York, NY 10001 (tel. 212-587-4025, World Wide Web http://www.abffe.org). Its president is Chris Finan.

Association of Research Libraries

21 Dupont Circle N.W., Washington, DC 20036
202-296-2296, e-mail arlhq@arl.org
World Wide Web http://www.arl.org

Lee Anne George
Publications Program Officer

The Association of Research Libraries (ARL) is a nonprofit organization of 124 research libraries in North America. Its mission is to influence the changing environment of scholarly communication and the public policies that affect research libraries and the diverse communities they serve. ARL pursues this mission by advancing the goals of its member research libraries, providing leadership in public and information policy to the scholarly and higher education communities, fostering the exchange of ideas and expertise, facilitating the emergence of new roles for research libraries, and shaping a future environment that leverages its interests with those of allied organizations.

New Strategic Plan

Following a year-long review involving several rounds of member input, the ARL board in November adopted an ARL Strategic Plan for 2010–2012. The new plan emphasizes advocacy in three strategic directions: Influencing Public Policies, Reshaping Scholarly Communications, and Transforming Research Libraries. The development of the new plan was led by members of ARL's Strategic Plan Review Task Force, whose work resulted in a set of priorities that provide direction for ARL efforts over the next three years. The new Strategic Plan is available online at http://www.arl.org/arl/governance/strat-plan.

Influencing Public Policies

A primary goal of ARL's Public Policies program is to influence legislative action that is favorable to the research library and higher education communities. To achieve this goal, the program helps ARL members keep abreast of the legislative landscape, as well as rapidly changing issues, players, regulations, and community priorities. Program staff track the activities of state and federal legislatures as well as regulatory and government agencies in North America and abroad. The program analyzes, responds to, and seeks to influence public initiatives on information, intellectual property, and telecommunications policies. In addition, the program promotes funding for numerous agencies and national institutions and advances ARL members' interests on these issues. The Public Policies program monitors Canadian information policies, such as copyright and intellectual property and access to government information, through the Canadian Association of Research Libraries (CARL).

Copyright and Intellectual Property

In December 2008 ARL collaborated with others in the public and private sectors on additional policy statements on copyright and privacy concerns for the incoming Obama administration's consideration. On copyright and intellectual property issues, ARL joined with other associations on a policy statement titled "Balanced Copyright Preserves Right to Innovate." The document states: "Innovation is the key to lifting America out of this recession. While copyright promotes creativity, many of the specific measures adopted or recently proposed to protect copyright in the digital age actually impede innovative technologies and services. Administration policy must, in an open and transparent manner, safeguard the copyright balance and protect the right to innovate in order to ensure the vitality of the information-driven economy."

The Library Copyright Alliance (LCA), of which ARL is a member, issued a statement titled "A Pro-Library Copyright Agenda," which lists key copyright issues of importance to the library community that require focus by the new administration. Finally, ARL joined with others in the public sector in a letter regarding the importance of protecting privacy. The policy statements and letter can be found at http://www.arl.org/pp/index.shtml and http://epic.org.

Digital Millennium Copyright Act

LCA and the Music Library Association (MLA) filed comments in the Digital Millennium Copyright Act (DMCA) Section 1201 rulemaking that the U.S. Copyright Office conducts every three years to consider possible exemptions for libraries, educational institutions, and users to legitimately circumvent technological protection measures when trying to access a copyrighted work. In the previous Section 1201 rulemaking, the Library of Congress granted an exemption for "audiovisual works included in the educational library of a college or university's film or media studies department, when circumvention is accomplished for the purpose of making compilations of portions of those works for educational use in the classroom by media studies or film professors." LCA and MLA called for the exemption to be broadened in two important ways. First, they called for the exemption to apply to audiovisual works included in any college or university library, not just the library of the media studies department. Second, they said the exemption should apply to classroom uses by instructors in all subjects, not just media studies or film professors. The comments are available at http://www.arl.org/bm~doc/2dec2008_1201comments-1.pdf.

During a five-hour hearing on May 6, 2009, attorney Jonathan Band—representing ARL, the American Library Association (ALA), and the Association of College and Research Libraries (ACRL, a division of ALA)—testified in support of expanding the exemption to DMCA Section 1201. At the same hearing, a witness representing the Special Libraries Association, the Medical Library Association, and the American Association of Law Libraries called for the exemption to be broadened, but only to faculty of law and the health sciences. Band's testimony is available at http://www.arl.org/bm~doc/dmca-1201-testimony-6may09.pdf.

The U.S. Register of Copyrights did not meet the October 27 deadline for making recommendations to the Librarian of Congress concerning exemptions to DMCA Section 1201. As a result, current Section 1201 exemptions were extended until the Librarian of Congress issues a new regulation.

Fair Use

LCA filed comments on the European Commission's "Green Paper on Copyright in the Knowledge Economy." In its letter, LCA supported "the adoption of mandatory specific exceptions in all the areas raised by the green paper: libraries and museums, people with disabilities, teaching and research, and user-generated content." LCA also commented that "In addition to mandating the adoption of specific exceptions, the EU should also require enactment of a general fair use exception similar to that contained in section 107 of the U.S. Copyright Act. In a time of rapid technological change, the legislative process, particularly on a Union-wide basis, simply cannot keep pace with the new uses enabled by new technologies. A flexible and robust fair use provision allows the law to evolve quickly in response to the realities of the marketplace." The letter is available at http://www.librarycopyrightalliance.org/lcanew.htm.

Google Book Search Settlement

Members of the library community discussed the implications of the Google Book Search settlement in a meeting hosted on February 9, 2009, in Washington, D.C., by ARL, the ALA Washington Office, and ACRL. Under the settlement, Google and the American Association of Publishers (AAP) and the Authors Guild resolved their legal dispute over the scanning of millions of books provided by research libraries. At the time this report was prepared, the settlement still required approval of the presiding judge. Although this is a private settlement, the result has very real implications for public policy and the way libraries of all types will operate. Because of the complexity of the agreement, its potential long-term impact on libraries (and thus user interests), and the enormity of the book collection involved, many librarians have raised questions about the settlement's impact. Issues raised at the meeting that members believe are of key concern to libraries include access, privacy, intellectual freedom, equitable treatment, and terms of use.

In May 2009 ARL, ALA, and ACRL filed comments with the U.S. District Court for the Southern District of New York for the judge to consider in his ruling on the proposed Google settlement. The associations asked the judge to exercise vigorous oversight of the interpretation and implementation of the settlement to ensure the broadest possible benefit from the services the settlement enables. The associations asserted that although the settlement has the potential to provide public access to millions of books, many of the features of the settlement, including the absence of competition for the new services, could compromise fundamental library values, including equity of access to information, patron privacy, and intellectual freedom. The court can mitigate these possible negative effects by regulating the conduct of Google and the Book Rights Registry the settlement establishes. The brief, along with additional information about the settlement, is available at http://www.arl.org/pp/ppcopyright/google.

In "A Guide for the Perplexed Part II: The Amended Google-Michigan Agreement," Band reviewed the revised agreement between Google and the University of Michigan that allows Google to scan books from the university library for inclusion in Google's search database. The amended agreement addresses the provisions of the proposed settlement between Google and the plaintiffs in the Google Book Search litigation. Band's review is available at http://www.arl.org/ bm~doc/google-michigan-12jun09.pdf.

In July ARL, ACRL, and ALA sent a letter to William Cavanaugh, a deputy assistant attorney general with the Department of Justice (DOJ) Antitrust Division, asking that the division advise the court presiding over the Google Book Settlement to supervise the implementation of the settlement closely, particularly the pricing of institutional subscriptions and the selection of Book Rights Registry board members. The letter also recommended that the division actively monitor the parties' compliance with the settlement's provisions. In particular, the library groups urged the division to ask the court to review pricing of institutional subscriptions whenever the division concludes that the prices do not meet the economic objectives set forth in the settlement. In order to evaluate the price of an institutional subscription, the groups believe the division should have access to all relevant pricing information from Google and the Book Rights Registry. For more information, see http://www.arl.org/pp/ppcopyright/google/ googledoj.shtml.

In September ARL, ALA, and ACRL submitted a supplemental filing with the U.S. District Court for the Southern District of New York to address developments that had occurred since the groups submitted their filing on May 4, 2009. While the library associations' position had not changed since their initial filing, the groups believed that recent activity (such as an amended agreement reached between Google and the University of Michigan, the University of Texas–Austin, and the University of Wisconsin–Madison; Google's recent blog regarding privacy; and the library associations' communication with the Antitrust Division of DOJ), should be brought to the court's attention. In their supplemental filing, the library associations called upon the court to address concerns with the pricing review, to direct Google to provide more detail on privacy issues, and to broaden representation on the Books Rights Registry. Finally, both the Urban Libraries Council and the International Federation of Library Associations and Institutions (IFLA) filed letters with the court echoing many of the concerns raised by ARL, ALA, and ACRL. More information on the settlement and the filings is available at http://www.arl.org/pp/ppcopyright/google/index.shtml.

At a status hearing before the court on the proposed Google settlement, the parties—AAP, Google, and the Authors Guild—expressed optimism that a new agreement, which would satisfy the concerns of DOJ, could be negotiated by the court-ordered presentation date of November 9, 2009. The judge and the parties also agreed that future objections to the new settlement would be limited to the amended aspects. A spokesman for the publishers told reporters that he expected that the "core of the settlement" would be the same. The plaintiffs' lawyer, Michael Boni, told the judge he hoped to seek final approval of a new settlement by December 2009 or early January 2010.

In November LCA released "A Guide for the Perplexed Part III: The Amended Settlement Agreement," again written by Band. The guide describes the major changes in the amended settlement agreement (ASA), submitted to the court by Google, the Authors Guild, and AAP on November 13, 2009, with emphasis on those changes relevant to libraries. While many of the amendments will have little direct impact on libraries, the ASA significantly reduces the scope of the settlement because it excludes most books published outside the United States. In addition, the ASA gives the Book Rights Registry the authority to increase the number of free public access terminals in public libraries, which had initially been set at one per library building, among other changes. The court accepted the parties' recommended schedule and set January 28, 2010, as the deadline for class members to opt out of the ASA or to file objections, and February 4, 2010, as the deadline for DOJ to file its comments. The court scheduled the fairness hearing for February 18, 2010. The guide is available at http://www.arl.org/bm~doc/guide_for_the_perplexed_part3.pdf.

In December ARL, ALA, and ACRL sent another letter to DOJ expressing their views on how DOJ should respond to the Google Book Search ASA. The associations noted that "the most effective way to prevent the registry and Google from abusing the control they will have over the essential research facility enabled by the settlement would be for the court to regulate the parties' conduct under the settlement. Specifically, when requested, the court should review the pricing of the institutional subscription to ensure that it meets the economic objectives set forth in the settlement, i.e., '(1) the realization of revenue at market rates for each Book and license on behalf of Rightsholders and (2) the realization of broad access to the Books by the public, including institutions of higher education.'" The associations also expressed disappointment that DOJ had not considered representation by academic authors on the Book Rights Registry board, noting that "While the Statement of Interest articulates at great length concern about the adequacy of representation of foreign rightsholders, it contains no mention whatsoever of academic authors. The parties responded to the United States' solicitude for foreign rightsholders by mandating six seats on the Registry board for rightsholders from Australia, Canada, and the United Kingdom. But in the absence of any support from the United States for the interests of academic authors, the Amended Settlement Agreement reserves no seats for these scholars whose works constitute most of the books Google will scan and display." The letter is available at http://www.arl.org/bm~doc/antitrustdivasa-final.pdf.

In addition, ARL, with other organizations and individuals, wrote to Google concerning privacy issues relating to Google Book Search. Calling for "enforceable privacy protections," the signatories suggested that Google "commit to additional privacy protections and that such commitments be enforceable by the court presiding over the settlement." The letter is available at http://www.arl.org/pp/ppcopyright/google.

LCA Statement on Limitations and Exceptions

LCA made a statement on copyright limitations and exceptions for libraries and archives at the World Intellectual Property Organization (WIPO) Standing Committee on Copyright and Related Rights 18th Session, Geneva, May 27, 2009. In its statement, LCA noted that "Copyright law has supported the essential functions of libraries, but in many nations copyright law has not been updated sufficiently to allow for adequate uses of digital information. The absence of effective provisions addressing access to digital information constrains libraries from performing functions that copyright law has previously facilitated. At a time of dramatic technological change, the role of copyright limitations and exceptions has become unacceptably unbalanced." Also at the WIPO meeting, LCA, Electronic Information for Libraries (eIFL), and IFLA offered a longer "Statement of Principles on Copyright Limitations and Exceptions for Libraries and Archives." Both statements are available at http://www.wo.ala.org/districtdispatch/?p=2972.

Other Copyright Issues

In April 2009 ARL, ALA, and ACRL filed comments on the U.S. Copyright Office Notice of Inquiry concerning facilitating access to copyrighted works for the blind or persons with other disabilities. The associations stated that "The blind or persons with other disabilities should be afforded the same access to materials as sighted persons. While current copyright law goes a long way in meeting the information needs of the visually impaired, ARL, ACRL, and ALA also believe that more can be done to improve and expand access . . ." The filing is available at http://www.arl.org/bm~doc/cofilingblindfinal.pdf.

In September ARL and ALA released a statement titled "Performance of or Showing Films in the Classroom" that provides guidance on the digital delivery of content to the "physical" classroom. When the federal Technology, Education, and Copyright Harmonization (TEACH) Act was enacted in 2002, librarians hoped that it would provide some clarity on copyright exceptions for the digital delivery of content for distance education. However, understanding what is permitted under the TEACH Act in combination with DMCA and existing exceptions like fair use has become more difficult for many practitioners. The statement was written by Jonathan Band, legal counsel to ALA and ARL; Peter Jaszi, professor of law and faculty director of the Glushko-Samuelson Intellectual Property Clinic at American University Washington College of Law, and Kenneth D. Crews, director of the copyright advisory office at Columbia University. The statement is available at http://www.arl.org/pp/ppcopyright/webdigitalpsa.shtml.

ARL, ALA, and ACRL joined the Organization for Transformative Works and the Right to Write Fund in filing a friends-of-the-court brief asking the U.S. Court of Appeals for the Second Circuit to reverse the Federal District Court judge's ruling in *Salinger* v. *Colting*. In July the District Court ruled in favor of author J. D. Salinger, who claimed that Fredrik Colting, the author of *60 Years Later: Coming Through the Rye,* infringed his copyright on *Catcher in the Rye.* The court's preliminary injunction prohibits the publication and distribution of the book in the United States, which the groups believe implicates free speech rights of authors, publishers, and the public protected by the First Amendment. In their friends-of-the-court filing, the groups also asserted that the judge applied too narrow an interpretation of the fair use doctrine, which permits new, transformative works into the marketplace. The brief was written by Anthony Falzone, executive director, Fair Use Project, Stanford Law School, and is available at http://www.arl.org/bm~doc/salingeramicusbrief.pdf.

Public Access Policies

Digitization of Public Domain Collections

Linking job creation, access to the nation's cultural and scientific resources, and the value of making public domain resources broadly available, ARL called upon the incoming Obama administration to engage in a large-scale initiative to digitize public domain collections. The ARL policy statement notes that

> Deepening our understanding of our Nation and its culture and history, advancing scientific discovery, tackling environmental, economic issues and more, all depend on scientists, researchers, students, scholars, and members of the public accessing our Nation's cultural, historical, and scientific assets. A large-scale initiative to digitize and preserve the public domain collections of library, governmental, and cultural memory organizations will support research, teaching, and learning at all levels, will help stem the current economic crisis by equipping and employing workers in every state with 21st century skills, and will lay a foundation for innovation and national competitiveness in the decades ahead. The goal is to establish a universal, open library or a digital data commons.

The complete statement is available at http://www.arl.org/bm~doc/ibopenlibpsa2.pdf.

In a May 2009 letter to the chair and vice chair of the Joint Committee on Printing, ARL and ALA wrote in strong support for a project that will digitize the nation's historical public domain government works and make these broadly available to the public. The U.S. Government Printing Office (GPO) is seeking the approval of the Joint Committee on Printing to undertake a digitization project at no cost to the government that will ultimately provide GPO with preservation and access copies of these important government information resources. The letter is available at http://www.arl.org/bm~doc/ltjcp-5-05-09.pdf.

Financial Bailout Transparency

ARL joined OpentheGovernment.org and 79 other organizations focused on open government in a letter calling on Congress to improve oversight and transparency of the financial bailout activities. The signatories asked Congress to use both its oversight authority to make the financial bailout more accountable to the public and its legislative authority to make the bailout more transparent.

Access to Research

In June Sen. Joe Lieberman (I-Conn., chair of the Committee on Homeland Security and Governmental Affairs) and Sen. John Cornyn (R-Texas) introduced the Federal Research Public Access Act of 2009 (FRPAA), S. 1373. Provisions in the legislation would require that federal government agencies and departments with an annual extramural research budget of $100 million or more make publicly available over the Internet final electronic manuscripts of articles in peer-reviewed journals stemming from research funded by that agency. The legislation seeks to extend and expand access to these federally funded research resources and accelerate scientific discovery. This legislation reflects the growing trend by funders and campuses alike of adopting and implementing public access policies relating to federally funded research.

The proposed bill was welcomed by the Alliance for Taxpayer Access, a coalition of research institutions, consumers, patients, and others, including ARL, formed to support open public access to publicly funded research. For more information, see http://www.arl.org/pp/access/frpaa2009.shtml.

Federal Depository Library Program

In April 2009 ARL released "Strategic Directions for the FDLP," a white paper that provides an environmental context for the Federal Depository Library Program (FDLP), discusses the current opportunity to reframe FDLP, presents selected regional cooperative initiatives that demonstrate new directions for the program, and suggests that reframing FDLP presents a unique opportunity to explore cooperative print-management strategies. The paper noted that "The reframing of the FDLP presents the opportunity to create a new service model that will substantially increase and enhance access to and discovery of government information. The framework for the future will be based on access, discovery, management of the resources and tools, and delivery of these resources to users. Emerging social software, digital technologies, and broadband networks offer GPO, participating depository libraries, and other partners new ways to cooperate as they seek to build, sustain, and provide access to the digital collections of the future while preserving the print resources of historic importance." The white paper is available at http://www.arl.org/bm~doc/arlwpfdlptrans.pdf.

'Documents for a Digital Democracy'

In December ARL, COSLA, and Ithaka S+R released "Documents for a Digital Democracy: A Model for the Federal Depository Library Program in the 21st Century," which examines the essential role of FDLP in distributing, providing access to, and preserving government documents. The report also focuses on the transition of government information from print to digital and how this change in format impacts FDLP's long-term sustainability. Without a system-wide transformation of current practices, the ability to effectively distribute, provide access to, and preserve this essential information is in jeopardy. The report stresses that preservation and integrity, along with advanced access services, should be achieved through a combination of formalized partnerships and decentralized approaches. The report is available at http://www.arl.org/bm~doc/documents-for-a-digital-democracy.pdf.

Presidential Libraries

ARL, with 15 other not-for-profit organizations, filed comments with the National Archives and Records Administration (NARA) on developing alternative models for presidential libraries. NARA requested public comment on alternatives that "may involve changing how records are processed and made available." The joint letter states that it is critically important that "NARA take full account of the effect any alternative model may have on the public's ability to gain access to important historical documents and on NARA's obligation to provide the public with timely access to important historical documents." The letter is available at http://www.arl.org/bm~doc/nara-rfi-preslibraries-final.pdf.

CRS Publications

In May 2009 ARL joined more than 40 open-government advocates in a letter to the Senate Rules Committee requesting "public hearings on open government issues and to mark-up and pass S.R. 118," a Senate resolution that would improve public access to reports by the Congressional Research Service (CRS). The resolution would provide for online public access to CRS publications. Currently, CRS reports that are undertaken for individual members of Congress are accessible electronically only to members of Congress and their staff. Numerous sites on the Internet have harvested some of the CRS reports. S.R. 118 would establish a centralized electronic system that would permit public access to CRS publications in addition to the creation of an index of CRS resources. The letter is available at http://www.openthegovernment.org/otg/CRS%20Letter%202009-FINAL.pdf.

Deposit of Electronic Works

In August ARL and ALA filed comments with the Copyright Office in response to the request for comments concerning the Library of Congress's interest in changing the current practice of not mandating deposit of electronic works. The new regulation would establish a process for mandatory deposit of electronic works, beginning with serials that are only available digitally. In the filing, ARL and ALA stated that ". . . this initiative to preserve and provide access to journal literature is extremely important, especially in light of the increasing number of journals being published only online." The associations also commented that the "Library of Congress has a unique responsibility for building a national collection of works . . . thus we note that this proposed policy is 'unique' to the Library of Congress, especially given the conservative nature of the proposed exemption that allows for simultaneous access of the electronic works by only two on-site users. ALA and ARL understand the nature of this approach; however, we caution that this should not be considered precedent setting." The filing is available at http://www.arl.org/bm~doc/locdeposit.pdf.

Telecommunications Policies

Supporting an Open Internet

ARL joined with others in the public sector in a letter applauding the announcement by the Federal Communications Commission (FCC) that the agency would begin a public proceeding concerning how to ensure an open and nondiscriminatory Internet. As stated by FCC Chairman Julius Genachowski, "the rules are necessary to protect innovation on the Internet and preserve the openness that has allowed the Internet to blossom." The letter to FCC is available at http://www.publicknowledge.org/pdf/pubint-nn-letter-20091021.pdf.

ACTA Negotiations

ARL joined with others in the public and private sectors in a letter to the Office of the U.S. Trade Representative (USTR) regarding concerns with the Anti-

Counterfeiting Trade Act (ACTA). The United States, along with other countries, recently re-engaged in negotiations on ACTA. Signatories of the letter called for USTR to delete the Internet-related provisions of ACTA given their complexity, and to make ACTA negotiation documents publicly available, and suggested that USTR establish advisory committees to represent the interests of the Internet, civil society, and consumer constituencies. The letter is available at http://copyrightalliance.org/files/acta_letter_to_ambassador_kirk_final.pdf.

Privacy, Security, Civil Liberties

Several provisions of the USAPatriot Act were set to expire on December 31, 2009, unless Congress reauthorized them. This "sunsetting" provided lawmakers with an opportunity to revisit the act and address its perceived shortcomings. The Senate Judiciary Committee took up these issues with what ARL viewed as disappointing results. Sen. Russ Feingold's (D-Wis.) proposals for comprehensive reform, which ARL and ALA endorsed, were declined in favor of a minimal bill that would offer library patrons some limited protections for their offline activities but does little else to address deep concerns with the original USAPatriot Act. At the time this report was prepared, the full Senate had yet to vote on the bill.

In the House of Representatives, members of the House Judiciary Committee introduced the USAPatriot Amendments Act of 2009, H.R. 3845. This bill included several key reforms to restore important civil liberties without diminishing the government's ability to conduct legitimate national security investigations. The committee began mark-up of H.R. 3845 in November. ARL, with others in the public sector, wrote in support of H.R. 3845. ARL and ALA also wrote a letter thanking the sponsors of H.R. 3845 for including strong library provisions in the bill. For more information, see http://www.arl.org/pp/pscl/patriot.

Federal Funding

Support for NEH, GPO Programs

ARL and ALA submitted a statement in support of the fiscal year (FY) 2010 appropriations for the National Endowment for the Humanities (NEH), particularly the NEH Division of Preservation and Access. The document states

> With NEH's support, libraries engage in numerous activities to preserve and provide access to our local, state, national, and international cultural heritage. We also urge you to support the overall funding for NEH at the level of $230 million, an increase of $75 million. Additional appropriations would permit the Agency to address the high level of unmet needs by supporting a greater number of humanities projects. NEH funding is central to libraries across the country as this funding supports core activities, including the preservation of unique collections, the training of librarians to preserve these culturally valuable resources, and to making important research tools broadly available for use by the public.

The statement is available at http://www.arl.org/bm~doc/tstneh2010final.pdf.

ARL and ALA filed a statement in support of FY 2010 appropriations for the GPO with a particular focus on the Federal Depository Library Program and GPO technological initiatives. The associations "commend GPO for investing in technologies and systems to support enhanced access to electronic government information . . . [S]everal important information technology projects . . . are designed to expand and improve public access to government information . . . [and] reduce internal GPO costs as well as improve efficiency of service to participating FDLs." The statement is available at http://www.arl.org/bm~doc/gpo-approps-24apr09.pdf.

Other Issues

Position on New Archivist

On October 1, 2009, the Senate Committee on Homeland Security and Governmental Affairs conducted a confirmation hearing on the nomination of David S. Ferriero as Archivist of the United States. Sen. Thomas Carper (D-Del.), chair of the Subcommittee on Federal Financial Management, Government Information, Federal Services, and International Security, chaired the hearing. Carper's questions to Ferriero focused on issues concerning presidential libraries; the preservation, access, and security of electronic records; and the role of NARA in educating members of the public about U.S. history. ARL noted its strong support of the nomination in a letter to the chair and ranking member of the committee. The letter is available at http://www.arl.org/bm~doc/ltferrieronara.pdf.

The Senate Homeland Security and Governmental Affairs Committee approved the nomination on October 28, and the Senate confirmed the nomination on November 6.

Swine Flu Information

ARL created a Web page that provides information and links to Web sites related to H1N1, the so-called swine flu virus. This page is intended as a resource for libraries as they respond to institutional policies and national concerns regarding the H1N1 virus. ARL libraries were invited to share Web sites detailing their institutional policies. The Web page is at http://www.arl.org/pp/otherissues/h1n1/index.shtml.

Reshaping Scholarly Communication

ARL's Reshaping Scholarly Communication program works to develop effective, extensible, sustainable, and economically viable models of scholarly communication that provide barrier-free access to quality information in support of the mission of research institutions.

Digital Repositories

In January 2009 the ARL Digital Repository Issues Task Force released its final report, "The Research Library's Role in Digital Repository Services." The report provided a broad overview of the state of digital repository services, important issues, and key strategies for service development. In addition, it included a "horizon analysis" projecting key shifts in the digital repository landscape over the next seven years. The report identified key areas for research library engagement and called on research libraries to act to ensure an ongoing role in digital repository service development. The report is available at http://www.arl.org/bm~doc/repository-services-report.pdf.

Campus Outreach Initiative

To help promote successful campus outreach, ARL released a new guide on outreach to scholarly society leaders to assist libraries in developing positive, supportive relationships with leaders, editors, and members of academic scholarly societies affiliated with their institutions. See http://www.arl.org/sc/faculty/coi/coitalkpoints2009.shtml.

In addition, ARL compiled a list of resources useful to scholarly society leaders, editors, and members, and an archive of the August Webcast "Reaching Out to Leaders of Scholarly Societies at Research Institutions." To explore the full set of resources, see http://www.arl.org/sc/faculty/coi/index.shtml.

University's Role in Dissemination

In February 2009 ARL and three leading higher education associations—the Association of American Universities, the Coalition for Networked Information, and the National Association of State Universities and Land Grant Colleges—jointly issued "The University's Role in the Dissemination of Research and Scholarship—A Call to Action," which was addressed to campus leaders including presidents, provosts, chief information officers, heads of faculty governance bodies, deans, and other stakeholders. The statement offers a vision statement, key principles, and a number of strategies institutions can pursue. The primary recommendation is that "Campuses should initiate discussions involving administration and faculty about modifying current practices and/or its intellectual property policies such that the university retains a set of rights sufficient to ensure that broad dissemination of the research and scholarly work produced by its faculty occurs." The full statement is available at http://www.arl.org/bm~doc/disseminating-research-feb09.pdf.

The Market

ARL and the International Coalition of Library Consortia (ICOLC) contributed their separate perspectives on the global economic crisis and its effects on research libraries. The "ARL Statement on the Global Economic Crisis and Its Effect on Publishing and Library Subscriptions," released in February 2009, reinforced key elements of the earlier ICOLC statement and described the current budget situation and expectations for future funding for ARL member library collections. In addition, the ARL statement provided recommendations for publishers seeking to remain true to a commitment to promote the broad exchange of new scholarship and research. The recommendations addressed such issues as price discipline, contract terms, and preservation arrangements. The statement closed by calling on publishers—particularly small, not-for-profit publishers, which are of particular concern to the ARL community—to "consult widely with research libraries." The statement is available at http://www.arl.org/bm~doc/economic-statement-2009.pdf.

In June 2009 ARL issued a statement strongly encouraging its members to refrain from signing agreements with publishers or vendors, either individually or through consortia, that include nondisclosure or confidentiality clauses. In addition, the statement encouraged ARL members to share, upon request from other libraries, information contained in these agreements (save for trade secrets or proprietary technical details) for licensing content, licensing software or other tools, and for digitization contracts with third-party vendors. The statement is based on a resolution introduced by the Scholarly Communication Steering Committee and adopted by the ARL board. For more information, see http://www.arl.org/news/pr/nondisclosure-5june09.shtml.

Institute on Scholarly Communication

Early in 2009 the ARL/ACRL Institute on Scholarly Communication released a guide, "Developing a Scholarly Communication Program in Your Library," authored by Kris Fowler, Gail Persily, and Jim Stemper. The online guide offers both generic tools that can be adapted locally under a "creative commons" license and examples of how these tools have been implemented at other schools. See http://www.arl.org/sc/institute/fair/scprog.

In March 2009 the Institute on Scholarly Communication workshop "Scholarly Communication Outreach: Crafting Messages that Grab Faculty Attention" was held in Seattle with 70 librarians in attendance. Jon Wergin, professor of educational studies at Antioch University, facilitated the first program session and focused on researcher communication practices and skills for interviewing and listening. The second program session addressed message development and was led by Alane Wilson, executive director of the British Columbia Library Association. For more information, see http://www.arl.org/sc/institute/inst-events/0309workshop.shtml.

Transforming Research Libraries

The transformation of research libraries mirrors, to a large degree, the ongoing evolution of research institutions and the practices of research and scholarship. ARL's third, and newest, strategic direction focuses on articulating, promoting, and facilitating new and expanding roles for ARL libraries that support, enable, and enrich the transformations affecting research and research-intensive education.

Planning and Visioning

Respondents to an ARL survey described their work to provide learning and research spaces for their constituents. The "Innovative Spaces in ARL Libraries" survey produced 98 instances of special or noteworthy projects. In a series of reports prepared by Crit Stuart and Laura Iandoli, these instances are reported under 17 subtopics. An article summarizing these initiatives, "Learning and Research Spaces in ARL Libraries: Snapshots of Installations and Experiments," is also available in *Research Library Issues* (*RLI*) no. 264 (June 2009). The survey results and the article are available at http://www.arl.org/rtl/space/2008study/index.shtml.

ARL compiled a selection of resources for libraries engaged in planning for new roles. The guide provides an annotated collection of recent documents from various organizations that analyze trends and developments relevant to library leaders focused on preparing for the future. It is available at http://www.arl.org/rtl/plan. In addition, ARL announced the launch of a new research initiative, New Roles for New Times, that will produce a series of reports in 2010 and 2011.

A special issue of *RLI* (no. 265) addressed the topic of new roles for liaison librarians. The article addressed such themes as the need for new forms of relationship-building, particularly with faculty, to respond to the changing work of faculty and researchers and to constantly evolving learning outcomes, research processes, and communication practices. Issue 265 is available at http://arl.tizrapublisher.com/view/o4jrq/default.

Evolving E-Research

The ARL E-science Working Group surveyed e-science activities at ARL member institutions. Members reported on a wide range of institution-level and library-based activities that promote management and curation of scientific research data. Early findings of the survey were presented by Wendy Lougee at the October ARL Membership Meeting. The resources provided by surveyed libraries are collected at http://www.arl.org/rtl/eresearch/escien/esciensurvey/surveyresearch.shtml.

Special Collections

The ARL Working Group on Special Collections, formed in 2007, released "Special Collections in ARL Libraries: A Discussion Report" that identified key issues in the management and exposure of special collections material in the 21st century. The report included overviews of and recommendations in three areas: (1) Collecting Carefully, with Regard to Costs, and Ethical and Legal Concerns; (2) Ensuring Discovery and Access; and (3) The Challenge of Born-Digital Collections. The report highlighted the need for research library leadership to support actions that will increase the visibility and use of special collections and promote both existing and developing best practices in the stewardship of special collections. The report is available at http://www.arl.org/bm~doc/scwg-report.pdf.

Lisa Carter, head of the Special Collections Research Center at the North Carolina State University Libraries, was appointed ARL Visiting Program Officer to work with the Special Collections Working Group to promote the discussion report and plan the October forum.

ARL hosted a Webcast on "Transformative Issues for Special Collections in ARL Libraries" in July to offer an interactive opportunity for research library staff and administrators with responsibility for managing and providing access to unique collections in all formats to discuss and provide feedback on the discussion report. Alice Prochaska, chair of the Working Group, moderated a short discussion by a panel drawn from leaders in the special collections community. For more information and links to the conference archive, see http://www.arl.org/rtl/speccoll/SCwebcastjuly07.shtml.

In the fall ARL and CNI co-hosted a forum on "An Age of Discovery: Distinctive Collections in the Digital Age" that built on the work of the ARL Special Collections Working Group. To sustain the momentum of community interest in rethinking the roles of distinctive collections in the digital age that was evident at the forum, the December 2009 issue of *RLI* (no. 267) was devoted to this topic. This special issue included papers delivered at the forum by Clifford Lynch of CNI, Anne Kenney of Cornell, and Don Waters of the Mellon Foundation. *RLI* issue 267 is available at http://arl.tizrapublisher.com/view/prvp3/default.

Celebrating Research: Rare and Special Collections from the Membership of the Association of Research Libraries is a book and Web site profiling selected rare and special collections in major research libraries of North America. Originally published in 2007 on the occasion of ARL's 75th anniversary, the Web site was expanded in 2009 with the addition of profiles of collections from the Bibliothèques de l'Université de Montréal and Rice University. Montreal contributed a profile of the Gilles-Rioux Collection about Surrealism, a collection focused not only on surrealism but also on other themes affiliated with this cultural movement. The collection profile can be viewed at http://www.celebratingresearch.org/libraries/montreal/gilles-rioux.shtml. Rice contributed a profile of its collection, called the Robert L. Patten Research Materials on George Cruikshank, the man best known as the original illustrator of many of Charles Dickens's novels. To view the profile, visit http://www.celebrating research.org/libraries/rice/patten-cruikshank.shtml. The Celebrating Research Web site compendium now includes 120 collection profiles, each from a different ARL member library. The content of *Celebrating Research,* including image previews, is available at http://www.celebratingresearch.org.

Diversity, Leadership Development

ARL works closely with member libraries, graduate library and information programs, and other libraries and library associations to promote awareness of career opportunities in research libraries and support the success of library professionals from racial and ethnic groups currently under-represented in the profession. ARL's diversity programs support member libraries as they strive to reflect society's diversity in their staffing, collections, leadership, and programs. Central to the diversity agenda are programs that facilitate the recruitment, preparation, and advancement of librarians into leadership positions in research libraries. The themes and curricula of these programs introduce participants to major trends affecting research libraries and the communities they serve: the changing nature of scholarly communication, the influence of information and other public policies, and new and expanding library roles in support of research and scholarship.

Leadership Institute

Early in 2009 ARL hosted the fifth annual leadership institute for MLIS students. The institute included presentations from library leaders and former ARL diversity scholars that focused on issues relating to transitioning into, and building career networks in, research libraries. This annual event is a component of the ARL Diversity Programs, which include the Initiative to Recruit a Diverse Work Force, the Leadership and Career Development Program, and the Career Enhancement Program. For more information on the institute, see http://www.arl. org/diversity/leadinst.

Initiative to Recruit a Diverse Work Force

The Initiative to Recruit a Diverse Work Force (IRDW) offers stipend funding in support of MLIS education of up to $10,000 over two years to students from under-represented groups who are interested in careers in research libraries. The program is funded by the Institute of Museum and Library Services (IMLS) and by voluntary contributions from 52 ARL member libraries. The ARL Diversity Working Group awarded stipends to 17 students for graduate study during 2008–2010. In April 2009 these ARL diversity scholars were guests of the Purdue University Libraries for a two-day visit. The scholars toured the libraries and participated in multiple sessions on such topics as the "embedded librarianship" model at Purdue, new areas in academic librarianship, the role of special collections in research, and the tenure process for librarians in research institutions. For more information about IRDW, visit http://www.arl.org/diversity/init.

Leadership and Career Development

ARL's Leadership and Career Development Program (LCDP) is an 18-month fellowship that prepares midcareer librarians from under-represented racial and ethnic groups to take on increasingly demanding leadership roles in ARL member libraries. In April 2009 the current cohort of ten fellows participated in the Institute on Research, Teaching, and Learning at Yale University. University Librarian Alice Prochaska and the Yale Library's Diversity Committee hosted a day that included tours of the Sterling Memorial Library, the Beineke Rare Book and Manuscript Library, and the Divinity Library; opportunities to meet and network with the library staff; and presentations on the transforming roles in research, teaching, and learning. For more information, see http://www.arl. org/diversity/lcdp.

Career Enhancement

ARL's Career Enhancement Program (CEP), funded by IMLS and ARL member libraries, gives MLIS students from under-represented groups a robust fellowship experience that includes an internship in an ARL member library. The program reflects the commitment of ARL members to provide practical experience to MLIS graduate students and to create a diverse research library community that will better meet the challenges of changing demographics and the emphasis of global perspectives in higher education.

MLIS graduate students from under-represented groups who have successfully completed a minimum of 12 credit hours in an ALA-accredited program are eligible to apply. ARL's CEP Coordinating Committee selected 18 fellows to participate in the program's first year. Program components included a paid internship in one of the host ARL libraries, support to attend the ARL Leadership Institute, relocation and housing assistance, an academic stipend (for those who qualify), and other benefits. From June to August, the CEP fellows relocated to the cities of their host institutions and participated in 6- to 12-week paid internships. Participating host libraries were at the University at Albany–SUNY; the University of Arizona; Columbia University; the University of California, San Diego; the University of Kentucky; the National Library of Medicine; North Carolina State University; and the University of Washington. For more information see http://www.arl.org/diversity/cep.

Research Library Leadership Fellows

ARL selected 21 individuals to participate in the 2009–2010 ARL Research Library Leadership Fellows (RLLF) Program, an executive leadership program that meets the increasing demands for succession planning for research libraries with a new approach to preparing the next generation of deans and directors. This third offering of the program was designed and sponsored by seven ARL member libraries—Brigham Young, Florida, Georgia Tech, Houston, Michigan, Utah, and Western Ontario.

In mid-September eight fellows were the guests of the University of Florida and the George A. Smathers Libraries in Gainesville. The site visit included programs on library development and university relations, visits to campus museums, and an event at the Center for Latin American Studies. In late September the program presented the first in a series of Internet seminars exploring strategic concerns facing the long-term development of research libraries. The program addressed the topic of the "Sustainability of Digital Resources." An archive of the presentation is available at http://www.infiniteconferencing.com/Events/ARL/093009ARL/recording-playback.html.

In November the libraries of the University of Utah and Brigham Young University hosted an institute in Salt Lake City and Provo that included an array of formal programs, tours, discussions with library directors and university administrators, and social events aimed at providing the RLLF fellows with opportunities to explore the operations of the two host institutions and some of the major strategic issues they are facing.

The roster of 2009–2010 fellows and additional information about the program are available at http://www.arl.org/leadership/rllf.

Diversity Programs Webcast

ARL's Diversity Programs hosted a Webcast in December on "The E-Science Imperative: The Future of Data Management in Academic Libraries." Program participants from the Leadership and Career Development Program as well as ARL diversity scholars were in attendance for a program presented by Wendy Lougee, university librarian at the University of Minnesota, and Scott Brandt, associate dean for research at Purdue University Libraries. An archive of the

Webcast is available at http://www.infiniteconferencing.com/Events/ARL/
120809ARL/recording-playback.html.

Library Statistics and Assessment

The ARL Statistics and Assessment program focuses on describing and measuring the performance of research libraries and their contributions to research, scholarship, and community service. The need to focus on outcomes, value, and impact has increased over the years and the new ARL strategic plan calls for accelerated action in the library assessment area. The program is a strategic enabling capability that supports member and other libraries in transforming their operations and maintaining relevance by demonstrating their value in the research and education process. The strong leadership role the program has provided in the development, testing, and application of academic library performance measures, statistics, and management tools is recognized through a widely used suite of assessment services.

The program provides analysis and reports of quantitative and qualitative indicators of library collections, personnel, and services by using a variety of evidence-gathering mechanisms. The program hosts the StatsQUAL (Statistics and Service Quality) suite of services that focus on developing new approaches for describing and evaluating library service effectiveness, return on investment, digital library services, the impact of networked electronic services, diversity, leadership, and organizational climate, among others. StatsQUAL tools include LibQUAL+, ClimateQUAL, MINES for Libraries, DigiQUAL, and ARL Statistics. More information is available at http://www.arl.org/stats.

A new Web site for LibQUAL+ was launched as the culmination of two years of redesign and experimentation to offer an improved assessment service. One of the major improvements is the ability to offer to library users a shorter version of the survey known as LibQUAL+ Lite. A series of randomized control trial experimental studies confirmed that the new protocol is promising, effective, and useful as it reduces respondent burden and improves response rates. LibQUAL+ Lite and long scores are essentially equivalent and there is no need for score conversion. The low effect sizes regarding the difference in the scores for total scores, dimension scores, and linking item scores indicate that there was little, if any, practical difference between responses in the long and "lite" forms. The latest research, in the form of Martha Kyrillidou's 2009 dissertation, will be available through the IDEALS institutional repository at the University of Illinois at Urbana-Champaign. Libraries have used LibQUAL+ data successfully to implement organizational improvements, and best practices were shared in person and online via "share fairs" during the year. For more information see http://www.libqual.org.

The need to focus on organizational climate improvement is also articulated via ClimateQUAL: Organizational Climate and Diversity Assessment Service. ClimateQUAL aims to: (a) foster a culture of healthy organizational climate and diversity, (b) help libraries better understand staff perceptions of organizational climate and diversity, (c) facilitate the ongoing collection and interpretation of staff feedback, (d) identify best practices in managing organizational climate, and

(e) enable libraries to interpret and act upon data. Since 2007 a group of more than 20 libraries joined the ClimateQUAL effort led by ARL and the University of Maryland. This community of libraries implemented the survey and comes together at the ALA Midwinter Meeting and Annual Conference to share best practices in terms of improving organizational climate as measured by perceptions of diversity, teamwork, learning, innovation, fairness, and leadership. A private ClimateQUAL blog allows sharing information among the community of participating libraries. The ClimateQUAL Web site provides information and useful resources for past, current, and potential participants at http://www.climatequal.org.

ARL has also made a concerted effort to articulate the value and use of evidence for decision making regarding digital resources. Measuring the Impact of Networked Electronic Services (MINES for Libraries) is an online, transaction-based survey that collects data on the purpose of use of electronic resources and the demographics of users. As libraries implement access to electronic resources through portals, collaborations, and consortial arrangements, the MINES for Libraries protocol offers a convenient way to collect information from users in an environment in which they no longer need to physically enter the library in order to access resources. The survey is based on methods developed to determine the indirect costs of conducting grant-funded research and development activities, and was adopted as part of ARL's New Measures program in 2003. More than 50 libraries have implemented the protocol in the last five years, some through ARL and some through indirect cost studies.

IMLS Leadership Grant

The value of the library and its services is the focus of an IMLS grant award that focuses on articulating and measuring the value proposition of libraries. The University of Tennessee, in collaboration with the University of Illinois at Urbana-Champaign Libraries and ARL, was awarded an IMLS leadership grant for its project "Value, Outcomes, and Return on Investment of Academic Libraries (Lib-Value)."

Lib-Value addresses academic librarians' growing need to demonstrate the return on investment and value of the library to the institution. Lib-Value will provide evidence and a set of tested methodologies and tools to assist academic librarians in these areas. The three-year grant of $1 million engages two well-known researchers in the library field as consultants, Bruce Kingma of Syracuse University and Donald W. King of the University of North Carolina at Chapel Hill. The project is also engaging an advisory committee of noted return-on-investment researchers. The results of the study will provide evidence and a set of tested methodologies and tools to help academic librarians demonstrate how the library provides value to its constituents and return on investment to its funders, and to measure which products and services are of most value to enhancing the university's mission.

The project will greatly expand upon earlier studies to consider multiple measures of value that the academic library brings to teaching/learning, research, and social/professional/public engagement functions of the academic institution.

Library Scorecards

The value of libraries is tied to the articulation of a clear vision and mission. During 2009 ARL initiated a project that focuses on mission-driven performance metrics. A year-long effort to assist, train, facilitate, and refine the implementation of library scorecards at ARL member libraries led to articulation and/or refinement of purpose statements, strategy maps, and metrics among the participating libraries.

Four member institutions participated in this project: Johns Hopkins, McMaster, Washington, and Virginia. Three librarians from each institution attended three half-day training sessions led by Accelerant, a strategy management group specializing in the implementation of scorecards in the nonprofit environment. The work of this group is building upon the foundation set by Robert S. Kaplan and David P. Norton, who wrote *The Balanced Scorecard: Translating Strategy into Action* (Harvard Business School). This project is an investment in helping libraries make a stronger case for the value they deliver by developing metrics that are tied to strategy. Lessons learned from this experience will be shared with the larger community.

Preservation Issues

Building on the need to rethink preservation activities, as well as the ARL Preservation Statistics, ARL released a report that provided a current picture of preservation activities in ARL member libraries and made recommendations about how libraries should characterize and measure those activities. The report by ARL Visiting Program Officer Lars Meyer, "Safeguarding Collections at the Dawn of the 21st Century: Describing Roles and Measuring Contemporary Preservation Activities in ARL Libraries," considered activities traditionally captured by ARL's preservation statistics as well as a host of emerging activities largely centered on developing digital collections and involving collaborative efforts. The report is available at http://www.arl.org/bm~doc/safeguarding-collections.pdf.

In September ARL hosted the Webcast "Preservation: Evolving Roles and Responsibilities of Research Libraries" to offer a brief overview of the key findings in the report. The Webcast archive is available at http://arlwebcastarchive.blip.tv.

Qualitative Descriptions

Another way to articulate the transformation of libraries is through the qualitative narrative descriptions ARL libraries were called upon to provide in 2009. For a decade ARL has promoted innovative methods of describing and evaluating the value of research libraries through its New Measures Initiative. However, when ARL directors were interviewed in 2005 and asked to describe a research library in the 21st century, there was general sentiment that greater flexibility is needed in describing the research library today in qualitative terms. Textual narrative descriptions of collections, services, collaborative relations, and other programs, as well as physical spaces were deemed necessary if the essence of a research library today is to be described and evaluated.

A series of pilot activities led to a general call to the membership to provide profile descriptions of their libraries in 2009. The profiles stand alone as descriptive information and are currently being analyzed. The Statistics and Assessment Committee will also use the profiles to identify similarities and differences among libraries and to identify elements that will be measured for the purposes of an alternative to the expenditure-focused Library Investment Index. The narratives are publicly available at http://directors.arl.org/wiki/institution-profiles.

Publications

Annual electronic and print publications describe salary compensation and collection, staffing, expenditures, and service trends for research libraries. The series includes the *ARL Annual Salary Survey, ARL Statistics, ARL Academic Law Library Statistics, ARL Academic Health Sciences Library Statistics, ARL Preservation Statistics,* and *ARL Supplementary Statistics.* A revamped data collection interface will incorporate the ARL Interactive Statistics and replace the facility originally developed by the Geostat Center of the University of Virginia. The interactive facility allows libraries to produce ranked lists and pick from more than 30 variables for data reports and ratios. This site is at http://fisher.lib.virginia.edu/arl/index.html.

Funding

Every year ARL studies the proportion of the university budget devoted to libraries for its member libraries; this ratio continues to decline. For the 40 ARL libraries tracked since 1982, this figure was 2.13 percent in 2006–2007, a slight decrease from 2.21 percent in the previous year. For the 17 libraries tracked since 1966, this figure was 2.09 percent in 2006–2007, down from 2.16 percent in the previous year. Possible explanations of this trend include

- The need for universities to invest greater amounts in technologies and other infrastructure
- The increased collaboration that is taking place in libraries through consortia and centralized purchasing
- The embedding of the library functions within the teaching, learning, and research processes through widespread availability of information

Updated graphs are available at http://www.arl.org/bm~doc/charts.xls. The machine-readable datafiles since 1982 are available at http://www.arl.org/stats/annualsurveys/eg.

SPEC Surveys

The SPEC survey program gathers information on current research library operating practices and policies, and "hot topics," and publishes the SPEC Kit series as guides for libraries as they face ever-changing management issues. Six SPEC Kits were published in 2009: *SPEC Kit 310 Author Addenda, SPEC Kit 311 Public Access Policies, SPEC Kit 312 Public Engagement, SPEC Kit 313 E-book Collections, SPEC Kit 314 Processing Decisions for Manuscripts and Archives, and SPEC Kit 315 Leave and Professional Development Benefits.* Links to the tables of contents and executive summaries of SPEC Kits are available at http://www.arl.org/resources/pubs/spec/complete.shtml.

Performance Measurement In Britain and Ireland

In August 2009 ARL published "Library Performance Measurement in the UK and Ireland," which describes the state-of-the-art methods of performance measurement from Society of College, National, and University Libraries (SCONUL) member libraries in the United Kingdom and Ireland. This survey was a joint initiative between SCONUL and ARL and was based on an ARL SPEC survey published as SPEC Kit 303 Library Assessment in 2007. The intention of this survey was to produce a similar publication focused on activities in British and Irish academic institutions, and reflects a matching SCONUL desire to provide tools, techniques, and data for performance measurement and improvement through its Working Group on Performance Improvement. This publication includes the complete survey results and documentation from respondents in the form of performance standards, survey Web sites, performance reports, and job descriptions. The report is available at http://www.arl.org/bm~doc/LibraryperformanceUKIreland.pdf.

ARL Assessment Forum and Conference

Evaluation and accountability procedures can play a valuable role in providing information critical to the support of budget reduction and program review. The ARL Assessment Forum in 2009 discussed how libraries are using assessment results, statistics, performance measures/metrics, and other management information data to support planning and decision making relating to budget cuts. The forum brings together the library assessment community. It meets every two years during the Library Assessment Conference. ARL issued a call for proposals for the next conference, to take place in Baltimore in October 2010. For more information, see http://www.libraryassessment.org.

Communications and Alliances

ARL's Communications and Alliances capability is engaged in many activities that support its strategic directions. These include acquainting ARL members with current, important developments of interest to research libraries; influencing policy and decision-makers within the higher education, research, and scholarly communities; educating academic communities about issues relating to scholarly communication and research libraries; and providing the library community with information about activities in which research libraries are engaged.

Using print and electronic media as well as direct outreach, the communications capability disseminates information about ARL to the higher education and scholarly communities, as well as to ARL member institutions, and publishes a full range of resources to assist library and higher education communities in their efforts to improve the delivery of scholarly communication. ARL makes many of its titles available electronically; some are available in excerpted form for preview before purchase and others are available in their entirety. See http://www.arl.org/resources/pubs.

News about ARL activities and publications is available through the arl-announce list, distributed widely to the library and higher education communities. To subscribe, visit http://www.arl.org/resources/emaillists.

Governance and Membership Meetings

The ARL Board of Directors formed a Strategic Plan Review Task Force to undertake a review of the ARL Strategic Plan to assure that the association is focused properly and that strategies within programs meet member needs. Following a year-long review involving several rounds of member input, the board adopted an ARL Strategic Plan for 2010–2012. The new plan emphasizes advocacy in three strategic directions: Influencing Public Policies, Reshaping Scholarly Communications, and Transforming Research Libraries. The new strategic plan is available at http://www.arl.org/arl/governance/strat-plan.

To support the work of the Strategic Plan Review Task Force, ARL senior staff identified trends that are likely to affect research libraries and the work of the association. The assessment considered challenges and opportunities and included findings prepared for the review by the Canadian Association of Research Libraries. The resulting report, "Transformational Times: An Environmental Scan," is available at http://www.arl.org/arl/governance/plan-review.shtml.

The ARL board also formed a Financial Strategies Review Task Force to examine current policies guiding ARL's financial strategies and to assess the extent to which the policies are adequate for achieving the directions in the updated ARL strategic plan.

Late in 2008 OCLC posted a new policy to replace the 20-year-old guidelines that governed how derived records were handled by participating libraries. The release of the policy elicited serious concern from the ARL community and from the broader library community as well. As a result, ARL established an ad hoc task force to analyze the policy, compare it to the previous guidelines, provide an analysis of the impact of the change, and identify issues of particular interest to research libraries. The ARL Ad Hoc Task Force to Review the Proposed OCLC Policy for Use and Transfer of WorldCat Records issued a report that called on OCLC to develop a new policy to replace the one released in 2008. The task force report included a brief overview of the policy and the task force's understanding of the policy's intent. This was followed by an explication of specific issues and the task force's findings regarding both the policy itself and the implementation process. The report concluded with recommendations for OCLC and the library community. The report is available at http://www.arl.org/bm~doc/oclc-report-jan09.pdf.

In spring 2009 ARL surveyed member library representatives about the impact of the economic environment on library budgets. The survey focused on ARL library plans and actions for the library's base budget that were implemented in FY 2008–2009. ARL Executive Director Charles B. Lowry reported the results of the survey at meetings of the ARL Membership, the Society for Scholarly Publishing, the Association of American University Presses, and the SPARC Forum at ALA. Interest was high, especially from the publishing market. Lowry's presentation at the SPARC Forum, "Rough Waters: Navigating Hard Times in the Scholarly Communication Marketplace," was videotaped and is available along with slides reporting the data at http://www.arl.org/sparc/meetings/ala09. The survey was repeated in the fall to collect information about library budget plans for 2009–2010.

A total of 102 ARL member library representatives participated in ARL's 154th Membership Meeting May 20–22, 2009, in Houston. The program theme, Transformational Times, was developed by ARL President Thomas C. Leonard (University of California, Berkeley) in consultation with the ARL Board of Directors to focus on sustained, collaborative actions that will transform libraries in ways that help navigate the current financial shoals and, more importantly, redefine what research libraries are and do in an environment where information is defined principally in terms of networked access.

ARL President Tom Leonard (University of California, Berkeley) convened the 155th ARL Membership Meeting October 14–15 in Washington, D.C. At the meeting, 107 ARL member library representatives took part in sessions examining new models for Federal Depository Library collections; potential library roles for supporting public access initiatives; the science, technology, and innovation agenda of the Obama administration; and the value and potential of distinctive collections in the digital age. The meeting also included an optional visit to the Library of Congress National Audiovisual Conservation Center in Culpeper, Virginia. Speakers' remarks, slides, and audio recordings are available at http://www.arl.org/resources/pubs/mmproceedings/155mm-proceedings.shtml.

At the business meeting, member library representatives ratified the ARL board's election of Carol Mandel (New York University) as ARL vice president/president-elect and elected three new members of the board: Carol Pitts Diedrichs (Kentucky/Ohio State), Deborah Jakubs (Duke), and Wendy Lougee (Minnesota). Members also voted to extend a membership invitation to the University of Calgary. At the conclusion of the business meeting, outgoing ARL President Leonard presented the gavel to his successor, Brinley Franklin (University of Connecticut).

Immediately following the Membership Meeting, ARL and CNI co-hosted a Forum on "An Age of Discovery: Distinctive Collections in the Digital Age." Building on the work of the ARL Special Collections Working Group, the overall goal of the forum was to focus attention on the opportunities available in the digital environment for leveraging the strengths of special collections, making them more widely accessible. Two hundred library directors and special collections librarians and archivists gathered at the forum to consider the value proposition of and innovative possibilities inherent in collections of rare books, archives, and other unique materials. Forum participants also explored the potential for expanding use of these resources via digital technologies and collaborative strategies. Text, slides, and audio recordings from presentations delivered at the forum are available at http://www.arl.org/resources/pubs/fallforumproceedings/forum09proceedings.shtml.

SPARC—The Scholarly Publishing and Academic Resources Coalition

21 Dupont Circle, Suite 800, Washington, DC 20036
202-296-2296, fax 202-872-0884, e-mail sparc@arl.org
World Wide Web http://www.arl.org/sparc

Heather Joseph
Executive Director

SPARC (the Scholarly Publishing and Academic Resources Coalition) promotes expanded sharing of scholarship in the networked digital environment. It believes that faster and wider sharing of outputs of the research process increases the impact of research, fuels the advancement of knowledge, and increases the return on research investments.

SPARC was launched in 1997 by the Association of Research Libraries to act on libraries' concern that the promise of the Internet to dramatically improve scholarly communication was inhibited by pricing and access barriers in the journals marketplace. SPARC has been an innovative leader in the rapidly expanding international movement to make scholarly communication more responsive to the needs of researchers, students, the academic enterprise, funders, and the public.

Today SPARC is supported by a membership of more than 220 academic and research libraries and works in cooperation with its affiliates, SPARC Europe and SPARC Japan. Together, SPARC North America, SPARC Europe, and SPARC Japan represent more than 800 libraries worldwide.

SPARC is a catalyst for action. Its pragmatic agenda focuses on collaborating with other stakeholders to stimulate the emergence of new scholarly communication norms, practices, and policies that leverage the networked digital environment to support research, expand the dissemination of research findings, and reduce financial pressures on libraries.

Strategy

SPARC's strategy focuses on reducing barriers to the access, sharing, and use of scholarship. SPARC's highest priority is advancing the understanding and implementation of policies and practices that ensure open access to scholarly research outputs. While much of SPARC's focus to date has been on journal literature, its evolving strategy reflects an increasing focus on open access to research outputs and digital data of all kinds, in all subject areas. SPARC's role in stimulating change centers on three key program areas:

- Educating stakeholders about the problems facing scholarly communication and the opportunities for them to play a role in achieving positive change
- Advocating policy changes that advance scholarly communication and explicitly recognize that dissemination of scholarship is an essential, inseparable component of the research process

- Incubating demonstrations of new publishing and sustainability models that benefit scholarship and academe

Priorities

SPARC actions during 2009 were designed to advance the viability and acceptance of a more open system of scholarship, with a primary focus on open access models for publishing and archiving the results of scholarly research. In particular, as interest in public access to the results of federally funded research continued to accelerate, SPARC worked to deploy a focused and disciplined advocacy strategy while remaining sufficiently agile to capitalize on emerging market opportunities that aligned with its objectives.

SPARC's program activity recognizes that cultural, economic, and technical differences exist in various disciplines and that, in some areas, the interests of scholarship may best be served in the near term by equitable fee-based publishing solutions. Its programs aim at building a broader understanding of opportunities for change in all fields, and place an emphasis on identifying areas of common advantage to all stakeholders in the scholarly communications community—particularly scholarly and scientific researchers, universities and colleges, and university presses and society publishers.

Key Program Activities and Outcomes

Advocacy and Policy Front

During 2009 SPARC led the policy advocacy work of the Open Access Working Group (OAWG), an alliance of leading organizations that support open access, and served as the organizational focal point for the Alliance for Taxpayer Access (ATA). It also retained and supervised work of a public policy consulting firm to help realize activities that track with SPARC and OAWG's focused objectives.

As legislative and policy proposals impacting open access were explored in Washington, D.C., SPARC played an active role. It supported initiatives promoting the adoption of positive government-wide policies on public access to the published results of publicly funded research. In a victory for open access, language in the fiscal year (FY) 2009 Labor, Health, and Human Services (LHHS) Appropriations Bill made the landmark National Institutes of Health (NIH) public access policy permanent. The NIH policy requires that manuscripts stemming from agency-funded research be deposited in the online archive of the National Library of Medicine—PubMed Central—so that they can be made publicly available no later than 12 months after publication in a journal.

SPARC supported the introduction of the Federal Research Public Access Act (FRPAA) in the Senate and educated members of the House of Representatives about the bill, in anticipation of a House introduction in early 2010. Introduced by Senators Joe Lieberman (I-Conn.) and John Cornyn (R-Texas) in June 2009, the Federal Research Public Access Act would require that research results stemming from the funding of 11 federal agencies be made publicly available no later than six months of publication in a journal.

Momentum for public access to publicly funded research across U.S. science and technology agencies was given another boost when the White House Office of Science and Technology Policy called for public comment to inform potential executive action on public access policies. In response to the request for information and in support of the expansion of the successful NIH policy across agencies, SPARC provided extensive guidance to its members and the community. SPARC also worked proactively to identify and counter activity opposing public access policies.

SPARC staff attended and actively participated in national and international advisory committee meetings where public access policies were discussed. As an original signatory on the Cape Town Declaration for Open Education Resources (OER), SPARC helped to inform development of a new OER advocacy coalition and forged new relationships with the OER community.

During 2009 SPARC developed a good working relationship with the Committee for Economic Development (CED), a Washington, D.C.-based think tank whose board of trustees includes several dozen university and college presidents as well as leaders in private industry. SPARC staff spoke at a National Press Club launch event for a CED report, "Harnessing Openness to Improve Research, Teaching, and Learning in Higher Education," alongside representatives from the secretary of education's office and the White House Office of Science and Technology Policy.

In response to media requests for information on public access issues, SPARC provided materials to journalists and expert sources for interviews. SPARC sources have been quoted in *The Scientist, Library Journal,* and the *Chronicle of Higher Education.* Its staff has also authored articles for various publications. For examples of SPARC in the press, see http://www.arl.org/sparc/media/inthenews/index.html.

Because change in scholarly communication is needed on a system-wide scale, SPARC continued to amplify its impact by working in collaboration with such global allies as SPARC Europe, the Canadian Association of Research Libraries, and various national and regional library associations.

Campus Education

On college and university campuses, SPARC continued to encourage and aid libraries' grassroots advocacy efforts to support open access with presentations, consulting, and new or enhanced resources. In 2009 SPARC provided more than three dozen presentations and Webcasts to library, publishing, and higher education institutions in the United States and abroad. Its staff met with faculty members, department heads, deans, and campus administrators on SPARC member campuses, at the request of SPARC member organizations, to provide information and advice on campus open access advocacy and other scholarly communication issues.

During the year SPARC created and deployed a new, targeted set of Web resources designed to support campus decision making on the process of faculty adoption of open access policies. It also established a group of faculty and library experts that provides ongoing advice and support for campus open access policy development and adoption. SPARC began work on Web resources designed to assist institutions interested in setting up funds in support of open access publishing. These resources were expected to debut in 2010.

In October 2009, in partnership with an expanded suite of organizations in the United States and internationally, SPARC sponsored the first International Open Access Week to raise awareness and highlight the research community's deep commitment to open access. Expanded from one day to a week to accommodate a wider level of participation, Open Access Week inspired events on more than 200 campuses in more than 30 countries. It was a platform for key new reports on the economic and social impacts of open access as well as the announcement of millions of dollars of new support for open access publishing.

Open Access Week activities helped strengthen ongoing education efforts and new policies were announced. The National Center for Atmospheric Research, whose researchers shared the 2007 Nobel Peace Prize for their work on climate change research, announced the first open access policy by a National Science Foundation-funded agency. Open Access Week also marked the launch of the Committee on Economic Development report "Harnessing Openness to Improve Research, Teaching and Learning in Higher Education," containing key recommendations relating to open access policies, and Trinity University in San Antonio announced its faculty open access policy.

The week-long event spurred the commitment of significant new funds to support open access publication. The Wellcome Trust, a major funder of biomedical research, announced that it would provide an additional £2 million over the next 12 months to support open access publication. The announcement followed commitments by a growing number of research universities to establish similar open access publishing funds.

There was a groundswell of support for open access by college and university students during Open Access Week. More than 5.5 million students are represented by organizations that signed the "Student Statement on the Right to Research" by October, calling for the adoption of open access policies throughout the academy.

The event was widely covered in the press and blogosphere, and contributed to significantly raising the profile of open access as an issue. SPARC has set 2010 Open Access Week for October 18–24.

To further spread the word, SPARC released "Open Access 101," a short animated video for use on campus illustrating the basic concept and its benefits. In 2009 SPARC also supported Peter Suber's work on the monthly *SPARC Open Access Newsletter*. SPARC created new members-only communication channels to connect directors with leaders in scholarly communication. It hosted two invitation-only conversations with Mike Carroll (intellectual property attorney and Creative Commons board member) and David Shulenburger (vice president for academic affairs at the Association of Public and Land-grant Universities). The popular SPARC Innovator Series continued in 2009, highlighting the efforts of key individuals and institutions in successfully promoting positive change in the scholarly communications. Profiled in 2009 were R. Preston McAfee of open textbook fame and Mike Rossner of Rockefeller University Press.

SPARC-ACRL Forum

A major component of SPARC's community outreach occurs twice a year at meetings of the American Library Association (ALA) when SPARC works with the Association of College and Research Libraries (ACRL, an ALA division) and its scholarly communication committee to bring current issues to the attention of the community. The 2009 midwinter SPARC-ACRL Forum focused on "The transformative potential of Open Educational Resources (OER)" and featured Richard Baraniuk, an architect of the Cape Town Open Education Declaration, founder of Connexions (an environment for collaboratively developing, freely sharing, and rapidly publishing scholarly content on the Web) and professor of electrical and computer engineering at Rice University; David Wiley, "chief openness officer" for Flat World Knowledge, associate professor of instructional psychology and technology at Brigham Young University, and another leader of the Cape Town Declaration; Nicole Allen, leader of the Student Public Interest Research Group's "Make Textbooks Affordable" campaign; and Mark Nelson, digital content strategist for the National Association of College Stores. The annual meeting addressed "Rough Waters: Navigating Hard Times in the Scholarly Communication Marketplace."

Headlining the event was Charles B. Lowry, executive director of the Association of Research Libraries (ARL), who reported on current fiscal year reductions to library budgets among ARL members and the continuing impact next fiscal year. Lowry was joined by Ivy Anderson, director of collection development and management, California Digital Library; Emma Hill, executive editor of the *Journal of Cell Biology* at Rockefeller University Press; and James Neal, vice president for information services and university librarian at Columbia University. The moderator, representing the ACRL Scholarly Communications Committee, emphasized the importance of current challenges and opportunities for libraries of all types and sizes.

Student Campaign

SPARC in 2009 greatly expanded its program to partner with student groups and educate the next generation of academics on issues relating to scholarly communication. It increased the scope and number organizations in the student Right to Research Coalition, which now includes organizations representing more than 6 million students. New members of the coalition include the largest student organizations in the United States and Canada (the United States Student Association and the Canadian Federation of Students) along with the National Association of Graduate and Professional Students and the International Association of Political Science Students.

All of the newly involved organizations signed the "Student Statement on the Right to Research," which serves as a point of coalescence for campus action on open access. In the statement, students express frustration with the current academic publishing system that does not allow full access to government-funded research. They make the point that students rely on access to academic journal literature for their research and education, yet many colleges have struggled with the high costs of journal subscriptions, restricting access for students and scientists alike. The statement closes with a call to action, urging universities, governments and other research funders, researchers, and additional student organizations to support open access.

SPARC held a first Student Leadership Summit in Washington, D.C., during 2009, bringing together active leaders from the new coalition to create and deploy ongoing campus education and an action agenda. Staff worked directly with coalition members on developing and enacting advocacy activities on campus and on Capitol Hill.

To further support student efforts, SPARC gave presentations at several national meetings of coalition member organizations. Work began on constructing a Right to Research Coalition Web site and supporting resources. To help students articulate the characteristics they value about the open Web and electronic communication using new media and technology, SPARC sponsored the third annual SPARKY Awards contest, which was cosponsored by Campus MovieFest, Open Video Alliance, New Media Consortium, the Center for Social Media, Students for Free Culture, and ACRL, among others.

Publisher Partnership Programs

SPARC supports and promotes useful examples of open access or other innovative publishing initiatives and participates in programs that highlight areas of common concern to libraries and not-for-profit publisher communities where collaborative action can be beneficial.

In 2009 SPARC published a paper by Raym Crow, senior consultant, SPARC Consulting Group, on the variety of business models currently used to support open access journal-publishing ventures. The paper, *Income Models for Open Access: An Overview of Current Practice,* examines the use of supply-side revenue streams (article processing fees and advertising) and demand-side models (versioning and use-triggered fees). It describes the models, evaluates the viability and financial potential of each, and gives examples of journals currently employing the various approaches. The paper was supplemented by an extensive Web resource that invites community discussion on models described as well as contributions relating to new and other models.

Crow also undertook an analysis of active university press-library publishing ventures, and published a paper of current collaborative projects. In conjunction with the research, SPARC established a Web resource in support of such collaborations, "Campus-Based Publishing Partnerships: A Guide to Critical Issues." The guide is designed to help partnering organizations establish practical governance and administrative structures, identify funding models, define objectives, and demonstrate the value of the collaboration to university administrators. The aim is to help libraries, presses, and other campus units structure successful partnerships. It reviews current library-press initiatives, describes the potential benefits of partnerships, and provides an overview of the financial and operating criteria for launching and sustaining a successful collaboration. The resource was designed in consultation with an editorial board representing university presses and libraries.

SPARC worked closely with representatives of the SCOAP3 initiative to educate the general community on the potential benefits of the proposed project and encourage library participation. It also supported efforts by the Stanford

Encyclopedia of Philosophy to build an endowment sufficient to sustain perpetual open access publication. As of March 2009, that project was nearly 80 percent toward achieving its goal of self-sustainability.

SPARC continued to assist both BioOne and Project Euclid in evolving sound, sustainable business practices needed to become leading platforms for digital dissemination of independent journals.

Business Consulting Services

SPARC provides ongoing consulting support to the library and publishing communities. Subsidized advisory services were made available to more than a dozen organizations and alternative publishing ventures in 2009.

Governance

SPARC is guided by a steering committee. Current committee members are David Carlson (chair), Southern Illinois University at Carbondale; Jun Adachi, Japanese National Institute of Informatics (for SPARC Japan); Lars Bjørnshauge, Lund University (for SPARC Europe); Faye Chadwell, Oregon State University Libraries; Maggie Farrell, University of Wyoming; Lorraine Harricombe, University of Kansas; Thomas Hickerson, University of Calgary; Paula Kaufman, University of Illinois at Urbana-Champaign; Rick Luce, Emory University; Jonathan Miller, Rollins College; Patricia Renfro, Columbia University; Lee Van Orsdel, Grand Valley State University; Jean Shipman, University of Utah; and Vicki Williamson, University of Saskatchewan.

Council on Library and Information Resources

1752 N St. N.W., Suite 800, Washington, DC 20036
202-939-4754; fax 202-939-4765
World Wide Web http://www.clir.org

Kathlin Smith
Director of Communications

The Council on Library and Information Resources (CLIR) is an independent nonprofit organization that works at the intersection of libraries, scholarship, and technology. CLIR helps organize, structure, and sustain the collaborative effort needed to realize a new digital environment for research, teaching, and learning.

CLIR is supported by fees from sponsoring institutions, grants from public and private foundations, contracts with federal agencies, and donations from individuals. CLIR's Board of Directors establishes policy, oversees the investment of funds, sets goals, and approves strategies for their achievement. In 2009 the CLIR board appointed new members Paul Courant, university librarian and dean of libraries, and professor of economics and of information at the University of Michigan; and Winston Tabb, dean of university libraries and museums, and vice provost for the arts at Johns Hopkins University. A full listing of CLIR board members is available at http://www.clir.org/about/board.html.

G. Sayeed Choudhury, Michael Keller, and Elliott Shore continued their affiliations with CLIR as senior presidential fellows in 2009. Choudhury is associate dean for library digital programs and director of the Digital Research and Curation Center at the Sheridan Libraries, Johns Hopkins University. Keller is university librarian, director of academic information resources, founder and publisher of HighWire Press, and publisher of the Stanford University Press. Shore is chief information officer and director of libraries, and professor of history at Bryn Mawr College.

Developments in 2009

DLF Rejoins CLIR

The Digital Library Federation (DLF), which was created as a CLIR program in 1995 and became independent in 2006, merged back into CLIR in July 2009. As a program within CLIR, DLF will build upon its original mission to pioneer the use of electronic technology to extend collections and services, while refocusing on issues and challenges specific to the second decade of the 21st century. The 2009 DLF Fall Forum, held in Long Beach, California, November 11–12, focused on innovation in library technology and gave participants a chance to share their views about the potential role of the new DLF program. CLIR expected to name a DLF senior program officer in spring 2010.

During 2009 CLIR continued programmatic activity within the framework of the three-year agenda established in March 2007 (http://www.clir.org/activities/agenda.htm). The agenda deepens CLIR's traditional work in scholarly communications, preservation, leadership, and the emerging library, while also strengthening their interconnections. It integrates CLIR's work more tightly with efforts to develop a cyberinfrastructure that will promote, sustain, and advance research and teaching in the humanities and social sciences. These activities are described below.

Deep Collaboration

In early 2009 CLIR began to convene meetings with a small group of research library directors who were intently motivated to experiment with new models of collaboration, usually among two or three institutions, that could redefine the concept of the research library and produce more cost-effective services and programs to improve support of research and teaching. Topics explored in these meetings include building campus cyberinfrastructures, developing connections between institutional repositories, collectively negotiating with commercial and external entities in large-scale digitization, cooperative cataloging, participating in academic and research computing roles on campus, and exploring print repository and "insurance" models, among others. As a direct consequence of the meetings, participating universities have submitted to a variety of funding sources grant proposals reflecting the topics under discussion.

Try, Use, Fail, Learn

CLIR has initiated a series of activities to promote digital scholarship through advanced computing. The activities, organized under the rubric of TrUFL (Try, Use, Fail, Learn), are directed toward four principal objectives: fostering collaboration; providing access to resources (including data, tools, capacities, and funding); supporting education and training; and enhancing communication.

To this end, CLIR supported two conferences in 2009. The first, in March, focused on the proposed Scaife Digital Library, a resource to support research in classics including undergraduate research. The second, in May, addressed machine-augmented access to multilingual corpora with particular reference to Arabic. The latter was undertaken in partnership with Tufts University and with support from the U.S. Department of Education.

In September CLIR was awarded funding from the Institute for Museum and Library Services (IMLS) to work with Tufts University on "Collaborative Planning to Support an Infrastructure for Humanities Scholarship." The project will engage scholars and academic librarians in examining the services and digital objects classicists have developed, their anticipated future needs, and the roles of libraries and other curatorial institutions in fostering the infrastructure on which the core intellectual activities of classics and many other institutions depend. In June CLIR received funding from the Andrew W. Mellon Foundation for an 18-month effort to identify and evaluate nonclassified tools developed in the intelligence community that might be useful to humanities scholars.

Open Access Feasibility Study

CLIR is partnering with Johns Hopkins University and the University of Michigan on a study to examine the feasibility of developing, operating, and sustaining an open access repository of articles from National Science Foundation (NSF)-

sponsored research. The study, funded by a $300,000 grant from NSF to Johns Hopkins Sheridan Libraries, is expected to be completed by September 2010.

The study will evaluate several approaches to establishing a repository, delineate the advantages and disadvantages of each approach, and present a recommendation to NSF. More information is available at http://releases.jhu.edu/2009/10/02/sheridan-libraries-awarded-20-million-grant.

Task Force on Digital Preservation

CLIR—along with the Library of Congress, the National Archives and Records Administration, and the United Kingdom's Joint Information Systems Committee—is an institutional participant in the Blue Ribbon Task Force on Economically Sustainable Digital Preservation and Access. The task force was created in 2007 to identify sustainable economic models for providing access to the ever-growing amount of digital information in the public interest. Funded by NSF and the Andrew W. Mellon Foundation, the task force is co-chaired by Fran Berman, director of the San Diego Supercomputer Center at the University of California, San Diego, and Brian Lavoie, research scientist and economist in OCLC's Office of Research. The task force's 17 members represent a cross section of fields and disciplines, including information and computer sciences, economics, entertainment, library and archival sciences, government, and business.

The task force's first-year report, issued in December 2008, is available at http://brtf.sdsc.edu/biblio/BRTF_Interim_Report.pdf. The group was to issue its final report early in 2010. The document will propose recommendations for sustainable economic models to support access to and preservation of digital data in the public interest.

Scholarly Communication Institute

CLIR continues to serve on the planning committee for the Scholarly Communication Institute (SCI), which in 2009 focused on spatial technologies and methodologies. SCI began in 2003 with the goal of providing an opportunity for scholars and leaders in scholarly disciplines and societies, academic libraries, information technology, and higher education administration to design, test, and implement strategies that advance the humanities through the use of innovative technologies. Since 2006 the University of Virginia has hosted SCI, which is now under the direction of Abby Smith-Rumsey. Information about SCI is available at http://www.uvasci.org.

Effects of Mass Digitization on Scholarship

With funding from the Andrew W. Mellon Foundation and in partnership with Georgetown University, CLIR continued work on a project to assess the utility to scholars of several large-scale digitization efforts. The project focuses on Google Book Search, Microsoft's Live Search Books, ACLS Humanities E-Book project, Internet Archive's text search, and the antecedent Project Gutenberg as the main sources for analysis of digitized content. CLIR commissioned four scholars from historical and literary areas of study to summarize key methodological considerations in conducting research in their disciplines, and to assess each mass digitization project under scrutiny. Their research served as the basis of a meeting in September 2009 to discuss the findings and recommendations, and to determine next steps. CLIR was to issue a public report early in 2010.

Preserving Recorded-Sound Heritage

Since 2004 CLIR has conducted work under contract with the Library of Congress and the National Recording Preservation Board in support of an ongoing study of the state of recorded-sound preservation and restoration. Recent reports have focused on copyright, with the aim of giving libraries and archives practical information on preservation and access rights, while also highlighting issues that need to be addressed at the national policy level. In March 2009 CLIR and the Library of Congress copublished *Copyright and Related Issues Relevant to Digital Preservation and Dissemination of Unpublished Pre-1972 Sound Recordings by Libraries and Archives* by June M. Besek. In September 2009 CLIR and LC copublished *Protection for Pre-1972 Sound Recordings under State Law and Its Impact on Use by Nonprofit Institutions: A Ten-State Analysis,* prepared by the Program on Information Justice and Intellectual Property, Washington College of Law, American University, under the supervision of Peter Jaszi with the assistance of Nick Lewis.

National Digital Information Infrastructure and Preservation Program

In 2009 CLIR continued to work with the Library of Congress's National Digital Information Infrastructure and Preservation Program (NDIIPP), assisting with the Blue Ribbon Task Force on Sustainable Digital Preservation and Access and with the preparation of the final report to Congress.

Faculty Research Behavior Workshops

During the year CLIR continued to offer faculty research behavior workshops, which teach library and information technology professionals ethnographic techniques that enable them to understand faculty members' work practices and how library and information services can address real faculty needs. Led by Nancy Foster, an anthropologist at the University of Rochester, the workshops have been well received, with a waiting list that continues to grow. At the time this report was prepared, CLIR had offered workshops at Wesleyan University, Kenyon College, Cornell University, George Washington University, the University of Rochester, New York University, the University of Miami, and the University of California, Berkeley.

In November CLIR launched a new series of workshops, patterned on the faculty research behavior workshops, that focus on the work practices of undergraduate students.

Leadership Through New Communities of Knowledge

In June 2009 CLIR received funding from IMLS to collaborate with the Council of Independent Colleges in launching a three-year program, "Leadership Through New Communities of Knowledge." The program will offer an array of professional development opportunities for library staff at small and midsize private colleges and universities. Program activities include convening workshops to help librarians strengthen leadership skills and enabling staff from less affluent institutions to experience work environments at other types of institutions, such as those affiliated with the Oberlin Group of libraries. In addition, the program will identify new topics for workshops to meet particular needs of library staff at small liberal arts colleges. The program will emphasize liberal arts colleges that are not well connected to the mainstream of American librarianship, including those that are members of the American International Consortium of Academic Libraries.

Frye Leadership Institute

The tenth annual Frye Leadership Institute was held May 31–June 11, 2009, at Emory University in Atlanta. The institute, which CLIR sponsors with EDU-CAUSE and Emory University, was created to develop leaders who can guide and transform academic information services for higher education. The program has trained more than 450 librarians, faculty members, and information technology experts.

Since the Frye leadership Institute welcomed its first class a decade ago, significant change has occurred in higher education. Advances in technology demand that we reconsider how a library is defined, how information technology services are organized, and how the college and university are conceptualized. A new academic ecology is emerging that has powerful implications for the organization, discovery, and communication of knowledge. This emerging academic ecology should be reflected in both the substance and the process of the Frye Leadership Institute. In 2010 the institute will take a year's hiatus so that the sponsors can develop a vigorous new program for Frye that addresses higher education's leadership needs in an era of unprecedented change.

Future of Digital Scholarship

In April 2009 CLIR and Emory University cohosted a two-day symposium, "The Future of Digital Scholarship: Preparation, Training, Curricula." The symposium brought together experts in digital scholarship—broadly construed as research, publications using digital media, and digital projects—to examine what skills are needed to undertake digital scholarship in the humanities and social sciences. Participants discussed the types of specialized coursework available to prepare students for digital research, additional types of training that would be useful, and whether specialized preparation for digital scholarship provides doctoral graduates with a competitive advantage in seeking tenure-track and other kinds of appointments in academia. A report of the meeting will be made available in 2010.

CLIR Chief Information Officers Group

CLIR facilitates a semiannual forum at which chief information officers (CIOs) of merged library and computing units in liberal arts colleges discuss issues affecting teaching and learning on their campuses. The CIOs' March 2009 meeting focused on results from MISO (Merged Information Services Organizations), a Web-based quantitative survey that measures how students, faculty, and staff use and evaluate the services and resources of colleges and universities with merged library and computing units. The CIOs have also explored strategic and tactical issues concerning cloud computing, specifically the services that have moved to the cloud and the impediments to moving more services there. In addition, members shared information about their information technology governance structures and trends in the use of technology in teaching.

Awards

Cataloging Hidden Special Collections and Archives

In November 2009 CLIR made the second round of awards in its Cataloging Hidden Special Collections and Archives program. Fourteen projects nationwide received a total of $4 million. Created in 2008 with funding from the Andrew W. Mellon Foundation, the program supports the identification and cataloging of special collections and archives of high scholarly value that are difficult or impossible to locate. Award recipients create descriptive information for their hidden collections that will eventually be linked to and interoperable with all other projects funded by this grant program.

Postdoctoral Fellowship in Academic Libraries

Now in its sixth year, the CLIR Postdoctoral Fellowship Program aims to prepare librarians and scholars for work at the intersections of scholarship, teaching, and librarianship in the emerging research environment. In 2009 eight fellows were hosted at institutions across the United States, working on projects that exploit current information technology to forge, renovate, and strengthen connections between academic library collections and their users. Host libraries benefit from the expertise of accomplished humanists and social scientists who invigorate approaches to collection use and teaching, contribute field-specific knowledge, and provide insight into the future of scholarship. Fellows have consulted on integrating library materials and resources into the classroom, designed and implemented metadata standards, curated exhibitions in libraries and museums, organized conferences and colloquia, taught courses in academic departments, authored successful grant proposals for host institutions, managed archives, created Web portals, and more.

Mellon Dissertation Fellowships

During 2009, 16 graduate students were selected to receive Mellon Dissertation Fellowships. The fellowships, now in their ninth year, are intended to help graduate students in the humanities and related social science fields pursue original-source doctoral research and gain skill and creativity in using primary source materials in libraries, archives, museums, and related repositories. The fellowships carry stipends of up to $25,000 each to support dissertation research for periods of up to 12 months. The program has supported 97 graduate students carrying out their dissertation research in a variety of public and private libraries and archives.

Zipf Fellowship in Information Management

Named in honor of A. R. Zipf, a pioneer in information management systems, the $10,000 Zipf fellowship is awarded annually to a student who is enrolled in graduate school in the early stages of study and shows exceptional promise for leadership and technical achievement in information management. The 2009 recipient was Hollie White, a doctoral student in information science at the University of North Carolina at Chapel Hill. She holds master's degrees in library and information science from the University of Illinois at Urbana-Champaign and in English from the University of Georgia. White's dissertation research focuses on the role that knowledge organization plays in large data and information environments.

Rovelstad Scholarship

Now in its seventh year, the Rovelstad Scholarship in International Librarianship provides travel funds for a student of library and information science to attend the annual meeting of the World Library and Information Congress. Katie Henningsen, a master's degree candidate at the Palmer School of Library and Information Science at Long Island University, was the 2009 recipient. The program is supported by funds from Mathilde and Howard Rovelstad.

CLIR Sponsors' Symposium

On December 16, 2009, CLIR hosted its tenth annual Sponsors' Symposium, titled "A Virtual Compass: Digital Technology and Resources as an Impetus for Change in Higher Education." The symposium examined the influence of digital technology and resources in changing curricula, strengthening scholarly communities around new research environments, facilitating the rethinking of library design and the university physical plant, and conceiving new methodological approaches to data gathering and analysis in the sciences. Special tribute was paid to Patricia Battin, first president of the Commission on Preservation and Access, for her contributions to the field of library and information services.

Publications

Archival Management Software: A Report for the Council on Library and Information Resources, by Lisa Spiro. January 2009.

The author describes and analyzes some of the major technologies that are available to librarians, curators, and archivists for cataloging archival collections, and the implications of deploying these systems for existing workflows.

Copyright and Related Issues Relevant to Digital Preservation and Dissemination of Unpublished Pre-1972 Sound Recordings by Libraries and Archives, by June M. Besek. Commissioned for and sponsored by the National Recording Preservation Board, Library of Congress. March 2009.

This report addresses the question of what libraries and archives are legally empowered to do to preserve and make accessible for research their holdings of unpublished pre-1972 sound recordings. Using examples of specific types of sound recordings, the author (1) describes the different bodies of law that protect pre-1972 sound recordings, (2) explains the difficulty in defining the precise contours of the law, and (3) provides guidance for libraries evaluating their activities with respect to these sound recordings.

Working Together or Apart: Promoting the Next Generation of Digital Scholarship. Report of a workshop cosponsored by the Council on Library and Information Resources and the National Endowment for the Humanities. March 2009.

In September 2008 CLIR, in cooperation with the National Endowment for the Humanities, held a symposium to which some 30 leading scholars were invited to address two questions:

- How do the new media advance and transform the analysis and interpretations of text, images, and other sources of interest to the humanities and social sciences and enable new expression and pedagogy?
- What questions and challenges do those processes of inquiry pose for research in computer science as well as in the humanities and social sciences?

White papers were commissioned to help frame the issues. This report contains the final versions of those papers, as well as an account of the day's discussion and a summary of a report by Diane Zorich on digital humanities centers.

Supporting Digital Tools for Humanists: Investigating Tool Infrastructure, by Katie Shilton. May 2009.

Drawing on a survey of 38 digital tools designed for use by the humanities community, this report explores the relationship between the accessibility of digital humanities tools and tools' supporting infrastructure.

Protection for Pre-1972 Sound Recordings under State Law and Its Impact on Use by Nonprofit Institutions: A Ten-State Analysis, prepared by the Program on Information Justice and Intellectual Property, Washington College of Law, American University, under the supervision of Peter Jaszi with the assistance of Nick Lewis. Commissioned for and sponsored by the National Recording Preservation Board, Library of Congress. September 2009.

This study examines criminal and civil laws of ten states, as well as judicial decisions and common law, pertaining to sound recordings fixed before 1972. The authors provide a brief history of the formulation of these laws and examine the laws and court cases that may determine the extent to which nonprofit institutions may preserve and disseminate pre-1972 recordings.

Association for Library and Information Science Education

ALISE Headquarters, 65 E. Wacker Place, Suite 1900, Chicago, IL 60601-7246
312-795-0996, fax 312-419-8950, e-mail contact@alise.org
World Wide Web http://www.alise.org

Linda C. Smith
President 2009–2010

The Association for Library and Information Science Education (ALISE) is an independent, nonprofit professional association. Its mission is to promote excellence in research, teaching, and service for library and information science (LIS) education through leadership, collaboration, advocacy, and dissemination of research.

The association was founded in 1915 as the Association of American Library Schools (AALS). In 1983 it changed its name to its present form to reflect more accurately its mission, goals, and membership.

Membership

Membership categories are personal and institutional. Personal members can include anyone who has an interest in the objectives of the association; personal membership categories are full-time (faculty member, administrator, librarian, researcher, or other interested individual); part-time (retired or part-time faculty member); and doctoral student. Institutional members are schools with programs accredited by the American Library Association (ALA) and other U.S. and Canadian schools that offer a graduate degree in library and information science or a cognate field. International affiliate institutional membership is open to any school outside the United States or Canada that offers a program to educate persons for the practice of librarianship or other information work at the professional level as defined or accepted by the country in which the school is located.

Structure and Governance

Operational groups within ALISE include the board of directors; committees; the council of deans, directors, and program chairs; school representatives; and special interest groups. Since 2006 ALISE has been managed by the Medical Library Association, with Kathleen Combs serving as ALISE executive director.

The board of directors consists of seven elected officers serving three-year terms. Officers for 2009–2010 are Linda C. Smith (University of Illinois at Urbana-Champaign), president; Lorna Peterson (University at Buffalo, the State University of New York), vice president/president-elect; Michèle V. Cloonan (Simmons College), past president; Jean Preer (Indiana University), secretary/treasurer; Melissa Gross (Florida State University), director for membership services; Susan Roman (Dominican University), director for external relations; and Andrew Wertheimer (University of Hawaii at Manoa), director for special interest groups. At the end of the January 2010 ALISE Annual Conference, Cloonan and Gross concluded their terms of service on the board and newly elected officers Lynne Howarth (University of Toronto), vice president/president-elect, and Ann Carlson Weeks (University of Maryland), director for membership services, joined the board. The board establishes policy, sets goals and strategic directions, and provides oversight for the management of the association. Face-to-face meetings are held in January in conjunction with the ALISE Annual Conference and in April to focus on strategic planning. For the remainder of the year, business is conducted through teleconferences and electronic mail.

Committees have important roles in carrying out the work of the association. Beginning in fall 2008, an open call for volunteers to serve on committees has been used to ensure broader participation in committee service, with members for the coming year appointed by the vice president/president-elect. Principal areas of activity include awards, budget and finance, conference program planning, governance, membership, nominations, publications, recruitment, research competitions, and tellers (see http://www.alise.org for a full list). Each committee is given an ongoing term of reference to guide its work as well as the specific charges for the year. Task forces can be charged to carry out tasks outside the scope of the existing standing committees. A Code of Ethics for Library and Information Science Educators Task Force, chaired by Toni Carbo (Drexel University), has been working since 2007. The task force presented a complete draft of "Ethical Guidelines for Library and Information Science Educators" at the 2010 Annual Conference with the expectation of completing the document over the coming year in response to feedback from ALISE members.

The ALISE Council of Deans, Directors, and Program Chairs consists of the chief executive officers of each ALISE institutional member school. The group convenes at the Annual Conference and can discuss issues via electronic mail in the interim. Stephen Bajjaly (Wayne State University) served as its chairperson for 2009–2010. This group provided input in formulating the ALISE comments submitted June 22, 2009, on the recommendations of the ALA Library Education Task Force in its final report issued January 13, 2009, to the ALA Executive Board for referral to the ALA Committee on Accreditation (http://www.oa.ala. org/accreditation/?page_id=61). This response sought to represent the interests of ALISE institutional members who have ALA-accredited programs or who may seek ALA accreditation in the future.

Within each institutional member school, a school representative is named to serve as a direct link between the membership and the ALISE board. These individuals communicate to the faculty of their school about ALISE and the organization's events and initiatives and provide input on membership issues to the ALISE board.

Special Interest Groups (SIGs) enable members with shared interests to communicate and collaborate, with a particular emphasis on programs at the Annual Conference. New SIGs are established as new areas of interest emerge among ALISE members. The 19 current SIGs, grouped by broad theme, are Assistant/ Associate Deans and Directors; Doctoral Students; New Faculty; Part-time and Adjunct Faculty; Curriculum; Distance Education; Teaching Methods; Archival/ Records Management Education; Gender Issues; Historical Perspectives; Information Ethics; Information Policy; International Library Education; Multicultural, Ethnic, and Humanistic Concerns; Preservation Education; Research; School Library Media; Technical Services Education; and Youth Services. SIGs are also exploring ways to connect members between conferences. For example, under the leadership of co-conveners Lauren Mandel (Florida State University) and Richard Urban (University of Illinois at Urbana-Champaign), the ALISE Doctoral Students Special Interest Group has sought to enhance communication among LIS doctoral students through both a blog (http://alisedocsig.wordpress.com) and a Facebook page.

Publications

The ALISE publications program has four components.

The *Journal of Education for Library and Information Science* (*JELIS*) is a peer-reviewed quarterly journal edited by Michelle Kazmer and Kathleen Burnett of Florida State University. In 2009 the 50th anniversary volume published a number of research articles, brief communications and discussions of research in progress, and the ALISE 2009 Best Conference Papers. The journal will continue to showcase outstanding contributed papers presented at each Annual Conference.

The editors have launched a companion Web site at http://jelis.org. Their goal is to raise the visibility of the journal and to create an interactive Web site that will engage the ALISE membership and others interested in LIS education in scholarly conversation.

ALISE has signed contracts for *JELIS* coverage in databases produced by H. W. Wilson, Gale, EBSCO, and JSTOR. With donations from the University of Illinois Library, JSTOR is adding retrospective coverage of the journal (originally published as *Journal of Education for Librarianship*) beginning with the first volume.

The *ALISE Directory of LIS Programs and Faculty in the United States and Canada* is published annually. It is now available only in electronic form to members through the ALISE Web site. Listings of faculty for each school include indications of teaching and research areas, using codes from the LIS Research Areas Classification Scheme that ALISE maintains. In consultation with the membership advisory committee and ALISE school representatives, board member Melissa Gross led a review and updating of this scheme in 2009. This resulted in the introduction of some new categories and re-labeling of some existing categories to better reflect the scope of research and teaching in ALISE member schools.

The *ALISE Library and Information Science Education Statistical Report* publishes data collected in cooperation with the ALA Committee on Accreditation. It is an annual compilation of statistical data on curriculum, faculty, students, income and expenditures, and continuing professional education. Since his appointment as ALISE statistical data manager in 2008, Danny Wallace (University of Alabama) has worked to bring publication of the annual volumes up to date. He is also planning ahead for enhancements to move from static annual reports to ongoing maintenance of a database that could support customized reporting. He recently submitted a grant proposal to the Institute of Museum and

Library Services seeking support for the design, development, and implementation of a sophisticated database system for managing all aspects of the annual statistical data-gathering process and retrospective inclusion of data for all years since 1980.

The ALISE Web site keeps members informed with posting of updates on association activities and with issues of *ALISE News,* published three times a year. Information compiled from each ALISE Annual Conference and made available on the Web site includes abstracts of papers and posters presented.

Annual Conference

The ALISE Annual Conference is held each year immediately before the ALA Midwinter Meeting. The 2010 conference drew nearly 500 attendees to Boston January 12–15 to explore the theme "Creating a Culture of Collaboration." The program co-chairpersons, Eileen Abels (Drexel University) and Deborah Barreau (University of North Carolina–Chapel Hill), put together an array of program sessions, including keynote speaker Thomas Malone, Patrick J. McGovern Professor of Management at the MIT Sloan School of Management, on "The Future of Collaboration." Two Work-in-Progress poster sessions and the Doctoral Student Research Poster Session offered opportunities to discuss a wide range of research. The Birds-of-a-Feather brown bag lunch fostered discussion of teaching various content areas. Scheduled sessions included presentation of papers, panel discussions, and SIG-sponsored programs. The first day of the conference was devoted to continuing professional development, with a workshop on online pedagogy, "Keys to Successful Online Collaboration," sponsored by the Web-based Information Science Education consortium in the morning and the ALISE Academy in the afternoon. This initiative, in its second year, is a continuing education opportunity designed to provide support and inspiration to members at all stages of their careers. Trudi Bellardo Hahn (University of Maryland) worked with her committee to plan three workshops: Launching the Research Agenda (Suzie Allard, University of Tennessee); Launching a Teaching Career (Scott Nicholson, Syracuse University); and Refreshing and Boosting a Teaching Career (Christine Jenkins and Sue Searing, University of Illinois). In addition, conference planners sought to stimulate post-conference research and teaching collaborations through the networking opportunities afforded by the conference.

The ALISE Annual Conference has an active placement service, facilitating support for job candidates through curriculum vita and portfolio reviews and scheduled interviews. Despite the economic downturn, representatives from several institutional member schools conducted interviews for open positions.

Grants and Awards

ALISE seeks to stimulate research and recognize accomplishments through its grants and awards programs. Research competitions include the ALISE Research Grant Competition, the ALISE/Bohdan S. Wynar Research Paper Competition, the ALISE/Dialog Methodology Paper Competition, the ALISE/Eugene Garfield

Doctoral Dissertation Competition, the ALISE/Linworth Youth Services Paper Award, and the OCLC/ALISE Library and Information Science Research Grant Competition.

Support for conference participation is provided by the University of Washington Information School Youth Services Graduate Student Travel Award and the Doctoral Student to ALISE Award. Awards recognizing outstanding accomplishments include the ALISE/Norman Horrocks Leadership Award (for early-career leadership), the ALISE/Pratt-Severn Faculty Innovation Award, the ALISE Service Award, the ALISE Award for Teaching Excellence, and the ALISE Award for Professional Contribution. Winners are recognized at an awards reception at the Annual Conference. [Winners of the ALISE awards are listed in "Library Scholarship and Award Recipients, 2009" in Part 3—*Ed.*]

Collaboration with Other Organizations

ALISE seeks to collaborate with other organizations on activities of mutual interest. ALISE is represented on the ALA Committee on Education (COE) by its director for external relations, Susan Roman. The association jointly sponsored a forum with COE at the 2010 ALA Midwinter Meeting on Learning Outcomes: Methodologies for Connecting Communities.

ALISE 2009–2010 President Linda Smith serves on the LSTA (Library Services and Technology Act) Reauthorization Subcommittee of the ALA Committee on Legislation. This provides an opportunity to advocate for continuing funding of the IMLS Laura Bush 21st Century Librarian Grant program, which has benefited many ALISE institutional members since the first awards were made in 2003.

Several ALISE institutional members collaborate on staffing an ALISE booth anchoring the LIS Education Pavilion area of the exhibit hall at the ALA Annual Conference each summer.

Along with ALA, ALISE is now one of a growing number of organizations that are members of the National Women's History Museum National Coalition.

ALISE is seeking to build more international connections. Toward that end, it is partnering with the International Federation of Library Associations and Institutions (IFLA) Sections on Education and Training (SET) and Library Theory and Research (LTR) and the European Association for Library and Information Education and Research (EUCLID) to organize an IFLA satellite meeting hosted by the Swedish School of Library and Information Science in Borås on August 8 and 9. The theme is "Cooperation and Collaboration in Teaching and Research: Trends in Library and Information Studies Education."

ALISE board members have served on the advisory committee for the IMLS-funded WILIS (Workforce Issues in Library and Information Science) project for which Joanne Gard Marshall (University of North Carolina–Chapel Hill) is principal investigator. ALISE is also contributing to the next phase of the study that is gathering data for several more programs beyond the six North Carolina programs that participated in the initial study (http://www.wilis.unc. edu).

Given the number of ALISE institutional members that have received grants from the IMLS Laura Bush 21st Century Librarian Program, ALISE was pleased to host a forum on measuring the program's impacts at the 2010 Annual Conference, led by IMLS staff members Carlos Manjarrez and Charles Thomas. The purpose of the forum was to provide input to shape the scope of work for the upcoming evaluation of the program.

Conclusion

As ALISE looks ahead to celebrating its centennial in 2015, the ALISE board is working with ALISE headquarters staff and the University of Illinois Archives (where the ALISE archives are housed) to ensure that records documenting the work of the association will continue to be maintained. Through its programs and the work of its personal and institutional members, ALISE is well positioned to provide leadership for library and information science education in the 21st century.

International Reports

International Federation of Library Associations and Institutions

P.O. Box 95312, 2509 CH The Hague, Netherlands
Tel. 31-70-314-0884, fax 31-70-383-4827
E-mail ifla@ifla.org
World Wide Web http://www.ifla.org

Beacher Wiggins
Director for Acquisitions and Bibliographic Access, Library of Congress

Library of Congress Representative to the Standing Committee
of the IFLA Section on Bibliography, 2005–2009

The International Federation of Library Associations and Institutions (IFLA) is the preeminent international organization representing librarians, other information professionals, and library users. During 2009 IFLA promoted high standards of provision and delivery of library and information services; encouraged widespread understanding of the value of good library and information services; and represented the interests of its members around the world. Throughout the year, IFLA promoted an understanding of libraries as cultural heritage resources that are the patrimony of every nation.

World Library and Information Congress

The World Library and Information Congress/75th IFLA General Conference and Council attracted 3,931 registered participants from 150 countries to Milan, Italy, August 23–27, 2009. The conference theme, "Libraries Create Futures: Building on Cultural Heritage," was brought to life by keynote speaker Nicoletta Maraschio, the first woman to be president of the Accademia della Crusca, founded in 1583 and still a leader in supporting research in Italian linguistics and multiculturalism. A series of "tableaux vivants" highlighted the preservation of cultural heritage from early Roman times up to contemporary digital technology.

Seventeen satellite meetings permitted intensive focus on special topics. The far-flung satellite meetings included "Service Strategies for Libraries" in Athens; "The Present Becomes the Past: Harvesting, Archiving and Presenting Today's Digitally Produced Newspapers" in Stockholm; "P3 Conference: Better Strategies for Print-Disabled People Through Partnerships with Publishers and Public Libraries" in Mechelen, Belgium, and Maastricht, the Netherlands; and "Early

Printed Books as Material Objects" in Munich. Additional satellite meetings filled the schedule in Italian cities from Bologna to Palermo.

The 2010 World Library and Information Congress—originally planned for Brisbane, Australia—will take place in Gothenburg (Göteborg), Sweden, August 10–15, followed by congresses in San Juan, Puerto Rico, in 2011 and Helsinki in 2012.

Conference of Directors of National Libraries

The Conference of Directors of National Libraries (CDNL) is an independent association that meets in conjunction with the IFLA World Library and Information Congress to promote cooperation on matters of common interest to national libraries around the world. The CDNL chair is Penny Carnaby, chief executive of the National Library of New Zealand, which hosts the CDNL secretariat. At the 2009 meeting, CDNL explored its long-term vision of a global, distributed digital library.

Response to War and Natural Disaster

In 1996 IFLA was a founding member of the International Committee of the Blue Shield (ICBS) to protect cultural property in the event of natural and human disasters. Its current partners in ICBS are the International Council on Archives, the International Council on Monuments and Sites, the International Council of Museums, and the Co-ordinating Council of Audiovisual Archives Associations. In 2009 the ICBS continued its concern for the preservation of cultural heritage in the ongoing aftermath of war in Iraq and of natural disasters such as the massive earthquake in Bam, Iran, in 2003, the Asian tsunami of December 2004, and Hurricane Katrina in August 2005. The IFLA North American regional center for preservation and conservation, hosted at the Library of Congress, continued to develop a network of colleague institutions to provide a safety net for library collections during emergencies. Rescue work for Sri Lankan and other South Asian libraries in the wake of the tsunami will continue for years to come.

Bibliographic Control

IFLA has worked steadily over the decades to improve bibliographic control, through practical workshops, support of the International Standard Bibliographic Description, and research that seeks to establish basic principles of bibliographic control and to identify areas where cataloging practice in different cultures can be harmonized to make library catalogs less expensive to produce and easier for patrons to use.

During 2009 IFLA reshaped its core activity ICABS, the IFLA-CDNL Alliance for Bibliographic Standards, into ICADS, the IFLA-CDNL Alliance for Digital Strategies, with a broader mission that also encompasses issues relating to long-term archiving, digital preservation, and rights metadata. The founding members of ICADS are the British Library, the Biblioteca Nacional de Portugal, the Deutsche Nationalbibliothek, the Library of Congress, the National Library of Australia, the National Library of New Zealand, the Koninklijke Bibliotheek (Netherlands), and the Conference of Directors of National Libraries (CDNL).

Closely related to ICADS is the separate IFLA UNIMARC Core Activity (UCA), which maintains, develops, documents, and promotes the four UNIMARC formats for bibliographic, authority, classification, and holdings data. Since 2003, when it succeeded IFLA's former Universal Bibliographic Control and International MARC program, UCA has been hosted by the National Library of Portugal. Under UCA, the Permanent UNIMARC Committee maintains the formats and also advises ICADS on matters relating to UNIMARC.

The Statement of International Cataloguing Principles was issued for worldwide review in 2008. The statement was approved by all the participants and by IFLA in January 2009. It is freely available on the IFLA Website (http://www.ifla.org) and was published in print by K. G. Saur in time for the Milan conference in August 2009. The statement was the final product of the International Meeting of Experts on an International Cataloging Code (IME ICC), a series of five regional invitational conferences planned by the IFLA Cataloguing Section to explore similarities and differences in current national and regional cataloging rules, in an attempt to clarify where variations for languages and cultural differences may be needed and where rules might be the same. The first meeting was held in Frankfurt in 2003 for experts from Europe and North America; the second took place in Buenos Aires, the third in Cairo, the fourth in Seoul, and the fifth in Pretoria, South Africa. The goal of IME ICC was to increase the ability to share cataloging information worldwide by promoting standards for the content of bibliographic and authority records used in library catalogs. At the Milan conference in 2009, Barbara Tillett, chief of the Policy and Standards Division at the Library of Congress, received the IFLA Scroll in recognition of her work on the statement.

Copyright Issues

The IFLA Committee on Copyright and Other Legal Matters (CLM) works to ensure a proper balance between the claims of intellectual property rights holders and the needs of library users worldwide. During 2009 CLM developed a list of 12 basic "Core Exceptions to Copyright" law that are essential if libraries throughout the world are to fulfill their mission of providing open access to information and knowledge for all people. The next step is to urge the World Intellectual Property Organization (WIPO) to recognize the 12 core exceptions.

At the Milan conference, a special panel presentation, "The Google Books Settlement: Love It or Leave It," educated conference attendees on the pros and cons of the proposal settlement, under which Google would continue to digitize books that were out of print but under copyright, and would fund a Book Rights Registry to compensate authors and publishers. Panelists Jonathan Band, an intellectual property lawyer and advocate who writes at policybandwith.com, Jon Orwant of Google Book Search, and Jim Neal, university librarian at Columbia University, examined the proposal from the perspectives of lawyers, Google and its partners, and libraries.

FAIFE

One of IFLA's core activities is Freedom of Access to Information and Freedom of Expression, or FAIFE, which is defined in Article 19 of the United Nations Universal Declaration of Human Rights as a basic human right.

Under FAIFE's leadership, in December 2008 the IFLA Governing Board endorsed the IFLA Manifesto on Transparency, Good Government, and Corruption, which asserts that "libraries are in their very essence transparency institutions" that counter corruption and deceit in government, and the IFLA Statement on Access to Personally Identifiable Information in Historical Records. The latter strikes a balance between individual privacy rights and long-term preservation of and access to historical documents such as census records, military service records, and wills and testaments—the raw data of historical and biographical research. In 2009 FAIFE conducted training courses, based on the IFLA Manifesto, in Russia, Peru, and the Philippines.

Grants and Awards

The federation continues to collaborate with corporate partners and national libraries to maintain programs and opportunities that would otherwise not be possible, especially for librarians and libraries in developing countries. The Jay Jordan IFLA/OCLC Early Career Development Fellowships bring library and information science professionals from countries with developing economies who are in the early stages of their careers to the OCLC headquarters in Dublin, Ohio, for four weeks of intensive experience in librarianship, followed by a week at OCLC's offices in Leiden, the Netherlands. The six fellows for 2009 were from Armenia, Kenya, Pakistan, Serbia, Uganda, and Zambia. As announced at the Milan conference, the fellows for 2010 will be from Azerbaijan, China, Egypt, Jamaica, Kenya, and Pakistan. The American Theological Library Association is the third sponsor of the program, and one of the fellows must be a theological librarian. Since its inception in 2001, the program has supported 50 librarians from developing countries.

The Frederick Thorpe Awards, established in 2003, are administered by the IFLA Libraries for the Blind Section and the Ulverscroft Foundation of Leicester, England, which Frederick Thorpe founded to support visually impaired people. The Ulverscroft Foundation renewed the program as the Ulverscroft/IFLA Best Practice Awards (Frederick Thorpe Awards) in 2006, 2007, and 2008, with no award in 2009. In September 2009 the Ulverscroft Foundation announced that it would renew its support for the awards the next year.

The Bill and Melinda Gates Foundation Access to Learning Award for 2009 was presented to the Fundación Empresas Publicas de Medellín (EPM Foundation) in Colombia for its network of public libraries. This annual award presents up to $1 million to libraries, library agencies, or comparable organizations outside the United States that have been innovative in providing free public access to information. The EPM Foundation was selected for the 2009 award, presented at the Milan conference, for its innovative use of technology in public libraries and its demonstration of ways in which libraries can contribute to the revitalization of a local community.

The IFLA International Marketing Award includes a stipend and travel to the annual IFLA Conference. In 2002, 2003, and 2004, IFLA and 3M Library Systems cosponsored the marketing awards. After a hiatus in 2005, IFLA cosponsored the awards with SirsiDynix in 2006 and 2007. The Emerald Group has sponsored the award since 2008. The Harry Campbell Conference Attendance Grant supports travel to the IFLA Conference from a developing country that has not had conference participants in recent years. The Dr. Shawky Salem Conference Grant supports conference attendance from an Arab country.

The Guust van Wesemael Literacy Prize of €3,000 is awarded biennially to a school or public library in a country with a developing economy. The recipient in 2009 was the Instituto Dois Irmãos, which works in the *favela* or depressed neighborhood of Rocinha, Rio de Janeiro, Brazil.

Membership and Finances

IFLA has more than 1,600 members in 150 countries. Initially established at a conference in Edinburgh, Scotland, in 1927, it has been registered in the Netherlands since 1971 and has headquarters facilities at the Koninklijke Bibliotheek (Royal Library) in The Hague. Although IFLA did not hold a General Conference outside Europe and North America until 1980, there has since been steadily increasing participation from Asia, Africa, South America, and Australia. The federation now maintains regional offices for Africa (in Pretoria); Asia and Oceania (in Singapore); and Latin America and the Caribbean (in Rio de Janeiro). The organization has seven official working languages—Arabic, Chinese, English, French, German, Russian, and Spanish—and offers a range of membership categories: international library associations, national library associations, other associations (generally regional or special library associations), institutions, institutional sub-units, one-person libraries, school libraries, personal affiliates, and student affiliates. Association and institution members have voting rights in the IFLA General Council and IFLA elections, and may nominate candidates for IFLA offices. Institutional sub-units, one-person libraries, school libraries, and personal affiliates do not have voting rights but may submit nominations for any IFLA office; personal affiliates may run for office. Except for personal and student affiliates, membership fees are keyed to the UNESCO Scale of Assessment and the United Nations list of least developed countries, to encourage participation regardless of economic circumstances. The IFLA Core Activity Fund is supported by national libraries worldwide.

UNESCO has given IFLA formal associate relations status, the highest level of relationship accorded to nongovernmental organizations. In addition, IFLA has observer status with the United Nations, WIPO, the International Organization for Standardization, and the World Trade Organization, and associate status with the International Council of Scientific Unions. The federation continues several follow-up activities with the World Summit on the Information Society—most recently convened in Tunis, Tunisia, in 2005—to ensure that libraries have a role in providing information and knowledge to all people.

More than two dozen corporations in the information industry have formed working relationships with IFLA as Corporate Partners, providing financial and in-kind support. Gold Corporate Partners that contributed more than €3,006 to IFLA in 2009 were OCLC, SirsiDynix, and publishers De Gruyter Saur, Elsevier, Emerald, nbd/biblion, ProQuest, and Sage.

The IFLA Foundation (Stichting IFLA) was established in 2007. The foundation accepts private donations and also is funded by all other IFLA income. It gives funding priority to proposals and projects that promise to have a long-term impact in developing and strengthening IFLA, are clearly related to at least one of IFLA's Three Pillars, and are not likely to be funded by other bodies.

The Bill and Melinda Gates Foundation's Global Libraries Program announced that beginning in 2009 it would donate $1.5 million directly to IFLA over the next three years to enable the IFLA Foundation to continue its advocacy for the world's libraries and its promotion of worldwide public access to Internet resources.

IFLA's Three Pillars: Society, Members, and Profession

The operational model for IFLA is based on the three pillars of society, membership, and professional matters. A review of IFLA's core activities conducted in 2003 and 2004 showed that all of the federation's core functions related to three strategic factors: the societal contexts in which libraries and information services operate; the membership of the federation; and the library profession.

Although the three pillars and the infrastructure of IFLA are interdependent, they can be roughly analyzed as follows: The Society Pillar focuses on the role and impact of libraries and information services in society. Activities supported by the Society Pillar include FAIFE, CLM, Blue Shield, IFLA's presence at the World Summit on the Information Society, and the advocacy office at IFLA headquarters—all activities that preserve memory, feed development, enable education and research, and support international understanding and community well-being. The Profession Pillar focuses on IFLA's role as the global voice for libraries and information services. The Members Pillar includes IFLA's member services, conferences, and publications.

The federation's operational infrastructure, consisting of IFLA headquarters, the IFLANET Web site, and the IFLA governance structure, support and receive strategic direction from the three pillars. The three pillars enable IFLA to promote its four core values: freedom of access to information and expression, as stated in Article 19 of the Universal Declaration of Human Rights; the belief that such access must be universal and equitable to support human well-being; delivery of high-quality library and information services in support of that access; and the commitment to enabling all members of IFLA to participate without regard to citizenship, disability, ethnic origin, gender, geographical location, political philosophy, race, or religion.

In 2007 and 2008 IFLA built further on the foundation of the three pillars with a new revision of the IFLA Statutes and a restructuring that reassigns the various sections to five new divisions. The new structure took effect in August 2009 at the Milan conference to reflect the increasing ease of global communications and the needs of an increasingly global membership.

Personnel, Structure, and Governance

The secretary general of IFLA is Jennefer Nicholson, former executive director of the Australian Library and Information Association. She succeeded Peter Johan Lor, who retired on September 5, 2008. Sjoerd M. J. Koopman is IFLA's coordinator of professional activities, an IFLA headquarters position. The editor of the quarterly *IFLA Journal* is J. Stephen Parker. In 2008 IFLA hired Stuart Hamilton as its first senior policy adviser for advocacy, also a headquarters position. The IFLA conference officer is Josche Ouwerkerk.

The current president of IFLA is Ellen R. Tise, senior director for library and information services, University of Stellenbosch, South Africa. She began developing the theme of her presidency with a brainstorming session in Québec City on the question "How can libraries and IFLA drive access to knowledge?" with a recognition that knowledge is generated only when information must be absorbed, processed, and internalized by individuals. "Libraries Driving Access to Knowledge" became her presidential theme when she began her two-year term as president in August 2009 at the close of the 75th World Library and Information Congress in Milan. She called for libraries and librarians to become more user-oriented and active in advocacy. Librarians must create partnerships with other societal stakeholders, other cultural heritage communities, and commercial and private enterprises and must promote awareness of the library as space and place.

Claudia Lux, director general, Zentral- und Landesbibliothek Berlin, was president from August 2007 until August 2009. With support from the German Foreign Ministry and the Goethe Institut, Lux hosted three international conferences in Berlin on free access to information during her term. The final conference took place February 19–20, 2009, on the topic "Access to Knowledge Infrastructures: Networking Through Libraries." President Lux also responded to the worldwide economic downturn of 2008 and 2009, particularly with a panel session at the Milan conference on libraries' short-term economic future.

The current president-elect of IFLA is Ingrid Parent, who had a long career at Library and Archives Canada before becoming university librarian at the University of British Columbia in Vancouver. She has adopted the theme "Convergence: Ensuring Access and Diversity for a Shared Future."

The current treasurer is Barbara Schleihagen, executive director, Deutsche Bibliotheksverband.

Under the revised 2008 IFLA Statutes, the 19 members of IFLA's Governing Board (plus the secretary general, ex officio) are responsible for the federation's general policies, management, and finance. Additionally, the board represents the federation in legal and other formal proceedings. The board is composed of the president, president-elect, treasurer, ten directly elected members, the chair of the IFLA Professional Committee, the chairs of each IFLA division, and the chair of the Standing Committee of the Management of Library Associations Section, currently Janice Lachance, chief executive officer of the U.S.-based Special Libraries Association. Current members, in addition to Tise, Parent, Schleihagen, Nicholson, and Lachance, are Helena Asamoah-Hassan (Ghana), Danielle Mincio (Switzerland), Tone Eli Moseid (Norway), Pascal Sanz (France), Donna Scheeder (United States), Paul Whitney (Canada), and Qiang Zhu (China), plus the chair and eight members of the professional committee, named below. In addition, Jesus Lau of the Universidad Veracruzana in Mexico and Sinikka Sipila of the Finnish Library Association were co-opted to the governing board in 2009 to provide special expertise.

The governing board delegates responsibility for overseeing the direction of IFLA between board meetings, within the policies established by the board, to the IFLA Executive Committee, which includes the president, president-elect, treasurer, chair of the professional committee, two members of the governing board (elected every two years by members of the board from among its elected members), and IFLA's secretary general, ex officio. The current elected governing board members of the executive committee are Lau and Sanz.

The IFLA Professional Committee monitors the planning and programming of professional activities carried out by IFLA's two types of bodies: professional groups—five divisions, forty-eight sections, and discussion groups—and core activities (formerly called core programs). The professional committee is composed of one elected officer from each division, plus a chair elected by the outgoing committee; the president, the president-elect, and the coordinator of professional activities, who serves as secretary; the chairs of the CLM and FAIFE committees, and two elected members of the governing board, currently Asamoah-Hassan and Moseid. Patrice Landry, chief of classification and indexing, Swiss National Library, chairs the professional committee.

The five divisions of IFLA and their representatives on the professional committee are I: Library Types (Steve W. Witt, United States); II: Library Collections (Ann Okerson, United States); III: Library Services (Judith J. Field, United States); IV: Support of the Profession (Michael Heaney, United Kingdom); and V: Regions (Buhle Mbambo-Thata, South Africa). The chair of the Copyright and Legal Matters Committee is Winston Tabb (United States). The chair of the Freedom of Access to Information and Freedom of Expression Committee is Kai Ekholm (Finland). A total of 44 sections focus on topical interests, such as statistics and evaluation, library theory and research, and management and marketing, or on particular types of libraries or parts of the world.

The six core activities are Action for Development through Libraries (ALP, formerly Advancement of Librarianship); Preservation and Conservation (PAC); IFLA-CDNL Alliance for Digital Strategies (ICADS); IFLA UNIMARC Core Activity, which maintains and develops the Universal MARC Format, UNIMARC; Free Access to Information and Freedom of Expression (FAIFE); and Copyright and Other Legal Matters (CLM). Two other longstanding IFLA projects are the IFLA World Wide Web site IFLANET and the IFLA Voucher Scheme, which replaced the IFLA Office for International Lending. The voucher scheme enables libraries to pay for international interlibrary loan requests using vouchers purchased from IFLA rather than actual currency or credit accounts. By eliminating bank charges and invoices for each transaction, the voucher scheme reduces the administrative costs of international library loans and allows libraries to plan budgets with less regard to short-term fluctuations in the value of different national currencies. The voucher scheme has also encouraged participating libraries to voluntarily standardize their charges for loans at the rate of one voucher for up to 15 pages.

To ensure an arena within IFLA for discussion of new social, professional, or cultural issues, the professional committee approves the formation of special interest groups for a limited time period. There currently are discussion groups for Access to Information Network/Africa (ATINA); Agricultural Libraries; E-Learning; E-Metrics; Environmental Sustainability and Libraries; Indigenous Matters; Libraries and Web 2.0; Library and Information Science Education in Developing Countries; Library History; National Organizations and International Relations; New Professionals; and Women, Information, and Libraries.

Canadian Libraries in 2009:
Copyright, Access, Economy Among Major Issues

Karen Adams
Director of Libraries, University of Manitoba

Introduction

The Conservative minority federal government led by Prime Minister Stephen Harper continued through 2009. This government planned a deficit of C$34 billion in 2009–2010, based on allocating C$16 billion to an infrastructure program to stimulate the economy.[1] On December 30, 2009, the governor general prorogued Parliament, following the prime minister's request.[2] The prorogation ended the legislative session and enabled the Conservatives to avoid a confidence vote that might have created a Liberal-New Democratic Party coalition. Parliament resumed on March 3, 2010.[3]

Canada's gross domestic product fell 1.7 percent from November 2008 to November 2009, with the largest losses in manufacturing, industrial production, and mining/oil and gas extraction. Some service industries enjoyed modest growth, including finance, insurance, and real estate; education; health care and social assistance; and public administration.[4]

By December the Canadian dollar had recovered to US$.955.[5]

Libraries of all types saw an impact on their operating budgets, although federal and provincial infrastructure funds supported capital projects in several provinces. In April the government of Alberta announced a 39 percent increase in public library funding, with C$7 million going directly to library boards and systems.[6] In the neighboring province of British Columbia, the provincial government ended a summer of speculation by announcing a 22 percent cut in funding to public libraries, citing health care and education priorities.[7] On average, provincial grants represented 10 percent of library operating budgets in that province. Vancouver City Council responded in December by raising property taxes 2.6 percent in order to avoid cuts to library services and hours.[8] The British Columbia province-wide virtual reference service was discontinued,[9] but then extended to June of 2010 in recognition of the fact that school children were the primary users of the service.[10] In Manitoba, the provincial government announced an increase of C$5.8 million to public libraries to support operating and collections costs, and the acquisition of technology.[11] Early in 2009 the Ontario government announced C$5 million to license electronic resources, made available through all publicly funded libraries.[12] Joint federal and provincial infrastructure grants totaling nearly C$41 million were awarded for renovation and construction of public libraries.[13] In addition to that total, Toronto (Ontario) Reference Library was awarded C$3 million in federal funds for architectural renovations.[14] In Quebec, provincial funding of C$4.85 million was awarded to convert a historic church into a new library.[15] On the east coast, the federal government awarded C$18.3 million, the province C$13 million, and the municipal government C$23.7 million toward a new Halifax Central Library.[16]

Following its previous fiscal year announcement of C$15 million, the Ontario government allocated an additional C$10 million for school libraries to purchase new books from Ontario-based suppliers.[17] However, the Toronto District School Board cut its teacher-librarian staffing.[18] In New Brunswick, the government reversed its decision to cut 588 jobs for library assistants and student support staff across the province's schools.[19]

Copyright

It was another year of intense activity around copyright in 2009, with the year again ending without changes to the federal legislation. Throughout the year the business and entertainment lobbyists (groups such as the Canadian Motion Picture Distributors Association, the Canadian Recording Industry Association, Microsoft/Entertainment Software Association, and the Canadian Chamber of Commerce) held regular meetings with politicians and senior officials who were influential in the copyright file.[20] The gaming industry, through the Entertainment Software Association of Canada, entered the fray in April, seeking stronger protection of intellectual property.[21] In early February Canadian Heritage Minister James Moore indicated that new copyright legislation might be released in the fall.[22] In July Tony Clement, minister of industry, and James Moore, minister of Canadian heritage and official languages, announced a nationwide copyright consultation process that began in July and concluded in September.[23] In addition to meetings, anyone could participate through a Web site.[24] However, no bill resulted.

Interest in the Anti-Counterfeiting Trade Agreement (ACTA) continued to grow, supported by a roundtable consultation in April. During the consultation, government reassured participants that ACTA was not about such matters as extending the term of protection for copyright, weakening privacy laws, or filtering Internet traffic for infringing copyright works,[25] but the fact that the draft text had still not been made public remained a concern. For example, reports in November indicated that Internet service providers might be required to filter material believed to be infringing copyright and to report the names of customers associated with these activities.[26]

Canadians also followed the Google Book settlement with interest, with the result that representatives of the Canadian library community (the Canadian Association of Research Libraries, the Canadian Library Association, the Canadian Research Knowledge Network, and the Canadian Urban Libraries Council) met with representatives of Google, Inc. in June.[27]

A long-standing copyright class action suit was resolved, with three Canadian publishers ending the suit by agreeing to pay C$11 million to freelance writers. The suit initially challenged the republication in electronic media of articles originally published in print. The Supreme Court had ruled in 2006 that if the reproductions were complete and accurate, no extra payments to the authors were required. The continuing suit sought compensation for work sold through databases where the reproductions were not true to the original.[28]

The Copyright Board issued a new K–12 education tariff in June, covering the years 2005–2008. The tariff set out a rate of C$5.16 per student, with a 10 percent discount applied in the first four years, requiring school boards to pay

C$4.64 per student to Access Copyright, the Canadian print collective. The full tariff became effective in 2009; it represented a 111 percent increase over the previous tariff of C$2.45 per student.[29]

Another copyright collective, the Neighbouring Rights Collective, sought payment from gyms for the use of music on their premises. Gyms already paid a tariff to the Society of Composers, Authors, and Music Publishers of Canada; the second fee would go to performing artists and record companies.[30]

The Conference Board of Canada (CCB), a well-respected research group, withdrew three reports on copyright and intellectual property after line-by-line review to compare their work with reports from the International Intellectual Property Alliance (IIPA), a coalition of U.S.-based publisher, entertainment, film, and music associations. CCB reports repeated whole paragraphs from the IIPA documents and contained unverified data with respect to the amount of piracy taking place in Canada.[31]

In Hamilton, Ontario, four people were charged with selling infringing copies of movies on DVD at local flea markets.[32] Other intellectual property cases involved pirated DVDs[33] and pirated video games.[34]

Access to Information

In July, as part of its economic stimulus package, the federal government announced a C$225 million (over three years) program, Broadband Canada, to fund 50 percent of the costs of providing broadband access to the 81 percent of rural homes that didn't have it.[35] However, the fall 2008 pre-election promise was to spend C$500 million.[36] The federal government partnered with the province of Ontario to make C$110 million available to build a broadband network in eastern Ontario.[37] Before the formation of Broadband Canada, C$1.7 million was awarded to bring broadband to 43 communities in Gaspésie, Quebec.[38] Communities in Nunavut saw improvements to the existing network that allowed more subscribers to join.[39]

Prince Edward Island announced completion of its province-wide broadband rollout costing C$8.2 million.[40] New Brunswick used C$13 million of its own funds pursuing its goal of making available affordable high-speed Internet access to every resident regardless of location. The program also decreased costs for rural and low-density region residents.[41] In Saskatchewan, crown corporation SaskTel committed C$200 million to expanding its networks to provide high-speed Internet everywhere in the province, and cellular coverage to 98 percent of its residents.[42]

The federal government's Community Access Program continued to support existing sites, many of them in rural public libraries, with priority still being given to those on the wrong side of the digital divide.[43]

Canada's privacy commissioner was instrumental in forcing Facebook to improve its privacy safeguards to make it more compliant with Canadian privacy legislation. One of the issues was the capability of third-party software developers (creating such applications as games and quizzes for the site) to see virtually all of the personal information of users. Facebook planned changes so that users will have control over the information that an application can access; the application will have to get express consent for each category of personal information it wants to use.[44]

Early in the year, the National Research Council announced a 70 percent cut to Canada's national science library, the Canada Institute for Scientific and Technical Information (NRC-CISTI). In addition to the impact on the national library's service, NRC-CISTI's publishing arm will be privatized.[45] On the positive side, NRC-CISTI continued with its plan to establish PubMed Central Canada (PMC Canada) as a national digital repository of peer-reviewed health and life sciences literature. This supported the policy on access to research outputs of the Canadian Institutes of Health Research (CIHR), which requires grant recipients to have their publications freely accessible online within six months of publication.[46] In British Columbia, the provincial agency supporting health research, the Michael Smith Foundation for Health Research, adopted a policy similar to that of CIHR on access to research outputs.[47] At the institutional level, the University of Ottawa launched a comprehensive open access program that included an institutional repository, an author fund, a fund to put digital educational materials online, support for the University of Ottawa Press's commitment to publishing open access books, and a research grant on the subject of open access.[48]

A less positive development on the open access front saw the publisher of the *Canadian Medical Association Journal* announce its intention to move from open access back to a subscription model.[49]

Censorship

Censorship was a minor focus during 2009, with most of the cases emanating from schools in Toronto. In January Margaret Atwood's *The Handmaid's Tale* was challenged by a parent on the grounds of foul language, anti-Christian overtones, violence, and sexual degradation. The student involved was assigned another book.[50] A similar resolution followed a complaint about Harper Lee's *To Kill a Mockingbird.*[51]

In Ottawa, three books on sex education were challenged but retained by the public library.[52]

Vancouver Public Library cancelled a booking by Exit International, a right-to-die organization, on the grounds that the event risked breaching the Criminal Code; the workshop was held in a church instead.[53]

Studies

Early in the year, Booknet Canada announced an increase in first quarter 2009 retail book sales compared with 2008, reporting volume up 6.7 percent and value up 5 percent despite the faltering economy and the anticipated post-Christmas slump.[54]

Interest in data on various aspects of Internet use continued. June 2009 data from the Organisation for Economic Co-operation and Development (OECD) indicated that Canada ranked first among G7 countries in terms of the number of broadband users per hundred population, and was tenth in the world. However, Canada was fourteenth in terms of monthly costs and twenty-fourth out of thirty in terms of speed.[55] The Canadian Council on Learning (CCL) found that 85 percent of Canadian households had access to broadband services in 2007, with the greatest access in Ontario and Quebec and the lowest in Alberta and New Brunswick. CCL also found that dial-up access was more prevalent than broadband in rural and remote communities, with only 17 percent of aboriginal communities having broadband access.[56] Two studies looked at what Canadians did when they went online. MSN and Harris/Decima found that 8 out of 10 Canadians spend at least an hour a day online for personal reasons, and 45 percent spend three hours or more online daily—possibly because 9 out of 10 Canadians have more than one online account to check and update.[57] Hitwise used April 2009 data to determine that the largest category of Canadian use of the Internet was search engines, followed by social networking and forums. Least-used categories were music and government.[58]

The Public Interest Advocacy Centre and Environics Research held focus groups to determine public awareness of net neutrality issues, and found that while consumers were not aware of the debate around net neutrality, they were concerned about such related issues as universal access, privacy, censorship, and the commercialization of the Internet.[59]

Two provinces conducted studies of libraries. In Ontario, the government commissioned a report, "Third Generation Public Libraries," intended to position public libraries for 2020. The report found that public libraries have strong roles in literacy and learning, innovation, community, and prosperity.[60] Also in Ontario, the Ontario Library Association commissioned a study of school libraries, "Exemplary School Libraries in Ontario," which documented four major challenges that prevent school libraries from becoming exemplary: funding, the absence of provincial policy to ensure libraries in every school, lack of awareness on the part of personnel in the educational system on how school libraries can contribute to better education, and the need for teacher-librarians to cover preparation time for other teachers. The study also found that since 1997–1998 there has been a 31 percent drop in the percentage of elementary schools with teacher-librarians.[61] In Quebec, the provincial government conducted the first-ever province-wide survey of Quebecers with respect to the library system. Findings included the importance of libraries as a cultural resource; mechanisms for improving service, such as longer open hours; and the expectation that enhanced digital libraries can improve access and services. About 40 percent of Quebecers are regular library users.[62]

The National Research Council's CISTI completed and released a gap analysis of Canada's stewardship of research data. The study found that significant amounts of data were being lost. Major areas where the gap between what exists and the ideal state included funding, well-defined roles and responsibilities, the existence of trusted digital repositories, skills and training, reward and recognition systems, and preservation.[63]

Following the fall 2008 event, the Canadian Library Association released the document *National Summit on Library Human Resources: Report*. The report outlined priority themes for action: a national internship program, leadership development programs or institutes, a competencies-based approach (list of competencies, curriculum, and training related to these competencies), an online or distance education program, and a national recruitment campaign.[64]

Events

In Prince Edward Island, the Montague Public Library opened new library space, which increased the library by a factor of five. Community volunteers moved the collections to the new space, which is home to a "reading lighthouse" for children.[65]

The Augustana campus of the University of Alberta opened its new library in September 2009 after two years of construction. The new library has 100 computer workstations, and has a view of the campus ravine.[66]

In February the University of Alberta became the first Canadian governing member of CLOCKSS (Controlled Lots of Copies Keeps Stuff Safe), a multi-site dark archive of digital content.[67] Also on the digital front, on June 1, 2009, Canadiana.org launched the digital collection builder, an open source software that provides tools to enable organizations of all sizes to provide access to digitized collections. Funding for the project came from the federal government.[68] Earlier in the year, the National Business Archives of Canada was launched in Toronto as a nonprofit organization with a goal of commemorating the events that have shaped Canadian business history, beginning with the incorporation of the Hudson's Bay Company in 1670.[69]

The National Film Board of Canada made a number of its films freely available on its Web site, as well as sending DVD sets of selected films on the history of Quebec City to schools and public libraries across Canada.[70]

Supporters of the Portrait Gallery of Canada who had been hoping that the federal government would provide a new building and distinct identity for the gallery— possibly outside Ottawa—were disappointed[71] with the announcement that the collection would continue as a program of Library and Archives Canada (LAC).[72]

In June LAC also announced a moratorium on buying print collections. Current Canadian publications have been subject to legal deposit, but LAC normally spent approximately C$1 million a year on works that predate legal deposit or were published outside Canada.[73]

The economy affected BookExpo Canada, the annual trade show of the Canadian book industry. The June event was cancelled following the withdrawal of three major Canadian publishers and noting the decline in the number of booksellers as Chapters/Indigo continued to replace independent booksellers.[74] Funding cuts also ended the Audio-Visual Preservation Trust, whose mission had been the preservation of historic Canadian music and film.[75] At the same time, LAC began construction of a new C$17 million storage facility for nitrate-based film and for photo negatives.[76]

Richmond Hill (Ontario) Central Library was closed for two weeks because of flooding, probably caused by the library's hot-water heating system. Some 30,000 books suffered water damage.[77] Whitehorse (Yukon) Public Library unveiled its plans for a new library with twice the current usable space, to be completed in 2012.[78]

The University of Guelph hosted Ontario's first "Living Library" over two days in March. The "books" in the Living Library were people who might encounter prejudice, stereotyping, or social exclusion.[79]

Toronto Public Library received its largest donation ever in the form of a C$3 million gift from the Bluma Appel Community Trust in support of the

Toronto Public Library Foundation's "re:vitalize" campaign. The new 16,800 square foot state-of-the-art event space at the Toronto Reference Library was named the Bram & Bluma Appel Salon.[80]

The Bibliothèque et Archives Nationales du Québec (BAnQ) acquired a unique set of letters dating from 1686, detailing life in New France from the perspective of a merchant. BAnQ planned to digitize them.[81]

The Inuvik Centennial Library (Northwest Territories) continued its unique history local project of collecting funeral and memorial literature, funded by a donation received in 2002. Communities involved included Inuvik, the Beaufort Delta, and Tuktoyaktuk.[82]

And the Lyn Public Library (Ontario) received an overdue dictionary from across the Canada/U.S. border—only 110 years late. The fine came to more than $9,000 but it was waived.[83]

Initiatives

NRC Canada Institute for Scientific and Technical Information (NRC-CISTI) announced its collaboration with Google Scholar to provide access to scientific, technical, and medical (STM) journal articles from NRC-CISTI's Discover collection through Google Scholar.[84]

The Saskatchewan Information and Library Services Consortium (SILS) went live in its first location, Saskatoon Public Library. The installation of the single integrated library system in all public libraries has a completion date of year end 2010. This will support the use of a single library card across those libraries.[85]

The Ontario Council of University Libraries announced its geospatial portal, which will provide storage capacity for large geospatial and health data sets for all Ontario universities, along with the capacity to do further research and analysis of the data.[86]

In British Columbia, a consortium of public libraries, schools, the Association of Book Publishers of British Columbia, the Educational Resources Acquisition Consortium, and the British Columbia Electronic Library Network announced a project, Best of B.C. Books Online, that will purchase electronic rights to nonfiction books published in the province and make them available to schools and libraries.[87]

In September libraries in Nova Scotia, as part of their Libraries Nova Scotia project, launched their BARA (Borrow Anywhere Return Anywhere) initiative. Participants include public, community college, and university libraries.[88]

Schools in Calgary announced plans to include iPods and other smart phones in their classrooms and libraries, with the goal of teaching students to use them productively as a learning tool.[89]

Libraries in York (New Brunswick) Regional Library successfully tested Playaway Audio Books, a compact audio format each containing a single title, and continued to build that collection.[90]

The Saint John (New Brunswick) Free Public Library launched a service from the bus terminal that let bus riders take a book with them. The goal of the service was to promote reading and the sharing of books with other readers/riders.[91]

A unique fund-raising event in Kingsville (Ontario) saw some 80 people build a house to be sold to the public, with the profits supporting local community facilities, including the public library.[92]

Sources

1. http://www.ic.gc.ca/eic/site/ic1.nsf/eng/h_04567.html.

2. http://www.parl.gc.ca/common/index.asp?language=e.

3. http://www.parl.gc.ca/common/index.asp?language=e.

4. http://www.statcan.gc.ca/daily-quotidien/100129/dq100129a-eng.htm.

5. http://www.bankofcanada.ca/en/rates/exchange-avg.html.

6. http://alberta.ca/home/NewsFrame.cfm?ReleaseID=/acn/200904/25715AF69E6BB-BADC-ACB8-B247942628738419.html.

7. http://www.libraryjournal.com/article/ca6685299.html.

8. http://www.theglobeandmail.com/news/national/property-tax-boost-to-help-libraries/article1406335.

9. http://www.bcla.bc.ca/page/news/ezlist_item_9876d4e5-5660-4990-af2b-b32d89fb46ad.aspx?_s=http%3a%2f%2fwww.bcla.bc.ca%2fpage%2fnews.aspx.

10. http://www.bcla.bc.ca/page/news/ezlist_item_21b7a642-a318-46be-a27e-347a10fdc731.aspx?_s=http%3a%2f%2fwww.bcla.bc.ca%2fpage%2fnews.aspx.

11. http://www.gov.mb.ca/chc/press/top/2009/05/2009-05-07-091900-5782.html.

12. http://www.accessola.com/olba/bins/content_page.asp?cid=66-827-2861.

13. http://accessola.com/olba/bins/content_page.asp?cid=2051-3647.

14. http://www.theglobeandmail.com/news/national/toronto/toronto-reference-library-gets-3-million-federal-boost/article1327716.

15. http://www.banq.qc.ca/a_propos_banq/communiques/2009/com_2009_11_11.html?bnq_langue=en.

16. http://www.apla.ca/bulletin/73/2.ns.

17. http://www.news.ontario.ca/edu/en/2009/09/one-million-new-books-in-school-libraries.html.

18. http://www.accessola3.com/index.php?autocom=blog&blogid=9&showentry=599.

19. http://www.cbc.ca/canada/new-brunswick/story/2009/07/10/library-jobs.html.

20. http://www.ocl-cal.gc.ca/eic/site/lobbyist-lobbyiste1.nsf/eng/h_nx00274.html.

21. http://www.canada.com/story_print.html?id=1523774&sponsor=.

22. http://www.straight.com/article-200814/james-moore-says-copyright-reform-bill-likely-fall.

23. http://www.jamesmoore.ca/EN/news_releases/government_of_canada_launches_national_consultations_on_copyright_modernization.

24. http://copyright.econsultation.ca/topics-sujets/show-montrer/29.

25. http://www.international.gc.ca/trade-agreements-accords-commerciaux/fo/discussion_summary-resume.aspx?lang=eng.

26. http://www.calgaryherald.com/business/Canada+talks+over+copyright+laws+with+bite/2189494/story.html.

27. http://www.carl-abrc.ca/publications/elert/2009/elert332-e.html.

28. http://www.theglobeandmail.com/servlet/story/RTGAM.20090505.wsettle05art2141/BNStory/National/home.

29. http://www.cb-cda.gc.ca/decisions/2009/20090626-nr-e.pdf.

30. http://www.cbc.ca/arts/story/2009/08/25/gym-royalty.html?ref=rss.

31. http://license.icopyright.net/user/viewFreeUse.act?fuid=NzA1OTczMw%3D%3D.

32. http://www.rcmp-grc.gc.ca/on/news-nouvelles/2009/09-01-28-ham-fep-pelf-eng.htm.

33. http://www.rcmp-grc.gc.ca/on/news-nouvelles/2009/09-05-06-gta-rgt-fes-pelf-eng.htm.

34. http://www.rcmp-grc.gc.ca/on/news-nouvelles/2009/09-11-05-gta-rgt-fes-pelf-eng.htm.

35. http://www.pm.gc.ca/eng/media.asp?id=2703.

36. http://www.cbc.ca/news/canadavotes/story/2008/10/11/broadband-conservative.html.

37. http://www.news.ontario.ca/omafra/en/2009/07/canada-and-ontario-invest-in-broadband-access-for-eastern-ontario.html.

38. http://news.gc.ca/web/article-eng.do?m=/index&nid=430139.

39. http://www.leonaaglukkaq.ca/EN/8931/102504.

40. http://www.itu.int/ITU-D/ict/newslog/Bell+Aliant+Completing+Prince+Edward+Broadband+Rollout+Launches+Rural+Broadband+Fund+Canada.aspx.

41. http://www.dailybusinessbuzz.ca/2009/06/09/nb-timeline-released-for-high-speed-internet.

42. http://www.gov.sk.ca/news?newsId=3483cf76-a6f7-47fc-9eaa-7ddbbc30cf4f.

43. http://www.ic.gc.ca/eic/site/cap-pac.nsf/eng/home.

44. http://www.priv.gc.ca/media/nr-c/2009/let_090827_e.cfm.

45. http://datalibre.ca/2009/03/17/cuts-to-cisti-mean-less-access-to-science-data.

46. http://www.nrc-cnrc.gc.ca/eng/news/nrc/2009/07/06/pubmed-cisti.html.

47. http://www.earlham.edu/~peters/fos/2009/08/new-oa-mandate-from-bc-canada-health.html.

48. http://oa.uottawa.ca.

49. http://www.cmaj.ca/cgi/content/full/181/11/E245.

50. http://www.cbc.ca/arts/books/story/2009/01/16/atwood-complaint.html?ref=rss.

51. http://www.parentcentral.ca/parent/article/705792.

52. http://www.canada.com/news/Chief+librarian+defends+purchase+instruction+books/1842563/story.html.

53. http://www.cbc.ca/canada/british-columbia/story/2009/11/04/bc-right-to-die-exit-international.html.

54. http://www.booknetcanada.ca/mambo/index.php?option=com_content&task=view&id=431&Itemid=232.

55. http://www.oecd.org/document/4/0,3343,en_2649_34225_42800196_1_1_1_1,00.html.

56. http://www.ccl-cca.ca/CCL/Reports/CLI/CLI2009/2009Factsheet13.htm.

57. http://news.microsoft.ca/press_releases_consumer/archive/2009/03/11/canadians-are-connected-but-not-happy-with-their-fragmented-online-world.aspx.

58. http://weblogs.hitwise.com/us-heather-hopkins/2009/05/how_canadians_spend_their_time.html.

59. http://www.piac.ca/telecom/canadian_consumers_need_more_net_neutrality.

60. http://www.culture.gov.on.ca/english/library/newman_study.htm.

61. http://www.peopleforeducation.com/school-libraries.

62. http://www.banq.qc.ca/portal/dt/a_propos_banq/communiques/2009/com_2009_11_11.jsp?bnq_langue=en.

63. http://data-donnees.gc.ca/eng/news/gap_analysis.html.

64. http://www.cla.ca/AM/Template.cfm?Section=Home&TEMPLATE=/CM/ContentDisplay.cfm&CONTENTID=7131.

65. www.apla.ca/bulletin/73/2.pe.

66. http://www.library.ualberta.ca/augustana/newlibrary.

67. http://blogs.library.ualberta.ca:80/libnews/?p=1105.

68. http://www.canadianheritage.gc.ca/pc-ch/infoCntr/cdm-mc/index-eng.cfm?action=doc& DocIDCd=CR090442.

69. http://www.businessarchives.ca.

70. http://www.nfb.ca.

71. http://www.cbc.ca:80/arts/story/2009/09/10/ottawa-portrait-gallery-of-canada-cancelled. html.

72. http://www.collectionscanada.gc.ca/whats-new/013-415-e.html.

73. http://www.cbc.ca/arts/story/2009/06/18/pei-archives-paper-digital.html#socialcomments.

74. http://www.cbc.ca/arts/books/story/2009/02/02/bookexpo-cancelled.html?ref=rss.

75. http://www.thestar.com/entertainment/article/733276—trust-folds-puts-canuck-film-music-in-peril.

76. http://www.cbc.ca/arts/film/story/2009/08/04/film-preservation.html?FORM=ZZNR2.

77. http://www.theliberal.com/article/88643.

78. http://whitehorsestar.com/archive/story/new-library-to-offer-21st-century-services.

79. http://www.uoguelph.ca/news/2009/02/post_178.html.

80. http://www.revitalizetrl.ca/news_releases.php.

81. http://www.ledevoir.com/2009/05/28/252442.html.

82. http://www.nnsl.com/frames/newspapers/artpage2010/aug21_09mem-arts.html.

83. http://www.theweek.com/article/index/95426/A_9000_library_fine_and_more.

84. http://cisti-icist.nrc-cnrc.gc.ca/eng/ibp/cisti/newsletters/cisti-news/2009april.html#a1.

85. http://www.slaforum.sk.ca/index.php/slaforum/article/view/116.

86. http://130.15.161.74/library/news/story/09/07/13/ontario-council-university-libraries-ocul-announces-new-geospatial-data-.

87. http://www.theglobeandmail.com/news/technology/article971319.ece.

88. http://librariesns.ca/content/borrow-anywhere-return-anywhere-bara.

89. http://www.cbc.ca/canada/calgary/story/2009/10/09/calgary-school-libraries-ipods.html.

90. http://www.apla.ca/node/226.

91. http://www.cbc.ca/canada/new-brunswick/story/2009/07/29/nb-bus-library-402.html.

92. http://www.cbc.ca/canada/windsor/story/2009/09/17/kingsville-extremebuild-091909.html.

Canadian Library Association

328 Frank St., Ottawa, ON K2P 0X8
613-232-9625, fax 613-563-9895
E-mail info@cla.ca
World Wide Web http://www.cla.ca

Kelly Moore
Executive Director

The Canadian Library Association/Association Canadienne des Bibliothèques (CLA) is Canada's major national professional association for the library and information community. It is predominantly English-language, with selected activities also in French. Its mission reads: "CLA is my advocate and public voice, educator and network. We build the Canadian library and information community and advance its information professionals."

Founded in 1946, CLA is a federally incorporated not-for-profit organization. It is governed by a 12-person executive council, which is advised by appointed standing committees and as-needed task forces.

Membership is composed both of individuals (librarians and other information professionals and library board trustees) and of institutions (mainly libraries, but also suppliers to the library and information community).

Much of CLA's work is done through its five divisions:

- Canadian Association of College and University Libraries (CACUL), which includes the Community and Technical College Libraries (CTCL) section
- Canadian Association of Public Libraries (CAPL), which includes the Canadian Association of Children's Librarians (CACL) section
- Canadian Library Trustees Association (CLTA)
- Canadian Association for School Libraries (CASL)
- Canadian Association of Special Libraries and Information Services (CASLIS)

There are CLA Student Chapters at six English-language library and information science post-graduate programs in Canada, and there is a student chapter at one library technician program.

To facilitate sharing of information in specific areas of interest, CLA has 19 interest groups focusing on topics as diverse as access to government information, action for literacy, library and information needs of native people, and new librarians and information professionals.

Governance

In May 2009 the role of CLA president was assumed by John Teskey, director of libraries at the University of New Brunswick. He succeeded Ken Roberts, chief librarian of the Hamilton Public Library, who had served as president since May 2008.

Serving as officers for 2009–2010 in addition to Teskey are Vice President Keith Walker, Treasurer Ingrid Langhammer, and CLA Executive Director Kelly Moore.

Major Activities

CLA continues to lead a variety of national advocacy initiatives and to offer professional development opportunities. Major activities have focused on these two elements, with additional efforts directed at a number of other important issues.

Advocacy and Public Awareness

Canada Post decided to maintain the Library Book Rate for 2010 with no increase in costs. CLA supported MP Merv Tweed (Brandon-Souris) on the introduction of his private member's bill (C-322) to create legislation supporting the rate, and CLA continues to encourage members to sign petitions for Tweed to present to Parliament.

CLA met with members of parliament and officials and staff in federal government ministries to raise awareness of key issues, including copyright and infrastructure resources for libraries. It also worked in concert with staff at Library and Archives Canada and the Canadian National Institute for the Blind on the development of the Initiative for Equitable Library Access.

CLA has been monitoring national and international developments in the area of copyright and related rights. The Canadian government introduced new copyright legislation in 2009, but it did not make it through Parliament; CLA was awaiting reintroduction of the bill in 2010.

The association continued to spearhead Canadian Library Month/Le Mois Canadien des Bibliothèques, partnering with provincial, regional, and territorial library associations and governments. Under the theme "Your Library Your World" with the tagline "Now More Than Ever," this bilingual collection of events helped raise awareness during 2009 of all types of libraries—public, academic, school, and special—and their roles in difficult economic times. Governor General Michaëlle Jean applauded library staff and volunteers and the "wonderful adventure" of reading.

New Position Statement

Being the voice of the Canadian library and information community involves CLA in setting out formal positions on issues of importance to that community. The association adopted one new position statement on April 20, 2009, advocating that any appointments to the position of Librarian and Archivist of Canada be a librarian or an archivist with recognized professional qualifications.

Continuing Professional Development

CLA's major contribution to continuing professional development continues to be its National Conference, which took place in May 2009 in Montreal.

International Activities

Following on from the successful World Library and Information Congress of the International Federation of Library Associations and Institutions (IFLA) in Quebec City in August 2008, CLA has maintained strong contact with the international library community. CLA President John Teskey and Executive Director Kelly Moore attended the 2009 IFLA Congress in Milan, Italy, as did a large number of CLA members who are engaged in IFLA's professional units. The Canadian library community celebrated the election of Ingrid Parent as Canada's first president-elect of IFLA; she will assume presidency of the federation in August 2011. CLA provided support to IFLA for various international advocacy initiatives, including work on the adoption by UNESCO of the IFLA Multicultural Library Manifesto, and efforts with WIPO on copyright issues.

Communications

As information professionals, Canadian librarians depend on timely and attractive publications and resources from their professional association; and those outside the community look to the major national association as a significant source of information.

CLA's bimonthly publication, *Feliciter,* published since 1956, continues to explore core themes in the library community: e-resources and the digital divide, retirement and second careers, information literacy and security. The *CLA Digest* is a biweekly e-newsletter for members, with links to more in-depth news.

Awards and Honors

CLA recognized individuals from the library and information community with awards and honors in 2009.

CLA's most significant award is for Outstanding Service to Librarianship. It is presented only when there is a candidate worthy to receive it. In 2009 CLA presented the award to Barbara Clubb, city librarian for the Ottawa Public Library.

The 2009 CLA Award for the Advancement of Intellectual Freedom was presented to Kim Bolan, longtime reporter for the *Vancouver Sun.* Since 1988, the award has recognized outstanding contributions to intellectual freedom of individuals and groups, both in and outside the library community.

The CLA/Ken Haycock Award—established in honor of educator, administrator, advocate, and former CLA President Ken Haycock—honors an individual for demonstrating exceptional success in enhancing public recognition and appreciation of librarianship. The 2009 recipient was Karen Lindsay, a teacher-librarian at Reynolds Secondary School in Victoria, B.C.

The CLA/Information Today Award for Innovative Technology went to the Pictou-Antigonish Regional Library. The award was given in recognition of *Lobster Fishing on the Susan B,* a digital story book.

The CLA/3M Canada Award for Achievement in Technical Services was presented to the University of Prince Edward Island Robertson Library's "Open Sourcing the Serials Workflow" project.

The CLA 26th annual Student Article contest was won by Manuela Boscenco for "Strictly Business: Providing Access to Digital Images."

Conclusion

CLA celebrated a number of successes in 2009 in the areas of advocacy and professional development, which members identified as priorities. Through achieving tangible success with government on some key files, continued progress in increasing public awareness of the role and importance of libraries and literacy, and taking public positions on critical issues in the library and information community, CLA more than fulfilled its mission during the year.

Special Libraries Association

331 South Patrick St., Alexandria, VA 22314
703-647-4900, fax 703-647-4901
E-mail sla@sla.org
World Wide Web http://www.sla.org

Janice R. Lachance
Chief Executive Officer

Founded in 1909 and headquartered in Alexandria, Virginia, the Special Libraries Association (SLA) is a global organization for information professionals and their strategic partners. As an international professional association, SLA represents thousands of information experts and knowledge managers in more than 80 countries who collect, analyze, evaluate, package, and disseminate information to facilitate strategic decision making.

SLA's 11,000 members work in various settings including Fortune 500 companies, not-for-profit organizations, consulting firms, government agencies, technical and academic institutions, museums, law firms, and medical facilities. SLA promotes and strengthens its members through learning, advocacy, and networking initiatives.

Alignment Project

In 2009 SLA completed the research phase of the SLA Alignment Project, a two-year extensive look at how employers value and view knowledge managers, information professionals, and special librarians and the services they provide. A multidisciplinary team unveiled research that will not only help refine the current positioning of the profession in the marketplace but will also provide a framework for discussing the inherent value in the profession and SLA in a clear and cohesive voice. The results of this intensive research will be used to shape the benefits and services provided by the association, as well as the strategy, mission, vision, and values of SLA.

SLA's History

SLA was founded in 1909 by John Cotton Dana and a group of librarians who believed that libraries serving business, government, social agencies, and the academic community were very different from other libraries. The founders believed that these libraries operated using a different philosophy and more-diverse resources than the typical public or school library.

These "special"—or more aptly, "specialized"—libraries at first were distinguished by being subject collections with a specialized clientele, but gradually it was recognized that their chief characteristic was that they existed to serve the organization of which they were a part. Their purpose was not education per se, but the delivery of practical, focused, and even filtered information to the executives and other clients within their organizations. Specialist librarians are unique in their relationship with their users and customers, and are proactive partners in information and knowledge management.

Over the past century, SLA members have been working on the technological edge, moving into knowledge services, and adapting to new roles to keep up with the times. They are entrepreneurial, embracing change and using their knowledge and vision to further the goals of their organizations. Corporate information professionals synthesize strategic information to help executives make the decisions necessary for business to thrive. Government information professionals organize and deliver information for congressional, parliamentary, judicial, and executive leaders to make policy decisions. Academic special librarians organize, digitize, and deliver research information so that professors and students can advance knowledge.

SLA's strengths in serving its membership are in three areas: learning, networking, and advocacy. These are the underpinnings that prompted the information pioneers of 1909 to come together in a cooperative association, and they are still the fundamental benefits SLA provides the information pioneers of the 21st century.

SLA's Core Values

The association's core values are

- Leadership—Strengthening members' roles as information leaders in their organizations and communities, including shaping information policy, and ethical use and gathering of information
- Service—Responding to clients' needs, adding qualitative and quantitative value to information services and products
- Innovation and continuous learning—Embracing innovative solutions for the enhancement of services and intellectual advancement within the profession
- Results and accountability—Delivering measurable results in the information economy and members' organizations; the association and its members are expected to operate with the highest level of ethics and honesty
- Collaboration and partnering—Providing opportunities to meet, communicate, collaborate, and partner within the information industry and the business community

Chapters, Divisions, and Caucuses

SLA chapter membership provides a network of information professionals for members in their local community or region, while SLA division membership links them to information professionals within their topical area of expertise. SLA membership includes membership in one chapter and in one division. For a small fee, members can join additional chapters, divisions, and caucuses. A caucus is an informal network of discipline or interest not covered in other divisions.

SLA has 58 regional chapters in the United States, Canada, Europe, Asia, and the Middle East; 27 divisions representing a variety of industries; and 11 special-interest caucuses.

SLA is organized into 57 regional chapters that elect officers, issue bulletins or meeting announcements, hold three to nine program meetings during a year, and initiate special projects. Members may affiliate with the chapter nearest to their own preferred mailing address (either business or residence).

SLA divisions represent subject interests, fields, or types of information-handling techniques. Each division elects officers and publishes a bulletin or newsletter. Most conduct professional programs during the association's annual conferences. The association added an Academic Division in 2008 and a Taxonomy Division in 2009.

Governance

SLA is governed by a board of directors elected by the membership. The board and the association both operate on a calendar year, with newly elected officers, as well as chapter and division leaders, taking office in January. SLA's president for 2010 is Anne Caputo of Dow Jones, and its president-elect is Cindy Romaine of Romainiacs Intelligent Research. Janice R. Lachance is the association's chief executive officer. [Additional officers are listed in SLA's directory entry in Part 6 of this volume—*Ed.*].

Programs and Services

Click University

SLA's Click University (Click U), launched in 2005, is an online learning community focusing on continuing professional education for librarians, information professionals, and knowledge workers. Click U is primarily designed to give SLA members state-of-the-art learning opportunities in partnership with today's information industry experts. Courses on software and technology, management, communications, and leadership are designed to enhance the skills acquired through traditional library education. Click U and its programs are available only to SLA members. The majority of the Webinars offered through Click U are offered free of charge, included as part of membership benefits. Those offerings that carry an additional fee are noted as "Click U Premium," including Click U at Annual Conference and Click U Certificate Programs.

Click U is constantly adding programs and courses on topics ranging from public speaking to copyright law.

Innovation Laboratory

The SLA Innovation Laboratory is a resource for members to discover new technologies. The laboratory offers a wide variety of Web 2.0 software learning tools (including wikis, blogs, and such social networking sites as Twitter, Facebook, and LinkedIn) to help information professionals become more business-savvy and technologically adept.

Click U Certificate Programs (Premium)

Click U provides certificate programs for information professionals looking to take the next step into a new career and utilize their traditional information skills in fields such as competitive intelligence, knowledge management, and copyright management.

Click U @ Annual Conference (Premium)

SLA offers in-person training and continuing education at the SLA Annual Conference and INFO-EXPO. SLA Workshops (half day) or Learning Forums (full day) are designed to educate and inspire participants to make an impact in their organizations.

Advocacy

SLA serves the profession by advocating publicly on the value and values of the profession. Its activities range from communicating with executives and hiring professionals on the important role information professionals play in the workplace to sharing the membership's views and opinions with government officials worldwide.

Public Policy Program

Government bodies and related international organizations play a critical role in establishing the legal and social framework within which SLA members conduct information services. Because of the importance of governments and international organizations to its membership, SLA maintains an active public policy program. SLA staff and the association's Public Policy Advisory Council monitor and proactively work to shape legislation and regulatory proposals that affect the association's membership.

SLA supports government policies that

- Strike a fair and equitable balance among the rights and interests of all parties in the creation, distribution, and use of information and other intellectual property
- Strengthen the library and information management operations of government agencies
- Promote access to government public information through the application of modern technologies and sound information management practices
- Encourage the development and application of new information and communications technologies to improve library services, information services, and information management
- Protect individual intellectual freedom and the confidentiality of library records, safeguard freedom of expression, and oppose government censorship
- Foster international exchange of information

With regard to the actions of government bodies and related international organizations in the policy areas listed above, the association will

- Monitor executive, legislative, and judicial actions and initiatives at the national and international level, and to the extent practical at the sub-national level
- Educate key decision-makers on the concerns of SLA's membership
- Provide timely updates to the membership on critical issues and actions
- Encourage members to influence actions by expressing their opinions
- Develop cooperative relationships with other like-minded organizations, so as to expand SLA's visibility and impact

Legislative Action Center

SLA uses a Legislative Action Center tool on its Web site that allows all members to monitor legislation as well as activities at the U.S. federal level. The Legislative Action Center allows for automated and electronic proactive outreach to elected officials in an effort to shape legislation and regulatory proposals that affect the association's membership.

Employment and Career Services

The online SLA Career Center includes a variety of services to meet the career needs of members, including career coaching, articles and resources, and career disruption assistance mentoring. It includes a job bank that serves the needs of employers as well as SLA members looking for employment.

SLA Career Connection combines the power of the Web with the power of the face-to-face meeting. By participating online in SLA Career Connection, job seekers and employers are able to connect online and then meet face-to-face at the next SLA Annual Conference.

Information Center

The SLA Information Center provides access to resources to assist members in their day-to-day tasks and management decisions, and in their roles as SLA leaders. Among its resources are Information Portals (links to articles, Web sites, books and other resources on more than 40 topics); News Connections (the latest industry news, summarized by topic); recent reports on information industry issues; research and surveys to help with benchmarking and strategic planning; and the SLA Podcast Center, which contains audio files from SLA Career Center experts as well as tips from the SLA magazine *Information Outlook*. SLA's Leadership Center guides members through the resources created on best practices, training, guidelines, and responsibilities, and offers links to resources relevant to the operation and management of special libraries, from information portals to research and surveys.

Professional and Student Networks

SLA's student groups, located throughout the world, are affiliated with accredited graduate schools of library and information science. Through membership in SLA, students gain professional experience and make industry contacts.

Publications, Blogs, and Newsletters

SLA's monthly magazine, *Information Outlook,* provides news, features, and evaluation of trends in information management. SLA also gives members a weekly e-newsletter, *SLA Connections,* which covers breaking information industry news as well as association news and updates on Click University. In addition, SLA has a number of association blogs designed to keep members informed about important SLA and professional news.

SLA-TV

In 2009 the association launched its own Internet television network, SLA-TV (http://www.slatv.org). The online network will be an integral part of how SLA connects with its members worldwide. SLA-TV currently has numerous videos, including stories of SLA's award recipients, messages from elected leaders, and video contest submissions. SLA-TV is designed to be an online community and a resource that will further advance the association's mission to promote and strengthen its members through learning, advocacy, and networking initiatives.

SLA Awards and Honors

The SLA awards and honors program was created in 1948 to honor exceptional individuals, achievements, and contributions to the association and the information profession. The program's purpose is to bring attention to the important work of special librarians and information professionals within the corporate and academic setting.

The association offers 11 different awards annually and recently added the SLA Rising Star Award, which is granted annually to no more than five professionals with less than five years of experience in the profession. The Rising Star 2009 recipients were Michelle Dollinger, PricewaterhouseCoopers; Julie Fleischhacker, General Mills; Margaret Ostrander, Thomson Reuters; Abby Thorne, Bluegrass Community and Technical College; and Norah Xiao, University of Southern California, Los Angeles.

[For a list of the winners of SLA's other awards and grants, see "Library Scholarship and Award Recipients, 2009" in Part 3—*Ed.*]

Research

SLA funds surveys and projects, endowment fund grants, and research studies related to all aspects of information management.

Scholarships

Each year SLA awards scholarships to at least five students who have demonstrated their ability and desire to contribute to the special librarian and information management field. SLA's scholarship program consists of awards for graduate study leading to a master's degree, graduate study leading to a Ph.D., and for post-M.L.S. study.

Grants

SLA offers grants for research projects for the advancement of library sciences, the support of programs developed by SLA chapters, divisions, or committees, and the support of the association's expanding international agenda. Additionally, grants, scholarships, and stipends are offered by many of SLA's chapters and divisions.

Events and Conferences

SLA's Annual Conference and INFO-EXPO brings together thousands of information professionals and provides a forum for discussion on issues shaping the information industry. The conference offers more than 400 events, programs, panel discussions, and seminars, and includes an exhibit hall with more than 300 participating companies.

Despite tough economic conditions, sweeping layoffs, and shrinking travel and professional development budgets, members of SLA turned out in record numbers to participate in the association's 2009 Annual Conference in Washington, D.C., June 14–17. Final attendance totaled 5,856 registrants, a 16 percent increase over 2008. Of that number, 1,130 participants were first-time SLA conference participants.

The association's 2010 Annual Conference was scheduled for June 13–15 at the Ernest N. Morial Convention Center in New Orleans, with the theme "Entering SLA's Next Century: Let the Good Times Roll!"

Part 2
Legislation, Funding, and Grants

Legislation

Legislation and Regulations Affecting Libraries in 2009

Emily Sheketoff
Executive Director, Washington Office, American Library Association

American Recovery and Reinvestment Act (ARRA)

In February 2009 Congress passed the American Recovery and Reinvestment Act (ARRA), which released an unprecedented level of federal spending—$787 billion—into the U.S. economy in an effort to combat the effects of the faltering economy. Since that time, the American Library Association (ALA) Washington Office has dedicated much of its work to educating the library community about this bill and to influencing the decision-makers tasked with implementing this very complex legislation.

The Washington Office began its mission by centralizing information on how these provisions can benefit libraries by establishing a Web site (http://www.ala.org/knowyourstimulus), that offers news and information on the stimulus, including application information and frequently asked questions.

Libraries could benefit from specific provisions in the stimulus, including $13 billion for Title I of the Elementary and Secondary Education Act (ESEA), $650 million for Enhancing Education Through Technology, $7.2 billion for broadband, $53.6 billion for the State Fiscal Stabilization Fund, an additional $120 million for the Senior Community Service Employment Program, and an additional $130 million for the Rural Community Facilities Program.

Some libraries received part of the funding slotted for the State Fiscal Stabilization Fund and Title I of ESEA as well as rural community development and education funding, all of which went toward employment, construction, equipment, and technologies. Many libraries were also able to hire seniors through the Senior Community Service Employment Program.

Funding for broadband proved to be the biggest opportunity for libraries; the extent to which this opportunity will impact them is yet to be determined as the process is still ongoing. More information on this portion of the bill is under the "Telecommunications and the Internet" portion of this report.

Library Services and Technology Act

In December 2009 President Barack Obama signed omnibus legislation that included the Labor, Health and Human Services, and Education appropriations. The final version of the legislation included a slight increase for Library Services and Technology Act (LSTA) funding.

LSTA received a $213.5 million appropriation for fiscal year (FY) 2010, a 0.63 percent increase over FY 2009. Of that amount, $172.5 million was designated for the Grants to States program, the primary source of federal funding for libraries. This amount is a $1 million increase.

While the increase in funding is modest, this outcome was a win for libraries. However, lobbying and engaging grassroots advocacy for increasing LSTA to $450 million remains a primary goal of the ALA Office of Government Relations (OGR) for 2010.

School Libraries

In late August 2009 ALA filed comments with the Department of Education on the stimulus program Race to the Top. In collaboration with the American Association of School Librarians' Legislative Committee, ALA suggested that 21st century school library programs provide students with more than just books selected to hone readers' developing skills and instill a love of reading. The comments asserted that while reading and books are mainstays of the school library program, today's school libraries are also sophisticated learning environments that provide the skills necessary to succeed in the workplace—but only when staffed by qualified professionals trained to collaborate with teachers and engage students meaningfully with information that matters to them both in the classroom and outside it.

ALA believes that taking action to fund school library programs with state-licensed school librarians is imperative. Research and experience indicate that doing so leads to improved results for students, long-term gains in school and school system capacity, and increased productivity and effectiveness. ALA takes the position that states must invest in school library programs headed by state-licensed school librarians in order to articulate an innovative, comprehensive, coordinated commitment to reform. With the much-anticipated reauthorization of ESEA—now called the No Child Left Behind Act—coming up in the second session of the 111th Congress, the ALA Office of Government Relations was aggressively lobbying the administration and Congress on this point.

Higher Education

Student Aid and Fiscal Responsibility Act of 2009

In September 2009 OGR lobbied for the inclusion of community college libraries in the Student Aid and Fiscal Responsibility Act of 2009 (H.R. 3221), a bill to establish two new competitive grant programs giving states and junior and community colleges an opportunity to apply for funds to launch initiatives to improve graduation- and employment-related outcomes.

The original bill's language did not explicitly include community college libraries as potential recipients of the grants, which ALA believes is essential to highlight the role libraries play in preparing students to successfully obtain and retain employment and to encourage community colleges to pursue the grants to invest in their libraries and the services and resources they offer.

Working with Rep. Raúl Grijalva (D-Ariz.), who championed an amendment to include community college libraries, OGR successfully secured this text in the bill, which passed the House of Representatives on September 17. OGR continued to work to ensure that comparable language was included in the drafting of a Senate version of the bill.

Copyright

Google Book Search Settlement Agreement

In late October 2008 Google, the Authors Guild, and the Association of American Publishers (AAP) proposed a major settlement agreement resolving the class action lawsuit brought by book authors and publishers in response to Google's Book Search digitization project, which involves the scanning of millions of books. A month later, ALA and the Association of Research Libraries (ARL) released *A Guide for the Perplexed: Libraries and the Google Library Project Settlement* by attorney Jonathan Band to help the library community digest this complex settlement and understand the implications for libraries.

Members of the library community and others discussed the implications of the proposed settlement in a meeting hosted by the ALA Washington Office, ARL, and the Association of College and Research Libraries (ACRL) in February 2009 in Washington, D.C. The three associations filed a brief in May 2009 with the U.S. District Court for the Southern District of New York in response to the settlement agreement. In the filing, the library associations did not oppose approval of the settlement, but asked the judge "to exercise vigorous oversight of the interpretation and implementation of the settlement to ensure the broadest possible benefit from the services the settlement enables."

The associations also asserted that although the settlement had the potential to provide public access to millions of books, many of its features—including the absence of competition for new services—could compromise fundamental library values including equity of access to information, patron privacy, and intellectual freedom.

In June ALA, ACRL, and ARL released *A Guide for the Perplexed, Part II: The Amended Google-Michigan Agreement* in response to the University of Michigan entering into an amended agreement that would govern the relationship between Google and the university if the proposed Google Book Search settlement is approved. At the time this report was prepared, final settlement had not yet been reached.

Privacy

USAPatriot Act

In November 2009 the House of Representatives Judiciary Committee passed the USAPatriot Act Amendments Act of 2009 (H.R. 3845). ALA believes this legislation could lead to comprehensive reform of the nation's surveillance laws. However, the committee failed to approve a bill that would secure comprehensive reform.

H.R. 3845 would restore reader privacy by curbing the use of secret court orders and National Security Letters to obtain library and bookstore records about patron and customer activity. Other key protections in the bill include improved judicial review of investigations, new protections for librarians and others who receive "gag orders" from the government, and more oversight of how USAPatriot Act powers are being used.

The House committee also approved an amendment from Rep. Tammy Baldwin (D-Wis.) calling for the president to periodically review secret surveillance programs to determine whether they should remain classified. The committee rejected several amendments that would have watered down or eliminated the bill's civil liberties protections. H.R. 3845 goes much further toward restoring civil liberties than the Senate Judiciary Committee's bill, S. 1692, which passed committee in October 2009.

On December 16, Congress extended the sunset deadline for Section 215 and the other two expiring provisions, the roving wiretaps and "lone wolf" sections, from December 31, 2009, to February 28, 2010. ALA will continue to monitor House activities.

Consumer Product Safety Improvement Act

In August 2008 Congress passed the Consumer Product Safety Improvement Act (CPSIA) in an attempt to ensure that children's products are free of dangerous levels of lead and phthalates.

This law was initially set to go into effect February 10, 2009, and was to be enforced by the Consumer Product Safety Commission (CPSC). That same month, however, the commission issued a one-year stay of implementation.

Under the current opinion released by the CPSC General Counsel, this law would apply to ordinary, paper-based children's books (created for children under the age of 12).

As ALA has emphasized since the enactment of CPSIA, concern for safety is a top priority in providing materials to children. On August 26, CPSC issued its final rule on children's products containing lead. In the rule, CPSC confirmed that libraries had no independent obligation to test library books for lead under the law. Meanwhile, CPSC announced a second stay of implementation, postponing the date to February 2011.

In the 2010 omnibus appropriations bill passed by Congress in December 2009, Congress asked CPSC to release a report regarding difficulties encountered with enforcing CPSIA. The report notes that older books have emerged as a particular problem due to the retroactive nature of the law, adding that the retroactive applicability of the lead limits creates problems for libraries.

Additionally, the report reaffirms the commission's belief that Congress did not intend to impose the strict lead ban—as imposed by section 101(a) of CPSIA—for ordinary books. However, the report states that CPSC does not have the flexibility needed to grant an exclusion for ordinary books. "In order to address this issue, Congress may, with some limitations, choose to consider granting an exclusion for ordinary children's books and other children's paper-based printed materials," the report states.

Congress will respond to the CPSC report, and the ALA Washington Office will continue to engage grassroots advocacy and keep membership informed of developments on this issue.

Telecommunications and the Internet

American Recovery and Reinvestment Act

After the passage of the American Recovery and Reinvestment Act (ARRA), ALA launched an intensive campaign to guide membership through the application process for the Commerce Department's National Telecommunications and Information Administration (NTIA) Broadband Technology Opportunities Program (BTOP) and the U.S. Department of Agriculture's Rural Utilities Service (RUS) Broadband Initiatives Program. The Washington Office held Web seminars and conference calls and also produced and distributed instructional documents.

Additionally, ALA's Office for Information Technology Policy (OITP) regularly filed formal comments to the administering agencies and took other opportunities to represent the needs of libraries and to influence the unprecedented process such as participating in coalitions and attending meetings with members of Congress and the Federal Communications Commission (FCC).

In early 2009 OITP coordinated the development and submission of two sets of comments to federal agencies concerning broadband policy. In response to a request for information from NTIA and RUS, extensive comments were generated concerning the design of the broadband funding programs mandated in ARRA. These comments emphasized libraries as community "anchor institutions" that need high-speed broadband to provide essential user services. The comments also addressed funding mechanisms, including the problematic nature of the 20 percent match, given the financial constraints faced by most libraries.

In 2010, as the final round of funding for broadband is awarded, ALA will continue to focus on this issue.

During 2009 FCC solicited input on its creation of a National Broadband Plan. OITP submitted on behalf of the library community comments that emphasized the same themes as comments submitted to NTIA and RUS regarding the ARRA broadband programs.

New OITP Policy Brief Series

OITP established a new series of policy briefs in 2009 that will be substantive works on the order of 10 to 30 pages each when published. The first, *Fiber to the*

Library: How Public Libraries Can Benefit, was issued as a print version in November. Several other policy briefs are in process and were expected to be published in the first half of 2010.

The purpose of *Fiber to the Library: How Public Libraries Can Benefit* is to assist libraries in understanding the benefits of fiber optic technology and to suggest strategies they can consider when exploring how to obtain fiber connectivity. The paper provides background information and arguments that may be useful in library community applications to the Department of Commerce's Broadband Technology Opportunities Program.

Funding Programs and Grant-Making Agencies

National Endowment for the Humanities

1100 Pennsylvania Ave. N.W., Washington, DC 20506
800-634-1121 or 202-606-8400
TDD (hearing impaired) 202-606-8282 or 866-372-2930 (toll free)
E-mail Info@neh.gov, World Wide Web http://www.neh.gov

Founded in 1965, the National Endowment for the Humanities (NEH) is an independent grant-making institution of the United States government dedicated to supporting research, education, preservation, and public programs in the humanities. It is the largest funder of humanities programs in the United States.

NEH grants enrich classroom learning, create and preserve knowledge, and bring ideas to life through public television, radio, new technologies, museum exhibitions, and programs in libraries and other community places. Recipients typically are cultural institutions, such as museums, archives, libraries, colleges, universities, public television and radio stations, and individual scholars. NEH grants:

- Strengthen teaching and learning in the humanities in schools and colleges
- Preserve and provide access to cultural and educational resources
- Provide opportunities for lifelong learning
- Facilitate research and original scholarship
- Strengthen the institutional base of the humanities

The endowment's mission is to enrich American cultural life by promoting the study of the humanities. According to the National Foundation on the Arts and the Humanities Act (1965):

> The term "humanities" includes, but is not limited to, the study of the following: language, both modern and classical; linguistics; literature; history; jurisprudence; philosophy; archaeology; comparative religion; ethics; the history, criticism, and theory of the arts; those aspects of social sciences which have humanistic content and employ humanistic methods; and the study and application of the humanities to the human environment with particular attention to reflecting our diverse heritage, traditions, and history, and to the relevance of the humanities to the current conditions of national life.

The act provided for the establishment of the National Foundation on the Arts and the Humanities in order to promote progress and scholarship in the humanities and the arts in the United States. The act included the following findings:

- The arts and the humanities belong to all the people of the United States.
- The encouragement and support of national progress and scholarship in the humanities and the arts, while primarily matters for private and local initiative, are also appropriate matters of concern to the federal government.
- An advanced civilization must not limit its efforts to science and technology alone, but must give full value and support to the other great branches of scholarly and cultural activity in order to achieve a better understanding of the past, a better analysis of the present, and a better view of the future.
- Democracy demands wisdom and vision in its citizens. It must therefore foster and support a form of education, and access to the arts and the humanities, designed to make people of all backgrounds and locations masters of technology and not its unthinking servants.
- It is necessary and appropriate for the federal government to complement, assist, and add to programs for the advancement of the humanities and the arts by local, state, regional, and private agencies and their organizations. In doing so, the government must be sensitive to the nature of public sponsorship. Public funding of the arts and humanities is subject to the conditions that traditionally govern the use of public money. Such funding should contribute to public support and confidence in the use of taxpayer funds. Public funds provided by the federal government ultimately must serve public purposes the Congress defines.
- The arts and the humanities reflect the high place accorded by the American people to the nation's rich culture and history and to the fostering of mutual respect for the diverse beliefs and values of all persons and groups.

What NEH Grants Accomplish

Since its founding, NEH has awarded more than 66,724 competitive grants.

Interpretive Exhibitions

Interpretive exhibitions provide opportunities for lifelong learning in the humanities for millions of Americans. Since 1967 the endowment has awarded nearly $259 million in grants for interpretive exhibitions, catalogs, and public programs, which are among the most highly visible activities supported by the agency. During 2010 more than 20 reading, viewing, and discussion programs, exhibitions, Web-based programs, and other public education programs will employ various delivery mechanisms at venues across the nation.

Renewing Teaching

Over the years more than 75,000 high school and college teachers have deepened their knowledge of the humanities through intensive summer study supported by NEH; tens of thousands of students benefit from the expertise the teachers bring back to the classroom.

Reading and Discussion Programs

Since 1982 the endowment has supported reading and discussion programs in the nation's libraries, bringing people together to discuss works of literature and history. Scholars in the humanities provide thematic direction for the discussion programs. Using selected texts and themes such as "Work," "Family," "Diversity," and "Not for Children Only," these programs have attracted more than 2 million Americans to read and talk about what they've read.

Preserving the Nation's Heritage

The National Digital Newspaper Program supports the conversion of microfilm of historically important U.S. newspapers into fully searchable digital files. Developed in partnership with the Library of Congress, this complex, long-term project ultimately will make more than 30 million pages of newspapers accessible online.

Stimulating Private Support

More than $1.66 billion in humanities support has been generated by the NEH Challenge Grants program, which requires most grant recipients to raise $3 in nonfederal funds for every dollar they receive.

Presidential Papers

Ten presidential papers projects have received support from the endowment, from Washington to Eisenhower. Matching grants for the ten projects have leveraged $7.6 million in nonfederal contributions.

New Scholarship

NEH grants enable scholars to do in-depth study: Jack Rakove explored the making of the Constitution in his *Original Meanings* and James McPherson chronicled the Civil War in his *Battle Cry of Freedom*. Both won the Pulitzer Prize, as have 14 other recipients of NEH grants.

History on Screen

Since 1967 the endowment has awarded nearly $282 million to support the production of films for broad public distribution, including the Emmy Award-winning series *The Civil War,* the Oscar-nominated films *Brooklyn Bridge, The Restless Conscience,* and *Freedom on My Mind,* and film biographies of John and

Abigail Adams, Ernest Hemingway, Dolley Madison, and Eugene O'Neill. These films help Americans learn about the events and people that shaped the nation. Recently, two NEH-funded films on World War II, *The Rape of Europa* and the Ken Burns series *The War,* received critical acclaim. *The Rape of Europa* tells the epic story of the systematic theft, deliberate destruction, and, in some cases, miraculous survival of Europe's art treasures during the war, and the seven-episode series *The War* details the experiences of American soldiers and their families through eyewitness testimony.

Library of America

Millions of books have been sold as part of the Library of America series, a collection of the riches of the nation's literature. Begun with NEH seed money, the more than 200 published volumes include works by Henry Adams, Edith Wharton, William James, Eudora Welty, W. E. B. DuBois, and many others.

The Library of America also received a $150,000 grant for the publication of *American Poetry: The Seventeenth and Eighteenth Centuries* (two volumes) and an expanded volume of selected works by Captain John Smith—a key figure in the establishment of the first permanent English settlement in North America, at Jamestown, Virginia—and other early American narratives.

Science and the Humanities

The scientific past is being preserved with NEH-supported editions of the letters of Charles Darwin, the works of Albert Einstein, and the 14-volume papers of Thomas A. Edison. Additionally, NEH and the National Science Foundation (NSF) have joined forces in Documenting Endangered Languages (DEL), a multiyear effort to preserve records of key languages before they become extinct.

Learning Under the Tent

Across the country, state humanities councils bring a 21st century version of Chautauqua to the public, embracing populations of entire towns, cities, even regions. Scholars portray such significant figures as Meriwether Lewis, Sojourner Truth, Willa Cather, Teddy Roosevelt, and Sacagawea, first speaking as the historic character and then giving audiences the opportunity to ask questions. The give-and-take between the scholar/performer and the audiences provides an entertaining, energetic, and thought-provoking exchange about experiences and attitudes in the present and the past.

Special Initiatives

We the People

We the People grants foster the teaching, study, and understanding of American history and culture. Under this program, NEH invites scholars, teachers, filmmakers, curators, librarians, and others to submit grant applications that explore significant events and themes in the nation's history and culture and that advance knowledge of the principles that define the United States. Since its inception in 2002, We the People has provided support to more than 1,700 projects.

Proposals responding to the initiative can take the form of

- New scholarship
- Projects to preserve and provide access to documents and artifacts significant to the national heritage
- Professional development programs for teachers and educators at every level, from kindergarten through college
- Public programs in libraries, museums, and historical societies, including exhibitions, film, radio, and Internet-based programs

NEH will accept We the People proposals in all programs and at all deadlines. Proposals are expected to meet the guidelines of the program that best fits the character of the project. A list of programs and deadlines is available on the NEH Web site (http://www.neh.gov).

The main components of We the People are

- Landmarks of American History and Culture workshops for K–12 teachers and community college faculty at important historical sites
- Interpreting America's Historic Places grants to provide opportunities to learn more about American history and culture
- The National Digital Newspaper Program, which is digitizing historically important U.S. newspapers and making them available in a searchable online database
- Picturing America, which provides schools and teachers with high-quality poster reproductions of some of the nation's greatest art, along with materials that help educators incorporate these art works into their teaching of history, literature, art history, and architecture
- The We the People Bookshelf, a set of classic books for young readers on American themes to schools and libraries for use in local programs

Picturing America

In February 2008 NEH launched Picturing America, an initiative designed to promote the teaching, study, and understanding of American history and its culture in K–12 schools and public libraries. Part of the We the People program, Picturing America is a free resource that provides an innovative way for people of all ages to explore the history and character of the United States through some of the nation's greatest works of art, including Emanuel Leutze's *Washington Crossing the Delaware* and Norman Rockwell's *Freedom of Speech.*

Picturing America features 40 high-quality reproductions (24 by 36 inches) of American art, an illustrated teachers' resource book, and a comprehensive Web site (http://picturingamerica.neh.gov) with additional information about the artwork and the artists. More than 76,000 schools, public libraries, and Head Start centers have taken advantage of this resource.

EDSITEment

As a gateway to more than 200 peer-reviewed Web sites, EDSITEment (http://www.edsitement.neh.gov) offers resources for teachers, students, and parents searching for high-quality material on the Internet in the subject areas of literature and language arts, foreign languages, art and culture, and history and social studies.

More than 400,000 visitors a month use EDSITEment's online lesson plans, now numbering over 400, in all areas of the humanities. EDSITEment's digital resources also help educators enhance their teaching and engage students with interactive technology tools that hone critical-thinking skills.

Federal-State Partnership

NEH's Office of Federal-State Partnership links the endowment with the nationwide network of 56 humanities councils, which are located in each state, the District of Columbia, Puerto Rico, the U.S. Virgin Islands, the Northern Mariana Islands, American Samoa, and Guam. Each humanities council funds humanities programs in its own jurisdiction.

Directory of State Humanities Councils

Alabama

Alabama Humanities Foundation
1100 Ireland Way, Suite 101
Birmingham, AL 35205-7001
205-558-3980, fax 205-558-3981
http://www.ahf.net

Alaska

Alaska Humanities Forum
421 W. First Ave., Suite 300
Anchorage, AK 99501
907-272-5341, fax 907-272-3979
http://www.akhf.org

Arizona

Arizona Humanities Council
Ellis-Shackelford House
1242 N. Central Ave.
Phoenix, AZ 85004-1887
602-257-0335, fax 602-257-0392
http://www.azhumanities.org

Arkansas

Arkansas Humanities Council
407 President Clinton Ave., Suite 201
Little Rock, AR 72201

501-221-0091, fax 501-221-9860
http://www.arkhums.org

California

California Council for the Humanities
312 Sutter St., Suite 601
San Francisco, CA 94108
415-391-1474, fax 415-391-1312
http://www.calhum.org

Colorado

Colorado Humanities
1490 Lafayette St., Suite 101
Denver, CO 80218
303-894-7951, fax 303-864-9361
http://www.coloradohumanities.org

Connecticut

Connecticut Humanities Council
37 Broad St.
Middletown, CT 06457
860-685-2260, fax 860-704-0429
http://www.ctculture.org

Delaware

Delaware Humanities Forum

100 W. Tenth St., Suite 1009
Wilmington, DE 19801
302-657-0650, fax 302-657-0655
http://www.dhf.org

District of Columbia

Humanities Council of Washington, D.C.
925 U St. N.W.
Washington, DC 20001
202-387-8393, fax 202-387-8149
http://wdchumanities.org

Florida

Florida Humanities Council
599 Second St. S.
St. Petersburg, FL 33701-5005
727-873-2000, fax 727-873-2014
http://www.flahum.org

Georgia

Georgia Humanities Council
50 Hurt Plaza S.E., Suite 595
Atlanta, GA 30303-2915
404-523-6220, fax 404-523-5702
http://www.georgiahumanities.org

Hawaii

Hawaii Council for the Humanities
First Hawaiian Bank Bldg.
3599 Waialae Ave., Room 25
Honolulu, HI 96816
808-732-5402, fax 808-732-5432
http://www.hihumanities.org

Idaho

Idaho Humanities Council
217 W. State St.
Boise, ID 83702
208-345-5346, fax 208-345-5347
http://www.idahohumanities.org

Illinois

Illinois Humanities Council
17 N. State St., No. 1400
Chicago, IL 60602-3296
312-422-5580, fax 312-422-5588
http://www.prairie.org

Indiana

Indiana Humanities Council
1500 N. Delaware St.
Indianapolis, IN 46202
317-638-1500, fax 317-634-9503
http://www.indianahumanities.org

Iowa

Humanities Iowa
100 Oakdale Campus N310 OH
University of Iowa
Iowa City, IA 52242-5000
319-335-4153, fax 319-335-4154
http://www.humanitiesiowa.org

Kansas

Kansas Humanities Council
112 S.W. Sixth Ave., Suite 210
Topeka, KS 66603
785-357-0359, fax 785-357-1723
http://www.kansashumanities.org

Kentucky

Kentucky Humanities Council
206 E. Maxwell St.
Lexington, KY 40508
859-257-5932, fax 859-257-5933
http://www.kyhumanities.org

Louisiana

Louisiana Endowment for the Humanities
938 Lafayette St., Suite 300
New Orleans, LA 70113-1027
504-523-4352, fax 504-529-2358
http://www.leh.org

Maine

Maine Humanities Council
674 Brighton Ave.
Portland, ME 04102-1012
207-773-5051, fax 207-773-2416
http://www.mainehumanities.org

Maryland

Maryland Humanities Council
108 W. Centre St.
Baltimore, MD 21201-4565

410-685-0095, fax 410-685-0795
http://www.mdhc.org

Massachusetts

Mass Humanities
66 Bridge St.
Northampton, MA 01060
413-584-8440, fax 413-584-8454
http://www.masshumanities.org

Michigan

Michigan Humanities Council
119 Pere Marquette Drive, Suite 3B
Lansing, MI 48912-1270
517-372-7770, fax 517-372-0027
http://michiganhumanities.org

Minnesota

Minnesota Humanities Center
987 E. Ivy Ave.
St. Paul, MN 55106-2046
651-774-0105, fax 651-774-0205
http://www.minnesotahumanities.org

Mississippi

Mississippi Humanities Council
3825 Ridgewood Rd., Room 311
Jackson, MS 39211
601-432-6752, fax 601-432-6750
http://www.mshumanities.org

Missouri

Missouri Humanities Council
543 Hanley Industrial Court, Suite 201
St. Louis, MO 63144-1905
314-781-9660, fax 314-781-9681
http://www.mohumanities.org

Montana

Humanities Montana
311 Brantly
Missoula, MT 59812-7848
406-243-6022, fax 406-243-4836
http://www.humanitiesmontana.org

Nebraska

Nebraska Humanities Council

Lincoln Center Bldg., Suite 500
215 Centennial Mall South
Lincoln, NE 68508
402-474-2131, fax 402-474-4852
http://www.nebraskahumanties.org

Nevada

Nevada Humanities
1034 N. Sierra St.
Reno, NV 89507
775-784-6587, fax 775-784-6527
http://www.nevadahumanities.org

New Hampshire

New Hampshire Humanities Council
19 Pillsbury St.
Concord, NH 03302-2228
603-224-4071, fax 603-224-4072
http://www.nhhc.org

New Jersey

New Jersey Council for the Humanities
28 W. State St., 6th Floor
Trenton, NJ 08608
609-695-4838, fax 609-695-4929
http://www.njch.org

New Mexico

New Mexico Humanities Council
MSC06 3570
1 University of New Mexico
Albuquerque, NM 87131-0001
505-277-3705, fax 505-277-6056
http://www.nmhum.org

New York

New York Council for the Humanities
150 Broadway, Suite 1700
New York, NY 10038
212-233-1131, fax 212-233-4607
http://www.nyhumanities.org

North Carolina

North Carolina Humanities Council
122 N. Elm St., Suite 601
Greensboro, NC 27401
336-334-5325, fax 336-334-5052
http://www.nchumanities.org

North Dakota

North Dakota Humanities Council
418 E. Broadway, Suite 8
P.O. Box 2191
Bismarck, ND 58502
701-255-3360, fax 701-223-8724
http://www.nd-humanities.org

Ohio

Ohio Humanities Council
471 E. Broad St., Suite 1620
Columbus, OH 43215-3857
614-461-7802, fax 614-461-4651
http://www.ohiohumanities.org

Oklahoma

Oklahoma Humanities Council
Festival Plaza
428 W. California Ave., Suite 270
Oklahoma City, OK 73102
405-235-0280, fax 405-235-0289
http://www.okhumanitiescouncil.org

Oregon

Oregon Council for the Humanities
813 S.W. Alder St., Suite 702
Portland, OR 97205
503-241-0543, fax 503-241-0024
http://www.oregonhum.org

Pennsylvania

Pennsylvania Humanities Council
325 Chestnut St., Suite 715
Philadelphia, PA 19106-2607
215-925-1005, fax 215-925-3054
http://www.pahumanities.org

Rhode Island

Rhode Island Council for the Humanities
385 Westminster St., Suite 2
Providence, RI 02903
401-273-2250, fax 401-454-4872
http://www.rihumanities.org

South Carolina

Humanities Council of South Carolina
2711 Middleburg Drive, Suite 308

P.O. Box 5287
Columbia, SC 29254
803-771-2477, fax 803-771-2487
http://www.schumanities.org

South Dakota

South Dakota Humanities Council
1215 Trail Ridge Rd., Suite A
Brookings, SD 57006
605-688-6113, fax 605-688-4531
http://web.sdstate.edu/humanities

Tennessee

Humanities Tennessee
306 Gay St., Suite 306
Nashville, TN 37201
615-770-0006, fax 615-770-0007
http://www.humanitiestennessee.org

Texas

Humanities Texas
1410 Rio Grande St.
Austin, TX 78701
512-440-1991, fax 512-440-0115
http://www.humanitiestexas.org

Utah

Utah Humanities Council
202 W. 300 North
Salt Lake City, UT 84103
801-359-9670, fax 801-531-7869
http://www.utahhumanities.org

Vermont

Vermont Humanities Council
11 Loomis St.
Montpelier, VT 05602
802-262-2626, fax 802-262-2620
http://www.vermonthumanities.org

Virginia

Virginia Foundation for the Humanities and
    Public Policy
145 Ednam Drive
Charlottesville, VA 22903-4629
434-924-3296, fax 434-296-4714
http://www.virginiafoundation.org

Washington

Humanities Washington
1204 Minor Ave.
Seattle, WA 98101
206-682-1770, fax 206-682-4158
http://www.humanities.org

West Virginia

West Virginia Humanities Council
1310 Kanawha Blvd. E., Suite 800
Charleston, WV 25301
304-346-8500, fax 304-346-8504
http://www.wvhumanities.org

Wisconsin

Wisconsin Humanities Council
222 S. Bedford St., Suite F
Madison, WI 53703-3688
608-262-0706, fax 608-263-7970
http://www.wisconsinhumanities.org

Wyoming

Wyoming Humanities Council
1315 E. Lewis St.
Laramie, WY 82072-3459
307-721-9243, fax 307-742-4914
http://uwadmnweb.uwyo.edu/humanities

American Samoa

Amerika Samoa Humanities Council
P.O. Box 5800
Pago Pago, AS 96799

684-633-4870, fax 684-633-4873

Guam

Guam Humanities Council
222 Chalan Santo Papa
Reflection Center, Suite 106
Hagatna, Guam 96910
671-472-4460, fax 671-472-4465
http://www.guamhumanitiescouncil.org

Northern Mariana Islands

Northern Mariana Islands Council for the
    Humanities
P.O. Box 506437
Saipan, MP 96950
670-235-4785, fax 670-235-4786
http://www.nmihumanities.org

Puerto Rico

Fundación Puertorriqueña de las
    Humanidades
109 San José St.
Box 9023920
San Juan, PR 00902-3920
787-721-2087, fax 787-721-2684
http://www.fphpr.org

Virgin Islands

Virgin Islands Humanities Council
1826 Kongens Gade 5-6, Suite 2
St. Thomas, VI 00802-6746
340-776-4044, fax 340-774-3972
http://www.vihumanities.org

NEH Overview

Division of Education Programs

Through grants to educational institutions and professional development programs for scholars and teachers, this division supports and strengthens the study
and teaching of the humanities at all levels of education.

Grants support the development of curriculum and materials, faculty study programs among educational institutions, and conferences and networks of institutions.

Eligible applicants: Public and private elementary and secondary
schools, school systems, colleges and universities,
nonprofit academic associations, and cultural institutions, such as libraries and museums

Application deadlines:	Humanities Initiatives at Historically Black Colleges and Universities, Humanities Initiatives at Institutions with High Hispanic Enrollment, and Humanities Initiatives at Tribal Colleges and Universities, June 15, 2010; Picturing America School Collaboration Projects, October 7, 2010; Enduring Questions Course Grants, September 15, 2010
Contact:	202-606-8500, e-mail education@neh.gov

Seminars and Institutes

Grants support summer seminars and institutes in the humanities for college and school teachers. These faculty development activities are conducted at colleges and universities across the country, as well as at appropriate locations abroad. Those wishing to participate in seminars should submit their seminar applications to the seminar director.

Eligible applicants:	Individuals and institutions of higher learning, as well as cultural institutions
Application deadlines:	Participants, March 2, 2010, for summer seminars and institutes in 2011; directors, March 2, 2010, for summer seminars and institutes in 2011

Landmarks of American History and Culture

Grants for Landmarks workshops provide support to school teachers and to community college faculty. These professional development workshops are conducted at or near sites important to American history and culture (such as presidential residences or libraries, colonial-era settlements, major battlefields, historic districts, and sites associated with major writers or artists) to address central themes and issues in American history, government, literature, art history, and other related subjects in the humanities.

Eligibility:	Individuals, institutions of higher learning, cultural institutions
Application deadlines:	School teacher and community college faculty participants, March 16, 2010, for summer workshops in 2010; directors, March 16, 2010, for summer workshops in 2011
Contact:	202-606-8463, e-mail sem-inst@neh.gov

Division of Preservation and Access

Grants are made for projects that will create, preserve, and increase the availability of resources for research, education, and public programming in the humanities.

Projects may encompass books, journals, newspapers, manuscript and archival materials, maps, still and moving images, sound recordings, and objects of material culture held by libraries, archives, museums, historical organizations, and other repositories.

Preservation and Access Projects

Support may be sought to preserve the intellectual content and aid bibliographic control of collections; to compile bibliographies, descriptive catalogs, and guides to cultural holdings; and to create dictionaries, encyclopedias, databases, and electronic archives. Applications may also be submitted for education and training projects dealing with issues of preservation or access; for research and development leading to improved preservation and access standards, practices, and tools; and for projects to digitize historic American newspapers and to document endangered languages. Grants are also made to help smaller cultural repositories preserve and care for their humanities collections.

Proposals may combine preservation and access activities within a single project.

Eligible applicants: Nonprofit institutions, cultural organizations, state agencies, and institutional consortia

Application deadlines: May 18, July 1, July 15, September 15, and November 16, 2010

Contact: 202-606-8570, e-mail preservation@neh.gov

Division of Public Programs

Public programs bring the humanities to large audiences through libraries and museums, television and radio, historic sites, and digital media. Programs foster public understanding of major historical events and figures.

Grants support development and production of television, radio, and digital media programs; planning and implementation of museum exhibitions; interpretation of historic sites; production of related publications, multimedia components, and educational programs; and the planning and implementation of reading and discussion programs, lectures, symposia, and interpretive exhibitions of books, manuscripts, and other library resources.

Eligible applicants: Nonprofit institutions and organizations, including public television and radio stations and state humanities councils

Application deadlines: Planning, implementation, development, production: August 18, 2010, and January 2011

Contact: 202-606-8269, e-mail publicpgms@neh.gov

Division of Research Programs

The Division of Research Programs makes awards to support original scholarship in all areas of the humanities, funding individuals as well as teams of researchers and institutions. Funded projects may involve research, writing, or editing, as well as efforts to publish (online or on paper) materials of historical or literary significance.

Fellowships and Stipends

Grants provide support for scholars to undertake full-time independent research and writing in the humanities. Grants are available for a maximum of one year and a minimum of two months of summer study.

Eligible applicants:	Individuals
Application deadlines:	Fellowships, May 4, 2010; Fellowships at Digital Humanities Centers, September 15, 2010; Teaching Development Fellowships, October 4, 2010; Summer Stipends, October 4, 2010
Contact:	202-606-8200, e-mail (fellowships) fellowships@neh.gov, (summer stipends) stipends@neh.gov

Research

Grants provide up to three years of support for collaborative research in the preparation for publication of editions, translations, and other important works in the humanities, and in the conduct of large or complex interpretive studies including archaeology projects and humanities studies of science and technology. Grants also support research opportunities offered through independent research centers and international research organizations.

Eligible applicants:	Individuals, institutions of higher education, nonprofit professional associations, scholarly societies, and other nonprofit organizations
Application deadlines:	Collaborative Research and Scholarly Editions, October 28, 2010; fellowship programs at independent research institutions, August 19, 2010
Contact:	202-606-8200, e-mail research@neh.gov

Office of Challenge Grants

Nonprofit institutions interested in developing new sources of long-term support for educational, scholarly, preservation, and public programs in the humanities can be assisted in these efforts by an NEH Challenge Grant. Grantees are required to raise $3 in nonfederal donations for every federal dollar offered. Both federal and nonfederal funds may be used to establish or increase institutional endowments and therefore guarantee long-term support for a variety of humanities needs. Funds also may be used for limited direct capital expenditures where such needs are compelling and clearly related to improvements in the humanities.

Eligible applicants:	Nonprofit postsecondary, educational, research, or cultural institutions and organizations working within the humanities.
Application deadlines:	Challenge Grants, May 5, 2010; We the People Challenge Grants, February 3, 2011
Contact:	202-606-8309, e-mail challenge@neh.gov

Office of Digital Humanities

The Office of Digital Humanities (ODH) promotes the use of technology to ask new questions. Responding to needs that may have arisen only recently, it makes grants and sponsors efforts that show how new media and technology are reshaping traditional disciplines in the humanities. The future of scholarly publishing, the impact of open access, the development of new digital tools, and the relevance of supercomputing all fall within the domain of its grant-making and other activities.

ODH coordinates the endowment's efforts in the area of digital scholarship. Currently NEH has numerous programs throughout the agency that are actively funding digital scholarship, including Humanities Collections and Resources, Institutes for Advanced Topics in the Digital Humanities, Digital Humanities Challenge Grants, Digital Humanities Start-Up Grants, and many others. The endowment is also actively working with other funding partners, both within the United States and abroad, to better coordinate spending on digital infrastructure for the humanities.

Eligible applicants:	Nonprofit postsecondary, educational, research, or cultural institutions and organizations working within the humanities
Application deadlines:	Digital Humanities Start-Up Grants, March 23, 2010; Institutes for Advanced Topics in the Digital Humanities, February 17, 2011
Contact:	202-606-8401, e-mail odh@neh.gov

Institute of Museum and Library Services Office of Library Services

1800 M St. N.W., Ninth Floor, Washington, DC 20036-5802
202-653-4657, fax 202-653-4625
World Wide Web http://www.imls.gov

Anne-Imelda M. Radice
Director

Mary L. Chute
Deputy Director for Libraries

Mission

The Institute of Museum and Library Services (IMLS) is the primary source of federal support for the nation's 123,000 libraries and 17,500 museums. The institute's mission is to support the development of strong libraries and museums that connect people to information and ideas. IMLS works at the national level and in coordination with state and local organizations to sustain heritage, culture, and knowledge; enhance learning and innovation; and support professional development.

Overview

Libraries and museums help create vibrant, energized learning communities. Our achievement as individuals, and our success as a society, depend on learning continually, adapting to change readily, and evaluating information critically.

Museums and libraries—as stewards of cultural heritage, information, and ideas—traditionally have played a vital role in helping people experience, explore, discover, and make sense of the world. Through building technological infrastructure and strengthening community relationships, libraries and museums can offer the public unprecedented access and expertise in transforming information overload into knowledge.

The role of IMLS is to provide leadership and funding for libraries and museums, resources these institutions need to fulfill their mission of becoming centers of learning crucial to achieving personal fulfillment, a productive work force, and an engaged citizenry.

Specifically, the Museum and Library Services Act authorizes IMLS to support the following activities:

Library Services and Technology Act (LSTA)

- To promote improvements in library services in all types of libraries to better serve the people of the United States
- To facilitate access to resources and in all types of libraries for the purpose of cultivating an educated and informed citizenry

- To encourage resource sharing among all types of libraries for the purpose of achieving economical and efficient delivery of library services to the public

Museum Services Act

- To encourage and support museums in carrying out their public service role of connecting the whole society to cultural, artistic, historic, natural, and scientific understandings that constitute its heritage
- To encourage and support museums in carrying out their educational role as core providers of learning and in conjunction with schools, families, and communities
- To encourage leadership, innovation, and applications of the most current technologies and practices to enhance museum services
- To assist, encourage, and support museums in carrying out their stewardship responsibilities to achieve the highest standards in conservation and care of the cultural, historic, natural, and scientific heritage of the United States to benefit future generations
- To assist, encourage, and support museums in achieving the highest standards of management and service to the public, and to ease the financial burden borne by museums as a result of their increasing use by the public
- To support resource sharing and partnerships among museums, libraries, schools, and other community organizations

Fiscal Year 2009

In fiscal year (FY) 2009, Congress appropriated $225,770,010 for the programs and administrative support authorized by LSTA. The Office of Library Services within IMLS, under the policy direction of the IMLS director and deputy director, administers LSTA programs. The office comprises the Division of State Programs, which administers the Grants to States program, and the Division of Discretionary Programs, which administers the National Leadership Grants for Libraries program, the Laura Bush 21st Century Librarian program, the Native American Library Services program, and the Native Hawaiian Library Services program. IMLS also presents annual awards to libraries through the National Medal for Museum and Library Service program. Additionally, IMLS is one of the sponsoring organizations supporting the Coming Up Taller awards (in conjunction with the President's Committee on the Arts and the Humanities, the National Endowment for the Arts, and the National Endowment for the Humanities), the Big Read program (in partnership with the National Endowment for the Arts), and Save America's Treasures (in partnership with the National Park Service, the National Trust for Historic Preservation, Heritage Preservation, the National Endowment for the Arts, and the National Park Foundation).

Impact of Museum and Library Services

A general provision of the Museum and Library Services Act states that "the IMLS director shall carry out and publish analyses of the impact of museum and library services. Such analyses

- Shall be conducted in ongoing consultation with state library administrative agencies; state, regional, and national library and museum organizations; and other relevant agencies and organizations
- Shall identify national needs for, and trends of, museum and library services provided with funds made available under subchapters II and III of this chapter
- Shall report on the impact and effectiveness of programs conducted with funds made available by the Institute in addressing such needs
- Shall identify, and disseminate information on, the best practices of such programs to the agencies and entities described"

Library Statistics

The presidential budget request for FY 2009 included funds for IMLS to continue administering the Public Libraries Survey (PLS) and the State Library Agencies Survey (StLAS), which had been transferred to IMLS from the National Center for Education Statistics (NCES) effective October 1, 2008. FY 2009 marked the first year that IMLS administered the two surveys over a full collection cycle, from survey planning to collection and dissemination. Responding to concerns from the professional community, IMLS has reduced by six months the time it takes to release survey results. In addition to producing annual reports reporting the survey data, IMLS introduced new, shorter research products to highlight report findings. These new reports leverage the survey data to address a wide range of public policy priorities, including education, employment, community and economic development, and telecommunications policy.

In the Library Statistics section of the IMLS Web site (http://www.imls.gov/statistics), visitors can link to data search tools, the latest available data for each survey, other publications, data files, and survey definitions.

Public Libraries Survey

Descriptive statistics for more than 9,000 public libraries are collected and disseminated annually through a voluntary census, the Public Libraries Survey (PLS). The survey is conducted through the Public Library Statistics Cooperative (PLSC, formerly the Federal-State Cooperative System, or FSCS). IMLS will complete the 13th collection of this data in FY 2010.

PLS collects identifying information about public libraries and each of their service outlets, including street address, mailing address, Web address, and telephone number. The survey collects data about public libraries, including data on staffing, type of legal basis, type of geographic boundary, type of administrative structure, type of interlibrary relationship, type and number of public service outlets, operating revenue and expenditures, capital revenue and expenditures, size of collection (including number of electronic books and databases), current serial subscriptions (including electronic), and such service measures as number of reference transactions, interlibrary loans, circulation, public service hours, library visits, circulation of children's materials, number of children's programs, children's program attendance, total number of library programs, total attendance at library programs, number of Internet terminals used by the general public, and number of users of electronic resources per year.

PLS also collects several data items about outlets, including the location of an outlet relative to a metropolitan area, number of books-by-mail-only outlets, number of bookmobiles by bookmobile outlet, and square footage of the outlet.

The 50 states and the District of Columbia have participated in data collection from the survey's inception in 1989. In 1993 Guam, the Commonwealth of the Northern Mariana Islands, Puerto Rico, and the U.S. Virgin Islands were added. The first release of Public Libraries Survey data occurred with the release of the updated Compare Public Libraries Tool on the Library Statistics section of the IMLS Web site (http://www.imls.gov/statistics). The data used in this Web tool are final, but do not include imputations for missing data (imputation is a statistical means for providing an estimate for each missing data item).

Final imputed data files that contain FY 2007 data on more than 9,000 responding libraries and identifying information about their outlets were made available in November 2008 on the Library Statistics section of the IMLS Web site. The FY 2007 data were aggregated to state and national levels in the report *Public Libraries in the United States: Fiscal Year 2007,* released in June 2009 on the IMLS Web site. The Compare Public Libraries Tool and the Find Public Libraries Tool were updated with FY 2007 data. FY 2008 data were expected to be available on these tools in spring 2010.

An important new feature of the public library data tools is the availability of geographic identifiers for all administrative entities and outlets. These geocodes allow researchers to link the PLS data to other data sets using standard geographic information system (GIS) tools, which increases the utility of the data file for a wider set of research and analysis questions.

State Library Agencies Survey

The State Library Agencies Survey (StLAS) collects and disseminates information about the state library agencies in the 50 states and the District of Columbia. A state library agency is the official unit of state government charged with statewide library development and the administration of federal funds under LSTA. The agencies' administrative and developmental responsibilities affect the operation of thousands of public, academic, school, and special libraries. They provide important reference and information services to state government and sometimes also provide service to the general public. State library agencies often administer the state library as well as special operations such as state archives and libraries for the blind and physically handicapped, and the state Center for the Book.

The survey began in 1994 and was administered by the National Center for Education Statistics (NCES) until 2007. The FY 2008 StLAS collected data on the following areas: direct library services; adult literacy and family literacy; library development services; resources assigned to allied operations such as archive and records management; organizational and governance structure within which the agency operates; electronic networking; staffing; collections; and expenditures. The FY 2008 survey was the 15th in the series. These data are edited electronically, and before FY 1999 missing data were not imputed; beginning with FY 1999 data, however, national totals included imputations for missing data. Another change is that beginning with FY 1999 data, the StLAS became a Web-based data collection system. The most recent data available are for FY 2008. The survey database and report were released in December 2009.

National Medal for Museum and Library Service

The National Medal for Museum and Library Service honors outstanding institutions that make significant and exceptional contributions to their communities. Selected institutions demonstrate extraordinary and innovative approaches to public service, exceeding the expected levels of community outreach and core programs generally associated with their services. The medal includes a prize of $10,000 to each recipient and an awards ceremony held in Washington, D.C.

The winners of the 2009 National Medal for Museum and Library Service were Braille Institute Library Services, Los Angeles; Children's Museum of Pittsburgh; Cincinnati Museum Center at Union Terminal; Gail Borden Public Library, Elgin, Illinois; Indianapolis Museum of Art; Multnomah County Library, Portland, Oregon; Museum of Science and Industry, Tampa; Pritzker Military Library, Chicago; Stark County District Library, Canton, Ohio; and Tennessee Aquarium, Chattanooga.

State-Administered Programs

In FY 2009 approximately 76 percent of the annual federal appropriation under LSTA was distributed through the Grants to States program to the state library administrative agencies according to a population-based formula. The formula consists of a minimum amount set by law plus a supplemental amount based on population. Population data were based on the information available from the Bureau of Census Web site on October 1, 2008. The 2003 reauthorization required that base allotments of $340,000 to the states and $40,000 to the Pacific Territories be increased to $680,000 for the states and $60,000 for the Pacific Territories. Full funding to carry out this requirement was achieved for the first time in FY 2009.

For FY 2009 the Grants to States program total appropriation was $171,500,000 (see Table 1). State agencies may use the appropriation for statewide initiatives and services. They may also distribute the funds through competitive subgrants or cooperative agreements to public, academic, research, school, or special libraries. For-profit and federal libraries are not eligible applicants. LSTA state grant funds have been used to meet the special needs of children, parents, teenagers, the unemployed, senior citizens, and the business community, as well as adult learners. Many libraries have partnered with com-

Table 1 / Library Services and Technology Act, State Allotments, FY 2009
Total Distributed to States: $171,500,000[1]

State	Federal Funds from IMLS (66%)[2]	State Matching Funds (34%)	Total Federal and State Funds
Alabama	$2,731,303	$1,407,035	$4,138,338
Alaska	982,953	506,370	1,489,323
Arizona	3,489,664	1,797,706	5,287,370
Arkansas	1,936,529	997,606	2,934,135
California	16,882,275	8,696,930	25,579,205
Colorado	2,834,875	1,460,390	4,295,265
Connecticut	2,232,404	1,150,026	3,382,430
Delaware	1,063,308	547,765	1,611,073
Florida	8,769,895	4,517,825	13,287,720
Georgia	4,910,727	2,529,768	7,440,495
Hawaii	1,248,864	643,354	1,892,218
Idaho	1,344,613	692,679	2,037,292
Illinois	6,376,914	3,285,077	9,661,991
Indiana	3,492,560	1,799,198	5,291,758
Iowa	2,004,457	1,032,599	3,037,056
Kansas	1,910,465	984,179	2,894,644
Kentucky	2,560,041	1,318,809	3,878,850
Louisiana	2,582,970	1,330,621	3,913,591
Maine	1,263,854	651,076	1,914,930
Maryland	3,170,341	1,633,206	4,803,547
Massachusetts	3,538,865	1,823,052	5,361,917
Michigan	5,144,352	2,650,121	7,794,473
Minnesota	2,983,854	1,537,137	4,520,991
Mississippi	1,973,756	1,016,783	2,990,539
Missouri	3,285,618	1,692,591	4,978,209
Montana	1,104,574	569,023	1,673,597
Nebraska	1,466,582	755,512	2,222,094
Nevada	1,817,110	936,087	2,753,197
New Hampshire	1,263,243	650,762	1,914,005
New Jersey	4,530,049	2,333,662	6,863,711
New Mexico	1,553,168	800,117	2,353,285
New York	9,233,751	4,756,781	13,990,532
North Carolina	4,696,318	2,419,315	7,115,633
North Dakota	963,555	496,377	1,459,932
Ohio	5,762,731	2,968,680	8,731,411
Oklahoma	2,283,382	1,176,288	3,459,670
Oregon	2,341,066	1,206,004	3,547,070
Pennsylvania	6,190,856	3,189,229	9,380,085
Rhode Island	1,148,886	591,850	1,740,736
South Carolina	2,633,725	1,356,767	3,990,492
South Dakota	1,032,923	532,112	1,565,035
Tennessee	3,408,976	1,756,139	5,165,115
Texas	11,275,657	5,808,672	17,084,329
Utah	1,852,547	954,342	2,806,889
Vermont	955,372	492,161	1,447,533
Virginia	4,098,398	2,111,296	6,209,694
Washington	3,547,140	1,827,315	5,374,455

West Virginia	1,483,188	764,067	2,247,255
Wisconsin	3,162,937	1,629,392	4,792,329
Wyoming	911,745	469,687	1,381,432
District of Columbia	940,761	484,634	1,425,395
Puerto Rico	2,427,058	1,250,303	3,677,361
American Samoa	88,735	45,712	134,447
Northern Marianas	98,393	50,687	149,080
Guam	137,958	71,069	209,027
Virgin Islands	108,687	55,990	164,677
Pacific Territories[3]	265,072	136,552	401,624
Total	$171,500,000	$88,348,487	$259,848,487

1 The amount available to states is based on the estimated appropriation for FY 2009.

2 Calculation is based on minimum set in the law (P.L. 108-81).
Population data is from the Bureau of Census (BOC) estimates. Data used in the state allotment table are the most current published population estimates available the first day of the fiscal year. Therefore, the population data used in the 2009 table is what was available on the BOC Web site (http://www.census.gov/popest/states/index.html) on October 1, 2008. Population data for American Samoa, Northern Marianas, Guam, Virgin Islands, Marshall Islands, Federated States of Micronesia, and Palau can be accessed at http://www.census.gov/cgi-bin/ipc/idbrank.pl. This table reflects what was available on October 1, 2008.

3 Aggregate allotments (including administrative costs) for Palau, Marshall Islands, and Federated States of Micronesia are awarded on a competitive basis to eligible applicants, and are administered by Pacific Resources for Education and Learning (PREL).

munity organizations to provide a variety of services and programs, including access to electronic databases, computer instruction, homework centers, summer reading programs, digitization of special collections, access to e-books and adaptive technology, bookmobile service, and development of outreach programs to the underserved. The act limits the amount of funds available for administration at the state level to 4 percent and requires a 34 percent match from nonfederal state or local funds.

Grants to the Pacific Territories and the Freely Associated States (FAS) are funded under a Special Rule, 20 USCA 9131(b)(3), which authorizes a small competitive grants program in the Pacific region and the U.S. Virgin Islands. There are seven eligible entities: Guam, American Samoa, the Commonwealth of Northern Mariana Islands, the Federated States of Micronesia, the Republic of the Marshall Islands, the Republic of Palau, and the U.S. Virgin Islands. The funds for this grant program are taken from the allotment amounts for the Federated States of Micronesia, the Republic of the Marshall Islands, and Palau. The territories (Guam, American Samoa, Commonwealth of the Northern Mariana Islands, and the U.S. Virgin Islands) receive their allotments through the Grants to States program and, in addition, may apply for funds under the competitive program. In FY 2009 a total of $265,072 was available for the seven entities. This amount included a set-aside of 5 percent for Pacific Resources for Education and Learning (PREL), based in Hawaii, to facilitate the grants review process. Therefore, the total amount awarded in FY 2009 was $251,816.

The LSTA-funded programs and services delivered by each state library administrative agency support the purposes and priorities set forth in legislation. The individual agencies set goals and objectives for their state regarding the expenditure of Grants to States funds within the statutorily required five-year plan on file with IMLS. These goals and objectives are determined through a planning process that includes statewide needs assessments.

On a rotating basis, IMLS Grants to States program staff members conduct site visits to the state agencies to provide technical support and to monitor the states' success in administering the LSTA program. In 2009 program officers visited eight agencies, in Hawaii, Kansas, Kentucky, North Carolina, South Carolina, South Dakota, Washington, and Wisconsin. Each site visit includes a critical review of the administration of the LSTA program at the agency as well as trips into the field to visit libraries that are recipients of subgrants or beneficiaries of statewide LSTA projects.

Discretionary Grants Programs

IMLS began administering the discretionary grants programs of LSTA in 1998. In FY 2009 a total of $40,679,000 was allocated for discretionary programs, distributed as follows: National Leadership Grants, $12,437,000; Laura Bush 21st Century Librarian Program, $24,525,000; Native American Library Services, $3,186,000; Native Hawaiian Library Services, $531,000.

National Leadership Grants for Libraries

The National Leadership Grants for Libraries program provides funding for research and innovative model programs to enhance the quality of library services nationwide. National Leadership Grants are competitive and intended to produce results useful for the broader library community.

During 2009 IMLS awarded 30 National Leadership Grants totaling $12,009,544. A total of 101 applications were received, requesting more than $39,000,000. Projects were funded in four categories: Advancing Digital Resources, Demonstration, Research, and Library and Museum Community Collaboration (see Table 2). In addition, IMLS offered Collaborative Planning Grants of up to $100,000 in all categories of the National Leadership Grants program. Collaborative Planning Grants enable project teams from libraries, museums, or other partner organizations to work together on the planning of a collaborative project in any of the National Leadership Grant categories. Partnerships with museums are not required for any projects except those in the Library and Museum Community Collaboration category.

Advancing Digital Resources (Maximum Award $1 Million)

This award category supports the creation, use, preservation, and presentation of significant digital resources as well as the development of tools to manage digital assets, incorporating new technologies or new technology practice. IMLS supported projects that

- Developed and disseminated new tools to facilitate management, preservation, sharing, and use of digital resources
- Increased community access to institutional resources through innovative use of existing technology-based tools

(text continues on page 302)

Table 2 / National Leadership Grants for Libraries, FY 2009

Advancing Digital Resources

Georgia Institute of Technology Research Corporation $850,505

The GALILEO Knowledge Repository: Advancing the Access and
Management of Scholarly Digital Content

The Georgia Institute of Technology—in partnership with the University of Georgia, Georgia
State University, the Medical College of Georgia, Georgia Southern University, Valdosta State
University, Albany State University, North Georgia College and State University, and the College of Coastal Georgia—will build a statewide institutional repository (IR) called the
GALILEO Knowledge Repository. The partners will also host a national symposium on
statewide and consortial repositories, create instructional materials, conduct consortial IR
training, and offer consulting services.

Regents of the University of California, Los Angeles $249,342

The Next Generation Sheet Music Consortium

The university will partner with Indiana University to develop tools and services to meet the
needs both of data providers (libraries, museums, historical societies, and other curators of
sheet music collections) and users of sheet music (musicologists, performers, cultural and
art historians, and so forth) as identified from a needs analysis that was funded by a 2007
planning grant from the IMLS National Leadership Grants program.

University of North Carolina at Chapel Hill $249,623

Closing the Digital Curation Gap: An International Collaboration to Integrate
Best Practice, Research, and Education

The university's School of Information and Library Science will be the U.S. lead, working in
partnership with the Joint Information Systems Committee (JISC), a funding body in the United Kingdom for information technology, and its funded entities, the Strategic Content
Alliance, and the Digital Curation Centre. The partnership will establish a baseline of digital
curation practice and knowledge, especially for small to medium-sized cultural heritage institutions in the United States and Britain through surveys, interviews, and case studies.

President and Fellows of Harvard College $823,016

A Policy Based Archival Replication System for Libraries, Archives, and
Museums Using a Virtual Private LOCKSS

Harvard will develop and distribute a production-ready open source tool for verified distributed replication of digital collection data based on an existing prototype, working with the
Odum Institute for Research (University of North Carolina at Chapel Hill), the Roper Center
for Public Opinion (University of Connecticut), and the Interuniversity Consortium for Political
and Social Research (University of Michigan). The tool will allow any library, museum, or
archive to audit replication of their content across an existing LOCKSS (Lots of Copies Keep
Stuff Safe) network and will allow groups of collaborating institutions to automatically and verifiably replicate each others' content.

Washington University, St. Louis $376,426

The St. Louis Freedom Suits Legal Encoding Project

The Washington University Libraries, in partnership with the Missouri History Museum and
other contributors within and outside the university, will digitize, transcribe, and encode the
St. Louis Circuit Court Historical Records Project and supplementary materials. Creating a
full-text searchable collection of these documents and enhancing their use will provide new
means of understanding the roles of slaves, lawyers, abolitionists, the state of Missouri, and
others involved in these cases.

Table 2 / National Leadership Grants for Libraries, FY 2009 *(cont.)*

WGBH Educational Foundation $487,681

The Boston TV News Digital Library: 1960–2000

The WGBH Media Library and Archives—in collaboration with Northeast Historic Film, Cambridge Community Television, and the Boston Public Library—will develop the first online resource offering a city's commercial, noncommercial, and community cable TV news heritage. The purpose of the collaboration is to use, test, and demonstrate open source tools to assist custodians of similar resources, while creating an online library offering 40 years of urban moving-image materials, resulting in approximately 70,000 news records.

Regents of the University of California, Santa Cruz $615,175

Creating a Virtual Terrapin Station: Blending Traditional and Socially Constructed Archives for Research, Teaching

The university will digitize materials from its Grateful Dead archive and make them available in a unique Web site, the Virtual Terrapin Station, which will provide access to Grateful Dead archive materials and tools to facilitate public contributions to the archive. This project will enable the university to convert a significant part of a traditional archive to digital form and make it available online while simultaneously experimenting with the impact of fostering, creating, and curating a large, socially constructed archive.

Educational Broadcasting Corporation, Thirteen/WNET $976,549

Refining a Digital Production Workflow in Public Television to Aggregate Video Assets for Educational Use

The corporation will create a set of media asset management-based tools that will allow multiple groups of users to package digital video content easily for distribution over multiple non-broadcast channels. This project will make the corporation's digital content more widely available for cross-platform use, lead public broadcast organizations toward adopting systemwide technical standards and metadata schemata, and make important broadcast material available for classroom use.

Regents of the University of Michigan $247,262

Rescuing and Archiving Social Science Data

The Interuniversity Consortium for Political and Social Research, the world's largest social science data archive, will work with members of the institutional repositories community to preserve and reuse legacy social science data. The project will salvage many important legacy studies and their supporting datasets by converting them to new formats, and will develop tools and workflows to improve the archiving of current data.

George Washington University $399,290

Cultural Imaginings: The Creation of the Arab World in the Western Mind

The libraries of George Washington University and Georgetown University will digitize their jointly held collections of Western literature on the Middle East and works by Middle Eastern and North African authors, comprising more than 2,500 volumes. The collections will be freely accessible to scholars and the general public worldwide.

Advancing Digital Resources: Planning Grants

Wheaton College $86,770

Publishing TEI Documents for Small Liberal Arts Colleges: Planning a Service, Building a Community

The Text Encoding Initiative (TEI) has become the main vehicle for transcribing and encoding primary source and archival texts. The long-term goal of this project is to identify and develop an implementation plan to allow scholars and archivists from a wide array of liberal arts schools to store and display their TEI-enhanced digitized texts. Project participants will

Table 2 / National Leadership Grants for Libraries, FY 2009 *(cont.)*

conduct a survey of smaller colleges to identify peers who work with TEI and would benefit from joining in a community investment in the collection tool.

Bridgeport Roman Catholic Diocesan Corp. $50,000

Creating Global Learning and Cultural Centers Through Advancing Digital Resources in Our School Libraries

Working with the State Library of Connecticut, the corporation will investigate strategies to enhance parochial school libraries and build strategic partnerships with other school libraries and public libraries.

Pennsylvania State University Libraries $82,702

The Pennsylvania Home Front in the Civil War

Under a one-year planning grant, the university libraries and the Penn State George and Ann Richards Civil War Era Center—in partnership with the Pennsylvania Historical and Museum Commission, the State Library of Pennsylvania, the Historical Society of Pennsylvania, and the Historical Society of Western Pennsylvania—will lay the groundwork for a multiyear library-archive-scholar collaboration to digitize primary source materials held in Pennsylvania archives and special collections.

Demonstration

Association of Southeastern Research Libraries $328,329

ASERL Collaborative Federal Depository Project

The Association of Southeastern Research Libraries (ASERL), in partnership with the University of Kentucky and the University of South Carolina, will create collaborative centers of excellence among federally designated regional depository libraries, to improve access to federal government publications and create a model for improving depository library services and operations.

University of Guam $401,118

Information Literacy for Future Island Leaders

The university library will create a comprehensive system of graduate student support through new bibliographic instruction classes, research services, and digital resources. The library team will design services and instruction to support graduate programs and research using both traditional and digital resources. The project will demonstrate and test methods of advanced academic research assistance and instructional tools that can serve as models for libraries seeking to respond to student research needs.

University of Hawaii at Manoa $249,918

Pathways to Excellence and Achievement in Research and Learning (PEARL)

University faculty and librarians will design, implement, and assess a team-based model of professional development for high school librarians and teachers collaborating to help high school students construct rigorous, inquiry-focused, capstone research projects. The project will produce a training guide that can be used to create similar professional development programs, including training agendas, instructional materials, and recommended resources.

King County (Washington) Library System $998,556

Empowered by Open Source

King County Library System will partner with Peninsula Library System in San Mateo, California; Orange County Library System in Orlando, Florida; and Ann Arbor (Michigan) District Library to create and develop critical infrastructure components that have traditionally been provided by integrated library system (ILS) vendors, and will establish a peer-to-peer support model for open source libraries.

Table 2 / National Leadership Grants for Libraries, FY 2009 *(cont.)*

Demonstration: Planning Grants

University of Texas at Brownsville and Texas Southmost College $99,276

Planning for the Development of a Border Studies Resource Center

The university and college—working with the Colegio de la Frontera Norte in Matamoros, Tamaulipas, Mexico—will develop a plan to create a Border Studies Resource Center to serve institutions of higher education and others on both sides of the U.S.-Mexico border. It also will plan for the development of a digital repository of border studies-related research and resources.

University of Washington, Seattle $92,744

Project VIEWS: Valuable Initiatives in Early Learning that Work Successfully

This project's purpose is to plan to extend the local model of successful early-learning services and partnerships in Washington's public libraries into an exemplary, evaluated model that could be utilized nationally to support children's success in school through public library leadership. The University of Washington Information School is collaborating with the Florida State University College of Information, the Washington Early Learning Public Library Partnership (involving 21 urban, suburban, and rural library systems), and the Washington Foundation for Early Learning.

OCLC/WebJunction $80,537

Online Patron Instruction in Public Libraries

WebJunction is partnering with San Francisco Public Library to develop a plan for the creation of online patron instruction in public libraries. This project will conduct preliminary research on the "state of the library industry" for patron instruction; assess needs of both patrons and library staff; pilot a small set of patron-facing online programming in San Francisco public libraries; and produce a final evaluation of the effectiveness and efficiencies of the online programs and of the resulting behavioral changes in both patrons and library staff.

Research

Image Permanence Institute, Rochester Institute of Technology $580,174

Research on Energy-Saving Opportunities in Libraries

This project will investigate a promising method for libraries to achieve significant reductions in energy use without compromising the preservation quality of collection environments through a carefully monitored and risk-managed shutdown of air-handling units during unoccupied hours. Five partner libraries will help determine through actual experiment and documentation whether it is feasible to save energy in this manner.

University of Tennessee $1 million

Value, Outcomes, and Return on Investment of Academic Libraries (Lib-Value)

Lib-Value addresses academic librarians' growing need to demonstrate the return on investment and value of the library to the institution and will help guide library management in the redirection of library funds to important products and services for the future.

University of North Texas $631,720

Classification of Government Web Sites in the End-of-Term Archive: Extending Depository Libraries' Collection Development Practices

The university is partnering with the Internet Archive to investigate needs in the area of government information. Government information is represented in many library collections and has a well-established classification scheme, the Superintendent of Documents (SuDocs) Classification Numbering System. The project will classify, in accord with the SuDocs sys-

Table 2 / National Leadership Grants for Libraries, FY 2009 *(cont.)*

tem, the materials in the 2008–2009 End-of-Term Web, collected by the University of North Texas, which represents the entirety of the federal government's public Web presence before and after the 2009 change in presidential administrations.

University of North Carolina at Chapel Hill $492,463

Policy-Driven Repository Interoperability (PoDRI)

The university and the DuraSpace organization (formerly DSpace and the Fedora Commons) are partnering in a project to investigate the feasibility of interoperability mechanisms between repositories at the policy level. The project focuses on the integration of an object model and a policy-aware distributed data model with Fedora and iRODS as representative open source software for each model.

Lawrence Berkeley National Laboratory, University of California $673,344

Advancing Optical Scanning of Mechanical Sound Carriers: Connecting to Collections and Collaborations

Working with the Library of Congress, the laboratory will partner with the Phoebe Hearst Museum of Anthropology, the University of Chicago's South Asia Library, the Berlin Phonogramm Archive, the Smithsonian Institution's National Museum of American History, the Edison National Historic Site, and the University of Applied Science in Fribourg, Switzerland, to build on the success of the "3D/PRISM" or "IRENE-3D" project previously funded by IMLS. The project's goals are to enable institutions that hold rare early sound recordings made on wax cylinders to be recovered and digitally remastered even when the original cylinder is cracked or broken and can no longer be played.

Research: Planning Grants

Council on Library and Information Resources $96,879

Collaborative Planning (Co-Plan) to Support an Infrastructure for Humanities Scholarship

The Council on Library and Information Resources, in partnership with Tufts University, will lead a collaborative planning process engaging scholars and academic librarians to examine the services and digital objects classicists have developed, their future research needs, and the roles of libraries and other curatorial institutions in fostering the infrastructure on which the core intellectual activities of classics and many other disciplines depend.

Library and Museum Community Collaboration

Queens Museum of Art $433,596

Inviting Institutions: A Collaborative Approach to Family Programming for Audiences with Special Needs

The Queens (New York) Museum of Art, in partnership with Queens Library and Quality Services for the Autistic Community, will develop and implement a model community-based art therapy program for Spanish-speaking families of children with autism spectrum disorders. The goal is to make libraries and museums and their services more inviting to these non-English-speaking families. Over the three-year grant period, the project will produce 25 scheduled activities for families of children with autism spectrum disorders as well as two exhibitions of artwork by students with the disorders.

MATRIX Center for Humane Arts, Letters, and Social Sciences, Michigan State University $319,284

Oral History in the Digital Age

The university, through the MATRIX Center and the university museum, will partner with the Smithsonian Institution's Center for Folklife and Cultural Heritage, the Library of Congress's American Folklife Center, the American Folklore Society, and the Oral History Association to recommend standards and best practices for digital oral history.

Table 2 / National Leadership Grants for Libraries, FY 2009 *(cont.)*

Library and Museum Community Collaboration: Planning Grants

Ohio Historical Society $49,964

Building Connections: A Collaborative Planning Project

The society—in a planning grant partnership with the Kent State University School of Library and Information Science, the Ohio Humanities Council, and the Ohio Association of Historical Societies and Museums—will develop a sustainable and replicable model for cultural heritage organizations and schools of library and information science. Its goal is to solidify and formalize connections between partners and create unique learning opportunities emphasizing the commonalities between skill sets needed for staff in different types of cultural organizations.

Minnesota Children's Museum $50,000

Supporting Early Literacy Learning: A Model Partnership Between a Children's Museum and Public Libraries

In partnership with the Dakota County Library System, Hennepin County Library System, Saint Paul Public Library System, and other partners in the region, the museum will develop and test an innovative early literacy program. The project will explore new directions in which libraries and museums can bring their unique expertise together for new successful collaborations.

(continued from page 296)

- Increased community access to institutional resources by improving practice in use, dissemination, and support of existing technology-based tools
- Developed or advanced participation in museum and/or library communities using social technologies in new ways
- Developed new approaches or tools for digital curation

Demonstration (Maximum Award $1 Million)

Demonstration projects use available knowledge to address key needs and challenges facing libraries and museums, and transform that knowledge into formal practice. Funded projects

- Demonstrated and/or tested new practices in library and/or museum operations
- Demonstrated how libraries and/or museums serve their communities by fostering public value and implementing systemic changes in the field
- Established and/or tested standards and tools for innovative learning
- Demonstrated and/or tested an expansion of preservation or conservation practices

Research (Maximum Award $1 Million)

Research grants support projects that have the potential to improve library and museum practice, resource use, programs, and services. Both basic and applied research projects are encouraged. Funded projects

- Evaluated the impact of library or museum services
- Investigated how learning takes place in libraries and museums, and how use of library and/or museum resources enhance learning

- Investigated how to improve the quality, effectiveness, or efficiency of library or museum management programs or services
- Investigated ways to enhance the archiving, preservation, management, discovery, and use of digital assets and resources
- Investigated or conducted research to add new knowledge or make improvements in the conservation and preservation of collections

Library and Museum Community Collaboration (Maximum Award $1 Million)

This award category helps to create new opportunities for libraries and museums to engage with each other, and with other organizations as appropriate, to support the educational, economic, and social needs of their communities. A partnership of at least one eligible library entity and one eligible museum entity is required. Additional partners are encouraged where appropriate. Both research and implementation projects are eligible. Grant funds supported innovative collaborative projects, whether they were new partnerships or were building on an existing collaboration. Funded projects

- Addressed community civic and educational needs
- Increased the organizations' capacity to serve as effective venues and resources for learning
- Used technology in innovative ways to serve audiences more effectively

Collaborative Planning Grants (Maximum Award $100,000)

This category enables project teams from libraries, museums, and other partnering organizations to fully develop ideas for a National Leadership Grant project among project partners and should result in such products as plans, prototypes, or proofs of concept that could lead to a National Leadership Grant proposal. Collaborative Planning Grants support a variety of activities including partnership development, literature searches, project formation, and other planning efforts. These planning grants may also be used for workshops or convenings to support discussion by library and/or museum experts. These meetings should consider issues of national importance in the library and/or museum field, and result in a broadly disseminated report identifying the national challenges discussed, with recommendations for proposed research or solutions to address the challenges. Workshop/convening recommendations could lead to one or more National Leadership Grant proposals for project grants.

Laura Bush 21st Century Librarian Program

The Laura Bush 21st Century Librarian Program (maximum award $1 million) was established in 2003 as the Librarians for the 21st Century program; the name was changed in 2006 in accordance with the provisions of IMLS's congressional appropriation. The program provides competitive funding to support projects to recruit and educate the next generation of librarians and library leaders, build institutional capacity in graduate schools of library and information science and develop faculty who will help in this endeavor, conduct needed research on the

(text continues on page 308)

Table 3 / Laura Bush 21st Century Librarian Program, FY 2009

Doctoral Programs

University of Tennessee $711,727

Through previous and ongoing projects, the university's School of Information Sciences and College of Communication have identified a serious shortage of doctoral-level educators qualified to train librarians in working with scientific data and information. To address the shortage, the school will recruit and provide six IMLS-funded fellowships for students to earn a doctoral degree in library and information science with a specialization in scientific data and information.

Master's Programs

Colorado Seminary $917,891

In a project to prepare more librarians qualified to work with very young children in achieving early literacy, the University of Denver's Library and Information Science Program will partner with the Arapahoe Library District, the Colorado State Library, Colorado Libraries for Early Literacy, and Douglas Libraries. IMLS-funded fellowships will be awarded to support ten students earning master's degrees in librarianship with a specialization in early childhood literacy.

Denver Public Library $988,355

Building on the success of two previous initiatives, the library will partner with the Colorado Association of Libraries, REFORMA–Colorado, and the University of Denver to produce 18 additional librarians with the language skills, experience, and cultural awareness needed to serve these communities. This project will focus particularly on creating new librarians to serve Hispanic communities.

Louisiana State University and A&M College $763,901

Libraries in southern Louisiana continue to experience staffing shortages as a result of the damage caused to local communities by Hurricane Katrina in 2005. The university's School of Library and Information Science—in collaboration with the State Library of Louisiana, the state Department of Education, the New Orleans Public Library, Terrebonne Parish Public Library, Calcasieu Parish Public Library, the New Orleans Recovery School District, the Algiers Charter School Association, Jefferson Parish School System, and Southern University at New Orleans—will partner to help alleviate the shortage of librarians by recruiting, educating, and placing 30 new librarians in various libraries.

Montana State Library $730,659

The library—in partnership with the Idaho Commission for Libraries, the South Dakota State Library, and the Wyoming State Library—will recruit and provide IMLS-funded scholarships to educate 50 librarians and school library media specialists to work in that region's rural communities.

Sam Houston State University $898,195

The university's Department of Library Science will partner with the Texas Education Agency's Regional Education Centers 1, 2, and 20 to recruit and provide scholarships to 40 students studying to be certified school library media specialists. This project addresses a critical need for school library media specialists to serve the region's growing Hispanic student population.

Serra Cooperative Library System, San Diego $708,138

The library system, serving 14 public library systems in two highly diverse and multilingual southern California counties, will recruit and provide scholarships to 20 people to enable them to pursue a master's of library science degree through San Jose State University's School of Library and Information Science. Project partners include the Desert Valley Library Media Association and the San Diego Chapter of REFORMA.

Table 3 / Laura Bush 21st Century Librarian Program, FY 2009 *(cont.)*

University of Maryland at College Park $770,943

The University of Maryland at College Park's College of Information Studies, in partnership with the University of Illinois at Chicago, will create a new librarianship specialization in government information services to address challenges presented by changes in the ways governments produce and make information available to the public.

University of Oklahoma $414,545

The university's academic libraries and its School of Library and Information Studies will partner with academic libraries at East Central University, Langston University, Oklahoma Christian University, Oklahoma State University, Rose State College, and Southern Nazarene University to recruit and educate 15 new academic librarians qualified to work with underserved and minority groups.

University of Southern Mississippi $429,388

The university's School of Library and Information Science and the university libraries will partner with the Mississippi Library Association and the Mississippi Library Commission to increase the number of minority librarians in the state. Through targeted recruiting of minority undergraduates in Mississippi's universities and colleges, the project will award IMLS-funded scholarships to support ten students earning a master's degree in librarianship.

University of Tennessee $567,660

The university's School of Information Sciences will team with the Clinch-Powell Regional Library, Sevier County Public Library System, and the Watauga Regional Library to provide 15 IMLS-funded scholarships to enable well-qualified technology support professionals already working in the region's libraries to earn a master's degree in librarianship.

University of Wisconsin–Whitewater $989,495

The University of Wisconsin System School Education Consortium (UWSSEC) is a collaborative venture of five state university campuses, in Whitewater, Madison, Eau Claire, Superior, and Oshkosh. To address a statewide shortage of school library media specialists, UWSSEC will partner with the Wisconsin Department of Public Instruction and the Wisconsin Educational Media and Technology Association to train 50 school library media specialists for the state's rural and high-need urban public schools.

University System of Georgia $680,327

The Georgia Public Library Service and Valdosta State University's Department of Information Studies will prepare 45 students to be public librarians with expertise in community building. This program of study will emphasize the crafting of library services around specific community improvement initiatives in a way that builds social and human capital.

Research

Florida State University $309,344

Marcia Mardis at Florida State University will investigate how school libraries can successfully integrate open source science, technology, engineering, and mathematics (STEM) materials into their collections and services. This project will enhance school library media specialists' collection-building practices regarding STEM materials, particularly those offered free of charge on the Internet.

Research: Early Career Development

University of Maryland at College Park $348,325

Jean Dryden of the university's College of Information Studies will examine the copyright practices of libraries, archives, and museums in the digitization of their holdings and the impact of these practices on their users. This research will aid libraries, archives, and museums as they continue to develop best practices that will make their holdings more widely available to the public while still protecting the legitimate interests of rights holders.

Table 3 / Laura Bush 21st Century Librarian Program, FY 2009 *(cont.)*

University of Maryland at College Park $387,541

As the population ages, the need increases for trusted sources of health-related information and services. Bo Xie of the university's College of Information Studies will design a public library-based program to provide high-quality, Internet-based health information to seniors from diverse backgrounds.

University of Tennessee–Knoxville $321,178

Vandana Singh of the university's School of Information Sciences will compare the level of technical support required by open source integrated library systems (the computer systems used to acquire, manage, and circulate library materials) and off-the-shelf, proprietary versions of these systems.

University of Texas at Austin $215,862

Lynn Westbrook of the university's School of Information will investigate public library service to victims of domestic violence. Approaching the task from the viewpoint of users and their needs, rather than from an examination of existing library services, this project will seek to develop, test, and implement an assessment mechanism that public libraries can use to determine how well they serve these individuals.

Preprofessional Programs

Brooklyn Public Library $497,179

Brooklyn, New York, is one of the most ethnically diverse counties in the United States; nearly 37 percent of its 2.5 million residents are foreign-born. To better serve multicultural, low-income youth in this community, the Brooklyn Public Library will establish a multicultural intern program that will mesh with existing library multilingual outreach and services and will provide opportunities for both interns and librarians to share ideas and learn how to better serve a wide range of ethnic communities.

Northern Kentucky University Research Foundation $999,558

Northern Kentucky University, partnering with Bluegrass Community and Technical College and the Kentucky Department of Libraries and Archives, will provide scholarships for undergraduate degrees to 50 library staff members working in the high-poverty rural sections of eastern and far western Kentucky.

University of Illinois at Urbana-Champaign $506,910

The Library Access Midwest Program (LAMP) is a collaboration of schools of library and information science and academic libraries that seeks to build a more diverse academic library work force. As constituents of LAMP, the University of Illinois at Urbana-Champaign, the University of Wisconsin–Madison, Dominican University, Michigan State University, Marquette University, the University of Chicago, the University of Illinois at Chicago, the University of Iowa, the University of Wisconsin–Milwaukee, and Wayne State University will recruit 20 undergraduates, with an emphasis on those from ethnic minority backgrounds, to participate in activities and events designed to increase their awareness of career opportunities in library and information science.

Programs to Build Institutional Capacity

Simmons College $455,639

The Graduate School of Library and Information Science at Simmons College will partner with a wide range of New England cultural institutions to incorporate museum informatics and data stewardship into its existing program of study. The project will provide scholarships and intensive internships to 30 students.

Syracuse University $706,200

Partnering with the libraries of Cornell University, Syracuse seeks to educate a new generation of science librarians by developing a digital curation curriculum that will emphasize the

Table 3 / Laura Bush 21st Century Librarian Program, FY 2009 *(cont.)*

management and preservation of science-related information. In addition to curriculum planning, the project will recruit and provide scholarships to students with a background in the sciences.

University of North Carolina at Chapel Hill $803,258

The university's School of Information and Library Science and Government—partnering with the National Archives and Records Administration, the University Archives, and the State Archives of North Carolina—will further develop a dual master's degree program in public administration and library or information science with an emphasis on digital curation.

University of Pittsburgh $991,311

The university's School of Information Sciences, partnering with the university's Health Sciences Library System, will create a 15-credit, post-master's certificate of advanced studies in health sciences librarianship. This project will provide scholarships for an initial cohort of 27 students.

Continuing Education

Arizona Board of Regents, University of Arizona $910,846

Since 2007 the university's School of Information Resources and Library Science has offered the online DigIn graduate certificate program to train library professionals to create, collect, and manage digital information. In partnership with the Georgia Institute of Technology, the Sedona Conference, and the Arizona State Library, Archives, and Public Records, the school will recruit and provide scholarships to between 80 and 90 new students to earn the DigIn certificate. Recruitment efforts will target geographically, culturally, and ethnically diverse students, with the goal of diversifying the work force of digital information management experts.

Board of Trustees, University of Illinois at Urbana-Champaign $364,925

The university's Graduate School of Library and Information Science will increase the number of qualified youth services librarians by offering eight scholarships over three years to qualified and diverse students admitted to the school's Certificate of Advanced Studies program. The program provides continuing education for professionals already working in libraries.

Council on Library and Information Resources $713,108

The council, partnering with the Council of Independent Colleges, will build the skills of liberal arts college librarians working in institutions belonging to such organizations as the Appalachian College Association and the United Negro College Fund, as well as other colleges and universities serving predominantly minority and underserved student bodies.

Illinois State Library $418,758

Building on a successful state-based program, the library will develop a continuing-education initiative to build technology and leadership skills among that state's librarians. The replicable model, consisting of team- and project-based learning, will build a sustainable technology immersion program combining intermittent face-to-face meetings and online sessions over nine months.

Montana State University $251,695

The university's Tribal College Librarians Institute (TCLI) is an annual week-long conference of continuing education and professional development experiences for information professionals serving Native American communities. IMLS support over a three-year period will support TCLI during the summers of 2010, 2011, and 2012.

New York Public Library Astor, Lenox, and Tilden Foundations $577,941

Partnering with libraries at Yale, Rutgers, and the University of Connecticut at Storrs, New York Public Library will implement a preservation administration fellowship program designed to give recently graduated preservation librarians an opportunity to put theory into

Table 3 / Laura Bush 21st Century Librarian Program, FY 2009 *(cont.)*

practice while benefiting from the mentoring of experienced professionals. A total of eight fellows will spend nine-month residencies rotating through various preservation units such as collections care, conservation treatment, and audio and moving image preservation.

OCLC/WebJunction $250,000

In this one-year project, WebJunction, in partnership with the State Library of North Carolina, will develop a series of regional workshops to train librarians in the provision of information services in communities suffering from the economic downturn. The workshop will emphasize skills needed by job-seekers, including résumé preparation, interviewing skills, and job search strategies, to provide coordinated assistance to individuals and families who have been affected by the recession. The project team will deliver the training to state library agency staffs that will then customize that training for librarians in their home states.

Oklahoma Department of Libraries $889,610

Over a three-year period, the Oklahoma Department of Libraries will work with a national advisory group of tribal cultural leaders to sponsor five national educational opportunities for staff members serving in tribal archives, libraries, and museums.

Old Dominion University Research Foundation $661,154

The university, in partnership with the Library of Virginia, will establish a continuing-education center for librarians to acquire skills and perspectives to serve the state's increasingly diverse population.

Pacific Resources for Education and Learning $581,642

Pacific Resources for Education and Learning (PREL), based in Hawaii, serves libraries, archives, and museums in U.S.-affiliated Pacific region territories including American Samoa, the Commonwealth of the Northern Mariana Islands, the Federated States of Micronesia, Guam, the Republic of the Marshall Islands, and the Republic of Palau. Building on two previous IMLS-funded continuing-education and leadership training initiatives in this region, the new PREL Strategic Learning Communities project will recruit and train 80 information professionals in each territory over a three-year period.

Peninsula Library System $170,025

The library system, in San Mateo, California—partnering with state library agencies in California, Idaho, Oregon, and Washington—will develop and offer a fellowship program to practicing librarians designed to improve library services to older adults.

University of Denver $575,666

The university's Penrose Library and School of Library and Information Science, partnering with the Bibliographic Center for Research and the Denver Art Museum, will co-host with IMLS the WebWise Conferences to be held in 2010 in Denver and 2011 in Washington, D.C. The annual WebWise Conference, one of IMLS's signature activities, brings together library, archives, and museum professionals to address major issues facing their institutions in the digital realm.

University of Maryland $25,000

The university will host and cosponsor, along with the American Library Association's Library Research Round Table, Library Research Seminar V in October 2010. This grant will support ten student, ten junior faculty, and ten library practitioner attendees, as well as plenary speakers.

(continued from page 303)

demographics and needs of the profession, and support programs of continuing education and training in library and information science for librarians and library staff.

In FY 2009 IMLS awarded 38 grants totaling $22,503,899 for the program (see Table 3). A total of 116 applications requesting $64,286,631 were received. The 2009 priorities for program funding were

Doctoral Programs

- To develop faculty to educate the next generation of library professionals; in particular, to increase the number of students enrolled in doctoral programs that will prepare faculty to teach master's degree students who will work in school, public, and academic libraries
- To develop the next generation of library leaders; in particular, to increase the number of students enrolled in doctoral programs that will prepare them to assume positions as library managers and administrators

Master's Programs

- To educate the next generation of librarians; in particular, to increase the number of students enrolled in nationally accredited graduate library programs preparing for careers of service in libraries

Research

- *Early Career Development Program*—To support the early career development of new faculty members who are likely to become leaders in library and information science by supporting innovative research by untenured, tenure-track faculty
- *Research*—To provide the library community with information needed to support successful recruitment and education of the next generation of librarians; in particular, through funded research, to establish baseline data on professional demographics and job availability, and to evaluate current programs in library education for their capacity to meet the identified needs; and to conduct research and establish ongoing research capacity in the field of library and information science, particularly the evaluation of library and information services, assessment of the value and use of public libraries and their services by the public, and assessment of the public value and use of the Internet

Preprofessional Programs

- To recruit future librarians; in particular, to attract promising junior high school, high school, or college students to consider careers in librarianship through statewide or regional pilot projects employing recruitment strategies that are cost effective and measurable, and to introduce high school or college students to potential careers in library and information science by employing them to assist with library disaster recovery or service operation in areas that have suffered major disasters (participation of at least one library, as the applicant or as an official partner, in a location certified by the Federal Emergency Management Agency as a major disaster area in 2005 or 2006 is required)

Programs to Build Institutional Capacity

- To develop or enhance curricula within graduate schools of library and information science; in particular, to develop or enhance courses or programs of study for library, museum, and archives professionals in the creation, management, preservation, presentation, and use of digital assets; to broaden curricula by incorporating perspectives from other disciplines and fields of scholarship; to develop or enhance programs of study that address knowledge, skills, abilities, and issues of common interest to libraries, museums, archives, and data repositories; and to develop projects or programs in data curation as training programs for graduate students in library and information science

Continuing Education

- To increase professional development and library and archive staff knowledge, skills, and abilities through programs of continuing formal education, informal education, and training

Native American Library Services

The Native American Library Services program provides opportunities for improved library services to native American communities. The program offers three types of support to serve the range of needs of Indian tribes and Alaska Native villages and corporations.

In FY 2009 IMLS distributed $3,436,312 in grants for American Indian tribes and Alaska Native villages and corporations. This included some funds recovered from previous budget years and reallocated to the 2009 awards.

The program offers three types of support:

- Basic library services grants in the amount of $5,000, which support core library operations on a noncompetitive basis for all eligible Indian tribes and Alaska Native villages and corporations that apply for such support. IMLS awarded basic grants to 31 tribes in 2009.
- Basic library services grants with a supplemental education/assessment option of $1,000, totaling $6,000. IMLS awarded basic grants with the education/assessment option to 177 tribes. The purpose of the education/assessment option is to provide funding for library staff to attend continuing-education courses and/or training workshops on-site or off-site, for library staff to attend or give presentations at conferences relating to library services, and/or to hire a consultant for an on-site professional library assessment.
- Enhancement grants, which support new levels of library service for activities identified under LSTA. Of the 43 applications received, IMLS awarded 17 enhancement grants for a total of $2,219,312 (see Table 4).

(text continues on page 313)

Table 4 / Native American Library Services Enhancement Grants, FY 2009

Bear River Band of the Rohnerville Rancheria $135,571

In response to a community survey and assessment, the organization will hire a library consultant to catalog and automate the existing collection and train current and new local staff in the ongoing operation of the library.

Ahtna, Inc. $149,840

Ahtna, Inc. and the Ahtna Heritage Foundation plan to digitize and make available more than 280 hours of cassette recordings and more than 150 hours of VHS recordings of cultural significance to the Ahtna community.

Assiniboine and Sioux Tribes of the Fort Peck Indian Reservation $140,718

The Fort Peck Tribal Library, located at Fort Peck Community College, will enhance its technological capabilities by purchasing 12 computers and workstations and providing wireless access points for laptop computers in the library. To encourage more preteens and teens to read, the library will invest in graphic novels, popular science fiction titles, and bestsellers.

Chilkat Indian Village $149,993

For the benefit of Alaska's Chilkat Indian Village, the Klukwan Community and School Library, Xux' Daaka Hídí, will implement its "Enhancing Literacy; Preserving History" project, which will take a broad approach to literacy by enhancing skills for tribal members of all ages in reading, writing, and technology, as well as increasing cultural knowledge.

Chilkoot Indian Association $149,998

The Haines Borough Public Library, in partnership with the Chilkoot Indian Association, will harness the power of Tlingit cultural skills and knowledge to improve family and community sustainability in this isolated Alaskan location.

Chippewa Cree Indians of Rocky Boy's Reservation $92,566

The members of the tribe will receive an array of new library services through the Stone Child College Library, which also serves as the Rocky Boy Community Library. Culturally appropriate programming designed to encourage more library use by community members will include a youth book club, an adult book club, a storytelling series for children, a teen writing group, and visits by Native American authors.

Fort Belknap Indian Community $147,961

The Fort Belknap College Library will administer this project to expand library services to remote communities on the reservation. The Kills at Night Community Center in Hays and the Enemy Killer Community Center in Lodgepole will each receive two new computers with Internet access.

Jamestown S'Klallam Tribe $145,733

The Jamestown S'Klallam Tribe in Washington state plans to convert tribal and private archival materials with cultural content to digital format to provide public access through a tribally owned and managed Web site that interfaces with existing online museums and libraries.

Lac Courte Oreilles Band of Lake Superior Chippewa Indians $146,115

The band will receive a grant to allow the Lac Courte Oreilles Ojibwe College Community Library of Hayward, Wisconsin, to provide targeted services and materials to meet the critical needs of the community in the areas of traditional culture, health, and the environment.

Table 4 / Native American Library Services Enhancement Grants, FY 2009 (cont.)

Makah Indian Tribe $149,999

On behalf of the tribe, the Makah Cultural and Research Center in Neah Bay, Washington, will initiate the "We Are All Family" project to enhance access to family genealogy and ancestral history information for Makah community members.

Oglala Sioux Tribe $150,000

On behalf of the tribe, the Oglala Lakota College Learning Resource Center will implement "Woksape Tipi Taniyohila Kici" (House of Wisdom for Everyone), an outreach project that will provide additional resources and services at the college's branch libraries in the nine main communities on South Dakota's Pine Ridge Reservation.

Omaha Tribe of Nebraska $48,500

The Omaha Tribal Library, which serves as the public library for the Omaha Reservation and as the academic library for the Nebraska Indian Community College, will purchase furniture, shelving, and security gates for its new library space. New acquisitions will enhance the Native American, juvenile, and adult collections by providing materials of interest to community members. Library staff will initiate a youth reading incentive program, story hour/activity hour for preschool children and their families, and cultural awareness workshops.

Organized Village of Kasaan $121,145

The Organized Village of Kasaan's Cultural Learning Center and Library in Ketchikan, Alaska, is implementing a project to ensure long-term sustainability of the Kasaan library as a community resource by creating collaborative relationships with other organizations, including government and private entities, libraries, and tribal organizations.

Pascua Yaqui Tribe of Arizona $150,000

Based on a recent community needs assessment, the tribe's newly established Dr. Fernando Escalante Community Library and Resource Center will enhance its services to the community by focusing on intergenerational exchange and family involvement in the center and by creating a gathering place that promotes cultural learning for the community as a whole.

Pueblo of Santa Clara $150,000

The Pueblo of Santa Clara Community Library in Espanola, New Mexico, will implement a series of activities that promotes reading readiness among children up to 5 years of age using the American Library Association's Every Child Ready to Read program to train parents, teachers, and library tutors how to impart preliteracy skills to Tewa children at home, in school, and at the library.

Pueblo of Pojoaque $132,466

The Pueblo of Pojoaque Public Library in Santa Fe, New Mexico, will focus on literacy skills for preschool children and school-age children through the third grade as well as their parents, using the Every Child Ready to Read program.

Ute Mountain Tribe $75,854

Colorado's White Mesa Library, serving the small Ute Mountain Tribe community of White Mesa, plans to greatly improve the physical environment of the library with new furnishings that will create a welcoming space that allows for group activities as well as privacy. Twelve new computers will bring the computer lab up to date, and a new multimedia collection and increased Native American and Utah history resources will enhance the variety of offerings to community members.

Winnebago Tribe of Nebraska $118,424

On behalf of the tribe, the Little Priest Tribal College/Winnebago Public Library will expand and enhance library services to senior and disabled citizens living on the Winnebago Reservation.

(continued from page 310)
Native Hawaiian Library Services

The Native Hawaiian Library Services program provides opportunities for improved library services through grants to nonprofit organizations that primarily serve and represent Native Hawaiians, as the term "Native Hawaiian" is defined in section 7207 of the Native Hawaiian Education Act (20 U.S.C. 7517). In FY 2009 a single Native Hawaiian Library Services grant was awarded, to Alu Like, Inc., of Honolulu in the amount of $531,000.

Partnerships

The Big Read

A program of the National Endowment for the Arts (NEA) offered in partnership with IMLS and in cooperation with Arts Midwest, The Big Read is designed to restore reading to the center of American culture. The program offers grants to organizations in local communities to engage citizens in the reading of literature by exploring and discussing a single book within their communities. Organizations selected to participate receive a grant, financial support to attend a national orientation meeting, educational and promotional materials for broad distribution, an organizer's guide for developing and managing Big Read activities, and additional resources. IMLS's contribution was made through the Laura Bush 21st Century Librarian Program.

NEA inaugurated The Big Read as a pilot project in 2006 with ten communities featuring four books. The program expanded to include more communities in the United States, programming in four other countries, and more than 20 additional book selections. By 2010 more than 800 U.S. communities will have hosted a Big Read since the program's 2007 national launch. For more information, see http://www.neabigread.org.

Picturing America

Picturing America, an initiative of the National Endowment for the Humanities (NEH), promotes the teaching, study, and understanding of American art, history, and culture. IMLS has been a key partner in this initiative. The project has distributed large, high-quality, laminated color reproductions of 40 iconic works of American art, along with a comprehensive teacher's resource guide, to libraries and schools. More than 76,000 sets of Picturing America color reproductions were distributed to schools and public libraries across the country. IMLS continues to work with NEH and its partner, the American Library Association (ALA), on ways to leverage these materials for robust cultural programming and partnership opportunities, and to build the capacity of public librarians to use the materials in meaningful and effective ways.

IMLS funds supported the distribution of Picturing America to public libraries nationwide, as well as supporting the online portal (http://www.programminglibrarian.org) that hosts resources to assist public librarians in using the Picturing America materials. ALA hosted five online training programs to help public librarians maximize the impact of the materials. All of these online programs are available in an archived format on the Web portal. ALA continues to add content to the site, including resources for adult programs, reading lists and support materials on Picturing America-related themes, poetry programming resources developed in cooperation with the Academy of American Poets, and film viewing and discussion lists developed by ALA's Video Round Table.

Coming Up Taller

The Coming Up Taller awards recognize outstanding community arts and humanities programs that celebrate the creativity of young people by providing them with learning opportunities and chances to contribute to their communities. These awards focus national attention on exemplary programs currently fostering the creative and intellectual development of children and youth through education and practical experience in the arts and the humanities.

Accompanied by a $10,000 cash amount, these awards not only offer recognition but also contribute significant financial support. The program is a project of the President's Committee on the Arts and the Humanities in partnership with IMLS, NEA, and NEH. It was started in 1998. Each year, ten cash awards are presented to Coming Up Taller honorees, plus a certificate and funding for recipients to attend a leadership conference. Libraries and museums are encouraged to apply. For more information, see http://www.cominguptaller.org.

IMLS/NEH Digital Partnership

IMLS continued a partnership with NEH to promote development of the digital humanities through the Digital Humanities Start-up Grants.

Evaluation of IMLS Programs

IMLS encourages grant projects with strong evaluation components. In 2007 the institute awarded a grant of $362,490 through the Laura Bush 21st Century Librarian program to the Indiana University School of Library and Information Science to offer, enhance, and revise the online instructor-mediated courseware Shaping Outcomes (http://www.shapingoutcomes.org/course). The course was developed and tested through a three-year collaborative agreement between IMLS and Indiana University-Purdue University Indianapolis's museum studies program and School of Library and Information Science. IMLS grantees and prospective applicants may enroll in the mediated course for a small fee or may use the unmediated online tutorial at no charge to improve their approaches to project planning, grant preparation, and measurement of results to successfully address the needs of audiences and users.

In addition to outcome-based evaluation support for grantees, IMLS has instituted a new series of in-depth evaluations of its own programs on a rolling basis. In FY 2008 IMLS funded Himmel and Wilson Library Consultants to study service trends in the LSTA Grants to States program. That study resulted in a report titled *A Catalyst for Change: LSTA Grants to States Program Activities and the Transformation of Library Services to the Public*. The report was the subject of presentations at the ALA Annual Conference, has been widely dissem-inated, and has been particularly useful to state library administrative agencies and IMLS's congressional oversight committees. During FY 2008 IMLS also funded RMC Associates to conduct a five-year evaluation of the Museums for America program. In FY 2010 IMLS is funding an evaluation of the Laura Bush 21st Century Librarian program.

Research Sponsored and Conducted by IMLS

In July 2009 IMLS published *Partnership for a Nation of Learners: Joining Forces, Creating Value.* The report is the product of an evaluation of IMLS's partnership with the Corporation for Public Broadcasting (CPB). Together, IMLS and CPB supported 20 projects and created a Web site to encourage libraries, museums, and public broadcasting stations to work together to address issues of community concern. The new publication and Web site offer "how to" guidance on creating effective community collaborations with museums, libraries, and public broadcasters. The report profiles high-performing partnerships that tackled such issues as substance abuse in Alaska, educating families about childhood asthma in Boston, and conserving water in Utah. These profiles illustrate how vital community organizations responded to important local issues and achieved outcomes that might be unattainable for a single organization. To assist muse-ums, libraries, and other organizations that are considering partnering, the publi-cation's "lessons learned" section details tips and best practices.

In partnership with the Bill and Melinda Gates Foundation, IMLS funded the University of Washington Information School to conduct a national study of pub-lic access computing (PAC) in U.S. libraries (http://cis.washington.edu/usimpact). The study, which includes a national household survey, a Web-based survey of PAC users, and site visits to both rural and urban communities, will provide the first national portrait of public access computer use in public libraries. The study data were collected in the spring and summer of 2009, with a final report issued in early 2010.

IMLS staff is also actively engaged in research relevant to the library and information science field. In spring 2009 IMLS released a short report on the role libraries play in the deployment of broadband service in rural, suburban, and urban areas in the United States. In December IMLS released *Service Trends in U.S. Public Libraries, 1997–2007,* analyzing ten years of public library survey data. The brief identified important changes public libraries have made to address patron needs in an increasingly "Internet-centric" environment and explored ser-vice differences in urban and rural communities. The analysis documents the pos-itive impact that service changes by U.S. public libraries are having on visitation and circulation.

Future research from the IMLS Office of Policy, Planning, Research and Com-munication (OPPRC) will examine library services in a variety of contexts, from small towns and remote rural areas to central cities and suburbs. OPPRC also will look at the intersection of library service with other public policy priorities including education, employment, immigration, and public health.

Conferences and Activities

Grants to States Conference

The ninth Grants to States Conference was held in Washington, D.C., November 19–21, 2008, and the tenth was scheduled for 2010. At the 2008 conference, 101 participants represented the State Library Administrative Agencies in the 50 states, the District of Columbia, Puerto Rico, and the Virgin Islands. The conference included a two-day grants management course on the cost principles that are a primary area of federal grants administration. Another feature was a panel presentation with a question-and-answer session on the findings of the LSTA Grants to States trends analysis.

WebWise

The tenth WebWise Conference on Libraries and Museums in the Digital World was held February 25–27, 2009, in Washington, D.C. The theme, "Digital Debates," provided a forum for discussion of the issues cultural heritage institutions face as they contemplate an increasingly online world. Sessions included discussions about institutions and online communities, rights and responsibilities of institutions for their collections and users, and the merits and challenges of collaboration while maintaining institutional identity. The conference cosponsor was Wolfsonian–Florida International University, with support from the John D. and Catherine T. MacArthur Foundation.

IMLS Web Site and Publications

The IMLS Web site (http://www.imls.gov) provides information on the various grant programs, the National Medal for Museum and Library Service, funded projects, application forms, and staff contacts. It also highlights model projects developed by libraries and museums throughout the country and provides information about IMLS-sponsored conferences, publications, and studies. Through an electronic newsletter, *Primary Source,* IMLS provides information on grant deadlines and opportunities. Information on subscribing to the IMLS newsletter is located on the Web site.

The following recent publications are available at the Web site: the 2010 *Grant and Award Opportunities* booklet; *Museums, Libraries, and 21st Century Skills*; *A Catalyst for Change: LSTA Grants to States Program Activities and the Transformation of Library Services to the Public*; *The Future of Museums and Libraries: A Discussion Guide*; *Partnership for a Nation of Learners: Joining Forces, Creating Value*; the *2009 National Medal for Museum and Library Service* brochure; and guidelines for each of the grant programs.

Additional Grants

In addition to the grants described above, funds from this program in 2009 supported the following activities and projects: the Salzburg Conference ($150,000); the American Association of State and Local History for the Connecting to Collections Bookshelf Project ($359,178); Heritage Preservation in support of the Connecting to Collections Project forums ($215,072); the Connecting to Collections Project's Statewide Planning Grants ($454,103); the Big Read project sponsored in conjunction with the National Endowment for the Arts ($500,000); support for state library agency activities associated with the National Book Festival, through Chief Officers of State Library Agencies (COSLA) ($91,500); the Pavilion of the States at the National Book Festival, in cooperation with the Library of Congress ($100,000); the University of North Carolina at Chapel Hill in the expansion of a project to track the careers of graduates of schools of library and information science ($101,248).

Part 3
Library/Information Science Education, Placement, and Salaries

Library Employment Sources on the Internet

Catherine Barr
Contributing Editor

The continuing recession during 2009 affected the library field in many ways. There were reports of lower starting salaries although mid-career salaries seemed to be holding steady or even increasing. Job searches were longer, and new and forthcoming library school graduates were gloomy about their prospects.

Library Journal's annual "Placements and Salaries" report for 2009 was titled "LJ's 2009 Placements and Salaries Survey Shows Tough Library Job Market." [See the full report in Part 3—*Ed.*]

The American Library Association (ALA)-Allied Professional Association reported 2009 data (http://www.ala-apa.org/news/news.html#2009survey) showing that the median salary for public and academic librarians with ALA-accredited master's degrees, at $54,500, was up 2 percent from the previous year. And the Special Library Association's 2009 Salary Survey (http://www.sla.org/content/SLA/pressroom/pressrelease/10pr/pr1002.cfm) posted an increase from the previous year of more than $2,000 in the average salary of an information professional in the United States, to $73,880.

For the first time in several years, "librarian" was not included as one of the best careers in the 2010 *U.S. News & World Report*'s annual survey. In the 2009 report (http://www.usnews.com/articles/business/best-careers/2008/12/11/best-careers-2009-librarian.html), median national pay was given as $51,400 and job satisfaction and prestige received a higher rating than job outlook. Special librarianship was again selected in 2009 as the "smart specialty" and the fastest-growing sector in an "underrated" field.

In response to the difficulties facing both new and mid-career librarians, ALA created a new site called Get a Job! (http://www.getajob.ala.org). A work in progress, this site—with the subtitle "ALA's Toolkit for Getting a Job in a Tough Economy"—organizes helpful information under headings such as "Especially in a Tough Job Market." Podcasts and stories offer real-life experiences, and users can ask questions and contribute comments.

The following is not a comprehensive list of the hundreds of job-related sites on the Internet of interest to librarians and information professionals. These are, however, the best starting places for a general job search in this area. Many offer additional information that will be helpful to those considering a career in librarianship, including advice on conducting a successful search, writing résumés, preparing for interviews, and negotiating salaries.

Before spending a lot of time on any Web site, users should check that the site has been updated recently and that out-of-date job listings no longer appear. The Directory of Organizations in Part 6 of this volume may also prove useful.

Background Information

The Bureau of Labor Statistics of the U.S. Department of Labor provides a thorough overview of the work of a librarian, necessary qualifications, and the job and salary outlook at http://www.bls.gov/oco/ocos068.htm. Similar pages are available for archivists, curators, and museum technicians (http://www.bls.gov/oco/ocos065.htm) and for library technicians and library assistants (http://www.bls.gov/oco/ocos316.htm).

The American Library Association provides a user-friendly overview of librarianship at all levels—from page and library assistants to managers and directors—at LibraryCareer.org (http://www.ala.org/ala/educationcareers/careers/librarycareerssite/home.cfm), and Info*Nation: Choose a Career in Libraries (http://www.cla.ca/infonation/welcome.htm) is an excellent Canadian site that describes the work of librarians, combining brief information on a variety of career options with statements by individual librarians about why they love their jobs. These two sites will be particularly useful for young people considering a possible career in librarianship.

Also of interest to aspiring librarians is Rachel Singer Gordon's article in the September 15, 2009, *Library Journal* (http://www.libraryjournal.com/article/CA605244.html)—"How to Become a Librarian—Updated." In this, she covers all the basics and recommends paths to the profession.

Finally, How to Apply for a Library Job (http://www.liswiki.com/wiki/HOWTO:Apply_for_a_library_job) offers thoughtful advice and practical interview tips.

General Sites/Portals

American Library Association: Education and Careers http://www.ala.org/ala/educationcareers/index.cfm
Maintained by ALA. A useful source of information on library careers, education and professional development, scholarships, and salaries.

ALA JobLIST http://joblist.ala.org
Sponsored by ALA and the Association of College and Research Libraries. This site incorporates the former job sites of *American Libraries* magazine and *C&RL News*. Registration is free for jobseekers, who can post their résumés and search jobs by library type, date, state, institution name, salary range, and other parameters. Employers can choose from a menu of print and electronic posting combinations.

Canadian Library Association: Library Careers http://www.cla.ca/AM/Template.cfm?Section=Library_Careers
The Canadian Library Association lists Canadian job openings here (select Job Search) and provides guidance on recognition of foreign credentials.

Employment Resources: Organizations and Associations http://slisweb.sjsu.edu/resources/employment.htm

Maintained by San José State University's School of Library and Information Science. Gives links to organizations that will be of interest to students at the university, including a number of California sites. A related page, Professional Associations in the Information Sciences (http://slisweb.sjsu.edu/resources/orgs. htm), is a comprehensive listing of associations in the United States and abroad. And excellent information on conducting job searches and professional development in general can be found at http://slisgroups.sjsu.edu/alumni/jobseekers/index.html.

LibGig   http://www.libgig.com
This professional networking site offers jobs, "who's hiring" job alerts, résumé consultation, career profiles, news, blogs, and a Job Market full of current advice (http://libgig.com/jobmarket).

Library Job Postings on the Internet   http://www.libraryjobpostings.org
Compiled by Sarah (Nesbeitt) Johnson of Booth Library, Eastern Illinois University, coauthor of *The Information Professional's Guide to Career Development Online* (Information Today, Inc., 2002); there is a link to the book's companion Web site. Provides links to library employment sites in the United States and abroad, with easy access by location and by category of job.

LIScareer.com: Career Strategies for Librarians   http://www.liscareer.com
Relaunched in 2009, this helpful site is maintained by Priscilla Shontz and offers "practical career development advice for new librarians and information professionals, MLS students, and those considering a library-related career." There are no job listings, but the site offers interesting articles in the areas of career exploration, education, job searching, experience, networking, mentoring, interpersonal skills, leadership, publishing and presenting, and work/life balance. This is an excellent place to begin research on library jobs. Shontz also offers career consulting services via this site. Shontz and Richard Murray are coeditors of *A Day in the Life: Career Options in Library and Information Science* (Libraries Unlimited, 2007). Shontz is also the author of *The Librarian's Career Guidebook* (Scarecrow, 2004) and *Jump Start Your Career in Library and Information Science* (Scarecrow, 2002).

Lisjobs.com—Jobs for Librarians and   http://www.lisjobs.com
Information Professionals
Maintained by Rachel Singer Gordon, author of books including *What's the Alternative? Career Options for Librarians and Info Pros* (Information Today, Inc., 2008), *Information Tomorrow: Reflections on Technology and the Future of Public and Academic Libraries* (Information Today, Inc., 2007), *The NextGen Librarian's Survival Guide* (Information Today, Inc., 2006), and *The Accidental Library Manager* (Information Today, Inc., 2005).

This newly updated site includes a searchable database of job listings (RSS feed available), links to job banks, and useful job hunting and career development resources. Job seekers can post résumés for a small fee. The site also features information on scholarships and funding for continuing education, and a section called "Career Q&A with the Library Career People," which provides detailed answers to users' questions.

The Riley Guide: http://www.rileyguide.com
Employment Opportunities and Job Resources on the Internet
Compiled by Margaret F. Dikel, a private consultant and coauthor with Frances Roehm of *The Guide to Internet Job Searching* (McGraw-Hill, 2006). A general site rich in advice for the job seeker, from résumé writing and how to target a new employer to tips on networking and interviewing. Links to job sites are organized by type of opportunity; Information Delivery, Design, and Management is found under Humanities, Social Sciences, and Personal Services.

Sites by Sector

Public Libraries

Public library openings can be found at all the general sites/portals listed above.

Careers in Public Librarianship   http://www.ala.org/ala/mgrps/divs/
                                               pla/placareers/index.cfm
The Public Library Association offers information on public librarianship, with a section on the experiences of PLA members.

School Libraries

School library openings can be found at many of the sites listed above. Sites with interesting material for aspiring school librarians include those listed below.

AASL: Recruitment to School Librarianship   http://www.ala.org/
           ala/mgrps/divs/aasl/aasleducation/recruitmentlib/aaslrecruitment.cfm
The American Association of School Librarians hosts this site, which describes the role of school librarians, salary and job outlooks, and mentoring programs; provides testimonials from working library media specialists; and offers state-by-state information on licensure, scholarships, library education, job hunting, mentoring, and recruitment efforts.

General education sites usually include school library openings. Among sites with nationwide coverage is:

Education America   http://www.educationamerica.net
Library openings can be searched by geographic location.

Special and Academic Libraries

AALL Career Center   http://www.aallnet.org/careers
Maintained by the American Association of Law Librarians, this site, with an online job board, also links to the excellent Careers in Law Librarianship site (http://www.lawlibrarycareers.org), which answers the question "Is a career as a law librarian right for you?"

Association of College and Research Libraries
See ALA JobLIST above.

ALISE: Job Placement   http://www.alise.org
The Association for Library and Information Science Education posts jobs (under the heading Job Placement) for deans, directors, and faculty, organized by position and alphabetically by school.

ASIS&T: Careers   http://www.asist.org/careers.html
The Careers page maintained by the American Society for Information Science and Technology offers access to a Jobline, Placement Center, and Continuing Education information.

Association of Research Libraries: http://www.arl.org/resources/
Career Resources   careers/index.shtml
In addition to listings of openings at ARL member institutions and at other organizations, there is information on ARL's diversity programs plus a database of research library residency and internship programs.

Chronicle of Higher Education   http://chronicle.com/jobs
Listings can be browsed, with geographical options, under the category "Library/ information sciences" (found under "Professional fields") or searched by simple keyword such as "library." Articles and advice on job searching are also available.

EDUCAUSE Job Posting Service   http://www.educause.edu/jobpost
EDUCAUSE member organizations post positions "in the broad field of information technology in higher education."

HigherEdJobs.com   http://www.higheredjobs.com
The category "Libraries" is found under Administrative Positions.

Major Orchestra Librarians' Association   http://www.mola-inc.org
A nice site for a field that might be overlooked. The Resources section includes an introduction to the work of an orchestra librarian.

Medical Library Association: http://www.mlanet.org/career/index.html
Career Development
The Medical Library Association offers much more than job listings here, with brochures on medical librarianship, a video, career tips, and a mentor program.

Music Library Association Job Openings   http://www.musiclibraryassoc.org/
                                 employmentanded/joblist/openings.shtml
Along with job postings and a résumé review service, this site features an article titled "Music Librarianship—Is It for You?" and a listing of resources for both beginning and mid-career music librarians.

SLA: Career Center   http://www.sla.org/content/jobs/index.cfm
In addition to salary information and searchable job listings that are available to all users, the Special Libraries Association provides many services for association members.

Government

Library of Congress   http://www.loc.gov/hr/employment
Current job openings, internships, fellowships, and volunteering.

National Archives and Records Administration   http://www.archives.gov/
careers/
In addition to information on employment opportunities, internships, and volunteering, NARA provides profiles of employees and interns, describing the kinds of work they do.

Serials

NASIG Jobs   http://jobs.nasig.org
Managed by the North American Serials Interest Group. Accepts serials-related job postings.

Library Periodicals

American Libraries
See ALA JobList above.

Library Journal   http://www.libraryjournal.com
Job listings are found under the Careers tab.

School Library Journal   http://www.schoollibraryjournal.com
Click on the Jobs tab for access to a general list of job openings (jointly maintained with *Library Journal*; you must filter by Children's/Young Adult to access school positions.

Employment Agencies/Commercial Services

A number of employment agencies and commercial services in the United States and abroad specialize in library-related jobs. Among those that keep up-to-date listings on their Web sites are:

Advanced Information Management   http://www.aimusa.com
Specializes in librarians and support staff in a variety of types of libraries across the country.

ASLIB   http://www.aslib.co.uk/recruitment
Lists jobs available in Britain.

Library Associates   http://www.libraryassociates.com
An easy-to-use list of openings that can be sorted by function, department, and location.

TPFL: The Information People: http://www.tfpl.com/permanent_recruitment/
Recruitment and Executive Search   candidates/pjobs.cfm
Specializes in jobs in the fields of knowledge management, library and information management, records management, and Web and content management. Jobs around the world are listed, with the majority in the United Kingdom.

Listservs

Many listservs allow members to post job openings on a casual basis.

jESSE   http://web.utk.edu/~gwhitney/jesse.html
This worldwide discussion group focuses on library and information science education; LIS faculty position announcements frequently appear here.

LIBJOBS   http://www.ifla.org/en/mailing-lists
LIBJOBS is a mailing list for librarians and information professionals seeking employment. It is managed by the International Federation of Library Associations and Institutions (IFLA). Subscribers to this list receive posted job opportunities by e-mail.

PUBLIB   http://lists.webjunction.org/publib
Public library job openings often appear on this list.

Blogs

The Blogging Libraries Wiki (http://www.blogwithoutalibrary.net/links/index.php?title=Welcome_to_the_Blogging_Libraries_Wiki) provides lists of library blogs in the following fields: Academic Libraries, Public Libraries, School Libraries, Special Libraries, Internal Library Communication, Library Associations, and Library Director.

Beyond the Job   http://www.beyondthejob.org
Compiled by Sarah Johnson and Rachel Singer Gordon, this blog focuses on job-hunting advice and professional development.

Career Q&A with the Library Career People   http://www.lisjobs.com/
                                                      careerqa_blog
This attractive and user-friendly blog is maintained by librarians Tiffany Allen and Susanne Markgren and is intended to "create an enlightening discussion forum of professional guidance and advice for librarians, library staff, and those thinking of entering the profession." Categories include job satisfaction, job seeking, and professional development.

Placements and Salaries 2009: Jobs and Pay Take a Hit

Stephanie Maatta, Ph.D.

Assistant Professor, University of South Florida
School of Library and Information Sciences, Tampa

"It's a recession, baby!" was the common refrain among the graduates of 2008. This was a record year for the number of graduates participating in our annual survey, with 2,089 respondents, representing approximately 31.7 percent of the approximate 6,500 library and information science (LIS) graduates. They had stories to tell, providing evidence both of hard times in the job market and some successes and satisfaction.

Even before the economic crisis of 2009, 2008 graduates were hit hard. Job searches averaged almost five months, and unemployment postgraduation rose to 5.9 percent in 2008, compared with 4.7 percent in 2007. Average starting salaries dipped slightly overall, dropping 1.8 percent to $41,579, after 18 years of increases. Part-time placements increased from 16.3 percent of the placements in 2007 to 18.3 percent of 1,817 graduates reporting jobs in 2008, after holding steady for two years. Similarly, 13.5 percent of the 2008 graduates either remained in or found nonprofessional positions, compared with 11.3 percent in 2007.

The decreasing salaries, declining number of full-time positions overall, and the increase in part-time jobs and unemployment in 2008 appear to be the precursor to what will undoubtedly be a seriously depressed job market for graduates in the near future, with widespread hiring freezes and budget cuts across all types of libraries and information agencies.

Fewer Full-Time Jobs

While the total percentage of graduates reporting that they found jobs appears to have held steady between 2007 and 2008, the status of those jobs is more telling. In 2007, 87.9 percent of the graduates reported employment, including both full-time and part-time placements, compared with 2008, when 87.3 percent of graduates reported employment of any sort. The noticeable difference is in the percentage of full-time placements; 89.2 percent of the 2007 graduates reported full-time employment, while 69.8 percent were employed full-time in 2008.

There also appeared to be a serious decline in the total number of jobs reported in some types of libraries and information agencies (full-time and part-time combined), with special libraries dropping by 36 percent compared with 2007, public libraries by 21.4 percent, and other agencies by 11.3 percent.

In a few exceptions, academic libraries, government libraries, and library cooperatives had improved full-time placements compared with 2007, ranging from an increase of 13.4 percent for academic jobs to 43.8 percent with library cooperatives. In general, however, the total number of overall placements in government libraries and co-ops remained low.

Adapted from *Library Journal*, October 15, 2009.

Following regional patterns of unemployment and economic instability, starting salaries in the Midwest ($39,047, or 3.1 percent below 2007) and the Southeast ($39,694, or 4.5 percent below the previous year) declined after several years of forward momentum. Starting salaries in the West, while consistently higher than other regions, also fell 4.2 percent to $48,593, after averages above $50,000 in 2007. Average starting salaries for graduates who sought jobs in other types of agencies outside of libraries also declined by 8.3 percent from $51,349 in 2007 to $47,934 in 2008, with jobs in the private sector suffering as much as placements in public agencies.

Indicative of a struggling economy, full-time placements in public libraries declined by 12.5 percent in 2008, and salaries inched up less than 1 percent. Men in the Southeast were hardest hit by falling public library salaries, tumbling 6.7 percent to an average of $34,680. Yet a contraindication was that public libraries in the Midwest, an area struck hard by climbing unemployment, had the best growth rate in placements (12.9 percent from 2007 to 2008) although salaries remained flat, while the Northeast had a significant drop in reported positions (approximately 29 percent fewer) despite 2.5 percent growth in public library salaries.

Jobs in special libraries also disappeared, with approximately 36 percent fewer full-time positions reported in 2008, and salaries were on average 7.3 percent lower than last year.

Approximately 42.3 percent of the graduates who responded to questions about employers indicated that they returned to their current employer upon graduation, down slightly from 2007 (43.8 percent). While it is difficult to determine whether they received promotions or moved into new positions upon earning a master's degree, more graduates indicated they held nonprofessional positions when returning to a current employer (20.1 percent in 2008 compared with 16.75 percent in 2007). The increase in nonprofessional positions reflects a decision by graduates to take a job of any sort rather than face unemployment.

Pockets of Good News

Amid a challenging job market, there were positive signs. LIS graduates reporting minority status continued to experience positive salary growth, gaining an average of 2.5 percent from 2007 ($43,928 in 2008 compared with $42,831 in 2007); their starting salaries averaged 5.3 percent higher than those for all graduates in 2008. While salaries in the rest of the United States declined, the graduates finding positions in the Northeast negotiated better-than-average salaries starting at $43,854, which was 3.2 percent higher than in 2007 and 5.2 percent higher than the national average of $41,579 for LIS graduates in 2008.

Other positive notes were that academic libraries appeared to continue to experience growth in full-time numbers (as mentioned above, they were up approximately 13.4 percent from 2007), though salaries held steady, rising by less than 1 percent to $41,151 from $40,911. Academic library salaries benefited from the second year of increased earnings in the Northeast (up 5.5 percent in 2007 and another 4.3 percent in 2008), though salaries for similar placements in the Southeast plummeted by almost 9 percent.

(text continues on page 332)

Table 1 / Status of 2008 Graduates*

	Number of Schools Reporting	Number of Graduates Responding	Permanent Professional	Temporary Professional	Non-professional	Total	Graduates Outside of Profession	Unemployed or Status Unreported
Northeast	12	532	275	42	70	387	72	72
Southeast	9	325	182	17	31	230	40	54
Midwest	10	756	488	52	56	596	64	94
Southwest	6	235	165	8	27	200	18	17
West	3	128	67	17	22	106	12	10
Total	40	2,089	1,239	142	216	1,597	220	268

* Table based on survey responses from schools and individual graduates. Figures will not necessarily be fully consistent with some of the other data reported. Tables do not always add up, individually or collectively, since both schools and individuals omitted data in some cases.

Table 2 / Placements and Full-Time Salaries of 2008 Graduates/Summary by Region*

	Number of Placements	Salaries			Low Salary		High Salary		Average Salary			Median Salary		
Region		Women	Men	Total	Women	Men	Women	Men	Women	Men	All	Women	Men	All
Northeast	269	206	63	269	$17,680	$27,000	$95,000	$130,000	$43,079	$46,387	43,854	$41,205	$44,500	$42,000
Southeast	297	207	53	260	13,500	10,000	85,000	96,000	39,462	40,599	39,694	38,700	38,500	38,550
Midwest	467	327	80	407	10,000	32,000	125,000	68,199	38,736	40,455	39,047	38,000	39,000	38,000
Southwest	192	137	33	170	13,000	17,663	60,000	80,000	38,997	42,299	40,000	39,060	43,000	40,000
West	142	92	34	126	13,260	24,000	86,000	112,808	46,515	54,217	48,593	46,544	49,500	47,750
International	20	8	3	11	25,000	20,000	137,000	55,800	60,456	41,933	58,022	55,000	50,000	50,000
Combined	1,475	977	266	1,243	10,000	10,000	137,000	130,000	40,898	44,172	41,579	40,000	42,000	40,000

* All international salaries converted to U.S. dollars based on conversion rates for August 24, 2009. This table represents only salaries and placements reported as full-time. Some data were reported as aggregate without breakdown by gender or region. Comparison with other tables will show different numbers of placements.

Table 3 / 2008 Total Graduates and Placements by School*

Schools	Graduates			Employed		
	Women	Men	Total	Women	Men	Total
Alabama	89	20	109	11	4	15
Albany	70	27	97	16	4	20
Arizona	100	22	122	21	5	26
Buffalo	99	29	128	25	5	30
Denver	35	3	38	11	1	12
Dominican	262	70	332	155	30	185
Drexel	252	91	343	50	20	70
Florida State	572	221	793	49	20	69
Hawaii	49	12	61	7	1	8
Illinois	180	45	225	66	17	83
Indiana	179	45	224	46	10	56
Iowa**	19	7	26	15	5	20
Kent State	165	65	230	65	25	90
Kentucky	57	18	75	19	5	24
Long Island	118	24	142	32	2	35
Louisiana State**	10	4	14	6	4	10
Maryland	89	30	119	22	3	25
Michigan***	74	47	121	53	31	84
Missouri–Columbia	74	10	84	2	—	2
N.C.–Chapel Hill**	19	7	26	14	1	15
North Texas	301	72	373	74	18	92
Oklahoma	58	17	75	13	3	16
Pittsburgh	176	44	220	17	7	24
Pratt***	120	44	164	—	—	—
Rhode Island	71	9	80	13	—	13
Rutgers	107	36	143	16	6	22
San José	366	66	432	99	11	110
Simmons	223	61	284	155	36	191
Southern Connecticut	105	26	131	21	7	28
South Carolina	149	33	182	24	6	30
South Florida	129	37	166	23	3	26
St. John's	16	3	19	5	2	7
Syracuse	125	19	144	17	4	21
Tennessee	62	13	75	45	10	55
Texas (Austin)	50	19	69	29	7	36
Texas Woman's	186	7	193	36	1	37
UCLA	50	19	69	1	—	1
Wayne State	162	33	195	38	4	42
Wisconsin (Madison)	77	15	92	54	9	63
Wisconsin (Milwaukee)	136	38	174	32	6	38
Total	5,181	1,408	6,589	1,458	363	1,823

* Tables do not always add up, individually or collectively, since both schools and individuals omitted data in some cases.
** For schools that did not fill out the institutional survey, data were taken from graduate surveys, thus there is not full representation of their graduating classes.
*** Some schools completed the institutional survey, but responses were not received from graduates; or schools conducted their own survey and provided reports. This table represents placements of any kind. Comparison with other tables will show different numbers of placements.
Other categories: Students: 30 women, 10 men, with a total of 46. Unemployed: 92 women, 32 men, with a total of 128. Unknown: 3,631 women, 1,013 men, with a total of 4,638.

(continued from page 329)

After several years of concern over falling salaries, graduates entering children's and youth/teen services finally experienced growth. While still below the overall average starting salary for the 2008 graduates, children's librarians earned 3.7 percent more than their peers in the previous year ($39,486 vs. $38,029). Graduates seeking opportunities in youth/teen services fared even better: salaries rose 5.7 percent to $38,104 from $35,929 in 2007.

The Minority Report

Professionwide there continues to be a strong emphasis on recruiting a diverse work force in all areas, whether by region, position, or library type. Funding agencies, such as the Institute of Museum and Library Services (IMLS), American Library Association (ALA) Office of Diversity, and others, have continued to disseminate grants and scholarships to recruit, retain, and promote minority candidates despite a lean economy. In 2008 approximately 11.2 percent of the LIS graduates claimed minority status, midrange between the 9 percent and almost 13 percent in previous years. And these graduates report successful job hunts and better-than-average salaries.

Minority graduates in 2008 were paid a higher than average starting salary of $43,928, improving by $1,097 or 2.5 percent. In part, the salary growth can be attributed to an increase in salaries for graduates entering "other" agencies (private industry, for example), which topped $50,776 in 2008 (5.9 percent higher than 2007). As a subgroup of graduates, minority men garnered the highest salary increases between 2007 and 2008, improving 4.5 percent to $46,952 (11.4 percent above the national average for 2008), while the salaries for all men slid down 2.3 percent to $45,192. The most significant salary growth for minority graduates occurred in the Northeast, improving 21 percent.

Regional Stresses

Historically, region has played a critical role in the level of salaries that LIS graduates obtain. Jobs in the West and in the Northeast typically carry fatter paychecks and more opportunities. In 2008, although salaries declined nationwide, this pattern held. And, despite falling numbers, there were pockets of improvement for LIS graduates regionally. In the Southwest, for example, women in academic libraries received an average of 7.1 percent higher salaries ($38,828) compared with 2007, and women in the West kept a similar pace, improving by 7.8 percent to $47,452.

Compared with 2007, part-time placements were up in the Midwest (34.9 percent in 2008 vs. 24 percent in 2007) and the Southeast (9.3 percent in 2008, 7.3 percent in 2007). The West, on the other hand, showed a decrease in part-time positions (13.1 percent in 2008 compared with 18 percent in 2007), as did the Southwest (dropping from 8.2 percent in 2007 to 6.9 percent in 2008).

Economic troubles hit the West hard, especially California, with starting salaries reversing the gains made previously, slipping from $50,736 to $48,593. But the news was not all bad. Salaries for public and academic librarians both saw improvement, jumping a healthy 5.8 percent and 13 percent, respectively. While notoriously among the lowest-paying of library types, public library salaries in the West were competitive in 2008, averaging $46,727, or 19.6 percent higher than public library salaries nationwide (coming in at $37,556).

The Northeast, while showing evidence of unemployment and part-time jobs among the graduate pool, experienced overall salary growth in 2008. In fact, the Northeast was the only region to experience any overall salary growth for LIS graduates in 2008, although the number of reported placements was down. Jobs may be paying better, but there are fewer of them to go around.

Venus and Mars on the Job

By the numbers there is a consistent 80–20 split between women and men in the LIS work force, and for many years a gender gap has existed between salaries achieved by these same women and men. This past year was no exception, with men averaging salaries that were 7.4 percent higher than women, with only a marginal closing of the gap from the previous 7.7 percent. Among graduates reporting minority status, the gap was even wider, with men's salaries 8.0 percent higher than those obtained by women, but in the plus column minority men realized a 4.5 percent improvement in salaries, heading up from $44,828 in 2007 to $46,952 in 2008, in an economic environment when most salaries were down.

Clearly the type of library impacts overall salaries, and it is most noticeable among women. For example, public libraries continue to offer the lowest average salaries, with a national average of $37,556, and while women make up the largest proportion of the employment pool (82 percent in 2008), their salaries are lower than average at $37,361. In the public library, women outnumber men in children's and youth services, cataloging, and circulation, which are at the lower end of the salary scale.

By comparison, women comprised 93 percent of the placements in school library media centers in 2008 and won salaries that were 8.8 percent higher than those of the men ($45,116 compared with $41,362).

Evidence of the gender gap also emerges when looking at prior professional positions and background. Women entering their second (sometimes third) profession in 2008 garnered salaries that were 3.3 percent higher than the national average ($43,005 compared with $41,579); men with a similar profile received salaries 8.3 percent higher ($45,354 compared with $41,579). Dollar for dollar, these same graduates saw a 5.5 percent difference between the starting salaries for men and women. Backgrounds for second-career women included education, human and social services, retail management, and the ministry; backgrounds for men included law, education, business, computer sciences, and engineering. On the wage scale, backgrounds in science, technology, and engineering appear to provide more salary momentum than those in the service industries.

Academic Library Review

Of the 1,817 jobs reported in the current survey period, academic libraries comprised 29.3 percent of the overall placements. This was up approximately 13.4

percent from 2007. With the increase in placements came an increase in salaries in some regions of the United States, including a solid 3.9 percent in the Southwest, 4.7 percent in the Northeast, and an impressive 13 percent in the West. This seems to run counter to some of the stories shared during the survey period of across-the-board hiring freezes, nonprofessional staffing, and salary cuts. However, salaries in academic libraries in the Southeast and Midwest, areas severely impacted by the economic recession, fell below 2007 levels. New academic librarians in the Southeast lost 8.99 percent in salary, slipping to $38,722, while those in the Midwest dropped 3.5 percent.

Background and experience played out in salary for academic librarians, too. Nearly 41 percent of the graduates who got academic library jobs also reported that LIS was not their first professional position. Their backgrounds included other advanced and professional degrees (master's, J.D.s, and Ph.D.s), as well as specialized subject areas like medicine, computer sciences, and engineering. For these graduates, starting salaries averaged $43,298 (approximately 5.2 percent higher than all academic librarians) compared with $39,517 for those whom LIS was the first professional position.

Public Libraries

As in the past, public libraries continue to be a popular choice for LIS job seekers. In 2008 positions in public libraries made up approximately 29.6 percent of all reported placements, including full-time and part-time positions, up about 5.4 percent from 2007. However, the reports of full-time placement were down by approximately 12.5 percent. While remaining among the lowest offered, in 2008 salaries for new public librarians held steady, growing by less than 1 percent, when salaries for other types of libraries declined. Public library positions in the Northeast and in the West helped to balance the rise and fall of salaries with increases of 2.6 percent and 5.8 percent, respectively, from 2007. Even in the Southeast and Midwest where unemployment rates soared and salaries slumped, salaries for public librarians barely moved between 2007 and 2008.

Part-time employment in public libraries is a growing fact of life in the current economic environment. In 2008 approximately 18.3 percent of the LIS graduates held part-time jobs, both within and outside of the profession. Of these part-time workers, 45.3 percent were employed in public libraries; this is a steep increase in the number of part-time positions compared with 2007 when 40 percent of new public librarians were part-time.

Like other types of jobs within the LIS professions, the search for public library positions was time-consuming and often frustrating. A repeated comment among LIS graduates seeking public library jobs was that there were too few professional jobs with adequate salaries; they also indicated sending out many résumés and rarely landing an interview. Yet graduates also struck some high notes. Approximately 48.6 percent of public librarians returned to their former employer upon graduation, many indicating they had expectations of promotion to professional staff from support staff. For some, the promotion did not come through as employers faced the decision to cut staff and hours; some also reported that jobs had turned into part-time positions, accompanied by a loss of benefits. For others, the degree paid off in promotion to professional staffing complemented by higher salaries. For those who did not return to a former public library employer, the job search was a little shorter than some others experienced, averaging 4.1 months compared with the overall average of 4.9.

Public, Private, or Other

While often used as a catchall for organizations and types of jobs that defy description, other categories of employment provide interesting opportunities for LIS graduates. The "other" classification encompasses three types of agencies: nonprofit organizations, such as social service agencies; private industry or corporate business; and those organizations that fall outside of LIS, such as retail, public relations, or hospital administration. In 2008 approximately 15.5 percent of the LIS graduates found employment in other agencies, down slightly from 16.3 percent in 2007. (This downward trend reflects similar patterns in library and information agencies of all types.)

As in the past, jobs in the other agencies represent a diversity of positions, ranging from information policy to business analysis. Several of the graduates employed in nonprofit agencies described their jobs as donor research, identifying potential corporate and individual donors for fund raising. Social networking and social media cropped up, too. Usability testing, user experience design and analysis, and knowledge management have become standard fare within the "other" category. Private industry shows a strong emphasis on information technology, research analysis, and consulting. This category also represents jobs in archives, museums, and research foundations not affiliated with universities or corporate entities.

The type of "other" organization in which a graduate seeks employment greatly impacts the level of salary likely to be obtained. Similarly to 2007, salaries diverged widely between nonprofits and private industry, $41,488 to $58,194, respectively (a solid 40 percent difference). The gap between women and men widened in 2008, with women earning 17.2 percent less than men in other agencies; in 2007, the salary differential was 12.5 percent.

I's, L's and O's

Discussions about the merits between library science (LS) and information science (IS) programs have not abated. The arguments still simmer and erupt as schools drop LS from their names and professional organizations attempt to guide curriculum. In 2008 graduates were once again asked to self-define whether their jobs fell into LS, IS, or some other designation. Of the 1,650 graduates who responded to the question, the clear majority believed their jobs were decidedly LS (71.9 percent—which was down slightly from 2008), 11.3 percent claimed the IS designation, and the rest described their positions as falling into other areas, most frequently as archives or education (classroom teachers and higher education). The "other" category also served as a designation for many of the positions that fell outside of the LIS professions.

(text continues on page 338)

Table 4 / Placements by Average Full-Time Salary of Reporting 2008 Graduates*

	Average Salary			Median Salary		Low Salary		High Salary		Salaries		Total Placements
	Women	Men	All	Women	Men	Women	Men	Women	Men	Women	Men	
Syracuse	$51,536	$44,525	$49,978	$42,000	$43,300	$38,000	$36,500	$95,000	$55,000	14	4	21
Michigan	46,929	55,217	49,576	43,500	52,000	24,000	30,000	125,000	82,500	49	23	79
Long Island	48,981	48,000	48,878	48,000	48,000	32,000	45,000	72,000	51,000	17	2	25
San Jose	48,127	54,857	48,863	45,000	49,000	13,260	45,000	137,000	78,000	57	7	73
Maryland	44,529	72,000	48,112	42,000	90,000	32,000	36,000	60,000	90,000	20	3	24
N.C.-Chapel Hill	46,304	61,000	47,435	46,500	61,000	34,026	61,000	60,000	61,000	12	1	13
Albany	50,743	39,650	47,330	49,000	39,000	42,589	32,600	58,000	48,000	9	4	15
Southern Connecticut	46,347	47,153	46,508	46,600	45,000	24,960	41,460	74,000	55,000	12	3	20
Illinois	44,467	48,615	45,297	44,000	48,000	25,480	38,000	92,000	63,000	52	13	75
Rutgers	43,874	47,850	44,810	45,000	44,500	20,800	40,000	76,000	62,400	13	4	19
Texas Woman's	44,484	40,000	44,305	44,000	40,000	28,125	40,000	63,000	40,000	24	1	33
St. John's	47,333	34,000	44,000	49,000	34,000	44,000	34,000	49,000	34,000	3	1	5
Drexel	38,140	50,073	43,022	39,500	44,500	17,680	24,000	62,000	112,808	26	18	54
Simmons	42,480	42,973	42,574	41,500	42,500	13,000	16,000	73,000	65,000	85	20	112
Arizona	43,028	40,750	42,572	39,500	41,500	25,000	30,000	68,000	50,000	16	4	22
Wisconsin-Milwaukee	40,555	50,333	41,888	39,000	52,000	29,000	45,000	52,200	54,000	19	3	25
Texas (Austin)	41,067	42,143	41,310	39,000	38,000	18,000	20,000	70,000	67,000	24	7	33
Wayne State	41,903	34,301	40,734	40,000	37,700	25,000	10,000	117,000	51,804	22	4	28
Indiana	39,794	41,050	40,039	39,000	40,200	16,000	30,333	75,000	48,000	33	8	46
South Florida	39,722	40,417	39,822	40,750	41,000	22,000	37,000	52,000	43,250	18	3	26
North Texas	39,457	38,846	39,338	40,000	40,592	19,000	21,500	56,600	56,000	58	14	81

Rhode Island	39,290	—	39,290	39,950	—	20,000	—	62,000	—	10	—	10
South Carolina	38,856	39,469	38,995	37,500	39,000	32,000	30,000	52,000	47,000	17	5	25
Louisiana State	38,014	40,375	38,958	35,500	39,500	23,000	38,500	63,000	44,000	6	4	9
Florida State	37,081	44,795	38,887	36,000	35,000	13,500	29,500	70,000	116,100	36	11	63
Kent State	37,945	40,608	38,790	40,000	39,500	11,295	24,000	65,000	58,000	43	20	66
Pittsburgh	37,763	40,657	38,643	35,900	40,000	24,900	35,000	54,000	45,000	16	7	22
Wisconsin–Madison	37,539	45,288	38,469	38,165	46,750	20,000	30,000	55,000	54,225	44	6	56
Alabama	35,863	44,850	38,431	35,992	42,700	20,925	36,000	50,000	58,000	10	4	14
Denver	38,474	36,000	38,199	39,000	36,000	26,500	36,000	45,000	36,000	8	1	9
Tennessee	36,974	40,450	37,782	35,000	36,000	24,000	22,000	85,000	72,500	33	10	48
Iowa	38,000	36,667	37,429	36,000	40,000	30,000	25,000	50,000	45,000	4	3	9
Buffalo	37,384	36,800	37,263	36,000	36,000	20,800	29,000	56,000	43,000	19	5	24
Oklahoma	36,348	38,000	36,498	35,000	38,000	26,000	38,000	50,000	38,000	10	1	13
Dominican	36,489	35,760	36,358	36,000	35,000	10,000	12,800	75,000	55,000	114	25	157
Hawaii	36,216	36,000	36,189	39,000	36,000	14,000	36,000	64,000	36,000	7	1	7
UCLA	34,000	—	34,000	34,000	—	34,000	—	34,000	—	1	—	1
Missouri–Columbia	31,750	—	31,750	31,750	—	23,500	—	40,000	—	2	—	2
Kentucky	31,169	33,250	31,724	29,000	33,500	18,000	31,000	49,500	35,000	11	4	20

* This table represents only placements and salaries reported as full-time. Some individuals or schools omitted some information, rendering information unusable. Comparisons with other tables will show different numbers of placements and salaries.

337

Table 5 / Average Salary Index Starting Library Positions, 1998–2008

Year	Library Schools	Average Starting Salary	Dollar Increase in Average Salary	Salary Index	BLS-CPI*
1998	47	$31,915	$1,645	180.38	164.3
1999	37	33,976	2,061	192.03	168.7
2000	37	34,871	895	197.26	175.1
2001	40	36,818	1,947	208.09	177.1
2002	30	37,456	638	211.70	179.9
2003	43	37,975	519	214.63	184.0
2004	46	39,079	1,104	220.87	188.9
2005	37	40,115	1,036	226.73	195.3
2006	45	41,014	899	231.81	201.6
2007	43	42,361	1,347	239.42	207.3
2008	40	41,579	(782)	235.00	215.3

* U.S. Department of Labor, Bureau of Labor Statistics, Consumer Price Index, All Urban Consumers (CPI-U), U.S. city average, all items, 1982–1984=100. The average beginning professional salary for that period was $17,693.

(continued from page 335)

The LS vs. IS designation continues to represent more than curriculum standards and pedagogical philosophies. In a dollar for dollar comparison, graduates who described their jobs as information science earned 15 percent more on average than those claiming library science. IS-defined positions earned an average starting salary of $46,310 compared with LS positions, which earned $40,221. Jobs described as "other" obtained salaries slightly above LS, averaging $41,638, and significantly less than IS-defined jobs (a difference of 11.2 percent). In a surprising twist to the LS vs. IS debate, the graduate who earned the top salary in 2008 of $137,000 was self-defined as library science.

IS designation did not provide immunity to a poor economy. In fact, jobs described as IS declined approximately $2,000 annually (4.4 percent lower) compared with the 2007 salary levels of $48,354, while LS job salaries remained flat. The drop in salary was much steeper than the national average of 1.8 percent, suggesting that this segment of the information industry was impacted by the credit crisis and falling stock prices as well as severely reduced funding for educational institutions and public agencies. However, the information science jobs continued to have some of the best levels of compensation, 11.4 percent higher salaries than the national average ($41,579) for all of the LIS graduates in 2008. And, once again, a degree from an iSchool Caucus member did influence salary, with seven of the 12 reporting institutions climbing well above the average starting salaries overall (ranging from 3.3 percent higher than average to an eye-popping 16.8 percent more, see Table 4).

From the Front Line

For the LIS graduates of 2008, this year was fraught with many challenges along with some triumphs. In general, the economic recession erased any gains that graduates made in 2007, with the notable exception of the Northeast. Some

Table 6 / Salaries of Reporting Professionals* by Area of Job Assignment

Assignment	No.	Percent of Total	Low Salary	High Salary	Average Salary	Median Salary
Acquisitions	25	1.42	$20,800	$52,525	$38,184	$38,000
Administration	110	6.23	10,000	137,000	41,809	38,000
Adult Services	61	3.46	11,295	58,000	36,442	36,250
Archives	81	4.59	25,000	60,000	40,397	40,000
Automation/Systems	24	1.36	20,000	82,500	48,922	47,750
Cataloging and Classification	104	5.89	18,000	70,000	36,812	36,750
Children's Services	78	4.42	13,260	56,000	39,486	39,530
Circulation	82	4.65	17,680	69,000	33,648	31,500
Collection Development	24	1.36	28,000	55,000	42,675	42,500
Database Management	22	1.25	10,000	50,000	39,606	40,400
Electronic or Digital Services	56	3.17	25,480	69,000	42,121	41,500
Government Documents	11	0.62	17,663	40,000	31,583	32,500
Indexing/Abstracting	4	0.23	35,000	55,000	45,000	45,000
Info Technology	73	4.14	23,500	130,000	51,010	48,000
Instruction	59	3.34	22,880	112,808	42,314	41,500
Interlibrary Loans/ Document Delivery	22	1.25	20,540	63,000	37,910	36,000
Knowledge Management	11	0.62	33,000	116,100	60,178	50,000
Metadata	7	0.40	35,000	55,000	44,800	49,000
Other	160	9.07	10,400	125,000	41,983	40,000
Preservation/ Conservation	5	0.28	19,000	48,100	34,620	38,000
Reference/Info Services	363	20.57	13,500	68,000	40,368	40,000
Research Services	8	0.45	37,500	60,000	47,167	44,000
School Library Media Specialist	193	10.93	13,000	10,000	45,261	43,000
Serials	8	0.45	31,000	64,000	41,629	39,500
Solo Librarian	43	2.44	18,000	66,000	38,042	37,000
Technical Services	9	0.51	27,000	53,909	38,652	38,000
Usability/Usability Testing	7	0.40	40,000	80,000	60,533	60,000
Web Services	4	0.23	61,000	61,000	61,000	61,000
Youth Services	99	5.61	20,000	59,000	38,104	37,700
Total	1,765		10,000	137,000	41,542	40,000

* This table represents placements of any type reported by job assignment, but only salaries reported as full-time.
Some individuals omitted placement information, rendering some information unusable. Comparison with other tables will show different numbers of placements.

reported that during the job hunt, employers told them that it would be three to five years before their organizations realized any substantial improvements in funding along with the ability to hire professional staff. Other job seekers suffered huge disappointments when, after successful interviews, they were told that the search had been canceled owing to hiring freezes or loss of funding for positions. A growing number of graduates remained in or accepted nonprofessional

(text continues on page 342)

Table 7 / Comparison of Salaries by Type of Organization*

	Total Placements	Salaries		Low Salary		High Salary		Average Salary			Median Salary		
		Women	Men	Women	Men	Women	Men	Women	Men	All	Women	Men	All
Public Libraries													
Northeast	64	49	8	$20,000	$33,000	$68,000	$45,000	$39,544	$40,308	$39,651	$39,250	$42,230	$40,000
Southeast	63	48	15	13,500	25,900	63,000	48,000	36,257	34,680	35,882	36,000	35,000	36,000
Midwest	153	115	16	11,295	25,000	71,700	50,700	34,897	37,150	35,118	35,000	35,500	35,000
Southwest	47	33	7	20,000	23,500	50,000	52,000	35,451	38,741	35,980	36,000	40,000	36,000
West	40	27	12	13,260	27,000	61,000	58,000	47,667	44,612	46,727	48,500	44,500	48,000
All Public	387	276	58	11,295	23,500	71,700	58,000	37,361	38,650	37,556	36,433	37,225	37,000
School Libraries													
Northeast	60	53	4	22,424	36,000	95,000	44,100	49,242	40,555	48,632	48,000	41,060	47,000
Southeast	36	31	1	19,000	35,000	62,000	35,000	40,290	35,000	40,125	38,000	35,000	37,781
Midwest	58	45	8	16,000	25,000	100,000	55,000	45,604	43,651	45,309	42,600	43,500	43,000
Southwest	46	39	1	13,000	38,000	60,000	38,000	43,849	38,000	43,703	43,849	38,000	45,000
West	15	14	—	16,915	—	56,700	—	41,053	—	41,053	41,000	—	41,000
Canada/International	3	2	—	36,000	—	70,000	—	53,000	—	53,000	53,000	—	53,000
All School	225	184	15	13,000	25,000	100,000	55,000	45,116	41,362	44,839	44,000	41,120	44,000
College/University Libraries													
Northeast	102	59	25	20,800	27,000	73,000	60,000	43,752	42,518	43,385	42,000	42,250	42,000
Southeast	98	77	12	15,000	12,800	69,000	72,500	38,372	41,338	38,722	39,000	40,500	39,500
Midwest	134	100	24	10,000	27,000	55,000	51,700	38,753	38,938	38,789	40,000	39,400	40,000
Southwest	62	43	16	19,000	17,663	53,909	56,000	38,828	38,410	38,715	40,000	39,500	40,000
West	39	25	11	32,000	35,000	69,000	112,808	47,452	59,003	50,982	47,087	54,225	48,050
Canada/International	7	2	2	60,000	20,000	137,000	50,000	98,500	35,000	66,750	98,500	35,000	55,000
All Academic	445	308	90	10,000	12,800	137,000	112,808	40,749	42,523	41,151	40,000	41,500	40,000
Special Libraries													
Northeast	22	15	5	17,680	42,000	63,000	65,000	37,850	49,000	40,435	35,000	45,000	40,500
Southeast	14	9	4	19,000	18,000	52,000	42,000	40,833	33,750	38,654	45,000	37,500	42,000
Midwest	29	22	5	20,000	24,000	75,000	47,500	35,914	35,180	35,778	34,000	33,000	33,000
Southwest	10	8	2	27,000	48,500	43,000	63,000	37,438	55,750	41,100	38,750	55,750	40,750
West	12	9	1	23,000	45,000	65,000	45,000	42,907	45,000	43,116	40,000	45,000	42,500

Type / Region													
Canada/International	1												
All Special	89	63	18	17,680	18,000	75,000	65,000	38,206	42,189	39,091	38,000	42,000	39,500
Government Libraries													
Northeast	5	4		20,800	21,000	60,574		39,844		39,844	39,000	28,500	39,000
Southeast	25	22	2	21,000	36,500	67,500	36,000	45,611	44,833	44,185	48,100	45,000	48,050
Midwest	7	3	3	11,000	30,000	38,000	53,000	23,180	44,667	34,007	20,540	50,000	37,250
Southwest	7	4	3	30,000	48,000	42,000	54,000	36,250	48,000	39,857	36,500	48,000	38,000
West	8	5	1	25,000		78,000	48,000	41,693		42,594	33,500		35,000
Canada/International	1												
All Government	54	39	10	11,000	21,000	78,000	56,000	41,731	42,950	41,980	40,000	46,500	40,000
Library Cooperatives/Networks													
Northeast	5	1	4	23,500	34,000	23,500	62,400	23,500	46,685	42,048	23,500	45,170	43,339
Southeast	1		1										
Midwest	7	6		26,500	41,000	48,000	41,000	37,750	41,000	38,214	39,000	41,000	40,000
Southwest	2	1		27,000		27,000		27,000		27,000	27,000		27,000
West	1	1		85,000		85,000		85,000		85,000	85,000		85,000
All Co-Op./Networks	16	9	5	23,500	34,000	85,000	62,400	40,222	45,548	42,124	38,000	43,339	40,500
Vendors													
Northeast	3	3		35,000		36,000		35,333		35,333	35,000		35,000
Southeast	2	2		34,000		85,000		59,500		59,500	59,500		59,500
Midwest	5	3	2	10,400	42,000	39,000	50,000	27,800		35,080	34,000	46,000	39,000
Southwest													
West	1		1		50,000		50,000		50,000	50,000		50,000	50,000
All Vendors	11	8	3	10,400	42,000	85,000	50,000	38,550	47,333	40,945	35,000	50,000	36,000
Other Organizations													
Northeast	47	22	17	25,000	36,000	60,000	13,000	40,586	55,471	47,053	35,000	50,000	45,600
Southeast	43	17	18	23,000	10,000	60,000	96,000	41,453	47,806	44,676	40,000	45,000	43,500
Midwest	74	33	23	25,480	25,000	125,000	68,199	47,164	43,405	45,660	42,000	40,000	40,000
Southwest	18	9	4	18,000	38,000	50,000	80,000	35,722	57,125	42,308	36,000	55,250	38,000
West	26	10	8	33,000	24,000	86,000	90,000	51,000	64,500	57,000	46,500	75,000	55,000
Canada/International	8	4	1	25,000	55,800	85,000	55,800	52,362	55,800	53,049	49,723	55,800	50,000
All Other	231	96	71	18,000	10,000	125,000	130,000	44,166	51,758	47,394	40,000	48,000	44,000

* This table represents only full-time salaries and placements reported by type. Some individuals omitted placement information, rendering some information unusable. Comparison with other tables will show different numbers of total placements owing to completeness of the data reported by individuals and schools.

(continued from page 339)
positions as clerks and library assistants (13.5 percent in 2008 compared with 11.3 percent in 2007), and, as noted previously, part-time positions increased.

For other graduates, the transitions from graduate student to employed professional was much smoother. Approximately 42.3 percent of the 1,784 who responded to questions about previous employment remained with their current employer while completing the master's degree. While this did not guarantee the likelihood of promotion or better salary, it did mean continued employment in a poor economic environment.

In 2008 the number of graduates who found employment prior to graduation fell from a high of 42 percent in 2007 to 22.9 percent in 2008. This reverses a trend that began in 2003 when 30 percent of the graduates were employed before completing their master's degree. Once again, graduates began the job search well in advance of graduation day, by as much as two semesters earlier.

Graduates reported sending out 30-40 résumés before being offered even one interview opportunity. The average length of the search was longer than in previous years at just under five months, though it has been slowly creeping up over time. The comments most frequently made by the LIS graduates was that employers are looking for experience (two to three years professional experience) and that the number of entry-level jobs is dropping. Some graduates expressed the wish that they had not pursued an LIS degree at this time and in hindsight say they would have chosen another field if they had known how truly difficult the job market was for librarians and other information professionals.

Other graduates reported successful, quick job searches. Most attribute their success to prior experience as well as personal contacts. Among their strategies, they count the assistance of LIS faculty in identifying appropriate positions and keeping in touch with former classmates about open positions. They also did their homework and were well prepared when going into a job interview, understanding the agency and the position they were seeking and well practiced in interviewing skills. Overwhelmingly, they advised others not to underestimate the value of completing an internship. It not only provided practical skills, but it also put them in the running for available positions at the institution where they were interning.

Not surprisingly, the LIS programs' view on the job search is less dire than that of the graduates. Approximately 54 percent of the participating schools said that it was no more difficult to place graduates in 2008 than it had been in previous years, down from 60 percent last year. However, 15 of the participating programs indicated that the number of jobs available decreased on average 22.5 percent from 2007. In particular they saw fewer jobs in school library media centers and in special libraries. This reflects the placement trends described by the graduates.

The reality is probably somewhere between the graduates' view and that of the LIS schools. The economic recession was well illustrated in the declining salaries and position counts, especially in agencies reliant upon public funding and in regions hit heavily by high unemployment. And, given the number of potential library system closings and continued economic hardships, it is likely that the 2009 graduating class will experience similar frustrations along with some triumphs.

Accredited Master's Programs in Library and Information Studies

This list of graduate programs accredited by the American Library Association is issued by the ALA Office for Accreditation. Regular updates and additional details appear on the Office for Accreditation's Web site at http://www.ala.org/Template.cfm?Section=lisdirb&Template=/cfapps/lisdir/index.cfm. More than 150 institutions offering both accredited and nonaccredited programs in librarianship are included in the 63rd edition (2010–2011) of *American Library Directory* (Information Today, Inc.)

Northeast: Conn., D.C., Md., Mass., N.J., N.Y., Pa., R.I.

Catholic University of America, School of Lib. and Info. Science, 620 Michigan Ave. N.E., Washington, DC 20064. Kimberly Kelley, dean. Tel. 202-319-5085, fax 202-219-5574, e-mail cua-slis@cua.edu, World Wide Web http://slis.cua.edu. Admissions contact: Timothy Steelman. Tel. 202-319-5085, e-mail grayl@cua.edu.

Clarion University of Pennsylvania, College of Educ. and Human Services, Dept. of Lib. Science, 210 Carlson Lib. Bldg., 840 Wood St., Clarion, PA 16214. Andrea Miller, chair. Tel. 866-272-5612, fax 814-393-2150, World Wide Web http://www.clarion.edu/libsci. Admissions contact: Lois Dulavitch. Tel. 866-272-5612, e-mail ldulavitch@clarion.edu.

Drexel University, College of Info. Science and Technology, 3141 Chestnut St., Philadelphia, PA 19104-2875. David E. Fenske, dean. Tel. 215-895-2474, fax 215-895-2494, e-mail info@ischool.drexel.edu, World Wide Web http://www.ischool.drexel.edu. Admissions contact: Matthew Lechtenburg. Tel. 215-895-1951, e-mail matthew.lechtenberg@ischool.drexel.edu.

Long Island University, Palmer School of Lib. and Info. Science, C. W. Post Campus, 720 Northern Blvd., Brookville, NY 11548-1300. Mary L. Westermann-Cicio, dean pro tem. Tel. 516-299-2866, fax 516-299-4168, e-mail palmer@cwpost.liu.edu, World Wide Web http://www.cwpost.liu.edu/palmer. Admissions contact: Rose-mary Chu. Tel. 516-299-2487, e-mail rchu@liu.edu.

Pratt Institute, School of Info. and Lib. Science, 144 W. 14 St., New York, NY 10011. Tula Giannini, dean. Tel. 212-647-7682, fax 202-367-2492, e-mail infosils@pratt.edu, World Wide Web http://www.pratt.edu/sils. Admissions contact: Claire Moore.

Queens College, City Univ. of New York, Grad. School of Lib. and Info. Studies, Rm. 254, Rosenthal Lib., 65-30 Kissena Blvd., Flushing, NY 11367-1597. Virgil L. P. Blake, dir. Tel. 718-997-3790, fax 718-997-3797, e-mail gc_gslis@qc.cuny.edu, World Wide Web http://www.qc.edu/gslis. Admissions contact: Roberta Brody. E-mail roberta_brody@qc.edu.

Rutgers University, School of Communication and Info., Dept. of Lib. and Info. Science, 4 Huntington St., New Brunswick, NJ 08901-1071. Claire R. McInerney, chair. Tel. 732-932-7500 ext. 8218, fax 732-932-6916, e-mail scilsmls@comminfo.rutgers.edu, World Wide Web http://www.comminfo.rutgers.edu. Admissions contact: Kay Cassell. Tel. 732-932-7500 ext. 8264.

Saint John's University, College of Liberal Arts and Sciences, Div. of Lib. and Info. Science, 8000 Utopia Pkwy., Queens, NY 11439. Jeffery E. Olson, dir. Tel. 718-990-6200, fax 718-990-2071, e-mail dlis@stjohns.edu, World Wide Web http://www.stjohns.edu/libraryscience. Admissions contact: Deborah Martinez. Tel. 718-990-6209.

Simmons College, Grad. School of Lib. and Info. Science, 300 The Fenway, Boston, MA 02115. Michele Cloonan, dean. Tel. 617-521-2800, fax 617-521-3192, e-mail gslis@simmons.edu, World Wide Web http://www.simmons.edu/gslis.

Southern Connecticut State University, School of Communication, Info., and Lib. Science, 501 Crescent St., New Haven, CT 06515. Chang Suk Kim, chair. Tel. 203-392-5781, fax 203-392-5780, e-mail ils@southernct.edu, World Wide Web http://www.southernct.edu/ils. Admissions contact: Kathy Muldowney.

Syracuse University, School of Info. Studies, 343 Hinds Hall, Syracuse, NY 13244. Elizabeth D. Liddy, dean. Tel. 315-443-2911, fax 315-443-6886, e-mail ischool@syr.edu, World Wide Web http://www.ischool.syr.edu. Admissions contact: R. David Lankes. Tel. 315-443-2911, e-mail mslis@syr.edu.

University at Albany, State Univ. of New York, College of Computing and Info., Dept. of Info. Studies, Draper 113, 135 Western Ave., Albany, NY 12222. Terrence A. Maxwell, chair. Tel. 518-442-5110, fax 518-442-5367, e-mail infostudies@albany.edu, World Wide Web http://www.albany.edu/cci/informationstudies/index.shtml. Admissions contact: Frances Reynolds. E-mail reynolds@albany.edu.

University at Buffalo, State Univ. of New York, Graduate School of Educ., Lib. and Info. Studies, 534 Baldy Hall, Box 1020, Buffalo, NY 14260. Dagobert Soergel, chair. Tel. 716-645-2412, fax 716-645-3775, e-mail ub-lis@buffalo.edu, World Wide Web http://www.gse.buffalo.edu/programs/mls. Admissions contact: Radhika Suresh. Tel. 716-645-2110, e-mail gse-info@buffalo.edu.

University of Maryland, College of Info. Studies, 4105 Hornbake Bldg., College Park, MD 20742. Jennifer Preece, dean. Tel. 301-405-2033, fax 301-314-9145, e-mail lbscgrad@deans.umd.edu, World Wide Web http://www.clis.umd.edu. Admissions tel. 301-405-2038, e-mail lbscgrad@deans.umd.edu.

University of Pittsburgh, School of Info. Sciences, 135 N. Bellefield Ave., Pittsburgh, PA 15260. Richard C. Cox, chair. Tel. 800-672-9435, fax 412-624-5231, e-mail lisinq@mail.sis.pitt.edu, World Wide Web http://www.sis.pitt.edu. Admissions contact: Shabana Reza. Tel. 412-624-3988.

University of Rhode Island, Grad. School of Lib. and Info. Studies, Rodman Hall, 94 W. Alumni Ave., Kingston, RI 02881. Gale Eaton, dir. Tel. 401-874-2878, fax 401-874-4964, e-mail gslis@etal.uri.edu, World Wide Web http://www.uri.edu/artsci/lsc.

Southeast: Ala., Fla., Ga., Ky., La., Miss., N.C., S.C., Tenn., P.R.

Florida State University, College of Communication and Info., School of Lib. and Info. Studies, 142 Collegiate Loop, P.O. Box 3062100, Tallahassee, FL 32306-2100. Corinne Jorgensen, dir. Tel. 850-644-5775, fax 850-644-9763, World Wide Web http://slis.fsu.edu. Admissions contact: Delores Bryant. Tel. 850-645-3280, e-mail delores.bryant@cci.fsu.edu.

Louisiana State University, School of Lib. and Info. Science, 267 Coates Hall, Baton Rouge, LA 70803. Beth Paskoff, dean. Tel. 225-578-3158, fax 225-578-4581, e-mail slis@lsu.edu, World Wide Web http://slis.lsu.edu. Admissions contact: LaToya Coleman Joseph. E-mail lcjoseph@lsu.edu.

North Carolina Central University, School of Lib. and Info. Sciences, P.O. Box 19586, Durham, NC 27707. Irene Owens, dean. Tel. 919-530-6485, fax 919-530-6402, World Wide Web http://www.nccuslis.org. Admissions contact: Tysha Jacobs. Tel. 919-530-7320, e-mail tjacobs@nccu.edu.

University of Alabama, College of Communication and Info. Sciences, School of Lib. and Info. Studies, 515 Gorgas Lib., Capstone Drive, Box 870252, Tuscaloosa, AL 35487-0252. Elizabeth Aversa, dean. Tel. 205-348-4610, fax 205-348-3746, e-mail info@slis.ua.edu, World Wide Web http://www.slis.ua.edu. Admissions contact: Beth Riggs.

University of Kentucky, School of Lib. and Info. Science, 320 Little Lib., Lexington,

KY 40506-0224. Jeffrey T. Huber, dir. Tel. 859-257-8876, fax 859-257-4205, e-mail ukslis@uky.edu, World Wide Web http://www.uky.edu/CIS/SLIS. Admissions contact: Will Buntin. Tel. 859-257-3317, e-mail wjbunt0@uky.edu.

University of North Carolina at Chapel Hill, School of Info. and Lib. Science, CB 3360, 100 Manning Hall, CB 3360, Chapel Hill, NC 27599-3360. Barbara B. Moran, dean. Tel. 919-962-8366, fax 919-962-8071, e-mail info@ils.unc.edu, World Wide Web http://www.sils.unc.edu. Admissions contact: Lara Bailey.

University of North Carolina at Greensboro, School of Educ., Dept. of Lib. and Info. Studies, 349 Curry Bldg., Greensboro, NC 27402-6170. Lee Shiflett, chair. Tel. 336-334-3477, fax 336-334-5060, World Wide Web http://lis.uncg.edu. Admissions contact: Cindy Felts. E-mail cpfelts@uncg.edu.

University of Puerto Rico, Info. Sciences and Technologies, P.O. Box 21906, San Juan, PR 00931-1906. Luisa Vigo-Cepeda, acting dir. Tel. 787-763-6199, fax 787-764-2311, e-mail egcti@uprrp.edu, World Wide Web http://egcti.upr.edu. Admissions contact: Migdalia Dávila-Perez. Tel. 787-764-0000 ext. 3530, e-mail migdalia.davila @upr.edu.

University of South Carolina, College of Mass Communications and Info. Studies, School of Lib. and Info. Science, 1501 Greene St., Columbia, SC 29208. Samantha K. Hastings, dir. Tel. 803-777-3858, fax 803-777-7938, e-mail hastings@sc.edu, World Wide Web http://www.libsci.sc.edu. Admissions contact: Tilda Reeder. Tel. 800-304-3153, e-mail tildareeder@sc.edu.

University of South Florida, College of Arts and Sciences, School of Lib. and Info. Science, 4202 E. Fowler Ave., CIS 1040, Tampa, FL 33620. James Andrews, interim dir. Tel. 813-974-3520, fax 813-974-6840, e-mail lisinfo@cas.usf.edu, World Wide Web http://slisusf.edu. Admissions contact: Wendy Steiger. E-mail wsteiger@cas.usf.edu.

University of Southern Mississippi, College of Educ. and Psychology, School of Lib. and Info. Science, 118 College Drive, No. 5146, Hattiesburg, MS 39406-0001. M. J. Norton, dir. Tel. 601-266-4228, fax 601-266-5774, e-mail slis@usm.edu, World Wide Web http://www.usm.edu/slis. Admissions tel. 601-266-5137, e-mail graduatestudies@usm.edu.

University of Tennessee, College of Communication and Info., School of Info. Sciences, 451 Communication Bldg., Knoxville, TN 37996. Edwin M. Cortez, dir. Tel. 865-974-2148, fax 865-974-4967, World Wide Web http://www.sis.utk.edu. Admissions contact: Tanya Arnold. E-mail tnarnold@utk.edu.

Valdosta State University, Dept. of Info. Studies, 1500 N. Patterson St., Valdosta, GA 31698-0133. Wallace Koehler, dir. Tel. 229-333-5966, fax 229-259-5055, e-mail mlis@valdosta.edu, World Wide Web http://www.valdosta.edu/mlis. Admissions contact: Sheila Peacock.

Midwest: Ill., Ind., Iowa, Kan., Mich., Mo., Ohio, Wis.

Dominican University, Grad. School of Lib. and Info. Science, 7900 W. Division St., River Forest, IL 60305. Susan Roman, dean. Tel. 708-524-6845, fax 708-524-6657, e-mail gslis@dom.edu, World Wide Web http://www.gslis.dom.edu. Admissions contact: Dianna K. Wiggins. Tel. 708-524-6848, e-mail dwiggins@dom.edu.

Emporia State University, School of Lib. and Info. Management, 1200 Commercial, Campus Box 4025, Emporia, KS 66801. Gwen Alexander, dean. Tel. 620-341-5203, fax 620-341-5233, e-mail sliminfo@emporia.edu, World Wide Web http://slim.emporia.edu. Admissions contact: Candace Boardman. Tel. 620-341-6159, e-mail sliminfo@emporia.edu.

Indiana University, School of Lib. and Info. Science, 1320 E. 10 St., LI011, Bloomington, IN 47405-3907. Blaise Cronin, dean. Tel. 812-855-2018, fax 812-855-6166, e-mail slis@indiana.edu, World Wide Web http://www.slis.iu.edu. Admissions contact: Rhonda Spencer.

Kent State University, School of Lib. and Info. Science, P.O. Box 5190, Kent, OH

44242-0001. Richard E. Rubin, dir. Tel. 330-672-2782, fax 330-672-7965, e-mail inform@slis.kent.edu, World Wide Web http://www.slis.kent.edu. Admissions contact: Cheryl Tennant.

University of Illinois at Urbana-Champaign, Grad. School of Lib. and Info. Science, 501 E. Daniel St., Champaign, IL 61820-6211. John Unsworth, dean. Tel. 217-333-3280, fax 217-244-3302, e-mail gslis@Illinois.edu, World Wide Web http://www.lis.uiuc.edu. Admissions contact: Penny Ames. Tel. 217-333-7197, e-mail pames@illinois.edu.

University of Iowa, School of Lib. and Info. Science, 3087 Main Lib., Iowa City, IA 52242-1420. James K. Elmborg, dir. Tel. 319-335-5707, fax 319-335-5374, e-mail slis@uiowa.edu, World Wide Web http://slis.uiowa.edu/~slisweb. Admissions contact: Kit Austin. E-mail caroline-austin@uiowa.edu.

University of Michigan, School of Info., 304 West Hall Bldg., 1085 S. University Ave., Ann Arbor, MI 48109-1092. Martha Pollack, dean. Tel. 734-763-2285, fax 734-764-2475, e-mail si.admissions@umich.edu, World Wide Web http://www.si.umich.edu. Admissions contact: Laura Elgas. E-mail si.admissions@umich.edu.

University of Missouri, College of Educ., School of Info. Science and Learning Technologies, 303 Townsend Hall, Columbia, MO 65211. John Wedman, dir. Tel. 877-747-5868, fax 573-884-0122, e-mail sislt@missouri.edu, World Wide Web http://sislt.missouri.edu. Admissions tel. 573-882-4546.

University of Wisconsin–Madison, College of Letters and Sciences, School of Lib. and Info. Studies, Rm. 4217, H. C. White Hall, 600 N. Park St., Madison, WI 53706. Christine Pawley, dir. Tel. 608-263-2900, fax 608-263-4849, e-mail uw-slis@slis.wisc.edu, World Wide Web http://www.slis.wisc.edu. Admissions contact: Andrea Poehling. Tel. 608-263-2909, e-mail student-services@slis.wisc.edu.

University of Wisconsin–Milwaukee, School of Info. Studies, P.O. Box 413, Milwaukee, WI 53211. Johannes Britz, dean. Tel.

414-229-4707, fax 414-229-6699, e-mail soisinfo@uwm.edu, World Wide Web http://www4.uwm.edu/sois. Admissions tel. 414-229-4707.

Wayne State University, Lib. and Info. Science Program, 106 Kresge Lib., Detroit, MI 48202. Stephen T. Bajjaly, dir. Tel. 313-577-1825, fax 313-577-7563, e-mail asklis@wayne.edu, World Wide Web http://www.lisp.wayne.edu. Admissions contact: Matthew Fredericks. Tel. 313-577-2446, e-mail aj8416@wayne.edu.

Southwest: Ariz., Okla., Texas

Texas Woman's University, School of Lib. and Info. Studies, P.O. Box 425438, Denton, TX 76204-5438. Ling Hwey Jeng, dir. Tel. 940-898-2602, fax 940-898-2611, e-mail slis@twu.edu, World Wide Web http://www.twu.edu/library-studies. Admissions contact: Brenda Mallory. E-mail bmallory@mail.wu.edu.

University of Arizona, College of Social and Behavioral Sciences, School of Info. Resources and Lib. Science, 1515 E. 1 St., Tucson, AZ 85719. P. Bryan Heidorn, dir. Tel. 520-621-3565, fax 520-621-3279, e-mail sirls@email.arizona.edu, World Wide Web http://www.sir.arizona.edu. Admissions contact: Geraldine Fragoso.

University of North Texas, College of Info., Dept. of Lib. and Info. Sciences, 1155 Union Circle, No. 311068, Denton, TX 76203-5017. Herman L. Totten, dean. Tel. 940-565-2445, fax 940-565-3101, e-mail slis@unt.edu, World Wide Web http://www.unt.edu/slis. Admissions contact: John Pipes. Tel. 940-565-3562, e-mail john.pipes@unt.edu.

University of Oklahoma, School of Lib. and Info. Studies, College of Arts and Sciences, Rm. 120, 401 W. Brooks, Norman, OK 73019-6032. Kathy Latrobe, dir. Tel. 405-325-3921, fax 405-325-7648, e-mail slisinfo@ou.edu, World Wide Web http://www.ou.edu/cas/slis. Admissions contact: Maggie Ryan.

University of Texas at Austin, School of Info., 1616 Guadalupe St., Suite 5.202,

Austin, TX 78701-1213. Andrew Dillon, dean. Tel. 512-471-3821, fax 512-471-3971, e-mail info@ischool.utexas.edu, World Wide Web http://www.ischool.utexas.edu. Admissions contact: Carla Criner. Tel. 512-471-5654, e-mail criner@ischool.utexas.edu.

West: Calif., Colo., Hawaii, Wash.

San José State University, School of Lib. and Info. Science, 1 Washington Sq., San José, CA 95192-0029. Ken Haycock, dir. Tel. 408-924-2490, fax 408-924-2476, e-mail office@slis.sjsu.edu, World Wide Web http://slisweb.sjsu.edu. Admissions contact: Scharlee Phillips. Tel. 408-924-2417, e-mail sphillip@slis.sjsu.edu.

University of California, Los Angeles, Graduate School of Educ. and Info. Studies, Dept. of Info. Studies, Box 951520, Los Angeles, CA 90095-1520. Gregory Leazer, interim chair. Tel. 310-825-8799, fax 310-206-3076, e-mail info@gseis.ucla.edu, World Wide Web http://is.gseis.ucla.edu. Admissions contact: Susan Abler. Tel. 310-825-5269, e-mail abler@gseis.ucla.edu.

University of Denver, Morgridge College of Educ., Lib. and Info. Science Program, JMAC Bldg., 2450 S. Vine St., Denver, CO 80208. Mary Stansbury, chair. Tel. 303-871-2747, fax 303-871-2709, World Wide Web http://www.du.edu/lis. Admissions contact: Nick Heckart. E-mail nheckart@du.edu.

University of Hawaii, College of Natural Sciences, Lib. and Info. Science Program, 2550 McCarthy Mall, Honolulu, HI 96822. Peter Jacso, chair. Tel. 808-956-7321, fax 808-956-3548, e-mail slis@hawaii.edu, World Wide Web http://www.hawaii.edu/slis.

University of Washington, The Info. School, 370 Mary Gates Hall, Box 352840, Seattle, WA 98195-2840. Harry Bruce, dean. Tel. 206-685-9937, fax 206-616-3152, e-mail info@ischool.washington.edu, World Wide Web http://www.ischool.washington.edu. Admissions contact: Admissions coordinator. Tel. 206-543-1794, e-mail mlis@ischool.washington.edu.

Canada

Dalhousie University, School of Info. Management, Kenneth C. Rowe Management Bldg., Halifax, NS B3H 3J5. Fiona Black, dir. Tel. 902-494-3656, fax 902-494-2451, e-mail sim@dal.ca, World Wide Web http://www.sim.management.dal.ca. Admissions contact: JoAnn Watson. E-mail mlis@dal.ca.

McGill University, School of Info. Studies, 3661 Peel St., Montreal, PQ H3A 1X1. France Bouthillier, dir. Tel. 514-398-4204, fax 514-398-7193, e-mail sis@mcgill.ca, World Wide Web http://www.mcgill.ca/sis. Admissions contact: Kathryn Hubbard, Tel. 514-398-4204 ext. 0742.

Université de Montréal, École de Bibliothéconomie et des Sciences de l'Information, C.P. 6128, Succursale Centre-Ville, Montreal, QC H3C 3J7. Jean-Michel Salaun, dir. Tel. 514-343-6400, fax 514-343-5753, e-mail ebsiinfo@ebsi.umontreal.ca, World Wide Web http://www.ebsi.umontreal.ca. Admissions contact: Alain Tremblay. Tel. 514-343-6044, e-mail alain.tremblay.1@umontreal.ca.

University of Alberta, School of Lib. and Info. Studies, 3-20 Rutherford S., Edmonton, AB T6G 2J4. Ann Curry, dir. Tel. 780-492-4578, fax 780-492-2430, e-mail slis@ualberta.ca, World Wide Web http://www.slis.ualberta.ca. Admissions contact: Morgen Zoeller. Tel. 780-492-4140, e-mail slisadmissions@ualberta.ca.

University of British Columbia, School of Lib., Archival, and Info. Studies, Irving K. Barber Learning Center, Suite 470, 1961 East Mall, Vancouver, BC V6T 1Z1. Edie Rasmussen, dir. Tel. 604-822-2404, fax 604-822-6006, e-mail slais@interchange.ubc.ca, World Wide Web http://www.slais.ubc.ca. Admissions contact: Michelle Mallette. E-mail slaisad@interchange.ubc.ca.

University of Toronto, Faculty of Info., Rm. 211, 140 George St., Toronto, ON M5S 3G6. Seamus Ross, dean. Tel. 416-978-

3202, fax 416-978-5762, e-mail inquire@ ischool.utoronto.ca, World Wide Web http://www.ischool.utoronto.ca. Admissions contact: Judy Dunn. Tel. 416-978-3934, e-mail judy.dunn@utoronto.ca.

University of Western Ontario, Grad. Programs in Lib. and Info. Science, Faculty of Info. and Media Studies, Rm. 240, North Campus Bldg., 1151 Richmond St., London, ON N6A 5B7. Thomas Carmichael, dean. Tel. 519-661-4017, fax 519-661-3506, e-mail mlisinfo@uwo.ca, World Wide Web http://fims.uwo.ca. Admissions contact: Shelley Long.

Library Scholarship Sources

For a more complete list of scholarships, fellowships, and assistantships offered for library study, see *Financial Assistance for Library and Information Studies,* published annually by the American Library Association (ALA). The document is also available on the ALA Web site at http://www.ala.org/ala/educationcareers/education/financialassistance/index.cfm.

American Association of Law Libraries. (1) A varying number of scholarships of a minimum of $1,000 for graduates of an accredited law school who are degree candidates in an ALA-accredited library school; (2) a varying number of scholarships of varying amounts for library school graduates working on a law degree and non-law graduates enrolled in an ALA-accredited library school; (3) the George A. Strait Minority Stipend of $3,500 for varying numbers of minority librarians working toward a library or law degree; and (4) a varying number of $500 scholarships for law librarians taking courses relating to law librarianship. For information, write to: Scholarship Committee, AALL, 53 W. Jackson Blvd., Suite 940, Chicago, IL 60604.

American Library Association. (1) The Marshall Cavendish Scholarship of $3,000 for a varying number of students who have been admitted to an ALA-accredited library school; (2) the David H. Clift Scholarship of $3,000 for a varying number of students who have been admitted to an ALA-accredited library school; (3) the Tom and Roberta Drewes Scholarship of $3,000 for a varying number of library support staff; (4) the Mary V. Gaver Scholarship of $3,000 for a varying number of individuals specializing in youth services; (5) the Miriam L. Hornback Scholarship of $3,000 for a varying number of ALA or library support staff; (6) the Christopher J. Hoy/ERT Scholarship of $5,000 for a varying number of students who have been admitted to an ALA-accredited library school; (7) the Tony B. Leisner Scholarship of $3,000 for a varying number of library support staff; (8) the Peter Lyman Memorial/SAGE Scholarship in New Media of $2,500 for a student admitted to an ALA accredited library school and specializing in new media; (9) the Cicely Phippen Marks Scholarship of $3,000 for a varying number of students admitted to an ALA-accredited program and specializing in federal librarianship; (10) Spectrum Initiative Scholarships of $6,500 for a varying number of minority students admitted to an ALA-accredited library school. For information, write to: ALA Scholarship Clearinghouse, 50 E. Huron St., Chicago, IL 60611, or see http://www.ala.org/scholarships.

ALA/Association for Library Service to Children. (1) The Bound to Stay Bound Books Scholarship of $7,000 each for four students who are U.S. or Canadian citizens, who have been admitted to an ALA-accredited program, and who will work with children in a library for one year after graduation; (2) the Frederic G. Melcher Scholarship of $6,000 each for two U.S. or Canadian citizens admitted to an ALA-accredited library school who will work with children in school or public libraries for one year after graduation. For information, write to: ALA Scholarship Clearinghouse, 50 E. Huron St., Chicago, IL 60611, or see http://www.ala.org/scholarships.

ALA/Association of College and Research Libraries and Thomson Reuters. (1) The ACRL Doctoral Dissertation Fellowship of $1,500 for a student who has completed all coursework, and submitted a dissertation proposal that has been accepted, in the area of academic librarianship; (2) the Samuel Lazerow Fellowship of $1,000 for a research, travel, or writing project in acquisitions or technical services in an academic or research library; (3) the ACRL and Coutts Nijhoff International West European Specialist Study Grant of $3,000 to pay travel expenses, room, and board for a ten-day trip to Europe for an ALA member (selection is based on proposal outlining purpose of trip). For information, write to: Megan Griffin, ALA/ACRL, 50 E. Huron St., Chicago, IL 60611.

ALA/Association of Specialized and Cooperative Library Agencies. Century Scholarship of up to $2,500 for a varying number of disabled U.S. or Canadian citizens admitted to an ALA-accredited library school. For information, write to: ALA Scholarship Clearinghouse, 50 E. Huron St., Chicago, IL 60611, or see http://www.ala.org/scholarships.

ALA/International Relations Committee. The Bogle Pratt International Library Travel Fund grant of $1,000 for a varying number of ALA members to attend a first international conference. For information, write to: Michael Dowling, ALA/IRC, 50 E. Huron St., Chicago, IL 60611.

ALA/Library and Information Technology Association. (1) The LITA/Christian Larew Memorial Scholarship of $3,000 for a disabled U.S. or Canadian citizen admitted to an ALA-accredited library school; (2) the LITA/OCLC Minority Scholarship in Library and Information Technology of $3,000 and (3) the LITA/LSSI Minority Scholarship of $2,500, each for a minority student admitted to an ALA-accredited program. For information, write to: ALA Scholarship Clearinghouse, 50 E. Huron St., Chicago, IL 60611, or see http://www.ala.org/scholarships.

ALA/Public Library Association. The Demco New Leaders Travel Grant Study Award of up to $1,500 for a varying number of PLA members with MLS degrees and five years or less experience. For information, write to: PLA Awards Program, ALA/PLA, 50 E. Huron St., Chicago, IL 60611.

American-Scandinavian Foundation. Fellowships and grants for 25 to 30 students, in amounts from $3,000 to $18,000, for advanced study in Denmark, Finland, Iceland, Norway, or Sweden. For information, write to: Exchange Division, American-Scandinavian Foundation, 58 Park Ave., New York, NY 10026, or see http://www.amscan.org/fellowships_grants.html.

Association for Library and Information Science Education (ALISE). A varying number of research grants of up to $2,500 each for members of ALISE. For information, write to: Association for Library and Information Science Education, Box 7640, Arlington, VA 22207.

Association of Jewish Libraries. The AJL Scholarship Fund offers up to two scholarships of $1,000 each for MLS students who plan to work as Judaica librarians. For information, write to: Lynn Feinman, 92nd St. Y Library, 1395 Lexington Ave., New York, NY 10128, e-mail lfeinman@92Y.org.

Association of Seventh-Day Adventist Librarians. The D. Glenn Hilts Scholarship of $1,200 for a member of the Seventh-Day Adventist Church in a graduate library program. For information, write to: Lee Wisel, Association of Seventh-Day Adventist Librarians, Columbia Union College, 7600 Flower Ave., Takoma Park, MD 20912.

Beta Phi Mu. (1) The Sarah Rebecca Reed Scholarship of $2,000 for a person accepted in an ALA-accredited library program; (2) the Frank B. Sessa Scholarship of $1,250 for a Beta Phi Mu member for continuing education; (3) the Harold Lancour Scholarship of $1,750 for study in a foreign country relating to the applicant's work or schooling; (4) the Blanche E. Woolls Scholarship for School Library Media Service of $2,250 for a person accepted in an ALA-accredited library program; (5) the Eugene Garfield Doctoral Dissertation Scholarship of $3,000 for a person who has approval of a dissertation topic. For information, write to: Christie Koontz, Executive Director, Beta Phi Mu, College of Information, Florida State University, 101H Louis Shores Building, 142 Collegiate Loop, Tallahassee, FL 32306-2100.

Canadian Association of Law Libraries. The Diana M. Priestly Scholarship of $2,500 for a student with previous law library experience or for entry to an approved Canadian law school or accredited Canadian library school. For information, write to: Janet Mass, Chair, CALL/ACBD Scholarship and Awards Committee, Gerard V. La Forest Law Library, University of New Brunswick, Bag Service 44999, Fredericton, NB E38 6C9.

Canadian Federation of University Women. (1) The Alice E. Wilson Award of $6,000 for five mature students returning to graduate studies in any field, with special consideration given to those returning to study after at least three years; (2) the Margaret McWilliams Pre-Doctoral Fellowship of $13,000 for a student who has completed at least one full year as a full-time student in doctoral-level studies; (3) the Marion Elder Grant Fellowship of $11,000 for a full-time student at any level of a doctoral program; (4) the CFUW Memorial Fellowship of $11,000 for a female student who has completed at least a year in full-time doctoral program and is currently enrolled full time in Canada or abroad; (5) the Beverly Jackson Fellowship of $2,000 for a student over the age of 35 at the time of application who is enrolled in graduate studies at an Ontario university; (6) the 1989 Ecole Polytechnique Commemorative Award of $7,000 for graduate studies in any field; (7) the Bourse Georgette LeMoyne award of $7,000 for graduate study in any field at a Canadian university (the candidate must be studying in French); (8) the Margaret Dale Philp Biennial Award of $3,000 for studies in the humanities or social sciences; (9) the Canadian Home Economics Association Fellowship of $6,000 for a student enrolled in a postgraduate program in Canada. For information, write to: Fellowships Program Manager, Canadian Federation of University Women, 305-251 Bank St., Suite 305, Ottawa, ON K2P 1X3, Canada, or see http://www.cfuw.org.

Canadian Library Association. (1) The World Book Graduate Scholarship in Library and Information Science of $2,500; (2) the CLA Dafoe Scholarship of $5,000; and (3) the H. W. Wilson Scholarship of $2,000—each scholarship is given to a Canadian citizen or landed immigrant to attend an accredited Canadian library school; (4) the Library Research and Development Grant of $1,000 for a member of the Canadian Library Association, in support of theoretical and applied research in library and information science. For information, write to: CLA Membership Services Department, Scholarships and Awards Committee, 328 Frank St., Ottawa, ON K2P 0X8, Canada.

Catholic Library Association. (1) The World Book, Inc., Grant of $1,500 divided among a varying number of CLA members for continuing education in children's or school librarianship; (2) the Rev. Andrew L. Bouwhuis Memorial Scholarship of $1,500 for a student accepted into a graduate program in library science. For information, write to: Jean R. Bostley, SSJ, Scholarship Chair, Catholic Library Association, 100 North St., Suite 224, Pittsfield, MA 01201-5109.

Chinese American Librarians Association. (1) The Sheila Suen Lai Scholarship and (2) the C. C. Seetoo/CALA Conference Travel Scholarship each offer $500 to a Chinese descendant who has been accepted in an ALA-accredited program. For information, write to: MengXiong Liu, Clark Library, San José State University, 1 Washington Sq., San Jose, CA 95192-0028.

Church and Synagogue Library Association. The Muriel Fuller Memorial Scholarship of $200 (including texts) for a correspondence course offered by the association. For information, write to: CSLA, 2920 S.W. Dolph Court, Suite 3A, Portland, OR 97280-0357.

Council on Library and Information Resources. (1) The Rovelstad Scholarship in International Librarianship, to enable a student enrolled in an accredited LIS program to attend the IFLA Annual Conference; (2) the A. R. Zipf Fellowship in Information Management of $10,000, awarded annually to a U.S. citizen enrolled in graduate school who shows exceptional promise for leadership and technical achievement. For more information, write to: A. R. Zipf Fellowship, Council on Library and Information Resources, 1755 Massachusetts Ave. N.W., Suite 500, Washington, DC 20036.

Massachusetts Black Librarians' Network. Two scholarships of at least $500 and

$1,000 for minority students entering an ALA-accredited master's program in library science with no more 12 semester hours completed toward a degree. For information, write to: Pearl Mosley, Chair, Massachusetts Black Librarians' Network, 17 Beech Glen St., Roxbury, MA 02119.

Medical Library Association. (1) The Cunningham Memorial International Fellowship of $3,500 for each of two health sciences librarians from countries other than the United States and Canada; (2) a scholarship of $5,000 for a person entering an ALA-accredited library program, with no more than one-half of the program yet to be completed; (3) a scholarship of $5,000 for a minority student for graduate study; (4) a varying number of Research, Development, and Demonstration Project Grants of $100 to $1,000 for U.S. or Canadian citizens who are MLA members; (5) the MLA Doctoral Fellowship of $2,000 for doctoral work in medical librarianship or information science; (6) the Rittenhouse Award of $500 for a student enrolled in an ALA-accredited library program or a recent graduate working as a trainee in a library internship program; (7) Continuing Education Grants of $100 to $500 for U.S. or Canadian citizens who are MLA members. For information, write to: Professional Development Department, Medical Library Association, 65 E. Wacker Place, Suite 1900, Chicago, IL 60601-7298.

Mountain Plains Library Association. A varying number of grants of up to $600 each for MPLA members with at least two years of membership, for continuing education. For information, write to: Judy Zelenski, MPLA Executive Secretary, 14293 W. Center Drive, Lakewood, SD 80228.

Society of American Archivists. (1) The Colonial Dames Awards, two grants of $1,200 each for specific types of repositories and collections; (2) the SAA Mosaic Scholarship, $5,000, for two minority students who are U.S. citizens or permanent residents pursuing graduate education in archival science. For information, write to: Debra Noland, Society of American Archivists, 521 S. Wells St., 5th fl., Chicago, IL 60607.

Southern Regional Education Board. A varying number of grants of varying amounts to cover in-state tuition for graduate or postgraduate study in an ALA-accredited library school for residents of various southern U.S. states (qualifying states vary year by year). For information, write to: Academic Common Market, c/o Southern Regional Education Board, 592 Tenth St. N.W., Atlanta, GA 30318-5790.

Special Libraries Association. (1) Three $6,000 scholarships for students interested in special-library work; (2) the Plenum Scholarship of $1,000 and (3) the ISI Scholarship of $1,000, each also for students interested in special-library work; (4) the Affirmative Action Scholarship of $6,000 for a minority student interested in special-library work; and (5) the Pharmaceutical Division Stipend Award of $1,200 for a student with an undergraduate degree in chemistry, life sciences, or pharmacy entering or enrolled in an ALA-accredited program. For information on the first four scholarships, write to: Scholarship Committee, Special Libraries Association, 331 South Patrick St., Alexandria, VA 22314-3501. For information on the Pharmaceutical Stipend, write to: Susan E. Katz, Awards Chair, Knoll Pharmaceuticals Science Information Center, 30 N. Jefferson St., Whippany, NJ 07981.

Library Scholarship and Award Recipients, 2009

Compiled by the Staff of the Library and Book Trade Almanac

Scholarships and awards are listed by organization.

American Association of Law Libraries (AALL)

AALL Scholarships. *Winners:* (Library Degree for Law School Graduates) Cindy Guyer, Mindy Rush Chipman, Errol Adams, Thomas Sneed, Tina Brooks, Ian Bourgoine; (Library Degree for Non-Law School Graduates) Phanelson Braxton.

AALL and Thomson West George A. Strait Minority Scholarship. *Winners:* Maria Femenia, Tiffany Paige, Sarah Nolan.

Joseph L. Andrews Bibliographic Award. *Winner:* William H. Manz for *Guide to State Legislation, Legislative History, and Administrative Materials* (Hein).

James F. Connolly LexisNexis Scholarship. To a law librarian interested in pursuing a law degree and who has demonstrated an interest in government publications. *Winner:* Caitlin Connelly Smith.

Marian Gould Gallagher Distinguished Service Award. To recognize extended and sustained service to law librarianship. *Winners:* Patrick E. Kehoe, Elizabeth Ann Puckett.

LexisNexis/John R. Johnson Memorial Scholarships. *Winners:* Donna Bowman, Marianne Sterna, Ellen Qualey, Joanne Gialelis.

American Institute for the Conservation of Historic and Artistic Works (AIC).

Forbes Medal for Distinguished Contribution to the Field of Conservation. *Winner:* Not awarded in 2009.

American Library Association (ALA)

ALA/Information Today Library of the Future Award ($1,500). For a library, consortium, group of librarians, or support organization for innovative planning for, applications of, or development of patron training programs about information technology in a library setting. *Donor:* Information Today, Inc. *Winner:* Indianapolis-Marion County (Indiana) Public Library for its "The Learning Curve @ Central Library" project.

ALA Presidential Citations for International Library Innovation. To libraries outside United States for significant contributions to the people they serve. *Winners:* Hester J. Hodgdan Libraries-for-All Program, San Juan del Sur, Nicaragua; Lubuto Library Project, Lusaka, Zambia; Tongji University Library, Shanghai, China

Leo Albert Spectrum Scholarship. To a designated Spectrum Scholarship recipient. *Donor:* Leo Albert. *Winner:* Rebecca "Nicci" Cobb.

Hugh C. Atkinson Memorial Award. For outstanding achievement (including risk taking) by academic librarians that has contributed significantly to improvements in library automation, management, and/or development or research. *Offered by:* ACRL, ALCTS, LLAMA, and LITA divisions. *Winner:* Ray English.

Carroll Preston Baber Research Grant (up to $3,000). For innovative research that could lead to an improvement in library services to any specified group(s) of people. *Donor:* Eric R. Baber. *Winner:* Not awarded in 2009.

Beta Phi Mu Award ($1,000). For distinguished service in library education. *Donor:* Beta Phi Mu International Library Science Honorary Society. *Winner:* C. James Schmidt.

Bogle-Pratt International Library Travel Fund Award ($1,000). To ALA member(s) to attend their first international conference. *Donors:* Bogle Memorial Fund and

Pratt Institute School of Information and Library Science. *Winner:* Jessica Brooks.

W. Y. Boyd Literary Novel Award. *Winner:* See "Literary Prizes, 2009" in Part 5.

David H. Clift Scholarship ($3,000). To worthy U.S. or Canadian citizens enrolled in an ALA-accredited program toward an MLS degree. *Winner:* Rachel Channer.

Eileen Cooke State and Local James Madison Award. To recognize individuals or groups who have championed public access to government information. *Winner:* Not awarded in 2009.

Melvil Dewey Medal ($2,000). To an individual or group for recent creative professional achievement in library management, training, cataloging and classification, and the tools and techniques of librarianship. *Donor:* OCLC/Forest Press. *Winner:* James G. Neal.

Tom and Roberta Drewes Scholarship ($3,000). To a library support staff member pursuing a master's degree. *Donor:* Quality Books. *Winner:* Carol Ann Geary.

EBSCO/ALA Conference Sponsorship Award ($1,000). To enable ten librarians to attend the ALA Annual Conference. *Donor:* EBSCO. *Winners:* Elizabeth A. Boyson, Karen W. Brown, Debra Cox Rollins, Lynne T. Holloway, Tami Miller-Earick, Carol A. Reichardt, Kristin Stout, Vitalija Svencionyte, Breanna Weston, Jill L. Woolums.

Equality Award ($1,000). To an individual or group for an outstanding contribution that promotes equality in the library profession. *Donor:* Scarecrow Press. *Winner:* Karen Downing.

Elizabeth Futas Catalyst for Change Award ($1,000). A biennial award to recognize and honor a librarian who invests time and talent to make positive change in the profession of librarianship. *Donor:* Elizabeth Futas Memorial Fund. *Winner:* Not awarded in 2009.

Loleta D. Fyan Public Library Research Grant (up to $10,000). For projects in public library development. *Donor:* Fyan Estate. *Winner:* Not awarded in 2009.

Gale Cengage Learning Financial Development Award ($2,500). To a library organization for a financial development project to secure new funding resources for a public or academic library. *Donor:* Gale Cengage Learning. *Winner:* Flagler County (Florida) Public Library.

Mary V. Gaver Scholarship ($3,000). To a student pursuing an MLS degree and specializing in youth services. *Winner:* Laura Elena Ochoa Podell.

Louise Giles Spectrum Scholarship. To a designated Spectrum Scholarship recipient. *Donor:* Louise Giles. *Winner:* Umesh Thakkar.

William R. Gordon Spectrum Scholarship. To a designated Spectrum Scholarship recipient. *Donor:* William R. Gordon and friends. *Winner:* Janee Jackson.

Greenwood Publishing Group Award for Best Book in Library Literature ($5,000). To recognize authors of U.S. or Canadian works whose books improve library management principles and practice. *Donor:* Greenwood Publishing Group. *Winner:* Jean Preer for *Library Ethics* (Libraries Unlimited).

Ken Haycock Award for Promoting Librarianship ($1,000). For significant contribution to public recognition and appreciation of librarianship through professional performance, teaching, or writing. *Winner:* Not awarded in 2009.

Honorary ALA Membership. To recognize outstanding contributions of lasting importance to libraries and librarianship. *Honoree:* Judith F. Krug (posthumously).

Miriam L. Hornback Scholarship ($3,000). To an ALA or library support staff person pursuing a master's degree in library science. *Winner:* Janet E. Yost.

Paul Howard Award for Courage ($1,000). Awarded biennially to a librarian, library board, library group, or an individual for exhibiting unusual courage for the benefit of library programs or services. *Donor:* Paul Howard Memorial Fund. *Winners:* Judith Flint, Amy Grasmick, and Christine Lesinski of Kimball Public Library, Randolph, Vermont.

John Ames Humphry/OCLC/Forest Press Award ($1,000). To an individual for significant contributions to international librarianship. *Donor:* OCLC/Forest Press. *Winner:* Patricia Oyler.

Tony B. Leisner Scholarship ($3,000). To a library support staff member pursuing a master's degree program. *Donor:* Tony B. Leisner. *Winner:* Justine Johnson.

Joseph W. Lippincott Award ($1,000). To a librarian for distinguished service to the profession. *Donor:* Joseph W. Lippincott III. *Winner:* Beverly P. Lynch.

Peter Lyman Memorial/Sage Scholarship in New Media ($2,500). *Donor:* Sage Publications. *Winner:* Stacy Kitsis.

James Madison Award. To recognize efforts to promote government openness. *Winner:* Thomas M. Susman, director, American Bar Association Government Affairs Office.

Marshall Cavendish Excellence in Library Programming Award ($2,000). To recognize either a school library or public library that demonstrates excellence in library programming by providing programs that have community impact and respond to community need. *Donor:* Marshall Cavendish. *Winner:* Nashville (Tennessee) Public Library for "Bringing Books to Life."

Marshall Cavendish Scholarship ($3,000). To a worthy U.S. or Canadian citizen to begin an MLS degree in an ALA-accredited program. *Winner:* Ryan David Stoops.

Grolier Foundation Award. See Scholastic Library Publishing Award.

Medical Library Association/National Library of Medicine Spectrum Scholarship. To a designated Spectrum Scholarship recipient or recipients. *Donors:* Medical Library Association, National Library of Medicine. *Winners:* Shalu Gillum, Mark Miller.

Schneider Family Book Awards. *Winners:* See "Literary Prizes, 2009" in Part 5.

Scholastic Library Publishing Award (formerly the Grolier Foundation Award) ($1,000). For stimulation and guidance of reading by children and young people. *Donor:* Scholastic Library Publishing. *Winner:* Kathleen T. Horning.

Spectrum Doctoral Fellowships. To provide full tuition support and stipends to minority U.S. and Canadian LIS doctoral students. *Donor:* Institute of Museum and Library Services. *Winners:* Not awarded in 2009.

Spectrum Initiative Scholarships ($5,000). Presented to minority students admitted to ALA-accredited library schools. *Donors:* ALA and Institute of Museum and Library Services. *Winners:* Reginald Allen, Rachel Arteaga, Emilia Askari, Anjali Bhasin, Hsiaojane "Anna" Chen, Victoria Chu, Rebecca "Nicci" Cobb, Kaela Cordova, Halima Davis, Tiara Farley, Stephen Xavier Flynn, Simone Fujita, Shalu Gillum, Larissa Estes Hammond, Youngmie Han, Alyss Hardin, Aaisha Haykal, Chinasa Izeogu, Janee Jackson, Boutsaba Janetvilay, Everett Kanehiro, Daisy Larios, Brian Leaf, Mai Youa Lee, Alicia K. Long, Michelle K May, Candelaria "Candy" Mendoza, Mark Miller, Cristina Mitra, Winifred Mixon, Mayumi Miyaoka, Jessica M. Navarro, Zoya Nazari, Holly Nguyen, Laura Elena Ochoa Podell, Yukie Ohta, Rumit Pancholi, Rita Puig, Neeri Rao, Trevar Riley-Reid, Miranda Rivers, Margarita "Maggie" Shawcross, Yasmeen Shorish, Susan Song, Jessamyn Sudhakaran, Sharon K. Tani, Trena N. Taylor, Umesh Thakkar, Christina M. Thompson, Sofia Vazquez-Duran.

Sullivan Award for Public Library Administrators Supporting Services to Children. To a library supervisor/administrator who has shown exceptional understanding and support of public library services to children. *Donor:* Peggy Sullivan. *Winner:* Clara Nalli Bohrer.

Howard M. and Gladys B. Teeple Spectrum Scholarship. To a designated Spectrum Scholarship recipient. *Donor:* Religion and Ethics Institute. *Winner:* Christina M. Thompson.

Dr. Betty J. Turock Spectrum Scholarship. To a designated Spectrum Scholarship recipient. *Winner:* Trevar Riley-Reid.

H. W. Wilson Library Staff Development Grant ($3,500). To a library organization for a program to further its staff development goals and objectives. *Donor:* H. W. Wilson Company. *Winner:* Office of Library Services, New York City Department of Education.

Women's National Book Association Award. To a living American woman who derives part or all of her income from books and allied arts and who has done meritorious work in the world of books. *Winner:* To be awarded next in 2010.

Women's National Book Association/Ann Heidbreder Eastman Grant ($500). To a librarian to take a course or participate in an institute devoted to aspects of publishing as a profession or to provide reimbursement for such study completed within the past year. *Winner:* Molly Krichten.

World Book/ALA Information Literacy Goal Awards ($5,000). To promote exemplary information literacy programs in both public and school libraries. *Donor:* World Book. *Winners:* Brockport (New York) Central School District for its "Information Literacy Continuum"; Troy (Michigan) Public Library for "Information Literacy for the Job Seeker."

ALA/Allied Professional Association

SirsiDynix Award for Outstanding Achievement in Promoting Salaries and Status for Library Workers. *Donor:* SirsiDynix. *Winners:* Anderson County Library Board, Clinton, Tennessee ($2,000); Lynn Sutton ($1,500); Mohamed Ismail ($1,500),

American Association of School Librarians (AASL)

AASL/ABC-CLIO Leadership Grant (up to $1,750). For planning and implementing leadership programs at state, regional, or local levels to be given to school library associations that are affiliates of AASL. *Donor:* ABC-CLIO. *Winner:* Not awarded in 2009.

AASL/Baker & Taylor Distinguished Service Award ($3,000). For outstanding contributions to librarianship and school library development. *Donor:* Baker & Taylor Books. *Winner:* Not awarded in 2009.

AASL Collaborative School Library Media Award ($2,500). For expanding the role of the library in elementary and/or secondary school education. *Donor:* Highsmith, Inc. *Winners:* Maureen O'Neill and Dennis Jutras of Baltimore Polytechnic Institute for "Beyond National History Day."

AASL Crystal Apple Award. To an individual, individuals, or group for a significant

impact on school libraries and students. *Winner:* Target Brands, Inc.

AASL Distinguished School Administrators Award ($2,000). For expanding the role of the library in elementary and/or secondary school education. *Donor:* ProQuest. *Winner:* Melanie Goffen Horowitz.

AASL/Frances Henne Award ($1,250). To a school library media specialist with five or fewer years in the profession to attend an AASL regional conference or ALA Annual Conference for the first time. *Donor:* Greenwood Publishing Group. *Winner:* Jill Mantel.

AASL Innovative Reading Grant ($2,500). To support the planning and implementation of an innovative program for children that motivates and encourages reading, especially with struggling readers. *Sponsor:* Capstone Publishers. *Winner:* Cathleen Friedmann, Metairie Park Country Day School, Metairie, Louisiana.

Information Technology Pathfinder Award ($1,000 to the specialist and $500 to the library). To library media specialists for innovative approaches to microcomputer applications in the school library media center. *Donor:* Follett Software Company. *Winners:* (elementary) Jennifer Gorup; (secondary) Melanie Le Jeune.

Intellectual Freedom Award ($2,000 plus $1,000 to the media center of the recipient's choice). To a school library media specialist and AASL member who has upheld the principles of intellectual freedom. *Donor:* ProQuest. *Winner:* Not awarded in 2009.

National School Library Media Program of the Year Award ($10,000). To school districts and two single schools for excellence and innovation in outstanding library media programs. *Donor:* Follett Library Resources. *Winners:* (district) Livonia (New York) Central School District; (single schools) Robert E. Clow Elementary School, Napierville, Illinois; Blue Valley North High School, Overland Park, Kansas.

Association for Library Collections and Technical Services (ALCTS)

ALCTS/LBI George Cunha and Susan Swartzburg Preservation Award ($1,250). To recognize cooperative preservation projects and/or individuals or groups that foster collaboration for preservation goals. *Donor:* LBI. *Winner:* Ann Russell.

ALCTS Presidential Citations for Outstanding Service. *Winners:* Magda El-Sherbini, Andy Hart, Dale Swensen.

Hugh C. Atkinson Memorial Award. *See under* American Library Association.

Ross Atkinson Lifetime Achievement Award. To recognize the contribution of an ALCTS member and library leader who has demonstrated exceptional service to ALCTS and its areas of interest. *Donor:* EBSCO. *Winner:* Cindy Hepfer.

Paul Banks and Carolyn Harris Preservation Award ($1,500). To recognize the contribution of a professional preservation specialist who has been active in the field of preservation and/or conservation for library and/or archival materials. *Donor:* Preservation Technologies. *Winner:* Barclay W. Ogden.

Best of *LRTS* Award ($250). To the author(s) of the year's best paper published in the division's official journal. *Winners:* Karen Schmidt, Wendy Allen Shelburne, and David Steven Vess for "Approaches to Selection, Access, and Collection Development in the Web World: A Case Study with Fugitive Literature."

Blackwell's Scholarship Award ($2,000 scholarship to the U.S. or Canadian library school of the recipients' choice). To honor the author(s) of the year's outstanding monograph, article, or original paper in the field of acquisitions, collection development, and related areas of resource development in libraries. *Donor:* Blackwell's. *Winners:* Karen Schmidt, Wendy Allen Shelburne, and David Steven Vess for "Approaches to Selection, Access, and Collection Development in the Web World: A Case Study with Fugitive Literature," published in *Library Resources & Technical Services,* vol. 52, no. 3.

Coutts Award for Innovation in Electronic Resources Management ($2,000). To recognize significant and innovative contributions to electronic collections management and development practice. *Donor:* Coutts Information Services. *Winner:* Judy Luther and Selden Lamoreux.

First Step Award (Wiley Professional Development Grant) ($1,500). For librarians new to the serials field to attend the ALA Annual Conference. *Donor:* John Wiley & Sons. *Winner:* Not awarded in 2009.

Leadership in Library Acquisitions Award ($1,500). For significant contributions by an outstanding leader in the field of library acquisitions. *Donor:* Harrassowitz. *Winner:* Trisha Davis.

Margaret Mann Citation (includes $2,000 award to the U.S. or Canadian library school of the winner's choice). To a cataloger or classifier for achievement in the areas of cataloging or classification. *Donor:* Online Computer Library Center. *Winner:* Francis L. Miksa.

Outstanding Collaboration Citation. For outstanding collaborative problem-solving efforts in the areas of acquisition, access, management, preservation, or archiving of library materials. *Winner:* Not awarded in 2009.

Esther J. Piercy Award ($1,500). To a librarian with no more than ten years' experience for contributions and leadership in the field of library collections and technical services. *Donor:* YBP Library Services. *Winner:* Laurel Tarulli.

Support Staff Travel Grants (up to $1,000). To enable support staff to attend an ALA Annual Conference. *Winners:* Not awarded in 2009.

Ulrich Serials Librarianship Award ($1,500). For distinguished contributions to serials librarianship. *Sponsor:* Ulrich's. *Winner:* Brian Green.

Association for Library Service to Children (ALSC)

ALSC/Book Wholesalers, Inc. BWI Summer Reading Program Grant ($3,000). To an ALSC member for implementation of an outstanding public library summer reading program for children. *Donor:* Book Wholesalers, Inc. *Winner:* Madison (Ohio) Public Library.

ALSC/Booklist/YALSA Odyssey Award. To the producer of the best audiobook for children or young adults available in English in the United States. *Sponsor: Booklist. Winner:* Recorded Books for *The Absolutely*

True Diary of a Part-Time Indian, written and narrated by Sherman Alexie.

ALSC/Candlewick Press "Light the Way: Library Outreach to the Underserved" Grant ($3,000). To a library conducting exemplary outreach to underserved populations, presented in honor of author Kate DiCamillo. *Donor:* Candlewick Press. *Winner:* To be awarded next in 2010.

May Hill Arbuthnot Honor Lectureship. To an author, critic, librarian, historian, or teacher of children's literature who prepares a paper considered to be a significant contribution to the field of children's literature. *Winner:* Kathleen T. Horning, director, University of Wisconsin–Madison Cooperative Children's Book Center.

Mildred L. Batchelder Award. *Winner:* See "Literary Prizes, 2009" in Part 5.

Louise Seaman Bechtel Fellowship ($4,000). For librarians with 12 or more years of professional-level work in children's library collections, to read and study at the Baldwin Library, University of Florida. *Donor:* Bechtel Fund. *Winner:* Linda Martin.

Pura Belpré Award. *Winners:* See "Literary Prizes, 2009" in Part 5.

Bookapalooza Program Awards. To provide three libraries with a collection of materials that will help transform their collection. *Winners:* Fletcher (Oklahoma) Public School Library, Laguna (New Mexico) Public Library, and Henry Whittemore Elementary School Library, Waltham, Massachusetts.

Bound to Stay Bound Books Scholarships ($7,000 each). For men and women who intend to pursue an MLS or advanced degree and who plan to work in the area of library service to children. *Donor:* Bound to Stay Bound Books. *Winners:* Jessica Ammons, Megan Bannen, Kristin Edstrom, Jennifer Raymond.

Randolph Caldecott Medal. *Winner:* See "Literary Prizes, 2009" in Part 5.

Andrew Carnegie Medal. To the U.S. producers of the most distinguished video for children in the previous year. *Sponsor:* Carnegie Corporation of New York. *Winners:* Paul R. Gagne and Melissa Reilly of Weston Woods Studios for Christine King

Farris's *March On! The Day My Brother Martin Changed the World.*

Carnegie-Whitney Awards (up to $5,000). For the preparation of print or electronic reading lists, indexes, or other guides to library resources that promote reading or the use of library resources at any type of library. *Donors:* James Lyman Whitney and Andrew Carnegie Funds. *Winners:* Anne Bailey for http://www.bookpublishing forum.com; Rose Bland for *Clinical Trials 101: Resources for Alzheimer's Patients and Their Caregivers;* Liza Palmer for *Avant-Garde Film: An Index to Films and Publications, 1905–2005;* Priscilla Matthews for *Mystery Series Characters in Short Stories: An Index to Collections and Specific Short Stories with Specific Series Characters;* Rana Salzmann for *The Planner's Bibliography: An Annotated List of Electronic and Print Resources for Practicing Planners, Scholars, and Students of Planning;* Gail Staines for *Horses in Cultures: A Searchable Database of Works of Fiction.*

Distinguished Service Award ($1,000). To recognize significant contributions to, and an impact on, library services to children and/or ALSC. *Winner:* Jane Botham.

Theodor Seuss Geisel Award. *Winner:* See "Literary Prizes, 2009" in Part 5.

Maureen Hayes Author/Illustrator Visit Award (up to $4,000). For an honorarium and travel expenses to enable a library talk to children by a nationally known author/illustrator. *Sponsor:* Simon & Schuster Children's Publishing. *Winners:* Maria Kramer and Chuck Ashton, Redwood City (California) Public Library.

Frederic G. Melcher Scholarship ($6,000). To two students entering the field of library service to children for graduate work in an ALA-accredited program. *Winners:* Heidi Knuth, Mary Bridget Maddan.

John Newbery Medal. *Winner:* See "Literary Prizes, 2009" in Part 5.

Penguin Young Readers Group Awards ($600). To children's librarians in school or public libraries with ten or fewer years of experience to attend the ALA Annual Conference. *Donor:* Penguin Young Readers Group. *Winners:* Cheryl Lee, Katherine

T. McCabe, Heather Karrick Perkinson, Sarah Polace.

Robert F. Sibert Medal. *Winner:* See "Literary Prizes, 2009" in Part 5.

Tandem Library Books Literature Program Award ($1,000 toward ALA Annual Conference attendance). To an ALSC member for the development of an outstanding reading or literature program for children. *Donor:* Tandem Library Books. *Winner:* Award discontinued.

Laura Ingalls Wilder Medal. *Winner:* See "Literary Prizes, 2009" in Part 5.

Association of College and Research Libraries (ACRL)

ACRL Academic or Research Librarian of the Year Award ($5,000). For outstanding contribution to academic and research librarianship and library development. *Donor:* YBP Library Services. *Winner:* Gloriana St. Clair.

ACRL Distinguished Education and Behavioral Sciences Librarian Award ($1,500). To an academic librarian who has made an outstanding contribution as an education and/or behavioral sciences librarian through accomplishments and service to the profession. *Donor:* John Wiley & Sons. *Winner:* Gary Lare.

ACRL/DLS Haworth Press Distance Learning Librarian Conference Sponsorship Award ($1,200). To an ACRL member working in distance-learning librarianship in higher education. *Winner:* Jack Fritts.

ACRL Doctoral Dissertation Fellowship ($1,500). To a doctoral student in the field of academic librarianship whose research has potential significance in the field. *Donor:* Thomson Reuters. *Winner:* Krystyna K. Matusiak for "Use of Digital Resources in an Academic Environment: A Qualitative Study of Students' Perceptions, Experiences, and Digital Literacy Skills."

ACRL Special Presidential Recognition Award. To recognize an individual's special career contributions to ACRL and the library profession. *Winners:* founding members of the Institute for Information Literacy Steering Committee and faculty.

ACRL/WSS Award for Career Achievement in Women's Studies Librarianship ($1,000). *Donor:* Greenwood Publishing Group. *Winner:* Linda Krikos.

ACRL/WSS Award for Significant Achievement in Women's Studies Librarianship ($1,000). *Donor:* Greenwood Publishing Group. *Winner:* Ken Middleton, Middle Tennessee State University, for development of "Discovering American Women's History Online," a Web-based historical research tool.

Hugh C. Atkinson Memorial Award. *See under* American Library Association.

Community College Learning Resources Leadership/Library Achievement Awards ($500). To recognize outstanding achievement in library programs or leadership. *Sponsor:* EBSCO Information Services. *Winners:* (leadership) Kenley Neufeld; (programs) Diana Fitzwater.

Coutts Nijhoff International West European Specialist Study Grant ($3,000). Supports research pertaining to West European studies, librarianship, or the book trade. *Sponsor:* Coutts Information Services. *Winner:* Gordon Bruce Anderson, University of Minnesota, for his proposal to complete the Svenskamerikanska Bibliografi (Swedish American Bibliography).

Miriam Dudley Instruction Librarian Award ($1,000). For a contribution to the advancement of bibliographic instruction in a college or research institution. *Winner:* Trudi E. Jacobson.

Excellence in Academic Libraries Awards ($3,000). To recognize outstanding community college, college, and university libraries. *Donor:* Blackwell's Book Services. *Winners:* (university) University of Minnesota–Twin Cities; (college) Hollins University, Roanoke, Virginia; (community college) Moraine Valley Community College, Palos Hills, Illinois.

Instruction Section Innovation Award ($3,000). To librarians or project teams in recognition of a project that demonstrates creative, innovative, or unique approaches to information literacy instruction or programming. *Donor:* LexisNexis. *Winners:* Abby Clobridge and David Willson Del

Testa for the Bucknell University World War II Poster Project.

Marta Lange/CQ Press Award ($1,000). To recognize an academic or law librarian for contributions to bibliography and information service in law or political science. *Donor:* CQ Press. *Winner:* Lynne M. Rudasill.

Samuel Lazerow Fellowship for Research in Acquisitions or Technical Services ($1,000). To foster advances in acquisitions or technical services by providing librarians a fellowship for travel or writing in those fields. *Sponsor:* Thomson Reuters. *Winner:* Sara Marcus for her research project on the change of terms and terminology over several editions of the *Sears List of Subject Headings.*

Katharine Kyes Leab and Daniel J. Leab Exhibition Catalog Awards (citations). For the best catalogs published by American or Canadian institutions in conjunction with exhibitions of books and/or manuscripts. *Winners:* (category I–expensive) Getty Research Institute for *China on Paper: European and Chinese Works from the Late Sixteenth to the Early Nineteenth Century*; (category II–moderately expensive) Stanford University Libraries' Department of Special Collections for *Experiments in Navigation: The Art of Charles Hobson*; (category III–inexpensive) Rare Books and Special Collections Department, Thomas Cooper Library, University of South Carolina, for *Scottie Fitzgerald: The Stewardship of Literary Memory*; (category IV–brochures) Book Club of California for *The Book Art of Edward Gorey*; (category V–electronic exhibition) Modern Books and Manuscripts unit, Harvard University Houghton Library, for "Public Poet, Private Man: Henry Wadsworth Longfellow at 200."

Oberly Award for Bibliography in the Agricultural or Natural Sciences. Awarded biennially for the best English-language bibliography in the field of agriculture or a related science in the preceding two-year period. *Donor:* Eunice Rockwood Oberly Memorial Fund. *Winner:* International Rice Research Institute's Rice Database.

Ilene F. Rockman Instruction Publication of the Year Award ($3,000). To recognize an outstanding publication relating to instruction in a library environment in the past two years. *Sponsor:* Emerald Group. *Winners:* Kenneth J. Burhanna, Julie A. Gedeon, Mary L. Jensen, Carolyn Radcliff, and Joseph A. Salem, Jr. of Kent State University for *Practical Guide to Information Literacy Assessment for Academic Librarians* (Libraries Unlimited).

Association of Library Trustees, Advocates, Friends and Foundations (ALTAFF)

ALTAFF/Baker & Taylor Awards. To recognize library friends groups for outstanding efforts to support their libraries. *Winners:* (public library group with assistance from paid staff) Friends of the Florence County (South Carolina) Library; (public library group without assistance from paid staff) Friends of the San Benito County (California) Free Library, Friends of the Orangevale (California) Library, Friends of the Cedar Rapids (Iowa) Public Library, Friends of Henderson (Nevada) Libraries.

ALTAFF/Gale Outstanding Trustee Conference Grant Award ($750). *Donor:* Gale Research. *Winner:* Elisa Bruce.

ALTAFF Literacy Award (citation). To a library trustee or an individual who, in a volunteer capacity, has made a significant contribution to addressing the illiteracy problem in the United States. *Winner:* Award discontinued.

ALTAFF Major Benefactors Honor Award (citation). To individuals, families, or corporate bodies that have made major benefactions to public libraries. *Winner:* Not awarded in 2009.

ALTAFF Public Service Award. To a legislator who has been especially supportive of libraries. U.S. Sen. Barbara Boxer (D-Calif.)

Trustee Citations. To recognize public library trustees for individual service to library development on the local, state, regional, or national level. *Winners:* David H. Goldsmith, Shirley Ann Bruursema.

Association of Specialized and Cooperative Library Agencies (ASCLA)

ASCLA Cathleen Bourdon Service Award. To recognize an ASCLA personal member for outstanding service and leadership to the division. *Winner:* Not awarded in 2009.

ASCLA Century Scholarship ($2,500). For a library school student or students with disabilities admitted to an ALA-accredited library school. *Winner:* Amy Lynn Sonnie.

ASCLA Exceptional Service Award. To recognize exceptional service to patients, the homebound, inmates, and to medical, nursing, and other professional staff in hospitals. *Winner:* Not awarded in 2009.

ASCLA Leadership and Professional Achievement Award. To recognize leadership and achievement in the areas of consulting, multitype library cooperation, statewide service and programs, and state library development. *Winner:* Not awarded in 2009.

Francis Joseph Campbell Award. For a contribution of recognized importance to library service for the blind and physically handicapped. *Winner:* U.S. Secretary of Transportation Ray LaHood.

KLAS/National Organization on Disability Award for Library Service to People with Disabilities ($1,000). To a library organization to recognize an innovative project to benefit people with disabilities. *Donor:* Keystone Systems. *Winner:* Margaret Kolaya, Scotch Plains (New Jersey) Public Library, and Daniel Weiss, Fanwood (New Jersey) Memorial Library for "Libraries and Autism: We're Connected."

Black Caucus of the American Library Association (BCALA)

BCALA Trailblazer's Award. Presented once every five years in recognition of outstanding and unique contributions to librarianship. *Winner:* To be awarded next in 2010.

DEMCO/BCALA Excellence in Librarianship Award ($500). To a librarian who has made significant contributions to promoting the status of African Americans in the library profession. *Winner:* Jerome Offord, Jr.

E. J. Josey Scholarship Awards ($2,000). To two African American students enrolled in or accepted by ALA accredited MLIS programs. *Winners:* Sandra Eddie, Teneka Taylor.

Ethnic and Multicultural Information and Exchange Round Table (EMIERT)

David Cohen/EMIERT Multicultural Award ($300). To recognize articles of significant research and publication that increase understanding and promote multiculturalism in North American libraries. *Donor:* Routledge. *Winner:* Not awarded in 2009.

Gale/EMIERT Multicultural Award ($1,000). For outstanding achievement and leadership in serving the multicultural/multiethnic community. *Donor:* Gale Research. *Winner:* Not awarded in 2009.

Exhibits Round Table (ERT)

Christopher J. Hoy/ERT Scholarship ($5,000). To an individual or individuals who will work toward an MLS degree in an ALA-accredited program. *Donor:* Family of Christopher Hoy. *Winner:* Jade Torres-Morrison.

Federal and Armed Forces Librarians Round Table (FAFLRT)

FAFLRT Achievement Award. For achievement in the promotion of library and information service and the information profession in the federal government community. *Winner:* Donna Scheeder, Library of Congress.

Adelaide del Frate Conference Sponsorship Award ($1,000). To encourage library school students to become familiar with federal librarianship and ultimately seek work in federal libraries; for attendance at ALA Annual Conference and activities of the Federal and Armed Forces Librarians Round Table. *Winner:* Ken Kozel.

Distinguished Service Award (citation). To honor a FAFLRT member for outstanding and sustained contributions to the association and to federal librarianship. *Winner:* Fran Perros, U.S. Department of State Ralph J. Bunche Library.

Cicely Phippen Marks Scholarship ($1,500). To a library school student with an interest in working in a federal library. *Winner:* Michelle Demeter.

Gay, Lesbian, Bisexual, and Transgendered Round Table (GLBT)

Stonewall Book Awards. *Winners:* See "Literary Prizes, 2009" in Part 5.

Government Documents Round Table (GODORT)

James Bennett Childs Award. To a librarian or other individual for distinguished lifetime contributions to documents librarianship. *Winner:* Andrea Sevetson.

Bernadine Abbott Hoduski Founders Award. To recognize documents librarians who may not be known at the national level but who have made significant contributions to the field of local, state, federal, or international documents. *Winner:* Eleanor Chase.

LexisNexis Documents to the People Award. To an individual, library, organization, or noncommercial group that most effectively encourages or enhances the use of government documents in library services. *Winner:* Daniel Cornwall.

NewsBank/Readex Catharine J. Reynolds Award. Grants to documents librarians for travel and/or study in the field of documents librarianship or area of study benefiting performance as documents librarians. *Donor:* NewsBank and Readex Corporation. *Winner:* Aimée Quinn.

W. David Rozkuszka Scholarship ($3,000). To provide financial assistance to an individual who is currently working with government documents in a library while completing a master's program in library science. *Winner:* Justin Joque.

Intellectual Freedom Round Table (IFRT)

John Phillip Immroth Memorial Award for Intellectual Freedom ($500). For notable contribution to intellectual freedom fueled by personal courage. *Winners:* Karen MacPherson and Alanna Natanson.

Eli M. Oboler Memorial Award. See "Literary Prizes, 2009" in Part 5.

ProQuest/SIRS State and Regional Achievement Award ($1,000). To an innovative and effective intellectual freedom project covering a state or region during the calendar year. *Donor:* ProQuest Social Issues Resource Series (SIRS). *Winners:* "Celebrate the Freedom to Read" Oregon, a coalition made up of the American Civil Liberties Union of Oregon, the Intellectual Freedom Committees of the Oregon Library Association, and the Oregon Association of School Libraries.

Library and Information Technology Association (LITA)

Hugh C. Atkinson Memorial Award. *See under* American Library Association.

Ex Libris Student Writing Award ($1,000 and publication in *Information Technology and Libraries*). For the best unpublished manuscript on a topic in the area of libraries and information technology written by a student or students enrolled in an ALA-accredited library and information studies graduate program. *Donor:* Ex Libris. *Winner:* T. Michael Silver for "Monitoring Network and Service Availability with Open-Source Software."

LITA/Brett Butler Entrepreneurship Award ($5,000). To recognize a librarian or library for demonstrating exemplary entrepreneurship by providing innovative products or services through the application of information technology. *Winner:* John Blyberg.

LITA/Christian Larew Memorial Scholarship ($3,000). To encourage the entry of qualified persons into the library and information technology field. *Sponsor:* Informata. com. *Winner:* Nicholas Taylor.

LITA/Library Hi Tech Award ($1,000). To an individual or institution for a work that shows outstanding communication for continuing education in library and information technology. *Donor:* Emerald Press. *Winner:* Meredith Farkas.

LITA/LSSI Minority Scholarship in Library and Information Science ($2,500). To encourage a qualified member of a principal minority group to work toward an MLS degree in an ALA-accredited program with emphasis on library automation. *Donor:* Library Systems and Services. *Winner:* Diane Kay Doctor.

LITA/OCLC Frederick G. Kilgour Award for Research in Library and Information Technology ($2,000 and expense-paid attendance at the ALA Annual Conference). To bring attention to research relevant to the development of information technologies. *Donor:* OCLC. *Winner:* William H. Mischo.

LITA/OCLC Minority Scholarship in Library and Information Technology ($3,000). To encourage a qualified member of a principal minority group to work toward an MLS degree in an ALA-accredited program with emphasis on library automation. *Donor:* OCLC. *Winner:* Victoria Chu.

Library History Round Table (LHRT)

Phyllis Dain Library History Dissertation Award ($500). To the author of a dissertation treating the history of books, libraries, librarianship, or information science. *Winner:* Karen J. Cook for "Freedom Libraries in the 1964 Mississippi Freedom Summer Project: A History."

Donald G. Davis Article Award (certificate). For the best article written in English in the field of U.S. and Canadian library history. *Winner:* To be awarded next in 2010.

Eliza Atkins Gleason Book Award. Presented every third year to the author of the best book in English in the field of library history. *Winner:* To be awarded next in 2010.

Justin Winsor Prize Essay ($500). To an author of an outstanding essay embodying original historical research on a significant subject of library history. *Winner:* Richard LeComte for "Writers Blocked: The Debate Over Public Lending Right During the 1980s."

Library Leadership and Management Association (LLAMA)

Hugh C. Atkinson Memorial Award. *See under* American Library Association.

Diana V. Braddom Fundraising and Financial Development Section Scholarship ($1,000).

To enable attendance at the ALA Annual Conference. *Donor:* Diana V. Braddom. *Winner:* Alicia A. Antone. (Award discontinued in 2009.)

John Cotton Dana Library Public Relations Awards ($5,000). To libraries or library organizations of all types for public relations programs or special projects ended during the preceding year. *Donors:* H. W. Wilson Company and H. W. Wilson Foundation. *Winners:* Baltimore County (Maryland) Public Library, Gwinnett County (Georgia) Public Library, Houston (Texas) Public Library, Library Foundation of the Multnomah County (Oregon) Library, St. Paul (Minnesota) Public Library, Ypsilanti (Michigan) District Library.

LLAMA Group Achievement Award. *Winner:* LLAMA Mentoring Committee.

LLAMA Leadership Award. *Winner:* Not awarded in 2009.

LLAMA Library Design Awards. To recognize excellence in library design. *Sponsors:* LLAMA and American Institute of Architects. *Winners:* richard+bauer architecture for Arabian Library, Scottsdale (Arizona) Public Library; Tod Williams Billie Tsien Architects for C. V. Starr East Asian Library, University of California, Berkeley; Perkins Eastman for Chongqing (China) Library; Pei Partnership Architects for Biblioteca Central Estatal Wigberto Jiménez Moreno, León, Guanajuato, Mexico; 1100 Architect for New York Public Library's Francis Martin Library, Bronx; Marlon Blackwell Architect for Gentry (Arkansas) Public Library; Pelli Clarke Pelli Architects and Architectural Alliance for Minneapolis Central Library; Gould Evans Associates + Wendell Burnette Architects for Palo Verde Library / Maryvale Community Center, Phoenix.

LLAMA President's Award. *Winner:* Not awarded in 2009.

Library Research Round Table (LRRT)

Ingenta Research Award (up to $6,000). To sponsor research projects about acquisition, use, and preservation of digital information; the award includes $1,000 to support travel to a conference to present the results of that research. *Sponsor:*

Ingenta. *Winner:* Carol Anne Germain for "Maintaining persistent scholarship: An analysis of the accessibility rate of cited electronic resources within doctoral dissertations."

Jesse H. Shera Award for Distinguished Published Research ($500). For a research article on library and information studies published in English during the calendar year. *Winner:* Lynn Westbrook for "Understanding Crisis Information Needs in Context: The Case on Intimate Partner Violence Survivors."

Jesse H. Shera Award for Support of Dissertation Research ($500). To recognize and support dissertation research employing exemplary research design and methods. *Winner:* Not awarded in 2009.

New Members Round Table (NMRT)

NMRT/Marshall Cavendish Award (tickets to the Newbery/Caldecott/Wilder Banquet at the ALA Annual Conference). *Winners:*. Jennifer Baker, Jan Hamilton, Ken Kozel.

Shirley Olofson Memorial Award ($1,000). To an individual to help defray costs of attending the ALA Annual Conference. *Winner:* Candice Anne Wing-Yee Mack.

Student Chapter of the Year Award. To an ALA student chapter for outstanding contributions to ALA. *Winner:* ALA student chapter at San José State University.

3M Professional Development Grant. To new NMRT members to encourage professional development and participation in national ALA and NMRT activities. *Donor:* 3M. *Winners:* Linda Crook, Mark Danley, Pamela Taylor.

Office for Diversity

Achievement in Diversity Research Honor. To an ALA member who has made significant contributions to diversity research in the profession. *Winner:* Not awarded in 2009.

Diversity Research Grants ($2,500). To the authors of research proposals that address critical gaps in the knowledge of diversity issues within library and information science. *Winners:* Clayton Copeland for "Library and Information Center Accessi-

bility: The Differently-able Patron's Perspective"; Diana Tedone and Zoe Jarocki for "Bringing the Library to the People: Addressing the Job Related Information Needs of Day Laborers"; Stephanie Maatta Smith, Laurie J. Bonnici, and Muriel K. Wells for "ICT Readiness Index: Measuring the Preparedness of Libraries to Serve Patrons With Disabilities in the Context of Economic Challenge."

Office for Information Technology Policy

L. Ray Patterson Copyright Award. To recognize an individual who supports the constitutional purpose of U.S. copyright law, fair use, and the public domain. *Sponsor:* Freedom to Read Foundation. *Winner:* Jack Bernard.

Office for Intellectual Freedom

Freedom to Read Foundation Roll of Honor (citation): To recognize individuals who have contributed substantially to the foundation. *Winner:* Robert P. Doyle.

Office for Literacy and Outreach Services (OLOS)

Jean E. Coleman Library Outreach Lecture. *Sponsor:* OLOS Advisory Committee. *Winner:* Kathleen Mayo.

Diversity Fair Awards. To outreach librarians for their institutions' diversity-in-action initiatives. *Winners:* (first place) Greensboro (North Carolina) Public Library for "LifeVerse"; (second place) Multnomah County (Oregon) Library for "Partnerships to Support Adult Reading Programs"; (third place) Birmingham (Alabama) Public Library for "Ready to Read."

Estela and Raúl Mora Award ($1,000 and plaque). For the most exemplary program celebrating Día de Los Niños/Día de Los Libros. *Winners:* San Francisco Public Library, Topeka and Shawnee County (Kansas) Public Library.

Public Awareness Committee

Scholastic Library Publishing National Library Week Grant ($3,000). To libraries or library associations of all types for a public awareness campaign in connection with National Library Week in the year the grant is awarded. *Sponsor:* Scholastic Library Publishing. *Winner:* Moline (Illinois) Public Library.

Public Library Association (PLA)

Advancement of Literacy Award (plaque). To a publisher, bookseller, hardware and/or software dealer, foundation, or similar group that has made a significant contribution to the advancement of adult literacy. *Donor: Library Journal. Winner:* Project Read, San Francisco Public Library.

Baker & Taylor Entertainment Audio Music/ Video Product Grant ($2,500 worth of audio music or video products). To help a public library to build or expand a collection of either or both formats. *Donor:* Baker & Taylor. *Winner:* Curtis Memorial Library, Brunswick, Maine.

Gordon M. Conable Award ($1,500). To a public library staff member, library trustee, or public library for demonstrating a commitment to intellectual freedom and the Library Bill of Rights. *Sponsor:* LSSI. *Winner:* Scottsdale (Arizona) Public Library.

Demco New Leaders Travel Grants (up to $1,500). To PLA members who have not attended a major PLA continuing-education event in the past five years. *Winners:* Odette Batis, Sarah Hammershaimb, Leslie Partridge, Craig L. Scott, Carolyn Sears.

EBSCO Excellence in Small and/or Rural Public Service Award ($1,000). Honors a library serving a population of 10,000 or less that demonstrates excellence of service to its community as exemplified by an overall service program or a special program of significant accomplishment. *Donor:* EBSCO Information Services. *Winner:* John C. Fremont Library District, Florence, Colorado.

Highsmith Library Innovation Award ($2,000). To recognize a public library's innovative achievement in planning and implementing a creative community service program. *Donor:* Highsmith. *Winner:* Princeton (New Jersey) Public Library.

Allie Beth Martin Award ($3,000). To honor a public librarian who has demonstrated

extraordinary range and depth of knowledge about books or other library materials and has distinguished ability to share that knowledge. *Donor:* Baker & Taylor. *Winner:* Barbara Clubb.

Polaris Innovation in Technology John Iliff Award ($1,000). To a library worker, librarian, or library for the use of technology and innovative thinking as a tool to improve services to public library users. *Sponsor:* Polaris. *Winner:* Gail Borden Public Library, Elgin, Illinois.

Charlie Robinson Award. Honors a public library director who, over a period of seven years, has been a risk taker, an innovator, and/or a change agent in a public library. *Donor:* Baker & Taylor. *Winner:* Donna Nicely.

Public Programs Office

Sara Jaffarian School Library Program Award ($4,000). To honor a K–8 school library that has conducted an exemplary program or program series in the humanities. *Donors:* Sara Jaffarian and ALA Cultural Communities Fund. *Winner:* Carroll Academy for International Studies, Houston, for "Learning about the World with a Global Perspective."

Reference and User Services Association (RUSA)

ABC-CLIO Online History Award ($3,000). A biennial award to recognize professional achievement in historical reference and librarianship. *Donor:* ABC-CLIO. *Winner:* Ken Middleton, Middle Tennessee State University, for his development of "Discovering American Women's History Online," a Web-based historical research tool.

ALA/RUSA Zora Neale Hurston Award. To recognize the efforts of RUSA members in promoting African American literature. *Sponsored by:* Harper Perennial Publishing. *Winner:* Miriam Rodriguez, Dallas Public Library.

Virginia Boucher-OCLC Distinguished ILL Librarian Award ($2,000). To a librarian for outstanding professional achievement, leadership, and contributions to interlibrary loan and document delivery. *Winner:* Barbara Coopey

BRASS Emerald Research Grant Awards ($5,000). To ALA members seeking support to conduct research in business librarianship. *Donor:* Emerald Group Publishing. *Winners:* Ann Fiegan, Bryna Coonin.

BRASS Gale Cengage Learning Student Travel Award ($1,000). To enable a student enrolled in an ALA-accredited master's program to attend an ALA Annual Conference. *Donor:* Gale Cengage Learning. *Winner:* Frans Jozef Velasco Albarillo.

BRASS Public Librarian Support Award ($1,000). To support the attendance at the ALA Annual Conference of a public librarian who has performed outstanding business reference service. *Donor:* Morningstar. *Winner:* Not awarded in 2009.

Sophie Brody Medal. *Winner:* See "Literary Prizes, 2009" in Part 5.

Gale Cengage Award for Excellence in Business Librarianship ($3,000). For distinguished activities in the field of business librarianship *Donor:* Gale Cengage Learning. *Winner:* Michael Halperin.

Gale Cengage Award for Excellence in Reference and Adult Library Services ($3,000). To recognize a library or library system for developing an imaginative and unique library resource to meet patrons' reference needs. *Donor:* Gale Cengage Learning. *Winner:* University of Kentucky Libraries.

Genealogical Publishing Company/History Section Award ($1,500). To encourage and commend professional achievement in historical reference and research librarianship. *Donor:* Genealogical Publishing Company. *Winner:* Ruth A. Carr.

MARS Achievement Recognition Certificate. For excellence in service to the Machine-Assisted Reference Section. *Winner:* Carole Pilkinton.

Margaret E. Monroe Library Adult Services Award (citation). To a librarian for impact on library service to adults. *Winner:* Not awarded in 2009.

Isadore Gilbert Mudge–Gale Cengage Award ($5,000). For distinguished contributions

to reference librarianship. *Donor:* Gale Cengage Learning. *Winner:* Nancy Huling.

Reference Service Press Award ($2,500). To the author or authors of the most outstanding article published in *RUSQ* during the preceding two volume years. *Donor:* Reference Service Press. *Winner:* Pixey Anne Mosley for "Assessing User Interactions at the Desk Nearest the Front Door."

John Sessions Memorial Award (plaque). To a library or library system in recognition of work with the labor community. *Donor:* Department of Professional Employees, AFL/CIO. *Winner:* Wirtz Labor Library, U.S. Department of Labor.

Louis Shores–Greenwood Publishing Group Award ($3,000). To an individual, team, or organization to recognize excellence in reviewing of books and other materials for libraries. *Donor:* Greenwood Publishing Group. *Winner:* Williamsburg (Virginia) Regional Library for its Web site "Blogging for a Good Book."

Standard and Poor's Award for Outstanding Service to Minority Business Communities ($2,000). To a librarian or library to recognize creation of an innovative service to a minority business community or achievement of recognition from that community for providing outstanding service. *Winner:* African-American Research Library and Cultural Center, part of the Broward County (Florida) Libraries Division.

STARS-Atlas Systems Mentoring Award ($1,000). To a library practitioner new to the field of interlibrary loan, resource sharing, or electronic reserves, to attend an ALA Annual Conference. *Donor:* Atlas Systems. *Winner:* Beverly Rossini.

Social Responsibilities Round Table (SRRT)

Jackie Eubanks Memorial Award ($500). To honor outstanding achievement in promoting the acquisition and use of alternative media in libraries. *Donor:* SRRT Alternatives in Publication Task Force. *Winner:* Not awarded in 2009.

Coretta Scott King Awards. *Winners:* See "Literary Prizes, 2009" in Part 5.

Young Adult Library Services Association (YALSA)

Alex Awards. *Winners:* See "Literary Prizes, 2009" in Part 5.

Baker & Taylor/YALSA Scholarship Grants ($1,000). To young adult librarians in public or school libraries to attend an ALA Annual Conference for the first time. *Donor:* Baker & Taylor. *Winners:* Laurie Amster-Burton, Kate Toebbe.

BWI/YALSA Collection Development Grants ($1,000). To YALSA members who represent a public library and work directly with young adults, for collection development materials for young adults. *Donor:* Book Wholesalers, Inc. *Winners:* Lexie Robinson, Wini Ashooh.

Margaret A. Edwards Award. *Winner:* See "Literary Prizes, 2009" in Part 5.

Great Books Giveaway (books, videos, CDs, and audiocassettes valued at a total of $25,000). *Winners:* Lincoln County Public Libraries, Libby, Montana; Creekside High School, Fairburn, Georgia; Jackson (Michigan) District Library.

Frances Henne/YALSA/VOYA Research Grant ($1,000). To provide seed money to an individual, institution, or group for a project to encourage research on library service to young adults. *Donors: Voice of Youth Advocates* and Scarecrow Press. *Winners:* Amy Alessio and Marc Aronson.

Michael L. Printz Award. *Winner:* See "Literary Prizes, 2009" in Part 5.

YALSA/Greenwood Publishing Group Service to Young Adults Achievement Award ($2,000). Awarded biennially to a YALSA member who has demonstrated unique and sustained devotion to young adult services. *Donor:* Greenwood. *Winner:* Not awarded in 2009.

YALSA/MAE Award ($500 for the recipient plus $500 for his or her library). For an exemplary young adult reading or literature program. *Sponsor:* Margaret A. Edwards Trust. *Winner:* Valerie H. Nicholson, Eva Perry Regional Library, Apex, North Carolina.

YALSA William C. Morris YA Debut Award. *Winner:* See "Literary Prizes, 2009" in Part 5.

YALSA/Sagebrush Award. See YALSA/MAE Award.

YALSA Spectrum Scholarship. To a designated Spectrum Scholarship recipient. *Winner:* Cristina Mitra.

American Society for Information Science and Technology (ASIS&T)

ASIS&T Award of Merit. For an outstanding contribution to the field of information science. *Winner:* Carol Tenopir.

ASIS&T Best Information Science Book. *Winner:* James Boyle for *The Public Domain: Enclosing the Commons of the Mind* (Yale University Press).

ASIS&T Proquest Doctoral Dissertation Award ($1,000 plus expense-paid attendance at ASIS&T Annual Meeting). *Winner:* Luanne Freund for "Exploiting Task-Document Relations in Support of Information Retrieval in the Workplace."

ASIS&T Research in Information Science Award. For a systematic program of research in a single area at a level beyond the single study, recognizing contributions in the field of information science. *Winner:* Not awarded in 2009.

ASIS&T Special Award. To recognize long-term contributions to the advancement of information science and technology and enhancement of public access to information and discovery of mechanisms for improved transfer and utilization of knowledge. *Winner:* Not awarded in 2009.

James M. Cretsos Leadership Award. *Winner:* Cassidy Sugimoto.

Watson Davis Award. For outstanding continuous contributions and dedicated service to the society. *Winner:* Edie Rasmussen.

Pratt-Severn Best Student Research Paper Award. To recognize the outstanding work of a current student in a degree-granting program in the information field. *Sponsor:* Pratt Institute. *Winner:* Katie O'Leary for "Information Seeking in the Context of a Hobby: A Case Study of a Young Adult with Asperger's Syndrome."

Thomson ISI Citation Analysis Research Grant. *Winner:* Cassidy Sugimoto for "Measuring Interdisciplinarity: An Exploration of a Novel Metric Applied to ILS Dissertations."

Thomson ISI Doctoral Dissertation Proposal Scholarship. *Winner:* Heather Piwowar for "Foundational Studies for Measuring the Impact, Prevalence, and Patterns of Publicly Shared Viomedical Research Data."

Thomson ISI Outstanding Information Science Teacher Award ($500). *Winner:* Diane Kelly.

John Wiley Best *JASIST* Paper Award. *Winners:* Ofer Bergman, Ruth Beyth-Marom, and Rafi Nachmias for "The User-Subjective Approach to Personal Information Management Systems Design: Evidence and Implementations."

Art Libraries Society of North America (ARLIS/NA)

ARLIS/NA Conference Attendance Award ($1,000). *Winner:* Rodica Tanjala Krauss.

ARLIS/NA Internship Award. To provide financial support for students preparing for a career in art librarianship or visual resource librarianship. *Winner:* Adrienne Lai.

ARLIS/NA Student Conference Attendance Award. *Winner:* Meredith Kahn.

ARLIS/NA Worldwide Books Award for Electronic Resources. *Winners:* Lynda Bunting, Skye Lacerte, and Julie Yamashita for the online exhibition "MOCA Exhibition Archive."

ARLIS/NA Worldwide Books Award for Publications. Hee-Gwone Yoo and Kristen Regina for *Visual Resources from Russia and Eastern Europe in the New York Public Library: A Checklist* (Ross).

Andrew Cahan Photography Award ($1,000). To encourage conference participation of art information professionals in the field of photography. *Winner:* Not awarded in 2009.

Distinguished Service Award. To honor an individual whose exemplary service in art librarianship, visual resources curatorship, or a related field has made an outstanding national or international contribution to art information and/or art librarianship. *Winner:* Patricia Barnett.

Melva J. Dwyer Award. To the creators of exceptional reference or research tools relating to Canadian art and architecture. *Winners:* Serena Keshavjee, editor, and Herbert Enns, designer, for *Winnipeg Modern: Architecture 1945–1975* (University of Manitoba).

Gerd Muehsam Award. To one or more graduate students in library science programs to recognize excellence in a graduate paper or project. *Winner:* Maureen Whalen for "What's Wrong with This Picture? An Examination of Art Historians' Attitudes About Electronic Publishing Opportunities."

George Wittenborn Memorial Book Award. See "Literary Prizes, 2009" in Part 5.

Asian/Pacific Americans Libraries Association (APALA)

APALA Scholarship ($1,000). For a student of Asian or Pacific background who is enrolled, or has been accepted into, a master's or doctoral degree program in library and/or information science at an ALA-accredited school. *Winner:* Vivian Wong.

APALA Travel Award ($500). To a library professional possessing a master's-level degree in library and/or information science to attend the ALA Annual Conference. *Winner:* Sally Ma.

Association for Library and Information Science Education (ALISE)

ALISE Award for Teaching Excellence in the Field of Library and Information Science Education. *Winner:* Ana Cleveland.

ALISE/Dialog Methodology Paper Competition ($500). To stimulate communication on research methodologies at ALISE annual conferences. *Sponsor:* Dialog. *Winners:* Heather Archibald and Lisa Given, University of Alberta, for "Visual Traffic Sweeps (VTS): A research Method for Mapping user Activities in the Library Space."

ALISE/Eugene Garfield Doctoral Dissertation Award ($500). *Winner:* Charles Kamau Maina, University of Western Ontario, for "The Traditional Knowledge Protection Debate: Identifying and Listening to the Voices of Traditional Knowledge Holders."

ALISE Professional Contribution to Library and Information Science Education Award. *Winner:* Ken Haycock.

ALISE Research Grant Awards (one or more grants totaling $5,000): *Winners:* Kyungwon Koh, Sung Jae Park, and Kathleen Burnett, Florida State University, for "Online Collaborative Learning in the Web 2.0 Era."

ALISE/University of Washington Information School Youth Services Graduate Student Travel Award ($750). To support the costs associated with travel to and participation in the ALISE Annual Conference. *Winner:* Minjie Chen.

Doctoral Students to ALISE Grant ($500). To support the attendance of one or more promising LIS doctoral students at the ALISE Annual Conference. *Winner:* Sarah Sutton, Texas Woman's University.

OCLC/ALISE Library and Information Science Research Grant Program. To promote independent research that helps librarians integrate new technologies into areas of traditional competence and contributes to a better understanding of the library environment. *Winners:* Kathryn La Barre and Carol Tilley, Michael Khoo, Bill Kules.

Service to ALISE Award. *Winner:* Connie Van Fleet.

Association of Jewish Libraries (AJL)

AJL Scholarships ($1,000). For students enrolled in accredited library schools who plan to work as Judaica librarians. *Winners:* Alla Markova, Klara Maidenberg.

Association of Research Libraries

ARL Diversity Scholarships (stipend of up to $10,000). To a varying number of MLS students from under-represented groups who are interested in careers in research libraries. *Sponsors:* ARL member libraries and the Institute of Museum and Library Services. *Winners (2009–2011):* Anissa Ali, Langston Bates, Johnnie Blunt, Roy Brooks, Jeffery Cruz, Kiyomi Deards, Marcela Estevez, Emmanuel Faulkner, Roland Garcia-Milian, Xiaomei Gu, Stacy Harris, Christina Herd, Jennifer Huck, Sheetija Kathuria, Samip Mallick, Yasmin Mathew, Myrna Elsa Morales, Derek Mosley, Laksamee Putnam, Umesh Thakker.

Association of Seventh-Day Adventist Librarians

D. Glenn Hilts Scholarship ($1,200) for a member of the Seventh-Day Adventist Church in a graduate library program. *Winner:* Talea Anderson.

Beta Phi Mu

Beta Phi Mu Award. *See under* American Library Association.

Eugene Garfield Doctoral Dissertation Fellowships ($3,000). *Winners:* Linda Most for "The Rural Public Library as Place in North Florida: A Case Study"; Zhixian Yi for "The Management of Change in the Information Age: Approaches of Academic Library Directors in the United States"; Jennifer Crispin for "Discovering the Social Organization of School Library Work"; Bradley Wade Bishop for "Chat Reference and Location-Based Questions: A Multi-Method Evaluation of a Statewide Chat Reference Consortium."

Harold Lancour Scholarship for Foreign Study ($1,500). For graduate study in a foreign country related to the applicant's work or schooling. *Winner:* Jessie A. Howell.

Mary Jo Lynch Distinguished Lecture Award ($2,000). *Sponsors:* Florida State University Information Use Management and Policy Institute and Beta Phi Mu. *Winner:* Not awarded in 2009.

Sarah Rebecca Reed Scholarship ($2,000). For study at an ALA-accredited library school. *Winner:* Naomi Schemm.

Frank B. Sessa Scholarship for Continuing Professional Education ($1,250). For continuing education for a Beta Phi Mu member. *Winner:* Joshua Finnell.

Blanche E. Woolls Scholarship ($1,500). For a beginning student in school library media services. *Winner:* Christine J. Hartigan.

Bibliographical Society of America (BSA)

BSA Fellowships ($1,500–$6,000). For scholars involved in bibliographical inquiry and research in the history of the book trades and in publishing history. *Winners:* Carol Armbruster, John Craig, Gary Dyer, Nicholas Frankel, Elizabeth Fraser, Julian Hendrix, Susann Liebich, Nancy Marino, Norbert Schürer, Kathryn Veeman, Marta Vicente.

William L. Mitchell Prize for Research on Early British Serials ($1,000). Awarded triennially for the best single work published in the previous three years. *Winners:* Sharon M. Harris, Thomas Lockwood.

St. Louis Mercantile Library Prize in American Bibliography ($2,000). Awarded triennially to encourage scholarship in the bibliography of American history and literature. *Sponsor:* St. Louis Mercantile Library, University of Missouri, St. Louis. *Winner:* To be awarded next in 2011.

Justin G. Schiller Prize for Bibliographical Work on Pre-20th-Century Children's Books ($2,000). A triennial award to encourage scholarship in the bibliography of historical children's books. *Winner:* To be awarded next in 2010.

Canadian Library Association (CLA)

Olga B. Bishop Award ($200). To a library school student for the best paper on gov-

ernment information or publications. *Winner:* Not awarded in 2009.

CLA Award for the Advancement of Intellectual Freedom in Canada. *Winner:* Kim Bolan.

CLA Elizabeth Dafoe Scholarship ($5,000). *Winner:* Paul Burry.

CLA/Information Today Award for Innovative Technology. *Donor:* Information Today, Inc. *Winner:* Pictou-Antigonish Regional Library (PARL), Antigonish, Nova Scotia.

CLA Outstanding Service to Librarianship Award. *Donor:* R. R. Bowker. *Winner:* Barbara Clubb.

CLA Research and Development Grant ($1,000). *Winner:* Jean McKendry.

CLA Student Article Award. *Winner:* Manuela Boscenco for "Strictly Business: Providing Access to Digital Images."

CLA/3M Award for Achievement in Technical Services ($1,000). *Winner:* Robertson Library, University of Prince Edward Island.

CLA/YBP Award for Outstanding Contribution to Collection Development and Management ($1,000). To recognize a CLA/ACB member who has made an outstanding local, national, or international contribution in the field of library collection development or management. *Sponsor:* YBP Library Services. *Winner:* Carol Stephenson.

W. Kaye Lamb Award for Service to Seniors. *Winner:* To be awarded next in 2010.

H. W. Wilson Scholarship ($2,000). *Winner:* Carla Haug.

World Book Graduate Scholarship in Library Science ($2,500). *Winner:* Award discontinued in 2009.

Canadian Association for School Libraries (CASL)

CASL Follett International Teacher Librarian of the Year Award. *Winner:* Michele Farquharson.

CASL Margaret B. Scott Award of Merit. For the development of school libraries in Canada. *Winners:* Jocelyne Dion.

CASL Angela Thacker Memorial Award. For outstanding contribution to teacher-librarianship. *Winner:* British Columbia Teacher Librarians' Association Executive (Bonnie

Chapman, Lauren Craze, Heather Daly, Moira Ekdahl, Val Hamilton, Halia Hirniak, Amanda Hufton, Karen Lindsay, Bonnie McComb, Angie MacRitchie, Al Smith, Lynn Turner, Sylvia Zubke.

Canadian Association of College and University Libraries (CACUL)

CACUL/Robert H. Blackburn Distinguished Paper Award ($200). To acknowledge notable research published by CACUL members. *Winner:* Not awarded in 2009.

CACUL/Miles Blackwell Award for Outstanding Academic Librarian. *Sponsor:* Blackwell's. *Winner:* Gwen Zilm.

CACUL Innovation Achievement Award ($1,000). *Sponsor:* SirsiDynix. *Winner:* Hazel McCallion Academic Learning Centre, Mississauga Library, University of Toronto.

CTCL Award for Outstanding College Librarian. *Winner:* Katherine Wallis, Library Director of Georgian College, Barrie, Ontario.

CTCL Innovation Achievement Award. *Sponsor:* Micromedia ProQuest. *Winner:* Banff Centre Library for its "Streaming Audio" program.

Canadian Association of Public Libraries (CAPL)

CAPL/Brodart Outstanding Public Library Service Award. *Winner:* Judith Saltman.

Canadian Association of Special Libraries and Information Services (CASLIS)

CASLIS Award for Special Librarianship in Canada. *Winner:* Yvonne Earle.

Canadian Library Trustees Association (CLTA)

CLTA/Stan Heath Achievement in Literacy Award. For an innovative literacy program by a public library board. *Donor:* ABC Canada. *Winner:* Windsor (Ontario) Public Library.

CLTA Merit Award for Distinguished Service as a Public Library Trustee. *Winner:* Rod MacArthur.

Catholic Library Association

Regina Medal. For continued, distinguished contribution to the field of children's literature. *Offered by:* Catholic Library Association. *Winner:* Gail Gibbons.

Chinese-American Librarians Association (CALA)

CALA Distinguished Service Award. To a librarian who has been a mentor, role model, and leader in the fields of library and information science. *Winner:* John T. Ma.

CALA President's Recognition Award. *Winners:* Barbara Ford, Haipeng Li.

CALA Scholarship of Library and Information Science ($500). *Winner:* Silvia Lu.

Sheila Suen Lai Scholarship ($500). *Winner:* Danitta Wong.

C. C. Seetoo/CALA Conference Travel Scholarship ($500). For a student to attend the ALA Annual Conference and CALA program. *Winner:* Kam Yan Lee.

Sally T. Tseng Professional Development Grant ($1,000). *Winner:* Liana Zhou for "Sex Education and Its History, Progress, and Struggles in the United States: Thoughts and Analysis for Today's Chinese Sex Educators."

Huang Tso-ping and Wu Yao-yu Scholarship Memorial Research Grant ($200): *Winner:* May P. Y. Yan.

Church and Synagogue Library Association (CSLA)

CSLA Award for Outstanding Congregational Librarian. For distinguished service to the congregation and/or community through devotion to the congregational library. *Winner:* Mary Brown Baker.

CSLA Award for Outstanding Congregational Library. For responding in creative and innovative ways to the library's mission of reaching and serving the congregation and/or the wider community. *Winner:* Northern Colorado Faith Library, First United Methodist Church, Fort Collins.

CSLA Award for Outstanding Contribution to Congregational Libraries. For providing inspiration, guidance, leadership, or resources to enrich the field of church or synagogue librarianship. *Winner:* Not awarded in 2009.

Helen Keating Ott Award for Outstanding Contribution to Children's Literature. *Winner:* Dandi Daley Mackall, Tyndale House Publishers.

Pat Tabler Memorial Scholarship Award. *Winner:* Not awarded in 2009.

Coalition for Networked Information

Paul Evan Peters Award. Awarded biennially to recognize notable and lasting international achievements relating to high-performance networks and the creation and use of information resources and services that advance scholarship and intellectual productivity. *Sponsors:* Association of Research Libraries, EDUCAUSE. *Winner:* To be awarded next in 2010.

Paul Evan Peters Fellowship ($5,000 a year for two years). Awarded biennially to a student pursuing a graduate degree in librarianship or the information sciences. *Sponsors:* Association of Research Libraries, EDUCAUSE. *Winner:* To be awarded next in 2010.

Council on Library and Information Resources (CLIR)

CLIR Postdoctoral Fellowships in Scholarly Information Resources. *Current fellows:* Anne Bruder, Gloria Chacon, Daniel Chamberlain, Gabrielle Dean, Melissa Grafe, Timothy F. Jackson, Lori Jahnke, Noah Shenker, Heather Waldroup.

Mellon Fellowship Program for Dissertation Research in the Humanities in Original Sources (stipends of up to $20,000 to support dissertation research). *Current fellows:* Daniel Berger, Lydia Brandt, Jun Hee Cho, Martin Gutmann, Robert Herr, Kristine Hess, Nicholas Johnson, Erin Lambert, Pedro Monaville, Lindsay Moore, Virginia Myhaver, Jamie Rosenthal,

Danielle Terrazas Williams, Jaime Wadowiec, Kimberly Welch.

Rovelstad Scholarship in International Librarianship. To enable a student enrolled in an accredited LIS program to attend the IFLA World Library and Information Congress. *Winner:* Katie Henningsen.

A. R. Zipf Fellowship in Information Management ($10,000). To a student enrolled in graduate school who shows exceptional promise for leadership and technical achievement. *Winner:* Hollie White.

Bill and Melinda Gates Foundation

Access to Learning Award ($1 million). To public libraries or similar organizations outside the United States for innovative programs that provide the public free access to information technology. *Administered by:* Gates Foundation Global Libraries initiative. *Winner:* Fundación Empresas Publicas de Medellín (EPM Foundation) in Colombia, for its network of public libraries.

Institute of Museum and Library Services

National Medal for Museum and Library Service. For extraordinary civic, educational, economic, environmental, and social contributions ($10,000). *Winners:* (libraries) Braille Institute Library Services, Los Angeles; Gail Borden Public Library, Elgin, Illinois; Multomah County Library, Portland, Oregon; Pritzker Military Library, Chicago; Stark County District Library, Canton, Ohio.

International Association of School Librarians (IASL)

Ken Haycock and Jean Lowrie Leadership Development Grants ($1,000). To enable applicants in developing nations to attend their first IASL Annual Conference. *Winners:* Not awarded in 2009.

International Federation of Library Associations and Institutions (IFLA)

De Gruyter Saur/IFLA Research Paper Award (€1,000). For the best unpublished research paper on a topic of importance to publishing and access to information by an author or authors with no more than eight years of professional experience in library and information services. *Sponsors:* IFLA and De Gruyter Saur. *Winner:* To be awarded first in 2010.

Dr. Shawky Salem Conference Grant (up to $1,900). To enable an expert in library and information science who is a national of an Arab country to attend the IFLA Conference for the first time. *Winner:* Domingua Abboud, Mariam and Youssef Library, Notre Dame University–Louaize Zouk Mosbeh, Lebanon.

Frederick Thorpe Individual Awards (up to £5,000 total). To librarians working in libraries for the blind. *Donor:* Ulverscroft Foundation. *Winners:* Not awarded in 2009.

Frederick Thorpe Organizational Award (up to £15,000). To a library organization for development of service delivery to the visually impaired. *Winners:* Not awarded in 2009.

Medical Library Association (MLA)

Virginia L. and William K. Beatty MLA Volunteer Service Award. To recognize a medical librarian who has demonstrated outstanding, sustained service to the Medical Library Association and the health sciences library profession. *Winner:* Not awarded in 2009.

Estelle Brodman Award for the Academic Medical Librarian of the Year. To honor significant achievement, potential for leadership, and continuing excellence at mid-career in the area of academic health sciences librarianship. *Winner:* Not awarded in 2009.

Lois Ann Colaianni Award for Excellence and Achievement in Hospital Librarian-

ship. To a member of MLA who has made significant contributions to the profession in the area of overall distinction or leadership in hospital librarianship. *Winner:* Not awarded in 2009.

Cunningham Memorial International Fellowships. Six-month grant and travel expenses in the United States and Canada for one or more foreign librarians. *Winners:* Hasbullah Atan, Stanslaus Ngadaya.

Louise Darling Medal. For distinguished achievement in collection development in the health sciences. *Winner:* Not awarded in 2009.

Janet Doe Lectureship. *Winner:* Ana D. Cleveland.

EBSCO/MLA Annual Meeting Grants (up to $1,000). *Winners:* Jamie L. Furrh, Andrea Harrow, Trey Lemley and Heidi Schroeder.

Ida and George Eliot Prize. For an essay published in any journal in the preceding calendar year that has been judged most effective in furthering medical librarianship. *Donor:* Login Brothers Books. *Winners:* Daniel E. Banks, Runhua Shi, Donna F. Timm, Kerri Ann Christopher, David Charles Duggar, Marianne Comegys, and Jerry McLarty for "Decreased Hospital Length of Stay Associated with Presentation of Cases at Morning Report with Librarian Support."

Carla J. Funk Governmental Relations Award ($500). To recognize a medical librarian who has demonstrated outstanding leadership in the area of governmental relations at the federal, state, or local level, and who has furthered the goal of providing quality information for improved health. *Winner:* Marianne Comegys.

Murray Gottlieb Prize. For the best unpublished essay on the history of medicine and allied sciences written by a health sciences librarian. *Donors:* Ralph and Jo Grimes. *Winner:* Trenton Boyd for "The Lost History of American Veterinary Medicine: The Need for Preservation."

T. Mark Hodges International Service Award. To honor outstanding achievement in promoting, enabling, or delivering improved health information internationally. *Winner:* Donna B. Flake.

Hospital Libraries Section/MLA Professional Development Grants. *Winners:* Lois Culler, Lisa A. Marks.

David A. Kronick Traveling Fellowship ($2,000). *Sponsor:* Bowden-Massey Foundation. *Winner:* Kathryn Mary Piorun.

Joseph Leiter NLM/MLA Lectureship. *Winner:* Ben Young.

Donald A. B. Lindberg Research Fellowship ($9,945). *Winner:* Sujin Kim for "A Study of Microscopic Imaging Description through Captions Published in Academic Biomedical Journals."

Lucretia W. McClure Excellence in Education Award. To an outstanding eduator in the field of health sciences librarianship and informatics. *Winner:* K. Ann McKibbon.

Majors/MLA Chapter Project of the Year Award. *Sponsor:* J. A. Majors Co. *Winner:* Pacific Northwest Chapter of MLA for "Awakening the Searcher Within: An Online Seminar on Expert Searching."

Medical Informatics Section Career Development Grant ($1,500). To support a career development activity that will contribute to advancement in the field of medical informatics. *Winners:* Kristine M. Alpi.

MLA Award for Distinguished Public Service. *Winner:* Not awarded in 2009.

MLA Continuing Education Awards. *Winner:* Lauren Maggio.

MLA Fellowships. For sustained and outstanding contributions to health sciences librarianship and to the advancement of the purposes of MLA. *Honorees:* Holly Shipp Buchanan, Gary D. Byrd, Logan Ludwig, Jean Pugh Shipman, M. J. Tooey.

MLA Honorary Membership. *Honoree:* Carla J. Funk, executive director, MLA.

MLA/NLM Spectrum Scholarships (total of $6,500). To support minority students in their goals to become health sciences information professionals. *Winners:* Shalu Gillum, Mark Miller.

MLA Research, Development, and Demonstration Project Grants ($100 to $1,000). To provide support for research, development, or demonstration projects that will help to promote excellence in the field of health sciences librarianship and information sciences. *Winner:* Naomi Broering.

MLA Scholarship (up to $5,000). For graduate study at an ALA-accredited library school. *Winner:* Elaine Hicks.

MLA Scholarship for Minority Students (up to $5,000). For graduate study at an ALA-accredited library school. *Winner:* Vivian Okyere.

Marcia C. Noyes Award. For an outstanding contribution to medical librarianship. *Winner:* Wayne J. Peay.

President's Award. To an MLA member for a notable or important contribution made during the past association year. *Winner:* Clinton "Marty" Thompson, Jr.

Rittenhouse Award. For the best unpublished paper on medical librarianship submitted by a student enrolled in, or having been enrolled in, a course for credit in an ALA-accredited library school or a trainee in an internship program in medical librarianship. *Donor:* Rittenhouse Medical Bookstore. *Winner:* Not awarded in 2009.

Thomson Reuters/Frank Bradway Rogers Information Advancement Award. To recognize outstanding contributions for the application of technology to the delivery of health science information, to the science of information, or to the facilitation of the delivery of health science information. *Sponsor:* Thomson Reuters. *Winner:* Robert T. Mackes.

Thomson Reuters/MLA Doctoral Fellowship ($2,000). To encourage superior students to conduct doctoral work in an area of health sciences librarianship or information sciences and to provide support to individuals who have been admitted to candidacy. *Sponsor:* Thomson Reuters. *Winner:* Not awarded in 2009.

Music Library Association

Carol June Bradley Award. To support studies that involve the history of music libraries or special collections. *Winner:* Stephen Mantz.

Vincent H. Duckles Award. For the best book-length bibliography or other research tool in music. *Winners:* David Williams and C. Matthew Balensuela for *Music Theory from Boethius to Zarlino: A Bibliography and Guide* (Pendragon).

Dena Epstein Award for Archival and Library Research in American Music. To support research in archives or libraries internationally on any aspect of American music. *Winners:* Lara Housez, Maria Cristina Fava.

Kevin Freeman Travel Grants. To colleagues who are new to the profession to enable them to attend the association's annual meeting. *Winners:* Veronica Alzalde, Dominique, Bourassa, Janet McKinney, Laurie Neuerburg.

Walter Gerboth Award. To members of the association who are in the first five years of their professional library careers, to assist research-in-progress in music or music librarianship. *Winner:* Mark Puente.

Richard S. Hill Award, For the best article on music librarianship or article of a music-bibliographic nature. *Winner:* Edward Komara for "Culture Wars, Canonicity, and a Basic Music Library" in *Notes.*

MLA Citation. Awarded in recognition of contributions to the profession over a career. *Winner:* Linda Solow Blotner.

Eva Judd O'Meara Award. For the best review published in *Notes. Winner:* Louis Niebur for "The BBC Radiophonic Workshop: Recent Reissues of British Electronic Music from 1955-1996."

National Library Service for the Blind and Physically Handicapped, Library of Congress

Library of the Year Awards ($1,000). *Winners:* (network library of the year) Perkins Library for the Blind, Watertown, Massachusetts; (network subregional library of the year) Miami-Dade (Florida) Public Library System.

REFORMA (National Association to Promote Library and Information Services to Latinos and the Spanish-Speaking)

REFORMA scholarships ($1,500). To students who qualify for graduate study in library science and who are citizens or permanent residents of the United States. *Winners:* Laura R. Castillo, Alma E. Garcia, Erin M. Kirkbride, Lisa M. Lopez, Maria Elena Olmedo,

Arnulfo D. Trejo Librarian of the Year Award. To recognize a librarian who has promoted and advocated services to the Spanish-speaking and Latino communities and made outstanding contributions to REFORMA. *Winner:* Susan Luevano.

K. G. Saur Verlag (Munich, Germany)

Award for Best *Libri* Student Paper (€500). To recognize the most outstanding article published in *LIBRI* during the preceding year. *Donor:* K. G. Saur Verlag. *Winner:* Elizabeth Platzer, Karl Franzens University, Graz, Austria, for "A Critical Review of User Acceptance Research in the Area of Mobile Services," published December 2009.

Society of American Archivists (SAA)

C. F. W. Coker Award for Description. To recognize creators of tools that enable archivists to produce more effective finding aids. *Winners:* Timothy Mulligan (compiler) and Rebecca L. Collier, Judith Koucky, and Patrick R. Osborn (editors) for *World War II: Guide to Records Relating to U.S. Military Participation* (National Archives and Records Administration).

Colonial Dames of America Scholarship (up to $1,200). To enable new archivists to attend the Modern Archives Institute of the National Archives and Records Administration. *Winners:* Maria Day, Amanda Klaus.

Distinguished Service Award. To recognize an archival institution, education program, nonprofit organization, or governmental organization that has given outstanding service to its public and has made an exemplary contribution to the archives profession. *Winner:* National Historical Publications and Records Commission

(NHPRC), the grant-making affiliate of the National Archives and Records Administration (NARA).

Fellows' Ernst Posner Award. For an outstanding essay dealing with a facet of archival administration, history, theory, or methodology, published in *American Archivist*. *Winner:* Geoffrey Yeo for "Concepts of Record (2): Prototypes and Boundary Objects."

F. Gerald Ham Scholarship ($7,500). To recognize an individual's past performance in a graduate archival studies program and his or her potential in the field. *Winner:* Andy (Jonathan) Uhrich.

Philip M. Hamer and Elizabeth Hamer Kegan Award. For individuals and/or institutions that have increased public awareness of a specific body of documents. *Winner:* Ward M. Canaday Center for Special Collections, University of Toledo (Ohio), for its exhibit and publication "From Institutions to Independence: A History of People with Disabilities in Northwest Ohio."

Oliver Wendell Holmes Award. To enable overseas archivists already in the United States or Canada for training to attend the SAA annual meeting. *Winner:* Ricardo L. Punzalan.

J. Franklin Jameson Award. For individuals and/or organizations that promote greater public awareness of archival activities and programs. *Winner:* Ross King, chair, Georgia Historical Records Advisory Board.

Sister M. Claude Lane, O.P., Memorial Award. For a significant contribution to the field of religious archives. *Winner:* Robert Johnson-Lally.

Waldo Gifford Leland Prize. For writing of superior excellence and usefulness in the field of archival history, theory, or practice. *Winner:* Philip C. Bantin for *Understanding Data and Information Systems for Recordkeeping* (Neal-Schuman).

Theodore Calvin Pease Award. For the best student paper. *Winner:* Kathleen Fear for "User Understanding of Metadata in Digital Image Collections."

Donald Peterson Student Scholarship Award (up to $1,000). To enable a student or recent graduate to attend the SAA Annual Meeting. *Winner:* Jessica Sedgwick.

Harold T. Pinkett Minority Student Award. To encourage minority students to consider careers in the archival profession, and to promote minority participation in SAA. *Winners:* Krystal Appiah, I-Ting Emily Chu.

Preservation Publication Award. To recognize an outstanding work published in North America that advances the theory or the practice of preservation in archival institutions. *Winner: AIC Guide to Digital Photography and Conservation Documentation,* produced by the American Institute for Conservation of Historic and Artistic Works (AIC).

SAA Fellows. Highest individual distinction awarded to a limited number of members for their outstanding contribution to the archival profession. *Honored:* David Carmicheal, Edward Galvin, Nancy McGovern, Sheryl Vogt.

SAA Mosaic Scholarship ($5,000). To minority students pursuing graduate education in archival science. *Winners:* Janet Ceja, Harrison Inefuku.

SAA Spotlight Award. To recognize the contributions of individuals who work for the good of the profession and of archival collections, and whose work would not typically receive public recognition. *Winners:* Not awarded in 2009.

Special Libraries Association (SLA)

Diversity Leadership Development Award ($1,000 stipend). *Sponsor:* EBSCO. *Winners:* Regina Beard, Julia Leggett, Nora Martin, Eric Schwarz, Nedelina Tchangalova.

Dow Jones Leadership Award ($2,000). For excellence in special librarianship. *Winner:* Barbie Keiser.

SLA John Cotton Dana Award. For exceptional support and encouragement of special librarianship. *Winner:* Richard Geiger.

SLA Fellows. *Honored:* Ellie Briscoe, Stacey Greenwell, Nancy Minter, Pam Rollo, Tony Stankus.

SLA Hall of Fame Award. For outstanding performance and distinguished service to SLA. *Winners:* Donna Scheeder, Barbara Semonche.

SLA/J. J. Keller Innovations in Technology Award ($1,000). *Winner:* Diane Brenes.

SLA Research Grant (incorporating the Steven I. Goldspiel Memorial Research Grant Fund) (up to $25,000). To support outstanding research. *Winner:* Tao Jin for his proposal "Understanding the Value of Corporate Libraries in Competitive Intelligence Practices."

Rose L. Vormelker Award. *Winner:* David Shumaker.

H. W. Wilson Company Award ($500). For the most outstanding article in the past year's *Information Outlook. Donor:* H. W. Wilson Company. *Winner:* Award discontinued.

Other Awards of Distinction

I Love My Librarian Awards ($5,000). To recognize librarians for service to their communities, schools, and campuses. Winners are nominated by library patrons. *Sponsors:* Carnegie Corporation of New York and the *New York Times. Winners:* (public librarians) Sol A. Gomez, Laura Grunwerg, Karen Martines, Dwight McInvaill; (school library media specialists) Lucy Hansen, Dana Thomas, Carolyn Wheeler; (college, community college, and university librarians) Alice K. Juda, Séamus Ó'Scanláin, Oceana Wilson.

IGI Global Library Technology Excellence Award. To honor an individual for commitment to the utilization and understanding of technological resources within the academic and research communities. *Sponsor:* IGI Global. *Winner:* Chia-Wen Tsai.

Part 4
Research and Statistics

Library Research and Statistics

Research and Statistics on Libraries and Librarianship in 2009

Denise M. Davis

Director, Office for Research and Statistics, American Library Association

This article concentrates on longitudinal research and some new studies employing quantitative and observational methods. It highlights library statistics for the year, including the American Library Association (ALA)/American Association of School Librarians (AASL) study School Libraries Count! and two issues briefs from the Public Library Funding and Technology Access Study. The topic is Web 2.0 and social networking research, and four projects focused in these areas published in 2009 are described.

Winners of research awards and grants conferred by ALA and its divisions, and by the American Society for Information Science and Technology, the Association for Library and Information Science Education, and the Medical Library Association, also are highlighted.

Facts and Figures

Public Libraries

The Institute of Museum and Library Services (IMLS) made a useful addition to its annual summary of public library statistics in *Public Libraries in the United States: Fiscal Year 2007* by including fiscal year (FY) 1998–2007 trend graphs and maps to the Findings section of the report (http://harvester.census.gov/imls/pubs/pls/pub_detail.asp?id=122#). These easy-to-read graphics provide helpful information to library staff and advocates, enhancing understanding of change over time. For instance, Figure 5, "Percentage of Operating Revenue from Local Sources FY 1998–FY 2007" clearly presents the increase in local revenue support from about 77.5 percent of total operating revenue in FY 1998 to slightly more than 84 percent in FY 2007, while Figure 6 presents the decline in state support to public libraries—a useful juxtaposition.

Two issues briefs released by ALA in 2009, and compiled from the 2008–2009 report *Libraries Connect Communities 3: Public Library Funding and Technology Access Study,* are *U.S. Public Libraries and E-Government Services* and *Supporting Learners in Public Libraries.*

U.S. Public Libraries and E-Government Services, published in June, describes the role of libraries in connecting people with essential government resources, including unemployment benefits, federal and state emergency assistance, and tax filing. Detailed in the brief are the increased use of online government information and services, the critical role of public libraries in helping provide access to and assistance in using these resources, and the challenges that must be addressed to improve e-government at the local, state, and federal levels. It is available at http://www.ala.org/ala/research/initiatives/plftas/issuesbriefs/IssuesBrief-Egov.pdf.

Supporting Learners in Public Libraries, published in March and updated in October, describes the role of public libraries as key agencies in supporting the educational and learning needs of every person in the community. It includes data supporting libraries as providers of vital resources for early literacy development, homework help, home schooling, continuing education, and lifelong avocations. The issues brief is available at http://www.ala.org/ala/research/initiatives/plftas/issuesbriefs/SupportingLearnersRev2009-NewR.pdf.

Academic Libraries

High marks go to the National Center for Education Statistics (NCES) for timeliness of the release of the biennial report on academic libraries, *Academic Libraries: 2008,* within nine months of closing the survey. Compared with earlier survey release timelines, the achievement is monumental. One change to the report was a disaggregation of the full-time equivalent (FTE) enrollment ranges from three to six—less than 1,000, 1,000 to 2,999, 3,000 to 4,999, 5,000 to 9,999, 10,000 to 19,999, and, 20,000 or more. There also is a new table, "Information Resources Expenditures and Total Expenditures per FTE Enrollment, Librarians and Other Professional Staff" (Table 20) in the supplemental document.

Some highlights of the report:

- Visits were up, but circulation and service transactions (reference and so forth) were down compared with FY 2006. Academic libraries reported that in a typical week they had more than 20.3 million visits, answered more than 1.1 million reference questions, and provided more than 498,000 informational services more than 8.9 million students and faculty. Visits to academic libraries increased about 1.5 million from FY 2006, as did services to groups by about 27,000.

- Expenditures for electronic books, serial back files, and other materials increased from $93.8 million in FY 2006 to $133.6 million in FY 2008, and expenditures for electronic current serial subscriptions rose from $691.6 million in FY 2006 to $1 billion in FY 2008.

- Circulation transactions from academic library general collections were 138.1 million in 2008, an overall decline of 6 million from FY 2006. Of that decline, 3.3 million—about half—was at doctorate-level institutions, but institutions at the less-than-four-year level also saw a decrease in FY 2008 circulation of more than 62,000.

The full report is available at http://nces.ed.gov/pubsearch/pubsinfo.asp? pubid=2010348.

School Libraries

School Libraries Count!—an annual longitudinal study from the American Association of School Librarians (AASL)—details "changes in the field to gain understanding of the state of school library media programs nationally." The AASL research is a voluntary survey of public and private K–12 schools; the national estimates published annually are compiled from a stratified random sample of all responding libraries.

The 2009 survey report, presenting data from 5,824 responses, down from nearly 7,000 in 2008, is available at http://www.ala.org/ala/mgrps/divs/aasl/ researchandstatistics/slcsurvey/slcsurvey.cfm, as are reports from 2007 and 2008.

Social Networking and Web 2.0

Research on social networking seemed to increase in 2009. A literature search showed that since 1993 fewer than 200 articles had appeared in peer-reviewed journals and of those, about 27 percent were published prior to 2004 and nearly 35 percent in 2008 and 2009. The growth of key terms was evident in the more current citations. Terms like "microblogging" are new, and branded terms like Twitter and Flickr also are indexed.

Zeth Lietzau of the Colorado State Library's Library Research Service has been studying Web technologies available on public library Web sites, what he refers to as Web 2.0. What is special about Lietzau's work is that he identifies characteristics of early adopters of Web technologies. The results of his 2009 research were to be available in 2010, and results from the spring 2008 research are reported in *A Closer Look: U.S. Public Libraries and the Use of Web Technologies* (October 2009), available at http://www.lrs.org/public/webtech. Public libraries are generally slow technology adopters, and only about one-third offered a blog, e-mail reference, or chat reference, according to his report. Lietzau determined that early adopters outpaced their peers in almost every statistical input and output measure—they had more funding, more staff, higher visit counts and circulation, and so forth. Collection count was the only metric not exceeded by early adopters versus their peers.

Lietzau developed a 29-point scale to determine the significance of adoption of Web 2.0 technologies. The average score was 14 and the highest score was 18, achieved by Hennepin County Library, Minneapolis. It is important to note that because of the predominance of urban libraries offering Web 2.0 technologies, a more substantial proportion of library users had access to these services than appears to be the case if one looks only at the numbers of libraries providing such services (see table below). For the purposes of his study, Lietzau identified the top 20 percent (80th percentile) of libraries scored as "early adopters." His study provides detailed comparison of early adopters and non-adopters for revenue, staffing, collections, and services. The following chart is excerpted from his report and presents the estimates of public library patrons served by 12 Web 2.0 technologies.

Chart 7 / Estimated Percentage of U.S. Library Patrons Served by Various Web 2.0 Technologies

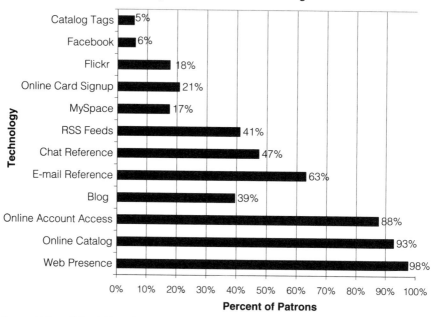

Source: Lietzau, Zeth. *A Closer Look: U.S. Public Libraries and the Use of Web Technologies.* (October 2009).

Lietzau provides detail on the study methodology and includes the survey instrument as an appendix to the 2009 report.

Lorri Mon and Berahim Randeree of Florida State University, in "On the Boundaries of Reference Services: Questioning and Library 2.0" (*Journal of Education for Library and Information Science* 50(3): 164–175, Summer 2009) responded to criticism of library and information science (LIS) education's failure to prepare students in Web 2.0 technology training. Mon and Randeree contacted a sample of more than 800 public libraries in 2008 and received about 240 responses (about 30 percent of the sample) to a series of questions to reveal what Web 2.0 skills demand there was in the public library work force. In 2007 Mon and Randeree had surveyed LIS graduate students about their experiences with and perceptions of Web 2.0 technologies. What they found from public libraries was that blogging, social networking, RSS feeds, and Wikis were the most highly reported Web 2.0 technologies. The researchers also provide demographic data on student (undergraduate and graduate) respondents.

Loosely comparing results from the Lietzau and Mon-Randeree research, it was curious that Lietzau identified about 30 percent of libraries with a Web 2.0 presence, and about 30 percent of libraries surveyed by Mon and Randeree responded with details of their Web 2.0 adoption. About twice as many libraries in the Mon-Randeree study identified blogging than were observed by Lietzau. It is recommended that these two studies be considered together to get a fuller picture of the public library Web 2.0 landscape, at least as it was in 2008–2009.

Two user-behavior studies are worth reviewing. The first is by I-Ping Chiang, Chun-Yao Huang, and Chien-Wen Huang: "Characterizing Web Users' Degree of Web 2.0-ness" (*Journal of the American Society of Information Science and Technology* 60(7): 1349–1357, July 2009); the second is by Pietro Panzarasa, Tore Opsahl, and Kathleen M. Carley: "Patterns and Dynamics of Users' Behavior and Interaction: Network Analysis of an Online Community" (*Journal of the American Society of Information Science and Technology* 60(5): 911–932, May 2009).

The Chiang-Huang-Huang research utilized a panel of respondents and focused on Web 2.0 user attributes and the degree of "Web 2.0-ness" of a Web site, based on click streams ("quantifiable metrics such as behavioral volume, behavioral speed, and behavioral concentration") (Chiang et al., p. 1352). The research team found that the stronger skills were held by those who viewed more pages and did so more rapidly than others. Gender and age also were determinants of Web 2.0-ness. The references provided in this article are particularly valuable to anyone interested in exploring this topic further.

The Panzarasa-Opsahl-Carley research utilized online community network data (longitudinal) to understand user behavior and level of interaction, and the extent to which longevity of participation influences overall interaction within the network and how the "hub-dominated structure" of the network influences the longevity of the social network.

Awards and Grants That Honor and Support Excellent Research

The professional library associations offer many awards and grants to recognize and encourage research. The 2009 awards and grants here are listed under the name of the sponsoring association, and in the case of ALA by the awarding division, in alphabetical order. More-detailed information about the prizes and prize winners can be found at the various associations' Web sites.

American Library Association

Jesse H. Shera Award for Excellence in Published Research
Winner: Lynn Westbrook, for "Understanding Crisis Information Needs in Context: The Case on Intimate Partner Violence Survivors" (*Library Quarterly* 78 (3): 237–261).

American Society for Information Science and Technology

ASIS&T Best Information Science Book Award
Winner: James Boyle for *The Public Domain: Enclosing the Commons of the Mind* (Yale University Press).

John Wiley Best *JASIST* Paper Award
Winners: Ofer Bergman, Ruth Beyth-Marom, and Rafi Nachmias for "The User-Subjective Approach to Personal Information Management Systems Design: Evidence and Implementations."

ProQuest Doctoral Dissertation Award
Winner: Luanne Freund for "Exploiting Task-Document Relations in Support of Information Retrieval in the Workplace."

Thomson ISI Citation Analysis Research Grant
Winner: Cassidy Sugimoto for "Measuring Interdisciplinarity: An Exploration of a Novel Metric Applied to ILS Dissertations."

Thomson ISI Doctoral Dissertation Proposal Scholarship
Winner: Heather Piwowar for "Foundational Studies for Measuring the Impact, Prevalence, and Patterns of Publicly Shared Biomedical Research Data."

Association of College and Research Libraries

Coutts Nijhoff International West European Specialist Study Grant
Winner: Gordon Bruce Anderson, University of Minnesota, for his proposal to work toward the completion of a long-standing project, the Svenskamerikanska Bibliografi (Swedish American Bibliography).

Doctoral Dissertation Fellowship
Winner: Krystyna K. Matusiak, University of Wisconsin–Milwaukee Libraries, for "Use of Digital Resources in an Academic Environment: A Qualitative Study of Students' Perceptions, Experiences, and Digital Literacy Skills."

Ilene F. Rockman Instruction Publication of the Year Award
Winners: Carolyn Radcliff, Mary Lee Jensen, Joseph A. Salem, Jr., Kenneth J. Burhanna, and Julie A. Gedeon, Kent State University, for *A Practical Guide to Information Literacy Assessment for Academic Librarians* (Libraries Unlimited).

Samuel Lazerow Fellowship for Research in Collections and Technical Services in Academic and Research Libraries
Winner: Sara Marcus, Queensborough Community College, for her research project on the change of terms and terminology over several editions of the Sears List of Subject Headings.

Association for Library and Information Science Education

ALISE/Eugene Garfield Doctoral Dissertation Competition
Winner: Xiaojun Yuan, Rutgers University, for "Supporting Multiple Information-Seeking Strategies in a Single System Framework."

Library and Information Technology Association

LITA/OCLC Frederick G. Kilgour Award for Research in Library and Information Technology
Winner: William H. Mischo, head of the Grainger Engineering Library and Information Center at the University of Illinois at Urbana-Champaign Library.

Medical Library Association

Donald A. B. Lindberg Research Fellowship

Winner: Sujin Kim, School of Library and Information Science, University of Kentucky–Lexington for "A Study of Microscopic Imaging Description through Captions Published in Academic Biomedical Journals."

Ida and George Eliot Prize

Winners: Daniel E. Banks, Runhua Shi, Donna F. Timm, Kerri Ann Christopher, David Charles Duggar, Marianne Comegys, and Jerry McLarty, for "Decreased Hospital Length of Stay Associated with Presentation of Cases at Morning Report with Librarian Support."

Janet Doe Lectureship

Winner: Ana D. Cleveland, College of Information, Library Science, and Technologies, University of North Texas–Denton.

Library Purchasing Power Has Held Steady Over Time

Robert E. Molyneux

In last year's *Library and Book Trade Almanac,* I discussed the effects of inflation on U.S. public libraries[1] and concluded that those libraries, at least, were losing ground to inflation. Alas, my analysis was incorrect and I am revisiting the subject and analyzing public libraries and a set of academic libraries for which we have data back to 1908. Here, I examine three sets of data and find that the purchasing power of the expenditures in inflation-adjusted terms in the last year exceeded those of the first year.

Brief Inflation Overview

Measuring inflation and its effects is difficult, and I will discuss the matter in a bit more detail in a section later in this article.

Inflation can be seen as a disease that money gets where the value of a nation's currency slowly wastes away over time—the currency loses value. As each dollar (say) is worth less, it takes more to purchase goods and services. Inflation, then, appears to most as an increase in prices.

Prices can rise or fall for other reasons than a mismanaged currency—for example, in response to changes in supply or demand of an economy's goods and services. If there is a freeze in Florida, the price of citrus crops will likely rise because there will be fewer oranges and grapefruits and consumers will have to pay more to get the few there are. This kind of rise is not inflation, but is the price mechanism adjusting to changes in supply and demand.

Currencies can also deflate; that is, the currency increases in value and prices fall in response. Depressions are often seen as deflationary events.

Money functions as a means of exchange and a store of value. As inflation grips a currency, the store of value function lessens, although the currency can continue to be used in exchange. There is an extensive literature on inflation's causes, so we can leave that matter to others.

Inflation and Libraries

Supporting libraries and the functions they perform is among the noblest acts done by a civilization, because through this method civilizations seek to pass on knowledge gained to others who will follow. Such support is a profound act of optimism. However, libraries are easily damaged by such ignoble acts of civilization as wars, vagaries of budgets, and inflation.

From the founding of the nation through the early part of the 20th century, the U.S. dollar managed to appreciate in value slightly. However, since then, the

Robert E. Molyneux has worked on compiling, documenting, and analyzing library data for more than 25 years and has taught a variety of library school classes dealing with the integration of computers and networking technology in libraries. He is vice president for business development at Equinox Software, Inc.

dollar has lost about 95 percent of its value. What can we measure about the effect this loss of value has on libraries?

We will need data and a means of measuring inflation. For reasons discussed above, we will use the Consumer Price Index (CPI-U) for All Urban Consumers, annual average. This series begins in 1913.

The first set of data we will look at comes from the Association of Research Libraries (ARL) and the Gerould data.[2] The latter is a series that began in 1907–1908 academic year and continued through 1961–1962. The ARL data began in 1961–1962 and continue to this day. Both series are available from ARL (http://www.arl.org/stats/annualsurveys/arlstats/index.shtml). Twelve university libraries have submitted data for all those years and have data on the expenditures for library materials and binding.[3] After the data for the 1961–1962 academic year, ARL disaggregated the expenditures for materials and those for binding. For this chart, this variable has been reconstructed by adding the two separate figures together for each institution.

Figure 1 shows a line chart of two numbers over time. The solid line is expenditures in current dollars—that is, as reported each year—and the dotted line is the 1913 "constant dollars." This number is a calculated amount that attempts to convert the current dollars—as reported in the statistics—to one with the purchasing power of a 1913 dollar. The horizontal axis is years with the second half of the academic year given. That is, 1909–1910 data are plotted above "1910." The vertical axis reaches to $15 million to plot the "current dollars." "Constant dollars" are not nearly so impressive—its largest number is under $700,000.

The notch at 2005 is a result, largely, of the fact that data from the University of Michigan libraries—one of the largest of the 12—are missing for a few years, thus dragging the average down.

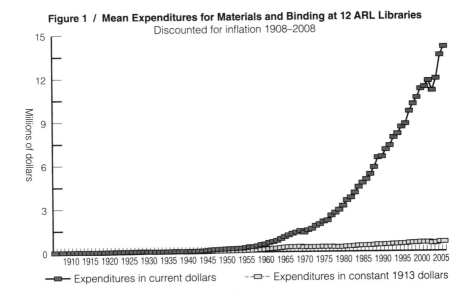

Figure 1 / Mean Expenditures for Materials and Binding at 12 ARL Libraries
Discounted for inflation 1908–2008

These latter "constant dollars" are a construct made by a method discussed later that is used to discount the effects of inflation. The method is at best approximate, but it does show that the expenditure of these libraries in reported "current" dollars has gone up a great deal in the century of data we have. The calculated "constant" dollars begins in 1913 and the dotted line representing this number is overlayed on this chart.

What about these constant dollars? Let's examine them in more detail. Figure 2 has these calculated figures. The notch at 2005 is seen here, too. The plateau in the late 1960s through the 1980s has been seen before in several places and appears to be a result of the recession and other economic factors. As I have discussed elsewhere, it appears that libraries are lagging indicators of an economy. The line goes up and down over time, but shows an increase over time. That means that the constant dollars for materials and binding go up, overall, but have periods where inflation takes its toll on purchasing power.

Figure 2 / Mean Expenditures for Materials and Binding at 12 ARL Libraries

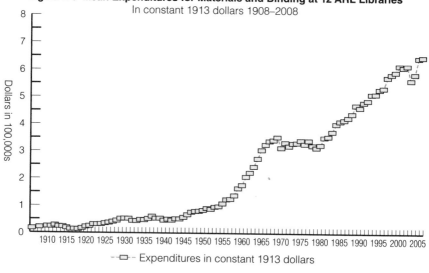

In constant 1913 dollars 1908–2008

--□-- Expenditures in constant 1913 dollars

In the Gerould data for the 1907–1908 academic year, these 12 libraries expended an actual average of $16,561 for materials and binding; in the last year, just under $650,000 of the calculated "constant" 1913 dollars. By this measure, for this variable measuring one aspect of the purchasing of these libraries, these libraries handily beat inflation over the period with a few ups and downs along the way.

It is important to take a moment and consider what these charts do not tell us.

- The 12 ARL libraries for which we have data are not a randomly chosen group of libraries. In fact, they are among the finest libraries in the world and they got that way through years of generous support from their institutions. Also, the individual institutions are not analyzed—rather it is the average values of these 12. We cannot conclude from these data much about the individual institutions.

- Note also that this variable is not really the one we want to measure the impact of inflation. Of course, ideally we would want all data, but that has not been given to us since the Garden of Eden. We receive incomplete data and we draw meaning from them only through the sweat of our brows. We get missing data, problem data, not-quite-what-we-were-looking-for data: that is, bad data. It is the high purpose of the discipline of statistics to help us make sense of the universe in spite of the flaws. That said, we would really like to have total expenditures. That number is first available from the ARL series in 1963 and we will take that up presently.

- This long run of data is something to ponder in thinking about measuring inflation. Among the many difficulties in measuring inflation is the fact that the world changes. In 1907–1908, when James Thayer Gerould started the collection of these data, there were no computers, e-books, Internet, and so forth. It is uncertain how to assess changes in information technology on the figures we see here. The library world does not have sufficient research resources to help us answer these kinds of questions. In any case, this general question of changes in technology presents a difficulty in measurement of inflation's effects.

- Libraries adjust to the world around them. In previous discussions of trends in public libraries in the *Library and Book Trade Almanac,* the data have revealed changes in allocation of resources in apparent response to economic factors. If budgets are tight, a library might not fill a vacant position; if e-books are cheaper than a hardcover book, then the library may buy more e-books. With expenditures for materials and binding, we are seeing a secondary variable, one that might change in response to other aspects of these libraries.

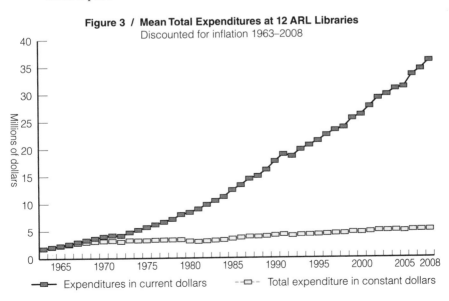

Figure 3 / Mean Total Expenditures at 12 ARL Libraries
Discounted for inflation 1963–2008

Expenditures in current dollars   Total expenditure in constant dollars

Figure 3 presents data from the 12 libraries for total expenditures. The first year for which we have this variable is the 1962–1963 academic year. The structure of this graph is similar to that seen in Figure 1: the current dollars in a solid line start out at the same level as the 1963 "constant" dollars (dotted line) but quickly run up to about $36 million.

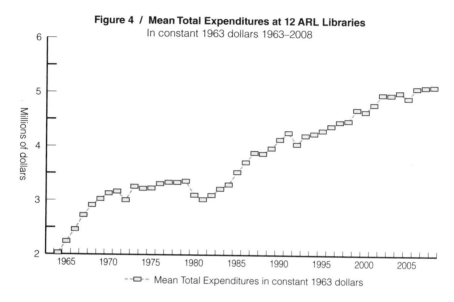

Figure 4 / Mean Total Expenditures at 12 ARL Libraries
In constant 1963 dollars 1963–2008

- -□- - Mean Total Expenditures in constant 1963 dollars

Figure 4, like Figure 2, shows us the calculated constant dollar figure. In 1962–1963 the mean total expenditures at these 12 libraries were just under $1.8 million and in 2007–2008 just over $5 million in constant dollars. By this important measure, for these libraries, and with caveats noted, these libraries beat inflation in the purchasing power of the total expenditures they had.

Figure 5 presents summary data for total expenditures by U.S. public libraries in the 1992–2007 fiscal years, in the graphic form we have seen before. In this case, the sum of the total expenditures for the several states is plotted. The current dollar figure—the sum of the total expenditures for all public libraries in the United States—is more than $10 billion. The constant dollar figure for 1992 is $4.5 billion and for 2007 is $6.9 billion. In other words, the purchasing power of total expenditures for all public libraries in the United States—with the caveats given—has kept ahead of inflation.[4]

Measuring Inflation

Measuring inflation's effects is quite difficult. In the library world, probably the first source to examine is *Measuring Inflation in Public Libraries: A Comparison of Two Approaches.*[5] This publication presents a detailed discussion of two methodologies for analyzing inflation's impact on public libraries—if we had data that we do not have. It does discuss the research of Kent Halstead, whose

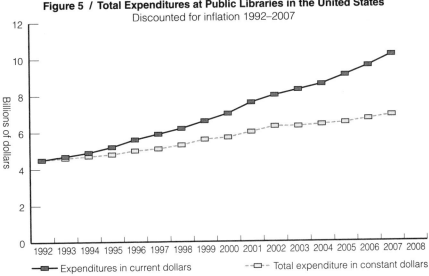

Figure 5 / Total Expenditures at Public Libraries in the United States
Discounted for inflation 1992–2007

Expenditures in current dollars · Total expenditure in constant dollars

work with ARL was the most professional examination of this question. The data he published was available in the *Bowker Annual Library and Book Trade Almanac* for a number of years. Halstead has since retired and the infrastructure to implement either method suggested in *Measuring Inflation* does not currently exist. This lack of infrastructure is a fact that undergirds all data analysis in the library field.

A careful reading of *On the Accuracy of Economic Observations* by Oskar Morgenstern[6] would provide analysts a set of cautionary thoughts about what is possible with the data we have—not just in libraries but data about the economy at large—and the phenomena we are trying to get a handle on. The best data that exist do not overcome all the difficulties in measuring inflation and its impact on institutions or sectors of the economy.

Given these difficulties, how were these calculations done?

With the Gerould data, we have 12 libraries that reported their expenditures for materials and binding for the 1907–1908 academic year and most years subsequently. The mean figure for this variable that year for these libraries is $16,561. By the 2007–2008 academic year, the mean figure for the (now disaggregated) figures of expenditures for library materials plus the expenditure for binding is more than $14 million. Given the inflation over the last century, are these figures remotely comparable? Has the purchasing power of libraries kept up with inflation?

Again, we do not have perfect data. We do, however, have the Consumer Price Index (CPI) and that allows us to make an approximation.

When one talks about the CPI, there is talk of a "market basket" of goods. Libraries buy many things. Different libraries buy different things. Your library might buy more X and another might buy more Y. In other words, each library has a different market basket of goods and services it purchases. As a result, the effects of inflation on libraries will vary. There are about 9,200 public libraries in the United States,[7] 100,000 school library media centers, depending on how you count them, 3,000-plus academic libraries. Given the complexity of analyzing the spending patterns of each of those libraries, our first approximation will assume each library has the same spending patterns or close enough to get a broad picture. We will do the best we can given the data we have available.

Here is the first approximation:

The Consumer Price Index raw data are currently here: ftp://ftp.bls.gov/pub/special.requests/cpi/cpiai.txt.

Taking the annual average of these data gives us a place to start. Are all libraries urban? No, of course not. But the annual figures give is a base to work from. Now what?

The annual average price level given in 1913 is 9.9 and in 2008 is 215.3. What does that mean? In 1913 and 2008 the reported figures for the mean expenditures for materials and binding at these libraries in the Gerould/ARL series are, respectively, $23,386 and $14,090,521. If the value of the U.S. dollar from 1913 to 2008 went down about 95 percent, have these 12 libraries done better than inflation?

Glad you asked! Let's look at the CPI Inflation Calculator which is a bit more accessible: http://www.bls.gov/data/inflation_calculator.htm.

In 1913 the mean expenditures for this variable for our 12 libraries are $23,386. The inflation calculator tells us this amount is the equivalent in purchasing power of a bit under $508,600 for 2008. Where did *this* number come from?

Let's compare the average expenditures for materials and binding from 1913 ($23,386) with the figure for 1914 ($27,768). For this year, the money spent rose $4,382 (27,768-23,386). That was a healthy increase of nearly 19 percent over the 1913 figure. The CPI-U for 1913 is 9.9, while in 1914 it was 10. According to this measure, then, the value of the dollar in 1914 was 99 percent (9.9/10) of the 1913 dollar.

Now let's compare these figures. In inflation-adjusted terms (as is being calculated here), to compare the 1914 figure with the 1913 figure we would multiply the 1914 figure by .99 to take into account the decline in the dollar.

	Current dollars	Constant 1913 dollars
1913	23,386	
1914	27,768	27,490

We compare the current (the figures as reported in that year) 1913 dollars with our estimate of the 1914 dollars corrected for inflation. Given that these estimated "constant" 1913 dollars in 1914 are greater than the reported 1913 figure, we can say that these libraries had an increase in expenditures for materials and binding from 1913 through 1914 in "constant dollars."

Another way to make this comparison is to use the CPI Inflation Calculator and enter the 23,386 figure in 1913 and 1914 in the second block and the calculator will report that 23,386 has the same buying power as 23,622.22 in 1914. Because $27,490 is higher, this method confirms that these libraries had an increase in their purchasing power for this one variable over these two years.

What about 1913 to 2008? The calculation is the same. The percentage change in the dollar figures is huge, but have these libraries had an increase in their purchasing power? As we saw above, the CPI-U for 1913 is 9.9 and we can now use the 2008 figure of 215.3. The decline in the value of the dollar is 9.9/215.3 or .046—that is, this calculation gives us a figure that the 2008 dollar is 4.6 percent of the value of the 1913 dollar.

	Current dollars	Constant 1913 dollars
1913	23,386	
2008	14,090,521	648,164

Again, we see that the purchasing power of the declining dollars kept ahead of inflation and by a considerable amount.

By calculating this percentage for each year, we can multiply the current dollars for any year times the percentage estimate of that year's figure to get an estimate of that number in terms of the base year's "constant dollars." That is where the "current" figures referred to in the text and figures come from.

Notes

1. 2009, 54th edition, "Library Budget Dollars Shrinking in Real Terms—Are We Eating Our Seed Corn?"

2. Robert E. Molyneux, *The Gerould Statistics,* Washington, D.C., ARL, 1986.

3. The 12 ARL libraries that are analyzed here are those at these institutions: University of California, Berkeley; University of Illinois, Urbana-Champaign; Indiana University; University of Iowa; University of Kansas; University of Michigan; University of Minnesota; University of Missouri; University of Nebraska; Ohio State University; University of Washington; University of Wisconsin.

4. Summary public library data used in Chart 5: Robert E. Molyneux, Library Data Archive, State Summary/State Characteristics Longitudinal Data File (PUSUM); http://drdata.lrs.org/pusum.

5. U.S. Department of Education, Office of Educational Research and Improvement, NCES 1999-326: Washington, D.C., 1999.

6. Morgenstern, Oskar, *On the Accuracy of Economic Observations,* Princeton University Press, 1963.

7. The FY 2007 data published by the Institute of Museum and Library Services are for 9,214 public libraries in the United States and 3 in Guam. http://harvester.census.gov/imls/pubs/Publications/fy2007_pls_report.pdf.

A Perfect Storm Brewing:
Budget Cuts Threaten Public Library Services at
Time of Increased Demand

Public Library Funding and Technology Access Study
ALA Office for Research and Statistics, 50 East Huron Street, Chicago, IL 60611-2795
800-545-2433

In a world where knowledge is power, libraries help make everyone more powerful. With more than 16,600 locations serving people of all ages in communities of all sizes, America's public libraries have a wide reach and a vital mission to connect people with the resources they need to thrive.

In the grip of one of the most severe recessions since the Great Depression, more Americans are turning to their libraries not only for free access to books, magazines, CDs, and DVDs, but also for a lifeline to technology training and online resources for employment, continuing education, and government resources. In January 2009 more than 25 million Americans reported using their public library more than 20 times in the last year, up from 20.3 million Americans in 2006. It is likely this trend continued or increased through the remainder of 2009.

This level of use and reliance on public libraries was recently confirmed by new research conducted by the American Library Association (ALA) and the Center for Library and Information Innovation (CLII) at the University of Maryland. Initial findings from the study suggest a "perfect storm" of growing community demand for library resources converging with budget cuts closing library doors and reducing the staff available to assist library patrons. The study finds:

- More people are relying on public libraries for technology use, particularly to find employment and connect to online government services
- The vast majority of public libraries support job seeking with specialized electronic resources, software, and personal assistance from library staff
- A majority of states report cuts in state funding to public libraries and to the state library agencies that support libraries and statewide library programs
- The top challenge affecting public libraries' ability to help job seekers is a lack of adequate staff to effectively help patrons with their job-seeking needs
- Almost 15 percent of public libraries report operating hours decreased over the past fiscal year

Library Technology Use Jumps

America's public libraries serve as community technology hubs for millions of people every day. Two-thirds of libraries report that they provide the only free access to computers and the Internet in their communities. In 2009 libraries also overwhelmingly reported an increase in usage of public library computers over the previous fiscal year. More than three-quarters of all public libraries reported increased computer use (Figure A1).

Figure A1 / Use of Public Library Internet Workstations, by Metropolitan Status

Use of Workstations	Metropolitan Status			
	Urban	Suburban	Rural	Overall
Use of workstations increased since last fiscal year	79.0% (n=2,114)	77.6% (n=4,203)	73.2% (n=5,527)	75.7% (n=11,844)
Use of workstations decreased since last fiscal year	2.8% (n=75)	3.5% (n=191)	2.9% (n=216)	3.1% (n=482)
Use of workstations have stayed the same since last fiscal year	16.8% (n=450)	18.1% (n=980)	23.1% (n=1,744)	20.3% (n=3,174)

Weighted missing values, n=336

For example, the Appleton (Wisconsin) Public Library reports its public computer use is up as much as 52 percent over 2008. "It really took a jump as the recession hit us," said Library Director Terry Dawson, as reported in the December 12 *Post-Crescent* newspaper. "It's something we're seeing on a national level with more employers requiring electronic applications to apply for a job. With this economy, more people are losing their high-speed Internet subscriptions, and they are relying on the library now."

Seventy-one percent of public library survey respondents report they've also witnessed increased use of the library's wireless Internet access. More than 82 percent of public libraries currently offer wireless access, up from 76.4 percent last year (Figure A2).

Similarly, close to half (45.6 percent) of all public libraries reported increased use of their electronic resources (which encompass a range of Internet-based services, including jobs databases, online test preparation services, invest-

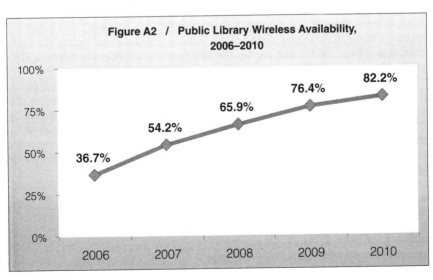

Figure A2 / Public Library Wireless Availability, 2006–2010

36.7% 54.2% 65.9% 76.4% 82.2%
2006 2007 2008 2009 2010

ment tools, reference sources, and downloadable books and audio) and more than one-quarter reported increased use of patron technology training classes.

In all cases, urban libraries reported the greatest surge in patron demand for technology services: 77 percent reported increased wireless use; 61 percent reported increased use of electronic resources; and 40 percent reported increased use of patron technology classes. Urban libraries also were the most likely to report their hours of service had decreased since the last fiscal year—illustrating the "perfect storm" that many public libraries and their communities are facing in fiscal year (FY) 2010 with increased demand for services and fewer resources available to meet those demands (Figure A3).

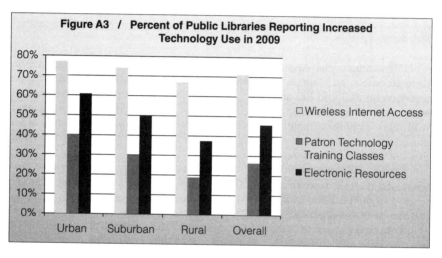

Figure A3 / Percent of Public Libraries Reporting Increased Technology Use in 2009

Job Seeking Takes Center Stage

With more businesses—including a majority of America's leading retailers—requiring applicants to apply online, job-seeking resources are among the most critical and most in demand among the technology resources available in U.S. public libraries.

A vast majority of public libraries help patrons complete online job applications (67 percent); provide access to job databases and other online resources (88 percent) and civil service exam materials (75 percent); and offer software or other resources (69 percent) to help patrons create résumés and other employment materials. Forty-two percent of urban libraries report offering classes related to job seeking, and about 27 percent collaborate with outside agencies or individuals to help patrons complete online job applications (Figure A4).

Bethany Pisanchyn of Clarks Summit (Pennsylvania) is one of many people who recently turned to the library when she was looking for work as a music teacher. "Over last summer, I found myself at the Abington Community Library for many hours a day, four to five days a week. One may ask what would cause me to do something like that, and I would quickly respond, 'finding a job.'" Pisanchyn applied to more than 70 schools using library computers after her home computer stopped working and she was unable to afford to replace it.

Figure A4 / Job Seeking Services of the Public Library Outlets, by Metropolitan Status

Job Seeking Roles and Services	Metropolitan Status			
	Urban	Suburban	Rural	Overall
The library provides access to jobs databases and other job opportunity resources	89.3% (n=2,336)	91.6% (n=4,717)	85.3% (n=6,068)	88.2% (n=13,121)
The library provides access to civil service exam materials	85.7% (n=2,240)	78.9% (n=4,063)	68.0% (n=4,840)	74.9% (n=11,144)
The library offers software and other resources to help patrons create résumés and other employment materials	81.2% (n=2,124)	68.7% (n=3,535)	64.5% (n=4,591)	68.9% (n=10,251)
The library helps patrons complete online job applications	67.4% (n=1,762)	63.8% (n=3,287)	69.4% (n=4,937)	67.1% (n=9,986)
The library offers classes (either by librarians or others working with the library) on job seeking strategies, interview tips, etc.	42.0% (n=1,099)	30.7% (n=1,583)	13.6% (n=969)	24.5% (n=3,650)
The library collaborates with outside agencies or individuals to help patrons complete online job applications	32.9% (n=860)	20.6% (n=1,062)	22.3% (n=1,586)	23.6% (n=3,507)
The library collaborates with outside agencies or individuals to help patrons develop business plans and other materials to start businesses	26.5% (n=694)	13.2% (n=680)	10.5% (n=745)	14.2% (n=2,119)
The library helps patrons develop business plans and other materials to start businesses	22.1% (n=578)	14.0% (n=719)	9.5% (n=675)	13.3% (n=1,972)
Other	4.7% (n=123)	3.0% (n=152)	3.2% (n=228)	3.4% (n=504)

Will not total 100%, as categories are not mutually exclusive.
Weighted missing values, n=1.099

"The library was able to offer me a wealth of valuable resources that are not only free but also extremely helpful in my job search. The library offered me up-to-date computers with fast Internet service and printing capabilities. I also was given valuable advice and assistance from the friendly library staff. One of the staff members actually informed me of the resource that ultimately led me to finding a job in my field. There are many people in the library like me who are in there all the time and need the services. I even built a curriculum for my new teaching job using library materials."

With 16,604 public library buildings nationwide, the impact public library staff and services can have in meeting the needs faced by unemployed and under-employed people is significant. With public computers, Internet, Wi-Fi, electronic resources, technology training, and staff to help support and guide users to job information, libraries are well-positioned to support employment and economic development—particularly in collaboration with other community and government agencies, including Department of Labor ONESTOP centers and other work force development agencies.

"The numbers of people that need services are larger than our capacity," said Nancy Borrell, executive director of DavidsonWorks, the Davidson County, North Carolina, work force development board. "The library (Davidson County

Public Library) is a natural partner—they are located in all corners of the county and have the space, computers, and trained library staff we need. We're reaching areas of the county we've never been able to reach before."

E-Government Role Expands

As many government agencies eliminate print forms and even close satellite offices, U.S. public libraries are on the front lines of connecting people with essential government resources. Continuing a trend begun with the 2006–2007 survey, libraries report an increased range of e-government services for patrons.

Figure A5 / E-Government Roles and Services of the Public Library Outlets, by Metropolitan Status

E-Government roles and services	Metropolitan Status			
	Urban	Suburban	Rural	Overall
Staff provide as needed assistance to patrons for understanding how to access and use e-government Web sites	91.2% (n=2,300)	88.8% (n=4,317)	87.9% (n=5,918)	88.8% (n=12,535)
Staff provide assistance to patrons applying for or accessing e-government services	75.9% (n=1,913)	78.6% (n=3,820)	79.9% (n=5,383)	78.7% (n=11,116)
Staff provide assistance to patrons for completing government forms	71.4% (n=1,800)	65.2% (n=3,168)	65.1% (n=4,386)	66.3% (n=9,354)
Staff provide assistance to patrons for understanding government programs and services	45.6% (n=1,149)	45.6% (n=2,215)	40.7% (n=2,742)	43.3% (n=6,106)
The library is partnering with government agencies, non-profit organizations, and others to provide e-government services	26.4% (n=666)	21.2% (n=1,030)	17.8% (n=1,201)	20.5% (n=2,898)
The library has at least one staff member with significant knowledge and skills in provision of e-government services	31.5% (n=794)	16.2% (n=789)	15.4% (n=1035)	18.5% (n=2,618)
The library developed guides, tip sheets, or other tools to help patrons use e-government Web sites and services	23.3% (n=588)	18.7% (n=907)	14.2% (n=957)	17.4% (n=2,452)
The library offers training classes regarding the use of government Web sites, understanding government programs, and completing electronic forms	22.9% (n=578)	7.3% (n=357)	4.8% (n=321)	8.9% (n=1,256)
The library is working with government agencies (local, state, or federal) to help agencies improve their Web sites and/or e-government services	11.0% (n=277)	8.2% (n=398)	6.0% (n=405)	7.7% (n=1,080)
The library offered translation services for forms and services in other languages	11.1% (n=279)	6.6% (n=321)	4.2% (n=280)	6.2% (n=880)
Other	4.8% (n=121)	3.3% (n=159)	4.4% (n=298)	4.1% (n=578)

There was a 23 percent jump in libraries reporting that they provide assistance to patrons applying for or accessing e-government services. Almost 79 percent of libraries report this is the case, compared with 54 percent last year (Figure A5).

"For anyone without a computer, you're really out of luck without the library," said Elsie Werdin, who spent almost two weeks on the telephone trying to get the information she needed to enroll herself and her husband in a Medicare plan that would cover her husband's expensive medications. With assistance from the Pasco County Library System (Florida) e-government librarian, she was able to complete an online Medicare enrollment form in less than 30 minutes. The Pasco library provided e-government services to more than 9,100 people from October 2008 to March 31, 2009, up 177 percent over the same period a year earlier.

Two-thirds of public libraries provide assistance to patrons completing government forms; and one in five public libraries is partnering with other agencies to provide e-government services, up from 13.4 percent one year ago.

"People come in every day to apply for unemployment. They could also go to the unemployment office, but the lines are long there, and there is no one to help them navigate," said an Indiana public library director. "The library's hours also are more conducive since they can look for work all day, then come to the library at night."

Library Funding Under Threat

At the same time demand for critical services has climbed, many state and local libraries are facing growing funding challenges. Among the more complex challenges are state library's reallocation of financial support of public libraries from state sources to already stretched federal sources, or the disappearance of support altogether. As part of the *Public Library Funding and Technology Access Study*, the ALA surveyed the 51 Chief Officers of State Library Agencies (50 states and the District of Columbia) in November 2009.

Twenty-four states reported cuts in state funding for public libraries between FY 2009 and FY 2010. Of these, nearly half indicated the cuts were greater than 11 percent—almost four times the number that reported this was the case in the previous fiscal year. Also:

- Seven states and the District of Columbia do not provide state funding
- Eleven states reported there had been no change between FY 2009 and FY 2010
- Three states reported an increase in funding
- One state had not yet begun FY 2010

For many states, FY 2010 cuts come on top of state funding cuts made between FY 2008 and FY 2009. In January 2009, 41 percent of responding states reported declining state funding for public libraries. Georgia, for instance, saw state funding reductions greater than 7 percent each year for the past three fiscal years.

Cuts at the state level frequently were compounded by cuts at the local level and cuts in the state library agency budget. When considering current local funding to public libraries, a majority of state libraries reported decreases in the 5 to 10 percent range. Seventeen states (37 percent) reported they believed a majority of libraries in their states had received cuts in funding in FY 2010, compared with FY 2009.

Washoe County (Nevada) Public Library, for instance, has lost nearly 40 percent of its operating budget over the past two fiscal years. At the same time the county is reporting declines in property and sales taxes, the Nevada State Library and Archives reports state funding declines greater than 11 percent in both of the last two fiscal years. As a result, Washoe County Public Library has cut its operating hours 25 percent, and staffing is down 30 percent.

Nearly three-quarters of state library agencies reported their budgets had been reduced, decreasing their ability to support public libraries in their states, including lost staff to provide consultation and continuing education; reduced state expenditures for library collections, subscriptions, databases, and new or replacement equipment; eliminated reciprocal borrowing; and more. This is consistent with a separate survey conducted by the Chief Officers of State Library Agencies (COSLA), which found that 77 percent (31 of 40 respondents) of state library agencies experienced a budget cut in the current fiscal year.

The South Carolina State Library's budget, for instance, has been reduced 37 percent since fiscal year 2008. State aid to public libraries has been reduced from $2.25 per capita in FY 2008 to $1.32 in FY 2010. The reduction to state aid in FY 2010 was offset by (one-time) American Recovery and Reinvestment Act (ARRA) funds in the amount of $0.42 per capita. State Library agency staff positions are down 23 percent. With staff numbers decreasing, programs may have to be curtailed or eliminated, according to state library staff.

Fewer Hours, Staff to Meet Demand

Thirteen states (28 percent) reported they were aware of public library closures in their states the past 12 months. Twelve states reported closures of five or fewer libraries; and one state (Indiana) reported more than five closures.

The 2009 national survey of public libraries also found a significant increase in the number of libraries reporting a decrease in the hours they are available to serve their communities. Nearly one-quarter of urban libraries and 14.5 percent of all libraries (up from 4.5 percent last year) report operating hours have decreased since the previous fiscal year. Nationally, this translates to lost hours at more than 2,400 public library branches, and the trend is likely to continue in 2010 unless funding is restored or new funds identified (Figure A6).

Decreased funding also is impacting staffing levels at many public libraries at a time when patron demand is vastly increasing. The No. 1 challenge affecting libraries' ability to help job seekers is a lack of adequate staff to effectively help patrons with their job-seeking needs. Almost 60 percent of libraries strongly agreed or agreed with the statement that the library does not have enough staff to help patrons. About 52 percent agreed or strongly agreed that library staff does

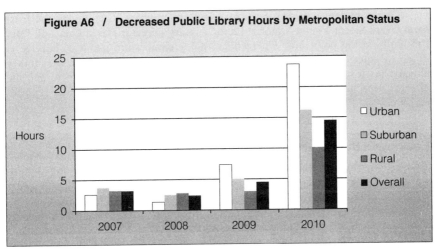

Figure A6 / Decreased Public Library Hours by Metropolitan Status

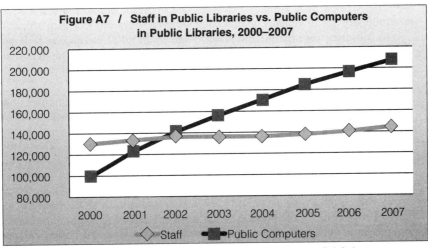

Figure A7 / Staff in Public Libraries vs. Public Computers in Public Libraries, 2000–2007

Institute of Museum and Library Services, http://harvester.census.gov/imls/index.asp

not have the necessary skills to meet patron demand, and about 36 percent agreed or strongly agreed the library has too few public computers to meet demand.

In 2008, 90 percent of libraries provided formal technology training classes or one-on-one assistance to library patrons using public Internet computers. Budget cuts at Broward County (Florida) Library System, however, included 12 instructors who previously taught technology classes. The library system has lost 28 percent of its funding and one-third of its staff positions over the past three years, while circulation has increased 27 percent over the same period.

Along with a 90 percent increase in the number of computers available in U.S. public libraries between 2000 and 2007 (Figure A7), Americans visit their public libraries 1.4 billion times and check out almost 2.2 billion items each year, according to recent data from the Institute of Museum and Library Services.

"(When budget cutting), I try to select areas where it would do the least harm," said Sierra Vista (Arizona) Public Library Director David Gunckel. "But I'm really at the point now where none of my choices are painless. Service is going to deteriorate in some way." With a hiring freeze in place, the library already has lost 70 staff hours per week compared with one year ago, and the director expects longer lines, fewer new materials, putting off computer replacements beyond five years, and reducing operating hours.

Looking to the Future

America's public libraries are first responders in a time of economic uncertainty and are, and should continue to be, part of both national and community-level responses to supporting employment and economic development efforts.

Some libraries and their communities already have been selected to benefit from one-time federal stimulus funding (ARRA).

- The Arizona State Library, Archives and Public Records received a $1.3 million grant to enhance public computing facilities in more than 80 public libraries throughout the state. More than 1,000 computers will be added in a state where more than 90 percent of public libraries reported they do not have enough public computers to meet demand some or all of the time.
- The city of Boston will use stimulus funding to expand computer and Internet capacity at the Boston Public Library and its 26 branches.

State libraries also are teaming with other state agencies to cost-effectively train librarians to assist newly unemployed residents.

- In North Carolina, which has had one of the highest unemployment rates in the country, the State Library collaborated with the Employment Security Commission and the Department of Commerce to train librarians, create an online job search toolkit, and expand job-related library collections.
- The Tennessee State Library and Archives purchased résumé software for 100 libraries in the state; awarded six Library Services and Technology Act (LSTA) grants to create job-training centers in public libraries in collaboration with local agencies, such as adult education centers and career centers; and partnered with the Tennessee Department of Labor and Workforce Development to provide training for library staff. "Our local communities are hurting. One county was devastated—with 27 percent unemployment. Public libraries are stepping up to the plate and becoming anchors of the community—offering services many people don't have available at home," said Assistant State Librarian for Planning and Development Jane Pinkston.

Community, government agency, and library collaborations are one of many keys to aiding families in weathering the economic storm. Together, they have the opportunity to

- Increase awareness of the 21st century services and resources available in public libraries
- Ensure sustained funding and staffing for public libraries
- Improve coordination and implementation of e-government and economic development activities at all levels of government
- Recognize public libraries as anchor institutions that connect people to the Internet, technology training and assistance, trained staff, and rich electronic and print collections.

Libraries are part of the solution for those struggling to regain their footing in uncertain economic times. Keeping library doors open with sufficient staffing is vital to ensuring that every person has equal access to essential employment, continuing education, and government resources.

Note: The *Public Library Funding and Technology Access Study,* funded by ALA and the Bill and Melinda Gates Foundation, provides current national information on public library funding and technology use and services. The foregoing article presents selected preliminary findings from the 2009–2010 study's public library and state library agency surveys. The 2009–2010 public library survey was available for completion between September 7, 2009, and November 13, 2009, and produced 7,393 responses, for a response rate of 82.4 percent. Forty-five states and the District of Columbia responded to the state library agency survey in November 2009, for a total response rate of 90 percent. For more information, see http://www.ala.org/plinternetfunding.

Number of Libraries in the United States and Canada

Statistics are from *American Library Directory* (*ALD*) *2009–2010* (Information Today, Inc., 2009). Data are exclusive of elementary and secondary school libraries.

Libraries in the United States

Public Libraries	17,064*
Public libraries, excluding branches	9,757†
Main public libraries that have branches	1,430
Public library branches	7,307
Academic Libraries	3,768*
Community college	1,167
Departmental	203
Medical	11
Religious	10
University and college	2,601
Departmental	1,389
Law	183
Medical	247
Religious	235
Armed Forces Libraries	289*
Air Force	84
Medical	6
Army	133
Medical	26
Marine Corps	11
Navy	61
Law	1
Medical	13
Government Libraries	1,150*
Law	403
Medical	162
Special Libraries (excluding public, academic, armed forces, and government)	7,609*
Law	912
Medical	1,496
Religious	537
Total Special Libraries (including public, academic, armed forces, and government)	8,906
Total law	1,499
Total medical	1,961
Total religious	1,048
Total Libraries Counted(*)	29,880

Libraries in Regions Administered by the United States

Public Libraries	29 *
Public libraries, excluding branches	11 †
Main public libraries that have branches	3
Public library branches	18
Academic Libraries	37 *
Community college	5
Departmental	3
Medical	0
University and college	32
Departmental	22
Law	3
Medical	2
Religious	1
Armed Forces Libraries	2 *
Air Force	1
Army	1
Navy	0
Government Libraries	6 *
Law	1
Medical	2
Special Libraries (excluding public, academic, armed forces, and government)	7 *
Law	3
Medical	1
Religious	1
Total Special Libraries (including public, academic, armed forces, and government)	16
Total law	7
Total medical	5
Total religious	2
Total Libraries Counted(*)	81

Libraries in Canada

Public Libraries	2,056 *
Public libraries, excluding branches	825 †
Main public libraries that have branches	133
Public library branches	1,231
Academic Libraries	349 *
Community college	86
Departmental	13
Medical	0
Religious	4
University and college	263

Departmental	175
Law	16
Medical	21
Religious	34
Government Libraries	297*
Law	36
Medical	7
Special Libraries (excluding public, academic, armed forces, and government)	953*
Law	106
Medical	179
Religious	26
Total Special Libraries (including public, academic, armed forces, and government)	1,071
Total law	158
Total medical	207
Total religious	94
Total Libraries Counted(*)	3,655

Summary

Total U.S. Libraries	29,880
Total Libraries Administered by the United States	81
Total Canadian Libraries	3,655
Grand Total of Libraries Listed	33,616

Note: Numbers followed by an asterisk are added to find "Total libraries counted" for each of the three geographic areas (United States, U.S.-administered regions, and Canada). The sum of the three totals is the "Grand total of libraries listed" in *ALD*. For details on the count of libraries, see the preface to the 62nd edition of *ALD—Ed.*

†Federal, state, and other statistical sources use this figure (libraries *excluding* branches) as the total for public libraries.

Highlights of IMLS and NCES Surveys

The Institute of Museum and Library Services (IMLS) and the National Center for Education Statistics (NCES) collect and disseminate statistical information about libraries in the United States and its outlying areas. Two major surveys are conducted by NCES, the Academic Libraries Survey and the School Library Media Centers Survey; two others, the Public Libraries Survey and the State Library Agencies Survey, were formerly conducted by NCES, but are now handled by IMLS.

Both IMLS and NCES also conduct surveys on related topics, such as the recent NCES survey Educational Technology in Public School Districts included here.

This article presents highlights from four of the most recently conducted surveys. For more information, see "National Center for Education Statistics Library Statistics Program" in Part 1 and "Institute of Museum and Library Services Library Programs" in Part 2.

Public Libraries

The following are highlights from the publication *Public Libraries Survey, Fiscal Year 2007,* released in June 2009 by IMLS.

Number of Public Libraries and Population of Legal Service Area

- There were 9,214 public libraries (administrative entities) in the 50 states and the District of Columbia in fiscal year (FY) 2007, slightly up from 9,208 in FY 2006. Public libraries are widely distributed across the United States; 98 percent of counties have at least one administrative entity or library outlet.
- Public library service areas encompassed 97 percent of the total population of the states and the District of Columbia in FY 2007, either in legally established geographic service areas or in areas under contract. This was the same percentage of the nation's population served during the prior fiscal year.
- Twelve percent of the public libraries served 73 percent of the population of legally served areas in the United States during FY 2007; each of these public libraries had a legal service area population of 50,000 or more.

Service Outlets

- Eighty-one percent of public libraries had one single direct-service outlet in FY 2007 (an outlet that provides service directly to the public). Nineteen percent had more than one direct-service outlet. Both of these percentages were equal to their FY 2006 levels. Types of direct-service outlets include central library outlets, branch library outlets, and bookmobile outlets.

• A total of 1,544 public libraries (17 percent) had one or more branch library outlets, with a total of 7,564 branch outlets. The total number of central library outlets was 9,040. The total number of stationary outlets (central library outlets and branch library outlets) was 16,604. Nine percent of public libraries had one or more bookmobile outlets, with a total of 808 bookmobiles.

• Ten percent of public libraries had an average number of weekly public service hours per outlet of less than 20 hours, 38 percent had weekly public service hours per outlet of 20–39 hours, and 52 percent had weekly public service hours per outlet of 40 hours or more.

Legal Basis and Interlibrary Relationships

• The majority of public libraries (85 percent) are public agencies connected to some form of local government. In FY 2007, 53 percent of public libraries were part of a municipal government, 15 percent were separate government units known as library districts, 10 percent were part of a county/parish, 3 percent had multijurisdictional legal basis under an intergovernmental agreement, 2 percent were part of a school district, 1 percent were part of a city/county, and 2 percent reported their legal basis as "other." Fifteen percent of public libraries were operated by nonprofit associations/agencies; this means that they were privately controlled, but met the legal definition of a public library in the states in which they were located.

• Although the majority of public libraries reported single jurisdictions, many belong to broader service networks. Seventy-five percent of public libraries were members of a federation or cooperative service, while 23 percent were not. One percent served as the headquarters of a federation or cooperative service.

Library Services

• In FY 2007 total nationwide circulation of public library materials was 2.2 billion, or 7.4 materials circulated per capita; these were slight increases from the 2.1 billion total materials and 7.3 materials per capita that were circulated during FY 2006. Among the 50 states and the District of Columbia, Ohio had the highest per capita circulation at 15.9, while the District of Columbia had the lowest, at 2.5, during FY 2007.

• The growth in per capita circulation from FY 2006 to FY 2007 was a continuation of the steady growth that has occurred since FY 2000. Per capita circulation grew from 6.4 materials per person to 7.4 materials per person from FY 2000 to FY 2007, an increase of 16 percent.

• Nationwide, 49.9 million library materials were loaned by public libraries to other libraries. This was a 14 percent increase over FY 2006 total (43.7 million).

- Nationwide, reference transactions in public libraries totaled 292 million, or 1.0 reference transactions per capita. This was a small decrease from the 295 million reference transactions that occurred during FY 2006.
- Nationwide, visits to public libraries totaled 1.4 billion, or 4.9 library visits per capita, a small increase from the 4.8 visits per capita that were made during FY 2006. As in the case of per capita circulation, this is a continuation of a larger, longer upward trend. Per capita visitation increased from 4.2 to 4.9 between FY 1998 and FY 2007, an overall increase of 17 percent.
- Ohio had the highest per capita visitation rate at 7.6 visits per person; Mississippi had the lowest at 2.8 visits per person. The states with the highest rates of library visitation were not concentrated in any particular region of the country and included the Pacific Northwest states of Washington and Oregon, the midwestern states of Iowa and Illinois, and the northeastern states of Massachusetts and Vermont. The states with the lowest rates of per capita visitation were mostly clustered in the Southeast.

Children's Services

- Nationwide circulation of children's materials during FY 2007 was 739.7 million, or 34 percent of total circulation. While the absolute number increased from 728.1 million the prior year, the percentage of total circulation that children's circulation composed was basically unchanged from its FY 2006 level of 35 percent. Attendance at children's programs was 59.0 million in FY 2007, up from 57.6 million the prior year.

Electronic Services

- Nationwide, uses of public-use Internet terminals totaled 357 million, or 1.2 uses per capita, in FY 2007. This was a 7 percent increase in total uses from the previous year, but per capita uses remained unchanged.
- Internet terminals available for public use in public libraries nationwide numbered 208,000, or 3.6 per 5,000 people. This represents increases from the previous year's figures of 196,000 total terminals and 3.4 terminals per 5,000 people. The average number of Internet terminals available for public use per stationary outlet was 12.5, a 6 percent increase from FY 2006.
- The increase in the number of Internet PCs per 5,000 people from FY 2006 to FY 2007 continued the longer-term trend of providing more Internet terminals for library patrons. The number of Internet PCs per 5,000 people grew from 1.9 in FY 2000 to 3.6 in FY 2007, an increase of 89 percent.

Collections

- Nationwide, public libraries had 812.5 million print materials in their collections, or 2.8 volumes per capita, in FY 2007. This was a slight increase from the nationwide total of 807.2 million print materials in FY 2006, but the number of volumes per capita remained the same. By state, the number of print materials per capita ranged from 1.5 in Arizona to 5.5 in Maine during FY 2007.

- Public libraries nationwide held 45.9 million audio materials in FY 2007, an 8 percent increase from the previous year. They held 46.3 million video materials in FY 2007, an increase of 6 percent over the previous year.

Staffing

- Public libraries had a total of 145,000 paid full-time-equivalent (FTE) staff in FY 2007, an increase of 5,000 over the previous year. There were 12.4 paid FTE staff persons per 25,000 people in FY 2007, virtually the same number as there were in FY 2006 (12.2 FTE). Library staffing levels were fairly stable during the study time period, ranging from 11.9 (FY 1998) to a high of 12.4 (FY 2007).
- Librarians accounted for 33 percent of total FTE staff; 67 percent were in other positions. More than two-thirds of the librarians—68 percent—had master's degrees from programs of library and information studies accredited by the American Library Association (ALA-MLS degrees).
- Forty-eight percent of all public libraries, or 4,408 libraries, had librarians with ALA-MLS degrees in FY 2007, practically the same percentage as in FY 2006.

Operating Revenue and Expenditures

Operating Revenue

- In FY 2007, 84 percent of public libraries' total operating revenue of $11.0 billion came from local sources, 7 percent from state sources, 0.4 percent from federal sources, and 9 percent from other sources, such as monetary gifts and donations, interest, library fines, fees, and grants.
- FY 2007 total operating revenue grew by 7 percent from the prior year. The percentage distribution of operating revenue sources also changed slightly over the period; state sources fell from 9 percent in FY 2006 to 7 percent in FY 2007, while local sources of revenue became somewhat more prominent, increasing from 82 percent to 84 percent. The share of operating revenue from federal and other sources remained more or less unchanged.
- Nationwide, the average total per capita operating revenue for public libraries was $37.66 in FY 2007. Of that, $31.68 was from local sources, $2.52 was from state sources, $0.16 from federal sources, and $3.29 from other sources.
- Per capita operating revenue from local sources in FY 2007 was under $3.00 for 5 percent of public libraries, $3.00 to $14.99 for 25 percent of libraries, $15.00 to $29.99 for 32 percent of libraries, and $30.00 or more for 38 percent of libraries.

- Since FY 2001, local revenue has composed an increasingly large proportion of overall operating revenues. That year 77 percent of public library operating revenue came from local sources. The local contribution to operating revenue grew to 81.5 percent in FY 2004 and held steady for the next two fiscal years, before increasing to 84 percent in FY 2007. This increase in the proportion of operating revenue from local sources has been paralleled by a decrease in the proportion of funds from state sources. From FY 1998 to FY 2001, the state funding contribution held steady around 12.7 percent, but since FY 2001, the percentage has steadily fallen, down to 6.7 percent in FY 2007. This shift has occurred because of large absolute increases in operating revenue at the local level combined with absolute decreases in funding at the state level. A total of $7.44 billion (in 2007 dollars) came from local sources in FY 2001; by FY 2007 this figure had grown to $9.25 billion. At the same time, $1.22 billion of operating revenues were covered by states in FY 2001, but by FY 2007 this figure had decreased to $740 million. Operating revenue from federal sources (0.6 percent in FY 2001, 0.4 percent in FY 2007) and "other" sources (9.4 percent in FY 2001, 8.7 percent in FY 2007) remained comparatively flat over the same time period.

Operating Expenditures

- Total operating expenditures for public libraries were $10.2 billion in FY 2007, up from $9.6 billion in FY 2006. Of this, 66 percent was expended for paid staff and 13 percent for the library collection. The remaining 21 percent was used on a variety of "other" expenditures.
- Nationwide, the average per capita operating expenditure for public libraries was $34.95. The highest average per capita operating expenditure was $75.12 (District of Columbia), and the lowest was $14.75 (Mississippi).
- Expenditures for library collection materials in electronic format were 11 percent of total operating expenditures for public libraries, up from 10 percent in FY 2006.
- Twenty-five percent of public libraries had operating expenditures of less than $50,000, 42 percent expended $50,000 to $399,999, and 34 percent expended $400,000 or more.
- Per capita operating expenditures have trended upward since FY 1998, rising from $29.66 that year to their FY 2007 level of $34.95, an increase of 18 percent.

State Library Agencies

The following are highlights from the publication *State Library Agencies: Fiscal Year 2008,* released in December 2009 by IMLS.

- State library agencies (StLAs) play important roles in promoting basic literacy in the communities they serve. From 1999 to 2008, more than two-thirds of state library agencies funded literacy programs in public libraries. In 2001, a total of 47 state library agencies funded such programs. During 2002–2007, the number of states funding such programs fluctuated between 39 and 40, before dropping slightly to 38 in 2008.

- In the three most recent data years (2006–2008), all but one state library agency provided financial support to summer reading programs.

- State library agencies fund library services for hard-to-reach populations, from services to persons with physical or learning disabilities to bookmobiles and services for migrant workers and non-English-speakers. The high point for such expenditures during the study period came in 2002–2004, when $49.6–$57.0 million in Library Services and Technology Act (LSTA) funds were spent serving these populations. Since then, LSTA expenditures for such services have dropped off considerably.

- In 2008 state library agencies gave $809 million in financial aid to public libraries; this number was nearly identical to the amount awarded in 1999 ($810 million), but there was much fluctuation in between these two points. By 2000 the figure had risen to $846 million, before reaching a high of $977 million in 2001. By 2004 the figure had fallen to $791 million, and remained in that range until 2007, when it rose to $834 million.

- As part of their role as coordinator of library services in their states, many StLAs purchase database licenses for public libraries, school library media centers, and library cooperatives. In 2008, 50 StLAs bought statewide database licenses for their public libraries, 42 purchased statewide database licenses for school library media centers (elementary and secondary school libraries), and 35 purchased statewide database licenses for library cooperatives.

- State library agencies also facilitate access to the Internet for public libraries. The majority of states do this in a direct manner; in 2008, 29 StLAs provided public libraries with direct funding for Internet access, while 32 states provided libraries with equipment for Internet access. States are moving away from furnishing funds for direct Internet access, however; in 1999, 41 StLAs performed this function, and in 2008 only 29 did.

- All state library agencies provided access to directories, databases, or online catalogs via the Internet in 2008. All 51 StLAs also managed a Web site, file server, bulletin board(s), or electronic mailing list(s) in 2008. In fact, all states have performed these last two functions since 2002.

- State library agencies also facilitate maintenance of and access to public library collections, through digitization efforts and preservation/conservation services. In 2008, 33 StLAs funded or facilitated digitization or digital programs or services to public libraries or library cooperatives. Such measures include any program or activity that provides for the digitization of documents, publications, or sets of records or artifacts to be made available for public use.

- Eighteen StLAs provided collection preservation or conservation services to public libraries, either directly or by contract in 2008.

- The number of continuing education events funded by StLAs increased from just over 3,900 in 1999 to more than 7,100 in 2008, an increase of 82 percent. Attendance at continuing education events rose from just under 96,000 in 1999 to a high of more than 134,000 in 2007, before decreasing to just over 114,000 in 2008. Despite the considerable drop-off from 2007 to 2008, attendance at StLA-funded continuing education events still increased by 19 percent during the study period.

- State library agencies directly provide a diverse range of services to state governments. In 12 states (Alaska, Arizona, California, Connecticut, Florida, Kansas, Kentucky, Nevada, Oklahoma, Tennessee, Texas, and Virginia), the state library agency performed services to at least one of the following: the primary state legislative research organization (4 states); state archives (10 states), state records management services (10 states); state history museum/art gallery (3 states).

- StLAs' revenue was basically the same at the beginning of the study period as it was at the end—$1.19 billion in 1999, and just under $1.20 billion in 2008. Revenues rose dramatically immediately after 1999, reaching the period's high point of $1.40 billion in 2001. Between 2001 and 2004, StLA revenues fell to $1.18 billion, a decrease of 15.7 percent. Since 2004, StLA revenues have fluctuated between $1.15 billion and $1.20 billion.

- The vast majority of the revenues used to run state library agencies come from the states themselves. In 2008, the most recent data year, 83.9 percent of StLA revenues came from states, with 13.4 percent coming from the federal government and 2.8 percent coming from other sources. The lowest share of state contributions to StLA revenue came during 2004, when 81.2 percent of revenues came from the states; the highest came during 2001, when the corresponding percentage was 85.5 percent. The highest year of proportional federal contributions was during 2004, when 15.3 percent of StLA revenues came from federal sources. The lowest was during 2001, when federal contributions accounted for 12.7 percent of StLA revenues.

Academic Libraries

The following are highlights from the First Look publication *Academic Libraries, 2008,* released in December 2009 by NCES.

Services

- During FY 2008, there were about 138.1 million circulation transactions from academic libraries' general collections.

- Academic libraries loaned some 11.1 million documents to other libraries in FY 2008. Academic libraries also borrowed approximately 10.7 million documents from other libraries and commercial services. Documents from commercial services accounted for about 936,000 of the documents borrowed.

- The majority of academic libraries, 2,530, were open between 60 and 99 hours during a typical week in FY 2008. Another 683 academic libraries were open between 40 and 59 hours per typical week, and 532 were open more than 100 hours per typical week.

- During a typical week in the fall of 2008, approximately 1.1 million academic library reference transactions were conducted, including computer searches.

Collections

- At the end of FY 2008, there were 226 academic libraries that held 1 million or more books, serial backfiles, and other paper materials including government documents.
- Academic libraries held approximately 102.5 million e-books and about 3.6 million electronic reference sources and aggregation services at the end of FY 2008.
- In FY 2008 academic libraries added approximately 24.0 million books, serial backfiles, and other paper materials including government documents.

Staff

- Academic libraries reported 93,438 full-time-equivalent (FTE) staff working in academic libraries during the fall of 2008.
- Academic libraries reported 27,030 FTE librarians during the fall of 2008. Librarians accounted for about 29 percent of the total number of FTE staff in academic libraries during the fall of 2008.

Expenditures

- Academic libraries' expenditures totaled approximately $6.8 billion during FY 2008.
- During FY 2008 academic libraries spent about $3.3 billion on salaries and wages, representing approximately 49 percent of total library expenditures.
- Academic libraries spent about $2.7 billion on information resources during FY 2008.
- Academic libraries spent approximately $133.6 million for electronic books, serial backfiles, and other materials in FY 2008.
- Expenditures for electronic current serial subscriptions were about $1.0 billion.
- During FY 2008 academic libraries spent approximately $113.4 million for bibliographic utilities, networks, and consortia.

Electronic Services

- In fall 2008 some 72 percent of academic libraries provided library reference service by e-mail or the Web.
- Nearly half (49 percent) reported providing technology to assist patrons with disabilities in fall 2008.

Information Literacy

- During FY 2008 some 46 percent of academic libraries reported that their postsecondary institution defined information literacy or the information-literate student.
- During FY 2008 about 33 percent of academic libraries reported that their postsecondary institution had incorporated information literacy into its mission.

Educational Technology in Public Schools

The following are highlights from the First Look publication *Educational Technology in Public School Districts,* released in December 2009 by NCES.

- School districts reported information on local area networks connecting computers within a school, district networks connecting schools to the district, and connections to the Internet. Ninety-seven percent of districts had a local area network in all schools and 2 percent had it in some schools. Eighty-one percent of districts provided a district network to all schools, and 3 percent provided it to some schools. Of the districts surveyed, 100 percent of those with a district network were connected to the Internet.
- Districts reported that 92 percent of public schools were connected to a district network. Among these schools, the types of connections from schools to districts included direct fiber (55 percent), T1 or DS1 lines (26 percent), and wireless connections (16 percent).
- Among the 84 percent of districts with a district network, the types of connections from districts to Internet service provider(s) included T1 or DS1 lines (42 percent), direct fiber (37 percent), wireless connections (18 percent), broadband cable (13 percent), and T3 or DS3 lines (12 percent). Direct fiber connections were reported by a larger percentage of city districts than by suburban, town, or rural districts (62 percent versus 49 percent, 46 percent, and 24 percent, respectively). Relatively more rural districts than city districts reported T1 or DS1 connections (51 percent versus 18 percent).
- Sixty-seven percent of districts had a formal computer replacement plan reflected in long-term budget planning. An asset recovery program for computers was used by 37 percent of districts for all computers and by 22 percent for some computers. Districts treated older computers that could no longer serve their original purpose by recycling or disposing of them (91 percent), repurposing them for less-demanding tasks (85 percent), and upgrading memory or components to extend their useful life (83 percent).
- The percentage of districts that offered access to online district resources to all elementary or all secondary teachers was 92 percent. The percentage that offered access to electronic administrative tools to all teachers was 87 percent for elementary and 95 percent for secondary. The percentage that

offered server space for posting Web pages or class materials to all teachers was 82 percent for elementary and 83 percent for secondary.

• The percentage of districts that offered online access to the library catalogue to all students was 72 percent for elementary and 82 percent for secondary. The percentage that offered electronic storage space on a server to all students was 62 percent for elementary and 83 percent for secondary.

• Districts had written policies on acceptable student use of e-mail (84 percent), social networking Web sites (76 percent), wikis and/or blogs (52 percent), and other Internet use (92 percent).

• Districts reported employing an individual responsible for educational technology leadership who was devoted to this role full time (51 percent) or part time (32 percent). Seventeen percent of districts reporting no one in this role, with more small districts than large districts reported no one with this function (21 percent of districts with an enrollment size less than 2,500 compared with 5 percent of districts with an enrollment size of 10,000 or more).

• Districts reported offering teachers professional development in topics such as integrating technology into instruction (95 percent), using Internet resources and communication tools for instruction (91 percent), and Internet safety (89 percent). Fifty-five percent of districts required teachers to take professional development in Internet safety.

• Eighty-three percent of district respondents agreed with the statement "Teachers are interested in using technology in classroom instruction," while 58 percent agreed that "Teachers are sufficiently trained to integrate technology into classroom instruction." Forty-two percent of respondents agreed that "Funding for educational technology is adequate," and 83 percent agreed that "Funding for educational technology is being spent in the most appropriate ways."

Library Acquisition Expenditures, 2008–2009: U.S. Public, Academic, Special, and Government Libraries

The information in these tables is taken from *American Library Directory* (*ALD*) *2009–2010* (Information Today, Inc., 2009). The tables report acquisition expenditures by public, academic, special, and government libraries.

The total number of libraries in the United States and in regions administered by the United States listed in this 62nd edition of *ALD* is 29,670, including 17,093 public libraries, 3,805 academic libraries, 7,616 special libraries, and 1,156 government libraries.

Understanding the Tables

Number of libraries includes only those U.S. libraries in *ALD* that reported annual acquisition expenditures (1,265 public libraries, 548 academic libraries, 105 special libraries, and 30 government libraries). Libraries that reported annual income but not expenditures are not included in the count. Academic libraries include university, college, and junior college libraries. Special academic libraries, such as law and medical libraries, that reported acquisition expenditures separately from the institution's main library are counted as independent libraries.

The amount in the *total acquisition expenditures* column for a given state is generally greater than the sum of the categories of expenditures. This is because the total acquisition expenditures amount also includes the expenditures of libraries that did not itemize by category.

Figures in *categories of expenditure* columns represent only those libraries that itemized expenditures. Libraries that reported a total acquisition expenditure amount but did not itemize are only represented in the total acquisition expenditures column.

Table 1 / Public Library Acquisition Expenditures

State	Number of Libraries	Total Acquisition Expenditures	Books	Other Print Materials	Periodicals/ Serials	Manuscripts & Archives	AV Equipment	AV Materials	Microforms	Electronic Reference	Preservation
Alabama	10	17,488,725	1,082,041	6,541	17,284	0	0	144,841	1,963	21,828	200
Alaska	7	302,429	162,281	7,000	24,889	0	0	23,071	500	16,418	0
Arizona	18	13,386,061	3,564,707	4,779,439	283,471	0	0	2,415,794	50,656	2,238,126	8,868
Arkansas	10	2,762,808	1,892,849	22,064	156,110	0	1,105	386,295	1,640	271,975	8,270
California	51	73,856,036	33,391,998	1,470,789	3,766,576	4,500	0	9,665,718	83,381	7,660,282	85,785
Colorado	26	11,657,120	3,750,258	2,200	429,074	0	17,200	2,297,109	1,081	807,444	264
Connecticut	40	6,863,010	3,313,492	664,448	357,877	0	0	576,402	107,673	987,332	21,489
Delaware	1	93,277	0	0	0	0	0	0	0	0	0
District of Columbia	0	0	0	0	0	0	0	0	0	0	0
Florida	21	29,131,262	13,286,789	535,836	2,325,599	0	0	4,937,237	238,545	1,827,860	0
Georgia	12	9,231,285	2,403,147	1,068	145,535	0	2,026	592,143	990	415,913	1,698
Hawaii	1	5,030,113	0	0	275,320	0	0	0	54,902	1,580,296	0
Idaho	5	374,169	91,323	135	12,006	0	0	9,459	900	5,843	0
Illinois	85	28,878,699	7,994,506	77,327	672,218	10,000	58,720	2,305,901	50,039	2,489,853	14,735
Indiana	56	24,768,857	11,163,934	65,231	1,500,125	0	87,601	3,896,285	157,783	684,103	98,162
Iowa	35	5,553,568	1,215,593	18,937	138,368	0	11,025	348,022	668	92,023	0
Kansas	26	7,680,786	2,357,435	138,997	812,631	0	23,600	801,687	2,950	649,324	400
Kentucky	17	4,069,657	1,803,954	2,486	78,438	0	15,329	685,422	13,685	323,207	0
Louisiana	7	6,307,976	2,437,122	5,000	299,118	3,000	77,168	797,547	54,882	544,823	0
Maine	23	1,203,947	598,588	1,000	155,372	2,000	5,350	84,280	1,200	198,780	1,000
Maryland	2	3,057,536	1,832,335	0	115,097	0	0	908,338	0	201,766	0
Massachusetts	63	15,607,907	2,419,716	54,600	271,844	0	2,036	721,004	11,824	342,959	3,200
Michigan	50	20,389,083	6,581,011	3,653	453,027	0	30,000	1,542,037	23,500	750,630	12,673
Minnesota	27	16,685,762	4,595,455	3,045	185,747	0	2,000	1,338,244	5,406	477,305	968

State											
Mississippi	8	3,799,584	394,010	0	15,512	0	0	145,058	6,014	1,419,207	0
Missouri	27	18,569,579	2,099,519	0	180,934	0	21,197	615,995	1,058	792,466	4,523
Montana	11	636,975	360,880	6,491	79,881	0	5,500	121,797	1,000	39,761	1,500
Nebraska	19	1,584,248	822,853	368,663	11,308	278	47	22,591	40	197,302	96
Nevada	4	215,285	128,500	1,193	10,558	0	0	19,634	200	20,000	0
New Hampshire	52	2,667,153	1,001,670	2,500	144,772	0	3,328	244,589	31,642	120,181	12,550
New Jersey	53	55,909,045	8,849,322	75,919	1,017,865	0	2,500	2,170,691	115,000	1,390,185	18,500
New Mexico	4	854,164	646,372	427	53,122	0	0	106,571	11,799	35,873	0
New York	80	28,087,774	13,849,933	357,406	1,287,820	3,000	70,588	2,701,813	46,593	1,591,056	7,028
North Carolina	17	9,500,712	6,497,358	1,125,765	203,382	0	1,200	607,745	9,040	586,267	0
North Dakota	12	1,149,137	383,694	59,085	57,284	0	2,000	48,566	3,000	46,527	1,000
Ohio	44	49,483,300	18,454,537	23,830	3,660,378	1,031	134,787	9,268,061	539,127	6,532,172	383,438
Oklahoma	8	11,021,027	5,012,907	2,647	833,193	0	0	1,296,142	4,300	776,963	0
Oregon	28	3,320,554	1,770,214	13,352	208,443	0	0	291,819	5,647	157,835	0
Pennsylvania	49	10,078,402	4,204,184	253,211	1,114,558	0	34,208	1,044,681	517,193	997,742	189,582
Rhode Island	5	487,258	304,709	5,673	41,236	0	0	76,874	0	55,266	3,500
South Carolina	11	9,674,357	5,136,775	3,343	67,269	5,000	7,500	1,314,243	0	718,207	10,832
South Dakota	14	1,739,678	839,750	0	89,838	0	0	264,814	50	115,387	0
Tennessee	15	6,216,908	2,777,841	0	155,306	0	10,100	273,861	1,200	232,822	1,657
Texas	64	24,133,910	10,201,324	424,883	1,090,943	0	272,155	2,204,054	62,423	1,558,587	9,895
Utah	8	4,341,069	1,344,887	1,203	97,363	245,000	0	484,110	30,367	108,754	72,000
Vermont	34	973,118	353,617	221	20,381	0	0	40,396	276	17,797	500
Virginia	21	8,442,516	3,476,357	14,962	507,655	6,278	0	1,305,706	36,651	635,210	4,800
Washington	22	30,944,587	2,668,713	490,238	98,941	0	54,230	644,065	4,100	510,158	900
West Virginia	11	3,266,972	1,074,760	1,000	43,280	9,000	24,000	133,196	0	729,233	0
Wisconsin	43	6,237,608	3,259,335	8,822	178,944	0	456	991,509	9,920	570,352	1,200
Wyoming	8	706,650	384,571	0	45,106	0	6,000	69,384	55	28,074	0
Puerto Rico	0	0	0	0	0	0	0	0	0	0	0
Total	1,265	598,421,643	202,237,126	11,100,630	23,790,998	289,087	982,956	60,984,801	2,300,863	42,571,474	981,213
Estimated % of Acquisition Expenditures			33.80	1.85	3.98	0.05	0.16	10.19	0.38	7.11	0.16

421

Table 2 / Academic Library Acquisition Expenditures

State	Number of Libraries	Total Acquisition Expenditures	Books	Other Print Materials	Periodicals/ Serials	Manuscripts & Archives	AV Equipment	AV Materials	Microforms	Electronic Reference	Preservation
					Categories of Expenditure (in U.S. dollars)						
Alabama	10	12,106,942	1,333,266	4,017	3,896,030	0	10,000	94,548	133,535	824,874	94,014
Alaska	4	4,895,613	360,433	0	846,408	0	300	59,887	14,307	888,392	18,827
Arizona	6	1,276,290	510,192	8,235	298,120	0	3,465	68,347	26,131	288,791	6,009
Arkansas	6	11,601,443	1,646,915	0	6,624,194	0	0	94,323	180,909	2,960,144	94,958
California	42	62,633,499	8,040,344	537,034	12,413,755	2,000	34,578	333,242	299,837	7,106,579	415,724
Colorado	11	25,028,946	3,241,544	899,571	9,546,870	0	0	77,040	935	8,241,363	69,462
Connecticut	9	7,430,707	1,725,974	358	3,606,705	0	0	146,378	122,980	1,382,769	88,965
Delaware	1	48,419	40,000	0	8,419	0	0	0	0	0	0
District of Columbia	3	11,350,148	1,959,391	0	5,999,323	0	0	7,468	75,165	1,004,179	94,154
Florida	19	20,823,144	3,724,299	360,609	9,013,743	0	0	415,193	179,345	5,773,181	256,711
Georgia	10	11,241,653	740,616	0	1,408,311	0	0	94,373	81,870	1,068,437	43,202
Hawaii	0	0	0	0	0	0	0	0	0	0	0
Idaho	4	9,428,579	832,363	0	3,584,197	2,470	0	28,897	0	879,501	56,780
Illinois	28	35,804,020	2,557,927	9,966	4,927,065	0	33,598	323,966	51,390	2,670,403	166,123
Indiana	15	21,988,239	3,575,800	24,211	12,783,058	0	8,952	153,006	31,328	1,497,322	90,635
Iowa	14	24,379,104	3,217,846	264,492	12,943,524	0	31,139	72,711	39,578	2,496,492	143,699
Kansas	7	863,767	281,665	22,000	196,096	0	5,918	9,465	3,500	303,469	375
Kentucky	13	21,198,377	2,069,121	11,300	9,338,187	32,109	2,825	119,492	193,222	4,674,389	203,176
Louisiana	7	4,905,861	505,811	33,426	3,275,170	3,427	3,720	6,199	68,382	863,339	36,718
Maine	2	3,653,112	1,052,979	0	2,285,741	0	0	34,164	0	251,231	28,997
Maryland	9	8,587,386	608,001	9,286	2,607,080	11,983	0	55,665	15,748	549,302	51,755
Massachusetts	17	164,747,414	2,058,338	47,407	3,477,123	0	57,000	167,169	10,042	7,865,901	97,348
Michigan	12	17,369,383	2,116,176	64,011	5,498,255	20,000	6,778	130,939	114,070	4,998,636	141,971
Minnesota	11	7,312,389	1,635,168	0	3,145,998	0	25,375	127,116	38,099	1,401,340	70,049

State											
Mississippi	2	476,289	74,104	0	146,629	0	0	11,050	0	84,006	10,500
Missouri	15	10,213,379	762,592	0	2,442,816	3,863	10,223	116,812	125,636	568,237	57,042
Montana	2	84,680	32,067	0	17,184	0	0	7,069	0	15,000	0
Nebraska	6	11,634,714	474,146	101,451	2,124,750	0	34,909	127,515	82,297	480,368	58,695
Nevada	0	0	0	0	0	0	0	0	0	0	0
New Hampshire	3	7,369,284	1,012,724	0	3,980,222	0	0	0	20,416	1,189,794	71,271
New Jersey	10	7,161,236	1,402,166	71,023	1,796,058	0	0	58,800	83,376	1,339,234	22,619
New Mexico	4	1,126,450	44,000	0	1,700	0	20,000	24,000	0	5,000	0
New York	37	98,241,095	9,618,515	338,780	15,984,001	29,390	140,338	506,370	214,310	12,630,323	386,120
North Carolina	18	35,436,565	9,115,078	14,548	17,734,904	2,300	9,810	364,710	235,379	1,178,762	103,358
North Dakota	3	4,721,383	334,210	0	2,057,007	0	0	22,734	684	989,749	22,732
Ohio	23	21,641,405	4,222,142	29,193	6,960,024	2,461	9,813	195,297	149,333	3,343,673	231,330
Oklahoma	7	4,085,094	609,648	56,186	2,355,978	2,000	0	145,430	0	86,137	5,850
Oregon	12	17,190,144	1,224,008	3,104	3,909,936	0	47,564	96,511	0	1,277,808	95,375
Pennsylvania	20	11,300,812	1,951,423	9,500	4,565,256	1,314	22,960	116,179	147,604	1,520,303	69,135
Rhode Island	5	6,089,745	619,357	2,100	956,593	9,500	55,407	44,958	21,021	566,652	23,538
South Carolina	10	5,144,778	688,719	108,196	1,126,281	20,000	5,000	60,905	97,945	1,157,288	52,623
South Dakota	4	3,400,979	283,332	0	665,928	0	1,950	14,475	12,509	617,698	18,765
Tennessee	10	17,740,472	826,491	300	1,754,985	0	0	69,545	57,828	2,456,405	18,023
Texas	30	52,038,011	9,464,484	18,140	18,753,243	0	13,000	209,199	262,724	3,196,068	247,197
Utah	3	1,144,673	437,900	0	478,773	0	1,000	66,500	3,500	157,000	0
Vermont	5	1,735,964	434,918	0	770,312	3,000	5,000	39,960	2,477	342,066	10,500
Virginia	20	31,501,965	6,104,988	618,144	12,049,753	2,000	40,536	211,343	113,825	5,392,185	99,466
Washington	11	8,839,356	1,442,503	11,644	5,075,788	0	4,000	104,130	30,413	823,486	7,228
West Virginia	9	1,285,873	316,578	11,741	353,110	12,696	19,000	38,013	35,507	493,688	3,071
Wisconsin	12	8,831,742	2,459,869	8,095	5,429,669	0	26,153	106,717	74,554	659,141	60,548
Wyoming	2	7,344,506	3,458,937	0	2,201,321	0	0	13,200	0	863,481	0
Puerto Rico	5	5,691,238	654,121	1,000	4,454,122	5,000	18,227	32,638	0	514,235	9,500
Total	548	870,146,267	101,903,189	3,699,068	235,869,715	165,513	708,538	5,423,648	3,451,711	99,937,821	3,954,138
Estimated % of Acquisition Expenditures		11.71	0.43	27.11	0.02	0.08	0.62	0.40	11.49	0.45	

Table 3 / Special Library Acquisition Expenditures

State	Number of Libraries	Total Acquisition Expenditures	Books	Other Print Materials	Periodicals/ Serials	Manuscripts & Archives	AV Equipment	AV Materials	Microforms	Electronic Reference	Preservation
										Categories of Expenditure (in U.S. dollars)	
Alabama	1	1,375	250	0	525	0	0	0	0	500	100
Alaska	0	0	0	0	0	0	0	0	0	0	0
Arizona	4	20,324	0	0	0	0	0	0	0	0	0
Arkansas	0	0	0	0	0	0	0	0	0	0	0
California	8	347,298	46,398	1,000	164,059	0	2,500	1,100	0	24,741	7,500
Colorado	0	0	0	0	0	0	0	0	0	0	0
Connecticut	0	0	0	0	0	0	0	0	0	0	0
Delaware	0	0	0	0	0	0	0	0	0	0	0
District of Columbia	3	877,714	124,027	0	57,110	0	0	261	25,000	13,000	504,877
Florida	5	78,300	42,150	1,000	27,200	0	0	0	0	5,000	2,100
Georgia	0	0	0	0	0	0	0	0	0	0	0
Hawaii	0	0	0	0	0	0	0	0	0	0	0
Idaho	0	0	0	0	0	0	0	0	0	0	0
Illinois	9	2,731,891	95,910	500	138,181	200	1,900	1,000	1,500	72,000	4,700
Indiana	1	3,075	275	0	120	500	0	0	680	0	1,500
Iowa	2	203,058	35,362	0	12,408	0	0	0	155,288	0	0
Kansas	2	12,581	4,400	4,000	4,081	0	0	0	0	0	100
Kentucky	0	0	0	0	0	0	0	0	0	0	0
Louisiana	0	0	0	0	0	0	0	0	0	0	0
Maine	1	200	0	0	0	0	0	0	0	0	0
Maryland	3	166,950	23,150	0	130,450	50	0	0	0	12,000	100
Massachusetts	3	81,891	0	0	0	0	0	0	0	0	0
Michigan	1	12,000	3,000	500	3,600	0	0	400	0	0	0
Minnesota	2	54,850	21,350	5,000	11,500	0	0	1,000	0	16,000	0

State											
Mississippi	0	0	0	0	0	0	0	0	0	0	0
Missouri	2	68,745	24,000	0	30,145	0	0	0	600	14,000	0
Montana	1	17,348	15,848	0	0	0	0	0	0	1,500	0
Nebraska	1	2,000	800	0	1,200	0	0	0	0	0	0
Nevada	0	0	0	0	0	0	0	0	0	0	0
New Hampshire	2	69,000	16,000	2,000	4,000	15,000	0	0	0	22,000	9,000
New Jersey	3	39,100	17,000	0	10,900	0	0	6,000	0	2,200	3,000
New Mexico	1	2,600	0	300	500	0	500	0	0	0	1,300
New York	14	364,181	71,547	2,050	28,220	20,000	727	2,462	1,000	1,475	8,200
North Carolina	0	0	0	0	0	0	0	0	0	0	0
North Dakota	1	8,098	2,660	0	3,975	0	0	0	0	0	1,463
Ohio	9	1,606,083	138,643	550	672,538	1,200	150	501	500	775,108	12,293
Oklahoma	3	101,050	15,000	1,250	36,800	12,000	20,000	1,000	3,000	12,000	0
Oregon	1	600	200	0	0	0	0	0	0	400	0
Pennsylvania	6	483,061	44,827	68,798	87,355	30,238	0	13,602	10,000	202,965	19,376
Rhode Island	1	75,313	44,726	0	5,000	15,387	0	0	0	0	10,200
South Carolina	1	29,600	14,000	0	5,000	0	0	6,000	3,000	0	0
South Dakota	0	0	0	0	0	0	0	0	0	0	0
Tennessee	0	0	0	0	0	0	0	0	0	0	0
Texas	5	809,759	44,337	31,992	15,859	0	1,474	1,587	0	10,000	0
Utah	1	75,000	5,000	5,000	10,000	0	5,000	0	0	50,000	0
Vermont	0	0	0	0	0	0	0	0	0	0	0
Virginia	4	374,910	99,159	12,600	48,530	40,373	48,265	5,380	3,000	27,975	89,628
Washington	1	1,500	0	0	0	0	0	0	0	0	0
West Virginia	1	11,000	4,000	0	5,000	0	0	500	0	1,500	0
Wisconsin	2	128,400	11,200	0	74,000	0	0	0	0	43,000	0
Wyoming	0	0	0	0	0	0	0	0	0	0	0
Total	105	8,858,855	965,219	136,540	1,588,256	134,948	80,516	40,793	203,568	1,307,364	675,437
Estimated % of Acquisition Expenditures			10.9	1.54	17.93	1.52	0.91	0.46	2.30	14.76	7.62

425

Table 4 / Government Library Acquisition Expenditures

State	Number of Libraries	Total Acquisition Expenditures	Books	Other Print Materials	Periodicals/ Serials	Manuscripts & Archives	AV Equipment	AV Materials	Microforms	Electronic Reference	Preservation
					Categories of Expenditure (in U.S. dollars)						
Alabama	2	626,295	243,777	0	575	0	0	0	0	381,472	471
Alaska	0	0	0	0	0	0	0	0	0	0	0
Arizona	0	0	0	0	0	0	0	0	0	0	0
Arkansas	0	0	0	0	0	0	0	0	0	0	0
California	8	2,523,766	792,275	177,758	493,722	0	7,472	38	9,804	319,789	4,432
Colorado	0	0	0	0	0	0	0	0	0	0	0
Connecticut	0	0	0	0	0	0	0	0	0	0	0
Delaware	0	0	0	0	0	0	0	0	0	0	0
District of Columbia	0	0	0	0	0	0	0	0	0	0	0
Florida	1	19,545	3,750	0	14,170	0	0	1,625	0	0	0
Georgia	0	0	0	0	0	0	0	0	0	0	0
Hawaii	0	0	0	0	0	0	0	0	0	0	0
Idaho	0	0	0	0	0	0	0	0	0	0	0
Illinois	0	0	0	0	0	0	0	0	0	0	0
Indiana	0	0	0	0	0	0	0	0	0	0	0
Iowa	0	0	0	0	0	0	0	0	0	0	0
Kansas	2	827,975	306,783	0	330,366	0	0	0	0	185,543	5,283
Kentucky	0	0	0	0	0	0	0	0	0	0	0
Louisiana	2	1,042,318	28,500	0	123,000	0	500	1,000	0	15,000	0
Maine	0	0	0	0	0	0	0	0	0	0	0
Maryland	3	8,909,000	273,000	21,800	6,103,000	0	0	7,700	0	2,500,000	3,500
Massachusetts	1	78,000	0	0	0	0	0	0	0	0	0
Michigan	1	35,000	0	0	0	0	0	0	0	0	0
Minnesota	1	60,000	8,000	0	16,000	0	0	0	0	36,000	0

State											
Mississippi	1	2,500	0	0	0	0	0	0	0	0	0
Missouri	0	0	0	0	0	0	0	0	0	0	0
Montana	1	425,961	328,391	0	0	0	0	0	0	97,570	0
Nebraska	0	0	0	0	0	0	0	0	0	0	0
Nevada	1	768,769	562,656	0	10,803	0	0	0	3,151	186,357	5,802
New Hampshire	0	0	0	0	0	0	0	0	0	0	0
New Jersey	0	0	0	0	0	0	0	0	0	0	0
New Mexico	0	0	0	0	0	0	0	0	0	0	0
New York	0	0	0	0	0	0	0	0	0	0	0
North Carolina	0	0	0	0	0	0	0	0	0	0	0
North Dakota	0	0	0	0	0	0	0	0	0	0	0
Ohio	1	69,800	24,000	0	17,600	0	7,500	1,000	0	2,500	0
Oklahoma	0	0	0	0	0	0	0	0	0	0	0
Oregon	0	0	0	0	0	0	0	0	0	0	0
Pennsylvania	3	468,000	0	0	0	0	0	0	0	0	0
Rhode Island	1	43,425	9,961	0	31,764	0	0	814	886	0	0
South Carolina	0	0	0	0	0	0	0	0	0	0	0
South Dakota	0	0	0	0	0	0	0	0	0	0	0
Tennessee	1	125,000	0	0	0	0	0	0	0	0	0
Texas	0	0	0	0	0	0	0	0	0	0	0
Utah	0	0	0	0	0	0	0	0	0	0	0
Vermont	0	0	0	0	0	0	0	0	0	0	0
Virginia	1	63,090	13,355	0	42,453	0	0	6,271	0	1,011	0
Washington	0	0	0	0	0	0	0	0	0	0	0
West Virginia	1	275,000	5,000	0	120,000	0	0	0	0	150,000	0
Wisconsin	0	0	0	0	0	0	0	0	0	0	0
Wyoming	0	0	0	0	0	0	0	0	0	0	0
Puerto Rico	0	0	0	0	0	0	0	0	0	0	0
Total	30	15,737,149	2,355,671	199,558	7,302,878	0	15,472	18,448	12,955	3,494,656	19,017
Estimated % of Acquisition Expenditures			14.97	1.27	46.41	0.00	0.10	0.12	0.08	22.21	0.12

Public Library State Rankings, 2007

State	Library Visits per Capita*	Reference Transactions per Capita	Circulation Transactions per Capita	Interlibrary Loans per 1,000 Population	Internet Terminals per Outlet
Alabama	45	27	46	32	13
Alaska	28	50	33	27	49
Arizona	39	38	28	45	3
Arkansas	46	43	44	44	39
California	37	28	40	24	14
Colorado	13	11	6	22	10
Connecticut	4	7	15	15	23
Delaware	21	44	11	12	18
District of Columbia***	43	5	51	50	28
Florida	36	3	37	38	1
Georgia	41	18	45	29	8
Hawaii	33	42	41	51	35
Idaho	16	34	17	25	38
Illinois	6	8	16	6	29
Indiana	3	19	3	35	5
Iowa	11	45	12	19	46
Kansas	9	9	7	11	41
Kentucky	35	33	32	40	11
Louisiana	47	12	48	34	21
Maine	18	40	25	9	48
Maryland	27	10	13	31	2
Massachusetts	14	26	20	4	34
Michigan	25	22	24	7	12
Minnesota	23	20	9	13	27
Mississippi	51	49	50	47	37
Missouri	24	14	14	26	20
Montana	34	51	34	16	42
Nebraska	2	24	10	33	44
Nevada	42	47	36	36	25
New Hampshire	26	46	21	18	51
New Jersey	22	17	30	14	17
New Mexico	32	23	35	42	30
New York	17	4	23	8	24
North Carolina	38	6	38	49	6
North Dakota	31	35	27	17	47
Ohio	1	1	1	5	9
Oklahoma	30	32	29	41	32
Oregon	10	31	2	2	33
Pennsylvania	40	41	39	10	31
Rhode Island	20	29	31	3	19
South Carolina	44	15	42	43	7
South Dakota	19	37	22	23	45
Tennessee	48	39	49	48	26
Texas	49	36	43	39	4
Utah	5	2	4	46	22
Vermont	7	30	26	20	50

State	Library Visits per Capita*	Reference Transactions per Capita	Circulation Transactions per Capita	Interlibrary Loans per 1,000 Population	Internet Terminals per Outlet
Virginia	29	21	18	37	16
Washington	12	16	5	30	15
West Virginia	50	48	47	28	43
Wisconsin	15	25	8	1	36
Wyoming	8	13	19	21	40

State	Internet Terminals per 5,000 Population**	Book and Serial Volumes per Capita	Audio Materials per 1,000 Population	Video Materials per 1,000 Population	Current Serials (Print) Subscriptions per 1,000 Population
Alabama	12	40	41	43	49
Alaska	25	18	22	6	11
Arizona	46	51	45	41	47
Arkansas	41	39	48	47	42
California	49	43	46	42	46
Colorado	22	36	19	16	29
Connecticut	16	10	11	7	15
Delaware	47	37	34	27	22
District of Columbia***	48	19	37	35	18
Florida	35	49	36	30	38
Georgia	37	48	51	50	51
Hawaii	50	31	42	46	40
Idaho	20	23	24	29	34
Illinois	23	16	6	11	8
Indiana	4	9	2	2	7
Iowa	5	11	10	9	3
Kansas	6	5	13	3	9
Kentucky	31	42	38	39	36
Louisiana	9	30	47	33	20
Maine	7	1	18	8	13
Maryland	38	32	25	32	28
Massachusetts	26	3	14	13	16
Michigan	10	22	17	24	26
Minnesota	19	25	23	26	27
Mississippi	33	44	50	48	45
Missouri	14	20	26	28	14
Montana	17	24	33	31	32
Nebraska	2	2	7	14	5
Nevada	51	50	29	25	44
New Hampshire	21	7	15	12	2
New Jersey	27	17	27	21	24
New Mexico	18	26	30	36	23
New York	30	15	3	18	6
North Carolina	32	47	49	51	43
North Dakota	13	12	28	23	19
Ohio	11	14	1	1	1
Oklahoma	29	38	40	45	41

State	Internet Terminals per 5,000 Population**	Book and Serial Volumes per Capita	Audio Materials per 1,000 Population	Video Materials per 1,000 Population	Current Serials (Print) Subscriptions per 1,000 Population
Oregon	36	27	12	19	30
Pennsylvania	44	34	16	34	33
Rhode Island	15	13	31	17	25
South Carolina	34	41	44	40	35
South Dakota	3	8	20	15	17
Tennessee	43	45	35	49	50
Texas	40	46	43	44	48
Utah	45	33	5	20	31
Vermont	1	4	8	4	4
Virginia	39	35	32	38	37
Washington	28	29	21	22	21
West Virginia	42	28	39	37	39
Wisconsin	24	21	9	5	10
Wyoming	8	6	4	10	12

State	Paid FTE Staff per 25,000 Population	Paid FTE Librarians per 25,000 Population	ALA-MLS Librarians per 25,000 Population	Other Paid FTE Staff per 25,000 Population	Total Operating Income per Capita
Alabama	40	31	42	42	47
Alaska	29	30	26	27	14
Arizona	44	46	33	36	37
Arkansas	45	44	50	37	45
California	47	48	25	41	28
Colorado	14	27	15	10	7
Connecticut	8	7	2	11	9
Delaware	42	32	39	43	31
District of Columbia***	6	10	1	5	1
Florida	41	43	23	33	25
Georgia	49	51	36	39	43
Hawaii	34	38	11	28	41
Idaho	27	36	48	18	35
Illinois	4	16	9	3	4
Indiana	3	11	8	2	12
Iowa	19	3	30	38	29
Kansas	5	1	18	12	13
Kentucky	28	13	40	40	27
Louisiana	23	22	32	23	18
Maine	16	6	14	29	30
Maryland	15	14	16	15	10
Massachusetts	18	9	5	24	19
Michigan	24	25	12	21	16
Minnesota	30	34	21	25	22
Mississippi	35	20	51	47	51
Missouri	10	33	35	6	17
Montana	43	23	46	50	44

State	Paid FTE Staff per 25,000 Population	Paid FTE Librarians per 25,000 Population	ALA-MLS Librarians per 25,000 Population	Other Paid FTE Staff per 25,000 Population	Total Operating Income per Capita
Nebraska	12	8	28	19	21
Nevada	33	49	43	17	24
New Hampshire	9	2	10	32	20
New Jersey	11	28	6	9	5
New Mexico	32	26	31	35	36
New York	7	15	4	7	3
North Carolina	46	50	34	34	42
North Dakota	39	19	45	49	46
Ohio	1	12	7	1	2
Oklahoma	36	24	37	45	38
Oregon	26	35	19	16	11
Pennsylvania	37	40	24	31	39
Rhode Island	13	17	3	13	15
South Carolina	38	41	22	30	40
South Dakota	22	18	44	26	34
Tennessee	51	47	49	48	50
Texas	50	45	38	46	48
Utah	31	42	41	22	33
Vermont	20	5	27	44	32
Virginia	25	39	17	14	26
Washington	17	37	13	8	8
West Virginia	48	29	47	51	49
Wisconsin	21	21	20	20	23
Wyoming	2	4	29	4	6

State	State Operating Income per Capita	Local Operating Income per Capita	Other Income per Capita	Operating Expenditures per Capita	Collection Expenditures per Capita
Alabama	28	45	31	46	47
Alaska	31	12	34	15	29
Arizona	45	31	45	38	31
Arkansas	99	42	42	47	43
California	27	25	30	25	40
Colorado	48	6	10	11	9
Connecticut	37	9	5	6	12
Delaware	8	35	18	30	27
District of Columbia***	51	1	50	1	1
Florida	18	23	41	31	28
Georgia	9	47	48	44	46
Hawaii	1	51	35	41	42
Idaho	34	33	17	39	41
Illinois	13	3	9	4	4
Indiana	10	14	13	8	3
Iowa	32	26	24	24	19
Kansas	21	11	11	14	14
Kentucky	19	27	22	36	32

State	State Operating Income per Capita	Local Operating Income per Capita	Other Income per Capita	Operating Expenditures per Capita	Collection Expenditures per Capita
Louisiana	17	18	19	27	39
Maine	43	37	3	26	38
Maryland	5	17	6	12	6
Massachusetts	23	20	16	16	13
Michigan	29	13	23	18	21
Minnesota	26	22	21	20	26
Mississippi	11	50	39	51	50
Missouri	36	16	14	21	7
Montana	38	40	36	45	44
Nebraska	39	19	25	23	17
Nevada	24	36	2	32	15
New Hampshire	49	15	20	17	23
New Jersey	30	2	26	5	8
New Mexico	20	34	32	34	24
New York	12	4	1	3	10
North Carolina	16	41	43	42	45
North Dakota	25	44	28	43	37
Ohio	2	10	7	2	2
Oklahoma	33	32	49	37	35
Oregon	42	8	15	10	18
Pennsylvania	4	46	12	35	34
Rhode Island	3	28	8	13	22
South Carolina	14	39	46	40	33
South Dakota	47	30	33	33	30
Tennessee	46	48	47	49	51
Texas	44	43	51	48	48
Utah	40	29	38	29	16
Vermont	50	38	4	28	36
Virginia	15	24	40	22	20
Washington	41	5	29	7	5
West Virginia	6	49	44	50	49
Wisconsin	35	21	37	19	25
Wyoming	7	7	27	9	11

State	Staff Expenditures per Capita	Salary and Wages Expenditures per Capita	Average Rank	Rank of Ranks
Alabama	45	43	37.95	43
Alaska	14	17	24.86	25
Arizona	39	39	38.50	45
Arkansas	48	48	46.50	51
California	26	29	34.55	38
Colorado	13	12	16.64	11
Connecticut	5	3	10.77	5
Delaware	30	31	29.05	30
District of Columbia***	1	1	21.00	21

State	Staff Expenditures per Capita	Salary and Wages Expenditures per Capita	Average Rank	Rank of Ranks
Florida	32	34	30.68	33
Georgia	43	44	39.86	46
Hawaii	38	26	36.23	41
Idaho	36	35	29.95	31
Illinois	7	5	9.55	3
Indiana	10	10	8.77	2
Iowa	22	22	20.86	20
Kansas	17	15	12.05	7
Kentucky	41	41	31.95	35
Louisiana	33	33	27.50	29
Maine	25	23	21.68	22
Maryland	12	13	17.23	12
Massachusetts	15	9	16.23	9
Michigan	20	20	19.59	16
Minnesota	19	18	22.55	24
Mississippi	51	51	43.68	49
Missouri	24	25	20.18	18
Montana	44	45	36.91	42
Nebraska	23	24	18.23	14
Nevada	31	30	32.77	37
New Hampshire	16	14	20.27	19
New Jersey	4	6	16.18	8
New Mexico	34	38	30.50	32
New York	3	4	10.05	4
North Carolina	42	42	38.00	44
North Dakota	46	46	32.68	36
Ohio	2	2	4.32	1
Oklahoma	37	36	36.18	40
Oregon	11	16	19.50	15
Pennsylvania	35	37	31.64	34
Rhode Island	9	11	16.27	10
South Carolina	40	40	34.91	39
South Dakota	29	28	26.50	26
Tennessee	49	49	46.18	50
Texas	47	47	43.05	48
Utah	28	32	27.00	28
Vermont	27	27	22.36	23
Virginia	21	21	26.64	27
Washington	8	8	17.50	13
West Virginia	50	50	41.95	47
Wisconsin	18	19	19.68	17
Wyoming	6	7	11.82	6

FTE = full-time equivalent

* Per capita is based on the unduplicated population of legal service areas.

** Average number of public-use terminals per 5,000 population.

***The District of Columbia, while not a state, is included in the state rankings. Special care should be taken in comparing the data to state data.

Source: Compiled by Julia C. Miller from *Public Libraries Survey Fiscal Year 2007*, Institute of Museum and Library Services (2009).

Library Buildings 2009: The Constant Library

Bette-Lee Fox

Managing Editor, *Library Journal*

Can it be only two years, as Alan Jay Lerner once wrote, "since the whole [economic] rigmarole began"? Yet libraries have weathered to varying degrees the unreliability of funding, especially with regard to programming, materials, and hours. Money earmarked years ago is seeing construction through to conclusion; state support has helped out in some cases, defaulted in others. Private contributions seem to have fallen in the wake of personal concerns.

Lots of environmental features are included in this year's 170 public library and 40 academic library building projects. All were completed between July 1, 2008, and June 30, 2009.

Despite the economy, the larger focus remains the constancy of the library as a place for learning and entertainment, for bringing individuals—readers, students, researchers, gamers, dreamers—together in a space created just for them, the heart of a community, a campus, a landscape.

This year's expenditures on public and academic projects totaled more than $1.1 billion. The following are some noteworthy examples.

The new Tanimura and Antle Family Memorial Library at California State University, Monterey Bay, addresses "the challenges of building in a fragile world while creating a beautiful and functional learning environment." At the U.S. Military Academy at West Point, New York, the architects were given the responsibility of "provid[ing] new structures that equal the high standards established by its historic buildings."

The Hyman Forum at Goucher College Athenaeum in Maryland is a performance space "whose character changes from day to day—and sometimes hour to hour." The renovated space at Duke University's Perkins Library in Durham, North Carolina, the 24,000 square foot learning center called The Link, "dazzles everyone who walks in."

The main branch of the Yuma County (Arizona) Library has so much natural illumination that some staff "have yet to turn the lights on" in their offices. The Kendale Lakes Branch, Miami, Florida, has a 24-foot-high corridor that "connects the pedestrian-friendly main entrance to a county-run park." The Pinecrest Branch Library in Florida is on the site of the former Parrot Jungle tourist attraction, and is said to combine "modern architecture with old-world charm."

The German Township Branch of St. Joseph County Public Library in Indiana "emulates a whimsical cottage in the woods," while the Oldham County Public Library in Kentucky "was designed to replicate a park lodge." The Finksburg Branch Library in Maryland is shaped "to fit into the undulating edge of the wetlands." The Saddlebrook Joint-Use Facility in Omaha "embodies the philosophy of lifelong learning and fitness."

The Arkansas Studies Institute, Little Rock, melds 1882 and 1914 buildings in "a new 21st-century structure [to] function as one entity." The original librari-

Adapted from *Library Journal,* December 2009.

an of the Guilford Free Library in Connecticut (built 1933) still volunteers in its refurbished Historical Room; she's 101 years old. An interactive learning center at Waukegan Public Library in Illinois "reinforces the parent as the child's first 'teacher.'" The McPherson Public Library in Kansas has eight stained-glass windows. The Leland Township Public Library in Michigan worked with existing space to "totally reinvent itself." What could be more timely than the unveiling of the new Kansas City (Missouri) Public Library business and career center? The Flesh Public Library in Piqua, Ohio, moved to a renovated 1891 hotel that "hosted presidential speeches . . . a civil rights sit-in . . . and the end of Prohibition in Piqua."

Whether new or reconditioned, historic Carnegie or more contemporary, shooting for LEED "green building" certification or not, this year's library projects have one thing in common: establishing themselves as the flagship, hub, oasis, crossroads, anchor, intersection, civic presence, fabric, destination, living room, and "important campus place" to the constituents of their communities and institutions while meeting the needs and sensibilities of 21st-century library service.

Table 1 / New Academic Library Buildings, 2009

Institution	Project Cost	Gross Square Feet	Square Foot Cost	Construction Cost	Equipment Cost	Book Capacity	Architect
Mathewson-IGT Knowledge Center, University of Nevada, Reno	$107,512,000	296,766	$266.29	$79,026,000	$15,903,000	2,100,000	Hershenow + Klippenstein; Dekker/Perich/Sabatini
Learning Commons, Harrisburg University of Science and Technology, PA	73,000,000	373,173	167.48	62,500,000	10,500,000	10,500	Burt, Hill
Tanimura and Antle Family Memorial Library, California State University, Monterey Bay	69,500,000	136,150	427.43	58,194,000	4,228,000	152,000	EHDD Architecture
Jefferson Hall Library and Learning Center, U.S. Military Academy at West Point	62,000,000	141,000	312.06	44,000,000	12,000,000	700,000	Holzman Moss Architecture STV Inc.
Athenaeum, Goucher College, Baltimore	47,500,000	103,000	373.79	38,500,000	2,900,000	450,000	RMJM
Bass Library/Community Resource Center, Lorain County Community College, Elyria, OH	26,807,000	86,000	248.93	21,408,375	1,840,000	150,000	Sasaki Associates w/ Osborn Engineering
Charleston Campus Library, College of Southern Nevada, Las Vegas*	25,000,000	78,110	256.05	20,000,000	5,000,000	150,000	Domingo Cambeiro Corp.
Century College Library, Century Community and Technical College, White Bear Lake, MN	19,000,000 **	28,200	235.00	6,627,000	966,995	120,000	DLR Group
Legacy Library, Marietta College, OH	17,500,000	53,000	283.02	15,000,000	2,500,000	277,000+	Burgess & Niple; Jim Butz
Miriam B. and James Mulva Library, St. Norbert College, De Pere, WI	17,500,000	80,000	172.50	13,800,000	1,478,225	466,008	RMJM; Performa Inc.
Pell Marine Science Library, University of Rhode Island/GSO, Narragansett	15,000,000	42,000	325.83	13,685,000	0	28,100	Burt, Hill
Library Media Center, Peninsula College, Port Angeles, WA	12,500,000	27,500	385.64	10,605,000	768,421	71,117	Schacht Aslani Architects
Frank and Laura Lewis Library, LaGrange College, GA	n.a.	45,000	249.96	11,248,000	670,000	190,000	Perry Dean Rogers
Sarah D. and L. Kirk McKay Jr. Archives Center, Florida Southern College, Lakeland	3,500,000	10,100	n.a.	n.a.	25,000+	n.a.	Straughn Trout Architects
Brown School of Business and Leadership Library, Stevenson University, Owings Mills, MD	1,020,780	4,815	173.00	832.995	135.652	12,000	J.T. Fishman & Associates
Peter B. Lewis Library, Princeton University	n.a.	87,000	n.a.	n.a.	n.a.	325,000	Gehry Partners, LLP

* Costs for new classroom building include 24,000 square foot library.
** Refers to cost of total project; other figures refer just to the library portion.

Table 2 / Academic Library Buildings, Additions and Renovations, 2009

Institution	Status	Project Cost	Gross Square Feet	Square Foot Cost	Construction Cost	Equipment Cost	Book Capacity	Architect
William Oxley Thompson Memorial Library, Ohio State University, Columbus	Total	$108,700,000	307,000	$246.58	$75,700,000	$8,800,000	1,250,000	GUND Partnership; Acock Associates Architects
	New	n.a.	90,000	n.a.	n.a.	n.a.	n.a.	
	Renovated	n.a.	217,000	n.a.	n.a.	n.a.	n.a.	
Henry Madden Library, Fresno State University, CA	Total	105,000,000	327,920	299.21	98,116,000	6,884,000	2,800,000	A.C. Martin; RMJM
	New	87,323,250	242,999	335.80	81,598,171	5,725,079	2,500,000	
	Renovated	17,676,750	84,921	194.51	16,517,829	1,158,921	300,000	
Morris Library, Southern Illinois University, Carbondale	Total	48,000,000	322,673	137.91	44,500,000	3,500,000	2,350,000	PSA-Dewberry; Woollen, Molzan & Partners
	New	n.a.	50,000	n.a.	n.a.	n.a.	n.a.	
	Renovated	n.a.	272,673	n.a.	n.a.	n.a.	n.a.	
Vera P. Shiffman Medical Library, Wayne State University, Detroit*	Total	n.a.	34,257	n.a.	n.a.	884,650	297,085	SHW Group
	New	n.a.	12,521	n.a.	n.a.	186,750	112,085	
	Renovated	n.a.	21,736	1,610.23	35,000,000	697,900	185,000	
Zach S. Henderson Library, Georgia Southern University, Statesboro	Total	25,003,639	236,000	98.86	23,330,739	1,672,900	1,223,948	Cogdell & Mendrala Architects
	New	n.a.	101,000	n.a.	n.a.	n.a.	800,000	
	Renovated	n.a.	135,000	n.a.	n.a.	n.a.	423,948	
Loyola-Notre Dame Library, Loyola College/College of Notre Dame of Maryland, Baltimore	Total	20,049,640	115,000	147.99	17,019,024	1,557,616	630,000	RMJM; Penza Bailey Architects
	New	n.a.	26,000	n.a.	n.a.	n.a.	n.a.	
	Renovated	n.a.	89,000	n.a.	n.a.	n.a.	n.a.	
Research and Information Commons, Daemen College, Amherst, NY	Total	15,000,000	51,000	261.78	13,350,755	966,520	170,112	Perry Dean Rogers
	New	n.a.	49,000	n.a.	n.a.	n.a.	n.a.	
	Renovated	n.a.	2,000	n.a.	n.a.	n.a.	n.a.	
Robert Hutchings Goddard Library, Clark University, Worcester, MA	Total	n.a.	126,000	96.03	13,000,000	1,500,000	375,000	Perry Dean Rogers
	New	n.a.	13,000	500.00	6,500,000	750,000	0	
	Renovated	n.a.	113,000	57.52	6,500,000	750,000	375,000	
Henry Clay Hofheimer II Library, Virginia Wesleyan College, Norfolk	Total	5,788,610	45,863	109.51	5,022,187	143,591	200,000	Cho Benn Holback & Associates
	New	560,902	5,447	114.73	624,945	17,867	0	
	Renovated	5,227,708	40,416	108.80	4,397,242	125,724	200,000	
Paul Meek Library, University of Tennessee at Martin	Total	135,325	2,196	50.91	111,800	23,525	450	University of Tennessee at Martin Physical Plant Building Services
	New	83,707	966	69.16	66,800	16,907	0	
	Renovated	51,618	1,230	36.59	45,000	6,618	450	

* Figures include the new School of Medicine

Table 3 / Academic Library Buildings, Renovations Only, 2009

Institution	Project Cost	Gross Square Feet	Square Foot Cost	Construction Cost	Equipment Cost	Book Capacity	Architect
Bancroft Library (Doe Annex), University of California, Berkeley	$64,000,000	129,651	$354.80	$46,000,000	$1,500,000	600,000+	Ratcliff; Noll & Tam
Law Commons: Daniel F. Cracchiolo, Law Library and James E. Rogers College of Law, University of Arizona, Tucson	21,000,000	113,694	126.66	14,400,000	1,450,000	275,000+	GouldEvans
J. Michael Goodson Law Library, Duke University Law School, Durham, NC	15,400,000	85,000	134.11	11,400,000	1,100,000	625,000	Shepley Bulfinch
Dr. C.C. and Mabel L. Criss Library, University of Nebraska at Omaha	12,725,888	187,254	46.85	8,773,640	3,241,202	1,000,000	HDR
Perkins Library, Duke University, Durham, NC	7,100,000	25,000	208.00	5,200,000	1,550,000	n.a.	Shepley Bulfinch
Mikkelsen Library, Augustana College, Sioux Falls, SD	6,825,000	58,635	97.21	5,700,000	1,125,000	300,000	TSP
UWM Libraries, University of Wisconsin–Milwaukee	4,900,000	52,816	68.16	3,600,000	710,000	n.a.	The Kubala Washatko Architects
Dexter Library, Northland College, Ashland, WI	2,500,000	22,000	85.23	1,875,000	300,000	85,000	MS&R, Ltd.
Gettysburg Campus Learning Commons, Gettysburg Campus of HACC, Central Pennsylvania's Community College	2,350,331	9,645	223.03	2,151,102	199,229	6,200	JMZ Architects
Gordon McKay Library, Harvard University, Cambridge, MA	2,263,000	2,560	742.19	1,900,000	173,000	20,280	Douglas Okun & Associates
Hannah V. McCauley Library, Ohio University, Lancaster	1,800,000	15,000	93.33	1,400,000	365,000	53,100	WSA Studio, Architects
Van Ingen Art Library, Vassar College, Poughkeepsie, NY	1,500,000	5,000	286.00	1,430,000	50,000	65,000+	Platt Byard Dovell White
Louis Calder Memorial Library, Miller School of Medicine, University of Miami, FL	1,084,145	45,745	14.95	684,017	400,128	n.a.	not reported
Arrigoni Library/Technology Center, Iona College, New Rochelle, NY	162,000	4,000	40.50	162,000	0	10,000	Iona College/Dimitris Halaris

Table 4 / New Public Library Buildings, 2009

Community	Pop. ('000)	Code	Project Cost	Construction Cost	Gross Square Feet	Square Foot Cost	Equipment Cost	Architect
Arizona								
Peoria	158	B	$10,579,556	$8,470,000	22,500	$376.44	$704,556	richärd+bauer
Phoenix	76	B	12,282,400	8,189,340	25,000	327.57	990,380	Will Bruder+Partners
Phoenix	48	B	6,893,470	5,409,950	12,400	436.29	552,580	richärd+bauer
Queen Creek	23	O	18,201,634	13,695,733	47,000	291.39	573,820	PSA-Dewberry/DFDG
Yuma	28	B	6,267,405	5,200,000	22,398	232.16	450,000	Welles/Pugsley…
Yuma	88	MS	27,966,227	18,042,381	79,491	226.97	3,464,669	VCBO; Oakland
Arkansas								
Jacksonville	30	B	5,488,157	4,026,058	13,500	298.23	344,224	WER Architects
California								
Alhambra	90	M	33,747,140	30,054,512	45,296	663.51	2,222,500	CWA AIA
Chino Hills	79	O	13,400,000	12,400,000	27,975	443.25	n.a.	LPA
Fowler	8	B	3,931,986	2,851,414	8,660	329.26	447,498	Fresno County
Highland	62	B	14,853,433	13,301,743	30,000	443.40	482,140	STK Architecture
Lawndale	34	B	17,785,950	9,412,500	17,360	542.19	2,101,600	Gruen Associates
Los Angeles	73	B	11,764,650	10,500,000	14,500	724.14	365,650	Tetra Design
Portola Valley	7	O	3,885,680	3,055,000	6,450	473.69	325,680	Siegel Strain; Goring
Redwood City	11	B	18,633,652	15,364,086	22,000	698.37	859,542	Anderson Brulé
San Francisco	11	B	6,690,800	3,451,255	6,427	536.99	500,000	Stoner Meek; Noll & Tam
Colorado								
Bennett	3	B	2,596,650	1,880,000	7,000	268.57	282,650	Humphries Poli
Centennial	31	B	2,003,799	1,353,417	17,561	77.07	370,300	SEM Architects
Crawford	2	B	970,606	744,798	4,800	155.17	35,791	Tom Lindblom
Denver	23	B	7,567,927	5,377,811	30,000	179.26	355,706	Bennett Wagner…
Durango	51	M	19,418,755	12,336,559	42,908	287.51	1,554,000	Barker Rinker Seacat
Fort Collins	50	B	6,200,000	4,000,000	16,600	240.96	800,000	Aller Lingle…; studiotrope
Mancos	3	M	3,060,711	2,509,269	7,500	334.57	157,397	Humphries Poli
Penrose	5	M	884,993	744,857	6,900	107.95	10,010	Art C. Klein Constr.

Symbol Code: B=Branch Library; BS=Branch and System Headquarters; M=Main Library; MS=Main and System Headquarters; S=System Headquarters; O=combined use space; n.a.=not available.

Table 4 / New Public Library Buildings, 2009 *(cont.)*

Community	Pop. ('000)	Code	Project Cost	Construction Cost	Gross Square Feet	Square Foot Cost	Equipment Cost	Architect
Connecticut								
Darien	20	M	27,301,918	16,254,724	55,750	291.56	2,352,493	Peter Gisolfi Assocs.
Delaware								
Wilmington	45	B	8,982,000	6,300,000	22,500	280.00	800,000	ikon.5 architects
Florida								
Fort Lauderdale	70	B	4,331,386	3,588,922	10,000	358.90	393,784	Russell Partnership
Lake Worth	16	B	14,981,609	11,297,153	29,000	389.56	1,262,118	Slattery & Associates
Miami	56	B	5,413,769	3,773,600	15,000	251.57	81,807	N&J Construction
Miramar	112	B	9,654,105	7,437,555	30,000	247.90	1,003,700	Cartaya & Associates
Naples	90	B	12,671,313	6,519,813	30,000	217.33	2,651,800	Schenkel Shultz
Naranja	31	B	7,494,387	6,363,376	15,000	424.23	740,390	C.G. Chase Construction
Pinecrest	19	B	3,661,345	3,582,000	15,000	238.88	79,345	Bea Architects
Seffner	30	B	4,427,000	3,000,000	15,000	200.00	740,000	FleischmanGarcia
Tampa	64	O	7,525,083	5,533,695	29,687	186.40	1,230,000	Harvard Jolly
West Palm Beach	100	M	31,091,316	23,958,511	85,000	281.86	3,358,642	Song + Assocs.
Georgia								
Decatur	57	B	5,084,580	4,179,861	18,000	232.21	394,278	Houser Walker
Idaho								
Boise	212	B	4,900,000	3,606,185	15,300	235.70	641,535	Fletcher Farr Ayotte
Illinois								
Byron	7	M	8,372,214	6,621,076	27,640	239.54	395,350	PSA-Dewberry/BCA
Chicago	25	B	12,575,251	9,659,339	16,350	590.79	143,403	Ilekis Associates
Dunlap	6	M	2,500,000	1,796,820	12,300	146.08	462,140	apaceDesign
Elgin	134	B	4,656,620	3,816,809	10,000	381.68	378,122	Engberg Anderson
Indiana								
Michigantown	5	B	957,803	697,752	4,000	174.43	15,000	H.L. Mohler & Assocs.
South Bend	48	B	4,865,737	2,794,504	15,569	179.49	723,982	Arkos Design Inc.

Symbol Code: B=Branch Library; BS=Branch and System Headquarters; M=Main Library; MS=Main and System Headquarters; S=System Headquarters; O=combined use space; n.a.=not available.

Marshalltown	26	MS	9,054,600	6,283,198	35,710	175.95	1,252,684	FEH Associates
Kansas								
Bonner Springs	10	M	4,027,058	3,153,716	20,125	156.71	291,070	Treanor Architects
Kentucky								
Brownsville	12	M	1,535,641	1,400,000	10,500	133.33	35,641	Alliance Corporation
Lagrange	56	MS	7,222,459	5,763,183	30,000	192.11	603,321	Robert Ehmet Hayes
Louisiana								
Alexandria	25	B	1,982,000	1,452,400	10,500	138.33	131,600	Alliance Design
Lafayette	56	B	11,728,615	8,458,235	37,600	224.95	929,609	The Sellers Group
Maryland								
Finksburg	18	B	6,400,000	5,000,000	13,805	362.19	370,000	Lukmire Partnership
Thurmont	6	B	8,550,995	6,825,458	26,432	258.23	1,045,000	PSA-Dewberry
Massachusetts								
Mattapan	37	B	17,149,399	12,070,690	20,630	585.10	404,256	Wm. Rawn Assocs.
Michigan								
Dexter	16	M	9,136,723	6,925,000	30,000	230.83	749,250	HB+M | Architects
Lakeview	10	M	2,300,000	1,605,855	15,000	107.06	179,647	C2AE
Otsego	13	M	4,732,738	3,813,000	18,415	207.06	527,083	Thomson Architectural
Minnesota								
Rosemount	30	B	7,137,655	5,080,013	23,420	216.91	623,893	Durrant
Saint Cloud	107	MS	30,000,000	23,058,750	118,025	195.37	2,087,600	MS&R, Ltd.
Nebraska								
Omaha	487	O	3,700,000	2,000,000	14,900	134.23	1,120,000	BCDM Architects
Nevada								
Las Vegas	56	B	22,074,000	17,700,000	45,555	388.54	1,384,000	JMA Architecture
New Hampshire								
Gilford	7	M	3,695,500	2,771,000	14,400	192.43	172,000	Architectural Studio
Hudson	25	M	4,183,658	3,723,566	19,488	191.07	194,566	Adams & Smith LLC
New York								
New York	44	B	4,649,311	3,735,641	13,000	287.36	341,459	Gensler Architects
North Dakota								

Symbol Code: B=Branch Library; BS=Branch and System Headquarters; M=Main Library; MS=Main and System Headquarters; S=System Headquarters; O=combined use space; n.a.=not available.

Table 4 / New Public Library Buildings, 2009 (cont.)

Community	Pop. ('000)	Code	Project Cost	Construction Cost	Gross Square Feet	Square Foot Cost	Equipment Cost	Architect
Fargo	101	M	11,850,831	9,014,106	57,950	155.55	1,078,581	MS&R, Ltd.
Ohio								
Doylestown	11	B	1,627,598	967,055	5,224	185.12	68,293	HB+M	Architects
Oklahoma								
Sperry	8	B	1,270,531	956,386	5,000	191.28	44,660	Beck Design
Oregon								
Portland	15	B	125,836	71,909	4,641	15.49	49,141	TI Design
Pennsylvania								
Pittsburgh	19	B	3,956,442	2,480,319	8,334	297.61	326,261	Pfaffmann + Associates
Williamsport	29	MS	5,950,000	4,400,000	26,400	166.67	1,000,000	Larson Design Group
Tennessee								
Gatlinburg	40	O	1,767,082	1,303,576	8,000	162.95	238,568	Trotter & Associates
Texas								
Austin	11	B	5,829,000	3,939,000	14,000	281.36	515,000	Studio8 Architects
Austin	25	B	6,970,000	3,825,000	10,738	356.21	605,000	Limbacher + Godfrey
Azle*	15	M	n.a.	n.a.	30,261	n.a.	280,000	Magee Architects
Dickinson	22	M	2,449,441	2,227,390	12,229	182.14	40,860	Hall Barnum Lucchesi
Virginia								
Berryville**	15	O	n.a.	1,000,000	5,000	200.00	225,000	L.B. Baughan
Mechanicsville	45	B	5,785,000	3,725,000	16,170	230.36	430,000	Lukmire Partnership
Portsmouth	99	B	6,715,420	4,357,709	20,804	209.46	608,345	HBA
Washington								
Battle Ground	52	B	4,271,517	3,146,880	14,356	219.20	320,994	Hennebery Eddy
West Virginia								
Salt Rock	10	B	1,222,600	993,900	5,000	198.78	100,000	Edward Tucker Architects
Sutton	5	M	446,213	342,277	5,500	62.23	40,387	VanNostrand Architects

* Except for automated systems, project was supported by a single donor
** Library in shared government building; figures not available
Symbol Code: B=Branch Library; BS=Branch and System Headquarters; M=Main Library; MS=Main and System Headquarters; S=System Headquarters; O=combined use space; n.a.=not available.

Table 5 / Public Library Buildings, Additions and Renovations, 2009

Community	Pop. ('000)	Code	Project Cost	Construction Cost	Gross Square Feet	Square Foot Cost	Equipment Cost	Architect
Alabama								
Hoover	67	M	$1,998,636	$1,598,949	4,828	$331.18	$219,256	Evan Terry Associates
Arizona								
Somerton	13	B	2,868,259	2,617,684	5,980	437.74	87,000	LEA Archs.; DPE Constr.
Yuma	88	B	4,253,794	3,752,523	22,605	166.00	141,749	Studio Ma
Arkansas								
Little Rock	2,700	B	22,789,164	16,104,326	65,746	244.95	1,193,246	Polk Stanley Architects
Magnolia	25	MS	3,225,000	1,100,000	25,615	42.94	1,550,000	Trull-Hollensworth
Walnut Ridge	17	MS	121,335	80,331	8,500	9.45	37,591	Brackett Krennerich
California								
Borrego Springs	4	B	207,242	149,955	3,787	39.60	51,287	CSI General Inc.
Carlsbad	11	B	6,140,000	4,343,122	11,393	381.21	390,268	Manuel Oncina Architects
Castaic	21	B	591,606	488,307	6,985	69.91	103,229	L.A. County Real Estate
Courtland	1	B	410,010	325,010	960	338.55	35,000	Rainforth Grau
Descanso	3	B	263,152	185,035	455	406.67	13,152	Zagronik + Thomas
Elk Grove	68	B	8,164,580	2,464,380	13,785	178.77	820,000	Group 4 Architecture
Glendale	34	B	1,249,904	586,919	2,190	268.00	519,001	Osborn Architects
Milpitas	65	B	38,468,781	30,378,315	60,074	505.68	1,677,508	Group 4 Architecture
Rancho Cucamonga	180	B	2,200,000	1,600,000	22,000	72.73	400,000	Pitassi Architects
San Francisco	47	B	14,495,759	10,486,144	13,900	754.40	750,000	SF Bureau of Architecture
Torrance	142	M	1,362,977	729,443	20,000	36.47	458,733	Deems Lewis McKinley
Colorado								
Colorado Springs	52	B	2,307,938	1,699,691	14,060	120.89	483,012	Humphries Poli
Pueblo West	27	B	6,760,000	5,200,000	28,000	185.71	577,000	Humphries Poli
Steamboat Springs	16	M	16,614,026	12,955,736	35,345	366.55	1,151,667	MS&R, Ltd.
Windsor	18	M	1,592,000	1,300,000	11,222	115.84	200,000	Thorp Associates
Connecticut								
Greenwich	8	B	5,674,355	4,546,654	10,400	437.18	322,064	Peter Gisolfi Associates
Guilford	23	M	8,000,000	5,400,000	34,000	158.82	1,000,000	Tuthill & Wells

Symbol Code: B=Branch Library; BS=Branch and System Headquarters; M=Main Library; MS=Main and System Headquarters; S=System Headquarters; O=combined use space; n.a.=not available.

Table 5 / Public Library Buildings, Additions and Renovations, 2009 *(cont.)*

Community	Pop. ('000)	Code	Project Cost	Construction Cost	Gross Square Feet	Square Foot Cost	Equipment Cost	Architect
District of Columbia								
Washington	15	B	642,406	422,925	4,600	91.94	109,463	Core Architects
Washington	2	MS	577,125	396,174	4,500	88.03	151,509	Atelier Architects
Washington	18	B	1,960,000	1,835,000	5,500	333.64	n.a.	Martinez + Johnson
Florida								
Alachua	16	B	1,500,000	1,200,000	11,950	100.42	200,000	Skinner Vignola McLean
Boynton Beach	65	M	9,390,370	7,482,039	62,864	119.01	1,291,321	SchenkelSchultz
Safety Harbor	24	M	5,121,556	4,404,331	25,000	176.17	332,328	Long & Associates
Stuart	24	B	3,965,129	3,296,888	21,504	153.31	419,367	Stephen Boruff, AIA
Georgia								
Tucker	37	B	3,111,581	2,495,498	15,000	166.37	261,873	RWH Design
Illinois								
Charleston	21	MS	8,209,990	5,964,000	29,000	205.66	994,000	PSA-Dewberry/BCA
Chatham	15	M	3,419,510	2,619,488	29,100	90.02	392,052	apaceDesign
Streamwood	67	M	23,700,000	20,940,583	96,846	216.23	793,849	Frye Gillan Molinaro
Waukegan	90	M	330,000	230,000	2,200	104.55	70,000	Product Arch + Design
Indiana								
Auburn	13	B	355,905	197,000	3,200	61.56	96,405	WKM Architects
Highland	24	B	1,102,153	836,952	10,000	83.70	128,915	Carras-Szany-Kuhn
Kansas								
McPherson	14	M	3,904,601	2,804,840	27,427	102.27	719,125	DMA Architects
Kentucky								
Glasgow	42	M	2,546,000	865,000	14,534	59.52	264,000	5253 Design Group
Scottsville	19	M	2,865,099	2,387,038	12,899	185.06	337,061	Pearson & Peters
Louisiana								
Dularge	3	B	553,526	472,969	2,525	187.31	38,844	cheramie + bruce
Maine								
Belfast	9	M	810,000	510,000	7,000	72.86	90,000	Maine Group
Maryland								
Taneytown	22	B	1,600,000	1,350,000	14,283	94.52	153,000	BMK Architects

Symbol Code: B=Branch Library; BS=Branch and System Headquarters; M=Main Library; MS=Main and System Headquarters; S=System Headquarters; O=combined use space; n.a.=not available.

Massachusetts							
Mattapoisett	7	M	5,635,177	5,182,021	14,600	354.93	36,056	Durland Van Voorhis
Middleton	8	M	7,516,379	5,792,047	18,200	318.24	563,577	Durland Van Voorhis
Milton	26	M	13,418,000	9,900,000	39,000	253.85	849,000	Schwartz/Silver
Northborough	15	M	7,105,465	6,200,000	26,200	236.64	323,142	Johnson Roberts
Michigan							
Bloomfield Hills	77	M	24,687,095	18,035,347	108,500	166.22	5,400,000	Fanning Howey; RDA
Grand Haven	36	M	10,720,577	6,965,513	50,000	139.31	1,576,390	Troyer Group
Leland	6	M	422,500	202,000	5,000	40.40	137,000	Riemenschneider; Graves; Easling
Minnesota							
Eagan	67	BS	2,125,500	1,536,803	30,000	51.22	398,697	MS&R
Missouri							
Cape Girardeau	35	M	8,733,857	6,437,739	39,430	163.27	1,168,542	Clark Enersen Partners
Kansas City	605	M	538,500	288,000	2,800	102.86	205,500	Helix Architecture
St. Charles	63	B	2,766,832	2,420,865	28,681	84.41	265,287	Cornerstone Architecture
New Jersey							
Glen Ridge	7	M	1,294,000	957,000	10,431	91.75	200,000	Arcari + Iovino
Monroe Township	33	M	6,496,000	5,626,000	24,000	234.42	300,000	Arcari + Iovino
Randolph	26	M	380,544	184,813	4,250	43.49	150,530	Tiina Vaska
New York							
Bay Shore	32	M	12,465,639	9,504,422	33,207	286.22	873,297	Beatty, Harvey, Coco
Broad Channel	3	B	761,353	525,236	1,750	300.13	145,340	Integrated Design
Bronx	60	O	1,220,000	802,036	16,773	47.82	80,717	1100 Architect PC
Brooklyn	35	B	7,806,000	6,500,000	25,785	252.08	750,000	Li/Saltzman Architects
Cortland	29	M	92,532	84,105	14,000	6.00	0	Crawford & Stearns
Elmsford	44	M	20,392,021	17,292,021	46,000	375.91	1,000,000	Beatty, Harvey, Coco
Glens Falls	54	M	18,800,000	11,415,091	52,500	217.43	2,047,403	Ann Beha Architects
New York	217	M	812,000	812,000	2,700	300.74	0	Gensler Architects
Staten Island	33	O	512,000	358,701	7,500	47.83	42,352	Andrew Berman Architects
Ohio							
Barnesville	8	O	340,574	190,811	2,583	73.87	3,999	Davis Architectural
Beaver	3	B	255,316	173,208	900	192.45	56,511	TRIAD Architects
Columbus	61	B	1,979,809	1,207,001	25,481	47.36	563,128	DesignGroup
Delta	9	M	137,150	96,386	500	192.77	n.a.	Spring Valley Architects

Symbol Code: B=Branch Library; BS=Branch and System Headquarters; M=Main Library; MS=Main and System Headquarters; S=System Headquarters; O=combined use space; n.a.=not available.

Table 5 / Public Library Buildings, Additions and Renovations, 2009 *(cont.)*

Community	Pop. ('000)	Code	Project Cost	Construction Cost	Gross Square Feet	Square Foot Cost	Equipment Cost	Architect
North Olmsted	n.a.	B	800,000	732,000	2,100	348.57	68,000	RCU Architects
Oak Harbor	10	M	415,775	321,612	6,713	47.90	13,000	HB+M | Architects
Piqua	20	M	21,672,917	16,019,518	85,000	188.46	452,990	PSA-Dewberry
Toledo	20	B	419,127	323,386	1,357	238.31	68,254	Vetter Design Group
Worthington	61	MS	1,734,072	1,023,682	42,446	24.11	520,928	DesignGroup
Youngstown	24	BS	5,007,513	3,856,112	24,824	155.34	217,611	HB+M | Architects
Oklahoma								
Tulsa	n.a.	B	1,678,745	1,558,565	5,000	311.71	n.a.	Kinslow, Keith & Todd
Pennsylvania								
Philadelphia	1,000	M	243,000	183,500	5,000	36.70	0	Moshe Safdie Assocs.
Rhode Island								
Bristol	23	M	9,185,677	7,401,177	28,357	261.00	455,000	a.i. designs
Texas								
Houston*	2	B	5,702,000	5,175,000	13,010	397.77	527,000	Glassman Shoemake...
Houston	114	B	3,548,672	2,354,710	10,409	226.22	516,848	m Architects
Pasadena	163	MS	5,044,533	4,307,907	44,300	97.24	338,754	Dansby & Miller
Virginia								
Fredericksburg	121	B	4,745,000	3,950,000	10,675	370.02	425,000	Lukmire Partnership
Leesburg	340	B	9,135,000	7,200,000	42,970	167.56	1,200,000	Lukmire Partnership
Washington								
Liberty Lake**	7	M	2,685,000	675,000	8,700	n.a.	50,000	Bernardo Wills
Pasco	52	O	340,797	176,349	15,046	11.72	120,137	Arculus
Wisconsin								
Beloit	47	M	8,710,248	7,068,150	63,419	111.45	810,170	Engberg Anderson
Wyoming								
Cody	27	MS	5,925,880	4,990,655	41,450	120.40	411,507	CTA Architects
Lander	10	MS	6,640,500	4,938,617	25,603	192.89	624,522	GSG Architecture
Pinedale	7	MS	5,742,103	4,876,500	13,898	350.88	225,603	Carney Architects

* Project total includes unknown design costs paid for by the Clayton Library Friends

** Building also houses the city police station

Symbol Code: B=Branch Library; BS=Branch and System Headquarters; M=Main Library; MS=Main and System Headquarters; S=System Headquarters; O=combined use space; n.a.=not available.

Table 6 / Public Library Buildings, Six-Year Cost Summary

	Fiscal 2004	Fiscal 2005	Fiscal 2006	Fiscal 2007	Fiscal 2008	Fiscal 2009
Number of new buildings	99	91	81	82	95	80
Number of ARRs*	102	94	79	86	88	90
Sq. ft. new buildings	3,178,027	2,349,670	2,050,087	2,245,929	2,235,853	1,772,434
Sq. ft. ARRs	2,096,243	1,530,382	1,505,326	2,300,619	1,782,204	1,942,810
New Buildings						
Construction cost	$655,261,309	$420,241,028	$421,856,723	$491,240,609	$539,109,943	$486,722,590
Equipment cost	72,422,017	57,152,920	51,541,695	60,666,368	73,468,236	54,212,351
Site cost	30,873,801	43,892,631	43,897,019	37,089,067	36,331,029	37,658,061
Other cost	157,419,044	75,384,007	90,240,356	105,271,399	86,508,406	75,202,090
Total—Project cost	916,026,171	596,670,586	611,502,793	705,543,661	736,767,614	656,020,880
ARRs—Project cost	326,410,267	235,915,173	293,982,768	426,681,990	334,871,847	482,214,848
New & ARR Project Cost	$1,242,436,438	$832,585,759	$905,485,561	$1,132,225,651	$1,071,639,461	$1,138,235,728
Fund Sources						
Federal, new buildings	$3,765,492	$3,657,196	$9,733,136	$9,701,152	$6,797,857	$17,049,910
Federal, ARRs	6,202,088	3,692,293	4,150,883	2,971,210	7,733,967	7,873,278
Federal, total	$9,967,580	$7,349,489	$13,884,019	$12,672,362	$14,531,824	$24,923,188
State, new buildings	$115,846,277	$28,458,752	$26,218,139	$65,941,808	$47,484,015	$63,038,118
State, ARRs	24,889,690	12,816,996	28,803,122	23,951,016	25,725,016	40,827,176
State, total	$140,735,967	$41,275,748	$55,021,261	$89,892,824	$73,209,031	$103,865,294
Local, new buildings	$703,245,493	$537,391,416	$534,202,531	$560,754,782	$620,037,382	$518,738,443
Local, ARRs	237,027,037	193,115,934	236,808,805	369,691,281	258,453,050	392,376,170
Local, total	$940,272,530	$730,507,350	$771,011,336	$930,446,063	$878,490,432	$911,114,613
Gift, new buildings	$93,284,817	$27,464,751	$43,422,990	$71,784,153	$62,835,806	$58,532,660
Gift, ARRs	58,402,733	26,579,726	24,780,729	31,906,464	43,718,655	42,456,942
Gift, total	$151,687,550	$54,044,477	$68,203,719	$103,690,617	$106,554,461	$100,989,602
Total funds used	$1,242,663,627	$833,177,064	$908,120,335	$1,136,701,866	$1,072,785,748	$1,140,892,697

* ARR: Additions, Renovations, and Remodels

Book Trade Research and Statistics

2009: Another Year of Readjustment Across the Publishing Industry

Jim Milliot

Co-Editorial Director, *Publishers Weekly*

The year began with a steady drumbeat of bad news about layoffs, reorganizations, and pay and hiring freezes and ended with talk of little else but the industry's digital future. In between, 2009 was dominated by the impact of the continuing recession.

Debate over the Google Book Search settlement—reached in the fall of 2008 between Google and the Association of American Publishers (AAP) and the Authors Guild—began to heat up as the June date for the final hearing drew closer. With opposition to the deal from authors, agents, foreign governments, and others mounting, the parties asked that the final fairness hearing be extended by four months, to October 7. When the Department of Justice announced it was reviewing the deal as well, another extension was granted. While the judge did eventually give his preliminary approval to the agreement, a final hearing was put off until February 2010.

One reason for the close scrutiny of the Google deal was that the agreement began to outline different business models concerning how authors and publishers might be compensated in the digital future, and all parties wanted to make sure their interests were protected. That concern over new business models was also reflected in other skirmishes that developed between authors and publishers as 2009 moved along. What to pay authors for e-books became a major topic when Macmillan introduced a new contract that called for paying authors 20 percent of net proceeds from sales of digital editions, down from what had been a de facto industry standard of 25 percent. Agents and authors objected, arguing for something closer to a 50-50 split.

The question of who owns the rights to publish older backlist titles came to the forefront late in 2009 when Random House Chairman Markus Dohle wrote a letter to agents saying it was the company's belief that its older contracts, signed before 1994, gave Random the right to publish the titles as e-books. Authors and agents objected again, insisting that authors owned the rights. Random did not spell out what royalty it was prepared to pay for e-book editions of backlist titles. Earlier in 2009 authors and agents agreed that the text-to-speech function incorporated into Amazon's Kindle electronic book-reading device was a copyright violation since Amazon added the capability without asking permission from copyright holders. Somewhat surprisingly, Amazon agreed to remove the function from the Kindle while it worked out the rights issues.

A price war broke out in the fall as Amazon and Walmart sought to be the lowest-price source for books bought online. The two lowered the price of certain new titles to less than $9, prompting the American Booksellers Association to ask the Justice Department to investigate the two for predatory pricing. As both retailers were selling bestsellers for below cost, it appeared that Amazon and Walmart were using bestselling books as "loss leaders." Amazon's pricing of e-books at $9.99 was a source or frustration for publishers all year. Publishers are worried that the low e-book price will kill sales of hardcover books, which still generate a great deal of revenue that permits publishers to pay meaningful advances to authors and to cover other expenses.

Another question that became a major issue in 2009 was when e-books should be released. Despite concerns that e-books might cut into hardcover sales, in most cases publishers were releasing e-book editions simultaneously with the hardcover edition. That began to change late in 2009 when Simon & Schuster announced it would delay releasing e-book editions of 35 frontlist titles for four months after the publication of the hardcover edition. Other publishers announced similar plans, as well as some other tactics for releasing e-books. One strategy that was gaining traction was to create enhanced e-books that would be released at the same time as the hardcover but priced close to the level of the print edition; three or four months later, regular e-book editions would be released at lower prices.

Growth in Online Retailing

Online retailing continued to make significant gains in 2009, led by Amazon, which continued to report solid revenue growth even as its major physical bookstore rivals reported sluggish—and, in some cases, declining—sales. To focus on their most profitable areas—superstores—both Barnes & Noble and Borders downsized their mall businesses. B&N had been exiting the smaller-store format for years and scheduled the closing of all of its B. Dalton outlets for early 2010. Borders has a much larger small-format footprint through its Waldenbooks specialty group, but it too made moves to reduce its presence in shopping malls. The company planned to close 180 small-format stores by the end of January 2010, leaving it with about 150.

Reducing the number of mall outlets was only one of the steps Borders took to return to profitability. In January 2009 the company replaced CEO George Jones with Ron Marshall, who quickly overhauled the management ranks of the nation's second-largest bookseller. Within a few months of taking over, Marshall implemented cost cuts in Borders' headquarters and store staff. Borders eliminated 136 jobs in its Ann Arbor offices, 12 percent of the corporate work force, and about 800 jobs in the field.

During the year, many publishers increased their online selling efforts. Tor Books, for example, started selling its own titles and those of other science fiction/fantasy publishers through Tor.com.

Ramifications of the recession reverberated throughout the year. Reader's Digest filed for prepackaged bankruptcy in mid-2009 and as part of a deal to emerge from Chapter 11 the company reached an agreement with its lenders to refinance its debt. Under the refinancing, the investment of Ripplewood Holdings, the equity firm that bought Reader's Digest, was wiped out and other lenders traded their debt for equity. Earlier in 2009 the company laid off about 8 percent of its work force as part of its strategy to downsize its operations.

Another company that had to cope with heavy debt because of an acquisition was Houghton Mifflin Harcourt. Barry O'Callaghan, who led the group that acquired Houghton Mifflin and then Harcourt, agreed to a debt restructuring under which his stake in the company was significantly reduced and most of HMH's lenders traded debt for a share of the company.

Pearson overhauled its DK Publishing and Rough Guides divisions in response to declining sales of reference print products, including travel guides. As a result, Gary June, DK chief executive, moved to another spot at Pearson and the company transferred some back office operations from Britain to India. There were also some job losses in DK's U.S. office.

After a disappointing holiday season in 2008, the three-year-old regional distributor BookStream closed in January 2009. Weak 2008 holiday sales were also the final blow for the Milwaukee-area bookstore chain Harry W. Schwartz, which closed its four outlets. Two stores were reopened by former Schwartz employees.

One company that emerged from bankruptcy in 2009 was the printing giant Quebecor. After rejecting an acquisition offer from R. R. Donnelley, Quebecor completed its financial restructuring in the fall, at which time it changed its name to World Color Press. Meanwhile, the Christian bookselling chain Berean Christian Stores had a quick trip into bankruptcy and was acquired by an investor.

With the Canadian industry split on the need for a traditional trade show, Reed Exhibitions canceled BookExpo Canada in early 2009. In response, the Canadian Booksellers Association put together a much smaller summer conference in Toronto and made plans for a slightly more ambitious event in May 2010.

The recession resulted in a number of publishers choosing to sit out the 2009 BookExpo America, and organizers of the annual trade show continued to explore ways to make the annual event more relevant to a changing industry.

Self-Publishing Expands

Self-publishing continued to expand in 2009, and with its growth came controversy. The leader in the field, AuthorSolutions, inked partnerships with Thomas Nelson and Harlequin for joint ventures to form self-publishing units at the two houses. The Nelson deal drew little reaction, but several writers' groups objected to the Harlequin venture, which was named Harlequin Horizons. Various writers' groups, including the Romance Writers Association, criticized the deal, saying it misled would-be authors into thinking they were being published by Harlequin while also draining resources from Harlequin's traditional authors. Harlequin changed the name of the venture to DellArte Press, but the writer organizations were not appeased and called for the publisher to drop the venture entirely. This had not happened by early 2010.

Among all the other issues it had to deal with, the book industry was gearing up for the loss of Oprah Winfrey's talk show, which is scheduled to go off the air in 2011. Selection for the Oprah Book Club meant instant bestseller status, and her show provided an invaluable promotional platform for hundreds of authors. It is estimated Winfrey helped to generate $500 million for the publishing industry.

Reorganizations

The last of the series of reorganizations at the major houses in 2009 came in February when HarperCollins integrated the Collins division into its general books group, a move that eliminated at least 60 jobs and resulted in the departure of three high-ranking executives—Steve Ross and Lisa Gallagher, who oversaw Collins, and Brenda Bowen, who was in the process of starting up her own children's book imprint. Harper's Spanish-language imprint Rayo also took a big hit with its two top executives, Rene Alegria and Cecilia Molinari (publisher and managing editor, respectively), leaving.

Following a major reorganization at Random House in December 2008, Crown Publishing Group was split into two groups in late fall 2009 with all of its trade publishing imprints remaining as part of Crown while the Random House Audio and Random House Information Group businesses moved under their own umbrella. Jenny Frost, who had led Crown, left the company, and the Crown publishing imprints were placed under Maya Mavyee, who had been at Doubleday Canada. Random was looking for someone to oversee the audio and information operations.

Bonnie Ammer resigned as executive vice president, international sales, for Random House. Madeline McIntosh was named to the new position of president of sales, operations, and digital starting December 1. She had worked at Random in different executive capacities before leaving to work for Amazon in Europe. McIntosh reports directly to Random Chairman Markus Dohle.

Simon & Schuster appointed industry veteran Jonathan Merkh publisher of its religious imprint, Howard Books. A month after his appointment, Merkh transplanted the unit from Louisiana to Nashville with a few employees making the move.

McGraw-Hill Education eliminated 340 positions as it combined its el-hi basal and supplemental operations. Getty Publications laid off 10 people, 20 percent of its staff. After naming Debra Lande publisher of Klutz, Scholastic reduced the staff by 11 positions. The Aperture Foundation reduced its work force by 20 percent and cut its book list. HCI Communications laid off 35 people mainly from its manufacturing/production division. Oxford University Press laid off 60 people between its New York City editorial offices and Cary, North Carolina, warehouse.

Ingram formed the Ingram Content Group and moved its Ingram Digital into the group, joining Ingram Book Company and Lightning Source.

Digital Developments

New developments in digital publishing and bookselling occurred throughout the year and began to accelerate as 2009 moved along. The reason for interest in all things digital was seen in the monthly sales report from the Association of American Publishers—the spectacular growth in the sale of e-books. Through November, sales of e-books from the 12 publishers that report results to AAP jumped 185 percent to $150 million. Although e-books remained a small part of overall revenue, the segment is easily the most dynamic sector of the industry.

One reason for the growth of e-books was the growing acceptance by the public of using digital devices to read consumer books. Amazon reported that its dedicated e-reader, the Kindle, was the best-selling product at the company during the 2009 holiday season. In an attempt to compete with Amazon in the digital book space, Barnes & Noble announced the launch of its own e-reader at an October press conference. Priced the same as the Kindle, at $259, B&N's "nook" started shipping in late November and the device quickly became out of stock. B&N was able to get devices to customers before Christmas for those who ordered the nook by November 20 and planned to ship other orders early in 2010. The company also expected to begin selling the nook in its stores, a key to its strategy, early in 2010. Amazon was not remaining idle, however, and on October 19 it began shipping its International Kindle to more than 100 countries (it debuted in Canada in November). The company also launched the Kindle DX, a bigger, higher-priced e-reader designed to read textbooks and newspapers. Other e-readers in the market in 2009 included several devices from Sony as well as the Cooler, a device from a British manufacturer. More e-readers were introduced at the January 2010 Consumer Electronics Show.

The availability of the Kindle in other countries raised questions about the integrity of territorial rights. Amazon said it will only sell e-books in the various countries where appropriate rights have been acquired. The question of who can buy what in open market territories is more complicated; many contracts define "open market" differently, and in many cases American and British publishers have nonexclusive rights to sell to certain markets.

Shortcovers, launched as an e-bookstore in February by Canada's largest bookstore chain, Indigo Books & Music, was spun off from the company in December, changed its name to Kobo, and said it would develop its own e-reading device. It also struck a deal with Borders to sell e-books through the Borders.com site. Baker & Taylor formed a digital publishing division and signed deals with LibreDigital, Overdrive, and Donnelley to facilitate digital distribution. Scribd, the self-described "YouTube for books," signed an agreement with Simon & Schuster to create an S&S storefront on Scribd to sell e-books. Scribd draws about 30 million monthly visitors to its site, which features millions of print posts. To ease concerns of publishers and authors over piracy, Scribd developed a system to take down any material posted without permission of the copyright holder. In an effort to combat digital piracy, a number of publishers, including John Wiley and Hachette, signed with Attributor, a company that searches online for illegally posted material.

Mergers and Acquisitions

The biggest acquisition of 2009 was Disney's $4 billion purchase of Marvel Enterprises. The deal was completed at the end of 2010 and matches Marvel's characters with Disney's huge film and television businesses. It also brings Marvel's relatively small publishing operation into the Disney fold.

Baker & Taylor bought Blackwell Book Service North America (BNA) from British-based Blackwell as well as its James Bennett subsidiary in Australia. B&T is integrating BNA into its YBP Library Services unit.

Barnes & Noble, Inc. acquired Barnes & Noble College Booksellers, in a deal valued at $596 million, from B&N Chairman Len Riggio. The deal includes rights to the B&N name, which it had licensed from B&N College Booksellers. B&N said the acquisition of the college operation will add a reliable source of cash flow while providing growth opportunities for both the college and trade units. Earlier in the year, B&N acquired the e-bookstore Fictionwise for $13 million as part of its strategy to expand in the e-bookselling business.

To deepen its e-book presence, Amazon bought Lexcycle, the parent company of Stanza, the popular e-book reading app for the iPhone. An investment group led by CEO Barry Lipsky made a $19 million bid to buy Franklin Electronic Publishers; the transaction was still pending at the close of 2009.

In one of the few deals involving trade publishers, Random House acquired Ten Speed Press. AuthorSolutions cemented its place as the largest self-publisher in the country with its acquisition of Xlibris. Among some smaller acquisitions, Quick Publishing of St. Louis bought VanderWyk & Burnham of Acton, Massachusetts, and Kaplan Publishing bought the assets of the Cleveland Clinic Press. British-based Nicholas Brealey acquired the business book publisher Davies-Black. In a deal involving two agencies, William Morris merged with Endeavor.

Launched and Closed

Kirkus Reviews, the pre-publication review magazine, was set to be closed by parent company Nielsen at the end of the year, although there were ongoing negotiations to try to find a way to save the publication. In January, *Kirkus* announced that it had been acquired by a new company, Kirkus Media, created by investor Herbert Simon and headed by Marc Winkelman.

At the beginning of 2009, the *Washington Post* closed its stand-alone Sunday book review, *Book World. Post* reviews now run in an online *Book World* while print coverage appears in the paper's Outlook and Style & Art sections. Bloomberg Press, the small book-publishing arm of financial giant Bloomberg L.P., stopped acquiring new books late in 2009 and was winding down operations in early 2010. The press had nine employees and released about 28 books annually on business and investing.

Graphic Arts Center Publishing, one of the biggest independent publishers in the Northwest, filed for Chapter 7 liquidation in late fall and quickly began selling off its assets, including 350 active backlist titles, to pay creditors. Graphic Arts had emerged from bankruptcy earlier in the decade with help from Ingram, which distributed the company's products and was one of its largest creditors. Arcade

Publishing filed for bankruptcy early in 2009 following the death of cofounder Dick Seaver. In early fall, the bankruptcy court approved a plan to seek a buyer for Arcade's assets, which included 250 active backlist titles. Struggling Weinstein Books signed a deal with Perseus Books Group under which Perseus will undertake most publishing activities, including distribution, while Weinstein editors continue to acquire titles. Blu Sky Media, distributor for 72 small presses, closed in late summer, citing the recession and tight credit policies.

Former HarperCollins CEO Jane Friedman returned to the business as cofounder of Open Road Integrated Media. Jeff Sharp, an independent movie producer who had been in partnership with Harper, joined Friedman to launch the new venture, which was backed by $3 million in funding. Open Road will help to promote e-books from other publishers as well as publish its own e-books in a combination of original e-books and digital editions of titles previously published in print. Penguin's Dutton and Riverhead imprints started a new imprint, Redeemer, devoted to books from evangelical preacher Timothy Keller and his Redeemer Presbyterian Church.

After losing his position as head of Sterling's Union Square Books imprint, Philip Turner founded his own imprint and struck a deal with Rowman & Littlefield in which R&L would "host" his imprint, and its sister company, National Book Network, would distribute his titles. Turner hoped to form more hosting deals with other publishers. Ben LeRoy, founder of Bleak House, left the company to start Tyrus Books. Encyclopaedia Britannica teamed with Rosen Educational Services to launch Britannica Educational Publishing, which will release books and curriculum-correlated materials for the library and school market. Red Wheel/Weiser/Conari signed a joint operating pact with Hampton Roads Publishing under which Red Wheel took over distribution as well as all back office functions. Publications International launched a new adult nonfiction imprint, West Side Publishing. The independent house MacAdam/Cage, which had stopped buying books as it struggled with cash flow problems, received a cash infusion in November intended to allow the literary publisher to rebuild.

Harlequin started Carina Press, an imprint that will publish e-books only and sell them from the Harlequin Web site and third-party e-book retailers. Angela James, formerly with digital publisher Samhain Publishing, was named executive director. Another e-books-only publisher, Quartet Press, disbanded before it had a chance to release its first title. The company was backed by industry veteran Don Linn and attributed the shutdown to higher-than-expected costs and launch delays. Former Ingram executive and consultant Peter Clifton launched Filedby.com, a company that hosts Web pages for authors. More than 1.8 million pages were available at launch. In children's publishing, Capstone Publishers collaborated with Sports Illustrated Kids to launch a series of books for the school and library market.

People

Former Congressman Tom Allen officially took over as president of the Association of American Publishers in April, succeeding former Congresswoman Pat Schroeder. Rocco Landesman was appointed head of the National Endowment for the Arts, succeeding Dana Gioia who stepped down. Michael Healy ended a three-year term as executive director of Book Industry Study Group to serve as director designate for the Book Rights Registry, a new rights clearinghouse created as part of the Google Book Search settlement. Scott Lubeck, whose background included positions with Wolters Kluwer and Perseus Books, was named Healy's successor at BISG in early 2010.

Following the appointment of Ron Marshall as CEO of Borders, the chain had nearly a complete turnover of executives. Late in 2009 Bill Dandy was named senior vice president, marketing, with Art Keeney, who had held that post, moving to senior vice president, store operations. Larry Norton, former Simon & Schuster sales executive, moved to senior vice president, merchandising, for adult trade and children's books. S&S named Michael Edwards, former president and CEO of Ellington Leather, as executive vice president and chief merchandise officer, succeeding Anne Kubek.

At the nation's third-largest bookstore chain, Books-A-Million, Clyde Anderson returned as CEO, succeeding Sandy Cochran, who joined Cracker Barrel Old Country Store. Anderson, who was BAM's CEO from 1992 to 2004, remained its chairman. Oren Teicher was named CEO of the American Booksellers Association, succeeding Avin Domnitz. Teicher had been chief operating officer of the organization, and Len Vlahos was promoted to succeed him in that position. Karin Taylor was let go as executive director of the New York Center for Independent Publishing because of budget pressures.

Barry O'Callaghan, chairman of Houghton Mifflin Harcourt parent company Educational Media & Publishing Group, replaced HMH CEO Tony Lucki. David Naggar, former Random House executive and president of iAmplify.com, moved to Amazon, where he was named vice president, Kindle content. Steve Rubin, one-time head of Doubleday Broadway and publisher at large for Random House, landed at Henry Holt as president and publisher of the Macmillan imprint. Dan Farley, who led Holt since early 2008, is devoting his full attention to Macmillan Children's Publishing. Maria Rodale, daughter of company founders Robert and Ardath Rodale, took over as CEO of Rodale on September 1, succeeding Steve Murphy; she had been chairman of the company since 2007. Chris Navratil left his position as publisher of Andrews McMeel's Accord Publishing division to become publisher of Running Press. Mark Gompertz, publisher of Simon & Schuster's Touchstone Fireside imprint, was named to the newly created post of executive vice president, digital publishing, for the entire company. He was succeeded by Stacy Creamer, who had been editor-in-chief of Broadway Books. Richard Nash left as editorial director of Soft Skull Press to launch his own company. Barbara Epler was named publisher of New Directions Publishing.

Nancy Paulsen, president and publisher of Putnam Books for Young Readers, plans to start her own imprint in 2011, publishing 12 to 15 picture books and middle grade and young adult novels. Kirsty Melville, executive vice president and publisher at Andrews McMeel Publishing, was named president of its book division. Erik Engstrom was named CEO of Reed Elsevier, succeeding Ian Smith, who had held the role only eight months. Lance Fensterman, general manager of BookExpo America (owned by Reed Elsevier), was promoted and given responsibility for the company's pop culture shows. Steve Rosato was named to succeed Fensterman. Lorena Jones, former publisher of Ten Speed Press, joined

Chronicle Books as publishing director. Chronicle also brought on Josalyn Moran as its new children's publishing director. Moran had been vice president, children's buying, at Barnes & Noble. Bruce Nichols, publisher of HarperCollins's Collins imprint, was named senior vice president and publisher, adult and reference, at Houghton Mifflin Harcourt.

John Wiley took the somewhat unusual step of naming successors for three top executives getting close to retirement. Mark Allin was named to succeed Stephen Kippur as head of the professional/trade segment when he retires July 31, 2010; Steven Miron was named to succeed Eric Swanson as head of the STMS group on October 31, 2010; and Joseph Heider was picked to take the place of Bonnie Lieberman as head of the higher education group upon Lieberman's retirement on April 30, 2011. Will Balliett left as editor-in-chief of Hyperion to become publisher of Thames & Hudson. DC Comics publisher and president Paul Levitz stepped down as part of a reorganization by parent company Warner Bros. DC Comics was renamed DC Entertainment, and Diane Nelson was named president with orders to integrate the comics unit with Warner's movie, TV, and production businesses. In distribution, Rich Freese, resigned as president of BookMasters Distribution Services, to return to National Book Network as president.

A number of well-known book industry figures died in 2009, included several who were still active in the industry. Richard Seaver, founder of Arcade Publishing, died of a heart attack in early January. Jean Srnecz, vice president at Baker & Taylor, died in a plane crash in February. Judith Krug, the American Library Association's First Amendment advocate, died in the spring. Marshall Smith, cofounder of the large remainder trade show CIROBE, died in a motel on his way back to his home following the 2009 event. Michael Viner, founder of Phoenix Books and a pioneer of the audiobooks industry as the founder of Dove Audio, died in the summer of cancer. Another pioneer, Wally Hunt, died in the fall; Hunt was a key figure in reviving the children's pop-up book industry and was the founder of Intervisual Books.

Bestsellers

No author dominated the bestsellers lists in 2009 the way Stephenie Meyer had in 2008 as more titles than ever landed on the hardcover and trade paperback bestsellers list of *Publishers Weekly.* Meyer, with *The Host,* spent 29 weeks on the adult fiction hardcover list, the longest run of any author. In hardcover nonfiction, Malcolm Gladwell stayed on the list for the entire year, as did William Young in trade paperback with *The Shack.* The top-selling adult fiction title in 2009 was Dan Brown's *The Lost Symbol,* his first book since the publication of blockbuster *The Da Vinci Code.* In nonfiction, while Barack Obama stayed on the bestseller list with *Dreams from My Father,* the biggest nonfiction seller in 2009 was from political rival Sarah Palin, whose *Going Rogue* was an immediate hit when it was released in the fall.

After losing market share in 2008, Random House, the country's largest trade book publisher, gained ground on the 2009 bestsellers lists. The company's market share increased by 3.7 percent in both the hardcover and paperback categories. The hardcover increase was enough to boost Random's No. 1 position in hardcover from 21.4 percent of bestsellers in 2008 to 25.4 percent in 2009; Random had 100 titles reach the *Publishers Weekly* hardcover bestsellers list in 2009. Penguin USA and Hachette Book Group each increased their market share by 2.1 percent in 2009, and Penguin edged out Hachette for the second most hardcover bestsellers in the year. While Hachette had relatively few hardcover bestsellers (39 compared with 73 for Penguin), its titles remained on the list for a long period of time. Simon & Schuster's market share slipped 2.9 percent in 2009, placing it fourth, ahead of HarperCollins, which had a 10.8 percent share of the hardcover bestseller list.

In paperback, Penguin had a dramatic decline in market share in 2009, but still had the most paperback bestsellers and the highest market share (although its hold on the list fell from 32.5 percent to 22.0 percent). Random House's share of the paperback bestsellers list bounced back to 21.0 percent from 17.3 percent, putting it just behind Penguin. Simon & Schuster's share of the paperback market rose 2.7 percent to 11.4 percent, making it the third-largest publisher of paperback bestsellers in 2009. With an increase of 1.5 percent, Hachette's share of paperback bestsellers was 10.0 percent, putting it in fourth place, while Harper-Collins's 8.2 percent of paperback bestseller put it fifth.

Prices of U.S. and Foreign Published Materials

Narda Tafuri

Editor, ALA ALCTS Library Materials Price Index Editorial Board

The Library Materials Price Index (LMPI) Editorial Board of the American Library Association's Association for Library Collections and Technical Services' Publications Committee continues to monitor prices for a range of library materials from sources within North America and from other key publishing centers around the world.

The U.S. Consumer Price Index (CPI) rose 2.7 percent in 2009, an increase substantially higher than the 0.1 percent registered in 2008 and primarily due to a surge in the gasoline index, which was up 53.5 percent. The index for all items less food and energy rose 1.8 percent in 2009, which matches the increase seen in 2008.

Periodicals, college books and audiobooks continue to outperform the CPI. The 2009 cost of hardcover and trade paperback books fell when compared with 2008, and while the overall cost of mass market paperback books rose compared with 2008 it did not outperform the CPI. This year, for the first time, the hardcover books, mass market paperbacks, trade paperbacks, and audiobooks tables are organized by BISAC subject categories. The percent change has been recalibrated in the chart below to reflect this change. CPI data are obtained from the Bureau of Labor Statistics Web site at http://www.bls.gov/cpi. For additional information on consumer price trends, readers are referred to U.S. Bureau of Labor Statistics Economic News Release: http://data.bls.gov/cgi-bin/print.pl/news.release/cpi.nr0.htm.

Two new indexes have been established by compiler Stephen Bosch to track changes in textbook and e-book prices. The base index year has been set to 2007. These indexes have been added in response to reader demand for this type of information. Inflation of textbook prices for 2008 has seen a substantial increase over 2007. It far exceeds the increases exhibited by North American Academic Books in general, as well as the CPI.

	Percent Change				
Index	2005	2006	2007	2008	2009
CPI	3.4	2.5	4.1	0.1	2.7
Periodicals	7.8	7.3	7.2	8.0	6.4
Serials services	n.a.	n.a.	n.a.	n.a.	n.a.
*Hardcover books	n.a	5.90	-3.36	2.81	-1.18
Academic books	6.4	2.9	1.1	3.9	n.a.
E-books	n.a.	n.a.	n.a.	-4.8	n.a.
Textbooks	n.a.	n.a.	n.a.	5.5	n.a.
College books	1.7	3.0	0.47	3.3	4.1
*Mass market paperbacks	n.a.	0.47	0.47	1.56	2.46
*Trade paperbacks	n.a.	1.06	27.29	-9.75	-3.12
*Audiobooks	n.a.	-9.61	8.44	11.39	8.91
Newspapers	-0.9	1.8	-2.0	4.1	n.a.

n.a. = not available
* = figures revised based on BISAC categories

Due to unavailability of data, it was not possible to generate Table 2 (U.S. Serials Services) or Table 9 (British Academic Books) this year. A decision was made by the LMPI Editorial Board last year to discontinue indexing newspapers (former Tables 8A and 8B). For historical information, readers should consult past editions of the *Library and Book Trade Almanac.*

U.S. Published Materials

Tables 1 through 7A indicate average prices and price indexes for library materials published primarily in the United States. These indexes are U.S. Periodicals (Table 1), U.S. Hardcover Books (Table 3), North American Academic Books (Table 4), North American Academic E-Books (Table 4A), North American Academic Textbooks (Table 4B), U.S. College Books (Table 5), U.S. Mass Market Paperback Books (Table 6), U.S. Paperback Books (Excluding Mass Market) (Table 7), and U.S. Audiobooks (Table 7A).

Periodical and Serials Prices

The LMPI Committee and Swets Information Services jointly produce the U.S. Periodical Price Index (USPPI) (Table 1). The subscription prices shown are publishers' list prices, excluding publisher discount or vendor service charges. This report includes 2008, 2009, and 2010 data indexed to the base year of 1984.

More extensive reports from the periodical price index were published annually in the April 15 issue of *Library Journal* through 1992, in the May issue of *American Libraries* from 1993 to 2002, and in the October 2003 issue of *Library Resources and Technical Services*. The full reports for the 1999 through 2006 studies are available on the Web site of the Association for Collections and Library Technical Services (ALCTS) at http://www.ala.org/ala/mgrps/divs/alcts/resources/collect/serials/uspi.cfm. Future editions of the USPPI will also be posted on the ALCTS Web site as they are completed.

Compiled by Brenda Dingley, Table 1 shows that U.S. periodical prices, excluding Russian translations, increased by 7.1 percent from 2008 to 2009, and by 6.4 percent from 2009 to 2010. This compares with the overall rate of inflation from the last (2008) report at 8 percent. Including the Russian translation category, the single-year increase for 2009 to 2010 was also 6.4 percent. These figures compare with the 7.2 percent increase for the entire sample in 2009, and the 8 percent increase in 2008. In 2009 the overall greatest price increases were in the social sciences, which averaged an 8.4 percent overall increase, with the sciences atypically posting the lowest overall increases at 6.5 percent. In 2010, as in most other years, the sciences posted the highest average increase, at 7.6 percent, followed by the social sciences at 7.4 percent, and the humanities at 6.3 percent. Unlike 2009, when both Zoology and Industrial Arts increased more than 10 percent, no category showed double-digit price increases in 2010. Sociology and Anthropology titles showed the steepest increases in 2010, at 9 percent, with Psychology titles following at 8.6 percent. These were followed by Political Science and Education, which both increased 8.5 percent, with the rest of the social sciences showing much lower increases. Among the science and

(text continues on page 464)

Table 1 / U.S. Periodicals: Average Prices and Price Indexes, 2008–2010
Index Base: 1984 = 100

Subject Area	1984 Average Price	2008 Average Price	2008 Index	2009 Average Price	2009 Index	2010 Average Price	2010 Index
U.S. periodicals excluding Russian translations	$54.97	$436.90	794.8	$467.82	851.1	$497.63	905.3
U.S. periodicals including Russian translations	72.47	559.96	772.7	603.85	833.3	642.62	886.8
Agriculture	24.06	169.99	706.5	181.40	754.0	201.60	837.9
Business and economics	38.87	245.27	631.0	263.64	678.3	287.64	740.0
Chemistry and physics	228.90	2,333.37	1,019.4	2,482.16	1,084.4	2,622.14	1,145.5
Children's periodicals	12.21	29.98	245.5	33.43	273.8	35.87	293.8
Education	34.01	240.80	708.0	258.73	760.8	276.33	812.5
Engineering	78.70	688.98	875.5	734.14	932.8	786.72	999.6
Fine and applied arts	26.90	84.94	315.8	89.40	332.4	94.10	349.8
General interest periodicals	27.90	60.11	215.5	63.91	229.1	66.70	239.1
History	23.68	106.55	450.0	113.94	481.2	123.57	521.8
Home economics	37.15	225.51	549.5	246.26	600.1	260.64	635.1
Industrial arts	30.40	170.51	560.9	172.22	566.5	188.27	619.3
Journalism and communications	39.25	182.41	464.8	192.89	491.4	210.49	536.3
Labor and industrial relations	29.87	201.12	673.3	220.96	739.8	234.50	785.1
Law	31.31	141.02	450.4	149.04	476.0	157.88	504.2
Library and information sciences	38.85	161.15	414.8	172.63	444.4	179.80	462.8
Literature and language	23.02	96.35	418.5	102.92	447.1	109.32	474.9
Mathematics, botany, geology, general science	106.56	925.61	868.6	991.88	930.8	1,024.13	961.1
Medicine	125.57	1,224.41	975.1	1,317.81	1,049.5	1,427.56	1,136.9
Philosophy and religion	21.94	99.33	452.8	107.44	489.7	117.24	534.3
Physical education and recreation	20.54	81.79	398.2	87.73	427.1	91.48	445.4
Political science	32.43	241.37	744.3	261.05	805.0	273.80	844.3
Psychology	69.74	631.79	905.9	686.52	984.4	726.87	1,042.3
Russian translations	381.86	3,080.51	806.7	3,390.04	887.8	3,580.13	937.6
Sociology and anthropology	43.87	367.59	837.9	400.08	912.0	432.76	986.5
Zoology	78.35	911.89	1,163.9	980.66	1,251.6	1,047.35	1,336.8
Total number of periodicals							
Excluding Russian translations	3,731	3,728		3,728		3,728	
Including Russian translations	3,942	3,910		3,910		3,912	

Compiled by Brenda Dingley, University of Missouri, Kansas City, based on subscription information supplied by Swets Information Services.

Table 3 / U.S. Hardcover Books: Average Prices and Price Indexes, 2006–2009
Index Base: 2005 = 100

BISAC Category	2005 Average Prices	2006 Final			2007 Final			2008 Final			2009 Preliminary		
		Volumes	Average Prices	Index	Volumes	Average Prices	Index	Volumes	Average Prices	Index	Volumes	Average Prices	Index
Antiques and collectibles	$71.07	212	$58.69	82.6	200	$65.02	91.5	195	$80.84	113.7	162	$48.24	67.9
Architecture	66.99	769	74.01	110.5	788	71.47	106.7	853	77.54	115.7	819	81.55	121.7
Art	62.33	1,567	68.12	109.3	1,651	82.55	132.4	1,681	84.79	136.0	1,659	72.51	116.3
Bibles	48.05	215	49.46	102.9	176	41.20	85.8	191	49.19	102.4	169	45.84	95.4
Biography and autobiography	46.20	1,793	50.60	109.5	1,825	52.75	114.2	1,714	57.55	124.6	1,670	49.53	107.2
Body, mind, and spirit	26.76	233	27.15	101.5	208	31.50	117.7	233	26.12	97.6	199	27.69	103.5
Business and economics	120.56	3,399	140.10	116.2	3,452	126.71	105.1	3,581	134.29	111.4	3,865	118.80	98.5
Children	23.14	12,372	23.47	101.4	14,959	24.07	104.0	13,235	27.35	118.2	11,977	24.69	106.7
Comics and graphic novels	32.75	279	32.21	98.3	324	33.46	102.2	462	32.65	99.7	747	32.34	98.7
Computers	113.07	904	112.98	99.9	769	116.67	103.2	731	146.42	129.5	799	153.53	135.8
Cooking	28.68	835	30.59	106.7	878	27.65	96.4	1,015	29.99	104.6	768	29.65	103.4
Crafts and hobbies	28.82	297	25.55	88.6	338	26.78	92.9	267	27.57	95.7	232	29.54	102.5
Design	59.41	287	86.99	146.4	385	87.10	146.6	358	62.22	104.7	317	66.47	111.9
Drama	60.81	50	88.36	145.3	84	66.77	109.8	192	53.65	88.2	78	82.92	136.4
Education	95.10	1,271	107.76	113.3	1,245	111.28	117.0	1,330	111.90	117.7	1,385	100.92	106.1
Family and relationships	25.37	348	28.78	113.5	324	26.68	105.2	301	29.37	115.8	301	33.61	132.5
Fiction	28.37	4,518	28.78	101.5	4,627	33.61	118.5	4,976	29.03	102.3	4,484	28.77	101.4
Foreign language study	116.89	209	107.19	91.7	211	113.35	97.0	146	110.68	94.7	109	133.51	114.2
Games	32.07	205	28.73	89.6	154	29.50	92.0	145	39.16	122.1	165	36.53	113.9
Gardening	38.20	164	52.40	137.2	189	37.56	98.3	149	42.41	111.0	140	36.79	96.3
Health and fitness	54.05	405	50.20	92.9	405	54.06	100.0	449	61.08	113.0	358	54.88	101.5
History	88.17	4,630	92.87	105.3	4,766	85.18	96.6	4,795	87.46	99.2	4,639	86.48	98.1
House and home	31.51	145	33.82	107.3	152	36.80	116.8	117	40.85	129.6	114	40.39	128.2
Humor	19.00	213	18.11	95.3	227	20.71	109.0	241	20.42	107.5	232	19.88	104.6

Language arts and disciplines	120.71	1,135	126.73	105.0	1,404	130.09	107.8	1,300	133.45	110.6	1,553	132.50	109.8
Law	155.28	1,373	177.73	114.5	1,409	167.87	108.1	1,516	163.59	105.3	1,535	162.20	104.5
Literary collections	74.92	278	86.95	116.1	472	139.70	186.5	383	89.75	119.8	374	87.08	116.2
Literary criticism	123.84	1,584	104.51	84.4	1,823	102.68	82.9	1,707	106.08	85.7	1,877	107.68	86.9
Mathematics	144.88	1,098	125.88	86.9	1,029	122.66	84.7	916	127.81	88.2	908	113.31	78.2
Medical	156.54	3,054	160.58	102.6	3,118	153.14	97.8	3,076	154.91	99.0	3,001	163.23	104.3
Music	77.63	391	79.21	102.0	486	76.07	98.0	485	69.34	89.3	526	73.91	95.2
Nature	67.75	426	69.53	102.6	447	63.67	94.0	435	62.58	92.4	409	65.10	96.1
Performing arts	71.74	508	73.57	102.5	577	80.10	111.7	618	81.63	113.8	554	79.53	110.9
Pets	25.45	205	21.55	84.7	225	24.12	94.8	181	29.39	115.5	167	24.71	97.1
Philosophy	127.22	939	105.63	83.0	1,007	94.62	74.4	973	98.56	77.5	1,015	93.79	73.7
Photography	56.77	851	99.96	176.1	895	66.57	117.3	882	82.64	145.6	800	79.27	139.6
Poetry	36.58	330	39.50	108.0	351	42.30	115.6	339	42.50	116.2	287	42.89	117.3
Political science	103.39	2,230	95.01	91.9	2,315	99.59	96.3	2,492	97.13	93.9	2,718	100.14	96.9
Psychology	93.85	1,098	96.99	103.3	1,112	103.14	109.9	1,063	101.94	108.6	1,028	100.37	106.9
Reference	202.23	706	207.30	102.5	644	266.10	131.6	613	290.72	143.8	538	269.53	133.3
Religion	62.29	2,467	68.45	109.9	2,510	65.68	105.4	2,449	68.04	109.2	2,303	71.04	114.0
Science	203.44	3,358	201.47	99.0	3,214	213.59	105.0	3,171	204.74	100.6	3,223	182.60	89.8
Self-help	22.43	350	26.82	119.6	326	24.14	107.6	322	25.67	114.4	311	23.35	104.1
Social science	96.17	2,760	111.30	115.7	2,932	108.85	113.2	2,948	97.93	101.8	3,119	95.95	99.8
Sports and recreation	38.77	701	39.30	101.4	670	39.62	102.2	746	41.47	107.0	583	39.25	101.2
Study aids	105.28	44	78.87	74.9	21	87.52	83.1	17	78.49	74.6	24	112.83	107.2
Technology and engineering	187.80	1,980	167.50	89.2	1,947	156.46	83.3	2,145	158.80	84.6	2,470	156.21	83.2
Transportation	68.68	328	53.20	77.5	287	57.40	83.6	312	64.24	93.5	244	72.47	105.5
Travel	37.11	394	43.97	118.5	754	53.63	144.5	457	34.80	93.8	365	44.08	118.8
True crime	29.28	81	30.00	102.5	97	28.44	97.1	94	26.32	89.9	91	29.37	100.3
Young adult	50.17	2,313	48.80	97.3	2,749	50.68	101.0	2,256	49.41	98.5	2,294	34.25	68.3
Totals	$80.36	66,302	$85.10	105.9	71,158	$82.24	102.3	69,253	$84.55	105.2	67,705	$83.55	104.0

Compiled by Catherine Barr from data supplied by Baker & Taylor.

(continued from page 460)

technology categories, Agriculture titles showed the greatest price increases, at 8.4 percent, followed by Zoology at 8.2 percent, Home Economics at 8.1 percent, and Medicine at 8 percent. In 2009 Children's Literature, which in most years is the category that increases at the lowest rate, saw the highest inflationary increase of any single category, at 11.5 percent. In 2010 Children's Literature returned to a more usual form, showing the second-lowest increase at 4.1 percent, with the lowest category being General Interest periodicals, at 4 percent.

Book Prices

Tables 3 (hardcover books), 6 (mass market paperbacks), 7 (other paperbacks), and 7A (audiobooks), prepared by Catherine Barr, are once again derived from data provided by book wholesaler Baker & Taylor. This year, however, they use the Book Industry Study Group's BISAC categories. Updates to the Baker & Taylor database have resulted in slightly different results for earlier years and therefore these tables provide all-new data for 2005 forward. For more information on the BISAC categories, visit http://www.bisg.org.

Book prices were mixed in 2008 and preliminary figures indicated a similar situation for 2009. List prices for hardcover books (Table 3) rose 2.81 percent in 2008 and the preliminary 2009 average price ($83.55) remaining above a dip in 2007 ($82.24). Mass market paperback prices (Table 6) continued to show slow but steady increases, up 0.47 percent in 2007, a further 1.56 percent in 2008, and an additional 2.46 percent in early 2009 reporting. Trade paperback prices (Table 7), on the other hand, rose a strong 27.29 percent in 2007 but declined by 9.75 percent in 2008 and a further 3.12 percent in preliminary 2009 figures. Audiobook prices (Table 7A) were up 8.44 percent in 2007, 11.39 percent in 2008, and were showing a strong 8.91 percent increase in preliminary data for 2009.

The North American Academic Books Price Indexes (Tables 4, 4A, and 4B) are prepared by Stephen Bosch. The most significant news concerning the North American Academic Books Price Index (NAABPI) for 2008 is the addition of two indexes, one for e-books (Table 4A) and another for textbooks (Table 4B). Both of these areas were of high interest to users. Based on that input the indexes will debut with the base index year of 2007. In the academic market, it has always been assumed that e-books are more expensive than their print counterparts as the $9.95 versions of e-books available to consumers through channels such as Amazon are not available to libraries. The new index clearly points out the difference in price—the average price of an e-book in 2008 was $102.80 and the average price for print books was $70.64. Due to customer demands, vendors offer multiple platforms and pricing models for e-books and consequently there can be multiple prices for the same title. Only the first instance of a unique ISBN is included in the data, so if the same book was treated by a vendor from one e-book aggregator and then treated again from another aggregator only the first instance of the e-book is in the index. As electronic access is where the market is going, it is appropriate to have e-books as a separate index. It is also important to note that the e-book market is changing rapidly. This is reflected in the large swing in numbers of titles between 2007 and 2008. One vendor reported a huge jump in numbers in 2007 due to adding "catch-up" titles to their database. Increases in the costs of textbooks have been a hot topic on many campuses. The index for textbooks will try to document price change in this area.

The average price of print North American Academic Books in 2008 (Table 4) increased by 3.9 percent as compared with the 2007 average price. Over the past years the average prices had been trending higher (6.4 percent in 2005–2006), and this year the increase has continued. The number of titles treated this year declined slightly from 2007 (from 72,965 to 72,159). The drop in title count was fairly even across all price bands except for titles costing more than $120.00, which actually saw an increase. One driver in the 2008 price increase is the higher number of titles published at the high end of the price spectrum. Unlike all other price bands the >$120 area shows steady growth in the number of titles overall during the past four years. See Figure 1.

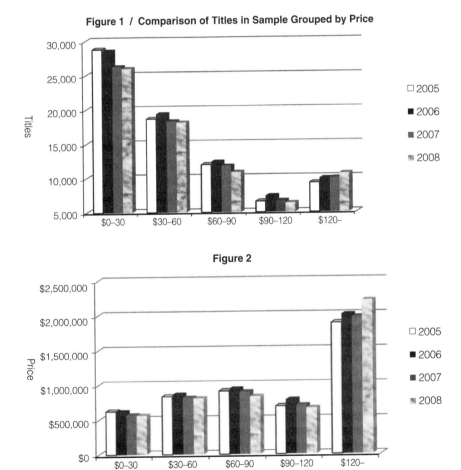

Figure 1 / Comparison of Titles in Sample Grouped by Price

Figure 2

The impact on pricing from the titles in the >$120 price band is confirmed if you look at the actual dollar values in groups (sum of all prices for titles in the group). It is clear that the increase in the top end of the index was the main component in the overall increase in the index for 2008. Although the $0–30 price area has the largest number of titles, dollar-wise it is the smallest portion as far as total cost (sum of all prices) goes in the index, and has been declining over the past four years. The increase in the prices in the upper end of the index was what added to the overall level of increase. See Figure 2.

The data used for this index are derived from all titles treated by Blackwell Book Services (BBS) and YBP in their approval plans during the calendar years listed. The index does include paperback editions as supplied by these vendors, and this inclusion of paperbacks as distributed as part of the approval plans has clearly influenced the prices reflected in the index figures. It is safe to say that the recent purchase of BBS by YBP means that this index in all likelihood will be very different next year.

E-books are now being treated in a separate index (Table 4A) and the impact on the index of separating out e-books will have to be monitored. Currently the vast majority of titles are published in both print and "e" versions, so the number of titles in the print index should not be affected until the industry moves toward more e-publishing with print as an added component to the electronic version. It is safe to say that in the future the number of titles in the print-only index should decline. At the same time, pricing for e-books should rise especially as we see more scientific, technical, and medical (STM) publishers move to publishing primarily "e" versions of their books. Many e-book pricing models add extra charges of as much as 50 percent to the retail price. This pricing model is reflected in the higher prices for e-books. The overall price for e-books did show a decline from 2007 to 2008, but as the number of titles treated had a huge variation it is not really possible to draw sound conclusions about pricing trends in e-books.

The first year of the price index for textbooks (Table 4B) shows a 5.5 percent increase for overall prices between 2007 and 2008. This increase is higher than the increase seen for the broader print index and the overall prices are also higher. These are indicators that the angst experienced by students as they purchase their texts may well be justified as prices appear to be increasing at a faster clip and the overall cost is 31 percent higher. It will take a little more time and data before any real trends can be identified.

Analysis of the data in the overall print index (Table 4) as it was processed still indicates that the overlap titles that are excluded from the index tend to be more expensive than the unique titles processed by each vendor. This fact will tend to hold down the average prices in the index. In all cases, the average price of a book for each vendor is 4 percent to 6 percent higher than the aggregate average price. This shows that when the titles are combined in the aggregate index the unique titles each vendor handles tend to be cheaper than the titles that overlap. This makes sense because publications from small publishers tend to be cheaper than those from mainstream publishers, and the small publishers will tend to make up more of the unique titles handled by each vendor. All vendors will carry the full title list from Macmillan or Oxford University Press, but a small regional press may not be supplied by all vendors. Current trends reported by vendors indicate that increases are going to grow in 2009 and there should also be increases in the titles and formats available.

Price changes vary, as always, among subject areas. This year there were several double-digit increases in subject areas and several areas saw prices decrease. If you look at the top areas for price increases, 2008 shows that STM areas did not show the largest price increases as these were in the Social Sciences and the general areas (A, Z). The areas showing double-digit increases were General Works, Library and Information Science, and Geography. Outside of Science most of the higher increases were seen in subject areas from the Social Sciences. It is interesting to note that some areas that showed high increases last year (Geology) are now at the other end of the spectrum of price increases.

It is good to remember that price indexes become less accurate at describing price changes the smaller the sample becomes. General Works and Library and Information Science are small samplings and showed very large increases, but to then conclude that all books in the area increased at similar rates is not correct. These areas have a small sample size (<500 titles) and the inclusion of just a few large, expensive items can have a major impact on prices for the category. In these areas there will be a lot of encyclopedias and other large reference works, so price volatility is expected. The inclusion of a few expensive items can really affect the overall average price when the number of titles in an area is small.

This compilation of the U.S. College Books Price Index (Table 5), prepared by Frederick C. Lynden, contains price and indexing information for the years 2007 through 2009 (index base year of 1989), and also the percentage change between 2008 and 2009. Data for the index was compiled from 6,632 reviews of books published in *Choice* during 2009; expensive titles ($500 or more) were omitted from the analysis, thus the total number of titles reported is smaller. As with the "North American Academic Books: Average Prices and Price Indexes" data, which appear annually in the *Library and Book Trade Almanac,* this index includes some paperback prices; as a result, the average price of books is less than if only hardcover books were included. Table 5 reports the number of titles, dollar amounts, percentages, and average price for books in 2009 in each *Choice* subject category. In 2009 the percentage of titles in the Humanities titles dropped while the percentage of titles in Science and Technology and the Social and Behavioral Sciences remained consistent.

The average price for Humanities titles in 2009 increased by 4.25 percent over the previous year. The average price for Science and Technology titles increased by more than 5 percent (5.44 percent) whereas the price for Social and Behavioral Sciences titles increased by 7.54 percent. Since 1989 there has been an overall average book price increase of 65 percent when reference books are included (and 65 percent when reference books are not included).

For 2009 the overall average price for books in the Humanities, Sciences, and Social and Behavioral Sciences (including reference books) was $67.18, a large increase of 4.12 percent over the average 2008 book price of $64.52. Calculated separately, reference books showed a 5.62 percent decrease from the previous year (2008). This decline is due to the large number of expensive sets, removed from the price study. Since 1989 there has been a 210 percent increase in the average price of reference books. Without reference books included, the

(text continues on page 481)

Table 4 / North American Academic Books: Average Prices and Price Indexes 2006–2008
Index Base: 1989 = 100

Subject Area	LC Class	1989		2006		2007		2008			
		No. of Titles	Average Price	No. of Titles	Average Price	No. of Titles	Average Price	No. of Titles	Average Price	% Change 2007–2008	Index
General works	A	333	$134.65	97	$72.40	109	$74.80	94	$99.84	33.5%	74.1
Philosophy and religion	B	3,518	29.06	5,745	59.32	5,448	56.25	5,458	58.59	4.1	201.6
Psychology	BF	890	31.97	1,010	55.27	1,027	59.04	1,011	64.67	9.5	202.3
History	C-D-E-F	5,549	31.34	7,296	52.54	6,838	55.45	6,916	60.12	8.4	191.8
Geography	G	396	47.34	788	80.11	706	80.60	723	89.52	11.1	189.1
Anthropology	GN	406	32.81	368	67.94	416	67.88	371	68.13	0.4	207.6
Physical education and recreation	GV	814	20.38	1,226	41.23	1,134	42.58	1,210	43.35	1.8	212.7
Business and economics	H	5,979	41.67	7,485	71.64	6,534	72.44	6,228	78.88	8.9	189.3
Sociology	HM	2,742	29.36	4,856	60.55	4,440	62.64	4,177	64.14	2.4	218.4
Political science	J	1,650	36.76	2,300	65.94	2,195	66.69	2,182	69.46	4.2	189.0
Law	K	1,252	51.10	2,701	87.26	2,788	98.78	2,956	105.83	7.1	207.1
Education	L	1,685	29.61	3,011	56.86	2,822	58.83	2,923	61.44	4.4	207.5
Fine and applied arts	M-N	3,040	40.72	4,652	52.77	4,761	53.28	4,873	54.10	1.5	132.9
Literature and language	P	10,812	24.99	12,551	45.69	12,595	44.91	12,678	43.97	-2.1	176.0
Science (general)	Q	433	56.10	416	84.02	328	92.59	337	101.57	9.7	181.1

Subject	LC	No. titles	Avg. price	No. titles	Avg. price	No. titles	Avg. price	No. titles	Avg. price	% change	Index
Mathematics and computer science	QA	2,707	44.68	3,365	76.47	2,939	79.16	2,992	82.92	4.7	185.6
Physics and astronomy	QB	1,219	64.59	1,285	104.67	1,100	101.91	1,007	109.68	7.6	169.8
Chemistry	QD	577	110.61	484	176.72	485	175.33	399	186.81	6.5	168.9
Geology	QE	303	63.49	203	100.12	191	118.23	201	103.36	-12.6	162.8
Zoology	QH,L,P,R	1,967	71.28	2,235	107.34	2,006	110.43	1,843	106.92	-3.2	150.0
Botany	QK	251	69.02	239	115.31	178	107.34	175	112.37	4.7	162.8
Medicine	R	5,028	58.38	6,550	85.21	5,757	86.01	5,632	91.63	6.5	157.0
Agriculture	S	897	45.13	963	65.14	995	76.22	911	79.70	4.6	176.6
Engineering and technology	T	4,569	64.94	5,666	98.67	5,156	100.13	4,955	103.12	3.0	158.8
Industrial arts	TT	175	23.89	237	32.54	248	36.01	221	39.05	8.4	163.4
Home economics	TX	535	27.10	683	41.23	686	43.62	658	42.16	-3.3	155.6
Military and naval science	U-V	715	33.57	643	58.96	603	56.40	527	60.83	7.9	181.2
Library and information science	Z	857	44.51	479	62.89	480	66.85	501	84.90	27.0	190.8
Average for all subjects		59,299	$41.69	77,534	$67.29	72,965	$68.01	72,159	$70.64	3.9%	169.4

Compiled by Stephen Bosch, University of Arizona, from electronic data provided by Blackwell Book Services and YBP Library Services. The data represents all titles (includes hardcover, trade, and paperback books, as well as annuals) treated for all approval plan customers serviced by the vendors. This table covers titles published or distributed in the United States and Canada during the calendar years listed.

This index does not include paperback editions. The inclusion of these items does impact pricing in the index.

Table 4A / North American Academic EBooks: Average Prices and Price Indexes 2007–2008

Index Base: 2007 = 100

Subject Area	LC Class	2007		2008			
		No. of Titles	Average Price	No. of Titles	Average Price	% Change 2007–2008	Index
General works	A	67	$107.08	25	$105.28	-1.7%	98.3
Philosophy and religion	B	4,154	92.86	3,355	97.33	4.8	104.8
Psychology	BF	1,185	81.55	668	83.98	3.0	103.0
History	C-D-E-F	5,058	90.95	3,157	77.91	-14.3	85.7
Geography	G	946	128.02	495	114.59	-10.5	89.5
Anthropology	GN	418	104.00	191	100.58	-3.3	96.7
Physical education and recreation	GV	660	93.21	392	63.87	-31.5	68.5
Business and economics	H	10,391	95.53	5,017	82.53	-13.6	86.4
Sociology	HM	4,681	95.31	2,797	86.20	-9.6	90.4
Political science	J	2,786	99.72	1,536	89.23	-10.5	89.5
Law	K	2,046	102.10	1,360	106.66	4.5	104.5
Education	L	2,769	104.24	1,277	97.76	-6.2	93.8
Fine and applied arts	M-N	1,310	82.41	868	74.64	-9.4	90.6
Literature and language	P	6,430	89.65	4,713	92.25	2.9	102.9
Science (general)	Q	502	112.29	321	107.49	-4.3	95.7
Mathematics and computer science	QA	4,445	101.58	2,164	105.78	4.1	104.1
Physics and astronomy	QB	2,063	139.14	1,142	141.80	1.9	101.9
Chemistry	QD	954	208.92	452	223.52	7.0	107.0
Geology	QE	223	134.63	162	148.89	10.6	110.6
Zoology	QH,L,P,R	3,561	148.52	1,806	152.63	2.8	102.8
Botany	QK	291	164.92	150	163.46	-0.9	99.1
Medicine	R	7,905	120.89	4,095	116.12	-3.9	96.1
Agriculture	S	1,003	124.99	569	134.57	7.7	107.7
Engineering and technology	T	7,487	130.89	3,317	129.88	-0.8	99.2
Industrial arts	TT	19	52.61	17	56.14	6.7	106.7
Home economics	TX	272	105.75	147	87.54	-17.2	82.8
Military and naval science	U-V	740	80.95	357	74.30	-8.2	91.8
Library and information science	Z	339	75.57	184	107.91	42.8	142.8
Average for all subjects		72,705	$107.99	40,734	$102.80	-4.8	95.2

Compiled by Stephen Bosch, University of Arizona, from electronic data provided by Blackwell Book Services and YBP Library Services. The data represents all Ebook titles treated for all approval plan customers serviced by the vendors. This table covers titles published or distributed in the United States and Canada during the calendar years listed.

Table 4B / North American Academic Text Books: Average Prices and Price Indexes 2007–2008

Index Base: 2007 = 100

Subject Area	LC Class	2007		2008			
		No. of Titles	Average Price	No. of Titles	Average Price	% Change 2007–2008	Index
General works	A	11	$76.79	2	$52.00	-32.3%	67.7
Philosophy and religion	B	267	48.87	268	53.27	9.0	109.0
Psychology	BF	196	86.19	225	86.82	0.7	100.7
History	C-D-E-F	180	62.87	215	65.02	3.4	103.4
Geography	G	105	91.86	128	98.16	6.9	106.9
Anthropology	GN	75	74.77	57	82.35	10.1	110.1
Physical education and recreation	GV	75	70.95	104	63.81	-10.1	89.9
Business and economics	H	1,096	90.48	1,125	99.13	9.6	109.6
Sociology	HM	647	70.66	673	72.24	2.2	102.2
Political science	J	208	68.65	217	71.95	4.8	104.8
Law	K	404	88.85	533	89.69	0.9	100.9
Education	L	489	61.83	508	66.49	7.6	107.6
Fine and applied arts	M-N	143	63.70	155	67.93	6.6	106.6
Literature and language	P	705	59.96	618	63.39	5.7	105.7
Science (general)	Q	42	103.09	50	83.06	-19.4	80.6
Mathematics and computer science	QA	1,052	84.40	1,056	84.87	0.6	100.6
Physics and astronomy	QB	350	105.25	325	108.87	3.4	103.4
Chemistry	QD	162	127.60	148	123.33	-3.4	96.6
Geology	QE	35	115.15	39	119.33	3.6	103.6
Zoology	QH,L,P,R	455	104.59	415	107.00	2.3	102.3
Botany	QK	18	105.94	29	121.21	14.4	114.4
Medicine	R	1,804	104.04	1,930	113.46	9.1	109.1
Agriculture	S	134	120.96	114	119.15	-1.5	98.5
Engineering and technology	T	1,050	104.79	1,186	109.34	4.3	104.3
Industrial arts	TT	20	69.50	23	81.36	17.1	117.1
Home economics	TX	67	66.60	61	99.77	49.8	149.8
Military and naval science	U-V	12	89.44	21	91.03	1.8	101.8
Library and information science	Z	37	60.87	60	68.88	13.2	113.2
Average for all subjects		9,843	$88.05	10,285	$92.86	5.5	105.5

Compiled by Stephen Bosch, University of Arizona, from electronic data provided by Blackwell Book Services and YBP Library Services. The data represents all textbook titles treated for all approval plan customers serviced by the vendors. This table covers titles published or distributed in the United States and Canada during the calendar years listed. This index does include paperback editions. The inclusion of these items does impact pricing in the index.

Table 5 / U.S. College Books: Average Prices and Price Indexes 1989, 2007–2009
Index Base: 1989 = 100

Subject	1989 No. of Titles	1989 Avg. Price per Title	2007 No. of Titles	2007 Avg. Price per Title	2007 Indexed to 1989	2007 Indexed to 2006	2008 No. of Titles	2008 Avg. Price per Title	2008 Indexed to 1989	2008 Indexed to 2007	2009 No. of Titles	2009 Avg. Price per Title	2009 Indexed to 1989	2009 Indexed to 2008	2009 Indexed Percent to Change 2008–2009
General	19	$40.19	n.a.	n.a.	n.a.	n.a.	n.a.	n.a.	n.a.	n.a.	n.a.	n.a.	n.a.	n.a.	n.a.
Humanities	21	32.33	61	$55.00	170.12	99.19	73	$56.95	176.15	103.55	80	$55.38	171.30	97.24	-2.76
Art and Architecture	276	55.56	152	57.55	103.58	108.05	150	57.84	104.10	100.50	161	58.30	104.93	100.80	0.80
Fine Arts	n.a.	n.a.	226	61.02	n.a.	104.34	116	68.77	n.a.	112.70	88	64.79	n.a.	94.21	-5.79
Architecture	n.a.	n.a.	75	57.00	n.a.	105.42	50	77.12	n.a.	135.30	55	62.38	n.a.	80.89	-19.11
Photography	24	44.11	48	51.76	117.34	102.82	18	46.64	105.74	90.11	30	54.44	123.42	116.72	16.72
Communication	42	32.70	93	58.83	179.91	115.33	98	54.17	165.66	92.08	90	61.00	186.54	112.61	12.61
Language and Literature	110	35.17	95	54.88	156.04	87.37	70	64.77	184.16	118.02	73	60.76	172.76	93.81	-6.19
African and Middle Eastern	n.a.	n.a.	24	49.58	n.a.	88.25	26	49.03	n.a.	98.89	30	48.68	n.a.	99.29	-0.71
Asian and Oceanian	n.a.	n.a.	40	54.07	n.a.	96.19	25	62.27	n.a.	115.17	23	55.94	n.a.	89.83	-10.17
Classical	75	43.07	27	77.23	179.31	112.02	29	81.64	189.55	105.71	29	74.51	173.00	91.27	-8.73
English and American	547	30.27	401	57.70	190.62	100.59	420	58.83	194.35	101.96	382	62.74	207.27	106.65	6.65
Germanic	38	32.18	29	61.66	191.61	94.88	29	66.89	207.86	108.48	25	65.85	204.63	98.45	-1.55
Romance	97	30.30	89	51.28	169.24	90.14	70	53.94	178.02	105.19	70	63.77	210.46	118.22	18.22
Slavic	41	27.92	15	67.01	240.01	155.91	20	44.41	159.06	66.27	16	55.17	197.60	124.23	24.23
Other	63	25.09	n.a.	n.a.	n.a.	n.a.	n.a.	n.a.	n.a.	n.a.	n.a.	n.a.	n.a.	n.a.	n.a.
Performing Arts	20	29.41	25	50.55	171.88	70.89	29	54.42	185.04	107.66	34	55.77	189.63	102.48	2.48
Film	82	33.00	133	52.44	158.91	100.85	159	58.12	176.12	110.83	163	66.89	202.70	115.09	15.09
Music	156	35.34	145	53.60	151.67	109.34	157	56.97	161.21	106.29	116	54.62	154.56	95.88	-4.12
Theater and Dance	58	34.18	43	51.20	149.80	88.86	41	64.11	187.57	125.21	48	62.44	182.68	97.40	-2.60
Philosophy	185	37.25	187	58.64	157.42	97.52	183	58.00	155.70	98.91	198	70.02	187.97	120.72	20.72
Religion	174	33.49	232	50.73	151.48	109.17	250	48.32	144.28	95.25	213	50.23	149.99	103.95	3.95
Total Humanities	2,009	$36.09	2,140	$56.09	155.42	101.78	2,013	$58.37	161.73	104.06	1,924	$60.85	168.61	104.25	4.25

	99	$46.90	65	$46.46	99.06	105.23	109	$53.68	114.46	115.54	89	$64.47	137.46	120.10	20.10
Science and Technology															
History of Science and Technology	74	40.56	95	47.73	117.68	116.24	96	46.72	115.19	97.88	90	61.47	151.55	131.57	31.57
Astronautics and Astronomy	22	50.56	71	50.37	99.62	92.32	68	50.64	100.16	100.54	82	54.41	107.61	107.44	7.44
Biology	97	51.01	138	58.18	114.06	83.53	145	71.31	139.80	122.57	140	72.10	141.34	101.11	1.11
Botany	29	63.91	48	55.62	87.03	76.13	85	77.65	121.50	139.61	82	86.09	134.71	110.87	10.87
Zoology	53	49.21	76	76.36	155.17	115.42	94	67.63	137.43	88.57	107	64.28	130.62	95.05	-4.95
Chemistry	21	70.76	76	116.67	164.88	105.54	70	109.05	154.11	93.47	50	103.32	146.01	94.75	-5.25
Earth Science	34	79.44	54	79.63	100.24	130.22	95	73.74	92.82	92.60	111	77.25	97.24	104.76	4.76
Engineering	87	66.74	90	90.31	135.32	83.08	90	95.23	142.69	105.45	101	102.62	153.76	107.76	7.76
Health Sciences	94	34.91	151	52.75	151.10	92.94	156	56.29	161.24	106.71	191	52.90	151.53	93.98	-6.02
Information and Computer Science	70	40.35	55	63.55	157.50	89.38	90	75.86	188.00	119.37	82	93.54	231.82	123.31	23.31
Mathematics	60	48.53	90	65.38	134.72	92.21	98	68.98	142.14	105.51	117	67.75	139.60	98.22	-1.78
Physics	22	43.94	81	79.13	180.09	116.49	65	63.43	144.36	80.16	47	64.30	146.34	101.37	1.37
Sports and Physical Education	18	27.46	20	37.52	136.64	92.89	65	38.72	141.01	103.20	56	51.82	188.71	133.83	33.83
Total Science	780	$49.54	1,110	$66.15	133.53	98.64	1,326	$67.34	135.93	101.80	1,345	$71.00	143.32	105.44	5.44
Social and Behavioral Sciences	92	$37.09	102	$60.65	163.52	121.35	108	$60.31	162.60	99.44	95	$64.92	175.03	107.64	7.64
Anthropology	96	39.94	96	67.55	169.13	118.28	142	56.41	141.24	83.51	125	68.14	170.61	120.79	20.79
Business Management and Labor	145	35.72	132	50.78	142.16	104.72	151	53.01	148.40	104.39	150	54.88	153.64	103.53	3.53
Economics	332	40.75	261	63.37	155.51	108.96	263	62.36	153.03	98.41	292	63.56	155.98	101.92	1.92
Education	71	34.50	159	51.75	150.00	96.69	163	52.71	152.78	101.86	170	58.33	169.07	110.66	10.66
History, Geography and Area Studies	59	42.10	105	49.33	117.17	89.71	111	51.33	121.92	104.05	102	53.59	127.29	104.40	4.40
Africa	44	34.85	29	54.94	157.65	95.90	29	62.02	177.96	112.89	24	63.61	182.53	102.56	2.56
Ancient History	n.a.	n.a.	57	71.50	n.a.	101.19	48	80.66	n.a.	112.81	44	63.06	n.a.	78.18	-21.82
Asia and Oceania	76	34.75	83	56.04	161.27	104.42	86	54.73	157.50	97.66	82	71.83	206.71	131.24	31.24
Central and Eastern Europe	n.a.	n.a.	60	55.80	n.a.	107.99	60	57.24	n.a.	102.58	60	68.85	n.a.	120.28	20.28
Latin America and Caribbean	42	37.23	56	52.06	139.83	92.68	71	53.15	142.76	102.09	60	55.14	148.11	103.74	3.74

Table 5 / U.S. College Books: Average Prices and Price Indexes 1989, 2007–2009 (cont.)

Index Base: 1989 = 100

Subject	1989		2007				2008				2009				
	No. of Titles	Avg. Price per Title	No. of Titles	Avg. Price per Title	Indexed to 1989	Indexed to 2006	No. of Titles	Avg. Price per Title	Indexed to 1989	Indexed to 2007	No. of Titles	Avg. Price per Title	Indexed to 1989	Indexed to 2008	Percent Change 2008–2009
Middle East and North Africa	30	36.32	45	64.82	178.47	125.06	45	50.17	138.13	77.40	44	68.44	188.44	136.42	36.42
North America	349	30.56	406	42.53	139.17	104.99	382	45.07	147.48	105.97	396	49.3	161.32	109.39	9.39
United Kingdom	n.a.	n.a.	73	56.88	n.a.	97.93	91	58.62	n.a.	103.06	62	64.55	n.a.	110.12	10.12
Western Europe	287	42.08	168	48.88	116.16	84.99	134	65.03	154.54	133.04	144	69.55	165.28	106.95	6.95
Political Science	28	33.56	37	60.88	181.41	126.54	6	54.30	161.80	89.19	3	103.00	306.91	189.69	89.69
Comparative Politics	236	37.82	228	58.17	153.81	98.93	207	60.16	159.07	103.42	185	70.93	187.55	117.90	17.90
International Relations	207	35.74	156	53.02	148.35	93.86	166	59.46	166.37	112.15	171	66.19	185.20	111.32	11.32
Political Theory	59	37.76	60	60.41	159.98	108.49	81	62.43	165.33	103.34	89	61.13	161.89	97.92	-2.08
U.S. Politics	212	29.37	160	46.88	159.62	95.79	218	49.15	167.35	104.84	218	50.30	171.26	102.34	2.34
Psychology	179	36.36	130	59.19	162.79	100.32	125	61.59	169.39	104.05	122	65.45	180.01	106.27	6.27
Sociology	178	36.36	257	57.14	157.15	109.78	237	61.09	168.01	106.91	258	59.86	164.63	97.99	-2.01
Behavioral Sciences	2,722	$36.43	2,860	$54.46	149.49	102.79	2,924	$56.40	154.82	103.56	2,896	$60.65	166.48	107.54	7.54
Total General Humanities	5,511	$38.16	6,110	$57.15	149.76	101.62	6,263	$59.35	155.53	103.85	6,165	$62.97	165.02	106.10	6.10
Science and Social Science Reference	636	$61.02	33	$136.26	n.a.	147.71	20	$72.36	n.a.	53.10	39	$93.36	153.00	129.02	29.02
General	n.a.	n.a.	139	114.51	n.a.	86.88	144	102.95	n.a.	89.90	115	112.72	n.a.	109.49	9.49
Humanities	n.a.	n.a.	64	96.76	n.a.	65.60	89	145.94	n.a.	150.83	85	117.06	n.a.	80.21	-19.79
Science and Technology	n.a.	n.a.	253	143.28	n.a.	99.03	198	162.60	n.a.	113.48	185	150.72	n.a.	92.69	-7.31
Total Reference	636	$61.02	489	$128.54	210.65	93.93	451	$136.26	223.30	106.01	424	$128.60	210.75	94.38	-5.62
Grand Total	6,147	$40.52	6,599	$62.44	154.10	100.47	6,714	$64.52	159.23	103.33	6,589	$67.18	165.79	104.12	4.12

Table 6 / U.S. Mass Market Paperback Books: Average Prices and Price Indexes, 2006–2009

Index Base: 2005 = 100

BISAC Category	2005 Average Prices	2005 Volumes	2006 Final Volumes	2006 Final Average Prices	2006 Final Index	2007 Final Volumes	2007 Final Average Prices	2007 Final Index	2008 Final Volumes	2008 Final Average Prices	2008 Final Index	2009 Preliminary Volumes	2009 Preliminary Average Prices	2009 Preliminary Index
Antiques and collectibles	$7.69	9	9	$7.82	101.7	9	$7.99	103.9	10	$8.59	111.7	9	$8.66	112.6
Architecture	n.a.	n.a.	n.a.	n.a.	n.a.	n.a.	n.a.	n.a.	n.a.	n.a.	n.a.	n.a.	n.a.	n.a.
Art	n.a.	n.a.	n.a.	n.a.	n.a.	n.a.	n.a.	n.a.	n.a.	n.a.	n.a.	n.a.	n.a.	n.a.
Bibles	n.a.	n.a.	n.a.	n.a.	n.a.	n.a.	n.a.	n.a.	n.a.	n.a.	n.a.	n.a.	n.a.	n.a.
Biography and autobiography	7.83	13	13	7.91	101	9	7.87	100.6	8	7.87	100.4	13	7.48	95.6
Body, mind and spirit	7.11	29	29	7.13	100.2	22	7.62	107.2	14	7.13	100.3	13	7.99	112.4
Business and economics	12.47	n.a.	n.a.	n.a.	n.a.	n.a.	n.a.	n.a.	1	7.99	64.1	1	9.99	80.1
Children	5.29	277	277	5.61	106.0	284	5.61	106.1	239	5.94	112.3	234	6.10	115.3
Comics and graphic novels	8.47	n.a.	n.a.	n.a.	n.a.	n.a.	n.a.	n.a.	n.a.	n.a.	n.a.	n.a.	n.a.	n.a.
Computers	n.a.	n.a.	n.a.	n.a.	n.a.	n.a.	n.a.	n.a.	n.a.	n.a.	n.a.	n.a.	n.a.	n.a.
Cooking	7.50	1	1	6.99	93.2	n.a.	n.a.	n.a.	n.a.	n.a.	n.a.	n.a.	n.a.	n.a.
Crafts and hobbies	n.a.	n.a.	n.a.	n.a.	n.a.	n.a.	n.a.	n.a.	n.a.	n.a.	n.a.	n.a.	n.a.	n.a.
Design	n.a.	n.a.	n.a.	n.a.	n.a.	n.a.	n.a.	n.a.	n.a.	n.a.	n.a.	n.a.	n.a.	n.a.
Drama	6.32	6	6	6.46	102.2	4	6.47	102.4	2	5.99	94.8	3	5.98	94.6
Education	n.a.	n.a.	n.a.	n.a.	n.a.	n.a.	n.a.	n.a.	n.a.	n.a.	n.a.	n.a.	n.a.	n.a.
Family and relationships	6.98	5	5	7.77	111.4	3	8.32	119.2	n.a.	n.a.	n.a.	2	5.99	85.8
Fiction	6.34	4,316	4,316	6.33	99.9	4,227	6.40	100.9	4,162	6.48	102.2	4,029	6.64	104.7
Foreign language study	n.a.	1	1	5.99	n.a.	4	6.74	n.a.	5	6.19	n.a.	4	6.99	n.a.
Games	7.14	9	9	6.65	93.1	19	5.54	77.6	13	5.45	76.4	5	4.99	69.9
Gardening	n.a.	n.a.	n.a.	n.a.	n.a.	n.a.	n.a.	n.a.	n.a.	n.a.	n.a.	n.a.	n.a.	n.a.
Health and fitness	7.43	33	33	7.23	97.3	18	7.49	100.8	18	7.66	103.1	14	7.70	103.7
History	7.90	16	16	7.74	98.0	13	7.76	98.2	3	5.83	73.8	5	7.69	97.4
House and home	5.99	n.a.	n.a.	n.a.	n.a.	n.a.	n.a.	n.a.	n.a.	n.a.	n.a.	n.a.	n.a.	n.a.
Humor	6.99	3	3	7.32	104.8	4	7.49	107.2	3	6.32	90.5	n.a.	n.a.	n.a.
Language arts and disciplines	6.99	n.a.	n.a.	n.a.	n.a.	n.a.	n.a.	n.a.	n.a.	n.a.	n.a.	n.a.	n.a.	n.a.
Law	6.99	1	n.a.	n.a.	n.a.	n.a.	n.a.	n.a.	n.a.	n.a.	n.a.	n.a.	n.a.	n.a.
Literary collections	n.a.	n.a.	1	7.95	n.a.	n.a.	n.a.	n.a.	1	4.99	n.a.	1	7.95	n.a.

Table 6 / U.S. Mass Market Paperback Books: Average Prices and Price Indexes, 2006–2009 (cont.)

Index Base: 2005 = 100

BISAC Category	2005 Average Prices	2005 Volumes	2006 Final Average Prices	2006 Final Volumes	2006 Final Index	2007 Final Average Prices	2007 Final Volumes	2007 Final Index	2008 Final Average Prices	2008 Final Volumes	2008 Final Index	2009 Preliminary Average Prices	2009 Preliminary Volumes	2009 Preliminary Index
Literary criticism	$7.95	n.a.	n.a.	n.a.	n.a.	n.a.	n.a.	n.a.	$7.95	1	100	$7.99	1	100.5
Mathematics	n.a.	n.a.	n.a.	n.a.	n.a.	n.a.	n.a.	n.a.	n.a.	n.a.	n.a.	n.a.	n.a.	n.a.
Medical	7.83	4	$6.62	4	84.5	$6.87	4	87.7	7.50	1	95.8	8.99	1	114.8
Music	7.95	n.a.	n.a.	n.a.	n.a.	n.a.	n.a.	n.a.	n.a.	n.a.	n.a.	n.a.	n.a.	n.a.
Nature	n.a.	n.a.	n.a.	n.a.	n.a.	n.a.	n.a.	n.a.	n.a.	n.a.	n.a.	n.a.	n.a.	n.a.
Performing arts	8.23	2	8.49	2	103.2	8.64	3	105.0	9.99	1	121.4	9.99	1	121.4
Pets	n.a.	n.a.	n.a.	n.a.	n.a.	n.a.	n.a.	n.a.	7.99	1	n.a.	n.a.	n.a.	n.a.
Philosophy	7.49	5	7.58	5	101.2	7.78	5	103.9	5.95	2	79.4	n.a.	n.a.	n.a.
Photography	n.a.	1	6.99	1	n.a.	n.a.	n.a.	n.a.	n.a.	n.a.	n.a.	n.a.	n.a.	n.a.
Poetry	5.75	2	5.95	2	103.5	5.95	1	103.5	4.95	2	86.1	6.95	5	120.9
Political science	n.a.	2	7.45	2	n.a.	6.99	1	n.a.	7.99	2	n.a.	5.95	1	n.a.
Psychology	7.97	3	7.99	3	100.3	7.97	2	100.0	n.a.	n.a.	n.a.	n.a.	n.a.	n.a.
Reference	6.85	11	10.13	11	147.9	6.49	3	94.8	7.16	3	104.5	7.49	3	109.4
Religion	9.96	6	7.65	6	76.8	6.99	2	70.2	7.74	4	77.7	6.98	3	70.0
Science	n.a.	1	7.99	1	n.a.	n.a.	n.a.	n.a.	6.95	1	n.a.	n.a.	n.a.	n.a.
Self-help	12.45	13	7.43	13	59.7	7.80	6	62.7	9.64	3	77.5	7.99	2	64.2
Social science	7.08	1	7.99	1	112.9	7.99	1	112.9	n.a.	n.a.	n.a.	n.a.	n.a.	n.a.
Sports and recreation	7.62	2	7.99	2	104.9	7.49	2	98.3	7.99	3	104.9	6.99	3	91.7
Study aids	n.a.	n.a.	n.a.	n.a.	n.a.	n.a.	n.a.	n.a.	n.a.	n.a.	n.a.	n.a.	n.a.	n.a.
Technology and engineering	n.a.	n.a.	n.a.	n.a.	n.a.	n.a.	n.a.	n.a.	n.a.	n.a.	n.a.	n.a.	n.a.	n.a.
Transportation	12.95	n.a.	7.99	n.a.	n.a.	n.a.	n.a.	n.a.	n.a.	n.a.	n.a.	14.00	1	108.1
Travel	n.a.	1	n.a.	1	n.a.	n.a.	1	n.a.	6.95	1	n.a.	4.95	1	n.a.
True crime	7.19	44	7.43	44	103.4	7.42	51	103.2	7.35	53	102.2	7.44	51	103.5
Young adult	6.46	200	6.93	200	107.2	6.79	159	105.2	7.10	142	109.9	7.65	94	118.3
Totals	$6.34	5,017	$6.37	5,017	100.4	$6.40	4,856	101.0	$6.50	4,699	102.5	$6.66	4,500	105.0

Compiled by Catherine Barr from data supplied by Baker & Taylor.

n.a. = not available

Table 7 / U.S. Paperback Books (Excluding Mass Market): Average Prices and Price Indexes, 2006–2009

Index Base: 2005 = 100

BISAC Category	2005		2006 Final		2007 Final			2008 Final			2009 Preliminary		
	Average Prices	Volumes	Average Prices	Index	Volumes	Average Prices	Index	Volumes	Average Prices	Index	Volumes	Average Prices	Index
Antiques and collectibles	$24.80	282	$24.86	100.2	275	$121.12	488.4	239	$27.08	109.2	192	$27.28	110.0
Architecture	38.90	597	38.67	99.4	717	40.17	103.3	694	41.89	107.7	645	42.24	108.6
Art	31.28	1,515	32.20	102.9	1,692	34.43	110.1	1,581	37.55	120.0	1,472	36.54	116.8
Bibles	36.87	470	38.07	103.3	291	40.08	108.7	363	49.29	133.7	273	40.31	109.3
Biography and autobiography	19.19	2,108	19.87	103.5	2,278	20.92	109.0	2,211	20.31	105.8	2,437	20.29	105.8
Body, mind and spirit	17.48	991	17.17	98.2	1,045	17.67	101.1	1,072	18.47	105.7	963	18.03	103.2
Business and economics	71.12	6,206	70.83	99.6	11,053	106.82	150.2	5,937	73.97	104.0	5,817	59.50	83.7
Children	11.11	9,409	10.28	92.6	9,136	10.43	93.9	9,099	10.79	97.1	9,678	11.10	99.9
Comics and graphic novels	12.75	1,998	13.61	106.7	2,167	15.18	119.1	2,407	14.15	110.9	2,263	15.35	120.4
Computers	57.01	3,112	61.44	107.8	3,809	79.96	140.3	3,279	87.12	152.8	3,771	96.01	168.4
Cooking	18.30	992	19.06	104.1	1,068	17.98	98.2	1,271	18.84	102.9	964	19.64	107.3
Crafts and hobbies	18.49	1,024	19.12	103.4	906	20.31	109.8	943	19.98	108.1	853	21.07	113.9
Design	32.87	352	32.67	99.4	415	35.91	109.3	381	34.18	104.0	376	35.41	107.7
Drama	16.40	449	18.07	110.2	578	18.16	110.7	521	18.66	113.8	580	21.41	130.5
Education	35.10	4,031	37.42	106.6	4,166	36.98	105.3	3,929	37.21	106.0	3,119	38.12	108.6
Family and relationships	17.10	1,033	18.05	105.5	983	18.23	106.6	951	17.78	104.0	928	19.40	113.5
Fiction	15.74	8,119	16.19	102.9	9,517	17.74	112.7	9,480	16.30	103.6	9,874	17.23	109.5
Foreign language study	41.90	1,356	39.13	93.4	1,209	34.78	83.0	1,405	30.19	72.0	898	30.22	72.1
Games	16.53	965	16.11	97.5	847	16.90	102.2	800	17.08	103.3	778	17.69	107.0
Gardening	20.59	250	20.29	98.5	241	19.86	96.5	368	18.93	92.0	254	21.49	104.4
Health and fitness	22.81	1,612	24.88	109.1	1,539	22.39	98.2	1,373	24.19	106.1	1,345	24.12	105.7
History	33.53	5,854	33.23	99.1	6,743	35.19	105.0	5,856	31.85	95.0	6,075	30.90	92.2
House and home	19.33	330	20.21	104.6	327	20.72	107.2	295	20.23	104.6	227	21.99	113.8
Humor	12.96	482	13.95	107.6	477	13.29	102.5	463	13.49	104.1	479	13.56	104.6
Language arts and disciplines	49.14	1,992	53.78	109.4	2,022	51.59	105.0	1,654	53.38	108.6	1,952	59.96	122.0
Law	60.92	3,129	53.90	88.5	2,857	80.75	132.5	3,781	115.14	189.0	2,667	73.67	120.9
Literary collections	28.07	361	28.89	102.9	559	43.66	155.5	540	35.23	125.5	577	33.54	119.5

Table 7 / U.S. Paperback Books (Excluding Mass Market): Average Prices and Price Indexes, 2006–2009 (cont.)

Index Base: 2005 = 100

BISAC Category	2005		2006 Final			2007 Final			2008 Final			2009 Preliminary		
	Average Prices	Volumes	Average Prices		Index	Volumes	Average Prices	Index	Volumes	Average Prices	Index	Volumes	Average Prices	Index
Literary criticism	$31.99	1,453	$36.48		114.0	1,577	$36.60	114.4	1,446	$36.57	114.3	1,689	$37.12	116.1
Mathematics	75.77	963	70.25		92.7	989	74.91	98.9	961	61.82	81.6	850	65.79	86.8
Medical	64.27	4,045	63.30		98.5	4,153	69.32	107.9	3,986	74.82	116.4	3,886	74.77	116.3
Music	22.66	2,851	25.00		110.3	2,659	26.95	118.9	2,921	21.67	95.6	2,723	23.24	102.5
Nature	26.90	707	26.81		99.7	698	25.98	96.6	604	25.42	94.5	615	26.64	99.0
Performing arts	27.85	979	32.09		115.2	1,100	30.43	109.3	991	31.01	111.3	957	33.36	119.8
Pets	18.86	331	17.97		95.3	321	17.53	93.0	292	18.70	99.2	301	19.02	100.8
Philosophy	31.40	1,101	33.31		106.1	1,619	32.69	104.1	1,271	30.93	98.5	1,415	33.62	107.1
Photography	27.74	511	28.32		102.1	480	31.94	115.1	535	32.87	118.5	530	30.12	108.6
Poetry	16.09	1,710	15.73		97.7	1,863	17.19	106.8	1,784	16.50	102.5	1,649	16.82	104.6
Political science	45.65	2,885	38.29		83.9	3,663	59.46	130.3	3,142	37.58	82.3	3,205	37.05	81.2
Psychology	45.74	1,457	44.63		97.6	1,575	45.22	98.9	1,377	41.37	90.4	1,231	40.55	88.6
Reference	52.54	1,472	62.93		119.8	1,276	65.70	125.0	1,353	68.97	131.3	1,281	89.59	170.5
Religion	20.54	5,628	20.92		101.8	5,549	20.51	99.8	5,796	20.12	98.0	5,695	21.19	103.1
Science	71.05	2,236	69.76		98.2	2,346	74.30	104.6	2,099	70.80	99.6	2,384	74.82	105.3
Self-help	16.36	1,017	16.75		102.4	1,216	16.92	103.4	1,148	17.17	105.0	1,073	17.58	107.5
Social science	36.83	3,898	39.55		107.4	4,061	38.53	104.6	4,037	40.16	109.0	3,789	39.46	107.1
Sports and recreation	21.82	1,478	23.02		105.5	1,381	22.74	104.2	1,331	23.77	108.9	1,235	23.27	106.7
Study aids	30.90	1,142	31.16		100.8	682	32.02	103.6	880	32.14	104.0	692	30.14	97.6
Technology and engineering	85.80	1,964	86.42		100.7	2,689	139.50	162.6	2,583	154.07	179.6	2,625	153.13	178.5
Transportation	40.19	666	35.64		88.7	414	35.30	87.8	430	39.28	97.7	446	38.06	94.7
Travel	19.18	2,915	19.81		103.3	3,449	21.03	109.6	3,077	20.33	106.0	2,756	20.48	106.8
True crime	17.71	105	17.74		100.2	154	18.65	105.3	144	18.17	102.6	155	19.09	107.8
Young adult	14.06	2,583	14.39		102.3	3,108	13.85	98.5	2,555	13.76	97.9	2,242	14.06	100.0
Totals	$33.90	103,116	$34.26		101.1	113,939	$43.61	128.6	105,636	$39.36	116.1	102,881	$38.13	112.5

Compiled by Catherine Barr from data supplied by Baker & Taylor.

Table 7A / U.S. Audiobooks: Average Prices and Price Indexes, 2006–2009
Index Base: 2005 = 100

BISAC Category	2005 Average Prices	2006 Final Volumes	2006 Final Average Prices	2006 Final Index	2007 Final Volumes	2007 Final Average Prices	2007 Final Index	2008 Final Volumes	2008 Final Average Prices	2008 Final Index	2009 Preliminary Volumes	2009 Preliminary Average Prices	2009 Preliminary Index
Antiques and collectibles	n.a.	n.a.	n.a.	n.a.	1	$11.95	n.a.	n.a.	n.a.	n.a.	1	$74.95	n.a.
Architecture	$68.95	3	$36.66	53.2	n.a.	n.a.	n.a.	2	$37.47	54.3	n.a.	n.a.	n.a.
Art	57.51	3	33.63	58.5	5	40.18	69.9	5	40.99	71.3	8	67.36	117.1
Bibles	47.08	52	45.51	96.7	34	51.45	109.3	20	41.83	88.9	10	66.97	142.2
Biography and autobiography	37.68	378	37.93	100.7	453	44.53	118.2	641	47.05	124.9	704	50.07	132.9
Body, mind and spirit	26.74	73	30.33	113.4	81	33.52	125.4	83	38.28	143.2	81	39.79	148.8
Business and economics	42.11	242	37.28	88.5	295	34.17	81.1	426	39.54	93.9	443	45.88	109.0
Children	26.57	534	27.14	102.1	876	28.80	108.4	733	31.09	117.0	826	36.16	136.1
Comics and graphic novels	n.a.	n.a.	n.a.	n.a.	n.a.	n.a.	n.a.	n.a.	n.a.	n.a.	n.a.	n.a.	n.a.
Computers	41.39	2	27.45	66.3	n.a.	n.a.	n.a.	4	31.23	75.4	5	46.99	113.5
Cooking	14.45	13	15.72	108.8	7	35.40	245.0	4	14.71	101.8	14	44.70	309.3
Crafts and hobbies	n.a.	n.a.	n.a.	n.a.	10	26.96	n.a.	9	42.20	n.a.	4	38.72	n.a.
Design	n.a.	n.a.	n.a.	n.a.	n.a.	n.a.	n.a.	n.a.	n.a.	n.a.	n.a.	n.a.	n.a.
Drama	23.45	40	26.59	113.4	27	29.74	126.8	48	36.67	156.4	162	34.22	145.9
Education	27.46	35	28.42	103.5	27	40.39	147.1	17	29.78	108.5	22	49.23	179.3
Family and relationships	24.58	34	28.05	114.1	47	31.52	128.3	73	36.73	149.4	54	39.41	160.3
Fiction	41.47	3,131	39.96	96.4	3,644	44.08	106.3	4,379	48.43	116.8	6,335	52.12	125.7
Foreign language study	70.04	424	42.05	60.0	314	41.17	58.8	394	37.63	53.7	242	41.60	59.4
Games	32.68	2	34.95	106.9	n.a.	n.a.	n.a.	1	14.95	45.7	6	14.12	43.2
Gardening	n.a.	n.a.	n.a.	n.a.	3	30.62	n.a.	2	39.97	n.a.	n.a.	n.a.	n.a.
Health and fitness	26.61	70	28.16	105.8	60	31.89	119.8	83	33.32	125.2	85	45.39	170.6
History	41.61	294	41.04	98.6	480	48.35	116.2	577	54.71	131.5	453	57.38	137.9
House and home	25.00	2	29.54	118.2	1	29.95	119.8	n.a.	n.a.	n.a.	n.a.	n.a.	n.a.
Humor	29.60	56	31.15	105.2	59	30.31	102.4	65	36.20	122.3	72	40.87	138.1
Language arts and disciplines	60.84	34	32.21	52.9	31	55.43	91.1	14	36.96	60.7	17	45.88	75.4
Law	55.32	49	75.23	136.0	24	59.46	107.5	18	54.21	98.0	8	49.97	90.3
Literary collections	24.71	5	26.18	105.9	16	28.73	116.2	16	38.91	157.5	21	32.03	129.6

Table 7A / U.S. Audiobooks: Average Prices and Price Indexes, 2006–2009 *(cont.)*
Index Base: 2005 = 100

BISAC Category	2005		2006 Final			2007 Final			2008 Final			2009 Preliminary		
	Average Prices	Volumes	Volumes	Average Prices	Index	Volumes	Average Prices	Index	Volumes	Average Prices	Index	Volumes	Average Prices	Index
Literary criticism	$26.41	25	25	$23.57	89.2	18	$35.63	134.9	35	$49.61	187.8	21	$42.31	160.2
Mathematics	n.a.	n.a.	n.a.	n.a.	n.a.	1	89.99	n.a.	n.a.	n.a.	n.a.	n.a.	n.a.	n.a.
Medical	153.72	23	23	42.62	27.7	20	68.55	44.6	25	96.61	62.8	13	60.55	39.4
Music	29.83	170	170	24.77	83.0	121	27.58	92.5	144	29.46	98.8	97	37.14	124.5
Nature	28.92	8	8	26.71	92.4	21	33.07	114.3	27	39.18	135.5	38	46.56	161.0
Performing arts	25.78	32	32	32.44	125.8	18	25.38	98.4	39	38.32	148.6	21	46.23	179.3
Pets	33.05	11	11	28.33	85.7	10	29.28	88.6	20	34.05	103.0	23	43.51	131.6
Philosophy	35.30	63	63	26.52	75.1	24	40.01	113.3	37	41.33	117.1	37	52.06	147.5
Photography	n.a.	n.a.	n.a.	n.a.	n.a.	n.a.	n.a.	n.a.	n.a.	n.a.	n.a.	n.a.	n.a.	n.a.
Poetry	22.87	80	80	21.57	94.3	54	24.30	106.2	45	25.88	113.2	50	35.88	156.9
Political science	42.66	108	108	30.71	72.0	151	40.97	96.0	174	44.16	103.5	184	48.98	114.8
Psychology	35.70	11	11	29.18	81.7	30	36.19	101.4	31	37.38	104.7	54	51.94	145.5
Reference	21.20	20	20	14.89	70.2	7	34.10	160.8	15	32.78	154.6	6	46.32	218.5
Religion	26.52	360	360	26.50	99.9	377	27.07	102.1	313	30.20	113.9	439	31.88	120.2
Science	39.86	41	41	35.86	90.0	30	39.73	99.7	61	48.59	121.9	64	47.59	119.4
Self-help	23.58	167	167	25.87	109.7	297	27.61	117.1	207	29.98	127.1	296	38.03	161.3
Social science	35.73	61	61	32.29	90.4	63	35.52	99.4	55	40.17	112.4	79	50.36	140.9
Sports and recreation	28.46	21	21	27.79	97.7	45	38.44	135.1	57	39.75	139.7	40	46.28	162.6
Study aids	41.85	23	23	58.52	139.8	9	43.36	103.6	18	67.10	160.3	21	33.92	81.0
Technology and engineering	61.47	5	5	36.77	59.8	12	33.88	55.1	10	52.09	84.7	6	52.49	85.4
Transportation	28.00	3	3	42.97	153.5	n.a.	n.a.	n.a.	n.a.	n.a.	n.a.	3	36.66	130.9
Travel	41.91	13	13	22.35	53.3	45	46.24	110.3	39	44.73	106.7	18	50.20	119.8
True crime	35.97	23	23	48.20	134.0	30	41.90	116.5	59	51.41	142.9	47	49.77	138.4
Young adult	35.68	240	240	42.84	120.1	273	39.87	111.7	269	45.52	127.6	47	44.21	123.9
Totals	$40.49	6,984	6,984	$36.60	90.4	8,151	$39.69	98.0	9,294	$44.21	109.2	11,671	$48.15	118.9

Compiled by Catherine Barr from data supplied by Baker & Taylor.

(continued from page 467)
2009 average book price was $62.97, a major 6.1 percent increase over the average 2008 price of $59.35.

Questions regarding this index should be addressed to the author: Frederick Lynden, Retired Director, Scholarly Communication and Library Research, Brown University Library, Providence, RI 02912 (e-mail Flynden@stanford alumni.org).

Prices of Other Media

The Library Materials Price Index Editorial Board is continuing to work on developing a price index for electronic journals. It is hoped that a pricing model and index can be developed for next year's article.

Foreign Prices

The dollar lost some ground against the euro, the British pound sterling, and the Canadian dollar, yet continued to prove stronger when compared with 2007 exchange rates. The dollar continued its decline against the Japanese yen. The volatility of world economies is quite apparent.

Dates	12/31/05*	12/31/06*	12/30/07*	12/31/08*	12/31/09*
Canada	1.1680	1.1720	0.9990	1.1910	1.0510
Euro	0.8470	0.7590	0.6800	0.7310	0.6950
U.K.	0.5820	0.5120	0.4860	0.6570	0.6160
Japan	117.9400	119.5300	110.8800	92.6500	92.3900

* Data from Financial Management Services. U.S. Treasury Department, http://fms.treas.gov/intn.html.

We were unable to update the price index for British Academic Books this year because of discrepancies in the data. Data will be reviewed over the coming year and the table will either be re-established or dropped. No other foreign price indexes are available at this time. Readers are referred to past editions of the *Library and Book Trade Almanac* for historical information.

Using the Price Indexes

Librarians are encouraged to monitor trends in the publishing industry and changes in economic conditions when preparing budget forecasts and projections. The ALA ALCTS Library Materials Price Index Editorial Board endeavors to make information on publishing trends readily available by sponsoring the annual compilation and publication of price data contained in Tables 1 to 7A. The indexes cover newly published library materials and document prices and rates of percent changes at the national and international level. They are useful benchmarks against which local costs can be compared, but because they reflect retail prices in the aggregate, they are not a substitute for cost data that reflect the collecting patterns of individual libraries, and they are not a substitute for specific cost studies.

Differences between local prices and those found in national indexes arise partially because these indexes exclude discounts, service charges, shipping and handling fees, and other costs that the library might incur. Discrepancies may also relate to a library's subject coverage; mix of titles purchased, including both current and backfiles; and the proportion of the library's budget expended on domestic or foreign materials. These variables can affect the average price paid by an individual library, although the individual library's rate of increase may not differ greatly from the national indexes.

LMPI is interested in pursuing studies that would correlate a particular library's costs with the national prices. The group welcomes interested parties to its meetings at ALA Annual and Midwinter conferences.

The Library Materials Price Index Editorial Board consists of compilers Catherine Barr, Ajaye Bloomstone, Stephen Bosch, Stephanie Braunstein, Brenda Dingley, Virginia Gilbert, Frederick Lynden, and editor Narda Tafuri.

Book Title Output and Average Prices: 2006–2009

Catherine Barr
Contributing Editor

Constance Harbison
Baker & Taylor

The economic difficulties of the past two years are showing clearly in the publishing market. American book title output slowed in 2008 and preliminary figures for 2009 indicate a continuing pullback in production. After growing by 3.7 percent in 2005, 0.5 percent in 2006, and 8.9 percent in 2007, the number of titles published dropped by 5.5 percent in 2008 and preliminary figures for 2009— publishers were still submitting late 2009 titles in early 2010—showed a further decline of 2.5 percent.

The figures in this edition of the *Library and Book Trade Almanac* were provided by book wholesaler Baker & Taylor and this year, for the first time, are based on the Book Industry Study Group's BISAC categories. The BISAC juvenile category (fiction and nonfiction) has been divided into children's and young adult. Final figures for 2005 through 2007 have been restated, reflecting updates to the Baker & Taylor database.

For more information on the BISAC categories, visit http://www.bisg.org.

Output by Format and by Category

Title output fell in every format except audiobooks in 2008, with hardcover titles and editions falling by 1,905 (2.68 percent) following a gain of 4,856 (7.32 percent) in 2007. Hardcovers priced at less than $81—nearly 70 percent of the hardcover market—fell by 1,270 titles (2.64 percent) in 2008 after increasing by 4,134 (9.41 percent) in 2007. Mass market paperback output fell by 157 titles (3.23 percent) in 2008, following on a drop of 161 titles (3.21 percent) in 2007. Trade paperbacks registered a decrease of 8,303 titles (7.29 percent) in 2008 after a strong increase of 10,823 titles (10.5 percent) in 2007. Output of audiobooks, however, continued its steady rise, up 1,143 titles or 14.02 percent in 2008 following the increase of 1,167 titles (16.71 percent) registered in 2007. This growth is caused in part by the introduction of new formats. Preliminary data for 2009 show an even steeper rise, up more than 25 percent. Preliminary 2009 figures for other formats show continuing declines.

Fiction, a key category, showed resilience in 2008. Overall output was up 0.9 percent and hardcover fiction (less than $81) was up 10.5 percent. In the paperback sector, mass market fiction was down 1.54 percent and trade fiction was down 0.39 percent. Audiobook fiction, on the other hand, soared, with a 20.17 increase in titles in 2008 and an astonishing 44.67 surge in preliminary 2009 figures. Trade paperback fiction also was stronger for 2009.

The important juveniles category is broken into children's (PreK–6) and young adult (YA; grades 7–12) titles. Both these sectors showed mostly disappointing results in 2008. For children's books, hardcover titles priced at less than

Table 1 / American Book Production, 2004–2009

BISAC Category	2005 Final	2006 Final	2007 Final	2008 Final	2009 Preliminary
Antiques and collectibles	486	503	485	445	363
Architecture	1,187	1,366	1,504	1,548	1,469
Art	2,881	3,083	3,347	3,261	3,136
Bibles	655	684	467	554	444
Biography and autobiography	4,101	3,916	4,116	3,935	4,119
Body, mind, and spirit	1,282	1,258	1,276	1,319	1,176
Business and economics	10,352	9,689	14,593	9,593	9,751
Children	22,039	22,115	24,440	22,603	21,878
Comics and graphic novels	2,321	2,277	2,491	2,869	3,011
Computers	4,405	4,020	4,590	4,014	4,579
Cooking	2,072	1,842	1,957	2,294	1,744
Crafts and hobbies	1,282	1,322	1,247	1,212	1,083
Design	602	640	800	739	693
Drama	617	505	666	714	662
Education	5,558	5,322	5,428	5,277	4,486
Family and relationships	1,522	1,389	1,317	1,256	1,235
Fiction	17,822	17,059	18,471	18,638	18,396
Foreign language study	1,595	1,568	1,431	1,550	1,015
Games	1,137	1,181	1,022	958	949
Gardening	463	414	431	517	396
Health and fitness	2,043	2,056	1,962	1,847	1,720
History	10,148	10,503	11,526	10,658	10,739
House and home	541	475	481	412	340
Humor	741	699	710	708	711
Language arts and disciplines	3,576	3,132	3,436	2,967	3,520
Law	3,152	4,547	4,318	5,363	4,236
Literary collections	711	640	1,031	922	954
Literary criticism	3,491	3,039	3,401	3,158	3,572
Mathematics	2,073	2,063	2,025	1,888	1,767
Medical	6,651	7,141	7,331	7,092	6,924
Music	3,335	3,241	3,149	3,408	3,246
Nature	1,125	1,133	1,145	1,039	1,027
Performing arts	1,600	1,489	1,681	1,610	1,516
Pets	643	536	546	474	467
Philosophy	2,032	2,044	2,631	2,246	2,433
Photography	1,190	1,363	1,375	1,417	1,330
Poetry	2,299	2,042	2,215	2,126	1,941
Political science	5,085	5,126	5,988	5,655	5,929
Psychology	2,316	2,564	2,698	2,456	2,277
Reference	2,094	2,203	1,933	1,975	1,829
Religion	8,079	8,128	8,065	8,276	7,997
Science	5,438	5,611	5,596	5,324	5,685
Self-help	1,488	1,381	1,548	1,474	1,387
Social science	6,359	6,662	6,997	6,998	6,899
Sports and recreation	2,171	2,185	2,054	2,081	1,823
Study aids	849	1,186	704	898	719

Technology and engineering	3,500	3,957	4,642	4,739	5,111
Transportation	837	994	701	742	691
Travel	2,612	3,313	4,206	3,542	3,127
True crime	211	230	303	291	297
Young adult	5,331	5,120	6,025	4,950	4,644
Totals	174,100	174,956	190,502	180,032	175,443

$81 fell 12.33 percent, mass market paperbacks were down 15.85 percent, and trade paperbacks were down 0.40 percent. YA titles showed similar trends—down 17.08 percent for hardcovers less than $81, 10.7 percent for mass market paperbacks, and down 17.8 percent for trade paperbacks. Even the audiobook sector was depressed, down 16.32 percent for children's titles (a still relatively undeveloped market) and down a more modest 1.47 percent for YA titles. Preliminary figures for 2009 promised a rebound in both audiobook categories, and the preliminary data for 2009 trade paperbacks showed a surprising increase for children's books, to surpass the level produced in 2006.

Comics and graphic novels—a category that can include both fiction and nonfiction—continued to show impressive increases, posting gains of 40 percent in hardcovers under $81 and 11.08 percent in trade paperbacks. The increase in hardcovers under $81 promised to be above 65 percent.

A review of overall output in nonfiction categories (Table 1) shows the usual variations. As expected, many categories lost ground in 2008. A few registered double-digit increases in title output—among them, cooking (up 17.22 percent), gardening (up 19.95 percent), law (up 24.2 percent), and study aids (up 27.56 percent); however, preliminary 2009 figures appeared to erase these gains entirely. Business and economics, which had surged in 2007, was closer to the 2006 level in 2008 and appeared to be holding steady in 2009. Computers, on the other hand, which saw a decline of more than 12 percent in 2008, seemed ready to top its 2007 level in 2009. And travel titles, which showed growth from 2005 through 2007, were down 15.79 percent in 2008 and a further 11.72 percent in preliminary 2009 figures.

Average Book Prices

Average book prices were mixed in 2008 and preliminary figures indicated a similar situation in 2009. List prices for hardcovers (Table 2) have fluctuated within a tight range, with even the preliminary 2009 average price ($83.55) remaining above a dip in 2007 ($82.24). Prices for hardcovers under $81 (Table 3) rose by 3.71 percent in 2008 and seem set for an increase of nearly 3.2 percent in 2009.

Mass market paperback prices (Table 4) continue to show slow but steady increases, up 0.5 percent in 2007 to $6.40, a further 1.56 percent in 2008 to $6.50, and an additional 2.46 percent in early 2009 reporting; trade paperback prices (Table 5), on the other hand, rose a strong 27.3 percent in 2007, to $43.61, but declined by 9.75 percent in 2008 and a further 3.1 percent in preliminary

(text continues on page 496)

Table 2 / Hardcover Average Per-Volume Prices, 2006–2009

BISAC Category	2006 Final			2007 Final			2008 Final			2009 Preliminary		
	Vols.	$ Total	Prices	Vols.	$ Total	Prices	Vols.	$ Total	Prices	Vols.	$ Total	Prices
Antiques and collectibles	212	$12,442.15	$58.69	200	$13,003.84	$65.02	195	$15,763.28	$80.84	162	$7,815.17	$48.24
Architecture	769	56,910.95	74.01	788	56,321.04	71.47	853	66,141.71	77.54	819	66,793.23	81.55
Art	1,567	106,748.37	68.12	1,651	136,283.82	82.55	1,681	142,524.38	84.79	1,659	120,298.57	72.51
Bibles	215	10,633.77	49.46	176	7,251.88	41.20	191	9,396.02	49.19	169	7,746.44	45.84
Biography and autobiography	1,793	90,717.36	50.60	1,825	96,276.98	52.75	1,714	98,643.35	57.55	1,670	82,712.99	49.53
Body, mind, and spirit	233	6,325.89	27.15	208	6,551.93	31.50	233	6,085.82	26.12	199	5,509.92	27.69
Business and economics	3,399	476,208.28	140.10	3,452	437,415.74	126.71	3,581	480,896.85	134.29	3,865	459,161.81	118.80
Children	12,372	290,343.34	23.47	14,959	360,012.83	24.07	13,235	362,043.14	27.35	11,977	295,707.57	24.69
Comics and graphic novels	279	8,985.21	32.21	324	10,840.21	33.46	462	15,084.50	32.65	747	24,157.27	32.34
Computers	904	102,135.69	112.98	769	89,715.87	116.67	731	107,032.74	146.42	799	122,674.13	153.53
Cooking	835	25,542.27	30.59	878	24,276.18	27.65	1,015	30,443.41	29.99	768	22,768.75	29.65
Crafts and hobbies	297	7,586.89	25.55	338	9,050.47	26.78	267	7,361.24	27.57	232	6,852.26	29.54
Design	287	24,964.97	86.99	385	33,532.68	87.10	358	22,273.82	62.22	317	21,070.92	66.47
Drama	50	4,418.20	88.36	84	5,608.74	66.77	192	10,300.98	53.65	78	6,467.89	82.92
Education	1,271	136,967.64	107.76	1,245	138,539.83	111.28	1,330	148,820.74	111.90	1,385	139,768.91	100.92
Family and relationships	348	10,016.96	28.78	324	8,644.62	26.68	301	8,839.56	29.37	301	10,115.82	33.61
Fiction	4,518	130,050.26	28.78	4,627	155,507.10	33.61	4,976	144,477.84	29.03	4,484	129,015.67	28.77
Foreign language study	209	22,401.82	107.19	211	23,915.86	113.35	146	16,159.40	110.68	109	14,552.68	133.51
Games	205	5,890.40	28.73	154	4,543.19	29.50	145	5,678.75	39.16	165	6,026.92	36.53
Gardening	164	8,593.15	52.40	189	7,099.09	37.56	149	6,318.83	42.41	140	5,151.27	36.79
Health and fitness	405	20,332.62	50.20	405	21,893.76	54.06	449	27,425.63	61.08	358	19,647.51	54.88
History	4,630	429,967.58	92.87	4,766	405,946.42	85.18	4,795	419,378.14	87.46	4,639	401,167.93	86.48
House and home	145	4,903.84	33.82	152	5,593.30	36.80	117	4,779.14	40.85	114	4,603.92	40.39
Humor	213	3,857.95	18.11	227	4,701.10	20.71	241	4,921.32	20.42	232	4,611.33	19.88

Category	Count	Amount	Value	Count	Amount	Value	Count	Amount	Value	Count	Amount	Value
Language arts and disciplines	1,135	143,835.35	126.73	1,404	182,644.90	130.09	1,300	173,479.85	133.45	1,553	205,774.57	132.50
Law	1,373	244,017.68	177.73	1,409	236,529.80	167.87	1,516	247,998.43	163.59	1,535	248,975.13	162.20
Literary collections	278	24,172.19	86.95	472	65,940.69	139.70	383	34,373.11	89.75	374	32,567.66	87.08
Literary criticism	1,584	165,548.11	104.51	1,823	187,184.88	102.68	1,707	181,073.91	106.08	1,877	202,106.47	107.68
Mathematics	1,098	138,219.37	125.88	1,029	126,215.07	122.66	916	117,073.40	127.81	908	102,886.86	113.31
Medical	3,054	490,396.51	160.58	3,118	477,496.29	153.14	3,076	476,516.50	154.91	3,001	489,838.71	163.23
Music	391	30,971.99	79.21	486	36,967.71	76.07	485	33,628.05	69.34	526	38,875.30	73.91
Nature	426	29,620.76	69.53	447	28,459.99	63.67	435	27,221.52	62.58	409	26,626.63	65.10
Performing arts	508	37,371.79	73.57	577	46,217.96	80.10	618	50,450.12	81.63	554	44,061.72	79.53
Pets	205	4,417.46	21.55	225	5,427.23	24.12	181	5,318.82	29.39	167	4,126.56	24.71
Philosophy	939	99,189.85	105.63	1,007	95,281.98	94.62	973	95,896.54	98.56	1,015	95,193.40	93.79
Photography	851	85,070.05	99.96	895	59,582.47	66.57	882	72,886.61	82.64	800	63,419.66	79.27
Poetry	330	13,035.24	39.50	351	14,845.72	42.30	339	14,406.45	42.50	287	12,309.81	42.89
Political science	2,230	211,878.60	95.01	2,315	230,550.20	99.59	2,492	242,055.07	97.13	2,718	272,188.35	100.14
Psychology	1,098	106,489.55	96.99	1,112	114,696.17	103.14	1,063	108,360.07	101.94	1,028	103,180.46	100.37
Reference	706	146,354.39	207.30	644	171,371.20	266.10	613	178,211.72	290.72	538	145,004.89	269.53
Religion	2,467	168,869.85	68.45	2,510	164,865.97	65.68	2,449	166,622.19	68.04	2,303	163,608.97	71.04
Science	3,358	676,528.20	201.47	3,214	686,473.09	213.59	3,171	649,242.37	204.74	3,223	588,519.23	182.60
Self-help	350	9,385.70	26.82	326	7,871.19	24.14	322	8,265.48	25.67	311	7,261.97	23.35
Social science	2,760	307,192.92	111.30	2,932	319,137.90	108.85	2,948	288,701.80	97.93	3,119	299,258.75	95.95
Sports and recreation	701	27,546.97	39.30	670	26,546.21	39.62	746	30,938.26	41.47	583	22,880.96	39.25
Study aids	44	3,470.46	78.87	21	1,838.00	87.52	17	1,334.40	78.49	24	2,707.80	112.83
Technology and engineering	1,980	331,644.90	167.50	1,947	304,618.30	156.46	2,145	340,632.86	158.80	2,470	385,847.61	156.21
Transportation	328	17,450.84	53.20	287	16,474.77	57.40	312	20,043.82	64.24	244	17,681.58	72.47
Travel	394	17,325.67	43.97	754	40,433.70	53.63	457	15,904.23	34.80	365	16,090.37	44.08
True crime	81	2,430.23	30.00	97	2,758.97	28.44	94	2,474.48	26.32	91	2,672.47	29.37
Young adult	2,313	112,871.35	48.80	2,749	139,330.93	50.68	2,256	111,464.02	49.41	2,294	78,570.11	34.25
Totals	66,302	$5,642,251.54	$85.10	71,158	$5,852,287.77	$82.24	69,253	$5,855,364.67	$84.55	67,705	$5,656,634.88	$83.55

Table 3 / Hardcover Average Per-Volume Prices, Less Than $81, 2006–2009

BISAC Category	2006 Final			2007 Final			2008 Final			2009 Preliminary		
	Vols.	$ Total	Prices	Vols.	$ Total	Prices	Vols.	$ Total	Prices	Vols.	$ Total	Prices
Antiques and collectibles	190	$7,916.71	$41.67	164	$6,880.05	$41.95	158	$6,091.85	$38.56	138	$5,108.84	$37.02
Architecture	574	28,629.21	49.88	579	28,797.91	49.74	613	31,148.56	50.81	571	29,629.60	51.89
Art	1,282	56,106.53	43.76	1,319	60,267.17	45.69	1,333	62,046.12	46.55	1,344	62,953.46	46.84
Bibles	193	7,307.01	37.86	171	6,591.96	38.55	177	6,708.32	37.90	159	6,198.60	38.98
Biography and autobiography	1,613	49,504.52	30.69	1,623	50,892.84	31.36	1,510	47,377.50	31.38	1,498	46,021.44	30.72
Body, mind, and spirit	222	4,478.09	20.17	195	4,763.98	24.43	222	4,861.07	21.90	188	4,178.62	22.23
Business and economics	1,375	54,980.64	39.99	1,503	59,611.00	39.66	1,615	66,649.41	41.27	1,859	75,004.79	40.35
Children	12,061	227,799.27	18.89	14,595	279,188.12	19.13	12,796	250,571.44	19.58	11,688	229,198.90	19.61
Comics and graphic novels	270	7,987.25	29.58	310	9,328.87	30.09	434	12,220.74	28.16	719	20,638.60	28.70
Computers	261	16,130.84	61.80	247	14,769.55	59.80	240	14,827.83	61.78	205	12,742.76	62.16
Cooking	808	21,135.48	26.16	864	22,518.11	26.06	987	26,659.53	27.01	759	21,919.07	28.88
Crafts and hobbies	295	7,371.94	24.99	335	8,795.47	26.26	266	7,276.24	27.35	228	6,447.31	28.28
Design	242	11,345.12	46.88	324	15,389.93	47.50	307	14,911.87	48.57	266	12,936.32	48.63
Drama	33	1,297.80	39.33	58	2,316.24	39.94	168	6,923.43	41.21	42	2,095.89	49.90
Education	676	35,467.69	52.47	648	35,228.48	54.36	625	35,825.96	57.32	663	37,192.77	56.10
Family and relationships	328	7,470.61	22.78	308	6,540.27	21.23	279	6,119.71	21.93	276	6,610.59	23.95
Fiction	4,473	121,050.96	27.06	4,466	122,128.45	27.35	4,935	136,931.49	27.75	4,459	125,520.92	28.15
Foreign language study	92	4,144.07	45.04	79	3,803.36	48.14	71	3,764.05	53.01	40	1,803.53	45.09
Games	203	5,700.45	28.08	151	4,221.25	27.96	139	4,415.85	31.77	160	5,278.92	32.99
Gardening	158	5,768.15	36.51	182	6,286.39	34.54	141	5,084.13	36.06	135	4,656.47	34.49
Health and fitness	335	9,817.50	29.31	350	10,054.34	28.73	342	10,366.78	30.31	292	10,084.54	34.54
History	2,976	127,328.22	42.79	3,013	130,476.75	43.30	3,210	139,908.95	43.59	3,106	139,677.64	44.97
House and home	142	4,618.94	32.53	145	4,883.90	33.68	110	3,874.20	35.22	109	4,063.97	37.28
Humor	213	3,857.95	18.11	224	4,092.22	18.27	238	4,483.44	18.84	230	4,411.33	19.18

Category	No.	Total	Avg.	No.	Total	Avg.	No.	Total	Avg.	No.	Total	Avg.
Language arts and disciplines	480	25,223.47	52.55	565	31,625.58	55.97	517	28,871.62	55.84	617	36,651.53	59.40
Law	276	14,760.97	53.48	309	16,280.97	52.69	331	17,692.70	53.45	293	16,718.87	57.06
Literary collections	169	7,582.95	44.87	215	8,925.14	41.51	265	12,426.71	46.89	241	11,137.76	46.21
Literary criticism	808	42,177.18	52.20	902	49,423.99	54.79	841	47,022.07	55.91	911	51,524.38	56.56
Mathematics	223	12,805.14	57.42	234	13,701.65	58.55	255	16,019.92	62.82	304	19,089.89	62.80
Medical	640	35,524.74	55.51	591	32,684.76	55.30	572	32,413.01	56.67	493	29,153.07	59.13
Music	245	10,055.24	41.04	315	12,872.91	40.87	351	15,137.90	43.13	350	15,306.47	43.73
Nature	301	11,714.48	38.92	338	12,825.60	37.95	342	12,455.23	36.42	299	10,836.00	36.24
Performing arts	332	15,977.84	48.13	351	17,790.33	50.68	378	18,878.72	49.94	336	16,322.98	48.58
Pets	204	4,307.46	21.12	221	4,954.33	22.42	179	4,356.83	24.34	164	3,831.61	23.36
Philosophy	394	20,592.64	52.27	433	23,065.71	53.27	489	26,490.89	54.17	471	25,432.80	54.00
Photography	779	32,075.95	41.18	833	35,558.62	42.69	793	34,612.03	43.65	702	31,275.47	44.55
Poetry	309	9,469.84	30.65	311	9,355.67	30.08	303	9,594.30	31.66	251	7,545.16	30.06
Political science	1,083	51,208.98	47.28	1,128	55,757.29	49.43	1,258	61,728.66	49.07	1,287	65,478.47	50.88
Psychology	500	24,393.58	48.79	487	24,857.24	51.04	460	23,722.51	51.57	511	27,160.03	53.15
Reference	349	12,077.81	34.61	297	11,236.10	37.83	270	9,210.17	34.11	228	8,498.41	37.27
Religion	1,760	53,303.84	30.29	1,762	53,473.09	30.35	1,762	55,636.12	31.58	1,589	54,383.67	34.23
Science	589	28,159.09	47.81	631	30,823.80	48.85	645	32,356.74	50.17	727	36,454.84	50.14
Self-help	339	6,980.70	20.59	318	7,035.21	22.12	311	6,884.98	22.14	308	6,517.27	21.16
Social science	1,362	67,770.81	49.76	1,496	76,093.02	50.86	1,657	86,305.63	52.09	1,713	91,097.98	53.18
Sports and recreation	651	19,611.99	30.13	630	19,560.31	31.05	690	22,765.11	32.99	545	17,719.06	32.51
Study aids	36	1,337.36	37.15	14	586.65	41.90	12	558.50	46.54	15	661.50	44.10
Technology and engineering	253	14,366.19	56.78	226	12,396.32	54.85	305	16,902.02	55.42	310	18,146.38	58.54
Transportation	297	11,802.79	39.74	245	9,542.87	38.95	259	10,541.22	40.70	197	8,260.73	41.93
Travel	371	11,666.27	31.45	733	28,686.75	39.14	439	12,882.88	29.35	347	11,060.17	31.87
True crime	79	2,025.23	25.64	95	2,511.47	26.44	94	2,474.48	26.32	89	2,492.47	28.01
Young adult	2,079	55,654.94	26.77	2,524	68,724.52	27.23	2,093	56,380.12	26.94	2,212	61,970.64	28.02
Totals	43,923	$1,429,842.43	$32.55	48,057	$1,568,176.51	$32.63	46,787	$1,583,369.54	$33.84	44,644	$1,559,102.49	$34.92

Table 4 / Mass Market Paperbacks Average Per-Volume Prices, 2006–2009

BISAC Category	2006 Final			2007 Final			2008 Final			2009 Preliminary		
	Vols.	$ Total	Prices	Vols.	$ Total	Prices	Vols.	$ Total	Prices	Vols.	$ Total	Prices
Antiques and collectibles	9	$70.42	$7.82	9	$71.91	$7.99	10	$85.90	$8.59	9	$77.91	$8.66
Architecture	n.a.	n.a.	n.a.	n.a.	n.a.	n.a.	n.a.	n.a.	n.a.	n.a.	n.a.	n.a.
Art	n.a.	n.a.	n.a.	n.a.	n.a.	n.a.	n.a.	n.a.	n.a.	n.a.	n.a.	n.a.
Bibles	n.a.	n.a.	n.a.	n.a.	n.a.	n.a.	n.a.	n.a.	n.a.	n.a.	n.a.	n.a.
Biography and autobiography	13	102.83	7.91	9	70.87	7.87	8	62.92	7.87	13	97.30	7.48
Body, mind, and spirit	29	206.67	7.13	22	167.74	7.62	14	99.86	7.13	13	103.87	7.99
Business and economics	n.a.	n.a.	n.a.	n.a.	n.a.	n.a.	1	7.99	7.99	1	9.99	9.99
Children	277	1,553.27	5.61	284	1,593.33	5.61	239	1,420.29	5.94	234	1,427.20	6.10
Comics and graphic novels	n.a.	n.a.	n.a.	n.a.	n.a.	n.a.	n.a.	n.a.	n.a.	n.a.	n.a.	n.a.
Computers	n.a.	n.a.	n.a.	n.a.	n.a.	n.a.	n.a.	n.a.	n.a.	n.a.	n.a.	n.a.
Cooking	1	6.99	6.99	n.a.	n.a.	n.a.	n.a.	n.a.	n.a.	n.a.	n.a.	n.a.
Crafts and hobbies	n.a.	n.a.	n.a.	n.a.	n.a.	n.a.	n.a.	n.a.	n.a.	n.a.	n.a.	n.a.
Design	n.a.	n.a.	n.a.	n.a.	n.a.	n.a.	n.a.	n.a.	n.a.	n.a.	n.a.	n.a.
Drama	6	38.74	6.46	4	25.88	6.47	2	11.98	5.99	3	17.93	5.98
Education	n.a.	n.a.	n.a.	n.a.	n.a.	n.a.	n.a.	n.a.	n.a.	n.a.	n.a.	n.a.
Family and relationships	5	38.87	7.77	3	24.97	8.32	n.a.	n.a.	n.a.	2	11.98	5.99
Fiction	4,316	27,326.41	6.33	4,227	27,051.87	6.40	4,162	26,965.85	6.48	4,029	26,741.63	6.64
Foreign language study	1	5.99	5.99	4	26.96	6.74	5	30.95	6.19	4	27.96	6.99
Games	9	59.85	6.65	19	105.28	5.54	13	70.87	5.45	5	24.95	4.99
Gardening	n.a.	n.a.	n.a.	n.a.	n.a.	n.a.	n.a.	n.a.	n.a.	n.a.	n.a.	n.a.
Health and fitness	33	238.65	7.23	18	134.84	7.49	18	137.82	7.66	14	107.86	7.70
History	16	123.84	7.74	13	100.87	7.76	3	17.48	5.83	5	38.46	7.69
House and home	n.a.	n.a.	n.a.	n.a.	n.a.	n.a.	n.a.	n.a.	n.a.	n.a.	n.a.	n.a.
Humor	3	21.97	7.32	4	29.96	7.49	3	18.97	6.32	n.a.	n.a.	n.a.

Subject	No.	List price	Avg. price	No.	List price	Avg. price	No.	List price	Avg. price	No.	List price	Avg. price
Language arts and disciplines	n.a.	n.a.	n.a.	n.a.	n.a.	n.a.	n.a.	n.a.	n.a.	n.a.	n.a.	n.a.
Law	n.a.	n.a.	n.a.	n.a.	n.a.	n.a.	n.a.	n.a.	n.a.	n.a.	n.a.	n.a.
Literary collections	1	7.95	7.95	n.a.	n.a.	n.a.	1	4.99	4.99	1	7.95	7.95
Literary criticism	n.a.	n.a.	n.a.	n.a.	n.a.	n.a.	1	7.95	7.95	1	7.99	7.99
Mathematics	n.a.	n.a.	n.a.	n.a.	n.a.	n.a.	n.a.	n.a.	n.a.	n.a.	n.a.	n.a.
Medical	4	26.47	6.62	4	27.47	6.87	1	7.50	7.50	1	8.99	8.99
Music	n.a.	n.a.	n.a.	n.a.	n.a.	n.a.	n.a.	n.a.	n.a.	n.a.	n.a.	n.a.
Nature	n.a.	n.a.	n.a.	n.a.	n.a.	n.a.	1	9.99	9.99	n.a.	n.a.	n.a.
Performing arts	2	16.98	8.49	3	25.93	8.64	1	7.99	7.99	1	9.99	9.99
Pets	n.a.	n.a.	n.a.	n.a.	n.a.	n.a.	2	11.90	5.95	n.a.	n.a.	n.a.
Philosophy	5	37.91	7.58	5	38.91	7.78	n.a.	n.a.	n.a.	n.a.	n.a.	n.a.
Photography	1	6.99	6.99	n.a.	n.a.	n.a.	2	9.90	4.95	5	34.75	6.95
Poetry	2	11.90	5.95	1	5.95	5.95	2	15.98	7.99	1	5.95	5.95
Political science	2	14.90	7.45	1	6.99	6.99	n.a.	n.a.	n.a.	n.a.	n.a.	n.a.
Psychology	3	23.97	7.99	2	15.94	7.97	3	21.48	7.16	3	22.48	7.49
Reference	11	111.44	10.13	3	19.48	6.49	4	30.96	7.74	3	20.93	6.98
Religion	6	45.90	7.65	2	13.98	6.99	1	6.95	6.95	n.a.	n.a.	n.a.
Science	1	7.99	7.99	n.a.	n.a.	n.a.	3	28.93	9.64	2	15.98	7.99
Self-help	13	96.55	7.43	6	46.82	7.80	n.a.	n.a.	n.a.	n.a.	n.a.	n.a.
Social science	1	7.99	7.99	1	7.99	7.99	3	23.97	7.99	3	20.97	6.99
Sports and recreation	2	15.98	7.99	2	14.98	7.49	n.a.	n.a.	n.a.	n.a.	n.a.	n.a.
Study aids	n.a.	n.a.	n.a.	n.a.	n.a.	n.a.	n.a.	n.a.	n.a.	n.a.	n.a.	n.a.
Technology and engineering	n.a.	n.a.	n.a.	n.a.	n.a.	n.a.	n.a.	n.a.	n.a.	n.a.	n.a.	n.a.
Transportation	n.a.	n.a.	n.a.	n.a.	n.a.	n.a.	1	6.95	6.95	1	14.00	14.00
Travel	1	7.99	7.99	n.a.	n.a.	n.a.	n.a.	n.a.	n.a.	1	4.95	4.95
True crime	44	327.07	7.43	51	378.49	7.42	53	389.47	7.35	51	379.49	7.44
Young adult	200	1,385.14	6.93	159	1,080.06	6.79	142	1,007.71	7.10	94	718.63	7.65
Totals	5,017	$31,947.62	$6.37	4,856	$31,087.47	$6.40	4,699	$30,523.50	$6.50	4,500	$29,960.09	$6.66

n.a. = not available

Table 5 / Trade Paperbacks Average Per-Volume Prices, 2006–2009

BISAC Category	2006 Final			2007 Final			2008 Final			2009 Preliminary		
	Vols.	$ Total	Prices	Vols.	$ Total	Prices	Vols.	$ Total	Prices	Vols.	$ Total	Prices
Antiques and collectibles	282	$7,009.93	$24.86	275	$33,306.69	$121.12	239	$6,471.72	$27.08	192	$5,237.48	$27.28
Architecture	597	23,085.58	38.67	717	28,801.97	40.17	694	29,074.36	41.89	645	27,246.86	42.24
Art	1,515	48,776.84	32.20	1,692	58,262.19	34.43	1,581	59,368.38	37.55	1,472	53,791.38	36.54
Bibles	470	17,894.36	38.07	291	11,662.34	40.08	363	17,891.83	49.29	273	11,005.48	40.31
Biography and autobiography	2,108	41,882.60	19.87	2,278	47,660.75	20.92	2,211	44,895.41	20.31	2,437	49,457.07	20.29
Body, mind, and spirit	991	17,017.93	17.17	1,045	18,462.36	17.67	1,072	19,799.35	18.47	963	17,366.52	18.03
Business and economics	6,206	439,588.34	70.83	11,053	1,180,679.39	106.82	5,937	439,177.68	73.97	5,817	346,122.80	59.50
Children	9,409	96,771.35	10.28	9,136	95,293.74	10.43	9,099	98,172.30	10.79	9,678	107,400.90	11.10
Comics and graphic novels	1,998	27,183.71	13.61	2,167	32,904.80	15.18	2,407	34,048.57	14.15	2,263	34,730.78	15.35
Computers	3,112	191,211.19	61.44	3,809	304,573.90	79.96	3,279	285,682.16	87.12	3,771	362,048.28	96.01
Cooking	992	18,905.52	19.06	1,068	19,200.62	17.98	1,271	23,940.09	18.84	964	18,935.19	19.64
Crafts and hobbies	1,024	19,577.66	19.12	906	18,399.77	20.31	943	18,840.65	19.98	853	17,969.52	21.07
Design	352	11,498.53	32.67	415	14,902.92	35.91	381	13,021.49	34.18	376	13,313.89	35.41
Drama	449	8,112.72	18.07	578	10,493.96	18.16	521	9,719.82	18.66	580	12,417.10	21.41
Education	4,031	150,831.49	37.42	4,166	154,046.24	36.98	3,929	146,190.54	37.21	3,119	118,902.32	38.12
Family and relationships	1,033	18,642.76	18.05	983	17,918.59	18.23	951	16,908.59	17.78	928	18,006.49	19.40
Fiction	8,119	131,443.18	16.19	9,517	168,794.52	17.74	9,480	154,544.25	16.30	9,874	170,152.53	17.23
Foreign language study	1,356	53,054.58	39.13	1,209	42,048.22	34.78	1,405	42,411.50	30.19	898	27,139.59	30.22
Games	965	15,547.98	16.11	847	14,314.60	16.90	800	13,664.44	17.08	778	13,763.74	17.69
Gardening	250	5,071.37	20.29	241	4,787.39	19.86	368	6,967.28	18.93	254	5,459.14	21.49
Health and fitness	1,612	40,101.97	24.88	1,539	34,458.41	22.39	1,373	33,213.71	24.19	1,345	32,440.41	24.12
History	5,854	194,534.04	33.23	6,743	237,306.47	35.19	5,856	186,490.43	31.85	6,075	187,741.15	30.90
House and home	330	6,669.67	20.21	327	6,774.33	20.72	295	5,966.45	20.23	227	4,992.00	21.99
Humor	482	6,723.02	13.95	477	6,337.84	13.29	463	6,245.21	13.49	479	6,494.25	13.56

Language arts and disciplines	1,992	107,131.02	53.78	2,022	104,307.32	51.59	1,654	88,284.87	53.38	1,952	117,047.07	59.96
Law	3,129	168,642.86	53.90	2,857	230,700.59	80.75	3,781	435,331.41	115.14	2,667	196,482.05	73.67
Literary collections	361	10,427.50	28.89	559	24,407.35	43.66	540	19,026.29	35.23	577	19,350.74	33.54
Literary criticism	1,453	53,008.17	36.48	1,577	57,723.82	36.60	1,446	52,882.23	36.57	1,689	62,703.96	37.12
Mathematics	963	67,652.63	70.25	989	74,089.98	74.91	961	59,407.06	61.82	850	55,919.79	65.79
Medical	4,045	256,045.09	63.30	4,153	287,874.33	69.32	3,986	298,247.53	74.82	3,886	290,554.40	74.77
Music	2,851	71,268.26	25.00	2,659	71,667.90	26.95	2,921	63,289.38	21.67	2,723	63,275.18	23.24
Nature	707	18,953.35	26.81	698	18,134.27	25.98	604	15,354.00	25.42	615	16,384.00	26.64
Performing arts	979	31,415.42	32.09	1,100	33,474.19	30.43	991	30,729.49	31.01	957	31,922.41	33.36
Pets	331	5,947.62	17.97	321	5,627.67	17.53	292	5,460.59	18.70	301	5,723.73	19.02
Philosophy	1,101	36,676.77	33.31	1,619	52,920.03	32.69	1,271	39,313.80	30.93	1,415	47,569.97	33.62
Photography	511	14,470.13	28.32	480	15,330.39	31.94	535	17,583.24	32.87	530	15,961.50	30.12
Poetry	1,710	26,891.41	15.73	1,863	32,019.27	17.19	1,784	29,429.78	16.50	1,649	27,742.72	16.82
Political science	2,885	110,464.32	38.29	3,663	217,800.56	59.46	3,142	118,071.58	37.58	3,205	118,729.43	37.05
Psychology	1,457	65,021.88	44.63	1,575	71,221.17	45.22	1,377	56,963.01	41.37	1,231	49,914.04	40.55
Reference	1,472	92,635.46	62.93	1,276	83,832.08	65.70	1,353	93,313.81	68.97	1,281	114,771.07	89.59
Religion	5,628	117,722.63	20.92	5,549	113,803.78	20.51	5,796	116,639.69	20.12	5,695	120,653.97	21.19
Science	2,236	155,991.22	69.76	2,346	174,316.32	74.30	2,099	148,609.73	70.80	2,384	178,369.63	74.82
Self-help	1,017	17,037.75	16.75	1,216	20,571.68	16.92	1,148	19,714.93	17.17	1,073	18,865.22	17.58
Social science	3,898	154,147.78	39.55	4,061	156,469.26	38.53	4,037	162,110.83	40.16	3,789	149,504.77	39.46
Sports and recreation	1,478	34,019.43	23.02	1,381	31,400.10	22.74	1,331	31,637.86	23.77	1,235	28,740.69	23.27
Study aids	1,142	35,580.58	31.16	682	21,836.71	32.02	880	28,279.44	32.14	692	20,859.27	30.14
Technology and engineering	1,964	169,735.29	86.42	2,689	375,124.65	139.50	2,583	397,972.78	154.07	2,625	401,974.99	153.13
Transportation	666	23,738.66	35.64	414	14,615.31	35.30	430	16,891.62	39.28	446	16,975.45	38.06
Travel	2,915	57,731.78	19.81	3,449	72,525.62	21.03	3,077	62,556.02	20.33	2,756	56,436.98	20.48
True crime	105	1,863.03	17.74	154	2,872.86	18.65	144	2,616.49	18.17	155	2,958.48	19.09
Young adult	2,583	37,158.82	14.39	3,108	43,036.58	13.85	2,555	35,166.01	13.76	2,242	31,525.66	14.06
Totals	103,116	$3,532,515.18	$34.26	113,939	$4,969,095.80	$43.61	105,636	$4,157,589.68	$39.36	102,881	$3,923,052.04	$38.13

Table 6 / Audiobook Average Per-Volume Prices, 2006–2009

BISAC Category	2006 Final			2007 Final			2008 Final			2009 Preliminary		
	Vols.	$ Total	Prices	Vols.	$ Total	Prices	Vols.	$ Total	Prices	Vols.	$ Total	Prices
Antiques and collectibles	n.a.	n.a.	n.a.	1	$11.95	$11.95	n.a.	n.a.	n.a.	1	$74.95	$74.95
Architecture	3	109.97	36.66	n.a.	n.a.	n.a.	2	74.94	37.47	n.a.	n.a.	n.a.
Art	3	100.90	33.63	5	200.89	40.18	5	204.96	40.99	8	538.86	67.36
Bibles	52	2,366.34	45.51	34	1,749.17	51.45	20	836.66	41.83	10	669.70	66.97
Biography and autobiography	378	14,337.87	37.93	453	20,173.61	44.53	641	30,161.85	47.05	704	35,246.77	50.07
Body, mind, and spirit	73	2,213.94	30.33	81	2,715.33	33.52	83	3,177.53	38.28	81	3,223.35	39.79
Business and economics	242	9,021.99	37.28	295	10,079.10	34.17	426	16,843.14	39.54	443	20,326.60	45.88
Children	534	14,491.00	27.14	876	25,229.59	28.80	733	22,787.18	31.09	826	29,871.18	36.16
Comics and graphic novels	n.a.	n.a.	n.a.	n.a.	n.a.	n.a.	n.a.	n.a.	n.a.	n.a.	n.a.	n.a.
Computers	2	54.90	27.45	n.a.	n.a.	n.a.	4	124.91	31.23	5	234.95	46.99
Cooking	13	204.38	15.72	7	247.78	35.40	4	58.83	14.71	14	625.78	44.70
Crafts and hobbies	n.a.	n.a.	n.a.	10	269.58	26.96	9	379.79	42.20	4	154.88	38.72
Design	n.a.	n.a.	n.a.	n.a.	n.a.	n.a.	n.a.	n.a.	n.a.	n.a.	n.a.	n.a.
Drama	40	1,063.65	26.59	27	803.01	29.74	48	1,760.14	36.67	162	5,543.24	34.22
Education	35	994.68	28.42	27	1,090.65	40.39	17	506.32	29.78	22	1,083.02	49.23
Family and relationships	34	953.57	28.05	47	1,481.66	31.52	73	2,681.09	36.73	54	2,128.13	39.41
Fiction	3,131	125,124.47	39.96	3,644	160,624.65	44.08	4,379	212,093.98	48.43	6,335	330,203.81	52.12
Foreign language study	424	17,828.49	42.05	314	12,928.46	41.17	394	14,826.58	37.63	242	10,067.68	41.60
Games	2	69.90	34.95	n.a.	n.a.	n.a.	1	14.95	14.95	6	84.74	14.12
Gardening	n.a.	n.a.	n.a.	3	91.85	30.62	2	79.94	39.97	n.a.	n.a.	n.a.
Health and fitness	70	1,971.36	28.16	60	1,913.20	31.89	83	2,765.84	33.32	85	3,858.22	45.39
History	294	12,064.93	41.04	480	23,208.18	48.35	577	31,569.53	54.71	453	25,992.25	57.38
House and home	2	59.08	29.54	1	29.95	29.95	n.a.	n.a.	n.a.	n.a.	n.a.	n.a.
Humor	56	1,744.40	31.15	59	1,788.54	30.31	65	2,353.30	36.20	72	2,942.36	40.87

Language arts and disciplines	34	1,095.29	32.21	31	1,718.18	55.43	14	517.38	36.96	17	779.97	45.88
Law	49	3,686.22	75.23	24	1,426.92	59.46	18	975.80	54.21	8	399.74	49.97
Literary collections	5	130.88	26.18	16	459.60	28.73	16	622.55	38.91	21	672.66	32.03
Literary criticism	25	589.13	23.57	18	641.35	35.63	35	1,736.31	49.61	21	888.57	42.31
Mathematics	n.a.	n.a.	n.a.	1	89.99	89.99	n.a.	n.a.	n.a.	n.a.	n.a.	n.a.
Medical	23	980.21	42.62	20	1,371.08	68.55	25	2,415.28	96.61	13	787.09	60.55
Music	170	4,211.09	24.77	121	3,337.78	27.58	144	4,241.96	29.46	97	3,602.55	37.14
Nature	8	213.68	26.71	21	694.44	33.07	27	1,057.98	39.18	38	1,769.38	46.56
Performing arts	32	1,038.07	32.44	18	456.75	25.38	39	1,494.32	38.32	21	970.78	46.23
Pets	11	311.65	28.33	10	292.79	29.28	20	681.06	34.05	23	1,000.67	43.51
Philosophy	63	1,671.06	26.52	24	960.23	40.01	37	1,529.12	41.33	37	1,926.21	52.06
Photography	n.a.	n.a.	n.a.	n.a.	n.a.	n.a.	n.a.	n.a.	n.a.	n.a.	n.a.	n.a.
Poetry	80	1,725.94	21.57	54	1,312.04	24.30	45	1,164.63	25.88	50	1,794.08	35.88
Political science	108	3,316.54	30.71	151	6,186.44	40.97	174	7,684.54	44.16	184	9,011.64	48.98
Psychology	11	321.01	29.18	30	1,085.65	36.19	31	1,158.63	37.38	54	2,805.00	51.94
Reference	20	297.80	14.89	7	238.70	34.10	15	491.73	32.78	6	277.90	46.32
Religion	360	9,541.09	26.50	377	10,205.68	27.07	313	9,452.23	30.20	439	13,993.95	31.88
Science	41	1,470.41	35.86	30	1,191.99	39.73	61	2,964.04	48.59	64	3,045.70	47.59
Self-help	167	4,319.64	25.87	297	8,200.73	27.61	207	6,205.85	29.98	296	11,256.89	38.03
Social science	61	1,969.95	32.29	63	2,237.70	35.52	55	2,209.62	40.17	79	3,978.46	50.36
Sports and recreation	21	583.66	27.79	45	1,729.93	38.44	57	2,265.59	39.75	40	1,851.20	46.28
Study aids	23	1,345.89	58.52	9	390.20	43.36	18	1,207.83	67.10	21	712.23	33.92
Technology and engineering	5	183.87	36.77	12	406.58	33.88	10	520.92	52.09	6	314.94	52.49
Transportation	3	128.90	42.97	n.a.	n.a.	n.a.	n.a.	n.a.	n.a.	3	109.97	36.66
Travel	13	290.57	22.35	45	2,080.75	46.24	39	1,744.45	44.73	18	903.55	50.20
True crime	23	1,108.62	48.20	30	1,256.85	41.90	59	3,033.48	51.41	47	2,339.03	49.77
Young adult	240	10,280.43	42.84	273	10,884.11	39.87	269	12,244.65	45.52	541	23,920.09	44.21
Totals	6,984	$255,587.42	$36.60	8,151	$323,493.61	$39.69	9,294	$410,921.41	$44.21	11,671	$561,982.72	$48.15

n.a. = not available

(continued from page 485)

2009 figures. Audiobook prices (Table 6) were up 8.44 percent in 2007, 11.4 percent in 2008 (to $44.21), and were showing a strong 8.91 percent increase in preliminary data for 2009.

Average book prices for fiction were mixed in 2008. Hardcover fiction titles priced at less than $81 increased 40 cents (1.46 percent) to $27.75. Mass market fiction increased 8 cents (1.25 percent) to $6.48, but trade fiction fell $1.44 (8.12 percent) to $16.30. Audiobook fiction rose a strong $4.34 (9.87 percent) to $48.43. Preliminary data for 2009 indicated that hardcover, mass market, and audiobook prices would continue to climb, and that trade paperbacks would make at least a partial recovery.

Prices for children's titles increased in 2008. Hardcover prices under $81 increased 45 cents (2.35 percent). Children's mass market paperbacks rose 33 cents (5.88 percent), trade paperbacks increased 36 cents (3.45 percent), and audiobooks were up by $2.29 (7.95 percent); all categories registered further increases in preliminary 2009 data.

Young adult prices showed more volatility in 2008. Prices in the hardcovers under $81 sector fell by 29 cents or 1.06 percent but looked set to recover in 2009 and exceed earlier years. Mass market paperback prices continued to rise with hikes of 31 cents or 4.57 percent in 2008 and 55 cents or 7.75 percent in 2009, while trade paperbacks registered a fall of 9 cents (0.65 percent) in 2008 but were up 30 cents (2.18 percent) for 2009. YA audiobooks were up $5.65 or 14.2 percent in 2008, but preliminary data for 2009 suggested a slight decline.

Hardcover categories (Table 2) showing substantial price increases in 2008 include antiques and collectibles (up 24.3 percent), Bibles (up 19.4 percent), computers (up 25.5 percent), games (up 32.75 percent), pets (up 21.83 percent), and photography (up 24.13 percent). Of these, however, only computers showed a further increase in 2009, and antiques and collectibles posted a dramatic decline of 40.32 percent.

The trade paperback sector saw substantial increases in the following categories in 2008: Bibles, up 22.99 percent but with a preliminary 2009 drop of 18.21 percent; and law, up a whopping 42.59 percent (on top of a 49.81 percent hike in 2007) but with a decline of 36.01 percent forecast for 2009. Categories with large declines included business and economics (down 30.75 percent), literary collections (down 19.3 percent), music (down 19.61 percent), and political science (down 36.8 percent); of these categories only music showed any improvement in 2009.

Audiobook prices generally continued their upward trend in 2008, with sharp increases in some small categories—drama (up 23.3 percent), humor (up 19.43 percent), literary collections (up 35.45 percent), and performing arts (up 51 percent, for example). More-established categories generally had less dramatic increases—biography and autobiography was up only 5.66 percent, history posted a 13.16 percent increase (both of these categories promising lower rates of increase for 2009), and, as previously discussed, the children, fiction, and YA categories registered 2008 increases of 7.95 percent, 9.87 percent, and 14.17 percent respectively.

Note: Restated total average prices for 2005 are as follows: Table 2, $80.36; Table 3, $31.88; Table 4, $6.34; Table 5, $33.90; Table 6, $40.49.

Book Sales Statistics, 2009: AAP Estimates

Association of American Publishers

Net sales by the U.S. publishing industry are estimated to have decreased 1.8 percent from 2008 to 2009. The 2009 grand total was $23.9 billion, down from $24.3 billion in 2008, according to figures released by the Association of American Publishers (AAP).

The AAP report, which uses data from the Bureau of the Census as well as sales data from 86 publishers, indicates a compound annual growth rate (CAGR) of 1.1 percent since 2002.*

Trade sales of adult and juvenile books were steady at $8.1 billion in 2009. Adult hardbound books showed healthy growth of 6.9 percent, reaching $2.6 billion in 2009; however adult paperbound books fell 5.2 percent to $2.2 billion. Hardbound books in the children's and young adult category fell 5.0 percent to $1.7 billion, while paperbound books in that category grew 2.2 percent to $1.5 billion.

Over the period from 2002 to 2009, the CAGR for hardbound books was 1.3 percent for adult books and 0.6 percent for juvenile books. Adult paperbound books grew 2.6 percent and juvenile paperbound 2.7 percent from the base year of 2002.

Mass market paperbacks decreased 4.0 percent to $1.0 billion and brought the category CAGR for the 2002–2009 period to -2.2 percent. Book clubs and mail order fell to $588 million, a decline of 2.0 percent.

Audiobook sales for 2009 totaled $192 million, down 12.9 percent on the previous year, but the 2002–2009 CAGR for this category is still healthy at 4.3 percent. E-books overtook audiobooks in 2009 with sales reaching $313 million, up 176.6 percent.

Religious book sales dropped 9.0 percent to $659 million in 2009. However, over the 2002–2009 period this sector has seen steady growth with a CAGR of 2.4 percent.

Educational sales in the elementary and high school (el-hi) category—books produced for K–12 education—fell 13.8 percent to $5.2 billion in 2009, and the 2002–2009 CAGR for this category was -1.4 percent. The higher education category, which includes sales of college textbooks, reached $4.3 billion in 2009, up 12.9 percent and with a comparable CAGR of 5.0 percent.

---

*For a complete list of the preliminary estimated book publishing industry net sales for 2009—and the compound annual growth rate (CAGR) from 2002 to 2009—prepared by Management Practice, Inc., visit the AAP Web site at http://www.publishers.org or this specific page: http://www. publishers.org./main/PressCenter/Archicves/2010_April/BookSalesEstimatedat23.9Billionin2009. htm. The online report includes figures for additional years and the CAGR for each category. For additional information, contact Tina Jordan at AAP's New York office (212-255-0200 ext. 263, tjordan@publishers.org).

Table 1 / Estimated Book Publishing Industry Net Sales, 2004–2009
(figures in thousands of dollars)

	2004		2005		2006		2007		2008		2009	
	$	% Change from 2003	$	% Change from 2004	$	% Change from 2005	$	% Change from 2006	$	% Change from 2007	$	% Change from 2008
Trade (total)	7,504,458	9.20	8,043,471	7.20	8,274,103	2.90	8,525,932	3.00	8,079,423	-5.20	8,067,524	-0.15
Adult hardbound	2,460,458	6.30	2,495,175	1.40	2,597,477	4.10	2,800,080	7.80	2,436,070	-13.00	2,604,159	6.90
Adult paperbound	1,917,590	2.80	2,099,187	9.50	2,277,618	8.50	2,282,173	0.20	2,364,331	3.60	2,241,386	-5.20
Juvenile hardbound	1,902,587	28.20	2,100,456	10.40	2,058,447	-2.00	2,048,155	-0.50	1,794,184	-12.40	1,704,475	-5.00
Juvenile paperbound	1,223,823	1.30	1,348,653	10.20	1,340,561	-0.60	1,395,524	4.10	1,484,838	6.40	1,517,504	2.20
Book clubs and mail order	706,634	-8.90	659,290	-6.70	639,511	-3.00	621,605	-2.80	600,470	-3.40	588,461	-2.00
Mass market paperbacks	1,089,580	-8.90	1,091,759	0.20	1,141,980	4.60	1,119,140	-2.00	1,085,566	-3.00	1,042,143	-4.00
Audiobooks	159,922	-0.70	206,299	29.00	182,162	-11.70	218,230	19.80	220,412	1.00	191,979	-12.90
Religious	883,145	5.60	829,273	-6.10	744,687	-10.20	783,411	5.20	723,872	-7.60	658,724	-9.00
E-books	30,271	53.10	43,832	44.80	54,396	24.10	67,233	23.60	113,220	68.40	313,167	176.60
Professional	3,334,154	2.00	3,300,812	-1.00	3,376,731	2.30	3,474,656	2.90	3,457,283	-0.50	3,357,022	-2.90
El-hi (K-12 education)	5,945,860	0.10	6,570,175	10.50	6,189,105	-5.80	6,356,211	2.70	6,076,538	-4.40	5,237,976	-13.80
Higher education	3,190,341	1.80	3,359,429	5.30	3,453,493	2.80	3,677,970	6.50	3,777,275	2.70	4,264,543	12.90
All other	161,629	5.00	158,558	-1.90	140,641	-11.30	115,185	-18.10	168,976	46.70	134,167	-20.60
Total	23,005,994	2.90	24,262,898	5.50	24,196,809	-0.30	24,959,573	3.20	24,303,035	-2.60	23,855,706	-1.80

Source: Adapted from the table published by the Association of American Publishers.

Global Recession Dampens U.S. Book Exports and Imports in 2009

Albert N. Greco

The Institute for Publishing Research
E-mail angreco@aol.com

For the first time since the end of the recession of 2001, U.S. book export revenues for physical books declined in 2009, falling from $2.187 billion to $1.987 billion (9.1 percent). Units fell 11.1 percent, from 460,703,000 in 2008 to 409,748,000 in 2009. Figures 1 and 2 illustrate these sharp declines.

Book publishing has been a major global business for decades, but clearly the impact of the global recession (especially in parts of Asia and the Pacific Rim and in Europe) adversely affected many U.S. book-publishing companies.

Meanwhile, a review of U.S. book imports showed the unsettled state of the U.S. economy. Imports had posted steady annual increases since 1970, but in 2009 the market for imported physical books declined precipitously. Revenues sustained a 21 percent decline (from $2.31 billion in 2008 to $1.75 billion in 2009). Units dropped 11.5 percent (from 926,324,000 in 2008 to 819,433,000 in 2009). Figures 3 and 4 outline these changes. What happened?

Consumers purchase books with discretionary dollars, and the ravages of the recession impacted negatively on book sales across the United States. A review of substantive economic indicators disclosed the effect of this recession on U.S. consumers and the U.S. book-publishing industry.

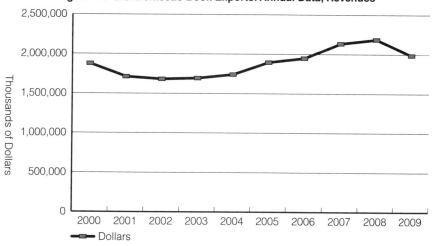

Figure 1 / U.S. Domestic Book Exports: Annual Data, Revenues

In this article, all numbers are rounded off to one or two decimal places and may not add up to 100 percent. Only physical books are analyzed in this research study; foreign rights and digital books are excluded. The author developed the 2008 and 2009 statistical data on trade books.

Figure 2 / U.S. Domestic Book Exports: Annual Data, Units

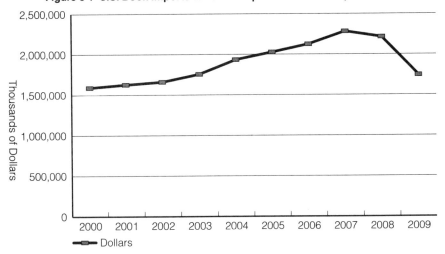

Figure 3 / U.S. Book Imports for Consumption: Annual Data, Revenues

Some measures of the depth of the recession:

- The nominal change in the gross domestic product between 2008 and 2009 was -1.3 percent.
- The unemployment rate topped 10.1 percent in 2009.
- The University of Michigan Consumer Confidence Index fell from 78.4 in January 2008 to 61.2 in January 2009, inching up slowly to 72.5 in December 2009.

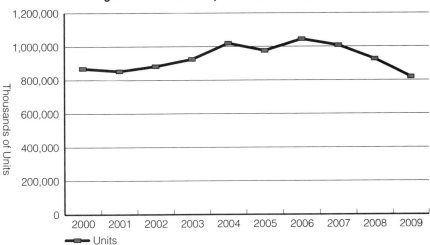

Figure 4 / U.S. Book Imports: Annual Data, Units

- The Federal Reserve Bank released data showing that the amount of consumer credit fell from $2.53 trillion in January 2008 to $2.46 trillion in December 2009 (2.8 percent).
- The Case-Shiller National Home Index, which topped 189.9 in the second quarter of 2006, fell in every quarter through the third quarter of 2009.
- Between 20 percent and 23 percent of all home mortgages were "under water" in 2009 (i.e., the value of the mortgage exceeded the value of the property).
- "Personal consumption expenditures" for durable goods declined in 2008 and again in 2009.

These events were well documented by the media (especially by extensive coverage in the *Wall Street Journal* and the *Financial Times*). The causes and impact of the recession were the subject of numerous useful books, including El-Erian's *When Markets Collide*; Knee, Greenwald, and Seave's *The Curse of the Mogul*; Gasparino's *The Sellout*; Reinhart and Rogoff's *This Time Is Different*; Patterson's *The Quants*; Kosman's *The Buyout of America*; Tett's *Fool's Gold*; and Shiller's *Irrational Exuberance.* Two excellent studies addressed some of these economic issues: Porter's *Competitive Strategy* and Ferguson's *The Ascent of Money.* A bibliography at the end of this article provides a complete list of these books, with annotations.

The impact on publishing was considerable. Annual bookstore sales declined 1.6 percent in 2008 and another 1.0 percent in 2009; sales of adult trade books were down 4.0 percent, mass market paperbacks 4 percent, religious books 7.9 percent, book clubs and book fairs 4 percent, and mail order sales 6 percent. Juvenile/young adult (YA) books were the only trade book sector posting positive results, increasing 5.1 percent (in part because the sale of "vampire"-themed books surged in 2008 and 2009).

U.S. Book Exports

The International Trade Administration, U.S. Department of Commerce, collects useful annual statistical data on book exports. Table 1 lists economic data on book exports and imports since 1970; information about the ratio between exports and imports is also listed in this table.

Table 1 / U.S. Trade in Books: 1970–2008
($ million)

Year	U.S. Book Exports	U.S. Book Imports	Ratio: U.S. Book Exports/Imports
1970	$174.9	$92.0	1.90
1975	269.3	147.6	1.82
1980	518.9	306.5	1.69
1985	591.2	564.2	1.05
1990	1,415.1	855.1	1.65
1995	1,779.5	1,184.5	1.50
1996	1,775.6	1,240.1	1.43
1997	1,896.6	1,297.5	1.46
1998	1,841.8	1,383.7	1.33
1999	1,871.1	1,441.4	1.30
2000	1,877.0	1,590.5	1.18
2001	1,712.3	1,627.8	1.05
2002	1,681.2	1,661.2	1.01
2003	1,693.6	1,755.9	0.96
2004	1,740.5	1,934.4	0.90
2005	1,894.3	2,026.3	0.93
2006	1,948.1	2,124.3	0.92
2007	2,135.2	2,281.3	0.94
2008	2,187.0	2,313.8	0.95
2009	1,987.3	1,746.1	1.13

Source: U.S. Department of Commerce, International Trade Administration. All totals are rounded off to one decimal point. Data for individual categories may not add to totals due to statistical rounding. Due to changes in the classification of "U.S. traded products" and what constitutes products classified as "books," data prior to 1990 are not strictly comparable with data beginning in 1990. All numbers are rounded off. Commerce often updates previously released data incorporating changes in collection methodologies.

Since 1970 the Department of Commerce has recorded some significant shifts in export revenues as a percentage of total U.S. book "shipments" (i.e., revenues). In 2009 the ratio stood at 6.0, the lowest total since 1985. Table 2 outlines total U.S. book shipments, exports, and the ratio covering the years 1970 to 2009.

For the past ten years, Canada has been the primary destination of all U.S. book exports, accounting for slightly more than 47 percent of all sales. The United Kingdom has been a distant second, with a 14.4 percent market share. Of the top ten export destinations, nine posted declines in 2009; only Hong Kong recorded a gain (30.7 percent). China did not make the list of top ten export countries in 2009. Table 3 outlines these trends.

**Table 2 / U.S. Book Industry Shipments
Compared with U.S. Book Exports: 1970–2009**
($ million)

Year	Total Shipments	U.S. Book Exports	Exports as a Percent of Total Shipments
1970	$2,434.2	$174.9	7.2%
1975	3,536.5	269.3	7.6
1980	6,114.4	518.9	8.5
1985	10,165.7	591.2	5.8
1990	14,982.6	1,415.1	9.4
1995	19,471.0	1,779.5	9.1
1996	20,285.7	1,775.6	8.8
1997	21,131.9	1,896.6	9.0
1998	22,480.0	1,841.8	8.2
1999	24,129.9	1,871.1	7.8
2000	25,235.0	1,877.0	7.4
2001	26,096.0	1,712.3	6.6
2002	27,203.0	1,681.2	6.2
2003	26,326.0	1,693.6	6.4
2004	27,903.0	1,740.5	6.2
2005	27,905.0	1,894.3	6.8
2006	28,236.0	1,948.1	6.9
2007	29,296.0	2,135.2	7.3
2008	31,812.4	2,187.0	6.9
2009	33,084.9	1,987.3	6.0

Source: U.S. Department of Commerce, International Trade Administration; and calculations by the author. Due to changes in the classification of U.S. traded products and what constitutes products classified as "books," data prior to 1990 are not strictly comparable with data beginning in 1990. All totals are rounded off to one decimal point. Data for individual categories may not add to totals due to statistical rounding. Commerce often updates previously released data incorporating changes in collection methodologies.

A broader overview of export activity outlines substantive trends. Table 4 lists data for 2006 through 2009 for the top 25 nations; additional information is provided for nations failing to make that cut-off.

In 2009, 16 of the top 25 countries bought fewer U.S. books, triggering a cumulative 8.4 percent decline. Eight nations posted impressive double-digit increases, paced by Hong Kong (30.7), Saudi Arabia (23 percent), and Ireland (20.5 percent). France posted a modest 5.1 percent increase. But the other 75-plus nations saw a staggering 18.4 percent decline.

Overall, exports sagged a disappointing 9.1 percent in 2009. Table 4 outlines this situation.

An analysis of the eight primary book categories indicated the unmistakably shaky composition of international sales in 2009. While the revenue and unit export markets for dictionaries and thesauruses, encyclopedias, religious books, and art books have been anemic for a number of years, declines in textbook revenues (7.1 percent) and units (13.2 percent) were odd in light of the preeminent position U.S. textbook publishers hold in various academic fields (especially scientific, technical, and medical; business administration; and a number of the humanities and social sciences). Unfortunately, the Department of Commerce did

Table 3 / Top Ten Export Destinations for U.S. Books: 2000–2009
($'000)

Country	2000	2001	2002	2003	2004	2005	2006	2007	2008	2009	Percent Change 2008–2009
Canada	756,667	727,698	742,619	776,441	812,833	866,173	918,250	962,509	999,309	934,517	-6.5%
United Kingdom	264,230	250,031	270,622	274,596	289,196	284,993	291,376	300,150	340,864	286,309	-16.0
Australia	116,302	66,010	70,806	76,067	78,549	100,769	107,754	110,922	110,922	93,885	-11.3
Mexico	73,886	63,804	64,938	68,132	66,087	102,658	71,316	79,685	78,578	74,430	-5.3
Japan	123,100	129,316	100,804	95,835	98,436	93,394	78,219	78,301	76,594	66,238	-13.5
Singapore	60,669	48,985	49,570	48,358	57,974	53,395	49,734	52,689	58,541	55,703	-4.8
Germany	34,341	34,007	29,081	34,128	27,174	35,789	38,298	76,176	44,837	42,457	-5.3
South Korea	36,793	35,499	29,131	24,698	26,670	38,557	33,432	44,400	42,922	40,234	-6.3
India	14,430	15,992	19,513	16,807	18,967	22,497	21,757	40,022	32,537	25,340	-22.1
Hong Kong	32,492	29,409	31,559	19,234	22,936	16,636	17,844	19,722	18,879	24,677	30.7

Source: U.S. Department of Commerce, International Trade Administration.

Individual shipments are excluded from the foreign trade data if valued under $2,500. All totals are rounded off to one decimal point. Data for individual categories may not add to totals due to statistical rounding. Commerce often updates previously released data incorporating changes in collection methodologies.

Table 4 / U.S. Book Exports to 25 Principal Countries: 2006–2009

Country	Value ($'000)				Percent Change 2008–2009
	2006	2007	2008	2009	
Canada	$918,250	$962,509	$999,309	$934,517	-6.5%
United Kingdom	291,376	300,150	340,864	286,309	-16.0
Australia	107,754	110,922	105,822	93,885	-11.3
Mexico	71,316	79,685	78,578	74,430	-5.3
Japan	78,219	78,301	76,594	66,238	-13.5
Singapore	49,734	52,689	58,541	55,703	-4.8
Germany	38,298	76,176	44,837	42,457	-5.3
South Korea	33,432	44,400	42,922	40,234	-6.3
India	21,757	40,022	32537	25,340	-22.1
Hong Kong	17,844	19,722	18,879	24,677	30.7
Philippines	19,131	18,883	19,997	21,281	6.4
China	25,777	29,715	28,058	20,640	-26.4
United Arab Emirates	5,483	9,999	17349	19,111	10.2
Brazil	13,758	21,676	21829	18,997	-13.0
South Africa	21,172	18,627	22,772	18,100	-20.5
Taiwan	16,144	18,663	15,065	17,182	14.1
Saudi Arabia	9,804	10,109	12,770	15,707	23.0
Netherlands	11,879	12,260	11,759	13,723	16.7
Malaysia	9,801	9,913	9,946	9,799	-1.5
Colombia	7,711	8,333	8,739	9,629	10.2
Nigeria	7,970	11,635	14,044	9,407	-33.0
France	7,487	7,803	8,089	8,505	5.1
Thailand	6,799	7,922	10,102	7,961	-21.1
New Zealand	11,731	14,385	12,000	7,905	-34.1
Ireland	4,946	5,511	5,580	6,725	20.5
Total, Top 25 Countries	$1,807,575	$1,970,011	$2,016,978	$1,848,463	-8.4
All Others	$140,528	$165,184	$170,071	$138,819	-18.4
Grand Total	$1,948,103	$2,135,195	$2,187,049	$1,987,282	-9.1

Source: U.S. Department of Commerce, International Trade Administration. Individual shipments are excluded from the foreign trade data if valued under $2,500. All totals are rounded off to one decimal point. Data for individual categories may not add to totals due to statistical rounding. Commerce often updates previously released data incorporating changes in collection methodologies.

not indicate whether these textbooks were K–12 or higher education; however, reliable sources indicate that these were higher education books.

Some modest slippage in technical, scientific, and professional books was anticipated in light of the movement of these publishers to digital e-books, but the 13.7 percent decline in revenues and 14.4 percent reduction in units were abnormally large in light of the current need for printed (not just digital) professional books in certain regions of the world.

The hardcover book category was also not defined by the U.S. Department of Commerce, but other datasets indicated that it included both adult and juvenile titles. This category experienced a modest 5.2 percent increase in revenues, but a more sturdy growth of 8.5 percent in unit sales. Mass market paperback sales sagged in the United States in 2009, yet global sales were strong—up 13.1 percent in revenues and 5.1 percent in units.

Table 5 provides an overview of these categories.

Table 5 / U.S. Exports of Books: 2009

Category	Value ($'000)	Percent Change 2008–2009	Units ('000)	Percent Change 2008–2009
Dictionaries and thesauruses	$1,605	-43.3%	306	-37.4%
Encyclopedias	3,497	-50.2	392	-51.4
Art books	17,109	-47.3	2,700	-45.7
Textbooks	476,625	-7.1	33,583	-13.2
Religious books	96,319	-9.1	34,958	-19.7
Technical, scientific, and professional	434,888	-13.7	28,636	-14.4
Hardcover books, n.e.s.	203,062	5.2	25,608	8.5
Mass market paperbacks	307,358	13.1	89,846	5.1

n.e.s = not elsewhere specified

Source: U.S. Department of Commerce, International Trade Administration. Individual shipments are excluded from the foreign trade data if valued under $2,500. All totals are rounded off to one decimal point. Data for individual categories may not add to totals due to statistical rounding. Commerce often updates previously released data incorporating changes in collection methodologies.

Mass market paperbacks have been one of the most durable and popular book categories. While reprints of successful adult trade and juvenile/YA novels have been a staple of this category (ever since Ian Ballantine launched Bantam Books in the summer of 1945), romance novels traditionally accounted for a significant percentage of title output. In 2009 mass market paperbacks recorded impressive tallies, with Canada remaining the destination for the largest number of units (and revenues). What is rather intriguing is the popularity of these books in Asia (Japan, China, Singapore, Thailand) as well as South Africa and Brazil.

These books have attractive price points and popular genre-driven formats, and U.S. publishers should cultivate this market in the coming years. Table 6 contains information about this category.

Table 6 / U.S. Exports of Mass Market Paperbacks (Rack Sized): Top Ten Markets 2009

Country	Value ($'000)	Percent Change 2008–2009	Units ('000)	Percent Change 2008–2009
Canada	$158,689	7.1%	47,728	-5.1%
United Kingdom	43,064	85.4	12,706	110.5
Australia	20,574	32.1	6,185	10.0
Japan	11,680	-9.1	3,900	-8.1
Philippines	11,007	1.3	3,461	-9.2
Singapore	10,875	117.9	2,287	107.9
South Africa	10,826	-19.5	2,625	-5.0
China	5,731	10.6	1,614	7.6
Brazil	4,100	14.6	800	8.6
Thailand	3,728	5.3	660	1.6

Source: U.S. Department of Commerce, International Trade Administration. All totals are rounded off to one decimal point. Data for individual categories may not add to totals due to statistical rounding. Commerce often updates previously released data incorporating changes in collection methodologies.

The digital transformation of book publishing has been well chronicled in the mass media and in book industry publications (especially in *Publishers Weekly*). While trade books have received almost all of the publicity, because of the emergence of highly seductive e-readers (including the iPad, the nook, the Kindle 1-2-DX, and the Sony Reader), two categories have moved aggressively into digital books—technical, scientific, and professional books, and higher education textbooks.

In 2009 printed technical, scientific, and professional books should have posted better revenue and unit numbers, but this was not the case. Revenues sagged in eight of the top ten export destinations, with seven drops in unit sales. In 2009 about 13 percent of sales in the United States in this category were for digital e-book downloads. Markets in Canada, the United Kingdom, and many other nations adopted digital reading platforms (computers, and to a lesser degree e-readers) in order to access this content. Yet while the majority of consumers and institutional users in other countries still rely on printed products (this is a category in transition), within a few years—possibly by 2013–2015—a significant proportion of technical, scientific, and professional books will be e-books, making the concept of a "book unit" an anachronism. Table 7 details the situation in this category.

Table 7 / U.S. Exports of Technical, Scientific, and Professional Books: Top Ten Markets 2009

Country	Value ($'000)	Percent Change 2008–2009	Units ('000)	Percent Change 2008–2009
Canada	$129,830	-22.7%	9,588	-23.8%
United Kingdom	92,344	-2.6	4,571	5.6
Japan	26,497	-17.2	1,413	-13.1
Mexico	23,134	63.6	2,257	68.3
Australia	21,753	-23.4	1,581	-18.8
Germany	16,385	-36.5	812	-41.0
Hong Kong	15,676	26.6	399	-5.9
Singapore	14,755	-9.7	2065	-35.5
India	10,159	-25.8	606	-9.7
Brazil	9,931	-14.5	696	-16.2

Source: U.S. Department of Commerce, International Trade Administration. All totals are rounded off to one decimal point. Data for individual categories may not add to totals due to statistical rounding. Commerce often updates previously released data incorporating changes in collection methodologies.

The second category moving rapidly toward digital e-books in the United States is the textbook business, both in higher education and K–12 education. In March 2010 McGraw-Hill announced that 95 percent of its higher education textbooks and 100 percent of its K–12 textbooks were available in digital formats. Peter C. Davis, president of McGraw-Hill Education, announced that "McGraw-Hill enthusiastically embraces the digital revolution, and believes that the creation and delivery of digital content is integral to the future of education."

In August 2007 the six largest higher education publishers created Coursesmart, a digital higher education textbook platform leasing books for six months at approximately 51 percent of the price of a printed textbook. As of 2010 the vast majority of higher education textbooks in the United States were available as digital e-textbooks. Accordingly, it is only a matter of time before the export of physical textbooks ends; the 2009 results, while more drastic that some anticipated, are a harbinger of future developments.

Reductions in revenues and units were recorded by about half of the top ten export nations, with exceptionally debilitating totals recorded in the United Kingdom (revenues down 37.2 percent, units down 52.4 percent). By 2015 "textbook units" will be replaced by "e-textbook downloads." See Table 8 for the details.

As bad as the religious book market was in the United States in 2009, export sales were abysmal. Export revenues were off in seven nations, with Nigeria (down 37.9 percent) and Australia (down 39.9 percent) leading the way. Unit

Table 8 / U.S. Exports of Textbooks: Top Ten Markets 2009

Country	Value ($'000)	Percent Change 2008–2009	Units ('000)	Percent Change 2008–2009
Canada	$108,956	-0.4%	7,128	4.6%
United Kingdom	89,816	-37.2	6,167	-52.4
Australia	34,666	-12.6	2,588	-19.1
South Korea	26,518	-16.8	1,811	-21.1
Singapore	25,368	-18.4	2,815	-12.6
Japan	23,682	4.4	1,320	13.7
Germany	18,665	203.4	1,208	158.3
Mexico	14,850	37.2	1,270	43.9
United Arab Emirates	12,968	43.2	790	45.6
Taiwan	9,983	41.6	520	81.4

Source: U.S. Department of Commerce, International Trade Administration. All totals are rounded off to one decimal point. Data for individual categories may not add to totals due to statistical rounding. Commerce often updates previously released data incorporating changes in collection methodologies.

Table 9 / U.S. Exports of Religious Books: Top Ten Markets 2009

Country	Value ($'000)	Percent Change 2008–2009	Units ('000)	Percent Change 2008–2009
Canada	$20,078	52.1%	4,428	25.9%
United Kingdom	14,064	-10.9	5,975	-8.5
Mexico	8,894	10.6	4,818	0.8
Nigeria	8,030	-37.9	2,186	-44.4
Australia	7,157	-39.9	1,914	-39.3
Argentina	2,336	-25.7	1,105	-45.5
Venezuela	2,320	-12.3	604	-36.0
Philippines	2,055	9.2	773	4.7
Guatemala	1,968	-16.4	645	-38.6
Colombia	1,670	-27.1	436	-28.5

Source: U.S. Department of Commerce, International Trade Administration. All totals are rounded off to one decimal point. Data for individual categories may not add to totals due to statistical rounding. Commerce often updates previously released data incorporating changes in collection methodologies.

Table 10 / U.S. Exports of Hardbound Books: Top Ten Markets 2009

Country	Value ($'000)	Percent Change 2008–2009	Units ('000)	Percent Change 2008–2009
Canada	$160,246	11.2%	19,401	12.3%
United Kingdom	12,552	17.6	2,031	7.4
India	4,498	-9.7	607	-14.3
Australia	3,938	40.4	669	60.3
Singapore	1,941	-44.6	349	-32.3
Japan	1,909	-17.2	212	-17.0
Mexico	1,840	24.0	307	57.5
Philippines	1,089	-26.6	111	-33.2
South Korea	107	16.7	184	40.0
New Zealand	817	-3.4	79	-2.3

Source: U.S. Department of Commerce, International Trade Administration. All totals are rounded off to one decimal point. Data for individual categories may not add to totals due to statistical rounding. Commerce often updates previously released data incorporating changes in collection methodologies.

Table 11 / U.S. Exports of Encyclopedias and Serial Installments: Top Ten Markets 2009

Country	Value ($'000)	Percent Change 2008–2009	Units ('000)	Percent Change 2008–2009
Canada	$1,297	-28.4%	150	-27.2%
South Africa	274	-12.6	21	-23.8
Philippines	273	-2.6	29	-15.6
United Kingdom	253	-32.1	23	-39.2
Australia	252	-53.4	20	-60.3
Taiwan	226	105.0	24	315.5
Mexico	168	-59.4	34	-63.1
Indonesia	123	-10.4	12	-23.5
Saudi Arabia	115	113.6	14	100.4
South Korea	104	275.7	15	488.5

Source: U.S. Department of Commerce, International Trade Administration. All totals are rounded off to one decimal point. Data for individual categories may not add to totals due to statistical rounding. Commerce often updates previously released data incorporating changes in collection methodologies.

sales were even worse, with hefty negative numbers recorded by Nigeria (down 44.4 percent), Australia (39.3 percent), Argentina (45.5 percent), and Venezuela (36 percent).

This was not a one-year decline. Rather it is a pattern that, left unaddressed, will escalate into a major melt-down in what had been a robust book category. Table 9 outlines the alarming picture.

The United States has long had a dominant position in hardcover fiction and nonfiction books in both adult and juvenile/YA sectors. Over the years, U.S. books have been well received in English and in translated versions, a fact evident in the 2009 results for Canada (revenues up 11.2 percent, units 12.3 percent), the United Kingdom (revenues up 17.6 percent, units 7.4 percent), South Korea (revenues up 16.7 percent, units 40 percent), Mexico (revenues up 24 percent, units 57.5 percent), and Australia (revenues up 40.4 percent, units 60.3 per-

Table 12 / U.S. Exports of Dictionaries (Including Thesauruses): Top Ten Markets 2009

Country	Value ($'000)	Percent Change 2008–2009	Units ('000)	Percent Change 2008–2009
Canada	$589	-45.8%	105	-36.3%
Mexico	124	-40.6	31	-47.6
Chile	114	165.3	21	149.9
Colombia	112	175.4	20	178.1
Brazil	64	114.2	9	-21.8
Costa Rica	50	88.0	11	12.7
Peru	27	121.0	6	29.8
Guatemala	26	74.4	5	18.6
United Kingdom	22	-93.5	3	-94.0
Singapore	21	-28.0	1	-67.1

Source: U.S. Department of Commerce, International Trade Administration. All totals are rounded off to one decimal point. Data for individual categories may not add to totals due to statistical rounding. Commerce often updates previously released data incorporating changes in collection methodologies.

Table 13 / U.S. Exports of Art and Pictorial Books: Top Ten Markets 2009

Country	Value ($'000)	Percent Change 2008–2009	Units ('000)	Percent Change 2008–2009
United Kingdom	$7,295	-66.9%	1,233	-64.8%
Canada	2,731	-12.0	242	-22.3
Mexico	1,106	119.0	206	196.1
Netherlands	797	1,405.2	163	2,784.0
Singapore	610	115.9	106	116.0
Chile	525	7,582.2	89	5,205.4
Australia	391	-28.6	64	716.7
United Arab Emirates	390	408.8	62	-33.5
South Korea	349	84.6	52	87.8
Germany	236	-72.9	46	-64.1

Source: U.S. Department of Commerce, International Trade Administration. All totals are rounded off to one decimal point. Data for individual categories may not add to totals due to statistical rounding. Commerce often updates previously released data incorporating changes in collection methodologies.

cent). Overall, however, the 2009 results for the other top ten countries were lackluster.

In the first quarter of 2010 some U.S. publishers started to investigate this situation, but few resources have been allocated to understand why this vibrant category sustained an erosion in international sales. See Table 10 for the 2009 results.

The two smallest and weakest book categories are the encyclopedia and serial installments cluster and the dictionaries and thesauruses clusters. Total revenues and unit sales have nearly reached the point of irrelevancy. Data can be found in Tables 11 and 12.

Art and pictorial books remain a small but important category. In 2009, while steep reversals were evident in sales to the United Kingdom, Canada,

Australia, and Germany, the results for the other top ten nations were exceptionally positive, if not borderline spectacular.

Gigantic increases were evident in sales to the Netherlands (revenues up 1,405.2 percent, units 2,784 percent) and Chile (revenues up 7,582.2 percent, units 5,205.4 percent). Additionally, Mexico, Singapore, and the United Arab Emirates all recorded triple-digit increases.

Publishers in other categories should use this category as a case study on how to market high-quality books with rather high suggested retail prices. Table 13 outlines this pattern.

U.S. Book Imports

At one time, it was the law of the land that a book had to be printed in the United States in order to receive a U.S. copyright (it was called the "manufacturing clause"). That policy ended in the late 1970s when the U.S. copyright law was amended. Since then, U.S. book printers, paper manufacturers, ink companies, and printing and graphic arts trade unions sustained losses in business and jobs as book manufacturing moved increasingly to other countries.

A review of the data covering the years 2000–2009 provided irrefutable evidence that a significant amount of book printing moved to foreign nations, primarily manufacturing operations in Asia and the Pacific Rim. Detailed discussions with publishing executives, and a drilling down through the complicated strata of statistics, revealed that the majority of these books are printed, and not printed-and-published, abroad. The reasons are twofold: first, to curtail skyrocketing unit manufacturing costs (e.g., printing, paper, and binding expenses); and second, to dampen increases in the suggested retail prices for books.

For a number of years, Canada was a U.S. source of printed books. However, exceptionally low manufacturing costs in China allowed it to benefit from the shift in the U.S. book-manufacturing business, and by 2001 China surpassed Canada as the place where books could be manufactured to high production standards at highly competitive prices—often 50 percent lower than the cost of printing a book in the United States. Table 14 lists the top ten sources of printed books.

Table 15 provides a slightly broader overview of this phenomenon, with 2006 through 2009 revenue data for the top 25 nations and the lump sum total for countries not in the top 25, plus grand total tallies. Again, the results for 2009 were rather feeble, with the entire pool of nations declining 17.4 percent.

Table 16 provides an overview of the eight major book categories. While the results for 2009 were disappointing—with all eight book categories showing declines in revenues and six in units, and in most instances severe declines—a broader evaluation is needed. A high percentage of higher education textbooks; technical, scientific, and professional books; and hardcover books are printed abroad. While the Commerce Department inexplicably did not separate out juvenile/YA books, a review of these books in major national bookstore chains revealed that almost all juvenile/YA books sold in the United States are printed abroad, primarily in Asian and Pacific Rim nations.

Table 14 / Top Ten Import Sources of Books 2000–2009
($'000)

Country	2000	2001	2002	2003	2004	2005	2006	2007	2008	2009	Percent Change 2008–2009
China	220,895	267,582	338,489	413,065	5335,241	605,229	724,742	815,677	806,695	711,438	-11.8 %
Canada	229,045	243,689	251,085	275,053	289,423	281,120	292,273	298,633	308,340	247,509	-19.7
United Kingdom	317,660	303,897	267,853	287,972	304,619	307,517	286,624	332,579	289,280	195,495	-32.4
Singapore	86,630	96,325	100,610	103,383	113,900	115,314	115,609	120,867	115,740	93,988	-18.8
Hong Kong	224,834	229,719	223,452	189,783	185,963	176,079	136,617	125,138	107,406	76,092	-29.2
Germany	57,345	53,092	55,993	52,055	7,353	68,211	76,657	82,088	88,075	56,780	-35.5
Japan	59,268	49,956	47,198	45,277	48,726	50,765	63,822	88,062	96,681	52,285	-45.9
South Korea	29,430	35,559	40,459	39,083	46,265	54,303	54,398	54,252	55,545	47,290	-14.9
Italy	94,983	87,779	83,360	84,167	78,567	69,463	69,571	69,393	62,430	40,800	-34.6
Mexico	24,656	19,272	18,627	21,828	22,627	40,956	47,089	32,380	30,667	29,559	-3.6

Source: U.S. Department of Commerce, International Trade Administration. All totals are rounded off to one decimal point. Data for individual categories may not add to totals due to statistical rounding. Commerce often updates previously released data incorporating changes in collection methodologies.

Table 15 / U.S. Book Imports from 25 Principal Countries: 2006–2009

Country	Value ($'000)				Percent Change 2008–2009
	2006	2007	2008	2009	
China	$724,742	$815,677	$806,695	$711,438	-11.8%
Canada	292,273	298,633	308,340	247,509	-19.7
United Kingdom	286,624	332,579	289,280	195,495	-32.4
Singapore	115,609	120,867	115,740	93,988	-18.8
Hong Kong	136,617	125,138	107,406	76,092	-29.2
Germany	76,657	82,088	88,075	56,780	-35.5
Japan	63,822	88,062	96,681	52,285	-45.9
South Korea	54,398	54,252	55,545	47,290	-14.9
Italy	69,571	69,393	62,430	40,800	-34.6
Mexico	47,089	32,380	30,667	29,559	-3.6
Colombia	22,102	36,274	31,159	27,479	-11.8
Spain	36,901	32,646	32,679	26,274	-19.6
India	14,222	16,439	16,161	19,180	18.7
France	31,006	25,562	22,503	17,222	-23.5
Malaysia	14,011	13,816	15,063	12,666	-15.9
Israel	12,874	14,309	13,686	11,122	-18.7
Thailand	19,476	18,747	15,454	9,345	-39.5
Netherlands	8,570	8,084	21,557	7,901	-63.4
Taiwan	8,860	9,866	10,303	7,820	-24.1
Australia	6,828	6,811	6,564	7,673	16.9
United Arab Emirates	6,748	6,075	6,578	6,095	-7.3
Switzerland	9,541	5,441	5,410	4,513	-16.6
Belgium	15,113	12,860	8,087	4,335	-46.4
Indonesia	3,431	3,254	6,145	3,249	-47.1
Brazil	5,994	5,882	2,380	3,163	32.9
Total Top 25 Countries	$2,083,079	$2,235,137	$2,174,609	$1,719,275	-20.9
All Others:	$41,227	$46,138	$39,203	$26,801	-31.6
Grand Total:	$2,124,306	$2,281,275	$2,113,812	$1,746,076	-17.4

Source: U.S. Department of Commerce, International Trade Administration. All totals are rounded off to one decimal point. Data for individual categories may not add to totals due to statistical rounding. Individual shipments are excluded from the foreign trade data if valued under $2,500. Commerce often updates previously released data incorporating changes in collection methodologies.

An analysis of specific book categories reveals the staggering amount of books printed abroad. In the textbook sector, Canada paced the top ten nations in total revenues, but China dominated in the total number of printed books imported into the United States. The emergence of the United Arab Emirates as a source of printed books is intriguing, indicating the growing interest and need for Arabic-language and Arabic-literature textbooks in the U.S. market. Four of the top ten nations were in Asia. Table 17 lists these developments.

The phenomenon of books printed, and not printed-and-published, abroad caught the attention of a remarkably small cluster of book industry researchers when China's position emerged after 2000. In spite of weak 2009 business patterns, China again totally dominated the eclectic religious book sector (which included Bibles, testaments, prayer books, and other religious books).

Table 16 / U.S. Imports of Books: 2009

Category	Value ($'000)	Percent Change 2008–2009	Units	Percent Change 2008–2009
Encyclopedias	$1,980	-65.0%	899	-51.8%
Textbooks	246,473	-15.6	40,780	-25.2
Religious books	122,195	-7.3	65,095	-5.4
Technical, scientific, and professional	177,169	-32.5	34,222	9.6
Hardcover books	528,402	-26.5	188,163	-19.1
Mass market paperbacks	84,415	-25.0	41,808	-26.3
Art and pictorial books (valued at more than $5.00)	26,394	-17.0	1,782	-24.7
Dictionaries and thesauruses	5,519	-28.4	2,395	7.1

Source: U.S. Department of Commerce, International Trade Administration. All totals are rounded off to one decimal point. Data for individual categories may not add to totals due to statistical rounding. Individual shipments are excluded from the foreign trade data if valued under $2,500. Commerce often updates previously released data incorporating changes in collection methodologies.

Table 17 / U.S. Imports of Textbooks: Top Ten Markets 2009

Country	Value ($'000)	Percent Change 2008–2009	Units ('000)	Percent Change 2008–2009
Canada	$68,651	-12.6%	11,799	-6.9%
United Kingdom	57,547	-14.3	3,510	-9.2
China	54,253	-19.2	14,606	-20.9
Hong Kong	16,823	-1.3	2,551	-51.9
Singapore	10,309	-6.0	2,988	-36.3
United Arab Emirates	3,940	187.1	289	125.4
Mexico	3,678	-46.0	541	-79.5
India	2,920	26.0	170	-27.4
Colombia	2,696	-46.1	736	-36.4
Germany	2,689	-50.5	134	-53.0

Source: U.S. Department of Commerce, International Trade Administration. All totals are rounded off to one decimal point. Data for individual categories may not add to totals due to statistical rounding. Commerce often updates previously released data incorporating changes in collection methodologies.

This is also a sector where Israel, Mexico, South Korea, and Colombia achieved success in the last decade. Belgium, long an important source of religious books, fell out of the top ten in 2009. See Table 18.

Seven of the top ten nations reported declines in the importation of printed technical, scientific, and professional books. There are two underlying reasons for this situation.

First, certain markets made the transition to a print and digital environment, including the United States. This explains to a great degree the decline in the importation of these printed books, with significant revenue declines from China, Japan, Germany, Canada, the United Kingdom, Mexico, and France.

Second, recent meetings sponsored by the Society for Scholarly Publishing and other organizations highlighted the impact of the "serials crisis" as the sec-

Table 18 / U.S. Imports of Bibles, Testaments, Prayer Books, and Other Religious Books: Top Ten Markets 2009

Country	Value ($'000)	Percent Change 2008–2009	Units ('000)	Percent Change 2008–2009
China	$37,174	6.5%	15,359	-2.5%
Colombia	19,896	16.9	10,096	0.4
South Korea	19,343	1.9	10,500	-10.5
Israel	9,402	-16.7	3,152	-10.6
Canada	4,910	-13.7	2,351	45.1
United Kingdom	3,994	-32.1	784	11.8
Spain	3,644	-3.0	649	10.9
Mexico	2,797	-2.0	3,470	3.5
Italy	2,647	-41.1	1,237	13.5
Hong Kong	2,440	-27.6	5,639	-11.8

Source: U.S. Department of Commerce, International Trade Administration. All totals are rounded off to one decimal point. Data for individual categories may not add to totals due to statistical rounding. Commerce often updates previously released data incorporating changes in collection methodologies.

Table 19 / U.S. Imports of Technical, Scientific, and Professional Books: Top Ten Markets 2009

Country	Value ($'000)	Percent Change 2008–2009	Units ('000)	Percent Change 2008–2009
China	$33,721	-13.5%	11,922	24.8%
Japan	28,403	-53.4	1,020	16.4
Germany	26,291	-41.0	1,104	-21.5
Canada	24,144	-33.0	4,341	-11.0
United Kingdom	22,653	-25.0	3,171	-7.5
Hong Kong	7,805	12.9	1,458	13.6
India	5,898	47.3	1,456	172.5
Singapore	5,710	27.8	1,551	30.8
Mexico	4,357	-22.5	3,208	1.0
France	3,566	-50.1	195	-28.7

Source: U.S. Department of Commerce, International Trade Administration. All totals are rounded off to one decimal point. Data for individual categories may not add to totals due to statistical rounding. Commerce often updates previously released data incorporating changes in collection methodologies.

ond reason for the decline. The "serials crisis" relates to sharp increases in the price of "serials" (i.e., scholarly journals)—for example, the journal *Brain Research* has an annual subscription price of $21,000—and the concomitant decline in book purchases by libraries and other institutions. Some excellent research studies released by the Association of Research Libraries highlighted this issue.

The end result has been the digital transformation of this technical, scientific, and professional category, with a preponderance of academics and researchers downloading content onto computers and eschewing traditional printed books. For example, Springer offers more than 33,000 technical, scientific, and professional e-books; the other major publishers in this sector (among them Elsevier, Kluwer, Sage, Wiley-Blackwell, Informa, Pearson, and McGraw-Hill) also offer a wide array of digital technical, scientific, and professional e-books.

This sector will continue to experience a movement away from print. Table 19 outlines these trends.

Why was there a complete decline in the hardbound and mass market paperback importation markets in 2009? Nine of the nations selling hardbound book in 2009 posted lower revenue numbers, and nine nations in the mass market paperback business generated lower revenues.

At first glance, some might believe it was due to the proliferation of e-readers. In reality, total trade (adult, juvenile/YA, religion) e-book sales in 2008 hovered around $78 million and reached approximately $155 million to $160 million in 2009. It is likely this sector will be in the $350 million to $450 million range in 2010. Trade e-book revenues represent, perhaps, 3 percent of the total trade sector. Price was not a cause of this debacle as these books can be printed abroad for rather modest manufacturing costs.

Table 20 / U.S. Imports of Hardbound Books: Top Ten Markets 2009

Country	Value ($'000)	Percent Change 2008–2009	Units ('000)	Percent Change 2008–2009
China	$312,453	-12.8%	134108	-11.3%
Singapore	42,250	-25.8	16988	-31.4
United Kingdom	36,712	-58.5	4505	-9.1
Hong Kong	23,405	-40.4	8052	-36.4
Canada	21,647	-38.2	4570	-34.9
Italy	19,971	-33.9	1914	-54.6
Spain	10,628	-14.2	1628	-12.7
Germany	9,131	-35.1	1244	-41.4
France	7,294	144.1	197	-38.3
South Korea	6,329	-31.9	4137	-33.4

Source: U.S. Department of Commerce, International Trade Administration. All totals are rounded off to one decimal point. Data for individual categories may not add to totals due to statistical rounding. Commerce often updates previously released data incorporating changes in collection methodologies.

Table 21 / U.S. Imports of Mass Market Paperbacks (Rack Size): Top Ten Markets 2009

Country	Value ($'000)	Percent Change 2008–2009	Units ('000)	Percent Change 2008–2009
China	$24,503	-30.2%	16,348	-20.1%
Canada	21,021	-6.2	10,832	-18.2
United Kingdom	18,716	-27.1	4,616	-28.1
Hong Kong	4,418	-35.2	2,783	-21.7
Italy	3,528	-23.1	1,103	-41.3
Singapore	3,498	-39.0	2,650	-47.2
Spain	2,178	-23.2	1,207	-23.8
Japan	1,146	-13.3	312	5.4
Malaysia	684	68.7	234	-23.9
Germany	636	-16.2	196	-64.1

Source: U.S. Department of Commerce, International Trade Administration. All totals are rounded off to one decimal point. Data for individual categories may not add to totals due to statistical rounding. Commerce often updates previously released data incorporating changes in collection methodologies.

Classical economic theory explained this situation: the irrefutable law of supply and demand. The supply of titles increased; the demand in the United States sagged because of the impact of the recession. The outlook for 2010 is equally bleak. It is likely that trade book sales, including hardbound and mass market paperbacks, will be off by somewhere in the 4 percent range. This means that the outlook for 2010 is equally bleak for certain other nations, including China (the largest source of printed hardcover and mass market paperbacks). Tables 20 and 21 outline these negative trends.

The plight of encyclopedias and serial installments and dictionaries and thesauruses has been well documented. Digital versions of these products are inexpensive and ubiquitous, often provided free of change on new computers. These two categories are likely to become appendices in future editions of this research report. See Tables 22 and 23.

Table 22 / U.S. Imports of Encyclopedias and Serial Installments: Top Ten Markets 2009

Country	Value ($'000)	Percent Change 2008–2009	Units ('000)	Percent Change 2008–2009
Mexico	$460	-44.8%	80	-5.0%
Singapore	280	-31.4	82	14.1
China	279	-91.0	64	95.4
Taiwan	264	239.0	411	1,076.2
United Arab Emirates	233	245.0	99	98.9
Germany	105	52.6	35	-41.4
Hong Kong	84	-67.4	13	-67.7
United Kingdom	83	15.7	3	-45.0
Canada	76	-82.3	89	25.2
Netherlands	32	5.3	13	146.6

Source: U.S. Department of Commerce, International Trade Administration. All totals are rounded off to one decimal point. Data for individual categories may not add to totals due to statistical rounding. Commerce often updates previously released data incorporating changes in collection methodologies.

Table 23 / U.S. Imports of Dictionaries and Thesauruses: Top Ten Markets 2009

Country	Value ($'000)	Percent Change 2008–2009	Units ('000)	Percent Change 2008–2009
China	$1,377	-43.6%	1,129	72.2%
United Kingdom	1,362	27.0	280	10.0
Italy	516	6.3	120	43.1
France	445	1137.8	99	1,761.3
Singapore	438	-51.5	122	-52.0
Spain	378	23.2	107	10.4
Canada	220	-51.4	201	-31.7
India	142	254.3	63	122.4
Colombia	140	-19.3	47	23.4
United Arab Emirates	87	-21.8	55	25.0

Source: U.S. Department of Commerce, International Trade Administration. All totals are rounded off to one decimal point. Data for individual categories may not add to totals due to statistical rounding. Commerce often updates previously released data incorporating changes in collection methodologies.

Table 24 / U.S. Imports of Art and Pictorial Books (Minimum Values $5):
Top Ten Markets 2009

Country	Value ($'000)	Percent Change 2008–2009	Units ('000)	Percent Change 2008–2009
Germany	$5,927	40.1%	421	20.2%
China	4,766	-22.9	375	-44.5
United Kingdom	4,567	51.6	225	15.9
Italy	3,768	-28.2	227	-26.2
Hong Kong	2,063	8.0	210	-1.4
Singapore	925	-50.4	95	-51.8
Netherlands	552	-63.0	25	-63.3
France	535	-76.0	18	-47.6
Spain	496	-20.1	25	-29.4
Canada	479	-65.5	27	-48.3

Source: U.S. Department of Commerce, International Trade Administration. All totals are rounded off to one decimal point. Data for individual categories may not add to totals due to statistical rounding. Commerce often updates previously released data incorporating changes in collection methodologies.

The situation of art and pictorial books (with a value of more than $5) is a bit more upbeat. While mainly posting declines in revenues and units, this remains a vital segment of the book-publishing industry, with respectable revenues even in 2009. Table 24 outlines the development of this category in 2009.

Imports from Asia and the Pacific Rim

A more-detailed analysis of the book importation business was needed. Eleven nations in Asia and the Pacific Rim were evaluated: China, Singapore, South Korea, Hong Kong, India, Malaysia, Taiwan, Thailand, Japan, Indonesia, and Australia. The United States imports books from dozens of countries, but these 11 accounted for the preponderance.

Table 25 details information about the years 2000–2004. During these years, China sent the United States more than 1 billion books (23.4 percent of all book imports). Overall, the United States imported 4.55 billion books, and these 11 countries accounted for 2.19 billion of them, or 48.1 percent of all imported books.

Table 26 addresses the years 2005–2009. During those five years, the importation of books accelerated, increasing from 4.55 billion in 2000–2004 to 4.77 billion in 2005–2009. Of that total, the 11 Asian and Pacific Rim nations sent the United States 2.85 billion books. This meant that these countries accounted for 59.8 percent of all imports. Again China dominated, with 40.4 percent of all book imports (1.93 billion units).

Between 2000 and 2009, China's book manufacturing companies sent the United States 2.99 billion books (32.1 percent of all imports); and these 11 nations produced more than 5 billion books (54.1 percent of the total). Table 27 lists the consolidated statistical data for 2000 to 2009.

Table 25 / Book Units Imported from Asia and the Pacific Rim: 2000–2004
('000)

	2000	2001	2002	2003	2004	Total
China	151,594	183,228	213,236	232,049	284,844	1,064,951
Singapore	34,945	40,582	44,076	45,085	50,762	215,450
South Korea	12,324	17,586	22,082	20,443	36,910	109,345
Hong Kong	130,582	121,142	117,091	102,881	107,997	579,693
India	1,436	3,782	2,777	4,015	9,993	22,003
Malaysia	5,739	5,245	8,111	9,330	6,142	34,567
Taiwan	8,637	6,648	6,827	6,966	6,562	35,640
Thailand	6,906	7,665	8,293	7,891	4,765	35,520
Japan	18,741	12,668	12,293	12,724	11,311	67,737
Indonesia	2,583	1,273	2,864	1,948	3,765	12,433
Australia	2,573	4,292	2,645	2,171	2,874	14,555
Total	376,060	404,111	440,295	445,503	525,925	2,191,894
Total All Imported Books	869,114	853,309	882,606	924,184	1,019,474	4,548,687
Eleven Nations: Percentage of All Imported Books	43.3%	47.4%	49.9%	48.2%	51.6%	48.2%

Source: U.S. Department of Commerce, International Trade Administration. All totals are rounded off to one decimal point. Data for individual categories may not add to totals due to statistical rounding. Commerce often updates previously released data incorporating changes in collection methodologies.

Table 26 / Book Units Imported from Asia and the Pacific Rim 2005–2009
('000)

	2005	2006	2007	2008	2009	Total
China	318,269	394,795	432,716	420,852	362,395	1,929,027
Singapore	47,467	47,948	52,607	53,522	41,237	242,781
South Korea	34,671	33,465	34,823	38,783	37,280	179,022
Hong Kong	96,742	65,752	60,140	47,097	33,692	303,423
India	7,628	6,723	7,392	5,713	7,143	34,599
Malaysia	6,796	5,950	6,836	7,287	6,096	32,965
Taiwan	6,626	6,762	6,732	6,411	5,776	32,307
Thailand	5,777	8,869	7,537	6,153	5,290	33,626
Japan	9,611	8,781	10,064	9,574	5,194	43,224
Indonesia	4,495	2,152	2,649	4,220	2,662	16,178
Australia	2,643	1,215	1,070	778	1,221	6,927
Total	540,725	582,412	622,566	600,390	507,986	2,854,079
Total All Imported Books	975,459	1,044,165	1,007,257	926,324	819,433	4,772,639
Eleven Nations: Percentage of All Imported Books	55.4%	55.8%	61.8%	64.8%	62.0%	59.8%

Source: U.S. Department of Commerce, International Trade Administration. All totals are rounded off to one decimal point. Data for individual categories may not add to totals due to statistical rounding. Commerce often updates previously released data incorporating changes in collection methodologies.

Table 27 / Book Units Imported from Asia and the Pacific Rim: 2000–2009
('000)

	2000–2009	Percent of Total Imports
China	$2,993,978	32.1%
Singapore	458,231	4.9
South Korea	288,367	3.1
Hong Kong	883,116	9.5
India	56,602	0.6
Malaysia	67,532	0.7
Taiwan	67,947	0.7
Thailand	69,146	0.7
Japan	110,961	1.2
Indonesia	28,611	0.3
Australia	21,482	0.2
Total	5,045,973	—
Total All Imported Books	9,321,326	—
Eleven Nations: Percentage of Total Imported Books	54.1%	

Source: U.S. Department of Commerce, International Trade Administration. All totals are rounded off to one decimal point. Data for individual categories may not add to totals due to statistical rounding. Commerce often updates previously released data incorporating changes in collection methodologies.

Book Prices

Sam Walton and other key management officials at Wal-Mart long maintained that the importation of consumer products from Asia and the Pacific Rim allowed them to keep prices low. Was this also true for the importation of books from Asia and the Pacific Rim?

The Bureau of Labor Statistics, U.S. Department of Labor, tracks monthly and annual consumer price index (CPI) statistics for a category called "recreational books." Upon closer analysis, this "recreational book" category is the trade book sector—adult, juvenile/YA, and mass market paperbacks.

The annual CPI for "recreational books" when compared with the CPI for all items for urban consumers revealed the following.

Table 28 / CPI for Recreational Books Compared with CPI All Items, Urban Consumers, 2000–2009

	Recreational Books		U.S. CPI All Urban Consumers	
	Annual CPI	Annual Percent Change	Annual CPI	Annual Percent Change
2000	100.700	0.70%	172.2	3.40%
2001	101.900	1.19	177.1	2.80
2002	105.000	3.04	179.9	1.60
2003	104.100	-0.86	184.0	2.30
2004	104.300	0.19	188.9	2.70
2005	103.900	-0.38	195.3	3.40
2006	103.300	-0.58	201.6	3.20
2007	104.120	0.79	207.3	2.80
2008	105.886	1.70	215.3	3.80
2009	106.885	0.94	214.5	-0.37

Between 2000 and 2009 the CPI for "recreational books" increased 6.14 percent. The national CPI grew 24.56 percent.

The importation of books, with more than 54 percent coming from 11 nations in Asia and the Pacific Rim, allowed U.S. book publishers to keep trade book prices low during this entire decade, providing substantial evidence that Sam Walton was right.

References

El-Erian, Mohamed. *When Markets Collide: Investment Strategies for the Age of Global Economic Change* (McGraw-Hill, 2008), pp. 265–288. El-Erian is a senior executive at PIMCO, and his comment on "Improved Risk Management" was based on his extensive work at PIMCO and Harvard.

Ferguson, Niall. *The Ascent of Money: A Financial History of the World* (Penguin, 2008), pp. 283–340. In this comprehensive work, which was turned into a PBS television program, Ferguson's evaluation of "From Empire to Chimerica" brings this history up to date.

Gasparino, Charles. *The Sellout: How Three Decades of Wall Street Greed and Government Mismanagement Destroyed the Global Financial System* (Harper Business, 2009). Gasparino, long a fixture on CNBC and now on Fox Business, is one of the America's best financial reporters. His material on "Bigger Is Better" (pages 87–102) is an excellent critique of Wall Street; his material on derivatives (page 96) is worth the price of the book.

Knee, Jonathan A., Bruce C. Greenwald, and Ava Seave. *The Curse of the Mogul: What's Wrong with the World's Leading Media Companies* (Penguin, 2009). Knee is a former investment banker, and he and his co-authors wrote convincing chapters on "The Landscape of Competitive Advantage" (pages 33–56) and "The Structure of Media Industries" (pages 57–66).

Kosman, Josh. *The Buyout of America: How Private Equity Will Cause the Next Great Credit Crisis* (Penguin, 2009). Kosman's chapter "How Private Equity Started" is lucid and valuable; pages 19–34.

Patterson, Scott. *The Quants: How a New Breed of Math Whizzes Conquered Wall Street and Nearly Destroyed It* (Crown Business, 2010). Patterson is a reporter at the *Wall Street Journal* and this is perhaps the best business study of Wall Street and the influence of the quants in the past ten years. "The August Factor" (pages 209–241), "The Doomsday Clock" (pages 242–261), and the coverage of Bear Stearns and Ralph Cioffi are first-rate.

Porter, Michael E. *Competitive Strategy: Techniques for Analyzing Industries and Competitors* (Free Press, 1980). Porter is a preeminent expert on competition. See his definitive and widely quoted coverage of "Generic Competitive Strategies," pages 34–46.

Reinhart, Carmen M., and Kenneth S. Rogoff. *This Time Is Different: Eight Centuries of Financial Folly* (Princeton University Press, 2009). While the historical material is somewhat ponderous, the statistical appendices are outstanding, especially the banking data (pages 344–392).

Shiller, Robert J. *Irrational Exuberance* (Princeton University Press, 2000). Shiller is co-author of the Case-Shiller housing index, a definitive analysis of housing prices in the United States. See the interesting and useful analysis "Efficient Markets, Random Walks, and Bubbles," pages 171–190.

Tett, Gillian. *Fool's Gold: How the Bold Dream of a Small Tribe at J.P. Morgan Was Corrupted by Wall Street Greed and Unleashed a Catastrophe* (Free Press, 2009). A reporter at the *Financial Times,* Tett has written a superb analysis of derivatives; see pages 3–22.

Number of Book Outlets in the United States and Canada

The *American Book Trade Directory* (Information Today, Inc.) has been published since 1915. Revised annually, it features lists of booksellers, wholesalers, periodicals, reference tools, and other information about the U.S. and Canadian book markets. The data shown in Table 1, the most current available, are from the 2010–2011 edition of the directory.

Table 1 / Bookstores in the United States and Canada, 2009

Category	United States	Canada
Antiquarian General	805	73
Antiquarian Mail Order	309	12
Antiquarian Specialized	147	4
Art Supply Store	67	2
College General	3,197	173
College Specialized	119	6
Comics	220	26
Computer Software	2	0
Cooking	277	11
Department Store	1,599	7
Educational*	185	37
Federal Sites†	221	1
Foreign Language*	22	3
General	3,631	606
Gift Shop	156	7
Juvenile*	116	21
Mail Order General	119	11
Mail Order Specialized	382	21
Metaphysics, New Age, and Occult	159	22
Museum Store and Art Gallery	495	32
Nature and Natural History	41	7
Newsdealer	29	2
Office Supply	15	2
Other‡	2,353	452
Paperback§	109	6
Religious*	2,026	168
Self Help/Development	22	7
Stationer	5	4
Toy Store	46	19
Used*	438	86
Totals	17,312	1,828

* Includes Mail Order Shops for this topic, which are not counted elsewhere in this survey.
† National Historic Sites, National Monuments, and National Parks.
‡ Stores specializing in subjects or services other than those covered in this survey.
§ Includes Mail Order. Excludes used paperback bookstores, stationers, drugstores, or wholesalers handling paperbacks.

The 19,140 stores of various types shown are located throughout the United States, Canada, and regions administered by the United States. "General" bookstores stock trade books and children's books in a general variety of subjects. "College" stores carry college-level textbooks. "Educational" outlets handle school textbooks up to and including the high school level. "Mail order" outlets sell general trade books by mail and are not book clubs; all others operating by mail are classified according to the kinds of books carried. "Antiquarian" dealers sell old and rare books. Stores handling secondhand books are classified as "used." "Paperback" stores have more than 80 percent of their stock in paperbound books. Stores with paperback departments are listed under the appropriate major classification ("general," "department store," "stationer," and so forth.). Bookstores with at least 50 percent of their stock on a particular subject are classified by subject.

Review Media Statistics

Compiled by the staff of the *Library and Book Trade Almanac*

Number of Books and Other Media Reviewed by Major Reviewing Publications 2008–2009

	Adult		Juvenile		Young Adult		Total	
	2008	2009	2008	2009	2008	2009	2008	2009
Booklist[1]	4,673	4,737	3,138	3,542	—	—	7,811	8,279
Bookmarks	716	692	—	—	20	—	736	692
BookPage[2]	533	758	77	109	20	34	630	901
Bulletin of the Center for Children's Books[3]	—	—	849	790	—	—	849	790
Chicago Sun Times	n.a.	n.a.	n.a.	n.a.	—	—	n.a.	n.a.
Chicago Tribune Sunday Book Section	400	350	250	200	50	50	675	600
Choice[4]	6,766	6,632	—	—	—	—	6,766	6,632
Horn Book Guide	—	—	3,324	3,272	1,154	1,101	4,478	4,373
Horn Book Magazine[5]	2	3	320	335	106	116	428	454
Kirkus Reviews[7]	2,532	2,311	2,096	2,155	—	—	4,628	4,466
Library Journal[8]	5,814	5,741	—	—	—	—	5,814	5,741
Los Angeles Times	n.a.	n.a.	—	—	—	—	n.a.	n.a.
Multicultural Review[6]	374	331	128	127	57	63	559	521
New York Review of Books	332	n.a.	—	—	—	—	332	n.a.
New York Times Sunday Book Review[7]	1,050	n.a.	115	n.a.	—	—	1,165	n.a.
Publishers Weekly[9]	6,284	6,352	1,030	1,243	—	—	7,912	7,595
School Library Journal[7]	280	172	4,853	5,528	—	—	5,133	5,700
Washington Post Book World	n.a.	860	n.a.	50	—	—	n.a.	910

n.a. = not available

1 All figures are for a 12-month period from September 1, 2008, to August 31, 2009 (vol. 105). YA books are included in the juvenile total. *Booklist* also reviewed 595 other media.

2 Of the total count, 25 were Web-only reviews.

3 All figures are for a 12-month period beginning September and ending July/August. YA books are included in the juvenile total.

4 All materials reviewed in *Choice* are scholarly publications intended for undergraduate libraries. *Choice* also reviewed 423 Internet sites, 4 CD-ROMs, 2 DVDs, and 2 e-books.

5 *Horn Book Magazine* also reviewed 20 audiobooks.

6 *MultiCultural Review* also reviewed 13 audio/video reviews in 2008, 3 in 2009.

7 YA books are included in the juvenile total.

8 In addition, *Library Journal* reviewed 414 audiobooks, 410 DVDs/videos, 108 magazines, 238 books in Collection Development, and 145 online databases, and previewed 1,215 books in "Prepub Alert," "Prepub Mystery," and "Prepub Audio."

9 Of the total of 7,595 reviews, 943 were online only. *Publishers Weekly* also reviewed 403 audiobooks.

Part 5
Reference Information

Bibliographies

The Librarian's Bookshelf

Mary Ellen Quinn

Editor, *Booklist/Reference Books Bulletin,* American Library Association

Most of the books on this selective bibliography have been published since 2007; a few earlier titles are retained because of their continuing importance.

General Works

American Library Directory, 2010–2011. 2v. Information Today, Inc., 2010. $319. Also available online.

Annual Review of Information Science and Technology (ARIST). Ed. by Blaise Cronin. Information Today, Inc., 2010. $124.95.

Charleston Conference Proceedings, 2008. Ed. by Beth R. Bernhardt and others. Libraries Unlimited, 2009. Paper $40.

Library and Book Trade Almanac, 2010 (Bowker Annual). Information Today, Inc., 2010. $219.

Encyclopedia of Library and Information Science. 2nd ed. Ed. by Miriam A. Drake. Taylor & Francis, 2003. $1,500. Also available online.

Library Literature and Information Science Full Text. H. W. Wilson (http://www.hwwilson.com).

Library Literature and Information Science Index. H. W. Wilson, 1921–. Also available online, 1984–.

Library Literature and Information Science Retrospective: 1905–1983. H. W. Wilson (http://www.hwwilson.com).

The Oxford Guide to Library Research. 3rd ed. By Thomas Mann. Oxford University Press, 2005. Paper $19.99.

The Whole Library Handbook 4. Ed. by George Eberhart. American Library Association, 2006. Paper $48.

Academic Libraries

The Academic Library and the Net Gen Student: Making the Connection. By Susan Gibbons. American Library Association, 2007. Paper $50.

The Academic Library Manager's Forms, Policies, and Procedures Handbook with CD-ROM. By Rebecca Brumley. Neal-Schuman, 2007. Paper and CD-ROM $155.

Academic Library Outreach: Beyond the Campus Walls. By Nancy Courtney. Libraries Unlimited, 2008. Paper $45.

Academic Library Trends and Statistics, 2008. Association of College and Research Libraries/American Library Association, 2009. 3 vols. $500. (Also available online at http://secure200.telusys.net/trendstat/ 2006.)

ARL Statistics. Association of Research Libraries. Annual. 1962– (http://www.arl.org/stats/annualsurveys/arlstats).

Convergence and Collaboration of Campus Information Services. Ed. by Peter Hernon and Ronald R. Powell. Libraries Unlimited, 2008. Paper $50.

Creating the Customer-Driven Academic Library. By Jeannette Woodward. American Library Association, 2008. Paper $58.

A Field Guide to the Information Commons. By Charles Forrest and Martin Halbert. Scarecrow, 2009. Paper $65.

Making a Difference: Leadership and Academic Libraries. By Peter Hernon and Nancy Rossiter. Libraries Unlimited, 2007. Paper $45.

Mistakes in Academic Library Management: Grievous Errors and How to Avoid Them. Ed. by Jack E. Fritts, Jr. Scarecrow, 2009. $39.95.

Starting, Strengthening, and Managing Institutional Repositories: A How-To-Do-It Manual. By Johathan A. Nabe. Neal-Schuman, 2010. Paper $85.

Transforming Library Service through Information Commons: Case Studies for the Digital Age. By D. Russell Bailey and Barbara Gunter Tierney. American Library Association, 2008. Paper $60.

Administration and Personnel

Crash Course in Library Supervision. By Dennis C. Tucker and Shelley Elizabeth Mosley. Libraries Unlimited, 2007. Paper $30.

Developing a Compensation Plan for Your Library. By Paula M. Singer and Laura L. Francisco. American Library Association, 2009. Paper $55.

Even More Ideas for Libraries and Friends. By Sally Gardner Reed and Beth Nawalinski Neal-Schuman, 2008. Paper $69.95.

Hiring, Training, and Supervising Library Shelvers. By Patricia Tunstall. American Library Association, 2010. Paper $48.

Human Resources for Results: The Right Person for the Right Job. By Jeanne Goodrich and Paula M. Singer. 2007. American Library Association, 2007. Paper $60.

Implementing for Results: Your Strategic Plan in Action. By Sandra Nelson. American Library Association, 2009. Paper $55.

Inside, Outside, and Online: Building Your Library Community. By Chrystie Hill.

American Library Association, 2009. Paper $48.

Library and Information Center Management. 7th ed. By Robert D. Stueart and Barbara B. Moran. Libraries Unlimited, 2007. Paper $50.

Library Board Strategic Guide: Going to the Next Level. By Ellen G. Moore and Patricia H. Fisher. Scarecrow, 2007. Paper $35.

The Library Security and Safety Guide to Prevention, Planning, and Response. By Miriam B. Kahn. American Library Association, 2008. Paper $52.

Management Basics for Information Professionals. 2nd ed. By G. Edward Evans and Patricia Layzell Ward. Neal-Schuman, 2007. Paper $65.

Moving Materials: Physical Delivery in Libraries. Ed. by Valerie Horton and Bruce Smith. American Library Association, 2010. Paper $70.

Our New Public, A Changing Clientele: Bewildering Issues or New Challenges for Managing Libraries? Ed. by Janes R. Kennedy, Lisa Vardaman, and Gerard B. McCabe. Libraries Unlimited, 2008. $45.

Privacy and Confidentiality Issues: A Guide for Libraries and Their Lawyers. By Theresa Chmara. American Library Association, 2009. Paper $40.

The Quality Library: Guide to Staff-Driven Improvement, Better Efficiency, and Happier Customers. By Sara Laughlin and Ray W. Wilson. American Library Association, 2008. Paper $55.

Staff Development Strategies That Work: Stories and Strategies from New Librarians. Ed. by Georgie L. Donovan and Miguel A. Figueroa. Neal-Schuman, 2008. Paper $75.

Strategic Planning for Results. By Sandra Nelson. American Library Association, 2008. Paper $72.

Streamlining Library Services: What We Do, How Much Time It Takes, What It Costs, and How We Can Do It Better. By Richard M. Dougherty. Scarecrow, 2008. Paper $45.

The Successful Library Trustee Handbook. By Mary Y. Moore. American Library Association, 2009. Paper $45.

Buildings and Space Planning

Designing a School Library Media Center for the Future. By Rolf Erikson and Carolyn Markuson. American Library Association, 2007. Paper $52.

Libraries Designed for Kids By Nolan Lushington. Neal-Schuman, 2008. Paper $85.

Library Furnishings: A Planning Guide. By Tish Murphy. McFarland, 2007. Paper $55.

Managing Your Library Construction Project. By Richard C. McCarthy. American Library Association, 2007. Paper $64.

Moving Your Library: Getting the Collection from Here to There. By Steven Carl Fortriede. American Library Association, 2010. Paper $70.

Planning New and Remodeled Archival Facilities. By Thomas P. Wilsted. Society of American Archivists, 2007. Paper $49.

Cataloging and Bibliographic Control

Beginning Cataloging. By Jean Weihs and Sheila S. Intner. Libraries Unlimited, 2009. $70.

FRBR: A Guide for the Perplexed. By Robert L. Maxwell. American Library Association, 2008. Paper $57.

Introduction to Cataloging and Classification. 10th ed. By Arlene G. Taylor. Libraries Unlimited, 2006. Paper $50.

Metadata. By Marcia Lei Zeng and Jian Qin. Neal-Schuman, 2008. Paper $65.

Moving Image Cataloging: How to Create and How to Use a Moving Image Catalog. By Martha M. Yee. Libraries Unlimited, 2007. Paper $45.

Radical Cataloging: Essays at the Front. Ed. by K. R. Roberto. McFarland, 2008. Paper $45.

Standard Cataloging for School and Public Libraries. 4th ed. By Sheila S. Intner and Jean Weihs. Libraries Unlimited, 2007. Paper $50.

Understanding FRBR: What It Is and How It Will Affect Our Retrieval Tools. By Arlene G. Taylor. Libraries Unlimited, 2008. Paper $45.

Children's and Young Adult Services and Materials

Children's Books: A Practical Guide to Selection. By Phyllis J. Van Orden and Sunny Strong. Neal-Schuman, 2007. Paper $59.95.

Children's Literature in Action: A Librarian's Guide. By Sylvia Vardell. Libraries Unlimited, 2008. Paper $50.

Connecting with Reluctant Teen Readers: Tips, Titles, and Tools. By Patrick Jones. Neal-Schuman, 2006. Paper $59.95.

Connecting Young Adults and Libraries. 4th ed. By Michele Gorman and Tricia Suellentrop. Neal-Schuman, 2009. Paper $85.

Core Collection for Children and Young Adults. By Rachel E. Schwedt and Janice DeLong. Scarecrow, 2008. $50.

The Guy-Friendly YA Library. By James Rollie Welch. Libraries Unlimited, 2007. Paper $40.

Managing Children's Services in the Public Library. 3rd ed. By Adele M. Fasick and Leslie E. Holt. Libraries Unlimited, 2007. Paper $45.

More Than MySpace: Teens, Librarians, and Social Networking. Ed. by Robyn M. Lupa. Libraries Unlimited, 2009. Paper $40.

The Newbery and Caldecott Awards 2009: A Guide to the Medal and Honor Books. Association for Library Service to Children/American Library Association, 2009. Paper $25.

Serving Urban Teens. By Paula Brehm-Heeger. Libraries Unlimited, 2008. Paper $40.

Sex, Brains, and Video Games: A Librarian's Guide to Teens in the Twenty-first Century. By Jennifer Burek Pierce. American Library Association, 2007. Paper $40.

Start to Finish YA Programs: Hip-Hop Symposiums, Summer Reading Programs, Virtual Tours, Poetry Slams, Teen Advisory Boards, Term Paper Clinics, and More!

By Ella W. Jones. Neal-Schuman, 2009. Paper $75.

Teen Spaces: The Step-by-Step Library Makeover. By Kimberly Bolan. American Library Association, 2009. Paper $36.

Collection Development

The Collection Program in Schools: Concepts, Practices, and Information Sources. 4th ed. By Kay Bishop. Libraries Unlimited, 2007. Paper $50.

Crash Course in Collection Development. By Wayne Disher. Libraries Unlimited, 2007. Paper $30.

Fundamentals of Collection Development and Management. 2nd ed. By Peggy Johnson. American Library Association, 2009. Paper $70.

The Kovacs Guide to Electronic Library Collection Development. By Diane K. Kovacs. Neal-Schuman, 2009. Paper $150.

Copyright

Intellectual Property: Everything the Digital-Age Librarian Needs to Know. By Timothy Lee Wherry. American Library Association, 2007. Paper $57.

Smart Copyright Compliance for Schools: A How-To-Do-It Manual. By Rebecca P. Butler. Neal-Schuman, 2009. Paper $75.

Electronic Library

Building Digital Libraries. By Terry Reese, Jr. and Kyle Banerjee. Neal-Schuman, 2008. Paper $75.

Going the Distance: Library Instruction for Remote Users. Ed. by Susan J. Clayton. Neal-Schuman, 2007. Paper $65.

Licensing Digital Content: A Practical Guide for Librarians. By Lesley Ellen Harris. American Library Association, 2009. Paper $57.

What Every Librarian Should Know about Electronic Privacy By Jeanette Woodward. Libraries Unlimited, 2008. Paper $40.

The Whole Digital Library Handbook. Ed. by Diane Kresh. American Library Association, 2007. Paper $50.

Evaluation of Library Services

Library Data: Empowering Practice and Persuasion. Ed. by Darby Orcutt. Libraries Unlimited, 2010. Paper $50.

The Evaluation and Measurement of Library Services. By Joseph R. Matthews. Libraries Unlimited, 2007. Paper $50.

Library Assessment in Higher Education. By Joseph R. Matthews. Libraries Unlimited, 2007. Paper $45.

Measuring Your Library's Value: How to Do a Cost-Benefit Analysis for Your Public Library. By Donald S. Elliot, Glen E. Holt, Sterling W. Hayden, and Leslie Edmonds Holt. American Library Association, 2007. Paper $60.

History

The History of Public Library Access for African Americans in the South, or, Leaving Behind the Plow. By David M. Battles. Scarecrow, 2008. Paper $44.

Libraries and Librarianship: Sixty Years of Challenge and Change, 1945–2005. By George Bobinski. Scarecrow, 2007. $40.

Librarianship in Gilded Age America: An Anthology of Writings, 1868–1901. Ed. by Leonard Schlup and Stephen H. Paschen. McFarland, 2009. Paper $45.

Information Literacy

Information Literacy Instruction: Theory and Practice. 2nd ed. By Esther S. Grassian and Joan R. Kaplowitz. Neal-Schuman, 2009. Paper $75.

Proven Strategies for Building an Information Literacy Program. Ed. by Susan Carol

Curzon and Lynn D. Lampert. Neal-Schuman, 2007. Paper $75.

Information Science

Fundamentals of Information Studies: Understanding Information and Its Environment. 2nd ed. By June Lester and Wallace C. Koehler, Jr. Neal-Schuman, 2007. Paper $65.

Intellectual Freedom

Access to Libraries and Information: Towards a Fairer World. Ed. by Theo J. D. Bothma. International Association of Library Associations and Institutions, 2007. Paper $79.44. Also available online.

Banned Books Resource Guide. Office for Intellectual Freedom/American Library Association, 2007. Paper $39.

The New Inquisition: Understanding and Managing Intellectual Freedom Challenges. By James LaRue. Libraries Unlimited, 2007. Paper $40.

Protecting Intellectual Freedom in Your Academic Library. By Barbara M. Jones. American Library Association, 2009. Paper $55.

Protecting Intellectual Freedom in Your School Library. By Pat R. Scales. American Library Association, 2009. Paper $55.

The Internet/Web

Going beyond Google: The Invisible Web in Learning and Teaching. By Jane Devine and Francine Egger-Sider. Neal-Schuman, 2008. Paper $65.

Librarian's Guide to Online Searching. By Suzanne S. Bell. Libraries Unlimited, 2009. Paper $45.

Making Library Web Sites Usable: A LITA Guide. Ed. by Tom Lehman and Terry Nikkel. Neal-Schuman, 2008. Paper $65.

Knowledge Management

Perspectives on Knowledge Management. Ed. by I. V. Malhan and Shivirama Rao K. Scarecrow, 2008. Paper. $65.

Librarians and Librarianship

A Day in the Life: Career Options in Library and Information Science. Ed. by Priscilla K. Schontz and Richard A. Murray. Libraries Unlimited, 2007. $45.

The ALA-APA Salary Survey 2009: Librarian—Public and Academic. ALA-Allied Professional Association and the ALA Office for Research and Statistics. American Library Association, 2009. Paper $90. Also available online.

ARL Annual Salary Survey, 2008–2009. Association of Research Libraries, 2009. Download from http://www.arl.org/stats/annualsurveys/salary/sal0809.shtml.

Information Technology in Librarianship: New Critical Approaches. Ed. by Gloria J. Leckie and John E. Buschman. Libraries Unlimited, 2009. Paper $50.

Introduction to the Library and Information Professions. By Roger C. Greer, Robert J. Grover, and Susan G. Fowler. Libraries Unlimited, 2007. Paper $60.

Leadership Basics for Librarians and Information Professionals. By G. Edward Evans and Patricia Layzell Ward. Scarecrow, 2007. $40.

Libraries in the Information Age: An Introduction and Career Exploration. By Denise K. Fourie and David R. Dowell. Libraries Unlimited, 2009. Paper $45.

Library Ethics. By Jean Preer. Libraries Unlimited, 2008. Paper $45.

Library World Records. 2nd ed. By Godfrey Oswald. McFarland, 2009. Paper $39.95.

The Portable MLIS: Insights from the Experts. Ed. by Ken Haycock and Brooke E. Sheldon. Libraries Unlimited, 2008. Paper $50.

Self-Examination: The Present and Future of Librarianship. By John M. Budd. Libraries Unlimited, 2008. Paper $60.

Service Learning: Linking Library Education and Practice. By Loriene Roy, Kelly Jensen, and Alex Hershey Meyers. American Library Association, 2009. Paper $65.

Library 2.0

Game On! Gaming at the Library. By Beth Gallaway. Neal-Schuman, 2009. Paper $55.

Gamers . . . In the Library?! By Eli Neilburger. American Library Association, 2007. Paper $46.

Library Mashups: Exploring New Ways to Deliver Library Data. Ed. by Nicole C. Engard. Information Today, Inc. 2009. Paper $39.50.

Library 2.0 and Beyond: Innovative Technologies and Tomorrow's Users. Ed. by Nancy Courtney. Libraries Unlimited, 2007. Paper $45.

Searching 2.0. By Michael Sauers. Neal-Schuman, 2009. Paper $65.

Social Software in Libraries: Building Collaboration, Communication, and Community Online. By Meredith G. Farkas. Information Today, Inc., 2007. Paper $39.50.

Special Collections 2.0: New Technologies for Rare Books, Manuscripts, and Archival Collections. By Beth M. Whittaker and Lynne M. Thomas. Libraries Unlimited, 2009. Paper $45.

Web 2.0 for Librarians and Information Professionals. By Ellyssa Kroski. Neal-Schuman, 2008. Paper $75.

Preservation

Leading and Managing Archives and Records Programs: Strategies for Success. Ed. by Bruce W. Dearstyne. Neal-Schuman, 2008. Paper $75.

Preservation in the Age of Large-Scale Digitization: A White Paper. By Oya Y. Rieger. Council on Library and Information Resources, 2008. Download from http://www.clir.org/pubs/abstract/pub141abst.html.

Public Libraries

The Customer-Focused Library: Re-Inventing the Public Library from the Outside-In. By Joseph R. Matthews. Libraries Unlimited, 2009. Paper $50.

Defining Relevancy: Managing the New Public Library. Ed. by Janet McNeil Hurlbert. Libraries Unlimited, 2008. Paper $45.

Introduction to Library Public Services. By G. Edward Evans and Thomas L. Carter. Libraries Unlimited, 2008. $65.

The PLA Reader for Public Library Directors and Managers. Ed. by Kathleen M. Hughes. Neal-Schuman, 2009. Paper $65.

Pop Goes the Library: Using Pop Culture to Connect with Your Whole Community. By Sophie Brookover and Elizabeth Burns. Information Today, Inc. 2008. Paper $39.50.

Public Libraries and Internet Service Roles: Measuring and Maximizing Internet Services. By Charles R. McClure and Paul T. Jaeger. American Library Association, 2008. Paper $65.

Public Library Data Service Statistical Report. Public Library Association/American Library Association, 2009. Paper $120.

The Public Library Policy Writer: A Guidebook with Model Policies on CD-ROM. By Jeanette C. Larson and Herman L. Totten. Neal-Schuman, 2008. Paper and CD-ROM $75.

The Small Public Library Survival Guide: Thriving on Less. By Herbert B. Landau. American Library Association. 2008. Paper $45.

The Thriving Library: Successful Strategies for Challenging Times. By Marylaine Block. Information Today, Inc., 2007. Paper $39.50.

Public Relations/Marketing

Bite-Sized Marketing: Realistic Solutions for the Overworked Librarian. By Nancy Dowd, Mary Evangelista, and Jonathan Silberman. American Library Association, 2010. Paper $48.

Building a Buzz: Libraries and Word-of-Mouth Marketing. By Peggy Barber and Linda Wallace. American Library Association, 2010. Paper $45.

Crash Course in Marketing for Libraries. By Susan Webreck Alman. Libraries Unlimited, 2007. Paper $30.

Creating Your Library Brand: Communicating Your Relevance and Value to Your Patrons. By Elizabeth Doucett. American Library Association, 2008. Paper $50.

The Library PR Handbook: High-Impact Communications. Ed. by Mark R. Gould. American Library Association, 2009. Paper $48.

Look, It's Books! Marketing Your Library with Displays and Promotions. By Gayle Skaggs. McFarland, 2008. Paper $49.95.

Merchandising Made Simple: Using Standards and Dynamite Displays to Boost Circulation. By Jenny LaPerriere and Trish Christiansen. Libraries Unlimited, 2008. Paper $36.

Readers' Advisory

A Few Good Books: Using Contemporary Readers' Advisory Strategies to Connect Readers with Books. By Stephanie L. Maatta. Neal-Schuman, 2009. Paper $69.95.

Nonfiction Readers' Advisory. By Neal Wyatt. American Library Association, 2007. Paper $53.

The Readers' Advisory Guide to Genre Fiction. By Joyce G. Saricks. American Library Association, 2009. Paper $65.

Research-Based Readers' Advisory. By Jessica E. Moyer. American Library Association, 2008. Paper $55.

Serving Teens through Readers' Advisory. By Heather Booth. American Library Association, 2007. Paper $42.

Reference Services

Conducting the Reference Interview. By Catherine Sheldrick Ross, Kristi Nilsen, and Marie L. Radford. Neal-Schuman, 2009. Paper $75.

Crash Course in Reference. By Charlotte Ford. Libraries Unlimited, 2008. Paper $30.

Guide to Reference. American Library Association. Online database at http://www.guidetoreference.org.

Reference and Information Services in the 21st Century: An Introduction. By Kay Ann Cassell and Uma Hiremath. Neal-Schuman, 2009. Paper $69.95.

Training Paraprofessionals for Reference Service. By Pamela J. Morgan. Neal-Schuman, 2008. Paper $65.

Virtual Reference Best Practices: Tailoring Services to Your Library. By M. Kathleen Kern. American Library Association, 2008. Paper $50.

Virtual Reference on a Budget: Case Studies. Ed. by Teresa Dalston and Michael Pullin. Linworth, 2008. Paper $39.95.

Virtual Reference Service: From Competencies to Assessment. Ed. by R. David Lankes, Scott Nicholson, Marie L. Radford, Joanne Silverstein, Lynn Westbrook, and Philip Nast. Neal-Schumann, 2008. Paper $75.

School Libraries/Media Centers

21st Century Learning in School Libraries. Ed. by Kristin Fontichiaro. Libraries Unlimited, 2009. Paper $40.

Collaborating with Administrators and Educational Support Staff. By Lesley S. J. Farmer. Neal-Schuman, 2007. Paper $65.

Enhancing Teaching and Leaning: A Leadership Guide for School Library Media Specialists. 2nd ed. By Jean Donham. Neal-Schuman, 2008. Paper $65.

Ensuring Intellectual Freedom and Access to Information in the School Library Media Program. By Helen R. Adams. Libraries Unlimited, 2008. Paper $40.

Facilities Planning for School Library Media and Technology Centers. By Steven M. Baule. Linworth, 2007. Paper $39.95.

Fundamentals of School Library Media Management. By Barbara Stein Martin and Marco Zannier. Neal-Schuman, 2009. Paper $59.95.

Leadership for Excellence: Insights of National School Library Media Programs of the Year Award Winners. Ed. by Joanne Carr. American Library Association, 2008. Paper $45.

Library 101: A Handbook for the School Library Media Specialist. By Claire Gatrell Stephens and Patricia Franklin. Libraries Unlimited, 2007. Paper $35.

Personal Learning Networks: Professional Development for the Isolated School Librarian. By Mary Ann Harlan. Libraries Unlimited, 2009. Paper $30.

The School Library Media Manager. 4th ed. By Blanche Woolls. Libraries Unlimited, 2008. Paper $45.

The School Library Media Specialist's Policy and Procedure Writer. By Elizabeth Downs. Neal-Schuman, 2010. Paper and CD-ROM $75.

School Reform and the School Library Media Specialist. By Sandra Hughes-Hassell and Violet H. Harada. Libraries Unlimited, 2007. Paper $40.

Teaching Generation M: A Handbook for Librarians and Educators. Ed. by Vibiana Bowman Cvetkovic and Robert J. Lackie. Neal-Schuman, 2009. Paper $85.

The Tech-Savvy Booktalker: A Guide for 21st-Century Educators. By Terence Cavanaugh and Nancy Keane. Libraries Unlimited, 2009. Paper $35.

Toward a 21st Century School Media Program. Ed. by Esther Rosenfeld and David V. Loertscher. Scarecrow, 2007. Paper $40.

Your School Library: Check It Out! By Lesley S. J. Farmer. Libraries Unlimited, 2009. Paper $35.

Services for Special Groups

Adult Learners Welcome Here. By Margaret Crowley Weibel. Neal-Schuman, 2007. Paper $75.

Crash Course in Serving Spanish-Speakers. By Salvador Avila. Libraries Unlimited, 2008. Paper $30.

Easy Information Sources for ESL, Adult Learners, and New Readers. By Rosemarie Riechel. Neal-Schuman, 2008. Paper $64.

Serving Latino Communities: A How-To-Do-It Manual. 2nd ed. By Camila Alire and Jacqueline Ayala. Neal-Schuman, 2007. Paper $59.95.

Serving New Immigrant Communities in the Library. By Sondra Cuban. Libraries Unlimited, 2007. Paper $40.

Technical Services

Fundamentals of Technical Services Management. By Sheila S. Intner, with Peggy Johnson. American Library Association, 2008. Paper $48.

More Innovative Redesign and Reorganization of Library Technical Services. By Bradford Lee Eden. Libraries Unlimited, 2008. Paper $50.

Technology

The Accidental Technology Trainer: A Guide for Libraries. By Stephanie Gerding. Information Today, Inc., 2007. Paper $29.50.

Core Technology Competencies for Librarians and Library Staff: A LITA Guide. Ed. by Susan M Thompson. Neal-Schuman, 2009. Paper $65.

Information Tomorrow: Reflections on Technology and the Future of Public and Academic Libraries. Ed. by Rachel Singer Gordon. Information Today, Inc., 2007. Paper $35.

Library Programs Online: Possibilities and Practicalities of Web Conferencing. By Thomas A. Peters. Libraries Unlimited, 2009. Paper $40.

Listen Up! Podcasting for Schools and Libraries. By Linda W. Braun. Information Today, Inc., 2007. Paper $29.50.

Neal-Schuman Library Technology Companion: A Basic Guide for Library Staff. 3rd ed. By John J. Burke. Neal-Schuman, 2009. Paper $65.

Periodicals

ARL
Advanced Technology Libraries
Against the Grain
American Archivist
American Libraries
Behavioral and Social Sciences Librarian
Booklist
Booklist Online
The Bottom Line: Managing Library Finances
Cataloging and Classification Quarterly
Catholic Library World
Children and Libraries: The Journal of the Association for Library Services to Children
CHOICE
CHOICE Reviews Online
Collection Management
College and Research Libraries
College and Undergraduate Libraries
Community and Junior College Libraries
Computers in Libraries
Congregational Libraries Today
IFLA Journal
Information Outlook
Information Technology and Libraries
Journal of Academic Librarianship
Journal of Education for Library and Information Science
Journal of Electronic Resources Librarianship
Journal of Information Ethics
Journal of Interlibrary Loan, Document Delivery and Information Supply
Journal of Library Administration
Journal of the American Society for Information Science and Technology
Journal of the Medical Library Association
Knowledge Quest
Law Library Journal
Legal Reference Services Quarterly
Libraries and the Cultural Record
Library Administration and Management
Library and Information Science Research (LIBRES)
Library Hi-Tech News
Library and Archival Security
Library Issues: Briefings for Faculty and Academic Administrators
Library Journal

Library Media Connection
The Library Quarterly
Library Resources and Technical Services
Library Technology Reports
Library Trends
Librarysparks
Marketing Library Services
Medical Reference Services Quarterly
MultiMedia and Internet @ Schools
Music Library Association Notes
Music Reference Services Quarterly
New Review of Children's Literature and Librarianship
portal: Libraries and the Academy
Public Libraries
Public Library Quarterly
Reference and User Services Quarterly
Reference Librarian
Resource Sharing & Information Networks
RSR: Reference Services Review
School Library Journal
School Library Media Research
Searcher: The Magazine for Database Professionals
Serials Librarian
Serials Review
Technical Services Quarterly
Technicalities
Video Librarian
Voice of Youth Advocates (VOYA)
World Libraries
Young Adult Library Services

Blogs

AASL Blog (http://www.aasl.ala.org/aaslblog)
ACRLog (http://acrlog.org)
ALA TechSource (http://www.alatechsource.org/blog)
Annoyed Librarian (http://www.libraryjournal.com/blog/580000658.html)
ASCL Blog (http://www.alsc.ala.org/blog)
Audiobooker. By Mary Burkey. (http://audiobooker.booklistonline.com)
Blue Skunk. By Doug Johnson (http://dougjohnson.squarespace.com)
Book Group Buzz (http://bookgroupbuzz.booklistonline.com)

Catalogablog. By David Bigwood (http://catalogablog.blogspot.com)

A Chair, a Fireplace, and a Tea Cozy. By Liz Burns, Melissa Rabey, and Carlie Webber (http://yzocaet.blogspot.com)

David Lee King. By David Lee King (http://www.davidleeking.com)

Early Word. By Nora Rawlinson (http://www.earlyword.com)

Free Range Librarian. By Karen G. Schneider (http://freerangelibrarian.com)

Hey Jude. By Judy O'Connell (http://heyjude.wordpress.com)

Information Wants to Be Free. By Meredith Farkas (http://meredith.wolfwater.com/wordpress)

Librarian.net. By Jessamyn West (http://www.librarian.net)

LibrarianInBlack. By Sarah Houghton-Jan (http://librarianinblack.net/librarianinblack)

Library Juice. By Rory Litwin (http://libraryjuicepress.com/blog)

LibraryBytes. By Helene Blowers (http://www.librarybytes.com)

Likely Stories. By Keir Graff (http://blog.booklistonline.com)

LibraryLaw Blog. By Mary Minow (http://blog.librarylaw.com)

LIS News. By Blake Carver (http://lisnews.org)

LITA Blog (http://litablog.org)

Lorcan Dempsey's Weblog. By Lorcan Dempsey (http://orweblog.oclc.org)

The 'M' Word—Marketing Libraries (http://themwordblog.blogspot.com)

NeverEndingSearch. By Joyce Valenza (http://www.schoollibraryjournal.com/blog/1340000334.html)

No Shelf Required. By Sue Polanka (http://www.libraries.wright.edu/noshelfrequired)

Phil Bradley's Weblog. By Phil Bradley (http://www.philbradley.typepad.com)

PLA Blog (http://plablog.org)

Points of Reference (http://pointsofreference.booklistonline.com)

Pop Goes the Library. By Sophie Brookover, Liz Burns, Melissa Rabey, Susan Quinn, John Klima, Carlie Webber, Karen Corday, and Eli Neiberger (http://www.popgoesthelibrary.com).

ResourceShelf. By Gary Price (http://www.resourceshelf.com)

RUSA Blog (http://rusa.ala.org/blog)

ShelfRenewal. By Karen Kleckner and Rebecca Vnuk (http://www.libraryjournal.com/blog/1760000776.html)

The Shifted Librarian. By Jenny Levine (http://www.theshiftedlibrarian.com)

Stephen's Lighthouse. By Stephen Abram (http://stephenslighthouse.syrsidynix.com)

Swiss Army Librarian. By Brian Herzog (http://www.swissarmylibrarian.net)

Tame the Web: Libraries and Technology. By Michael Stephens (http://tametheweb.com)

The Travelin' Librarian. By Michael Sauers (http://www.travelinlibrarian.info/home)

Walking Paper. By Aaron Schmidt (http://www.walkingpaper.org)

Walt at Random. By Walt Crawford (http://walt.lishost.org)

What I Learned Today. By Nicole C. Engard (http://www.web2learning.net)

YALSA Blog (http://yalsa.ala.org/blog)

Ready Reference

How to Obtain an ISBN

Andy Weissberg and Louise Timko
United States ISBN/SAN Agency

The International Standard Book Numbering (ISBN) system was introduced into the United Kingdom by J. Whitaker & Sons Ltd. in 1967 and into the United States in 1968 by R. R. Bowker. The Technical Committee on Documentation of the International Organization for Standardization (ISO TC 46) is responsible for the international standard.

The purpose of this standard is to "establish the specifications for the International Standard Book Number (ISBN) as a unique international identification system for each product form or edition of a monographic publication published or produced by a specific publisher." The standard specifies the construction of an ISBN, the rules for assignment and use of an ISBN, and all metadata associated with the allocation of an ISBN.

Types of monographic publications to which an ISBN may be assigned include printed books and pamphlets (in various product formats); electronic publications (either on the Internet or on physical carriers such as CD-ROMs or diskettes); educational/instructional films, videos, and transparencies; educational/instructional software; audiobooks on cassette or CD or DVD; braille publications; and microform publications.

Serial publications, printed music, and musical sound recordings are excluded from the ISBN standard as they are covered by other identification systems.

The ISBN is used by publishers, distributors, wholesalers, bookstores, and libraries, among others, in 217 countries and territories as an ordering and inventory system. It expedites the collection of data on new and forthcoming editions of monographic publications for print and electronic directories used by the book trade. Its use also facilitates rights management and the monitoring of sales data for the publishing industry.

The "new" ISBN consists of 13 digits. As of January 1, 2007, a revision to the ISBN standard was implemented in an effort to substantially increase the numbering capacity. The 10-digit ISBN identifier (ISBN-10) is now replaced by the ISBN 13-digit identifier (ISBN-13). All facets of book publishing are now expected to use the ISBN-13, and the ISBN agencies throughout the world are now issuing only ISBN-13s to publishers. Publishers with existing ISBN-10s need to convert their ISBNs to ISBN-13s by the addition of the EAN prefix 978 and recalculation of the new check digit:

ISBN-10: 0-8352-8235-X
ISBN-13: 978-0-8352-8235-2

When the inventory of the ISBN-10s has been exhausted, the ISBN agencies will start assigning ISBN-13s with the "979" prefix instead of the "978." There is no 10-digit equivalent for 979 ISBNs.

Construction of an ISBN

An ISBN currently consists of 13 digits separated into the following parts:

1 A prefix of "978" for an ISBN-10 converted to an ISBN-13
2 Group or country identifier, which identifies a national or geographic grouping of publishers
3 Publisher identifier, which identifies a particular publisher within a group
4 Title identifier, which identifies a particular title or edition of a title
5 Check digit, the single digit at the end of the ISBN that validates the ISBN-13

For more information regarding ISBN-13 conversion services provided by the U.S. ISBN Agency at R. R. Bowker, LLC, visit the ISBN Agency Web site at http://www.isbn.org, or contact the U.S. ISBN Agency at isbn-san@bowker.com.
Publishers requiring their ISBNs to be converted from the ISBN-10 to ISBN-13 format can use the U.S. ISBN Agency's free ISBN-13 online converter at http://isbn.org/converterpub.asp. Large list conversions can be requested by e-mailing isbnconversion@bowker.com. Publishers can also subscribe to view their ISBN online log book by accessing their personal account at http://www.bowkerlink.com.

Displaying the ISBN on a Product or Publication

When an ISBN is written or printed, it should be preceded by the letters ISBN, and each part should be separated by a space or hyphen. In the United States, the hyphen is used for separation, as in the following example: ISBN 978-0-8352-8235-2. In this example, 978 is the prefix that precedes the ISBN-13, 0 is the group identifier, 8352 is the publisher identifier, 8235 is the title identifier, and 2 is the check digit. The group of English-speaking countries, which includes the United States, Australia, Canada, New Zealand, and the United Kingdom, uses the group identifiers 0 and 1.

The ISBN Organization

The administration of the ISBN system is carried out at three levels—through the International ISBN Agency in the United Kingdom, through the national agencies, and through the publishing houses themselves. The International ISBN Agency, which is responsible for assigning country prefixes and for coordinating the worldwide implementation of the system, has an advisory panel that represents the International Organization for Standardization (ISO), publishers, and libraries. The International ISBN Agency publishes the *Publishers International ISBN Directory,* which is a listing of all national agencies' publishers with their assigned ISBN publisher prefixes. R. R. Bowker, as the publisher of *Books In Print* with its extensive and varied database of publishers' addresses, was the obvious place to initiate the ISBN system and to provide the service to the U.S. publishing industry. To date, the U.S. ISBN Agency has entered more than 180,000 publishers into the system.

ISBN Assignment Procedure

Assignment of ISBNs is a shared endeavor between the U.S. ISBN Agency and the publisher. Publishers can make online application through the ISBN Agency's Web site, or by phone or fax. After an application is received and processed by the agency, an ISBN Publisher Prefix is assigned, along with a computer-generated block of ISBNs that is mailed or e-mailed to the publisher. The publisher then has the responsibility to assign an ISBN to each title, keep an accurate record of each number assigned, and register each title in the Books In Print database at http://www.bowkerlink.com. It is the responsibility of the ISBN Agency to validate assigned ISBNs and keep a record of all ISBN publisher prefixes in circulation.

ISBN implementation is very much market-driven. Major distributors, wholesalers, retailers, and so forth recognize the necessity of the ISBN system and request that publishers register with the ISBN Agency. Also, the ISBN is a mandatory bibliographic element in the International Standard Bibliographical Description (ISBD). The Library of Congress Cataloging in Publication (CIP) Division directs publishers to the agency to obtain their ISBN prefixes.

Location and Display of the ISBN

On books, pamphlets, and other printed material, the ISBN shall be printed on the verso of the title leaf or, if this is not possible, at the foot of the title leaf itself. It should also appear on the outside back cover or on the back of the jacket if the book has one (the lower right-hand corner is recommended). The ISBN shall also appear on any accompanying promotional materials following the provisions for location according to the format of the material.

On other monographic publications, the ISBN shall appear on the title or credit frames and any labels permanently affixed to the publication. If the publication is issued in a container that is an integral part of the publication, the ISBN shall be displayed on the label. If it is not possible to place the ISBN on the item or its label, then the number should be displayed on the bottom or the back of the container, box, sleeve, or frame. It should also appear on any accompanying material, including each component of a multi-type publication.

Printing of ISBN in Machine-Readable Coding

All books should carry ISBNs in the EAN-13 bar code machine-readable format. All ISBN EAN-13 bar codes start with the EAN prefix 978 for books. As of January 1, 2007, all EAN bar codes should have the ISBN-13 appearing immediately above the bar code in eye-readable format, preceded by the acronym "ISBN." The recommended location of the EAN-13 bar code for books is in the lower right-hand corner of the back cover (see Figure 1).

Figure 1 / Printing the ISBN in Bookland/EAN Symbology

Five-Digit Add-On Code

In the United States, a five-digit add-on code is used for additional information. In the publishing industry, this code is used for price information. The lead digit of the five-digit add-on has been designated a currency identifier, when the add-on is used for price. Number 5 is the code for the U.S. dollar, 6 denotes the Canadian dollar, 1 the British pound, 3 the Australian dollar, and 4 the New Zealand dollar. Publishers that do not want to indicate price in the add-on should print the code 90000 (see Figure 2).

Figure 2 / Printing the ISBN Bookland/EAN Number in Bar Code with the Five-Digit Add-On Code

978 = ISBN Bookland/EAN prefix
5 = Code for U.S. $
2499 = $24.99

90000 means no information
in the add-on code

Reporting the Title and the ISBN

After the publisher reports a title to the ISBN Agency, the number is validated and the title is listed in the many R. R. Bowker hard-copy and electronic publications, including *Books in Print; Forthcoming Books; Paperbound Books in Print; Books in Print Supplement; Books Out of Print; Books in Print Online; Books in Print Plus-CD ROM; Children's Books in Print; Subject Guide to Children's Books in Print; Books Out Loud: Bowker's Guide to AudioBooks; Bowker's Complete Video Directory; Software Encyclopedia; Software for Schools;* and other specialized publications.

For an ISBN application and information, visit the ISBN Agency Web site at http://www.isbn.org, call the toll-free number 877-310-7333, fax 908-219-0188, or write to the United States ISBN Agency, 630 Central Ave., New Providence, NJ 07974.

The ISSN, and How to Obtain One

U.S. ISSN Center
Library of Congress

In the early 1970s the rapid increase in the production and dissemination of information and an intensified desire to exchange information about serials in computerized form among different systems and organizations made it increasingly clear that a means to identify serial publications at an international level was needed. The International Standard Serial Number (ISSN) was developed and became the internationally accepted code for identifying serial publications.

The ISSN is an international standard, ISO 3297: 2007, as well as a U.S. standard, ANSI/NISO Z39.9. The 2007 edition of ISO 3297 expands the scope of the ISSN to cover continuing resources (serials, as well as updating databases, looseleafs, and some Web sites).

The number itself has no significance other than as a brief, unique, and unambiguous identifier. The ISSN consists of eight digits in Arabic numerals 0 to 9, except for the last—or check—digit, which can be an X. The numbers appear as two groups of four digits separated by a hyphen and preceded by the letters ISSN—for example, ISSN 1234-5679.

The ISSN is not self-assigned by publishers. Administration of the ISSN is coordinated through the ISSN Network, an intergovernmental organization within the UNESCO/UNISIST program. The ISSN Network consists of national ISSN centers, coordinated by the ISSN International Centre, located in Paris. National ISSN Centers are responsible for registering serials published in their respective countries. The ISSN International Centre handles ISSN assignments for international organizations and for countries that do not have a national center. It also maintains and distributes the ISSN Register and makes it available online as the ISSN Portal. The ISSN Register contains bibliographic records corresponding to each ISSN assignment as reported by national ISSN centers. The database contains records for about 1.5 million ISSNs.

The ISSN is used all over the world by serial publishers to identify their serials and to distinguish their titles from others that are the same or similar. It is used by subscription services and libraries to manage files for orders, claims, and back issues. It is used in automated check-in systems by libraries that wish to process receipts more quickly. Copyright centers use the ISSN as a means to collect and disseminate royalties. It is also used as an identification code by postal services and legal deposit services. The ISSN is included as a verification element in interlibrary lending activities and for union catalogs as a collocating device. In recent years, the ISSN has been incorporated into bar codes for optical recognition of serial publications and into the standards for the identification of issues and articles in serial publications. Another growing use for the ISSN is in online systems where it can serve to connect catalog records or citations in abstracting and indexing databases with full-text journal content via OpenURL resolvers or reference linking services.

Because serials are generally known and cited by title, assignment of the ISSN is inseparably linked to the key title, a standardized form of the title derived from information in the serial issue. Only one ISSN can be assigned to a title in a particular medium. For titles issued in multiple media—e.g., print, online, CD-ROM—a separate ISSN is assigned to each medium version. If a title change occurs or the medium changes, a new ISSN must be assigned. Centers responsible for assigning ISSNs also construct the key title and create an associated bibliographic record.

A significant new feature of the 2007 ISSN standard is the Linking ISSN (ISSN-L), a mechanism that enables collocation or linking among different media versions of a continuing resource. The Linking ISSN allows a unique designation (one of the existing ISSNs) to be applied to all media versions of a continuing resource while retaining the separate ISSN that pertains to each version. When an ISSN is functioning as a Linking ISSN, the eight digits of the base ISSN are prefixed with the designation "ISSN-L." The Linking ISSN facilitates search, retrieval, and delivery across all medium versions of a serial or other continuing resource for improved ISSN functionality in OpenURL linking, search engines, library catalogs, and knowledge bases. The 2007 standard also supports interoperability by specifying the use of ISSN and ISSN-L with other systems such as DOI, OpenURL, URN, and EAN bar codes. ISSN-L was implemented in the ISSN Register in 2008. To help ISSN users implement the ISSN-L in their databases, two free tables are available from the ISSN International Centre's home page: one lists each ISSN and its corresponding ISSN-L; the other lists each ISSN-L and its corresponding ISSNs.

In the United States, the U.S. ISSN Center at the Library of Congress is responsible for assigning and maintaining the ISSNs for all U.S. serial titles. Publishers wishing to have an ISSN assigned should request an application form, or download one from the center's Web site, and mail, e-mail, or fax the form to the U.S. ISSN Center. Assignment of the ISSN is free, and there is no charge for use of the ISSN.

To obtain an ISSN for a U.S. publication, or for further information about ISSN in the United States, libraries, publishers, and other ISSN users should visit the U.S. ISSN Center's Web site, http://www.loc.gov/issn, or contact the U.S. ISSN Center, U.S. and Publisher Liaison Division, Library of Congress, 101 Independence Ave. S.E., Washington, DC 20540-4284 (telephone 202-707-6452, fax 202-707-6333, e-mail issn@loc.gov).

Non-U.S. parties should visit the ISSN International Centre's Web site at http://www.issn.org or contact the ISSN International Centre, 45 rue de Turbigo, 75003 Paris, France (telephone 33-1-44-88-22-20, fax 33-1-40-26-32-43, e-mail issnic@issn.org.

How to Obtain an SAN

Andy Weissberg and Louise Timko

United States ISBN/SAN Agency

SAN stands for Standard Address Number. The SAN system, an American National Standards Institute (ANSI) standard, assigns a unique identification number that is used to positively identify specific addresses of organizations in order to facilitate buying and selling transactions within the industry. It is recognized as the identification code for electronic communication within the industry.

For purposes of this standard, the book industry includes book publishers, book wholesalers, book distributors, book retailers, college bookstores, libraries, library binders, and serial vendors. Schools, school systems, technical institutes, and colleges and universities are not members of this industry, but are served by it and therefore included in the SAN system.

The purpose of the SAN is to ease communications among these organizations, of which there are several hundreds of thousands that engage in a large volume of separate transactions with one another. These transactions include purchases of books by book dealers, wholesalers, schools, colleges, and libraries from publishers and wholesalers; payments for all such purchases; and other communications between participants. The objective of this standard is to establish an identification code system by assigning each address within the industry a unique code to be used for positive identification for all book and serial buying and selling transactions.

Many organizations have similar names and multiple addresses, making identification of the correct contact point difficult and subject to error. In many cases, the physical movement of materials takes place between addresses that differ from the addresses to be used for the financial transactions. In such instances, there is ample opportunity for confusion and errors. Without identification by SAN, a complex record-keeping system would have to be instituted to avoid introducing errors. In addition, problems with the current numbering system—such as errors in billing, shipping, payments, and returns—are significantly reduced by using the SAN system. The SAN also eliminates one step in the order fulfillment process: the "look-up procedure" used to assign account numbers. Previously a store or library dealing with 50 different publishers was assigned a different account number by each of the suppliers. The SAN solved this problem. If a publisher prints its SAN on its stationery and ordering documents, vendors to whom it sends transactions do not have to look up the account number, but can proceed immediately to process orders by SAN.

Libraries are involved in many of the same transactions as book dealers, such as ordering and paying for books and charging and paying for various services to other libraries. Keeping records of transactions—whether these involve buying, selling, lending, or donations—entails operations suited to SAN use. SAN stationery speeds up order fulfillment and eliminate errors in shipping, billing, and crediting; this, in turn, means savings in both time and money.

History

Development of the Standard Address Number began in 1968 when Russell Reynolds, general manager of the National Association of College Stores (NACS), approached R. R. Bowker and suggested that a "Standard Account Number" system be implemented in the book industry. The first draft of a standard was prepared by an American National Standards Institute (ANSI) Committee Z39 subcommittee, which was co-chaired by Russell Reynolds and Emery Koltay of Bowker. After Z39 members proposed changes, the current version of the standard was approved by NACS on December 17, 1979.

Format

The SAN consists of six digits plus a seventh *Modulus 11* check digit; a hyphen follows the third digit (XXX-XXXX) to facilitate transcription. The hyphen is to be used in print form, but need not be entered or retained in computer systems. Printed on documents, the Standard Address Number should be preceded by the identifier "SAN" to avoid confusion with other numerical codes (SAN XXXXXXX).

Check Digit Calculation

The check digit is based on *Modulus 11,* and can be derived as follows:

1. Write the digits of the basic number. 2 3 4 5 6 7
2. Write the constant weighting factors associated with each position by the basic number. 7 6 5 4 3 2
3. Multiply each digit by its associated weighting factor. 14 18 20 20 18 14
4. Add the products of the multiplications. $14 + 18 + 20 + 20 + 18 + 14 = 104$
5. Divide the sum by *Modulus 11* to find the remainder. $104 \div 11 = 9$ plus a remainder of 5
6. Subtract the remainder from the *Modulus 11* to generate the required check digit. If there is no remainder, generate a check digit of zero. If the check digit is 10, generate a check digit of X to represent 10, since the use of 10 would require an extra digit. $11 - 5 = 6$
7. Append the check digit to create the standard seven-digit Standard Address Number. SAN 234-5676

SAN Assignment

R. R. Bowker accepted responsibility for being the central administrative agency for SAN, and in that capacity assigns SANs to identify uniquely the addresses of organizations. No SANs can be reassigned; in the event that an organization should cease to exist, for example, its SAN would cease to be in circulation entirely. If an organization using an SAN should move or change its name with no change in ownership, its SAN would remain the same, and only the name or address would be updated to reflect the change.

The SAN should be used in all transactions; it is recommended that the SAN be imprinted on stationery, letterheads, order and invoice forms, checks, and all other documents used in executing various book transactions. The SAN should always be printed on a separate line above the name and address of the organization, preferably in the upper left-hand corner of the stationery to avoid confusion with other numerical codes pertaining to the organization, such as telephone number, zip code, and the like.

SAN Functions

The SAN is strictly a Standard Address Number, becoming functional only in applications determined by the user; these may include activities such as purchasing, billing, shipping, receiving, paying, crediting, and refunding. It is the method used by Pubnet and PubEasy systems and is required in all electronic data interchange communications using the Book Industry Systems Advisory Committee (BISAC) EDI formats. Every department that has an independent function within an organization could have a SAN for its own identification.

For additional information or to make suggestions, write to ISBN/SAN Agency, R. R. Bowker, LLC, 630 Central Ave., New Providence, NJ 07974, call 877-310-7333, or fax 908-219-0188. The e-mail address is san@bowker.com. The SAN Web site for online applications is at http://www.isbn.org.

Distinguished Books

Notable Books of 2009

The Notable Books Council of the Reference and User Services Association, a division of the American Library Association, selected these titles for their significant contribution to the expansion of knowledge or for the pleasure they can provide to adult readers.

Fiction

Anthony, Jessica. *The Convalescent.* McSweeney's.

Atwood, Margaret. *The Year of the Flood.* Doubleday.

Baker, Nicholson. *The Anthologist.* Simon & Schuster.

Chaon, Dan. *Await Your Reply.* Ballantine.

Cleave, Chris. *Little Bee.* Simon & Schuster.

Dexter, Pete. *Spooner.* Grand Central.

Harding, Paul. *Tinkers.* Bellevue Literary Press.

Li, Yiyun. *The Vagrants.* Random.

McCann, Colum. *Let the Great World Spin.* Random.

Morrison, Toni. *A Mercy.* Knopf.

Powers, Richard. *Generosity: An Enhancement.* Farrar, Straus & Giroux.

Tóibín, Colm. *Brooklyn.* Scribner.

Nonfiction

Cullen, Dave. *Columbine.* Twelve.

Eggers, Dave. *Zeitoun.* McSweeney's.

Finkel, David. *The Good Soldiers.* Farrar, Straus & Giroux.

Grann, David. *The Lost City of Z: A Tale of Deadly Obsession in the Amazon.* Doubleday.

Guibert, Emmanuel. *The Photographer: Into War-torn Afghanistan with Doctors without Borders.* First Second.

Holmes, Richard. *The Age of Wonder: How the Romantic Generation Discovered the Beauty and Terror of Science.* Pantheon.

Keefe, Patrick Radden. *Snakehead: An Epic Tale of the Chinatown Underworld and the American Dream.* Doubleday.

McDougall, Christopher. *Born to Run: A Hidden Tribe, Superathletes, and the Greatest Race the World Has Never Seen.* Knopf.

Norman, Michael and Elizabeth M. Norman. *Tears in the Darkness: The Story of the Bataan Death March and Its Aftermath.* Farrar, Straus & Giroux.

Salisbury, Lainey and Aly Sujo. *Provenance: How a Con Man and a Forger Rewrote the History of Modern Art.* Penguin.

Small, David. *Stitches: A Memoir.* Norton.

Thompson, Nicholas. *The Hawk and the Dove: Paul Nitze, George Kennan, and the History of the Cold War.* Holt.

Poetry

Alexie, Sherman. *Face.* Hanging Loose.

Dunn, Stephen. *What Goes On: Selected and New Poems 1995–2009.* Norton.

Best Books for Young Adults

Each year a committee of the Young Adult Library Services Association YALSA, a division of the American Library Association, compiles a list of the best fiction and nonfiction appropriate for young adults ages 12 to 18. Selected on the basis of each book's proven or potential appeal and value to young adults, the titles span a variety of subjects as well as a broad range of reading levels.

Fiction

Anderson, Laure Halse. *Wintergirls.* Penguin.

Barnes, John. *Tales of the Madman Underground.* Penguin.

Boorhaem, Ellen. *The Unnameables.* Houghton Mifflin.

Bradley, Alan. *The Sweetness at the Bottom of the Pie.* Dell.

Bray, Libba. *Going Bovine.* Random.

Brennan, Sarah Rees. *Demon's Lexicon.* Simon & Schuster.

Brown, Jennifer. *Hate List.* Little, Brown.

Burg, Anne E. *All the Broken Pieces.* Scholastic.

Cashore, Kristin. *Fire.* Dial.

Chaltas, Talia. *Because I Am Furniture.* Penguin.

Clement-Moore, Rosemary. *Highway to Hell.* Random.

Collins, Suzanne. *Catching Fire.* Scholastic.

Cooper, Michelle. *A Brief History of Montmaray.* Random.

Crowley, Suzanne Carlisle. *The Stolen One.* HarperCollins.

Davies, Jacqueline. *Lost.* Marshall Cavendish.

Davis, Tanita. *Mare's War.* Random.

de la Pena, Matt. *We Were Here.* Random.

Dessen, Sarah. *Along for the Ride.* Penguin.

Dowd, Siobhan. *Solace of the Road.* Random.

Efaw, Amy. *After.* Penguin.

Forman, Gayle. *If I Stay.* Penguin.

Frost, Helen. *Crossing Stones.* Farrar, Straus & Giroux.

Garsee, Jeannine. *Say the Word.* Bloomsbury.

George, Jessica Day. *Princess of the Midnight Ball.* Bloomsbury.

Gill, David Macinnis. *Soul Enchilada.* HarperCollins.

Goodman, Alison. *Eon: Dragoneye Reborn.* Penguin.

Griffin, Paul. *The Orange Houses.* Penguin.

Halpern, Julie. *Into the Wild Nerd Yonder.* Macmillan.

Han, Jenny. *The Summer I Turned Pretty.* Simon & Schuster.

Hardinge, Frances. *The Lost Conspiracy.* HarperCollins.

Herlong, M. H. *The Great Wide Sea.* Penguin.

Hernandez, David. *No More Us for You.* HarperCollins.

Jinks, Catherine. *The Reformed Vampire Support Group.* Harcourt.

Johnson, Louanne. *Muchacho.* Random.

Katcher, Brian. *Almost Perfect.* Random.

Kelly, Jacqueline. *The Evolution of Calpurnia Tate.* Henry Holt.

King, A. S. *The Dust of 100 Dogs.* Llewellyn.

Knowles, Jo. *Jumping Off Swings.* Candlewick.

LaCour, Nina. *Hold Still.* Dutton.

Larbalestier, Justine. *Liar.* Bloomsbury.

Levine, Kristine. *The Best Bad Luck I Ever Had.* Putnam.

Lockhart, E. *The Treasure Map of Boys: Noel, Jackson, Finn, Hutch—And Me, Ruby Oliver.* Random.

Madigan, L. K. *Flash Burnout.* Houghton Mifflin.

Magoon, Kekla. *The Rock and the River.* Aladdin.

McCormick, Patricia. *Purple Heart.* HarperCollins.

McKernan, Victoria. *The Devil's Paintbox.* Random.

McKinley, Robin. *Fire: Tales of Elemental Spirits.* Putnam.

Miller-Lachmann, Lyn. *Gringolandia.* Curbstone.

Napoli, Donna Jo. *Alligator Bayou.* Random.

Northrop, Michael. *Gentlemen.* Scholastic.

Oaks, J. Adams. *Why I Fight.* Atheneum.

Pearson, Mary E. *The Miles Between*. Henry Holt.

Rapp, Adam. *Punkzilla*. Candlewick.

Runyon, Brent. *Surface Tension: A Novel in Four Summers*. Random.

Ryan, Carrie. *The Forest of Hands and Teeth*. Random.

Scott, Elizabeth. *Love You, Hate You, Miss You*. HarperCollins.

Smith, Andrew. *In the Path of Falling Objects*. Macmillan.

Smith, Sherri L. *Flygirl*. Putnam.

Standiford, Natalie. *How to Say Goodbye in Robot*. Scholastic.

Stead, Rebecca. *When You Reach Me*. Random.

Stiefvater, Maggie. *Lament: The Faerie Queen's Deception*. Llewell.

Stiefvater, Maggie. *Shiver*. Scholastic.

Stork, Francisco X. *Marcelo in the Real World*. Scholastic.

Stroud, Jonathan. *Heroes of the Valley*. Disney.

Tan, Shaun. *Tales from Outer Suburbia*. Scholastic.

Taylor, Laini. *Lips Touch: Three Times*. Scholastic.

Thompson, Kate. *Creature of the Night*. Roaring Brook.

Valentine, Jenny. *Broken Soup*. HarperCollins.

Vivian, Siobhan. *Same Difference*. Scholastic.

Warman, Jessica. *Breathless*. Walker.

Westerfeld, Scott. *Leviathan*. Simon & Schuster.

Williams, Carol Lynch. *The Chosen One*. Macmillan.

Williams-Garcia, Rita. *Jumped*. HarperCollins.

Wyatt, Melissa. *Funny How Things Change*. Farrar, Straus & Giroux.

Wynne-Jones, Tim. *The Uninvited*. Candlewick.

Yancey, Rick. *The Monstrumologist*. Simon & Schuster.

Yang, Gene Luen. *The Eternal Smile*. Roaring Brook.

Zarr, Sara. *Once Was Lost*. Little, Brown.

Zulkey, Claire. *An Off Year*. Penguin.

Nonfiction

Fleming, Candace. *The Great and Only Barnum: The Tremendous, Stupendous Life of Showman P. T. Barnum*. Random.

Gray, Theodore. *The Elements: A Visual Exploration of Every Known Atom in the Universe*. Black Dog & Leventhal.

Heiligman, Deborah. *Charles and Emma: The Darwins' Leap of Faith*. Henry Holt.

Hoose, Phillip M. *Claudette Colvin: Twice Toward Justice*. Farrar, Straus & Giroux.

Mann, Charles C. *Before Columbus: The Americas of 1491*. Simon & Schuster.

Murphy , Jim. *Truce: The Day the Soldiers Stopped Fighting*. Scholastic.

Partridge, Elizabeth. *Marching for Freedom: Walk Together, Children, and Don't You Grow Weary*. Penguin.

Small, David. *Stitches: A Memoir*. Norton.

Stone, Tanya Lee. *Almost Astronauts: 13 Women Who Dared to Dream*. Candlewick.

Swanson, James L. *Chasing Lincoln's Killer*. Scholastic.

Walker, Sally M. *Written in Bone: Buried Lives of Jamestown and Colonial Maryland*. Lerner.

Quick Picks for Reluctant Young Adult Readers

The Young Adult Library Services Association, a division of the American Library Association, annually chooses a list of outstanding titles that will stimulate the interest of reluctant teen readers. This list is intended to attract teens who, for whatever reason, choose not to read.

The list, compiled by a ten-member committee, includes fiction and nonfiction titles published from late 2008 through early 2010.

Fiction

Anderson, Laurie Halse. *Wintergirls*. Viking.

Baratz-Logsted, Lauren. *Crazy Beautiful*. Houghton Mifflin Harcourt.

Byrd, A. J. *Chasing Romeo* (BFF series No. 1). Kimani Tru.

Daniels, Babygirl. *Glitter* (Babygirl Drama No. 4). Urban.

Daniels, Babygirl. *Sister, Sister* (Babygirl Drama No. 3). Urban.

Daniels, Babygirl. *16 on the Block* (Babygirl Drama No. 1). Urban.

Daniels, Babygirl. *161/2 on the Block* (Babygirl Drama No. 2). Urban.

de la Pena, Matt. *We Were Here*. Random.

Divine, L. *Courtin' Jayd* (Drama High No. 6). Kensington.

Divine, L. *Hustlin'* (Drama High No. 7). Kensington.

Divine, L. *Keep It Movin'* (Drama High No. 8). Kensington.

Draper, Sharon M. *Just Another Hero*. Simon & Schuster.

Duck, Phillip Thomas. *Dirty Jersey*. Kimani Tru.

Duck, Phillip Thomas. *Dirty South*. Kimani Tru.

Efaw, Amy. *After*. Viking.

Elkeles, Simone. *Perfect Chemistry*. Walker.

Fahy, Thomas. *Sleepless*. Simon & Schuster.

Forman, Gail. *If I Stay*. Dutton.

Harmon, Michael. *Brutal*. Knopf.

Johnson, LouAnne. *Muchacho*. Random.

Kaye, Marilyn. *Better Late Than Never* (Gifted series No. 2). Kingfisher.

Kaye, Marilyn. *Here Today, Gone Tomorrow* (Gifted series No. 3). Kingfisher.

Kaye, Marilyn. *Out of Sight, Out of Mind* (Gifted series No. 1). Kingfisher.

Knowles, Jo. *Jumping Off Swings*. Candlewick.

McKayhan, Monica. *Deal With It* (Indigo No. 5). Kimani Tru.

McKayhan, Monica. *Jaded* (Indigo No. 4). Kimani Tru.

Norfleet, Celeste O. *Fast Forward* (Kenisha No. 2). Kimani Tru.

Pride, Felicia. *Patterson Heights*. Kimani Tru.

Lee, Darrien. *Denim Diaries Book 1: Sixteen Going on Twenty-One*. Urban.

Lee, Darrien. *Denim Diaries Book 2: Grown in Sixty Seconds*. Urban.

Lee, Darrien. *Denim Diaries Book 3: Queen of the Yard*. Urban.

Lee, Darrien. *Denim Diaries Book 4: Broken Promises*. Urban.

Lynch, Janet Nichols. *Messed Up*. Holiday House.

Mac, Carrie. *Jacked*. Orca.

McCaffrey, Kate. *In Ecstasy*. Annick.

McClintock, Norah. *Taken*. Orca.

McDaniel, Lurlene. *Breathless*. Delacorte.

Myers, Walter Dean. *Dope Sick*. Amistad.

Reger, Rob, and Jessica Gruner. *Emily the Strange: The Lost Days*. HarperCollins.

Ryan, Darlene. *Five Minutes More*. Orca.

Sarkar, Dona. *Shrink to Fit*. Kimani.

Sewell, Earl. *Decision Time* (Keysha No. 4). Kimani Tru.

Sewell, Earl. *Lesson Learned* (Keysha No. 3). Kimani Tru.

Sparks, Chandra Taylor. *The Pledge* (Worth-the-Wait No. 1). Kimani Tru.

Simone, Ni-Ni. *A Girl Like Me*. Kensington.

Simone, Ni-Ni. *If I Was Your Girl*. Kensington.

Simone, Ni-Ni. *Shortie Like Mine*. Kensington.

Singleton, Linda Joy. *Dead Girl Dancing* (Dead Girl No. 2). Llewellyn/Flux.

Singleton, Linda Joy. *Dead Girl in Love* (Dead Girl No. 3). Llewellyn/Flux.

Singleton, Linda Joy. *Dead Girl Walking* (Dead Girl No. 1). Llewellyn/Flux.

Smith, Alexander Gordon. *Lockdown: Escape from Furnace* (Lockdown No. 1). Farrar, Straus & Giroux.

Sniegoski, Thomas. *Legacy*. Delacorte.

Stiefvater, Maggie. *Shiver*. Scholastic.

Volponi, Paul. *Response*. Penguin.

Williams, Carol Lynch. *The Chosen One*. St. Martin's.

Graphic Novels

Chmakova, Svetlana. *Nightschool Volume 1* (Nightschool series). Yen.

Chmakova, Svetlana. *Nightschool Volume 2* (Nightschool series). Yen.

Shan, Darren, and Takahiro Arai *Cirque du Freak: The Manga Vol. 1*. Yen.

Shan, Darren, and Takahiro Arai. *Cirque du Freak: The Manga Vol. 2—The Vampire's Assistant*. Yen.

Shan, Darren, and Takahir Arai. *Cirque du Freak: The Manga Vol. 3—Tunnels of Blood*. Yen.

Nonfiction

Beckwith, Lois. *The Dictionary of High School B.S.: From Acne to Varsity, All the Funny, Lame, and Annoying Aspects of High School Life*. Orange Avenue.

Blackshaw, Ric, and Liz Farrelly. *Street Art Book: 60 Artists in Their Own Words*. HarperCollins.

Borgenicht, David. *The Worst-Case Scenario Survival Handbook: Middle School*. Chronicle.

Bright, J. E. *America's Next Top Model: Fierce Guide to Life—The Ultimate Source of Beauty, Fashion, and Model Behavior*. Universe.

Brown, Marvelyn. *The Naked Truth: Young, Beautiful and (HIV) Positive*. Amistad.

Cliver, Sean. *The Disposable Skateboard Bible*. Gingko.

Conley, Erin Elisabeth, Karen Macklin, and Jake Miller. *Crap: How to Deal with Annoying Teachers, Bosses, Backstabbers, and Other Stuff that Stinks*. Orange Avenue.

Cooper, Martha, and Henry Chalfant. *Subway Art: 25th Anniversary Edition*. Chronicle.

Davidson, Tony. *One-Track Mind: A Revealing Insight into the Obsessed Minds of Men*. Random.

Fagerstrom, Derek, and Lauren Smith. *Show Me How: 500 Things You Should Know—Instructions for Life from the Everyday to the Exotic*. Collins Design.

Garza, Mario. *Stuff on my Mutt*. Chronicle.

Gavin, Francesca. *Hell Bound: New Goth Art*. Laurence King.

Girdler, Chris. *The Travel Book: A Journey Through Every Country in the World*. Lonely Planet.

Gray, Amy. *How to Be a Vampire: A Fangs-on Guide for the Newly Undead*. Candlewick.

Happycat, Professor, and icanhascheezburger.com. *How to Take Over Teh Wurld: A LOLcat Guide 2 Winning*. Gotham.

Happycat, Professor, and icanhascheezburger.com. *I Can Has Cheezburger? A LOLcat Colleckshun*. Gotham.

Hardwicke, Catherine. *Twilight Director's Notebook: The Story of How We Made the Movie*. Little, Brown.

Hart, Carey, and Chris Palmer. *Inked*. Artisan/Workman.

Heimber, Justin, and David Gomberg. *Would You Rather . . . ? Gross Out—Over 300 Disgusting Dilemmas Plus Extra Pages to Make Up Your Own!* Falls Media.

Horvath, David. *Ugly Guide to Being Alive and Staying that Way: Hi! It's the Ugly-doll*. Random.

Jacoby, Annice. *Street Art San Francisco: Mission Muralismo*. Harry N. Abrams.

Janic, Susan. *Jonas Brothers Forever: The Unofficial Story of Kevin, Joe and Nick*. ECW.

Jenisch, Josh. *Art of the Video Game*. Quirk.

Komanoya, Rico. *Gothic Lolita Punk: Draw Like the Hottest Japanese Artists*. Collins Design.

Mawji, Nasim, Chris Doherty, and Burt Jensen. *Hollywoof! Celebrity Dogs Bite Back*. DK.

Miller, Kerry. *Passive Aggressive Notes: Painfully Polite and Hilariously Hostile Writings from Shared Spaces the World Over.* HarperCollins.

Minguet, Eva. *Tattoo Delirium* Collins Design.

Nardone, Tom. *Extreme Pumpkins II: Take Back Halloween and Freak Out a Few More Neighbors.* Penguin.

O'Meara, Stephen James. *Are You Afraid Yet? The Science Behind Scary Stuff.* Kids Can.

Oser, Bodhi. *Fuck the World.* Chronicle.

Pahlow, Mark. *Who Would Buy This? The Archie McPhee Story.* Accoutrements.

Palladini, Doug. *Vans: Off the Wall—Stories of Sole from Vans Originals.* Abrams.

Renn, Crystal. *Hungry: A Young Model's Story of Appetite, Ambition and the Ultimate Embrace of Curves.* Simon & Schuster.

Mega Traumarama! Real Girls and Guys Confess More of Their Most Mortifying Moments! Hearst.

Smith, John. *Inked: Clever, Odd and Outrageous Tattoos.* teNeues.

Smith, Larry, and Rachel Fershleiser. *I Can't Keep My Own Secrets: Six-Word Memoirs by Teens Famous and Obscure.* HarperCollins.

Shields, Brian, and Kevin Sullivan. *WWE Encyclopedia: The Definitive Guide to World Wrestling Entertainment.* Brady Games DK.

Stenning, Paul. *The Robert Pattinson Album.* Plexus.

Stutts, Ryan. *The Skateboarding Field Manual.* Firefly.

Su, Lac. *I Love Yous Are for White People: A Memoir.* Harper Perennial.

Turner, Tracey. *Deadly Perils and How to Avoid Them.* Walker.

The Vampire Book: The Legends, the Lore, the Allure. DK.

Von D, Kat. *High Voltage Tattoo.* HarperCollins.

Willams, Mel. *Robert Pattinson: Fated for Fame.* Simon & Schuster.

Willin, Melvyn. *Paranormal Caught on Film.* David and Charles.

Audiobooks for Young Adults

Each year a committee of the Young Adult Library Services Association, a division of the American Library Association, compiles a list of the best audiobooks for young adults ages 12 to 18. The titles are selected for their teen appeal and recording quality, and because they enhance the audience's appreciation of any written work on which the recordings may be based. While the list as a whole addresses the interests and needs of young adults, individual titles need not appeal to this entire age range but rather to parts of it.

Nonfiction

We Are the Ship: The Story of Negro League Baseball, by Kadir Nelson, read by Dion Graham. Brilliance Audio, 1 hour and 55 minutes, 3 discs (978-1-4233-7537-1).

Fiction

After Tupac and D Foster, by Jacqueline Woodson, read by Susan Spain. Brilliance Audio, 3 hours and 13 minutes, 3 discs (978-1-4233-9805-9).

Along for the Ride, by Sarah Dessen, read by Rachel Botchan. Recorded Books, 12 hours and 45 minutes, 11 discs (978-1-4407-3027-6).

Boys are Dogs, by Leslie Margolis, read by Ellen Grafton. Brilliance Audio, 5 hours, 4 discs (978-1-4233-7729-0).

Carter Finally Gets It, by Brent Crawford, read by Nick Podehl. Brilliance Audio, 8 hours and 27 minutes, 7 discs (978-1-4233-9181-4).

The Chosen One, by Carol Lynch Williams, read by Jenna Lamia. Macmillan Audio, 5 hours and 30 minutes, 5 discs (978-1-4272-0706-7).

Identical, by Ellen Hopkins, read by Laura Flanagan. High Bridge Audiobooks, 8 hours and 45 minutes, 7 discs (978-1-59887-735-9).

If I Stay, by Gayle Forman, read by Kirsten Potter. Listening Library, 4 hours and 48 minutes, 4 discs (978-0-7393-8084-0).

The Indigo Notebook, by Laura Resau, read by Justine Eyre. Listening Library, 8 hours and 25 minutes, 7 discs (978-0-3075-7981-2).

In the Belly of the Bloodhound: Being an Account of a Particularly Peculiar Adventure in the Life of Jacky Faber, by L. A. Meyer, read by Katherine Kellgren. Listen and Live Audio, 15 hours, 13 discs (978-1-59316-142-2).

The Killer's Cousin, by Nancy Werlin, read by Nick Podehl. Brilliance Audio, 6 hours, 5 discs (978-1-4233-8078-8).

Living Dead Girl, by Elizabeth Scott, read by Kate Reinders. Brilliance Audio, 2 hours and 54 minutes, 3 discs (978-1-4233-9751-9).

Marcelo in the Real World, by Francisco X. Stork, read by Lincoln Hoppe. Listening Library, 10 hours and 8 minutes, 8 discs (978-0-7393-7991-2).

The Monstrumologist, by Rick Yancey, read by Stephen Boyer. Recorded Books, 11 hours and 45 minutes, 10 discs (978-1-4407-3564-6).

My Bonny Light Horseman: Being the Account of the Further Adventures of Jacky Faber, in Love and War, by L. A. Meyer, read by Katherine Kellgren. Listen and Live Audio, 12 hours, 10 discs (978-1-59316-446-1).

Newes from the Dead, by Mary Hooper, read by Rosalyn Landor and Michael Page. Brilliance Audio, 7 hours and 27 minutes, 7 discs (978-1-4233-9230-9).

Peace, Locomotion by Jacqueline Woodson, read by Dion Graham. Brilliance Audio, 2 hours and 7 minutes, 2 discs (978-1-4233-9799-1).

Slumdog Millionaire, by Vikas Swarup, read by Christopher Simpson. BBC Audiobooks America, 10 hours and 47 minutes, 9 discs (978-0-7927-6162-4).

Solace of the Road, by Siobhan Dowd, read by Sile Bermingham. Listening Library, 7 hours and 5 minutes, 6 discs (978-0-7393-8591-3).

The Spectacular Now, by Tim Tharp, read by MacLeod Andrews. Brilliance Audio, 8 hours and 19 minutes, 7 discs (978-1-4233-9963-6).

Tree Girl: A Novel, by Ben Mikaelsen, read by Amber Sealey. Listening Library, 4 hours and 37 minutes, 4 discs (978-0-7393-7265-4).

Wildwood Dancing, by Juliet Marillier, read by Kim Mai Guest. Listening Library, 12 hours and 54 minutes, 11 discs (978-0-7393-7940-0).

Zen and the Art of Faking It, by Jordan Sonnenblick, read by Mike Chamberlain. Listening Library, 5 hours and 35 minutes, 5 discs (978-0-7393-7155-8).

The Reading List

Established in 2007 by the Reference and User Services Association (RUSA), a division of the American Library Association, this list highlights outstanding genre fiction that merits special attention by general adult readers and the librarians who work with them.

RUSA's Reading List Council, which consists of 12 librarians who are experts in readers' advisory and collection development, selects books in eight categories: Adrenaline (suspense, thrillers, and action adventure), Fantasy, Historical Fiction, Horror, Mystery, Romance, Science Fiction, and Women's Fiction.

Adrenaline

Gone Tomorrow by Lee Child (Delacorte).

Fantasy

Lamentation by Ken Scholes (Tor).

Historical Fiction

Agincourt by Bernard Cornwell (Harper).

Horror

Last Days by Brian Evenson (Underland).

Mystery

A Beautiful Place to Die by Malla Nunn (Atria).

Romance

What Happens in London by Julia Quinn (Avon).

Science Fiction

The Windup Girl by Paolo Bacigalupi (Night Shade).

Women's Fiction

Very Valentine by Adriana Trigiani (Harper)

Notable Recordings for Children

This list of notable CD recordings for children was selected by the Association for Library Service to Children, a division of the American Library Association. Recommended titles are chosen by children's librarians and educators on the basis of their originality, creativity, and suitability.

The Alvin Ho Collection: Books 1 and 2. Listening Library, 4 hours and 2 minutes. Grades 1–4. Timid Alvin braves the perils of school, piano lessons, bullies, and camping trips. Narrated by Everette Plen.

Chasing Lincoln's Killer. Scholastic, 3 hours and 58 minutes. Grades 4–9. The story of the assassination of Abraham Lincoln and the capture of his killer, John Wilkes Booth, is told using trial manuscripts, interviews, and other firsthand accounts.

The Chicken Chasing Queen of Lamar County. Recorded Books, 15 minutes. Ages 5–up. Sisi Aisha Johnson tells the story of the pursuit of Miss Hen.

The Chosen One. Macmillan Audio, 5 hours and 30 minutes. Grades 7–up. Kyra, 13, a member of a polygamist religious cult, is chosen to become the seventh wife of her 60-year-old uncle. Narrated by Jenna Lamia.

Diamond Willow. Recorded Books, 2 hours. Grades 3–6. Jennifer Ikeda and a full cast tell the story of a part-Athabascan Indian girl in the Alaskan wilderness.

A Dog on His Own. Full Cast Audio, 3 hours. Grades 2–4. A humorous story told by a stray dog, told by William Dufris.

Don't Let the Pigeon Drive the Bus. Weston Woods, 4 minutes. Ages 3–6. A determined pigeon tries to persuade listeners to let him drive in this read-along, narrated by author Mo Willems and Jon Scieszka.

Emperors of the Ice: A True Story of Disaster and Survival in the Antarctic, 1910–1913. Brilliance Audio, 5 hours and 7 minutes. Grades 5–9. Michael Page tells the story of the three-year Antarctic expedition led by Captain Robert Scott, from the perspective of assistant zoologist Apsley Cherry-Garrard.

European Playground. Putumayo Kids, 45 minutes. Ages 3–up. A collection of lively songs from across Europe reflecting the culture of each represented country.

Field Trip. Monkey Mama, 41 minutes. Grades K–6. The Seattle-based band Recess Monkey takes children on a magical field trip.

Heart of a Shepherd. Listening Library, 4 hours. Grades 3–7. Kirby Heyborne narrates a story about modern ranch life and the difficulties faced by military service families.

Henry's Freedom Box: A True Story from the Underground Railroad. Weston Woods, 10 minutes. Ages 6–10. The true story of Henry "Box" Brown, who escaped slavery by hiding himself in a wooden crate, is told by Jerry Dixon.

The Jesus Storybook Bible. Zonderkids, 3 hours and 22 minutes. All ages. Stories from the Old and New Testaments are told in short segments. The narrator is David Suchet.

Knuffle Bunny Too: A Case of Mistaken Identity. Weston Woods, 9 minutes. Ages 3–6. The bestselling book is performed by its author, Mo Willems, with his daughter Trixie and wife Cheryl. An interview with Willems is included.

Leviathan. Simon & Schuster, 8 hours and 30 minutes. Grades 6–9. In a science fiction tale set in the days leading up to World War I, two factions (the Clankers, who put their faith in machines, and the Darwinists, whose technology is based on the development of new species) prepare for war.

Louise, The Adventures of a Chicken. Live Oak Media, 19 minutes. Ages 4–8. Louise is a French chicken with wanderlust in this story by Kate DiCamillo, told by Barbara Rosenblat.

Mañana Iguana. Live Oak Media, 25 minutes. Ages 4–8. As Iguana plans a party, young listeners learn the days of the week in Spanish.

Music for Abraham Lincoln: Campaign Songs, Civil War Tunes, Laments for a President. Enslow Publishers, 59 minutes. All ages. The Civil War story of Abraham Lincoln in song.

Nelson Mandela's Favorite African Folktales. Hachette Audio, 3 hours. Grades 1–8. Africa's oral tradition is the theme of this collection of 22 folktales accompanied by music.

Peace, Locomotion. Brilliance Audio, 2 hours and 7 minutes. Grades 6–9. Twelve-year-old Lonnie finally starts feeling at home with his foster family while struggling to keep the memory of his parents alive. The narrator is Dion Graham.

Picnic Playground. Putumayo Kids, 32 minutes. All ages. Twelve songs represent foods and cultures from around the world.

Red Blazer Girls: The Ring of Rocamadour. Listening Library, 6 hours and 55 minutes. Grades 5–8. Tai Ricci narrates a tale of four 12-year-old girls embroiled in a mystery surrounding a scavenger hunt and a missing ring.

Riot. Listening Library, 2 hours and 36 minutes. Grades 5–9. Fifteen-year-old Claire, daughter of an Irish mother and a black father, faces great danger when working-class immigrants, enraged by the Civil War and the federal draft, riot in the streets of New York City.

The Scrambled States of America Talent Show. Weston Woods, 16 minutes. Ages 5–9. The states parade their talents in this full-cast read-along of Laurie Keller's book.

Songs from the Garden of Eden: Jewish Lullabies and Nursery Rhymes. Secret Mountain, 53 minutes. All ages. Songs and rhymes are performed by various artists, accompanied by traditional instruments. Lyrics are included.

A Soup Opera. Jim Gill Music and Books, 21 minutes. Ages 4–up. A sing-along brought to life in a book illustrated by David Moose and a fully orchestrated CD that includes narration, dialogue, and instrumentation.

The Tapestry, Book 1: The Hound of Rowan. Recorded Books, 11 hours and 45 minutes. Grades 4–8. Jeff Woodman tells the story of 12-year-old Max McDaniels, who discovers that he is a wizard and joins a school for young magicians.

We Are The Ship: The Story of Negro League Baseball. Brilliance Audio, 1 hour and 55 minutes. Grades 2–6. Dion Graham tells the story of the history of the Negro National League. An additional CD showcases Kadir Nelson's paintings from the print edition.

Wild Girl. Listening Library, 2 hours and 56 minutes. Grades 4–7. The story of 12-year-old Lidie, who leaves Brazil and struggles to fit in with her family in New York after years apart.

The Witch's Guide to Cooking with Children. Brilliance Audio, 2 hours and 50 minutes. Grades 4–6. Laura Merlington narrates this modern update of the Hansel and Gretel story.

Notable Children's Books

A list of notable children's books is selected each year by the Notable Children's Books Committee of the Association for Library Service to Children, a division of the American Library Association. Recommended titles are selected by children's librarians and educators based on originality, creativity, and suitability for children. [See "Literary Prizes, 2009" later in Part 5 for Caldecott, Newbery, and other award winners—*Ed.*]

Books for Younger Readers

Arnold, Tedd. *I Spy Fly Guy!* Illus. by the author. Scholastic.

Brown, Peter. *The Curious Garden.* Illus. by the author. Little, Brown.

Brun-Cosme, Nadine. *Big Wolf and Little Wolf.* Illus. by Olivier Tallec, trans. by Claudia Bedrick. Enchanted Lion.

Cousins, Lucy. *Yummy: Eight Favorite Fairy Tales.* Illus. by the author. Candlewick.

Crum, Shutta. *Thunder Boomer.* Illus. by Carol Thompson. Clarion.

Gerstein, Mordicai. *A Book.* Illus. by the author. Roaring Brook.

Hayes, Geoffrey. *Benny and Penny in the Big No-No!* Illus. by the author. Toon.

Henkes, Kevin. *Birds.* Illus. by Laura Dronzek. Greenwillow.

Johnston, Tony. *My Abuelita.* Illus. by Yuyi Morales. Harcourt.

McMullan, Kate. *Pearl and Wagner: One Funny Day.* Illus. by R. W. Alley. Dial.

Meschenmoser, Sebastian. *Waiting for Winter.* Illus. by the author. Kane Miller.

Mora, Pat. *Book Fiesta! Celebrate Children's Day/Book Day; Celebremos El Día de los Niños/El Día de los Libros.* Illus. by Rafael López. Rayo.

Mora, Pat. *Gracias/Thanks.* Illus. by John Parra. Lee & Low.

Mortenson, Greg, and Susan L. Roth. *Listen to the Wind: The Story of Dr. Greg and Three Cups of Tea.* Collages by Susan L. Roth. Dial.

Newbery, Linda. *Posy.* Illus. by Catherine Rayner. Atheneum.

Newman, Lesléa. *Mommy, Mama and Me.* Illus. by Carol Thompson. Tricycle.

Patricelli, Leslie. *Higher! Higher!* Illus. by the author. Candlewick.

Scanlon, Liz Garton. *All the World.* Illus. by Marla Frazee. Beach Lane.

Sidman, Joyce. *Red Sings from Treetops: A Year in Colors.* Illus. by Pamela Zagarenski. Houghton Mifflin.

Smith, Jeff. *Little Mouse Gets Ready.* Illus. by the author. Toon.

Yee, Wong Herbert. *Mouse and Mole: Fine Feathered Friends.* Illus. by the author. Houghton Mifflin.

Middle Readers

Barton, Chris. *The Day-Glo Brothers: The True Story of Bob and Joe Switzer's Bright Ideas and Brand-New Colors.* Illus. by Tony Persiani. Charlesbridge.

Bernier-Grand, Carmen T. *Diego: Bigger Than Life.* Illus. by David Diaz. Marshall Cavendish.

Bond, Rebecca. *In the Belly of an Ox: the Unexpected Photographic Adventures of Richard and Cherry Kearton.* Illus. by the author.

Bredsdorff, Bodil. *Eidi.* Trans. by Kathryn Mahaffy. Farrar, Straus & Giroux.

DiCamillo, Kate. *The Magician's Elephant.* Illus. by Yoko Tanaka. Candlewick.

Jenkins, Steve. *Down, Down, Down: A Journey to the Bottom of the Sea.* Houghton Mifflin.

Kajikawa, Kimiko. *Tsunami!* Illus. by Ed Young. Philomel.

Kelly, Jacqueline. *The Evolution of Calpurnia Tate.* Holt.

Lázaro, Georgina. *Federico García Lorca.* Illus. by Enrique S. Moreiro. Lectorum.

Lin, Grace. *Where the Mountain Meets the Moon*. Illus. by the author. Little, Brown.

Lowry, Lois. *Crow Call*. Illus. by Bagram Ibatoulline. Scholastic.

Metselaar, Menno, and Ruud van der Rol. *Anne Frank: Her Life in Words and Pictures from the Archives of the Anne Frank House*. Roaring Brook.

Mills, Claudia. *How Oliver Olson Changed the World*. Illus. by Heather Maione. Farrar, Straus & Giroux.

Nelson, Vaunda Micheaux. *Bad News for Outlaws: The Remarkable life of Bass Reeves, Deputy U.S. Marshal*. Illus. by R. Gregory Christie. Carolrhoda.

O'Connor, Barbara. *The Small Adventure of Popeye and Elvis*. Farrar, Straus & Giroux.

Phelan, Matt. *The Storm in the Barn*. Illus. by the author. Candlewick.

Philbrick, Rodman. *The Mostly True Adventures of Homer P. Figg*. Blue Sky.

Ruddell, Deborah. *A Whiff of Pine, A Hint of Skunk: A Forest of Poems*. Illus. by Joan Rankin. Simon & Schuster.

Ruelle, Karen Gray, and Deborah Durland DeSaix. *The Grand Mosque of Paris: A Story of How Muslims Rescued Jews during the Holocaust*. Illus. by the authors. Holiday.

Stead, Rebecca. *When You Reach Me*. Random.

Sturm, James, Andrew Arnold, and Alexis Frederick-Frost. *Adventures in Cartooning*. Illus. by the authors. First Second.

Talbott, Hudson. *River of Dreams: The Story of the Hudson River*. Illus. by the author. Putnam.

Thor, Annika. *A Faraway Island*. Trans. by Linda Schenck. Delacorte.

Turner, Pamela S. *The Frog Scientist*. Photographs by Andy Comins. Houghton Mifflin.

Weitzman, David L. *Pharaoh's Boat*. Illus. by the author. Houghton Mifflin.

Wing, Natasha. *An Eye for Color: The Story of Josef Albers*. Illus. by Julia Breckenreid. Holt.

Winter, Jonah. *You Never Heard of Sandy Koufax?!* Illus. by André Carrilho. Random.

Older Readers

Allen, Thomas B., and Roger MacBride Allen. *Mr. Lincoln's High-Tech War: How the North Used the Telegraph, Railroads, Surveillance Balloons, Ironclads, High-Powered Weapons, and More to Win the Civil War*. National Geographic.

Alvarez, Julia. *Return to Sender*. Knopf.

Baskin, Nora Raleigh *Anything But Typical*. Simon & Schuster.

Carmichael, Clay. *Wild Things*. Front Street.

Datlow, Ellen, and Terri Windling, eds. *Troll's Eye View: A Book of Villanous Tales*. Viking.

Fleming, Candace. *The Great and Only Barnum: The Tremendous, Stupendous Life of Showman P. T. Barnum*. Random.

Hardinge, Frances. *The Lost Conspiracy*. HarperCollins.

Hoose, Phillip. *Claudette Colvin: Twice Toward Justice*. Farrar, Straus & Giroux.

Lawrence, Iain. *The Giant-Slayer*. Delacorte.

Magoon, Kekla. *The Rock and the River*. Aladdin.

Marrin, Albert. *Years of Dust: The Story of the Dust Bowl*. Dutton.

Murphy, Jim. *Truce: The Day the Soldiers Stopped Fighting*. Scholastic.

Nelson, Marilyn. *Sweethearts of Rhythm: The Story of The Greatest All-Girl Swing Band in the World*. Illus. by Jerry Pinkney. Dial.

Partridge, Elizabeth. *Marching For Freedom: Walk Together, Children, and Don't You Grow Weary*. Viking.

Russel, Ching Yeung *Tofu Quilt*. Lee & Low.

Smith, Hope Anita. *Mother Poems*. Illus. by the author. Holt.

Stone, Tanya Lee. *Almost Astronauts: 13 Women Who Dared to Dream*. Candlewick.

Tan, Shaun. *Tales from Outer Suburbia*. Illus. by the author. Scholastic.

Uehashi, Nahoko. *Moribito II: Guardian of the Darkness*. Illus. by Yuko Shimizu, trans. by Cathy Hirano. Scholastic.

Walker, Sally M. *Written in Bone: Buried Lives of Jamestown and Colonial Maryland*. Carolrhoda.

Westerfeld, Scott. *Leviathan*. Illus. by Keith Thompson. Simon Pulse.

All Ages

Bryan, Ashley. *Ashley Bryan: Words to My Life's Song*. Photographs by Bill Meguinnesss. Atheneum.

Chin, Jason. *Redwoods*. Illus. by the author. Flash Point.

Floca, Brian. *Moonshot: The Flight of Apollo 11*. Illus. by the author. Atheneum.

Hughes, Langston. *My People*. Photographs by Charles R. Smith, Jr. Atheneum.

Pinkney, Jerry. *The Lion and the Mouse*. Illus. by the author. Little, Brown.

Rosenthal, Amy Krouse. *Duck! Rabbit!* Illus. by Tom Lichtenheld. Chronicle.

Rotner, Shelley, and Sheila M. Kelly. *Shades of People*. Photographs by Shelley Rotner. Holiday.

Notable Children's Videos

These DVD titles are selected by a committee of the Association for Library Service to Children, a division of the American Library Association. Recommendations are based on originality, creativity, and suitability for children.

Abraham Lincoln Comes Home. Spoken Arts, 10 minutes. Ages 8–11.

Crazy Hair Day. Weston Woods, 12 minutes. Ages 5–8.

Don't Let the Pigeon Drive the Bus! Weston Woods, 7 minutes. Ages 2–6.

Duck on a Bike. Weston Woods, 8 minutes. Ages 3–8.

Los Gatos Black on Halloween. Weston Woods, 9 minutes. Ages 4–8.

Getting to Know Thomas Jefferson. Getting to Know, Inc., 22 minutes. Ages 5–14.

The Gym Teacher from the Black Lagoon. Weston Woods, 9 minutes. Ages 4–8.

Henry's Freedom Box: A True Story from the Underground Railroad. Weston Woods, 12 minutes. Ages 7–10.

Knuffle Bunny Too: A Case of Mistaken Identity. Weston Woods, 11 minutes. Ages 2–7.

Teen Truth: An Inside Look at Body Image. Human Relations Media, 23 minutes. Ages 13–up.

Those Shoes. Nutmeg Media, 12 minutes. Ages 4–9.

Wipe Out. National Film Board of Canada, 51 minutes. Ages 13–up.

Great Interactive Software for Kids

This list is chosen by a committee of the Association for Library Service to Children, a division of the American Library Association. Titles are selected on the basis of their originality, creativity, and suitability for children.

ItzaBitza. Sabi, Inc. (http://www.ItzaBitza.com). Ages 7–12. Art comes to life in this drawing game, tailored for early readers, as the computer animates their drawings. Download.

Left Brain/Right Brain 2. Majesco Entertainment (http://www.majescoentertainment.com). A new version of a game designed to boost mental skills while challenging the user's non-dominant hand. All ages. Nintendo DS.

Professor Layton and the Curious Village. Nintendo (http://www.nintendo.com) All ages. Lots of puzzles and brainteasers are part of the quest to find a hidden treasure. Nintendo DS.

Zula World. (http://www.ZulaWorld.com). Ages 6–up. Learning about science, math, and astronomy while having fun. Based on the PBS cartoon "The Zula Patrol." Online.

Bestsellers of 2009

The View from the Top:
Sales Ranking of 2009's Bestselling Hardcover Books

Michael Coffey
Co-Editorial Director, *Publishers Weekly*

Where are we? Good question, and it is the reason that every March for decades we have presented the results of our survey of publishers' sales figures for the previous year.

We all love numbers. Agents, marketing departments, sales folk, funders—not to mention authors and their accountants—all depend on them. They tell us what happened and are as good as anything else as predictors of what may lie ahead.

Looking at the compilation of bestseller numbers from 2009 confirms what publishers said throughout 2009 and even into 2010—that bestsellers don't sell in the numbers that they did in the past. And the numbers are rich with anecdotal surprises and bald truths. In fiction, for example, Lisa See outsold John Sandford and John Irving and Wally Lamb; she sold as many as Margaret Atwood and E. L. Doctorow put together. Dan Brown "only" sold 5.5 million copies, but perhaps 4 million (an estimate) more than his nearest competitor, our perennial John Grisham. In nonfiction, can it be that Dick Morris almost outsold Chesley Sullenberger? (Yes.) And did Sarah Palin really outsell Ted Kennedy 3 to1? You betcha.

It is also clear from these numbers that Doubleday and Harper had the hot hands. Doubleday had Brown and Grisham in the two top fiction spots, Grisham again at No. 6, and Pat Conroy at No. 18. Harper's *Going Rogue* and *Act Like a Lady, Think Like a Man,* by Steve Harvey, copped the top two spots in nonfiction, followed by a couple of titles from Simon & Schuster's Threshold imprint—by Glenn Beck and Mark R. Levin.

What is also true and not to be overlooked is that all the hardcover books in these lists were successes. To sell a hundred thousand copies (the cutoff for this list) is to generate near $1 million for a publisher—no small feat, especially in these times. And these times do seem to be different.

Now is as good an occasion as any to take a look at trends over the years, as reflected in this, our annual snapshot of how books did.

Apples & Apples: Comparisons

In 2008 John Grisham won the day—or year—in fiction with *The Appeal.* As Doubleday doesn't allow Grisham's exact numbers to be stated publicly (nor, please note, do any of the S&S imprints; such titles are ranked appropriately from numbers supplied in confidence and marked with an asterisk), we can only

Adapted from *Publishers Weekly,* March 22, 2010.

say that it was something in excess of the 1.3 million copies racked up by second-place David Wroblewski for *The Story of Edgar Sawtelle*. Below Wroblewski, though, four other authors also topped a million in sales—Stephenie Meyer, James Patterson, Nicholas Sparks, and Janet Evanovich, with Glenn Beck and his *Christmas Sweater* tale almost making it.

In 2009 the action at the top of the fiction list was, on first blush, more robust. Dan Brown smoked everyone with his 5,543,643 copies sold of *The Lost Symbol*, with Grisham relegated to second with a number we can only say was near 2008's; and he was followed by 3-million-copy sellers—Kathryn Stockett, James Patterson, and John Grisham again, with Evanovich, another Stephenie Meyer, and a Stephen King knocking on the magic million-copy door. Not bad.

But deeper in the comparison of 2008 and 2009, we see weakening this year. Whereas in 2008 there were 156 fiction titles with sales of 100,000+, in 2009 there are were only 130, a drop of nearly 17 percent. For nonfiction, the decrease in titles reaching the 100,000 level was more pronounced, from 119 to 91, a plunge of more than 23 percent. A look back at figures from 2000, in which we tallied 112 fiction and 117 nonfiction titles that sold above 100,000 copies, would indicate a flattening of frontlist performance. Given that the industry has grown during these ten years, to more than $40 billion annually, one can only conclude that Chris Anderson had it right: the long tail created by online retailing, at the expense of bricks-and-mortar, has dampened frontlist sales but extended sales down the line.

Successful frontlist numbers fluctuate for fiction and nonfiction, but fiction is clearly winning the wrestling match between the two. Whereas in 2000 and 2004 the two categories had near identical numbers of 100,000+ titles, fiction now has by far the upper hand.

Many have observed that political ideologies are hardening in this country, with each side of the ideological spectrum speaking predominantly to themselves. Nowhere is this more evident than in nonfiction titles that really, really sell. In 2000, 2004, and 2008, the top 15 nonfiction sellers were predominantly lifestyle, feel-good, and self-help titles—remember *Who Moved My Cheese? The Guinness Book of World Records, Body for Life*, and *Dr. Phil's Relationship Rescue* (2000)? Or *The Purpose-Driven Life, The South Beach Diet, Atkins for Life*, and *The Ultimate Weight Solution* (2004)? Or 2008's *The Last Lecture, The Purpose of Christmas, You: Being Beautiful*, and the outlying *Outliers*? These were all top-fours in their respective years in nonfiction. But in 2009, a politically and culturally divisive year by most measures, please change the channel to Sarah Palin's memoir, Glenn Beck's thoughts on government, and Ted Kennedy's memoir, which bracket an old-school relationship book by Steve Harvey.

Perhaps it's not fair to say that a thinning of the top echelon in nonfiction is a result of polarized politics, but I'm going there anyway. And looking at the significant expansion in the last ten years in fiction titles making the grade—all the usual

Note: the figures that follow were provided by the publishers. They reflect sales in calendar year 2009 for books (minus returns) for books published in 2008 or 2009. An asterisk denotes a title whose sales figures were provided in confidence, to be used for ranking purposes only.

suspects (Grisham, Patterson, Brown, Grafton, Cornwell) being joined by a widen-ing royalty, particularly in romance and thrillers—perhaps escapism is on the rise as more and more people seek it out in books. That could only be a good thing.

Speaking of escapism—e-book sales were not included this year, but will be next year. No escaping that.

Hardcover Fiction Sales, 2009

1. *The Lost Symbol: A Novel* by Dan Brown. Doubleday (5,543,643).
2. **The Associate: A Novel* by John Grisham. Doubleday.
3. *The Help* by Kathryn Stockett. Putnam/Amy Einhorn (1,104,617).
4. *I, Alex Cross* by James Patterson. Little, Brown (1,040,976).
5. *The Last Song* by Nicholas Sparks. Grand Central. (1,032,829).
6. **Ford County* by John Grisham. Doubleday.
7. *Finger Lickin' Fifteen* by Janet Evanovich. St. Martin's (977,178).
8. *The Host: A Novel* by Stephenie Meyer. Little, Brown (912,165).
9. **Under the Dome* by Stephen King. Scribner.
10. *Pirate Latitudes* by Michael Crichton. Harper (855,638).
11. *Scarpetta* by Patricia Cornwell. Putnam (800,000).
12. *U Is for Undertow* by Sue Grafton. Putnam (706,154).
13. *The Scarpetta Factor* by Patricia Cornwell. Putnam (705,000).
14. *Shadowland* by Alyson Noel. St. Martin's (609,355).
15. *The 8th Confession* by James Patterson. Little, Brown (606,097).
16. *Arctic Drift* by Clive Cussler with Dirk Cussler. Putnam (588,247).
17. *South of Broad: A Novel* by Pat Conroy. Doubleday (565,156).
18. *Run for Your Life* by James Patterson. Little, Brown (557,356).
19. *True Blue* by David Baldacci. Grand Central (555,296).
20. *Swimsuit* by James Patterson. Little, Brown (553,138).
21. **Pursuit of Honor: A Novel* by Vince Flynn. Atria.
22. *Alex Cross's Trial* by James Patterson. Little, Brown (517,171).
23. *Black Hills* by Nora Roberts. Putnam (502,000).
24. *Breathless: A Novel* by Dean Koontz. Bantam (500,964).
25. *Dead and Gone: A Sookie Stackhouse Novel* by Charlaine Harris. Ace (500,135).
26. *Southern Lights: A Novel* by Danielle Steel. Delacorte (497,140).
27. *First Family* by David Baldacci. Grand Central (447,484).
28. *The Gathering Storm: Book 12 of the Wheel of Time* by Robert Jordan and Brandon Sanderson. Tor (437, 474).
29. *The Wrecker* by Clive Cussler. Putnam (387,309).
30. **Just Take My Heart* by Mary Higgins Clark. S&S

300,000+

Nine Dragons by Michael Connelly. Little, Brown (356,490).

An Echo in the Bone: A Novel by Diana Gabaldon. Delacorte (347,081).

*Handle with Care: A Novel by Jodi Picoult. Atria.

One Day at a Time by Danielle Steel. Delacorte (344,079).

The Girl Who Played with Fire by Stieg Larsson. Knopf (336,534).

The Lacuna by Barbara Kingsolver. Harper (321,980).

Matters of the Heart by Danielle Steel. Delacorte (315,640).

Kindred in Death by J. D. Robb. Putnam (315,000).

*The Secret by Rhonda Byrne. Atria.

Promises in Death by J. D. Robb. Putnam (305,000).

200,000+

The Scarecrow by Michael Connelly. Little, Brown (288,998).

A Touch of Dead by Charlaine Harris. Ace (270,002).

*Half Broke Horses by Jeannette Walls. Scribner.

Bad Moon Rising by Sherrilyn Kenyon. St. Martin's (252,180).

Long Lost by Harlan Cooper. Harper (250,839).

Relentless: A Novel by Dean Koontz. Bantam (250,278).

Wicked Prey by John Sandford. Putnam (249,028).

*Best Friends Forever: A Novel by Jennifer Weiner. Atria.

Gone Tomorrow by Lee Child. Delacorte (245,639).

*Her Fearful Symmetry by Audrey Niffenegger. Scribner.

Spartan Gold by Clive Cussler. Putnam (231,808).

Medusa by Clive Cussler. Putnam (229,784).

Corsair by Clive Cussler. Putnam (229,049).

Knock Out: An FBI Thriller by Catherine Coulter. Putnam (227,487).

Shanghai Girls: A Novel by Lisa See. Random (225,359).

The Doomsday Key by James Rollins. William Morrow (225,026).

Christmas Secret by Donna Van Liere. St. Martin's (216,773).

*The Christmas List by Richard Paul Evans. S&S.

Last Night in Twisted River: A Novel by John Irving. Random (214,712).

*Smash Cut by Sandra Brown. S&S.

Twenties Girl: A Novel by Sophie Kinsella. Dial (209,661).

Wishin' and Hopin' by Wally Lamb. Harper (207,260).

Deadlock by Iris Johansen. St. Martin's (206,836).

The Paris Vendetta: A Novel by Steve Berry. Ballantine (204,501).

Rough Country by John Sandford. Putnam (203,202).

The Perfect Christmas by Debbie Macomber. Harlequin (200,227).

100,000+

Black Ops by W.E.B. Griffin. Putnam (198,586).

Altar of Eden by James Rollins. William Morrow (196,734).

Blood Game by Iris Johansen. St. Martin's (195,769).

Robert Ludlum's The Bourne Deception by Eric Van Lustbader. Grand Central (195,029).

The Defector by Daniel Silva. Putnam (194,067).

The Strain by Guillermo Del Toro. William Morrow (191,627).

Deeper than Dead by Tami Hoag. Penguin (185,936).

True Colors by Kristin Hannah. St. Martin's (185,658).

*The White Queen by Philippa Gregory. Touchstone Fireside.

Paths of Glory by Jeffrey Archer. St. Martin's (183,418).

Evidence: An Alex Delaware Novel by Jonathan Kellerman. Ballantine (182,958).

Sizzle: A Novel by Julie Garwood. Ballantine (182,010).

Look Again by Lisa Scottoline. St. Martin's (180,175).

Summer on Blossom Street by Debbie Macomber. Harlequin (173,694).

Rainwater by Sandra Brown. S&S.

The Christmas Sweater by Glenn Beck. Threshold.

Heart and Soul by Maeve Binchy. Knopf (167,755).

Divine Misdemeanors: A Novel by Laurell K. Hamilton. Ballantine (166,102).

That Old Cape Magic by Richard Russo. Knopf (164,437).

Angel Time by Anne Rice. Knopf (153,520).

Skin Trade by Laurell K. Hamilton. Berkley (153,004).

Cemetery Dance by Douglas Preston and Lincoln Child. Grand Central (148,804).

Dune Road by Jane Green. Viking (148,570).

*The Apostle: A Thriller by Brad Thor. Atria.

Fool by Christopher Moore. William Morrow (146,098).

Tea Time for the Traditionally Built by Alexander McCall Smith. Pantheon (144,439).

The Honor of Spies by W.E.B. Griffin. Putnam (141,050).

Storm Cycle by Iris Johansen and Roy Johansen. St. Martin's (140,817).

Heat Wave by Richard Castle. Hyperion (140,110).

Return to Sullivans Island by Christopher Moore. William Morrow (139,020).

Ice: A Novel by Linda Howard. Ballantine (138,126).

Loitering with Intent by Stuart Woods. Putnam (136,381).

White Witch, Black Curse by Kim Harrison. Eos (135,659).

Knit the Season: A Friday Night Knitting Club Novel by Kate Jacobs. Putnam (135,329).

True Detectives: A Novel by Jonathan Kellerman. Ballantine (132,403).

The Angel's Game: A Novel by Carlos Ruiz Zafón. Doubleday (131,509).

Sidney Sheldon's Mistress of the Game by Sidney Sheldon. William Morrow (131,405).

Hothouse Orchid by Stuart Woods. Putnam (130,426).

*206 Bones by Kathy Reichs. Scribner.

No Less than Victory: A Novel of World War II by Jeff Shaara. Ballantine (125,221).

Lover Avenged: A Novel of the Black Dagger Brotherhood by J. R. Ward. NAL (125,126).

Blindman's Bluff by Faye Kellerman. William Morrow (124,110).

Guardian of Lies by Steve Martini. William Morrow (123,393).

Second Opinion by Michael Palmer. St. Martin's (123,166).

The Professional by Robert B. Parker. Putnam (122,593).

Dark Slayer by Christine Feehan. Berkley (121,082).

*Devil's Punchbowl by Greg Iles. Scribner.

The Neighbor by Lisa Gardner. Bantam (120,555).

The Year of the Flood: A Novel by Margaret Atwood. Doubleday (120,249).

The Book of Genesis Illustrated by R. Crumb. Norton (119,914).

Fried Up: Book One of the Dreamlight Trilogy by Jayne Ann Krentz. Putnam (118,775).

Don't Look Twice by Andrew Gross. William Morrow (117,239).

Pygmy by Chuck Palahniuk. Doubleday (117,202).

The Physick Book of Deliverance Dane by Katherine Howe. Voice (116,217).

*Divine Soul Mind Body Healing and Transmission System Special Edition: The Divine Way to Heal You, Humanity, Mother Earth, and All Universes by Zhi Gang Sha. Atria.

Turn Coat: A Novel of the Dresden Files by Jim Butcher. Roc (115,111).

A Change in Altitude: A Novel by Anita Shreve. Little, Brown (113,518).

Fire and Ice by J. A. Jance. William Morrow (112,453).

*Roadside Crosses by Jeffery Deaver. S&S.

*Nanny Returns: A Novel by Emma McLaughlin. Atria.

*Days of Gold: A Novel by Jude Deveraux. Atria.

Night and Day by Robert B. Parker. Putnam (110,678).

New York: The Novel by Edward Rutherfurd. Doubleday (110,022).

Fatally Flaky by Diane Mott Davidson. William Morrow (108,369).

First Lord's Fury by Jim Butcher. Ace (108,105).

Homer & Langley: A Novel by E. L. Doctorow. Random (105,265).

What I Did for Love by Susan Elizabeth Phillips. William Morrow (105,199).

The Guernsey Literary and Potato Peel Pie Society by Mary Ann Shaffer and Annie Barrows. Dial (104,284).

Burn: A Novel by Linda Howard. Ballantine (102,258).

The Disciple by Stephen Coonts. St. Martin's (100,272).

Prayers for Sale by Sandra Dallas. St. Martin's (100,202).

To Try Men's Souls by Newt Gingrich and William R. Forstchen. St. Martin's/Dunne (100,099).

Hardcover Nonfiction Sales, 2009

1. *Going Rogue: An American Life* by Sarah Palin. Harper (2,674,684).
2. *Act Like a Lady, Think Like a Man: What Men Really Think About Love, Relationships, Intimacy, and Commitment* by Steve Harvey. Harper (1,735,219).
3. *Arguing with Idiots: How to Stop Small Minds and Big Government* by Glenn Beck. Threshold.
4. *Liberty & Tyranny: A Conservative Manifesto* by Mark R. Levin.
5. *True Compass: A Memoir* by Edward M. Kennedy. Grand Central (870,402).
6. *Have a Little Faith: A True Story* by Mitch Albom. Hyperion (855,843).
7. *It's Your Time: Activate Your Faith, Achieve Your Dreams, and Increase in God's Favor* by Joel Osteen. Free Press.
8. *The Last Lecture* by Randy Pausch with Jeffrey Zaslow. Hyperion (610,033).
9. *Stones into Schools: Promoting Peace with Books Not Bombs* by Greg Mortenson. Viking (515,566).
10. *Superfreakonomics* by Steven D. Levitt and Stephen J. Dubner. William Morrow (487,977).
11. *Mastering the Art of French Cooking* by Julia Child. Knopf (10/61) (487,228).
12. *Master Your Metabolism: The 3 Diet Secrets to Naturally Balancing Your Hormones for a Hot and Healthy Body!* by Jillian Michaels. Crown (486,154).
13. *The Yankee Years* by Joe Torre and Tom Verducci. Doubleday (397,954).
14. *Open* by Andre Agassi. Knopf (11/09) (383,722).
15. *Time of My Life* by Patrick Swayze and Lisa Niemi. Atria.
16. *Paula Deen's the Deen Family Cookbook* by Paula Deen with Melissa Clark. S&S.
17. *Uncommon: Finding Your Path to Significance* by Tony Dungy with Nathan Whitaker. Tyndale (309,872).
18. *Highest Duty* by Chesley Sullenberger. William Morrow (306,413).
19. *Catastrophe* by Dick Morris. Harper (289,887).
20. *Fearless: Imagine Your Life Without Fear* by Max Lucado. Thomas Nelson (263,242).
21. *Always Looking Up: The Adventures of an Incurable Optimist* by Michael J. Fox. Hyperion (262,594).
22. *Where Men Win Glory: The Odyssey of Pat Tillman* by Jon Krakauer. Doubleday (254,482).

23. *A Bold Fresh Piece of Humanity* by Bill O'Reilly. Broadway (247,897).
24. *Born to Run* by Christopher McDougall. Knopf (219,370).
25. *Guilty: Liberal "Victims" and Their Assault on America* by Ann Coulter. Crown (208,336).
26. *The Book of Basketball: The NBA According to the Sports Guy* by Bill Simmons. ESPN (208,286).
27. *Knockout: Interviews with Doctors Who Are Curing Cancer—And How to Prevent Getting It in the First Place* by Suzanne Somers. Crown (207,000).
28. *Barefoot Contessa Back to Basics: Fabulous Flavor from Simple Ingredients* by Ina Garten. Crown (206,419).
29. *Down Home with the Neelys* by Patrick and Gina Neely. Knopf (201,631).
30. *Official Book Club Selection: A Memoir According to Kathy Griffin* by Kathy Griffin. Ballantine (200,713).

200,000+

Never Give Up! Relentless Determination to Overcome Life's Challenges by Joyce Meyer. FaithWords (200,288).

*Are You There, Vodka? It's Me, Chelsea by Chelsea Handler. Simon Spotlight.

*Last Words by George Carlin. Free Press.

100,000+

Eat This, Not That! Best and Worst Foods by David Zinczenko. Rodale (190,000).

Love and Respect: The Love She Most Desires; The Respect He Desperately Needs by Emerson Eggerichs. Thomas Nelson (189,412).

The Pioneer Woman Cooks by Ree Drummond. Morrow Cookbooks (188,484).

The Girls from Ames: A Story of Women and a Forty-Year Friendship by Jeffrey Zaslow. Gotham (174,190).

*Horse Soldiers by Doug Stanton. Scribner.

Traveling with Pomegranates: A Mother-Daughter Story by Sue Monk Kidd and Ann Kidd Taylor. Viking (171,070).

*High on Arrival by Mackenzie Phillips. Simon Spotlight.

The Hole in Our Gospel: The Answer That Changed My Life and Might Just Change the World by Richard Stearns. Thomas Nelson (167,235).

Martha Stewart's Dinner at Home: 52 Quick Meals to Cook for Family and Friends by Martha Stewart. Crown (164,267).

Living with Confidence in a Chaotic World: What on Earth Should We Do Now? by David Jeremiah. Thomas Nelson (164,095).

What in the World Is Going On? 10 Prophetic Clues You Can't Afford to Ignore by David Jeremiah. Thomas Nelson (163,261).

You Better Not Cry: Stories for Christmas by Augusten Burroughs. St. Martin's (160,429).

Julia's Kitchen Wisdom by Julia Child. Knopf (160,142).

When the Game Was Ours by Larry Bird and Earvin "Magic" Johnson with Jackie MacMullan. HMH (159,169).

Too Big to Fail: The Inside Story of How Wall Street and Washington Fought to Save the Financial System—and Themselves by Andrew Ross Sorkin. Viking (156,508).

The End of Overeating by David A. Kessler, M.D. Rodale (155,000).

I Can Make You Thin: The Revolutionary System Used by More Than 3 Million People by Paul McKenna. Sterling (152,824).

The Noticer: Sometimes All a Person Needs Is a Little Perspective by Andy Andrews. Thomas Nelson (151,752).

The National Parks by Dayton Duncan and Ken Burns. Knopf (150,845).

How to Raise the Perfect Dog: Through Puppyhood and Beyond by Cesar Millan with Melissa Jo Peltier. Crown (150,430).

The Audacity to Win: The Inside Story and Lessons of Barack Obama's Historic Victory by David Plouffe. Viking (147,202).

Gourmet Today: More Than 1,000 All-New Recipes for the Contemporary Kitchen Edited by Ruth Reichl. HMH (146,971).

*Mommywood by Tori Spelling. Simon Spotlight.

My Journey with Farrah by Alana Stewart. William Morrow (145,528).

In the President's Secret Service: Behind the Scenes with Agents in the Line of Fire and the Presidents They Protect by Ronald Kessler. Crown (145,200).

Flat Belly Diet Cookbook by Liz Vaccariello. Rodale (145,000).

*Jim Cramer's Getting Back to Even by James J. Cramer with Cliff Mason. S&S.

Total Money Makeover: A Proven Plan for Financial Success by Dave Ramsey. Thomas Nelson (141,444).

Resilience: Reflections on the Burdens and Gifts of Facing Life's Adversities by Elizabeth Edwards. Broadway (141,032).

The Deen Bros. Take It Easy: Quick and Affordable Meals the Whole Family Will Love by Jamie and Bobby Deen and Melissa Clark. Ballantine (137,994).

*The Greatest Show on Earth: The Evidence for Evolution by Richard Dawkins. Free Press.

Half the Sky: Turning Oppression into Opportunity for Women Worldwide by Nicholas Kristof & Sheryl WuDunn. Knopf (134,087).

*Unmasked: The Final Years of Michael Jackson by Ian Halperin. Simon Spotlight.

A Lion Called Christian: The True Story of the Remarkable Bond Between Two Friends and a Lion by Anthony Bourke and John Rendall. Broadway (130,286).

Dewey: The Small-Town Library Cat Who Touched the World by Vicki Myron with Bret Witter. Grand Central (130,038).

House of Cards: A Tale of Hubris and Wretched Excess on Wall Street by William D. Cohan. Doubleday (129,371).

The Big Burn: Teddy Roosevelt and the Fire That Saved America by Timothy Egan. HMH (128,651).

The Love Revolution by Joyce Meyer. FaithWords (127,506).

Your Best Life Begins Each Morning: Devotions to Start Every New Day of the Year by Joel Osteen. FaithWords (120,012).

Martha Stewart's Encyclopedia of Crafts and A-to-Z Guide with Detailed Instructions and Endless Inspiration. Martha Stewart Living Magazine. Crown (117,933).

Artisan Bread in Five Minutes by Jeff Hertzberg and Zoe Francois. St. Martin's/Dunne (117,352).

Moonwalk by Michael Jackson. Crown (115,562).

PostSecret: Confessions on Life, Death and God by Frank Warren. William Morrow (114,577).

Out of Captivity by Marc Gonsalves. William Morrow (113,361).

America on Purpose: The Improbable Adventures of an Unlikely Patriot by Craig Ferguson. Harper (112,710).

The G-Free Diet: A Gluten-Free Survival Guide by Elizabeth Hasselbeck. Hachette/Center Street (111,696).

*Have You Seen My Country Lately? America's Wake-Up Call by Jerry Doyle. Threshold.

*The Great Depression Ahead: How to Prosper in the Crash Following the Greatest Boom in History by Harry S. Dent. Free Press.

End the Fed by Ron Paul. Grand Central (110,048).

*Comeback 2.0 by Lance Armstrong. Touchstone Fireside.

Inside the Revolution: How the Followers of Jihad, Jefferson & Jesus Are Battling to Dominate the Middle East and Transform the World by Joel C. Rosenberg. Tyndale (107,304).

Columbine by Dave Cullen. Grand Central (106,193).

Good Eats: The Early Years by Alton Brown. Abrams (104,908).

Reinventing the Body, Resurrecting the Soul: How to Create a New You by Deepak Chopra. Harmony (104,540).

The Lost City of Z: A Tale of Deadly Obsession in the Amazon by David Grann. Doubleday (104,120).

Notes Left Behind by Brooke Desserich. William Morrow (104,043).

The Conscious Cook by Tal Ronnen. Morrow Cookbook (103,936).

Our Iceberg Is Melting: Changing and Succeeding in Any Conditions by John Kotter. St. Martin's (103,188).

Lidia Cooks from the Heart of Italy by Lidia Matticchio Bastianich. Knopf (102,537).

Here's the Deal by Howie Mandel with Josh Young. Bantam (102,321).

The Prodigal God: Recovering the Heart of the Christian Faith by Timothy Keller. Penguin (101,836).

Strength in What Remains by Tracy Kidder. Random (100,738).

Paperbacks: In Mass Market, Women on Top; in Trade, *The Shack* Abides

Michael Coffey

We asked publishers to report 2009 net sales for mass market, trade paperbacks, and the combined category of almanacs, atlases, and annuals. For mass market books, we asked for titles that sold 500,000 or more copies; for trade paper and the final category, titles at 100,000 or more.

At the top of the mass market heap is John Grisham, who topped the 2008 list with 2,185,722 copies sold for *The Appeal*. In 2009 he leads with 2,150,227 sold for *The Associate*. In each of the past two years, Grisham had the only mass market title to pass the 2 million mark. Of the next 20 authors, only Dean Koontz, James Rollins, and Dan Brown are men.

Dead On

If it was anyone's year in mass market format, though, her name was Sookie Stackhouse. Charlaine Harris's protagonist—and narrator—is a southern-born woman with telepathic powers and a little fairy blood running through her. A very popular HBO series, "True Blood," is based on Sookie's exploits, and in 2009 Harris had no fewer than eight titles that sold more than 500,000 copies each—collectively, they came to 5.8 million, making her publisher, Ace, very happy. Sookie made her first appearance in 2008, in *Dead Until Dark*, a TV tie-in that marked that year's only Charlaine Harris title above the 500,000 mark. Sookie's come along very fast.

The Shack, The Road

In trade paperback, *The Shack* was where it's at, just as in 2008 when this Windblown title by William P. Young, about meeting God in person in a rather rustic assignation, clocked 4,432,439 copies sold; in 2009 it fell off only slightly, to just under 3.6 million. Still, in 2009 it reigned supreme, as Eckhart Tolle's *The New Earth*, which two years ago sold more than 5 million, dropped out of our count completely.

In the helped-by-movie department, *The Time Traveler's Wife, Push*, and Cormac McCarthy's *The Road* benefited mightily. In fact, *The Road* just keeps on riding. In 2008 the Vintage trade paperback sold 750,000 copies; with the movie tie-in in 2009, it found more devotees, with almost 615,000 in sales.

Mass Market

2,000,000+

The Associate: A Novel by John Grisham. Rep. Dell (2,150,227)

1,000,000+

Cross Country by James Patterson. Grand Central (1,275,888)

Sail by James Patterson. Grand Central (1,251,364).

Tribute by Nora Roberts. Rep. Jove (1,250,361).

Fearless Fourteen by Janet Evanovich. Rep. St. Martin's (1,200,000).

The Quickie by James Patterson. Grand Central (1,167,569)

Scarpetta by Patricia Cornwell. Rep. Berkley (1,130,248).

The Whole Truth by David Baldacci. Grand Central (1,109,543)

Divine Justice by David Baldacci. Grand Central (1,021,344)

Sooner or Later by Debbie Macomber. Avon (1,000,000).

Mrs. Miracle by Debbie Macomber. Avon (1,000,000).

Dark Summer by Iris Johansen. Rep. St. Martin's (1,000,000).

750,000+

7th Heaven by James Patterson. Grand Central (994,030)

The Front by Patricia Cornwell. Rep. Berkley (915,192).

Sundays at Tiffany's by James Patterson. Grand Central (911,511)

Your Heart Belong to Me: A Novel by Dean Koontz. Rep. Bantam (887,394).

From Dead to Worse: A Sookie Stackhouse Novel by Charlaine Harris. Rep. Ace (877,000).

The Choice by Nicholas Sparks. Grand Central (870,116).

The Grand Finale by Janet Evanovich. Harper (850,000).

TailSpin by Catherine Coulter. Rep. Jove (840,210).

*Where Are You Now? A Novel by Mary Higgins Clark. Rep. Pocket.

Club Dead: A Sookie Stackhouse Novel by Charlaine Harris. Rep. Ace (802,469).

Plum Spooky by Janet Evanovich. Rep. St. Martin's (800,000).

The Last Oracle by James Rollins. Harper (800,000).

Deadlock by Iris Johansen. Rep. St. Martin's (780,000).

The Brass Verdict by Michael Connelly. Grand Central (768,417).

The Da Vinci Code by Dan Brown. Rep. Vintage/Anchor (759,982).

Dead to the World: A Sookie Stackhouse Novel by Charlaine Harris. Rep. Ace (750,388).

500,000+

A Good Woman: A Novel by Danielle Steel. Rep. Dell (733,557).

The Lovely Bones by Alice Sebold. Movie tie-in ed. Little, Brown (734,835).

Heat Lightning by John Sandford. Rep. Berkley (730,260).

Definitely Dead: A Sookie Stackhouse Novel by Charlaine Harris. Rep. Ace (730,013).

Silent Thunder by Iris and Roy Johansen. Rep. St. Martin's (725,000).

*Smoke Screen: A Novel by Sandra Brown. Rep. Pocket.

Dead as a Doornail: A Sookie Stackhouse Novel by Charlaine Harris. Rep. Ace (728,144).

*Angels & Demons by Dan Brown. Movie tie-in. Rep. Pocket.

Dead Until Dark: A Sookie Stackhouse Novel by Charlaine Harris. TV tie-in. Rep. Ace (700,516).

Phantom Prey by John Sandford. Rep. Berkley (700,191).

What Happens in London by Julia Quinn. Avon (700,000).

Honor Thyself by Danielle Steel. Rep. Dell (693,368).

Hold Tight by Harlan Coben. Rep. Signet (690,107).

Rogue by Danielle Steel. Rep. Dell (677,658).

92 Pacific Boulevard by Debbie Macomber. Mira (677,373).

*My Sister's Keeper: A Novel by Jodi Picoult. Movie tie-in. Rep. Pocket.

Fire and Ice: A Novel by Julie Garwood. Rep. Ballantine (655,836).

All Together Dead: A Sookie Stackhouse Novel by Charlaine Harris. Rep. Ace (655,046).

The Charlemagne Pursuit: A Novel by Steve Berry. Rep. Ballantine (651,373).

Dear John by Nicholas Sparks. Grand Central (645,978).

*Devil's Punchbowl: A Novel by Greg Iles. Rep. Pocket.

Promises in Death by J. D. Robb. Rep. Berkley (635,372).

Salvation in Death by J. D. Robb. Rep. Berkley (631,019).

While My Sister Sleeps by Barbara Delinsky. Rep. Vintage/Anchor (629,027).

The Untamed Bride by Stephanie Laurens. Avon (625,000).

Robert Ludlum's The Bourne Sanction by Eric Van Lustbader. Grand Central (615,719).

Plague Ship by Clive Cussler. Rep. Berkley (615,222).

*Lavender Morning by Jude Deveraux. Rep. Pocket.

The Road by Cormac McCarthy. Rep. Vintage/Anchor (605,322).

Odd Hours by Dean Koontz. Rep. Bantam (601,757).

*Just After Sunset: Stories by Stephen King. Rep. Pocket.

The Book of Lies by Brad Meltzer. Grand Central. (593,330).

Dean Koontz's Frankenstein: Dead & Alive: A Novel by Dean Koontz. Orig. Bantam (582,809).

*Dashing Through the Snow by Mary Higgins Clark and Carol Higgins Clark. Rep. Pocket.

Shutter Island by Dennis Lehane. Harper (575,000).

Dream Warrior by Sherrilyn Kenyon. Orig. St. Martin's (575,000).

Arctic Drift by Clive Cussler. Rep. Berkley (570,448).

Say Goodbye by Lisa Gardner. Rep. Bantam (568,515).

Living Dead in Dallas: A Sookie Stackhouse Novel by Charlaine Harris. Rep. Ace (557,282).

True Detectives: A Novel by Jonathan Kellerman. Rep. Ballantine (547,097).

The Treasure: A Novel by Iris Johansen. Rep. Bantam (540,413).

The Mercedes Coffin by Faye Kellerman. Harper (525,000).

Born of Fire by Sherrilyn Kenyon. Orig. St. Martin's (525,000).

Married in Seattle by Debbie Macomber. Mira (520,291).

Shadow of Power by Steve Martini. Harper (520,000).

Right Next Door by Debbie Macomber. Mira (515,992).

Tempt Me at Twilight by Lisa Kleypas. Orig. St. Martin's (515,000).

Where the Heart Lies by Stephanie Laurens. Avon (515,000).

Charmed & Enchanted by Nora Roberts. Silhouette (511,177).

Damage Control by J. A. Jance. Harper (510,000).

Executive Privilege by Phillip Margolin. Harper (510,000).

The Law of Love by Nora Roberts. Silhouette (509,464).

Twenty Wishes by Debbie Macomber. Mira (507,438).

Bones: An Alex Delaware Novel by Jonathan Kellerman. Rep. Ballantine (505,216).

Mastered by Love by Stephanie Laurens. Avon (505,000).

Born of Night by Sherrilyn Kenyon. Orig. St. Martin's (505,000).

The MacKade Brothers: Devin and Shane by Nora Roberts. Silhouette (504,277).

Terminal Freeze by Lincoln Child. Rep. Vintage/Anchor (501,607).

Fireside by Susan Wiggs. Mira (501,392).

Loitering with Intent by Stuart Woods. Rep. Signet (500,138).

Hidden Currents by Christine Feehan. Orig. Jove (500,044).

Worth the Risk by Nora Roberts. Silhouette (500,040).

Temptation and Surrender by Stephanie Laurens. Avon (500,000).

Born of Ice by Sherrilyn Kenyon. Orig. St. Martin's (500,000).

The Dark Tide by Andrew Gross. Avon (500,000).

Trade Paperbacks

1,000,000+

The Shack: Where Tragedy Confronts Eternity by William P. Young. Orig. Windblown (3,595,467).

Glenn Beck's Common Sense: The Case Against an Out-of-Control Government, inspired by Thomas Paine by Glenn Beck. Rep. Threshold.

The Time Traveler's Wife by Audrey Niffenegger. Rep. HMH (1,456,771).

Push by Sapphire. Rep. Vintage/Anchor (1,269,650).

The Guernsey Literary and Potato Peel Pie Society by Mary Ann Shaffer and Annie Barrows. Rep. Dial (1,105,469).

Vision in White by Nora Roberts. Orig. Berkley (1,100,427).

750,000+

Three Cups of Tea: One Man's Mission to Promote Peace . . . One School at a Time by Greg Mortenson. Penguin (973,280).

Bed of Roses by Nora Roberts. Orig. Berkley (950,024).

Eat This, Not That! Supermarkets by David Zinczenko. Rodale (950,000).

Pride and Prejudice and Zombies by Jane Austen and Seth Grahame-Smith. Quirk (794,333).

The Girl with the Dragon Tattoo by Stieg Larsson. Rep. Vintage/Anchor (777,382).

500,000+

Say You're One of Them by Uwem Akpan. Back Bay (708,033).

Olive Kitteridge by Elizabeth Strout. Rep. Random (702,993).

The Blindside: Evolution of a Game by Michael Lewis. Movie tie-in. Norton (676,645).

What to Expect When You're Expecting by Heidi Murkoff. Revised. Workman (670,595).

The Lucky One by Nicholas Sparks. Rep. Grand Central (628,127).

The Five Love Languages, How to Express Heartfelt Commitment to Your Mate by Gary Chapman. Reissue. Northfield (626,238).

The Road by Cormac McCarthy. Rep. Vintage/Anchor (614,879).

Sunday at Tiffany's by James Patterson. Rep. Grand Central (608,597).

Hungry Girl 200 Under 200: 200 Recipes Under 200 Calories by Lisa Lillien. Orig. St. Martin's (600,000).

7th Heaven by James Patterson. Rep. Grand Central (582,269).

Sarah's Key by Tatiana de Rosnay. Rep. St. Martin's (575,000).

My Sister's Keeper by Jodi Picoult. Movie tie-in ed. Washington Square Press.

Love the One You're With by Emily Giffin. Rep. St. Martin's (500,000).

250,000+

My Life in France by Julia Child with Alex Prud'homme. Rep. Vintage/Anchor (497,731).

America's Most Wanted Recipes by Ron Douglas. Atria.

Blink. Malcolm Gladwell by Back Bay. (476,532).

Firefly Lane by Kristin Hannah. Rep. St. Martin's (475,000).

Julie & Julia by Julie Powell. Movie tie-in ed. Back Bay. (472,790).

Eat This, Not That! 2010 by David Zinczenko. Rodale (450,000).

The Alchemist by Paulo Coehlo. HarperOne (450,000+).

The Reader by Bernhard Schlink. Rep. Vintage/Anchor (449,947).

The Lovely Bones by Alice Sebold. Movie tie-in ed. Back Bay (437,397).

The Tipping Point by Malcolm Gladwell. Back Bay (434,339).

*Handle with Care by Jodi Picoult. Washington Square Press.

The Lovely Bones by Alice Sebold. Back Bay (400,523).

When You Are Engulfed in Flames by David Sedaris. Back Bay (394,613).

Cook This, Not That by David Zinczenko. Rodale (385,000).

Eat, Pray, Love: One Woman's Search for Everything Across Italy, India, and Indonesia by Elizabeth Gilbert. Penguin (365,831).

Of Mice and Men by John Steinbeck. Penguin (365,502).

Unaccustomed Earth by Jhumpa Lahiri. Rep. Vintage/Anchor (362,055).

*The Glass Castle: A Memoir by Jeannette Walls. Rep. Scribner.

Eat This, Not That Restaurants by David Zinczenko. Rodale (355,000).

Run for Your Life by James Patterson. Rep. Grand Central (347,074).

Dreams from My Father: A Story of Race and Inheritance by Barack Obama. Rep. Crown (338,672).

Hello, Cupcake! Irresistibly Playful Creations Anyone Can Make by Karen Tack and Alan Richardson. Orig. HMH (334,074).

City of Thieves by David Benioff. Rep. Plume (333,675).

*My Sister's Keeper by Jodi Picoult. Washington Square Press.

What to Expect the First Year by Heidi Murkoff. Revised. Workman (326,615).

More Diners, More Drive-ins & Dives by Guy Fieri. Morrow Cookbooks (325,790).

The Elegance of the Hedgehog by Muriel Barbery, trans. by Alison Anderson. Europa (315,665).

Dear John by Nicholas Sparks. Media tie-in. Rep. Grand Central (312,719).

Testimony by Anita Shreve. Back Bay (308,019).

Same Kind of Different as Me: A Modern-day Slave, an International Art Dealer, and the Unlikely Woman Who Bound Them Together by Ron Hall and Denver Moore, with Lynn Vincent. Nelson (304,559).

Into the Wild by Jon Krakauer. Rep. Vintage/Anchor (299,147).

Rachael Ray's Book of Ten: More Than 300 Recipes to Cook Every Day by Rachael Ray. Orig. Crown (293,985).

A Summer Affair by Anita Shreve. Back Bay (291,920).

The House on Mango Street by Sandra Cisneros. Orig. Vintage/Anchor (284,025).

Martha Stewart's Cupcakes: 175 Inspired Ideas for Everyone's Favorite Treat. Martha Stewart Living Magazine. Orig. Crown (281,504).

Biggest Loser Family Cookbook by Devin Alexander and Melissa Roberson. Rodale (280,000).

The Zombie Survival Guide: Complete Protection for the Living Dead by Max Brooks. Orig. Crown (277,357)

My Horizontal Life: A Collection of One-Night Stands by Chelsea Handler. Bloomsbury (275,000).

The Kite Runner by Khaled Hosseini. Rep. Riverhead (272,273).

In Defense of Food: An Eater's Manifesto by Michael Pollan. Penguin (265,003).

Biggest Loser 30 Day Jumpstart by Cheryl Forberg, Melissa Roberson, and Lisa Wheeler. Rodale (265,000).

The Power of Now: A Guide to Spiritual Enlightenment by Eckhart Tolle. Rep. New World Library (262,101).

The Secret by Beverly Lewis. Bethany House (260,661).

Diners, Drive-ins and Dives by Guy Fieri. Morrow Cookbooks (259,955).

The Piano Teacher: A Novel by Janice Y.K. Lee. Penguin (258,779).

The Beach House by Jane Green. Rep. Plume (257,427).

The Brief Wondrous Life of Oscar Wao by Junot Díaz. Rep. Riverhead (254,742).

American Wife: A Novel by Curtis Sittenfeld. Rep. Random (252,697).

The Omnivore's Dilemma: A Natural History of Four Meals by Michael Pollan. Penguin (252,185).

A Thousand Splendid Suns by Khaled Hosseini. Rep. Riverhead (250,086).

Revolutionary Road by Richard Yates. Rep. Vintage/Anchor (251,338).

Our Choice by Al Gore. Rodale (250,000).

Flat Belly Diet Pocket Guide by Liz Vaccariello. Rodale (250,000).

100,000+

An Inconvenient Book: Real World Solutions to the World's Biggest Problems by Glenn Beck. Rep. Threshold.

Audition by Barbara Walters. Rep. Vintage/Anchor (239,660).

Things Fall Apart by Chinua Achebe. Rep. Vintage/Anchor (238,527).

The Middle Place by Kelly Corrigan. Rep. Voice (237,662).

The Gate House by Nelson DeMille. Rep. Grand Central (237,052).

This Side of Heaven: A Novel by Karen Kingsbury. Orig. Center Street (235,938).

The Missing by Beverly Lewis. Bethany House (234,865).

The No. 1 Ladies' Detective Agency by Alexander McCall Smith. Rep. Vintage/Anchor (231,719).

Cook Yourself Thin: Skinny Meals You Can Make in Minutes. Lifetime Television. Orig. Voice (228,574).

Knit Two by Kate Jacobs. Rep. Berkley (220,069).

In the Woods by Tana French. Penguin (219,138).

The Secret Life of Bees by Sue Monk Kidd. Penguin (210,768).

Water for Elephants by Sara Gruen. Algonquin (203,000).

The Shadow of the Wind by Carlos Ruiz Zafón. Penguin (202,856).

Likeness: A Novel by Tana French. Penguin (202,762).

Naturally Thin: Unleash Your SkinnyGirl and Free Yourself from a Lifetime of Dieting by Bethenny Frankel. Touchstone Fireside.

World War Z: An Oral History of the Zombie War by Max Brooks. Rep. Crown (199,435).

A Raisin in the Sun by Lorraine Hansberry. Rep. Vintage/Anchor (197,057).

Hotel on the Corner of Bitter and Sweet by Jamie Ford. Rep. Ballantine (195,241).

Public Enemies: America's Greatest Crime Wave and the Birth of the F.B.I. by Bryan Burrough. Penguin (191,937).

Making the Cut: The 30-Day Diet and Fitness Plan for the Strongest, Sexiest You by Jillian Michaels. Rep. Crown (190,764).

Certain Girls by Jennifer Weiner. Washington Square Press.

Netherland by Joseph O'Neill. Vintage/Anchor (185,479).

People of the Book: A Novel by Geraldine Brooks. Penguin (184,301).

The Inaugural Address, 2009: Together with Abraham Lincoln's First and Second Inaugural Addresses and the Gettysburg Address and Ralph Waldo Emerson's Self-Reliance by Barack Obama. Penguin (180,862).

The Friday Night Knitting Club by Kate Jacobs. Rep. Berkley (180,328).

Wolf Hall: A Novel by Hilary Mantel. Holt (180,000).

Nineteen Minutes by Jodi Picoult. Washington Square Press.

Battlefield of the Mind: Winning the Battle in Your Mind by Joyce Meyer. Orig. Faith Words (178,899).

Comfort Food by Kate Jacobs. Rep. Berkley (175,159).

Flat Belly Diet by Liz Vaccariello. Rodale (175,000).

American Lion: Andrew Jackson in the White House by Jon Meacham. Rep. Random (172,043).

I Am America (and So Can You!) by Stephen Colbert. Rep. Grand Central (170,819).

The Senator's Wife by Sue Miller. Vintage/Anchor (170,607).

Biggest Loser Simple Swaps by Cheryl Forberg and Melissa Roberson. Rodale (170,000).

The Curious Incident of the Dog in the Night-Time by Mark Haddon. Vintage/Anchor (169,587).

The Devil in the White City by Erik Larson. Vintage/Anchor (167,549)

A Mercy by Toni Morrison. Vintage/Anchor (166,349).

Are You There Vodka, It's Me, Chelsea by Chelsea Handler. Rep. Simon Spotlight.

The Miracle Ball Method by Elaine Petrone. Orig. Workman (165,956).

Hungry Girl: Recipes and Survival Strategies for Guilt-Free Eating in the Real World by Lisa Lillien. Orig. St. Martin's (165,000).

The White Tiger: A Novel by Aravind Adiga. Rep. Free Press.

Loving Frank: A Novel by Nancy Horan. Rep. Ballantine (162,460).

Hot, Flat, and Crowded 2.0: Why We Need a Green Revolution—and How It Can Renew America by Thomas L. Friedman. Reissue. Picador (160,000).

South Beach Diet Supercharged by Arthur Agatston. Rep. St. Martin's (160,000).

The Cake Mix Doctor Returns! by Anne Byrn. Orig. Workman (159,629).

Caring for Your Baby and Young Child: Birth to Age 5 by Steven P. Shelov and Tanya Remer Altmann. Rep. Bantam (158,080).

*Chasing Harry Winston: A Novel by Lauren Weisberger. Rep. Pocket.

The 19th Wife: A Novel by David Ebershoff. Rep. Random (151,212).

Girls in Trucks by Katie Crouch. Back Bay. (149,883).

Barefoot by Elin Hilderbrand. Back Bay (146,892).

Atlas Shrugged by Ayn Rand. Rep. Plume (148,695).

The Miracle at Speedy Motors by Alexander McCall Smith. Vintage/Anchor (148,032).

My Stroke of Insight: A Brain Scientist's Personal Journey by Jill Bolte Taylor. Rep. Plume (146,224).

Fireproof by Eric Wilson, Alex Kendrick, Stephen Kendrick. Thomas Nelson (146,106).

Lone Survivor by Marcus Luttrell. Back Bay(145,257).

The Other Queen by Philippa Gregory. Touchstone Fireside.

Rich Dad, Poor Dad: What the Rich Teach Their Kids About Money—That the Poor and the Middle Class Do Not! by Robert T. Kiyosaki with Sharon L. Lechter. Orig. Grand Central (142,621).

The Memory Keeper's Daughter by Kim Edwards. Penguin (141,490).

The Soloist: A Lost Dream. An Unlikely Friendship, and the Redemptive Power of Music by Steve Lopez. Movie tie-in. Rep. Berkley (140,156).

Home: A Novel by Marilynne Robinson. Rep. Picador (140,000).

Food Rules: An Eater's Manual by Michael Pollan. Penguin (138,770).

Up in the Air by Walter Kirn. Vintage/Anchor (137,062).

Me Talk Pretty One Day by David Sedaris. Back Bay (136,012)

The Stranger by Albert Camus. Vintage/Anchor (135,434).

*Become a Better You: 7 Keys to Improving Your Life Every Day by Joel Osteen. Rep. Free Press.

The Monster of Florence by Douglas Preston and Mario Spezi. Rep. Grand Central (134,690).

The Five People You Meet in Heaven by Mitch Albom. Rep. Hyperion (132,154).

The Reef by Nora Roberts. Reissue. Berkley (130,225).

Wolf at the Table: A Memoir of My Father by Augusten Burroughs. Rep. Picador (130,000).

A Lesson Before Dying by Ernest J. Gaines. Vintage/Anchor (129,716).

A Whole New Mind: Why Right-Brainers Will Rule the Future by Daniel H. Pink. Rep. Riverhead (128,397).

*Still Alice by Lisa Genova. Orig. Pocket.

*The Skinnygirl Dish: Easy Recipes for Your Naturally Thin Life by Bethenny Frankel. Touchstone Fireside.

Off Season by Anne Rivers Siddons. Rep. Grand Central (124,508).

The Pearl by John Steinbeck. Penguin (123,757).

Let the Great World Spin: A Novel by Colum McCann. Rep. Random (122,757).

What to Expect: The Toddler Years by Heidi Murkoff. Revised. Workman (122,248).

One Fifth Avenue by Candace Bushnell. Rep. Voice (121,443).

*The Bro Code by Barney Stinson. Touchstone Fireside.

*Stori Telling by Tori Spelling. Rep. Simon Spotlight.

*The Catcher in the Rye by J. D. Salinger. Back Bay.

Smart Guide to the Bible by Larry Richards. Thomas Nelson (120,210).

Fix-It and Forget It Cookbook: Feasting with Your Slow Cooker by Dawn J. Ranck and Phyllis Pellman Good. Orig. Good Books (118,423).

Captivating: Unveiling the Mystery of a Woman's Soul by John Eldridge and Stasi Eldridge. Thomas Nelson (117,758).

Wild at Heart: Discovering the Secret of a Man's Soul by John Eldridge. Thomas Nelson (115,450).

The Wednesday Letters by Jason F. Wright. Rep. Berkley (115,129).

Sleeping Arrangements by Madeleine Wickham. Rep. St. Martin's (115,000).

Nightlight. The Harvard Lampoon. Vintage/Anchor (114,343).

Against Medical Advice by James Patterson. Rep. Grand Central (114,303).

So You Don't Want to Go to Church Anymore: An Unexpected Journey by Wayne Jacobsen and Dave Coleman. Orig. Windblown Media (112,797).

*Vanishing Acts by Jodi Picoult. Washington Square Press.

The Principles, Practices & Priorities of a Winning Life by Tony Dungy with Nathan Whitaker. Rep. Tyndale (112,562).

Julie & Julia by Julie Powell. Back Bay (111,108).

World Without End by Ken Follett. Rep. NAL (110,328).

The Private Patient by P. D. James. Vintage/Anchor (110,041).

Secrets of a Shoe Addict by Beth Harbison. Rep. St. Martin's (110,000).

The Reason for God by Timothy Keller. Rep. Riverhead (108,741).

Getting Things Done: The Art of Stress-Free Productivity by David Allen. Penguin (107,092).

How Not to Look Old: Fast and Effortless Ways to Look 10 Years Younger, 10 Pounds Lighter, 10 Times Better by Charla Krupp. Rep. Grand Central (106,530).

The Post-American World by Fareed Zakaria. Rep. Norton (106,141).

The Zookeeper's Wife: A War Story by Diane Ackerman. Rep. Norton (106,141).

Nudge: Improving Decisions About Health, Wealth, and Happiness by Richard H. Thaler. Penguin (105,857).

Stuff White People Like: A Definitive Guide to the Unique Taste of Millions by Christian Lander. Orig. Random (105,628).

Irish Born by Nora Roberts. Orig. Berkley (105,328).

Look Me in the Eye: My Life with Asperger's by John Elder Robinson. Rep. Crown (104,988).

Physics of the Impossible by Michio Kaku. Vintage/Anchor (104,797).

God Is Not Great: How Religion Poisons Everything by Christopher Hitchens. Rep. Grand Central (104,446).

Cesar's Way: The Natural, Everyday Guide to Understanding and Correcting Common Dog Problems by Cesar Millan and Melissa Jo Peltier. Rep. Three Rivers (103,863).

Bananagrams! The Official Book. Puzzles by Joe Edley, created by Abe and Rena Nathanson. Orig. Workman (103,583).

1,000 Places to See Before You Die by Patricia Schultz. Orig. Workman (103,578).

The Almost Moon by Alice Sebold. Back Bay (103,178).

AAP New Mother's Guide to Breastfeeding. American Academy of Pediatrics, Joan Younger Meek with Sherill Tippins. Rep. Bantam (102,905).

Halo: Essential Tales of the Halo Universe. Various authors. Orig. Tor (102,779).

The Enchantress of Florence: A Novel by Salman Rushdie. Rep. Random (102,351).

Letter to My Daughter by Maya Angelou. Rep. Random (101,394).

Snuff by Chuck Palahniuk. Vintage/Anchor (101,352).

*The Tenth Circle by Jodi Picoult. Washington Square Press.

Why We Suck: A Feel Good Guide to Staying Fat, Loud, Lazy and Stupid by Denis Leary. Rep. Plume (101,093).

The Drunkard's Walk by Leonard Mlodinow. Vintage/Anchor (100,198).

Out Stealing Horses: A Novel by Per Petterson. Reissue. Picador (100,000).

Lush Life: A Novel by Richard Price. Rep. Picador (100,000).

Mere Christianity by C. S. Lewis. HarperOne (100,000+).

Eat This, Not That! For Kids by David Zinczenko. Rodale (100,000).

Children's Bestsellers:
YA Queen Stephenie Meyer Holds On to Top Spots

Diane Roback

Publishers Weekly

The Stephenie Meyer juggernaut rolls on. Though the queen of the vampire novel didn't release any new books in 2009, demand was still enormous, fueled by the *New Moon* film and the DVD release of 2008's *Twilight.* Combining the various hardcover, paperback, and movie tie-in editions, Meyer sold just under 26.5 million copies of her *Twilight* saga in 2009. That's a remarkably similar figure to last year's (27.5 million). Add in 912,000 copies sold of her adult novel, *The Host,* and it looks as if Meyer—and Little, Brown—had another very good year.

So did Jeff Kinney, chronicler of all things *Wimpy.* His two new additions to the *Diary of a Wimpy Kid* series sold 5.7 million, and his three backlist titles (including a do-it-yourself journal) sold another 3.8 million, for a total of 9.5 million copies.

These days the numbers game is all about series. The many paranormal series continue their prominence on bestseller lists, including PC and Kristin Cast's House of Night books (nearly 5.4 million copies sold, in various editions), Alyson Noël's Immortals series (1.6 million), L. J. Smith's The Vampire Diaries (1.6 million) and Night World (1.3 million), and Vampire Academy by Richelle Mead (1.2 million). In other series news, Rick Riordan's Percy Jackson books are still huge, with 3.3 million copies sold; James Patterson sold 3.2 million copies of his various lines for kids; and the multi-authored 39 Clues series sold 1.7 million copies.

But other kinds of titles find their way onto the lists too. There were new novels from Kate DiCamillo (352,000 copies) and Sarah Dessen (231,000 copies), and a *Hunger Games* sequel from Suzanne Collins (460,000 copies). And a few titles from celebrities could be spotted (Lauren Conrad, 477,000 copies sold; Miley Cyrus, 342,000 copies; Glenn Beck, 322,000 copies), though fewer than in previous years.

Children's Hardcover Frontlist

300,000+

1. *Dog Days* (Diary of a Wimpy Kid No. 4) by Jeff Kinney. Abrams/Amulet (3,102,504).

2. *The Last Straw* (Diary of a Wimpy Kid No. 3) by Jeff Kinney. Abrams/Amulet (2,621,952).

3. *Tempted* (House of Night No. 6) by PC and Kristin Cast. St. Martin's Griffin (1,108,400).

4. *The Last Olympian* (Percy Jackson and the Olympians No. 5) by Rick Riordan. Disney-Hyperion (1,059,566).

5. *Breaking Dawn Special Edition* by Stephenie Meyer. Little, Brown/Tingley (962,337).

6. *Hunted* (House of Night No. 5) *by* PC and Kristin Cast. St. Martin's Griffin (853,411).

7. *Twilight: Director's Notebook: The Story of How We Made the Movie Based on the Novel by Stephenie Meyer* by Catherine Hardwicke. Little, Brown (800,320).

8. *Witch & Wizard* by James Patterson and Gabrielle Charbonnet. Little, Brown (635,567).

9. *Shadowland* (The Immortals No. 3) by Alyson Noël. St. Martin's Griffin (500,746).

10. *Max* (Maximum Ride) by James Patterson. Little, Brown (465,401).

11. *Catching Fire* by Suzanne Collins. Scholastic Press (460,733).

12. *Watch the Skies* (Daniel X) by James Patterson and Ned Rust. Little, Brown (386,365).

13. *Fancy Nancy: Splendiferous Christmas* by Jane O'Connor, illus. by Robin Preiss Glasser. HarperCollins (375,677).

14. *L.A. Candy* by Lauren Conrad. HarperCollins (359,197).

15. *The Sword Thief* (The 39 Clues No. 3) by Peter Lerangis. Scholastic (355,745).

16. *The Magician's Elephant* by Kate DiCamillo, illus. by Yoko Tanaka. Candlewick (351,706).

17. *Miles to Go* by Miley Cyrus. Disney-Hyperion (341,668).

18. *Blood* Promise (Vampire Academy No. 4) by Richelle Mead. Penguin/ Razorbill (335,832).

19. **City of Glass* (The Mortal Instruments) by Cassandra Clare. S&S/ McElderry.

20. *Beyond the Grave* (The 39 Clues No. 4) by Jude Watson. Scholastic (329,333).

21. **The Christmas Sweater* by Glenn Beck, illus. by Brandon Dorman. S&S/Aladdin.

22. *Fancy Nancy: Explorer Extraordinaire!* by Jane O'Connor, illus. by Robin Preiss Glasser. HarperCollins (317,461).

23. *Goldilicious* by Victoria Kann. HarperCollins (313,005).

200,000+

24. *The Vampire Diaries: The Return: Nightfall* by L. J. Smith. HarperTeen (285,699).

25. *Percy Jackson: The Demigod Files* by Rick Riordan. Disney-Hyperion (281,942).

26. *Waddle!* by Rufus Butler Seder. Workman (257,747).

27. *In Too Deep* (The 39 Clues No. 6) by Jude Watson. Scholastic (255,042).

28. *The Black Circle* (The 39 Clues No. 5) by Patrick Carman. Scholastic (252,473).

29. *The Van Alan Legacy* (Blue Bloods) by Melissa de la Cruz. Disney-Hyperion (251,805).

30. *Along for the Ride* by Sarah Dessen. Viking (231,134).

31. *Moonlight on the Magic Flute* (Magic Tree House No. 41) by Mary Pope Osborne, illus. by Sal Murdocca. Random (226,199).

32. *A Good Night for Ghosts* (MTH No. 42) by Mary Pope Osborne, illus. by Sal Murdocca. Random (224,255).

33. *Toy Story.* Golden/Disney (207,910).

150,000+

34. **The Secret to Teen Power* by Paul Harrington. Simon Pulse.

35. *Crocodile Tears* (Alex Rider No. 8) by Anthony Horowitz. Philomel (176,157).

36. *Don't Judge a Girl by Her Cover* by Ally Carter. Disney-Hyperion (173,247).

37. *Baby Bear, Baby Bear, What Do You See?* (board book) by Bill Martin, Jr., illus. by Eric Carle. Holt (172,800).

38. *Mr. FancyPants!* Illus. by Caleb Meurer. Golden (162,944).

39. *Scat* by Carl Hiaasen. Knopf (162,785).

40. *Million-Dollar Throw* by Mike Lupica. Philomel (160,810).

41. **Dork Diaries: Tales from a Not-so-Fabulous Life* by Rachel Renée Russell. S&S/Aladdin.

42. **Soldiers of Halla* (Pendragon No. 10) by D. J. MacHale. S&S/Aladdin.

100,000+

43. **Cat* by Matthew Van Fleet, photos by Brian Stanton. S&S/Wiseman.

44. *Sunrise* (Warriors: Power of Three No. 6) by Erin Hunter. HarperCollins (147,856).

45. *Eragon's Guide to Alagaësia* by Christopher Paolini. Knopf (147,478).

46. *The Princess and the Frog.* Golden/Disney (147,012).

47. *Marked* (House of Night No. 1) by PC and Kristin Cast. St. Martin's Griffin (146,781).

48. *The Mysterious Benedict Society and the Prisoner's Dilemma* by Trenton Lee Stewart. Little, Brown (146,553).

49. *Marley Goes to School* by John Grogan, illus. by Richard Cowdrey. HarperCollins (144,034).

50. *The Sorceress* (The Secrets of the Immortal Nicholas Flamel) by Michael Scott. Delacorte (143,192).

51. *The Big Green Book of Beginner Books* by Dr. Seuss. Random (143,095).

52. *Cars: Look Out for Mater!* Golden/Disney (142,329).

53. *The Awakening* by Kelly Armstrong. HarperCollins (142,263).

54. *Return to the Hundred Acre Wood* by David Benedictus, illus. by Mark Burgess. Dutton (140,243).

55. **Paula Deen's Cookbook for the Lunch-Box Set* by Paula Deen with Martha Nesbit, illus. by Susan Mitchell. Simon & Schuster.

56. *Walt Disney's Classic Storybook*. Disney Press (134,609).

57. *Junie B.'s Essential Survival Guide to School* by Barbara Park, illus. by Denise Brunkus. Random (133,958).

58. *Charmed and Dangerous: The Clique Prequel* by Lisi Harrison. Little, Brown/Poppy (133,308).

59. *The Fourth Apprentice* (Warriors: Omen of the Stars No. 1) by Erin Hunter. HarperCollins (133,279).

60. *New Moon* (Collector's Edition) by Stephenie Meyer. Little, Brown/Tingley (131,773).

61. *Shiver* by Maggie Stiefvater. Scholastic Press (130,996).

62. *Fancy Nancy: Tea Parties* by Jane O'Connor, illus. by Robin Preiss Glasser. HarperCollins (128,417).

63. *Smoke Mountain* (Seekers No. 3) by Erin Hunter. HarperCollins (128,354).

64. *The Siege of Macindaw* (Ranger's Apprentice No. 6) by John Flanagan. Philomel (127,828).

65. *Wings* by Aprilynne Pike. HarperTeen (126,651).

66. *The Princess and the Frog* (Read-Aloud Storybook). Random/Disney (126,112).

67. *Thomas and the Great Discovery* by Schuyler Hooke, illus. by Tommy Stubbs. Golden (125,921).

68. *Great Bear Lake* (Seekers No. 2) by Erin Hunter. HarperCollins (124,142).

69. **Tricks* by Ellen Hopkins. S&S/McElderry.

70. *Bluestar's Prophecy* (Warriors Super Edition) by Erin Hunter, illus. by Wayne McLoughlin. HarperCollins (121,819).

71. *Fallen* by Lauren Kate. Delacorte (120,582).

72. **Hush, Hush* by Becca Fitzpatrick. Simon & Schuster.

73. **Leviathan* by Scott Westerfeld, illus. by Keith Thompson. Simon Pulse.

74. *Nubs: The True Story of a Mutt, a Marine and a Miracle* by Maj. Brian Dennis, Mary Nethery, and Kirby Larson. Little, Brown (118,508).

75. *Listen to the Wind* by Greg Mortensen, illus. by Susan Roth. Dial (118,124).

76. *Five Little Monkeys Storybook Treasury* by Eileen Christelow. HMH (117,729).

77. *3 Willows* by Ann Brashares. Delacorte (117,041).

78. *Julie Andrews' Collection of Poems, Songs, and Lullabies* by Julie Andrews Edwards and Emma Walton Hamilton, illus. by James McMullan. Little, Brown (116,676).

79. *Lego Star Wars: The Visual Dictionary* by Simon Beecroft. DK (116,393).

80. *Betrayed* (House of Night No. 2) by PC and Kristin Cast. St. Martin's Griffin (115,525).

81. *Chosen* (House of Night No. 3) by PC and Kristin Cast. St. Martin's Griffin (115,054).

82. *The Spirit of Christmas* by Nancy Tillman. Feiwel and Friends (115,000).

83. *Skippyjon Jones, Lost in Spice* by Judy Schachner. Dutton (114,844).

84. *Untamed* (House of Night No. 4) by PC and Kristin Cast. St. Martin's Griffin (113,561).

85. *Hannah Montana: In the Loop.* Disney Press (111,489).

86. **Dora's Christmas Carol* (board book) by Christine Ricci, illus. by Robert Roper. Simon Spotlight.

87. *Stargazer* by Claudia Gray. HarperTeen (109,223).

88. **Where Is Baby's Christmas Present?* (board book) by Karen Katz. Little Simon.

89. **The Wyrm King* (Beyond the Spiderwick Chronicles) by Holly Black and Tony DiTerlizzi, illus. by Tony DiTerlizzi. Simon & Schuster.

90. *Disney Princess: Dazzling Jewels, A Princess Book and Magnetic Play Set.* Disney Press (106,618).

91. *I Spy: A to Z* by Jean Marzollo, illus. by Walter Wick. Scholastic/Cartwheel (106,286).

92. *Dewey: There's a Cat in the Library!* by Vicki Myron, Bret Witter, and Steve James. Little, Brown (106,205).

93. *Fragile Eternity* by Melissa Marr. HarperCollins (105,023).

94. *Killer* (Pretty Little Liars No. 6) by Sara Shepard. HarperTeen (104,924).

95. *Silly Street* by Jeff Foxworthy, illus. by Steve Björkman. HarperCollins (103,638).

96. *Syren* (Septimus Heap No. 5) by Angie Sage, illus. by Mark Zug. HarperCollins/Tegen (103,416).

97. *The Maze Runner* by James Dashner. Delacorte (102,934).

98. *Day Is Done* by Peter Yarrow, illus. by Melissa Sweet. Sterling (102,896).

99. *Odd and the Frost Giants* by Neil Gaiman, illus. by Brett Helquist. HarperCollins (100,391).

100. **The Missing: Sent* by Margaret Peterson Haddix. Simon & Schuster.

Children's Hardcover Backlist

300,000+

1. *Breaking Dawn* by Stephenie Meyer. Little, Brown/Tingley, 2008 (4,686,713).

2. *Eclipse* by Stephenie Meyer. Little, Brown/Tingley, 2007 (4,305,594).

3. *New Moon* by Stephenie Meyer. Little, Brown/Tingley, 2006 (1,371,686).

4. *Diary of a Wimpy Kid* by Jeff Kinney. Abrams/Amulet, 2007 (1,365,987).

5. *Twilight* by Stephenie Meyer. Little, Brown/Tingley, 2006 (1,268,373).

6. *Rodrick Rules* by Jeff Kinney. Abrams/Amulet, 2008 (1,257,806).

7. *Diary of a Wimpy Kid Do-It-Yourself Book* by Jeff Kinney. Abrams/Amulet, 2008 (1,204,701).

8. *Goodnight Moon* (board book) by Margaret Wise Brown, illus. by Clement Hurd. HarperFestival, 1991 (653,140).

9. *Green Eggs and Ham* by Dr. Seuss. Random, 1960 (540,366).

10. *Brown Bear, Brown Bear, What Do You See?* (board book) by Bill Martin, Jr., illus. by Eric Carle. Holt, 1996 (534,500).

11. *Where the Wild Things Are* by Maurice Sendak. HarperCollins, 1988 (514,282).

12. *Oh, the Places You'll Go!* by Dr. Seuss. Random, 1990 (455,725).

13. *The Cat in the Hat* by Dr. Seuss. Random, 1957 (452,258).

14. *The Very Hungry Caterpillar* (board book) by Eric Carle. Philomel, 1994 (450,294).

15. *One Fish, Two Fish, Red Fish, Blue Fish* by Dr. Seuss. Random, 1960 (409,068).

16. *Gallop!* by Rufus Butler Seder. Workman, 2007 (385,877).

17. *The Maze of Bones* (The 39 Clues No. 1) by Rick Riordan. Scholastic, 2008 (378,293).

18. *The Hunger Games* by Suzanne Collins. Scholastic Press, 2008 (374,199).

19. *Biggest, Strongest, Fastest* by Steve Jenkins. Houghton, 1995 (362,585).

20. *Actual Size* by Steve Jenkins. Houghton, 2004 (341,984).

21. *What Do You Do with a Tail Like This?* by Steve Jenkins and Robin Page. Houghton, 2003 (341,548).

22. *The Graveyard Book* by Neil Gaiman, illus. by Dave McKean. Harper-Collins, 2008 (339,042).

23. *Dr. Seuss's ABC* (board book) by Dr. Seuss. Random, 1996 (328,264).

200,000+

24. *The Poky Little Puppy* by Janette Sebring Lowery, illus. by Gustaf Tenggren. Golden, 1996 (288,295).

25. *The Big Blue Book of Beginner Books* by P. D. Eastman. Random, 2008 (260,143).

26. *Mr. Brown Can Moo! Can You?* by Dr. Seuss. Random, 1996 (253,277).

27. *Thirteen Reasons Why* by Jay Asher. Razorbill, 2007 (240,807).

28. *Hop on Pop* by Dr. Seuss. Random, 1963 (240,196).

29. *I Love You Through and Through* (board book) by Bernadette Rossetti Shustak, illus. by Caroline Jayne Church. Scholastic/Cartwheel, 2005 (227,024).

30. *Are You My Mother?* by P. D. Eastman. Random, 1960 (226,766).

31. *Are You My Mother?* (board book) by P. D. Eastman. Random, 1998 (222,752).

32. *Disney Bedtime Favorites.* Disney Press, 2007 (220,329).

33. *Five Little Monkeys Jumping on the Bed* (board book) by Eileen Christelow. HMH, 1998 (211,017).

34. *The Polar Express* by Chris Van Allsburg. Houghton, 1985 (209,500).

35. *Dr. Seuss's ABC* by Dr. Seuss. Random, 1960 (208,359).

36. **The Going to Bed Book* (board book) by Sandra Boynton. Little Simon, 1982.

150,000+

37. *Fox in Socks* by Dr. Seuss. Random, 1965 (197,459).

38. *How Do I Love You?* by Marion Dane Bauer, illus. by Caroline Jayne Church. Scholastic/Cartwheel, 2008 (195,453).

39. *First 100 Words Bright Baby* (board book) by Roger Priddy. Priddy, 2005 (195,200).

40. **Moo, Baa, La La La!* (board book) by Sandra Boynton. Little Simon, 1982.

41. *Swing!* by Rufus Butler Seder. Workman, 2008 (190,180).

42. *Go, Dog. Go!* by P. D. Eastman. Random, 1961 (184,387).

43. *The Giving Tree* by Shel Silverstein. HarperCollins, 1964 (184,201).

44. *Treasury of Curious George* by H. A. Rey. HMH, 2004 (181,504).

45. *Baby Farm Animals* by Garth Williams. Golden, 1993 (179,001).

46. **Where Is Baby's Belly Button?* (board book) by Karen Katz. Little Simon, 2000.

47. *My First Read and Learn Bible.* Scholastic/Little Shepherd, 2006 (168,727).

48. *Barnyard Bath!* by Sandra Boynton. Workman, 1993 (167,420).

49. *One False Note* (The 39 Clues No. 2) by Gordon Korman. Scholastic, 2008 (166,127).

50. *Pinkalicious* by Victoria Kann. HarperCollins, 2006 (164,156).

51. *Clap Your Hands!* by Naomi Kleinberg, illus. by Joseph Ewers. Random, 2002 (163,653).

52. *Brisingr* by Christopher Paolini. Knopf, 2008 (161,944).

53. *Nursery Rhymes* by Roger Priddy. Priddy, 2006 (159,800).

54. *Ten Apples Up on Top!* by Dr. Seuss as Theo LeSieg. Random, 1961 (158,934).

55. *Pat the Bunny* by Dorothy Kunhardt. Golden Books, 2001 (158,009).

56. *The Monster at the End of This Book* by Jon Stone, illus. by Michael Smollin. Golden, 1999 (154,383).

100,000+

57. *Fancy Nancy* by Jane O'Connor, illus. by Robin Preiss Glasser. HarperCollins, 2005 (149,744).

58. **Toes, Ears, & Nose!* (board book) by Marion Dane Bauer, illus. by Karen Katz. Little Simon, 2003.

59. *Cars Puzzle Book.* Random/Disney, 2008 (147,005).

60. *Hand, Hand, Fingers, Thumb* by Al Perkins. Random, 1998 (145,934).

61. *Farm* (Baby Touch and Feel). DK, 2008 (144,990).

62. *Slide and Find: Trucks* (board book) by Roger Priddy. Priddy, 2007 (144,000).

63. *Baby Einstein: First Words.* Disney Press, 2008 (143,608).

64. *Happy Birthday to You!* by Dr. Seuss. Random, 1959 (142,412).

65. *If You Give a Cat a Cupcake* by Laura Numeroff, illus. by Felicia Bond. HarperCollins/Balzer+Bray, 2008 (140,242).

66. *How the Grinch Stole Christmas!* by Dr. Seuss. Random, 1957 (139,931).

67. *Baby Einstein: Mirror Me!* Disney Press, 2002 (137,310).

68. *Where Do Kisses Come From?* by Maria Fleming, illus. by Janice Kinnealy. Random/Golden, 1999 (136,473).

69. *Simple First Words, Let's Talk* (board book) by Roger Priddy. Priddy, 2007 (135,000).

70. *Where the Sidewalk Ends* (30th anniversary edition) by Shel Silverstein. HarperCollins, 2003 (133,732).

71. *I Love You Stinky Face* (board book) by Lisa McCourt, illus. by Cyd Moore. Scholastic/Cartwheel (133,368).

72. *Hop on Pop* (board book) by Dr. Seuss. Random, 2004 (131,946).

73. *Put Me in the Zoo* by Robert Lopshire. Random, 1960 (131,703).

74. *Fancy Nancy's Favorite Fancy Words* by Jane O'Connor, illus. by Robin Preiss Glasser. HarperCollins, 2008 (130,938).

75. *The House in the Night* by Susan Marie Swanson, illus. by Beth Krommes. Houghton, 2008 (130,858).

76. *Disney Princess Collection.* Disney Press, 2006 (129,789).

77. *I Can Read with My Eyes Shut!* by Dr. Seuss. Random, 1978 (128,433).

78. *Polar Bear, Polar Bear, What Do You Hear?* (board book) by Bill Martin, Jr., illus. by Eric Carle. Holt, 1997 (127,500).

79. *Purplicious* by Victoria Kann. HarperCollins, 2007 (126,362).

80. *On the Night You Were Born* by Nancy Tillman. Feiwel and Friends, 2006 (125,400).

81. *The Jolly Barnyard* by Annie North Bedford, illus. by Tibor Gergely. Golden, 2004 (123,127).

82. *Animals* (Baby Touch and Feel). DK, 2008 (122,852).

83. *Puppies and Kittens* (Baby Touch and Feel). DK, 2008 (120,269).

84. *If You Give a Mouse a Cookie* (25th anniversary edition) by Laura Numeroff, illus. by Felicia Bond. HarperCollins/Balzer+Bray, 1985 (119,864).

85. *Five Little Pumpkins* (board book). Illus. by Dan Yaccarino. HarperFestival, 1998 (119,236).

86. **Where Is Baby's Pumpkin?* (board book) by Karen Katz. Little Simon, 2006.

87. *Let's Go to the Farm* (Fisher-Price Little People) by Lori C. Froeb. Reader's Digest, 1997 (117,089).

88. *Cars.* Golden/Disney, 2006 (116,953)

89. *The Foot Book* (board book) by Dr. Seuss. Random, 1996 (116,573).

90. *There's No Place Like Space* by Tish Rabe, illus. by Aristides Ruiz. Random, 1999 (116,359).

91. *Fifteen Animals!* by Sandra Boynton. Workman, 2008 (116,092).

92. **Dora's Rainbow Egg Hunt* (board book) by Kirsten Larsen, illus. by Steven Savitsky. Simon Spotlight, 2006.

93. *The Lorax* by Dr. Seuss. Random, 1971 (115,611).

94. *Old, New, Red, Blue!* Random/Disney, 2006 (115,053).

95. *Pajama Time!* Sandra Boynton. Workman, 2001 (114,322).

96. *The Nose Book* (board book) by Al Perkins, illus. by Joe Mathieu. Random, 2003 (113,544).

97. *I Am Not Going to Get Up Today!* by Dr. Seuss, illus. by James Stevenson. Random, 1987 (112,059).

98. *The Battle of the Labyrinth* (Percy Jackson and the Olympians No. 4) by Rick Riordan. Disney-Hyperion, 2008 (111,216).

99. *Oh, the Things You Can Think!* by Dr. Seuss. Random, 1975 (110,639).

100. *My Little Golden Book About God* by Jane Werner Watson. Golden Christian, 2000 (110,586).

101. *There's a Wocket in My Pocket!* (board book) by Dr. Seuss. Random, 1996 (108,147).

102. *Bright Baby First Words* (board book) by Roger Priddy. Priddy, 2004 (107,600).

103. *Bright Baby Touch and Feel: Colors* (board book) by Roger Priddy. Priddy (107,600).

104. *Bright Baby Animals* (board book) by Roger Priddy. Priddy, 2004 (106,600).

105. *Go, Dog. Go!* (board book) by P. D. Eastman. Random, 1997 (106,294).

106. *The Runaway Bunny* (board book) by Margaret Wise Brown, illus. by Clement Hurd. HarperFestival, 1991 (106,290).

107. *Snuggle Puppy!* by Sandra Boynton. Workman, 2003 (105,692).

108. *The Shy Little Kitten* by Cathleen Schurr, illus. by Gustaf Tenggren. Golden, 1999 (105,680).

109. *Belly Button Book!* by Sandra Boynton. Workman, 2005 (105,509).

110. *Fancy Nancy: Bonjour, Butterfly* by Jane O'Connor, illus. by Robin Preiss Glasser. HarperCollins, 2008 (103,511).

111. *The Alphabet Book* (board book) by P. D. Eastman. Random, 2000 (103,281).

112. *If You Give a Moose a Muffin* by Laura Numeroff, illus. by Felicia Bond. HarperCollins/Balzer+Bray, 1991 (103,147).

113. *Fancy Nancy and the Posh Puppy* by Jane O'Connor, illus. by Robin Preiss Glasser. HarperCollins, 2007 (102,251).

114. *My First Counting Book* by Lilian Moore, illus. by Garth Williams. Golden, 2001 (101,988).

115. *Big Red Barn* (board book) by Margaret Wise Brown, illus. by Felicia Bond. HarperFestival, 1995 (101,604).

116. *From Head to Toe* (board book) by Eric Carle. HarperFestival, 1999 (100,726).

117. *Good Night, Gorilla* (board book) by Peggy Rathmann. Putnam, 1996 (100,204).

Children's Paperback Frontlist

300,000+

1. *Eclipse* by Stephenie Meyer. Little, Brown/Tingley (2,565,053).

2. *New Moon* (mass market media tie-in) by Stephenie Meyer. Little, Brown/Tingley (2,089,468).

3. *New Moon* (media tie-in) by Stephenie Meyer. Little, Brown/Tingley (1,664,364).

4. *Harry Potter and the Deathly Hallows* by J. K. Rowling, illus. by Mary Grandpré. Scholastic/Levine (1,085,698).

5. *New Moon: The Official Illustrated Movie Companion* by Mark Cotta Vaz. Little, Brown (845,961).

6. *The Dangerous Days of Daniel X* (mass market) by James Patterson. Little, Brown (639,755).

7. *The Final Warning* (*mass market*) by James Patterson. Little, Brown (622,795).

8. *Evermore* (The Immortals No. 1) by Alyson Noël. St. Martin's Griffin (615,961).

9. *The Battle of the Labyrinth* (Percy Jackson and the Olympians No. 4) by Rick Riordan. Disney-Hyperion (584,478).

10. *Blue Moon* (The Immortals No. 2) by Alyson Noël. St. Martin's Griffin (471,143).

11. *Night World No. 3: Huntress, Black Dawn, Witchlight* by L. J. Smith. Simon Pulse.

12. *Fancy Nancy: The Dazzling Book Report* by Jane O'Connor, illus. by Robin Preiss Glasser. HarperCollins (379,231).

13. *PS: I Loathe You* (The Clique No. 10) by Lisi Harrison. Little, Brown/Poppy (372,790).

14. *All the Lovely Bad Ones* by Mary Downing Hahn. HMH/Sandpiper (362,585).

15. *Fancy Nancy: Pajama Day* by Jane O'Connor, illus. by Robin Preiss Glasser. HarperCollins (355,692).

16. *City of Ashes* (The Mortal Instruments) by Cassandra Clare. S&S/McElderry.

17. *Three Cups of Tea* (young readers' edition) by Greg Mortenson. Puffin (324,004).

200,000+

18. *Fancy Nancy: Halloween. . . or Bust!* by Jane O'Connor, illus. by Robin Preiss Glasser. HarperFestival (246,565).

19. *Boys R Us* (The Clique No. 11) by Lisi Harrison. Little, Brown/Poppy (246,277).
20. *Lock and Key* by Sarah Dessen. Penguin/Speak (244,952).
21. **Thirst No. 1: The Last Vampire, Black Blood, Red Dice* by Christopher Pike. Simon Pulse.
22. *Transformers: Revenge of the Fallen: I Am Optimus Prime* by Jennifer Frantz, illus. by Guido Guidi. HarperCollins (240,903).
23. *The Absolutely True Diary of a Part-Time Indian* by Sherman Alexie. Little, Brown (238,034).
24. *Finding Nemo: Fish School.* Random/Disney (233,760).
25. *Disney Fairies: A Game of Hide-and-Seek.* Random/Disney (218,571).
26. *Hannah Montana The Movie: The Junior Novel.* Disney Press (216,173).
27. *Monday with a Mad Genius* (MTH No. 28) by Mary Pope Osborne, illus. by Sal Murdocca. Random (204,828).
28. *The Princess and the Frog: Kiss the Frog.* Random/Disney (200,139).

150,000+

29. *Fancy Nancy: The Show Must Go On* by Jane O'Connor, illus. by Robin Preiss Glasser. HarperCollins (193,398).
30. *Star Wars: Yoda in Action* by Heather Scott. DK (190,010).
31. *The Lemonade War* by Jacqueline Davies. HMH/Sandpiper (188,919).
32. **Dark Visions: The Strange Power, the Possessed, the Passion* by L. J. Smith. Simon Pulse
33. *The Princess and the Frog: Hoppily Ever After.* Random/Disney (185,835).
34. *Junie B., First Grader: Dumb Bunny* by Barbara Park, illus. by Denise Brunkus. Random (176,530).
35. *The Summoning* by Kelley Armstrong. HarperCollins (169,797).
36. *Dark Day in the Deep Sea* (MTH No. 39) by Mary Pope Osborne, illus. by Sal Murdocca. Random (167,269).
37. *Vampire Kisses: The Beginning* by Ellen Schreiber. HarperCollins/Tegen, (165,736).
38. *The Wednesday Wars* by Gary D. Schmidt. HMH/Sandpiper (164,583).
39. *Meet Rebecca* by Jacqueline Dembar Greene, illus. by Robert Hunt. American Girl (160,232).
40. *Alphas* by Lisi Harrison. Little, Brown/Poppy (160,122).
41. *Junie B., First Grader: Jingle Bells, Batman Smells! (P.S. So Does May)* by Barbara Park, illus. by Denise Brunkus. Random (159,905).
42. *The Mysterious Benedict Society and the Perilous Journey* by Trenton Lee Stewart. Little, Brown (159,759).
43. *Bakugan: Collector's Sticker Book.* Scholastic Licensed Publishing (159,742).
44. *Revelations* (Blue Bloods) by Melissa de la Cruz. Disney-Hyperion (157,891).

45. *Disney Princesses: Dancing Cinderella/Belle of the Ball.* Random/Disney (153,730).

100,000+

46. *The Vampire Diaries: The Awakening* by L. J. Smith. HarperTeen (146,842).
47. *Fancy Nancy: Heart to Heart* by Jane O'Connor, illus. by Robin Preiss Glasser. HarperFestival (146,644).
48. *Thomas and the Jet Engine* by Schuyler Hooke. Golden (146,137).
49. *Barbie and the Three Musketeers* by Mary Man-Kong. Random (139,834).
50. *Hannah Montana: The Movie: Country Girl.* Disney Press (138,503).
51. *Evernight* by Claudia Gray. HarperTeen (136,347).
52. *Toy Story 2: Friends Forever* by Melissa Lagonegro. Random/Disney (135,379).
53. **Happiness to Go!* (SpongeBob Squarepants). Simon Spotlight.
54. *Max* (Maximum Ride) by James Patterson. Little, Brown (132,622).
55. *National Geographic Kids Almanac 2010.* National Geographic (132,361).
56. *Disney Fairies: Tink's Treasure Hunt.* Random/Disney (127,578).
57. *Transformers: Revenge of the Fallen: Rise of the Decepticons* by Jennifer Frantz, illus. by Marcelo Matere. HarperCollins (124,367).
58. *Cars: A Day at the Races/Night Vision.* Random/Disney (122,929).
59. **Wicked: Resurrection* by Nancy Holder and Debbie Viguié. Simon Pulse.
60. *Transformers: Revenge of the Fallen: Operation Autobot* by Susan Korman. HarperFestival (122,162).
61. **Ni Hao, Kai-lan: Meet Kai-lan!* Adapted by Micki Matheis, illus. by Jason Frutcher and Aka Chikasawa. Simon Spotlight.
62. *Toy Story: Meet the Toys!* Golden/Disney (120,957).
63. *Barbie and the Three Musketeers.* Golden (120,527).
64. **Wonder Pets! You Can Fly, Bumblebee!* Simon Spotlight.
65. *L.A. Candy* by Lauren Conrad. HarperCollins (118,336).
66. *Up! Bird's Best Friend.* Random/Disney (117,062).
67. *Monsters vs. Aliens: Team Monster* by Gail Herman. HarperCollins (114,991).
68. **Glass* by Ellen Hopkins. S&S/McElderry.
69. **Dora Saves Crystal Kingdom.* Adapted by Molly Reisner, illus. by Dave Aikins. Simon Spotlight.
70. *Impossible* by Nancy Werlin. Penguin/Speak (112,418).
71. *A Cars Christmas* by Melissa Lagonegro. Random/Disney (112,139).
72. *The Garden of Eve* by K. L. Going. HMH/Sandpiper (111,662).
73. *The Princess and the Frog Junior Novelization.* Random/Disney (111,454).
74. *Transformers: Revenge of the Fallen: When Robots Attack!* by Ray Santos. HarperFestival (111,079).

75. *Marley's Big Adventure* by John Grogan, illus. by Richard Cowdrey. HarperCollins (109,323).

76. *Ink Exchange* by Melissa Marr. HarperCollins (109,179).

77. *Dirt on My Shirt: Selected Poems* by Jeff Foxworthy, illus. by Steve Björkman. HarperCollins (107,790).

78. *Ninth Grade Slays* (The Chronicles of Vladimir Tod No. 2) by Heather Brewer. Penguin/Speak (107,794).

79. *Hannah Montana: The Movie: Secret Crush.* Disney Press (107,453).

80. *Monsters vs. Aliens: The Junior Novel* by Susan Korman. HarperFestival (107,076).

81. *The Vampire Diaries: The Struggle* by L. J. Smith. HarperTeen (106,758).

82. *Barbie: Thumbelina* by Diane Wright Landolf. Random (106,283).

83. *Disney Fairies: Rosetta's Daring Day* by Lisa Papademetriou. Random/ Disney (105,409).

84. *The Twilight Companion: Completely Updated: The Unauthorized Guide to the Series* by Lois H. Gresh. St. Martin's Griffin (105,000).

85. *Barbie: Thumbelina* by Mary Man-Kong. Golden (104,992).

86. *Transformers: Revenge of the Fallen: The Junior Novel* by Dan Jolley. HarperFestival (104,400).

87. *The Quest Begins* (Seekers No. 1) by Erin Hunter. HarperCollins (104,059).

88. *Christmas in Camelot* (MTH No. 29) by Mary Pope Osborne, illus. by Sal Murdocca. Random (103,805).

89. **Grip of the Shadow Plague* (Fablehaven No. 3) by Brandon Mull. S&S/ Aladdin.

90. *Bear Hugs* by Alyssa Satin Capucilli, illus. by Jim Ishi. Golden (102,750).

91. *Super Friends: Going Bananas* by Ben Harper. Random (101,232).

92. *Eve of the Emperor Penguin* (MTH No. 40) by Mary Pope Osborne, illus. by Sal Murdocca. Random (101,094).

93. *Rumors: A Luxe Novel* by Anna Godbersen. HarperCollins (100,808).

94. **The Missing: Found* by Margaret Peterson Haddix. Simon & Schuster.

95. *Outcast* (Warriors: Power of Three No. 3) by Erin Hunter. HarperCollins (100,457).

96. *Stink and the Great Guinea Pig Express* by Megan McDonald, illus. by Peter H. Reynolds. Candlewick (100,267).

Children's Paperback Backlist

300,000+

1. *New Moon* by Stephenie Meyer. Little, Brown/Tingley, 2008 (4,516,304).

2. *Twilight* by Stephenie Meyer. Little, Brown/Tingley, 2006 (3,266,186).

3. *The Lightning Thief* (Percy Jackson and the Olympians No. 1) by Rick Riordan. Disney-Hyperion, 2006 (1,395,152).

4. *Twilight* (mass market media tie-in) by Stephenie Meyer. Little, Brown/ Tingley, 2008 (1,252,937).

5. *Where the Wild Things Are* by Maurice Sendak. HarperCollins, 1988 (1,168,006).

6. *Marked* (House of Night No. 1) by PC and Kristin Cast. St. Martin's Griffin, 2007 (955,601).

7. *Twilight* (media tie-in) by Stephenie Meyer. Little, Brown/Tingley, 2008 (926,741).

8. *Betrayed* (House of Night No. 2) by PC and Kristin Cast. St. Martin's Griffin, 2007 (800,190).

9. *Chosen* (House of Night No. 3) by PC and Kristin Cast. St. Martin's Griffin, 2008 (750,752).

10. *The Sea of Monsters* (Percy Jackson and the Olympians No. 2) by Rick Riordan. Disney-Hyperion, 2007 (685,656).

11. *Untamed* (House of Night No. 4) by PC and Kristin Cast. St. Martin's Griffin, 2008 (682,870).

12. *The Titan's Curse* (Percy Jackson and the Olympians No. 3) by Rick Riordan. Disney-Hyperion, 2008 (614,237).

13. *The Vampire Diaries: The Awakening and the Struggle* by L. J. Smith. HarperTeen, 2007 (582,978).

14. *Night World No. 1: Secret Vampire, Daughters of Darkness, Spellbinder* by L. J. Smith. Simon Pulse, 2008.

15. *The Giver* by Lois Lowry. Random (various imprints), 1999 (481,877).

16. *Harry Potter and the Half-Blood Prince* by J. K. Rowling, illus. by Mary Grandpré. Scholastic/Levine, 2006 (479,387).

17. *The Vampire Diaries: The Fury and the Dark Reunion* by L. J. Smith. HarperTeen, 2007 (465,437).

18. *City of Bones* (The Mortal Instruments) by Cassandra Clare. S&S/McElderry, 2008.

19. *The Book Thief* by Markus Zusak. Knopf, 2007 (435,587).

20. *Cloudy with a Chance of Meatballs* by Judy Barrett, illus. by Rob Barrett. S&S/Atheneum, 1982.

21. *Harry Potter and the Sorcerer's Stone* by J. K. Rowling, illus. by Mary Grandpré. Scholastic/Levine, 1999 (407,000).

22. *Love You Forever* by Robert Munsch, illus. by Sheila McGraw. Firefly, 1986 (392,514).

23. *Night World No. 2: Dark Angel, the Chosen, Soulmate* by L. J. Smith. Simon Pulse, 2008.

24. *Fancy Nancy Sees Stars* by Jane O'Connor, illus. by Robin Preiss Glasser. HarperCollins, 2008 (360,396).

25. *Dinosaurs Before Dark* (MTH No. 1) by Mary Pope Osborne, illus. by Sal Murdocca. Random, 1992 (348,786).

26. *Twilight: The Complete Illustrated Movie Companion* by Mark Cotta Vaz. Little, Brown, 2008 (348,102).

27. *The Boy in the Striped Pajamas* by John Boyne. Random/Fickling, 2007 (330,571).

28. *Harry Potter and the Chamber of Secrets* by J. K. Rowling, illus. by Mary Grandpré. Scholastic/Levine, 2000 (325,962).

29. *Harry Potter and the Order of the Phoenix* by J. K. Rowling, illus. by Mary Grandpré. Scholastic/Levine, 2004 (324,957).

30. *Harry Potter and the Prisoner of Azkaban* by J. K. Rowling, illus. by Mary Grandpré. Scholastic/Levine, 2001 (310,136).

31. *The Mysterious Benedict Society* by Trenton Lee Stewart. Little, Brown, 2008 (305,942).

32. *Vampire Academy* by Richelle Mead. Razorbill, 2007 (304,827).

200,000+

33. *Harry Potter and the Goblet of Fire* by J. K. Rowling, illus. by Mary Grandpré. Scholastic/Levine, 2002 (296,912).

34. *Cars: Race Team.* Random/Disney, 2008 (289,218).

35. *The Cat in the Hat: Cooking with the Cat* by Bonnie Worth, illus. by Christopher Moroney. Random, 2003 (276,215).

36. **Kissed by an Angel; The Power of Love; Soulmates* by Elizabeth Chandler. Simon Pulse, 2008.

37. *The Care & Keeping of You: The Body Book for Girls* by Valorie Schaefer, illus. by Norm Bendel. American Girl, 1998 (266,140).

38. *Frostbite* (Vampire Academy No. 2) by Richelle Mead. Razorbill, 2008 (260,257).

39. *Holes* by Louis Sachar. Random (various editions), 2000 (255,424).

40. *Mummies in the Morning* (MTH No. 3) by Mary Pope Osborne, illus. by Sal Murdocca. Random, 1993 (251,633).

41. *The Outsiders* by S. E. Hinton. Penguin/Speak, 1997 (250,920).

42. *The Knight at Dawn* (MTH No. 2) by Mary Pope Osborne, illus. by Sal Murdocca. Random, 1993 (250,292).

43. *Coraline* by Neil Gaiman, illus. by Dave McKean. HarperFestival, 2008 (240,138).

44. *Blue Bloods* by Melissa de la Cruz. Disney-Hyperion, 2007 (235,967).

45. *Biscuit* by Alyssa Satin Capucilli, illus. by Pat Schories. HarperCollins, 1997 (232,817).

46. *Shadow Kiss* (Vampire Academy No. 3) by Richelle Mead. Razorbill, 2008 (231,228).

47. *Disney Princesses: What Is a Princess?* Random/Disney, 2004 (230,944).

48. *Fancy Nancy: Poison Ivy Expert* by Jane O'Connor, illus. by Robin Preiss Glasser. HarperCollins, 2008 (230,479).

49. *A Wrinkle in Time* by Madeleine L'Engle. Macmillan/Square Fish, 2007 (229,500).

50. *Just Go to Bed* by Mercer Mayer. Random, 2001 (223,506).

51. *Pirates Past Noon* (MTH No. 4) by Mary Pope Osborne, illus. by Sal Murdocca. Random, 1994 (221,698).

52. *Fancy Nancy at the Museum* by Jane O'Connor, illus. by Robin Preiss Glasser. HarperCollins, 2008 (220,845).

53. *Amelia Bedelia* by Peggy Parish, illus. by Fritz Siebel. HarperCollins, 1992 (217,107).

54. *Inkheart* by Cornelia Funke. Scholastic/Chicken House, 2005 (216,838).

55. *Dinosaur Days* by Joyce Milton. Random, 1985 (214,485).

56. *Number the Stars* by Lois Lowry. Random (various editions), 1990 (214,167).

57. *Junie B. Jones and the Stupid Smelly Bus* (Junie B. Jones No. 1) by Barbara Park, illus. by Denise Brunkus. Random, 1992 (213,113).

58. *The Tale of Despereaux* by Kate DiCamillo, illus. by Timothy Basil Ering. Candlewick, 2006 (207,789).

150,000+

59. *Star Wars: Jabba the Hut* by Simon Beecroft. DK, 2008 (195,328).

60. *Little Engines Can Do Big Things.* Random House, illus. by Ted Gadecki. Random, 2000 (191,390).

61. *Star Wars: Anakin in Action* by Simon Beecroft. DK, 2008 (190,429).

62. *Fancy Nancy and the Boy from Paris* by Jane O'Connor, illus. by Robin Preiss Glasser. HarperCollins, 2008 (183,105).

63. *Masquerade* (Blue Bloods) by Melissa de la Cruz. Disney-Hyperion, 2008 (182,565).

64. **Hatchet* by Gary Paulsen. Simon & Schuster, 2006.

65. *Super Friends: Flying High.* Random, 2008 (176,203).

66. **Dora Saves the Snow Princess* by Phoebe Beinstein, illus. by Dave Aikins. Simon Spotlight, 2008.

67. *Maniac Magee* by Jerry Spinelli. Little, Brown, 1999 (172,741).

68. *Danny and the Dinosaur* (50th anniversary edition) by Syd Hoff. HarperCollins, 1978 (168,956).

69. **Dora: It's Sharing Day!* by Kirsten Larsen, illus. by Ron Zalme. Simon Spotlight, 2007.

70. *Night of the Ninjas* (MTH No. 5) by Mary Pope Osborne, illus. by Sal Murdocca. Random, 1995 (166,031).

71. *Barbie Loves Pets.* Illus. by Jiyoung An. Golden, 2007 (165,676).

72. *Because of Winn-Dixie* by Kate DiCamillo. Candlewick, 2006 (165,434).

73. *Into the Wild* (Warriors No. 1) by Erin Hunter. HarperCollins, 2003 (165,271).

74. *Junie B. Jones and Her Big Fat Mouth* (JBJ No. 3) by Barbara Park, illus. by Denise Brunkus. Random, 1993 (164,827).

75. *Frog and Toad Are Friends* by Arnold Lobel. HarperCollins, 1979 (164,401).

76. *The Berenstain Bears Forget Their Manners* by Stan and Jan Berenstain. Random, 1985 (163,029).

77. *Flat Stanley: His Original Adventure!* by Jeff Brown, illus. by Macky Pamintuan. HarperCollins, 2003 (162,805).

78. *Bakugan Handbook.* Scholastic Licensed Publishing, 2008 (162,021).

79. *Speak* by Laurie Halse Anderson. Penguin/Speak, 2006 (158,802).

80. *Junie B. Jones and Some Sneaky Peeky Spying* (JBJ No. 4) by Barbara Park, illus. by Denise Brunkus. Random, 1994 (158,213).

81. **Crank* by Ellen Hopkins. S&S/McElderry, 2004.

82. *Judy Moody* by Megan McDonald, illus by Peter H. Reynolds. Candlewick, 2002 (155,967).

83. **Go Ask Alice.* Anonymous. Simon Pulse, 2006.

84. *Disney Princesses: A Horse to Love.* Random/Disney, 2007 (153,421).

85. *Junie B. Jones and a Little Monkey Business* (JBJ No. 2) by Barbara Park, illus. by Denise Brunkus. Random, 1993 (153,087).

86. *Ramona Quimby, Age 8* by Beverly Cleary, illus. by Tracy Dockray. HarperCollins, 1992 (151,259).

87. *Just Listen* by Sarah Dessen. Penguin/Speak, 2008 (151,021).

100,000+

88. *Island of the Blue Dolphins* by Scott O'Dell. Random (various editions), 1987 (148,568).

89. *Tales of a Fourth Grade Nothing* by Judy Blume. Puffin, 2007 (148,079).

90. *Curious George and the Pancakes* by H. A. Rey. HMH/Sandpiper, 1998 (146,664).

91. *The Miraculous Journey of Edward Tulane* by Kate DiCamillo, illus. by Bagram Ibatoulline. Candlewick, 2002 (146,097).

92. *Where the Red Fern Grows* by Wilson Rawls. Random (various editions), 1996 (143,937).

93. *Goodnight Moon* (60th anniversary edition) by Margaret Wise Brown, illus. by Clement Hurd. HarperCollins, 1977 (143,770).

94. *Afternoon on the Amazon* (MTH No. 6) by Mary Pope Osborne, illus. by Sal Murdocca. Random, 1995 (143,714).

95. *Biscuit's Day at the Farm* by Alyssa Satin Capucilli, illus. by Pat Schories. HarperCollins, 2007 (143,560).

96. *The Angel Experiment* (Maximum Ride) by James Patterson. Little, Brown, 2007 (142,740).

97. *Dolphins at Daybreak* (MTH No. 9) by Mary Pope Osborne, illus. by Sal Murdocca. Random, 1993 (142,170).

98. *Junie B., First Grader: Toothless Wonder* (JBJ No. 20) by Barbara Park, illus. by Denise Brunkus. Random, 2003 (141,935).

99. *Transformers: Meet the Autobots* by Jennifer Frantz, illus. by Guido Guidi. HarperCollins, 2007 (140,357).

100. *The Fat Cat Sat on the Mat* by Nurit Karlin. HarperCollins, 1998 (140,278).

101. *The Berenstain Bears Learn About Strangers* by Stan and Jan Berenstain. Random, 1985 (140,028).

102. *Hoot* by Carl Hiaasen. Random (various editions), 2005 (140,002).

103. *The Lion, the Witch and the Wardrobe* by C. S. Lewis, illus. by Pauline Baynes. HarperCollins, 2002 (138,982).

104. *Grandma, Grandpa, and Me* (Little Critter) by Mercer Mayer. HarperFestival, 2007 (135,722).

105. *Midnight on the Moon* (MTH No. 8) by Mary Pope Osborne, illus. by Sal Murdocca. Random, 1996 (135,697).

106. **Uglies* by Scott Westerfeld. Simon Pulse, 2005.

107. *Bud, Not Buddy* by Christopher Paul Curtis. Random (various editions), 2002 (135,575).

108. *Monster* by Walter Dean Myers. HarperCollins/Amistad, 2001 (135,570).

109. *I'd Tell You I Love You, but Then I'd Have to Kill You* by Ally Carter. Disney-Hyperion, 2007 (134,736).

110. *The Adventures of Captain Underpants* by Dav Pilkey. Scholastic, 1997 (133,873).

111. **Behold, No Cavities!* (SpongeBob Squarepants) by Sarah Willson, illus. by Harry Moore. Simon Spotlight, 2007.

112. *Dragon of the Red Dawn* (MTH No. 37) by Mary Pope Osborne, illus. by Sal Murdocca. Random, 2008 (130,689).

113. *Junie B. Jones Is a Party Animal* (JBJ No. 10) by Barbara Park, illus. by Denise Brunkus. Random, 1997 (130,441).

114. **Frindle* by Andrew Clements, illus. by Brian Selznick. S&S/Atheneum, 1998.

115. *Ghost Town at Sundown* (MTH No. 10) by Mary Pope Osborne, illus by Sal Murdocca. Random, 1997 (129,440).

116. *Tuck Everlasting* by Natalie Babbitt. Macmillan/Square Fish, 2007 (126,300).

117. *The City of Ember* by Jeanne Du Prau. Random/Yearling, 2004 (126,121).

118. *I Spy a Dinosaur's Eye* by Jean Marzollo, illus. by Walter Wick. Scholastic/Cartwheel, 2003 (125,932).

119. *Curious George and the Puppies* by H. A. Rey. HMH/Sandpiper, 1998 (125,417).

120. *Junie B. Jones Has a Monster Under Her Bed* (JBJ No. 8) by Barbara Park, illus. by Denise Brunkus. Random, 1997 (125,075).

121. *Charlotte's Web* by E. B. White, illus. by Garth Williams. HarperCollins, 1974 (124,984).

122. *Bolt: My Hero.* Random/Disney, 2008 (124,456).

123. *The Mouse and the Motorcycle* by Beverly Cleary, illus. by Tracy Dockray. HarperCollins, 1990 (124,113).

124. *Junie B., First Grader: Aloha-ha-ha!* (JBJ No. 26) by Barbara Park, illus. by Denise Brunkus. Random, 2007 (123,684).

125. *Captain Underpants and the Perilous Plot of Professor Poopypants* by Dav Pilkey. Scholastic, 2000 (122,900).

126. *The Watsons Go to Birmingham—1963* by Christopher Paul Curtis. Random (various editions), 1997 (122,682).

127. **Wicked: Witch & Curse* by Nancy Holder and Debbie Viguié. Simon Pulse, 2008.

128. *The Secret Circle: The Initiation and the Captive, Part 1* by L. J. Smith. HarperTeen, 2008 (121,739).

129. *Stink* by Megan McDonald, illus. by Peter H. Reynolds. Candlewick, 2006 (120,553).

130. *Eragon* (The Inheritance Cycle) by Christopher Paolini. Random (various editions), 2006 (119,353).

131. *Frog and Toad Together* by Arnold Lobel. HarperCollins, 1979 (118,850).

132. *The Berenstain Bears Get the Gimmies* by Stan and Jan Berenstain. Random, 1988 (118,797).

133. *The Truth About Forever* by Sarah Dessen. Penguin/Speak, 2006 (118,258).

134. *Disney Fairies: The Fairy Berry Bake-Off.* Random/Disney, 2008 (117,686).

135. *Tonight on the Titanic* (MTH No. 17) by Mary Pope Osborne, illus. by Sal Murdocca. Random, 1999 (116,127).

136. *Judy Moody Gets Famous* by Megan McDonald, illus. by Peter H. Reynolds. Candlewick, 2003 (116,002).

137. *Eldest* (The Inheritance Cycle) by Christopher Paolini. Random (various editions), 2007 (115,519).

138. *Eighth Grade Bites* (The Chronicles of Vladimir Tod No. 1) by Heather Brewer. Penguin/Speak, 2008 (115,317).

139. *Captain Underpants and the Wrath of the Wicked Wedgie Woman* by Dav Pilkey. Scholastic, 2001 (114,620).

140. *Freak the Mighty* by Rodman Philbrick. Scholastic, 2001 (114,466).

141. *Junie B. Jones Is a Beauty Shop Guy* (JBJ No. 11) by Barbara Park, illus. by Denise Brunkus. Random, 1998 (114,336).

142. *Polar Bears Past Bedtime* (MTH No. 12) by Mary Pope Osborne, illus. by Sal Murdocca. Random, 1999 (113,879).

143. *Transformers Animated: Robot Roll Call* by Jennifer Frantz. HarperCollins, 2008 (113,622).

144. **Fablehaven* by Brandon Mull. S&S/Aladdin, 2007.

145. *Schooled* by Gordon Korman. Disney-Hyperion, 2008 (113,015).

146. *Cars: Roadwork.* Illus. by Art Mawhinney. Random/Disney, 2008 (112,776).

147. *The Cricket in Times Square* by George Selden, illus. by Garth Williams. Macmillan/Square Fish, 2008 (112,500).

148. *Sunset of the Sabertooth* (MTH No. 7) by Mary Pope Osborne, illus by Sal Murdocca. Random, 1996 (111,537).

149. *Frog and Toad All Year* by Arnold Lobel. HarperCollins, 1984 (111,046).

150. *Alexander and the Terrible, Horrible, No Good, Very Bad Day* by Judith Viorst, illus. by Ray Cruz. S&S/Atheneum, 1987.

151. *Fire and Ice* (Warriors No. 2) by Erin Hunter. HarperCollins, 2004 (110,708).

152. *Seedfolks* by Paul Fleischman, illus. by Judy Pedersen. HarperTeen, 1999 (110,534).

153. *Captain Underpants and the Invasion of the Incredibly Naughty Cafeteria Ladies from Outer Space* by Dav Pilkey. Scholastic, 1999 (110,042).

154. *Ivy and Bean* by Annie Barrows, illus. by Sophie Blackall. Chronicle, 2006 (108,987).

155. *The Boxcar Children Mysteries No. 1* by Gertrude Chandler Warner. Albert Whitman, 1942 (108,784).

156. *The Tail of Emily Windsnap* by Liz Kessler, illus. by Sarah Gibb. Candlewick, 2006 (108,549).

157. *Esperanza Rising* by Pam Muñoz Ryan. Scholastic, 2002 (107,881).

158. *Stargirl* by Jerry Spinelli. Random (various editions), 2002 (107,365).

159. *Junie B. Jones and That Meanie Jim's Birthday* (JBJ No. 6) by Barbara Park, illus. by Denise Brunkus. Random, 1996 (107,344).

160. *Marley & Me: Meet Marley* by Natalie Engel. HarperCollins, 2008 (106,932).

161. *Burned* by Ellen Hopkins. S&S/McElderry, 2007.

162. *The Luxe* by Anna Godbersen. HarperCollins, 2008 (106,579).

163. *The Alchemyst* (The Secrets of the Immortal Nicholas Flamel) by Michael Scott. Delacorte, 2008 (106,329).

164. *Captain Underpants and the Attack of the Talking Toilets* by Dav Pilkey. Scholastic, 1999 (106,319).

165. *The Magician* (The Secrets of the Immortal Nicholas Flamel) by Michael Scott. Delacorte, 2009 (106,126).

166. *Wake* by Lisa McMann. Simon Pulse, 2008.

167. *Wicked Lovely* by Melissa Marr. HarperCollins, 2008 (105,973).

168. *Junie B. Jones and the Yucky Blucky Fruitcake* (JBJ No. 5) by Barbara Park, illus. by Denise Brunkus. Random, 1995 (105,236).

169. *Impulse* by Ellen Hopkins. S&S/McElderry, 2008.

170. *Chicka Chicka Boom Boom* by Bill Martin, Jr. and John Archambault, illus. by Lois Ehlert. S&S/Beach Lane, 2000.

171. *Where's Waldo?* by Martin Handford. Candlewick, 2007 (104,563).

172. *Junie B. Jones Loves Handsome Warren* (JBJ No. 7) by Barbara Park, illus. by Denise Brunkus. Random, 1996 (103,800).

173. *Junie B. Jones Is Not a Crook* (JBJ No. 9) by Barbara Park, illus. by Denise Brunkus. Random, 1997 (103,541).

174. *Just Me and My Dad* by Mercer Mayer. Random, 2001 (103,455).

175. *Tangerine* by Edward Bloor. HMH/Sandpiper, 2006 (103,247).

176. *The Final Warning* (Maximum Ride) by James Patterson. Little, Brown, 2008 (103,107).

177. *Fever 1793* by Laurie Halse Anderson. Simon & Schuster, 2002.

178. *The Ruins of Gorlan* (Ranger's Apprentice No. 1) by John Flanagan. Puffin, 2006 (102,660).

179. *Junie B., First Grader (at last!)* (JBJ No. 18) by Barbara Park, illus. by Denise Brunkus. Random, 2002 (102,646).

180. *Harold and the Purple Crayon* (50th anniversary edition) by Crockett Johnson. HarperCollins, 1981 (102,359).

181. *I Spy a Penguin* by Jean Marzollo, illus. by Walter Wick. Scholastic/Cartwheel, 2005 (102,177).

182. *The Phantom Tollbooth* by Norton Juster, illus. by Jules Feiffer. Random/Yearling, 1988 (101,947).

183. *Milly and the Macy's Parade* by Shana Corey, illus. by Brett Helquist. Scholastic, 2006 (101,780).

184. *I Spy a School Bus* by Jean Marzollo, illus. by Walter Wick. Scholastic/Cartwheel, 2003 (101,764).

185. *School's Out Forever* (Maximum Ride) by James Patterson. Little, Brown, 2007 (101,637).

186. *Where's Waldo? The Ultimate Travel Collection* by Martin Handford. Candlewick, 2008 (101,422).

187. *Sammy the Seal* by Syd Hoff. HarperCollins, 1999 (101,336).

188. *Biscuit Goes to School* by Alyssa Satin Capucilli, illus. by Pat Schories. HarperCollins, 2003 (101,135).

189. **WonderPets! Join the Circus.* Simon Spotlight, 2008.

190. *Ramona the Pest* by Beverly Cleary, illus. by Tracy Dockray. HarperCollins, 1992 (100,717).

191. *Forest of Secrets* (Warriors No. 3) by Erin Hunter. HarperCollins, 2004 (100,214).

192. *The Secret Circle: The Captive Part II and the Power* by L. J. Smith. HarperTeen, 2008 (100,026).

Literary Prizes, 2009

Compiled by the staff of the *Library and Book Trade Almanac*

Jane Addams Children's Book Awards. For children's books that effectively promote the cause of peace, social justice, world community, and equality. *Offered by:* Women's International League for Peace and Freedom and the Jane Addams Peace Association. *Winners:* (younger children) Claire A. Nivola for *Planting the Trees of Kenya: The Story of Wangari Maathai* (Farrar, Straus & Giroux); (older children) Margarita Engle for *The Surrender Tree: Poems of Cuba's Struggle for Freedom* (Holt).

Aesop Prize. For outstanding work in children's folklore, both fiction and nonfiction. *Offered by:* American Folklore Society. *Winners:* Joe Hayes for *Dance, Nana, Dance (Baila, Nana, Baila)*, illustrated by Mauricio Trenard Sayago (Cinco Puntos); Kirsti McKinen, adapter, Pirkko-Liisa Surojegin, illustrator, and Kaarina Brooks, translator, for *The Kalevala: Tales of Magic and Adventure* (Simply Read); Nona Beamer, Caren Ke'ala Loebel-Fried, illustrator, and Kaliko Beamer-Trapp, translator, for *Naupaka* (Kamahoi).

Agatha Awards. For mystery novels written in the method exemplified by author Agatha Christie. *Offered by:* Malice Domestic Ltd. *Winners:* (novel) Louise Penny for *The Cruelest Month* (Minotaur); (first novel) G. M. Malliet for *Death of a Cozy Writer* (Midnight Ink); (children's/young adult novel) Chris Grabenstein for *The Crossroads* (Random); (nonfiction) Kathy Lynn Emerson for *How to Write Killer Historical Mysteries* (Perseverance); (short story) Dana Cameron for "The Night Things Changed" in *Wolfsbane and Mistletoe* (Penguin).

Alex Awards. To the authors of ten books published for adults that have high potential appeal to teenagers. *Sponsor:* Margaret Alexander Edwards Trust and *Booklist*. *Winners:* David Benioff for *City of Thieves* (Penguin); Michael Swanwick for *The Dragons of Babel* (Tor); Zoë Ferraris for

Finding Nouf (Houghton Mifflin); Hannah Tinti for *The Good Thief* (Dial); Stephen King for *Just After Sunset: Stories* (Simon & Schuster); Hillary Jordan for *Mudbound* (Algonquin); Todd Tucker for *Over and Under* (St. Martin's); Stephen G. Bloom and Peter Feldstein, photographer, for *The Oxford Project* (Welcome); Toby Barlow for *Sharp Teeth* (HarperCollins); Theresa Rebeck for *Three Girls and Their Brother* (Random).

Ambassador Book Awards: To honor an exceptional contribution to the interpretation of life and culture in the United States. *Offered by:* English-Speaking Union of the United States. *Winners:* (American studies) Christopher Benfey for *A Summer of Hummingbirds* (Penguin); (biography and autobiography) Donald Worster for *A Passion for Nature: The Life of John Muir* (Oxford University Press); (current affairs) Jane Mayer for *The Dark Side* (Doubleday); (fiction) Steven Millhauser for *Dangerous Laughter* (Knopf); (poetry) Alan Shapiro for *Old War* (Houghton Mifflin Harcourt); (special award) Toni Morrison.

American Academy of Arts and Letters Award of Merit ($10,000). To an American author of novels, poetry, short stories, or drama. *Offered by:* American Academy of Arts and Letters. *Winner:* novelist Denis Johnson.

American Academy of Arts and Letters Awards in Literature ($7,500). To honor writers of fiction and nonfiction, poets, dramatists, and translators of exceptional accomplishment. *Offered by:* American Academy of Arts and Letters. *Winners:* Rilla Askew; Michael Collier; Ron Currie, Jr.; Tracy Letts; D. Nurkse; Marie Ponsot; George Saunders; Susan Stewart.

American Academy of Arts and Letters Rome Fellowships. For a one-year residency at the American Academy in Rome for young writers of promise. *Offered by:*

American Academy of Arts and Letters. *Winners:* Peter Campion, Eliza Griswold.

American Book Awards. For literary achievement by people of various ethnic backgrounds. *Offered by:* Before Columbus Foundation. *Winners:* Houston A. Baker, Jr., for *Betrayal: How Black Intellectuals Have Abandoned the Ideals of the Civil Rights Era* (Columbia University Press); Danit Brown for *Ask for a Convertible* (Pantheon); Jericho Brown for *Please* (New Issues Poetry & Prose); José Antonio Burciaga for *The Last Supper of Chicano Heroes: Selected Works of José Antonio Burciaga,* Mimi R. Gladstein and Daniel Chacón, editors (University of Arizona Press); Claire Hope Cummings for *Uncertain Peril: Genetic Engineering and the Future of Seeds* (Beacon); Stella Pope Duarte for *If I Die in Juarez* (University of Arizona Press); Linda Gregg for *All of It Singing: New and Selected Poems* (Graywolf); Suheir Hammad for *Breaking Poems* (Cypher); Richard Holmes for *The Age of Wonder* (Pantheon); George E. Lewis for *A Power Stronger than Itself: The A.A.C.M. and American Experimental Music* (University of Chicago Press); Patricia Santana for *Ghosts of El Grullo* (University of New Mexico Press); Jack Spicer for *My Vocabulary Did This to Me: The Collected Poetry of Jack Spicer,* edited by Peter Gizzi and Kevin Killian (Wesleyan University Press); (lifetime achievement award) Miguel Algarin.

American Poetry Review/Honickman First Book Prize in Poetry ($3,000). To encourage excellence in poetry and to provide a wide readership for a deserving first book of poems. *Winner:* Laura McKee for *Uttermost Paradise Place* (American Poetry Review).

Américas Book Award for Children's and Young Adult Literature. To recognize U.S. works of fiction, poetry, folklore, or selected nonfiction that authentically and engagingly portray Latin America, the Caribbean, or Latinos in the United States. *Sponsored by:* Consortium of Latin American Studies Programs (CLASP). *Winners:* Yuyi Morales for *Just in Case: A Trickster Tale and Spanish Alphabet Book* (Roaring Brook); Margarita Engle for *The Surrender Tree: Poems of Cuba's Struggle for Freedom* (Holt).

Rudolfo and Patricia Anaya Premio Aztlan Literary Prize ($1,000). To honor a Chicano or Chicana fiction writer who has published no more than two books. *Offered by:* University of New Mexico. *Winner:* Patricia Santana for *Ghosts of El Grullo* (University of New Mexico Press).

Hans Christian Andersen Awards. Awarded biennially to an author and an illustrator whose body of work has made an important and lasting contribution to children's literature. *Offered by:* International Board on Books for Young People (IBBY). *Sponsor:* Nami Island, Inc. *Winners:* To be awarded next in 2010.

Anthony Awards. For superior mystery writing. *Offered by:* Boucheron World Mystery Convention. *Winners:* (novel) Michael Connelly for *The Brass Verdict* (Little, Brown); (first novel) Stieg Larsson for *The Girl With the Dragon Tattoo* (Knopf); (paperback original) Julie Hyzy for *State of the Onion* (Berkley); (short story) Sean Chercover for "A Sleep Not Unlike Death" in *Hardcore Hardboiled* (Kensington); (critical nonfiction work) Jeffrey Marks for *Anthony Boucher: A Biobibliography* (McFarland); (children's/young adult novel) Chris Grabenstein for *The Crossroads* (Random); (cover art) Peter Mendelsund for *The Girl With the Dragon Tattoo* by Stieg Larsson (Knopf).

Asian American Literary Awards. To Asian American writers for excellence in poetry, fiction, and creative nonfiction. *Sponsor:* Asian American Writers' Workshop. *Winners:* (poetry) Sesshu Foster for *World Ball Notebook* (City Lights); (fiction) Jhumpa Lahiri for *Unaccustomed Earth* (Knopf); (creative nonfiction) Leslie T. Chang for *Factory Girls: From Village to City in a Changing China* (Spiegel & Grau).

Asian American Writers' Workshop's Lifetime Achievement Award. *Winner:* Ajai Singh "Sonny" Mehta.

Asian/Pacific American Awards for Literature. For books that promote Asian/Pacific American culture and heritage. *Sponsor:*

Asian/Pacific American Librarians Association (APALA). *Winners:* (adult fiction) Jhumpa Lahiri for *Unaccustomed Earth* (Knopf); (adult nonfiction) Jennifer 8. Lee for *Fortune Cookie Chronicles: Adventures in the World of Chinese Food* (Twelve); (picture book) Mark Reibstein for *Wabi Sabi,* illustrated by Ed Young (Little, Brown); (youth literature) Many Ly for *Roots and Wings* (Delacorte).

Audio Publishers Association awards (Audies). To recognize excellence in audiobooks. *Winners:* (audiobook of the year) *The Graveyard Book* by Neil Gaiman, read by the author (HarperChildren's); (distinguished achievement in production) *Curse of the Blue Tattoo: Being an Account of the Misadventures of Jacky Faber, Midshipman and Fine Lady* by L. A. Meyer, read by Katherine Kellgren (Listen & Live); (audiobook adaptation) *English Majors: A Comedy Collection for the Highly Literate* by Garrison Keillor, read by the author and cast (HighBridge Audio); (audio drama) *The Odyssey* by Homer, read by Tim McInnerny, Amanda Redman, and cast (BBC Audiobooks America); (biography/memoir) *The Last Lecture* by Randy Pausch with Jeffrey Zaslow, read by Erik Singer (Hyperion); (business/educational) *The Little Red Book of Selling* by Jeffrey Gitomer, read by the author (Simon & Schuster); (children's titles for ages up to 8) *James Herriot's Treasury for Children* by James Herriot, read by Jim Dale (Macmillan); (children's titles for ages 8–12) *The Graveyard Book* by Neil Gaiman, read by the author (HarperChildren's); (classic) *Great Expectations* by Charles Dickens, read by Simon Vance (Tantor); (fiction—tie) *The Duma Key* by Stephen King, read by John Slattery (Simon & Schuster), *The Guernsey Literary and Potato Peel Pie Society* by Mary Ann Shaffer and Annie Barrows, read by Paul Boehmer, Susan Duerden, Rosalyn Landor, John Lee, and Juliet Mills (Books on Tape); (history) *Gandhi and Churchill* by Arthur Herman, read by John Curless (Recorded Books); (humor) *The Learners* by Chip Kidd, read by Bronson Pinchot (Blackstone); (inspirational/faith-based fiction) *Prague Counterpoint* by Bodie and Brock Thoene, read by Sean Barrett (FamilyAudioLibrary.com); (inspirational/faith-based nonfiction) *The Word of Promise Next Generation: New Testament* audio Bible, read by Sean Astin and cast (Thomas Nelson); (literary fiction) *Elmer Gantry* by Sinclair Lewis, read by Anthony Heald (Blackstone); (multi-voiced performance) *Mudbound* by Hillary Jordan, read by Joey Collins, Peter Jay Fernandez, Kate Forbes, Ezra Knight, Brenda Pressley, and Tom Stechschulte (Recorded Books); (mystery) *Voice of the Violin* by Andrea Camilleri, read by Grover Gardner (Blackstone); (narration by the author or authors) *When You Are Engulfed in Flames* by David Sedaris (Hachette); (nonfiction) *Hot, Flat, and Crowded* by Thomas Friedman, read by Oliver Wyman (Macmillan); (original work) *Louis Vuitton Soundwalk: Beijing* by Stephan Crasneanscki, read by Gong Li (Louis Vuitton/Soundwalk); (politics—judges' award) *Hot, Flat, and Crowded* by Thomas Friedman, read by Oliver Wyman (Macmillan); (romance) *The Dark Highlander* by Karen Marie Moning, read by Phil Gigante (Brilliance); (science fiction/fantasy) *Calculating God* by Robert J. Sawyer, read by Jonathan Davis (Audible); (short stories/collections) *Armageddon in Retrospect* by Kurt Vonnegut, read by Rip Torn and Mark Vonnegut (Penguin); (solo narration, female) Katherine Kellgren for *Curse of the Blue Tattoo: Being an Account of the Misadventures of Jacky Faber, Midshipman and Fine Lady* by L. A. Meyer (Listen & Live); (solo narration, male) John Lee for *The Count of Monte Cristo* by Alexandre Dumas (Blackstone); (Spanish language) *Por un Dia Mas* by Mitch Albom, read by Jose Manuel Vieira (FonoLibro); (teens) *Curse of the Blue Tattoo: Being an Account of the Misadventures of Jacky Faber, Midshipman and Fine Lady* by L. A. Meyer, read by Katherine Kellgren (Listen & Live); (thriller/suspense) *Child 44* by Tom Rob Smith, read by Dennis Boutsikaris (Hachette).

Bad Sex in Fiction Award (United Kingdom). *Sponsor: Literary Review. Winner:* Jonathan Littell for *The Kindly Ones* (Harper-Collins).

Bakeless Literary Publication Prizes. For promising new writers. *Offered by:* Bread Loaf Writers' Conference of Middlebury College. *Winners:* (fiction) Belle Boggs for *Mattaponi Queen* (Graywolf); (creative nonfiction) Kim Dana Kupperman for *I Just Lately Started Buying Wings: Missives from the Other Side of Silence* (Graywolf); (poetry) Nick Lantz for *We Don't Know We Don't Know: Poems* (Graywolf).

Bancroft Prizes ($10,000). For books of exceptional merit and distinction in American history, American diplomacy, and the international relations of the United States. *Offered by:* Columbia University. *Winners:* Thomas G. Andrews for *Killing for Coal: America's Deadliest Labor War* (Harvard University Press); Drew Gilpin Faust for *This Republic of Suffering: Death and the American Civil War* (Knopf); Pekka Hämäläinen for *The Comanche Empire* (Yale University Press).

Barnes & Noble Discover Great New Writers Awards. To honor a first novel and a first work of nonfiction by American authors. *Offered by:* Barnes & Noble, Inc. *Winners:* (fiction) Gin Phillips for *The Well and the Mine* (Hawthorne); (nonfiction) David Sheff for *Beautiful Boy: A Father's Journey Through His Son's Addiction* (Houghton Mifflin).

Mildred L. Batchelder Award. For an American publisher of a children's book originally published in a language other than English and subsequently published in English in the United States. *Offered by:* American Library Association, Association for Library Service to Children. *Winner:* Arthur A. Levine Books for *Moribito: Guardian of the Spirit,* written by Nahoko Uehashi and translated by Cathy Hirano.

Beacon of Freedom Award. For the best title introducing American history, from colonial times through the Civil War, to young readers. *Offered by:* Williamsburg (Virginia) Regional Library and the Colonial Williamsburg Foundation. *Winner:* Amy Butler for *Virginia Bound* (Clarion).

Pura Belpré Awards. To a Latino/Latina writer and illustrator whose work portrays,

affirms, and celebrates the Latino cultural experience in an outstanding work of literature for children and youth. *Offered by:* American Library Association, Association for Library Service to Children. *Winners:* (author) Margarita Engle for *The Surrender Tree: Poems of Cuba's Struggle for Freedom* (Holt); (illustrator) Yuyi Morales for *Just in Case* (Roaring Brook).

Curtis Benjamin Award. To an outstanding individual within the U.S. publishing industry who has shown exceptional innovation and creativity in the field of publishing. *Offered by:* Association of American Publishers. *Winner:* Not awarded in 2009.

Helen B. Bernstein Award. To a journalist who has written at book length about an issue of contemporary concern. *Offered by:* New York Public Library. *Winner:* Jane Mayer for *The Inside Story of How the War on Terror Turned into a War on American Ideals* (Doubleday).

Black Caucus of the American Library Association (BCALA) Literary Awards. *Winners:* (fiction) Diane McKinney-Whetstone for *Trading Dreams at Midnight* (HarperCollins); (nonfiction) Paula J. Giddings for *Ida: A Sword Among Lions* (HarperCollins); (first novelist award) Carleen Brice for *Orange Mint and Honey* (Ballantine); (outstanding contribution to publishing citation) Deborah Willis and Kevin Merida for *Obama: The Historic Campaign in Photographs* (HarperCollins).

Irma Simonton Black and James H. Black Award for Excellence in Children's Literature. To a book for young children in which the text and illustrations work together to create an outstanding whole. *Offered by:* Bank Street College of Education. *Winners:* Robie H. Harris and Michael Emberley, illustrator, for *Mail Harry to the Moon* (Little, Brown).

James Tait Black Memorial Prize (United Kingdom) (£10,000). To recognize literary excellence in biography and fiction. *Offered by:* University of Edinburgh. *Winners:* (fiction) Sebastian Barry for *The Secret Scripture* (Viking); (biography) Michael Holroyd for *A Strange Eventful History: The Dramatic Lives of Ellen Terry, Henry*

Irving, and Their Remarkable Families (Vintage).

Rebekah Johnson Bobbitt National Prize for Poetry ($10,000). *Offered by:* Library of Congress. *Winners:* Not awarded in 2009.

BookSense Book of the Year Awards. See Indies Choice Book Awards.

Booktrust Teenage Prize (United Kingdom) (£2,500). *Offered by:* Booktrust. *Winner:* Neil Gaiman for *The Graveyard Book* (HarperCollins).

Borders Original Voices Awards ($5,000). To recognize works by new and emerging writers. *Offered by:* Borders Group, Inc. *Winners:* (fiction) Steven Galloway for *The Cellist of Sarajevo* (Riverhead); (nonfiction) Eric Weiner for *The Geography of Bliss: One Grump's Search for the Happiest Places in the World* (Twelve); (young adult/independent reader) Tanya Landman for *I Am Apache* (Candlewick); (picture book) Adam Rubin and Daniel Salmieri, illustrator, for *Those Darn Squirrels!* (Clarion).

Boston Globe/Horn Book Awards. For excellence in children's literature. *Winners:* (fiction and poetry) Terry Pratchett for *Nation* (HarperCollins); (nonfiction) Candace Fleming for *The Lincolns: A Scrapbook Look at Abraham and Mary* (Random); (picture books) Margaret Mahy and Polly Dunbar (illustrator) for *Bubble Trouble* (Clarion).

W. Y. Boyd Literary Award ($5,000). For a military novel that honors the service of American veterans during a time of war. *Offered by:* American Library Association. *Winner:* Richard Bausch for *Peace* (Knopf).

Branford Boase Award (United Kingdom). To the author and editor of an outstanding novel for young readers by a first-time writer. *Winners:* B. R. Collins and Emma Matthewson (editor) for *The Traitor Game* (Bloomsbury).

Michael Braude Award for Light Verse ($5,000). *Offered by:* American Academy of Arts and Letters. *Winner:* Not awarded in 2009.

Bridport International Creative Writing Prizes (United Kingdom). For poetry and short stories. *Offered by:* Bridport Arts Centre. *Winners:* (poetry) (first prize,

£5,000) Dore Kiesselbach for "Non-invasive"; (second prize, £1,000) Nick MacKinnon for "By Tompion and Banger"; (third prize, £500) Lydia Fulleylove for "Night Drive"; (short story) (first prize, £5,000) Jenny Clarkson for "Something"; (second prize, £1,000) Natasha Soobramanien for "Some Nice Stories, And One Not"; (third prize, £500) N Nye for "The Queens from Houston."

British Fantasy Awards (United Kingdom). *Offered by:* British Fantasy Society. *Winners:* (novel—the August Derleth Fantasy Award) Graham Joyce, writing as William Heaney, for *Memoirs of a Master Forger* (Gollancz); (novella) Tim Lebbon for "The Reach of Children" (Humdrumming); (short fiction) Sarah Pinborough for "Do You See" in *Myth-Understandings* (Newcon); (collection) Allyson Bird for *Bull Running for Girls* (Screaming Dreams); (anthology) Stephen Jones, editor, for *The Mammoth Book of Best New Horror* No. 19 (Constable & Robinson); (artist) Vincent Chong; (comic/graphic novel) Joe Hill and Gabriel Rodriguez, artist, for *Locke and Key* (IDW); (nonfiction) Stephen Jones, editor, for *Basil Copper: A Life in Books* (PS Publishing).

Sophie Brody Medal. For the U.S. author of the most distinguished contribution to Jewish literature for adults published in the preceding year. *Donor:* Brodart Foundation. *Offered by:* Reference and User Services Association, American Library Association. *Winner:* Peter Manseau for *Songs for the Butcher's Daughter* (Free Press).

Cabell First Novelist Award ($5,000). For a first novel published in the previous year. *Offered by:* Virginia Commonwealth University. *Winner:* Deb Olin Unferth for *Vacation* (McSweeney's).

Caine Prize for African Writing (£10,000). For a short story by an African writer, published in English. *Winner:* EC Osondu for "Waiting," published in the online literary magazine *Guernica.*

Randolph Caldecott Medal. For the artist of the most distinguished picture book. *Offered by:* American Library Association, Association for Library Service to Children. *Winner:* Beth Krommes for *The House in the Night,* written by Susan Marie Swanson (Houghton Mifflin).

California Book Awards. To California residents to honor books of fiction, nonfiction, and poetry published in the previous year. *Offered by:* Commonwealth Club of California. *Winners:* (fiction) Adam Mansbach for *The End of the Jews* (Spiegel & Grau); (first fiction) Rachel Kushner for *Telex from Cuba* (Scribner); (poetry) August Kleinzahler for *Sleeping It Off in Rapid City* (Farrar, Straus & Giroux); (nonfiction) John Adams for *Hallelujah Junction: Composing an American Life* (Picador); (Californiana) William David Estrada for *The Los Angeles Plaza: Sacred and Contested Space* (University of Texas Press); (young adult) Ellen Klages for *White Sands, Red Menace*; (juvenile) Kadir Nelson for *We Are the Ship: The Story of Negro League Baseball* (Disney); (contribution to publishing) Gordon H. Chang, Mark Dean Johnson, and Paul J. Karlstrom for *Asian American Art: A History, 1850–1970* (Stanford General).

John W. Campbell Memorial Award. For science fiction writing. *Offered by:* Center for the Study of Science Fiction. *Winners:* (tie) Ian MacLeod for *Song of Time* (PS Publishing), Cory Doctorow for *Little Brother* (Tor).

Canadian Library Association Book of the Year for Children. *Sponsor:* Library Services Centre. *Winner:* Anne Laurel Carter for *The Shepherd's Granddaughter* (Groundwood).

Canadian Library Association Amelia Frances Howard-Gibbon Illustrator's Award. *Sponsor:* Library Services Centre. *Winner:* Dusan Petricic for *Mattland,* written by Hazel Hutchins and Gail Herbert (Annick).

Canadian Library Association Young Adult Canadian Book Award. *Winner:* Allan Stratton for *Chanda's Wars* (HarperCollins).

Center for Fiction First Novel Prize ($10,000). *Offered by:* Center for Fiction, Mercantile Library of New York. *Winner:* John Pipkin for *Woodsburner* (Doubleday).

Chicago Tribune Heartland Prize for Fiction ($7,500). *Offered by: Chicago Tribune.*

Winner: Jayne Anne Phillips for *Lark and Termite* (Knopf).

Chicago Tribune Heartland Prize for Nonfiction ($7,500). *Offered by: Chicago Tribune. Winner:* Nick Reding for *Methland* (Bloomsbury USA).

Chicago Tribune Literary Prize. For a lifetime of literary achievement by an author whose body of work has had great impact on American society. *Offered by: Chicago Tribune. Winner:* Tony Kushner.

Chicago Tribune Nelson Algren Award ($5,000). For short fiction. *Offered by: Chicago Tribune. Winner:* Anne Sanow for "The Grand Tour" in *Triple Time* (University of Pittsburgh Press).

Chicago Tribune Young Adult Literary Prize. To recognize a distinguished literary career. *Winner:* Neil Gaiman.

Children's Africana Book Awards. To recognize and encourage excellent children's books about Africa. *Offered by:* Outreach Council of the African Studies Association. *Winners:* (younger readers) Katie Smith Milway and Eugenie Fernandes for *One Hen: How One Loan Made a Big Difference* (Kids Can); (older readers) Marguerite Abouet and Clement Oubrerie for *Aya* (Drawn & Quarterly).

Children's Book Council of Australia Children's Book of the Year Awards. *Winners:* (picture book) Kylie Dunstan for *Collecting Colour* (Hachette); (Eve Pownall Book of the Year) Lincoln Hall for *Alive in the Death Zone* (Random); (early childhood) Bob Graham for *How to Heal a Broken Wing* (Walker); (younger readers) Glenda Millard and Stephen Michael King, illustrator, for *Perry Angel's Suitcase* (ABC); (older readers) Shaun Tan for *Tales from Outer Suburbia* (Allen & Unwin).

Children's Poet Laureate ($25,000). For lifetime achievement in poetry for children. Honoree holds the title for two years. *Offered by:* The Poetry Foundation. *Winner:* Mary Ann Hoberman (named in 2008).

Chinese-American Librarians Association Book Awards. *Winners:* (adult fiction) Fae Myenne Ng for *Steer Toward Rock* (Hyperion); (adult nonfiction), Ha Jin for *The Writer as Migrant* (University of Chicago Press); (young adult) Laurence Yep for

Dragon Road (HarperCollins); (children's book) Icy Smith for *Mei Ling in China City,* illustrated by Gayle Garner Roski (East West Discovery).

Cholmondeley Awards for Poets (United Kingdom) (£1,500). For a poet's body of work and contribution to poetry. *Winners:* Bernard O'Donoghue, Alice Oswald, Fiona Sampson, Pauline Stainer.

CILIP Carnegie Medal (United Kingdom). For the outstanding children's book of the year. *Offered by:* CILIP: The Chartered Institute of Library and Information Professionals (formerly the Library Association). *Winner:* Siobhan Dowd for *Bog Child* (David Fickling).

CILIP Kate Greenaway Medal (United Kingdom). For children's book illustration. *Offered by:* CILIP: The Chartered Institute of Library and Information Professionals. *Winner:* Catherine Rayner for *Harris Finds His Feet* (Little Tiger).

Arthur C. Clarke Award (United Kingdom). For the best science fiction novel published in the United Kingdom. *Offered by:* British Science Fiction Association. *Winner:* Ian R. MacLeod for *Song of Time* (PS Publishing).

David Cohen Prize (United Kingdom) (£40,000). Awarded biennially to a living British writer, novelist, poet, essayist, or dramatist in recognition of an entire body of work written in the English language. *Offered by:* David Cohen Family Charitable Trust. *Winner:* Seamus Heaney.

Matt Cohen Award (Canada) (C$20,000). To a Canadian author whose life has been dedicated to writing as a primary pursuit, for a body of work. *Offered by:* Writers' Trust of Canada. *Winner:* Paul Quarrington.

Commonwealth Writers' Prize (United Kingdom). To reward and encourage new Commonwealth fiction and ensure that works of merit reach a wider audience outside their country of origin. *Offered by:* Commonwealth Institute. *Winners:* (best book) (£10,000) Christos Tsiolkas, Australia, for *The Slap* (HarperCollins); (best first book) (£5,000) Mohammed Hanif, Pakistan, for *A Case of Exploding Mangoes* (Knopf).

Olive Cook Prize. See Tom-Gallon Trust Award and Olive Cook Prize.

Cork City–Frank O'Connor Short Story Award (€35,000). An international award for a collection of short stories. *Offered by:* Munster Literature Centre, Cork, Ireland. *Sponsor:* Cork City Council. *Winner:* Simon Van Booy for *Love Begins in Winter* (Harper).

Costa Book Awards (United Kingdom) (formerly the Whitbread Book Awards). For literature of merit that is readable on a wide scale. *Offered by:* Booksellers Association of Great Britain and Costa Coffee. *Winners:* (book of the year, £25,000) Christopher Reid for *A Scattering* (Arete); (novel, £5,000) Colm Tóibín for *Brooklyn* (Viking); (first novel, £5,000) Raphael Selbourne for *Beauty* (Tindal Street); (biography £5,000) Graham Farmelo for *The Strangest Man: The Hidden Life of Paul Dirac, Quantum Genius* (Faber); (poetry, £5,000) Christopher Reid for *A Scattering* (Arete); (children's, £5,000) Patrick Ness for *The Ask and the Answer* (Walker).

Crab Orchard Series in Poetry Open Competition ($3,500 and publication by Southern Illinois University Press). For poetry collections. *Winners:* Todd Hearon for *Strange Land,* Jennifer Richter for *Threshold.*

Crime Writers' Association (CWA) Dagger Awards (United Kingdom). (CWA Dagger in the Library, £1,500 to the author, £300 to a participating library's readers' group). To the author of crime fiction whose work is currently giving the greatest enjoyment to library users. *Winner:* Colin Cotterill; (CWA International Dagger, £1,000 for the author and £500 for the translator). For crime, thriller, suspense novels or spy fiction translated into English for publication in Britain. *Winners:* Fred Vargas and translator Sîan Reynolds for *The Chalk Circle Man* (Penguin); (CWA Short Story Dagger) *Winner:* Sean Chercover for "One Serving of Bad Luck" in *Killer Year* (Mira); (CWA Debut Dagger, £500) For a writer in the English language who has not yet had a novel published commercially. *Winner:* Catherine O'Keefe for *The Pathologist*; (CWA Cartier Diamond Dagger).

For sustained excellence in crime writing. *Winner:* Andrew Taylor.

Roald Dahl Funny Prize (United Kingdom) (£2,500). *Offered by:* Booktrust. *Winners:* (ages 6 and under) Sam Lloyd for *Mr Pusskins Best in Show* (Orchard); (ages 7 to 14) Philip Ardagh for *Grubtown Tales: Stinking Rich and Just Plain Stinky,* illustrated by Jim Paillot (Faber).

Benjamin H. Danks Award ($20,000). To a promising young writer or playwright, in alternate years. *Offered by:* American Academy of Arts and Letters. *Winner:* Not awarded in 2009.

Dartmouth Medal. For creating current reference works of outstanding quality and significance. *Donor:* Dartmouth College. *Winner:* Greenwood Press for *Pop Culture Universe* (first electronic recipient of the award).

Derringer Awards. To recognize excellence in short crime and mystery fiction. *Sponsor:* Short Mystery Fiction Society. *Winners:* (flash story, up to 1,000 words) Dee Stuart for "No Place Like Home" in *Mysterical-E*, Ruth McCarty for "No Flowers for Stacey" in *Deadfall*; (short story, 1,001 to 4,000 words) Michael Penncavage for "The Cost of Doing Business" in *Thuglit*; (long story, 4,001 to 8,000 words) Robert S. Levinson for "The Quick Brown Fox" in *Alfred Hitchcock Mystery Magazine*; (novelette, 8,001 to 17,500 words) O'Neil De Noux for "Too Wise" in *Ellery Queen Mystery Magazine*; (Edward D. Hoch Memorial Golden Derringer Award for Lifetime Achievement) Clark Howard.

Philip K. Dick Award. For a distinguished science fiction paperback published in the United States. *Sponsor:* Philadelphia Science Fiction Society. *Winners:* (tie) Adam-Troy Castro for *Emissaries from the Dead* (Eos), David Walton for *Terminal Mind* (Meadowhawk).

Dundee International Book Prize (Scotland) (£10,000). For an unpublished novel on any theme, in any genre. *Winner:* Chris Longmuir for *Dead Wood.*

Dundee Picture Book Award (Scotland) (£1,000). To recognize excellence in storytelling for children. *Winner:* Helen Stephens for *Fleabag* (Alison Green).

Educational Writers' Award (United Kingdom) (£2,000). For noteworthy educational nonfiction for children. *Offered by:* Authors' Licensing and Collecting Society and Society of Authors. *Winners:* Nick Sharratt, illustrator; Steve Alton, writer; and Sally Symes, designer, for *The Gooey, Chewy, Rumble, Plop Book* (Bodley Head).

Margaret A. Edwards Award ($2,000). To an author whose book or books have provided young adults with a window through which they can view their world and which will help them to grow and to understand themselves and their role in society. *Donor: School Library Journal. Winner:* Laurie Halse Anderson for *Catalyst* (Penguin), *Fever 1793* (Simon & Schuster), and *Speak* (Penguin).

Encore Award (United Kingdom) (£10,000). Awarded biennially for the best second novel of the previous two years. *Offered by:* Society of Authors. *Winner:* Julia Leigh for *Disquiet* (Faber).

European Union Prize for Literature (€5,000). To recognize outstanding European writing. *Sponsors:* European Commission, European Booksellers Federation, European Writers' Council, Federation of European Publishers. The initial 2009 round of the competition involved writers from Austria, Croatia, France, Hungary, Ireland, Italy, Lithuania, Norway, Poland, Portugal, Slovakia, and Sweden. *Winners:* (Austria) Paulus Hochgatterer for *Die Süsse des Lebens* (*The Sweetness of Life*) (Paul Zsolnay Verlag); (Croatia) Mila Pavicevic for *Djevojcica od Leda i Druge Bajke* (*Ice Girl and Other Fairytales*) (Naklada Boökovic); (France) Emmanuelle Pagano for *Les Adolescents Troglodytes* (*The Cave Teenagers*) (Editions P.O.L); (Hungary) Szécsi Noémi for *Kommunista Monte Cristo* (*Communist Monte Cristo*) (Tericum); (Ireland) Karen Gillece for *Longshore Drift* (Hachette); (Italy) Daniele del Giudice for *Orizzonte Mobile* (*Movable Horizon*) (Giulio Einaudi); (Lithuania) Laura Sintija Cerniauskaite for *Kvepavimas i Marmura* (*Breathing into Marble*) (Alma Littera); (Norway) Carl Frode Tiller for *Innsirkling* (*Encirclement*); (Poland) Jacek Dukaj for *Lód* (*Ice*) (Wydawnictwo

Literackie); (Portugal) Dulce Maria Cardoso for *Os Meus Sentimentos* (*My Feelings*) (Asa Editores); (Slovakia) Pavol Rankov for *Stalo sa Prvého Septembra (Alebo Inokedy)* (*It Happened on September the First [or Whenever]*) (Kalligram); (Sweden) Helena Henschen for *I Skuggan av ett Brott* (*The Shadow of a Crime*) (Brombergs).

Fairfax Prize ($10,000). For a body of work that has "made significant contributions to American and international culture." *Sponsors:* Fairfax County (Virginia) Public Library Foundation and George Mason University. *Winner:* E. L. Doctorow.

FIELD Poetry Prize ($1,000). For a book-length poetry collection. *Offered by: FIELD: Contemporary Poetry and Poetics. Winner:* Amy Newlove Schroeder for *The Sleep Hotel* (to be published by Oberlin College Press).

ForeWord Magazine Book of the Year Awards ($1,500). For independently published books. *Offered by: ForeWord* magazine. *Winners:* (fiction) Nilita Vachani for *HomeSpun* (Other); (nonfiction) Bill McKibben, editor, for *American Earth: Environmental Writing Since Thoreau* (Library of America).

E. M. Forster Award ($20,000). To a young writer from England, Ireland, Scotland, or Wales, for a stay in the United States. *Offered by:* American Academy of Arts and Letters. *Winner:* Paul Farley.

Forward Prizes (United Kingdom). For poetry. *Offered by: The Forward. Winners:* (best collection, £10,000) Don Paterson for *Rain* (Farrar, Straus & Giroux); (best first collection, £5,000) Emma Jones for *The Striped World* (Faber); (best single poem, £1,000) Robin Robertson for "At Roane Head."

H. E. Francis Short Story Competition ($1,000). *Sponsors:* Ruth Hindman Foundation and English Department, University of Alabama, Huntsville. *Winner:* Jacob Appel for "The Vermin Episode."

Josette Frank Award (formerly the Children's Book Award). For a work of fiction in which children or young people deal in a positive and realistic way with difficulties in their world and grow emotionally and morally. *Offered by:* Bank Street College of Education and the Florence M. Miller Memorial Fund. *Winner:* Jacqueline Woodson for *After Tupac & D Foster* (Putnam).

George Freedley Memorial Award. For the best English-language work about live theater published in the United States. *Offered by:* Theatre Library Association. *Winner:* Jayna Brown for *Babylon Girls: Black Women Performers and the Shaping of the Modern* (Duke University Press).

French-American Foundation Translation Prize ($10,000). For a translation or translations from French into English of a work of fiction and a work of nonfiction. *Offered by:* French-American Foundation. *Winners:* (fiction) Jody Gladding and Elizabeth Deshays for *Small Lives* by Pierre Michon (Archipelago); (nonfiction) Matthew Cobb and Malcolm DeBevoise for *Life Explained* by Michel Morange (Yale University Press).

Frost Medal. To recognize achievement in poetry over a lifetime. *Offered by:* Poetry Society of America. *Winner:* X. J. Kennedy.

Lewis Galantière Award. A biennial award for a literary translation into English from any language other than German. *Offered by:* American Translators Association. *Winner:* Not awarded in 2009.

Galaxy British Book Awards. *Offered by: Publishing News. Winners:* (Galaxy Book of the Year) Kate Summerscale for *The Suspicions of Mr. Whicher* (Bloomsbury); (Outstanding Achievement Award) Michael Palin; (Richard & Judy Best Read of the Year) Kate Atkinson for *When Will There Be Good News?* (Black Swan); (Borders Author of the Year) Aravind Adiga for *The White Tiger* (Atlantic); (Tesco Biography of the Year) Barack Obama for *Dreams From My Father* (Canongate); BooksDirect Crime Thriller of the Year) Stieg Larsson for *The Girl with the Dragon Tattoo* (Quercus); (Sainsbury's Popular Fiction Award) Sebastian Faulks for *Devil May Care* (Penguin); (Play.com Popular Nonfiction Award) Kate Summerscale for *The Suspicions of Mr. Whicher* (Bloomsbury); (Waterstone's New Writer of the Year) Tom Rob Smith for *Child 44* (Simon & Schuster); (WHSmith Children's Book of the Year) Stephenie Meyer for *Breaking Dawn* (Little, Brown).

Theodor Seuss Geisel Medal. For the best book for beginning readers. *Offered by:* American Library Association, Association for Library Service to Children. *Winner:* Mo Willems for *Are You Ready to Play Outside?* (Hyperion).

David Gemmell Legend Award for Fantasy. For the best full-length fantasy novel published for the first time in English during the year of nomination. *Winner:* Andrzej Sapkowski for *Blood of Elves* (Orbit).

Giller Prize (Canada) (C$50,000). For the best Canadian novel or short story collection written in English. *Offered by:* Giller Prize Foundation and Scotiabank. *Winner:* Linden MacIntyre for *The Bishop's Man* (Random).

Gival Press Novel Award ($3,000 and publication by Gival Press). *Winner:* David Winner for *The Cannibal of Guadalajara*.

Giverny Award. For an outstanding children's science picture book. *Offered by:* 15 Degree Laboratory. *Winners:* Jennifer Ward and Jamichael Henterly for *Forest Bright/Forest Night* (Dawn).

Goldberg Prize for Jewish Fiction by Emerging Writers ($2,500). To highlight new works by contemporary writers exploring Jewish themes. *Offered by:* Foundation for Jewish Culture. *Donor:* Samuel Goldberg & Sons Foundation. *Winner:* Irina Reyn for *What Happened to Anna K* (Simon & Schuster).

Golden Duck Awards for Excellence in Children's Science Fiction Literature. *Sponsored by:* Super-Con-Duck-Tivity. *Winners:* (picture book) Colin McNaughton for *We're Off To Look For Aliens* (Candlewick); (Eleanor Cameron Award for Middle Grades) Henry Melton for *Lighter Than Air* (Wire Rim); (Hal Clement Award for Young Adult Books) (tie) Suzanne Collins for *The Hunger Games* (Scholastic), Cory Doctorow for *Little Brother* (Tor).

Golden Kite Awards ($2,500). For children's books. *Offered by:* Society of Children's Book Writers and Illustrators. *Winners:* (fiction) Steve Watkins for *Down Sand Mountain* (Candlewick); (nonfiction)

Pamela S. Turner for *A Life in the Wild: George Schaller's Struggle to Save the Last Great Beasts* (Farrar, Straus & Giroux); (picture book text) Bonny Becker for *A Visitor for Bear*, illustrated by Kady MacDonald Denton (Candlewick); (picture book illustration) Hyewon Yum for *Last Night* (Farrar, Straus & Giroux).

Governor General's Literary Awards (Canada) (C$25,000, plus C$3,000 to the publisher). For works, in English and in French, of fiction, nonfiction, poetry, drama, and children's literature, and for translation. *Offered by:* Canada Council for the Arts. *Winners:* (fiction, English) Kate Pullinger for *The Mistress of Nothing* (McArthur); (fiction, French) Julie Mazzieri for *Le Discours sur la Tombe de l'Idiot* (Éditions José Corti); (poetry, English) David Zieroth for *The Fly in Autumn* (Harbour); (poetry, French) Hélène Monette for *Thérèse pour Joie et Orchestre* (Éditions du Boréal); (drama, English) Kevin Loring for *Where the Blood Mixes* (Talonbooks); (drama, French) Suzanne Lebeau for *Le Bruit des Os Qui Craquent* (Leméac Éditeur); (nonfiction, English) M. G. Vassanji for *A Place Within: Rediscovering India* (Doubleday); (nonfiction, French) Nicole V. Champeau for *Pointe Maligne: l'Infiniment Oubliée.* (Éditions du Vermillon); (children's literature, text, English) Caroline Pignat for *Greener Grass: The Famine Years* (Red Deer); (children's literature, text, French) Hervé Bouchard for *Harvey* (Éditions de la Pastèque); (children's literature, illustration, English) Jirina Marton for *Bella's Tree* (text by Janet Russell), (Groundwood); (children's literature, illustration, French) Janice Nadeau for *Harvey* (text by Hervé Bouchard) (Éditions de la Pastèque); (translation, English) Susan Ouriou for *Pieces of Me* by Charlotte Gingras (Kids Can); (translation, French) Paule Noyart for *Le Miel d'Harar* by Camilla Gibb (Leméac Éditeur);

Eric Gregory Awards (United Kingdom) (£3,500). For a published or unpublished collection by poets under the age of 30. *Winners:* Liz Berry for *The Patron Saint of Schoolgirls* (Harper); James Brookes for *The Stone Operation;* Swithun Cooper for

Touchpaper the Night; Alex McRae for *Joséphine's Giraffe*; Sam Riviere for *It Ain't Honest.*

Griffin Poetry Prizes (Canada) (C$100,000 total). To a living Canadian poet or translator and a living poet or translator from any country, which may include Canada. *Offered by:* Griffin Trust. *Winners:* (Canadian) A. F. Moritz for *The Sentinel* (House of Anansi); (international) C. D. Wright for *Rising, Falling, Hovering* (Copper Canyon); (lifetime achievement) Hans Magnus Enzensberger.

Gryphon Award ($1,000). To recognize a noteworthy work of fiction or nonfiction for younger children. *Offered by:* The Center for Children's Books. *Winner:* Nic Bishop for *Frogs* (Scholastic).

Guardian Children's Fiction Prize (United Kingdom) (£1,500). For an outstanding children's or young adult novel. *Offered by: The Guardian. Winner:* Mal Peet for *Exposure* (Candlewick).

Guardian First Book Award (United Kingdom) (£10,000). For recognition of a first book. *Offered by: The Guardian. Winner:* Petina Gappah for *An Elegy for Easterly* (Faber).

Gumshoe Awards. For crime fiction. *Offered by: Mysterious Ink* online magazine. *Winners:* (mystery) James Lee Burke for *The Tin Roof Blowdown* (Simon & Schuster); (thriller) Robert Crais for *The Watchman* (Simon & Schuster); (first novel) Sean Chercover for *Big City, Bad Blood* (William Morrow); (lifetime achievement) Donald E. Westlake.

Dashiell Hammett Prize. For a work of literary excellence in the field of crime writing. *Offered by:* North American Branch, International Association of Crime Writers. *Winner:* George Pelecanos for *The Turnaround* (Little, Brown).

O. B. Hardison, Jr. Poetry Prize ($10,000). To a U.S. poet who has published at least one book in the past five years, and has made important contributions as a teacher, and is committed to furthering the understanding of poetry. *Offered by:* Folger Shakespeare Library. *Winner:* Juliana Spahr.

Harvey Awards. To recognize outstanding work in comics and sequential art. *Winners:* (best syndicated strip or panel) Patrick McDonnell for *Mutts* (King Features); (best new series) Echo (Abstract Studios); (special award for humor in comics) Al Jaffee for *Tall Tales* (Abrams); (best biographical, historical, or journalistic presentation) Mark Evanier for *Kirby: King of Comics* (Abrams); (best anthology) Rantz Hoseley, editor, for *Comic Book Tattoo* (Image Comics); (best domestic reprint project) *Complete Peanuts* (Fantagraphics); (best continuing or limited series) *All-Star Superman* (DC Comics); (best writer) Grant Morrison for *All-Star Superman.*

R. R. Hawkins Award. For the outstanding professional/scholarly work of the year. *Offered by:* Association of American Publishers. *Winners:* Claudia Goldin and Lawrence F. Katz for *The Race Between Education and Technology* (Harvard University Press).

Anthony Hecht Poetry Prize ($3,000 and publication by Waywiser Press). For an unpublished first or second book-length poetry collection. *Winner:* Carrie Jerrell for *After the Revival.*

Robert A. Heinlein Award. For outstanding published works in science fiction and technical writings to inspire the human exploration of Space. *Sponsor:* Heinlein Society. *Winners:* Joe Haldeman, John Varley.

Drue Heinz Literature Prize ($15,000). For short fiction. *Winner:* Anne Sanow for *Triple Time* (University of Pittsburgh Press).

O. Henry Awards. See PEN/O. Henry Prize.

William Dean Howells Medal. In recognition of the most distinguished novel published in the preceding five years. *Offered by:* American Academy of Arts and Letters. *Winner:* To be awarded next in 2010.

Hugo Awards. For outstanding science fiction writing. *Offered by:* World Science Fiction Convention. *Winners:* (novel) Neil Gaiman for *The Graveyard Book* (HarperCollins); (novella) Nancy Kress for "The Erdmann Nexus" in *Asimov's*; (novelette) Elizabeth Bear for "Shoggoths in Bloom" in *Asimov's*; (short story) Ted Chiang for "Exhalation" in *Eclipse Two* (Night Shade); (related book) John Scalzi for *Your Hate Mail Will Be Graded: A Decade of Whatever, 1998–2008* (Subterranean); (graphic story) Kaja, Phil Foglio, and Cheyenne Wright for *Girl Genius, Volume 8: Agatha Heterodyne and the Chapel of Bones* (Airship Entertainment).

Hurston/Wright Legacy Awards. To writers of African American descent for a book of fiction, a book of nonfiction, and a book of poetry. *Offered by:* Hurston/Wright Foundation and Borders Books. *Winners:* (fiction) Uwem Akpan for *Say You're One of Them* (Little, Brown); (nonfiction) Frank B. Wilderson III for *Incognegro: A Memoir of Exile and Apartheid* (South End): (poetry) Myronn Hardy for *The Headless Saints* (New Issues).

Ignatz Awards. To recognize outstanding achievement in comics and cartooning. *Offered by:* Small Press Expo SPX Cartoons and Comic Arts Festival. *Winners:* (outstanding artist) Nate Powell for *Swallow Me Whole* (Top Shelf); (outstanding anthology or collection) Sammy Harkham, editor, for *Kramer's Ergot* No. 7 (Buenaventura); (outstanding graphic novel) Chris Ware for *Acme Novelty Library* No. 19 (Drawn & Quarterly); (outstanding story) Damien Jay for "Willy" in *Papercutter* No. 10 (Tugboat); (promising new talent) Colleen Frakes for *Woman King* (self-published); (outstanding series) Jordan Crane for Uptight (Fantagraphics).

IMPAC Dublin Literary Award (Ireland) (€100,000). For a book of high literary merit, written in English or translated into English. *Offered by:* IMPAC Corp. and the City of Dublin. *Winner:* Michael Thomas for *Man Gone Down* (Grove Atlantic).

Indies Choice Book Awards (formerly BookSense Book of the Year Awards). Chosen by owners and staff of American Booksellers Association member bookstores. *Winners:* (best indie buzz book—fiction) Mary Ann Shaffer and Annie Barrows for *The Guernsey Literary and Potato Peel Pie Society* (Dial); (best indie young adult buzz book—fiction) Neil Gaiman for *The Graveyard Book* (HarperCollins); (best conversation starter—nonfiction) Sarah Vowell for *The Wordy Shipmates* (Riverhead); (most engaging author) Sherman Alexie; (best author discovery) David Wroblewski for *The Story of Edgar Sawtelle* (Ecco); (best new picture book) Brian Lies for *Bats at the Library* (Houghton Mifflin).

International Prize for Arabic Fiction. To reward excellence in contemporary Arabic creative writing. *Sponsors:* Booker Prize Foundation, Emirates Foundation, Weidenfeld Institute for Strategic Dialogue. *Winner:* Youssef Ziedan for *Beelzebub* (Dar al Shorouk).

Iowa Poetry Prize. For book-length poetry collections by new or established poets. *Sponsor:* University of Iowa Press. *Winners:* Samuel Amadon for *Like a Sea*, Molly Brodak for *A Little Middle of the Night*.

IPPY Peacemaker Award. To honor the best book promoting world peace and human tolerance. *Offered by:* Jenkins Group and *Independent Publisher* online. *Winner:* Tom Cordaro for *Be Not Afraid: An Alternative to the War on Terror* (Pax Christi).

IRA Children's and Young Adult Book Awards. For first or second books in any language published for children or young adults. *Offered by:* International Reading Association. *Winners:* (primary fiction) Alison L. Randall for *The Wheat Doll* (Peachtree); (intermediate fiction) K. A. Nuzum for *The Leanin' Dog* (HarperCollins); (young adult fiction) Heidi Ayarbe for *Freeze Frame* (HarperCollins); (primary nonfiction) Jennifer Berne for *Manfish: The Story of Jacques Cousteau* (Chronicle); (intermediate nonfiction) Carlyn Beccia for *The Raucous Royals* (Houghton Mifflin); (young adult nonfiction) Moying Li for *Snow Falling in Spring* (Farrar, Straus & Giroux).

Rona Jaffe Foundation Writers' Awards ($25,000). To identify and support women writers of exceptional talent in the early stages of their careers. *Offered by:* Rona Jaffe Foundation. *Winners:* Krista Bremer, Vievee Francis, Janice N. Harrington, Lori Ostlund, Helen Phillips, Heidy Steidlmayer.

Jerusalem Prize (Israel). Awarded biennially to a writer whose works best express the theme of freedom of the individual in society. *Offered by:* Jerusalem International Book Fair. *Winner:* Haruki Murakami.

Samuel Johnson Prize for Nonfiction (United Kingdom) (£20,000). For an outstanding work of nonfiction. *Offered by:* British Broadcasting Corporation. *Winner:* Philip Hoare for *Leviathan: Or the Whale* (Fourth Estate).

Sue Kaufman Prize for First Fiction ($5,000). For a first novel or collection of short stories. *Offered by:* American Academy of Arts and Letters. *Winner:* Charles Bock for *Beautiful Children* (Random).

Ezra Jack Keats Awards. For children's picture books. *Offered by:* New York Public Library and the Ezra Jack Keats Foundation. *Winners:* (new writer award) Stian Hole for *Garmann's Summer,* illustrated by the author; (new illustrator award) Shadra Strickland for *Bird,* written by Zetta Elliot (Lee and Low).

Kerlan Award. To recognize singular attainments in the creation of children's literature and in appreciation for generous donation of unique resources to the Kerlan Collection for the study of children's literature. *Offered by:* Kerlan Children's Literature Research Collections, University of Minnesota. *Winner:* Jeanette Winter.

Coretta Scott King Book Awards. To an African American author and illustrator of outstanding books for children and young adults. *Offered by:* American Library Association, Social Responsibilities Roundtable. *Winners:* (author) Kadir Nelson for *We Are the Ship: The Story of Negro League Baseball* (Disney); (illustrator) Floyd Cooper for *The Blacker the Berry,* written by Joyce Carol Thomas (Harper-Collins).

Coretta Scott King/John Steptoe Award for New Talent. To offer visibility to a writer or illustrator at the beginning of a career. *Sponsor:* Coretta Scott King Book Award Committee. *Winner:* Shadra Strickland, illustrator, for *Bird* (Lee & Low).

Kiriyama Pacific Rim Book Prize ($30,000). For a book of fiction or a book of nonfiction that best contributes to a fuller understanding among the nations and peoples of the Pacific Rim. *Offered by:* Pacific Rim Voices. *Winner:* Not awarded in 2009.

Robert Kirsch Award for Lifetime Achievement. To a living author whose residence or focus is the American West, and whose contributions to American letters clearly merit body-of-work recognition. *Offered by: Los Angeles Times. Winner:* Robert Alter.

Lambda Literary Awards. To honor outstanding lesbian, gay, bisexual, and transgendered (LGBT) literature. *Offered by:* Lambda Literary Foundation. *Winners:* (anthology) Thomas Glave, editor, for *Our Caribbean* (Duke University Press); (bisexual) Jenny Block for *Open* (Seal); (children's/young adult) Bill Konigsberg for *Out of the Pocket* (Dutton); (drama) Carolyn Gage for *The Second Coming of Joan of Arc* (Outskirts); (gay debut fiction) Shawn Stewart Ruff for *Finlater* (Quote Editions); (gay erotica) Richard Labonte and James Lear, editors, for *Best Gay Erotica 2009* (Cleis); (gay fiction) Scott Heim for *We Disappear* (Harper Perennial); (gay memoir/biography) Sheila Rowbotham for *Edward Carpenter: A Life of Liberty and Love* (Verso); (gay mystery) Scott Sherman for *First You Fall* (Alyson); (gay poetry) (tie) Mark Doty for *Fire to Fire* (Harper), James Allen Hall for *Now You're the Enemy* (University of Arkansas Press); (gay romance) Larry Duplechan for *Got 'Til It's Gone* (Arsenal Pulp); (nonfiction) Jane Rule for *Loving the Difficult* (Hedgerow); (lesbian debut fiction) Magdalena Zurawski for *The Bruise* (University of Alabama Press); (lesbian erotica) Radclyffe and Karin Kallmaker for *In Deep Waters 2: Cruising the Strip* (Bold Strokes); (lesbian fiction) (tie) Emma Donoghue for *The Sealed Letter* (Houghton Mifflin Harcourt), Chandra Mayor for *All the Pretty Girls* (Conundrum); (lesbian memoir/biography) Maureen Seaton for *Sex Talks to Girls: A Memoir* (University of Wisconsin Press); (lesbian mystery) Josie Gordon for *Whacked* (Bella); (lesbian poetry) Judy Grahn for *Love Belongs to Those Who Do the Feeling* (Red Hen); (lesbian romance) Karin Kallmaker for

The Kiss That Counted (Bella); (LGBT studies) Regina Kunzel for *Criminal Intimacy: Prison and the Uneven History of Modern American Sexuality* (University of Chicago Press); (science fiction/fantasy/horror) Nicole Kimberling for *Turnskin* (Blind Eye); (transgender) Thea Hillman for *Intersex (For Lack of a Better Word)* (Manic D).

Harold Morton Landon Translation Award ($1,000). For a book of verse translated into English by a single translator. *Offered by:* Academy of American Poets. *Winner:* Avi Sharon for *C. P. Cavafy: Selected Poems* (Penguin).

Langum Charitable Trust Prize in American Historical Fiction ($1,000). To honor a book of historical fiction published in the previous year. *Winner:* Kathleen Kent for *The Heretic's Daughter* (Little, Brown).

Lannan Foundation Literary Fellowships. To recognize young and mid-career writers of distinctive literary merit who demonstrate potential for continued outstanding work. *Offered by:* Lannan Foundation. *Winners:* Valzhyna Mort, Sarah Lindsay.

James Laughlin Award. To commend and support a second book of poetry. *Offered by:* Academy of American Poets. *Winner:* Jennifer K. Sweeney for *How to Live on Bread and Music* (Perugia).

Claudia Lewis Award. For the year's best poetry book or books for young readers. *Offered by:* Bank Street College of Education and the Florence M. Miller Memorial Fund. *Winner:* Marguerita Engle for *The Surrender Tree: Poems of Cuba's Struggle for Freedom* (Holt).

Library of Congress Lifetime Achievement Award for the Writing of Fiction. For a distinguished body of work. *Offered by:* Library of Congress. *Winner:* Not awarded in 2009.

Ruth Lilly Fellowships ($15,000). To emerging poets to support their continued study and writing of poetry. *Offered by:* the Poetry Foundation. *Winners:* Malachi Black, Eric Ekstrand, Chloë Honum, Jeffrey Schultz, Joseph Spece.

Ruth Lilly Poetry Prize ($100,000). To a U.S. poet in recognition of lifetime achievement. *Offered by:* the Poetry Foundation. *Winner:* Fanny Howe.

Astrid Lindgren Memorial Award (Sweden) (approximately $690,000). In memory of children's author Astrid Lindgren, to honor outstanding children's literature and efforts to promote it. *Offered by:* Government of Sweden and the Swedish Arts Council. *Winner:* Tamer Institute for Community Education, a nonprofit organization that promotes reading among Palestinian children and young adults in the West Bank and the Gaza Strip.

Locus Awards. For science fiction writing. *Offered by:* Locus Publications. *Winners:* (science fiction novel) Neal Stephenson for *Anathem* (Morrow); (fantasy novel) Ursula K. Le Guin for *Lavinia* (Harcourt); (first novel) Paul Melko for *Singularity's Ring* (Tor); (young adult book) Neil Gaiman for *The Graveyard Book* (HarperCollins); (novella) Kelly Link for "Pretty Monsters" in *Pretty Monsters* (Canongate); (novelette) Paolo Bacigalupi for "Pump Six" in *Pump Six and Other Stories* (Night Shade); (short story) Ted Chiang for "Exhalation" in *Eclipse Two* (Night Shade); (anthology) Gardner Dozois, editor, for *The Year's Best Science Fiction: Twenty-Fifth Annual Collection* (St. Martin's); (nonfiction/art book) *Coraline: The Graphic Novel* by Neil Gaiman, adapted and illustrated by P. Craig Russell (HarperCollins).

Elizabeth Longford Prize for Historical Biography (United Kingdom) (£5,000). *Sponsors:* Flora Fraser and Peter Soros. *Winner:* Mark Bostridge for *Florence Nightingale: The Woman and Her Legend* (Viking).

Los Angeles Times Book Prizes. To honor literary excellence. *Offered by:* Los Angeles Times. *Winners:* (biography) Paula J. Giddings for *Ida: A Sword Among Lions: Ida B. Wells and the Campaign Against Lynching* (HarperCollins); (current interest) Barton Gellman for *Angler: The Cheney Vice Presidency* (Penguin); (fiction) Marilynne Robinson for *Home* (Farrar, Straus & Giroux); (Art Seidenbaum Award for First Fiction) Zoë Ferraris for *Finding Nouf* (Houghton Mifflin); (history) Mark Mazower for *Hitler's Empire:*

How the Nazis Ruled Europe (Penguin); (mystery/thriller) Michael Koryta for *Envy the Night* (St. Martin's); (poetry) Frank Bidart for *Watching the Spring Festival* (Farrar, Straus & Giroux); (science and technology) Leonard Susskind for *The Black Hole War: My Battle with Stephen Hawking to Make the World Safe for Quantum Mechanics* (Little, Brown); (young adult literature) Terry Pratchett for *Nation* (HarperCollins).

Amy Lowell Poetry Travelling Scholarship. For a U.S. poet to spend one year outside North America in a country the recipient feels will most advance his or her work. *Offered by:* Amy Lowell Poetry Travelling Scholarship. *Winner:* Brian Turner.

J. Anthony Lukas Awards. For nonfiction writing that demonstrates literary grace, serious research, and concern for an important aspect of American social or political life. *Offered by:* Columbia University Graduate School of Journalism and the Nieman Foundation for Journalism at Harvard. *Winners:* (book prize) ($10,000) Jane Mayer for *The Dark Side: The Inside Story of How the War on Terror Turned Into a War on American Ideals* (Doubleday); (Mark Lynton History Prize) ($10,000) Timothy Brook for *Vermeer's Hat: The Seventeenth Century and the Dawn of the Global World* (Bloomsbury); (work-in-progress) ($30,000) Judy Pasternak for *Yellow Dirt: The Betrayal of the Navajos* (Free Press).

Macavity Awards. For excellence in mystery writing. *Offered by:* Mystery Readers International. *Winners:* (novel) Deborah Crombie for *Where Memories Lie* (William Morrow); (first mystery) Stieg Larsson for *The Girl With the Dragon Tattoo* (Knopf); (nonfiction, critical) Frankie Bailey for *African American Mystery Writers* (McFarland); (short story) Dana Cameron for "The Night Things Changed" in *Wolfsbane and Mistletoe* (Penguin); (Sue Feder Memorial Award for Best Historical Mystery) Rhys Bowen for *A Royal Pain* (Berkley).

McKitterick Prize (United Kingdom) (£4,000). To an author over the age of 40 for a first novel, published or unpublished. *Winner:* Chris Hannan for *Missy* (Chatto).

James Madison Book Award ($10,000). To honor books representing excellence in bringing knowledge and understanding of American history to children ages 5 to 14. *Offered by:* James Madison Book Award Fund. *Winner:* Award discontinued in 2008.

Man Asian Literary Prize ($10,000 plus $3,000 for translator, if applicable). For an Asian novel as yet unpublished in English. *Sponsor:* Man Group. *Winner:* Su Tong for *The Boat to Redemption,* translated by Howard Goldblatt (Doubleday).

Man Booker International Prize (United Kingdom) (£60,000). Awarded biennially to a living author for a significant contribution to world literature. *Offered by:* Man Group. *Winner:* Alice Munro.

Man Booker Prize for Fiction (United Kingdom) (£50,000). For the best novel written in English by a Commonwealth author. *Offered by:* Booktrust and the Man Group. *Winner:* Hilary Mantel for *Wolf Hall* (Holt).

Lenore Marshall Poetry Prize ($25,000). For an outstanding book of poems published in the United States. *Offered by:* Academy of American Poets. *Winner:* Linda Gregg for *All of It Singing: New and Selected Poems* (Graywolf).

Mason Award ($10,000). To honor an author whose body of work has made extraordinary contributions to bringing literature to a wide reading public. *Sponsors:* George Mason University and Fall for the Book. *Winner:* Sherman Alexie.

Somerset Maugham Awards (United Kingdom). For works in any genre except drama by a writer under the age of 35, to enable young writers to enrich their work by gaining experience of foreign countries. *Winners:* (first, £3,000) Adam Foulds for *The Broken Word* (Cape); (awards, £1,000 each) Alice Albinia for *Empires of the Indus: The Story of a River* (John Murray); Rodge Glass for *Alasdair Gray: A Secretary's Biography* (Bloomsbury); Henry Hitchings for *The Secret Life of Words: How English Became English* (John Murray); Thomas Leveritt for *The Exchange*

Rate Between Love and Money (Harvill Secker); Helen Walsh for *Once Upon a Time in England* (Canongate).

Addison M. Metcalf Award. To a young writer of great promise. *Offered by:* American Academy of Arts and Letters. *Winner:* Ron Currie, Jr.

Vicky Metcalf Award for Children's Literature (Canada) (C$20,000). To a Canadian writer of children's literature for a body of work. *Offered by:* Metcalf Foundation. *Winner:* Marthe Jocelyn.

Midwest Booksellers Choice Awards. *Offered by:* Midwest Booksellers Association. *Winners:* (fiction) David Wroblewski for *The Story of Edgar Sawtelle* (HarperCollins); (nonfiction) Michael Perry for *Coop: A Year of Poultry, Pigs and Parenting* (HarperCollins); (poetry) Freya Manfred for *Swimming With a Hundred-Year-Old Snapping Turtle* (Red Dragonfly); (children's picture book) Kate DiCamillo for *Louise, The Adventures of a Chicken,* illustrated by Harry Bliss (HarperCollins); (children's literature) Neil Gaiman for *The Graveyard Book,* illustrated by Dave McKean (HarperCollins).

Moonbeam Spirit Awards. For books that show dedication and compassion about children, humanity, and literacy. *Offered by:* Jenkins Group and Independent Publisher Online. *Winners:* Stephen Kanter and Dory Kanter, illustrator, for *The Bear and the Blackberry* (Kantourian); Hana and Makena Couture for *My Dad Has Cancer*; Tauna Lee for *Once in a Blue Moon* (Morning Glory); Jeryl Abelmann, Miriam Kronish, and Chason Matthams, illustrator, for *Quickly: The Magic Spatula* (New Year).

William C. Morris YA Debut Award. To honor a debut book published by a first-time author writing for teens and celebrating impressive new voices in young adult literature. *Offered by:* Young Adult Library Services Association, American Library Association. *Donor:* William C. Morris Endowment. *Winner:* Elizabeth C. Bunce for *A Curse Dark as Gold* (Scholastic).

Gustavus Myers Awards. For outstanding books that extend understanding of the root causes of bigotry. *Offered by:* Gustavus Myers Center for the Study of Bigotry and Human Rights in North America. *Winners:* Not awarded in 2009.

Mythopoeic Fantasy Awards. To recognize fantasy or mythic literature for children and adults that best exemplifies the spirit of the Inklings, a group of fantasy writers that includes J. R. R. Tolkien, C. S. Lewis, and Charles Williams. *Offered by:* Mythopoeic Society. *Winners:* (children's) Kristin Cashore for *Graceling* (Graphia); (adult) Carol Berg for *Flesh and Spirit* and *Breath and Bone* (ROC).

National Book Awards. For the best books of the year published in the United States. *Offered by:* National Book Foundation. *Winners:* (fiction) Colum McCann for *Let the Great World Spin* (Random); (nonfiction) T. J. Stiles for *The First Tycoon: The Epic Life of Cornelius Vanderbilt* (Knopf); (young people's literature) Phillip Hoose for *Claudette Colvin: Twice Toward Justice* (Farrar, Straus & Giroux); (poetry) Keith Waldrop for *Transcendental Studies: A Trilogy* (University of California Press).

National Book Critics Circle Awards. For literary excellence. *Offered by:* National Book Critics Circle. *Winners:* (fiction) Roberto Bolaño for *2666* (Farrar, Straus & Giroux); (general nonfiction) Dexter Filkins for *The Forever War* (Knopf); (biography) Patrick French for *The World Is What It Is: The Authorized Biography of V. S. Naipaul* (Knopf); (poetry) (tie) Juan Felipe Herrera for *Half the World in Light* (University of Arizona Press), August Kleinzahler for *Sleeping It Off in Rapid City* (Farrar, Strauss & Giroux); (autobiography) Ariel Sabar for *My Father's Paradise: A Son's Search for His Jewish Past in Kurdish Iraq* (Algonquin); (criticism) Seth Lerer for *Children's Literature: A Reader's History from Aesop to Harry Potter* (University of Chicago Press); (Ivan Sandrof Lifetime Achievement Award) PEN American Center; (Nona Balakian Citation for Excellence in Reviewing) Ron Charles, *Washington Post Book World.*

National Book Festival Award for Creative Achievement. *Offered by:* Center for the

Book, Library of Congress. *Winner:* John Grisham.

National Book Foundation Literarian Award for Outstanding Service to the American Literary Community. *Offered by:* National Book Foundation. *Winner:* Dave Eggers.

National Book Foundation Medal for Distinguished Contribution to American Letters. To a person who has enriched the nation's literary heritage over a life of service or corpus of work. *Offered by:* National Book Foundation. *Winner:* Gore Vidal.

National Endowment for the Arts Translation Fellowships. To support the translation of works of poetry, fiction, and creative nonfiction into English. *Winners:* (poetry, $12,500) Olga Broumas, Eléna Rivera, Richard Tillinghast, Russell Valentino; (fiction, $25,000) Charlotte Mandell, Daniel Shapiro, Martha Tennent; (fiction, $12,500) Ellen Elias-Bursac, Tina Kover, Tess Lewis; (creative nonfiction, $25,000) Brian Henry; (creative nonfiction, $12,500) Sandra Kingery.

National Heritage Fellowship ($25,000). To honor traditional and folk artists, including writers, whose work contributes to the living cultural heritage of the United States. *Offered by:* Natonal Endowment for the Arts. *Winner:* (poetry) Joel Nelson.

National Translation Award ($2,500). To honor a translator whose work has made a valuable contribution to literary translation into English. *Offered by:* American Literary Translators Association. *Winner:* Norman Shapiro for *French Women Poets of Nine Centuries: The Distaff and the Pen* (Johns Hopkins University Press).

Nebula Awards. For science fiction writing. *Offered by:* Science Fiction and Fantasy Writers of America (SFWA). *Winners:* (novel) Ursula K. Le Guin for *Powers* (Harcourt); (novella) Catherine Asaro for "The Spacetime Pool" in *The Year's Best Science Fiction: Twenty-Sixth Annual Collection* (St. Martin's); (novelette) John Kessel for "Pride and Prometheus"; (short story) Nina Kiriki Hoffman for "Trophy Wives"; (script) Andrew Standon and Jim Reardon for "WALL-E"; (Andre Norton Award for Young Adult Science Fiction and Fantasy) Ysabeau S. Wilce for *Flora's Dare* (Harcourt); (Solstice Award) A. J. Budrys, Marty Greenberg, Kate Wilhelm; (Bradbury Award) Joss Whedon; (grand master) Harry Harrison; (author emerita) M. J. Engh.

Nestlé Children's Book Prizes (formerly Smarties Book Prizes) (United Kingdom). To encourage high standards and to stimulate interest in books for children. *Offered by:* Nestlé UK Ltd. *Winners:* Discontinued in 2008.

John Newbery Medal. For the most distinguished contribution to literature for children. *Offered by:* American Library Association, Association for Library Service to Children. *Winner:* Neil Gaiman for *The Graveyard Book,* illustrated by Dave McKean (HarperCollins).

Nobel Prize in Literature (Sweden). For the total literary output of a distinguished career. *Offered by:* Swedish Academy. *Winner:* Herta Müller.

Eli M. Oboler Memorial Award. Biennially, to an author of a published work in English or in English translation dealing with issues, events, questions, or controversies in the area of intellectual freedom. *Offered by:* Intellectual Freedom Round Table, American Library Association. *Winner:* To be awarded next in 2010.

Flannery O'Connor Awards for Short Fiction. For collections of short fiction. *Offered by:* University of Georgia Press. *Winners:* Jessica Treadway for "Please Come Back to Me," Linda L. Grover for "The Dance Boots."

Frank O'Connor Short Story Award. See Cork City–Frank O'Connor Short Story Award.

Oddest Book Title of the Year Award. *Sponsor: The Bookseller* magazine. *Winner: The 2009–2014 World Outlook for 60-Milligram Containers of Fromage Frais* (ICON Group)

Scott O'Dell Award for Historical Fiction. *Offered by: Bulletin of the Center for Children's Books,* University of Chicago. *Winner:* Laurie Halse Anderson for *Chains* (Simon & Schuster).

Sean O'Faoláin Short Story Competition (€1,500 and publication in the literary journal *Southword.*) *Offered by:* Munster

Literature Centre, Cork, Ireland. *Winner:* Alexa Beattie for "Cold Cut."

Orange Award for New Writers (United Kingdom). For a first novel or short story collection written by a woman and published in the United Kingdom. *Offered by:* Orange plc and Arts Council London. *Winner:* Francesca Kay for *An Equal Stillness* (George Weidenfeld & Nicholson).

Orange Prize for Fiction (United Kingdom) (£30,000). For the best novel written by a woman and published in the United Kingdom. *Offered by:* Orange plc. *Winner:* Marilynne Robinson for *Home* (Farrar, Straus & Giroux).

Orbis Pictus Award. For outstanding nonfiction for children. *Offered by:* National Council of Teachers of English. *Winners:* Shelley Tanaka and David Craig, illustrator, for *Amelia Earhart: The Legend of the Lost Aviator* (Abrams).

Orion Book Award ($3,000). To recognize books that deepen connection to the natural world, present new ideas about mankind's relationship with nature, and achieve excellence in writing. *Sponsors: Orion Magazine* and the Geraldine R. Dodge Foundation. *Winner:* Amy Irvine for *Trespass: Living at the Edge of the Promised Land* (North Point).

Pegasus Awards. For poetry. *Offered by:* The Poetry Foundation. (Neglected Master Award, $50,000). For the life's work of a significant but under-recognized American poet. *Winner:* Not awarded in 2009; (Emily Dickinson First Book Award, $10,000). To a writer over the age of 50 who has never published a book. *Winner:* Not awarded in 2009; (Randall Jarrell Award in Poetry Criticism, $10,000) *Winner:* Ange Mlinko; Mark Twain Poetry Award ($25,000). To recognize a poet's contribution to humor in American poetry. *Winner:* Not awarded in 2009. (Verse Drama Prize, $10,000) to honor a living poet who has written a previously unpublished, outstanding original verse drama in English. *Winner:* Not awarded in 2009.

PEN Award for Poetry in Translation ($3,000). For a book-length translation of poetry from any language into English and published in the United States. *Offered by:*

PEN American Center. *Winner:* Marilyn Hacker for her translation from French of *King of a Hundred Horsemen* by Marie Étienne (Farrar, Straus & Giroux).

PEN/Saul Bellow Award for Achievement in American Fiction ($25,000). Awarded biennially to a distinguished living American author of fiction. *Offered by:* PEN American Center. *Winner:* Cormac McCarthy.

PEN Beyond Margins Awards. For book-length writings by authors of color, published in the United States during the current calendar year. *Offered by:* PEN American Center. *Winners:* Uwem Akpan for *Say You're One of Them* (Little, Brown); Juan Felipe Herrera for *Half of the World in Light: New and Selected Poems* (University of Arizona); Lily Hoang for *Changing* (Fairy Tale Review).

PEN/Robert Bingham Fellowship ($35,000). To a writer whose first novel or short story collection represents distinguished literary achievement and suggests great promise. *Offered by:* PEN American Center. *Winner:* Donald Ray Pollock for *Knockemstiff* (Doubleday).

PEN/Jacqueline Bograd Weld Award for Biography ($10,000). To the author of a distinguished biography published in the United States during the previous calendar year. *Offered by:* PEN American Center. *Winner:* Richard Brody for *Everything Is Cinema: The Working Life of Jean-Luc Godard* (Metropolitan).

PEN/Faulkner Award for Fiction ($15,000). To honor the best work of fiction published by an American. *Winner:* Joseph O'Neill for *Netherland* (Vintage).

PEN/John Kenneth Galbraith Award ($10,000). For a distinguished book of general nonfiction. *Offered by:* PEN American Center. *Winner:* Steve Coll for *The Bin Ladens: An Arabian Family in the American Century* (Penguin).

PEN/Ernest Hemingway Foundation Award. For a distinguished work of first fiction by an American. *Offered by:* PEN New England. *Winner:* Michael Dahlie for *A Gentleman's Guide to Graceful Living* (Norton).

PEN/Nora Magid Award ($2,500). To honor a magazine editor whose high literary standards and taste have contributed significantly to the excellence of the publication he or she edits. *Offered by:* PEN American Center. *Winner:* Hannah Tinti, editor of *One Story*.

PEN/Malamud Award ($5,000). To an author or authors who have demonstrated long-term excellence in short fiction. *Offered by:* PEN American Center. *Winners:* Alistair MacLeod, Amy Hempel.

PEN/Ralph Manheim Medal for Translation. Given every three years to a translator whose career has demonstrated a commitment to excellence. *Winner:* Michael Henry Heim.

PEN/Nabokov Award ($20,000). To celebrate the accomplishments of a living author whose body of work, either written in or translated into English, represents achievement in a variety of literary genres. *Winner:* Not awarded in 2009.

PEN/Phyllis Naylor Working Writer Fellowship ($5,000). *Offered by:* PEN American Center. *Winner:* Carol Lynch Williams, author of the forthcoming "A Glimpse Is All I Can Stand."

PEN/O. Henry Prize. To strengthen the art of the short story. *Winners:* Graham Joyce for "An Ordinary Soldier of the Queen" in *Paris Review*; Kirsten Sundberg Lunstrum for "The Nursery" in *American Scholar*; E. V. Slate for "Purple Bamboo Park" in *New England Review* and "The Camera and the Cobra" in *Grain*; John Burnside for "The Bell Ringer" in the *New Yorker*; Mohan Sikka for "Uncle Musto Takes a Mistress" in *One Story*; L. E. Miller for "Kind" in *Missouri Review*; Alistair Morgan for "Icebergs" in *Paris Review*; Manuel Muñoz for "Tell Him about Brother John" in *Epoch*; Caitlin Horrocks for "This Is Not Your City" in *Third Coast*; Ha Jin for "The House Behind a Weeping Cherry" in the *New Yorker*; Paul Theroux for "Twenty-two Stories" in *Harper's*; Judy Troy for "The Order of Things" in *Epoch*; Nadine Gordimer for "A Beneficiary" in the *New Yorker*; Viet Dinh for "Substitutes" in *Five Points*; Karen Brown for "Isabel's Daughter" in *Florida Review*; Marisa Silver for "The Visitor" in the *New Yorker*; Paul Yoon for "And We Will Be Here" in *Ploughshares*; Andrew Sean Greer for

"Darkness" in *Zoetrope: All-Story*; Junot Díaz for "Wildwood" in the *New Yorker*.

PEN/Joyce Osterweil Award for Poetry ($5,000). A biennial award to recognize a new and emerging American poet. *Offered by:* PEN American Center. *Winner:* Jeffrey Yang for *An Aquarium* (Graywolf).

PEN/Laura Pels Foundation Awards for Drama. To recognize a master American dramatist and an American playwright in mid-career. *Offered by:* PEN American Center. *Winners:* (master playwright) Sam Shepard; (mid-career prize) Nilo Cruz.

PEN Prison Writing Awards. To provide support and encouragement to prison inmates whose writing shows merit or promise. *Offered by:* PEN American Center. *Winners:* (outstanding achievement) Charles P. Norman for "I Wore Chains to My Father's Funeral"; (poetry) Richard Miller for "Lepidoptera or Butterflies"; (essay) D. Babb for "The First O.J. Book"; (memoir) George Hughes for "Six Basement"; (fiction) Samuel Harris for "Shepherds of the Passaic"; (drama) Keith Sanders for "Every Day's Your Birthday."

PEN Translation Fund Grants. To support the translation of book-length works of fiction, creative nonfiction, poetry, or drama that have not previously appeared in English or have appeared only in an egregiously flawed translation. *Winners:* Eric Abrahamsen, Mee Chang, Robyn Creswell, Brett Foster, Geoffrey Michael Goshgarian, Tess Lewis, Fayre Makeig, Arvind Krishna Mehrotra, Frederika Randall, Daniel Shapiro, Chantal Wright.

PEN Translation Prize. To promote the publication and reception of translated world literature in English. *Winner:* Natasha Wimmer for her translation from Spanish of Roberto Bolaño's *2666* (Farrar, Straus & Giroux).

PEN/Voelcker Award for Poetry. Given in even-numbered years to an American poet at the height of his or her powers. *Offered by:* PEN American Center. *Winner:* Not awarded in 2009.

PEN/L. L. Winship Award. For books of fiction, poetry, or creative nonfiction with a New England subject or written by a New England author. *Offered by:* PEN New

England. *Winners:* (fiction) Margot Livesey for *The House on Fortune Street* (HarperCollins); (nonfiction) Patrick Tracey for *Stalking Irish Madness* (Bantam); (poetry) Nancy K. Pearson for *Two Minutes of Light* (Perugia).

Maxwell E. Perkins Award. To honor an editor, publisher, or agent who has discovered, nurtured, and championed writers of fiction in the United States. *Offered by:* Center for Fiction, Mercantile Library of New York. *Winner:* Gerald Howard.

Phoenix Award. To the author of an English-language children's book that failed to win a major award at the time of its publication 20 years earlier. *Winner:* Francesca Lia Block for *Weetzie Bat* (HarperColllins).

Edgar Allan Poe Awards. For outstanding mystery, suspense, and crime writing. *Offered by:* Mystery Writers of America. *Winners:* (novel) C. J. Box for *Blue Heaven* (St. Martin's); (first novel by an American author) Francie Lin for *The Foreigner* (Picador); (paperback original) Meg Gardiner for *China Lake* (New American); (critical/biographical) Harry Lee Poe for *Edgar Allan Poe: An Illustrated Companion to His Tell-Tale Stories* (Sterling); (fact crime) Howard Blum for *American Lightning: Terror, Mystery, the Birth of Hollywood, and the Crime of the Century* (Crown); (short story) T. Jefferson Parker for "Skinhead Central" in *The Blue Religion* (Little, Brown); (best young adult) John Green for *Paper Towns* (Dutton); (best juvenile) Tony Abbott for *The Postcard* (Little, Brown); (best play) Ifa Bayeza for "The Ballad of Emmett Till" (Goodman Theatre); (television episode teleplay) Patrick Harbinson for "Prayer of the Bone" from "Wire in the Blood" (BBC America); (motion picture screenplay) Martin McDonagh for "In Bruges" (Focus Features); (Robert L. Fish Memorial Award) Joseph Guglielmelli for "Buckner's Error" in *Queens Noir* (Akashic); (Simon & Schuster–Mary Higgins Clark Award) Bill Floyd for *The Killer's Wife* (St. Martin's); (grand masters) James Lee Burke, Sue Grafton.

Poets Out Loud Prize ($2,000 and publication by Fordham University Press). For a book-length poetry collection. *Sponsor:* Fordham University at Lincoln Center. *Winner:* Leslie Chang for *Things That No Longer Delight Me.*

Katherine Anne Porter Award ($20,000). Awarded biennially to a prose writer of demonstrated achievement. *Offered by:* American Academy of Arts and Letters. *Winner:* Not awarded in 2009.

Michael L. Printz Award. For excellence in literature for young adults. *Offered by:* American Library Association, Young Adult Library Services Association. *Winner:* Melina Marchetta for *Jellicoe Road* (HarperCollins).

V. S. Pritchett Memorial Prize (United Kingdom) (£1,000). For a previously unpublished short story. *Offered by:* Royal Society of Literature. *Winner:* Kate Clanchy for "The Not-Dead and the Saved."

Pritzker Military Library Literature Award ($100,000). To recognize a living author for a body of work that has profoundly enriched the public understanding of American military history. *Sponsor:* Tawani Foundation. *Winner:* Gerhard L. Weinberg.

Prix Aurora Awards (Canada). For science fiction writing. *Winners:* (long-form work in English) Edward Willett for *Marseguro* (DAW); (long-form work in French) Michèle Laframboise for *Les Vents de Tammerlan* (Éditions Médiaspaul); (short-form work in English) Randy McCharles for "Ringing in the Changes in Okotoks, Alberta" in *Tesseracts Twelve* (Edge Science Fiction); (short-form work in French) Jean-Louis Trudel for "Le Dôme de Saint-Macaire" in *Solaris*; (work in English, other) Karl Johanson, editor, for *Neo-Opsis*; (work in French, other) Joël Champetier, editor, for *Solaris.*

Prix Goncourt (France). For "the best imaginary prose work of the year." *Offered by:* Société des Gens des Lettres. *Winner:* Marie Ndiaye for *Three Powerful Women* (Gallimard).

Pulitzer Prizes in Letters ($10,000). To honor distinguished work dealing preferably with American themes. *Offered by:* Columbia University Graduate School of Journalism. *Winners:* (fiction) Elizabeth Strout for

Olive Kitteridge (Random); (general non-fiction) Douglas A. Blackmon for *Slavery by Another Name: The Re-Enslavement of Black Americans from the Civil War to World War II* (Doubleday); (biography or autobiography) Jon Meacham for *American Lion: Andrew Jackson in the White House* (Random); (history) Annette Gordon-Reed for *The Hemingses of Monticello: An American Family* (Norton); (poetry) W. S. Merwin for *The Shadow of Sirius* (Copper Canyon); (drama) Lynn Nottage for "Ruined" (Theatre Communications Group).

Quill Awards. To honor excellence in book publishing. *Offered by:* Reed Business Information and the NBC Universal Television Stations. *Winners:* Program suspended in 2008.

Raiziss/De Palchi Translation Award ($5,000 prize and a $25,000 fellowship). Awarded biennially for a translation into English of a significant work of modern Italian poetry by a living translator. *Offered by:* Academy of American Poets. *Winner:* Not awarded in 2009.

Raven Awards. For outstanding achievement in the mystery field outside the realm of creative writing. *Offered by:* Mystery Writers of America. *Winners:* Edgar Allan Poe Society and Poe House, Baltimore.

RBC Bronwen Wallace Award for Emerging Writers (Canada) ($5,000). For a writer under the age of 35 who has not yet been published in book form. *Sponsor:* RBC Foundation. *Winner:* Emily McGiffen.

Arthur Rense Poetry Prize ($20,000). Awarded triennially to an exceptional poet. *Offered by:* American Academy of Arts and Letters. *Winner:* To be awarded next in 2011.

John Llewellyn Rhys Prize (United Kingdom) (£5,000). For a work of literature by a British or Commonwealth author 35 or younger and published in the United Kingdom. *Offered by:* Booktrust. *Winner:* Evie Wyld for *After the Fire, a Still Small Voice* (Pantheon).

Harold U. Ribalow Prize. For Jewish fiction published in English. *Sponsor: Hadassah* magazine. *Winner:* Peter Manseau for *Songs for the Butcher's Daughter* (Free Press).

Rita Awards. *Offered by:* Romance Writers of America. *Winners:* (best first book) Tera Lynn Childs for *Oh. My. Gods.* (Dutton); (best contemporary series romance) Karen Templeton for *A Mother's Wish* (Harlequin); (best contemporary series romance: suspense/adventure) Kathleen Creighton for *Danger Signals* (Harlequin); (best contemporary single title romance) Rachel Gibson for *Not Another Bad Date* (HarperCollins); (best historical romance) Pam Rosenthal for *The Edge of Impropriety* (Penguin); (best inspirational romance) Susan May Warren for *Finding Stefanie* (Tyndale House); (best novel with strong romantic elements) Nora Roberts for *Tribute* (Penguin); (best paranormal romance) Gwyn Cready for *Seducing Mr. Darcy* (Simon & Schuster); (best Regency historical romance) Joanna Bourne for *My Lord and Spymaster* (Penguin); (best romance novella) Stephanie Laurens for "The Fall of Rogue Gerard" in *It Happened One Night* (HarperCollins); (best romantic suspense) Cindy Gerard for *Take No Prisoners* (Simon & Schuster); (best young adult romance) Rosemary Clement-Moore for *Hell Week* (Random); (Nora Roberts Lifetime Achievement Award) Alison Hart.

Rodda Book Award. To recognize a book that exhibits excellence in writing and has contributed significantly to congregational libraries through promotion of spiritual growth. The award is given to books for adults, young adults, and children on a three-year-rotational basis. *Offered by:* Church and Synagogue Library Association. *Winner:* Ariel Sabar for *My Father's Paradise: A Son's Search for His Jewish Past in Kurdish Iraq* (Algonquin).

Rogers Writers' Trust Fiction Prize (Canada) (C$25,000). To a Canadian author of a novel or short story collection. *Offered by:* Rogers Communications. *Winner:* Annabel Lyon for *The Golden Mean* (Random).

Sami Rohr Prize for Jewish Literature ($100,000). For emerging writers of Jewish literature. *Offered by:* Family of Sami Rohr. *Winner:* Sana Krasikov for her debut short story collection *One More Year* (Spiegel & Grau).

Rosenthal Family Foundation Award ($5,000). To a young novelist of considerable literary talent. *Offered by:* American Academy of Arts and Letters. *Winner:* Chris Adrian for *A Better Angel: Stories* (Picador).

Royal Society of Literature/Jerwood Awards for Nonfiction (United Kingdom). For authors engaged on their first major commissioned works of nonfiction. *Offered by:* Royal Society of Literature. *Winners:* Rachel Hewitt for the historical biography *Map of a Nation,* to be published by Granta; (£5,000) Matthew Hollis for his study of the poet Edward Thomas, *Edward Thomas—The Final Years,* to be published by Faber; (£5,000) poets Michael Symmons Roberts and Paul Farley for *Edgelands—Journeys into England's Last Wilderness,* to be published by Cape.

Royal Society of Literature Ondaatje Prize (£10,000). For a distinguished work of fiction, nonfiction or poetry evoking the spirit of a place. *Offered by:* Royal Society of Literature. *Winner:* Adam Nicolson for *Sissinghurst: An Unfinished History* (Harper).

Juan Rulfo International Latin American and Caribbean Prize (FIL Literature Prize) (Mexico) ($150,000). For lifetime achievement in any literary genre. *Offered by:* Juan Rulfo International Latin American and Caribbean Prize Committee. *Winner:* Rafael Cadenas.

Carl Sandburg Literary Award. To honor a significant body of work that has enhanced public awareness of the written word. *Sponsor:* Chicago Public Library Foundation. *Winner:* Salman Rushdie.

Schneider Family Book Awards ($5,000). To honor authors and illustrators for books that embody artistic expressions of the disability experience of children and adolescents. *Offered by:* American Library Association. *Donor:* Katherine Schneider. *Winners:* (ages 0–10) Robert Andrew Parker for *Piano Starts Here: The Young Art Tatum* (Random); (ages 11–13) Leslie Connor for *Waiting for Normal* (HarperCollins); (ages 13–18) Jonathan Friesen for *Jerk, California* (Penguin).

Scottish Book of the Year (£30,000). *Sponsor:* Scottish Arts Council. *Donor:* Scottish Mortgage Investment Trust. *Winner:* James Kelman for *Kieron Smith, Boy* (Houghton Mifflin Harcourt).

Shelley Memorial Award ($3,500). To a poet living in the United States who is chosen on the basis of genius and need. *Offered by:* Poetry Society of America. *Winners:* Ron Padgett and Gary Young.

Shenandoah/Glasgow Prize for Emerging Writers ($2,500). To a writer who has published one book of poetry. *Offered by:* *Shenandoah* literary magazine and Washington and Lee University. *Winner:* Aaron Baker for *Mission Work* (Mariner).

Robert F. Sibert Medal. For the most distinguished informational book for children. *Offered by:* American Library Association, Association for Library Service to Children. *Winner:* Kadir Nelson for *We Are the Ship: The Story of Negro League Baseball* (Disney).

Smarties Book Prizes. See Nestlé Children's Book Prizes.

Spur Awards. *Offered by:* Western Writers of America. *Winners:* (long novel) Thomas Cobb for *Shavetail* (Scribner); (short novel) Craig Johnson for *Another Man's Moccasins* (Viking/Penguin); (original mass market paperback) John D. Nesbitt for *Trouble At the Redstone* (Dorchester); (first novel) Carol A. Buchanan for *God's Thunderbolt: The Vigilantes of Montana* (Book Surge); (nonfiction biography) Meredith Mason Brown for *Frontiersman: Daniel Boone and the Making of America* (Louisiana State University Press); (nonfiction historical) Richard C. Rattenbury for *Hunting the American West: The Pursuit of Big Game for Life, Profit, and Sport, 1800–1900* (Boone and Crockett Club); (nonfiction contemporary) Linda Peavy and Ursula Smith for *Full-Court Quest: The Girls from Fort Shaw Indian School—Basketball Champions of the World* (University of Oklahoma Press); (short fiction story) Susan K. Salzer for "Cornflower Blue" (Untamed Ink); (short nonfiction) David A. Smith for "Owen Wister's Paladin of the Plains: The Virginian as a Cultural Hero" (South Dakota

State Historical Society); (juvenile fiction) Tanya Landman for *I Am Apache* (Candlewick); (juvenile nonfiction) Frank Keating and Mike Wimmer, artist, for *The Trial of Standing Bear* (Oklahoma Heritage Association); (storyteller award) Alison L. Randall and Bill Farnsworth, artist, for *The Wheat Doll* (Peachtree); (western documentary) Michelle Ferrari for "Kit Carson" (WGBH); (poem) Linda Hussa for "The Only Good Indian" (Black Rock); (audiobook) Stan Lynde for *Vendetta Canyon* (Books in Motion); (song) Jon Chandler for "Linwood" (Western Dog).

Wallace Stevens Award ($100,000). To recognize outstanding and proven mastery in the art of poetry. *Offered by:* Academy of American Poets. *Winner:* Jean Valentine.

Bram Stoker Awards. For superior horror writing. *Offered by:* Horror Writers Association. *Winners:* (novel) Stephen King for *Duma Key* (Scribner); (first novel) Lisa Mannetti for *The Gentling Box* (DarkHart); (long fiction) John R. Little for *Miranda* (Bad Moon); (short fiction): Sarah Langan for *The Lost* (Cemetery Dance); (fiction collection) Stephen King for *Just After Sunset* (Scribner); (anthology) Vince A. Liaguno and Chad Helder, editors, for *Unspeakable Horror* (Dark Scribe); (nonfiction) Lisa Morton for *A Hallowe'en Anthology: Literary and Historical Writings Over the Centuries* (McFarland); (poetry collection) Bruce Boston for *The Nightmare Collection* (Dark Regions); (lifetime achievement) F. Paul Wilson, Chelsea Quinn Yarbro.

Stonewall Book Awards. *Offered by:* Gay, Lesbian, Bisexual, and Transgendered Round Table, American Library Association. *Winners:* (Barbara Gittings Literature Award) Evan Fallenberg for *Light Fell* (Soho); (Israel Fishman Nonfiction Award) William N. Eskridge, Jr. for *Dishonorable Passions: Sodomy Laws in America, 1861–2003* (Viking).

The Story Prize. For a collection of short fiction. *Offered by: Story* magazine. *Winner:* Tobias Wolff for *Our Story Begins* (Knopf).

Flora Stieglitz Straus Award. For nonfiction books that serve as an inspiration to young readers. *Offered by:* Bank Street College

of Education and the Florence M. Miller Memorial Fund. *Winner:* Candace Fleming for *The Lincolns: A Scrapbook Look at Abraham and Mary* (Schwartz and Wade).

Mildred and Harold Strauss Livings ($50,000 a year for five years). To two writers of English prose literature to enable them to devote their time exclusively to writing. *Winners:* (2008) Madison Smartt Bell, William T. Vollman.

Sunburst Awards for Canadian Literature of the Fantastic (C$1,000). *Winners:* (adult) Andrew Davidson for *The Gargoyle* (Random); (young adult) Cory Doctorow for *Little Brother* (Tor).

Sunday Times Young Writer of the Year Award (£5,000) (United Kingdom) *Offered by:* Society of Authors. *Sponsor:* The *Sunday Times*. *Winner:* Ross Raisin for *God's Own Country* (Penguin).

Tanizaki Prize (Japan) (1 million yen, about $11,000). For a full-length work of fiction or drama of the highest literary merit by a professional writer. *Winner:* Not awarded in 2009.

Charles Taylor Prize for Literary Nonfiction (Canada) ($25,000). To honor a book of creative nonfiction widely available in Canada and written by a Canadian citizen or landed immigrant. *Offered by:* Charles Taylor Foundation. *Winner:* Tim Cook for *Shock Troops: Canadians Fighting the Great War, 1917–1918,* Volume Two (Viking Canada).

Sydney Taylor Children's Book Awards. For a distinguished contribution to Jewish children's literature. *Offered by:* Association of Jewish Libraries. *Winners:* (younger readers) Richard Michelson for *As Good as Anybody: Martin Luther King, Jr. and Abraham Joshua Heschel's Amazing March Toward Freedom,* illustrated by Raul Colon (Knopf); (older readers) Karen Hesse for *Brooklyn Bridge* (Macmillan); (teen readers) Valerie Zenatti for *A Bottle in the Gaza Sea* (Bloomsbury).

Sydney Taylor Manuscript Competition ($1,000). For the best fiction manuscript appropriate for readers ages 8–11, both Jewish and non-Jewish, revealing positive aspects of Jewish life, and written by an unpublished author. *Winner:* Nechama

Liss-Levinson for "When the Hurricane Came to New Orleans."

Theatre Library Association Award. For the best English-language book about recorded performance, including motion pictures, television, and radio. *Offered by:* Theatre Library Association. *Winner:* Mark Harris for *Pictures at a Revolution: Five Movies and the Birth of the New Hollywood* (Penguin).

Dylan Thomas Prize (United Kingdom) (£60,000). Awarded biennially to a writer under the age of 30 for a commercially published work of literature. *Offered by:* David Cohen Family Charitable Trust and the Arts Council of England. *Winner:* Not awarded in 2009.

Thriller Awards. *Offered by:* International Thriller Writers. *Winners:* (novel) Jeffery Deaver for *The Bodies Left Behind* (Simon & Schuster); (first novel) Tom Rob Smith for *Child 44* (Grand Central); (short story) Alexandra Sokoloff for "The Edge of Seventeen" in *The Darker Mask* (Tor).

Thurber Prize for American Humor ($5,000). For a humorous book of fiction or nonfiction. *Offered by:* Thurber House. *Winner:* Ian Frazier for *Lamentations of the Father* (Picador).

Tom-Gallon Trust Award and Olive Cook Prize (£1,000). For a short story. Each is awarded biennially in alternate years. *Winner:* (Tom-Gallon Award) Rosemary Mairs for "My Father's Hands."

Betty Trask Prize and Award (United Kingdom). To Commonwealth writers under the age of 35 for "romantic or traditional" first novels. *Offered by:* Society of Authors. *Winners:* (Betty Trask Prize, £12,000) Samantha Harvey for *The Wilderness* (Cape); (Betty Trask Award, £8,000) Eleanor Catton for *The Rehearsal* (Granta).

Kate Tufts Discovery Award ($10,000). For a first or very early book of poetry by an emerging poet. *Offered by:* Claremont Graduate School. *Winner:* Matthew Dickman for *All-American Poem* (American Poetry Review).

Kingsley Tufts Poetry Award ($100,000). For a book of poetry by a mid-career poet. *Offered by:* Claremont Graduate School.

Winner: Matthea Harvey for *Modern Life* (Graywolf).

21st Century Award. To honor recent achievement in writing by an author with ties to Chicago. *Sponsor:* Chicago Public Library Foundation. *Winner:* Patrick Somerville.

UKLA Children's Book Awards (United Kingdom). *Sponsor:* United Kingdom Literacy Association. *Winners:* (younger readers) Marcia Williams for *Archie's War* (Walker); (older readers) Siobhan Dowd for *Bog Child* (Random).

Ungar German Translation Award. Awarded biennially for a distinguished literary translation from German into English that has been published in the United States. *Offered by:* American Translators Association. *Winner:* Rodney Livingstone for *Theodor W. Adorno: One Last Genius* by Detlev Claussen (Harvard University Press).

Harold D. Vursell Memorial Award ($10,000). To a writer whose work merits recognition for the quality of its prose style. *Offered by* American Academy of Arts and Letters. *Winner:* Sharon Cameron.

Amelia Elizabeth Walden Award ($5,000). To honor a book relevant to adolescents that has enjoyed a wide teenage audience. *Sponsor:* Assembly on Literature for Adolescents, National Council of Teachers of English. *Winner:* Steve Kluger for *My Most Excellent Year: A Novel of Love, Mary Poppins, and Fenway Park* (Dial).

Kim Scott Walwyn Prize (United Kingdom). To recognize the professional achievements of women in publishing. *Offered by:* Booktrust. *Winner:* Kathy Rooney.

George Washington Book Prize ($50,000). To recognize an important new book about America's founding era. *Offered by:* Washington College and the Gilder Lehrman Institute of American History. *Winner:* Annette Gordon-Reed for *The Hemingses of Monticello: An American Family* (Norton).

Carole Weinstein Poetry Prize ($10,000). To poets with strong connections to central Virginia who have made a "significant recent contribution to the art of poetry." *Winners:* Eleanor Ross Taylor, Charles Wright.

Whitbread Book Awards. See Costa Book Awards.

E. B. White Read Aloud Awards. For children's books with particular appeal as read-aloud books. *Offered by:* Association of Booksellers for Children. *Winners:* (picture books) Bonny Becker and Kady MacDonald Denton, illustrator, for *A Visitor for Bear* (Candlewick); (older readers) Elise Broach and Kelly Murphy, illustrator, for *Masterpiece* (Holt).

Whiting Writers' Awards ($50,000). For emerging writers of exceptional talent and promise. *Offered by:* Mrs. Giles Whiting Foundation. *Winners:* (fiction) Adam Johnson, Nami Mun, Salvatore Scibona, Vu Tran; (nonfiction) Michael Meyer, Hugh Raffles; (poetry) Jericho Brown, Jay Hopler, Joan Kane; (plays) Rajiv Joseph.

Walt Whitman Award ($5,000). To a U.S. poet who has not published a book of poems in a standard edition. *Offered by:* Academy of American Poets. *Winner:* J. Michael Martinez for *Heredities* (LSU Press).

Richard Wilbur Award ($1,000 and publication by University of Evansville Press). Given biennially for a book-length poetry collection. *Winner:* Susan McLean for *The Best Disguise.*

Laura Ingalls Wilder Award. Awarded biennially to an author or illustrator whose books have made a substantial and lasting contribution to children's literature. *Offered by:* American Library Association, Association for Library Service to Children. *Winner:* Ashley Bryan.

Thornton Wilder Prize for Translation ($20,000). To a practitioner, scholar, or patron who has made a significant contribution to the art of literary translation. *Offered by:* American Academy of Arts and Letters. *Winner:* Gregory Rabassa.

Robert H. Winner Memorial Award. To a mid-career poet over 40 who has published no more than one book of poetry. *Offered by:* Poetry Society of America. *Winner:* Eliot Khalil Wilson for "The Tailor of Al Hamdaniyah."

George Wittenborn Memorial Book Awards. To North American art publications that represent the highest standards of content,

documentation, layout, and format. *Offered by:* Art Libraries Society of North America (ARLIS/NA). *Winner: Cai Guo-Qiang: I want to believe* (Guggenheim Museum), text by David Joselit, Miwon Kwon, Alexandra Munroe, and Wang Hui.

Thomas Wolfe Award and Lecture. To honor writers with distinguished bodies of work. *Offered by:* Thomas Wolfe Society and University of North Carolina at Chapel Hill. *Winner:* Roy Blount, Jr.

Thomas Wolfe Fiction Prize ($1,000). For a short story that honors Thomas Wolfe. *Offered by:* North Carolina Writers Network. *Winner:* Howard Carter for "Mr. Mason's Request."

Helen and Kurt Wolff Translator's Prize ($10,000). For an outstanding translation from German into English, published in the United States. *Offered by:* Goethe Institut Inter Nationes, Chicago. *Winner:* John Hargraves for his translation of Michael Krüger's *Turiner Komödie (The Executor—A Comedy of Letters)* (Harcourt).

World Fantasy Convention Awards. For outstanding fantasy writing. *Offered by:* World Fantasy Convention. *Winners:* (novel) Jeffrey Ford for *The Shadow Year* (Morrow), Margo Lanagan for *Tender Morsels* (Knopf); (novella) Richard Bowes for "If Angels Fight" in *F&SF* February 2008; (short story) Kij Johnson for "26 Monkeys, Also the Abyss" in *Asimov's* July 2008; (anthology) Ekaterina Sedia, editor, for *Paper Cities: An Anthology of Urban Fantasy* (Senses Five); (collection) Jeffrey Ford for *The Drowned Life* (HarperPerennial); (artist) Shaun Tan; (lifetime achievement) Ellen Asher, Jane Yolen.

Writers' Trust Shaughnessy Cohen Prize for Political Writing (Canada) (C$25,000). For a nonfiction book that captures a subject of political interest. *Sponsor:* CTVglobemedia. *Winner:* James Orbinski for *An Imperfect Offering: Humanitarian Action in the Twenty-first Century* (Walker).

Writers' Trust/McClelland & Stewart Journey Prize (Canada) (C$10,000). To a new, developing Canadian author for a short story or an excerpt from a novel in progress. *Offered by:* McClelland & Stewart and

James A. Michener. *Winner:* Yasuko Thanh for "Floating Like the Dead," published in *Vancouver Review.*

Writers' Trust Nonfiction Prize (Canada) (C$25,000). *Offered by:* Writers' Trust. *Winner:* Brian Brett for *Trauma Farm: A Rebel History of Rural Life* (Greystone).

Writers' Trust Notable Author (Canada) (C$25,000). To a writer in mid-career for a body of work. *Winner:* David Bergen.

Young Lions Fiction Award ($10,000). For a novel or collection of short stories by an American under the age of 35. *Offered by:* Young Lions of the New York Public Library. *Winner:* Salvatore Scibona for *The End* (Riverhead).

Morton Dauwen Zabel Award ($10,000). Awarded biennially to a progressive and experimental writer. *Offered by:* American Academy of Arts and Letters. *Winner:* Not awarded in 2009.

Zoetrope Short Fiction Prizes. *Offered by:* Zoetrope: All-Story. *Winners:* (first, $1,000) Ted Burton for "The Third Law of Dialectics"; (second, $500) Jenny Jianing Zhang for "You Fell into the River and I Saved You!"; (third, $250) Megan Mayhew Bergman for "The Two Thousand Dollar Sock."

Charlotte Zolotow Award. To the author of the best children's picture book published in the United States in the previous year. *Offered by:* Cooperative Children's Book Center, University of Wisconsin–Madison. *Winner:* Bob Graham for *How to Heal a Broken Wing* (Candlewick).

Part 6
Directory of Organizations

Directory of Library and Related Organizations

Networks, Consortia, and Other Cooperative Library Organizations

United States

Alabama

Alabama Health Libraries Assn., Inc. (ALHeLa), Lister Hill Lib., Univ. of Alabama, Birmingham 35294-0013. SAN 372-8218. Tel. 205-975-8313, fax 205-934-2230. *Pres.* Lee Vacovich.

Library Management Network, Inc. (LMN), 2132 6th Ave S.E., Suite 106, Decatur 35601. SAN 322-3906. Tel. 256-308-2529, fax 256-308-2533. *Systems Coord.* Charlotte Moncrief.

Marine Environmental Sciences Consortium, Dauphin Island Sea Laboratory, Dauphin Island 36528. SAN 322-0001. Tel. 251-861-2141, fax 251-861-4646, e-mail disl@disl.org. *Coord.* John Dindo.

Network of Alabama Academic Libraries, c/o Alabama Commission on Higher Education, Montgomery 36104. SAN 322-4570. Tel. 334-242-2211, fax 334-242-0270. *Dir.* Sue O. Medina.

Alaska

Alaska Library Network (ALN), P.O. Box 100585, Anchorage 99501-0585. SAN 371-0688. Tel. 907-269-6587. *Cataloger* Keri Canepa.

Arizona

Maricopa County Community College District/Library Technology Services, 2411 W. 14 St., Tempe 85281-6942. SAN 322-0060. Tel. 480-731-8774, fax 480-731-8787. *Dir. of Technical Services* Thomas Saudargas.

Arkansas

Arkansas Area Health Education Center Consortium (AHEC), Sparks Regional Medical Center, Fort Smith 72901-4992. SAN 329-3734. Tel. 479-441-5337, fax 479-441-5339. *Dir.* Grace Anderson.

Arkansas Independent Colleges and Universities, Firstar Bldg., 1 Riverfront Place, Suite 610, North Little Rock 72114. SAN 322-0079. Tel. 501-378-0843, fax 501-374-1523. *Pres.* Kearney E. Dietz.

Northeast Arkansas Hospital Library Consortium, 223 E. Jackson, Jonesboro 72401. SAN 329-529X. Tel. 870-972-1290, fax 870-931-0839. *Dir.* Karen Crosser.

South Arkansas Film Coop., c/o Malvern-Hot Spring County Lib., Malvern 72104. SAN 321-5938. Tel. 501-332-5441, fax 501-332-6679, e-mail hotspringcountylibrary@yahoo.com. *Dir.* Tammy Carter.

California

49-99 Cooperative Library System, c/o Southern California Lib. Cooperative, Monrovia 91016. SAN 301-6218. Tel. 626-359-6111, fax 626-359-0001. *Dir.* Rosario Garza.

Bay Area Library and Information Network (BayNet), C/o San Francisco Public Lib., San Francisco 94702. SAN 371-0610. Tel. 415-355-2826, e-mail infobay@baynetlibs. org. *Pres.* Linda Suzukie.

Bay Area Library and Information System (BALIS), 2471 Flores St., San Mateo 94403. Tel. 650-349-5538, fax 650-349-5089. *Exec. Dir.* Linda Crowe.

Berkeley Information Network (BIN), Berkeley Public Lib., Berkeley 94704. Tel. 510-981-6166; 510-981-6150, fax 510-981-6246. *Mgr.* Jane Scantlebury.

Califa, 32 W. 25 Ave., Suite 201, San Mateo 94403. Tel. 650-572-2746, fax 650-349-5089, e-mail califa@califa.org. *Exec. Dir.* Linda Crowe.

Central Assn. of Libraries (CAL), 605 N. El Dorado St., Stockton 95202-1999. SAN 322-0125. Tel. 209-937-8649, fax 209-937-8292. *Dir.* Darla Gunning.

Claremont University Consortium (CUC), 150 E. 8 St., Claremont 91711. Tel. 909-621-8026; 909-621-8150, fax 909-621-8681. *CEO* Robert Walton.

Consortium for Open Learning, 333 Sunrise Ave., No. 229, Roseville 95661-3480. SAN 329-4412. Tel. 916-788-0660, fax 916-788-0696. *Operations Mgr.* Sandra Scott-Smith.

Consumer Health Information Program and Services (CHIPS), 12350 Imperial Hwy., Norwalk 90650. SAN 372-8110. Tel. 562-868-4003, fax 562-868-4065, e-mail referenceservices@gw.colapl.org. *Libn.* Amy Beteilho.

Gold Coast Library Network, 3437 Empresa Drive, Suite C, San Luis Obispo 93401-7355. Tel. 805-543-6082, fax 805-543-9487. *Admin. Dir.* Maureen Theobald.

Kaiser Permanente Library System–Southern California Region (KPLS), Health Sciences Lib., Riverside 92505. SAN 372-8153. Tel. 951-353-3659, fax 951-353-3262, e-mail scal.rsvd-medical-library@ kp.org. *Dir.* William Paringer.

Monterey Bay Area Cooperative Library System (MOBAC), 2471 Flores St., San Mateo 94403. SAN 301-2921. Tel. 650-349-5538, fax 650-349-5089. *Exec. Dir.* Linda Crowe.

Mountain Valley Library System (MVLS), 55 E St., Santa Rosa 95404. Tel. 707-544-0142, fax 707-544-8411 ext. 101. *Exec. Dir.* Annette Milliron.

National Network of Libraries of Medicine–Pacific Southwest Region (NN/LM-PSR), Louise M. Darling Biomedical Lib., Los Angeles 90095-1798. SAN 372-8234. Tel. 310-825-1200, fax 310-825-5389, e-mail psr-nnlm@library.ucla.edu. *Dir.* Judy Consales.

Nevada Medical Library Group (NMLG), Barton Memorial Hospital Lib., South Lake Tahoe 96150. SAN 370-0445. Tel. 530-543-5844, fax 530-541-4697. *Senior Exec. Coord.* Laurie Anton.

Northern California Assn. of Law Libraries (NOCALL), 268 Bush St., No. 4006, San Francisco 94104. SAN 323-5777. E-mail admin@nocall.org. *Pres.* Coral Henning.

Northern California Consortium of Psychology Libraries (NCCPL), Argosy Univ., San Francisco Bay Area Campus, Alameda 94133. SAN 371-9006. Tel. 510-837-3715. *Pres.* Julie Griffith.

OCLC Western Service Center, 3281 E. Guasti Rd., Suite 560, Ontario 91761. SAN 370-0747. Tel. 909-937-3300, fax 909-937-3384, e-mail western@oclc.org. *Dir.* Pamela Bailey.

Peninsula Libraries Automated Network (PLAN), 2471 Flores St., San Mateo 94403-4000. SAN 371-5035. Tel. 650-349-5538, fax 650-349-5089. *Dir., Information Technology.* Monica Schultz.

San Bernardino, Inyo, Riverside Counties United Library Services (SIRCULS), 3581 Mission Inn Ave., Riverside 92501-3377. SAN 322-0222. Tel. 951-369-7995, fax 951-784-1158, e-mail sirculs@inlandlib. org. *Exec. Dir.* Kathleen F. Aaron.

San Francisco Biomedical Library Network (SFBLN), San Francisco General Hospital UCSF/ Barnett-Briggs Medical Lib., San Francisco 94110. SAN 371-2125. Tel. 415-206-6639, e-mail fishbon@ucsfmedctr. org.

Santa Clarita Interlibrary Network (SCIL-NET), Powell Lib., Santa Clarita 91321. SAN 371-8964. Tel. 661-259-3540 ext. 3420, fax 661-222-9159. *Libn.* John Stone.

Serra Cooperative Library System, 820 E St., San Diego 92101. SAN 372-8129. Tel. 619-232-1225, fax 619-696-8649, e-mail serral@serralib.org. *ILL/Document Delivery Services* Ralph DeLauro.

Southern California Library Cooperative (SCLC), 248 E. Foothill Blvd., Suite 101, Monrovia 91016-5522. SAN 371-3865. Tel. 626-359-6111, fax 626-359-0001, e-mail sclchq@socallibraries.org. *Dir.* Rosario Garza.

Substance Abuse Librarians and Information Specialists (SALIS), P.O. Box 9513, Berkeley 94709-0513. SAN 372-4042. Fax 510-985-6459, e-mail salis@salis.org. *Exec. Dir.* Andrea L. Mitchell.

Colorado

Automation System Colorado Consortium (ASCC), c/o Delta Public Lib., Delta 81416. Tel. 970-872-4317. *Technology Consultant* Connie Wolfrom.

BCR (Bibliographical Center for Research), 14394 E. Evans Ave., Aurora 80014-1408. SAN 322-0338. Tel. 303-751-6277, fax 303-751-9787, e-mail info@bcr.org. *Pres. and CEO* Brenda Bailey-Hainer.

Colorado Alliance of Research Libraries, 3801 E. Florida Ave., Suite 515, Denver 80210. SAN 322-3760. Tel. 303-759-3399, fax 303-759-3363. *Exec. Dir.* Alan Charnes.

Colorado Assn. of Law Libraries, P.O. Box 13363, Denver 80201. SAN 322-4325. Tel. 303-492-7535, fax 303-492-2707. *Pres.* Tracy Leming.

Colorado Council of Medical Librarians (CCML), P.O. Box 101058, Denver 80210-1058. SAN 370-0755. Tel. 303-724-2124, fax 303-724-2154. *Pres.* Gene Gardner.

Colorado Library Consortium (CLiC), 770 W. Hampden Ave., Suite 105, Centennial 80112. SAN 371-3970. Tel. 303-422-1150, fax 303-431-9752. *Dir.* Valerie Horton.

Connecticut

Bibliomation, 32 Crest Rd., Middlebury 06762. Tel. 203-577-4070, fax 203-577-4077. *CEO* Mike Simonds.

Capital Area Health Consortium, 270 Farmington Ave., Suite 352, Farmington 06032-1994. SAN 322-0370. Tel. 860-676-1110, fax 860-676-1303. *Pres.* Karen Goodman.

Connecticut Library Consortium, 234 Court St., Middletown 06457-3304. SAN 322-0389. Tel. 860-344-8777, fax 860-344-9199, e-mail clc@ctlibrarians.org. *Exec. Dir.* Christine Bradley.

Council of State Library Agencies in the Northeast (COSLINE), Connecticut State Lib., Hartford 06106. SAN 322-0451. Tel. 860-757-6510, fax 860-757-6503.

CTW Library Consortium, Olin Memorial Lib., Middletown 06459-6065. SAN 329-4587. Tel. 860-685-3889, fax 860-685-2661. *System Libn.* Steve Bischof.

Hartford Consortium for Higher Education, 950 Main St., Suite 314, Hartford 06103. SAN 322-0443. Tel. 860-906-5016, fax 860-906-5118. *Exec. Dir.* Rosanne Druckman.

LEAP, 110 Washington Ave., North Haven 06473. SAN 322-4082. Tel. 203-239-1411, fax 203-239-9458. *Exec. Dir.* Diana Sellers.

Libraries Online, Inc. (LION), 100 Riverview Center, Suite 252, Middletown 06457. SAN 322-3922. Tel. 860-347-1704, fax 860-346-3707. *Exec. Dir.* Alan Hagyard.

Library Connection, Inc., 599 Matianuck Ave., Windsor 06095-3567. Tel. 860-298-5322, fax 860-298-5328. *Exec. Dir.* George Christian.

North Atlantic Health Sciences Libraries, Inc. (NAHSL), Dana Medical Lib., Univ. of Vermont Medical School, Burlington 05405. SAN 371-0599. Tel. 508-656-3483, fax 508-656-0762. *Chair* Marianne Burke.

Delaware

Central Delaware Library Consortium, Dover Public Lib., Dover 19901. SAN 329-3696. Tel. 302-736-7030, fax 302-736-5087. *Dir.* Margery Kirby Cyr.

Delaware Library Consortium (DLC), Delaware Academy of Medicine, Newark 19713. SAN 329-3718. Tel. 302-733-1122, fax 302-733-3885, e-mail library@delamed.org. *Dir.* P J Grier.

District of Columbia

Computer Sciences Corporation/ERIC Project, 655 15th St. N.W., Suite 500, Washington 20005. SAN 322-161X. Tel. 202-741-4200, fax 202-628-3205. *Dir.* Lawrence Henry.

Council for Christian Colleges and Universities, 321 8th St. N.E., Washington 20002. SAN 322-0524. Tel. 202-546-8713, fax 202-546-8913, e-mail council@cccu.org. *Pres.* Paul R. Corts.

District of Columbia Area Health Science Libraries (DCAHSL), American College of Obstetrics and Gynecology Resource Center, Washington 20024. SAN 323-9918. Tel. 202-863-2518, fax 202-484-1595, e-mail resources@acog.org. *Pres.* Rudine Anderson.

FEDLINK/Federal Library and Information Network, c/o Federal Lib. and Info. Center Committee, Washington 20540-4935. SAN 322-0761. Tel. 202-707-4800, fax 202-707-4818, e-mail flicc@loc.gov. *Exec. Dir.* Roberta I. Shaffer.

Interlibrary Users Assn. (IUA), c/o Urban Institute Lib., Washington 20037. SAN 322-1628. Tel. 202-261-5534, fax 202-223-3043. *Pres.* Nancy L. Minter.

OCLC Eastern, 11 Dupont Circle N.E., Suite 550, Washington 20036-3430. SAN 321-5954. Tel. 202-331-5771, fax 202-331-5788, e-mail eastern@oclc.org. *Exec. Dir.* Irene M. Hoffman.

Transportation Research Board, 500 5th St. N.W., Washington 20001. SAN 370-582X. Tel. 202-334-2990, fax 202-334-2527. *Mgr., Info. Services* Barbara Post.

Veterans Affairs Library Network (VAL-NET), Lib. Programs Office 19E, Washington 20420. SAN 322-0834. *Dir. of Lib. Programs* Ginny DuPont.

Washington Theological Consortium, 487 Michigan Ave. N.E., Washington 20017-1585. SAN 322-0842. Tel. 202-832-2675, fax 202-526-0818, e-mail wtc@washtheocon.org. *Exec. Dir.* John Crossin.

Florida

Central Florida Library Cooperative (CFLC), 431 E. Horatio Ave., Suite 230, Maitland 32751. SAN 371-9014. Tel. 407-644-9050, fax 407-644-7023, e-mail contactus@cflc.net. *Exec. Dir.* Marta Westall.

College Center for Library Automation (CCLA), 1753 W. Paul Dirac Drive, Tallahassee 32310. Tel. 850-922-6044, fax 850-922-4869, e-mail servicedesk@cclaflorida.org. *Exec. Dir.* Richard Madaus.

Consortium of Southeastern Law Libraries (COSELL), Lawton Chiles Legal Information Center, Gainesville 32611. SAN 372-8277. Tel. 352-273-0710, fax 352-392-5093.

Florida Center for Library Automation (FCLA), 5830 N.W. 39 Ave., Gainesville 32606. Tel. 352-392-9020, fax 352-392-9185, e-mail fclmin@ufl.edu. *Dir.* James Corey.

Florida Library Information Network, R. A. Gray Bldg., Tallahassee 32399-0250. SAN 322-0869. Tel. 850-245-6600, fax 850-245-6744, e-mail library@dos.state.fl.us. *Lending Services Libn.* Linda Pulliam.

Miami Health Sciences Library Consortium (MHSLC), Miami VA Healthcare System, Miami 33125-1624. SAN 371-0734. Tel. 305-575-3187, fax 305-575-3118, e-mail vhamialibrary@va.gov. *Pres.* Devica Samsundar.

Northeast Florida Library Information Network (NEFLIN), 2233 Park Ave., Suite 402, Orange Park 32073. Tel. 904-278-5620, fax 904-278-5625, e-mail office@neflin.org. *Exec. Dir.* Brad Ward.

Panhandle Library Access Network (PLAN), Five Miracle Strip Loop, Suite 8, Panama City Beach 32407-3850. SAN 370-047X. Tel. 850-233-9051, fax 850-235-2286. *Exec. Dir.* William P. Conniff.

SEFLIN/Southeast Florida Library Information Network, Inc, Wimberly Lib., Office 452, Boca Raton 33431. SAN 370-0666. Tel. 561-208-0984, fax 561-208-0995. *Exec. Dir.* Tom Sloan.

Southwest Florida Library Network (SWFLN), Bldg. III, Unit 7, Fort Myers 33913. Tel. 239-225-4225, fax 239-225-4229, e-mail swfln@fgcu.edu. *Exec. Dir.* Sondra Taylor-Furbee.

Tampa Bay Library Consortium, Inc., 1202 Tech Blvd., Suite 202, Tampa 33619. SAN 322-371X. Tel. 813-740-3963; 813-622-

8252, fax 813-628-4425. *Exec. Dir.* Charlie Parker.

Tampa Bay Medical Library Network (TABAMLN), Florida Hospital College of Health Sciences, Orlando 32803-1226. SAN 322-0885. Tel. 407-303-9798, fax 407-303-9408. *Pres.* Deanna Stevens.

Georgia

Assn. of Southeastern Research Libraries (ASERL), c/o LYRASIS, Atlanta 30309-2955. SAN 322-1555. Tel. 404-892-0943, fax 404-892-7879. *Exec. Dir.* John Burger.

Atlanta Health Science Libraries Consortium, Fran Golding Medical Lib. at Scottish Rite, Atlanta 30342-1600. Tel. 404-785-2157, fax 404-785-2155. *Pres.* Kate Daniels.

Atlanta Regional Council for Higher Education (ARCHE), 50 Hurt Plaza, Suite 735, Atlanta 30303-2923. SAN 322-0990. Tel. 404-651-2668, fax 404-880-9816, e-mail arche@atlantahighered.org. *Pres.* Michael Gerber.

Georgia Interactive Network for Medical Information (GAIN), c/o Mercer Univ. School of Medicine, Macon 31207. SAN 370-0577. Tel. 478-301-2515, fax 478-301-2051, e-mail gain.info@gain.mercer. edu. *Dir.* Jan H. LaBeause.

Georgia Online Database (GOLD), c/o Public Lib. Services, Atlanta 30345-4304. SAN 322-094X. Tel. 404-235-7200, fax 404-235-7201. *Lib. Services Mgr.* Elaine Hardy.

LYRASIS, 1438 W. Peachtree St. N.W., Suite 200, Atlanta 30309-2955. SAN 322-0974. Tel. 404-892-0943, fax 404-892-7879. *Exec. Dir.* Kate Nevins.

Metro Atlanta Library Assn. (MALA), P.O. Box 14948, Atlanta 30324. SAN 378-2549. Tel. 678-915-7207, fax 678-915-7471, e-mail mala-a@comcast.net. *Pres.* Steven Vincent.

Hawaii

Hawaii Library Consortium (HLC), c/o Hawaii Business Research Lib., Kihei 96753. Tel. 808-875-2408. *Pres.* Sonia I. King.

Hawaii-Pacific Chapter, Medical Library Assn. (HPC-MLA), Health Sciences Lib., Honolulu 96813. SAN 371-3946. Tel. 808-692-0810, fax 808-692-1244. *Chair* A. Lee Adams.

Idaho

Canyon Owyhee Library Group, Ltd. (COLG), 203 E. Owyhee Ave., Homedale 83628. Tel. 208-454-2221, 337-4613, fax 208-337-4933. *Coord.* Glynda Pflieger.

Cooperative Information Network (CIN), 8385 N. Government Way, Hayden 83835-9280. SAN 323-7656. Tel. 208-772-5612, fax 208-772-2498, e-mail hay@cin.kcl. org. *Fiscal Agent* John W. Hartung.

Idaho Health Information Assn. (IHIA), c/o Eastern Idaho Regional Medical Center, Idaho Falls 83403. SAN 371-5078. Tel. 208-529-6077, fax 208-529-7014. *Dir.* Kathy Fatkin.

Library Consortium of Eastern Idaho (LCEI), 5210 Stuart Ave., Chubbuck 83202. SAN 323-7699. Tel. 208-237-2192. *Chair* Linda Rasmussen.

LYNX Consortium, c/o Boise Public Lib., Boise 83702-7195. SAN 375-0086. Tel. 208-384-4238, fax 208-384-4025, e-mail askalibrarian@cityofboise.org.

Illinois

Alliance Library System, 600 High Point Lane, East Peoria 61611. SAN 371-0637. Tel. 309-694-9200, fax 309-694-9230. *Exec. Dir.* Kitty Pope.

American Theological Library Assn. (ATLA), 300 S. Wacker Drive, Suite 2100, Chicago 60606-5889. SAN 371-9022. Tel. 312-454-5100, fax 312-454-5505, e-mail atla@ atla.com. *Exec. Dir.* Dennis A. Norlin.

Areawide Hospital Library Consortium of Southwestern Illinois (AHLC), c/o St. Elizabeth Hospital Health Sciences Lib., Belleville 62222. SAN 322-1016. Tel. 618-234-2120 ext. 2011, fax 618-222-4614.

Assn. of Chicago Theological Schools (ACTS), Wiggin Lib. at Meadville/Lombard Theological School, Chicago 60637. SAN 370-0658. Tel. 773-256-3000 ext. 225. *Chair* Neil Gerdes.

Capital Area Consortium, 701 N. 1 St., Springfield 62781. *Coord.* Lynne Ferrell.

Center for Research Libraries, 6050 S. Kenwood, Chicago 60637-2804. SAN 322-1032. Tel. 773-955-4545, fax 773-955-4339. *Pres.* Bernard F. Reilly.

Chicago and South Consortium, Jackson Park Hospital and Medical Center, Chicago 60649-3993. SAN 322-1067. Tel. 773-947-7653. *Coord.* Andrew Paradise.

Chicago Area Museum Libraries (CAML), c/o Lib., Field Museum, Chicago 60605-2496. SAN 371-392X. Tel. 312-665-7887, fax 312-665-7893. *Assoc. Libn., Reference and Circulation Services* Christine Giannoni.

Committee on Institutional Cooperation, 1819 S. Neil St., Suite D, Champaign 61820-7271. Tel. 217-333-8475, fax 217-244-7127, e-mail cic@staff.cic.net. *Dir.* Barbara Mcfadden Allen.

Consortium of Academic and Research Libraries in Illinois (CARLI), 100 Trade Center Drive, Suite 303, Champaign 61820. SAN 322-3736. Tel. 217-244-7593, fax 217-244-7596, e-mail support@carli.illinois.edu. *Exec. Dir.* Susan Singleton.

Council of Directors of State University Libraries in Illinois (CODSULI), Southern Illinois Univ. School of Medicine Lib., Springfield 62702-4910. SAN 322-1083. Tel. 217-545-0994, fax 217-545-0988.

East Central Illinois Consortium, Booth Lib., Eastern Illinois Univ., Charleston 61920. SAN 322-1040. Tel. 217-581-7549, fax 217-581-7534. *Mgr.* Stacey Knight-Davis.

Fox Valley Health Science Library Consortium, c/o Delnor-Community Hospital, Geneva 60134. SAN 329-3831. Tel. 630-208-4299.

Heart of Illinois Library Consortium, 511 N.E. Greenleaf, Peoria 61603. SAN 322-1113. *Chair* Leslie Menz.

Illinois Library and Information Network (ILLINET), c/o Illinois State Lib., Springfield 62701-1796. SAN 322-1148. Tel. 217-782-2994, fax 217-785-4326. *Dir.* Anne Craig.

Illinois Office of Educational Services, 2450 Foundation Drive, Suite 100, Springfield 62703-5464. SAN 371-5108. Tel. 217-786-3010, fax 217-786-3020, e-mail info@ioes.org. *Dir.* Rebecca Woodhull.

LIBRAS, Inc., North Park Univ., Chicago 60625-4895. SAN 322-1172. Tel. 773-244-5584, fax 773-244-4891. *Pres.* Mark Vargas.

Metropolitan Consortium of Chicago, Chicago School of Professional Psychology, Chicago 60610. SAN 322-1180. Tel. 312-329-6633, fax 312-644-6075. *Coord.* Margaret White.

National Network of Libraries of Medicine–Greater Midwest Region (NN/LM-GMR), c/o Lib. of Health Sciences, Univ. of Illinois at Chicago, Chicago 60612-4330. SAN 322-1202. Tel. 312-996-2464, fax 312-996-2226. *Dir.* Kathryn Carpenter.

Network of Illinois Learning Resources in Community Colleges (NILRC), 719 William St., River Forest 60305-1925. Tel. 608-523-4094, fax 608-523-4072. *Exec. Dir.* John W. Berry.

Quad Cities Libraries in Cooperation (QuadLINC), 220 W. 23 Ave., Coal Valley 61240. SAN 373-093X. Tel. 309-799-3155 ext. 3254, fax 309-799-7916.

System Wide Automated Network (SWAN), c/o Metropolitan Lib. System, Burr Ridge 60527-5783. Tel. 630-734-5000, fax 630-734-5050. *Dir.* Aaron Skog.

Indiana

Central Indiana Health Science Libraries Consortium, Indiana Univ. School of Medicine Lib., Indianapolis 46202. SAN 322-1245. Tel. 317-274-8358, fax 317-274-4056. *Officer* Elaine Skopelja.

Collegiate Consortium Western Indiana, c/o Cunningham Memorial Lib., Terre Haute 47809. SAN 329-4439. Tel. 812-237-3700, fax 812-237-3376. *Interim Dean* Alberta Comer.

Consortium of College and University Media Centers (CCUMC), Indiana Univ., Bloomington 47405-1223. SAN 322-1091. Tel. 812-855-6049, fax 812-855-2103, e-mail ccumc@ccumc.org. *Exec. Dir.* Aileen Scales.

Consortium of Foundation Libraries, IUPUI Univ. Lib., Indianapolis 46202. SAN 322-2462. Tel. 317-278-2329. *Chair* Brenda Burk.

Evansville Area Library Consortium, 3700 Washington Ave., Evansville 47750. SAN

322-1261. Tel. 812-485-4151, fax 812-485-7564. *Coord.* Jane Saltzman.

Indiana Cooperative Library Services Authority (INCOLSA), 6202 Morenci Trail, Indianapolis 46268-2536. SAN 322-1296. Tel. 317-298-6570, fax 317-328-2380. *Exec. Dir.* Michael Piper.

Indiana State Data Center, Indiana State Lib., Indianapolis 46202. SAN 322-1318. Tel. 317-232-3733, fax 317-232-3728. *Coord.* Katie Springer.

Northeast Indiana Health Science Libraries Consortium (NEIHSL), Univ. of Saint Francis Vann Lib., Fort Wayne 46808. SAN 373-1383. Tel. 260-399-7700 ext. 6065, fax 260-399-8166. *Coord.* Lauralee Aven.

Northwest Indiana Health Science Library Consortium (NIHSLC), c/o N.W. Center for Medical Education, Gary 46408-1197. SAN 322-1350. Tel. 219-980-6852; 219-980-6709, fax 219-980-6524; 219-980-6566. *Coord. Lib. Services* Corona Wiley.

Iowa

Consortium of User Libraries (CUL), Lib. for the Blind and Physically Handicapped, Des Moines 50309-2364. Tel. 515-281-1333, fax 515-281-1378; 515-281-1263. *Pres.* Karen Keninger.

Dubuque Area Library Information Consortium, c/o Burton Payne Lib., N.E. Iowa Community College, Peosta 52068. Tel. 563-556-5110 ext. 269, fax 563-557-0340. *Coord.* Deb Seiffert.

Iowa Private Academic Library Consortium (IPAL), c/o Buena Vista Univ. Lib., Storm Lake 50588. SAN 329-5311. Tel. 712-749-2127, 712-749-2203, fax 712-749-2059, e-mail library@bvu.edu. *Univ. Libn.* Jim Kennedy.

Linn County Library Consortium, Russell D. Cole Lib., Mount Vernon 52314-1012. SAN 322-4597. Tel. 319-895-4259. *Pres.* Aileen Chang-Matus.

Polk County Biomedical Consortium, c/o Broadlawns Medical Center Lib., Des Moines 50314. SAN 322-1431. Tel. 515-282 2394, fax 515-282 5634. *Treas.* Elaine Hughes.

Quad City Area Biomedical Consortium, Great River Medical Center Lib., West

Burlington 52655. SAN 322-435X. Tel. 319-768-4075, fax 319-768-4080. *Coord.* Judy Hawk.

Sioux City Library Cooperative (SCLC), c/o Sioux City Public Lib., Sioux City 51101-1203. SAN 329-4722. Tel. 712-255-2933 ext. 255, fax 712-279-6432. *Chair* Betsy Thompson.

State of Iowa Libraries Online (SILO), State Lib. of Iowa, Des Moines 50319. SAN 322-1415. Tel. 515-281-4105, fax 515-281-6191. *State Libn.* Mary Wegner.

Kansas

Associated Colleges of Central Kansas (ACCK), 210 S. Main St., McPherson 67460. SAN 322-1474. Tel. 620-241-5150, fax 620-241-5153.

Dodge City Library Consortium, c/o Comanche Intermediate Center, Dodge City 67801. SAN 322-4368. Tel. 620-227-1609, fax 620-227-4862.

Kansas Regents Library Database Consortium (RLDC), c/o Emporia State Univ., Emporia 66801. Tel. 620-341-5480, e-mail rldc@ku.edu. *Chair* Cynthia Akers.

State Library of Kansas/Statewide Resource Sharing Div., 300 S.W. 10 Ave., Room 343 N., Topeka 66612-1593. SAN 329-5621. Tel. 785-296-3875, fax 785-368-7291. *Dir.* Patti Butcher.

Kentucky

Assn. of Independent Kentucky Colleges and Universities (AIKCU), 484 Chenault Rd., Frankfort 40601. SAN 322-1490. Tel. 502-695-5007, fax 502-695-5057. *Pres.* Gary S. Cox.

Eastern Kentucky Health Science Information Network (EKHSIN), c/o Camden-Carroll Lib., Morehead 40351. SAN 370-0631. Tel. 606-783-6860, fax 606-784-2178. *Lib. Dir.* Tammy Jenkins.

Kentuckiana Metroversity, Inc., 109 E. Broadway, Louisville 40202. SAN 322-1504. Tel. 502-897-3374, fax 502-895-1647.

Kentucky Medical Library Assn., VA Medical Center, Lib. Serices 142D, Louisville 40206-1499. SAN 370-0623. Tel. 502-

287-6240, fax 502-287-6134. *Head Libn.* Gene M. Haynes.

Kentucky Virtual Library (KVL), 1024 Capital Center Drive, Suite 320, Frankfort 40601. Tel. 502-573-1555, fax 502-573-0222, e-mail kyvl@ky.gov. *Dir.* Enid Wohlstein.

Southeastern Chapter of the American Assn. of Law Libraries (SEAALL), c/o Univ. of Kentucky Law Lib., Lexington 40506-0048. Tel. 859-257-8347, fax 859-323-4906. *Pres.* Amy Osborne.

Theological Education Assn. of Mid America (TEAM-A), Southern Baptist Theological Seminary, Louisville 40280. SAN 377-5038. Tel. 502-897-4807, fax 502-897-4600. *Dir., Info. Resources* Ken Boyd.

Louisiana

Central Louisiana Medical Center Library Consortium (CLMLC), 2495 Shreveport Hwy., 142D, Alexandria 71306. Tel. 318-619-9102, fax 318-619-9144, e-mail clmlc8784@yahoo.com. *Coord.* Miriam J. Brown.

Health Sciences Library Assn. of Louisiana (HSLAL), LSUHSC Lib., Shreveport 71103. SAN 375-0035. *Pres.* Donna Timm.

Loan SHARK, State Lib. of Louisiana, Baton Rouge 70802. SAN 371-6880. Tel. 225-342-4920, 342-4918, fax 225-219-4725. *Head, Access Services* Kytara A. Gaudin.

LOUIS/Louisiana Library Network, Info. Technology Services, Baton Rouge 70803. *Exec. Dir.* Ralph Boe.

Louisiana Government Information Network (LaGIN), c/o State Lib. of Louisiana, Baton Rouge 70802. SAN 329-5036. Tel. 225-342-4920, e-mail lagin@pelican.state.lib.la.us. *Coord.* Virginia Smith.

New Orleans Educational Telecommunications Consortium, 2 Canal St., Suite 2038, New Orleans 70130. SAN 329-5214. Tel. 504-524-0350, fax 504-524-0327, e-mail noetc@noetc.org. *Exec. Dir.* Michael Adler.

Maine

Health Science Library Information Consortium (HSLIC), 211 Marginal Way, No 245, Portland 04101. SAN 322-1601. Tel.

207-795-2561, fax 207-795-2569. *Chair* Kathy Brunjes.

Maryland

Maryland Assn. of Health Science Librarians (MAHSL), VA Medical HealthCare System Medical Lib., Baltimore 21201. SAN 377-5070. Tel. 401-605-7093. *Co-Pres.* Brittany Rice.

Maryland Interlibrary Loan Organization (MILO), c/o Enoch Pratt Free Lib., Baltimore 21201-4484. SAN 343-8600. Tel. 410-396-5498, fax 410-396-5837, e-mail milo@prattlibrary.org. *Mgr.* Emma E. Beaven.

National Network of Libraries of Medicine (NN/LM), National Lib. of Medicine, Bethesda 20894. SAN 373-0905. Tel. 301-496-4777, fax 301-480-1467. *Dir.* Angela Ruffin.

National Network of Libraries of Medicine–Southeastern Atlantic Region (NN/LM-SEA), Univ. of Maryland Health Sciences and Human Services Lib., Baltimore 21201-1512. SAN 322-1644. Tel. 410-706-2855, fax 410-706-0099, e-mail hshsl-nlmsea@hshsl.umaryland.edu. *Dir.* Mary J. Tooey.

Regional Alcohol and Drug Abuse Resource Network (RADAR), National Clearinghouse on Alcohol and Drug Info., Rockville 20852. SAN 377-5569. Tel. 301-468-2600, fax 301-468-6433.

U.S. National Library of Medicine (NLM), 8600 Rockville Pike, Bethesda 20894. SAN 322-1652. Tel. 301-594-5983, fax 301-402-1384, e-mail custserv@nlm.nih.gov. *Coord.* Martha Fishel.

Washington Research Library Consortium (WRLC), 901 Commerce Drive, Upper Marlboro 20774. SAN 373-0883. Tel. 301-390-2031, fax 301-390-2020. *Dir. of Lib. Services* Bruce Hulse.

Massachusetts

Boston Biomedical Library Consortium (BBLC), c/o Dana Farber Cancer Trust, Boston 02115. SAN 322-1725. *Pres.* Christine Fleuried.

Boston Library Consortium, Inc., McKim Bldg., Boston 02117. SAN 322-1733. Tel. 617-262-0380, fax 617-262-0163, e-mail admin@blc.org. *Exec. Dir.* Barbara G. Preece.

Boston Regional Library System (BRLS), c/o Boston Public Lib., Boston 02117. Tel. 617-859-2380, fax 617-424-8617, e-mail brl@bpl.org. *Regional Program Admin.* Michael Colford.

Cape Libraries Automated Materials Sharing Network (CLAMS), 270 Communication Way, Unit 4E, Hyannis 02601. SAN 370-579X. Tel. 508-790-4399, fax 508-771-4533. *Exec. Dir.* Gayle Simundza.

Catholic Library Assn., 100 North St., Suite 224, Pittsfield 01201-5109. SAN 329-1030. Tel. 413-443-2252, fax 413-442-2252, e-mail cla@cathla.org. *Exec. Dir.* Jean R. Bostley, SSJ.

Central and Western Massachusetts Automated Resource Sharing (C/W MARS), 67 Millbrook St., Suite 201, Worcester 01606. SAN 322-3973. Tel. 508-755-3323 ext. 30, fax 508-755-3721. *Exec. Dir.* Joan Kuklinski.

Cooperating Libraries of Greater Springfield (CLGS), Springfield College, Springfield 01109. SAN 322-1768. Tel. 413-748-3609, fax 413-748-3631. *Coord.* Lynn Coakley.

Fenway Libraries Online, Inc. (FLO), c/o Wentworth Institute of Technology, Boston 02115. SAN 373-9112. Tel. 617-442-2384, fax 617-442-1519. *Exec. Dir.* Walter Stine.

Massachusetts Health Sciences Libraries Network (MAHSLIN), Brigham and Women''s Hospital Medical Lib., Boston 02115. SAN 372-8293. Tel. 617-632-2489. *Chair* Christine Fleuriel.

Merrimack Valley Library Consortium, 1600 Osgood St., North Andover 01845. SAN 322-4384. Tel. 978-557-1050, fax 978-557-8101, e-mail netmail@mvlc.org. *Exec. Dir.* Lawrence Rungren.

Metrowest Massachusetts Regional Library System (METROWEST), 135 Beaver St., Waltham 02452. Tel. 781-398-1819, fax 781-398-1821. *Admin.* Sondra H. Vandermark.

Minuteman Library Network, 10 Strathmore Rd., Natick 01760-2419. SAN 322-4252. Tel. 508-655-8008, fax 508-655-1507. *Exec. Dir.* Susan McAlister.

National Network of Libraries of Medicine–New England Region (NN/LM-NER), Univ. of Massachusetts Medical School, Shrewsbury 01545-2732. SAN 372-5448. Tel. 508-856-5979, fax 508-856-5977. *Dir.* Elaine Martin.

Nelinet, Inc., 153 Cordaville Rd., Suite 200, Southborough 01772. SAN 322-1822. Tel. 508-460-7700 ext. 1934, fax 508-460-9455. *Exec. Dir.* Arnold Hirshon.

North of Boston Library Exchange, Inc. (NOBLE), 26 Cherry Hill Drive, Danvers 01923. SAN 322-4023. Tel. 978-777-8844, fax 978-750-8472. *Exec. Dir.* Ronald A. Gagnon.

Northeast Consortium of Colleges and Universities in Massachusetts (NECCUM), Merrimack College, North Andover 01845. SAN 371-0602. Tel. 978-556-3400, fax 978-556-3738. *Pres.* Richard Santagati.

Northeastern Consortium for Health Information (NECHI), Lowell General Hospital Health Science Lib., Lowell 01854. SAN 322-1857. Tel. 978-937-6247, fax 978-937-6855. *Libn.* Donna Beales.

SAILS, Inc., 547 W. Groves St., Suite 4, Middleboro 02346. SAN 378-0058. Tel. 508-946-8600, fax 508-946-8605. *Pres.* Robin Glasser.

Southeastern Massachusetts Consortium of Health Science Libraries (SEMCO), Youngdahl Lib., Norwood Hospital, Norwood 02062. SAN 322-1873. Tel. 781-278-6243, fax 781-769-9622. *Chair* Denise Corless.

Southeastern Massachusetts Regional Library System (SEMLS), 10 Riverside Drive, Lakeville 02347. Tel. 508-923-3531, fax 508-923-3539, e-mail semls@semls.org. *Admin.* Cynthia A. Roach.

West of Boston Network (WEBNET), Horn Lib., Babson College, Babson Park 02457. SAN 371-5019. Tel. 781-239-4308, fax 781-239-5226. *Pres.* Marilyn Bregoli.

Western Massachusetts Health Information Consortium, Baystate Medical Center Health Sciences Lib., Springfield 01199. SAN 329-4579. Tel. 413-794-1291, fax 413-794-1974. *Pres.* Susan La Forter.

Michigan

Detroit Area Consortium of Catholic Colleges, c/o Sacred Heart Seminary, Detroit 48206. SAN 329-482X. Tel. 313-883-8500, fax 313-883-8594. *Acting Dir.* Chris Spilker.

Detroit Area Library Network (DALNET), 6th Floor SEL, 5048 Gullen Mall, Detroit 48202. Tel. 313-577-6789, fax 313-577-1231. *Dir.* Steven K. Bowers.

Kalamazoo Consortium for Higher Education (KCHE), Kalamazoo College, Kalamazoo 49006. SAN 329-4994. Tel. 269-337-7220, fax 269-337-7219. *Pres.* Eileen B. Wilson-Oyelaran.

Lakeland Library Cooperative, 4138 Three Mile Rd. N.W., Grand Rapids 49534-1134. SAN 308-132X. Tel. 616-559-5253, fax 616-559-4329. *Dir.* Sandra Wilson.

Michigan Health Sciences Libraries Assn. (MHSLA), 1407 Rensen St., Suite 4, Lansing 48910. SAN 323-987X. Tel. 517-394-2774, fax 517-394-2675. *Pres.* Sheila Bryant.

Michigan Library Consortium (MLC), 1407 Rensen St., Suite 1, Lansing 48910-3657. SAN 322-192X. Tel. 517-394-2420, fax 517-394-2096, e-mail reception@mlcnet. org. *Assoc. Dir.* Ruth Dukelow.

PALnet, 1040 W Bristol Rd., Flint 48507. Tel. 810-766-4070. *Dir.* Stephanie C. John.

Southeastern Michigan League of Libraries (SEMLOL), Lawrence Technological Univ., Southfield 48075. SAN 322-4481. Tel. 248-204-3000, fax 248-204-3005. *Treas.* Gary Cocozzoli.

Southwest Michigan Library Cooperative (SMLC), c/o Niles District Lib., Niles 49120-2620. SAN 371-5027. Tel. 269-683-8545, fax 269-657-4494. *Pres.* Jennifer Ray.

Suburban Library Cooperative (SLC), 44750 Delco Blvd., Sterling Heights 48313. SAN 373-9082. Tel. 586-685-5750, fax 586-685-3010. *Interim Dir.* Arthur M. Woodford.

The Library Network (TLN), 13331 Reeck Rd., Southgate 48195-3054. SAN 370-596X. Tel. 734-281-3830, fax 734-281-1905. *Dir.* James Pletz.

Upper Peninsula of Michigan Health Science Library Consortium, c/o Marquette Health System Hospital, Marquette 49855. SAN 329-4803. Tel. 906-225-3429, fax 906-225-3524. *In Charge* Janis Lubenow.

Upper Peninsula Region of Library Cooperation, Inc., 1615 Presque Isle Ave., Marquette 49855. SAN 329-5540. Tel. 906-228-7697, fax 906-228-5627. *Treas.* Suzanne Dees.

Valley Library Consortium, 3210 Davenport Ave., Saginaw 48602-3495. Tel. 989-497-0925, fax 989-497-0918. *Exec. Dir.* Karl R. Steiner.

Minnesota

Capital Area Library Consortium (CALCO), c/o Minnesota Dept. of Transportation, Lib. MS155, Saint Paul 55155. SAN 374-6127. Tel. 651-296-5272, fax 651-297-2354. *Libn.* Shirley Sherkow.

Central Minnesota Libraries Exchange (CMLE), Miller Center, Room 130-D, Saint Cloud 56301-4498. SAN 322-3779. Tel. 320-308-2950, fax 320-654-5131, e-mail cmle@stcloudstate.edu. *Dir.* Patricia A. Post.

Cooperating Libraries in Consortium (CLIC), 1619 Dayton Ave., Suite 204, Saint Paul 55104. SAN 322-1970. Tel. 651-644-3878, fax 651-644-6258. *System Admin.* Deb Bergeron.

Metronet, 1619 Dayton Ave., Suite 314, Saint Paul 55104. SAN 322-1989. Tel. 651-646-0475, fax 651-649-3169, e-mail information@metrolibraries.net. *Exec. Dir.* Ann Walker Smalley.

Metropolitan Library Service Agency (MELSA), 1619 Dayton Ave., No. 314, Saint Paul 55104-6206. SAN 371-5124. Tel. 651-645-5731, fax 651-649-3169, e-mail melsa@melsa.org. *Exec. Dir.* Chris D. Olson.

MINITEX Library Information Network, 15 Andersen Lib., Univ. of Minnesota–Twin Cities, Minneapolis 55455-0439. SAN 322-1997. Tel. 612-624-4002, fax 612-624-4508. *Dir.* William DeJohn.

Minnesota Library Information Network (MnLINK), Univ. of Minnesota–Twin Cities, Minneapolis 55455-0439. Tel. 612-

624-8096, fax 612-624-4508. *Info. Specialist* Nick Banitt.

Minnesota Theological Library Assn. (MTLA), Luther Seminary Lib., Saint Paul 55108. SAN 322-1962. Tel. 651-641-3447. *Chair* David Stewart.

North Country Library Cooperative, 5528 Emerald Ave., Mountain Iron 55768-2069. SAN 322-3795. Tel. 218-741-1907, fax 218-741-1908. *Dir.* Linda J. Wadman.

Northern Lights Library Network, 103 Graystone Plaza, Detroit Lakes 56501-3041. SAN 322-2004. Tel. 218-847-2825, fax 218-847-1461, e-mail nloffice@nlln.org. *Dir.* Ruth Solie.

SMILE (Southcentral Minnesota Inter-Library Exchange), 1400 Madison Ave., No. 622, Mankato 56001. SAN 321-3358. Tel. 507-625-7555, fax 507-625-4049, e-mail smile @tds.lib.mn.us. *Dir.* Nancy Katharine Steele.

Southeastern Libraries Cooperating (SELCO), 2600 19th St. N.W., Rochester 55901-0767. SAN 308-7417. Tel. 507-288-5513, fax 507-288-8697. *Exec. Dir.* Ann Hutton.

Southwest Area Multicounty Multitype Interlibrary Exchange (SAMMIE), 109 S. 5 St., Suite 30, Marshall 56258-1240. SAN 322-2039. Tel. 507-532-9013, fax 507-532-2039, e-mail info@sammie.org. *Dir.* Robin Chaney.

Twin Cities Biomedical Consortium (TCBC), c/o Fairview Univ. Medical Center, Minneapolis 55455. SAN 322-2055. Tel. 612-273-6595, fax 612-273-2675. *Mgr.* Colleen Olsen.

West, P.O. Box 64526, Saint Paul 55164-0526. SAN 322-4031. Tel. 651-687-7000, fax 651-687-5614, e-mail west.customer. service@thomson.com.

Mississippi

Central Mississippi Library Council (CMLC), c/o Millsaps College Lib., Jackson 39210. SAN 372-8250. Tel. 601-974-1070, fax 601-974-1082. *Admin./Treas.* Tom Henderson.

Mississippi Electronic Libraries Online (MELO), Mississippi State Board for Community and Junior Colleges, Jackson 39211. Tel. 601-432-6518, fax 601-432-

6363, e-mail melo@colin.edu. *Dir.* Audra Kimball.

Missouri

Greater Western Library Alliance (GWLA), 5109 Cherry St., Kansas City 64110. Tel. 816-926-8765, fax 816-926-8790. *Exec. Dir.* Joni Blake.

Health Sciences Library Network of Kansas City (HSLNKC), Univ. of Missouri–Kansas City Health Sciences Lib., Kansas City 64108-2792. SAN 322-2098. Tel. 816-235-1880, fax 816-235-6570. *Dir.* Peggy Mullaly-Quijas.

Kansas City Library Consortium (KCLC), Kansas City Public Lib., Kansas City 64105-1702. Tel. 816-701-3400 ext. 3520, fax 816-701-3401, e-mail kclcsupport@ kclibrary.org. *Coord.* Donna Whitner.

Kansas City Metropolitan Library and Information Network, 15624 E. 24 Hwy., Independence 64050. SAN 322-2101. Tel. 816-521-7257, fax 816-461-0966. *Exec. Dir.* Susan Burton.

Missouri Library Network Corp. (MLNC), 8045 Big Bend Blvd., Suite 202, Saint Louis 63119-2714. SAN 322-466X. Tel. 314-918-7222, fax 314-918-7727, e-mail support@mlnc.org. *Exec. Dir.* Tracy Byerly.

Saint Louis Regional Library Network, 341 Sappington Rd., Saint Louis 63122. SAN 322-2209. Tel. 314-395-1305.

Nebraska

ICON Library Consortium, McGoogan Lib. of Medicine, Univ. of Nebraska, Omaha 68198-6705. Tel. 402-559-7099, fax 402-559-5498.

Southeast Nebraska Library System, 5730 R St., Suite C-1, Lincoln 68505. SAN 322-4732. Tel. 402-467-6188, fax 402-467-6196. *Pres.* Glenda Willnerd.

Nevada

Desert States Law Library Consortium, Wiener-Rogers Law Lib., William S. Boyd School of Law, Las Vegas 89154-1080. Tel. 702-895-2400, fax 702-895-2416. *Collection Development Libn.* Matthew Wright.

Information Nevada, Interlibrary Loan Dept., Nevada State Lib. and Archives, Carson City 89701-4285. SAN 322-2276. Tel. 775-684-3328, fax 775-684-3330.

New Hampshire

Carroll County Library Cooperative, c/o Freedom Lib., Freedom 03836. SAN 371-8999. Tel. 603-367-8545, fax 603-539-5176, e-mail librarian@madison.lib.nh.us. *Dir.* Elizabeth Rhymer.

GMILCS, Inc., 1701B Hooksett Rd., Hooksett 03106. Tel. 603-485-4286, fax 603-485-4246, e-mail helpdesk@gmilcs.org. *Chair* Dianne Hathaway.

Health Sciences Libraries of New Hampshire and Vermont, Breene Memorial Lib., New Hampshire Hospital, Concord 03246. SAN 371-6864. Tel. 603-527-2837, fax 603-527-7197. *Admin. Coord.* Marion Allen.

Librarians of the Upper Valley Coop. (LUV Coop), c/o Hanover Town Lib., Etna 03750. SAN 371-6856. Tel. 603-643-3116. *Coord.* Barbara Prince.

Merri-Hill-Rock Library Cooperative, c/o Kimball Lib., Atkinson 03811-2299. SAN 329-5338. Tel. 603-362-5234, fax 603-362-4791. *Interim Dir.* Caroline Birr.

New England Law Library Consortium, Inc. (NELLCO), 9 Drummer Rd., Keene 03431. SAN 322-4244. Tel. 603-357-3385, fax 603-357-2075. *Exec. Dir.* Tracy L. Thompson.

New Hampshire College and University Council, Three Barrell Court, Suite 100, Concord 03301-8543. SAN 322-2322. Tel. 603-225-4199, fax 603-225-8108. *Pres.* Thomas R. Horgan.

Nubanusit Library Cooperative, c/o Peterborough Town Lib., Peterborough 03458. SAN 322-4600. Tel. 603-924-8040, fax 603-924-8041.

Scrooge and Marley Cooperative, 695 Main St., Laconia 03246. SAN 329-515X. Tel. 603-524-4775. *In Charge* Randy Brough.

New Jersey

Basic Health Sciences Library Network (BHSL), Overlook Hospital Health Science Lib., Summit 07902. SAN 371-4888.

Tel. 908-522-2886, fax 908-522-2274. *Coord.* Pat Regenberg.

Bergen Passaic Health Sciences Library Consortium, c/o Health Sciences Lib., Englewood Hospital and Medical Center, Englewood 07631. SAN 371-0904. Tel. 201-894-3069, fax 201-894-9049. *Coord.* Lia Sabbagh.

Burlington Libraries Information Consortium (BLINC), Five Pioneer Blvd., Westampton 08060. Tel. 609-267-9660, fax 609-267-4091, e-mail hq@bcls.lib.nj.us. *Coord.* Gale Sweet.

Central Jersey Regional Library Cooperative (CJRLC), 4400 Rte. 9 South, Suite 3400, Freehold 07728-4232. SAN 370-5102. Tel. 732-409-6484, fax 732-409-6492, e-mail carol@cjrlc.org. *Exec. Dir.* Connie S. Paul.

Central New Jersey Health Science Libraries Consortium (CNJHSLA), Saint Francis Medical Center Medical Lib., Trenton 08629. SAN 370-0712. Tel. 609-599-5068, fax 609-599-5773. *Libn.* Donna Barlow.

Cosmopolitan Biomedical Library Consortium (CBLC), Overlook Hospital Medical Lib., Summit 07902. SAN 322-4414. Tel. 908-522-2699, fax 908-522-2274. *Coord.* Pat Regenberg.

Health Sciences Library Assn. of New Jersey (HSLANJ), Saint Michaels Medical Center, Newark 07102. SAN 370-0488. Tel. 973-877-5471, fax 973-877-5378. *Dir.* Peter Cole.

Highlands Regional Library Cooperative, 400 Morris Ave., Suite 202, Denville 07834. SAN 329-4609. Tel. 973-664-1776, fax 973-664-1780. *Exec. Dir.* Joanne P. Roukens.

INFOLINK/Eastern New Jersey Regional Library Cooperative, Inc., 44 Stelton Rd., Suite 330, Piscataway 08854. SAN 371-5116. Tel. 732-752-7720, fax 732-752-7785. *Exec. Dir.* Cheryl O'Connor.

Integrated Information Solutions, 600 Mountain Ave., Room 1B 202, Murray Hill 07974. SAN 329-5400. Tel. 908-582-4840, fax 908-582-3146. *Mgr.* M. E. Brennan.

Libraries of Middlesex Automation Consortium (LMxAC), 1030 Saint Georges Ave.,

Suite 203, Avenel 07001. SAN 329-448X. Tel. 732-750-2525, fax 732-750-9392. *Exec. Dir.* Eileen Palmer.

Monmouth-Ocean Biomedical Information Consortium (MOBIC), Community Medical Center, Toms River 08755. SAN 329-5389. Tel. 732-557-8117, fax 732-557-8354. *Libn.* Reina Reisler.

Morris Automated Information Network (MAIN), c/o Morris County Lib., 30 East Hanover Ave., Whippany 07981. SAN 322-4058. Tel. 973-631-5353, fax 973-631-5366. *Dir.* Jeremy Jenynak.

Morris-Union Federation, 214 Main St., Chatham 07928. SAN 310-2629. Tel. 973-635-0603, fax 973-635-7827.

New Jersey Health Sciences Library Network (NJHSN), Overlook Hospital Lib., Summit 07902. SAN 371-4829. Tel. 908-522-2886, fax 908-522-2274. *Lib. Mgr.* Patricia Regenberg.

New Jersey Library Network, Lib. Development Bureau, Trenton 08608. SAN 372-8161. Tel. 609-278-2640 ext. 152, fax 609-278-2650. *Assoc. State Libn. for Lib. Development* Kathleen Moeller-Peiffer.

South Jersey Regional Library Cooperative, Paint Works Corporate Center, Gibbsboro 08026. SAN 329-4625. Tel. 856-346-1222, fax 856-346-2839. *Exec. Dir.* Karen Hyman.

Virtual Academic Library Environment (VALE), William Paterson Univ. Lib., Wayne 07470-2103. Tel. 973-720-3179, fax 973-720-3171. *Coord.* Judy Avrin.

New Mexico

Alliance for Innovation in Science and Technology Information (AISTI), 369 Montezuma Ave., No. 237, Santa Fe 87501. *Exec. Dir.* Corinne Lebrunn.

Estacado Library Information Network (ELIN), 509 N. Shipp, Hobby 88240. Tel. 505-397-9328, fax 505-397-1508. *System Admin.* Cristine Adams.

New Mexico Consortium of Academic Libraries, Dean's Office, Albuquerque 87131-0001. SAN 371-6872. *Pres.* Ruben Aragon.

New Mexico Consortium of Biomedical and Hospital Libraries, c/o St. Vincent Hospital, Santa Fe 87505. SAN 322-449X. Tel. 505-820-5218, fax 505-989-6478. *Chair* Albert Robinson.

New York

Academic Libraries of Brooklyn, Long Island Univ. Lib. LLC 517, Brooklyn 11201. SAN 322-2411. Tel. 718-488-1081, fax 718-780-4057.

Associated Colleges of the Saint Lawrence Valley, SUNY Potsdam, Potsdam 13676-2299. SAN 322-242X. Tel. 315-267-3331, fax 315-267-2389. *Exec. Dir.* Anneke J. Larrance.

Capital District Library Council (CDLC), 28 Essex St., Albany 12206. SAN 322-2446. Tel. 518-438-2500, fax 518-438-2872. *Exec. Dir.* Jean K. Sheviak.

Central New York Library Resources Council (CLRC), 6493 Ridings Rd., Syracuse 13206-1195. SAN 322-2454. Tel. 315-446-5446, fax 315-446-5590. *Exec. Dir.* Penelope J. Klein.

Connect NY, Rochester Institute of Technology, Rochester 14623. Tel. 585-475-2050. *Dir. of Technology* Chris Lerch.

Council of Archives and Research Libraries in Jewish Studies (CARLJS), 330 7th Ave., 21st flr., New York 10001. SAN 371-053X. Tel. 212-629-0500, fax 212-629-0508, e-mail fjc@jewishculture.org. *Operations Dir.* Michelle Moskowitz Brown.

Library Assn. of Rockland County (LARC), P.O. Box 917, New City 10956-0917. Tel. 845-359-3877. *Pres.* Sara Nugent.

Library Consortium of Health Institutions in Buffalo (LCHIB), Abbott Hall, SUNY at Buffalo, Buffalo 14214. SAN 329-367X. Tel. 716-829-3900 ext. 143, fax 716-829-2211, e-mail hubnet@buffalo.edu; ulb-lchib@buffalo.edu. *Exec. Dir.* Martin E. Mutka.

Long Island Library Resources Council (LILRC), 627 N. Sunrise Service Rd., Bellport 11713. SAN 322-2489. Tel. 631-675-1570. *Dir.* Herbert Biblo.

Medical and Scientific Libraries of Long Island (MEDLI), c/o Palmer School of Lib. and Info. Science, Brookville 11548. SAN 322-4309. Tel. 516-299-2866, fax 516-299-4168. *Chair* Mary Westermann-Cicio.

Metropolitan New York Library Council (METRO), 57 E. 11 St., 4th flr., New York 10003-4605. SAN 322-2500. Tel. 212-228-2320, fax 212-228-2598. *Exec. Dir.* Dottie Hiebing.

National Network of Libraries of Medicine–Middle Atlantic Region (NN/LM-MAR), NYU Medical Center, New York 10010. E-mail rml@library.med.nyu.edu. *Assoc. Dir.* Kathel Dunn.

New York State Higher Education Initiative (NYSHEI), 22 Corporate Woods Blvd., Albany 12211-2350. Fax 518-432-4346, e-mail nyshei@nyshei.org. *Exec. Dir.* Jason Kramer.

Northeast Foreign Law Libraries Cooperative Group, Columbia Univ. Lib., New York 10027. SAN 375-0000. Tel. 212-854-1411, fax 212-854-3295. *Coord.* Silke Sahl.

Northern New York Library Network, 6721 U.S. Hwy. 11, Potsdam 13676. SAN 322-2527. Tel. 315-265-1119, fax 315-265-1881, e-mail info@nnyln.org. *Exec. Dir.* John J. Hammond.

Nylink, 22 Corporate Woods, 3rd flr., Albany 12211. SAN 322-256X. Tel. 518-443-5444, fax 518-432-4346, e-mail nylink@nylink.org. *Exec. Dir.* David Penniman.

Research Library Assn. of South Manhattan, Bobst Lib., New York Univ., New York 10012. SAN 372-8080. Tel. 212-998-2477, fax 212-995-4366. *Dean of Lib.* Carol Mandel.

Rochester Regional Library Council, 390 Packetts Landing, Fairport 14450. SAN 322-2535. Tel. 585-223-7570, fax 585-223-7712, e-mail rrlc@rrlc.org. *Exec. Dir.* Kathleen M. Miller.

South Central Regional Library Council, Clinton Hall, Ithaca 14850. SAN 322-2543. Tel. 607-273-9106, fax 607-272-0740, e-mail scrlc@lakenet.org. *Exec. Dir.* Mary-Carol Lindbloom.

Southeastern New York Library Resources Council (SENYLRC), 21 S. Elting Corners Rd., Highland 12528-2805. SAN 322-2551. Tel. 845-883-9065, fax 845-883-9483. *Exec. Dir.* John L. Shaloiko.

SUNYConnect, Office of Lib. and Info. Services, Albany 12246. Tel. 518-443-5577, fax 518-443-5358. *Asst. Provost for Lib. and Info. Services* Carey Hatch.

United Nations System Electronic Information Acquisitions Consortium (UNSEIAC), c/o United Nations Lib., New York 10017. SAN 377-855X. Tel. 212-963-2026, fax 212-963-2608, e-mail unseiac@un.org. *Coord.* Noriko Gines.

Western New York Library Resources Council, 4455 Genesee St., Buffalo 14225. SAN 322-2578. Tel. 716-633-0705, fax 716-633-1736. *Exec. Dir.* Sheryl Knab.

North Carolina

Cape Fear Health Sciences Information Consortium, 1601 Owen Drive, Fayetteville 28301. SAN 322-3930. Tel. 910-671-5046, fax 910-671-5337. *Dir.* Katherine Mcginniss.

Dialog Corp., 11000 Regency Pkwy., Suite 10, Cary 27518. SAN 322-0176. Tel. 919-462-8600, fax 919-468-9890. *In Charge* Kevin Bonson.

North Carolina Area Health Education Centers, Univ. of North Carolina Health Sciences Lib., CB 7585, Chapel Hill 27599-7585. SAN 323-9950. Tel. 919-962-0700. *Dir.* Diana McDuffee.

North Carolina Community College System, 200 W. Jones St., Raleigh 27603-1379. SAN 322-2594. Tel. 919-807-7100, fax 919-807-7175; 919-807-7164. *Assoc. V.P. for Learning Technology Systems* Bill Randall.

North Carolina Library and Information Network, State Lib. of North Carolina, Raleigh 27601-2807. SAN 329-3092. Tel. 919-807-7400, fax 919-733-8748. *State Libn.* Mary L. Boone.

Northwest AHEC Library at Hickory, Catawba Medical Center, Hickory 28602. SAN 322-4708. Tel. 828-326-3662, fax 828-326-3484. *Dir.* Karen Lee Martinez.

Northwest AHEC Library at Salisbury, c/o Rowan Regional Medical Center, Salisbury 28144. SAN 322-4589. Tel. 704-210-5069, fax 704-636-5050.

Northwest AHEC Library Information Network, Wake Forest Univ. School of Medicine, Winston-Salem 27157-1060. SAN 322-4716. Tel. 336-713-7700, fax 336-713-7701. *Dir.* Mike Lischke.

Triangle Research Libraries Network, Wilson Lib., Chapel Hill 27514-8890. SAN 329-5362. Tel. 919-962-8022, fax 919-962-4452. *Dir.* Mona C. Couts.

Western North Carolina Library Network (WNCLN), c/o Appalachian State Univ., Boone 28608. SAN 376-7205. Tel. 828-262-2774, fax 828-262-3001. *Libn.* Catherine Wilkinson.

North Dakota

Central Dakota Library Network, Morton Mandan Public Lib., Mandan 58554-3149. SAN 373-1391. Tel. 701-667-5365. *Dir.* Kelly Steckler.

Mid-America Law Library Consortium (MALLCO), Univ. of North Dakota School of Law, Grand Forks 58202. SAN 371-6813. Tel. 701-777-2204, fax 701-777-4956. *Interim Dir.* Rhonda Schwartz.

Tri-College University Libraries Consortium, NDSU Downtown Campus, Fargo 58102. SAN 322-2047. Tel. 701-231-8170, fax 701-231-7205. *In Charge* Sonia Hohnadel.

Ohio

Assn. of Christian Librarians (ACL), P.O. Box 4, Cedarville 45314. Tel. 937-766-2255, fax 937-766-5499, e-mail info@acl. org. *Pres.* Linda Poston.

Central Ohio Hospital Library Consortium, 127 S Davis Ave., Columbus 43222. SAN 371-084X. Tel. 614-234-5214, fax 614-234-1257, e-mail library@mchs.com. *Dir.* Stevo Roksandic.

Christian Library Consortium (CLC), c/o ACL, Cedarville 45314. Tel. 937-766-2255, fax 937-766-5499, e-mail info@acl. org. *Coord.* Beth Purtee.

Cleveland Area Metropolitan Library System (CAMLS), 20600 Chagrin Blvd., Suite 500, Shaker Heights 44122-5334. SAN 322-2632. Tel. 216-921-3900, fax 216-921-7220. *Exec. Dir.* Michael G. Snyder.

Columbus Area Library and Information Council of Ohio (CALICO), c/o Westerville Public Lib., Westerville 43081. SAN 371-683X. Tel. 614-882-7277, fax 614-882-5369.

Consortium of Popular Culture Collections in the Midwest (CPCCM), c/o Popular Cul-

ture Lib., Bowling Green 43403-0600. SAN 370-5811. Tel. 419-372-2450, fax 419-372-7996. *Head Libn.* Nancy Down.

Five Colleges of Ohio, 102 Allen House, Gambier 43022. Tel. 740-427-5377, fax 740-427-5390, e-mail ohiofive@gmail. com. *Exec. Dir.* Susan Palmer.

Northeast Ohio Regional Library System (NEO-RLS), 4445 Mahoning Ave. N.W., Warren 44483. SAN 322-2713. Tel. 330-847-7744, fax 330-847-7704, e-mail nola @nolanet.org. *Exec. Dir.* William Martino.

Northwest Regional Library System (NOR-WELD), 181½ S. Main St., Bowling Green 43402. SAN 322-273X. Tel. 419-352-2903, fax 419-353-8310. *Dir.* Allan Gray.

OCLC Online Computer Library Center, Inc., 6565 Kilgour Place, Dublin 43017-3395. SAN 322-2748. Tel. 614-764-6000, fax 614-718-1017, e-mail oclc@oclc.org. *Pres./CEO* Jay Jordan.

Ohio Health Sciences Library Assn. (OHSLA), Medical Lib., South Pointe Hospital, Warrensville Heights 44122. Tel. 216-491-7454, fax 216-491-7650. *Pres.* Michelle Kraft.

Ohio Library and Information Network (Ohio-LINK), 2455 N. Star Rd., Suite 300, Columbus 43221. SAN 374-8014. Tel. 614-728-3600, fax 614-728-3610, e-mail info@ohiolink.edu. *Exec. Dir.* Thomas J. Sanville.

Ohio Network of American History Research Centers, Ohio Historical Society Archives-Lib., Columbus 43211-2497. SAN 323-9624. Tel. 614-297-2510, fax 614-297-2546, e-mail ohsref@ohiohistory.org; reference@ohiohistory.org. *Research* Louise Jones.

Ohio Public Library Information Network (OPLIN), 2323 W. 5 Ave., Suite 130, Columbus 43204. Tel. 614-728-5252, fax 614-728-5256, e-mail support@oplin.org. *Exec. Dir.* Stephen Hedges.

OHIONET, 1500 W. Lane Ave., Columbus 43221-3975. SAN 322-2764. Tel. 614-486-2966, fax 614-486-1527. *Exec. Officer* Michael P. Butler.

Rural Ohio Valley Health Sciences Library Network (ROVHSLN), Southern State Community College–South, Sardinia 45171.

Tel. 937-695-0307 ext. 3681, fax 937-695-1440. *Mgr.* Mary Ayres.

Southeast Regional Library System (SERLS), 252 W. 13 St., Wellston 45692. SAN 322-2756. Tel. 740-384-2103, fax 740-384-2106, e-mail dirserls@oplin.org. *Exec. Dir.* Mary Leffler.

SouthWest Ohio and Neighboring Libraries (SWON), 10815 Indeco Drive, Suite 200, Cincinnati 45241-2926. SAN 322-2675. Tel. 513-751-4422, fax 513-751-0463, e-mail info@swonlibraries.org. *Exec. Dir.* Anne K. Abate.

Southwestern Ohio Council for Higher Education (SOCHE), Miami Valley Research Park, Dayton 45420-4015. SAN 322-2659. Tel. 937-258-8890, fax 937-258-8899, e-mail soche@soche.org.

State Assisted Academic Library Council of Kentucky (SAALCK), c/o SWON Libs., Cincinnati 45241. SAN 371-2222. Tel. 513-751-4422, fax 513-751-0463, e-mail saalck@saalck.org. *Exec. Dir.* Anne Abate.

Theological Consortium of Greater Columbus (TCGC), Trinity Lutheran Seminary, Columbus 43209-2334. Tel. 614-384-4646, fax 614-238-0263. *Lib. Systems Mgr.* Ray Olson.

Oklahoma

Greater Oklahoma Area Health Sciences Library Consortium (GOAL), Resource Center, Mercy Memorial Health Center, Ardmore 73401. SAN 329-3858. Tel. 580-220-6625, fax 580-220-6599. *Pres.* Catherine Ice.

Oklahoma Health Sciences Library Assn. (OHSLA), HSC Bird Health Science Lib., Univ. of Oklahoma, Oklahoma City 73190. SAN 375-0051. Tel. 405-271-2285 ext. 48755, fax 405-271-3297. *Dir.* Clinton M. Thompson.

Oregon

Chemeketa Cooperative Regional Library Service, c/o Chemeketa Community College, Salem 97305-1453. SAN 322-2837. Tel. 503-399-5105, fax 503-399-7316, e-mail cocl@chemeketa.edu. *Coord.* Linda Cochrane.

Coastal Resource Sharing Network (CRSN), c/o Tillamook County Lib., Tillamook 97141. Tel. 503-842-4792, fax 503-815-8194, e-mail webmaster@beachbooks.org. *Pres.* Jill Tierce.

Coos County Library Service District, Tioga, 3rd flr., 1988 Newmark, Coos Bay 97420. SAN 322-4279. Tel. 541-888-1529, fax 541-888-1529. *Dir.* Mary Jane Fisher.

Gorge LINK Library Consortium, c/o Hood River County Lib., Hood River 97031. Tel. 541-387-4659; 541-386-2535, fax 541-386-3835, e-mail gorge.link@co.hood-river.or.us. *System Admin.* Jayne Guidinger.

Library Information Network of Clackamas County, 16239 S.E. McLoughlin Blvd., Suite 208, Oak Grove 97267-4654. SAN 322-2845. Tel. 503-723-4888, fax 503-794-8238, e-mail webmaster@lincc.org. *Mgr.* Joanna Rood.

Orbis Cascade Alliance, 1501 Kincaid, No. 4, Eugene 97401-4540. SAN 377-8096. Tel. 541-346-1832, fax 541-346-1968. *Chair* Lee Lyttle.

Oregon Health Sciences Libraries Assn. (OHSLA), Oregon Health and Science Univ. Lib., Portland 97239-3098. SAN 371-2176. Tel. 503-494-3462, fax 503-494-3322, e-mail library@ohsu.edu.

Portland Area Library System (PORTALS), Port Community College, SYLIB202, Portland 97219. Tel. 503-977-4571, fax 503-977-4977. *Coord.* Roberta Richards.

Southern Oregon Library Federation, c/o Klamath County Lib., Klamath Falls 97601. SAN 322-2861. Tel. 541-882-8894, fax 541-882-6166. *Dir.* Andy Swanson.

Southern Oregon Library Information System (SOLIS), 724 S. Central Ave., Suite 112, Medford 97501. Tel. 541-772-2141, fax 541-772-2144, e-mail solis_97501@yahoo.com. *System Admin.* Marian Stoner.

Washington County Cooperative Library Services, 111 N.E. Lincoln St., MS No. 58, Hillsboro 97124-3036. SAN 322-287X. Tel. 503-846-3222, fax 503-846-3220. *Mgr.* Eva Calcagno.

Pennsylvania

Associated College Libraries of Central Pennsylvania, P.O. Box 39, Grantham

17027. E-mail aclcp@aclcp.org. *Pres.* Gregory Crawford.

Berks County Library Assn. (BCLA), Reading Public Lib., Reading 19602. SAN 371-0866. Tel. 610-478-9035; 610-655-6350. *Pres.* Jennifer Balas.

Central Pennsylvania Consortium (CPC), Dickinson College, Carlisle 17013. SAN 322-2896. Tel. 717-245-1984, fax 717-245-1807, e-mail cpc@dickinson.edu. *Pres.* Katherine Haley Will.

Central Pennsylvania Health Sciences Library Assn. (CPHSLA), Office for Research Protections, Pennsylvania State Univ., University Park 16802. SAN 375-5290. Fax 814-865-1775. *Pres.* Tracie Kahler.

Cooperating Hospital Libraries of the Lehigh Valley Area, Estes Lib., Saint Luke's Hospital, Bethlehem 18015. SAN 371-0858. Tel. 610-954-3407, fax 610-954-4651. *Chair* Sharon Hrabina.

Delaware Valley Information Consortium (DEVIC), St. Mary Medical Center Medical Lib., Langhorne 19047. Tel. 215-710-2012, fax 215-710-4638, e-mail info@devic-libraries.net. *Dir.* Rita Haydar.

Eastern Mennonite Associated Libraries and Archives (EMALA), 2215 Millstream Rd., Lancaster 17602. SAN 372-8226. Tel. 717-393-9745, fax 717-393-8751. *Chair* Edsel Burdge.

Erie Area Health Information Library Cooperative (EAHILC), Nash Lib., Gannon Univ., Erie 16541. SAN 371-0564. Tel. 814-871-7667, fax 814-871-5566. *Chair* Deborah West.

Greater Philadelphia Law Library Assn. (GPLLA), Wolf, Block, Schorr and Solis-Cohen LLP Lib., 25th flr., Philadelphia 19103. SAN 373-1375. *Pres.* Monica Almendarez.

HSLC/Access PA (Health Science Libraries Consortium), 3600 Market St., Suite 550, Philadelphia 19104-2646. SAN 323-9780. Tel. 215-222-1532, fax 215-222-0416, e-mail support@hslc.org. *Exec. Dir.* Joseph C. Scorza.

Interlibrary Delivery Service of Pennsylvania (IDS), c/o Bucks County IU, No. 22, Doylestown 18901. SAN 322-2942. Tel. 215-348-2940 ext. 1620, fax 215-348-

8315, e-mail ids@bucksiu.org. *Admin. Dir.* Beverly J. Carey.

Keystone Library Network, Dixon Univ. Center, Harrisburg 17110-1201. Tel. 717-720-4088, fax 717-720-4453. *Coord.* Mary Lou Sowden.

Laurel Highlands Health Science Library Consortium, 361 Sunrise Rd., Dayton 16222. SAN 322-2950. Tel. 814-341-0242, fax 814-266-8230. *Dir.* Rhonda Yeager.

Lehigh Valley Assn. of Independent Colleges, 130 W. Greenwich St., Bethlehem 18018. SAN 322-2969. Tel. 610-625-7888, fax 610-625-7891. *Exec. Dir.* Tom A. Tenges.

Montgomery County Library and Information Network Consortium (MCLINC), 301 Lafayette St., 2nd flr., Conshohocken 19428. Tel. 610-238-0580, fax 610-238-0581, e-mail webmaster@mclinc.org. *Pres.* Carrie L. Turner.

Northeastern Pennsylvania Library Network, c/o Marywood Univ. Lib., Scranton 18509-1598. SAN 322-2993. Tel. 570-348-6260, fax 570-961-4769. *Exec. Dir.* Catherine H. Schappert.

Northwest Interlibrary Cooperative of Pennsylvania (NICOP), Mercyhurst College Lib., Erie 16546. SAN 370-5862. Tel. 814-824-2190, fax 814-824-2219. *Archivist* Earleen Glaser.

Pennsylvania Library Assn., 220 Cumberland Pkwy, Suite 10, Mechanicsburg 17055. Tel. 717-766-7663, fax 717-766-5440. *Exec. Dir.* Glenn R. Miller.

Philadelphia Area Consortium of Special Collections Libraries (PACSCL), c/o Historical Society of Pennsylvania, Philadelphia 19107. SAN 370-7504. Tel. 215-985-1445, fax 215-985-1446, e-mail pacsl@pacscl.org. *Exec. Dir.* Laura Blanchard.

Southeastern Pennsylvania Theological Library Assn. (SEPTLA), c/o Biblical Seminary, Hatfield 19440. SAN 371-0793. Tel. 215-368-5000 ext. 234. *Chair* Daniel LaValla.

State System of Higher Education Library Cooperative (SSHELCO), c/o Bailey Lib., Slippery Rock 16057. Tel. 724-738-2630, fax 724-738-2661. *Dir.* Philip Tramdack.

Susquehanna Library Cooperative (SLC), Stevenson Lib., Lock Haven Univ., Lock Haven 17745. SAN 322-3051. Tel. 570-484-2310, fax 570-484-2506. *Dean of Lib. and Info. Services.* Tara Lynn Fulton.

Tri-State College Library Cooperative (TCLC), c/o Rosemont College Lib., Rosemont 19010-1699. SAN 322-3078. Tel. 610-525-0796, fax 610-525-1939, e-mail office@tclclibs.org. *Coord.* Ellen Gasiewski.

Rhode Island

Library of Rhode Island Network (LORI), c/o Office of Lib. and Info. Services, Providence 02908-5870. SAN 371-6821. Tel. 401-574-9300, fax 401-574-9320. *Lib. Services Dir.* Howard Boksenbaum.

Ocean State Libraries (OSL), 300 Centerville Rd., Suite 103S, Warwick 02886-0226. SAN 329-4560. Tel. 401-738-2200, fax 401-736-8949, e-mail support@oslri.net. *Exec. Dir.* Joan Gillespie.

South Carolina

Charleston Academic Libraries Consortium (CALC), P.O. Box 118067, Charleston 29423-8067. SAN 371-0769. Tel. 843-574-6088, fax 843-574-6484. *Chair* Drucie Gullion.

Columbia Area Medical Librarians' Assn. (CAMLA), School of Medicine Lib., Univ. of South Carolina, Columbia 29209. SAN 372-9400. Tel. 803-733-3361, fax 803-733-1509. *Pres.* Roz Anderson.

Partnership Among South Carolina Academic Libraries (PASCAL), 1333 Main St., Suite 305, Columbia 29201. Tel. 803-734-0900, fax 803-734-0901. *Exec. Dir.* Rick Moul.

South Carolina AHEC, c/o Medical Univ. of South Carolina, Charleston 29425. SAN 329-3998. Tel. 843-792-4431, fax 843-792-4430. *Exec. Dir.* David Garr.

South Carolina State Library/South Carolina Library Network, 1430 and 1500 Senate St., Columbia 29201. SAN 322-4198. Tel. 803-734-8666, fax 803-734-8676, e-mail reference@statelibrary.sc.gov. *Dir. of Lib. and Info. Services.* Mary Morgan.

South Dakota

South Dakota Library Network (SDLN), 1200 University, Unit 9672, Spearfish 57799-9672. SAN 371-2117. Tel. 605-642-6835, fax 605-642-6472, e-mail help@sdln.net. *Dir.* Warren Wilson.

Tennessee

Consortium of Southern Biomedical Libraries (CONBLS), Meharry Medical College, Nashville 37208. SAN 370-7717. Tel. 615-327-6728, fax 615-327-6448. *Chair* Barbara Shearer.

Knoxville Area Health Sciences Library Consortium (KAHSLC), Univ. of Tennessee Preston Medical Lib., Knoxville 37920. SAN 371-0556. Tel. 865-305-9525, fax 865-305-9527. *Pres.* Cynthia Vaughn.

Mid-Tennessee Health Science Librarians Assn., VA Medical Center, Nashville 37212. SAN 329-5028. Tel. 615-327-4751 ext. 5523, fax 615-321-6336.

Tennessee Health Science Library Assn. (THeSLA), Holston Valley Medical Center Health Sciences Lib., Kingsport 37660. SAN 371-0726. Tel. 423-224-6870, fax 423-224-6014. *Coord., Lib. Services* Sharon M. Brown.

Tri-Cities Area Health Sciences Libraries Consortium (TCAHSLC), James H. Quillen College of Medicine, East Tennessee State Univ., Johnson City 37614. SAN 329-4099. Tel. 423-439-6252, fax 423-439-7025. *Dir.* Biddanda Ponnappa.

Wolf River Library Consortium, c/o Germantown Community Lib., Germantown 38138-2815. Tel. 901-757-7323, fax 901-756-9940. *Dir.* Melody Pittman.

Texas

Abilene Library Consortium, 3305 N. 3 St., Suite 301, Abilene 79603. SAN 322-4694. Tel. 325-672-7081, fax 325-672-7082. *Coord.* David Bavousett.

Amigos Library Services, Inc., 14400 Midway Rd., Dallas 75244-3509. SAN 322-3191. Tel. 972-851-8000, fax 972-991-6061, e-mail amigos@amigos.org. *Exec. Dir.* Bonnie Juergens.

Council of Research and Academic Libraries (CORAL), P.O. Box 290236, San Antonio 78280-1636. SAN 322-3213. Tel. 210-458-4885. *Coord.* Rosemary Vasquez.

Del Norte Biosciences Library Consortium, El Paso Community College, El Paso 79998. SAN 322-3302. Tel. 915-831-4149, fax 915-831-4639. *Coord.* Becky Perales.

Harrington Library Consortium, 413 E. 4 Ave., Amarillo 79101. SAN 329-546X. Tel. 806-378-6037, fax 806-378-6038. *Dir.* Donna Littlejohn.

Health Libraries Information Network (Health LINE), Univ. of Texas Southwestern Medical Center Lib., Dallas 75390-9049. SAN 322-3299. Tel. 214-648-2626, fax 214-648-2826.

Houston Area Library Automation Network (HALAN), Houston Public Lib., Houston 77002. Tel. 832-393-1411, fax 832-393-1427, e-mail website@hpl.lib.tx.us. *Chief* Judith Hiott.

Houston Area Research Library Consortium (HARLiC), c/o Univ. of Houston Libs., Houston 77204-2000. SAN 322-3329. Tel. 713-743-9807, fax 713-743-9811. *Pres.* Dana Rooks.

National Network of Libraries of Medicine–South Central Region (NN/LM-SCR), c/o HAM-TMC Library, Houston 77030-2809. SAN 322-3353. Tel. 713-799-7880, fax 713-790-7030, e-mail nnlm-scr@exch.library.tmc.edu. *Dir.* Elizabeth K. Eaton.

Northeast Texas Library System (NETLS), 4845 Broadway Blvd., Garland 75043-7016. SAN 370-5943. Tel. 972-205-2566, fax 972-205-2767. *Major Resource Center Dir.* Claire Bausch.

South Central Academic Medical Libraries Consortium (SCAMeL), c/o Lewis Lib.-UNTHSC, Fort Worth 76107. SAN 372-8269. Tel. 817-735-2380, fax 817-735-5158. *Assoc. V.P. for Info. Resources/Treas.* Bobby Carter.

Texas Council of Academic Libraries (TCAL), VC/UHV Lib., Victoria 77901. SAN 322-337X. Tel. 361-570-4150, fax 361-570-4155. *Chair* Joe Dahlstrom.

Texnet, P.O. Box 12927, Austin 78711. SAN 322-3396. Tel. 512-463-5406, fax 512-936-2306, e-mail ill@tsl.state.tx.us.

Western Council of State Libraries, Inc., Texas State Lib. and Archives Commission, Austin 78711-2927. Tel. 512-463-5460, fax 512-463-5436. *Pres.* Peggy D. Rudd.

Utah

National Network of Libraries of Medicine–MidContinental Region (NN/LM-MCR), Spencer S. Eccles Health Sciences Lib., Univ. of Utah, Salt Lake City 84112-5890. SAN 322-225X. Tel. 801-587-3412, fax 801-581-3632. *Dir.* Wayne J. Peay.

Utah Academic Library Consortium (UALC), Univ. of Utah, Salt Lake City 84112-0731. SAN 322-3418. Tel. 801-581-3386; 801-581-6594, fax 801-585-3033, e-mail ualcmail@library.utah.edu. *Dir.* Rita Reusch.

Utah Health Sciences Library Consortium, c/o Spencer S. Eccles Health Sciences Lib., Univ. of Utah, Salt Lake City 84112-5890. SAN 376-2246. Tel. 801-585-5743, fax 801-581-3632. *Chair* John Bramble.

Vermont

Vermont Resource Sharing Network, c/o Vermont Dept. of Libs., Montpelier 05609-0601. SAN 322-3426. Tel. 802-828-3261, fax 802-828-1481. *Libn.* Gerrie Denison.

Virgin Islands

Vilinet/Virgin Islands Library and Information Network, c/o Div. of Libs., Archives, and Museums, Saint Thomas 00802. SAN 322-3639. Tel. 340-773-5715, fax 340-773-3257, e-mail info@vilinet.net. *Territorial Dir. of Libs., Archives, and Museums* Ingrid Bough.

Virginia

American Indian Higher Education Consortium (AIHEC), 121 Oronoco St., Alexandria 22314. SAN 329-4056. Tel. 703-838-0400, fax 703-838-0388, e-mail info@aihec.org.

Defense Technical Information Center, 8725 John J. Kingman Rd., Suite 0944, Fort Belvoir 22060-6218. SAN 322-3442. Tel. 703-767-8180, fax 703-767-8179. *Admin.* R. Paul Ryan.

Lynchburg Area Library Cooperative, c/o Sweet Briar College Lib., Sweet Briar 24595. SAN 322-3450. Tel. 434-381-6315, fax 434-381-6173.

Lynchburg Information Online Network (LION), 2315 Memorial Ave., Lynchburg 24503. SAN 374-6097. Tel. 434-381-6311, fax 434-381-6173. *Dir.* John G. Jaffee.

NASA Libraries Information System–NASA Galaxie, NASA Langley Research Center, MS 185-Technical Lib., Hampton 23681-2199. SAN 322-0788. Tel. 757-864-2356, fax 757-864-2375, e-mail tech-library@ larc.nasa.gov. *Coord.* Manjula Ambur.

Richmond Academic Library Consortium (RALC), James Branch Cabell Lib., Virginia Commonwealth Univ., Richmond 23284. SAN 322-3469. Tel. 804-828-1110; 804-828-1107, fax 804-828-1105; 804-828-0151. *Univ. Libn.* John E. Ulmschneider.

Southside Virginia Library Network (SVLN), Longwood Univ., Farmville 23909-1897. SAN 372-8242. Tel. 434-395-2431; 434-395-2433, fax 434-395-2453. *Dir.* Wendell Barbour.

Southwestern Virginia Health Information Librarians (SWVAHILI), Carilion Health Sciences Lib., Roanoke 24033. SAN 323-9527. Tel. 540-433-4166, fax 540-433-3106. *Chair* George Curran.

United States Army Training and Doctrine Command (TRADOC)/Lib. Program Office, U.S. Army Hq TRADOC, Fort Monroe 23651. SAN 322-418X. Tel. 757-788-2155, fax 757-788-5544. *Dir.* Amy Loughran.

Virginia Independent College and University Library Assn., c/o Mary Helen Cochran Lib., Sweet Briar 24595. SAN 374-6089. Tel. 434-381-6139, fax 434-381-6173. *Dir.* John Jaffee.

Virginia Tidewater Consortium for Higher Education (VTC), 4900 Powhatan Ave., Norfolk 23529. SAN 329-5486. Tel. 757-683-3183, fax 757-683-4515, e-mail lgdotolo@aol.com. *Pres.* Lawrence G. Dotolo.

Virtual Library of Virginia (VIVA), George Mason Univ., Fairfax 22030. Tel. 703-993-4652, fax 703-993-4662. *Dir.* Katherine Perry.

Washington

Cooperating Libraries in Olympia (CLIO), Evergreen State College Library, L2300, Olympia 98505. SAN 329-4528. Tel. 360-867-6260, fax 360-867-6790. *Dean, Lib. Services* Lee Lyttle.

Inland NorthWest Health Sciences Libraries (INWHSL), P.O. Box 10283, Spokane 99209-0283. SAN 370-5099. Tel. 509-368-6973, fax 509-358-7928. *Treas.* Robert Pringle.

National Network of Libraries of Medicine–Pacific Northwest Region (NN/LM-PNR), T-344 Health Sciences Bldg., Univ. of Washington, Seattle 98195. SAN 322-3485. Tel. 206-543-8262, fax 206-543-2469, e-mail nnlm@u.washington.edu. *Dir.* Neil Rambo.

Palouse Area Library Information Services (PALIS), c/o Neill Public Lib., Pullman 99163. SAN 375-0132. Tel. 509-334-3595, fax 509-334-6051. *Dir.* Andriette Pieron.

Washington Idaho Network (WIN), Foley Center Lib., Gonzaga Univ., Spokane 99258. Tel. 509-323-6545, fax 509-324-5398, e-mail winsupport@gonzaga.edu. *Pres.* Eileen Bell-Garrison.

West Virginia

Mid-Atlantic Law Library Cooperative (MALLCO), College of Law Lib., Morgantown 26506-6135. SAN 371-0645. Tel. 304-293-7641, fax 304-293-6020. *Lib. Dir.* Camille M. Riley.

Wisconsin

Arrowhead Health Sciences Library Network, Wisconsin Indianhead Technical College, Shell Lake 54817. SAN 322-1954. Tel. 715-468-2815 ext. 2298, fax 715-468-2819. *Coord.* Judy Lyons.

Fox River Valley Area Library Consortium (FRVALC), c/o Polk Lib., Univ. of Wisconsin–Oshkosh, Oshkosh 54901. SAN 322-3531. Tel. 920-424-3348; 920-424-4333, fax 920-424-2175. *Coord.* Erin Czech.

Fox Valley Library Council, c/o OWLS, Appleton 54911. SAN 323-9640. Tel. 920-832-6190, fax 920-832-6422. *Pres.* Joy Schwarz.

Library Council of Southeastern Wisconsin, Inc., 814 W. Wisconsin Ave., Milwaukee 53233-2309. SAN 322-354X. Tel. 414-271-8470, fax 414-286-2798. *Exec. Dir.* Susie M. Just.

North East Wisconsin Intertype Libraries, Inc. (NEWIL), 515 Pine St., Green Bay 54301. SAN 322-3574. Tel. 920-448-4412, fax 920-448-4420. *Dir.* Mark Merrifield.

Northwestern Wisconsin Health Science Library Consortium, c/o Gundersen Lutheran Medical Center, Lacrosse 54601. Tel. 608-775-5410, fax 608-775-6343. *Treas.* Eileen Severson.

South Central Wisconsin Health Science Library Consortium, c/o Fort Healthcare Medical Lib., Fort Atkinson 53538. SAN 322-4686. Tel. 920-568-5194, fax 920-568-5195. *Coord.* Carrie Garity.

Southeastern Wisconsin Health Science Library Consortium, Veterans Admin. Center Medical Lib., Milwaukee 53295. SAN 322-3582. Tel. 414-384-2000 ext. 42342, fax 414-382-5334. *Coord.* Janice Curnes.

Southeastern Wisconsin Information Technology Exchange, Inc. (SWITCH), 6801 N. Yates Rd., Milwaukee 53217-3985. SAN 371-3962. Tel. 414-351-2423, fax 414-228-4146. *Coord.* William A. Topritzhofer.

University of Wisconsin System School Library Education Consortium (UWSSLEC), Graduate and Continuing Educ., Univ. of Wisconsin–Whitewater, Whitewater 53190. Tel. 262-472-1463, fax 262-472-5210, e-mail lenchoc@uww.edu. *Co-Dir.* E. Anne Zarinnia.

Wisconsin Library Services (WILS), 728 State St., Room 464, Madison 53706-1494. SAN 322-3612. Tel. 608-265-0580; 608-263-4981; 608-265-4167, fax 608-262-6067; 608-263-3684. *Dir.* Kathryn Schneider Michaelis.

Wisconsin Public Library Consortium (WPLC), c/o South Central Lib. System, Madison 53718. *Dir.* Phyllis Davis.

Wisconsin Valley Library Service (WVLS), 300 N. 1 St., Wausau 54403. SAN 371-3911. Tel. 715-261-7250, fax 715-261-7259. *Dir.* Marla Rae Sepnafski.

WISPALS Library Consortium, c/o Gateway Technical College, Kenosha 53144-1690. Tel. 262-564-2602, fax 262-564-2787.

Wyoming

WYLD Network, c/o Wyoming State Lib., Cheyenne 82002-0060. SAN 371-0661. Tel. 307-777-6339, fax 307-777-6289, e-mail wyldstaff@will.state.wy.us. *State Libn.* Lesley Boughton.

Canada

Alberta

The Alberta Library (TAL), 6-14, 7 Sir Winston Churchill Sq., Edmonton T5J 2V5. Tel. 780-414-0805, fax 780-414-0806, e-mail admin@thealbertalibrary.ab.ca. *CEO* Lucy Pana.

NEOS Library Consortium, Cameron Lib., 5th flr., Edmonton T6G 2J8. Tel. 780-492-0075, fax 780-492-8302. *Mgr.* Margaret Law.

British Columbia

British Columbia Academic Health Council (BCAHC), 402-1770 W. 7 Ave., Vancouver V6J 4Y6. Tel. 604-739-3910 ext. 228, fax 604-739-3931, e-mail info@bcahc.ca. *CEO* George Eisler.

British Columbia Electronic Library Network (BCELN), WAC Bennett Lib., 7th flr., Simon Fraser Univ., Burnaby V5A 1S6. Tel. 778-782-7003, fax 778-782-3023, e-mail office@eln.bc.ca. *Exec. Dir.* Anita Cocchia.

British Columbia College and Institute Library Services, Langara College Lib., Vancouver V5Y 2Z6. SAN 329-6970. Tel.

604-323-5639, fax 604-323-5544, e-mail cils@langara.bc.ca. *Dir.* Mary Anne Epp.

Council of Prairie and Pacific University Libraries (COPPUL), 2005 Sooke Rd., Victoria V9B 5Y2. Tel. 250-391-2554, fax 250-391-2556, e-mail coppul@royalroads. ca. *Exec. Dir.* Alexander Slade.

Electronic Health Library of British Columbia (e-HLbc), c/o Bennett Lib., Burnaby V5A 1S6. Tel. 778-782-5440, fax 778-782-3023, e-mail info@ehlbc.ca. *Coord.* JoAnne Newyear-Ramirez.

Public Library InterLINK, c/o Burnaby Public Lib.–Kingsway Branch, Burnaby V5E 1G3. SAN 318-8272. Tel. 604-517-8441, fax 604-517-8410, e-mail info@interlink libraries.ca. *Operations Mgr.* Rita Avigdor.

Manitoba

Manitoba Government Libraries Council (MGLC), c/o Instructional Resources Unit, Winnipeg R3G 0T3. SAN 371-6848. Tel. 204-945-7833, fax 204-945-8756. *Chair* John Tooth.

Manitoba Library Consortium, Inc. (MLCI), c/o Lib. Admin., Univ. of Winnipeg, Winnipeg R3B 2E9. SAN 372-820X. Tel. 204-786-9801, fax 204-783-8910. *Chair* Judy Inglis.

Nova Scotia

Maritimes Health Libraries Assn. (MHLA-ABSM), W. K. Kellogg Health Sciences Lib., Halifax B3H 1X5. SAN 370-0836. Tel. 902-494-2483, fax 902-494-3750. *Libn.* Shelley McKibbon.

NOVANET, 1550 Bedford Hwy., No 501, Bedford B4A 1E6. SAN 372-4050. Tel. 902-453-2470, fax 902-453-2369, e-mail office@novanet.ns.ca. *Mgr.* Bill Slauenwhite.

Ontario

Bibliocentre, 31 Scarsdale Rd., North York M3B 2R2. SAN 322-3663. Tel. 647-722-9300, fax 647-722-9301. *Operations Dir.* Andre Paradis.

Canadian Assn. of Research Libraries (Association des Bibliothèques de Recherche du Canada), Morisset Hall, Room 238, Ottawa K1N 9A5. SAN 323-9721. Tel. 613-562-5385, fax 613-562-5297, e-mail carladm@ uottawa.ca. *Exec. Dir.* Brent Roe.

Canadian Health Libraries Assn. (CHLA-ABSC), 39 River St., Toronto M5A 3P1. SAN 370-0720. Tel. 416-646-1600, fax 416-646-9460, e-mail info@chla-absc.ca. *Pres.* Susan Powelson.

Canadian Research Knowledge Network (CRKN), Preston Sq., Tower 2, Ottawa K1S IN4. Tel. 613-907-7040, fax 866-903-9094. *Exec. Dir.* Deb deBruijn.

Consortium of Ontario Libraries (COOL), 111 Peter St., Suite 902, Toronto M5V 2H1. Tel. 416-961-1669, fax 416-961-5122. *Dir.* Barbara Franchetto.

Hamilton and District Health Library Network, c/o St Josephs Healthcare Hamilton, Sherman Lib., Room T2305, Hamilton L8N 4A6. SAN 370-5846. Tel. 905-522-1155 ext. 3410, fax 905-540-6504. *Coord.* Jean Maragno.

Health Science Information Consortium of Toronto, c/o Gerstein Science Info. Center, Univ. of Toronto, Toronto M5S 1A5. SAN 370-5080. Tel. 416-978-6359, fax 416-971-2637. *Exec. Dir.* Miriam Ticoll.

Ontario Council of University Libraries (OCUL), 130 Saint George St., Toronto M5S 1A5. Tel. 416-946-0578, fax 416-978-6755. *Exec. Dir.* Kathy Scardellato.

Ontario Health Libraries Assn. (OHLA), c/o Lakeridge Health, Oshawa L1G 2B9. SAN 370-0739. Tel. 905-576-8711 ext. 3334, fax 905-721-4759.

Ontario Library Consortium (OLC), Owen Sound and North Grey Union Public Lib., Owen Sound N4K 4K4. *Pres.* Judy Armstrong.

Parry Sound and Area Access Network, c/o Parry Sound Public Lib., Parry Sound P2A 1E3. Tel. 705-746-9601, fax 705-746-9601, e-mail pspl@vianet.ca. *Chair* Laurine Tremaine.

Perth County Information Network (PCIN), c/o Stratford Public Lib., Stratford N5A 1A2. Tel. 519-271-0220, fax 519-271-3843, e-mail webmaster@pcin.on.ca. *CEO* Sam Coglin.

Shared Library Services (SLS), South Huron Hospital, Exeter N0M 1S2. SAN 323-

9500. Tel. 519-235-5168, fax 519-235-4476, e-mail shha.sls@shha.on.ca. *Libn.* Linda Wilcox.

Southwestern Ontario Health Libraries and Information Network (SOHLIN), St. Joseph's Health Care London–Regional Mental Health Staff Libs., St. Thomas N5P 3V9. Tel. 519-631-8510 ext. 49685. *Pres.* Elizabeth Russell.

Toronto Health Libraries Assn. (THLA), 3409 Yonge St., Toronto M4N 2L0. SAN 323-9853. Tel. 416-485-0377, fax 416-485-6877, e-mail medinfoserv@rogers. com. *Pres.* Graziela Alexandria.

Quebec

Assn. des Bibliothèques de la Santé Affiliées a l'Université de Montréal (ABSAUM), c/o Health Lib., Univ. of Montreal, Montreal H3C 3J7. SAN 370-5838. Tel. 514-343-6826, fax 514-343-2350. *Dir.* Monique St-Jean.

Canadian Heritage Information Network (CHIN), 15 Eddy St., 4th flr., Gatineau K1A 0M5. SAN 329-3076. Tel. 819-994-1200, fax 819-994-9555, e-mail service@ chin.gc.ca. *CEO* Gabrielle Blais.

National Library and Information-Industry Associations, United States and Canada

American Association of Law Libraries

Executive Director, Kate Hagan
105 W. Adams St., Suite 3300, Chicago, IL 60603
312-939-4764, fax 312-431-1097, e-mail khagan@aall.org
World Wide Web http://www.aallnet.org

Object

The American Association of Law Libraries (AALL) is established for educational and scientific purposes. It shall be conducted as a nonprofit corporation to promote and enhance the value of law libraries to the public, the legal community, and the world; to foster the profession of law librarianship; to provide leadership in the field of legal information; and to foster a spirit of cooperation among the members of the profession. Established 1906.

Membership

Memb. 5,000+. Persons officially connected with a law library or with a law section of a state or general library, separately maintained. Associate membership available for others. Dues (Indiv.) $218; (Retired) $55; (Student) $55. Year. July 1–June 30.

Officers

Pres. Catherine Lemann, Alaska State Court Law Lib., Anchorage, AK 99501. Tel. 907-264-0583, fax 907-264-0599, e-mail clemann @courts.state.ak.us; *V.P.* Joyce Manna Janto, Univ. of Richmond School of Law Lib., 28 Westhampton Way, Richmond, VA 23173-0002. Tel. 804-289-8223, fax 804-289-8683, e-mail jjanto@richmond.edu; *Secy.* Ruth J. Hill. E-mail rhill@sulc.edu; *Treas.* David S. Mao. E-mail dmao@crs.loc.gov; *Past Pres.* James E. Duggan, Tulane Univ. Law Lib. E-mail duggan@tulane.edu

Executive Board

Carol Bredemeyer, Christine L Graesser, Marcus L. Hochstetler, Janet McKinney, Jean M. Wenger, Sally H. Wise.

American Library Association

Executive Director, Keith Michael Fiels
50 E. Huron St., Chicago, IL 60611
800-545-2433, 312-280-1392, fax 312-440-9374
World Wide Web http://www.ala.org

Object

The mission of the American Library Association (ALA) is to provide leadership for the development, promotion, and improvement of library and information services and the profession of librarianship in order to enhance learning and ensure access to information for all. Founded 1876.

Membership

Memb. (Indiv.) 59,423; (Inst.) 3,208; (Corporate) 234; (Total) 62,865 (as of November 2009). Any person, library, or other organization interested in library service and librarians. Dues (Indiv.) 1st year, $65; 2nd year, $98; 3rd year and later, $130; (Trustee and Assoc. Memb.) $59; (Lib. Support Staff) $46; (Student) $33; (Foreign Indiv.) $78; (Other) $46; (Inst.) $110 and up, depending on operating expenses of institution.

Officers (2009–2010)

Pres. Camila Alire, Dean Emerita, Univ. of New Mexico and Colorado State Univ. E-mail calire@att.net; *Pres.-Elect* Roberta Stevens, Outreach Projects and Partnerships Officer, Lib. of Congress. E-mail roberta@robertastevens.com; *Past Pres.* Jim Rettig, Univ. Libn., Boatwright Memorial Lib., Univ. of Richmond. Tel. 804-289-8456, fax 804-289-8757, e-mail jrettig@richmond.edu; *Treas.* Rod Hersberger, Dean, Univ. Lib., California State Univ.–Bakersfield. E-mail rhersberger@csub.edu.

Executive Board

Diane R. Chen (2011), Joseph M. Eagan (2011), Patricia M. Hogan (2012), Em Claire Knowles (2011), Charles E. Kratz, Jr. (2010), Stephen L. Matthews (2012), Larry Romans (2010), Courtney L. Young (2012).

Endowment Trustees

Daniel J. Bradbury (chair), John Vitali (2010), Robert A. Walton (2011); *Exec. Board Liaison* Rod Hersberger; *Staff Liaison* Gregory L. Calloway.

Divisions

See the separate entries that follow: American Assn. of School Libns.; Assn. for Lib. Collections and Technical Services; Assn. for Lib. Service to Children; Assn. for Lib. Trustees, Friends, and Advocates; Assn. of College and Research Libs.; Assn. of Specialized and Cooperative Lib. Agencies; Lib. Leadership and Management Assn.; Lib. and Info. Technology Assn.; Public Lib. Assn.; Reference and User Services Assn.; Young Adult Lib. Services Assn.

Publications

ALA Handbook of Organization (ann.).
American Libraries (10 a year; memb.; organizations $70; foreign $80; single copy $7.50).
Booklist (22 a year; U.S. and possessions $109.95; foreign $126.95; single copy $9).

Round Table Chairs

(ALA staff liaison in parentheses)

Continuing Library Education Network and Exchange. To be appointed (Darlena Davis).

Ethnic and Multicultural Information Exchange. Homa Naficy (Elliot Mandel).

Exhibits. Kathy Young (Deidre I. Ross).

Federal and Armed Forces Libraries. Richard Huffine (Patricia May).

Gay, Lesbian, Bisexual, Transgendered. Nancy Silverrod, Dale McNeill (Elliot Mandel).

Government Documents. Amy West (Rosalind Reynolds).

Intellectual Freedom. Robert Holley (Nanette Perez).

International Relations. Patricia Oyler (Michael Dowling).

Library History. Bernadette A. Lear (Denise M. Davis).

Library Instruction. (Darlena Davis).

Library Research. Nasha White (Denise M. Davis).

Library Support Staff Interests. AnnaMarie Kehnast (Darlena Davis).

Map and Geography. Katherine Weimer (Danielle M. Alderson).

New Members. Courtney Young (Kimberly Sanders).

Social Responsibilities. Alison Lewis (Elliot Mandel).

Staff Organizations. Leon S. Bey (Darlena Davis).

Video. Justin Michael Wadland (Danielle M. Alderson).

Committee Chairs

(ALA staff liaison in parentheses)

Accreditation (Standing). To be appointed (Karen L. O'Brien).

American Libraries Advisory (Standing). John C. Sandstrom (Leonard Kniffel).

Appointments (Standing). Roberta Stevens (Eileen Hardy).

Awards (Standing). Susan Stroyan (Cheryl Malden).

Budget Analysis and Review (Standing). James Neal (Gregory L. Calloway).

Chapter Relations (Standing). Susan S. DiMattia (Michael P. Dowling).

Committee on Committees (Elected Council Committee). Roberta Stevens (Eileen Hardy).

Conference Committee (Standing). Fred E. Goodman (Deidre I. Ross).

Conference Program Coordinating Team. Rhonda Putney (Deidre I. Ross).

Constitution and Bylaws (Standing). Thomas Wilding (JoAnne M. Kempf).

Council Orientation (Standing). Barbara Genco (Lois Ann Gregory-Wood).

Diversity (Standing). Ismail Abdullahi (Wendy Prellwitz).

Education (Standing). Lynn Silipigni Connaway (Lorelle R. Swader).

Election (Standing). Veronda J. Pitchford (Al Companio).

Human Resource Development and Recruitment (Standing). Hector Escobar (Lorelle R. Swader).

Information Technology Policy Advisory (Standing). Vivian M. Pisano (Alan Inouye).

Intellectual Freedom (Standing). Martin L. Garner (Nanette Perez).

International Relations (Standing). Beverly Lynch (Michael P. Dowling).

Legislation (Standing). Mario Anibal Ascencio (Lynne E. Bradley).

Literacy (Standing). Mark E. Pumphrey (Dale P. Lipschultz).

Literacy and Outreach Services Advisory (Standing). Angela J. Barnes (Miguel A. Figueroa).

Membership (Standing). Theresa S. Byrd (John F. Chrastka, Cathleen Bourdon).

Organization (Standing). Jan W. Sanders (Eileen Hardy).

Orientation, Training, and Leadership Development. Teri Switzer (Lorelle Swader).

Policy Monitoring (Standing). Janet Swan Hill (Lois Ann Gregory-Wood).

Professional Ethics (Standing). Nancy Zimmerman (Angela Maycock).

Public and Cultural Programs Advisory (Standing). Carolyn A. Anthony (Deborah Anne Robertson).

Public Awareness (Standing). Leslie Burger (Mark R. Gould).

Publishing (Standing). Erlene Bishop Killeen (Donald E. Chatham).

Research and Statistics (Standing). Kyung-Sun Kim (Denise M. Davis).

Resolutions. William L. Turner, Jr. (Lois Ann Gregory-Wood).

Rural, Native, and Tribal Libraries of All Kinds. Susan J. Hanks (Miguel A. Figueroa).

Scholarships and Study Grants. Aisha A. Harvy (Lorelle R. Swader).

Status of Women in Librarianship (Standing). Mary Callaghan Zunt (Lorelle R. Swader).

Web Site Advisory. Michael Stephens (Sherri L. Vanyek).

American Library Association
American Association of School Librarians

Executive Director, Julie A. Walker
50 E. Huron St., Chicago, IL 60611
312-280-4382, 800-545-2433, ext. 4382, fax 312-280-5276,
e-mail aasl@ala.org, World Wide Web http://www.aasl.org.

Object

The mission of the American Association of School Librarians (AASL) is to advocate excellence, facilitate change, and develop leaders in the school library media field. AASL works to ensure that all members of the field collaborate to provide leadership in the total education program; participate as active partners in the teaching/learning process; connect learners with ideas and information; and prepare students for lifelong learning, informed decision making, a love of reading, and the use of information technologies.

Established in 1951 as a separate division of the American Library Association.

Membership

Memb. 8,500+. Open to all libraries, school library media specialists, interested individuals, and business firms, with requisite membership in ALA.

Officers (2009–2010)

Pres. Cassandra Barnett; *Pres.-Elect* Nancy Everhart; *Treas.* Floyd Pentlin; *Past Pres.* Ann M. Martin.

Board of Directors

Rosina Alaimo, Alice Bryant, Cara Cavin, Linda Collins, Valerie B. Diggs, Gail M. Formanack, Susan Garvin, Maribel Garza-Castro, Louis Greco, Carl Harvey, Allison G. Kaplan, Dennis J. LeLoup, Sylvia K. Norton, Ann Perham, Allison Roberts, Paul K. Whitsitt.

Publications

AASL Hotlinks (mo.; electronic, memb.).

Knowledge Quest (5 a year; $50, $60 outside U.S.A.). *Ed.* Debbie Abilock. E-mail kq@abilock.net.

School Library Media Research (electronic, free, at http://www.ala.org/aasl.slmr). *Eds.* Jean Donham. E-mail jean.donham@uni.edu; Carol L. Tilley. E-mail ctilley@uiuc.edu.

Committee Chairs

AASL/ACRL Joint Information Literacy Committee. Robert Roth, Stephanie Sterling-Brasley.

AASL/ALSC/YALSA Interdivisional Committee on School/Public Library Cooperation. Mari J. Hardacre.

AASL/ELMSS Executive Committee. Laura Summers.

AASL/ISS Executive Committee. Cheryl Steele.

AASL/SPVS Executive Committee. Susan Thorniley.

Advocacy. Sherry R. Crow.

Affiliate Assembly. Sandra Dobbins Andrews.

Alliance for Association Excellence. Floyd Pentlin.

American University Press Book Selection. Jo Ann Carr.

Annual Conference 2009. Debra Logan, Karen Gavigan.

Appointments. Cyndi Phillip.

Awards. Diane Hughes.

Best Web Sites for Teaching and Learning. Pam Berger.

Blog Editorial Board. Angela P. Branyon, Wendy Stephens.

Bylaws and Organization. Dolores D. Gwaltney.

Intellectual Freedom. Linda Corey.

Knowledge Quest Editorial Board. Debbie Abilock.

Legislation. Mirah Dow.

National Conference 2009. Jay Bansbach, Ann Marie Pipkin.

National Institute 2010. Hilda K. Weisburg.

NCATE Coordinating Committee. Judy T. Bivens.

Nominating. J. Linda Williams.

Publications. Nancy Dickinson.

Research/Statistics. Barbara J. Ray.

SLMR Editorial Board. Jean Donham, Carol Tilley.

Web Site Resource Guides Editorial Board. To be appointed.

Task Force Chairs

Diversity in the Organization. Pauletta Brown Bracy.

Planned Giving Initiative. To be appointed.

Standards and Guidelines Implementation. Susan Ballard.

Awards Committees and Chairs

ABC-CLIO Leadership Grant. Frances R. Roscello.

Collaborative School Library Media Award. To be appointed.

Distinguished School Administrator Award. To be appointed.

Distinguished Service Award. To be appointed.

Frances Henne Award. Catherine E. Marriott.

Information Technology Pathfinder Award. To be appointed.

Innovative Reading Grant. Nancy L. Baumann.

Intellectual Freedom Award. To be appointed.

National School Library Media Program of the Year Award. Terri G. Kirk.

American Library Association
Association for Library Collections and Technical Services

Executive Director, Charles Wilt
50 E. Huron St., Chicago, IL 60611
800-545-2433 ext. 5030, fax 312-280-5033, e-mail cwilt@ala.org
World Wide Web http://www.ala.org/alcts

Object

The Association for Library Collections and Technical Services (ALCTS) envisions an environment in which traditional library roles are evolving. New technologies are making information more fluid and raising expectations. The public needs quality information anytime, anyplace. ALCTS provides frameworks to meet these information needs.

ALCTS provides leadership to the library and information communities in developing principles, standards, and best practices for creating, collecting, organizing, delivering, and preserving information resources in all forms. It provides this leadership through its members by fostering educational, research, and professional service opportunities. ALCTS is committed to quality information, universal access, collaboration, and lifelong learning.

Standards—Develop, evaluate, revise, and promote standards for creating, collecting, organizing, delivering, and preserving information resources in all forms.

Best practices—Research, develop, evaluate, and implement best practices for creating, collecting, organizing, delivering, and preserving information resources in all forms.

Education—Assess the need for, sponsor, develop, administer, and promote educational programs and resources for lifelong learning.

Professional development—Provide opportunities for professional development through research, scholarship, publication, and professional service.

Interaction and information exchange—Create opportunities to interact and exchange information with others in the library and information communities.

Association operations—Ensure efficient use of association resources and effective delivery of member services.

Established 1957; renamed 1988.

Membership

Memb. 4,500. Any member of the American Library Association may elect membership in this division according to the provisions of the bylaws.

Officers (2009–2010)

Pres. Mary M. Case, Univ. of Illinois–Chicago Lib., 801 S. Morgan St., Chicago, IL 60661 Tel. 312-996-2716, fax 312-413-0424, e-mail marycase@uic.edu; *Pres.-Elect* Cynthia Whitacre, OCLC, 6565 Kilgour Place, Dublin, OH 43017. Tel. 614-764-6183, fax 614-718-7397, email whitacrc@oclc.org; *Past Pres.* Dina Giambi, Univ. of Delaware Lib., 181 S. College Ave., Newark, DE 19717. Tel. 302-831-2829, fax 302-831-1046, mail dinag@udel.edu; *Councilor* Diane Dates Casey, Governors State Univ. Lib., 1

University Pkwy., University Park, IL 60466. Tel. 708-534-4110, fax 708-534-4564, e-mail d-casey@govst.edu.

Address correspondence to the executive director.

Board of Directors

Karen E. K. Brown, Beth Picknally Camden, Mary M. Case, Diane Dates Casey, Katharine Farrell, Connie Foster, Dina Giambi, Qiang Jin, Arthur Miller, Susan Mueller, Rebecca Mugridge, Carolynne Myall, Mary Page, Kathy Tezla, Mary Beth Thomson, Mary Beth Weber, Cynthia Whitacre, Charles Wilt.

Publications

ALCTS Newsletter Online (bi-mo.; free; posted at http://www.ala.org/alcts). *Ed.* Mary Beth Weber, Cataloging Dept., Rutgers Univ. Libs., 47 Davidson Rd., Piscataway, NJ 08854. Tel. 732-445-0500, fax 732-445-5888, e-mail mbfecko@rci.rutgers.edu.

Library Resources and Technical Services (q.; memb. $75; nonmemb. $85; international $95). *Ed.* Peggy Johnson, Univ. of Minnesota Libs., 499 Wilson Lib., 309 19th Ave. S., Minneapolis, MN 55455. Tel. 612-624-2312, fax 612-626-9353, e-mail m-john@tc.umn.edu.

Section Chairs

Acquisitions. Katharine Farrell.
Cataloging and Classification. Qiang Jin.
Collection Management and Development. Kathy Tezla.
Continuing Resources. Connie Foster.
Preservation and Reformatting. Karen E. K. Brown.

Committee Chairs

Hugh C. Atkinson Memorial Award (ALCTS/ACRL/LAMA/LITA). Barbara Ford.
Ross Atkinson Lifetime Achievement Award Jury. Wiliam Garrison.
Best of *LRTS* Award Jury. Xudong Jin.

Blackwell's Scholarship Award Jury. Hildegund Calvert.

Budget and Finance. Mary Beth Thomson.

Continuing Education. Pamela Bluh.

Fund Raising. Susan Davis.

International Relations. Susan Matveyeva.

Leadership Development. Melinda Flannery.

LRTS Editorial Board. Peggy Johnson.

Membership. Deborah Ryszka.

Nominating. Pamela Bluh.

Organization and Bylaws. Arthur Miller.

Outstanding Collaboration Citation Jury. Mary Jo Venetis.

Esther J. Piercy Award Jury. Ann Vidor.

Planning. Carolynne Myall.

Program. Joyce McDonough.

Publications. Sion Romaine.

Interest Groups

Authority Control (ALCTS/LITA). Amy McNeely.

Automated Acquisitions/In-Process Control Systems. Sharon Marshall, Michael Zeoli.

Creative Ideas in Technical Services. Emily Anne Prather-Rodgers.

Electronic Resources. Amira Aaron.

FRBR. Tami Morse McGill.

MARC Formats (ALCTS/LITA). Richard Leigh.

New Members. Keisha Manning.

Newspapers. Errol Somay.

Out of Print. John Riley.

Public Libraries Technical Services. Marlene Harris.

Role of the Professional in Academic Research Technical Service Departments. Sandra Macke, Robert Rendall.

Scholarly Communications. Terry Owen.

Technical Services Directors of Large Research Libraries. Beth Picknally Camden.

Technical Services Managers in Academic Libraries. Annie Wu.

Technical Services Workflow Efficiency. Robin Champieux.

American Library Association
Association for Library Service to Children

Executive Director, Aimee Strittmatter
50 E. Huron St., Chicago, IL 60611
312-280-2163, 800-545-2433 ext. 2163, fax 312-280-5271, e-mail alsc@ala.org
World Wide Web http://www.ala.org/alsc

Object

The core purpose of the Association for Library Service to Children (ALSC) is to create a better future for children through libraries. Its primary goal is to lead the way in forging excellent library services for all children. ALSC offers creative programming, information about best practices, continuing education, a prestigious award and media evaluation program, and professional connections. Founded 1901.

Membership

Memb. 4,216. Open to anyone interested in library services to children. For information on dues, see ALA entry.

Address correspondence to the executive director.

Officers

Pres. Thom Barthelmess; *V.P./Pres.-Elect* Julie Corsaro; *Past Pres.* Pat Scales; *Fiscal Officer* Tali Balas; *Division Councilor* Rhonda Puntney.

Directors

Mary Fellows, Marge Loch-Wouters, Cecelia McGowan, Leslie Molnar, Elizabeth Orsburn, Jennifer Ralston, Ellen Riordan, Tim Wadham.

Publications

Children and Libraries: The Journal of the Association for Library Service to Children (q.; memb.; nonmemb. $40; foreign $50).

ALSConnect (q., electronic; memb. Not available by subscription.)

Committee Chairs

AASL/ALSC/YALSA Interdivisional Committee on School/Public Library Cooperation. Maria Hardacre.

ALSC/*Booklist*/YALSA Odyssey Award Selection 2009. Sharon Grover.

Arbuthnot Honor Lecture 2010. Kristi Jemtegaard.

Arbuthnot Honor Lecture 2011. Carol Edwards.

Mildred L. Batchelder Award 2010. Annette Goldsmith.

Pura Belpré Award 2010. Lucía González.

Budget. Andrew Medlar.

Randolph Caldecott Award 2010. Rita Auerbach.

Andrew Carnegie Award 2010. Joan Kindig.

Children and Libraries Advisory Committee. Sharon Deeds.

Children and Technology. Amber Creger.

Distinguished Service Award 2010. Cynthia K. Richey.

Early Childhood Programs and Services. Melanie Huggins.

Education. Sarah Howard.

Theodor Seuss Geisel Award 2010. Susan Veltfort.

Grant Administration Committee. Linda Ernst.

Great Interactive Software for Kids. Angelique Kopa.

Great Web Sites. Meagan Albright.

Intellectual Freedom. Michael Santangelo.

Legislation. To be appointed.

Liaison with National Organizations. Marna Elliott, Dennis LeLoup.

Library Service to Special Population Children and Their Caregivers. Barbara Klipper.

Local Arrangements (Washington, D.C.). Christopher Borawski, Micki Freeny.

Managing Children's Services. Sarah English.

Membership. Tony Carmack.

John Newbery Award 2010. Katie O'Dell.

Nominating 2010. Kathleen T. Horning.

Notable Children's Books. Eliza Dresang.

Notable Children's Recordings. Janet Weber.

Notable Children's Videos. Sue Rokos.

Oral History. Floyd Dickman.

Organization and Bylaws. Julie Dietzel-Glair, Susan Pine.

Preconference Planning (Washington, DC). Wendy Lukehart.

Program Coordinating. Diane Janoff.

Public Awareness. Michele Farley.

Quicklists Consulting. Victor Schill, Maureen White.

Charlemae Rollins President's Program 2010. Eliza Dresang, Susannah Richards.

Scholarships. Ellen Spring.

School Age Programs and Service. Renee McGrath.

Robert F. Sibert Award 2010. Vicky Smith.

Special Collections and Bechtel Fellowship. Mary Beth Dunhouse, Nancy J. Johnson.

Laura Ingalls Wilder Award 2011. Megan Schliesman.

American Library Association
Association for Library Trustees, Advocates, Friends, and Foundations

Executive Director Sally Gardner Reed
109 S. 13 St., Suite 3N, Philadelphia, PA 19107
Tel. 312-280-2161, fax 215-545-3821, e-mail sreed@ala.org
World Wide Web http://www.ala.org/ala/mgrps/divs/altaff/index.cfm

Object

The Association for Library Trustees, Advocates, Friends, and Foundations (ALTAFF) was founded in 1890 as the American Library Trustee Association (ALTA). It was the only division of the American Library Association dedicated to promoting and ensuring outstanding library service through educational programs that develop excellence in trusteeship and promote citizen involvement in the support of libraries. In 2008 the members of ALTA voted to expand the division to more aggressively address the needs of friends of libraries and library foundations, and through a merger with Friends of Libraries USA (FOLUSA) became ALTAFF. ALTA had become an ALA division in 1961.

Membership

Memb. 5,200. Open to all interested persons and organizations. For dues and membership year, see ALA entry.

Officers (2009–2010)

Pres. Rose Mosley; *V.P./Pres.-Elect* Rodrique Gauvin; *Councilor* Shirley Bruursema; *Past Co.-Pres.* Margaret Danhof, Peggy Barber.

Publications

The Voice for America's Libraries (q.; memb.).
101+ Great Ideas for Libraries and Friends.
Even More Great Ideas for Libraries and Friends.
The Complete Trustee Handbook.

Committee Chairs

ALTAFF Leaders Orientation. Terry Higgins.
Annual Conference Program. Tanya Butler.
Library Issues. Joan Ress Reeves.
Newsletter and Web Site Advisory. Dave Hargett.
Nominating. Margaret Danhof.
PLA Conference Program. Margaret Schuster.
President's Events. Kim D. Johnson.
Regional Development. Claire Gritzer.

American Library Association
Association of College and Research Libraries

Executive Director, Mary Ellen K. Davis
50 E. Huron St., Chicago, IL 60611-2795
312-280-2523, 800-545-2433 ext. 2523, fax 312-280-2520, e-mail acrl@ala.org
World Wide Web http://www.ala.org/acrl

Object

The Association of College and Research Libraries (ACRL) leads academic and research librarians and libraries in advancing learning and scholarship. Founded 1938.

Membership

Memb. 12,780. For information on dues, see ALA entry.

Officers

Pres. Lori Goetsch, Dean of Libs., 504 Hale Lib., Kansas State Univ., Manhattan, KS 66506. Tel. 785-532-7400, fax 785-532-7415, e-mail lgoetsch@ksu.edu; *Pres.-Elect* Lisa Janicke Hinchliffe, Coord. for Info. Literacy, Univ. of Illinois, Urbana, IL 61801-3607. Tel. 217-333-1323, fax 217-244-4358, e-mail ljanicke@illinois.edu; *Past Pres.* Erika C. Linke, Assoc. Dean, Univ. Libs., Carnegie Mellon Univ., 5000 Forbes Ave., Pittsburgh, PA 15213-3890. Tel. 412-268-7800, fax 412-268-2793, e-mail el08@andrew.cmu.edu; *Budget and Finance Chair* Janice D. Welburn, Dean, Univ. Lib., Marquette Univ., P.O. Box 3141, Milwaukee, WI 53201-3141. Tel. 414-288-7840, fax 414-288-7214, e-mail janice.welburn@marquette.edu; *ACRL Councilor* Locke J. Morrisey, Head, Collections/Reference and Research Services, Gleeson Lib., Univ. of San Francisco, San Francisco, CA 94117-1080. Tel. 415-422-5399, e-mail morrisey@usfca.edu.

Board of Directors

Officers; Mary M. Carr, Lisabeth A. Chabot, Elizabeth A. Dupuis, Linda Kopecky, Michael J. LaCroix, John Lehner, Debbie L. Malone, Ann Campion Riley.

Publications

Choice (12 a year; $340; Canada and Mexico $390; other international $460). *Ed.* Irving Rockwood.
Choice Reviews-on-Cards (available only to subscribers of *Choice* and/or *Choice Reviews Online*; $425; Canada and Mexico $475; other international $555).
ChoiceReviews Online 2.0; ($425).
College & Research Libraries (*C&RL*) (6 a year; memb.; nonmemb. $70; Canada and other PUAS countries $75; other international $80). *Ed.* Joseph J. Branin.
College & Research Libraries News (*C&RL News*) (11 a year; memb.; nonmemb. $46; Canada and other PUAS countries $52; other international $57). *Ed.* David Free.
Publications in Librarianship (formerly ACRL Monograph Series) (occasional). *Ed.* Craig Gibson.
RBM: A Journal of Rare Books, Manuscripts, and Cultural Heritage (s. ann.; $42; Canada and other PUAS countries $47; other international $58). *Ed.* Beth M. Whittaker.

Committee and Task Force Chairs

AASL/ACRL Information Literacy (interdivisional). Stephanie Sterling-Brasley.
Academic/Research Librarian of the Year Award. Barbara Baxter Jenkins.
ACRL Academic Library Trends and Statistics Survey. William Miller.
ACRL/LLAMA Interdivisional Committee on Building Resources. Susan McCarthy Campbell.
ACRLog Advisory Board. To be appointed.

Appointments. Beth S. Woodard.

Assessment. Steve Hiller.

Hugh C. Atkinson Memorial Award. Barbara J. Ford.

Budget and Finance. Janice Welburn.

Choice Editorial Board. Edward Warro.

Colleagues. Frank A. D'Andraia, Julia M. Gelfand.

College & Research Libraries Editorial Board. Joseph Branin.

College & Research Libraries News Editorial Board. Gordon Aamot.

Advocacy. Jean Zanoni.

Copyright. Dwayne K. Buttler.

Council of Liaisons. Susan Kroll.

Doctoral Dissertation Fellowship. Brian J. Doherty.

Ethics. Alan R. Mattlage.

Excellence in Academic Libraries Award (Nominations). Kenley E. Neufeld.

Excellence in Academic Libraries Award (Selection). Julie B. Todaro.

Friends Fund. Beth McNeil.

Friends Fund Disbursement. Jane E. Schillie.

Government Relations. Jonathan Miller.

Immersion Program. Jennifer L. Dorner.

Information Literacy Coordinating. Debra Gilchrist.

Information Literacy Standards. To be appointed.

Information Literacy Web Site. Keith E. Gresham.

Intellectual Freedom. Paul J. Beavers.

International Relations. Ravindra N. Sharma.

E. J. Josey Spectrum Scholar Mentor. Carolyn H. Allen.

Samuel Lazerow Fellowship. Bradford L. Eden.

Leadership Recruitment and Nomination. Patricia A. Kreitz.

Marketing Academic and Research Libraries. Toni L. Tucker.

Membership Advisory. Susanna D. Boylston.

National Conference Coordinating Committee (Philadelphia). Pamela Snelson.

New Publications Advisory. Joan K. Lippincott.

President's Program Planning Committee, 2010. Jane E. Schillie.

President's Program Planning Committee, 2011. Steven J. Bell, Lisa Janicke Hinchliffe.

Professional Development Coordinating. Patricia A. Promis.

Publications Coordinating. Tim Gritten.

Publications in Librarianship Editorial Board. Craig Gibson.

Racial and Ethnic Diversity. Melanee Vicedo.

RBM Editorial Board. Beth Whittaker.

Research Coordinating. Eric L. Frierson.

Research Planning and Review. Ryan Johnson.

Research Program. Ruth A. Vondraceck.

Resources for College Libraries Editorial Board. Brian E. Coutts.

Scholarly Communications. Daniel R. Lee.

Standards and Accreditation. Virginia S. O'Herron.

Status of Academic Librarians. Sandra Lee Hawes.

Discussion Group Chairs

Balancing Baby and Book. Cynthia Dudenhoffer.

Consumer and Family Studies. Lore Guilmartin.

Continuing Education/Professional Development. Elizabeth Avery.

Copyright. Shannon Baird.

Heads of Public Services. Kathryn M. Crowe.

Information Commons. Scott B. Mandernack, Michael Whitchurch.

Librarianship in For-Profit Educational Institutions. Catherine J. Sawyer.

Libraries and Information Science Collections. Rebecca Vargha.

Media Resources. Joe Clark.

MLA International Bibliography. Kathleen Matthews Kluegel.

New Members. Allie K. Flanary.

Personnel Administrators and Staff Development Officers. Andrea Wigbels Stewart, Eileen Marie Theodore-Shusta.

Philosophical, Religious, and Theological Studies. Colin McCaffrey.

Popular Cultures. Sarah M. Sogigian.

Regional Campus Libraries. Patricia M. Duck.

Scholarly Communications. Daniel R. Lee.

Senior Administrators. Charles Gilreath.

Undergraduate Libraries. Jill Morrison McKinstry.

Interest Group Conveners

Academic Library Services to International Students. Dawn Amsberry.
Health Sciences. Carissa Ann Tomlinson.
Image Resources. Denise Hattwig.
Numeric and Geospatial Data Services in Academic Libraries. Jennifer Darragh.
Residency Programs. Gerald Holmes.
Universal Accessibility. Adina Joyce Mulliken.
Virtual Worlds. Rhonda Trueman.

Section Chairs

African American Studies Librarians. Vivian Njeri Fisher.
Anthropology and Sociology. Elizabeth A. Cooper.
Arts. William S. Hemmig.
Asian, African, and Middle Eastern. Anjana H. Bhatt.
College Libraries. Dawn R. Thistle.
Community and Junior College Libraries. Mary Ann Sheble.
Distance Learning. Michele D. Behr.
Education and Behavioral Sciences. Lori S. Mestre.
Instruction. Clara Fowler.
Law and Political Science. Erik Sean Estep.
Literatures in English. Angela Courtney.
Rare Books and Manuscripts. Deborah J. Leslie.
Science and Technology. Maliaca Oxnam.
Slavic and East European. Jon C. Giullian.
University Libraries. Miriam Leslie Madden.
Western European Studies. Sarah E. How.
Women's Studies. Kayo Denda.

American Library Association
Association of Specialized and Cooperative Library Agencies

Executive Director, Susan Hornung
50 E. Huron St., Chicago, IL 60611-2795
312-280-4398, 800-545-2433 ext. 4395, fax 312-280-5273
E-mail shornung@ala.org
World Wide Web http://www.ala.org/ascla

Object

The Association of Specialized and Cooperative Library Agencies (ASCLA) enhances the effectiveness of library service by providing networking, enrichment, and educational opportunities for its diverse members, who represent state library agencies, libraries serving special populations, multitype library organizations, and independent librarians. Within the interests of these library organizations, ASCLA has specific responsibility for

1. Development and evaluation of goals and plans for state library agencies, specialized library agencies, and multitype library cooperatives to facilitate the implementation, improvement, and extension of library activities designed to foster improved user services, coordinating such activities with other appropriate units of the American Library Association (ALA)

2. Representation and interpretation of the role, functions, and services of state library agencies, specialized library agencies, multitype library cooperatives, and independent librarians within and outside the profession, including contact with national organizations and government agencies

3. Development of policies, studies, and activities in matters affecting state library agencies, specialized library agencies, multitype library cooperatives, and independent librarians relating to (a) state and local library legislation, (b) state grants-in-aid and appropriations, and (c) relationships among state, federal, regional, and local governments, coordinating such

activities with other appropriate ALA units

4. Establishment, evaluation, and promotion of standards and service guidelines relating to the concerns of this association

5. Identifying the interests and needs of all persons, encouraging the creation of services to meet these needs within the areas of concern of the association, and promoting the use of these services provided by state library agencies, specialized library agencies, multitype library cooperatives, and independent librarians

6. Stimulating the professional growth and promoting the specialized training and continuing education of library personnel at all levels in the areas of concern of this association and encouraging membership participation in appropriate type-of-activity divisions within ALA

7. Assisting in the coordination of activities of other units within ALA that have a bearing on the concerns of this association

8. Granting recognition for outstanding library service within the areas of concern of this association

9. Acting as a clearinghouse for the exchange of information and encouraging the development of materials, publications, and research within the areas of concern of this association

Membership

Memb. 900. For information on dues, see ALA entry.

Board of Directors (2009–2010)

Pres. Brenda K. Bailey-Hainer, Bibliographical Center for Research, 14394 E. Evans Ave., Aurora, CO 80014-1408. Tel. 303-751-6277 ext. 117, fax 303-751-9787, e-mail bbailey@bcr.org; *Pres.-Elect* Diana Reese, Colorado State Lib., 201 E. Colfax Ave., Denver, CO 80203-1704. Tel. 303-866-6341, fax 303-866-6940, e-mail reese_d@cde.state.co.us; *Past Pres.* Carol Ann Desch, New York State Lib., 10C50 Cultural Educ. Center, Albany, NY 12230-0001. Tel. 518-474-7196, fax 518-486-5254, e-mail cdesch@mail.nysed.gov; *Div. Councilor* Kendall French Wiggin, Connecticut State Lib., 231 Capitol Ave., Hartford, CT 06106-1569. Tel. 860-757-6510, fax 860-757-6503, e-mail kwiggin@cslib.org.

Sections

Independent Librarian's Exchange (ILEX); Interlibrary Cooperation and Networking (ICAN); Libraries Serving Special Populations (LSSPS); LSSPS Board Representative; State Library Agency (SLAS).

Publication

Interface (q.; memb.). *Ed.* Emily Inlow-Hood. E-mail emily.inlow@gmail.com.

Committees

Accessibility Assembly; Awards; Legislation; Membership; Promotion; Nominating; Planning and Budget; President's Program; Publications; Standards Review.

American Library Association
Library Leadership and Management Association

Executive Director, Kerry Ward
50 E. Huron St., Chicago, IL 60611
312-280-5032, 800-545-2433 ext. 5032, fax 312-280-5033, e-mail kward@ala.org
World Wide Web http://www.ala.org/lama

Object

The Library Leadership and Management Association (LLAMA) Strategic Plan (2006–2010) sets out the following:

Mission: The Library Leadership and Management Association encourages and nurtures current and future leaders, and develops and promotes outstanding leadership and management practices.

Vision: LLAMA will be the foremost organization developing present and future leaders in library and information services.

Image: LLAMA is a welcoming community where aspiring and experienced leaders from all types of libraries, as well as those who support libraries, come together to gain skills in a quest for excellence in library management, administration, and leadership.

In addition

- LLAMA will be an organization in which value to its members drives decisions.

- LLAMA will expand and strengthen leadership and management expertise at all levels for all libraries.

- LLAMA will facilitate professional development opportunities to enhance leadership and management.

- LLAMA will be the preeminent professional organization that develops and supports library leaders and managers.

Established 1957.

Membership

Memb. 4,800. For information on dues, see ALA entry.

Officers (July 2009–June 2010)

Pres. Gina Millsap; *V.P.* Gail Kennedy; *Secy.* Emily A. Bergman; *Div. Councilor* Charles Forrest; *Past Pres.* Molly Raphael.

Address correspondence to the executive director.

Publications

Library Leadership and Management (q.; memb.; nonmemb. $65; foreign $75). *Ed.* Gregg Sapp.

Committee Chairs

Budget and Finance. Teri R. Switzer.
Continuing Education. Richard Moniz.
Financial Advancement. Andrea Lapsley.
Leadership Development. Susan Considine.
Marketing Communications. Tracy Hull.
Membership. Catherine Friedman.
Mentoring. Neely Tang.
Nominating. W. Bede Mitchell.
Organization. Yolanda Cooper.
Program. Philip Tramdack.
Publications Editorial Advisory Board. Diane Bisom.
Strategic Planning Action. Nanette Donohue, Anne Edwards.
Web Site Advisory Board. Marsha Iverson.

American Library Association
Library and Information Technology Association

Executive Director, Mary C. Taylor
50 E. Huron St., Chicago, IL 60611
312-280-4267, 800-545-2433
E-mail mtaylor@ala.org, World Wide Web http://www.lita.org

Object

As a center of expertise about information technology, the Library and Information Technology Association (LITA) leads in exploring and enabling new technologies to empower libraries. LITA members use the promise of technology to deliver dynamic library collections and services.

LITA educates, serves, and reaches out to its members, other ALA members and divisions, and the entire library and information community through its publications, programs, and other activities designed to promote, develop, and aid in the implementation of library and information technology.

Membership

Memb. 3,703. For information on dues, see ALA entry.

Officers (2009–2010)

Pres. Michelle L. Frisque; *V.P./Pres.-Elect* Karen Starr; *Past Pres.* Andrew K. Pace.

Directors

Officers; Mary Alice Ball, Mona C. Couts, Colleen Cuddy, Aaron Dobbs, Bonnie Postlethwaite, Lorre B. Smith, Maurice York; *Councilor* Colby Mariva Riggs; *Bylaws and Organization* Dale Poulter; *Exec. Dir.* Mary C. Taylor.

Publication

Information Technology and Libraries (*ITAL*) (q.; memb.; nonmemb. $65; single copy $30). *Ed.* Marc Truitt. For information or to send manuscripts, contact the editor.

Committee Chairs

Assessment and Research. Bonnie Postlethwaite.

Budget Review. Andrew Pace.

Bylaws and Organization. Dale Poulter.

Committee Chair Coordinator. Holly Yu.

Education. Mandy Havert, Danielle Cunniff Plumer.

Executive. Michelle Frisque.

International Relations. Frank Cervone.

ITAL Editorial Board. Marc Truitt.

LITA/Ex Libris Student Writing Award. Krista Clumpner.

LITA/Library Hi Tech Award. Aimee Fifarek.

LITA/LSSI and LITA/OCLC Minority Scholarships. Regina Koury.

LITA National Forum 2010. Jenny Reiswig.

LITA/OCLC Kilgour Award. Patrick Mullin.

LITA/Christian Larew Scholarship. David Bretthauer.

Membership Development. Donald W. Lemke.

Nominating. Bonnie Postlethwaite.

Program Planning. Jason Griffey.

Publications. Kristin Antelman.

Technology and Access. David J. Nutty.

Top Technology Trends. Gregg Silvis.

Web Coordinating. Jean Rainwater.

Interest Group Coordinators

Authority Control in the Online Environment (LITA/ALCTS). Amy McNeely.

Blogs, Interactive Media, Groupware, and Wikis. Jonathan David Blackburn.

Digital Library Technologies. Michael Robert Bolam.

Distance Learning. Lauren Marie Pressley.

Electronic Resources Management (LITA/ ALCTS). Chan Li.

Emerging Technologies. Patrick Joseph Griffis.

Heads of Library Technology. Mark A. Stoffan.

Imagineering. Cara V. W. Kinsey.

Interest Groups Coordinator. Aaron Dobbs.

Internet Resources and Services. Xan Arch.

JPEG 2000 in Archives and Libraries. Peter Murray.

Library Consortia Automated Systems. Jon Mark Bolthouse.

Next Generation Catalog. Raymond P. Schwartz.

Open Source Systems. Karen G. Schneider.

Public Libraries Technology. Rob Cullin.

RFID Technology. Vicki Terbovich.

Standards. Judy J. Jeng.

American Library Association
Public Library Association

Executive Director, Barbara A. Macikas
50 E. Huron St., Chicago, IL 60611
312-280-5752, 800-545-2433 ext. 5752, fax 312-280-5029, e-mail pla@ala.org
World Wide Web http://www.pla.org

The Public Library Association (PLA) has specific responsibility for

1. Conducting and sponsoring research about how the public library can respond to changing social needs and technical developments

2. Developing and disseminating materials useful to public libraries in interpreting public library services and needs

3. Conducting continuing education for public librarians by programming at national and regional conferences, by publications such as the newsletter, and by other delivery means

4. Establishing, evaluating, and promoting goals, guidelines, and standards for public libraries

5. Maintaining liaison with relevant national agencies and organizations engaged in public administration and human services, such as the National Association of Counties, the Municipal League, and the Commission on Postsecondary Education

6. Maintaining liaison with other divisions and units of ALA and other library organizations, such as the Association for Library and Information Science Education and the Urban Libraries Council

7. Defining the role of the public library in service to a wide range of user and potential user groups

8. Promoting and interpreting the public library to a changing society through legislative programs and other appropriate means

9. Identifying legislation to improve and to equalize support of public libraries

PLA enhances the development and effectiveness of public librarians and public library services. This mission positions PLA to

- Focus its efforts on serving the needs of its members

- Address issues that affect public libraries

- Commit to quality public library services that benefit the general public

The goals of PLA are

- Advocacy and recognition: public libraries will be recognized as the destination for a wide variety of valuable services and their funding will be a community priority.

- A literate nation: PLA will be a valued partner of public library initiatives to create a nation of readers.

- Staffing and recruitment: public libraries will be recognized as exciting places to work and will be staffed by skilled professionals who are recognized as the information experts, are competitively paid, and reflect the demographics of their communities.

- Training and knowledge transfer: PLA will be nationally recognized as the leading source for continuing education opportunities for public library staff and trustees.

Membership

Memb. 11,000+. Open to all ALA members interested in the improvement and expansion of public library services to all ages in various types of communities.

Officers (2009–2010)

Pres. Sari Feldman, Cuyahoga County Public Lib., 2111 Snow Rd., Parma, OH 44134. Tel 216-749-9490, e-mail sfeldman@cuyahoga library.org; *Pres.-Elect* Audra L. Caplan, Harford County Public Lib. Belcamp, MD 21017. E-mail caplan@hcplonline.info; *Past Pres.* Carol Sheffer, Troy, New York. Tel. 518-233-1740, email csheffer@live.com.

Publication

Public Libraries (bi-mo.; memb.; nonmemb. $65; foreign $75; single copy $10). *Ed.* Kathleen Hughes, PLA, 50 E. Huron St., Chicago, IL 60611. E-mail khughes@ala. org.

Committee Chairs

Advancement of Literacy Award Jury. Melissa E. Jones.

Allie Beth Martin Award Jury. Cynthia Orr.

Annual Conference Program (2011). Alan Harkness.

Annual Conference Program (2010). Felton Thomas, Jr.

Baker & Taylor Entertainment Audio Music/Video Product Award Jury. Carol Sheffer.

Budget and Finance. Marilyn H. Boria.

Charlie Robinson Award Jury. Jeanne Goodrich.

DEMCO New Leaders Travel Grant Jury. Susan A. Alcantara-Antoine.

EBSCO Excellence in Small and/or Rural Public Library Service Award Jury. John D. Hales, Jr.

Endowment Task Force. Susan Hildreth.

Every Child Ready to Read Evaluation Task Force. Clara Nalli Bohrer.

Gordon M. Conable Award Jury. Anne L. Coriston.

Highsmith Library Innovation Award Jury. Fred J. Gitner.

Intellectual Freedom Advisory Group. Sara Dallas.

Leadership Development Task Force. Luis Herrera.

Legislative Advisory Group. Cathy Elizabeth Sanford.

National Conference Committee (2012) Karen Danczak-Lyons.

National Conference Local Arrangements (2010). Vailey B. Oehlke.

National Conference Program Committee (2012) Sara Dallas.

Nominating Committee (2011) Carol L. Sheffer.

PLDS Statistical Report Advisory Committee. Susan G. Waxter.

Polaris Innovation in Technology John Iliff Award Jury. Bruce Schauer.

Public Libraries Advisory Committee. Alan Harkness.

Spring Symposium Program Subcommittee. To be appointed.

American Library Association
Reference and User Services Association

Executive Director, Susan Hornung
50 E. Huron St., Chicago, IL 60611
Tel.800-545-2433 ext. 4395, 312-280-4395, fax 312-280-5273
E-mail shornung@ala.org
World Wide Web http://www.ala.org/rusa

Object

The Reference and User Services Association (RUSA) is the foremost organization of reference and information professionals who make the connections between people and the information sources, services, and collection materials they need. Responsible for supporting the delivery of reference/information services to all groups, regardless of age, in all types of libraries, RUSA facilitates the development and conduct of direct service to library users, the development of programs and guidelines for service to meet the needs of these users, and assists libraries in reaching potential users.

The specific responsibilities of RUSA are

1. Conduct of activities and projects within the association's areas of responsibility

2. Encouragement of the development of librarians engaged in these activities and stimulation of participation by members of appropriate type-of-library divisions

3. Synthesis of the activities of all units within the American Library Association that have a bearing on the type of activities represented by the association

4. Representation and interpretation of the association's activities in contacts outside the profession

5. Planning and development of programs of study and research in these areas for the total profession

6. Continuous study and review of the association's activities

Membership

Memb. 4,500+

Officers (July 2009–June 2010)

Pres. Susan J. Beck; *Pres.-Elect* Barry Trott; *Secy.* Theresa Mudrock; *Past Pres.* Neal Wyatt.

Directors-at-Large

Paul Brothers, Corinne M. Hill, Alesia M. McManus, Mary M. D. Parker, Amber A. Prentiss, Joseph A. Thompson, Jr.

Publication

RUSQ (q.; memb.). *Ed.* Diane M. Zabel, Schreyer Business Lib., Pennsylvania State Univ., 309 Paterno Lib., University Park, PA 16802. E-mail dxz2@psu.edu.

Sections

Business Reference and Services; Collection Development and Evaluation; History; Machine-Assisted Reference; Reference Services; Sharing and Transforming Access to Resources.

Committees

Access to Information; AFL/CIO Joint Committee on Library Services to Labor Groups; Awards Coordinating; Budget and Finance; Conference Program Coordinating; Membership; Margaret E. Monroe Adult Services Award; Isadore Gilbert Mudge Award; Nominating; Organization and Planning; President's Program Planning; Professional Development; Publications and Communications; Services Press Award; Services; John Sessions Memorial Award; Standards and Guidelines.

American Library Association
Young Adult Library Services Association

Executive Director, Beth Yoke
50 E. Huron St., Chicago, IL 60611
312-280-4390, 800-545-2433 ext. 4390, fax 312-280-5276
E-mail yalsa@ala.org, World Wide Web http://www.ala.org/yalsa
Blog http://yalsa.ala.org/blog, MySpace http://www.myspace.com/yalsa
Wiki http://wikis.ala.org/yalsa, Twitter http://twitter.com/yalsa
Facebook http://www.facebook.com/YALSA.

Object

In every library in the nation, quality library service to young adults is provided by a staff that understands and respects the unique informational, educational, and recreational needs of teenagers. Equal access to information, services, and materials is recognized as a right, not a privilege. Young adults are actively involved in the library decision making process. The library staff collaborates and cooperates with other youth-serving agencies to provide a holistic, community-wide network of activities and services that support healthy youth development. To ensure that this vision becomes a reality, the Young Adult Library Services Association (YALSA)

1. Advocates extensive and developmentally appropriate library and information services for young adults ages 12 to 18
2. Promotes reading and supports the literacy movement
3. Advocates the use of information and communications technologies to provide effective library service
4. Supports equality of access to the full range of library materials and services, including existing and emerging information and communications technologies, for young adults
5. Provides education and professional development to enable its members to serve as effective advocates for young people
6. Fosters collaboration and partnerships among its individual members with the library community and other groups involved in providing library and information services to young adults
7. Influences public policy by demonstrating the importance of providing library and information services that meet the unique needs and interests of young adults
8. Encourages research and is in the vanguard of new thinking concerning the provision of library and information services for youth

Membership

Memb. 5,600. Open to anyone interested in library services, literature, and technology for young adults. For information on dues, see ALA entry.

Officers

Pres. Linda Braun. E-mail lbraun@leonline.com; *V.P./Pres.-Elect* Kim Patton. E-mail kimpatton@kclibrary.org; *Past Pres.* Sarah Debraski. E-mail slcornish@gmail.com; *Division Councilor* Nick Buron. E-mail nick.h.buron@queenslibraryl.org; *Fiscal Officer* Mary Hastler. E-mail mhastler@bcpl. net; *Secy.* Francisca Goldsmith. E-mail fgoldsmith@gmail.com.

Directors

Jerene Battisti. E-mail jdbattisti@kcls.org; Michele Gorman. E-mail comixlibrarian@ aol.com; Shannon Peterson. E-mail speterson @krl.org; Dawn Rutherford. E-mail drutherford@sno-isle.org; Sara Ryan. E-mail ryansara@gmail.com; Stephanie Squicciarini.

E-mail stephanie.squicciarini@fairport library.org; Gail Tobin. E-mail gtobin@stdl. org; Cindy Welch. E-mail cwelch2@gmail. com; Sarajo Wentling. E-mail sjwentling@ yahoo.com.

Publications

Young Adult Library Services (q.) (memb.; nonmemb. $50; foreign $60). *Ed.* Sarah Flowers.

YAttitudes (memb.) *Ed.* Erin Downey Howerton.

AIIM—The Enterprise Content Management Association

President, John F. Mancini
1100 Wayne Ave., Suite 1100, Silver Spring, MD 20910
800-477-2446, 301-587-8202, fax 301-587-2711
E-mail aiim@aiim.org, World Wide Web http://www.aiim.org
European Office: The IT Centre, 8 Canalside, Lowesmoor Wharf, Worcester WR1 2RR,
England. Tel. 44-1905-727613, fax 44-1905-727609, e-mail info@aiim.org.uk

Object

AIIM is an international authority on enterprise content management, the tools and technologies that capture, manage, store, preserve, and deliver content in support of business processes. Founded in 1943 as the Association for Information and Image Management.

Officers

Chair Lynn Fraas, Crown Partners; *V. Chair* John Chickering, Fidelity Investments; *Treas.* Llewellyn Thomas, Albistur Consulting; *Past Chair* Robert W. Zagami, DataBank IMX.

Publication

AIIM E-DOC Magazine (bi-mo.; memb.).

American Indian Library Association (AILA)

President, Liana Juliano
World Wide Web http://www.ailanet.org

Objective

To improve library and information services for American Indians. Founded in 1979; affiliated with American Library Association 1985.

Membership

Any person, library, or other organization interested in working to improve library and information services for American Indians may become a member. Dues (Inst.) $30; (Indiv.) $15; (Student) $10.

Officers (July 2009–June 2010)

Pres. Liana Juliano, e-mail lj12116@yahoo. com; *V.P./Pres.-Elect* Jody Gray. E-mail grayjl@umn.edu; *Secy.* Heather Devine. E-mail heather@io.com; *Interim Treas.* Carlene Engstrom. E-mail carleneengstrom@yahoo. com; *Past. Pres.* Susan Hanks. E-mail shanks

@library.ca.gov; *Members at Large* Lisa Mitten. E-Mail mohawk6nations@yahoo. com; Holly Tomren. E-mail htomren@uci. edu; Kelly Webster. E-mail kellypster@ gmail.com.

Publication

AILA Newsletter (q.).

Committee Chairs

Children's Literature Award. Lisa Mitten.
Communications and Publications. Liana Juliano, Heather Devine.
Development and Fund Raising. Richenda Hawkins.
Nominating. Kelly Webster, Joan Howland.
Programming. Susan Hanks.
Scholarship Review Board. Holly Tomren.
Subject Access and Classification. Mario Klimiades.

American Merchant Marine Library Association

(An affiliate of United Seamen's Service)
Executive Director, Roger T. Korner
635 Fourth Ave., Brooklyn, NY 11232
Tel. 718-369-3818, e-mail ussammla@ix.netcom.com
World Wide Web http://uss-ammla.com

Object

Provides ship and shore library service for American-flag merchant vessels, the Military Sealift Command, the U.S. Coast Guard, and other waterborne operations of the U.S. government. Established 1921.

Officers

Pres. Edward R. Morgan; *V.P.s* Thomas J. Bethel, John M. Bowers, Capt. Timothy A. Brown, James Capo, David Cockroft, Ron Davis, Capt. Remo Di Fiore, Yoji Fujisawa, John Halas, Rene Lioeanjie, George E. Murphy, Capt. Gregorio Oca, Michael Sacco, John J. Sweeney; *Secy.* Donald E. Kadlac; *Treas.* William D. Potts; *Gen. Counsel* John L. DeGurse, Jr.; *Exec. Dir.* Roger T. Korner.

American Society for Information Science and Technology

Executive Director, Richard B. Hill
1320 Fenwick Lane, Suite 510, Silver Spring, MD 20910
301-495-0900, fax 301-495-0810, e-mail asis@asis.org
World Wide Web http://www.asis.org

Object

The American Society for Information Science and Technology (ASIS&T) provides a forum for the discussion, publication, and critical analysis of work dealing with the design, management, and use of information, information systems, and information technology.

Membership

Memb. (Indiv.) 3,500; (Student) 800; (Inst.) 250. Dues (Indiv.) $140; (Student) $40; (Inst.) $650 and $800.

Officers

Pres. Gary Marchionini, Univ. of North Carolina at Chapel Hill; *Pres.-Elect* Linda C. Smith, Univ. of Illinois at Urbana-Champaign; *Treas.* Vicki Gregory, Univ. of South Florida; *Past Pres.* Donald O. Case, Univ. of Kentucky.

Address correspondence to the executive director.

Board of Directors

Dirs.-at-Large Deborah Barreau, France Bouthillier, Prudence Dalrymple, Efthimis Efthimiadis, Barbara Wildemuth.

Publications

ASIS&T Thesaurus of Information Science, Technology, and Librarianship, 3rd edition, ed. by Alice Redmond-Neal and Marjorie M. K. Hlava.
Computerization Movements and Technology Diffusion: From Mainframes to Ubiqui- *tous Computing,* ed. by Margaret S. Elliott and Kenneth L. Kraemer.
Covert and Overt: Recollecting and Connecting Intelligence Service and Information Science, ed. by Robert V. Williams and Ben-Ami Lipetz.
Editorial Peer Review: Its Strengths and Weaknesses, by Ann C. Weller.
Electronic Publishing: Applications and Implications, ed. by Elisabeth Logan and Myke Gluck.
Evaluating Networked Information Services: Techniques, Policy and Issues, by Charles R. McClure and John Carlo Bertot.
From Print to Electronic: The Transformation of Scientific Communication, by Susan Y. Crawford, Julie M. Hurd, and Ann C. Weller.
Historical Information Science: An Emerging Unidiscipline, by Lawrence J. McCrank.
Historical Studies in Information Science, ed. by Trudi Bellardo Hahn and Michael Buckland.
The History and Heritage of Scientific and Technological Information Systems, ed. by W. Boyd Rayward and Mary Ellen Bowden.
Information and Emotion: The Emergent Affective Paradigm in Information Behavior Research and Theory, ed. by Diane Nahl and Dania Bilal.
Information Management for the Intelligent Organization: The Art of Environmental Scanning, 3rd edition, by Chun Wei Choo.
Information Representation and Retrieval in the Digital Age, by Heting Chu.
Intelligent Technologies in Library and Information Service Applications, by F. W. Lancaster and Amy Warner.
Introductory Concepts in Information Science, by Melanie J. Norton.
Knowledge Management for the Information Professional, ed. by T. Kanti Srikantaiah and Michael E. D. Koenig.

Knowledge Management in Practice: Connections and Context, ed. by T. Kanti Srikantaiah and Michael E. D. Koenig.

Knowledge Management Lessons Learned: What Works and What Doesn't, ed. by T. Kanti Srikantaiah and Michael E. D. Koenig.

Knowledge Management: The Bibliography, compiled by Paul Burden.

Proceedings of ASIS&T Annual Meetings.

Statistical Methods for the Information Professional, by Liwen Vaughan.

Theories of Information Behavior, ed. by Karen E. Fisher, Sanda Erdelez, and Lynne E. F. McKechnie.

The Web of Knowledge: A Festschrift in Honor of Eugene Garfield, ed. by Blaise Cronin and Helen Barsky Atkins.

The above publications are available from Information Today, Inc., 143 Old Marlton Pike, Medford, NJ 08055.

American Theological Library Association

300 S. Wacker Drive, Suite 2100, Chicago, IL 60606-6701
Tel. 888-665-2852, 312-454-5100, fax 312-454-5505, e-mail atla@atla.com
World Wide Web http://www.atla.com/atlahome.html

Mission

The mission of the American Theological Library Association (ATLA) is to foster the study of theology and religion by enhancing the development of theological and religious libraries and librarianship. In pursuit of this mission, the association undertakes

- To foster the professional growth of its members, and to enhance their ability to serve their constituencies as administrators and librarians
- To advance the profession of theological librarianship, and to assist theological librarians in defining and interpreting the proper role and function of libraries in theological education
- To promote quality library and information services in support of teaching, learning, and research in theology, religion, and related disciplines and to create such tools and aids (including publications) as may be helpful in accomplishing this
- To stimulate purposeful collaboration among librarians of theological libraries and religious studies collec-

tions, and to develop programmatic solutions to information-related problems common to those librarians and collections

Membership

(Inst.) 252; (International Inst.) 16; (Indiv.) 437; (Student) 67; (Lifetime) 96; (Affiliates) 75.

Officers

Pres. David R. Stewart, Luther Seminary, 2481 Como Ave., St. Paul, MN 55108. Tel. 651-641-3592, fax 651-641-3280, e-mail dstewart@luthersem.edu; *V.P.* Roberta A. Schaafsma, Perkins School of Theology, Southern Methodist Univ., P.O. Box 750476, Dallas, TX 75275-0476. Tel. 214-768-1867, fax 214-768-4295, e-mail schaafsm@smu.edu; *Secy.* Eileen Crawford, Vanderbilt Univ. Divinity Lib., 419 21st Ave. S., Nashville, TN 37240-0007. Tel. 615-343-9880, fax 615-343-2918, e-mail eileen.k.crawford@vanderbilt.edu.

Directors

H. D. Sandy Ayer, Carisse Mickey Berryhill, M. Patrick Graham, Carrie M. Hackney, Duane Harbin, William J. Hook, Saundra Lipton, Allen W. Mueller, James C. Pakala, Laura C. Wood.

Publications

ATLA Indexes in MARC Format (q.)

ATLA Religion Database, 1949– (q., on EBSCO, OCLC, Ovid)
ATLASerials, 1949– (q., full-text, on EBSCO, OCLC, Ovid)
Catholic Periodical and Literature Index (q., on EBSCO)
Old Testament Abstracts (ann. on EBSCO)
New Testament Abstracts (ann. on EBSCO)
Proceedings (ann.; memb.; nonmemb. $55). *Ed.* Sara Corkery.
Research in Ministry: An Index to Doctor of Ministry Project Reports (ann.) online.

Archivists and Librarians in the History of the Health Sciences

President, Stephen J. Greenberg, Coord. of Public Services, History of Medicine Div., National Lib. of Medicine
301-435-4995, e-mail greenbes@mail.nih.gov
World Wide Web http://www.alhhs.org

Object

The association was established exclusively for educational purposes, to serve the professional interests of librarians, archivists, and other specialists actively engaged in the librarianship of the history of the health sciences by promoting the exchange of information and by improving the standards of service.

Membership

Memb. 170. Dues $15 (Americas), $21 (other countries).

Officers

Pres. Stephen J. Greenberg. E-mail greenbes @mail.nih.gov; *Secy./Treas.* Arlene Shaner. E-mail ashaner@nyam.org; *Membs.-at-Large* Christopher Lyons, Howard Rootenberg, Jack Eckert, Dawn McInnis; *Past Pres.* Lisa A. Mix. E-mail lisa.mix@library.ucsf.edu.

Publication

Watermark (q.; memb.). *Ed.* Christopher Lyons, Osler Lib. of the History of Medicine, McGill Univ. E-mail christopher. lyons@mcgill.ca.

ARMA International

Executive Director, Marilyn Bier
11880 College Blvd., Suite 450, Overland Park, KS 66210
Tel. 888-301-3324, 913.217.6002, fax 913.341.3742
World Wide Web http://www.arma.org

Object

To advance the practice of records and information management as a discipline and a profession; to organize and promote programs of research, education, training, and networking within that profession; to support the enhancement of professionalism of the membership; and to promote cooperative endeavors with related professional groups.

Membership

Memb. 11,000. Annual dues $150 for international affiliation (student/retired $25). Chapter dues vary.

Officers (July 2009–June 2010)

Pres./Chair Douglas Allen, Global 360, 3103 Sasparilla Cove, Austin, TX 78748. Tel. 512-791-8027; *Pres.-Elect* Nicholas De Laurentis, State Farm, 3 State Farm Plaza S, L3, Bloomington, IL 61791-0001. Tel. 309-735-3500; *Treas.* Fred Pulzello, 26 Holt Court, Glen Rock, NJ 07452. Tel. 201-723-5865; *Past Pres.* John Frost, IBM Corp., 12408 John Simpson Court, Austin, TX 78732. Tel. 877-622-9929.

Directors

Beverly Bishop, Galina Datskovsky, Pamela Duane, Michael Guentzel, Komal Gulich, John Isaza, Samantha Lofton, Susan Lord, Mike Marsh, Sean Tanner, Juana Walker, Jesse Wilkins.

Publication

Information Management (*IM*) (bi-mo.).

Art Libraries Society of North America (ARLIS/NA)

President, Amy Lucker
Executive Management, Technical Enterprises, Inc., Scott Sherer, Pres.
7044 S. 13 St., Oak Creek, WI 53154
Tel. 414-768-8000, fax 414-768-8001, e-mail sherer@techenterprises.net

Object

To foster excellence in art librarianship and visual resources curatorship for the advancement of the visual arts. Established 1972.

Membership

Memb. 1,100. Dues (Inst./Business Affiliate) $145; (Indiv.) $85; (Student) $45; (Retired/Unemployed) $45; (Sustaining) $250; (Sponsor) $500; (Overseas) $65. Year. Jan. 1–Dec. 31. Membership is open to all those interested in visual librarianship, whether they be professional librarians, students, library assistants, art book publishers, art book dealers, art historians, archivists, architects, slide and photograph curators, or retired associates in these fields.

Officers

Pres. Amy Lucker, Institute of Fine Arts Lib., 1 E. 78 St., New York, NY 10075. Tel. 212-992-5826, e-mail amy.lucker@nyu.edu; *V.P./Pres.-Elect* Marilyn Russell, Haskell Indian Nations Univ., 155 Indian Ave., Lawrence, KS 66046. Tel. 785-832-6661, e-mail mrussell@haskell.edu; *Secy.* V. Heidi Hass, Morgan Lib. and Museum, 225 Madison Ave., New York, NY 10016-3403. Tel. 212-590-0381, fax 212-768-5681, e-mail vhhass@themorgan.org; *Treas.* Edward Goodman, Avery Lib., Columbia Univ., 1172 Amsterdam Ave., MC 0301, New York, NY 10027. Tel. 212-854-8407, fax 212-854-8904, e-mail goodman@columbia.edu; *Past Pres.* Ken Soehner, Thomas J. Watson Lib., Metropolitan Museum of Art, 1000 Fifth Ave., New York, NY 10028. Tel. 212-570-3934, fax 212-570-3847, e-mail ken.soehner @metmuseum.org.

Address correspondence to Scott Sherer, Technical Enterprises, Inc., 7044 S. 13 St., Oak Creek, WI 53154.

Publications

ARLIS/NA Update (bi-mo.; memb.).

Art Documentation (2 a year; memb., subscription).
Handbook and List of Members (ann.; memb.).
Occasional papers (price varies).
Miscellaneous others (request current list from headquarters).

Committee Chairs

ARLIS/NA and VRA Summer Educational Institute for Visual Resources and Image Management. Jeanne Keefe, Alix Reiskind, Kathe Albrecht.
Awards. Susan Moon.
Cataloging Advisory. Sarah Quimby.
Communications and Publications. Jonathan Franklin.
Development. Barbara Rockenbach.
Distinguished Service Award. Betsy Peck-Learned.
Diversity. Krista Ivy, Martha González Palacios.
Finance. Fran Scott.
International Relations. Kristen Regina.
Membership. Shalimar Fojas White.
Gerd Muehsam Award. Tony White.
Nominating. Allen Townsend.
Professional Development. Sarah Falls.
Public Policy. Marc Gartler.
Strategic Planning. Ken Soehner.

Asian/Pacific American Librarians Association

Executive Director, Gary Colmenar
E-mail colmenar@library.ucsb.edu
World Wide Web http://www.apalaweb.org

Object

To provide a forum for discussing problems and concerns of Asian/Pacific American librarians; to provide a forum for the exchange of ideas by Asian/Pacific American librarians and other librarians; to support and encourage library services to Asian/Pacific American communities; to recruit and support Asian/Pacific American librarians in the library/information science professions; to seek funding for scholarships in library/information science programs for Asian/Pacific Americans; and to provide a vehicle whereby Asian/Pacific American librarians can cooperate with other associations and organizations having similar or allied interests. Founded in 1980; incorporated 1981; affiliated with American Library Association 1982.

Membership

Open to all librarians and information specialists of Asian/Pacific descent working in U.S. libraries and information centers and other related organizations, and to others who support the goals and purposes of the association. Asian/Pacific Americans are defined as people residing in North America who self-identify as Asian/Pacific American. Dues (Inst.) $50; (Indiv.) $20; (Students/Unemployed Libns.) $10.

Officers (July 2009–June 2010)

Pres. Sherise Kimura, Gleeson Lib., Univ. of San Francisco. E-mail kimura@usfca.edu; *V.P./Pres.-Elect* Florante Peter Ibanez, William M. Rains Lib., Loyola Law School, Los Angeles. E-mail florante.Ibanez@lls.edu; *Secy.* Liladhar Pendse, Charles E. Young Research Lib., UCLA. E-mail lpendse@library.ucla.edu; *Treas.* Angela Boyd, Davidson Lib., Univ. of California, Santa Barbara.

E-mail aboyd@library.ucsb.edu; *Past Pres.* Michelle Baildon, MIT Humanities Lib. E-mail baildon@mit.edu.

Publication

APALA Newsletter (q.).

Committee Chairs

Constitution and Bylaws. Ben Wakashige.
Finance and Fund Raising. Angela Yumiko Boyd.
Literary Awards. Dora Ho.
Membership. Jade Alburo.
Newsletter and Publications. Suhasini Kumar, Gary Colmenar.
Nomination. Michelle Baildon.
Program. Sherise Kimura.
Publicity. Ven Basco.
Research and Travel. Alanna Aiko Moore.
Scholarships. Heawon Paick.
Web. Andrienne Z. Gaerlan, Holly Yu.

Association for Library and Information Science Education

Executive Director, Kathleen Combs
ALISE Headquarters, 65 E. Wacker Place, Suite 1900, Chicago, IL 60601-7246
312-795-0996, fax 312-419-8950, e-mail contact@alise.org
World Wide Web http://www.alise.org

The Association for Library and Information Science Education (ALISE) is an independent, nonprofit professional association whose mission is to promote excellence in research, teaching, and service for library and information science (LIS) education through leadership, collaboration, advocacy, and dissemination of research. Its enduring purpose is to promote research that informs the scholarship of teaching and learning for library and information science, enabling members to integrate research into teaching and learning. The association provides a forum in which to share ideas, discuss issues, address challenges, and shape the future of education for library and information science. Founded in 1915 as the Association of American

Library Schools, it has had its present name since 1983.

Membership

600+ in four categories: Personal, Institutional, International Affiliate Institutional, and Associate Institutional. Personal membership is open to anyone with an interest in the association's objectives.

Officers (2010–2011)

Pres. Lorna Peterson, Univ. at Buffalo. E-mail lpeterso@buffalo.edu; *V.P./Pres.-Elect* Lynn

Horwarth, Univ. of Toronto; *Past Pres.* Linda C. Smith, Univ. of Illinois at Urbana-Champaign; *Secy.-Treas.* Jean Preer, Indiana Univ., Indianapolis; *Dirs.* Susan Roman, Dominican Univ., Anne Weeks, Univ. of Maryland, Andrew Wertheimer, Univ. of Hawaii.

Publications

Journal of Education for Library and Information Science (JELIS) (q.). *Co-Eds.* Kathleen Burnett, Michelle Kazmer.

ALISE News (q.)

Association of Academic Health Sciences Libraries

Executive Director, Louise S. Miller
2150 N. 107 St., Suite 205, Seattle, WA 98133
206-367-8704, fax 206-367-8777, e-mail aahsl@sbims.com
World Wide Web http://www.aahsl.org

Object

The Association of Academic Health Sciences Libraries (AAHSL) is composed of the directors of libraries of more than 140 accredited U.S. and Canadian medical schools belonging to the Association of American Medical Colleges. Its goals are to promote excellence in academic health science libraries and to ensure that the next generation of health practitioners is trained in information-seeking skills that enhance the quality of health care delivery, education, and research. Founded in 1977.

Membership

Memb. 140+. Regular membership is available to nonprofit educational institutions operating a school of health sciences that has full or provisional accreditation by the Association of American Medical Colleges. Regular members are represented by the chief administrative officer of the member institution's health sciences library. Associate membership (and nonvoting representation) is available to organizations having an interest in the purposes and activities of the association.

Officers (2009–2010)

Pres. Connie Poole, School of Medicine Lib., Southern Illinois Univ.; *Pres.-Elect* Pat Thibodeau, Medical Center Lib., Duke Univ.; *Secy./Treas.* Paul Schoening, Bernard Becker Medical Lib., Washington Univ. School of Medicine; *Past Pres.* Julia Sollenberger, Univ. of Rochester Medical Center.

Directors

Jim Bothmer, Health Science Lib., Creighton Univ.; Sandra Franklin, Woodruff Health Sciences Center Lib., Emory Univ.; M. J. Tooey, Health Sciences and Human Services Lib., Univ. of Maryland, Baltimore.

Association of Independent Information Professionals (AIIP)

8550 United Plaza Blvd., Suite 1001, Baton Rouge, LA 70809
225-408-4400, fax 225-408-4422, e-mail office@aiip.org
World Wide Web http://www.aiip.org

Object

AIIP's members are owners of firms providing such information-related services as online and manual research, document delivery, database design, library support, consulting, writing, and publishing. The objectives of the association are

- To advance the knowledge and understanding of the information profession
- To promote and maintain high professional and ethical standards among its members
- To encourage independent information professionals to assemble to discuss common issues
- To promote the interchange of information among independent information professionals and various organizations
- To keep the public informed of the profession and of the responsibilities of the information professional

Membership

Memb. 650+.

Officers (2009–2010)

Pres. Marcy Phelps, Phelps Research. Tel. 303-239-0657; *Pres.-Elect* Margaret King, InfoRich Group. Tel. 484-461-8100; *Secy.* Vada Repta, Precision Research Link. Tel. 217-637-0349; *Treas.* Cliff Kalibjian, Mr. Health Search. Tel. 925-830-8439; *Past Pres.* Edward Vawter, QD Information Service. Tel. 503-999-7347.

Publications

AIIP Connections (q.).
Membership Directory (ann.).
Professional paper series.

Association of Jewish Libraries

P.O. Box 1118, Teaneck, NJ 07666
212-725-5359, e-mail ajlibs@osu.edu
World Wide Web http://www.jewishlibraries.org

Object

The Association of Jewish Libraries (AJL) promotes Jewish literacy through enhancement of libraries and library resources and through leadership for the profession and practitioners of Judaica librarianship. The association fosters access to information, learning, teaching, and research relating to Jews, Judaism, the Jewish experience, and Israel.

Goals

- Maintain high professional standards for Judaica librarians and recruit qualified individuals into the profession
- Facilitate communication and exchange of information on a global scale
- Encourage quality publication in the field in all formats and media

- Stimulate publication of high-quality children's literature
- Facilitate and encourage establishment of Judaica library collections
- Enhance information access for all through application of advanced technologies
- Publicize the organization and its activities in all relevant venues
- Stimulate awareness of Judaica library services among the public at large
- Promote recognition of Judaica librarianship within the wider library profession
- Encourage recognition of Judaica library services by other organizations and related professions
- Ensure continuity of the association through sound management, financial security, effective governance, and a dedicated and active membership

Membership

Memb. 1,100. Dues $50; (Student/Retired) $30. Year. July 1–June 30.

Officers (July 2009–June 2010)

Pres. Susan Dubin; *V.P./Pres.-Elect* David Hirsch; *V.P. Memb.* Laurie Haas; *V.P. Publications* Deborah Stern; *Treas.* Schlomit Schwarzer; *Recording Secy.* Elana Gensler; *Corresponding Secy.* Rachel Glasser; *Treas.* Sheryl Stahl; *Past Pres.* Laurel S. Wolfson.

Address correspondence to the association.

Publications

AJL Newsletter (q.). *Ed.* Libby K. White, Baltimore Hebrew Univ., 5800 Park Heights Ave., Baltimore, MD 21215.
Judaica Librarianship (irreg.). *Ed.* Zachary M. Baker, Green Lib. 321, ASRG, Stanford Univ. Libs., Stanford, CA 94305-6004.

Division Presidents

Research Libraries, Archives, and Special Libraries. Elliot H. Gertel, Univ. of Michigan. Synagogue, School, and Center Libraries. Etta D. Gold, Temple Beth Am, Miami.

Association of Research Libraries

Executive Director, Charles B. Lowry
21 Dupont Circle N.W., Suite 800, Washington, DC 20036
202-296-2296, fax 202-872-0884, e-mail arlhq@arl.org
World Wide Web http://www.arl.org

Object

The Association of Research Libraries (ARL) is a nonprofit organization of 124 research libraries in North America. Its mission is to influence the changing environment of scholarly communication and the public policies that affect research libraries and the diverse communities they serve. ARL pursues this mission by advancing the goals of its member research libraries, providing leadership in public and information policy to the scholarly and higher education communities, fostering the exchange of ideas and expertise, facilitating the emergence of new roles for research libraries, and shaping a future environment that leverages its interests with those of allied organizations.

Membership

Memb. 124. Membership is institutional. Dues: $23,704 for 2010.

Officers

Pres. Brinley Franklin, Univ. of Connecticut; *V.P./Pres.-Elect* Carol A. Mandel, New York Univ.; *Past Pres.* Thomas C. Leonard, Univ. of California, Berkeley

Board of Directors

Colleen Cook, Texas A&M Univ.; Barbara Dewey, Univ. of Tennessee; Carol Pitts Diedrichs, Univ. of Kentucky; Brinley Franklin, Univ. of Connecticut; Deborah Jakubs, Duke Univ.; Tom Leonard, Univ. of California, Berkeley; Wendy Pradt Lougee, Univ. of Minnesota; Charles B. Lowry (ex officio), ARL; Carol A. Mandel, New York Univ.; Sarah Michalak (ex officio), Univ. of North Carolina at Chapel Hill; James Mullins, Purdue Univ.; James G. Neal (ex officio), Univ. of Columbia; Winston Tabb, Johns Hopkins Univ.; Karin Trainer, Princeton Univ.; Paul Wiens, Queens Univ.; Sandra Yee, Wayne State Univ.

Publications

Research Library Issues: A Bimonthly Report from ARL, CNI, and SPARC (bi-mo.).
ARL Academic Health Sciences Library Statistics (ann.).
ARL Academic Law Library Statistics (ann.).
ARL Annual Salary Survey (ann.).
ARL Preservation Statistics (ann.).
ARL Statistics (ann.).
ARL Supplementary Statistics (ann.).
SPEC Kits (6 a year).

Committee and Working Group Chairs

Diversity and Leadership. Nancy Baker, Univ. of Iowa.
Fair Use and Related Exemptions Working Group. Mary Case, Univ. of Illinois, Chicago.
Membership. Paula Kaufman, Univ. of Illinois at Urbana-Champaign.

Influencing Public Policies. Sarah Michalak, Univ. of North Carolina at Chapel Hill.
Regional Federal Depository Libraries Working Group. Joan Giesecke, Univ. of Nebraska.
Transforming Research Libraries. Barbara Dewey, Univ. of Tennessee.
Reshaping Scholarly Communication. Carole Moore, Univ. of Toronto.
Special Collections Working Group, Anne Kenney, Cornell Univ.
Statistics and Assessment. William Potter, Univ. of Georgia.

ARL Membership

Nonuniversity Libraries

Boston Public Lib., Canada Inst. for Scientific and Technical Info., Center for Research Libs., Lib. and Archives Canada, Lib. of Congress, National Agricultural Lib., National Lib. of Medicine, New York Public Lib., New York State Lib., Smithsonian Institution Libs.

University Libraries

Alabama; Albany (SUNY); Alberta; Arizona; Arizona State; Auburn; Boston College; Boston Univ.; Brigham Young; British Columbia; Brown; Buffalo (SUNY); Calgary; California, Berkeley; California, Davis; California, Irvine; California, Los Angeles; California, Riverside; California, San Diego; California, Santa Barbara; Case Western Reserve; Chicago; Cincinnati; Colorado; Colorado State; Columbia; Connecticut; Cornell; Dartmouth; Delaware; Duke; Emory; Florida; Florida State; George Washington; Georgetown; Georgia; Georgia Inst. of Technology; Guelph; Harvard; Hawaii; Houston; Howard; Illinois, Chicago; Illinois, Urbana-Champaign; Indiana; Iowa; Iowa State; Johns Hopkins; Kansas; Kent State; Kentucky; Laval; Louisiana State; Louisville; McGill; McMaster; Manitoba; Maryland; Massachusetts; Massachusetts Inst. of Technology; Miami (Florida); Michigan; Michigan State; Minnesota; Missouri; Montreal; Nebraska, Lincoln; New Mexico; New York; North

Carolina; North Carolina State; Northwestern; Notre Dame; Ohio; Ohio State; Oklahoma; Oklahoma State; Oregon; Pennsylvania; Pennsylvania State; Pittsburgh; Princeton; Purdue; Queen's (Kingston, Ontario); Rice; Rochester; Rutgers; Saskatchewan; South Carolina; Southern California; Southern Illinois; Stony Brook (SUNY); Syracuse; Temple; Tennessee; Texas; Texas A&M; Texas Tech; Toronto; Tulane; Utah; Vanderbilt; Virginia; Virginia Tech; Washington; Washington (Saint Louis): Washington State; Waterloo; Wayne State; Western Ontario; Wisconsin; Yale; York.

Association of Vision Science Librarians

Chair, 2010–2012, Gale A. Oren, Kellogg Eye Center, Univ. of Michigan,
1000 Wall St., Ann Arbor, MI 48105
Tel. 734-763-9468, fax 734-936-9050, e-mail goren@umich.edu
World Wide Web http://www.avsl.org

Object

To foster collective and individual acquisition and dissemination of vision science information, to improve services for all persons seeking such information, and to develop standards for libraries to which members are attached. Founded in 1968.

Membership

Memb. (U.S.) 62; (International) 60.

Publications

Core List of Audio-Visual Related Serials.

Guidelines for Vision Science Libraries.

Opening Day Book, Journal and AV Collection—Visual Science.

Publication Considerations in the Age of Electronic Opportunities.

Standards for Vision Science Libraries.

Union List of Vision-Related Serials (irreg.).

Meetings

Annual meeting held in the fall, mid-year mini-meeting with the Medical Library Association in the spring.

Beta Phi Mu
(International Library and Information Studies Honor Society)

Executive Director, Christie Koontz
College of Communication and Information,
Florida State University, Tallahassee, FL 32306-2100
850-644-3907, fax 850-644-9763, e-mail ckoontz@ci.fsu.edu
World Wide Web http://www.beta-phi-mu.org

Object

To recognize distinguished achievement in and scholarly contributions to librarianship, information studies, or library education, and to sponsor and support appropriate professional and scholarly projects related to these fields. Founded at the University of Illinois in 1948.

Membership

Memb. 36,000. Open to graduates of library school programs accredited by the American Library Association who fulfill the following requirements: complete the course requirements leading to a fifth year or other advanced degree in librarianship with a scholastic average of 3.75 where A equals 4 points (this provision shall also apply to planned programs of advanced study beyond the fifth year that do not culminate in a degree but that require full-time study for one or more academic years) and rank in the top 25 percent of their class; and receive a letter of recommendation from the faculty of their respective library schools attesting to their professional promise.

Officers

Pres. Sue Stroyan, Ames Lib., Illinois Wesleyan Univ., Bloomington, IL 61701; *V.P./ Pres.-Elect* John M. Budd, Univ. of Missouri, 303 Townsend Hall, Columbia, MO 65211; *Treas.* David Whisenant, College Center for Lib. Automation, 1753 W. Paul Dirac Drive, Tallahassee, FL 32310; *Exec. Dir.* Christie Koontz, College of Info., Florida State Univ., Tallahassee, FL 32306-2100. Tel. 850-644-

3907, fax 850-644-9763, e-mail betaphimuinfo @admin.fsu.edu.

Directors

Dirs. Kaye Bray, Alice Calabrese-Berry, Daria DeCooman, George Gaumond, Eloise May, Ron Miller, Beth Paskoff, Sue Searing, Diana L. Vogelsong.

Publications

Beta Phi Mu Monograph Series. Book-length scholarly works based on original research in subjects of interest to library and information professionals. Available from Greenwood Press, 130 Cremona Drive, Santa Barbara, CA 93117.

Chapbook Series. Limited editions on topics of interest to information professionals.

The Pipeline (electronic only). *Ed.* John Paul Walters.

Chapters

Alpha. Univ. of Illinois, Grad. School of Lib. and Info. Science; *Gamma.* Florida State Univ., College of Communication and Info.; *Epsilon.* Univ. of North Carolina, School of Info. and Lib. Science; *Theta.* Pratt Inst., Grad. School of Lib. and Info. Science; *Iota.* Catholic Univ. of America, School of Lib. and Info. Science; Univ. of Maryland, College of Info. Studies; *Lambda.* Univ. of Oklahoma, School of Lib. and Info. Studies; *Mu.* Univ. of Michigan, School of Info; *Xi.* Univ. of Hawaii, Grad. School of Lib. and Info. Studies; *Omicron.* Rutgers Univ., Grad. School of Communication, Info. and Lib. Studies; *Pi.* Univ. of Pittsburgh, School of

Info. Sciences; *Rho.* Kent State Univ., School of Lib. and Info. Science; *Sigma.* Drexel Univ., College of Info. Science and Technology; *Upsilon.* Univ. of Kentucky, School of Lib. and Info. Science; *Phi.* Univ. of Denver, Grad. School of Lib. and Info. Science; *Chi.* Indiana Univ., School of Lib. and Info. Science; *Psi.* Univ. of Missouri at Columbia, School of Lib. and Info. Science; *Omega.* San Jose State Univ., School of Lib. and Info. Science; *Beta Alpha.* Queens College, City College of New York, Grad. School of Lib. and Info. Studies; *Beta Beta.* Simmons College, Grad. School of Lib. and Info. Science; *Beta Delta.* State Univ. of New York at Buffalo, Dept. of Lib. and Info. Studies; *Beta Epsilon.* Emporia State Univ., School of Lib. and Info. Management; *Beta Zeta.* Louisiana State Univ., Grad. School of Lib. and Info. Science; *Beta Eta.* Univ. of Texas at Austin, Grad. School of Lib. and Info. Science; *Beta Iota.* Univ. of Rhode Island, Grad. School of Lib. and Info. Studies; *Beta Kappa.* Univ. of Alabama, Grad. School of Lib. and Info. Studies; *Beta Lambda.* Univ. of North Texas, College of Info.; Texas Woman's Univ., School of Lib. and Info. Sciences; *Beta Mu.* Long Island Univ., Palmer Grad. School of Lib. and Info. Science; *Beta Nu.* Saint John's Univ., Div. of Lib. and Info. Science; *Beta*

Xi. North Carolina Central Univ., School of Lib. and Info. Sciences; *Beta Omicron.* Univ. of Tennessee at Knoxville, Grad. School of Info. Sciences; *Beta Pi.* Univ. of Arizona, Grad. School of Info. Resources and Lib. Science; *Beta Rho.* Univ. of Wisconsin at Milwaukee, School of Info.; *Beta Sigma.* Clarion Univ. of Pennsylvania, Dept. of Lib. Science; *Beta Tau.* Wayne State Univ., Lib. and Info. Science Program; *Beta Phi.* Univ. of South Florida, Grad. School of Lib. and Info. Science; *Beta Psi.* Univ. of Southern Mississippi, School of Lib. and Info. Science; *Beta Omega.* Univ. of South Carolina, College of Lib. and Info. Science; *Beta Beta Alpha. Beta Beta Gamma.* Dominican Univ., Grad. School of Lib. and Info. Science; *Beta Beta Epsilon.* Univ. of Wisconsin at Madison, School of Lib. and Info. Studies; *Beta Beta Zeta.* Univ. of North Carolina at Greensboro, Dept. of Lib. and Info. Studies; *Beta Beta Theta.* Univ. of Iowa, School of Lib. and Info. Science; *Beta Beta Iota.* State Univ. of New York, Univ. at Albany, School of Info. Science and Policy; *Beta Beta Kappa.* Univ. of Puerto Rico, Grad. School of Info. Sciences and Technologies; *Pi Lambda Sigma.* Syracuse Univ., School of Info. Studies; *Beta Beta Mu.* Valdosta State Univ., School of Lib. and Info. Science.

Bibliographical Society of America

Executive Secretary, Michèle E. Randall
P.O. Box 1537, Lenox Hill Sta., New York, NY 10021
212-452-2710 (tel./fax), e-mail bsa@bibsocamer.org
World Wide Web http://www.bibsocamer.org

Object

To promote bibliographical research and to issue bibliographical publications. Organized 1904.

Membership

Memb. Dues (Indiv.) $65; (Sustaining) $250; (Contributing) $100; (Student) $20); (Inst.) $75; (Lifetime) $1,200. Year. Jan.–Dec.

Officers

Pres. John Neal Hoover. E-mail jhoover@umsl.edu; *V.P.* Claudia Funke. E-mail claudia funke@mac.com; *Secy.* David R. Whitesell. E-mail whitesel@fas.harvard.edu; *Treas.* G. Scott Clemons. E-mail scott.clemons@bbh.com; *Past Pres.* John Bidwell. E-mail jbidwell@morganlibrary.org.

Council

(2010) Eugene S. Flamm, James N. Green, Arthur L. Schwarz, Carolyn L. Smith; (2011) Douglas F. Bauer, John Crichton, Joan Friedman, Gregory A. Pass; (2012) David L. Gants, Barbara Shailor, Daniel Slive, David Supino.

Publication

Papers of the Bibliographical Society of America (q.; memb.). *Ed.* Trevor Howard-Hill, Thomas Cooper Lib., Univ. of South Carolina, Columbia, SC 29208. Tel./fax 803-777-7046, e-mail ralphcrane@msn. com.

Bibliographical Society of Canada
(La Société Bibliographique du Canada)

President, Anne Dondertman
P.O. Box 575, Postal Station P, Toronto, ON M5S 2T1
World Wide Web http://www.library.utoronto.ca/bsc/bschomeeng.html

Object

The Bibliographical Society of Canada is a bilingual (English/French) organization that has as its goal the scholarly study of the history, description, and transmission of texts in all media and formats, with a primary emphasis on Canada, and the fulfillment of this goal through the following objectives:

- To promote the study and practice of bibliography: enumerative, historical, descriptive, analytical, and textual
- To further the study, research, and publication of book history and print culture
- To publish bibliographies and studies of book history and print culture
- To encourage the publication of bibliographies, critical editions, and studies of book history and print culture
- To promote the appropriate preservation and conservation of manuscript, archival, and published materials in various formats
- To encourage the utilization and analysis of relevant manuscript and archival sources as a foundation of bibliographical scholarship and book history
- To promote the interdisciplinary

nature of bibliography, and to foster relationships with other relevant organizations nationally and internationally

- To conduct the society without purpose of financial gain for its members, and to ensure that any profits or other accretions to the society shall be used in promoting its goal and objectives

Membership

The society welcomes as members all those who share its aims and wish to support and participate in bibliographical research and publication.

Officers

Pres. Anne Dondertman; *1st V.P.* Paul Aubin; *2nd V.P.s* Randall Speller, Janet Friskney; *Secy.* Greta Golick. E-mail gretagolick@ rogers.com; *Assoc. Secy.* Roger Meloche; *Treas.* Tom Vincent.

Publications

Papers of the Bibliographical Society of Canada / Cahiers de la Société Bibliographique du Canada (s. ann).

The Bulletin / Le Bulletin (s. ann).

For a full list of the society's publications, see http://www.library.utoronto.ca/bsc/publicationseng.html.

Committee Chairs

Awards. Randall Speller.
Fellowships. Isabelle Robitaille.
Publications. Patricia Fleming.

Black Caucus of the American Library Association

President, Karolyn S. Thompson, Univ. Libs., Univ. of Southern Mississippi, 118 College Drive, No. 5053, Hattiesburg, MS 39406-0001
Tel. 601-266-5111, fax 601-266-4410, e-mail karolyn.thompson@usm.edu
World Wide Web http://www.bcala.org

Mission

The Black Caucus of the American Library Association (BCALA) serves as an advocate for the development, promotion, and improvement of library services and resources to the nation's African American community and provides leadership for the recruitment and professional development of African American librarians. Founded in 1970.

Membership

Membership is open to any person, institution, or business interested in promoting the development of library and information services for African Americans and other people of African descent and willing to maintain good financial standing with the organization. The membership is currently composed of librarians and other information professionals, library support staff, libraries, publishers, authors, vendors, and other library-related organizations in the United States and abroad. Dues (Corporate) $200; (Institutional) $60; (Regular) $45; (Student) $10.

Officers

Pres. Karolyn S. Thompson. E-mail karolyn.thompson@usm.edu; *V.P./Pres.-Elect* Jos N. Holman. Tel. 765-429-0118, e-mail jholman@tcpl.lib.in.us; *Secy.* Eboni Curry. Tel. 202-727-1248, e-mail eboni.curry@dc.gov; *Treas.* Stanton F. Biddle. E-mail treasurer@bcala.

org; *Past Pres.* Wanda K. Brown. E-mail brownw@wfu.edu.

Executive Board

Talia Abdullah, Gladys Smiley Bell, Vivian Bordeaux, Lisa Boyd, Jannie Cobb, Denyvetta Davis, Sharon Epps, LaVerne Gray, S. D. Harris, Gerald Holmes, Julius Jefferson, Jr., Alys Jordan, Carolyn Norman, Kelvin Watson, Joel White.

Publication

BCALA Newsletter (bi-mo; memb.). *Interim Ed.* S. D. Harris. E-mail sdh.newsletter@bcala.org.

Committee Chairs

Affiliated Chapters. Sylvia Sprinkle-Hamlin, Lainey Westbrooks.
Affirmative Action. Howard F. McGinn, Darren Sweeper.
ALA Relations. Allene Hayes.
Awards. Richard Bradberry, ayo dayo.
Budget/Audit. Bobby Player.
Constitution and Bylaws. D. L. Grant, Gerald Holmes.
Fund Raising. Makiba J. Foster, Kelvin Watson.
History. Sibyl E. Moses.
International Relations. Vivian Bordeaux, Eboni M. Stokes.

E. J. Josey Scholarship. Billy Beal, Joyce E. Jelks.

Literary Awards. Virginia Toliver, Joel White.

Membership. Rudolph Clay, Allison M. Sutton.

Newsletter. George Grant, S. D. Harris.

Nominations/Elections. Wanda K. Brown.

Programs. Jos Holman.

Public Relations. Barbara E. Martin.

Recruitment and Professional Development. Jannie R. Cobb, Andrew P. Jackson (Sekou Molefi Baako).

Services to Children of Families of African Descent. Karen Lemmons.

Smiley Fund. Gladys Smiley Bell.

Technology Advisory. H. Jamane Yeager.

Dr. John C. Tyson Award. Alys Jordan, Esmeralda M. Kale.

Awards

BCALA Literary Awards.

BCALA Trailblazer's Award.

DEMCO/ALA Black Caucus Award for Excellence in Librarianship.

Distinguished Service Award.

E. J. Josey Scholarship Award.

Smiley Student Fund.

John Tyson Award.

Canadian Association for Information Science
(L'Association Canadienne des Sciences de l'Information)

President, Catherine Johnson
Faculty of Info. and Media Studies, Univ. of Western Ontario, 203 North Campus Bldg.,
1151 Richmond St., London, ON N6A 5B7
World Wide Web http://www.cais-acsi.ca

Object

To promote the advancement of information science in Canada and encourage and facilitate the exchange of information relating to the use, access, retrieval, organization, management, and dissemination of information.

Membership

Institutions and individuals interested in information science and involved in the gathering, organization, and dissemination of information (such as information scientists, archivists, librarians, computer scientists, documentalists, economists, educators, journalists, and psychologists) and who support CAIS's objectives can become association members. Dues (Inst.) $165; (Personal) $75; (Senior) $40; (Student) $40.

Directors

Pres. Catherine Johnson, Univ. of Western Ontario; *V.P.* Nadia Caidi, Univ. of Toronto; *Treas.* Ali Shiri, Univ. of Alberta; *Dir., Communications* Dinesh Rathi, Univ. of Alberta; *Dir., Membership* Clément Arsenault, Univ. de Montréal; *Secy.* Heather O'Brien, Univ. of British Columbia; *Past Pres.* Joan Bartlett, McGill Univ.

Publication

Canadian Journal of Information and Library Science. Ed. Heidi Julien, Univ. of Alberta.

Canadian Association of Research Libraries
(Association des Bibliothèques de Recherche du Canada)

Brent Roe, Executive Director
Morisset Hall, 65 University St., Suite 239
University of Ottawa, Ottawa, ON K1N 9A5.
Tel. 613-562-5385, fax 613.562.5297, e-mail carl@uottawa.ca
World Wide Web http://www.carl-abrc.ca

Membership

The Canadian Association of Research Libraries (CARL), established in 1976, is the leadership organization for the Canadian research library community. The association's members are the 28 major academic research libraries across Canada together with Library and Archives Canada, the Canada Institute for Scientific and Technical Information (CISTI), and the Library of Parliament. Membership is institutional, open primarily to libraries of Canadian universities that have doctoral graduates in both the arts and the sciences. CARL is an associate member of the Association of Universities and Colleges of Canada (AUCC) and is incorporated as a not-for-profit organization under the Canada Corporations Act.

CARL strives to enhance the capacity of Canada's research libraries to partner in research and higher education, seeking effective and sustainable scholarly communication and public policy encouraging research and broad access to scholarly information. CARL's strategic directions for 2010–2012 focus on the continuing transformation of scholarly communication, advocacy for a favorable federal public policy environment, and the strengthening and promotion of Canada's research libraries.

Officers

Pres. (2009–2011) Ernie Ingles, 5-07 Cameron Lib., Univ. of Alberta, Edmonton AB T6G 2J8; *V.P./Pres.-Elect (2009–2011)* Thomas Hickerson, MacKimmie Lib. Tower, Univ. of Calgary, 2500 University Drive N.W., Calgary AB T2N 1N4; *Secy. (2008–*

2010) Margaret Haines, Maxwell MacOdrum Lib., Carleton Univ., 1125 Colonel By Drive, Ottawa ON K1S 5B6; *Treas. (2009–2011)* Lorraine Busby, Queen Elizabeth II Lib., Memorial Univ. of Newfoundland, St. John's, NF A1C 5S7; *Dirs.* Sylvie Belzile, Services des Bibliothèques et Archives, Univ. of Sherbrooke, 2500 Blvd. Université, Sherbrooke QC J1K 2R1; Lynn Copeland, WAC Bennett Lib., Simon Fraser Univ., 8888 University Drive, Burnaby BC V5A 1S6.

Member Institutions

Univ. of Alberta, Univ. of British Columbia, Brock Univ., Univ. of Calgary, Carleton Univ., CISTI (Canada Institute for Scientific and Technical Information), Concordia Univ., Dalhousie Univ., Univ. of Guelph, Université Laval, Univ. of Manitoba, Lib. and Archives Canada, Lib. of Parliament, McGill Univ., McMaster Univ., Memorial Univ. of Newfoundland, Université de Montréal, Univ. of New Brunswick, Univ. of Ottawa, Université du Québec à Montréal, Queen's Univ., Univ. of Regina, Univ. of Saskatchewan, Université de Sherbrooke, Simon Fraser Univ., Univ. of Toronto, Univ. of Victoria, Univ. of Waterloo, Univ. of Western Ontario, Univ. of Windsor, York Univ.

Publications

For a full list of publications, see http://www.carl-abrc.ca/publications/publications-e.html.

Canadian Library Association
(Association Canadienne des Bibliothèques)

Executive Director, Kelly Moore
328 Frank St., Ottawa, ON K2P 0X8
613-232-9625 ext. 306, fax 613-563-9895, e-mail kmoore@cla.ca
World Wide Web http://www.cla.ca

Object

The Canadian Library Association (CLA) is its members' advocate and public voice, educator, and network. It builds the Canadian library and information community by promoting, developing, and supporting library and information services and advancing today's information professionals, through cooperation with all who share its values. The association represents Canadian librarianship to the federal government and media, carries on international liaison with other library associations and cultural agencies, offers professional development programs, and supports such core library values as intellectual freedom and access to information, particularly for disadvantaged populations. Founded in 1946, CLA is a not-for-profit voluntary organization governed by an elected executive council.

Membership

Memb. (Indiv.) 1,800; (Inst.) 500. Open to individuals, institutions, library boards, and groups interested in librarianship and in library and information services.

Officers

Pres. John Teskey, Univ. of New Brunswick Libs.; *V.P./Pres.-Elect* Keith Walker, Medicine Hat Community College; *Treas.* Ingrid Langhammer.

Publications

Feliciter: Linking Canada's Information Professionals (6 a year; magazine/journal).
CLA Digest (bi-weekly; electronic newsletter).

Divisions

Canadian Association for School Libraries (CASL).
Canadian Association of College and University Libraries (CACUL).
Canadian Association of Public Libraries (CAPL).
Canadian Association of Special Libraries and Information Services (CASLIS).
Canadian Library Trustees Association (CLTA).

Catholic Library Association

Executive Director, Jean R. Bostley, SSJ
100 North St., Suite 224, Pittsfield, MA 01201-5178
413-443-2252, fax 413-442-2252, e-mail cla@cathla.org
World Wide Web http://www.cathla.org

Object

The promotion and encouragement of Catholic literature and library work through cooperation, publications, education, and information. Founded in 1921.

Membership

Memb. 1,000. Dues $45–$500. Year. July–June.

Officers (2008–2010)

Pres. Nancy K. Schmidtmann, 174 Theodore Drive, Coram, NY 11727; *V.P./Pres.-Elect* Malachy R. McCarthy, Claretian Missionaries Archives, 205 W. Monroe St., Chicago, IL 60606; *Past Pres.* Catherine M. Fennell, Gertrude Kistler Memorial Lib., Rosemont College, 1400 Montgomery Ave., Rosemont, PA 19010.

Address correspondence to the executive director.

Executive Board

Officers; Sara B. Baron, Regent Univ. Lib., 1000 Regent University Drive, Virginia Beach, VA 23464; Jean Elvekrog, 401 Doral Court, Waunakee, WI 53597; Cait C. Kokolus, St. Charles Borromeo Seminary, 100 E. Wynnewood Rd., Wynnewood, PA 19096; Frances O'Dell, OSF, Barry Univ. Lib., 11300 N.E. 2 Ave., Miami Shores, FL 33161; Annette B. Thibodeaux, Archbishop Chapelle H.S., 8800 Veterans Blvd., Metairie, LA 70003.

Publications

Catholic Library World (q.; memb.; nonmemb. $60). *General Ed.* Mary E. Gallagher, SSJ.

Catholic Periodical and Literature Index (*CLPI*) (q.; $400 calendar year; abridged ed., $125 calendar year. To be available as an online subscription only (1981–present), through EBSCO, from 2010. *Ed.* Deborah A. Winarski.

Center for the Study of Rural Librarianship

Dept. of Lib. Science, Clarion Univ. of Pennsylvania, 840 Wood St., Clarion, PA 16214.
Tel. 814-393-2014, fax 814-393-2150, e-mail jkrueger@clarion.edu or csrl@clarion.edu
World Wide Web http://jupiter.clarion.edu/~csrl/csrlhom.htm

Object

The Center for the Study of Rural Librarianship (CSRL) is a research, publishing, consultative, and continuing education facility established in the Department of Library Science at Clarion University of Pennsylvania in 1978. Its mission is to extend knowledge relative to the nature and role of rural and small libraries worldwide, whose defining characteristics are a limited budget and a diverse clientele. CSRL is concerned with the development and use of information technology in rural communities, and its recent endeavors include library outreach and, particularly, bookmobile services in the United States and overseas.

Its objectives are

- To stimulate imaginative thinking relative to rural library services
- To identify problems endemic with library services—for those currently being served and those who are not yet served
- To provide consultative services in designing new service patterns in rural libraries
- To conduct and/or coordinate research relative to identifiable library problems
- To stimulate continuing education
- To coordinate physical and human resources which could be lent to analyze library services
- To collect data relevant to the needs of rural libraries

Two professional associations are affiliated with CSRL: the Association for Rural and Small Libraries and the Association of Bookmobile and Outreach Services.

The Association for Rural and Small Libraries (ARSL) (http://www.webjunction. org/arsl) includes members among public, school, small urban branch, special, corporate, and small academic libraries. The association's mission is to provide a network of people and materials to support rural and small library staff, volunteers, and trustees to integrate the library thoroughly with the life and work of the community it serves.

The Association of Bookmobile and Outreach Services (ABOS) (http://www.abos-outreach.org) encompasses libraries of all types. The association's mission is to support and encourage government officials, library administrators, trustees, and staff in the provision of quality bookmobile and outreach services to meet diverse community information and programming needs.

Membership in ARSL and ABOS and attendance at their annual conferences are open to all individuals and institutions seeking to champion rural libraries and outreach services. Both associations are supported by CSRL in cooperation with the H. W. Wilson Foundation.

Publications

CSRL has published the journal *Rural Libraries* since 1980 and the journal *Bookmobile and Outreach Services* since 1998. Both are printed twice a year, with annual subscription rates of $20 for domestic and $30 for international subscribers. Back copies are available at $10 each, and selected full-text articles are available at http://www.clarion. edu/rural. CSRL also publishes a variety of monographs, bibliographies, and other resources.

CSRL maintains listservs for ARSL and ABOS to provide forums for discussion, sharing of best practices and success stories, relevant library news, and professional networking.

Chief Officers of State Library Agencies

Association Director, Laura Singler-Adams
201 E. Main St., Suite 1405, Lexington, KY 40507
859-514-9151, fax 859-514-9166, e-mail lsingler-adams@amrms.com
World Wide Web http://www.cosla.org

Object

Chief Officers of State Library Agencies (COSLA) is an independent organization of the chief officers of state and territorial agencies designated as the state library administrative agency and responsible for statewide library development. Its purpose is to identify and address issues of common concern and national interest; to further state library agency relationships with federal government and national organizations; and to initiate cooperative action for the improvement of library services to the people of the United States.

COSLA's membership consists solely of these top library officers, variously designated as state librarian, director, commissioner, or executive secretary. The organization provides a continuing mechanism for dealing with the problems and challenges faced by these officers. Its work is carried on through its members, a board of directors, and committees.

Officers (2008–2010)

Pres. Susan McVey, Dir., Dept. of Libs., 200 N.E. 18 St., Oklahoma City, OK 73105-3298. Tel. 405-521-2502, fax 405-525-7804, e-mail smcvey@oltn.odl.state.ok.us; *V.P./Pres.-Elect* Lamar Veatch, State Libn., Georgia Public Lib. Service, 1800 Century Place, Suite 150, Atlanta, GA 30345-4304. Tel. 404-235-7200, fax 404-235-7201, e-mail lveatch@georgialibraries.org; *Secy.* Donna Jones Morris, Dir./State Libn., Utah State Lib., 250 N. 1950 W., Suite A, Salt Lake City, UT 84116-7901. Tel. 801-715-6777, fax 801-715-6767, e-mail dmorris@utah.gov; *Treas.* Ann Joslin, State Libn., State Lib., 325 W. State St., Boise, ID 83702. Tel. 208-334-2150, ann.joslin@libraries.idaho.gov; *Dirs.* Jan Walsh, State Libn., Washington State Lib. Div., Office of the Secy. of State, 6880 Capitol Blvd., Tumwater, WA 98504-2460. Tel. 360-704-5253, fax 360-586-7575, e-mail jwalsh@secstate.wa.gov; Jeanne Sugg, State Libn. and Archivist, Tennessee State Lib. and Archives, 403 Seventh Ave. N., Nashville, TN 37243-0312. Tel. 615-741-7996, fax 615-532-9293, e-mail jeanne.sugg@state.tn.us.

Chinese American Librarians Association

Executive Director, Haipeng Li
E-mail haipeng.li@oberlin.edu
World Wide Web http://www.cala-web.org

Object

To enhance communications among Chinese American librarians as well as between Chinese American librarians and other librarians; to serve as a forum for discussion of mutual problems and professional concerns among Chinese American librarians; to promote Sino-American librarianship and library services; and to provide a vehicle whereby Chinese American librarians can cooperate with other associations and organizations having similar or allied interests.

Membership

Memb. 1,100+. Open to anyone who is interested in the association's goals and activities. Dues (Regular) $30; (International/Student/Nonsalaried) $15; (Inst.) $100; (Affiliated) $100; (Life) $300.

Officers

Pres. (2009–2010) Xudong Jin. E-mail xdjin @owu.edu; *V.P./Pres.-Elect (2009–2010)* Zhijia Shen. E-mail zhijia@u.washington. edu; *V.P./Pres.-Elect (2010–2011)* Min Chou. E-mail minchou.njcu@gmail.com; *Exec. Dir. (2009–2010)* Haipeng Li. E-mail haipeng4cala@gmail.com; *Treas. (2008–2010)* Shuyong Jiang. E-mail shyjiang@uiuc.edu; *Past Pres.* Sha Li Zhang. E-mail slzhang@ uncg.edu.

Publications

Journal of Library and Information Science (2 a year; memb.; online). *Ed. (2008–2011)* Min Chou, Congressman Frank J. Guarini Lib., New Jersey City Univ. E-mail minchou.njcu@gmail.com.
Membership Directory (memb.).
Newsletter (2 a year; memb.; online). *Eds.* Priscilla Yu. E-mail pcyu@illinois.edu; Sai Deng. E-mail sai.deng@wichita.edu.
Occasional Paper Series (OPS) (occasional, online). *Ed. (2009–2012)* Xue-Ming Bao. E-mail baoxuemi@shu.edu.

Committee Chairs

Alire Initiative Task Force. Nancy Hershoff, Dora Ho.
Annual Conference, Local Arrangements. Yuan Yao, Ding Ye.
Annual Conference, Program Planning (2009–2010). Zhijia Shen.
Annual Conference, Program Planning. (2010–2011). Min Chou.
Awards. Li Fu.
Best Book Award. Miao Jin.
Constitution and Bylaws. Karen Wei.
Finance. Ruan Lian.
International Relations. Guoqing Li, Qi Chen.
Membership. Elaine Dong, Songqian Lu.
Mentorship Program. Wenwen Zhang.
Nominating. Sha Li Zhang.
Public Relations/Fund Raising. Maria Yuen-Hung Fung, Hong Xu.
Publications. Hong Miao.

Church and Synagogue Library Association

2920 S.W. Dolph Court, Suite 3A, Portland, OR 97219-4055
503-244-6919, 800-542-2752, fax 503-977-3734, e-mail CSLA@worldaccessnet.com
World Wide Web http://www.cslainfo.org

Object

The Church and Synagogue Library Association (CSLA) provides educational guidance in the establishment and maintenance of congregational libraries.

Its purpose is to act as a unifying core for congregational libraries; to provide the opportunity for a mutual sharing of practices and problems; to inspire and encourage a sense of purpose and mission among congregational librarians; to study and guide the development of congregational librarianship toward recognition as a formal branch of the library profession. Founded in 1967.

Membership

Memb. 1,300. Dues (Inst.) $200; (Affiliated) $100; (Congregational) $70 ($75 foreign); (Indiv.) $50 ($55 foreign).

Officers (July 2009–July 2010)

Pres. Rusty Tryon; *Pres.-Elect* Marjorie Smink; *2nd V.P.* Barbara Stowers; *Treas.* Bill Anderson; *Admin.* Judith Janzen; *Past Pres.*

J. Theodore Anderson; *Ed., Congregational Libraries Today* Jeri Zulli, 5 Dorm Court, East Setauket NY 11733; *Book Review Ed.* Monica Tenney, 399 Blenheim Rd., Columbus, OH 43214-3219. E-mail motenney@aol.com.

Executive Board

Officers; committee chairs.

Publications

Bibliographies (4; price varies).
Congregational Libraries Today (q.; memb.; nonmemb. $50; Canada $60).
CSLA Guides (14; price varies).

Committee Chairs

Awards. Jeri Baker.
Conference. Alrene Hall, Jane Hope.
Library Services. Esther Beirbaum.
Nominations and Elections. Jane Hope.
Publications. Dorothy Lewis.

Coalition for Networked Information

Executive Director, Clifford A. Lynch
21 Dupont Circle, Suite 800, Washington, DC 20036
202-296-5098, fax 202-872-0884, e-mail info@cni.org
World Wide Web http://www.cni.org

Mission

The Coalition for Networked Information (CNI) is an organization to advance the transformative promise of networked information technology for the advancement of scholarly communication and the enrichment of intellectual productivity.

Membership

Memb. 219. Membership is institutional. Dues $6,600. Year. July–June.

Steering Committee

Richard P. West, California State Univ. (*Chair*); Daniel Cohen, George Mason Univ.; Timothy Lance, NYSERNet; Charles B. Lowry, Assn. of Research Libs.; Richard E. Luce, Emory Univ.; Clifford A. Lynch, CNI; Deanna B. Marcum, Lib. of Congress; Diana G. Oblinger, EDUCAUSE; Patti Orr, Baylor Univ.; Sherrie Schmidt, Arizona State Univ.; George O. Strawn, National Science Foundation; Donald J. Waters, Andrew W. Mellon Foundation.

Publication

CNI-Announce (subscribe by e-mail to cni-announce-subscribe@cni.org).

Council on Library and Information Resources

1752 N St. N.W., Suite 800, Washington, DC 20036
202-939-4750, fax 202-939-4765
World Wide Web http://www.clir.org

Object

In 1997 the Council on Library Resources (CLR) and the Commission on Preservation and Access (CPA) merged and became the Council on Library and Information Resources (CLIR). CLIR's mission is to expand access to information, however recorded and preserved, as a public good. CLIR identifies and defines the key emerging issues relating to the welfare of libraries and the constituencies they serve, convenes the leaders who can influence change, and promotes collaboration among the institutions and organizations that can achieve change. The council's interests embrace the entire range of information resources and services from traditional library and archival materials to emerging digital formats. It assumes a particular interest in helping institutions cope with the accelerating pace of change associated with the transition into the digital environment.

CLIR is an independent, nonprofit organization. While maintaining appropriate collaboration and liaison with other institutions and organizations, the council operates independently of any particular institutional or vested interests. Through the composition of its board, it brings the broadest possible perspective to bear upon defining and establishing the priority of the issues with which it is concerned.

Board

CLIR's Board of Directors currently has 15 members.

Officers

Chair Stephen Nichols; *Pres.* Charles Henry. E-mail chenry@clir.org; *Treas.* Herman Pab-bruwe.

Address correspondence to headquarters.

Publications

Annual Report.

CLIR Issues (bi-mo.).

Technical reports.

Council on Library/Media Technicians

Executive Director, Margaret Barron
PMB 168, 28262 Chardon Rd., Willoughby Hills, OH 44092
216-261-0776, e-mail margaretrbarron@aol.com
World Wide Web http://colt.ucr.edu

The Council on Library/Media Technicians (COLT), an affiliate of the American Library Association, is an international organization that works to address the issues and concerns of library and media support staff personnel.

Since 1967 COLT has addressed issues covering such areas as technical education, continuing education, certification, job description uniformity, and the more elusive goals of gaining recognition and respect for the professional work that its members do.

Objectives

COLT's objectives are

- To function as a clearinghouse for information relating to library support staff personnel

- To advance the status, employment, and certification of library staff

- To promote effective communication and cooperation with other organizations whose purposes and objectives are similar to those of COLT

COLT's Web site, http://colt.ucr.edu, provides information on library technician programs, a speaker exchange listing for help in organizing workshops and conferences, bibliographies on needed resources, and jobline resource links.

COLT holds an annual conference, generally immediately preceding the American Library Association Annual Conference.

Membership

Membership is open to all library employees. Dues (Inst.) $70 ($95 foreign); (Indiv.) $45 ($70 foreign); (Student) $35. Year Jan.–Dec.

Officers

Pres. Jackie Hite. E-mail jmhite0@dia.mil; *V.P./Pres.-Elect.* Chris Egan. E-mail egan@rand.org; *Secy.* Robin Martindill. E-mail rmartind@sdccd.edu; *Treas.* Stan Cieplinski. E-mail stan.cieplinski@domail.maricopa.edu; *Past Pres.* Jackie Lakatos. E-mail jlakatos@lemontlibrary.org; *Exec. Dir.* Margaret Barron, PMB 168, 28262 Chardon Rd., Willoughby Hills, OH 44092.

Federal Library and Information Center Committee

Executive Director, Roberta I. Shaffer
Library of Congress, Washington, DC 20540-4935
202-707-4800
World Wide Web http://www.loc.gov/flicc

Object

The Federal Library and Information Center Committee (FLICC) makes recommendations on federal library and information policies, programs, and procedures to federal agencies and to others concerned with libraries and information centers. The committee coordinates cooperative activities and services among federal libraries and information centers and serves as a forum to consider issues and policies that affect federal libraries and information centers, needs and priorities in providing information services to the government and to the nation at large, and efficient and cost-effective use of federal library and information resources and services. Furthermore, the committee promotes improved access to information, continued development and use of the Federal Library and Information Network (FEDLINK), research and development in the application of new technologies to federal libraries and information centers, improvements in the management of federal libraries and information centers, and relevant education opportunities. Founded in 1965.

Membership

Libn. of Congress, Dir. of the National Agricultural Lib., Dir. of the National Lib. of Medicine, Dir. of the National Lib. of Educ., representatives of each of the cabinet-level executive departments, and representatives of each of the following agencies: National Aeronautics and Space Admin., National Science Foundation, Smithsonian Institution, U.S. Supreme Court, National Archives and Records Admin., Admin. Offices of the U.S. Courts, Defense Technical Info. Center, Government Printing Office, National Technical Info. Service (Dept. of Commerce), Office of Scientific and Technical Info. (Dept. of Energy), Exec. Office of the President, Dept. of the Army, Dept. of the Navy, Dept. of the Air Force, and chair of the FEDLINK Advisory Council. Fifteen additional voting member agencies are selected on a rotating basis by the voting members of FEDLINK. These rotating members serve three-year terms. One representative of each of the following agencies is invited as an observer to committee meetings: Government Accountability Office, General Services Admin., Joint Committee on Printing, Office of Mgt. and Budget, Office of Personnel Mgt., and U.S. Copyright Office.

Officers

Chair Deanna Marcum, Assoc. Libn. for Lib. Services, Lib. of Congress; *Co-Chair* Kathryn Mendenhall; *V. Chair* Elaine Cline; *Exec. Dir.* Roberta I. Shaffer.

Address correspondence to the executive director.

Publication

FEDLINK Technical Notes (bi-mo.).

Medical Library Association

Executive Director, Carla Funk
65 E. Wacker Place, Suite 1900, Chicago, IL 60601-7298
312-419-9094, fax 312-419-8950, e-mail info@mlahq.org
World Wide Web http://www.mlanet.org

Object

The Medical Library Association (MLA) is a nonprofit educational organization composed of health sciences information professionals and organized exclusively for scientific and educational purposes. It is dedicated to the support of health sciences research, education, and patient care. MLA fosters excellence in the professional achievement and leadership of health sciences library and information professionals to enhance the quality of health care, education, and research.

Membership

Memb. (Inst.) 850+; (Indiv.) 3,600+, in 43 countries. Institutional members are medical and allied scientific libraries. Individual members are people who are (or were at the time membership was established) engaged in professional library or bibliographic work in medical and allied scientific libraries or people who are interested in medical or allied scientific libraries. Members can be affiliated with one or more of MLA's more than 20 special-interest sections and its regional chapters.

Officers

Pres. Connie Schardt. E-mail schar005@mc.duke.edu; *Pres-Elect* Ruth Holst. E-mail rholst@uic.edu; *Past Pres.* Mary L. Ryan. E-mail ryanmaryl@uams.edu.

Directors

Jane Blumenthal (2011), Judy Burnham (2011), Gary A. Freiberger (2010), Cynthia Henderson (2012), Julia Kochi (2011), Ann McKibbob (2012), Beverly Murphy (2011), Paula Raimondo (2010), Laurie L. Thompson (2010).

Publications

Journal of the Medical Library Association (q.; $163).

MLA News (10 a year; $58).

Miscellaneous (request current list from association headquarters).

Music Library Association

8551 Research Way, Suite 180, Middleton, WI 53562
608-836-5825, e-mail mla@areditions.com
World Wide Web http://www.musiclibraryassoc.org

Object

The Music Library Association provides a professional forum for librarians, archivists, and others who support and preserve the world's musical heritage. To achieve this mission, it

- Provides leadership for the collection and preservation of music and information about music in libraries and archives
- Develops and delivers programs that promote continuing education and professional development in music librarianship
- Ensures and enhances intellectual access to music for all by contributing to the development and revision of national and international codes, formats, and other standards for the bibliographic control of music
- Ensures and enhances access to music for all by facilitating best practices for housing, preserving, and providing access to music
- Promotes legislation that strengthens music library services and universal access to music
- Fosters information literacy and lifelong learning by promoting music reference services, library instruction programs, and publications
- Collaborates with other groups in the music and technology industries, government, and librarianship, to promote its mission and values

Membership

Memb. 1,274. Dues (Inst.) $125; (Indiv.) $90; (Retired or Assoc.) $60; (Paraprofessional) $45; (Student) $35. (Foreign, add $10.) Year. July 1–June 30.

Officers

Pres. Ruthann B. McTyre, 2000 Voxman Music Bldg., Univ. of Iowa, Iowa City 52242-1795. Tel. 319-335-3088, fax 319-335-2637, e-mail ruthann-mctyre@uiowa.edu; *Rec. Secy.* Karen Little. E-mail klittle@louisville.edu; *Treas./Exec. Secy.* Michael Rogan. E-mail michael.rogan@tufts.edu; *Past Pres.* Philip R. Vandermeer, Music Lib., Wilson Lib. CB3906, Univ. of North Carolina at Chapel Hill, Chapel Hill 27514. Tel. 919-966-1113, fax 919-843-0418, e-mail vanderme@email.unc.edu.

Members-at-Large

Members-at-Large (2008–2010) Paul Cary, Lois Kuyper-Rushing, Nancy Lorimer; (2009–2011) Linda Fairtile, Stephen Mantz, Jenn Riley.

Publications

MLA Index and Bibliography Series (irreg.; price varies).
MLA Newsletter (q.; memb.).
MLA Technical Reports (irreg.; price varies).
Music Cataloging Bulletin (mo.; online subscription only, $35).
Notes (q.; indiv. $85; inst. $100).

National Association of Government Archives and Records Administrators

90 State St., Suite 1009, Albany, NY 12207
518-463-8644, fax 518-463-8656, e-mail nagara@caphill.com
World Wide Web http://www.nagara.org

Object

Founded in 1984, NAGARA is a growing nationwide association of local, state, and federal archivists and records administrators, and others interested in improved care and management of government records. NAGARA promotes public awareness of government records and archives management programs, encourages interchange of information among government archives and records management agencies, develops and implements professional standards of government records and archival administration, and encourages study and research into records management problems and issues.

Membership

Most NAGARA members are federal, state, and local archival and records management agencies.

Officers

Pres. Tracey Berezansky, Alabama Dept. of Archives and History, P.O. Box 300100, Montgomery, AL 36130-0100. Tel. 334-353-4604, fax 334-353-4321, e-mail tracey. berezansky@archives.alabama.gov; *V.P.* Paul R. Bergeron, City Clerk, 229 Main St., Nashua, NH 03060. Tel. 603-589-3010, fax 603-589-3029, e-mail bergeronp@nashuanh. gov; *Secy.* Caryn Wojcik, Government

Records Archivist, Michigan Historical Center, 3400 N. Grand River Ave., P.O. Box 30026, Lansing, MI 48909. Tel. 517-335-8222, fax 517-321-3408, e-mail wojcikc@ michigan.gov; *Treas.* Nancy Fortna, National Archives and Records Administration, Seventh and Pennsylvania Ave. N.W., Room G-13 NWCC, Washington, DC 20408-0001. Tel. 202-357-5288, e-mail nancy.fortna@ nara.gov; *Past Pres.* Mary Beth Herkert, Archives Div., Offices of the Secy. of State, 800 Summer St. N.E., Salem, OR 97310. Tel. 503-373-0701, fax 503-373-0953, e-mail mary.e.herkert@state.or.us.

Directors

Jim Corridan, Indiana Commission on Public Records; Bonnie Curtin, Federal Trade Commission; John Paul Deley, Office of Info. Technology; Ken Feith, Metro Archives; Sandy Hart, McKinney, Texas; Sandra Jaramillo, New Mexico State Records Center and Archives; Douglas K. King, Sedgwick County (Kansas) Government.

Publications

Clearinghouse (q.; memb.).
Crossroads (q.; memb.).
Government Records Issues (series).
Preservation Needs in State Archives.
Program Reporting Guidelines for Government Records Programs.

National Church Library Association

Executive Director, Susan Benish
275 S. 3 St., Suite 204, Stillwater, MN 55082
651-430-0770, e-mail info@churchlibraries.org
World Wide Web http://www.churchlibraries.org

Object

The National Church Library Association (NCLA), formerly the Lutheran Church Library Association, is a nonprofit organization that serves the unique needs of congregational libraries and those who manage them. NCLA provides inspiration, solutions, and support to church librarians in the form of printed manuals and guidelines, booklists, the quarterly journal *Libraries ALIVE,* national conferences, a mentoring program, online support, and personal advice. Regional chapters operate throughout the United States.

Membership

Memb. $55. Year. Jan.–Jan.

Officers

Pres. Charles Mann; *V.P.* Phyllis Wendorf; *Secy.* Chris Magnusson; *Treas.* Sherry Acquino; *Past Pres.* Karen Gieseke.

Address correspondence to the executive director.

Directors

Kathleen Bowman, Deanna Gordon, Carol Spaulding, Melissa Taylor, Diane Volzer.

Publication

Libraries ALIVE (q.; memb.).

National Federation of Advanced Information Services

Executive Director, Bonnie Lawlor
1518 Walnut St., Suite 1004, Philadelphia, PA 19102
215-893-1561, fax 215-893-1564,e-mail nfais@nfais.org
World Wide Web http://www.nfais.org

Object

The National Federation of Advanced Information Services (NFAIS) is an international nonprofit membership organization composed of leading information providers. Its membership includes government agencies, nonprofit scholarly societies, and private sector businesses. NFAIS is committed to promoting the value of authoritative content. It serves all groups that create, aggregate, organize, or facilitate access to such information. In order to improve members' capabilities and to contribute to their ongoing success, NFAIS provides opportunities for education, advocacy, and a forum in which to address common interests. Founded in 1958.

Membership

Memb. 60. Full members are organizations whose main focus is any of the following activities: information creation, organization, aggregation, dissemination, access, or retrieval. Organizations are eligible for associate member status if they do not meet the qualifications for full membership.

Officers (2009–2010)

Pres. Terence Ford; *Pres.-Elect* Judith Russell; *Secy.* Barbara Dobbs Mackenzie; *Treas.* Keith MacGregor; *Past Pres.* David Brown.

Directors

David Gillikin, Ellen Herbst, Donna Jenkins, Lucian Parziale, Rafael Sidi, Suzanne BeDell, Lynn Willis.

Staff

Exec. Dir. Bonnie Lawlor. E-mail blawlor@nfais.org; *Dir., Planning and Communications* Jill O'Neill. E-mail jilloneill@nfais.org; *Customer Service* Margaret Manson. E-mail mmanson@nfais.org.

Publications

For a detailed list of NFAIS publications, see the NFAIS Web site, http://www.nfais.org.

National Information Standards Organization

Managing Director, Todd Carpenter
1 N. Charles Ave., Suite 1905, Baltimore, MD 21201
301-654-2512, fax 410-685-5278, e-mail nisohq@niso.org
World Wide Web http://www.niso.org

Object

NISO, the National Information Standards Organization, a nonprofit association accredited by the American National Standards Institute (ANSI), identifies, develops, maintains, and publishes technical standards to manage information in our changing and ever-more-digital environment. NISO standards apply both traditional and new technologies to the full range of information-related needs, including discovery, retrieval, repurposing, storage, metadata, business information, and preservation.

Experts from the information industry, libraries, systems vendors, and publishing participate in the development of NISO standards. The standards are approved by the consensus body of NISO's voting membership, which consists of more than 80 voting members representing libraries, publishers, vendors, government, associations, and private businesses and organizations. In addition, approximately 30 libraries are NISO Library Standards Alliance members. NISO is supported by its membership and corporate grants. NISO is a nonprofit educational organization. It is accredited by ANSI and serves as the U.S. Technical Advisory Group to ISO/TC 46 Information and Documentation as well as the secretariat for ISO/TC 46/SC 9, Identification and Description.

Membership

Memb. 80+. Open to any organization, association, government agency, or company willing to participate in and having substantial concern for the development of NISO standards. Libraries may support NISO as members of the Library Standards Alliance.

Officers

Chair Chuck Koscher, CrossRef, 40 Salem St., Lynnfield, MA 01940. Tel. 781-295-0072 ext. 26, fax 781-295-0077, e-mail ckoscher@crossref.org; *V. Chair/Chair-Elect* Janice Fleming, American Psychological Assn., 750 First St. N.E., Washington, DC 20002-4242. Tel. 202-336-5500, e-mail jfleming@apa.org; *Past Chair* Oliver Pesch,

EBSCO Info. Services, P.O. Box 1943, Birmingham, AL 35201. Tel. 205-981-4086, fax 205 991-1210, e-mail opesch@ebsco.com; *Treas.* Barbara Preece, Boston Lib. Consortium, 700 Boylston St., Boston, MA 02117. Tel. 617-262-6244, fax 617-262-0163, e-mail bpreece@blc.org.

Directors

Nancy Barnes, Nancy Davenport, John Harwood, Bruce Heterick, Charles Lowry, Heather Reid, Bruce Rosenblum, Winston Tabb, Mike Teets.

Publications

Information Standards Quarterly ($130/year, foreign $165, back issues $40).
NISO Newsline (free monthly e-letter released on the first Wednesday of each month. See the NISO Web site for details on subscribing and archived issues).

For other NISO publications, see the article "National Information Standards Organization (NISO) Standards" later in Part 6.

NISO published standards, recommended practices, and technical reports are available free of charge as downloadable pdf files from the NISO Web site (http://www.niso.org). Standards in hard copy are available for sale on the Web site.

Patent and Trademark Depository Library Association

World Wide Web http://www.ptdla.org

Object

The Patent and Trademark Depository Library Association (PTDLA) provides a support structure for the 84 patent and trademark depository libraries (PTDLs) affiliated with the U.S. Patent and Trademark Office (USPTO). The association's mission is to discover the interests, needs, opinions, and goals of the PTDLs and to advise USPTO in these matters for the benefit of PTDLs and their users, and to assist USPTO in planning and implementing appropriate services. Founded in 1983 as the Patent Depository Library Advisory Council; name changed to Patent and Trademark Depository Library Association in 1988; became an American Library Association affiliate in 1996.

Membership

Open to any person employed in a patent and trademark depository library whose responsibilities include the patent collection. Affiliate membership is also available. Dues $25.

Officers (2009–2010)

Pres. Andrew Wohrley. E-mail wohrlaj@auburn.edu; *V.P./Pres-Elect* Rob Klein. E-mail kleinr@mdpls.org; *Secy.* Marian Armour Gemmen. E-mail marmour@wvu.edu; *Treas.* Jim Miller. E-mail jmiller2@umd.edu; *Past Pres.* Karon King. E-mail karon.king@lib.state.ia.us.

Regional Representatives

Region 1, Martin Wallace. E-mail martin.wallace@umit.maine.edu; Region 2, Connie Wu. E-mail conniewu@rci.rutgers.edu; Region 3, John Meier. E-mail meier@psu.edu; Region 4, Jan Comfort. E-mail comforj@clemson.edu; Region 5, Hal Mendelsohn. E-mail hmendels@mail.ucf.edu; Region 6, Esther Crawford. E-mail crawford@rice.edu;

Region 7, Ran Raider. E-mail ran.raider@wright.edu; Region 8, Nancy Spitzer; Region 9, Suzanne Reinman. E-mail suzanne.reinman@okstate.edu; Region 10, Walt Johnson. E-mail wjohnson@mplib.org; Region 11, Patrick Ragains. E-mail ragains@unr.edu; Region 12, Marjory Cameron. E-mail mcameron@ci.sunnyvale.ca.us.

Publications

PTDLA Newsletter. Ed. Suzanne Holcombe. E-mail suzanne.reinman@okstate.edu.

Intellectual Property (IP), Journal of the PTDLA. Electronic at http://www.ptdla.org/ipjournal.html. *Ed.* Michael White.

REFORMA (National Association to Promote Library and Information Services to Latinos and the Spanish-Speaking)

President, Loida García Febo
National Office Manager, Sandra Rios Balderrama
P.O. Box 4386, Fresno, CA 93744
Tel. 480-734-4460, e-mail reformaoffice@riosbalderrama.com
World Wide Web http://www.reforma.org

Object

Promoting library services to the Spanish-speaking for nearly 40 years, REFORMA, an affiliate of the American Library Association, works in a number of areas to promote the development of library collections to include Spanish-language and Latino-oriented materials; the recruitment of more bilingual and bicultural professionals and support staff; the development of library services and programs that meet the needs of the Latino community; the establishment of a national network among individuals who share its goals; the education of the U.S. Latino population in regard to the availability and types of library services; and lobbying efforts to preserve existing library resource centers serving the interest of Latinos.

Membership

Memb. 800+. Any person who is supportive of the goals and objectives of REFORMA.

Officers

Pres. Loida García Febo, Queens Lib., 89-11 Merrick Blvd., Jamaica, NY 11209. Tel. 718-990-0891, fax 718-297-3404, e-mail loida garciafebo@gmail.com; *Pres.-Elect* Lucía M. González, 16410 Miami Drive, Apt. 404, North Miami Beach, FL 33162. Tel. 305-335-8215, e-mail inotherwordsllc@gmail.com; *Secy.* Siobhan Champ-Blackwell; *Treas.* Robin Imperial; *Memb.-at-Large* Toni Anaya; *Past Pres.* Luis Chaparro, El Paso Community College, P.O. Box 20500, El Paso, TX 79998. Tel. 915-831-2132, fax 915-831-2886, e-mail lchapa13@epcc.edu.

Committees

Pura Belpré Award. Lucía M. González.
Children's and Young Adult Services. Alma Ramos-McDermott, Jamie Campbell Naidoo.
Education. Tess Tobin.
Finance. Luis Chaparro.
International Relations. Miguel Garcia Colon.
Legislative. Sol Gomez.
Membership. Daniel Berdaner.
Nominations. Xima Avalos.
Organizational Development. Yolanda Valentín.
Public Relations. Jessica Hernandez.
Recruitment and Mentoring. Toni Anaya.
Translations. Armando Trejo.

Publication

REFORMA Newsletter (s. ann; memb.).

Meetings

General membership and board meetings take place at the American Library Association Midwinter Meeting and Annual Conference.

Society for Scholarly Publishing

Executive Director, Ann Mehan Crosse
10200 W. 44 Ave., Suite 304, Wheat Ridge, CO 80033
303-422-3914, fax 303-422-8894, e-mail info@sspnet.org
World Wide Web http://www.sspnet.org

Object

To draw together individuals involved in the process of scholarly publishing. This process requires successful interaction of the many functions performed within the scholarly community. The Society for Scholarly Publishing (SSP) provides the leadership for such interaction by creating opportunities for the exchange of information and opinions among scholars, editors, publishers, librarians, printers, booksellers, and all others engaged in scholarly publishing.

Membership

Memb. 900. Open to all with an interest in the scholarly publishing process and dissemination of information. Dues (New Member) $135; (Indiv. Renewal) $150; (Libn.) $75; (Early Career) $75; (New Student) $30; (Supporting) $1,350; (Sustaining) $3,275. Year. Jan. 1–Dec. 31.

Executive Committee

Pres. Raymond Fastiggi, Rockefeller Univ. Press. E-mail fastigg@rockefeller.edu; *Pres.-Elect* Lois Smith, Human Factors and Ergonomics Society. E-mail lois@hfes.org; *Past Pres.* October Ivins, Ivins eContent Solutions. E-mail october.ivins@mindspring.com; *Secy./Treas.* Mady Tissenbaum, *Journal of Bone and Joint Surgery.* E-mail madyt@jbjs.org.

Meetings

An annual meeting is held in late May/early June. SSP also conducts a Fall Seminar Series (November), Librarian Focus Group 303-422-3914 (February) and the IN Conference (September).

Society of American Archivists

Executive Director, Nancy Perkin Beaumont
17 N. State St., Suite 1425, Chicago, IL 60602
866-722-7858, 312-606-0722, fax 312-606-0728, e-mail nbeaumont@archivists.org
World Wide Web http://www.archivists.org

Object

Provides leadership to ensure the identification, preservation, and use of records of historical value. Founded in 1936.

Membership

Memb. 5,438. Dues (Indiv.) $77 to $216, graduated according to salary; (Assoc.) $77, domestic; (Student or Bridge) $44; (Inst.) $247; (Sustaining Inst.) $484.

Officers (2009–2010)

Pres. Peter Gottlieb, Wisconsin Historical Society, 816 State St., No. 422, Madison, WI 53706-1488. Tel. 608-264-6480, 608-264-6486, e-mail peter.gottlieb@wisconsin history.org; *V.P.* Helen Tibbo, School of Lib. and Info. Science, Univ. of North Carolina at Chapel Hill, 201 Manning Hall CB 3360, Chapel Hill, NC 27599-3360. E-mail tibbo@ email.unc.edu; *Treas.* Aimee Felker, Univ. of California, Los Angeles, 10920 Wilshire Blvd., Suite 530, Los Angeles, CA 90024

Staff

Exec. Dir. Nancy Perkin Beaumont; *Dir., Memb. and Technical Services* Brian P. Doyle; *Publishing Dir.* Teresa Brinati; *Educ. Dir.* Solveig DeSutter; *Dir., Finance and Admin.* Thomas Jurczak.

Publications

American Archivist (2 a year; individual print edition, $120; individual online edition, $120; print and online, $145; institutional, $145 print, $145 online, $170 print and online). *Ed.* Mary Jo Pugh; *Reviews Ed.* Amy Cooper Cary.

Archival Outlook (bi-mo.; memb.). *Ed.* Teresa Brinati.

Software and Information Industry Association

1090 Vermont Ave. N.W., Washington, DC 20005
Tel. 202-289-7442, fax 202-289-7097
World Wide Web http://www.siia.net

Membership

Memb. 520 companies. Formed January 1, 1999, through the merger of the Software Publishers Association (SPA) and the Information Industry Association (IIA). Open to companies involved in the creation, distribution, and use of software, information products, services, and technologies. For details on membership and dues, see the SIIA Web site.

Staff

Pres. Kenneth Wasch. E-mail kwasch@ siia.net.

Board of Directors

Suresh Balasubramanian, Adobe Systems, Inc.; Cynthia Braddon, McGraw-Hill; Daniel Burton, Salesforce.com; Joseph T. FitzGerald, Symantec; Kenneth J. Glueck, Oracle; Kathy Hurley, Pearson School and Pearson Foundation; Steve Manzo, Reed Elsevier; Randy Marcinko, Marcinko Enterprises; Bernard McKay, Intuit; Fiona O'Carroll, Houghton Mifflin Harcourt; Tom B. Rabon, Jr., Red Hat; Alan Scott; Timothy Sheehy (chair), IBM; Ken Wasch, SIIA.

SPARC

Executive Director, Heather Joseph
21 Dupont Circle, Suite 800, Washington, DC 20036
202-296-2296, fax 202-872-0884, e-mail sparc@arl.org
World Wide Web http://www.arl.org/sparc

SPARC, the Scholarly Publishing and Academic Resources Coalition, is an international alliance of academic and research libraries working to correct imbalances in the scholarly publishing system. Developed by the Association of Research Libraries, SPARC has become a catalyst for change. Its pragmatic focus is to stimulate the emergence of new scholarly communication models that expand the dissemination of scholarly research and reduce financial pressures on libraries. Action by SPARC in collaboration with stakeholders—including authors, publishers, and libraries—builds on the unprecedented opportunities created by the networked digital environment to advance the conduct of scholarship.

SPARC's role in stimulating change focuses on

- Advocating policy changes that harness the potential of technology to advance scholarly communication and that explicitly recognize that dissemination is an essential, inseparable component of the research process
- Educating stakeholders about the problems facing scholarly communication and the opportunities for change
- Incubating real-world demonstrations of business and publishing models that advance changes benefiting scholarship and academe.

SPARC is a visible advocate for changes in scholarly communication that benefit more than the academic community alone. Founded in 1997, SPARC has expanded to represent more than 800 academic and research libraries in North America, the United Kingdom, Europe, and Japan.

Membership

SPARC membership is open to North American and international academic and research institutions, organizations, and consortia that share an interest in creating a more open and diverse marketplace for scholarly communication. Dues are scaled by membership type and budget. For more information, visit SPARC's Web site at http://www.arl.org/sparc, SPARC Europe at http://www.sparceurope.org, or SPARC Japan at http://www.nii.ac.jp/sparc.

Publications

Campus-Based Publishing Partnerships: A Guide to Critical Issues (2009) by Raym Crow.

Income Models for Open Access: An Overview of Current Practice (2009) by Raym Crow.

The Right to Research: The Student Guide to Opening Access to Scholarship (2008), part of a campaign to engage students on the issue of research access.

Greater Reach for Research: Expanding readership through digital repositories (2008), the initiative to educate faculty on the benefits of open repositories and emerging research access policies.

Author Rights (2006), an educational initiative and introduction to the SPARC Author Addendum, a legal form that enables authors of journal articles to modify publishers' copyright transfer agreements and allow authors to keep key rights to their articles.

Open Access News Blog, daily updates on the worldwide movement for open access to science and scholarship, written by Peter Suber and cosponsored by SPARC.

SPARC Open Access Newsletter, a monthly roundup of developments relating to open access publishing written by Peter Suber.

SPARC e-news, SPARC's monthly newsletter featuring SPARC activities, an industry roundup, upcoming workshops and events, and articles relating to developments in scholarly communication.

Publishing Cooperatives: An Alternative for Society Publishers (2006) by Raym Crow.

Sponsorships for Nonprofit Scholarly and Scientific Journals: A Guide to Defining and Negotiating Successful Sponsorships (2005) by Raym Crow.

A more complete list of SPARC publications, including brochures, articles, and guides, is available at http://www.arl.org/sparc.

Special Libraries Association (SLA)

Chief Executive Officer, Janice R. Lachance
331 S. Patrick St., Alexandria, VA 22314
703-647-4900, fax 703-647-4901, e-mail sla@sla.org
World Wide Web http://www.sla.org

Mission

To advance the leadership role of the association's members in putting knowledge to work for the benefit of decision-makers in corporations, government, the professions, and society; to shape the destiny of today's information- and knowledge-based society.

Membership

Memb. 11,000. Dues (Organizational) $650; (Indiv.) $99–$160; (Student/Retired/Salary Less Than $18,000 a year) $35.

Officers (January 2009–December 2010)

Pres. Anne Caputo, Dow Jones. E-mail acaputo@dowjones.com; *Pres.-Elect* Cindy Romaine, Romainiacs Intelligence Research. E-mail cindy.romaine@romainiacs.com;

Treas. Dan Trefethen, Boeing. E-mail daniel. b.trefethen@boeing.com; *Chapter Cabinet Chair* Ruth Wolfish, IEEE. E-mail r.wolfish @ieee.org; *Chapter Cabinet Chair-Elect* Liz Blankson-Hemans, Dialog. E-mail liz. blankson-hemans@dialog.com; *Div. Cabinet Chair* Ann Sweeney, European Union Delegation, Washington. E-mail ann.sweeney@ ec.europa.eu; *Div. Cabinet Chair-Elect* Mary Ellen Bates, Bates Info. Services. E-mail mbates@batesinfo.com

Directors

Officers; Deb Hunt, Daniel Lee, Nettie Seaberry, Ty Webb.

Publication

Information Outlook (mo.) (memb., nonmemb. $125/yr.)

Theatre Library Association

c/o The New York Public Library for the Performing Arts,
40 Lincoln Center Plaza, New York, NY 10023
E-mail info@tla-online.org, World Wide Web http://www.tla-online.org

Object

To further the interests of collecting, preserving, and using theater, cinema, and performing arts materials in libraries, museums, and private collections. Founded in 1937.

Membership

Memb. 307. Dues (Indiv.) $20–$40, (Inst.) $40–$50. Year. Jan. 1–Dec. 31.

Officers

Pres. Kenneth Schlesinger, Lehman College, City Univ. of New York; *V.P.* Susan Brady, Yale Univ.; *Exec. Secy.* David Nochimson, New York Public Lib.; *Treas.* Colleen Reilly, Slippery Rock Univ.

Executive Board

William Boatman, Phyllis Dircks, John Frick, Nancy Friedland, Stephen Johnson, Beth Kattelman, Stephen Kuehler, Francesca Marini, Karen Nickeson, Brook Stowe, Angela Weaver, Sarah Zimmerman; *Honorary* Louis A. Rachow, Marian Seldes; *Legal Counsel* Georgia Harper; *Past Pres.* Martha S. LoMonaco.

Publications

Broadside (3 a year; memb.). *Ed.* Angela Weaver.
Performing Arts Resources (occasional; memb.).
Membership Directory (annual; memb.). *Ed.* David Nochimson.

Committee Chairs

Book Awards. Brook Stowe.
Conference Planning. Susan Brady.
Finance and Fund Raising. Colleen Reilly.
Membership. Beth Kerr.
Nominating. Martha S. LoMonaco.
Professional Award. Phyllis Dircks.
Publications. Robert W. Melton.
Strategic Planning. Susan Brady.
Web Site. David Nochimson.

Urban Libraries Council

125 S. Wacker Drive, Suite 1050, Chicago, IL 60606
312-676-0999, fax 312-676-0950, e-mail info@urbanlibraries.org
World Wide Web http://www.urbanlibraries.org

Object

The object of the Urban Libraries Council (ULC) is to strengthen the public library as an essential part of urban life; to identify and make known the opportunities for urban libraries; to facilitate the exchange of ideas and programs of member libraries and other libraries; to develop programs that enable libraries to act as a focus of community development and to supply the informational needs of the new urban populations; to conduct research and educational programs that will benefit urban libraries and to solicit and accept grants, contributions, and donations essential to their implementation.

ULC's Foresight 2020 initiative, launched in 2008, is teaching libraries how to spot trends and adapt quickly, putting them in a proactive mode regardless of how their environment changes.

Membership

Membership is open to public libraries serving populations of 100,000 or more located in a Standard Metropolitan Statistical Area and to corporations specializing in library-related materials and services. The organization also offers associate memberships.

Officers (2009–2010)

Chair Raymond Santiago, Miami-Dade Public Lib. System, 101 W. Flagler St., Miami, FL 33130; *V. Chair/Chair-Elect* Melinda Cervantes, Santa Clara (California) Lib. System; *Secy./Treas.* Dorothy Ridings, 505 Altagate Rd., Louisville, KY 40206; *Past Chair* Patrick A. Losinski, Columbus Metropolitan Lib., 96 S. Grant, Columbus, OH 43215.

Officers serve one-year terms, members of the executive board two-year terms. New officers are elected and take office at the summer annual meeting of the council.

Executive Board

Susan M. Adams, Ruth Neil Anna, Ginnie Cooper, Charles Higueras, Jan Harder, Jody Kretzmann, Okeima Ranaldo Lawrence, Robert Martin, Dennis B. Martinez, Joan M. Prince, Rivkah Sass, Keith B. Simmons.

Key Staff

Chief Operating Officer Susan Benton; *V.P. Finance* Angela Goodrich; *V.P. Membership and Communications* Veronda J. Pitchford; *Office Mgr.* Jeanie Ramsey.

State, Provincial, and Regional Library Associations

The associations in this section are organized under three headings: United States, Canada, and Regional. Both the United States and Canada are represented under Regional associations.

United States

Alabama

Memb. 1,200. Term of Office. Apr. 2009–Apr. 2010. Publication. *The Alabama Librarian* (q.).

Pres. Dennis Nichols, Homewood Public Lib., 1721 Oxmoor Rd., Homewood 35209. Tel. 205-332-6620, e-mail dnichols@bham.lib.al.us; *Pres.-Elect* Jodi Poe, Houston Cole Lib., Jacksonville State Univ., 700 Pelham Rd. N., Jacksonville 36265. Tel. 256-782-8103, e-mail jpoe@jsu.edu; *Secy.* Barbara Curry, Autauga-Prattville Public Lib. Tel. 334-324-4521, e-mail bcurry@appl.info; *Treas.* Neil Foulger, Alabama State Univ., 915 S. Jackson St., Montgomery 36101. Tel. 334-356-9422, e-mail nfoulger@alasu.edu; *Past Pres.* Eve Engle Kneeland, Auburn Public Lib., 479 E. Thach Ave., Auburn 36839. Tel. 334-501-3196, e-mail eengle@auburn alabama.org.

Address correspondence to the association, 9154 Eastchase Pkwy., Suite 418, Montgomery 36117. Tel. 334-414-0113, e-mail administrator@allanet.org.

World Wide Web http://allanet.org.

Alaska

Memb. 450+. Publication. *Newspoke* (q.).

Pres. Mary Jo Joiner. E-mail mjoiner@ci.kenai.ak.us; *V.P.–Committees* M. J. Grande. E-mail mjgrande@juneau.lib.ak.us; *V.P.–Conference* Susan Mitchell. E-mail afsm1@uaa.alaska.edu; *Secy.* Joyce McCombs. E-mail deltalibrary@wildak.net; *Treas.* Catherine Powers; *Past Pres.* Jane Fuerstenau. E-mail ifjef@uaa.alaska.edu; *Exec. Officer* Mary Jennings. E-mail maryj@gci.net.

Address correspondence to the secretary, Alaska Lib. Assn., P.O. Box 81084, Fairbanks 99708. Fax 877-863-1401, e-mail akla@akla.org.

World Wide Web http://www.akla.org.

Arizona

Memb. 1,000. Term of Office. Nov. 2009–Nov. 2010. Publication. *AzLA Newsletter* (mo.).

Pres. Cynthia Landrum, Glendale Public Lib., 5959 W. Brown St., Glendale 85302. Tel. 623-930-3566, e-mail clandrum@glendaleaz.com; *Pres.-Elect* Nancy Ledeboer, Pima County Public Lib., 101 N. Stone Ave., Tucson 85701-1501. Tel. 520-594-5601, fax 520-594-5621, e-mail nancy.ledeboer@pima.gov; *Secy.* McKay Wellikson, Central Arizona College, 8470 N. Overfield Rd., Coolidge 85228. Tel. 520-494-5416, e-mail mckay.wellikson@centralaz.edu; *Treas.* Linda Renfro, Blue Ridge Unified School Dist. Tel. 928-368-6119, e-mail lrenfro@brusd.k12.az.us; *Past Pres.* Denise C. Keller, Pinal County Lib. Dist., P.O. Box 2974, Florence 85232. Tel. 520-866-6457, fax 520-866-6533, e-mail denise.keller@pinalcountyaz.gov; *Exec. Dir.* Debbie J. Hanson. Tel. 480-609-3999, e-mail admin@azla.org.

Address correspondence to the executive director, AzLA, 1030 E. Baseline Rd., Suite 105-1025, Tempe 85283.

World Wide Web http://www.azla.org.

Arkansas

Memb. 600. Term of Office. Jan.–Dec. 2010. Publication. *Arkansas Libraries* (bi-mo.).

Pres. Connie Zimmer, Arkansas Tech Univ., 305 W. Q St., Russellville 72801. Tel. 479-968-0434, e-mail czimmer@atu.edu; *V.P./Pres.-Elect* Shawn Pierce, Lonoke/Prairie County Regional Lib., 2504 S. Tyler St., Little Rock 72204. Tel. 501-676-6608, e-mail spierce@lpregional.lib.ar.us; *Secy./Treas.* Jamie Melson, Main Lib., Central Arkansas Lib. System, 100 Rock St., Little Rock 72201. Tel. 501-918-3074, fax 501-376-1830, e-mail jamiem@cals.lib.ar.us;

Past Pres. Jerrie Townsend, Phillips Community College, 2807 Hwy. 165 S., Box A, Stuttgart 72160. Tel. 870-673-4201 ext. 1818, e-mail jtownsend@pccua.edu; *Exec. Admin.* Barbara Martin, P.O. Box 958, Benton 72018-0958. Tel. 501-860-7585, fax 501-776-9709, e-mail arlib2@sbcglobal.net.

Address correspondence to the executive administrator.

World Wide Web http://www.arlib.org.

California

Memb. 2,500. Publication. *Clarion* (s. ann.).

Pres. Kim Bui-Burton, Monterey Public Lib. Tel. 831-646-5601, e-mail buiburto@ci.monterey.ca.us; *V.P./Pres.-Elect* Paymaneh Maghsoudi, Whittier Public Lib. Tel. 562-464-3452, e-mail pmaghsoudi@whittierpl.org; *Treas.* Jackie Griffin, Ventura County Lib. Tel. 805-477-7333, e-mail jackie.griffin@ventura.org; *Past Pres.* Barbara Roberts, Palm Springs Public Lib. Tel. 760-322-8375, e-mail Barbara.Roberts@palmsprings-ca.gov; *Interim Exec. Dir.* Claudia Foutz, California Lib. Assn., 950 Glenn Drive, Suite 150, Folsom 95630. Tel. 916-932-2200, fax 932-2209, e-mail cfoutz@cla-net.org.

Address correspondence to the executive director.

World Wide Web http://www.cla-net.org.

Colorado

Memb. 1,000+. Publication. *Colorado Libraries* (q.).

Pres. Rochelle Logan. Tel. 303-688-7603, e-mail rlogan@dclibraries.org; *V.P./Pres.-Elect* Teri Switzer. E-mail switzer@uccs.edu; *Secy.* Denise Muniz. E-mail dmuniz@broomfield.org; *Treas.* Nicolle Steffen. E-mail steffen_n@cde.state.co.us; *Past Pres.* Jody Howard. E-mail jodyhoward@comcast.net; *Exec. Dir.* Kathleen Noland, Colorado Assn. of Libs., 12081 W. Alameda Pkwy., No. 427, Lakewood 80228. Tel. 303-463-6400, e-mail kathleen@cal-webs.org.

Address correspondence to the executive director.

World Wide Web http://www.cal-webs.org.

Connecticut

Memb. 1,000+. Term of Office. July 2009–June 2010. Publication. *Connecticut Libraries* (11 a year). *Ed.* Tom Newman, Middletown Lib. Service Center. Tel. 860-704-2200, fax 860-704-2228, e-mail tnewman@cslib.org.

Pres. Randi Ashton-Pritting, Univ. of Hartford Libs. Tel. 860-768-4268, fax 860-768-4274, e-mail pritting@hartford.edu; *V.P./Pres.-Elect* Debbie Herman, Central Connecticut State Univ. Tel. 860-832-2084, fax 860-832-2118, e-mail hermand@ccsu.edu; *Treas.* Alison Wang, Naugatuck Community College, Waterbury. Tel. 203-575-8250, e-mail awang@nvcc.commnet.edu; *Past Pres.* Kathy Leeds, Wilton Lib. Assn. Tel. 203-762-7196, fax 203-834-1166, e-mail kathy_leeds@wiltonlibrary.org; *Coord.* Pam Najarian, Connecticut Lib. Assn., P.O. Box 75, Middletown 06457. Tel. 860-346-2444, fax 860-344-9199, e-mail cla@ctlibrarians.org.

Address correspondence to the coordinator.

World Wide Web http://www.ctlibraryassociation.org.

Delaware

Memb. 200+. Term of Office. Apr. 2009–Apr. 2010. Publication. *DLA Bulletin* (online only).

Pres. Margaret P. Dillner, Educ. Resource Center at Univ. of Delaware Lib., 012 Willard Hall, Newark 19716-2940. Tel. 302-831-6308, fax 302-831-8404, e-mail mpd@udel.edu; *V.P.* Margery Cyr, Dover Public Library. Tel. 302-736-7032, e-mail margery.cyr@lib.de.us; *Secy.* Mary Jane Mallonee, Widener Law Lib., 4601 Concord Pike, Wilmington 19803. Tel. 302-477-2244, e-mail mmallonee@widener.edu; *Treas.* Pauly Iheanacho, Univ. of Delaware Lib., 181 S. College Ave., Newark 19717-5267. Tel. 302-831-6946, fax 302-831-1631, e-mail pinacho@udel.edu; *Past Pres.* Rebecca C. Knight, Univ. of Delaware Lib., 181 S. College Ave., Newark 19717-5267. Tel. 302-831-1631, e-mail knight@udel.edu.

Address correspondence to the association, Box 816, Dover 19903-0816. E-mail dla@dla.lib.de.us.

World Wide Web http://www2.lib.udel.edu/dla/index.htm.

District of Columbia

Memb. 300+. Term of Office. July 2009–June 2010. Publication. *Capital Librarian* (s. ann.).

Pres. Angela Fisher Jaffee; *V.P./Pres.-Elect* Richard Huffine; *Secy.* Barbara Conaty; *Treas.* Carol Bursik; *Past Pres.* M-J Oboroceanu.

Address correspondence to the association, Box 14177, Benjamin Franklin Sta., Washington 20044. Tel. 202-872-1112.

World Wide Web http://www.dcla.org.

Florida

Memb. (Indiv.) 1,100+. Term of Office. May 2009–April 2010. Publication. *Florida Libraries* (s. ann.). *Ed.* Gloria Colvin, 2505 Blarney Drive, Tallahassee 32309. Tel. 850-645-1680, e-mail gpcolvin@yahoo.com.

Pres. Wendy Breeden, Lake County Public Resources Dept., 2401 Woodlea Rd., Tavares 32778. Tel. 352-253-6180, e-mail wbreeden@lakeline.lib.fl.us; *V.P./Pres.-Elect* John J. Callahan III, Palm Beach County Lib. System, 3650 Summit Blvd., West Palm Beach 33406-4198; *Secy.* Gladys Roberts, Polk County Lib. Cooperative, 2150 S. Broadway Ave., Bartow 33830-7138. Tel. 863-519-7958; *Treas.* Alan Kornblau, Delray Beach Public Lib., 100 W. Atlantic Ave., Delray Beach 33444-3662. Tel. 561-266-9488, e-mail alan.kornblau@delraylibrary.org; *Past Pres.* Mercedes Clement, Daytona State College, 1200 W. International Speedway Blvd., Daytona Beach 32120. Tel. 386-506-3440, e-mail clemenm@daytonastate.edu; *Exec. Dir.* Faye Roberts, P.O. Box 1571, Lake City 32056-1571. Tel. 386-438-5795, e-mail faye.roberts@comcast.net.

Address correspondence to the executive director.

World Wide Web http://www.flalib.org.

Georgia

Memb. 800+. Publication. *Georgia Library Quarterly. Ed.* Susan Cooley, Sara Hightower Regional Lib., 205 Riverside Pkwy., Rome 30161. Tel. 706-236-4609, fax 706-236-4631, e-mail scooley@romelibrary.org.

Pres. Carol Stanley, Athens Technical College, 1317 Athens Hwy, Elberton, GA 30635. Tel. 706-213-2116, e-mail cstanley@athenstech.edu; *1st V.P./Pres.-Elect* Carolyn Fuller, Henry County Public Lib. Tel. 770-954-2806, e-mail cfuller@mail.henry.public.lib.ga.us; *2nd V.P.* Judith Brook, Swilley Lib., Mercer Univ.–Atlanta. Tel. 678-547-6280, e-mail brook_jd@mercer.edu; *Secy.* Jeff Heck, Reese Lib., Augusta State Univ. Tel. 706-737-1745, e-mail jheck@aug.edu; *Treas.* Cathy Jeffrey, Clayton State Univ. Tel. 678-466-4336, e-mail cathyjeffrey@clayton.edu; *Past Pres.* Jim Cooper, West Georgia Regional Lib. Tel. 770-836-6711, e-mail cooperj@wgrl.net.

Address correspondence to the president, c/o Georgia Lib. Assn., P.O. Box 793, Rex 30273-0793.

World Wide Web http://gla.georgialibraries.org.

Hawaii

Memb. 320. Publication. *HLA Newsletter* (3 a year).

Pres. Sheryl Lynch, Kapolei Public Lib. Tel. 808-693-7050, e-mail sheryll@imail.librarieshawaii.org; *Secy.* Loraine Oribio, Tokai Univ. E-mail loribio@tokai.edu; *Treas.* Carrie Young, Pacific Rim Christian College. E-mail carriey@prbc-hawaii.edu; *Past Pres.* Becky DeMartini, Brigham Young Univ.–Hawaii. Tel. 808-675-3946, e-mail rathgebb@byuh.edu.

Address correspondence to the president.

Idaho

Memb. 420. Term of Office. Oct. 2009–Oct. 2010.

Pres. Bette Ammon, Coeur d'Alene Public Lib., 702 E. Front, Coeur d'Alene 83814. E-mail bammon@cdalibrary.org; *V.P./Pres.-Elect* Ben Hunter, Univ. of Idaho Lib., P.O. Box 442350, Moscow 83844-2350. Tel. 208-

885-5858, e-mail bhunter@uidaho.edu; *Secy.* Phil Homan, Idaho State Univ., 921 S. 8 Ave., Stop 8089, Pocatello 83209-8089. Tel. 208-282-3047, e-mail homaphil@isu.edu; *Treas.* Steve Poppino, College of Southern Idaho, 315 Falls Ave., Twin Falls 83383-1238. Tel. 208-732-6504, fax 208-732-3087, e-mail spoppino@csi.edu; *Past Pres.* Susan Tabor-Boesch, Wood River Middle School, 900 N. 2 Ave., Hailey 83333. Tel. 208-578-5030 ext. 2323, e-mail staborboesch@blaineschools.org.

Address correspondence to the association, P.O. Box 8533, Moscow 83844.

World Wide Web http://www.idaho libraries.org.

Illinois

Memb. 3,000. Term of Office. July 2009–July 2010. Publication. *ILA Reporter* (bimo.).

Pres. Carole A. Medal, Gail Borden Public Lib. Dist., 270 N. Grove Ave., Elgin 60120-5505. Tel. 847-429-4699, fax 847-742-0485, e-mail cmedal@gailborden.info; *V.P./Pres.-Elect* Gail Bush, Center for Teaching Through Children's Books, National-Louis Univ., 5202 Old Orchard Rd., Suite 300, Skokie 60077. Tel. 224-233-2522, fax 224-233-2522, e-mail gail.bush@nl.edu; *Treas.* Theodore C. Schwitzner, Milner Lib., Illinois State Univ., Campus Box 8900, Normal 61790-8900. Tel. 309-438-3449, fax 309-438-5132, e-mail redm.andmlibrarian@yahoo.com; *Past Pres.* Donna Dziedzic, Naperville Public Lib., 200 W. Jefferson, Naperville 60540. Tel. 630-961-4100 ext. 6151, fax 630-637-6149, e-mail ddziedzic@naperville-lib.org; *Exec. Dir.* Robert P. Doyle, 33 W. Grand Ave., Suite 301, Chicago 60654. Tel. 312-644-1896, fax 312-644-1899, e-maildoyle@ila.org.

Address correspondence to the executive director.

World Wide Web http://www.ila.org.

Indiana

Memb. 3,000+. Publication. *Indiana Libraries* (s. ann.). *Ed.* Karen Evans, Cunningham Memorial Lib., Indiana State Univ., 650 Sycamore St., Terre Haute 47809. Tel. 812-237-8824, fax 812-237-2567, e-mail kevans4@isugw.indstate.edu.

Pres. Nancy Dowell, Vigo County Public Lib., 1 Library Sq., Terre Haute 47807. Tel. 812-232-1113, fax 812-235-1439, e-mail ndowell@vigo.lib.in.us; *V.P.* John Borneman, Tipton County Public Lib., 10373 W. 650 North, Sharpsville 46068. E-mail john borneman@gmail.com; *Secy.* Kim Carr, Burris Laboratory School, 2000 University Ave., Muncie 47306. Tel. 765-468-8878, e-mail 01kjcarr@bsu.edu; *Treas.* Jim Cline, Porter County Public Lib. System, 103 E. Jefferson St., Valparaiso 46383-4820. Tel. 219-462-0524, fax 219-477-4866, e-mail jcline@pcpls.lib.in.us; *Past Pres.* Cheryl Truesdell, Helmke Lib., Indiana Univ. Purdue Univ.–Fort Wayne, 2101 E. Coliseum Blvd., Fort Wayne 46805. Tel. 260-481-6506, fax 260-481-6509, e-mail truesdel@ipfw.edu; *Exec. Dir.* Susan Akers. Tel. 317-257-2040 ext. 101, e-mail sakers@ilfonline.org.

Address correspondence to Indiana Lib. Federation, 941 E. 86 St., Suite 260, Indianapolis 46240. Tel. 317-257-2040, fax 317-257-1389, e-mail ilf@indy.net.

World Wide Web http://www.ilfonline.org.

Iowa

Memb. 1,700. Publication. *The Catalyst* (bimo.). *Ed.* Laurie Hews.

Pres. Ellen Neuhaus, Rod Lib., Univ. of Northern Iowa, 1227 W. 27 St., Cedar Falls 50613. Tel. 319-273-3739, fax 319-273-2913, e-mail ellen.neuhaus@uni.edu; *V.P./Pres.-Elect* Dale H. Ross, Ames Public Lib., 515 Douglas Ave., Ames 50010. Tel. 515-233-2998, e-mail dross24704@aol.com; *Secy.* Marilyn Murphy, Busse Center Lib., Mount Mercy College, 1330 Elmhurst Drive N.E., Cedar Rapids 52402. Tel. 319-363-8213 ext. 1244, fax 319-363-9060, e-mail marilyn@mmc.mtmercy.edu; *Past Pres.* Barbara Peterson, Council Bluffs Public Lib., 400 Willow Ave., Council Bluffs 51503. Tel. 712-323-7553, fax 712-323-1269, e-mail bpeterson@cbpl.lib.ia.us; *Exec. Dir.* Laurie Hews. Tel. 515-273-5322, fax 515-309-4576, e-mail lhews@mcleodusa.net.

Address correspondence to the association, 3636 Westown Pkwy., Suite 202, West Des Moines 50266.

World Wide Web http://www.iowalibrary association.org.

Kansas

Memb. 1,500. Term of Office. July 2009–June 2010. Publication. *KLA Connects* (q.). *Ed.* Royce Kitts. E-mail roycekitts@gmail.com.

Pres. Denise Smith, Stanton County Lib., 103 E. Sherman, P.O. Box 480, Johnson City 67855. Tel. 620-492-2302, fax 620-492-2203, e-mail dolliesmith@hotmail.com; *1st V.P.* Emily Sitz, Southwest Kansas Lib. System, 100 Military Ave., Suite 210, Dodge City 67801. Tel. 620-225-1231, e-mail esitz @swkls.org; *2nd V.P.* Royce Kitts, Tonganoxie Public Lib., 303 S. Bury, Tonganoxie 66086. Tel. 913-845-3281, fax 913-845-2962, director@tonganoxielibrary.org; *Secy.* Joyce Armstrong, Hamilton County Lib., 102 W. Ave. C, P.O. Box 1307, Syracuse 67878. Tel. 620-384-5622, fax 620-384-5623, e-mail hamcolib@yahoo.com; *Treas.* Cynthia Berner Harris, Wichita Public Lib., 223 S. Main, Wichita 67202. Tel. 316-261-8520, fax 316-219-6320, e-mail cberner@wichita.gov; *Past Pres.* Laura Loveless, West Wyandotte Branch, Kansas City Public Lib., 1737 N. 82, Kansas City 66112. Tel. 913-596-5800, fax 913-596-5809, e-mail llove@kckpl.lib.ks.us; *Exec. Dir.* Rosanne Siemens, Kansas Lib. Assn., 1020 S.W. Washburn, Topeka 66604. Tel. 785-580-4518, fax 785-580-4595, e-mail kansaslibraryassociation@yahoo.com.

Address correspondence to the executive director.

World Wide Web http://www.kslibassoc.org.

Kentucky

Memb. 1,900. Term of Office. Oct. 2009–Oct. 2010. Publication. *Kentucky Libraries* (q.).

Pres. Emmalee Hoover, Dixie Heights H.S., 3010 Dixie Hwy., Edgewood 41017. Tel. 859-341-7650, e-mail emmalee.hoover@kenton.kyschools.us; *Pres.-Elect* Leoma Dunn, Thomas More College Lib., 333 Thomas More Pkwy., Crestview Hills 41017.

Tel. 859-344-3524, e-mail leoma.dunn@thomasmore.edu; *Secy.* Terry Buckner, Learning Resource Center, Bluegrass Community and Technical College, 460 Cooper Drive, 222B Oswald Bldg., Lexington 40506. Tel. 859-246-6397, e-mail terry.buckner@kctcs.edu; *Past Pres.* Debbe Oberhausen, Crescent Hill Branch, Louisville Free Public Lib., 2762 Frankfort Ave., Louisville 40206. Tel. 502-574-1793, e-mail debra.oberhausen@lfpl.org; *Exec. Secy.* Tom Underwood, 1501 Twilight Trail, Frankfort 40601. Tel. 502-223-5322, fax 502-223-4937, e-mail info@kylibasn.org.

Address correspondence to the executive secretary.

World Wide Web http://www.kylibasn.org.

Louisiana

Memb. 1,100+. Term of Office. July 2009–June 2010. Publication. *Louisiana Libraries* (q.).

Pres. Melanie Sims. Tel. 225-578-8815, fax 225-578-5773, e-mail melanie.sims@law.lsu.edu; *1st V.P./Pres.-Elect* Randy DeSoto. Tel. 985-651-6733, fax 985-652-8005, e-mail radesoto@stjohn.lib.la.us; *Secy.* Leslie Carloss. Tel. 337-942-5404 ext. 104, fax 337-942-5922, e-mail vanyar@bellsouth.net; *Past Pres.* Melissa Hymel. Tel. 225-638-7593, fax 225-638-9847, e-mail mkhymel@yahoo.com

Address correspondence to Louisiana Lib. Assn., 8550 United Plaza Blvd., Suite 1001, Baton Rouge 70809. Tel. 225-922-4642, fax 225-408-4422, e-mail office@llaonline.org.

World Wide Web http://www.llaonline.org.

Maine

Memb. 950. Term of Office. (Pres., V.P.) July 2009–July 2010. Publication. *MLA-To-Z* (q., online).

Pres. Sonja Plummer-Morgan, Mark and Emily Turner Memorial Lib., 39 Second St., Presque Isle 04769. Tel. 207-764-2571; *V.P./Pres.-Elect* Andi Jackson-Darling, Falmouth Memorial Lib., 5 Lunt Rd., Falmouth 04105. Tel. 207-781-2351; *Past Pres.* Molly Larson, Rockport Public Lib., P.O. Box 8, Rockport 04856-0008. Tel. 207-236-3642, e-mail mlarson@rockport.lib.me.us.

Address correspondence to the association, P.O. Box 634, Augusta 04332-0634. Tel. 207-441-1410.

World Wide Web http://mainelibraries.org.

Maryland

Memb. 1,100. Term of Office. July 2009–July 2010. Publications. *Happenings* (mo.); *The Crab* (q.).

Pres. James Fish, Baltimore County Public Lib. Tel. 410-887-6160, e-mail jfish@bcpl. net; *V.P./Pres.-Elect* Glennor Shirley, Dept. of Labor, Licensing, and Regulation. Tel. 410-767-9761, e-mail gshirley@dllr.state. md.us; *Past Pres.* Darrell Batson, Frederick County Public Libs. Tel. 301-600-1613, e-mail dbatson@fredco-md.net; *Exec. Dir.* Margaret Carty.

Address correspondence to the association, 1401 Hollins St., Baltimore 21223. Tel. 410-947-5090, fax 410-947-5089, e-mail mla@mdlib.org.

World Wide Web http://mdlib.org.

Massachusetts

Memb. (Indiv.) 1,000; (Inst.) 100. Term of Office. July 2009–June 2010. Publication. *Bay State Libraries* (4 a year).

Pres. Susan R. McAlister, Minuteman Lib. Network, 10 Strathmore Rd., Natick 01760. Tel. 508-655-8008 ext. 237, fax 508-655-1507, e-mail smcalister@minlib.net; *V.P.* Jacqueline Rafferty, Paul Pratt Memorial Lib., 35 Ripley Rd., Cohasset 02025. Tel. 781-383-1348, fax 781-383-3024, e-mail jrafferty@ocln.org; *Secy.* Margaret Cardello, Central Massachusetts Regional Lib. System, 8 Flagg Rd., Shrewsbury 01545. Tel. 508-757-4110 ext. 306, fax 508-757-4370, e-mail mcardello@cmrls.org; *Treas.* Bernadette D. Rivard, Bellingham Public Lib., 100 Blackstone St., Bellingham 02019. Tel. 508-966-1660, e-mail brivard@bellinghamma.org; *Past Pres.* Richard Callaghan, Bedford Free Public Lib., 7 Mudge Way, Bedford 01730. Tel. 781-275-9440, fax 781-275-3590, e-mail rcallaghan@minlib.net; *Exec. Mgr.* Elizabeth Hacala, Massachusetts Lib. Assn., P.O. Box 535, Bedford 01730. Tel. 781-275-7729, fax 781-998-0393, e-mail mlaoffice@masslib.org.

Address correspondence to the executive manager.

World Wide Web http://www.masslib.org.

Michigan

Memb. (Indiv.) 2,000+. Term of Office. July 2009–June 2010. Publications. *Michigan Librarian Newsletter* (6 a year), *Michigan Library Association Forum* (s. ann., online).

Pres. Larry Neal, Clinton Macomb Public Lib.; *Pres.-Elect* Christine Berro, Portage Dist. Lib.; *Secy.* Cathy Wolford, DALNET; *Treas.* Ed Repik, Howell Carnegie Dist. Lib.; *Past Pres.* Kathy Irwin, Univ. of Michigan–Dearborn Lib.

Address correspondence to Gretchen Couraud, Exec. Dir., Michigan Lib. Assn., 1407 Rensen St., Suite 2, Lansing 48910. Tel. 517-394-2774 ext. 224, e-mail couraudg@mlcnet.org.

World Wide Web http://www.mla.lib.mi. us.

Minnesota

Memb. 1,100. Term of Office. (Pres., Pres.-Elect) Jan.–Dec. 2010.

Pres. Kathleen James. E-mail kathleen@melsa.org; *Pres.-Elect* Robin Ewing. E-mail rlewing@stcloudstate.edu; *Secy.* Lynne Young. E-mail lynne.young@ci.northfield. mn.us; *Treas.* Mic Golden. E-mail grrlgolden@yahoo.com; *Past Pres.* Ken Behringer. E-mail ken.behringer@co.dakota.mn.us.

Address correspondence to the association, 1821 University Ave. W., Suite S256, Saint Paul 55104. Tel. 651-999-5343, fax 651-917-1835, e-mail office@mnlibraryassociation.org.

World Wide Web http://www.mnlibrary association.org.

Mississippi

Memb. 650. Term of Office. Jan.–Dec. 2010. Publication. *Mississippi Libraries* (q.).

Pres. Ann Branton, Univ. Libs., Univ. of Southern Mississippi. Tel. 601-266-4350, e-mail ann.branton@usm.edu; *V.P.* Jennifer A. Smith, Warren County–Vicksburg Public Lib. Tel. 601-636-6411, e-mail jensmith@warren.lib.ms.us; *Secy.* Ruth Ann Gibson, Speed Lib., Mississippi College. Tel. 601-

925-3433, e-mail gibson@mc.edu; *Treas.* Molly Signs McManus, Millsaps-Wilson College Lib. Tel. 601-974-1086, e-mail signsmj@millsaps.edu; *Past Pres.* Jan Willis, Lee-Itawama Lib. System. Tel. 662-841-9029, e-mail jwillis@li.lib.ms.us; *Exec. Secy.* Mary Julia Anderson, P.O. Box 13687, Jackson 39236-3687. Tel. 601-981-4586, fax 601-981-4501, e-mail info@misslib.org.

Address correspondence to the executive secretary.

World Wide Web http://www.misslib.org.

Missouri

Memb. 800+. Term of Office. Jan.–Dec. 2010. Publication. *MO INFO* (bi-mo.). *Ed.* Margaret Booker.

Pres. Sharon McCaslin, Fontbonne Univ., 6800 Wydown Blvd., St. Louis 63105. Tel. 314-889-4567, fax 314-719-8040, e-mail smccaslin@fontbonne.edu; *Pres.-Elect* Susan Wray, Blue Springs North Branch, Mid-Continent Public Lib., 850 N.W. Hunter Drive, Blue Springs 64015. Tel. 816-224-8772, e-mail swray@mcpl.lib.mo.us; *Secy.* Sarah Erwin, Kirkwood Public Lib., 140 E. Jefferson, Kirkwood 63122. Tel. 314-821-5770, fax 314-822-3755, e-mail serwin@kirkwood publiclibrary.org; *Treas.* Susan Burton, KCMLIN, 15624 E. 24 Hwy., Independence 64050. Tel. 816-521-7267, fax 816-461-0966, e-mail susanburton@kcmlin.org; *Past Pres.* Kimberlee Ried, National Archives and Records Admin., 2312 E. Bannister Rd., Kansas City 64131. Tel. 816-268-8072, fax 816-268-8037, e-mail mlaprez09@gmail.com; *Exec. Dir.* Margaret Booker, Missouri Lib. Assn., 3212-A LeMone Industrial Blvd., Columbia 65201. Tel. 573-449-4627, fax 573-449-4655, e-mail mla001@more.net.

Address correspondence to the executive director.

World Wide Web http://www.molib.org.

Montana

Memb. 600. Term of Office. July 2009–June 2010. Publication. *Focus* (bi-mo.).

Pres. Eva English, Fort Belknap College Lib., P.O. Box 159, Harlem 59526-0159. Tel. 406-353-2607 ext. 262, fax 406-353-2898, e-mail evaenglish@yahoo.com; *V.P.* Samantha Pierson, Lincoln County Public Lib., 220 W. 6 St., Libby 59427. Tel. 406-293-2778, fax 406-293-4235, e-mail spierson@lincoln countylibraries.com; *Secy./Treas.* Dee Ann Redman, Parmly Billings Lib., 510 N. Broadway, Billings 59101-1196. Tel. 406-657-8258, e-mail redmand@ci.billings.mt.us; *Past Pres.* Della Dubbe, Glacier County Lib., 21 First Ave. S.E., Cut Bank 59427. Tel. 406-873-4572, fax 406-873-4845, e-mail glibrary@northerntel.net; *Exec. Asst.* Debra Kramer, P.O. Box 1352, Three Forks 59752. Tel. 406-285-3090, fax 406-285-3091, e-mail debkmla@hotmail.com.

Address correspondence to the executive assistant.

World Wide Web http://www.mtlib.org.

Nebraska

Term of Office. Jan.–Dec. 2010. Publication. *Nebraska Library Association Quarterly* (*NLAQ*) (q.).

Pres. Scott Childers, UNL. E-mail schilder1 @unl.edu; *V.P./Pres.-Elect* Christine Walsh, Kearney Public Lib. E-mail cwalsh@kearney gov.org; *Secy.* Joanne Ferguson Cavanaugh, Omaha Public Lib. E-mail jferguson@omaha publiclibrary.org; *Treas.* Julie Hector, Lincoln City Libs. E-mail j.hector@lincoln libraries.org; *Past Pres.* Pam Bohmfalk, Hastings Public Lib. E-mail pbohmfal@ hastings.lib.ne.us; *Exec. Dir.* Michael Straatmann. E-mail nlaexecutivedirector@gmail. com.

Address correspondence to the executive director.

World Wide Web http://www.nebraska libraries.org.

Nevada

Memb. 450. Term of Office. Jan.–Dec. 2010. Publication. *Nevada Libraries* (q.).

Pres. Joan Vaughan, Henderson Libs. E-mail jevaughan@hdpl.org; *V.P./Pres.-Elect* Barbara Mathews, Churchill County Lib. E-mail blmathew@clan.lib.nv.us; *Treas.* Ed Feldman, Henderson Libs. E-mail efeldman @hdpl.org; *Past Pres.* Jeanette Hammons, Elko County Lib. E-mail jmhammon@

clan.lib.nv.us; *Exec. Secy.* Lisa Phelan, Henderson Libs. E-mail lphelan@hdpl.org. Address correspondence to the executive secretary.

World Wide Web http://www.nevada libraries.org.

New Hampshire

Memb. 700. Publication. *NHLA News* (q.). *Pres.* Judith Haskell, Hampton Falls Free Lib., 7 Drinkwater Rd., Hampton Falls 03844-2116. Tel. 603-926-3682, e-mail judyhaskell @comcast.net; *V.P./Pres.-Elect* Mary White, Howe Lib., 13 South St., Hanover 03755. Tel. 603-643-4120, e-mail mary.h.white@ thehowe.org; *Secy.* Kate Russell, Regina Lib., Rivier College, 420 S. Main St., Nashua 03060. Tel. 603-897-8683, e-mail krussel@ rivier.edu; *Treas.* Carl Heidenblad, Nesmith Lib., 8 Fellows Rd., Windham 03087. Tel. 603-432-7154, e-mail cheidenblad@nesmith library.org; *Past Pres.* Steve Butzel, Portsmouth Public Lib., 175 Parrott Ave., Portsmouth 03801. Tel. 603-766-1711, e-mail skbutzel@lib.cityofportsmouth.com.

Address correspondence to the association, c/o LGC, P.O. Box 617, Concord 03302-0617.

World Wide Web http://webster.state.nh. us/nhla.

New Jersey

Memb. 1,800. Term of Office. July 2009–June 2010. Publication. *New Jersey Libraries Newsletter* (q.). *Pres.* Susan Briant, Haddonfield Public Lib., 60 Haddon Ave., Haddonfield 08033. Tel. 856-429-1304, fax 856-429-3760, e-mail sbriant@haddonfieldlibrary.org; *V.P.* Mary Romance, West Orange Public Lib., 46 Mount Pleasant Ave., West Orange 07052. Tel. 973-736-0191, fax 973-324-9817, e-mail mromance@westorangelibrary.org; *2nd V.P.* Jayne Beline, Parsippany Lib., 449 Halsey Rd., Parsippany 07054. Tel. 973-887-5150, fax 973-887-0062, e-mail jayne.beline@ mainlib.org; *Secy.* Nancy Weiner, Chang Lib., William Paterson Univ., 300 Pompton Rd., Wayne 07470. Tel. 973-720-2161, e-mail weinern@wpunj.edu; *Treas.* Keith McCoy, Roselle Public Lib., 104 W. 4 Ave., Roselle 07203. Tel. 908-245-2166, fax 908-298-8881, e-mail wkmccoy@lmxac.org; *Past Pres.* Heidi Lynn Cramer, Newark Public Lib., 5 Washington St., P.O. Box 630, Newark 07101. Tel. 973-733-7837, fax 973-733-8539, e-mail hcramer@npl.org; *Exec. Dir.* Patricia Tumulty, NJLA, P.O. Box 1534, Trenton 08607. Tel. 609-394-8032, fax 609-394-8164, e-mail ptumulty@njla.org.

Address correspondence to the executive director.

World Wide Web http://www.njla.org.

New Mexico

Memb. 580. Term of Office. Apr. 2009–Apr. 2010. Publication. *New Mexico Library Association Newsletter* (6 a year). *Pres.* Dan Kammer. E-mail dkammer@ nmsu.edu; *V.P.* Barbara Lovato-Gassman. E-mail bgassman@unm.edu; *Secy.* Kathleen Teaze. E-mail kteaze@las-cruces.org; *Treas.* Tracy Thompson. E-mail thomptd@nmsu. edu; *Past Pres.* Cassandra Osterloh. E-mail cassandra.osterloh@gmail.com; *Admin.* Lorie Christian. E-mail admin@nmla.org.

Address correspondence to the association, Box 26074, Albuquerque 87125. Tel. 505-400-7309, fax 505-891-5171, e-mail admin@ nmla.org.

World Wide Web http://www.nmla.org.

New York

Memb. 3,000. Term of Office. Oct. 2009–Oct. 2010. Publication. *NYLA Bulletin* (4 a year). *Ed.* Michael J. Borges. *Pres.* Kathy Miller. Tel. 585-223-7570, e-mail kmiller@rrlc.org; *Past Pres.* Josh Cohen. Tel. 845-471-6060 ext. 17, e-mail jcohen@midhudson.org; *Treas.* Penelope Klein. Tel. 315-446-5446, e-mail pklein@ clrc.org; *Pres.-Elect* Marcia Eggleston. Tel. 315-250-0352, e-mail megglest@nncsk12.org; *Exec. Dir.* Michael J. Borges.

Address correspondence to the executive director, New York Lib. Assn., 6021 State Farm Rd., Guilderland 12084. Tel. 800-252-6952 (toll-free), 518-432-6952, fax 518-427-1697, e-mail director@nyla.org.

World Wide Web http://www.nyla.org.

North Carolina

Memb. 1,100. Term of Office. Oct. 2009–Oct. 2011. Publications. *North Carolina Library Association E-news* (bi-mo.). *Ed.* Marilyn Schuster, Local Documents/Special Collections, Univ. of North Carolina–Charlotte. E-mail mbschust@email.uncc.edu; *North Carolina Libraries Online* (2 a year). *Ed.* Ralph Scott, Joyner Lib., East Carolina Univ., Greenville 27858. Tel. 252-328-0265, e-mail scottr@ecu.edu.

Pres. Sherwin Rice, Bladen Community College, P.O. Box 266, Dublin 28332. Tel. 910-879-5641, e-mail srice@bladen.cc.nc.us; *V.P./Pres.-Elect* Wanda Brown, Wake Forest Univ., Box 7777 Reynolda Sta., Winston-Salem 27109. Tel. 336-758-5094, e-mail brownw@wfu.edu; *Secy.* Laura Davidson, Meredith College, 3800 Hillsborough St., Raleigh 27607; *Treas.* Andrea Tullos, Orange County Lib., P.O. Box 8181, Hillsboro 27278. E-mail atullos@co.orange.nc.us; *Past Pres.* Phil Barton, Rowan Public Lib., 714 Brookmont Ave., Salisbury 28146-7293. Tel. 704-633-5462, e-mail pbarton2@carolina.rr.com; *Admin. Asst.* Kim Parrott, North Carolina Lib. Assn., 1841 Capital Blvd., Raleigh 27604. Tel. 919-839-6252, fax 919-839-6253, e-mail nclaonline@ibiblio.org or nclaonline@gmail.com.

Address correspondence to the administrative assistant.

World Wide Web http://www.nclaonline.org.

North Dakota

Memb. (Indiv.) 330; (Inst.) 9. Term of Office. Sept. 2009–Sept. 2010. Publication. *The Good Stuff* (q.). *Ed.* Marlene Anderson, Bismarck State College Lib., Box 5587, Bismarck 58506-5587. Tel. 701-224-5578.

Pres. Laurie L. McHenry, Thormodsgard Lib., Univ. of North Dakota, 2968 2nd Ave. N Stop 9004, Grand Forks 58202-9004. Tel. 701-777-3475, fax 701-777-4956, e-mail mchenry@law.und.edu; *Pres.-Elect* Rita Ennen, Stoxen Lib., Dickinson State Univ., 166 S. College Ave, Dickinson 58601-4605. Tel. 701-483-2883, fax 701-483-2006, e-mail rita.ennen@dickinsonstate.edu; *Secy.* Chandra Hirning, Rasmussen College Lib., 1701 E. Century Ave., Bismarck 58503-0658. Tel.

701-530-9600, fax 701-530-9604, e-mail chandra.hirning@rasmussen.edu; *Treas.* Michael Safratowich, Harley French Lib. of the Health Sciences, Univ. of North Dakota, Box 9002, Grand Forks 58202-9002. Tel. 701-777-2602, fax 701-777-4790, e-mail msafrat@medicine.nodak.edu; *Past Pres.* Phyllis Ann K. Bratton, Raugust Lib., Jamestown College, 6070 College Lane, Jamestown 58405-0002. Tel. 701-252-3467 ext. 2433, fax 701-253-4446, e-mail pbratton@jc.edu.

Address correspondence to the president.

World Wide Web http://www.ndla.info.

Ohio

Memb. 2,700+. Term of Office. Jan.–Dec. 2010. Publication. *Access* (weekly, online only).

Pres. Beverly Cain, Portsmouth Public Lib., 1220 Gallia St., Portsmouth 45662. Tel. 740-353-5990, e-mail bcain@yourppl.org; *V.P./Pres.-Elect* Molly Carver, Bellevue Public Lib., 224 E. Main St., Bellevue 44811-1409. Tel. 419-483-4769 ext. 14, e-mail mcarver@bellevue.lib.oh.us; *Secy./Treas.* David Jennings, Akron-Summit County Public Lib., 55 S. Main St., Akron 44326. Tel. 330-643-9000, e-mail djennings@akronlibrary.org; *Past Pres.* Scott Shafer, Lima Public Lib., 650 W. Market St., Lima 45801. Tel. 419-228-5113, e-mail shafers@limalibrary.com; *Exec. Dir.* Douglas S. Evans.

Address correspondence to the executive director, OLC, 1105 Schrock Rd., Suite 440, Columbus 43229-1174. Tel. 614-410-8092, fax 614-410-8098, e-mail olc@olc.org.

World Wide Web http://www.olc.org.

Oklahoma

Memb. (Indiv.) 1,000; (Inst.) 60. Term of Office. July 2009–June 2010. Publication. *Oklahoma Librarian* (bi-mo.).

Pres. Charles Brooks. E-mail charlesbrooks@utulsa.edu; *V.P./Pres.-Elect* Leslie Langley; *Secy.* Stacy Schrank; *Treas.* Lynda Reynolds; *Past Pres.* Kathy Latrobe; *Exec. Dir.* Kay Boies, 300 Hardy Drive, Edmond 73013. Tel. 405-525-5100, fax 405-525-5103, e-mail kboies@sbcglobal.net.

Address correspondence to the executive director.

World Wide Web http://www.oklibs.org.

Oregon

Memb. (Indiv.) 1,000+. Publications. *OLA Hotline* (bi-w.), *OLA Quarterly*.
Pres. Connie Anderson-Cohoon, Southern Oregon Univ. E-mail anderson@sou.edu; *V.P./Pres.-Elect* Rob Everett, Springfield Public Lib. E-mail reverett@ci.springfield.or.us; *Secy.* Lorie Vik, Eugene Public Lib. E-mail lorie.a.vik@ci.eugene.or.us; *Treas.* Liisa Sjoblom, Deschutes Public Lib. E-mail liisas@dpls.lib.or.us; *Past Pres.* Mary Ginnane, Eugene Public Lib. E-mail mary.j.ginnane@ci.eugene.or.us.
Address correspondence to Oregon Lib. Assn., P.O. Box 3067, La Grande 97850. Tel. 541-962-5824, e-mail olaweb@olaweb.org.
World Wide Web http://www.olaweb.org.

Pennsylvania

Memb. 1,900+. Term of Office. Jan.–Dec. 2010. Publication. *PaLA Bulletin* (10 a year).
Pres. Margie Stern, Delaware County Lib. System. Tel. 610-891-8622, e-mail mstern@delco.lib.pa.us; *1st V.P.* Robin Lesher, Adams County Lib. System. Tel. 717-334-5716, e-mail robinl@adamslibrary.org; *2nd V.P.* Paula Gilbert, Martin Memorial Lib. Tel. 717-846-5300, e-mail pgilbert@yorklibraries.org; *3rd V.P.* Carrie Turner, Cheltenham Township Lib. System. Tel. 215-885-0457, e-mail cturner@mclinc.org; *Past Pres.* Joe Fennewald, Penn State–Hazleton. Tel. 570-450-3172, e-mail jaf23@psu.edu; *Exec. Dir.* Glenn R. Miller, Pennsylvania Lib. Assn., 220 Cumberland Pkwy., Suite 10, Mechanicsburg 17055. Tel. 717-766-7663, fax 717-766-5440, e-mail glenn@palibraries.org.
Address correspondence to the executive director.
World Wide Web http://www.palibraries.org.

Rhode Island

Memb. (Indiv.) 350+; (Inst.) 50+. Term of Office. June 2009–June 2011. Publication. *Rhode Island Library Association Bulletin.*
Pres. Laura Marlane, Providence Community Lib., South Providence Lib., 441 Prairie Ave., Providence 02905. Tel. 401-467-2700 ext. 1610, e-mail president@rilibraryassoc.org; *V.P./Pres.-Elect* Eileen Dyer, Cranston Public Lib., 140 Sockanossett Cross Rd., Cranston 02920. Tel. 401-943-9080 ext. 117, e-mail vicepresident@rilibraryassoc.org; *Secy.* Jenifer Bond, Douglas and Judith Krupp Lib., Bryant Univ., Smithfield 02917. Tel. 401-232-6299, e-mail secretary@rilibraryassoc.org; *Treas.* Cindy Lunghofer, East Providence Public Lib., 41 Grove Ave., East Providence 02914. Tel. 401-434-2453, e-mail treasurer@rilibraryassoc.org; *Past Pres.* Christopher La Roux, Greenville Public Lib., 573 Putnam Pike, Greenville 02828. Tel. 401-949-3630.
Address correspondence to Rhode Island Library Assn., P.O. Box 6765, Providence 02940.
World Wide Web http://www.rilibraryassoc.org.

South Carolina

Memb. 550+. Term of Office. Jan.–Dec. 2010. Publication. *News and Views.*
Pres. Rayburne Turner, Charleston County Public Lib., 2261 Otranto Rd., North Charleston 29406. Tel. 843-572-4094, fax 843-572-4190, e-mail turner@ccpl.org; *1st V.P./Pres.-Elect* Adam Haigh, Jackson Lib., Lander Univ., 320 Stanley Ave., Greenwood 29649. Tel. 864-388-8029, fax 864-388-8816, e-mail ahaigh@lander.edu; *2nd V.P.* Karen Brown, Thomas Cooper Lib., Univ. of South Carolina, Columbia 29208. Tel. 803-777-4267, fax 803-777-4661, e-mail kwbrown@gwm.sc.edu; *Secy.* Briget Livingston, Chapin Memorial Lib., 400 14th Ave., North Myrtle Beach 29577. Tel. 843-918-1275; *Treas.* Jeronell Bradley, Florence Darlington Technical College. Tel. 843-661-8032, e-mail jeronell.bradley@fdtc.edu; *Past Pres.* Libby Young, Furman Univ., 10 W. Earle St., Greenville 29609. Tel. 864-294-2260, fax 864-294-3004, e-mail libby.young@furman.edu; *Exec. Secy.* Donald Wood, SCLA, P.O. Box 1763, Columbia 29202. Tel. 803-252-1087, fax 803-252-0589. E-mail scla@capconsc.com.
Address correspondence to the executive secretary.
World Wide Web http://www.scla.org.

South Dakota

Memb. (Indiv.) 454; (Inst.) 69. Term of Office. Oct. 2009–Oct. 2010. Publication. *Book Marks* (q.).

Pres. Kay Christensen, Augustana College Lib., Sioux Falls. E-mail kay.christensen@ augie.edu; *V.P./Pres.-Elect* Paula DeMars, Hill City Community Lib., Hill City. E-mail pdemars@hillcitysd.org; *Recording Secy.* Julie Erickson, South Dakota State Lib. E-mail julie.erickson@state.sd.us; *Past Pres.* Nancy Sabbe, Madison Public Lib., Madison. E-mail nsabbe@sdln.net; *Exec. Secy./Treas.* Laura Olson. E-mail sdla@svtv.com.

Address correspondence to the executive secretary, SDLA, 28363 472nd Ave., Worthing 57077-5722. Tel. 605-343-3750, e-mail bkstand@rap.midco.net.

World Wide Web http://www.sdlibrary association.org.

Tennessee

Memb. 600+. Term of Office. July 2009–June 2010. Publications. *Tennessee Librarian* (q.), *TLA Newsletter* (bi-mo.) Both online only at http://www.tnla.org.

Pres. Kevin Reynolds. E-mail kreynold@ sewanee.edu; *V.P./Pres.-Elect* Susan Earl. E-mail susan.earl@nashville.gov; *Recording Secy.* James Staub. E-mail james.staub@ nashville.gov; *Past Pres.* Sue Szostak, Motlow. E-mail szostaksue1947@gmail.com; *Exec. Dir.* Annelle R. Huggins, Tennessee Lib. Assn., Box 241074, Memphis 38124. Tel. 901-485-6952, e-mail arhuggins1@ comcast.net

Address correspondence to the executive director.

World Wide Web http://tnla.org.

Texas

Memb. 7,300+. Term of Office. Apr. 2009–Apr. 2010. Publications. *Texas Library Journal* (q.), *TLACast* (9 a year).

Pres. Patrick Heath. E-mail patrickheath@ windstream.net; *Pres.-Elect* Maribel Garza-Castro, St. John's School. E-mail mgarzacastro @sjs.org; *Treas.* Jane Clausen, Lubbock Public Lib. E-mail jclausen@mail.ci.Lubbock. tx.us; *Past Pres.* Melody Kelly, Univ. of North Texas. E-mail melody.kelly@unt.edu; *Exec. Dir.* Patricia H. Smith, TXLA, 3355 Bee Cave Rd., Suite 401, Austin 78746-6763. Tel. 512-328-1518, fax 512-328-8852, e-mail pats@txla.org or tla@txla.org.

Address correspondence to the executive director.

World Wide Web http://www.txla.org.

Utah

Memb. 650. Term of Office. May 2009–May 2010. Publication. *Utah Libraries News* (bi-mo.) (online at http://www.ula.org/newsletter).

Pres. Ruby Cheesman, Bingham Creek Lib., Salt Lake County Lib. Services, 4834 W. 9000 S., West Jordan 84081. Tel. 801-944-7688, fax 801-282-0943, e-mail rcheesman@slcolibrary.org; *V.P./Pres.-Elect* Andy Spackman, Harold B. Lee Lib., Brigham Young Univ., 1212 HBLL, Provo 84602. Tel. 801-422-3924, e-mail andy_spackman@ byu.edu; *Recording Secy.* Carol Ormond, Salt Lake County Lib. Services, Cottonwood Heights. Tel. 801-944-7515, fax 801-942-6323, e-mail cormond@slcolibrary.org; *Treas.* Steve Pfeiffer, Salt Lake City Public Lib., 1270 Brandonwood Drive, Murray 84123. Tel. 801-594-8611, e-mail spfeiffer@ slcpl.org; *Past Pres.* Steven D. Decker, Cedar City Public Lib., Cedar City 84720. Tel. 435-586-6661 ext. 1001, fax 435-865-7280, e-mail dsteve@cedarcity.org; *Exec. Secy.* Ranny Lacanienta, Harold B. Lee Lib., Brigham Young Univ., Provo 84602. Tel. 801-422-6278, fax 801-422-0466, e-mail ranny_lacanienta@byu.edu.

Address correspondence to the executive secretary, Utah Lib. Assn., P.O. Box 708155, Sandy 84070-8155.

World Wide Web http://www.ula.org.

Vermont

Memb. 400. Publication. *VLA News* (6 a year).

Pres. John K. Payne, Saint Michael's College, Box L, 1 Winooski Park, Colchester 05439. Tel. 802-654-2401, e-mail jpayne@ smcvt.edu; *V.P./Pres.-Elect* Marti Fiske, Dorothy Alling Memorial Lib., 21 Library Lane, Williston 05495. Tel. 802-878-4918, e-mail marti@williston.lib.vt.us; *Secy.* David

Sturges, Hartness Lib. System, Community College of Vermont, 1 Main St., Randolph Center 05061. Tel. 802-728-1231, e-mail dsturges@vtc.edu; *Treas.* Wynne Browne, Downs Rachlin Martin, St. Johnsbury 05819-0099. Tel. 802-473-4216, e-mail wbrowne@drm.com; *Past Pres.* Judah S. Hamer, 1571 Rte. 30, Cornwall 05753. Tel. 802-462-2096, e-mail jshamer@gmail.com.

Address correspondence to VLA, Box 803, Burlington 05402.

World Wide Web http://www.vermont libraries.org.

Virginia

Memb. 1,100+. Term of Office. Oct. 2009–Oct. 2010. Publications. *Virginia Libraries* (q.); *VLA Newsletter* (10 a year, online only).

Pres. John Moorman, Williamsburg Public Lib., 7770 Croaker Rd., Williamsburg 23188. Tel. 757-259-7777, e-mail jmoorman@wrl.org; *V.P./Pres.-Elect* Matthew Todd, NOVA, 3001 N. Beauregard St., Alexandria 22331. Tel. 703-845-6033, e-mail mtodd@nvcc.edu; *2nd V.P.* Diantha McCauley, Augusta County Lib., 1759 Jefferson Hwy., Fisherville 22939. Tel. 540-949-6354, e-mail diantha@augusta countylibrary.org; *Secy.* Connie Gilman, Chinn Park Regional Lib., 13065 Chinn Park Drive, Prince William 22192. Tel. 703-792-6199, e-mail cgilman@pwcgov.org; *Treas.* Matt Todd, Northern Virginia Community College, 3001 N. Beauregard St., Alexandria 22331. Tel. 703-845-6033, e-mail mtodd@nvcc.edu; *Past Pres.* Robin Benke, Univ. of Virginia–Wise, 116 Dotson Ave., Wise 24293. Tel. 276-328-0151, e-mail rbenke@virginia.edu; *Exec. Dir.* Linda Hahne, P.O. Box 8277, Norfolk 23503-0277. Tel. 757-583-0041, fax 757-583-5041, e-mail lindahahne@cox.net.

Address correspondence to the executive director.

World Wide Web http://www.vla.org.

Washington

Memb. 1,040+. Term of Office. Apr. 2008–Apr. 2010. Publication. *ALKI* (3 a year). *Ed.* Julie Miller, EWU Libs., 816 F St., Cheney 99004. Tel. 509-359-4949, julie.miller@mail.ewu.edu.

Pres. Tim Mallory, Timberland Regional Lib., 415 Tumwater Blvd. S.W., Tumwater 98501. Tel. 360-704-4502, fax 360-586-6838, e-mail tmallory@trlib.org; *V.P./Pres.-Elect* Brian Soneda, Mount Vernon City Lib., 315 Snoqualmie St., Mount Vernon 98273. Tel. 360-336-6209, e-mail brians@ci.mount-vernon.wa.us; *Secy.* Karen Highum, Allen Lib., Univ. of Washington, Box 35290, Seattle 98195-2900. Tel. 206-685-3981, e-mail khighum@msn.com; *Treas.* Katie Cargill, Eastern Washington Univ., 816 F St., Cheney 99004. Tel. 206-685-3981, e-mail kcargill@ewu.edu; *Past Pres.* Martha Parsons, WSU Energy Program Lib., 925 Plum St. S.E., Olympia 98501. Tel. 360-956-2159, fax 360-236-2159, e-mail president@wla.org; *Exec. Dir.* Dana Murphy-Love, WLA, 23607 Hwy. 99, Suite 2-C, Edmonds 98026. Tel. 425-967-0739, fax 425-771-9588, e-mail dana@wla.org.

Address correspondence to the executive director.

World Wide Web http://www.wla.org.

West Virginia

Memb. 650+. Publication. *West Virginia Libraries* (6 a year). *Ed.* Pam Coyle, Martinsburg Public Lib., 101 W. King St., Martinsburg 25401. Tel. 304-267-8933, fax 304-267-9720, e-mail pcoyle@martin.lib.wv.us.

Pres. Judy K. Rule, Cabell County Public Lib., 455 Ninth Street, Huntington 25701. Tel. 304-528-5700, e-mail jrule@cabell.lib.wv.us; *1st V.P./Pres.-Elect* Monica Brooks, 306 Drinko Lib., Marshall Univ., Huntington 25755. Tel. 304-696-6474, e-mail brooks@marshall.edu; *2nd V.P.* Emilee Seesee, Ritchie County Public Lib., 608 E. Main St., Harrisville 26362. Tel. 304-643-2717, e-mail seesee@mail.mln.lib.wv.us; *Secy.* Barbara LaGodna, WVU Libs., P.O. Box 6105, Morgantown 26506-6105. Tel. 304-293-9748, e-mail blagodna@wvu.edu; *Treas.* Beth Royall, Evansdale Lib., WVU, P.O. Box 6105, Morgantown 26506-6105. Tel. 304-293-9755, e-mail beth.royall@mail.wvu.edu; *Past Pres.* Brian Raitz, Parkersburg and Wood County Public Lib., 3100 Emerson Ave., Parkersburg 26104-2414. Tel. 304-420-4587 ext. 11, e-mail raitzb@park.lib.wv.us.

Address correspondence to the president.
World Wide Web http://www.wvla.org.

Wisconsin

Memb. 1,800. Term of Office. Jan.–Dec.
Publication. *WLA Newsletter* (q.).
Pres. Walter Burkhalter, Mid-Wisconsin
Federated Lib. System, 112 Clinton St., Hori-
con 53032. E-mail wburkh@mwfls.org;
Pres.-Elect Alberto Herrera, Jr., Raynor
Memorial Libs., Marquette Univ., P.O. Box
3141, Milwaukee 53201-3141. E-mail alberto.
herrera@marquette.edu; *Secy.* Tasha Saecker,
Elisha D. Smith Public Lib., 440 First St.,
Menasha 54952-3191. E-mail saecker@
menashalibrary.org; *Treas.* Jan Berg, DeFor-
est Public Lib., 203 Library St., DeForest
53532. E-mail bergjd@scls.lib.wi.us; *Past
Pres.* Pat Chevis, Stoughton Public Lib., 304
S. 4 St., Stoughton 53589. E-mail pchevis@
scls.lib.wi.us; *Exec. Dir.* Lisa K. Strand, Wisconsin Lib. Assn., 5250 E. Terrace Drive,
Suite A1, Madison 53718-8345. Tel. 608-
245-3640, fax 608-245-3646, e-mail strand@
scls.lib.wi.us.
Address correspondence to the association.
World Wide Web http://www.wla.lib.wi.us.

Wyoming

Memb. 450+. Term of Office. Oct. 2009–Oct.
2010.
Pres. Jamie Markus, Wyoming State Lib.
Tel. 307-777-5914, fax 307-777-6289, e-mail
jmarku@state.wy.us; *V.P.* Sue Knesel, Campbell County Public Lib. System. Tel. 307-
687-9229, fax 307-686-4009, e-mail sknesel
@will.state.wy.us; *Recording Secy.* Susan
Mark, Wyoming State Lib. Tel. 307-777-
5915, e-mail smark@state.wy.us; *Past Pres.*
Cynthia Twing, Johnson County Public Lib.
Tel. 307-684-5546, fax 307-684-7888, e-mail
ctwing@will.state.wy.us; *Exec. Secy.* Laura
Grott, Box 1387, Cheyenne 82003. Tel. 307-
632-7622, fax 307-638-3469, e-mail grottski
@aol.com.
Address correspondence to the executive
secretary.
World Wide Web http://www.wyla.org.

Canada

Alberta

Memb. 500. Term of Office. May 2010–Apr.
2011. Publication. *Letter of the LAA* (4 a
year).
Pres. Mary Jane Bilsland, Edmonton Public Lib. E-mail mjbilsland@epl.ca: *Past Pres.*
Renee Reaume, Univ. of Calgary. E-mail
renee.reaume@ucalgary.ca; *2nd V.P.* Diane
Clark, Univ. of Alberta. E-mail diane.clark@
ualberta.ca; *Treas.* Julia Reinhart, Shortgrass
Regional Lib. E-mail julia@shortgrass.ca;
Exec. Dir. Christine Sheppard, 80 Baker
Crescent N.W., Calgary T2L 1R4. Tel. 403-
284-5818, fax 403-282-6646, e-mail info@
laa.ca.
Address correspondence to the executive
director.
World Wide Web http://www.laa.ca.

British Columbia

Memb. 820. Term of Office. April 2009–
April 2010. Publication. *BCLA Browser. Ed.*
Sandra Wong.
Pres. Ken Cooley, McPherson Lib., Univ.
of Victoria, P.O. Box 1800, STN CSC, Victoria V8W 3H5. E-mail kcooley@uvic.ca;
V.P./Pres.-Elect Marjorie Mitchell, Okana-
gan Lib., Univ. of British Columbia, 3333
University Way, Kelowna V1V 1V7. Tel.
250-807-9147, fax 250-807-8057, e-mail
marjorie.mitchell@ubc.ca; *2nd V.P.* Adrienne Wass, Greater Victoria Public Lib., 735
Broughton St., Victoria V8W 3H2. Tel. 250-
413-0370, e-mail awass@gvpl.ca; *Treas.*
Christina de Castell, Vancouver Public Lib.,
350 W. Georgia St., Vancouver V6B 6B1. E-
mail christina.decastell@vpl.ca; *Past Pres.*
Lynne Jordon, Greater Victoria Public Lib.,
735 Broughton St., Victoria V8W 3H2. E-
mail ljordon@gvpl.ca; *Exec. Dir.* Alane Wilson. E-mail execdir@bcla.bc.ca.
Address correspondence to the association,
900 Howe St., Suite 150, Vancouver V6Z
2M4. Tel. 604-683-5354, fax 604-609-0707,
e-mail office@bcla.bc.ca.
World Wide Web http://www.bcla.bc.ca.

Manitoba

Memb. 500+. Term of Office. May 2009–May 2010. Publication. *Newsline* (mo.).

Pres. Betty Braaksma, Univ. of Manitoba Libs., E3-362 EITC, Univ. of Manitoba, Winnipeg R3T 2N2. Tel. 204-474-7193, e-mail betty_braaksma@umanitoba.ca; *V.P.* Sherri Vokey, Red River College, W201B-160 Princess St., Winnipeg R3B 1K9. Tel. 204-949-8477, e-mail svokey@rrc.mb.ca; *Treas.* Kristen Kruse, Univ. of Manitoba Libs., 219 Elizabeth Dafoe Lib., Winnipeg R3T 2N2. Tel. 204-474-7435, e-mail krusek @cc.umanitoba.ca; *Past Pres.* Carolyn Minor, Millennium Lib., 251 Donald St., Winnipeg R3C 3P5. Tel. 204-986-4206.

Address correspondence to the association, 606-100 Arthur St., Winnipeg R3B 1H3. Tel. 204-943-4567, e-mail manitobalibrary@ gmail.com.

World Wide Web http://www.mla.mb.ca.

Ontario

Memb. 5,200+. Publications. *Access* (q.); *Teaching Librarian* (3 a year).

Pres. Mary Ann Mavrinac, Hazel McCallion Academic Learning Centre, Univ. of Toronto at Mississauga. E-mail maryann. mavrinac@utoronto.ca; *V.P./Pres.-Elect* Tanis Fink, Seneca Libs. E-mail tanis.fink@ senecac.on.ca; *Treas.* Paul Takala, Hamilton Public Lib. E-mail ptakala@hpl.ca; *Past Pres.* Peggy Thomas. E-mail peggythom@ gmail.com; *Exec. Dir.* Shelagh Paterson. E-mail spaterson@accessola.com.

Address correspondence to the association, 50 Wellington St. E., Suite 201, Toronto M5E 1C8. Tel. 416-363-3388, fax 416-941-9581, e-mail info@accessola.com.

World Wide Web http://www.accessola. com.

Quebec

Memb. (Indiv.) 100+. Term of Office. May 2009–April 2010. Publication. *ABQLA Bulletin* (3 a year).

Pres. Maria Luisa Morales; *V.P.* Anne Wade; *Secy.* Cathy Maxwell; *Exec. Secy./* *Treas.* Janet Ilavsky, P.O. Box 1095, Pointe-Claire H9S 4H9. Tel. 514-697-0146, e-mail abqla@abqla.qc.ca; *Past Pres.* Lisa Milner.

Address correspondence to the executive secretary.

World Wide Web http://www.abqla.qc.ca.

Saskatchewan

Memb. 200+. Term of Office. May 2009–May 2010. Publication. *Forum* (4 a year).

Pres. Barbara Kelly, Regina Public Lib., P.O. Box 2311, Regina S4P 3Z5. Tel. 306-777-6004, fax 306-949-7266, e-mail bkelly@ reginalibrary.ca; *V.P.* Jeff Mason, Regina Qu'Appelle Health Region, 0B—Health Sciences Lib., 1440 14th Ave., Regina S4P 0W5. Tel. 306-766-3833, fax 306-766-3839, e-mail jeff_mason@me.com; *Treas.* Brett Waytuck, Provincial Lib., Ministry of Educ., 1945 Hamilton St., Regina S4P 2C8. Tel. 306-787-8020, fax 306-787-2029, e-mail brett.waytuck@gov.sk.ca; *Exec. Dir.* Caroline Selinger, Saskatchewan Lib. Assn., 2010 Seventh Ave., No. 15, Regina S4R 1C2. Tel. 306-780-9413, fax 306-780-9447, e-mail slaexdir@sasktel.net.

Address correspondence to the executive director.

World Wide Web http://www.saskla.ca.

Regional

Atlantic Provinces: N.B., N.L., N.S., P.E.I.

Memb. (Indiv.) 200+; (Inst.) 26. Publications. *APLA Bulletin* (bi-mo.).

Pres. Donald Moses, Robertson Lib., Univ. of PEI, Charlottetown, PE C1A 4P3. Tel. 902-566-0479, fax 902-628-4305, e-mail dmoses@upei.ca; *V.P./Pres.-Elect* Sarah Gladwell, Saint John Free Public Lib., Saint John, NB E2L 4Z6. Tel. 506-643-7224, fax 506-643-7225, e-mail sarah.gladwell@gnb. ca; *V.P., Membership* Ann Smith, Vaughan Memorial Lib., Acadia Univ., Wolfville, NS B4P 2R6. Tel. 902-585-1723, fax 902-585-1748, e-mail apla_executive@yahoo.ca; *Secy.* Lori McCay-Peet, Centre for Management Informatics, Dalhousie Univ., Halifax, NS. B3H 4R2. Tel. 902-494-8392, e-mail mccay@dal.ca; *Treas.* Penny Logan, Capital Health, 1796 Summer St., Rm. 2212, Halifax, NS B3H 3A7. Tel. 902-473-4383, fax 902-473-8651, e-mail apla_executive@yahoo.ca; *Past Pres.* Su Cleyle, Queen Elizabeth II Lib., Memorial Univ. of Newfoundland, St. John's, NL A1B 3Y1. Tel. 709-737-3188, fax 709-737-2153, e-mail scleyle@mun.ca.

Address correspondence to Atlantic Provinces Lib. Assn., c/o School of Info. Mgt., Faculty of Mgt., Kenneth C. Rowe Mgt. Bldg., 6100 University Ave., Halifax, NS B3H 3J5.

World Wide Web http://www.apla.ca.

Mountain Plains: Ariz., Colo., Kan., Mont., Neb., Nev., N.Dak., N.M., Okla., S.Dak., Utah, Wyo.

Memb. 820. Term of Office. May 2009–May 2010. Publications. *MPLA Newsletter* (bi-mo.). *Ed./Advertising Mgr.* Judy Zelenski, 14293 W. Center Drive, Lakewood, CO 80228. Tel. 303-985-7795, e-mail mpla_execsecretary@operamail.com.

Pres. Eileen Wright, Billings Lib., Montana State Univ., 1500 University Drive, Billings, MT 59101. Tel. 406-657-1656, fax 406-657-2037, e-mail ewright@msubillings.edu; *V.P./Pres.-Elect* Elvita Landau, Brookings Public Lib., 515 Third St., Brookings, SD 57006. Tel. 605-692-9407, fax 605-692-9386, e-mail elandau@sdln.net; *Recording Secy.* Robin Brooks Clark, Sump Memorial Lib., 222 N. Jefferson, Papillion, NE 68046. Tel. 402-597-2042, fax 402-339-3918, e-mail robin.clark@sumplibrary.info; *Past Pres.* Robert Banks, Topeka and Shawnee County Public Lib., 1515 S.W. 10 Ave., Topeka, KS 66604. Tel. 785-580-4481, fax 785-580-4496, e-mail rbanks@mail.tscpl.org; *Exec. Secy.* Judy Zelenski, 14293 W. Center Drive, Lakewood, CO 80228. Tel. 303-985-7795, e-mail mpla_execsecretary@operamail.com.

Address correspondence to the executive secretary, Mountain Plains Lib. Assn.

World Wide Web http://www.mpla.us.

New England: Conn., Maine, Mass., N.H., R.I., Vt.

Memb. (Indiv.) 800. Term of Office. Nov. 2009–Oct. 2010. Publications. *New England Libraries* (annual), *NELA News* (electronic, mo.).

Pres. Rick Taplin, Minuteman Lib. Network, 10 Strathmore Rd., Natick, MA 01760. Tel. 508-655-8008 ext. 201, e-mail president @nelib.org; *V.P./Pres.-Elect* Jen Alvino Leo, e-mail vicepresident@nelib.org; *Secy.* Marija Sanderling, Lane Memorial Lib., 2 Academy Ave., Hampton, NH 03842. Tel. 603-926-3368, fax 603-926-1348, e-mail secretary@nelib.org; *Treas.* Karen Patterson. E-mail treasurer@nelib.org; *Past Pres.* Mary Ann Tricarico, New England Institute of Art, 10 Brookline Place West, Brookline, MA 02445. Tel. 800-903-4425, e-mail pastpresident@nelib.org; *Exec. Mgr.* Mary Ann Rupert, 31 Connor Lane, Wilton, NH 03086. Tel. 603-654-3533, fax 603-654-3526, e-mail executivemanager@nelib.org.

Address correspondence to the executive manager.

World Wide Web http://www.nelib.org.

Pacific Northwest: Alaska, Idaho, Mont., Ore., Wash., Alberta, B.C.

Memb. (Active) 172. Term of Office. Aug. 2009–Aug. 2010. Publication. *PNLA Quarterly.* *Ed.* Mary Bolin, 322B Love Lib., Univ. of Nebraska, P.O. Box 881140, Lincoln, NE 68588-4100. Tel. 402-472-4281, e-mail mbolin2@unlnotes.unl.edu.

Pres. Kathy Watson, Marshall Public Lib., 113 S. Garfield, Pocatello, ID 83204. Tel. 208-232-1263 ext. 30, fax 208-232-9266, e-mail kwatson@marshallpl.org; *1st V.P./Pres.-Elect* Samantha Hines, Mansfield Lib., Univ. of Montana, Missoula, MT 59812-9936. Tel. 406-243-4558. fax 406-243-4067, e-mail samantha.hines@umontana.edu; *2nd V.P.* Jason Openo, Edmonton Public Lib., 145 Whitemud Crossing Shopping Centre, 4211 106th St., Edmonton, AB T6J 6L7. Tel. 780-496-8348, e-mail jopeno@epl.ca; *Secy.* Brent Roberts, Montana State Univ.–Billings.

E-mail broberts@msubillings.edu; *Treas.* Katie Cargill, Eastern Washington Univ. Libs., 816 F St., Cheney, WA 99004. Tel. 509-359-2385, fax 509-359-2476, e-mail kcargill@mail.ewu.edu; *Past Pres.* Susannah Price, Boise Public Lib., 715 Capitol Blvd., Boise, ID 83702-7195. Tel. 208-384-4026, e-mail sprice@cityofboise.org.

Address correspondence to the president, Pacific Northwest Lib. Assn.

World Wide Web http://www.pnla.org.

Southeastern: Ala., Ark., Fla., Ga., Ky., La., Miss., N.C., S.C., Tenn., Va., W.Va.

Memb. 500. Publication. *The Southeastern Librarian (SELn)* (q.). *Ed.* Perry Bratcher, *SELn* Editor, 503A Steely Lib., Northern Kentucky Univ., Highland Heights, KY 41099. Tel. 859-572-6309, fax 859-572-6181, e-mail bratcher@nku.edu.

Pres. Kathleen R. T. Imhoff, 3617 Gloucester Drive, Lexington, KY 40510. Tel. 859-225-9310, e-mail kathleenrtimhoff@gmail.com; *1st V.P./Pres.-Elect* Michael Seigler, Smyrna Public Lib., 100 Village Green Circle, Smyrna, GA 30080. Tel. 770-431-2860, fax 770-431-2862, e-mail m.seigler@comcast.net; *Secy.* Elizabeth Doolittle, Univ. of Southern Mississippi, 730 E. Beach Blvd., Long Beach, MS 39560. Tel. 228-214-3455, e-mail elizabeth.doolittle@usm.edu; *Treas.* Gordon N. Baker, Clayton State Univ., 2000 Clayton State Blvd., P.O. Box 285, Morrow, GA 30260. Tel. 678-466-4325, e-mail gordon baker@clayton.edu; *Past Pres.* Faith A. Line, Anderson County Lib., P.O. Box 4047, 300 McDuffie St., Anderson, SC 29621. Tel. 864-260-4500, fax 864-260-4510, e-mail fline@andersonlibrary.org.

Address correspondence to Southeastern Lib. Assn., Admin. Services, P.O. Box 950, Rex, GA 30273-0950. Tel. 770-961-3520, fax 770-961-3712.

World Wide Web http://sela.jsu.edu.

State and Provincial Library Agencies

The state library administrative agency in each of the U.S. states will have the latest information on its state plan for the use of federal funds under the Library Services and Technology Act (LSTA). The directors and addresses of these state agencies are listed below.

Alabama

Rebecca Mitchell, Dir., Alabama Public Lib. Service, 6030 Monticello Drive, Montgomery 36130-6000. Tel. 334-213-3901, fax 334-213-3993, e-mail rmitchell@apls.state. al.us. World Wide Web http://www.apls. state.al.us.

Alaska

Linda Thibodeau, State Libn. and Dir., P.O. Box 110571, Juneau 99811. Tel. 907-465-2911, fax 907-465-2151, e-mail linda. thibodeau@alaska.gov. World Wide Web http://library.state.ak.us.

Arizona

GladysAnn Wells, Dir., State Libn., Arizona State Lib., Archives and Public Records, Rm. 200, 1700 W. Washington, Phoenix 85007. Tel. 602-926-4035, fax 602-256-7983, e-mail gawells@lib.az.us. World Wide Web http://www.lib.az.us.

Arkansas

Carolyn Ashcraft, State Libn., Arkansas State Lib., 1 Capitol Mall, 5th fl., Little Rock 72201. Tel. 501-682-1526, fax 501-682-1899, e-mail cashcraft@asl.lib.ar.us. World Wide Web http://www.asl.lib.ar.us.

California

Stacey Aldrich, State Libn., California State Lib., P.O. Box 942837, Sacramento 94237. Tel. 916-654-0174, fax 916-654-0064, e-mail saldrich@library.ca.gov. World Wide Web http://www.library.ca.gov.

Colorado

Eugene Hainer, Dir., Colorado State Lib., Rm. 309, 201 E. Colfax Ave., Denver 80203. Tel. 303-866-6733, fax 303-866-6940, e-mail hainer_g@cde.state.co.us. World Wide Web http://www.cde.state.co.us/index_library.htm.

Connecticut

Kendall F. Wiggin, State Libn., Connecticut State Lib., 231 Capitol Ave., Hartford 06106. Tel. 860-757-6510, fax 860-757-6503, e-mail kwiggin@cslib.org. World Wide Web http://www.cslib.org.

Delaware

Anne Norman, State Libn., Delaware Div. of Libs., 121 Duke of York St., Dover 19901. Tel. 302-739-4748 ext. 126, fax 302-739-6787, e-mail norman@lib.de.us. World Wide Web http://www.state.lib.de.us.

District of Columbia

Ginnie Cooper, Chief Libn., District of Columbia Public Lib., 901 G St. N.W., Suite 400, Washington 20001. Tel. 202-727-1101, fax 202-727-1129, e-mail ginnie.cooper@ dc.gov. World Wide Web http://www. dclibrary.org.

Florida

Judith A. Ring, State Libn., R. A. Gray Bldg., 500 S. Bronough St., Tallahassee 32399. Tel. 850-245-6600, fax 850-245-6735, e-mail jring@dos.state.fl.us. World Wide Web http://dlis.dos.state.fl.us/stlib.

Georgia

Lamar Veatch, State Libn., Georgia Public Lib. Services, 1800 Century Place N.E., Suite 150, Atlanta 30345. Tel. 404-235-7200, fax 404-235-7201, e-mail lveatch@georgia libraries.org. World Wide Web http://www. georgialibraries.org.

Hawaii

Richard Burns, State Libn., Hawaii State Public Lib. System, 44 Merchant St., Honolulu 96813. Tel. 808-586-3704, fax 808-586-3715, e-mail stlib@librarieshawaii.org. World Wide Web http://www.librarieshawaii.org.

Idaho

Ann Joslin, State Libn., Idaho Commission for Libs., 325 W. State St., Boise 83713. Tel. 208-334-2150, fax 208-334-4016, e-mail ann.joslin@libraries.idaho.gov. World Wide Web http://libraries.idaho.gov.

Illinois

Anne Craig, Dir., Illinois State Lib., Gwendolyn Brooks Bldg., 300 S. 2 St., Springfield 62701-1796. Tel. 217-782-2994, fax 217-785-4326, e-mail acraig@ilsos.net. World Wide Web http://www.cyberdriveillinois.com/departments/library/home.html.

Indiana

Roberta Brooker, Dir. and State Libn., Indiana State Lib., 140 N. Senate Ave., Indianapolis 46204. Tel. 317-232-3693, fax 317-232-3713, e-mail rbrooker@library.in.gov. World Wide Web http://www.in.gov/library.

Iowa

Mary Wegner, State Libn., State Lib. of Iowa, 1112 E. Grand Ave., Des Moines 50319. Tel. 515-281-4105, fax 515-281-6191, e-mail mary.wegner@lib.state.ia.us. World Wide Web http://www.statelibraryofiowa.org.

Kansas

Marc Galbraith, Interim State Libn., Capitol Bldg., Rm. 343-N, 300 S.W. 10 Ave., Topeka 66612. Tel. 785-296-3296, fax 785-296-6650, e-mail marcg@kslib.org. World Wide Web http://skyways.lib.ks.us/KSL.

Kentucky

Wayne Onkst, State Libn./Commissioner, Kentucky Dept. for Libs. and Archives, P.O. Box 537, Frankfort 40602-0537. Tel. 502-564-8300 ext. 312, fax 502-564-5773, e-mail wayne.onkst@ky.gov. World Wide Web http://www.kdla.ky.gov.

Louisiana

Rebecca Hamilton, State Libn., State Lib. of Louisiana, 701 N. 4 St., P.O. Box 131, Baton Rouge 70821-0131. Tel. 225-342-4923, fax 225-219-4804, e-mail rhamilton@crt.state.la.us. World Wide Web http://www.state.lib.la.us.

Maine

Linda Lord, State Libn., Maine State Lib., 64 State House Sta., Augusta 04333. Tel. 207-287-5600, fax 207-287-5624, e-mail linda.lord@maine.gov. World Wide Web http://www.maine.gov/msl.

Maryland

Irene Padilla, Asst. State Superintendent for Libs., State of Maryland, 200 W. Baltimore St., Baltimore 21201. Tel. 410-767-0435, fax 410-333-2507, e-mail ipadilla@msde.state.md.us. World Wide Web http://www.marylandpublicschools.org/MSDE/divisions/library.

Massachusetts

Robert Maier, Dir., Massachusetts Board of Lib. Commissioners, 98 N. Washington St., Suite 401, Boston 02114. Tel. 617-725-1860, fax 617-725-0140, e-mail robert.maier@state.ma.us. World Wide Web http://mblc.state.ma.us.

Michigan

Nancy Robertson, State Libn., Lib. of Michigan, P.O. Box 30007, Lansing 48909. Tel. 517-373-5504, fax 517-373-4480, e-mail nrobertson@michigan.gov. World Wide Web http://www.michigan.gov/libraryofmichigan.

Minnesota

Suzanne Miller, State Libn. and Dir., Minnesota Dept. of Educ., 1500 Hwy. 36 W., Roseville 55113-4266. Tel. 651-582-8251, fax 651-582-8752, e-mail suzanne.miller@

state.mn.us. World Wide Web http://education.state.mn.us/MDE/Learning_Support/Library_Services/index.html.

Mississippi

Sharman Smith, Exec. Dir., Mississippi Lib. Commission, 3881 Eastwood Drive, Jackson 39211. Tel. 601-432-4039, fax 601-432-4480, e-mail sharman@mlc.lib.ms.us. World Wide Web http://www.mlc.lib.ms.us.

Missouri

Margaret Conroy, State Libn., P.O. Box 387, Jefferson City 65102-0387. Tel. 573-526-4783, fax 573-751-3612, e-mail margaret.conroy@sos.mo.gov. World Wide Web http://www.sos.mo.gov/library.

Montana

Darlene Staffeldt, State Libn., Montana State Lib., 1515 E. 6 Ave., P.O. Box 201800, Helena 59620. Tel. 406-444-3115, fax 406-444-0266, e-mail dstaffeldt@mt.us. World Wide Web http://msl.mt.us.

Nebraska

Rod Wagner, Dir., Nebraska Lib. Commission, Suite 120, 1200 N St., Lincoln 68508. Tel. 402-471-4001, fax 402-471-2083, e-mail rod.wagner@nebraska.gov. World Wide Web http://www.nlc.state.ne.us.

Nevada

Daphne DeLeon, Admin., Nevada State Lib. and Archives, 100 N. Stewart St., Carson City 89701. Tel. 775-684-3317, fax 775-684-3311, e-mail ddeleon@nevadaculture.org. World Wide Web http://www.nevadaculture.org/docs/nsla.

New Hampshire

Michael York, State Libn., New Hampshire State Lib., 20 Park St., Concord 03301. Tel. 603-271-2397, fax 603-271-6826, e-mail michael.york@dcr.nh.gov. World Wide Web http://www.nh.gov/nhsl.

New Jersey

Norma Blake, State Libn., New Jersey State Lib., 185 W. State St., P.O. Box 520, Trenton 08625. Tel. 609-278-2640, fax 609-278-2652, e-mail nblake@njstatelib.org. World Wide Web http://www.njstatelib.org.

New Mexico

Susan Oberlander, State Libn., New Mexico State Lib., 1209 Camino Carlos Rey, Santa Fe 87507. Tel. 505-476-9762, fax 505-476-9761, e-mail susan.oberlander@state.nm.us. World Wide Web http://www.nmstatelibrary.org.

New York

Bernard Margolis, State Libn., Asst. Commissioner for Libs., New York State Lib., 310 Madison Ave., Albany 12230. Tel. 518-474-5930, fax 518-486-6880, e-mail bmargolis@mail.nysed.gov. World Wide Web http://www.nysl.nysed.gov.

North Carolina

Mary Boone, State Libn., State Lib. of North Carolina, 4640 Mail Service Center, Raleigh 27699. Tel. 919-807-7410, fax 919-733-8748, e-mail mary.boone@ncmail.net. World Wide Web http://statelibrary.dcr.state.nc.us.

North Dakota

Doris Ott, State Libn., North Dakota State Lib., 604 E. Boulevard Ave., Bismarck 58505. Tel. 701-328-2492, fax 701-328-2040, e-mail dott@nd.gov. World Wide Web http://www.library.nd.gov.

Ohio

Jo Budler, State Libn., State Lib. of Ohio, 274 E. 1 Ave., Columbus 43201. Tel. 614-644-6843, fax 614-466-3584, e-mail jbudler@sloma.state.ohio.us. World Wide Web http://www.library.ohio.gov.

Oklahoma

Susan McVey, Dir., Oklahoma Dept. of Libs., 200 N.E. 18 St., Oklahoma City 73105.

Tel. 405-521-2502, fax 405-521-1077, e-mail smcvey@oltn.odl.state.ok.us. World Wide Web http://www.odl.state.ok.us.

Oregon

James B. Scheppke, State Libn., Oregon State Lib., 250 Winter St. N.E., Salem 97301. Tel. 503-378-4367, fax 503-585-8059, e-mail jim.b.scheppke@state.or.us. World Wide Web http://oregon.gov/OSL.

Pennsylvania

Mary Clare Zales, State Libn., Office of Commonwealth Libs., 333 Market St., Harrisburg 17126. Tel. 717-787-2646, fax 717-772-3265, e-mail mzales@state.pa.us. World Wide Web http://www.statelibrary.state.pa.us.

Rhode Island

Howard Boksenbaum, Chief Lib. Officer, Rhode Island Office of Lib. and Info. Services, 1 Capitol Hill, Providence 02908-5803. Tel. 401-574-9301, fax 401-574-9320, e-mail howardbm@olis.ri.gov. World Wide Web http://www.olis.ri.gov.

South Carolina

David S. Goble, Dir. and State Libn., South Carolina State Lib., P.O. Box 11469, Columbia 29211. Tel. 803-734-8656, fax 803-734-8676, e-mail dgoble@statelibrary.sc.gov. World Wide Web http://www.statelibrary.sc.gov.

South Dakota

Dan Siebersma, State Libn., South Dakota State Lib., 800 Governors Drive, Pierre 57501. Tel. 605-773-3131, fax 605-773-6962, e-mail dan.siebersma@state.sd.us. World Wide Web http://www.sdstatelibrary.com.

Tennessee

Jeanne D. Sugg, State Libn. and Archivist, Tennessee State Lib. and Archives, 403 Seventh Ave. N., Nashville 37243. Tel. 615-741-7996, fax 615-532-9293, e-mail jeanne.sugg@tn.gov. World Wide Web http://www.Tennessee.gov/tsla.

Texas

Peggy Rudd, Dir./Libn., Texas State Lib. and Archives Commission, P.O. Box 12927, Austin 78711. Tel. 512-463-5460, fax 512-463-5436, e-mail prudd@tsl.state.tx.us. World Wide Web http://www.tsl.state.tx.us.

Utah

Donna Morris, State Libn./Dir., Utah State Lib. Div., Suite A, 250 N. 1950 W., Salt Lake City 84116. Tel. 801-715-6770, fax 801-715-6767, e-mail dmorris@utah.gov. World Wide Web http://library.utah.gov.

Vermont

Martha Reid, State Libn., Vermont Dept. of Libs., 109 State St., Montpelier 05609. Tel. 802-828-3265, fax 802-828-2199, e-mail martha.reid@mail.dol.state.vt.us. World Wide Web http://www.libraries.vermont.gov.

Virginia

Sandra Treadway, Libn. of Virginia, Lib. of Virginia, 800 E. Broad St., Richmond 23219. Tel. 804-692-3535, fax 804-692-3594, e-mail sandra.treadway@lva.virginia.gov. World Wide Web http://www.lva.virginia.gov.

Washington

Jan Walsh, State Libn., Washington State Lib., P.O. Box 42460, Tumwater 98504. Tel. 360-704-5253, fax 360-586-7575, e-mail jan.walsh@sos.wa.gov. World Wide Web http://www.secstate.wa.gov/library.

West Virginia

James D. Waggoner, Secy., West Virginia Lib. Commission, Cultural Center, 1900 Kanawha Blvd. E., Charleston 25305. Tel. 304-558-2041, fax 304-558-2044, e-mail jd.waggoner@wv.gov. World Wide Web http://librarycommission.lib.wv.us.

Wisconsin

Richard Grobschmidt, State Libn., Asst. Superintendent/Admin., P.O. Box 7841, Madison 53707. Tel. 608-266-2205, fax 608-267-1052, e-mail richard.grobschmidt@dpi. state.wi.gov. World Wide Web http://dpi.wi. gov/dltcl/index.html.

Wyoming

Lesley Boughton, State Libn., State of Wyoming, 2800 Central Ave., Cheyenne 82002. Tel. 307-777-5911, fax 307-777-6289, e-mail lbough@state.wy.us. World Wide Web http://will.state.wy.us.

American Samoa

Cheryl Polataivao, Territorial Libn., Government of American Samoa, Feleti Barstow Public Lib., P.O. Box 997687, Pago Pago, AS 96799. Tel./fax 684-633-5816, e-mail feletibarstow@yahoo.com. World Wide Web http://fbpl.org.

Federated States of Micronesia

Rufino Mauricio, Secy., National Archives, Culture, and Historic Preservation, P.O. Box PS 175, Palikir, Pohnpei, FM 96941. Tel. 691-320-2643, fax 691-320-5634, e-mail hpo@mail.fm. World Wide Web http://www. fsmgov.org.

Guam

Sandra Standley, Admin. Officer, Guam Public Lib. System, 254 Martyr St., Hagatna 96910. Tel. 671-475-4754, fax 671-477-0888, e-mail sandra.standley@gpls.guam. gov. World Wide Web http://gpls.guam.gov.

Northern Mariana Islands

Jennifer D. Rospel, Acting Dir., CNMI Joeten-Kiyu Public Lib., P.O. Box 501092, Saipan, MP 96950-1092. Tel. 670-235-7322, fax 670-235-7550, e-mail jspl.admin@gmai. com. World Wide Web http://www.cnmi library.com.

Palau

Mario Katosang, Minister of Educ., Republic of Palau, P.O. Box 189, Koror, PW 96940. Tel. 680-488-2973, fax 680-488-1465, e-mail mariok@palaumoe.net. World Wide Web http://www.palaugov.net/PalauGov/Executive/ Ministries/MOE/MOE.htm.

Puerto Rico

Sandra Castro, Dir., Lib. Services and Info. Services Program, Puerto Rico Dept. of Educ., P.O. Box 190759, San Juan, PR 00919-0759. Tel. 787-773-3564, fax 787-753-3570, e-mail castroas@de.gobierno.pr. World Wide Web http://de.gobierno.pr/dePortal/Escuelas/Bibli otecas/Bibliotecarios.aspx.

Republic of the Marshall Islands

Wilbur Heine, Secy. of Internal Affairs, Alele Museum and Public Lib., P.O. Box 629, Majuro, MH 96960. Tel. 692-625-8240, fax 692-625-3226, e-mail wilburheine@ yahoo.com. World Wide Web http://rmi government.org/index.jsp.

Virgin Islands

Ingrid A. Bough, Territorial Dir., Virgin Islands Div. of Libs., Archives, and Museums, 1122 Kings St., Christiansted, St. Croix VI 00802. Tel. 340-773-5715, fax 340-773-5327, e-mail ingrid.bough@dpnr.gov.vi. World Wide Web http://www.virginisland space.org/Division%20of%20Libraries/dlam what'snew.htm.

Canada

Alberta

Punch Jackson, Exec. Dir., Public Lib. Services Branch, Alberta Municipal Affairs, 803 Standard Life Centre, 10405 Jasper Ave., Edmonton T5J 4R7. Tel. 780-427-4871, fax 780-415-8594, e-mail libraries@gov.ab.ca. World Wide Web http://www.municipal affairs.alberta.ca/mc_libraries.cfm.

British Columbia

Jacqueline van Dyk, Dir., Public Lib. Services Branch, Ministry of Educ., P.O. Box

9831 Sta. Provincial Government, Victoria BC V8W 9T1. Tel. 250-356-1791, fax 250-953-3225, e-mail Jacqueline.vandyk@gov.bc.ca. World Wide Web http://www.bced.gov.bc.ca/pls.

Manitoba

Trevor Surgenor, Dir., Public Lib. Services, Manitoba Dept. of Culture, Heritage, and Tourism, 301-1011 Rosser Ave., Brandon R7A OL5. Tel. 204-726-6590, e-mail pls@gov.mb.ca. World Wide Web http://www.gov.mb.ca/chc/pls/index.html.

New Brunswick

Sylvie Nadeau, Exec. Dir., New Brunswick Public Lib. Service, Place 2000, 250 King St., P.O. Box 6000, Fredericton E3B 5H1. Tel. 506-453-2354, fax 506-444-4064, e-mail sylvie.nadeau@gnb.ca. World Wide Web http://www.gnb.ca/0003/index-e.asp.

Newfoundland and Labrador

Shawn Tetford, Exec. Dir., Provincial Info. and Lib. Resources Board, 48 St. George's Ave., Stephenville A2N 1K9. Tel. 709-643-0902, fax 709-643-0925, e-mail stetford@nlpl.ca. World Wide Web http://www.nlpl.ca.

Northwest Territories

Alison Hopkins, Territorial Libn., NWT Lib. Services, 75 Woodland Drive, Hay River X0E 1G1. Tel. 867-874-6531, fax 867-874-3321, e-mail alison_hopkins@gov.nt.ca. World Wide Web http://www.nwtpls.gov.nt.ca.

Nova Scotia

Jennifer Evans, Dir., Nova Scotia Provincial Lib., 2021 Brunswick St., P.O. Box 578, Halifax B3J 2S9. Tel. 902-424-2457, fax 902-424-0633, e-mail evansjl@gov.ns.ca. World Wide Web http://www.library.ns.ca.

Nunavut

Ron Knowling, Mgr., Nunavut Public Lib. Services, Box 270, Baker Lake X0C 0A0. Tel. 867-793-3358, fax 867-793-3360, e-mail rknowling@gov.nu.ca. World Wide Web http://www.publiclibraries.nu.ca.

Ontario

Aileen Carroll, Minister, Ontario Government Ministry of Culture, 900 Bay St., 5th fl., Mowat, Toronto M7A 1L2. Tel. 416-212-0644. World Wide Web http://www.culture.gov.on.ca/english/library/index.html. Ontario Lib. Service–North, 334 Regent St., Sudbury, ON P3C 4E2. Tel. 705-675-6467. World Wide Web http://www.olsn.ca. Southern Ontario Lib. Service, 111 Peter St., Suite 902, Toronto M5V 2H1. Tel. 416-961-1669 ext. 5118. World Wide Web http://www.sols.org.

Prince Edward Island

Harry Holman, Dir., Culture, Heritage and Libs., Province of Prince Edward Island, 16 Fitzroy St., Charlottetown, PE C1A 7N8. Tel. 902-368-4784, fax 902-368-4663, e-mail htholman@gov.pe.ca. World Wide Web http://www.gov.pe.ca/cca.

Quebec

Guy Berthiaume, Chair and CEO; Hélène Roussel, Dir. Gen. of Distribution, Bibliothèque et Archives Nationales du Québec (BAnQ), 475 Blvd. de Maisonneuve Est, Montreal H2L 5C4. Tel. 514-873-1100, fax 514-873-9312, e-mail pdg@banq.qc.ca or info@banq.qc.ca. World Wide Web http://www.banq.qc.ca/portal/dt/accueil.jsp.

Saskatchewan

Joylene Campbell, Provincial Libn., Saskatchewan Learning, 1945 Hamilton St., Regina S4P 2C8. Tel. 306-787-2972, fax 306-787-2029, e-mail jcampbell@library.gov.sk.ca. World Wide Web http://www.education.gov.sk.ca/Provincial-Library.

Yukon Territory

Julie Ourom, Dir., Public Libs., Community Development Div., Dept. of Community Services, Box 2703, Whitehorse Y1A 2C6. Tel. 867-667-5447, fax 867-393-6333, e-mail julie.ourom@gov.yk.ca. World Wide Web http://www.ypl.gov.yk.ca/index.html.

State School Library Media Associations

Alabama

Children's and School Libns. Div., Alabama Lib. Assn. Memb. 650. Publication. *The Alabama Librarian* (q.).

Chair Dorothy Hunt, Montgomery Public Schools, 1207 Charnwood Drive, Montgomery 36109. Tel. 334-272-9961, e-mail dorothy.hunt@mps.k12.al.us; *V. Chair/ Chair-Elect* Jana Fine, Tuscaloosa Public Lib., 1801 Jack Warner Pkwy., Tuscaloosa 35401. Tel. 205-391-9025, e-mail jfine@tuscaloosa-library.org; *Secy.* Cassie Johnson, Cullman County Public Lib., 910 Third Ave. S.E., Cullman 35055. Tel. 256-734-2720, e-mail johnsonc@ccpls.com; *Past Chair* Barbara Curry, Autauga-Prattville Public Lib., 254 Doster St., Prattville 36067. E-mail bcurry@appl.info.

Address correspondence to the association administrator, Alabama Lib. Assn., 9154 Eastchase Pkwy., Suite 418, Montgomery 36117. Tel. 334-414-0113, e-mail administrator@allanet.org.

World Wide Web http://allanet.org.

Alaska

Alaska Assn. of School Libns. Memb. 130. Publication. *The Puffin* (3 a year), online at http://www.akla.org/akasl/puffin/puffinhome.html. *Ed.* Piper Coulter, Ocean View Elementary. E-mail coulter_piper@asdk12.org.

Pres. Suzanne Metcalfe, Dimond H.S., Anchorage. E-mail metcalfe_suzanne@asdk12.org; *Pres.-Elect* Ann Morgester, Anchorage. E-mail morgester_ann@asdk12.org; *Secy.* Kari Sagel, Blatchley Middle School, Sitka. E-mail sagelk@mail.ssd.k12.ak.us; *Treas.* Janet Madsen, West Valley H.S., Fairbanks. E-mail jmadsen@northstar.k12.ak.us; *Past Pres.* Erika Drain, Mount Edgecomb H.S., Sitka. E-mail erikad@mehs.us.

World Wide Web http://www.akla.org/akasl.

Arizona

Teacher-Libn. Div., Arizona Lib. Assn. Memb. 1,000. Publication. *AZLA Newsletter.*

Chair Sally Roof, Madison Meadows Middle School, 225 W. Ocotillo Rd. Phoenix 85013. Tel. 602-664-7640, e-mail sroofhoff@cox.net; *Co-Chairs-Elect* Jean Kilker, 160 E. Estero Lane, Litchfield Park 85340. Tel. 602-764-2134 or 623-935-1464, e-mail jkilker@phxhs.k12.az.us or jean.kilker@gmail.com; Kerrlita Westrick, Verrado Middle School, 553 Plaza Circle, Litchfield Park 85340. Tel. 623-547-1324 or 623-935-1911, e-mail kerrlita@cox.net or westrick@lesd.k12.az.us; *Past Chair* Linda Renfro, Blue Ridge Unified School Dist. Tel. 928-368-6119, e-mail lrenfro@brusd.k12.az.us.

Address correspondence to the chairperson.

World Wide Web http://www.azla.affiniscape.com.

Arkansas

Arkansas Assn. of Instructional Media. Term of Office. Apr. 2009–Apr. 2010.

Pres. Diane Hughes. E-mail dianeallen hughes@gmail.com; *Pres.-Elect* Jana Dixon; *Secy.* Beth Stone. E-mail gjenkins@indian.dsc.k12.ar.us; *Treas.* Devona Pendergrass. E-mail dpendergrass@mtnhome.k12.ar.us; *Past Pres.* Lori Bush. E-mail lori.bush@lh.k12.ar.us.

Address correspondence to the president.

World Wide Web http://aaim.k12.ar.us.

California

California School Lib. Assn. Memb. 2,000. Publications. *CSLA Journal* (2 a year); *CSLA Bulletin* (9 a year).

Pres. Rosemarie Bernier, Alexander Hamilton Senior H.S., 2955 Robertson Blvd., Los Angeles 90034. Tel. 310-280-1430, e-mail rbernier@lausd.net; *Pres.-Elect* Diane Alexander, Heritage H.S., 540 Discovery Bay Blvd., Discovery Bay 94505. Tel. 925-634-

0037 ext. 6071, e-mail dapa@comcast.net; *Secy.* Nina Jackson, Franklin Classical Middle School, 540 Cerritos Ave., Long Beach 90802. E-mail catsandbooks999@hotmail.com; *Treas.* Sandra Patton, Lakewood H.S., 3461 Lilly Ave., Long Beach 90808-3214. Tel. 562-997-8000 ext. 3129, e-mail sgpatton@lbschools.net; *Past Pres.* Connie Hamner Williams, Petaluma H.S., 201 Fair St., Petaluma 94952. Tel. 707-778-4662, e-mail chwms@mac.com; *Exec. Dir.* Deidre Bryant, California School Lib. Assn., 950 Glenn Drive, Suite 150, Folsom 95630. Tel. 916-447-2684, fax 916-447-2695, e-mail diedreb@csla.net.

Address correspondence to the executive director.

World Wide Web http://www.csla.net.

Colorado

Colorado Assn. of School Libns. Memb. 300+. Term of Office. Nov. 2008–Oct. 2010.

Co-Pres. Nancy White, Academy School Dist. 20. E-mail nwhite@asd20.org; Diane Caro, Boulder Valley School Dist. E-mail diane.caro@bvsd.org; *Pres.-Elect* Yvonne Miller, Douglas County Schools. E-mail yvonne.miller@dcsdk12.org; *Secy.* Molly Gibney, Mount View Elementary. E-mail mgibney@comcast.net; *Past Pres.* Susan Gilbert, Clear Lake Middle School. Tel. 720-542-4606, e-mail gilbert.susan@comcast.net; *Exec. Dir.* Kathleen Noland, Colorado Assn. of School Libns., 3030 W. 81 Ave., Westminster 80031. Tel. 303-433-4446, fax 303-458-0002, e-mail kathleen@cal-webs.org or executivedirector@cal-webs.org.

World Wide Web http://www.cal-webs.org/associations2.html.

Connecticut

Connecticut Assn. of School Libns. (formerly Connecticut Educ. Media Assn.). Memb. 1,000+. Term of Office. July 2009–June 2010. Publication. *CASLGram* (9 a year).

Pres. Lucia Rafala. E-mail lucia.rafala@new-haven.k12.ct.us; *V.P.* Mary Lou Cassotto. E-mail mlcassotto@aol.com; *Recording Secy.* Christopher Barlow. E-mail christoph

barlow@sbcglobal.net; *Treas.* Martha Djang. E-mail mdjang@hamdenhall.org; *Admin. Secy.* Anne Weimann, 25 Elmwood Ave., Trumbull 06611. Tel. 203-372-2260, e-mail anneweimann@gmail.com.

Address correspondence to the administrative secretary.

World Wide Web http://www.ctcasl.com.

Delaware

Delaware School Lib. Media Assn., Div. of Delaware Lib. Assn. Memb. 100+. Publications. *DSLMA Newsletter* (online; irreg.); column in *DLA Bulletin* (3 a year).

Pres. Sharon Lyons, Central Middle School, 211 Delaware Ave., Dover 19901. E-mail slyons@capital.k12.de.us.

Address correspondence to the president.

World Wide Web http://www.udel.edu/erc/dslma.

District of Columbia

District of Columbia Assn. of School Libns. Memb. 8. Publication. *Newsletter* (4 a year).

Pres. André Maria Taylor. E-mail divalibrarian2@aol.com; *V.P.* Vacant.

Address correspondence to André Maria Taylor, 330 10th St. N.E., Washington, DC 20002. Tel. 301-502-4203.

Florida

Florida Assn. for Media in Educ. Memb. 1,400+. Term of Office. Nov. 2009–Oct. 2010. Publication. *Florida Media Quarterly.* Ed. Rhoda Cribbs. E-mail rcribbs@pasco.k12.fl.us.

Pres. Cecelia Solomon. E-mail buckysmom@tampabay.rr.com; *Pres.-Elect* Pat Dedicos. E-mail dedicosp@duvalschools.org; *Secy.* Debbie Rothfield. E-mail coollibrarianchick@gmail.com; *Treas.* Joanne Seale. E-mail seale.joanne@brevardschools.org; *Past Pres.* Deb Svec. E-mail dsvec@bellsouth.net; *Exec. Dir.* Larry E. Bodkin, Jr. Tel. 850-531-8351, fax 850-531-8344, e-mail lbodkin@floridamedia.org.

Address correspondence to FAME, 2563 Capital Medical Blvd., Tallahassee 32308.

Tel. 850-531-8351, fax 850-531-8344, e-mail info@floridamedia.org.
World Wide Web http://www.florida media.org.

Georgia

Georgia Lib. Assn., School Lib. Media Div.
Chair Tim Wojcik, Our Lady of Mercy Catholic H.S. Tel. 770-461-2202, e-mail wojcikt@bellsouth.net; *Chair-Elect* Judi Repman, Georgia Southern Univ. Tel. 912-681-5394, e-mail jrepman@georgiasouthern.edu.
Address correspondence to Georgia Lib. Assn., School Lib. Media Div., P.O. Box 793, Rex, GA 30273.
World Wide Web http://gla.georgia libraries.org/div_media.htm.

Georgia Lib. Media Assn. Memb. 700+.
Term of Office. Jan.–Dec. 2010.
Pres. Valerie Ayer. E-mail valerie_ayer@dekalb.k12.ga.us; *Pres.-Elect* Betsy Razza. E-mail betsy_razza@dekalb.k12.ga.us; *Secy.* Ann Schaub. E-mail schaub@fulton.k12.ga.us; *Treas.* Nan Brown. E-mail brownnt@fulton.k12.ga.us; *Past Pres.* Susan Grigsby. E-mail susan.grigsby@gmail.com.
World Wide Web http://www.glma-inc.org.

Hawaii

Hawaii Assn. of School Libns. Memb. 145.
Term of Office. June 2009–May 2010. Publication. *HASL Newsletter* (3 a year).
Co-Pres. Grace Fujiyoshi. E-mail gracef@hawaii.rr.com; Linda Kim, Mililaniwaena Elementary. E-mail tklinda@hawaii.rr.com; *V.P., Programming* Nancy Shim. E-mail mauitutushim@gmail.com; *V.P., Membership* Helen Shima. E-mail hmicshima@hawaii.rr.com; *Corresponding Secy.* Vicki Kwiatkowski. E-mail vvitallo@yahoo.com; *Recording Secy.* Sandra Kugisaki-Ongie. E-mail stamp@hawaii.rr.com; *Treas.* Jo-An Goss. E-mail gossj002@hawaii.rr.com; *Past Pres.* Linda Marks, Kalihi Uka Elementary. E-mail flcadiz@aol.com.
Address correspondence to the association, P.O. Box 235284, Honolulu 96823.
World Wide Web http://hasl.ws.

Idaho

Educational Media Div., Idaho Lib. Assn.
Memb. 44. Term of Office. Oct. 2009–Oct. 2010.
Chair Susan Nickel, Capital H.S., 8055 Goddard Rd., Boise 83704. Tel. 208-854-4490 ext. 199, e-mail susan.nickel@boise schools.org; *V. Chair/Chair-Elect* Ken Cox, Meridian H.S., 1900 W. Pine Ave., Meridian 83642. Tel. 208-350-4175, e-mail cox.ken@meridianschools.org.
Address correspondence to the chairperson.
World Wide Web http://www.idaho libraries.org.

Illinois

Illinois School Lib. Media Assn. Memb. 1,200. Term of Office. July 2009–June 2010. Publications. *ISLMA News* (4 a year); *Linking for Learning: The Illinois School Library Media Program Guidelines* (new ed. 2010); *Powerful Libraries Make Powerful Learners: The Illinois Study.*
Pres. Gail Janz, Morris Community H.S., 1000 Union St., Morris 60450-1297. Tel. 815-941-5328, fax 815-941-5409, e-mail gjanz@mchs.grundy.k12.il.us; *Pres.-Elect* Jeremy Dunn, Dept. of Libs. and Info. Services, Medill Technical and Professional Development Center, 1326 W. 14 Place, Chicago 60608. Tel. 773-553-6215, fax 773-553-6211, e-mail jdunn4@cps.k12.il.us; *Past Pres.* Randee Hudson, Millburn School, 18550 W. Millburn Rd., Wadsworth 60083. Tel. 847-356-8331, fax 847-356-9722, e-mail rhudson@millburn24.net; *Exec. Secy.* Kay Maynard, ISLMA, P.O. Box 598, Canton 61520. Tel. 390-649-0911, fax 309-649-0916, e-mail islma@islma.org.
World Wide Web http://www.islma.org.

Indiana

Assn. for Indiana Media Educators. Publications. *Focus on Indiana Libraries* (mo.); *Indiana Libraries* (q.).
Pres. Vicki Builta, Anderson H.S., 4610 S. Madison Ave., Anderson 46013. Tel. 765-641-2037 ext. 1057, fax 765-641-2041, e-mail vbuilta@yahoo.com; *Pres.-Elect* Lael

Dubois, Plainfield H.S., 709 Stafford Rd., Plainfield 46168. Tel. 317-839-7711 ext. 1212, fax 317-838-3682, e-mail ldubois@plainfield.k12.in.us; *Secy.* Susie Highley, Creston Middle School, 10925 E. Prospect, Indianapolis 46239. Tel. 812-532-6806, fax 812-532-6891, e-mail shighley@warren.k12.in.us; *Treas.* Kristen Borrelli, Yost Elementary, 100 W. Beam St., Chesterton 46304. Tel. 219-983-3640, e-mail kristen.borrelli@duneland.k12.in.us; *Past Pres.* Jill Youngblood, Adelaide DeVaney Elementary, Terre Haute 47803. Tel. 812-462-4497, fax 812-462-4317, e-mail jey@vigoschools.org.

Address correspondence to the association, c/o Indiana Lib. Federation, 941 E. 86 St., Suite 260, Indianapolis 46240. Tel. 317-257-2040, fax 317-257-1389, e-mail ilf@indy.net.

World Wide Web http://www.ilfonline.org/AIME.

Iowa

Iowa Assn. of School Libns., subdivision of the Iowa Lib. Assn. Memb. 180+. Term of Office. Jan.–Jan. Publication. *IASL Journal* (online, 4 a year). *Co-Eds.* Karla Krueger. E-mail karla.krueger@uni.edu; Becky Johnson. E-mail bcjohnson@cr.k12.ia.us.

Pres. Karen Lampe. E-mail klampe@aea14.k12.ia.us; *V.P.* Erin Feingold. E-mail feingolde@se-polk.k12.ia.us; *Secy./Treas.* Diane Brown. E-mail ddbrown@muscatine.k12.ia.us; *Past Pres.* Cheryl Carruthers. E-mail ccarruthersa@aea267.k12.ia.us.

Address correspondence to the president.

World Wide Web http://www.iasl-ia.org.

Kansas

Kansas Assn. of School Libns. Memb. 600. Term of Office. Aug. 2009–July 2010. Publication. *KASL News* (online; q.).

Pres. Cindy Pfeiffer. Tel. 620-235-3240, e-mail cpfeiffer@usd250.org; *Pres.-Elect* Barb Bahm. Tel. 913-845-2627, e-mail bbahm@ton464.org; *Secy.* Kaylyn Keating. E-mail kaylynk@manhattan.k12.ks.us; *Treas.* Kim Nowak. Tel. 785-735-2870, e-mail knowak@ruraltel.net; *Past Pres.* Laura Soash. Tel. 316-794-4260, e-mail lnsoash@yahoo.com; *Exec. Secy.* Judith Eller, 8517 W.

Northridge, Wichita 67205. Tel. 316-773-6723, e-mail judell8517@sbcglobal.net.

Address correspondence to the executive secretary.

World Wide Web http://kasl.typepad.com/kasl.

Kentucky

Kentucky School Media Assn. (section of the Kentucky Lib. Assn.). Memb. 600+. Term of Office. Oct. 2009–Oct. 2010. Publication. *KSMA Newsletter* (q.).

Pres. Melissa Gardner. E-mail melissa.gardner@uky.edu; *Pres.-Elect* Jennifer Wetzel, Lone Oak Elementary. E-mail jennifer.wetzel@mccracken.kyschools.us; *Past Pres.* Fred Tilsley, Sandgap Elementary. E-mail fred.tilsley@jackson.kyschools.us.

Address correspondence to the president.

World Wide Web http://www.kysma.org.

Louisiana

Louisiana Assn. of School Libns. Memb. 230. Term of Office. July 2009–June 2010.

Pres. Annie Miers. Tel. 318-387-0567, e-mail miers@opsb.net; *1st V.P.* Elizabeth Dumas. Tel. 318-396-9693, e-mail dumas@opsb.net; *2nd V.P.* Paula Clemmons. Tel. 337-433-5246, e-mail pclemmons@episcopaldayschool.org; *Secy.* Janet Lathrop. Tel. 225-635-3898, e-mail lathropj@wfpsb.org.

Address correspondence to the association, c/o Louisiana Lib. Assn., 8550 United Plaza Blvd., Suite 1001, Baton Rouge 70809. Tel. 225-922-4642, fax 225-408-4422, e-mail office@llaonline.org.

World Wide Web http://www.llaonline.org/sig/lasl.

Maine

Maine School Lib. Assn. Memb. 230+.

Pres. Peggy Becksvoort, Falmouth Middle School. E-mail pbecksvoort@fps.k12.me.us; *V.P.* Eileen Broderick. E-mail ebroderick@rus10.org; *Secy.* Joyce Lucas, Winslow H.S. E-mail jlucas@winslowk12.org; *Treas.* Donna Chale, Warsaw Middle School. E-mail dchale@msad43.org; *Past Pres.* Jeff Small, Cony H.S., Augusta. E-mail jsmall@

augustaschools.org; *Exec. Secy.* Edna Comstock. E-mail masl@gwi.net.

Address correspondence to the president.

World Wide Web http://www.maslibraries.org.

Maryland

Maryland Assn. of School Libns. (formerly Maryland Educ. Media Organization). Term of Office. July 2009–June 2011.

Pres. Michele Forney, High Bridge Elementary, Prince Georges County Public Schools. E-mail michele.forney@pgcps.org; *Pres.-Elect* To be announced; *Secy.* Lori M. Carter, Howard County Public Schools. E-mail lori_carter@hcpss.org; *Treas.* Jennifer Harner, Rising Sun Elementary, Cecil County Public Schools. E-mail jharner@ccps.org; *Past Pres.* Elizabeth Napier, North Carroll H.S. E-mail eanapie@k12.carr.org.

Address correspondence to the association, Box 21127, Baltimore 21228.

World Wide Web http://maslmd.org.

Massachusetts

Massachusetts School Lib. Assn. Memb. 800. Term of Office. June 2009–May 2011. Publication. *MSLA Forum* (3 a year, one in print, two online).

Pres. Gerri Fegan, High Plain Elementary School, Andover. Tel. 978-623-8914, e-mail feganpkt@comcast.net; *Secy.* Judi Paradis, Plympton Elementary School, Waltham. Tel. 781-314-5767, e-mail judiparadis@gmail.com; *Treas.* Linda Friel. E-mail lafriel@comcast.net; *Past Pres.* Sandy Kelly, Carlisle School, Carlisle. Tel. 978-369-6550 ext. 3140, e-mail ms.sandyk@gmail.com; *Exec. Dir.* Kathy Lowe, Massachusetts School Lib. Assn., P.O. Box 658, Lunenburg 01462. Tel. 978-582-6967, e-mail klowe@maschoolibraries.org.

Address correspondence to the executive director.

World Wide Web http://www.ma schoolibraries.org.

Michigan

Michigan Assn. for Media in Educ. Memb. 1,200. Publications. *Media Spectrum* (2 a year); *MAME Newsletter* (4 a year).

Pres. Lynn Gordon, Clarkston Community Schools, 6850 Hubbard Rd., Clarkston 48348. Tel. 248-623-5513, fax 248-623-5554, e-mail gordonlm@clarkston.k12.mi.us; *Pres.-Elect* Rachel Markel, Bangor Public Schools, 309 S. Walnut St., Bangor 49013. Tel. 269-427-6800 ext. 3028, fax 269-427-6893, e-mail rmarkel@bangorvikings.org; *Secy.* Betty Mundy, St. Joseph Public Schools, 2831 W. Garden Lane, St. Joseph 49085. Tel. 269-926-3525, fax 269-926-3503, e-mail bmundy@sjschools.org; *Treas.* Bruce Popejoy, East Jackson Community Schools, 4340 Walz Rd., Jackson 49201. Tel. 517-764-6010, fax 517-764-6081, e-mail mameexhibits@aol.com; *Past Pres.* Kathleen McBroom, Dearborn Public Schools, 18700 Audette, Dearborn 48124. Tel. 313-827-3078, fax 313-827-3132, e-mail mcbroom@dearborn.k12.mi.us; *Exec. Dir.* Tim Staal, MAME, 1407 Rensen, Suite 3, Lansing 48910. Tel. 517-394-2808, fax 517-394-2096, e-mail tstaal@gmail.com.

Address correspondence to the executive director.

World Wide Web http://www.mame.gen.mi.us.

Minnesota

Minnesota Educ. Media Organization. Memb. 700. Term of Office. July 2009–July 2010. Publications. *MEMOrandom*; *MTNews*.

Pres. Dawn Nelson, Osseo Area Schools, Maple Grove 55369. Tel. 763-391-7163, e-mail nelsond@district279.org; *Pres.-Elect* Tori Jensen, Spring Lake Park H.S., Spring Lake Park 55432. Tel. 763-786-5571, e-mail tjense@district16.org; *Secy.* Mary Mehsikomer, Region 1/NW-LINKS, P.O. Box 1178, 810 4th Ave. S., Suite 220, Moorhead 56561. Tel. 218-284-3117, e-mail mary@region1.k12.mn.us; *Treas.* Gina Light, Eagle Creek Elementary, Shakopee 55379. Tel. 952-368-7253, e-mail gmlight@chaska.net; *Past Pres.* Leslie Yoder, St. Paul Public Schools, St. Paul 55108. Tel. 651-603-4923, e-mail leslie.yoder@spps.org; *Admin. Asst.* Deanna Sylte, P.O. Box 130555, Roseville 55113. Tel. 651-771-8672, e-mail admin@memoweb.org.

World Wide Web http://memoweb.org.

Mississippi

School Section, Mississippi Lib. Assn. Memb. 1,300.

Chair Melissa Moak, Mississippi School of the Arts. Tel. 601-823-1340, e-mail Melissa. moak@msa.k12.ms.us; *Exec. Secy.* Mary Julia Anderson.

Address correspondence to School Section, Mississippi Lib. Assn., P.O. Box 13687, Jackson 39236-3687. Tel. 601-981-4586, fax 601-981-4501, e-mail info@misslib.org.

World Wide Web http://www.misslib.org.

Missouri

Missouri Assn. of School Libns. Memb. 1,000. Term of Office. June 2009–June 2010. Publication. *Connections* (q.).

Pres. Maggie Newbold. E-mail mnewbold @fz.k12.mo.us; *1st V.P./Pres.-Elect* Patricia Antrim. E-mail antrim@ucmo.edu; *2nd V.P.* Curtis Clark. E-mail msmediacenter@ harrisonville.k12.mo.us; *Secy.* Michelle Schmitt. E-mail mschmitt@ladue.k12.mo.us; *Treas.* Georganna Krumlinde. E-mail krumling@troy.k12.mo.us; *Past Pres.* Gayla Strack. E-mail gayla.strack@raytownschools. org.

Address correspondence to the association, P.O. Box 2107, Jefferson City 65102. Tel. 573-893-4155, fax 573-635-2858, e-mail info @maslonline.org.

World Wide Web http://www.maslonline. org.

Montana

Montana School Lib. Media Div., Montana Lib. Assn. Memb. 200+. Publication. *FOCUS* (published by Montana Lib. Assn.) (q.).

Chair Julie Hainline, Missoula County Public Schools. Tel. 406-728-2400 ext.1062, e-mail jhainline@mcps.k12.mt.us; *Exec. Asst., Montana Lib. Assn.* Debra Kramer, P.O. Box 1352, Three Forks 59752. Tel. 406-285-3090, fax 406-285-3091, e-mail debkmla @hotmail.com.

World Wide Web http://www.mtlib.org.

Nebraska

Nebraska Educ. Media Assn. Memb. 370. Term of Office. July 2009–June 2010. Publication. *NEMA News* (q.).

Pres. Carrie Turner. E-mail carrieturner@ westside66.org; *Pres.-Elect* Betty Meyer; *Secy.* Sara Churchill; *Treas.* Lynne Wragge; *Past Pres.* Robin Schrack; *Exec. Secy.* Jean Hellman. E-mail nemacontact@gmail.com.

Address correspondence to the executive secretary.

World Wide Web http://www.school librariesrock.org.

Nevada

Nevada School and Children's Libs. Section, Nevada Lib. Assn. Memb. 120.

Chair Jennifer Jost, Las Vegas-Clark County Lib. Dist. E-mail jostj@lvccld.org; *Exec. Secy.* Lisa Phelan, Henderson Libs. E-mail lphelan@hdpl.org.

Address correspondence to the executive secretary.

World Wide Web http://www.nevada libraries.org/publications/handbook/nscls.html.

New Hampshire

New Hampshire Educ. Media Assn., Box 418, Concord 03302-0418. Memb. 250+. Term of Office. June 2009–June 2010. Publication. *Online News* (fall, winter, spring; online and print).

Pres. Kathy Lane, G. H. Hood Middle School, Derry 03038. E-mail klane@derry. k12.nh.us; *V.P.* Helen Burnham, Lincoln Street School, 25 Lincoln St., Exeter 03833. Tel. 603-775-8851, e-mail hburnham@ sau16.org; *Recording Secy.* Melissa Moore, Northwood Elementary, Northwood 03290-6206. Tel. 603-942-5488 ext. 313, e-mail mmoore@northwood.k12.nh.us; *Treas.* Jeff Kent, 43 E. Ridge Rd., Merrimack 03054. E-mail jkent@comcast.net; *Past Pres.* Sharon Silva, Mastricola Upper Elementary, 26 Baboosic Lake Rd., Merrimack 03054. Tel. 603-424-6221, e-mail sharon.silva@ merrimack.k12.nh.us.

Address correspondence to the president.

World Wide Web http://www.nhema.net.

New Jersey

New Jersey Association of School Librarians (NJASL). Memb. 1,100. Term of Office. Aug. 2009–July 2010.

Pres. Pat Massey. E-mail president@njasl. org; *V.P.* Fran King. E-mail vicepresident@ njasl.org; *Pres.-Elect* Judith Everitt. E-mail presidentelect@njasl.org; *Recording Secy.* Nancy Stroud. E-mail recordingsecretary@ njasl.org; *Corresponding Secy.* Amy Rominiecki. E-mail correspondingsecretary@ njasl.org; *Treas.* Michelle Marhefka. E-mail treasurer@njasl.org; *Membs.-at-Large* Karen Brill. E-mail memberatlarge1@njasl.org; Wendy Su. E-mail memberatlarge2@njasl. org; *Past Pres.* Angela Crockett Coxen. E-mail immediatepastpresident@njasl.org.

Address correspondence to Aliah Davis-McHenry, Assn. Mgr., NJASL, Box 610, Trenton 08607. E-mail associationmanager@ njasl.org.

World Wide Web http://www.njasl.org.

New York

School Lib. Media Section, New York Lib. Assn., 252 Hudson St., Albany 12210. Tel. 518-432-6952. Memb. 880. Term of Office. Oct. 2009–Oct. 2010. Publications. *SLMS-Gram* (q.); participates in *NYLA Bulletin* (mo. except July and Aug.).

Pres. Fran Roscello. E-mail fran@roscello associates.com; *V.P. Conferences* Karen Sperrazza. E-mail ksperrazza@gmail.com; *V.P. Communications* Ellen Rubin. E-mail erubin@wallkillcsd.k12.ny.us; *Secy.* Pauline Herr. E-mail pherr@acsdny.org; *Treas.* Patty Martire. E-mail pmartire@mtmorriscsd.org; *Past Pres.* Carole Kupelian. E-mail carolek@ twcny.rr.com.

World Wide Web http://www.nyla.org/ slms.

North Carolina

North Carolina School Lib. Media Assn. Memb. 1,180+. Term of Office. Oct. 2009–Oct. 2010.

Pres. Kelly Brannock, Wake County Public Schools, 3355 Wendell Blvd., Wendell 27591. Tel. 919-365-2660, fax 919-365-2666, e-mail ncslma.kelly@gmail.com;

V.P./Pres.-Elect Deanna Harris, Wake County Public Schools, 1111 S.E. Maynard Rd., Cary 27511. Tel. 919-466-4377, fax 919-466-4388, e-mail harris_deanna@hotmail. com; *Secy.* Robin Boltz. E-mail boltz@email. unc.edu; *Treas.* Tammy Young. E-mail tammy.young@bcsemail.org; *Past Pres.* Deb Christensen, Union County Public Schools, Monroe 28112. Tel. 704-296-3088, fax 704-296-3090, e-mail deb.christensen@ucps.k12. nc.us.

Address correspondence to the president.

World Wide Web http://www.ncslma.org.

North Dakota

School Lib. and Youth Services Section, North Dakota Lib. Assn. Memb. 100. Term of Office. Sept. 2009–Sept. 2010. Publication. *The Good Stuff* (q.).

Chair Beth Greff, Mandan Middle School. Tel. 701-663-7491, fax 701-667-0984, e-mail beth.greff@msd1.org.

Address correspondence to the chairperson.

World Wide Web http://ndlaonline.org.

Ohio

Ohio Educ. Lib. Media Assn. Memb. 1,000. Publications. *OELMA News* (3 a year); *Ohio Media Spectrum* (q.).

Pres. Marie Sabol. E-mail sabolm@ hudson.edu; *V.P.* Sarah Thornbery. E-mail sthornbery@springboro.org; *Secy.* Diane Smith. E-mail smithd@hudson.edu; *Treas.* Cynthia DuChane. E-mail duchane@infohio. org; *Past Pres.* Kathy Halsey. E-mail info woman@sbcglobal.net; *Dir. of Services* Kate Brunswick, 17 S. High St., Suite 200, Columbus 43215. Tel. 614-221-1900, fax 614-221-1989, e-mail kate@assnoffices.com.

Address correspondence to the director of services.

World Wide Web http://www.oelma.org.

Oklahoma

Oklahoma Assn. of School Lib. Media Specialists. Memb. 300+. Term of Office. July 2009–June 2010. Publication. *Oklahoma Librarian.*

Chair Cathy Carlson. E-mail cjcarlson@okcps.org; *Chair-Elect* Patty Zody; *Secy.* Carolyn McClure. E-mail mccluca@tulsaschools.org; *Treas.* Tina Ham. E-mail hamti@tulsaschools.org; *Past Chair* Sally Rice. E-mail sbratton@norman.k12.ok.us.

Address correspondence to the chairperson, c/o Oklahoma Lib. Assn., 300 Hardy Drive, Edmond 73013. Tel. 405-348-0506.

World Wide Web http://www.oklibs.org/oaslms.

Oregon

Oregon Educ. Media Assn. Memb. 600. Term of Office. July 2009–June 2010. Publication. *OEMA Newsletter* (online).

Pres. Carol Dinges. E-mail carol_dinges@lebanon.k12.or.us; *Pres.-Elect* Ruth Murray. E-mail murrayr@pdx.edu; *Secy.* Jenny Takeda. E-mail jenny_takeda@beavton.k12.or.us; *Treas.* Victoria McDonald. E-mail vmcdonald@lshigh.org; *Past Pres.* Merrie Olson. E-mail lolson43@msn.com; *Exec. Dir.* Jim Hayden, 6780 N.W. 25th Lane, Redmond 97756-8168. E-mail j23hayden@aol.com.

Address correspondence to the executive director.

World Wide Web http://www.oema.net.

Pennsylvania

Pennsylvania School Libns. Assn. Memb. 1,400+. Term of Office. July 2009–June 2010. Publication. *Learning and Media* (q.).

Pres. Nancy Smith Latanision. E-mail nanka5@ptd.net; *V.P./Pres.-Elect* Doug Francis. E-mail francisd@lasd.k12.pa.us; *Secy.* Connie Burlingame. E-mail cbgame@gmail.com; *Treas.* Natalie Hawley. E-mail nhawley@masd.info; *Past Pres.* Margaret Foster. E-mail mfoster@northallegheny.org.

Address correspondence to the president. World Wide Web http://www.psla.org.

Rhode Island

Rhode Island Educ. Media Assn. Memb. 350+. Term of Office. June 2009–May 2010.

Pres. Jamie Greene. E-mail greenej@bw.k12.ri.us; *V.P.* To be announced; *Secy.* Emily Brown. E-mail emilyruthbrown@gmail.com;

Treas. Jane Vincelette. E-mail jwv@cox.net; *Past Pres.* Zachary Berger. E-mail zmberger@gmail.com.

Address correspondence to the association, Box 470, East Greenwich 02818.

World Wide Web http://riedmedia.org.

South Carolina

South Carolina Assn. of School Libns. Memb. 1,100. Term of Office. June 2009–May 2010. Publication. *Media Center Messenger* (2 print issues a year; 8 online issues a year).

Pres. Amanda LeBlanc. E-mail aleblanc@greenville.k12.sc.us; *V.P./Pres.-Elect* Joe Myers. E-mail joemyers1961@yahoo.com; *Secy.* Lena Lee. E-mail lelee@richlandone.org; *Treas.* Randa Edmunds. E-mail edmundsr@sumter17.k12.sc.us; *Past Pres.* Valerie Byrd Fort. E-mail vfort@lexington1.net.

Address correspondence to the president.

World Wide Web http://www.scasl.net.

South Dakota

South Dakota School Lib. Media Assn., Section of the South Dakota Lib. Assn. and South Dakota Educ. Assn., 28363 472nd Ave., Worthing 57077. Tel. 605-372-0235. Memb. 140+. Term of Office. Oct. 2009–Oct. 2010.

Chair Muriel Deckert, Milbank Middle/H.S.

Tennessee

Tennessee Assn. of School Libns. Memb. 450. Term of Office. Jan.–Dec. 2010. Publication. *Footnotes* (q.).

Pres. Becky Jackman, Northeast H.S., 3701 Trenton Rd., Clarksville 37040. E-mail becky37042@gmail.com; *V.P./Pres.-Elect* Pam Renfrow, St. Agnes Academy-St. Dominic School, 4830 Walnut Grove Rd., Memphis 38117. E-mail prenfrow@ssa-sds.org; *Secy.* Alice Bryant, Harpeth Hall School, 3801 Hobbs Rd., Nashville 37215. E-mail awbryant@bellsouth.net; *Treas.* Elizabeth Frerking, Northwest H.S., 800 Lafayette Rd., Clarksville 37042. E-mail Beth.frerking@hughes.net; *Past Pres.* Bruce Hester, Northeast Middle School, 3703 Trenton Rd.,

Clarksville 37040. E-mail bruce.hester@cmcss.net.

Address correspondence to the president.

World Wide Web http://www.korrnet.org/tasl.

Texas

Texas Assn. of School Libns. (Div. of Texas Lib. Assn.). Memb. 4,000+. Term of Office. Apr. 2009–Apr. 2010.

Chair Cindy Buchanan, Aldine ISD. Tel. 281-985-7258, e-mail cbuchanan@aldine.k12.tx.us; *Chair-Elect* Susan Geye, Everman ISD. Tel. 817-568-3560, e-mail sgeye@yahoo.com; *Secy.* Karen Harrell, Spring Branch ISD. Tel. 713-365-5450, e-mail karen.harrell@springbranchisd.com; *Past Chair* Jackie Chetzron, Richardson ISD. Tel. 469-593-1624, e-mail jackie.chetzron@risd.org.

Address correspondence to Texas Lib. Assn., 3355 Bee Cave Rd., Suite 401, Austin 78746. Tel. 512-328-1518, fax 512-328-8852, e-mail tla@txla.org.

World Wide Web http://www.txla.org/groups/tasl.

Utah

Utah Educ. Lib. Media Assn. Memb. 500+. Term of Office. Mar. 2009–Feb. 2010. Publication. *UELMA Newsletter* (q.).

Pres. Lanell Rabner, Springville H.S., 1205 E. 900 S., Springville 84663. Tel. 801-489-2870, fax 801-489-2806, e-mail lanell.rabner@nebo.edu; *Pres.-Elect* Brent Jones, Fremont H.S., 1900 N. 4700 W., Plain City 84404. Tel. 801-453-4034, e-mail bjones@weber.k12.ut.us; *Secy.* Pat Gerstner, Timpview H.S., 3570 Timpview Drive, Provo 84604. Tel. 801-221-9720 ext. 3513, e-mail patg@provo.edu; *Past Pres.* Debbie Naylor, Lehi H.S., 180 N. 500 E., Lehi 84043. Tel. 801-768-7000 ext. 337, fax 801-768-7007, e-mail dnaylor@alpine.k12.ut.us; *Exec. Dir.* John L. Smith, High Ridge Media, 714 W. 1900 N., Clinton 84015. Tel. 801-776-6829, fax 801-773-8708, e-mail jlsutah@comcast.net.

Address correspondence to the executive director.

World Wide Web http://www.uelma.org.

Vermont

Vermont School Lib. Assn. (formerly Vermont Educ. Media Assn.). Memb. 220+. Term of Office. May 2009–May 2010. Publication. *VSLA News* (q.).

Pres. Marsha Middleton, North Country Union H.S., P.O. Box 725, 209 Veterans Ave., Newport 05855. Tel. 802-334-7921, ext. 3040, e-mail mmiddleton@ncuhs.org; *Pres.-Elect* Claire Buckley, South Burlington H.S., 550 Dorset St., South Burlington 05403. Tel. 802-652-7085, e-mail cbuckley@sbschools.net; *Secy.* Lindy Sargent, Newport Elementary, 166 Sias Ave., Newport 05855. Tel. 802-334-2455, e-mail sargentl@newportcityelementary.org; *Treas.* Donna Smyth, Proctor Elementary, 14 School St., Proctor 05765. Tel. 802-459-2225 ext. 2005, e-mail smythd@rcsu.org; *Past Pres.* Susan Monmaney, Main Street Middle School, 170 Main St., Montpelier 05602. E-mail susanm@mpsvt.org.

Address correspondence to the president.

World Wide Web http://vsla.info.

Virginia

Virginia Educ. Media Assn. Memb. 1,700. Term of Office. (Pres., Pres.-Elect) Nov. 2009–Nov. 2010 (other officers two years in alternating years). Publication. *Mediagram* (q.).

Pres. Charlie Makela, Arlington Public Schools, Arlington. E-mail cmakela@arlington.k12.va.us; *Pres.-Elect* Mary Keeling, Newport News Public Schools, Newport News. E-mail mary.keeling@nn.k12.va.us; *Secy.* Roxanne Mills, Smithfield. E-mail rmills@odu.edu; *Treas.* Frances Reeve, Longwood Univ., Farmville. E-mail reevefm@longwood.edu; *Past Pres.* Terri Britt, G. A. Treakle Elementary, Chesapeake. E-mail britttwe@cps.k12.va.us; *Exec. Dir.* Margaret Baker. Tel. 540-416-6109, fax 540-885-6174, e-mail vema.org@gmail.com.

Address correspondence to the association, P.O. Box 2015, Staunton 24402-2015.

World Wide Web http://www.vemaonline. org.

Washington

Washington Lib. Media Assn. Memb. 1,450+. Term of Office. Oct.–Oct. Publication. *The Medium* (3 a year).

Pres. Linda King. E-mail winesapple@ aol.com; *Pres.-Elect* To be announced; *V.P.* Gary Simundson. E-mail gsimunds@egreen. wednet.edu; *Secy.* Steve Coker. E-mail cokers @rainier.wednet.edu; *Treas.* Kate Pankiewicz. E-mail kate.pankiewicz@shorelineschools.org; *Past Pres.* Dave Sonnen. E-mail wlmadave@ gmail.com.

Address correspondence to the association, 10924 Mukilteo Speedway, PMB 142, Mukilteo 98275. E-mail wlma@wlma.org.

World Wide Web http://www.wlma.org.

West Virginia

School Lib. Div., West Virginia Lib. Assn. Memb. 50. Term of Office. Nov.–Nov. Publication. *WVLA School Library News* (5 a year).

Co-Chairs Karen Figgatt, Bonham Elementary, Rt. 1, Box 425A, Charleston 25312. Tel. 304-348-1912, fax 304-348-1367, e-mail kfiggatt@kcs.kana.k12.wv.us; Cathy Davis, East Fairmont Junior H.S., 1 Orion Lane, Fairmont 26554. Tel. 304-367-2123, e-mail ctdavis@access.k12.wv.us.

Address correspondence to the chairpersons.

Wisconsin

Wisconsin Educ. Media and Technology Assn. Memb. 1,100+. Publication. *WEMTA Dispatch* (q.).

Pres. Jo Ann Carr. E-mail carr@ education.wisc.edu; *Interim Pres.-Elect* Annette Smith. E-mail arsmith14@gmail. com; *Secy.* Vicki Santacroce. E-mail vsantacroce@ashwaubenon.k12.wi.us; *Treas.* Sandy Heiden. E-mail sheiden@seymour. k12.wi.us.

Address correspondence to Communicators of Wisconsin (COW), P.O. Box 44578, Madison 53744-4578. E-mail WEMTA@ wiscow.com.

World Wide Web http://www.wemaonline. org.

Wyoming

School Lib. Media Personnel Section, Wyoming Lib. Assn. Memb. 90+. Term of Office. Oct. 2009–Oct. 2010. Publication. *WLA Newsletter.*

Chair Barb Osborne, Highland Park Elementary. E-mail osborneb@scsd2.com; *Chair-Elect* Christi Hampton, Upton Elementary and H.S. E-mail champton@upton. weston7.k12.wy.us; *Secy.* Sarah Prielipp, Campbell County School Dist. E-mail sprielipp@ccsd.k12.wy.us; *Past Pres.* Peggy Jording, Newcastle Schools. E-mail jordingp @weston1.k12.wy.us.

Address correspondence to the chairperson.

World Wide Web http://www.wyla.org/ schools.

International Library Associations

International Association of Agricultural Information Specialists

Peter Ballantyne, President
E-mail peter.ballantyne@iaald.org
World Wide Web http://www.iaald.org

Object

The International Association of Agricultural Information Specialists (IAALD) facilitates professional development of and communication among members of the agricultural information community worldwide. Its goal is to enhance access to and use of agriculture-related information resources. To further this mission, IAALD will promote the agricultural information profession, support professional development activities, foster collaboration, and provide a platform for information exchange. Founded 1955.

Membership

Memb. 400+ in 80 countries. Dues (Inst.) US$110; (Indiv.) US$50.

Officers

Pres. Peter Ballantyne (Netherlands). E-mail peter.ballantyne@iaald.org; *1st V.P.* Stephen Rudgard (Italy). E-mail stephen.rudgard@fao.org; *Secy.-Treas.* Toni Greider (USA), P.O. Box 63, Lexington, KY 40588-0063. Tel. 859-254-0752, fax 859-257-8379, e-mail info@iaald.org.

Publication

Agricultural Information Worldwide (q.) (memb.).

International Association of Law Libraries

Jules Winterton, President
c/o Institute of Advanced Legal Studies, 17 Russell Square, London WC1B 5DR, England
World Wide Web http://www.iall.org

Object

The International Association of Law Libraries (IALL) is a worldwide organization of librarians, libraries, and other persons or institutions concerned with the acquisition and use of legal information emanating from sources other than their jurisdictions and from multinational and international organizations.

IALL's purpose is to facilitate the work of librarians who acquire, process, organize, and provide access to foreign legal materials. IALL has no local chapters but maintains liaison with national law library associations in many countries and regions of the world.

Membership

More than 800 members in more than 50 countries on five continents.

Officers

Pres. Jules Winterton, Institute of Advanced Legal Studies, Univ. of London, 17 Russell Sq., London WCIB 5DR, England. Tel. 44-20-7862-5884, fax 44-20-7862-5850, e-mail julesw@sas.ac.uk; *1st V.P.* Richard Danner, Duke Univ. School of Law, Box 90361, Durham, NC 27708-0361. Tel. 919-613-7115, fax 919-613-7237, e-mail danner@law.duke.edu; *Secy.* Jennefer Aston, Bar Council of Ireland, P.O. Box 4460, Dublin 7, Ireland. Tel. 353-1-817-5121, fax 353-1-817-5151, e-mail jaston@iol.ie; *Treas.* Ann Morrison, Dalhousie Law School, 6061 University Ave., Halifax, Nova Scotia B3H 4H9, Canada. Tel. 902-494-2640/6301, fax 902-494-6669, e-mail ann.morrison@dal.ca; *Past Pres.* Holger Knudsen, Max-Planck-Institut für Ausländisches und Internationales Privatrecht, Mittelweg 187, D-20148, Hamburg, Germany. Tel. 49-40-41900-226, fax 49-40-41900-288, e-mail knudsen@mpipriv.de.

Board Members

Ruth Bird, Bodleian Law Lib., Oxford Univ., England; Barbara Garavaglia, Univ. of Michigan Law Lib.; Ligita Gjortlere, Riga Graduate School of Law Lib., Riga, Latvia; Petal Kinder, High Court of Australia Lib., Canberra; Xinh Luu, Univ. of Virginia Law Lib.; Uma Narayan, Bombay High Court, Mumbai, India; Pedro Padilla-Rosa, Univ. of Puerto Rico Law Lib., San Juan, Puerto Rico; Anita Soboleva, JURIX (Jurists for Constitutional Rights and Freedoms), Moscow, Russia; Jeroen Vervliet, Peace Palace Lib., The Hague, Netherlands.

Publication

International Journal of Legal Information (3 a year; US$60 indiv.; US$95 institutions).

International Association of Music Libraries, Archives and Documentation Centres

c/o Roger Flury, IAML Secretary-General
Music Room, National Library of New Zealand
Box 1467, Wellington 6001, New Zealand
Tel. 64-4-474-3039, fax 64-4-474-3035, e-mail secretary@iaml.info
World Wide Web http://www.iaml.info

Object

The object of the International Association of Music Libraries, Archives, and Documentation Centres (IAML) is to promote the activities of music libraries, archives, and documentation centers and to strengthen the cooperation among them; to promote the availability of all publications and documents relating to music and further their bibliographical control; to encourage the development of standards in all areas that concern the association; and to support the protection and preservation of musical documents of the past and the present.

Membership

Memb. 2,000.

Board Members

Pres. Martie Severt, MCO Muziekbibliotheek, Postbus 125, NL-1200 AC Hilversum, Netherlands. E-mail m.severt@mco.nl; *V.P.s* James P. Cassaro, Theodore M. Finney Music Lib., Univ. of Pittsburgh, B28 Music Bldg., Pittsburgh, PA 15260. Tel. 412-624-4130, fax 412-624-4180, e-mail cassaro+@pitt.edu; Jon Bagues, ERESBIL, Archivo

Vasco de la Música C/ Alfonso XI, 2, Código postal 20100-Errenteria Guipuzcoa, Euskal Herria, Spain. Tel. 34-943-000-868, fax 34-943-529-706, e-mail jbagues@eresbil.com; Aurika Gergeleziu, Fine Arts Information Centre, National Lib. of Estonia, Tönismägi 2, EE15189 Tallinn, Estonia. Tel. 372-6307-159, fax 372-6311-410, e-mail aurika@nlib.ee; Jutta Lambrecht, WDR D&A/Recherche Leitung Musik und Notenarchiv, Appellhofplatz 1, D-50667 Cologne, Germany. Tel. 49-0-221-220-3376, fax 49-0-221-220-9217, e-mail jutta.lambrecht@wdr.de; *Treas.* Kathryn Adamson, Royal Academy of Music, Marylebone Rd., London NW1 5HT, England. Tel. 44-0-20-7873-7321, e-mail k.adamson@ram.ac.uk; *Past Pres.* Massimo Gentili-Tedeschi, Biblioteca Nazionale Braidense, Ufficio Ricerca Fondi Musicali, via Conservatorio 12, I-20122 Milan, Italy. Tel. 39-02-7601-1822, fax 39-02-7600-3097.

Publication

Fontes Artis Musicae (4 a year; memb.). *Ed.* Maureen Buja, Hong Kong Gold Coast Block 22, Flat 1-A, 1 Castle Peak Rd., Tuen Mun, NT, Hong Kong. Tel. 852-2146-8047, e-mail mbuja@earthlink.net.

Professional Branches

Archives and Documentation Centres. Marguerite Sablonnière, Bibliothèque Nationale de France, Département de la Musique, 58 rue de Richelieu, 75002 Paris, France.

Broadcasting and Orchestra Libraries. Angela Escott, Royal College of Music, Prince Consort Rd., London SW7 2BS, England.

Libraries in Music Teaching Institutions. Pia Shekhter, Academy of Music and Drama, Göteborg University, SE-405 30 Göteborg, Sweden.

Public Libraries. Hanneke Kuiper, Public Lib., Oosterdoksstraat 143, 1011 DK Amsterdam, Netherlands.

Research Libraries. Stanislaw Hrabia, Uniwersytet Jagiellonski Instytut Muzykologii Biblioteka, ul. Westerplatte 10 31-033 Krakow, Poland.

International Association of School Librarianship

Karen Bonanno, Executive Secretary
P.O. Box 83, Zillmere, Qld. 4034, Australia
Fax 617-3633-0570, e-mail iasl@iasl-online.org
World Wide Web http://www.iasl-online.org

Object

The mission of the International Association of School Librarianship (IASL) is to provide an international forum for those interested in promoting effective school library programs as viable instruments in the educational process. The association provides guidance and advice for the development of school library programs and the school library profession. IASL works in cooperation with other professional associations and agencies.

The objectives of IASL are to advocate the development of school libraries throughout all countries; to encourage the integration of school library programs into the instructional and curriculum development of the school; to promote the professional preparation and continuing education of school library personnel; to foster a sense of community among school librarians in all parts of the world; to foster and extend relationships between school librarians and other professionals connected with children and youth; to foster research in the field of school librarianship and the integration of its conclusions with pertinent knowledge from related fields; to promote the publication and dissemination of information about successful advocacy and program initiatives in school librarianship; to share information about programs and materials for children and youth throughout the international community; and to initiate and coordinate activities, conferences, and other projects in the field of school librarianship and information services. Founded 1971.

Membership

Approximately 700.

Officers and Executive Board

Pres. James Henri, Australia; *V.P.s* Barbara Combes, Australia; Lesley Farmer, USA; Diljit Singh, Malaysia; *Treas.* Peter Warning, Hong Kong; *Dirs.* Busi Dlamini, Africa–Sub-Sahara; Luisa Marquardt, Europe; Marlene Asselin, Canada; Blanche Woolls, USA; Pat Carmichael, Oceania; Betty Chu Wah Hing, East Asia; Ingrid Skirrow, International Schools; Katharina B. L. Berg, Latin America/Caribbean; Madhu Bhargava, Asia; Michelle Fitzgerald, North Africa/Middle East.

Publications

Selected papers from proceedings of annual conferences (all prices are exclusive of postage):

32nd Annual Conference, 2003, Durban, South Africa. *School Libraries: Breaking Down Barriers.* US$30.

34th Annual Conference, 2005, Hong Kong. *Information Leadership in a Culture of Change.* US$20.

35th Annual Conference, 2006, Lisbon, Portugal. *The Multiple Faces of Literacy: Reading. Knowing. Doing.* US$20.

36th Annual Conference, 2007, Taipei, Taiwan. *Cyberspace, D-world, E-learning: Giving Libraries and Schools the Cutting Edge.* US$20.

37th Annual Conference, 2008, Berkeley, California. *World Class Learning and Literacy through School Libraries* US$20.

38th Annual Conference 2009, Abano Terme, Italy. *Preparing Pupils and Students for the Future: School Libraries in the Picture.* US$20.

International Association of Scientific and Technological University Libraries

President, Ainslie Dewe, La Trobe University, Victoria, Australia

Object

The object of the International Association of Scientific and Technological University Libraries (IATUL) is to provide a forum where library directors can meet to exchange views on matters of current significance in the libraries of universities of science and technology. Research projects identified as being of sufficient interest may be followed through by working parties or study groups.

Membership

Memb. 239 (in 42 countries); Ordinary, Associate, Sustaining, Honorary. Membership fee 75–150 euros a year, sustaining membership 500 euros a year.

Officers and Executives

Pres. Ainslie Dewe, Univ. Libn., La Trobe University Lib., Victoria, Australia. E-mail a.dewe@latrobe.edu.au; *Secy.* Paul Sheehan, Dublin City Univ. Lib., Dublin 9, Ireland. E-mail paul.sheehan@dcu.ie; *Treas.* Reiner Kallenborn, Munich Technical Univ. Lib., Arcisstrasse 21, Munich 80230, Germany. E-mail kallenborn@ub.tum.de; *Past Pres.* Maria Heijne, Postbus 98, 2600 MG Delft, Netherlands. E-mail m.a.m.heijne@library.tudelft.nl.

Publication

IATUL Proceedings (on IATUL Web site, http://www.iatul.org) (ann.).

International Council on Archives

David Leitch, Secretary-General
60 rue des Francs-Bourgeois, 75003 Paris, France
Tel. 33-1-40-27-61-37, fax 33-1-42-72-20-65, e-mail ica@ica.org
World Wide Web http://www.ica.org

Object

The mission of the International Council on Archives (ICA) is to establish, maintain, and strengthen relations among archivists of all lands, and among all professional and other agencies or institutions concerned with the custody, organization, or administration of archives, public or private, wherever located. Established 1948.

Membership

Memb. Approximately 1,400 (representing about 190 countries and territories).

Officers

Secy.-Gen. David Leitch; *Deputy Secys.-Gen.* Didier Grange, Margaret Kenna, Christine Martinez; *Pres.* Ian E. Wilson, Libn. and Archivist of Canada Emeritus; *V.P.s* Lew Bellardo, Advisor to the Archivist of the United States; Martin Berendse, National Archivist, National Archives of the Netherlands; Ross Gibbs, National Archives of Australia; Abdullah A. Kareem El Reyes, National Centre for Documentation and Research, United Arab Emirates; Tomas Lidman, National Archives of Sweden; Christine Martinez, Archives de France; Hans Eyvind Naess, National Archives of Norway; Nolda C. Romer-Kenepa, National Archives of the Netherlands Antilles; Setareki Tale, Government Archives of Fiji; Henri Zuber, Service Archives Documentation (SARDO), SNCF.

Publications

Comma (memb.). (CD-ROM only since 2005.)
Flash (3 a year; memb.).
Guide to the Sources of the History of Nations (Latin American Series, 11 vols. pub.; Africa South of the Sahara Series, 20 vols. pub.; North Africa, Asia, and Oceania Series, 15 vols. pub.).
Guide to the Sources of Asian History (English-language series [India, Indonesia, Korea, Nepal, Pakistan, Singapore], 14 vols. pub.; national language series [Indonesia, Korea, Malaysia, Nepal, Thailand], 6 vols. pub.; other guides, 3 vols. pub.).

International Federation of Film Archives
(Fédération Internationale des Archives du Film)

Secretariat, rue Defacqz, 1, B-1000 Brussels, Belgium
Tel. 32-2-538-3065, fax 32-2-534-4774, e-mail info@fiafnet.org
World Wide Web http://www.fiafnet.org

Object

Founded in 1938, the International Federation of Film Archives (FIAF) brings together not-for-profit institutions dedicated to rescuing films and any other moving-image elements considered both as cultural heritage and as historical documents.

FIAF is a collaborative association of the world's leading film archives whose purpose has always been to ensure the proper preservation and showing of motion pictures. A total of 151 archives in more than 75 countries collect, restore, and exhibit films and cinema documentation spanning the entire history of film.

FIAF seeks to promote film culture and facilitate historical research, to help create new archives around the world, to foster training and expertise in film preservation, to encourage the collection and preservation of documents and other cinema-related materials, to develop cooperation between archives, and to ensure the international availability of films and cinema documents.

Officers

Pres. Hisashi Okajima; *Secy.-Gen.* Meg Labrum; *Treas.* Patrick Loughney; *Membs.* Vittorio Boarini, Guadalupe Ferrer, Sylvia Frank, Olga Futemma, Luca Giuliani, Lise Gustavson, Eric Le Roy, Michael Loebenstein, Vladimir Opela.

Address correspondence to Christian Dimitriu, Senior Administrator, c/o FIAF Secretariat. E-mail c.dimitriu@fiafnet.org.

Publications

Journal of Film Preservation.

International Index to Film Periodicals.

FIAF International Filmarchive database (OVID).

FIAF International Index to Film Periodicals (ProQuest).

For additional FIAF publications, see http://www.fiafnet.org.

International Federation of Library Associations and Institutions

Jennefer Nicholson, Secretary-General
P.O. Box 95312, 2509 CH The Hague, Netherlands
Tel. 31-70-314-0884, fax 31-70-383-4827
E-mail ifla@ifla.org, World Wide Web http://www.ifla.org

Object

The object of the International Federation of Library Associations and Institutions (IFLA) is to promote international understanding, cooperation, discussion, research, and development in all fields of library activity, including bibliography, information services, and the education of library personnel, and to provide a body through which librarianship can be represented in matters of international interest. IFLA is the leading international body representing the interests of library and information services and their users. It is the global voice of the library and information profession. Founded 1927.

Officers and Governing Board

Pres. Ellen Tise, Univ. of Stellenbosch; *Pres.-Elect* Ingrid Parent, Univ. of British Columbia; *Treas.* Barbara Schleihagen, Deutscher Bibliotheksverband e.v. (DBV); *Governing Board* Patrice Landry, Swiss National Lib.; Jesus Lau, Universidad Veracruzana; Pascal Sanz, Bibliothèque Nationale de France; Helena R. Asamoah-Hassan, Kwame Nkrumah Univ. of Science and Technology; Judith J. Field, Wayne State Univ.; Michael Heaney, Oxford Univ.; Buhle Mbambo-Thata, UNISA; Danielle Mincio, Bibliothèque Cantonale et Universitaire; Tone Eli Moseid, ABM-Utvikling; Ann Okerson, Yale Univ.; Donna Scheeder, Law Lib., Lib. of Congress; Sinikka Sipilä, Finnish Lib. Assn.; Paul Whitney, Vancouver Public Lib.; Steve W. Witt, Univ. of Illinois at Urbana-Champaign; Qiang Zhu, Peking Univ. Lib.; Janice Lachance, Special Libs. Assn.; *Secy.-Gen.* Jennefer Nicholson; *Dir., Professional Programmes* Sjoerd M. J. Koopman.

Publications

IFLA Annual Report.

IFLA Directory (bienn.).

IFLA Journal (4 a year).

IFLA Professional Reports.

IFLA Publications Series.

IFLA Series on Bibliographic Control.

International Cataloguing and Bibliographic Control (q.).

International Preservation News.

American Membership

Associations

American Assn. of Law Libs., American Lib. Assn., Assn. for Lib. and Info. Science Educ., Assn. of Research Libs., Chief Officers of State Lib. Agencies, Medical Lib. Assn., Special Libs. Assn., Urban Libs. Council.

Institutional Members

There are 129 libraries and related institutions that are institutional members or consultative bodies and sponsors of IFLA in the United States (out of a total of 1,157 members globally), and 110 individual affiliates (out of a total of 315 members globally).

International Organization for Standardization

Robert Steele, Secretary-General
ISO Central Secretariat, 1 ch. de la Voie-Creuse, Case postale 56, CH-1211 Geneva 20, Switzerland
41-22-749-01-11, fax 41-22-733-34-30, e-mail central@iso.org
World Wide Web http://www.iso.org

Object

The International Organization for Standardization (ISO) is a worldwide federation of national standards bodies, founded in 1947, at present comprising 162 members, one in each country. The object of ISO is to promote the development of standardization and related activities in the world with a view to facilitating international exchange of goods and services, and to developing cooperation in the spheres of intellectual, scientific, technological, and economic activity. The scope of ISO covers international standardization in all fields except electrical and electronic engineering standardization, which is the responsibility of the International Electrotechnical Commission (IEC). The results of ISO technical work are published as international standards.

Officers

Pres. Alan Morrison, Australia; *V.P. (Policy)* Sadao Takeda, Japan; *V.P. (Technical Management)* Jacob Holmblad, Denmark.

Technical Work

The technical work of ISO is carried out by 208 technical committees. These include:

ISO/TC 46–Information and documentation (Secretariat, Association Française de Normalization, 11 ave. Francis de Pressensé, 93571 Saint-Denis La Plaine, Cedex, France). Scope: Standardization of practices relating to libraries, documentation and information centers, indexing and abstracting services, archives, information science, and publishing.

ISO/TC 37–Terminology and language and content resources (Secretariat, INFO-TERM, Aichholzgasse 6/12, 1120 Vienna, Austria, on behalf of Österreichisches Normungsinstitut). Scope: Standardization of principles, methods, and applications relating to terminology and other language and content resources in the contexts of multilingual communication and cultural diversity.

ISO/IEC JTC 1–Information technology (Secretariat, American National Standards Institute, 25 W. 43 St., 4th fl., New York, NY 10036). Scope: Standardization in the field of information technology.

Publications

ISO Annual Report.

ISO CataloguePlus on CD-ROM (combined catalog of published standards and technical work program) (ann.).

ISO Focus (11 a year).

ISO International Standards.

ISO Management Systems (bi-mo.).

ISO Memento (ann.).

ISO Online information service on World Wide Web (http://www.iso.org).

Foreign Library Associations

The following is a list of regional and national library associations around the world. A more complete list can be found in *International Literary Market Place* (Information Today, Inc.).

Regional

Africa

Standing Conference of Eastern, Central, and Southern African Lib. and Info. Assns. (SCECSAL), c/o Botswana Lib. Assn., Private Bag 00392, Gaborone, Botswana. Fax 267-391-3501. *Chair* Kgomotso Radijeng. E-mail kgomotsor@bnpc.bw.

The Americas

Asociación de Bibliotecas Universitarias, de Investigación e Institucionales del Caribe (ACURIL) (Assn. of Caribbean Univ., Research, and Institutional Libs.), Box 23317, UPR Sta., San Juan, PR 00931-3317. Tel./fax 787-790-8054, e-mail acuril@uprrp.edu, World Wide Web http://acuril.uprrp.edu/que.htm. *Pres.* Pedro Padilla-Rosa; *Exec. Secy.* Oneida Rivera de Ortiz.

Seminar on the Acquisition of Latin American Lib. Materials (SALALM), c/o *Exec. Secy.* Hortensia Calvo, SALALM Secretariat, Latin American Lib., 422 Howard Tilton Memorial Lib., 7002 Freret St., New Orleans, LA 70118-5549. Tel. 504-247-1366, fax 504-247-1367, e-mail salalm@tulane.edu, World Wide Web http://www.salalm.org. *Pres.* John Wright. E-mail john_wright@byu.edu; *Exec. Secy.* Hortensia Calvo.

Asia

Congress of Southeast Asian Libns. (CONSAL), c/o Cultural Affairs Assistant, 7 Lang Ha St., Ba Dinh District, Hanoi, Vietnam. Tel. 4-3850-5000, fax 04-3825-3357, World Wide Web http://www.consal.org. *Secy.-Gen.* Bui Thi Thuy. E-mail btthuy@nlv.gov.vn.

The Commonwealth

Commonwealth Lib. Assn. (COMLA), Univ. of the West Indies, Bridgetown Campus, Learning Resources Center, P.O. Box 144, Mona, Kingston 7, Jamaica. Tel. 876-927-0083, fax 876-927-1926, e-mail nkpodo@uwimonal.edu.jm. *Pres.* Anthony Evans; *Exec. Secy.* Norma Y. Amenu-Kpodo.

Standing Conference on Lib. Materials on Africa (SCOLMA), Social Science Collections and Research, British Lib. St. Pancras, 96 Euston Rd., London NW1 2DB, England. Tel. 020-7412-7567, fax 020-7747-6168, e-mail scolma@hotmail.com, World Wide Web http://www.lse/ac/uk/library/scolma. *Chair* Barbara Spina, School of Oriental and African Studies, Univ. of London, Thornhaugh St., Russell Sq., London WC1H 0XG, England. Tel. 020-7898-4157, fax 020-7898-4159, e-mail bs24@soas.ac.uk.

National and State Libs. Australasia, c/o State Lib. of Victoria, 328 Swanston St., Melbourne, Vic. 3000. Tel. 3-8664-7512, fax 3-9639-4737, e-mail nsla@slv.vic.gov.au, World Wide Web http://www.nsla.org.au. *CEO* Anne-Marie Schwirtlich.

Europe

Ligue des Bibliothèques Européennes de Recherche (LIBER) (Assn. of European Research Libs.), P.O. Box 90153, 5000 LE Tilburg, Netherlands. Tel. 013-466-33-70, fax 013-466-21-46, World Wide Web http://www.libereurope.eu. *Pres.* Hans Geleijnse. E-mail hans.geleijnse@uvt.nl.

National

Argentina

Asociación de Bibliotecarios Graduados de la República Argentina (ABGRA) (Assn. of

Graduate Libns. of Argentina), Parana 918, 2do Piso, C1017AAT Buenos Aires. Tel. 11-4811-0043, fax 11-4816-2234, e-mail info@abgra.org.ar, World Wide Web http://www.abgra.org.ar. *Pres.* Ana Maria Peruchena Zimmermann; *Exec. Secy.* Rosa Emma Monfasani.

Australia

Australian Lib. and Info. Assn., Box 6335, Kingston, ACT 2604. Tel. 2-6215-8222, fax 2-6282-2249, e-mail enquiry@alia.org. au, World Wide Web http://www.alia.org. au. *Pres.* Roxanne Missingham. E-mail roxanne.missingham@alia.org.au; *V.P.* Derek Whitehead. E-mail derek.whitehead @alia.org.au; *Exec. Dir.* Sue Hutley. E-mail sue.hutley@alia.org.au.

Australian Society of Archivists, P.O. Box 77, Dickson, ACT 2602. Tel. 800-622-251, e-mail ozarch@velocitynet.com.au, World Wide Web http://www.archivists. org.au. *Pres.* Kim Eberhard; *V.P.* Jackie Bettington; *Secy.* Lynda Weller.

Austria

Österreichische Gesellschaft für Dokumentation und Information (Austrian Society for Documentation and Info.), c/o OCG, Wollzeile 1-3, 1010 Vienna. E-mail office@ oegdi.at, World Wide Web http://www. oegdi.at. *Chair* Gabriele Sauberer.

Vereinigung Österreichischer Bibliothekarinnen und Bibliothekare (Assn. of Austrian Libns.), Voralberg State Lib., Fluherstr. 4, 6900 Bregenz. E-mail voeb@mail.ub. tuwien.ac.at, World Wide Web http:// www.univie.ac.at/voeb/php. *Pres.* Harald Weigel; *Contact* Josef Pauser. E-mail josef.pauser@univie.ac.at.

Bangladesh

Lib. Assn. of Bangladesh, Central Public Lib. Bldg., Shahbagh, Dhaka 1000. Tel. 2-504-269, World Wide Web http://www.lab-bd.org. *Pres.* M. Abdussattar; *Gen. Secy.* Syed Ali Akbor.

Barbados

Lib. Assn. of Barbados, P.O. Box 827E, Bridgetown, Saint Michael.

Belgium

Archief- en Bibliotheekwezen in België (Belgian Assn. of Archivists and Libns.), Keizershaan 4, 1000 Brussels. Tel. 2-519-5393, fax 2-519-5610. *Pres.* Frank Daelemans. E-mail frank.daelemans@kbr.be.

Association Belge de Documentation/Belgische Vereniging voor Documentatie (Belgian Assn. for Documentation), chaussée de Wavre 1683, B-1160 Brussels. Tel. 2-675-58-62, fax 2-672-74-46, e-mail info@abd-bvd.be, World Wide Web http:// www.abd-bvd.be. *Pres.* Paul Heyvaert; *Secy.* Christopher Boon.

Association Professionnelle des Bibliothécaires et Documentalistes (Assn. of Libns. and Documentation Specialists), Place de la Wallonie, 15 6140 Fontaine-l'Eveque. Tel. 71-52-31-93, fax 71-52-23-07, e-mail biblio.hainaut@skynet.be, World Wide Web http://www.a-p-b-d.be. *Pres.* Laurence Boulanger; *Secy.* Fabienne Gerard.

Vlaamse Vereniging voor Bibliotheek-, Archief-, en Documentatiewezen (Flemish Assn. of Libns., Archivists, and Documentalists), Statiestraat 179, B-2600 Berchem, Antwerp. Tel. 3-281-44-57, e-mail vvbad @vvbad.be, World Wide Web http://www. vvbad.be. *Pres.* Johan Vannieuwenhuyze; *Exec. Dir.* Marc Storms.

Belize

Belize Lib. Assn., c/o Central Lib., Bliss Inst., P.O. Box 287, Belize City. Tel. 2-7267, fax 2-34246. *Pres.* H. W. Young; *Secy.* Robert Hulse.

Bolivia

Centro Nacional de Documentacion Cientifica y Tecnologica (National Scientific and Technological Documentation Center), Av. Mariscal Santa Cruz 1175, Esquina c Ayacucho, La Paz. Tel. 02-359-583, fax 02-359-586, e-mail iiicndct@huayna. umsa.edu.bo, World Wide Web http://

www.bolivian.com/industrial/cndct. *Contact* Ruben Valle Vera.

Bosnia and Herzegovina

Drustvo Bibliotekara Bosne i Hercegovine (Libns. Society of Bosnia and Herzegovina), Zmaja od Bosne 8B, 71000 Sarajevo. Tel. 33-275-301, fax 33-212-435, e-mail nubbih@nub.ba, World Wide Web http://www.nub.ba. *Pres.* Nevenka Hajdarovic. E-mail nevenka@nub.ba; *Dir.* Ismet Ovcina. E-mail ismet@nub.ba.

Botswana

Botswana Lib. Assn., Box 1310, Gaborone. Tel. 371-750, fax 371-748, World Wide Web http://www.bla.0catch.com. *Chair* Bobana Badisang.

Brazil

Associação dos Arquivistas Brasileiros (Assn. of Brazilian Archivists), Av. Presidente Vargas 1733, Sala 903, 20210-030 Rio de Janiero RJ. Tel. 21-2507-2239, fax 21-3852-2541, e-mail aab@aab.org.br, World Wide Web http://www.aab.org.br. *Pres.* Lucia Maria Velloso de Oliveira.

Brunei Darussalam

Persatuan Perpustakaan Kebangsaan Negara Brunei (National Lib. Assn. of Brunei), Perpustakaan Universiti Brunei Darussalam, Jl. Tungku Link, Gadong BE 1410. Tel. 2-249-001, fax 2-249-504, e-mail chieflib@lib.ubd.edu.bn, World Wide Web http://www.ppknbd.org.bn. *Pres.* Puan Nellie bte Dato Paduka Haji Sunny.

Cameroon

Association des Bibliothécaires, Archivistes, Documentalistes et Muséographes du Cameroun (Assn. of Libns., Archivists, Documentalists, and Museum Curators of Cameroon), B.P. 4609, Yaoundé, Nlongkak. Tel. 222-6362, fax 222-4785, e-mail abadcam@yahoo.fr. *Pres.* Hilaire Omokolo.

Chile

Colegio de Bibliotecarios de Chile AG (Chilean Lib. Assn.), Avda. Diagonal Paraguay 383, Torre 11, of. 122, 6510017 Santiago. Tel. 2-222-56-52, fax 2-635-50-23, e-mail cbc@bibliotecarios.cl, World Wide Web http://www.bibliotecarios.cl. *Pres.* Marcia Marinovic Simunovic.

China

Library Society of China, 33 Zhongguancun Nandajie, Beijing 100081. Tel. 10-8854-5563, fax 10-6841-7815, e-mail ztxhm-sc@nlc.gov.cn, World Wide Web http://www.nlc.gov.cn. *Secy.-Gen.* Gensheng Tang; *Pres.* Zhan Furui.

Colombia

Asociación Colombiana de Bibliotecólogos y Documentalistas (Colombian Assn. of Libns. and Documentalists), Calle 21, No. 6-58, Of. 404, Bogotá. Tel. 1-282-3620, fax 1-282-5487, World Wide Web http://www.ascolbi.org. *Pres.* Carlos Zapata.

Congo (Republic of)

Association des Bibliothécaires, Archivistes, Documentalistes et museologues du Congo (ABADOM), BP 3148, Kinshasa-Gombe. *Pres.* Desire Didier Tengeneza.

Costa Rica

Asociación Costarricense de Bibliotecarios (Costa Rican Assn. of Libns.), Apdo. 3308, San José. Tel. 234-9989, e-mail info@cesdepu.com, World Wide Web http://www.cesdepu.com.

Côte d'Ivoire

Direction des Archives Nationales et de la Documentation, BP V 126, Abidjan, Tel. 20-21-74-20, fax 20 21 75 78. *Dir.* Venance Bahi Gouro.

Croatia

Hrvatsko Knjiznicarsko Drustvo (Croatian Lib. Assn.), c/o National and Univ. Lib.,

Hrvatske bratske zajednice 4, 10 000 Zagreb. Tel./fax 385-1-615-93-20, e-mail hkd@nsk.hr, World Wide Web http://www.hkdrustvo.hr. *Pres.* Zdenka Sviben. E-mail z.sviben@kqz.hr.

Cuba

Asociación Cubana de Bibliotecarios (ASCUBI) (Lib. Assn. of Cuba), Biblioteca Nacional Jose Marti, Ave. Independencia 20 de Mayo, Plaza de la Revolucion, Havana. Tel. 7-555-442, fax 7-816-224, e-mail publiweb@bnjm.cu, World Wide Web http://binanet.bnjm.cu. *Pres.* Margarita Bellas Vilarino.

Cyprus

Kypriakos Synthesmos Vivliothicarion (Lib. Assn. of Cyprus), P.O. Box 1039, 1105 Nicosia. Tel. 22-404-849.

Czech Republic

Svaz Knihovniku a Informacnich Pracovniku Ceske Republiky (SKIP) (Assn. of Lib. and Info. Professionals of the Czech Republic), National Lib., Klementinum 190, 110 00 Prague 1. Tel. 221-663-379, fax 221-663-175, e-mail vit.richter@nkp.cz, World Wide Web http://skip.nkp.cz. *Pres.* Vit Richter.

Denmark

Arkivforeningen (Archives Society), c/o Rigsarkivet, Rigsdagsgarden 9, 1218 Copenhagen. Tel. 3392-3310, fax 3315-3239, World Wide Web http://www.arkivarforeningen.no. *Dir.* Lars-Jorgen Sandberg.

Danmarks Biblioteksforening (Danish Lib. Assn.), Vesterbrogade 20/5, 1620 Copenhagen V. Tel. 3325-0935, fax 3325-7900, e-mail dbf@dbf.dk, World Wide Web http://www.dbf.dk. *Dir.* Winnie Vitzansky.

Danmarks Forskningsbiblioteksforening (Danish Research Lib. Assn.), c/o Statsbiblioteket, Tangen 2, 8200, Århus N. Tel. 89-46-22-07, e-mail df@statsbiblioteket.dk, World Wide Web http://www.dfdf.dk. *Pres.* Claus Vesterager Pedersen; *Secy.* Hanne Dahl.

Dansk Musikbiblioteks Forening (Assn. of Danish Music Libs.), Falkoner Plads 3, DK-2000 Frederiksberg. E-mail erdu01@frederiksberg.dk, World Wide Web http://www.dmbf.nu. *Pres.* Ole Bisbjerg; *Secy.-Gen* Jane Mariegaard.

Kommunernes Skolebiblioteksforening (Assn. of Danish School Libs.), Aboulevard 5, 2 th, DK-1635 Copenhagen. Tel. 33-11-13-91, fax 33-11-13-90, e-mail ksbf@ksbf.dk, World Wide Web http://www.ksbf.dk. *Admin.* Gitte Frausing.

Dominican Republic

Asociación Dominicana de Bibliotecarios (Dominican Assn. of Libns.), c/o Biblioteca Nacional, Cesar Nicolás Penson 91, Plaza de la Cultura, Pichincha, Santo Domingo. Tel. 809-688-4086, fax 809-688-5841.

Ecuador

Asociación Ecuatoriana de Bibliotecarios (Ecuadoran Lib. Assn.), c/o Casa de la Cultura Ecuatoriana, Casilla 87, Quito. Tel. 9832-258-7666, fax 9832-258-8516, e-mail asoebfp@hotmail.com, World Wide Web http://www.reicyt.org.ec/aeb.

El Salvador

Asociación de Bibliotecarios Salvadoreños (ABES) (Association of Salvadorian Libns.), Colonia Militar, Pasaje Victor Manuel Guerra Ingles No. 510, San Salvador. Tel./fax 503-237-0875, World Wide Web http://www.abes.org.sv. *Pres.* Jose Raul Mojica.

Asociación General de Archivistas de El Salvador (Assn. of Archivists of El Salvador), Edificio Comercial San Fancisco No. 214, Ga. C Ote y 2a Ave. Nte, San Salvador. Tel. 222-94-18, fax 281-58-60, e-mail agnes@agn.gob.sv.

Ethiopia

Ye Ethiopia Betemetshaft Serategnoch Mahber (Ethiopian Lib. and Info. Assn.), P.O. Box 30530, Addis Ababa. Tel. 1-511-344, fax 1-533-368.

Finland

Suomen Kirjastoseura (Finnish Lib. Assn.), Runeberginkatu 15 A 23, 00100 Helsinki. Tel. 9-6221-340, fax 9-6221-466, e-mail fla@fla.fi, World Wide Web http://www. fla.fi. *Pres.* Markku Laukkanen.

France

Association des Archivistes Français (Assn. of French Archivists), 9 rue Montcalm, F-75018 Paris. Tel. 1-46-06-39-44, fax 1-46-06-39-52, e-mail secretariat@archivistes. org, World Wide Web http://www. archivistes.org. *Pres.* Christine Martinez; *Secy.* Agnès Dejob.

Association des Bibliothécaires Français (Assn. of French Libns.), 31 rue de Chabrol, F-75010 Paris. Tel. 1-55-33-10-30, fax 1-55-30-10-31, e-mail abf@abf.asso.fr, World Wide Web http://www.abf.asso.fr. *Pres.* Dominique Arot; *Gen. Secy.* Jacques Sauteron.

Association des Professionnels de l'Information et de la Documentation (Assn. of Info. and Documentation Professionals), 25 rue Claude Tillier, F-75012 Paris. Tel. 1-43-72-25-25, fax 1-43-72-30-41, e-mail adbs @adbs.fr, World Wide Web http://www. adbs.fr. *Pres.* Martine Sibertin-Blanc; *Secy.-Gen.* Marie Baudry de Vaux.

Germany

Arbeitsgemeinschaft der Spezialbibliotheken (Assn. of Special Libs.), c/o Herder-Institute eV, Bibliothek, Gisonenweg 5-7, 35037 Marburg. Tel. 6421-91-78-41, fax 6421-184-139, e-mail geschaeftsstelle@ aspb.de, World Wide Web http://www. aspb.de. *Chair* Juergen Warmbrunn. E-mail warmbrunn@herder-institut.de; *Dir.* Jadwiga Warmbrunn.

Berufsverband Information Bibliothek (Assn. of Info. and Lib. Professionals), Gartenstr. 18, 72764 Reutlingen. Tel. 7121-3491-0, fax 7121-3004-33, e-mail mail@bib-info.de, World Wide Web http://www.bib-info.de. *Pres.* Susanne Riedel. E-mail susanne.riedel@uni-bielefeld.de.

Deutsche Gesellschaft für Informationswissenschaft und Informationspraxis eV (German Society for Info. Science and Practice), Hanauer Landstr. 151-153, 60314 Frankfurt-am-Main 1. Tel. 69-43-03-13, fax 69-490-90-96, e-mail mail@dgi-info. de, World Wide Web http://www.dgd.de. *Pres.* Gabriele Beger.

Deutscher Bibliotheksverband eV (German Lib. Assn.), Str. des 17 Juni 114, 10623 Berlin. Tel./fax 30-644-98-99-10, e-mail dbv@bibliotheksverband.de, World Wide Web http://www.bibliotheksverband.de. *Pres.* Gudrun Heute-Bluhm; *Chair* Gabriele Beger. E-mail beger@dgi-info.de.

VdA—Verband Deutscher Archivarinnen und Archivare (Assn. of German Archivists), Woerthstr. 3, 36037 Fulda. Tel. 661-29-109-72, fax 661-29-109-74, e-mail info@vda.archiv.net, World Wide Web http://www.vda.archiv.net. *Chair* Robert Kretzschmar.

Verein Deutscher Bibliothekare eV (Society of German Libns.), Universitaetsbibliothek Augsburg, Universitaetsstr. 22, 86159 Augsburg. Tel. 821-598-5300, fax 821-598-5354, e-mail sekr@bibliothek.uni-augsburg.de, World Wide Web http:// www.vdb-online.org. *Chair* Ulrich Hohoff.

Ghana

Ghana Lib. Assn., Knust Lib., Kwame Nkrumah Univ. of Science and Technology, Kumasi. Tel. 51-60199, fax 51-60358, e-mail library@knust.edu.gh, World Wide Web http://librarygla.org. *Pres.* Valentina J. A. Bannerman. E-mail valnin@yahoo. com.

Greece

Enosis Hellinon Bibliothekarion (Greek Lib. Assn.), 4 Skoulenion St., 105 61 Athens. Tel. 210-322-6625, World Wide Web http://www.eebep.gr.

Guyana

Guyana Lib. Assn., P.O. Box 10240, Georgetown. Tel. 0226-2690, fax 0226-2699, e-mail natlib@sdnp.org.gy, World Wide Web http://www.natlib.gov.gy. *Pres.* Ivor Rodriguez; *Secy.* Gwyneth George.

Honduras

Asociación de Bibliotecarios y Archiveros de Honduras (Assn. of Libns. and Archivists of Honduras), 11a Calle, 1a y 2a Avdas., No. 105, Comayagüela DC, Tegucigalpa. *Pres.* Francisca de Escoto Espinoza; *Secy.-Gen.* Juan Angel R. Ayes.

Hong Kong

Hong Kong Lib. Assn., GPO Box 10095, Hong Kong. E-mail hkla@hkla.org, World Wide Web http://www.hkla.org. *Pres.* Michael Robinson. E-mail robinson@ ied.edu.hk.

Hungary

Magyar Könyvtárosok Egyesülete (Assn. of Hungarian Libns.), Budavari Palota F, epulet 439 szoba, Budapest. Tel./fax 1-311-8634, e-mail mke@oszk.hu, World Wide Web http://www.mke.oszk.hu. *Pres.* Klara Bakos; *Exec. Secy.* Ilona Molnar.

Iceland

Upplysing—Felag bokasafns-og upplysingafraeoa (Information—The Icelandic Lib. and Info. Science Assn.), Lagmula 7, 108 Reykjavik. Tel. 553-7290, fax 588-9239, e-mail upplysing@bokis.is, World Wide Web http://www.bokis.is. *Pres.* H. A. Hardarson; *Secy.* A. Agnarsdottir.

India

Indian Assn. of Special Libs. and Info. Centres, P-291, CIT Scheme 6M, Kankurgachi, Kolkata 700054. Tel. 33-2362-9651, e-mail iaslic19@iaslic1955.org, World Wide Web http://www.iaslic1955. org. *Gen. Secy.* Arun Kumar Chakraborty. E-mail akc@bic.boseinst.ernet.in.

Indian Lib. Assn., A/40-41, Flat 201, Ansal Bldg., Dr Mukerjee Nagar, Delhi 110009. Tel./fax 11-2765-1743, e-mail office@ila-india.org, World Wide Web http://www.

ila-india.org. *Pres.* J. N. Satpathi; *Gen. Secy.* Arun Kumar Chakraborty.

Indonesia

Ikatan Pustakawan Indonesia (Indonesian Lib. Assn.), Jl. Merdeka Selatan No. 11, 10110 Jakarta, Pusat. Tel./fax 21-385-5729, World Wide Web http://ipi.pnri.go. id. *Pres.* S. Kartosdono.

Ireland

Cumann Leabharlann Na h-Eireann (Lib. Assn. of Ireland), 53 Upper Mount St., Dublin. Tel. 1-6120-2193, fax 1-6121-3090, e-mail president@libraryassociation. ie, World Wide Web http://www.library association.ie. *Pres.* Deirdre Ellis-King.

Israel

Israel Libns. and Info. Specialists Assn., 9 Beit Hadfus St., Givaat Shaul, Jerusalem. Tel. 2-658-9515, fax 2-625-1628, e-mail icl@icl.org.il, World Wide Web http:// www.icl.org.il. *Pres.* Benjamin Schachter.

Israeli Assn. of Libs. and Info. Centers (ASMI), P.O. Box 3211, 47131 Ramat-Hasharon. Tel. 3-547-2644, fax 3-547-2649, e-mail asmi@asmi.org.il; World Wide Web http://www.asmi.org.il. *Chair* Shoshana Langerman.

Israeli Center for Libs., P.O. Box 801, 51108 Bnei Brak. Tel. 03-618-0151, fax 3-579-8048, e-mail icl@icl.org.il, World Wide Web http://www.icl.org.il. *Chair* Danny Bustin.

Italy

Associazione Italiana Biblioteche (Italian Lib. Assn.), C.P. 2461, 00185 Rome AD. Tel. 6-446-3532, fax 6-444-1139, e-mail aib@aib.it, World Wide Web http://www. aib.it. *Pres.* Mauro Guerrini.

Jamaica

Lib. and Info. Assn. of Jamaica., P.O. Box 125, Kingston 5. Tel./fax 876-927-1614, e-mail liajapresident@yahoo.com, World

Wide Web http://www.liaja.org.jm. *Pres.* Marva Bradford.

Japan

Joho Kagaku Gijutsu Kyokai (Info. Science and Technology Assn.), Sasaki Bldg., 7 Koisikawa-2, Bunkyo-ku, Tokyo 112-0002. Tel. 3-3813-3791, fax 3-3813-3793, e-mail infosta@infosta.or.jp, World Wide Web http://www.infosta.or.jp. *Pres.* T. Gondoh; *Gen. Mgr.* Yukio Ichikawa.

Nihon Toshokan Kyokai (Japan Lib. Assn.), 1-11-14 Shinkawa, Chuo-ku, Tokyo 104 0033. Tel. 3-3523-0811, fax 3-3523-0841, e-mail info@jla.or.jp, World Wide Web http://www.jla.or.jp. *Secy.-Gen.* Reiko Sakagawa.

Senmon Toshokan Kyogikai (Japan Special Libs. Assn.), c/o Japan Lib. Assn., Bldg. F6, 1-11-14 Shinkawa Chuo-ku, Tokyo 104-0033. Tel. 3-3537-8335, fax 3-3537-8336, e-mail jsla@jsla.or.jp, World Wide Web http://www.jsla.or.jp. *Pres.* Kousaku Inaba; *Exec. Dir.* Fumihisa Nakagawa.

Jordan

Arab Archives Institute, P.O. Box 815454m Amman. Tel. 962-79-986-0004, fax 962-6-465-6693, e-mail saeda@nol.com.jo. *Dir.* Sa'eda Kilani.

Jordan Lib. Assn., P.O. Box 6289, Amman. Tel./fax 6-462-9412, e-mail info@jorla.org, World Wide Web http://www.jorla.org. *Pres.* Anwar Akroush; *Secy.* Yousra Abu Ajamieh.

Kenya

Kenya Assn. of Lib. and Info. Professionals (formerly Kenya Lib. Assn.), P.O. Box 46031, 00100 Nairobi. Tel. 20-733-732-799, fax 20-811-455, World Wide Web http://www.klas.or.ke.

Korea (Democratic People's Republic of)

Lib. Assn. of the Democratic People's Republic of Korea, c/o Grand People's Study House, P.O. Box 200, Pyongyang. E-mail kyokoi@jaspul.org.

Korea (Republic of)

Korean Lib. Assn., San 60-1, Banpo-dong, Seocho-gu, Seoul 137-702. Tel. 2-535-4868, fax 2-535-5616, e-mail klanet@hitel.net, World Wide Web http://www.korla.or.kr. *Pres.* Ki Nam Shin; *Exec. Dir.* Won Ho Jo.

Laos

Association des Bibliothécaires Laotiens (Lao Lib. Assn.), c/o Direction de la Bibliothèque Nationale, Ministry of Info. and Culture, B.P. 704, Vientiane. Tel. 21-21-2452, fax 21-21-2408, e-mail bailane@laotel.com.

Latvia

Lib. Assn. of Latvia, Terbatas iela 75, Riga LV-1001. Tel./fax 6731-2792, e-mail lbb@lbi.lnb.lv, World Wide Web http://www.lnb.lv. *Pres.* Anna Maulina.

Lebanon

Lebanese Lib. Assn., P.O. Box 13-5053, Beirut 1102 2801. Tel. 1-786-456, e-mail kjaroudy@lau.edu.lb; World Wide Web http://www.llaweb.org/index.php. *Pres.* Fawz Abdalleh.

Lesotho

Lesotho Lib. Assn., Private Bag A26, Maseru 100. Tel./fax 340-601, e-mail mmc@doc.isas.nul.ls, World Wide Web http://www.sn.apc.org. *Chair* S. M. Mohai; *Secy.* N. Taole.

Lithuania

Lietuvos Bibliotekininku Draugija (Lithuanian Libns. Assn.), Sv Ignoto 6-108, 1120 Vilnius. Tel. 5-262-11-43, fax 5-275-03-40, e-mail lbd@vpu.lt, World Wide Web http://www.lbd.lt. *Pres.* Vida Garunkstyte; *Dir.* Emilija Banionyte.

Luxembourg

Assn. Luxembourgeoise des Bibliothécaires, Archivistes, et Documentalistes (ALBAD)

(Luxembourg Assn. of Libns., Archivists, and Documentalists), c/o National Lib. of Luxembourg, BP 295, L-2012 Luxembourg. Tel. 352-22-97-55-1, fax 352-47-56-72, World Wide Web http://www. albad.lu. *Pres.* Jean-Marie Reding. E-mail jean-marie.reding@bnl.etat.lu; *Secy.-Gen.* Michel Donven. E-mail michel.donven@ bnl.etat.lu.

Macedonia

Bibliotekarsko Drustvo na Makedonija (Union of Libns.' Assns. of Macedonia), Blvd. Gotse Delcev 6, 1000 Skopje. E-mail bdm@bdm.org.mk, World Wide Web http://www.bdm.org.mk. *Pres.* Suzana Kotovchevska; *Secy.* Kiril Angelov.

Malawi

Malawi Lib. Assn., P.O. Box 429, Zomba. Tel. 50-522-222, fax 50-523-225. *Chair* Geoffrey F. Salanje; *Secy.-Gen.* Francis F. C. Kachala. E-mail fkachala@chanco. unima.mw.

Malaysia

Persatuan Perpustakaan Malaysia (Lib. Assn. of Malaysia), P.O. Box 12545, 50782 Kuala Lumpur. Tel./fax 3-2694-7390, e-mail ppm55@po.jaring.my, World Wide Web http://www.ppm55.org.my. *Pres.* Putri Saniah Megat Abdul Rahman. E-mail psaniah@yahoo.com.

Mali

Association Malienne des Bibliothécaires, Archivistes et Documentalistes (Mali Assn. of Libns., Archivists, and Documentalists), c/o Nationale Archives du Mali, BP 159, Bamako. Tel. 229-9423, fax 222-5844, e-mail dnambko@afribone.net.ml.

Malta

Malta Lib. and Info. Assn. (MaLIA), c/o Univ. of Malta Lib., Msida MSD 2080. E-mail info@malia-malta.org, World Wide Web http://www.malia-malta.org. *Chair* Robert Mizzi.

Mauritania

Association Mauritanienne des Bibliothécaires, Archivistes et Documentalistes (Mauritanian Assn. of Libns., Archivists, and Documentalists), c/o Bibliothèque Nationale, B.P. 216, Nouakchott. Tel. 525-18-62, fax 525-18-68, e-mail bibliotheque-nationale@yahoo.fr.

Mauritius

Mauritius Lib. Assn., Ministry of Educ. Public Lib., Moka Rd., Rose Hill. Tel. 403-0200, fax 454-9553. *Pres.* Abdool Fareed Soogali.

Mexico

Asociación Mexicana de Bibliotecarios (Mexican Assn. of Libns.), Apdo. 12-800, Administración Postal Obreto Mundial, 03001 México DF 06760. Tel. 155-5575-3396, fax 155-5575-1135, e-mail correo@ ambac.org.mx, World Wide Web http:// www.ambac.org.mx. *Pres.* Hortensia Lobato Reyes; *Secy.* Marisela Castro Moreno.

Myanmar

Myanmar Lib. Assn., c/o National Lib., 85 Thirimingalar Ave., Yangon. Tel. 1-27-2058, fax 01-53-2927.

Nepal

Nepal Lib. Assn., GPO 2773, Kathmandu. Tel. 977-1-441-1318, e-mail info@nla.org. np, World Wide Web http://www.nla.org. np. *Contact* Rudra Prasad Dulal.

The Netherlands

Nederlandse Vereniging voor Beroepsbeoefenaren in de Bibliotheek-Informatie-en Kennissector (Netherlands Assn. of Libns., Documentalists, and Info. Specialists), Nieuwegracht 15, 3512 LC Utrecht. Tel. 30-231-1263, fax 30-231-1830, e-mail nvbinfo@wxs.nl, World Wide Web http:// www.nvbonline.nl. *Pres.* J. S. M. Savenije. E-mail b.savenije@library.uu.nl.

New Zealand

New Zealand Lib. Assn. (LIANZA), P.O. Box 12-212, Wellington 6144. Tel. 4-473-5834, fax 4-499-1480, e-mail office@lianza.org.nz, World Wide Web http://www.lianza.org.nz. *Pres.* Vye Perrone.

Nicaragua

Asociación Nicaraguense de Bibliotecarios y Profesionales a Fines (Nicaraguan Assn. of Libns.), Bello Horizonte, Tope Sur de la Rotonda 1/2 cuadra abajo, Casa J-11-57, Managua. Tel. 277-4159 ext. 335, e-mail info@anibipa.org.ni, World Wide Web http://www.anibipa.org.ni. *Pres.* Darling Vallecillo.

Nigeria

Nigerian Lib. Assn., c/o National Lib. of Nigeria, Sanusi Dantata House, Business Central District, Garki District, Abuja 900001. Tel. 8055-36-5245, fax 9-234-6773, e-mail info@nla-ng.org, World Wide Web http://www.nla-ng.org. *Pres.* A. O. Banjo; *Secy.* D. D. Bwayili.

Norway

Arkivarforeningen (Assn. of Archivists), Postboks 4015, Ulleval Sta., N-0806 Oslo. Tel. 22-02-28-22, fax 22-23-74-89, e-mail lasa@arkivverket.no, World Wide Web http://www.forskerforbundet.no.

Norsk Bibliotekforening (Norwegian Lib. Assn.), Postboks 6540, 0606 Etterstad. Tel. 23-24-34-30, fax 22-67-23-68, e-mail nbf@norskbibliotekforening.no, World Wide Web http://www.norskbibliotek forening.no. *Dir.* Berit Aaker.

Pakistan

Pakistan Lib. Assn., c/o National Lib. of Pakistan, Constitution Ave., Islamabad 44000. Tel. 51-921-4523, fax 51-922-1375, e-mail info@pla.org.pk, World Wide Web http://www.pla.org.pk.

Panama

Asociación Panameña de Bibliotecarios (Panama Lib. Assn.), c/o Biblioteca Interamericana Simón Bolivar, Estafeta Universitaria, Panama City.

Paraguay

Asociación de Bibliotecarios Graduados del Paraguay (Assn. of Paraguayan Graduate Libns.), Facultad Politecnica, Universidad Nacional de Asunción, 2160 San Lorenzo. Tel. 21-585-588, e-mail abigrap@pol.una.py, World Wide Web http://www.pol.una.py/abigrap. *Pres.* Emilce Noemi Sena Correa.

Peru

Asociación de Archiveros del Perú (Peruvian Assn. of Archivists), Av. Manco Capacc No. 1180, tercer piso, La Victoria. Tel. 1-472-8729, fax 1-472-7408, e-mail contactos@adapperu.com, World Wide Web http://www.adapperu.org. *Pres.* Juan Antonio Espinoza Morante.

Asociación Peruana de Bibliotecarios (Peruvian Assn. of Libns.), Bellavista 561 Miraflores, Apdo. 995, Lima 18. Tel. 1-474-869. *Pres.* Martha Fernandez de Lopez; *Secy.* Luzmila Tello de Medina.

Philippines

Assn. of Special Libs. of the Philippines, Rm. 301, National Lib. Bldg., T. M. Kalaw St., 2801 Ermita, Manila. Tel. 2-524-4611, World Wide Web http://www.aczafra.com/aslp. *Pres.* Jocelyn L. Ladlad. E-mail ladlad@dlsu.edu.ph.

Philippine Libns. Assn., Bldg. 3F, Rm. 301, National Lib. of the Philippines, T. M. Kalaw St., 1000 Ermita, Manila. Tel. 2-525-9401, fax 02-525-9401. *Pres.* Susima L. Gonzales.

Poland

Stowarzyszenie Bibliotekarzy Polskich (Polish Libns. Assn.), al Niepodleglosci 213, 02-086 Warsaw. Tel. 22-825-83-74, fax 22-825-53-49, e-mail biurozgsbp@wp.pl,

World Wide Web http://ebib.info. *Pres.* Elzbieta Stefanczyk; *Secy.-Gen.* Maria Burchard.

Portugal

Associação Portuguesa de Bibliotecários, Arquivistas e Documentalistas (Portuguese Assn. of Libns., Archivists, and Documentalists), R. Morais Soares, 43C, 1 Dto e Fte, 1900-341 Lisbon. Tel. 21-816-19-80, fax 21-815-45-08, e-mail bad@apbad.pt, World Wide Web http://www.apbad.pt. *Pres.* António José de Pina Falcão.

Puerto Rico

Sociedad de Bibliotecarios de Puerto Rico (Society of Libns. of Puerto Rico), P.O. Box 22898, Universidad de Puerto Rico, San Juan 00931-2898. Tel./fax 787-764-0000, World Wide Web http://www. sociedadbibliotecarios.org. *Pres.* Maria de los Angeles Lugo.

Russia

Rossiiskaya Bibliotechnaya Assotsiatsiya (Russian Lib. Assn.), 18 Sadovaya St., St. Petersburg 191069. Tel. 812-118-85-36, fax 812-110-58-61, e-mail rba@nlr.ru, World Wide Web http://www.rba.ru. *Pres.* Vladimir Zaitsev; *Exec. Secy.* Maya Shaparneva.

Senegal

Association Sénégalaise des Bibliothécaires, Archivistes et Documentalistes (Senegalese Assn. of Libns., Archivists, and Documentalists), Université Cheikh Anta Diop de Dakar, BP 3252, Dakar. Tel. 221-864-27-73, fax 221-824-23-79, e-mail asbad200@hotmail.com, World Wide Web http://www.ebad.ucad.sn/sites_heberges/as bad/index.htm. *Pres.* Djibril Ndiaye; *Secy.-Gen.* Bernard Dione.

Serbia and Montenegro

Jugoslovenski Bibliografsko Informacijski Institut, Terazije 26, 11000 Belgrade. Tel. 11-687-836, fax 11-687-760. *Dir.* Radomir Glavicki.

Sierra Leone

Sierra Leone Assn. of Archivists, Libns., and Info. Scientists, c/o COMAHS Lib. New England, Freetown. Tel. 22-22-0758. *V.P.* Oliver Harding.

Singapore

Lib. Assn. of Singapore, National Lib. Board, 100 Victoria St., No. 14-01, Singapore 188064. Tel. 6749-7990, fax 6749-7480, e-mail lassec@las.org.sg, World Wide Web http://www.las.org.sg. *Pres.* Puspa Yeow.

Slovenia

Zveza Bibliotekarskih Druõtev Slovenije (Union of Assns. of Slovene Libns.), Turjaöka 1, 1000 Ljubljana. Tel. 01-20-01-193, fax 01-42-57-293, e-mail zveza-biblio. ds-nuk@quest.arnes.si, World Wide Web http://www.zbds-zveza.si. *Pres.* Melita Ambroũic.

South Africa

Lib. and Info. Assn. of South Africa, P.O. Box 1598, Pretoria 0001. Tel. 12-337-6129, fax 12-337-6108, e-mail liasa@ liasa.org.za, World Wide Web http://www. liasa.org.za. *Pres.* R. More; *Secy.* J. Henning.

Spain

Asociación Española de Archiveros, Bibliotecarios, Museólogos y Documentalistas (ANABAD) (Spanish Assn. of Archivists, Libns., Curators, and Documentalists), Recoletos 5, 3 izda., 28001 Madrid. Tel. 91-575-17-27, fax 91-578-16-15, e-mail anabad@anabad.org, World Wide Web http://www.anabad.org. *Pres.* Pilar Gallego Cuadrado.

Sri Lanka

Sri Lanka Lib. Assn., Professional Center, 275/75 Stanley Wijesundara Mawatha, Colombo 7. Tel./fax 11-258-9103, e-mail slla@slltnet.lk, World Wide Web http://www.slla.org.lk. *Pres.* Piyadasa Ranasinge; *Gen. Secy.* K. G. G. Wijeweera.

Swaziland

Swaziland Lib. Assn., P.O. Box 2309, Mbabane H100. Tel. 404-2633, fax 404-3863, e-mail sdnationalarchives@realnet.co.sz, World Wide Web http://www.swala.sz. *Chair* Faith Mkhonta.

Sweden

Svensk Biblioteksförening (Swedish Lib. Assn.), World Trade Center D5, Box 70380, 107 24 S-Stockholm. Tel. 8-545-132-30, fax 8-545-132-31, e-mail info@biblioteksforeningen.org, World Wide Web http://www.biblioteksforeningen.org. *Secy.-Gen.* Niclas Lindberg.

Svensk Förening för Informationsspecialister (Swedish Assn. for Info. Specialists), Osquars backe 25, SE-100 44 Stockholm. Tel. 8-678-23-20, e-mail kansliet@sfis.nu, World Wide Web http://www.sfis.nu. *Pres.* Margareta Nelke. E-mail nelke@icatonce.com.

Svenska Arkivsamfundet (Swedish Assn. of Archivists), c/o Swedish Society Archives, Stockholm City Archives, Box 22063, 10422 Stockholm. Tel. 46-19-70-00, fax 46-19-70-70, e-mail info@arkivsamfundet.se, World Wide Web http://www.arkivsamfundet.se. *Pres.* Berndt Fredricksson. E-mail berndt.fredriksson@foreign.ministry.se.

Switzerland

Association des Bibliothèques et Bibliothécaires Suisses/Vereinigung Schweizerischer Bibliothekare/Associazione dei Bibliotecari Svizzeri (Assn. of Swiss Libs. and Libns.), Hallestr. 58, CH-3012 Bern. Tel. 31-382-42-40, fax 31-382-46-48, e-mail info@bis.info, World Wide Web http://www.bbs.ch. *Gen. Secy.* Barbara Kraeuchi. E-mail b.kraeuchi@bbs.ch.

Schweizerische Vereinigung für Dokumentation/Association Suisse de Documentation (Swiss Assn. of Documentation), Hallestr. 58, CH-3012 Bern. Tel. 31-382-42-40, fax 31-382-46-48. E-mail info@bis.info, World Wide Web http://www.svd-asd.org. *Gen. Secy.* Barbara Kraeuchi. E-mail b.kraeuchi@bbs.ch.

Verein Schweizer Archivarinnen und Archivare (Assn. of Swiss Archivists), Schweizerisches Bundesarchiv, Brunngasse 60, CH-3003 Bern 8. Tel. 31-312-72-72, fax 31-312-38-01, e-mail vsa-aas@smueller.ch, World Wide Web http://www.vsa-aas.org. *Pres.* Andreas Kellerhals. E-mail andreas.kellerhals@bar.admin.ch

Taiwan

Lib. Assn. of the Republic of China (LAROC), c/o National Central Lib., 20 Chung Shan S. Rd., Taipei 10001. Tel. 2-2331-2675, fax 2-2370-0899, e-mail lac@msg.ncl.edu.tw. *Secy.-Gen.* Teresa Wang Chang.

Tanzania

Tanzania Lib. Assn., P.O. Box 33433, Dar es Salaam. Tel./fax 22-277-5411, e-mail tla_tanzania@yahoo.com, World Wide Web http://www.tlatz.org. *Chair* Alli Mcharazo. E-mail amcharazo@hotmail.com.

Thailand

Thai Lib. Assn., 1346 Akarnsongkrau Rd. 5, Klongchan, Bangkapi, 10240 Bangkok. Tel. 02-734-9022, fax 02-734-9021, e-mail tla2497@yahoo.com, World Wide Web http://tla.or.th. *Pres.* Chutima Sacchanand; *Exec. Secy.* Suwadee Vichetpan.

Trinidad and Tobago

Lib. Assn. of Trinidad and Tobago, P.O. Box 1275, Port of Spain. Tel. 868-625-0620, e-mail latt@lycos.com, World Wide Web http://www.latt.org.tt. *Pres.* Lillibeth S. V. Ackbarali.

Tunisia

Association Tunisienne des Documentalistes, Bibliothécaires et Archivistes (Tunisian Assn. of Documentalists, Libns., and Archivists), Centre de Documentation Nationale, 8004 rue Kheredinne Pacha, 1002 Tunis. Tel. 7165-1924.

Turkey

Türk Kütüphaneciler Dernegi (Turkish Libns. Assn.), Necatibey Caddesi Elgun Sok 8/8, Kizilay, Ankara. Tel. 312-230-13-25, fax 312-232-04-53, e-mail tkd.dernek@gmail. com, World Wide Web http://www. kutuphaneci.org.tr. *Pres.* Ali Fuat Kartal; *Secy.* Hakan Anameric.

Uganda

Uganda Lib. and Info. Assn., P.O. Box 8147, Kampala. Tel. 141-256-77-467698. *Pres.* Innocent Rugambwa; *Gen. Secy.* Sarah Kaddu.

Ukraine

Ukrainian Lib. Assn., Lesia Ukrainka Kyiv Public Lib., Turgenivska Str. 83/85, 04050 Kyiv. E-mail pashkovavs@yahoo.com, World Wide Web http://www.uba.org.ua. *Pres.* Valentyna Pashkova.

United Kingdom

ASLIB, the Assn. for Info. Management, Holywell Centre, 1 Phipp St., London EC2A 4PS, England. Tel. 20-7613-3031, fax 20-7613-5080, e-mail aslib@aslib. com, World Wide Web http://www.aslib. co.uk. *Dir.* R. B. Bowes.

Bibliographical Society, Institute of English Studies, Senate House, Rm. 306, Malet St., London WC1E 7HU, England. Tel. 20-7611-7244, fax 20-7611-8703, e-mail secretary@bibsoc.org.uk, World Wide Web http://www.bibsoc.org.uk/bibsoc.htm. *Pres.* Elisabeth Leedham-Green.

Chartered Institute of Lib. and Info. Professionals (CILIP) (formerly the Lib. Assn.), 7 Ridgmount St., London WC1E 7AE, England. Tel. 20-7255-0500, fax 20-7255-

0651, e-mail info@cilip.org.uk, World Wide Web http://www.cilip.org.uk. *Chief Exec.* Bob McKee.

School Lib. Assn., Unit 2, Lotmead Business Village, Lotmead Farm, Wanborough, Swindon SN4 0UY, England. Tel. 1793-791-787, fax 1793-791-786, e-mail info@ sla.org.uk, World Wide Web http://www. sla.org.uk. *Pres.* Gervase Phinn; *Chief Exec.* Kathy Lemaire.

Scottish Lib. and Info. Council, 1st fl., Bldg. C, Brandon Gate, Leechlee Rd., Hamilton ML3 6AU, Scotland. Tel. 1698-458-888, fax 1698-283-170, e-mail slic@slainte.org. uk, World Wide Web http://www.slainte. org.uk. *Dir.* Elaine Fulton.

Society of Archivists, Prioryfield House, 20 Canon St., Taunton TA1 1SW, England. Tel. 1823-327-030, fax 1823-371-719, e-mail societyofarchivists@archives.org.uk, World Wide Web http://www.archives. org.uk. *Chair* Peter Emmerson; *Hon. Secy.* Jenny Moran.

Society of College, National, and Univ. Libs. (SCONUL) (formerly Standing Conference of National and Univ. Libs.), 102 Euston St., London NW1 2HA, England. Tel. 20-7387-0317, fax 20-7383-3197, e-mail info@sconul.ac.uk, World Wide Web http://www.sconul.ac.uk. *Secy.* Toby Bainton.

Uruguay

Agrupación Bibliotecológica del Uruguay (Uruguayan Lib. and Archive Science Assn.), Cerro Largo 1666, 11200 Montevideo. Tel. 2-400-57-40. *Pres.* Luis Alberto Musso.

Asociación de Bibliotecólogos del Uruguay, Eduardo V. Haedo 2255, 11200 Montevideo. Tel./fax 2-4099-989, e-mail abu@ adinet.com.uy, World Wide Web http:// www.abu.net.uy. *Pres.* Victor Aguirre Negro.

Venezuela

Colegio de Bibliotecólogos y Archivólogos de Venezuela (Venezuelan Lib. and Archives Assn.), Apdo. 6283, Caracas.

Tel. 212-572-1858. *Pres.* Elsi Jimenez de Diaz.

Vietnam

Hôi Thu-Vien Viet Nam (Vietnamese Lib. Assn.), National Lib. of Vietnam, 31 Trang Thi, 10000 Hanoi. Tel. 4-8254-927, fax 4-8-253-357, e-mail info@nlv.gov.vn, World Wide Web http://www.nlv.gov.vn.

Zambia

Zambia Lib. Assn., Great East Rd. Campus, P.O. Box 38636, 10101 Lusaka. Tel. 21-291-381, fax 21-1-292-702. *Chair* Benson Njobvu. E-mail bensonnjobvu@gmail.com.

Zimbabwe

Zimbabwe Lib. Assn., P.O. Box 3133, Harare. Tel. 4-692-741. *Chair* Driden Kunaka.

Directory of Book Trade and Related Organizations

Book Trade Associations, United States and Canada

For more extensive information on the associations listed in this section, see the annual edition of *Literary Market Place* (Information Today, Inc.).

AIGA—The Professional Assn. for Design (formerly the American Institute of Graphic Arts), 164 Fifth Ave., New York, NY 10010. Tel. 212-807-1990, fax 212-807-1799, e-mail aiga@aiga.org, World Wide Web http://www.aiga.org. *Pres.* Debbie Millman, Sterling Brands, 350 Fifth Ave., No. 1714, New York, NY 10118. Tel. 212-329-4609, e-mail debbie.m@sterling brands.com; *Exec. Dir.* Richard Grefe. E-mail grefe@aiga.org.

American Booksellers Assn., 200 White Plains Rd., Tarrytown, NY 10591. Tel. 800-637-0037, 914-591-2665, fax 914-591-2720, World Wide Web http://www.bookweb.org. *Pres.* Michael Tucker, Books Inc., 1501 Vermont St., San Francisco, CA 94107. Tel. 415-643-3400 ext. 18, fax 415-643-2043, e-mail mtucker@booksinc.net; *V.P./Secy.* Becky Anderson, Anderson's Bookshops, 123 W. Jefferson Ave., Naperville, IL 60540 . Tel. 630-355-2665, fax 630-355-3470, e-mail becky@ andersonsbookshop.com; *CEO* Oren Teicher. E-mail oren@bookweb.org.

American Literary Translators Assn. (ALTA), Univ. of Texas–Dallas, 800 W. Campbell Rd., Mail Sta. JO51, Richardson, TX 75080. Tel. 972-883-2093, fax 972-883-6303, World Wide Web http://www.utdallas.edu/alta. *Pres.* Barbara Harshav; *V.P.* Gary Racz; *Secy.* Sidney Wade; *Admin. Asst.* Lindy Jolly. E-mail lindy.jolly@utdallas.edu.

American Medical Publishers Committee (AMPC), c/o Sara Pinto, dir., Professional/Scholarly Publishing Div., Assn. of American Publishers, 71 Fifth Ave., New York, NY 10003-3004. Tel. 212-255-0200 ext. 257, fax 212-255-7007, e-mail spinto@ publishers.org.

American Printing History Assn., Box 4519, Grand Central Sta., New York, NY 10163-4519. World Wide Web http://www.printinghistory.org. *Pres.* Paul W. Romaine. *Exec. Secy.* Stephen Crook. E-mail sgcrook@printinghistory.org.

American Society for Indexing, 10200 W. 44 Ave., Suite 304, Wheat Ridge, CO 80033. Tel. 303-463-2887, fax 303-422-8894, e-mail info@asindexing.org, World Wide Web http://www.asindexing.org. *Pres.* Kate Mertes. E-mail president@asindexing.org; *V.P./Pres.-Elect* Francis Lennie; *Secy.* Lucie Haskins; *Treas.* Richard Shrout; *Past Pres.* Fred Leise; *Exec. Dir.* Annette Rogers. E-mail arogers@resourcenter.com.

American Society of Journalists and Authors, 1501 Broadway, Suite 302, New York, NY 10036. Tel. 212-997-0947, fax 212-937-3215, e-mail director@asja.org, World Wide Web http://www.asja.org. *Pres.* Salley Shannon. E-mail president@asja.org; *Exec. Dir.* Alexandra Owens.

American Society of Media Photographers, 150 N. 2 St., Philadelphia, PA 19106. Tel. 215-451-2767, fax 215-451-0880, e-mail mopsik@asmp.org, World Wide Web http://www.asmp.org. *Pres.* Richard Kelly; *Exec. Dir.* Eugene Mopsik.

American Society of Picture Professionals, 117 S. Saint Asaph St., Alexandria, VA 22314. Tel. 703-299-0219, fax 703-299-9910, e-mail cathy@aspp.com, World Wide Web http://www.aspp.com. *Pres.* Amy Wrynn; *Exec. Dir.* Cathy D.-P. Sachs.

American Translators Assn., 225 Reinekers Lane, Suite 590, Alexandria, VA 22314. Tel. 703-683-6100, fax 703-683-6122, e-mail ata@atanet.org, World Wide Web http://www.atanet.org. *Pres.* Nicholas Hartmann; *Pres.-Elect* Dorothee Racette; *Secy.* Virginia Perez-Santalla; *Treas.* Gabe Bokor; *Exec. Dir.* Walter W. Bacak, Jr. E-mail walter@atanet.org.

Antiquarian Booksellers Assn. of America, 20 W. 44 St., No. 507, New York, NY 10036-6604. Tel. 212-944-8291, fax 212-944-8293, e-mail inquiries@abaa.org, World Wide Web http://www.abaa.org. *Pres.* Stuart Bennett, Stuart Bennett Rare Books; *Exec. Dir.* Susan Benne. E-mail hq@abaa.org.

Assn. Media and Publishing (formerly Society of National Assn. Publications, or SNAP), 1760 Old Meadow Rd., Suite 500, McLean, VA 22102. Tel. 703-506-3285, fax 703-506-3266, e-mail info@associationmediaandpublishing.org, World Wide Web http://www.associationmediaandpublishing.org. *Pres.* Jim Vick; *V.P.* Ryan Johnson.

Assn. of American Publishers, 71 Fifth Ave., New York, NY 10003. Tel. 212-255-0200, fax 212-255-7007. *Washington Office* 50 F St. N.W., Washington, DC 20001-1564. Tel. 202-347-3375, fax 202-347-3690. *Pres./CEO* Tom Allen; *V.P.s* Allan Adler, Tina Jordan; *Dir., Communications and Public Affairs* Judith Platt; *Exec. Dir., School Div.* Jay Diskey; *Exec. Dir., Higher Education* Bruce Hildebrand; *Exec. Dir., International Copyright Enforcement* M. Luisa Simpson; *Exec. Dir., Digital, Environmental, and Accessibility Affairs* Edward McCoyd; *Chair* Will Ethridge, Pearson Education.

Assn. of American University Presses, 28 W. 36 St., Suite 602, New York, NY 10018. Tel. 212-989-1010, fax 212-989-0275, e-mail info@aaupnet.org, World Wide Web

http://aaupnet.org. *Pres.* Kathleen Keane, Johns Hopkins; *Pres.-Elect* Richard Brown, Georgetown; *Exec. Dir.* Peter J.Givler. E-mail pgivler@aaupnet.org.

Assn. of Booksellers for Children (ABC), 6538 Collins Ave., No. 168, Miami Beach, FL 33141. Tel. 617-390-7759, fax 617-344-0540, e-mail kristen@abfc.com, World Wide Web http://www.abfc.com. *Exec. Dir.* Kristen McLean.

Assn. of Canadian Publishers, 174 Spadina Ave., Suite 306, Toronto, ON M5T 2C2. Tel. 416-487-6116, fax 416-487-8815, World Wide Web http://www.publishers.ca. *Pres.* Rodger Touchie, Heritage Group, 3555 Outrigger Rd., Suite 301, Nanoose Bay, BC V9P 9K1. Tel. 250-468-5328, fax 250-468-5318, e-mail publisher@heritagehouse.ca; *V.P.* Margie Wolfe, Second Story Press, 20 Maud St., Suite 401, Toronto, ON M5V 2M5. Tel. 416-537-7850, fax 416-537-0588, e-mail margie@secondstorypress.ca; *Exec. Dir.* Carolyn Wood. Tel. 416-487-6116 ext. 222, e-mail carolyn_wood@canbook.org.

Assn. of Educational Publishers (AEP), 510 Heron Dr., Suite 201, Logan Township, NJ 08085. Tel. 856-241-7772, fax 856-241-0709, e-mail mail@aepweb.org, World Wide Web http://www.aepweb.org. *Pres.* Suzanne I. Barchers; *Pres.-Elect* Daniel Caton; *V.P.* Neal Goff; *Treas.* Kevin McAliley; *Past Pres.* Richard Casabonne; *CEO* Charlene F. Gaynor. E-mail cgaynor@aepweb.org.

Authors Guild, 31 E. 32 St., Seventh fl., New York, NY 10016. Tel. 212-563-5904, fax 212-564-5363, e-mail staff@authorsguild.org, World Wide Web http://www.authorsguild.org. *Pres.* Roy Blount, Jr.

Book Industry Study Group, 370 Lexington Ave., Suite 900, New York, NY 10017. Tel. 646-336-7141, fax 646-336-6214, e-mail info@bisg.org, World Wide Web http://www.bisg.org. *Co-Chairs* Andrew Weber, Random House; Dominique Raccah, Sourcebooks; *Deputy Exec. Dir.* Angela Bole. E-mail angela@bisg.org.

Book Manufacturers' Institute, 2 Armand Beach Drive, Palm Coast, FL 32137. Tel. 386-986-4552, fax 386-986-4553, e-mail info@bmibook.com, World Wide Web http://www.bmibook.org. *Exec. V.P./Secy.* Bruce W. Smith. Address correspondence to the executive vice president.

Bookbuilders of Boston, 44 Vinal Rd., Scituate, MA 02066. Tel. 781-378-1361, fax 419-821-2171, e-mail office@bbboston. org, World Wide Web http://www. bbboston.org. *Pres.* Kirsten Sims. E-mail kirsten.sims@perason.com; *1st V.P.* Mike Ribaudo. E-mail mike@kaseprinting.com; *2nd V.P.* Michael Mozina. E-mail mmozina @brillusa.com; *Treas.* Scott Payne; *Clerk* Gina Choe.

Bookbuilders West, 9328 Elk Grove Blvd., Suite 105-250, Elk Grove, CA 95624. Tel. 916-320-0638, e-mail operations@book builders.org, World Wide Web http:// www.bookbuilders.org. *Pres.* Michael O'Brien, Laserwords U.S. E-mail michael @laserwords.com; *V.P.* Andrea Helmbolt, Jossey-Bass. E-mail ahelmbol@wiley.com.

Canadian Booksellers Assn., 789 Don Mills Rd., Suite 700, Toronto, ON M3C1T5. Tel. 416-467-7883, fax 416-467-7886, e-mail enquiries@cbabook.org, World Wide Web http://www.cbabook.org. *Pres.* Stephen Criber, Univ. of Western Ontario Bookstore, London, Ontario; *Exec. Dir.* Susan Dayus. E-mail sdayus@cbabook. org.

Canadian ISBN Agency, c/o Published Heritage, Library and Archives Canada, 395 Wellington St., Ottawa, ON K1A 0N4. Tel. 866-578-7777 (toll-free) or 819-994-6872, fax 819-997-7517, World Wide Web http://www.collectionscanada.ca/isn/index -e.html.

Canadian Printing Industries Association, 151 Slater St., Suite 1110, Ottawa, ON K1P 5H3. Tel. 613-236-7208, fax 613-232-1334, e-mail belliott@cpia-aci.ca, World Wide Web http://www.cpia-aci.ca. *Pres.* Bob Elliott; *Chair* Dean McElhinney, Unicom Graphics Ltd.

Catholic Book Publishers Assn., 11703 Huebner Rd., Suite 106-622, San Antonio, TX 78230. Tel. 210-368-2055, fax 210-368-2601, e-mail cliffk@cbpa.org, World Wide Web http://cbpa.org and http://www. catholicsread.org. *Pres.* Jeff Thomas; *Exec. Dir.* Cliff Knighten.

Chicago Book Clinic, 310 W. Lake St., Suite 219, Elmhurst, IL 60126. Tel. 630-833-4220, fax 630-563-9181, e-mail klabounty @apexmanage.com, World Wide Web http://www.chicagobookclinic.org. *Pres.* Dawn Weinfurtner. E-mail dawnw@ friesens.com; *V.P.* Eric Platou. E-mail eric_platou@malloy.com; *Contact* Kimberly LaBounty, Apex Management and Special Events. E-mail klabounty@ apexmanage.com.

Children's Book Council, 12 W. 37 St., 2nd fl., New York, NY 10018-7480. Tel. 212-966-1990, fax 212-966-2073, e-mail cbc. info@cbcbooks.org, World Wide Web http://www.cbcbooks.org. *Chair* Megan Tingley; *V. Chair* Chip Gibson; *Secy.* Justin Chanda; *Treas.* Don Weisberg; *Exec. Dir.* Robin Adelson. E-mail robin. adelson@cbcbooks.org.

Copyright Society of the USA, 352 Seventh Ave., Suite 739, New York, NY 10001. World Wide Web http://www.csusa.org. *Pres.* Karen Frank; *V.P./Pres.-Elect* Corey Field; *Secy.* Joseph Salvo; *Treas.* Nancy Mertzel; *Admin.* Amy Nickerson. E-mail amy@csusa.org.

Council of Literary Magazines and Presses, 154 Christopher St., Suite 3C, New York, NY 10014. Tel. 212-741-9110, fax 212-741-9112, e-mail info@clmp.org, World Wide Web http://www.clmp.org. *Cochairpersons* Ira Silverberg, Nicole Dewey; *Exec. Dir.* Jeffrey Lependorf. E-mail jlependorf@clmp.org.

Educational Book and Media Assn. (formerly Educational Paperback Assn.), Box 1399, East Hampton, NY 11937. Tel. 609-502-8147, e-mail bcombs@edupaperback.org, World Wide Web http://www.edu paperback.org. *Pres.* Neil Jaffe; *V.P.* Dan Walsh; *Treas.* Gene Bahlman; *Exec. Secy.* Bobbie Combs.

Evangelical Christian Publishers Assn., 9633 S. 48 St., Suite 140, Phoenix, AZ 85044. Tel. 480-966-3998, fax 480-966-1944, e-mail info@ecpa.org, World Wide Web http://www.ecpa.org. *Pres./CEO* Mark W. Kuyper; *Chair* Mike Hyatt, Thomas Nelson Publishers.

Graphic Artists Guild, 32 Broadway, Suite 1114, New York, NY 10004. Tel. 212-791-

3400, fax 212-792-0333, e-mail admin@gag.org, World Wide Web http://www.graphicartistsguild.org. *Pres.* John Schmelzer. E-mail president@gag.org; *Exec. Dir.* Patricia McKiernan. E-mail admin@gag.org.

Great Lakes Independent Booksellers Assn., c/o *Exec. Dir.* Jim Dana, Box 901, 208 Franklin St., Grand Haven, MI 49417. Tel. 616-847-2460, fax 616-842-0051, e-mail info@gliba.org, World Wide Web http://www.gliba.org. *Pres.* Sally Bulthuis. E-mail poohs@iserv.net; *V.P.* Cynthia Compton. E-mail kidsbooks4@msn.com; *Past Pres.* Jill Miner. E-mail saturn_booksellers@hotmail.com.

Guild of Book Workers, 521 Fifth Ave., New York, NY 10175. Tel. 212-292-4444, e-mail communications@guildofbookworkers.org, World Wide Web http://www.guildofbookworkers.org. *Pres.* James Reid-Cunningham. E-mail president@guildofbookworkers.org; *V.P.* Andrew Huot. E-mail vicepresident@guildofbookworkers.org.

Horror Writers Assn., 244 Fifth Ave., Suite 2767, New York, NY 10001. E-mail hwa@horror.org, World Wide Web http://www.horror.org. *Pres.* Deborah LeBlanc. E-mail president@horror.org; *V.P.* Heather Graham. E-mail vp@horror.org; *Secy.* Vince Liaguno. E-mail secretary@horror.org; *Treas.* Lisa Morton. E-mail treasurer@horror.org.

IAPHC—The Graphic Professionals Resource Network (formerly the International Assn. of Printing House Craftsmen), 7042 Brooklyn Blvd., Minneapolis, MN 55429. Tel. 800-466-4274, 763-560-1620, fax 763-560-1350, World Wide Web http://www.iaphc.org. *Pres./CEO* Kevin Keane. E-mail kkeane1069@aol.com.

Independent Book Publishers Association (formerly PMA), 627 Aviation Way, Manhattan Beach, CA 90266. Tel. 310-372-2732, fax 310-374-3342, e-mail info@ibpa-online.org, World Wide Web http://www.ibpa-online.org. *Pres.* Florrie Binford Kichler; *Exec. Dir.* Terry Nathan.

International Standard Book Numbering U.S. Agency, 630 Central Ave., New Providence, NJ 07974. Tel. 877-310-7333, fax 908-219-0188, e-mail isbn-san@bowker.com, World Wide Web http://www.isbn.org. *Vice Pres., Identifier Services* Andy Weissberg; *Dir.* Louise Timko.

Jewish Book Council, 520 Eighth Ave., Fourth fl., New York, NY 10010. Tel. 212-201-2920, fax 212-532-4952, e-mail jbc@jewishbooks.org, World Wide Web http://www.jewishbookcouncil.org. *Pres.* Lawrence J. Krule; *Exec.Dir.* Carolyn Starman Hessel.

Library Binding Institute, 4400 PGA Blvd., Suite 600, Palm Beach Gardens, FL 33410. Tel. 561-745-6821, fax 561-775-0089, e-mail info@lbibinders.org, World Wide Web http://www.lbibinders.org. *Pres.* Mark Hancock, Utah Bookbinding. E-mail mark@utahbookbinding.com; *V.P.* Jack Tolbert, National Lib. Bindery Co. of Georgia. E-mail nlbga@mindspring.com; *Exec. Dir.* Debra Nolan. E-mail dnolan@lbibinders.org.

Magazine Publishers of America, 810 Seventh Ave., 24th fl., New York, NY 10019. Tel. 212-872-3700, e-mail mpa@magazine.org, World Wide Web http://www.magazine.org. *Pres./CEO* Nina Link. Tel. 212-872-3710, e-mail president@magazine.org.

Midwest Independent Publishers Assn., P.O. Box 65686, St. Paul, MN 55165. Tel. 651-917-0021 or 651-797-3801, World Wide Web http://www.mipa.org. *Pres.* Pat Morris, Ricochet Frog Press. E-mail patmorris@comcast.net; *V.P.* Corrine Dwyer, North Star Press. E-mail info@northstarpress.com.

Miniature Book Society. *Pres.* Mark Palkovic. E-mail mark.palkovic@uc.edu; *V.P.* Stephen Byrne. E-mail sb@finalscore.demon.co.uk; *Secy.* Edward Hoyenski. E-mail ehoyensk@library.unt.edu; *Treas.* Karen Nyman. E-mail karennyman@cox.net; *Past Pres.* Julian I. Edison. E-mail jiestl@mac.com. World Wide Web http://www.mbs.org.

Minnesota Book Publishers Roundtable. *Pres.* Alison Aten, Minnesota Historical Society Press/Borealis Books, 345 Kellogg Blvd. W., St. Paul 55102. Tel. 651-259-3203, fax 651-297-1345, e-mail alison.aten@mnhs.org; *V.P.* Dan Wallek, Lerner Publishing Group, 241 First Ave. N., Minneapolis 55401. Tel. 612-215-6220, fax 612-332-7615, e-mail dwallek@lerner books.com. World Wide Web http://www. publishersroundtable.org.

Mountains and Plains Independent Booksellers Assn., 19 Old Town Sq., Suite 238, Fort Collins, CO 80524. Tel. 970-484-5856, fax 970-407-1479, e-mail info@ mountainsplains.org, World Wide Web http://www.mountainsplains.org.

NAPL (formerly National Assn. for Printing Leadership), 75 W. Century Rd., Suite 100, Paramus, NJ 07652. Tel. 800-642-6275, 201-634-9600, fax 201-634-0324, e-mail info@napl.org, World Wide Web http://www.napl.org. *Pres./CEO* Joseph P. Truncale.

National Assn. of College Stores, 500 E. Lorain St., Oberlin, OH 44074-1294. Tel. 800-622-7498, 440-775-7777, fax 440-775-4769, e-mail info@nacs.org, World Wide Web http://www.nacs.org. *CEO* Brian Cartier. E-mail bcartier@nacs.org.

National Coalition Against Censorship (NCAC), 275 Seventh Ave., No. 1504, New York, NY 10001. Tel. 212-807-6222, fax 212-807-6245, e-mail ncac@ncac.org, World Wide Web http://www.ncac.org. *Exec. Dir.* Joan E. Bertin.

New Atlantic Independent Booksellers Assn. (NAIBA), 2667 Hyacinth St., Westbury, NY 11590. Tel. 516-333-0681, fax 516-333-0689, e-mail info@naiba.com. World Wide Web http://www.newatlanticbooks. com. *Pres.* Joe Drabyak, Chester County Book Co., 975 Paoli Pike, West Chester, PA 19380. Tel. 610-696-1661, fax 610-429-9006, e-mail jdrabyak@ccbmc.com; *V.P.* Lucy Kogler. Talking Leaves Inc., 951 Elmwood Ave., Buffalo, NY 14222. Tel. 716-884-9524, fax 716-332-3625, e-mail lucyk@tleavesbooks.com; *Exec. Dir.* Eileen Dengler.

New England Independent Booksellers Assn., 297 Broadway, Arlington, MA 02474. Tel. 781-316-8894, fax 781-316-2605, e-mail steve@neba.org, World Wide Web http:// www.newenglandbooks.org. *Pres.* Dick Hermans; *V.P.* Annie Philbrick; *Treas.* Lisa Sullivan; *Exec. Dir.* Steve Fischer.

New York Center for Independent Publishing (formerly the Small Press Center), 20 W.

44 St., New York, NY 10036. Tel. 212-764-7021, fax 212-840-2046, e-mail contact@smallpress.org, World Wide Web http://www.nycip.org. *Exec. Dir.* Karin Taylor.

North American Bookdealers Exchange (NABE), Box 606, Cottage Grove, OR 97424. Tel./fax 541-942-7455, e-mail nabe@bookmarketingprofits.com, World Wide Web http://bookmarketingprofits. com. *Dir.* Al Galasso.

Northern California Independent Booksellers Assn., Presidio National Park, 1007 General Kennedy Ave., P.O. Box 29169, San Francisco, CA 94129. Tel. 415-561-7686, fax 415-561-7685, e-mail office@nciba. com, World Wide Web http://www.nciba. com. *Pres.* Michael Barnard; *V.P.* Calvin Crosby; *Exec. Dir.* Hut Landon.

Pacific Northwest Booksellers Assn., 214 E. 12 Ave., Eugene, OR 97401-3245. Tel. 541-683-4363, fax 541-683-3910, e-mail info@pnba.org, World Wide Web http:// www.pnba.org. *Pres.* Libby Manthey, Riverwalk Books. E-mail riverwalkl@nwi. net; *Exec. Dir.* Thom Chambliss.

PEN American Center, Div. of International PEN, 588 Broadway, Suite 303, New York, NY 10012. Tel. 212-334-1660, fax 212-334-2181, e-mail pen@pen.org, World Wide Web http://www.pen.org. *Pres.* Anthony Appiah; *Exec. V.P.* Laurence J. Kirshbaum; *Exec. Dir.* Steven L. Isenberg. E-mail sisenberg@pen.org

Periodical and Book Assn. of America, 481 Eighth Ave., Suite 826, New York, NY 10001. Tel. 212-563-6502, fax 212-563-4098, e-mail info@pbaa.net, World Wide Web http://www.pbaa.net. *Pres.* Joe Gallo. E-mail jgallo@ffn.com; *Chair* William Michalopoulos. E-mail wmichalopoulos@ hfmus.com; *Exec. Dir.* Lisa W. Scott. E-mail lscott@pbaa.net or lisawscott@ hotmail .com.

Romance Writers of America, 14615 Benfer Rd., Houston, TX 77069. Tel. 832-717-5200, fax 832-717-5201, e-mail info@ rwanational.org, World Wide Web http:// www.rwanational.org. *Pres.* Michelle Monkou. E-mail monkourwabd@comcast.net; *Pres.-Elect* Dorien Kelly. E-mail Kelly

RWAbd@gmail.com; *Exec. Dir.* Allison Kelley. E-mail allison.kelley@rwa.org.

Science Fiction and Fantasy Writers of America, P.O. Box 877, Chestertown, MD 21620. E-mail execdir@sfwa.org, World Wide Web http://www.sfwa.org. *Pres.* Russell Davis. E-mail president@sfwa.org; *V.P.* Elizabeth Moon. E-mail vp@sfwa.org; *Secy.* Mary Robinette Kowal. E-mail secretary@sfwa.org; *Treas.* Amy Casil. E-mail treasurer@sfwa.org.

Small Publishers Assn. of North America (SPAN), 1618 W. Colorado Ave., Colorado Springs, CO 80904. Tel. 719-475-1726, e-mail info1@spannet.org, World Wide Web http://www.spannet.org.

Society of Children's Book Writers and Illustrators (SCBWI), 8271 Beverly Blvd., Los Angeles, CA 90048. Tel. 323-782-1010, fax 323-782-1892, e-mail scbwi@scbwi.org, World Wide Web http://www.scbwi.org. *Pres.* Stephen Mooser. E-mail stephen mooser@scbwi.org; *Exec. Dir.* Lin Oliver.

Society of Illustrators (SI), 128 E. 63 St., New York, NY 10065. Tel. 212-838-2560, fax 212-838-2561, e-mail info@society illustrators.org, World Wide Web http://www.societyillustrators.org.

Southern Independent Booksellers Alliance (SIBA), 3806 Yale Ave., Columbia, SC 29205. Tel. 800-331-9617, 803-779-0118, fax 803-779-0113, e-mail info@sibaweb.com, World Wide Web http://www.siba web.com.

Technical Assn. of the Pulp and Paper Industry, 15 Technology Pkwy. S., Norcross, GA 30092 (P.O. Box 105113, Atlanta, GA 30348). Tel. 770-446-1400, fax 770-446-6947, World Wide Web http://www.tappi.org. *Pres.* Larry N. Montague. E-mail lmontague@tappi.org; *Chair* Jeffrey J. Siegel; *V. Chair* Norman F. Marsolan.

Western Writers of America, c/o Paul A. Hutton, MSC06 3770, 1 Univ. of New Mexico, Albuquerque, NM 87131-0001. E-mail wwa@unm.edu, World Wide Web http://www.westernwriters.org. *Pres.* Johnny D. Boggs; *Exec. Dir.* Paul Hutton.

Women's National Book Assn., c/o Susannah Greenberg Public Relations, P.O. Box 237, FDR Sta., New York, NY 10150. Tel./fax 212-208-4629, e-mail publicity@bookbuzz.com, World Wide Web http://www.wnba-books.org. *Pres.* Joan Gelfand; *V.P./Pres.-Elect* Mary Grey James; *Secy.* Ruth Light; *Treas.* Margaret E. Auer.

International and Foreign Book Trade Associations

For Canadian book trade associations, see the preceding section, "Book Trade Associations, United States and Canada." For a more extensive list of book trade organizations outside the United States and Canada, with more detailed information, consult *International Literary Market Place* (Information Today, Inc.), which also provides extensive lists of major bookstores and publishers in each country.

International

African Publishers' Network, BP 3429, Abidjan 01, Côte d'Ivoire. Tel. 202-11801, fax 202-11803, e-mail apnetes@yahoo.com, World Wide Web http://www.freewebs. com/africanpublishers. *Chair* Mamadou Aliou Sow; *Exec. Secy.* Akin Fasemore.

Afro-Asian Book Council, 4835/24 Ansari Rd., Daryaganj, New Delhi 110002, India. Tel. 11-2325-8865, fax 11-2326-7437, e-mail afro@aabcouncil.org, World Wide Web http://www.aabcouncil.org. *Secy.-Gen.* Sukumar Das; *Dir.* Saumya Gupta.

Centro Régional para el Fomento del Libro en América Latina y el Caribe (CERLALC) (Regional Center for Book Promotion in Latin America and the Caribbean), Calle 70, No. 9-52, Bogotá DC, Colombia. Tel. 1-540-2071, fax 1-541-6398, e-mail libro@cerlalc.com, World Wide Web http://www.cerlalc.org. *Dir.* Carmen Barvo.

Federation of European Publishers, rue Montoyer 31, Boîte 8, 1000 Brussels, Belgium. Tel. 2-770-11-10, fax 2-771-20-71, e-mail info@fep-fee.eu, World Wide Web http://www.fep-fee.be. *Pres.* Frederico Motto; *Dir.-Gen.* Anne Bergman-Tahon.

International Assn. of Scientific, Technical, and Medical Publishers (STM), Prama House, 267 Banbury Rd., Oxford OX2 7HT, England. Tel. 44-1865-339-321, fax 44-1865-339-325, e-mail info@stm-assoc. org, World Wide Web http://www.stm-assoc.org. *Chair* Jerry Cowhig; *CEO* Michael Mabe.

International Board on Books for Young People (IBBY), Nonnenweg 12, 4003 Basel, Switzerland. Tel. 61-272-29-17, fax 61-272-27-57, e-mail ibby@ibby.org, World Wide Web http://www.ibby.org. *Dir. Memb. Services* Elizabeth Page.

International Booksellers Federation (IBF), rue de la Science 10, 1000 Brussels, Belgium. Tel. 2-223-49-40, fax 2-223-49-38, e-mail ibf.booksellers@skynet.be, World Wide Web http://www.ibf-booksellers.org. *Dir.* Françoise Dubruille.

International League of Antiquarian Booksellers (ILAB), Prinsengracht 445, 1016 HN Amsterdam, Netherlands. Tel. 20-627-22-85, fax 20-625-89-70, e-mail info@ilab.org, World Wide Web http://www.ilab.org. *Pres.* Michael Steinbach; *Gen. Secy.* Arnoud Gerits.

International Publishers Assn. (Union Internationale des Editeurs), ave. de Miremont 3, CH-1206 Geneva, Switzerland. Tel. 22-7-4-1820, fax 22-704-1821, e-mail secretariat@internationalpublishers.org, World Wide Web http://www.international publishers.org. *Pres.* Herman P Spruijt; *Secy.-Gen.* Jens Bammel.

National

Argentina

Cámara Argentina del Libro (Argentine Book Assn.), Av. Belgrano 1580, 4 piso, C1093AAQ Buenos Aires. Tel. 11-4381-8383, fax 11-4381-9253, e-mail cal@editores.org.ar, World Wide Web http://www.editores.org.ar. *Dir.* Norberto J. Pou.

Fundación El Libro (Book Foundation), Hipolito Yrigoyen 1628, 5 piso, C1089AAF Buenos Aires. Tel. 11-4370-0600, fax 11-4370-0607, e-mail fundacion@el-libro.com.ar, World Wide Web http://www.el-libro.com.ar. *Pres.* Horacio Garcia; *Dir.* Marta V. Diaz.

Australia

Australian and New Zealand Assn. of Antiquarian Booksellers, P.O. Box 7127, McMahons Point, NSW 2060. Tel. 2-9966-9925, fax 2-9966-9926, e-mail admin @anzaab.com, World Wide Web http:// www.anzaab.com. *Pres.* Peter Tinslay. E-mail peter@antiquebookshop.com.au.

Australian Booksellers Assn., 828 High St., Unit 9, Kew East, Vic. 3102. Tel. 3-9859-7322, fax 3-9859-7344, e-mail mail@aba. org.au, World Wide Web http://www. aba.org.au. *Pres.* Fiona Stager; *CEO* Barbara Cullen.

Australian Publishers Assn., 60/89 Jones St., Ultimo, NSW 2007. Tel. 2-9281-9788, fax 2-9281-1073, e-mail apa@publishers.asn. au, World Wide Web http://www. publishers.asn.au. *CEO* Maree McCaskill.

Austria

Hauptverband des Österreichischen Buchhandels (Austrian Publishers and Booksellers Assn.), Grünangergasse 4, A-1010 Vienna. Tel. 1-512-15-35, fax 1-512-84-82, e-mail sekretariat@hvb.at, World Wide Web http:// www.buecher.at. *Mgr.* Inge Kralupper.

Verband der Antiquare Österreichs (Austrian Antiquarian Booksellers Assn.), Grünangergasse 4, A-1010 Vienna. Tel. 1-512-15-35, fax 1-512-84-82, e-mail sekretariat@ hvb.at, World Wide Web http://www. antiquare.at. *Pres.* Norbert Donhofer.

Belarus

National Book Chamber of Belarus, 31a V Khoruzhei Str., 220002 Minsk. Tel. 17-289-33-96, fax 17-334-78-47, World Wide Web http://www.natbook.org.by/start_en. php. *Dir.* Elena V. Ivanova.

Belgium

Vlaamse Boekverkopersbond (Flemish Booksellers Assn.), Te Buelaerlei 37, 2140 Borgerhout. Tel. 03-230-89-23, fax 3-281-22-40, World Wide Web http://www.boek. be. *Chair* Jos Geysels; *Dir.* Geert Joris.

Bolivia

Cámara Boliviana del Libro (Bolivian Booksellers Assn.), Calle Capitan Ravelo No. 2116, 682 La Paz. Tel. 2-244-4239, fax 2-211-3264, e-mail contacto@cabolib.org.bo. *Pres.* Ernesto Martinez Acchini.

Brazil

Cámara Brasileira do Livro (Brazilian Book Assn.), Rua Cristiano Viana 91, Pinheiros 05411-000 Sao Paulo-SP. Tel./fax 11-3069-1300, e-mail cbl@cbl.org.br, World Wide Web http://www.cbl.org.br. *Pres.* Rosely Boschini; *Dir.* H. Carlos Dias.

Sindicato Nacional dos Editores de Livros (Brazilian Publishers Assn.), Rue da Ajuda 35-18 andar, 20040-000 Rio de Janeiro-RJ. Tel. 21-2533-0399, fax 21-2533-0422, e-mail snel@snel.org.br, World Wide Web http://www.snel.org.br. *Pres.* Paulo Roberto Rocco.

Chile

Cámara Chilena del Libro AG (Chilean Assn. of Publishers, Distributors, and Booksellers), Av. Libertador Bernardo O'Higgins 1370, Oficina 501, Santiago. Tel. 2-672-0348, fax 2-687-4271, e-mail prolibro @tie.cl, World Wide Web http://www. camlibro.cl. *Pres.* Eduardo Castillo Garcia.

Colombia

Cámara Colombiana del Libro (Colombian Book Assn.), Calle 35, No. 5A 05, Bogotá. Tel. 1-323-01-11, fax 1-285-10-82, e-mail camlibro@camlibro.com.co, World Wide Web http://www.camlibro.com.co.

Czech Republic

Svaz českých knihkupců a nakladatelů (Czech Publishers and Booksellers Assn.), P.O. Box 177, 110 01 Prague. Tel. 224-219-944, fax 224-219-942, e-mail sckn@sckn. cz, World Wide Web http://www.sckn.cz. *Pres.* Vladimir Pistorius.

Denmark

Danske Boghandlerforening (Danish Booksellers Assn.), Langebrogade 6 opgang J, 1 sal, 1411 Copenhagen K. Tel. 3254-2255, fax 3254-0041, e-mail ddb@bogpost.dk, World Wide Web http://www.bogguide. dk. *Pres.* Jesper Moller; *Dir.* Olaf Winslow.

Danske Forlæggerforening (Danish Publishers Assn.), Skindergade 7 st tv, DK 1159 Copenhagen K. Tel. 3315-6688, fax 3315-6588, e-mail danishpublishers@danish publishers.dk, World Wide Web http:// www.danskeforlag.dk. *Chair* Karsten Blauert; *V. Chair* Tine Smedegaard Andersen.

Ecuador

Cámara Ecuatoriana del Libro, Núcleo de Pichincha, Avda. Eloy Alfaro, N29-61 e Inglaterra Edf. Eloy Al, Quito. Tel. 2-553-311, fax 2-222-150, e-mail celnp@uio. satnet.net, World Wide Web http://celibro. org.ec. *Pres.* Fausto Coba Estrella.

Egypt

General Egyptian Book Organization, P.O. Box 235, Cornich El-Nil, Ramlat Boulaq, Cairo. Tel. 2-2577-531, fax 2-2764-276, e-mail info@egyptianbook.org.eg, World Wide Web http://www.egyptianbook.org.eg. *Chair* Nasser El Ansary.

Estonia

Estonian Publishers Assn., Roosikrantsi 6, 10119 Tallinn. Tel. 644-9866, fax 617-7550, e-mail kirjastusteliit@eki.ee, World Wide Web http://www.estbook.com. *Dir.* Kaidi Urmet.

Finland

Kirjakauppaliitto Ry (Booksellers Assn. of Finland), Fredrikinkatu 47, 00100 Helsinki. Tel. 9-6859-9110, fax 9-6859-9119, e-mail toimisto@kirjakauppaliitto.fi, World Wide Web http://www.kirjakauppaliitto.fi. *Pres.* Stig-Bjorn Nyberg; *Dir.* Olli Erakivi.

Suomen Kustannusyhdistys (Finnish Book Publishers Assn.), P.O. Box 177, Lön-nrotinkatu 11 A, FIN-00121 Helsinki. Tel. 358-9-228-77-250, fax 358-9-612-1226, World Wide Web http://www.publishers. fi/en. *Pres.* Veli-Pekka Elonen; *Dir.* Sakari Laiho.

France

Bureau International de l'Edition Française (BIEF) (International Bureau of French Publishing), 115 blvd. Saint-Germain, F-75006 Paris. Tel. 01-44-41-13-13, fax 01-46-34-63-83, e-mail accueil_bief@bief.org, World Wide Web http://www.bief.org. *CEO* Jean-Guy Boin. *New York Branch* French Publishers Agency, 853 Broadway, Suite 1509, New York, NY 10003-4703. Tel./fax 212-254-4540, e-mail lucinda@frenchrights.com, World Wide Web http://frenchpubagency.com.

Cercle de la Librairie (Circle of Professionals of the Book Trade), 35 rue Grégoire-de-Tours, F-75006 Paris. Tel. 01-44-41-28-33, fax 01-44-41-28-65, e-mail commercial @electre.com, World Wide Web http:// www.electre.com. *Pres.* Charles Henri Flammarion.

Syndicat de la Librairie Française, 27 rue Bourgon, F-75013 Paris. Tel. 01-53-62-23-10, fax 01-53-62-10-45, e-mail slf@ nerim.fr, World Wide Web http://www. syndicat-librairie.fr. *Pres.* Benoit Bougerol.

Syndicat National de la Librairie Ancienne et Moderne (National Assn. of Antiquarian and Modern Booksellers), 4 rue Gît-le-Coeur, F-75006 Paris. Tel. 1-43-29-46-38, fax 1-43-25-41-63, e-mail slam-livre@ wanadoo.fr, World Wide Web http://www. slam-livre.fr. *Pres.* Alain Marchiset.

Syndicat National de l'Edition (National Union of Publishers), 115 blvd. Saint-Germain, F-75006 Paris. Tel. 1-44-41-40-50, fax 01-44-41-40-77, World Wide Web http://www.sne.fr. *Pres.* Serge Eyrolles.

Germany

Börsenverein des Deutschen Buchhandels e.V. (Stock Exchange of German Booksellers), Grosser Hirschgraben 17-21, 60311 Frankfurt-am-Main. Tel. 069-1306-

0, fax 069-13-06-201, e-mail info@boev.de, World Wide Web http://www.boersenverein.de. *Pres.* Gottfried Honnefelder; *CEO* Alexander Skipis.

Verband Deutscher Antiquare e.V. (German Antiquarian Booksellers Assn.), Geschäftsstelle, Norbert Munsch, Seeblick 1, 56459 Elbingen. Tel. 6435-909-147, fax 6435-909-148, e-mail buch@antiquare.de, World Wide Web http://www.antiquare.de. *Pres.* Eberhard Koestler.

Greece

Hellenic Federation of Publishers and Booksellers, 73 Themistocleous St., 106 83 Athens. Tel. 2103-300-924, fax 2133-301-617, e-mail secretary@poev.gr, World Wide Web http://www.poev.gr. *Pres.* Dimitris Panteleskos, *Secy.-Gen.* Georgios Stefanou.

Hungary

Magyar Könyvkiadók és Könyvterjesztök Egyesülése (Assn. of Hungarian Publishers and Booksellers), Postfach 130, 1367 Budapest. Tel. 1-343-2540, fax 1-343-2541, e-mail mkke@mkke.hu, World Wide Web http://www.mkke.hu. *Dir.* Peter Laszlo Zentai.

Iceland

Félag Islenskra Bókaútgefenda (Icelandic Publishers Assn.), Baronsstig 5, 101 Reykjavik. Tel. 511-8020, fax 511-5020, e-mail baekur@simnet.is, World Wide Web http://www.bokatidindi.is.

India

Federation of Indian Publishers, Federation House, 18/1C Institutional Area, Aruna Asaf Ali Marg, New Delhi 110067. Tel. 11-2696-4847, fax 11-2686-4054, e-mail fip1@satyam.net.in, World Wide Web http://www.fipindia.org. *Pres.* Shakti Malik.

Indonesia

Ikatan Penerbit Indonesia (Assn. of Indonesian Book Publishers), Jl. Kalipasir 32, Jakarta 10330. Tel. 21-314-1907, fax 21-314-6050, e-mail kkapi@cbn.net.id, World Wide Web http://www.ikapi.org. *Pres.* Arselan Harahap; *Secy.-Gen.* Robinson Rusdi.

Ireland

Publishing Ireland (formerly CLÉ: The Irish Book Publishers' Assn.), Guinness Enterprise Centre, Dublin 8. Tel. 1-639-4868, e-mail info@publishingireland.com, World Wide Web http://www.publishingireland.com. *Pres.* Alan Hayes.

Israel

Book and Printing Center, Israel Export Institute, 29 Hamered St., P.O. Box 50084, Tel Aviv 61500. Tel. 3-514-2855, fax 3-514-2881, e-mail export-institute@export.gov.il, World Wide Web http://www.export.gov.il. *Dir.-Gen.* Yechiel Assia.

Book Publishers' Assn. of Israel, P.O. Box 20123, 61201 Tel Aviv. Tel. 3-561-4121, fax 3-561-1996, e-mail hamol@tbpai.co.il, World Wide Web http://www.tbpai.co.il. *Managing Dir.* Amnon Ben-Shmuel; *Chair* Racheli Edelman.

Italy

Associazione Italiana Editori (Italian Publishers Assn.), Corso di Porta Romana 108, 20122 Milan. Tel. 2-89-28-0800, fax 2-89-28-0860, e-mail aie@aie.it, World Wide Web http://www.aie.it. *Dir.* Ivan Cecchini.

Associazione Librai Antiquari d'Italia (Antiquarian Booksellers Assn. of Italy), Via Cassia 1020, Rome. Tel. 39-347-64-6-9147, fax 39-06-2332-8979, e-mail alai@alai.it, World Wide Web http://www.alai.it. *Pres.* Umberto Pregliasco.

Japan

Antiquarian Booksellers Assn. of Japan, 29 San-ei-cho, Shinjuku-ku, Tokyo 160-0008. Tel. 3-3357-1411, fax 3-3351-5855, e-mail abaj@abaj.gr.jp, World Wide Web http://www.abaj.gr.jp. *Pres.* Takehiko Sakai.

Japan Assn. of International Publications (formerly Japan Book Importers Assn.), c/o UPS, 1-32-5 Higashi-shinagawa, Shinagawa-ku, Toyko 140-0002. Tel. 3-5479-7269, fax 3-5479-7307, e-mail office@jaip.jp, World Wide Web http://www.jaip.gr.jp. *Exec. Dir.* Mark Gresham.

Japan Book Publishers Assn., 6 Fukuromachi, Shinjuku-ku, Tokyo 162-0828. Tel. 3-3268-1303, fax 3-3268-1196, e-mail rd@jbpa.or.jp, World Wide Web http://www.jbpa.or.jp. *Pres.* Norio Komine; *Exec. Dir.* Tadashi Yamashita.

Kenya

Kenya Publishers Assn., P.O. Box 42767, Nairobi 00100. Tel. 20-375-2344, fax 20-375-4076, e-mail info@kenyapublishers.org, World Wide Web http://www.kenyapublishers.org. *Chair* Nancy Karimi; *CEO* Robert Obudho.

Korea (Republic of)

Korean Publishers Assn., 105-2 Sagan-dong, Jongro-gu, Seoul 110-190. Tel. 2-735-2701-4, fax 2-738-5414, e-mail webmaster@kpa21.or.kr, World Wide Web http://www.kpa21.or.kr. *Pres.* Sok-Ghee Baek; *Secy.-Gen.* Jon Jin Jung.

Latvia

Latvian Publishers' Assn., Brivibas 109-4, LV-1001 Riga. Tel. 67-282-392, fax 7-280-549, e-mail lga@gramatizdeveji.lv, World Wide Web http://www.gramatizdeveji.lv. *Pres.* Tenis Nigulis; *Exec. Dir.* Dace Pugaca.

Lithuania

Lithuanian Publishers Assn., Ave. Jaksto 22-13, 01105 Vilnius. Tel./fax 5-261-77-40, e-mail lla@centras.lt, World Wide Web http://www.lla.lt. *Pres.* Eugenijus Kaziliunas.

Malaysia

Malaysian Book Publishers' Assn., No. 39 Jl. Nilam 1/2, Subang Sq., Subang High Tech Industrial Park, Batu 3, 40000 Shah Alam, Selangor. Tel. 3-5637-9044, fax 3-5637-9043, e-mail inquiry@cerdik.com.my, World Wide Web http://www.mabopa.com.my. *Pres.* Law King Hui.

Mexico

Cámara Nacional de la Industria Editorial Mexicana (Mexican Publishers' Assn.), Holanda No. 13, CP 04120, Mexico DF. Tel. 155-56-88-20-11, fax 155-56-04-31-47, e-mail difusion@caniem.com, World Wide Web http://www.caniem.com. *Pres.* Juan Luis Arzoz Arbide.

The Netherlands

KVB—Koninklijke Vereeniging van het Boekenvak (formerly Koninklijke Vereeniging ter Bevordering van de Belangen des Boekhandels) (Royal Dutch Book Trade Assn.), Postbus 15007, 1001 MA Amsterdam. Tel. 20-624-02-12, fax 20-620-88-71, e-mail info@kvb.nl, World Wide Web http://www.kvb.nl. *Exec. Dir.* C. Verberne.

Nederlands Uitgeversverbond (Royal Dutch Publishers Assn.), Postbus 12040, 1100 AA Amsterdam. Tel. 20-43-09-150, fax 20-43-09-179, e-mail info@nuv.nl, World Wide Web http://www.nuv.nl. *Pres.* Henk J. L. Vonhoff.

Nederlandsche Vereeniging van Antiquaren (Netherlands Assn. of Antiquarian Booksellers), Prinsengracht 15, 2512 EW The Hague. Tel. 70-364-98-40, fax 70-364-33-40, e-mail kok@xs4all.nl, World Wide Web http://nvva.nl. *Pres.* Ton Kok.

Nederlandse Boekverkopersbond (Dutch Booksellers Assn.), Postbus 32, 3720 AA Bilhoven. Tel. 30-22-87-956, fax 030-22-84-566, e-mail nbb@boekbond.nl, World Wide Web http://www.boekbond.nl.

New Zealand

Booksellers New Zealand, Box 13-248, Johnsonville, Wellington 6440. Tel. 4-478-5511, fax 4-478-5519, e-mail info@booksellers.co.nz, World Wide Web http://www.booksellers.co.nz. *CEO* Lincoln Gould.

Nigeria

Nigerian Publishers Assn., GPO Box 2541, Ibadan. Tel. 2-751-5352, e-mail info@ nigerianpublishers.org, World Wide Web http://www.nigerianpublishers.org. *Exec. Secy.* Olakunle Sogbein.

Norway

Norske Bokhandlerforening (Norwegian Booksellers Assn.), Øvre Vollgate 15, 0158 Oslo. Tel. 22-40-45-40, fax 22-41-12-89, e-mail post@bokogsamfunn.no, World Wide Web http://www.bokogsamfunn.no. *Dir.* Kristin Cecilie Slordahl.

Norske Forleggerforening (Norwegian Publishers Assn.), Øvre Vollgate 15, 0158 Oslo. Tel. 22-00-75-80, fax 22-33-38-30, e-mail dnf@forleggerforeningen.no, World Wide Web http://www.forleggerforeningen.no. *Contact* Kristin Cecilie Slordahl.

Peru

Cámara Peruana del Libro (Peruvian Publishers Assn.), Av. Cuba 427, Jesús María, Apdo. 10253, Lima 11. Tel. 1-472-9516, fax 1-265-0735, e-mail cp-libro@amauta. rcp.net.pe, World Wide Web http://www. cpl.org.pe. *Pres.* Gladys Diaz Carrera.

Philippines

Philippine Educational Publishers Assn., 84 P. Florentino St., Sta. Mesa Heights, Quezon City. Tel. 2-712-4106, fax 2-731-3448, e-mail dbuhain@cnl.net, World Wide Web http://nbdb.gov.ph/publindust. htm. *Pres.* Dominador D. Buhain.

Poland

Polskie Towarzystwo Wydawców Ksikązek (Polish Society of Book Editors), ul. Świętokrzyska 30, 00-116 Warsaw. Tel. 22-407-77-30, fax 22-850-34-76, e-mail ptwk@wp.pl, World Wide Web http:// www.wydawca.com.pl. *Dir.* Maria Kuisz.

Stowarzyszenia Księgarzy Polskich (Assn. of Polish Booksellers), ul. Mazowiecka 2/4, 00-054 Warsaw. E-mail skp@ksiegarze. org.pl, World Wide Web http://www. ksiegarze.org.pl. *Pres.* Tadeusz Hussak.

Portugal

Associação Portuguesa de Editores e Livreiros (Portuguese Assn. of Publishers and Booksellers), Av. dos Estados Unidas da America 97, 6 Esq., 1700-167 Lisbon. Tel. 21-843-51-80, fax 21-848-93-77, e-mail apel@apel.pt, World Wide Web http:// www.apel.pt. *Pres.* Graca Didier.

Russia

Assn. of Book Publishers of Russia, ul. B. Nikitskaya 44, 121069 Moscow. Tel. 495-202-1174, fax 495-202-3989, e-mail aski @rol.ru, World Wide Web http://www. aski.ru. *Pres.* Chechenev Constantine Vasilyevich; *Exec. Dir.* Solonenko Vladimir Constantinovich.

Rossiiskaya Knizhnaya Palata (Russian Book Chamber), Kremlin nab, 1/9, 119019 Moscow. Tel. 495-688-96-89, fax 495-688-99-91, e-mail bookch@postman.ru, World Wide Web http://www.bookchamber.ru.

Serbia and Montenegro

Association of Yugoslav Publishers and Booksellers, Kneza Milosa 25/1, 11000 Belgrade. Tel. 11-642-533, fax 11-686-539, e-mail ognjenl@eunet.yu. *Dir.* Zivadin Mitrovic; *Mgr.* Marina Radojicic.

Singapore

Singapore Book Publishers Assn., c/o Cannon International, Block 86, Marine Parade Central No. 03-213, Singapore 440086. Tel. 6344-7801, fax 6344-0897, e-mail twcsbpa@singnet.com.sg, World Wide Web http://www.publishers-sbpa.org.sg. *Pres.* Triena Ong.

Slovenia

Zdruzenie Zaloznikov in Knjigotrzcev Slovenije Gospodarska Zbornica Slovenije (Assn. of Publishers and Booksellers of Slovenia), Dimičeva 13, SI 1000 Ljubljana. Tel. 1-5898-000, fax 1-5898-100, e-mail info@ gzs.si, World Wide Web http://www. gzs.si. *Pres.* Milan Matos.

South Africa

Publishers Assn. of South Africa (PASA), P.O. Box 106, Green Point 8051. Tel. 21-425-2721, fax 21-421-3270, e-mail pasa@publishsa.co.za, World Wide Web http://www.publishsa.co.za. *Exec. Dir.* Dudley Schroeder; *Mgr.* Samantha Faure.

South African Booksellers Assn. (formerly Associated Booksellers of Southern Africa), P.O. Box 870, Bellville 7530. Tel. 21-945-1572, fax 21-945-2169, e-mail saba@sabooksellers.com, World Wide Web http://sabooksellers.com. *Chair and Pres.* Guru Redhi.

Spain

Federación de Gremios de Editores de España (Federation of Spanish Publishers Assns.), Cea Bermúdez 44-2 Dcha, 2003 Madrid. Tel. 915-345-195, fax 915-352-625, e-mail fgee@fge.es, World Wide Web http://www.federacioneditores.org. *Pres.* D. Jordi Ubedai Baulo; *Exec. Dir.* Antonio María Avila.

Sri Lanka

Sri Lanka Book Publishers Association, 53 Maligakanda Rd., Colombo 10. Tel. 74-304-546, fax 1-821-454, e-mail bookpub@sltnet.lk, World Wide Web http://www.bookpublishers.lk. *Gen. Secy.* Upali Wanigasooriya.

Sudan

Sudanese Publishers' Assn., c/o Institute of African and Asian Studies, Khartoum Univ., P.O. Box 321, Khartoum 11115. Tel. 11-77-0022. *Dir.* Al-Amin Abu Manga Mohamed.

Sweden

Svenska Förläggareföreningen (Swedish Publishers Assn.), Drottninggatan 97, S-11360 Stockholm. Tel. 8-736-19-40, fax 8-736-19-44, e-mail info@forlaggareforeningen.se, World Wide Web http://www.forlaggare.se. *Dir.* Kristina Ahlinder.

Switzerland

Association Suisse des Éditeurs de Langue Française (ASELF) (Swiss Assn. of English-Language Publishers), 2 ave. Agassiz, 1001 Lausanne. Tel. 21-319-71-11, fax 21-319-79-10, e-mail aself@centrezational.cl, World Wide Web http://www.culturactif.ch/editions/asef1.htm. *Secy. Gen.* Philippe Schibli.

Schweizerischer Buchhandler- und Verleger-Verband (Swiss German-Language Booksellers and Publishers Assn.), Alderstr. 40, Postfach, 8034 Zurich. Tel. 044-421-36-00, fax 044-421-36-18, e-mail sbvv@swissbooks.ch, World Wide Web http://www.swissbooks.ch. *Exec. Dir.* Martin Jann.

Thailand

Publishers and Booksellers Assn. of Thailand, 83/156 Soi Chinnakhet 2, Ngam Wong Wan Rd., Thung Song Hong, Lak Si, Bangkok 10210. Tel. 662-9549560-4, fax 662-9549565-6, e-mail info@pubat.or.th, World Wide Web http://www.pubat.or.th.

Uganda

Uganda Publishers and Booksellers Assn., P.O. Box 7732, Kampala. Tel. 41-259-163, fax 41-251-160, e-mail mbd@infocom.co.ug. *Contact* Martin Okia.

United Kingdom

Antiquarian Booksellers Assn., Sackville House, 40 Piccadilly, London W1J 0DR, England. Tel. 20-7439-3118, fax 20-7439-3119, e-mail admin@aba.org.uk, World Wide Web http://www.aba.org.uk. *Admin.* Clare Pedder; *Secy.* John Critchley.

Assn. of Learned and Professional Society Publishers, Blenheim House, 120 Church St., Brighton BN1 1AU, England. Tel. 1275-858-837, World Wide Web http://www.alpsp.org. *Chief Exec.* Ian Russell.

Booktrust, 45 East Hill, Wandsworth, London SW18 2QZ, England. Tel. 20-8516-2977, fax 20-8516-2978, e-mail query@booktrust.org.uk, World Wide Web http://www.booktrust.org.uk.

Educational Publishers Council, 29B Montague St., London WC1B 5BW, England. Tel. 20-7691-9191, fax 20-7691-9199, e-mail mail@publishers.org.uk, World Wide Web http://www.publishers.org.uk. *Chair* Kate Harris; *Dir.* Graham Taylor.

Publishers Assn., 29B Montague St., London WC1B 5BW, England. Tel. 20-7691-9191, fax 20-7691-9199, e-mail mail@publishers. org.uk, World Wide Web http://www. publishers.org.uk. *Pres.* Ian Hudson; *Chief Exec.* Simon Juden; *Dir.* Graham Taylor.

Scottish Book Trust, Sandeman House, Trunk's Close, 55 High St., Edinburgh EH1 1SR, Scotland. Tel. 131-524-0160, fax 131-524-0161, e-mail info@scottish booktrust.com, World Wide Web http:// www.scottishbooktrust.com. *CEO* Marc Lambert.

Welsh Books Council (Cyngor Llyfrau Cymru), Castell Brychan, Aberystwyth, Ceredigion SY23 2JB, Wales. Tel. 1970-624-151, fax 1970-625-385, e-mail castell-brychan@wbc.org.uk, World Wide Web http://www.cllc.org.uk. *Dir.* Gwerfyl Pierce Jones.

Uruguay

Cámara Uruguaya del Libro (Uruguayan Publishers Assn.), Colon 1476, Apdo. 102, 11 200 Montevideo. Tel. 82-916-93-74, fax 82-916-76-28, e-mail info@camaradel libro.com.uy, World Wide Web http://www. camaradellibro.com.uy. *Pres.* Alvaro Juan Risso Castellanos.

Venezuela

Cámara Venezolana del Libro (Venezuelan Publishers Assn.), Av. Andrés Bello, Centro Andrés Bello, Torre Oeste 11, piso 11, of. 112-0, Caracas 1050. Tel. 212-793-1347, fax 212-793-1368, e-mail unegi@ cavelibro.org, World Wide Web http:// www.cavelibro.org. *Pres.* Leonardo Ramos.

Zambia

Booksellers and Publishers Assn. of Zambia, P.O. Box 32379, Lusaka. Tel. 1-292-837, fax 1-253-952, e-mail bpaz@zamtel.zm, World Wide Web http://africanpublishers. org. *Contact* H. Mwacalimba.

Zimbabwe

Zimbabwe Book Publishers Assn., P.O. Box 3794, Harare. Tel./fax 4-754-256, e-mail engelbert@collegepress.co.zw.

National Information Standards Organization (NISO) Standards

Information Retrieval

Z39.2-1994 (R2001)	Information Interchange Format
Z39.47-1993 (R2003)	Extended Latin Alphabet Coded Character Set for Bibliographic Use (ANSEL)
Z39.50-2003	Information Retrieval (Z39.50) Application Service Definition and Protocol Specification
Z39.53-2001	Codes for the Representation of Languages for Information Interchange
Z39.64-1989	(R2002) East Asian Character Code for Bibliographic Use
Z39.76-1996	(R2002) Data Elements for Binding Library Materials
Z39.84-2005	Syntax for the Digital Object Identifier
Z39.88-2004	The OpenURL Framework for Context-Sensitive Services
Z39.89-2003	The U.S. National Z39.50 Profile for Library Applications

Library Management

Z39.7-2004	Information Services and Use: metrics and statistics for libraries and information providers—Data Dictionary
Z39.20-1999	Criteria for Price Indexes for Print Library Materials
Z39.71-2006	Holdings Statements for Bibliographic Items
Z39.73-1994 (R2001)	Single-Tier Steel Bracket Library Shelving
Z39.83-1-2008	NISO Circulation Interchange Part 1: Protocol (NCIP)
Z39.83-2-2008	NISO Circulation Interchange Protocol (NCIP) Part 2: Implementation Profile 1
Z39.93-2007	The Standardized Usage Statistics Harvesting Initiative (SUSHI) Protocol

Preservation and Storage

Z39.32-1996 (R2002)	Information on Microfiche Headers
Z39.48-1992 (R2002)	Permanence of Paper for Publications and Documents in Libraries and Archives
Z39.62-2000	Eye-Legible Information on Microfilm Leaders and Trailers and on Containers of Processed Microfilm on Open Reels
Z39.74-1996 (R2002)	Guides to Accompany Microform Sets

Z39.77-2001   Guidelines for Information About Preservation Products
Z39.78-2000 (R2006) Library Binding
Z39.79-2001   Environmental Conditions for Exhibiting Library and
                     Archival Materials
Z39.87-2006   Data Dictionary—Technical Metadata for Digital Still
                     Images

Publishing and Information Management

Z39.9-1992 (R2001)   International Standard Serial Numbering (ISSN)
Z39.14-1997 (R2002) Guidelines for Abstracts
Z39.18-2005   Scientific and Technical Reports—Preparation,
                     Presentation, and Preservation
Z39.19-2005   Guidelines for the Construction, Format, and Management
                     of Monolingual Controlled Vocabularies
Z39.23-1997 (R2002) Standard Technical Report Number Format and Creation
Z39.26-1997 (R2002) Micropublishing Product Information
Z39.29-2005   Bibliographic References
Z39.41-1997 (R2002) Printed Information on Spines
Z39.43-1993 (R2006) Standard Address Number (SAN) for the Publishing
                     Industry
Z39.56-1996 (R2002) Serial Item and Contribution Identifier (SICI)
Z39.82-2001   Title Pages for Conference Publications
Z39.85-2001   Dublin Core Metadata Element Set
Z39.86-2005   Specifications for the Digital Talking Book
ANSI/NISO/ISO   Electronic Manuscript Preparation and Markup
12083-1995 (R2002)

In Development/NISO Initiatives

NISO examines new areas for standardization, reports, and best practices on a continuing basis to support its ongoing standards development program. NISO working groups are exploring these areas:

- CORE (Cost of Resource Exchange) Working Group
- ERM Data Standards and Best Practices Review Working Group
- DAISY Standard (ANSI/NISO Z39.86 - 2005 Specifications for the Digital Talking Book) Revision Working Group
- I2 (Institutional Identifiers) Working Group
- KBART (Knowledge Bases and Related Tools) Working Group (NISO and UKSG)
- ONIX-PL (NISO and EDItEUR)
- NCIP (ANSI/NISO Z39.83-2008, NISO Circulation Interchange Protocol) Standing Committee
- OpenURL Quality Metrics Working Group
- Physical Delivery of Library Resources Working Group

- SERU (Shared Electronic Resource Understanding) Standing Committee
- SSO (Single Sign-On) Authentication Working Group
- Standardized Markup for Journal Articles Working Group
- SUSHI (ANSI/NISO Z39.93-2007 Standardized Usage Statistics Harvesting Initiative Protocol) Standing Committee

NISO Technical Reports, Recommended Practices, and Other Publications

Best Practices for Designing Web Services in the Library Context (RP-2006-01)

Environmental Guidelines for the Storage of Paper Records (TR01-1995)

A Framework of Guidance for Building Good Digital Collections

Guidelines for Indexes and Related Information Retrieval Devices (TR02-1997)

Guidelines to Alphanumeric Arrangement and Sorting of Numerals and Other Symbols (TR03-1999)

Information Standards Quarterly (*ISQ*) (NISO quarterly magazine)

Journal Article Versions (JAV): Recommendations of the NISO/ALPSP JAV Technical Working Group (RP-8-2008)

KBART: Knowledge Bases and Related Tools (RP-9-2010)

Metadata Demystified: A Guide for Publishers

Networked Reference Services: Question/Answer Transaction Protocol (TR04-2006)

NISO Metasearch XML Gateway Implementers Guide (RP-2006-02)

NISO Newsline (free monthly e-newsletter)

Ranking of Authentication and Access Methods Available to the Metasearch Environment (RP-2005-01)

RFID in U.S. Libraries (RP-6-2008)

The RFP Writer's Guide to Standards for Library Systems

Search and Retrieval Citation Level Data Elements (RP-2005-03)

Search and Retrieval Results Set Metadata (RP-2005-02)

SERU: A Shared Electronic Resource Understanding (RP-7-2008)

Streamlining Book Metadata Workflow

Understanding Metadata

Up and Running: Implementing Z39.50—Proceedings of a Symposium Sponsored by the State Library of Iowa

Z39.50: A Primer on the Protocol

Z39.50 Implementation Experiences

NISO standards are available online at http://www.niso.org/standards. Recommended Practices, Technical Reports, White Papers, and other publications are available on the NISO Web site at http://www.niso.org/publications.

For more information, contact NISO, 1 North Charles St., Baltimore, MD 21201. Tel. 301-654-2512, fax 410-685-5278, e-mail nisohq@niso.org, World Wide Web http://www.niso.org.

Calendar, 2010–2019

The list below contains information on association meetings or promotional events that are, for the most part, national or international in scope. State and regional library association meetings are also included. To confirm the starting or ending date of a meeting, which may change after the *Library and Book Trade Almanac* has gone to press, contact the association directly. Addresses of library and book trade associations are listed in Part 6 of this volume. For information on additional book trade and promotional events, see *Literary Market Place* and *International Literary Market Place,* published by Information Today, Inc., and other library and book trade publications such as *Library Journal, School Library Journal,* and *Publishers Weekly. American Libraries,* published by the American Library Association, maintains an online calendar at http://www.ala.org/ala/alonline/calendar/calendar.cfm. An Information Today events calendar can be found at http://www.infotoday.com/calendar.shtml.

2010

June

2–4	Society for Scholarly Publishing	San Francisco
2–5	Canadian Library Assn.	Edmonton, AB
6–8	Specialized Information Publishers Assn. (SIPA 2010)	Washington, DC
7–10	Assn. of Christian Librarians	St. Paul, MN
7–10	World Newspaper Congress	Beirut, Lebanon
8–12	International Conference on Enterprise Information Systems	Madiera, Portugal
9–13	Bookfest Bukarest	Bucharest, Romania
10–11	International Council for Scientific and Technical Information (ICSTI)	Helsinki, Finland
10–12	LOEX of the West	Calgary, AB
13–16	Special Libraries Assn.	New Orleans
16–18	International Conference on Electronic Publishing (ELPUB 2010)	Helsinki, Finland
16–19	American Theological Libraries Assn.	Louisville
17–20	Assn. of American University Presses	Salt Lake City
20–22	Global Information Technology Management Assn.	Washington, DC

June 2010 *(cont.)*

20–24	International Assn. of Technology University Libraries (IATUL)	West Lafayette, IN
22–24	Center for Intellectual Property (CIP) Symposium	Washington, DC
24–30	American Library Assn. Annual Conference	Washington, DC
27–30	International Society for Technology in Education	Denver
28–30	International Conference on Information Society (i-Society 2010)	London, England
28–30	International Conference on Knowledge Management and Knowledge Economy	Paris, France

July

4–7	Assn. of Jewish Libraries	Seattle
5–8	Fifth International Conference on Digital Information Management (ICDIM 2010)	Thunder Bay, ON
6–9	International Conference on Open Repositories	Madrid, Spain
7–9	International Symposium on Wikis (WikiSym)	Gdansk, Poland
25–27	Church and Synagogue Library Assn.	Houston
29–8/2	LIBER Annual General Conference	Åarhus, Denmark
30–8/2	Cape Town Book Fair	Cape Town, South Africa

August

2–4	CRM Evolution 2010	New York
4–9	BCALA Conference of African American Librarians	Birmingham
7–8	Marketing Libraries in a Web 2.0 World	Stockholm, Sweden
10–15	IFLA General Conference and Assembly	Göteborg, Sweden
10–15	Society of American Archivists	Washington, DC
11–13	Washington Library Assn./Pacific Northwest Library Assn.	Victoria, BC
30–9/3	Beijing International Book Fair	Beijing, China

September

1–6	Moscow International Book Fair	Moscow, Russia
6–10	European Conference on Digital Libraries	Glasgow, Scotland
15–19	Kentucky Library Assn.	Louisville
21–23	Society for Scholarly Publishing	Philadelphia
22–24	South Dakota Library Assn.	Sioux Falls
23–25	Assn. for Library Service to Children	Atlanta
26–28	Arkansas Library Assn./Southeastern Library Assn.	Little Rock
28–10/1	Illinois Library Assn.	Chicago

| 29–10/2 | North Dakota Library Assn. | Grand Forks |
| 30–10/3 | Library and Information Technology Association (LITA) National Forum | Atlanta |

October

6–8	Minnesota Library Assn.	Rochester
6–8	Missouri Library Assn.	Lake of the Ozarks
6–9	Idaho Library Assn.	Post Falls
6–9	Nevada Library Assn.	Henderson
6–10	Frankfurt Book Fair	Frankfurt, Germany
7–8	Maine Library Assn.	Camden
7–9	Colorado Assn. of Libraries	Loveland
7–16	Sharjah International Book Fair	Sharjah, UAE
12–14	Iowa Library Assn.	Coralville
12–15	West Virginia Library Assn.	Roanoke
13–15	Georgia Council of Media Organizations	Athens
13–15	Nebraska Library Assn./NEMA	Grand Island
14–15	Internet Librarian International	London, England
14–15	Streaming Media Europe	London, England
14–16	Assn. of Bookmobiles and Outreach Services/ Assn. for Rural and Small Libraries	Denver
17–19	New England Library Assn.	Boxborough, MA
17–22	Pacific Northwest Library Assn.	Schweitzer Resort, ID
19–22	Mississippi Library Assn.	Vicksburg
20–22	South Carolina Library Assn.	Myrtle Beach
21–22	Virginia Library Assn.	Portsmouth
22–27	ASIS&T	Pittsburgh
24–27	Pennsylvania Library Assn.	Lancaster
25–26	Internet@Schools West	Monterey, CA
25–27	Internet Librarian	Monterey, CA
28–31	Helsinki Book Fair	Helsinki, Finland
30–11/7	Istanbul Book Fair	Istanbul, Turkey

November

2–3	Streaming Media West	Los Angeles
2–5	Wisconsin Library Assn.	Wisconsin Dells
3–6	New York Library Assn.	Saratoga Springs
4–7	YALSA Young Adult Literature Symposium	Albuquerque
6–8	International Conference on the Book	St. Gallen, Switzerland
8–9	SPARC Digital Repositories Meeting	Baltimore
10–12	Michigan Library Assn.	Acme-Traverse City
12–15	California Library Assn.	Sacramento
15–17	Indiana Library Federation	Indianapolis
16–18	KMWorld 2010	Washington, DC
17–22	Montreal Book Fair	Montreal, QC

November 2010 *(cont.)*

27–12/5	Guadalajara International Book Fair	Guadalajara, Mexico

2011

January

7–11	American Library Assn. Midwinter Meeting	San Diego

March

22–25	Tennessee Library Assn.	Murfreesboro
22–27	Abu Dhabi International Book Fair	Abu Dhabi, UAE
28–31	Bologna Children's Book Fair	Bologna, Italy

April

5–9	Washington Library Assn.	Yakima
6–8	Kansas Library Assn.	Topeka
7–10	Assn. of College and Research Libraries	Philadelphia
11–13	London Book Fair	London, England
12–15	Texas Library Assn.	Austin

May

24–26	BookExpo America	New York

June

23–28	American Library Assn. Annual Conference	New Orleans

August

13–18	IFLA General Conference and Assembly	San Juan, Puerto Rico

September

24–27	Arkansas Library Assn.	Little Rock
28–10/1	Kentucky Library Assn.	Louisville

October

5–7	Minnesota Library Assn.	Duluth
13–15	Colorado Assn. of Libraries	Loveland
18–21	Illinois Library Assn.	Rosemont
19–21	Minnesota Library Assn.	Duluth
27–28	Virginia Library Assn.	Portsmouth
26–30	American Assn. of School Librarians	Minneapolis

November

1–4	Wisconsin Library Assn.	Milwaukee
2–5	New York Library Assn.	Saratoga Springs

2012

January

20–24	American Library Assn. Midwinter Meeting	Dallas

March

13–17	Public Library Assn.	Philadelphia

April

24–27	Texas Library Assn.	Houston

May

30–6/1	BookExpo America	New York

June

21–26	American Library Assn. Annual Conference	Anaheim

August

11–16	IFLA General Conference and Assembly	Helsinki, Finland

October

23–26	Wisconsin Library Assn.	La Crosse

2013

January

25–29	American Library Assn. Midwinter Meeting	Seattle

April

4–7	Assn. of College and Research Libraries	Indianapolis
8–12	Texas Library Assn.	San Antonio

June

27–7/2	American Library Assn. Annual Conference	Chicago

2014

January

24–28   American Library Assn. Midwinter Meeting   Philadelphia

April

8–11   Texas Library Assn.   Dallas

June

26 –1/7   American Library Assn. Annual Conference   Las Vegas

2015

January

23–27   American Library Assn. Midwinter Meeting   Chicago

April

10–17   Texas Library Assn.   Austin

June

25–30   American Library Assn. Annual Conference   San Francisco

2016

January

22–26   American Library Assn. Midwinter Meeting   Boston

June

23–28   American Library Assn. Annual Conference   Orlando

2017

January

20–24   American Library Assn. Midwinter Meeting   Atlanta

June

22–27   American Library Assn. Annual Conference   Chicago

2018

January

19–23   American Library Assn. Midwinter Meeting   Los Angeles

June

21–26   American Library Assn. Annual Conference   New Orleans

2019

January

25–29   American Library Assn. Midwinter Meeting   Seattle

June

27–7/2   American Library Assn. Annual Conference   New York

Acronyms

A

AALL. American Association of Law Libraries

AAP. Association of American Publishers

AASL. American Association of School Librarians

ABA. American Booksellers Association

ABC. Association of Booksellers for Children

ABFFE. American Booksellers Foundation for Free Expression

ACRL. Association of College and Research Libraries

ACTA. Anti-Counterfeiting Trade Act

AIC. American Institute for the Conservation of Historic and Artistic Works

AIIP. Association of Independent Information Professionals

AILA. American Indian Library Association

AJL. Association of Jewish Libraries

ALA. American Library Association

ALCTS. Association for Library Collections and Technical Services

ALIC. National Archives and Records Administration, Archives Library Information Center

ALISE. Association for Library and Information Science Education

ALS. National Center for Education Statistics, Academic Library Survey

ALSC. Association for Library Service to Children

ALTAFF. Association for Library Trustees, Advocates, Friends, and Foundations

AMMLA. American Merchant Marine Library Association

APA. Allied Professional Association

APALA. Asian/Pacific American Librarians Association

ARC. National Archives and Records Administration, Archival Research Catalog

ARL. Association of Research Libraries

ARLIS/NA. Art Libraries Society of North America

ARRA. American Recovery and Reinvestment Act

ASCLA. Association of Specialized and Cooperative Library Agencies

ASIS&T. American Society for Information Science and Technology

ATLA. American Theological Library Association

ATN. Academic books, AccessText Network

B

BARD. Internet/Web, Braille and Audio Reading Download

BCALA. Black Caucus of the American Library Association

BEA. BookExpo America

BEC. BookExpo Canada

BNA. Blackwell Book Service North America

BSA. Bibliographical Society of America

C

CACUL. Canadian Association of College and University Libraries

CAIS. Canadian Association for Information Science

CALA. Chinese-American Librarians Association

CAP. Canada, Community Access Program

CAPL. Canadian Association of Public Libraries

CARL. Canadian Association of Research
Libraries
CASL. Canadian Association for School
Libraries
CASLIS. Canadian Association of Special
Libraries and Information Services
CCB. Conference Board of Canada
CCL. Canadian Council on Learning
CDNL. Conference of Directors of National
Libraries
CFR. Code of Federal Regulations
CGP. Government Printing Office, *Catalog
of Government Publications*
CIHR. Canadian Institutes of Health
Research
CLA. Canadian Library Association
CLIR. Council on Library and Information
Resources
CLOCKSS. Canada, CLOCKSS (Controlled
Lots of Copies Keep Stuff Safe)
CLTA. Canadian Library Trustees
Association
CNI. Coalition for Networked Information
COLT. Council on Library/Media
Technicians
COPA. Child Online Protection Act
COSLA. Chief Officers of State Library
Agencies
CPSIA. Consumer Product Safety
Improvement Act
CRP. Association of American Publishers,
Campaign for Reader Privacy
CSLA. Church and Synagogue Library
Association
CSRL. Center for the Study of Rural
Librarianship
CUI. Government information, access to,
controlled unclassified information
CWA. Crime Writers' Association

D

DLF. Digital Library Federation
DMCA. Digital Millennium Copyright Act
DTIC. Defense Technical Information Center

E

EAR. National Technical Information
Service, Export Administration
Regulations

EDB. National Technical Information
Service, Energy Science and
Technology Database
EHRs. National Library of Medicine,
electronic health records
EMIERT. American Library Association,
Ethnic and Multicultural Information
and Exchange Round Table

F

FAFLRT. American Library Association,
Federal and Armed Forces Librarians
Round Table
FAIFE. International Federation of Library
Associations and Institutions,
Freedom of Access to Information and
Freedom of Expression
FBI. Federal Bureau of Investigation
FDLP. Government Printing Office, Federal
Depository Library Program
FDsys. FDsys (Federal Digital System)
FEDRIP. National Technical Information
Service, FEDRIP (Federal Research in
Progress Database)
FIAF. International Federation of Film
Archives
FLICC. Federal Library and Information
Center Committee
FOIA. Freedom of Information Act
FRPAA. Federal Research Public Access Act

G

GLBT. American Library Association, Gay,
Lesbian, Bisexual, and Transgendered
Round Table
GLIN. Global Legal Information Network
GODORT. American Library Association,
Government Documents Round Table
GPO. Government Printing Office
GSU. Georgia State University

I

IAALD. International Association of
Agricultural Information Specialists
IACs. Defense Technical Information Center,
Information Analysis Centers
IALL. International Association of Law
Libraries

IAML. International Association of Music Libraries, Archives, and Documentation Centres

IASL. International Association of School Librarianship

ICA. International Council of Archives

ICADS. ICADS (IFLA-CDNL Alliance for Digital Strategies)

ICBS. International Committee of the Blue Shield

IFLA. International Federation of Library Associations and Institutions

IFRT. American Library Association, Intellectual Freedom Round Table

IFTP. Association of American Publishers, International Freedom to Publish

IIPA. International Intellectual Property Alliance

ILS. Government Printing Office, Integrated Library System

IMLS. Institute of Museum and Library Services

ISBN. International Standard Book Number

ISCAP. Interagency Security Classification Appeals Panel

ISE. Government information, access to, Information Sharing Environment

ISO. International Organization for Standardization

ISOO. National Archives and Records Administration, Information Security Oversight Office

ISSN. International Standard Serial Number

ISTE. International Society for Technology in Education

L

LAC. Library and Archives Canada

LCA. Library Copyright Alliance

LCDP. Association of Research Libraries, Leadership and Career Development Program

LHHS. Labor, Health, and Human Services Appropriations Bill

LHRT. American Library Association, Library History Round Table

LIS. Library/information science; Library of Congress, Legislative Information Service

LITA. Library and Information Technology Association

LJ. Library Journal

LLAMA. Library Leadership and Management Association

LRRT. American Library Association, Library Research Round Table

LSCM. Government Printing Office, Library Services and Content Management

LSP. National Center for Education Statistics, Library Statistics Program

LSTA. Library Services and Technology Act

LTIS. Library Technical Information Service

M

MINES. Internet/Web, MINES for libraries

MLA. Medical Library Association; Music Library Association

N

NAGARA. National Association of Government Archives and Records Administrators

NAL. National Agricultural Library

NARA. National Archives and Records Administration

NATO. North Atlantic Treaty Organization

NCAST. National Archives Center for Advanced Systems and Technologies

NCBI. National Center for Biotechnology Information

NCES. National Center for Education Statistics

NCLA. National Church Library Association

NCLB. No Child Left Behind

NDC. National Archives and Records Administration, National Declassification Center

NDIIPP. National Digital Information Infrastructure and Preservation Program

NDNP. Newspapers, National Digital Newspaper Program

NEH. National Endowment for the Humanities

NFAIS. National Federation of Advanced Information Services

NHPRC. National Historical Publications and Records Commission

NIH. National Institutes of Health

NISO. National Information Standards
  Organization
NLE. National Library of Education
NLM. National Library of Medicine
NMRT. American Library Association, New
  Members Round Table
NPR. National Public Radio
NSDs. National Security Directives
NTIS. National Technical Information
  Service
NTRL. National Technical Information
  Service, National Technical Reports
  Library

O

OGD. Government information, access to,
  Open Government Directive
OGIS. Government Information Services,
  Office of
OPA. Internet/Web, OPA (Online Public
  Access)

P

PENS. Internet/Web, Public Law Electronic
  Notification Service
PGC. Portrait Gallery Canada
PIDB. Public Interest Declassification Board
PLA. Public Library Association
PMC. PubMedCentral
PTDLA. Patent and Trademark Depository
  Library Association
PW. Publishers Weekly

R

RDA. Standards, Resource Description and
  Access
RUSA. Reference and User Services
  Association

S

SAA. Society of American Archivists
SAN. Standard Address Number

SAR. National Library of Medicine,
  Sequence Read Archive
SBU. Government information, access to,
  Sensitive But Unclassified
SCI. Scholarly Communication Institute
SIIA. Software and Information Industry
  Association
SLA. Special Libraries Association
SPARC. SPARC (Scholarly Publishing and
  Academic Resources Coalition)
SRIM. National Technical Information
  Service, Selected Research in
  Microfiche
SRRT. American Library Association, Social
  Responsibilities Round Table
SSP. Society for Scholarly Publishing

T

TLA. Theatre Library Association
TrUFL. Council on Library and Information
  Resources, TrUFL (Try, Use, Fail,
  Learn)

U

ULC. Urban Libraries Council

V

VHP. History, Veterans History Project

W

WDL. World Digital Library
WIPO. World Intellectual Property
  Organization
WNC. World News Connection

Y

YALSA. Young Adult Library Services
  Association
YPG. Association of American Pubishers,
  Young to Publishing Group

Index of Organizations

Please note that many cross-references refer to entries in the Subject Index.

B

Subject Index

Please note that many cross-references refer to entries in the Index of Organizations.